16²⁵

A HISTORY OF
CHRISTIANITY

Volume II: A.D. 1500–A.D. 1975

Also available

A History of Christianity, Vol. I, to A.D. 1500

Other books by Kenneth Scott Latourette

The Chinese: Their History and Culture

Christianity in a Revolutionary Age (5 volumes)

Christianity Through the Ages

The Gospel, the Church and the World

A History of Christian Missions in China

A History of Early Relations Between the United States and China

A History of Japan

A History of the Expansion of Christianity (7 volumes)

A Short History of the Far East

A HISTORY OF CHRISTIANITY

KENNETH SCOTT LATOURETTE

STERLING PROFESSOR OF MISSIONS AND ORIENTAL HISTORY

AND FELLOW OF BERKELEY COLLEGE IN YALE UNIVERSITY

Volume II: A. D. 1500–A.D. 1975

HARPER & ROW, PUBLISHERS

New York, Hagerstown, San Francisco, London

To my colleagues past and present
of the faculty of the
Yale University Divinity School

A HISTORY OF CHRISTIANITY *Volume II: A.D. 1500—A.D. 1975.* Copyright © 1953, 1975 by
Harper & Row, Publishers, Inc. All rights reserved. Printed in the United States of America. No
part of this book may be used or reproduced in any manner whatsoever without written permission
except in the case of brief quotations embodied in critical articles and reviews. For information
address Harper & Row, Publishers, Inc., 10 East 53rd Street, New York, N.Y. 10022. Published
simultaneously in Canada by Fitzhenry & Whiteside Limited, Toronto.

First Harper & Row paperback edition published in 1975.

Volume II contains pages 684—1516 of the hardcover edition of A HISTORY OF CHRISTIANITY, as
well as a new chapter (62).

ISBN: 0-06-064953-4

LIBRARY OF CONGRESS CATALOG CARD NUMBER: 74-25693

89 90   20 19 18 17 16 15 14 13

CONTENTS

Volume II: A.D. 1500 to A.D. 1975

Volume II: A.D. 1500 to A.D. 1975

VIGOUR AMIDST STORM, A.D. 1914–A.D. 1952

INCREASING DISESTABLISHMENT, INCREASING DIVERSITY, GROWTH AND VITALITY, A.D. 1950–A.D. 1975

MAPS

FOREWORD

It seems especially fitting that a 1500-page summary of that religious movement constituting the greatest influence in the history of mankind should be written by a man who knew the Chinese intimately, the people constituting the largest bloc of population in the history of mankind. As a matter of fact, for twenty years Kenneth Scott Latourette taught every course Yale University offered on the Far East. Yet, curiously, it would be the Chinese who, of all major sectors of modern mankind, have made the least overt response to the Christian Church. In any case this book, in some respects, is his response to the Chinese.

He writes as a warm, sympathetic Christian. His many other books demonstrate his ability as an objective scholar. In this book he writes as a Christian to Christians, and while he does not overemphasize China, it is clear on every page that there is a constant concern for the way in which Christianity has, is, or will affect the *remainder of all humanity.*

But Latourette is no religious imperialist: a gentle man, he is most impressed, as he tells this massive story, when he is describing the gentlest of all Christ's servants. Nor is he a religious apologist. He exhibits a rare sensitivity and faithfulness in describing those ways, those times, those places in which Christians have fallen short of their ideals. If as a committed Christian he does not hesitate to expose weaknesses and shortcomings when he finds them, then as a loyal Baptist, he does not hesitate to give credit to church movements far removed from his own tradition.

In fact there is one bias that runs throughout all his books, and helps to explain his larger perspective. Unobtrusively, but consistently, he favors the minority, the man on the bottom, the movement without pedigree or official backing. While this bias does not lead him to attack the established movements, his narrative is much more than a story about the major Christian churches, or even about churches as such. He does not hesitate to describe events both within and without the "organized" Church. It is incredible but true that no other human being in history has achieved—or perhaps even earnestly sought to produce—this kind of appreciative, comprehensive account of the whole Christian story. Christianity for him is a movement of fascinating complexity, and he sees it in "relation to the total story of mankind." In many ways he actually describes the total story of mankind, demonstrating how hopeless it would be to try to understand that story without understanding the extensive influence of Jesus in that larger picture.

He wrote with a post-Vatican II breadth of spirit *prior* to that great series of meetings! Thus surprisingly the friendly climate of the 1970's does not outmode the attitudes he expresses in this remarkable summary. One wonders how anyone today could more effectively chronicle so many delicate situations down through history—both triumphs and failures of practically every branch of Christianity—and do so with such a combination of generosity and honesty. Thus the scope, the balance, and the modernity of his perspective leaves this treatment without parallel even in 1975. In trying to stretch the canvas he painted, over an additional quarter of a century—in an additional chapter—we have become painfully aware that no one today, unfortunately, is as comprehensively informed as Latourette customarily considered it his duty to be. Fortunately he himself helped with the task. The twenty pages of his Chapter 59 became a whole book of 468 pages in 1962, *The Twentieth Century Outside Europe* (Vol. V of *Christianity in a Revolutionary Age*), and takes us at least part of the way into the 1950–1975 period. In his sprightly, brief *Christianity Through the Ages* he leads the reader as far as 1964, covering 1914 to 1964 in the last twenty-five pages.

What makes these two volumes virtually an encyclopedia is the unusually detailed index which has close to 6000 entries, vastly more than the average book and as many as any of three recent dictionaries of the Christian movement. It is a splendid idea, too, for the entire index to be placed in each of the two volumes, since many topics run through both.

A by-product of exploding world development in the 1950–1975 period is the profusion of new books on the Christian movement which have appeared since Latourette completed this work in 1952. A very modest selection of these books is to be found in the supplemental bibliographies which have been added at the end of each volume.

Ralph D. Winter

PREFACE

Here is both an old and a new story.

It is old. Repeatedly across its nineteen and a half centuries the history of Christianity has been told and retold. In one or another of its aspects it has called forth a voluminous and massive literature.

This is as it should be. Christianity has become the most widespread of all religious faiths. It is by no means dominant. It never ceases to be challenged. There have been times when it has seemed to be waning. Some of the major attacks on it have been made in our day. Its ideals have never been fully attained. Indeed, it at least is debatable whether they ever can be fully realized within the span of history, so high are they, and so far beyond anything actual, either in man's collective life, in small groups, or even in individuals. The one life in which they were fully embodied came to a cross, so contrary were they to current practice in religion and the state. Yet, measured by its effects, Christianity has become the most potent single force in the life of mankind.

Moreover, by its very genius, Christianity is a concern of the historian. If the Christian faith is true, it should be either central or at least be consciously kept as the setting and the point of reference for all the work of the historian. It had its inception in events and in a life which are part of the historical record. From the very first generation of Christians, there have been those who have believed that the clue to the perplexing and paradoxical human drama is to be found in Christ, that the whole of the created universe groans in travail waiting for the revealing of the sons of God, the sons of whom Christ is the first-born, and that it is the purpose of God to sum up all things in Christ, both in the heavens and upon the earth, and to put "all things in subjection under his feet." If this conviction arises from fact, to be seen in its proper perspective the entire course of mankind on the planet must be surveyed with reference to Christ, from the incarnation in Jesus of Nazareth, through his teaching, deeds, life, and resurrection, and it is no accident but of the very stuff of history that chronology is measured as B.C.—before Christ—and A.D., *Anno Domini,* the year of the Lord of men and of history.

It is not surprising that, equipped with this insight, again and again through the centuries Christian scholars have addressed themselves to the history of their faith and in the light of it have endeavoured to understand the nature of man and the course of mankind's pilgrimage. Examples can be instanced from the first to the twentieth century.

The story of Christianity is not only old: it is also ever new. In each age it must be told afresh. That is not merely because in every era a chapter is added by the ongoing current of events. It is also because at every stage of mankind's march fresh perspective is gained. Each generation of historians can say of its predecessors: "Without us they cannot be made perfect." That is partly for the reason that every historian can utilize the work of those of his craft who have gone before him. It is also because from the vantage of a later day and in the fresh setting of his times the historian can interpret anew the road which the race has thus far traversed. No historian can hope to give the final or definitive account of the course of Christianity. Those who come after him will presumably have the same advantages which he possesses over those who have earlier essayed the task. In each generation there must be those who will undertake to review for their fellows the scroll as it has thus far been unrolled.

Certain outstanding features of the mid-twentieth century make necessary now an attempt to resurvey the course of Christianity. These cannot be stated in logical order, for it is not clear that they are tied together in that fashion. One of them, probably the most pronounced at first glance, is the fact that the human race is bound together physically more closely than ever before. Decade by decade, almost year by year, rapid means of transportation and communication reduce the size of the globe in time-distances and make neighbours of people who only yesterday were remote from one another. Closely allied to the shrinkage of the planet is the emergence of what in some respects is a world culture. Civilization everywhere has been coming to have common features. These include machines, the scientific theories and processes which are closely allied with machines, nationalism, the trend towards socialism and democracy in one or another of their various forms, and the demand for universal primary education. Significantly, the immediate sources of the movements which have brought all mankind into close physical juxtaposition and of the outstanding features of the nascent world culture are to be found in the Occident, and the Occident has long been the main stronghold of Christianity, the major part of what traditionally has been called Christendom.

It is not surprising, therefore, that hand in hand with the spread of other features of the culture of the Occident, Christianity should be widely disseminated. That dissemination has not come automatically. Most of it has been achieved through the minority who have been deeply committed to the Christian faith. To be sure, much of it has been by emigration from Europe of those who have been Christians by heredity, but even of these the large majority have been Christians only in name and in the new environment have tended to drift away from the religious patterns of their fatherlands. It has been earnest Christians, usually from among the emigrants and their children, but sometimes missionaries from the mother countries who have kept the faith alive in the migrants as they have moved into a new setting. The spread of Christianity among non-Occidental peoples has been very infrequently through merchants or government officials from the Occident, but has been overwhelmingly by those giving their entire time as missionaries and by the converts of these missionaries. By whatever process, Christianity is today more widely distributed geographically and more deeply rooted among more peoples than it or any other faith has ever been.

By a strange and striking contrast, Christianity has never been as extensively challenged as in the mid-twentieth century. Not only have such traditional rivals as Islam, Hinduism, and Buddhism continued to prove resistant, but also, within "Christendom" great defections have been occurring and fresh rivals, sprung from Christendom, the chief of them Communism, have been spreading throughout the globe and have been threatening all historic religions, notably Christianity itself. Sometimes it seems that from Christianity have been issuing the forces of its own destruction.

It is against this background and from the coign of vantage which the present age affords that we will attempt to look backward and retell the history of Christianity from its beginning to our day.

Any history of Christianity, if it is to be comprehensive, must endeavour to survey the course of all the many features of the human story which can be traced in whole or even in part to Christ. We must strive to understand the fashion in which the impulses which issued from Christ have shaped the current of mankind's life.

Most of this will have to do with what we usually term Christianity. Christianity is a religion and as such is one of many religions. Its distinctive feature is that, as its name implies, it has Jesus Christ at its very heart. Yet Christianity is a synthesis of what the Christian regards as the Gospel, God's gift to man in Christ, and of the human response to it. Christianity centres about Christ but it is compounded of the faith, Judaism, from which Jesus sprang and which prepared the way for him; of Jesus himself, his birth, life, teachings, deeds, death, and resurrection; of the faith of his immediate disciples in him; and of the several aspects of the many environments into which it has moved.

Obviously a well-rounded account of the history of Christianity will narrate the story of its geographic spread, taking account of the forms of the faith which spread, the reasons for the expansion, and the methods, agents, and agencies through which the spread took place. Much of the history of Christianity will concern itself with the visible Church, the institutionalized fellowship, or, rather, the congeries of institutions which arose because of Christ. It must tell something of the character, the life, and the work of the outstanding creators and leaders of these institutions. It must narrate the story of the divisions within the Christian community and of the efforts to heal the divisions and to realize that unity in love which is of the essence of the Christian Gospel. It must cover the development of Christian thought, especially what is called doctrine, the attempts of Christians to give intellectual formulation to their faith. Such a survey must also recount the development of both corporate and private worship. It must tell of the means which Christians have used in their endeavour to live to the full the ideals of their faith and to encourage others to do so. To this end it must take cognizance of the methods and forms of instruction in the Christian faith, the course of Christian asceticism and mysticism both within and outside monastic movements, and the standards and processes of the discipline applied to their members by the churches. There must be accounts of some of the outstanding Christians, especially of those who have been regarded by their fellows as approaching the Christian ideal and of those who have been widely influential either within the Christian fellowship or outside it. A well-balanced narrative of the course of Christianity must also seek to disclose what the faith has meant to the rank and file of those who bear the Christian name and of those, unknown to wide fame, who in communities, most of them small and obscure, have been radiating centres of the faith. An inclusive history must say something of the effect of Christianity upon its environment, not alone individuals, although these are the goal and the test of the Christian Gospel, but also the many social and political institutions, movements, customs, and intellectual and emotional currents which shape individuals. Space must be assigned to the effect of the environment upon Christianity, for the two interact: Christianity both moulds and to some degree is moulded by the setting in which it operates.

If it is not to be distorted, the history of Christianity must include all the varieties of the faith. It must embrace not only those forms which have had a wide following, but also minority groups. It must mention not merely the numerous churches and movements which are features of the current scene in whatever part of the world they are found, but in addition those offshoots of Christianity which have disappeared.

From its very beginning, the course of Christianity must be viewed against the background of the entire human race. The necessity of this perspective should be obvious, yet often it has been ignored. Since Christians have claimed that Christ is essential to a comprehension of the meaning of history, since the outlook of Christianity is universal in its scope, and since from the outset the ideal has been set before the followers of Jesus of winning all men to his discipleship, the historian must ask how far that understanding and that dream have been realized. His canvass, therefore, must be all mankind from the beginning to the present. In every major stage of his narrative, he who would survey the history of Christianity must strive to view it in its global setting.

This means, for example, that in those chapters in which we are telling the story of the first five centuries of Christianity, when that faith was winning the professed allegiance of the peoples of the Roman Empire and was developing institutions, patterns of thought, and forms of worship which have been normative for the majority of Christians from that time to the present, we must make it clear that most of mankind, both civilized and uncivilized, was not as yet so much as touched by the Gospel and was not aware of even the name of Jesus Christ. In the twelfth and thirteenth centuries, a period to which many are inclined to look back as the heyday of Christianity, we must be aware of the frequently forgotten fact that Europe, where the faith had its stronghold, and especially Western Europe, where most of the vigour was displayed, was not even as prominent in the total world scene as the Roman Empire had been a thousand years earlier, and that the major centres of wealth, population, and civilization were elsewhere. In that relatively brief span from the fifteenth into the twentieth century, when so-called Christian peoples were spreading throughout the globe and were bringing most of the human race under their control, and when, in connexion with that expansion, Christianity was having the greatest geographic extension which it had thus far enjoyed, we must endeavour to take into account all the chief movements of the day, both within and without "Christendom."

This perspective does not entail a comprehensive history of mankind. A universal history might be written from the standpoint of the Christian faith. Indeed, it has repeatedly been essayed, never more notably than by Augustine in his *De Civitate Dei*. It does, however, mean that from the very outset the effort must be made to place the story of Christianity in the setting of universal history.

If the history of Christianity is surveyed with an awareness of the total human drama, much more attention must be accorded the past few centuries than has been usual in such accounts. During the past four hundred and fifty years and especially in the last century and a half, Christianity has been more influential in the life of the human race than at any previous time.

This is contrary to an impression which has wide currency. Generally it is assumed that Christianity has been waning since the Renaissance and especially since the eighteenth century. The secularism of the present age, the extensive and often spectacular defections from the faith in so-called Christendom which have occurred in the past two centuries, and the emergence of communism and other new challenges to Christianity have appeared to justify the dismissal of Christianity by many intellectuals as an interesting phenomenon which has had its day but is now dying. Even many Christians, among them some prominent in the churches, have shared in this appraisal and have occasionally spoken of the present as the "post-Christian era."

The picture is by no means so simple. It supports neither the pessimists nor the unqualified optimists. On the one hand are the adverse phases which undoubtedly exist and to which the prophets of gloom call attention. On the other hand are the wide geographic spread of Christianity, the many movements issuing from the faith, more numerous than in any other stretch of time of corresponding length and evidence of extraordinary vitality, and effects upon more branches of the human family than in any other period. If we are to seek to understand the fashion in which the Christian Gospel operates we must pay particular attention to these later centuries.

At the proper place we must take account of frankly anti-Christian interpretations of history and inquire into their significance. They have appeared within what has traditionally been known as Christendom and have entailed a repudiation of Christianity by much of the latter's hereditary constituency. The contrast between this trend and the fact that parallel with it Christianity has grown in influence in the world as a whole presents a seeming paradox in which there may be a clue to the correct understanding of history. It is partly because of the fact that in these later centuries this paradox, always present, has become especially vivid and has displayed itself on a world-wide scale that we must devote a large proportion of our space to the centuries which lie immediately back of us and particularly to the past four or five generations.

At the very outset we must notice the severe limitations under which all must labour who seek to recount the history of Christianity. We should be given pause by the warning in the Christian Scriptures that what from their viewpoint is the true perspective differs so radically from what is customary that to attain it requires a basic reorientation which is best described as a new birth. One of the ancient Hebrew prophets represents God as declaring: "My thoughts are not your thoughts, neither are my ways your ways. . . . As the heavens are higher than the earth so are my ways higher than your ways, and my thoughts than your thoughts." In the New Testament we find the forceful declaration on no less authority than that of Jesus himself that unless one receives it as a little child, learning afresh from the very beginning, he cannot enter the kingdom of God—that order in which God's will is known and done. Putting it even more bluntly, Jesus said that unless a man be born again, not only can he not enter into the kingdom of God but he cannot even see it, presumably meaning that he does not recognize it even when it is before his eyes. Similarly Jesus rejoiced that true insight had been hidden from the wise and the prudent and had been given to babes, and Paul insisted that God has made foolish the wisdom of this world and that through the wisdom of God the world through its wisdom has failed to know God. So contrary is the perspective given by the Gospel that those trained in the viewpoint of the Greeks tended scornfully to dismiss it as foolishness, and the Jews who were stoutly loyal to what they believed to be what God had given them in their national heritage were either puzzled or enraged by it.

All this would appear to mean that from the Christian standpoint those events, movements, and institutions which usually attract the attention of men and therefore find a place in the records of the past which survive are not nearly as significant as some which are scarcely noticed and of which either little or no trace remains or which, if it is there, is normally passed over by the historian. Yet it is to events and institutions which caught the eye, and to men and women who seemed important to their contemporaries that the historian is chiefly confined, even when he is aware that, judged by Christian standards, many of them are not as significant as others whose memory has so faded that when he seeks for them he cannot discover them.

Fortunately many individuals and movements have appealed to those whose insights have been born of their Christian faith. For them, accordingly, documents have been cherished. Because of their involvement in phases of the world about them which non-Christians deem important, some men and movements have been given a place in records made and preserved by those who did not sympathize with them. Then, too, many individuals and institutions which have borne the Christian name have compromised their Christian principles by mingling with the sub-Christian or anti-Christian world about them to such an extent that the latter has paid them the doubtful compliment of so noticing them that accounts of them have been kept.

Because of these factors, any history of Christianity, when viewed from the Christian perspective, while perhaps having something of true insight, cannot but be distorted and defective.

Moreover, even if his records gave all that he could desire and his own judgement were fully clarified by the Christian faith, the historian of Christianity would still be partly frustrated. Of the essence of his faith is the conviction that the Gospel was in the plan of God before He created man and thus before history began, and that the human drama, whether for individuals, for the Church, or for the race as a whole is not and cannot be complete within history, but moves on beyond this bourne of time and space. At best the historian can only record what has thus far occurred within history. If he could see in detail what is to come and what and when the culmination is to be he could venture on interpretation with greater assurance. As it is, the full pattern is not yet perceived and for much of it he can only offer conjectures. We are reminded that both knowledge and prophecy shall be done away and that now we see as in a mirror, darkly. A profound Christian conviction is that only faith, hope, and love endure. These can be a matter of history, but we cannot understand the past fully because not yet has history been completed nor the final outcome seen of that love which the Christian believes to be the dominant characteristic of God Who made all this vast universe and Who continues to work in it.

No one can hope to write history without presuppositions. The professional historian of the nineteenth and twentieth centuries has aspired to be "objective" and to tell "what actually happened." Yet every attempt to view the human story, whether in some small segment or as a whole, involves a selection of events from the stream which constitutes the crude stuff of history. Back of the selection is a conviction of what is important. Governing this "value judgement" is, consciously or unconsciously, a philosophy. Underneath and conditioning any endeavour to determine what happened also lies a theory of knowledge, epistemology, with attempts to answer such questions as: Can we know? If so how do we know? How valid and how complete is our knowledge? There have been and still are many theories of knowledge, many different answers to these questions. Many interpretations—"philosophies"—of history have been or are held. Some are basically agnostic, declaring that there may be no pattern in history, that if there is we cannot discover it, that all one can confidently affirm about the various philosophies of history is that we cannot know which if any of them is true, and that we cannot be too sure even of the validity of agnosticism. Others are cyclical, viewing history as endlessly repeating itself. Others affirm progress in one form or another. The view associated with the name of Hegel is one of thesis, antithesis, and synthesis, the synthesis becoming a new thesis, marked by a new antithesis, issuing in a fresh synthesis, and so onwards, a combination of cycles and progress. The Hegelian philosophy contributed to the emergence of the dialectical materialistic view of history. The Hindu has traditionally regarded history, like human life itself, as illusion. The nineteenth and twentieth century effort to determine what actually happened consciously or unconsciously has assumed that we can know what happened. In general, historians of the various schools of that period have believed that they could discover relationships between events—causes and effects. More and more they have assumed that history is universal, that the race has a common origin, that increasingly mankind has become one, that what affects the individual affects all, and that what the individual does concerns the whole.

Here is not the place to endeavor to determine which if any of the several philosophies is true, or even to seek for valid criteria by which they can be judged. That effort would necessitate a separate and large treatise. At the outset, however, we must say as clearly as we know how that underlying the pages which follow there is a profound conviction that the Christian Gospel is God's supreme act on man's behalf and that the history of Christianity is the history of what God has done for man through Christ and of man's response.

If it is complained that this is not an "objective" approach, it must be remembered that pure objectivity does not exist, even in the natural sciences. One is either for or against Christianity: there is no neutral or strictly "objective" ground. Reason has a legitimate place. We must employ it in testing what are presented to us as facts and in searching for other facts. But truth is not attained by reason alone. The insight that is born of faith can bring illumination. Faith is not credulity and if that which is called faith ignores reason it does so to its peril. But uncritical confidence in reason as the sole or final criterion is a blind act of credulity which may be even more dangerous than a faith which disdains reason. Throughout the chapters which follow is the conviction that the faith which is stimulated by contact with the Christian Gospel, the faith which is the commitment to God of the whole man, body, mind, and spirit, the commitment which is the response in love to God Who is love and Who in His love has revealed Himself in Jesus Christ, opens the mind towards the true understanding of history. That we fail to understand history is due to our lack of such a commitment. That we understand it partly but imperfectly arises from a commitment which is real but incomplete. No one of us has made a full commitment. If we are honest with ourselves we know how limited our commitment is. We should, therefore, never claim infallibility for our interpretation of history. Yet so far as the faith which follows commitment has been given to us, we must seek in its light to perceive the road which man has thus far traversed.

Limitations both in the records and in the historian are inescapable in narrating the history of Christianity. Yet we can attempt it, being aware in part of our handicaps. That is what is essayed in the work to which this is the preface.

In entering upon this adventure we must, as we have suggested, see the history of Christianity in its relation to the total story of mankind. We must endeavour to view it in the setting of human history as a whole. To segregate it from the rest of the course of mankind is to do it violence. Ours must be a purview as inclusive as all mankind and from the beginning to the present.

Obviously this purpose cannot be adequately fulfilled in one or two volumes: a multi-volume work would be too small for the total sweep of time and events. However, there may be some value in the effort to summarize the story within the compass of a few hundred pages and in doing so to bring into prominence the highlights in the record of Christianity. It is hoped that such a survey will prove useful to the thoughtful student, whether he be clergyman or layman, Christian or non-Christian, and that it will be helpful as a text-book in colleges, universities, and theological schools.

The main outline of the book can be quickly discerned by reference to the table of contents. It corresponds to what the author believes to be the main divisions of the Christian story.

First of all is a section made up of three chapters which attempts to place Christianity in its setting, to see it in the stream of history, to point out the particular currents in that stream from which it had its rise, and to describe the portion of the world in which it was born. Next is an account of the beginnings of Christianity. This must centre around Jesus. It may seem to be a banality to say that Christianity cannot be understood apart from him. Yet repeatedly through the centuries and in our own day there have been those who have regarded Jesus as unimportant in the origin and initial growth of Christianity. In contrast with this view, the author is convinced that without Jesus Christianity is not only unintelligible: it would never have been. The fashion in which Jesus Christ has shaped the faith which bears his name and the degree to which his professed followers have embodied him or departed from him never ceases to be both fascinating and significant.

After its origin, the course of Christianity is treated by what the author deems to have been its major epochs. These, as he conceives them, are best seen as pulsations in the life of Christianity as reflected in its vigour and its influence upon the ongoing history of the race. The criteria which he believes to be valid for discerning these pulsations are, in the main, three—the expansion or recession of the territory in which Christians are to be found, the new movements issuing from Christianity, and the effect of Christianity as judged from the perspective of mankind as a whole. Precise dates can seldom if ever be fixed for the pulsations. The lines between the eras are fuzzy. One age has a way of running over into its successor or of being foreshadowed before it is born. The eras are realities, but there are no sharp breaks between them which can be identified by particular years. Advance and retreat often begin at different times in the several areas in which Christians are found and the first indications of revival are frequently seen before decline has been halted. Terminal dates are, therefore, only approximations. Yet approximate dates can be named.

In treating each of these periods we will endeavour to sketch first of all the contemporary world setting in which Christianity was found, with special emphasis upon conditions in the areas in which Christianity was strong. We will tell of the geographic spread of the faith, inquiring into the forms of

Christianity through which the expansion was effected, the reasons for the expansion, and the processes by which the spread took place. If there were territorial losses we will seek to describe them, their causes, and their extent. We will take account of the new movements in the institutional expressions of the faith, and will give brief accounts of the individuals who were more prominent in the Christian story. We will summarize the developments in the thought of Christians about their faith, in forms of worship, and in the means employed to mould the Christian constituency. We will also attempt to say something of the effect of Christianity on its environment and note, in turn, the effect of the environment on Christianity. Not always will these aspects be treated in precisely the order in which they are arranged in this paragraph but in one way or another they will be covered.

The first period or pulsation embraces roughly the initial five centuries. Within these years Christianity won the professed allegiance of the large majority of the population of the Roman Empire. During that time the Church came into being and its visible, institutional expressions took the forms which in their main outlines still characterize the churches in which the majority of Christians have their membership. The several books which compose the New Testament were written and assembled. Other literature was produced. Christians wrestled with the intellectual problems presented by their faith and in consequence Christian theology came into being. The main formulations then hammered out, together with the creeds in which they were summarized, have continued to be standard. Monasticism arose and spread. Forms of worship developed which have had lasting effects. Christianity made a marked impression upon the civilizations of the Mediterranean Basin but this was not as deep or as striking as was that upon other cultures in later periods. In these five centuries only a small fraction of the earth's surface and a minority of mankind were touched by the faith. The large majority of civilized mankind and almost all the uncivilized portions of the human race were not even aware of it. In consequence, Christianity became so closely associated as almost to be identified with a cultural tradition which was only one among several and it was threatened by the possibility of being a regional rather than the universal faith.

Between A.D. 500 and A.D. 950 Christianity suffered the greatest losses which it has ever encountered. Its very existence was threatened. The decay of the empire and the culture with which its phenomenal successes in its first five hundred years had almost identified it seemed to presage its demise. Christianity's very victory appeared to have become its doom. The invasion of the Mediterranean world by non-Christians, notably by Islam-bearing Arabs, tore from Christianity approximately half the areas which had been gained in the preceding period. The morale of the Christian communities declined to their lowest ebb. The story was not altogether one of loss. Additional peoples were brought to accept the faith, and outposts were established from Ireland to China and from Scotland and Scandinavia to Nubia. Some important developments occurred within the churches. Yet never again since those long, agonizing centuries has the prospect for Christianity appeared to be so bleak.

There followed, from A.D. 950 to A.D. 1350, four centuries of advance. The area across which Christianity was carried expanded. More significantly, striking developments occurred within the churches, the Christian faith produced outstanding personalities and important movements in thought and organization, and it helped to bring into being new cultures, notably in Western Europe.

Between A.D. 1350 and A.D. 1500 a decline was witnessed. Much territory was lost and disorganization and corruption appeared in the churches. Yet the recession was neither as prolonged nor as severe as the one between A.D. 500 and A.D. 950. A larger proportion of the territory covered was retained, a few advances into fresh areas were achieved, and vigorous movements issued from Christianity which were indications of vitality.

The two and a half centuries between A.D. 1500 and A.D. 1750 constituted an amazing epoch. A series of awakenings revitalized and largely altered the Christianity of Western Europe. That segment of the globe was entering a new era and Christianity had an important share in modifying the culture which emerged. To a less but still important extent changes were seen in some aspects of Eastern Christianity. Explorations, conquests, and intrepid missionaries carried Christianity over a larger proportion of the earth's surface than had previously been true of it or of any other religion.

From A.D. 1750 to A.D. 1815 a series of events and movements again menaced Christianity. The decay of Spain and Portugal, strong champions of the faith in the preceding two-and-a-half centuries, fresh intellectual movements, and a succession of wars and revolutions in Europe and America appeared to many to be about to bring Christianity to an end. However, viewed in retrospect, the years were more a pause than a recession. There were few actual losses of territory, and new movements, too small at their inception to attract general attention, were appearing and were later to bring Christianity to a new high level of vigour.

The century from A.D. 1815 to A.D. 1914 presented striking contrasts. Western civilization was again moving into a new age. Many of the forces which were moulding that civilization were either openly or tacitly hostile to Christianity. The faith was threatened in its chief strongholds. But new life in Christianity swelled to a flood. This was especially marked in the form of Christianity, Protestantism, which had come into being as recently as the sixteenth

century. It was also seen in what long had been the most active segment of
Christianity, the Roman Catholic Church. Christianity continued to be potent
in Occidental culture and among Occidental peoples. To an important degree
the Occident was still Christendom. Even more than between A.D. 1500 and
A.D. 1750 Christianity spread over the surface of the globe. It was an integral
feature of the new nations which were created by European peoples in the
Americas and Australasia. Especially through its share in shaping the United
States of America Christianity gained in the total world scene. For the first
time Christianity really penetrated Africa south of the Sahara and many of the
islands of the Pacific. It had an enlarging rôle in Asia. The fresh life within
Christianity had many expressions in various lands and wrought significant
changes in that religion. The faith also continued to shape the Occident and
had effects of varying importance upon the peoples and cultures to which it
was being carried.

The period which had its inception in A.D. 1914 and is still incomplete constitutes the latest division of our story. In spite of colossal threats and striking
losses, Christianity has moved forward. Never before at any one time have all
cultures been so shaken. The revolutions have centred in what was once termed
Christendom. Indeed, there is some reason for regarding them as the fruit,
directly or indirectly, of Christianity. Yet for the first time Christianity is
becoming really world-wide. It is entering into the lives of more peoples than
it or any other religion has ever done. Into the new and often terrifying stage
into which the human race, bewildered, is being ushered, Christianity is more
potent than in any earlier era. It is by no means dominant. Never has that
adjective been an accurate description of its place in the human scene. However, when the world is surveyed as a whole, it is more to be reckoned with
than at any previous time. It is an important factor in the world culture which
appears to be emerging.

Readers of *A History of the Expansion of Christianity* will be inclined to
regard the present work as a summary of the earlier one. The chronological pattern, already familiar to them through its volumes, will seem to confirm them
in that impression. Inevitably much that the author learned in the writing of
that survey has been carried over into the present one. But the book which
follows is by no means a condensation of its larger predecessor. It has a quite
different purpose. The one, as its title indicates, is an account of the spread of
Christianity. The chapters which follow endeavour to be a well-rounded
summary of the entire history of Christianity in all its phases and in its setting
in the human scene. In them expansion must have a place and at times be
prominent. However, it is only one aspect of a larger whole. It is a fresh effort
upon which we are embarked.

A bibliography will be attached to each chapter, usually with brief appraisals of the various titles cited. These bibliographies are by no means complete or exhaustive. To make them such would extend the book beyond all reasonable dimensions. Indeed, it would mean multiplying the work into many volumes, for the published material on the history of Christianity is enormous, and that in manuscript is even more extensive. What is attempted, rather, is a selection of the works which the reader or the student who wishes to go further in some of the subjects covered in the text may employ as references and as guides. Several of the books listed are original sources, or as near to original sources as can be obtained. More are secondary accounts based upon the sources or upon other secondary works. The larger proportion are in English, for this study is designed primarily for those who read that language. However, many are in other languages, partly because of their outstanding importance and partly because this book may be translated into other tongues and those who have it in those forms will not wish their reference material confined to English. Not every study consulted by the author in the preparation of this work has been listed. The author has, however, personally examined all those whose titles have been included in the bibliographies and the appraisals given are his own.

Specialists will probably wish that a larger documentation had been given for subjects in which they are particularly interested and may differ both from the estimates of individual books and from the presentation which has been made of the topics in which they are experts. The author can lay no claim to infallibility. He has attempted to avail himself of the best of the books, monographs, and articles of the specialists, to examine a fair proportion of the original sources, and by their use to make his pages as factually accurate as possible. He is painfully conscious, however, that he has not covered more than a small fraction of the pertinent material and that errors have almost certainly crept into what he has written. In questions of judgement and interpretation, moreover, many will almost certainly challenge much that is here put down. The author can only hope that what he has written will prove of some use to both general readers and specialists. He trusts that his survey may enable some who come after him to tell the story of Christianity with more accuracy and with greater insight than he has been able to command.

The author would express his gratitude to the many to whom he and this work are deeply indebted—to the thousands of scholars who have preceded him and from whose labours he has gleaned much of whatever of value these pages may contain, to students who have patiently submitted to having the material presented to them and by their questions have added much illumination, and to colleagues in Yale University and in many another institution of higher learning who have contributed of their knowledge. To no small degree they are in reality co-authors, although few if any of their exact words have been quoted. The title page would be quite too small to include all their names.

As again and again across the years, the author owes an incalculable debt to Mrs. Charles T. Lincoln for typing the manuscript and for suggestions in matters of style.

The author craves the privilege of dedicating this book to his colleagues, past and present, of the Yale University Divinity School. It seems almost invidious to single out any from that goodly company for special mention, for each has contributed, usually quite unwittingly, to these pages. However, the author is peculiarly under obligation to the three Deans under whom he has worked—Charles R. Brown, Luther A. Weigle, and Liston Pope—to Williston Walker, who first introduced him to the history of Christianity as a subject for serious study and whose writings have been of great assistance, to Roland H. Bainton, whose friendship and high standards of scholarship have been a continued inspiration and on whose vast erudition this book has again and again drawn, to Robert L. Calhoun, from whom the author has gained not a little of such knowledge of the history of Christian doctrine as he possesses, and to Raymond P. Morris, who as Librarian of the Yale University Divinity School has not only shown extraordinary skill and judgement in assembling and making accessible the pertinent literature but has also been unfailingly generous and wise in this counsel.

The author needs scarcely add that none of these many friends is to be held accountable for any errors which the book may contain or for any omissions of which it may be guilty.

REFORM AND EXPANSION
A.D. 1500 — A.D. 1750

[Chapter 29]

RETROSPECT AND PROSPECT

At the middle of the fifteenth century the civilized world and with it Christianity were being ushered into a new age. The Mongol Empire, which for nearly a century had been ruling the heart-land of Eurasia, was breaking up. With its disappearance the caravan routes across Asia became more insecure and China all but closed her doors to the outside world. Near the end of the century a Mongol, Timur (Tamerlane), was laying waste much of Central and Western Asia. The Ottoman Turks were building a huge realm, in 1453 overwhelmed the Byzantine Empire and established their capital at Constantinople, and threatened to engulf part or all of Western Europe. In Western Europe, where Christianity now had its main stronghold, the medieval structure of society and its associated culture were beginning to pass.

These changes brought heavy geographical losses to Christianity and confronted it with grave challenges. The Christian minorities which on the eve of 1350 had been found across Asia either shrank or disappeared. By 1500 Christianity was scarcely even a memory in China and Central Asia; in India it survived, but only in small, encysted minorities; and in Western Asia, including what had been an early major centre of the faith, Asia Minor, the Christian communities declined. The headquarters of Greek Orthodox Christianity, Constantinople, was in the hands of Moslem rulers and Saint Sophia, the main cathedral of that wing of the faith, had been converted into a mosque. The eastern shores of the Mediterranean, where once had been the chief scenes of Christian thought and activity, were ruled by Moslems. Of the five historic patriarchal sees of the Catholic Church, Jerusalem, Antioch, Alexandria, Constantinople, and Rome, all but the last were now under the Crescent.

Even in Western Europe, where those who professed the Christian faith remained politically in the ascendant, the threat was sobering. The institutions which had been erected as bulwarks of the faith—monasteries, the clergy, and especially the Papacy—were honeycombed with corruption. The populations remained nominally Christian, but in Italy, where was the administrative centre of the Western wing of the Catholic Church, Christian morality was widely flaunted and the intellectual currents, associated as they were with a revived admiration of pre-Christian art and literature, appeared to be setting in against the faith. The emerging nation-states were threatening even the imperfect unity in the Christian community which had been attained under the Holy Roman Empire and the Church of Rome. The Church had been associated with feudalism and a predominantly rural culture. Feudalism was passing and cities were growing. It was not at all clear that the Church could adjust itself to the new order and win it. It might slowly fade with the disappearance of the kind of society which it had earlier penetrated and with which it had become identified. Moreover, the tenuous bonds which held together the Western and Eastern branches of the Catholic Church had at last been severed. Christian unity, never all-inclusive, suffered further disruption.

Yet the losses were not as great nor was the prospect as grim as they had been during the great recession between the end of the fifth and the middle of the tenth century. Although over most of Asia the Christian communities died out, east of Mesopotamia they had never been more than small minorities. In contrast with that earlier period when about half of what might be called Christendom became subject to Moslems and the churches in it slowly withered, after 1350 the main body of Christendom remained. While the territorial gains were not as extensive nor ultimately as significant as had been those between 500 and 950, some advances were registered, notably in Russia, Lithuania, and against the Moslems in Spain.

Even more important was the vitality displayed within the churches. The vigorous monastic movements in Russia were evidence that in that land the Greek Orthodox form of the faith was not only firmly rooted but was sending out fresh shoots. Although in Western Europe no theological activity appeared which for depth and originality could compare with that of the Middle Ages and no new monastic orders came into being which for numbers and the impression made on the region equalled such earlier movements as the Benedictines, Cluniacs, Cistercians, Franciscans, and Dominicans, the period was by no means sterile. Christian mysticism was widespread and was probably more varied and perhaps richer than at any previous time. There were numerous attempts, some of them successful, at monastic reform. New communities, notably the Brethren of the Common Life and the Hieronymites, came into being. In Spain a wave of reform spread to much of the Church and Vincent Ferrer brought his fervour to thousands in that land, France, and Italy. In several countries preaching seems to have increased and to have reached more people than before. Humanism was being captured by the Christian faith. Wyclif and the Lollards, Hus and the Hussites were evidence that the faith was becoming the conscious property of thousands in England and Bohemia and was not being passively received from the South as had previously been the case. Catherine of Siena, Catherine of Genoa, and Savonarola were the most prominent among many who were proof that even in Italy, where Christian morality was widely flouted, the Christian faith was very much alive. In many places the Gospel was stirring the masses. A ground swell was appearing which in the sixteenth century was to become a flood tide. Under the impulse of that tide in the next two and a half centuries Christianity was to create new as well as to utilize old expressions and was to have a greater geographic expansion than it or any other religion had thus far displayed.

Chapter 30

CHRISTIANITY FROM A.D. 1500 TO A.D. 1750: THE WORLD SETTING

Not far from 1500 Christianity found itself in a new and rapidly changing world which faced it with as great a challenge as it had thus far known. Challenge in the face of what seemed overwhelming odds was not a new experience. The most widely used symbol of the Christian faith was the cross and until Easter morn broke, the cross seemed to mean stark defeat and complete frustration. Even after Easter and Pentecost had nerved the disciples to go forward, they were a small and obscure minority confronted with hostile and powerful competitors. When the majority of the population of the Roman Empire had been won, though to a largely uncomprehending and superficial allegiance, that realm was disintegrating. The slow death of the culture and state with which it had come to be identified and the accompanying incursions of non-Christian peoples, some of them bearers of a new and aggressive faith, Islam, meant for Christianity the strong possibility of extinction. Christianity survived, and, winning some of the most unpromising of the invaders, those from Northern Europe, became a major factor in the emergence of a new civilization, that of Western Europe, and was carried clear across the largest of the continental land masses, Eurasia. Then, in the fourteenth and fifteenth centuries, political changes extinguished Christianity in most of Asia and confined it almost entirely to Europe. In South-eastern Europe a resurgent Islam brought Christian communities under Moslem rulers and menaced the independence of Western Europe. In Western Europe the stage of civilization with which Christianity had been interwoven, seemingly inextricably, was passing and the ecclesiastical structure which Christians had developed was shot through and through with dry rot and inefficiency and appeared to be an anachronism. Yet vigorous life was making itself felt and was mounting. Past experience gave ground for hope that, far from perishing, Christianity would rise to the challenge of the new age and go forward. However, partly because the challenge differed substantially from the earlier ones, precedent was no infallible proof that it would be met.

In the sixteenth century the situation which confronted Christianity was compounded of several elements, some of them with parallels in the past, but others of them quite new. The chief old ones were the continuation of the Turkish invasion and the passing in Western Europe of what was known as the culture of the Middle Ages. For over a thousand years Christianity had been menaced by the invasions of non-Christian peoples and for over eight hundred years the most serious of these had been by peoples who held to Islam. Grave though it was, the advance of the Turks did not constitute a completely fresh problem. In the disintegration of a culture with which it had been closely associated Christianity was faced by what had become a familiar phenomenon. That had been seen in connexion with the decay of the Roman Empire and the Græco-Roman world. Moreover, the main features of the new order which was succeeding the medieval structure of Western Europe had begun to appear before the sixteenth century and had been among the causes of the recession of the fourteenth and fifteenth centuries.

Although in broad general terms the chief aspects of the new stage of Western civilization had become familiar by the beginning of the sixteenth century, some of the developments of these aspects were novel. Moreover, they were of prime importance for Europe and so for Christianity.

One group of developments came in connexion with the emergence of nationalism. We have seen that beginning at least as early as the fourteenth century nation states were beginning to threaten the partial unity which had been achieved in Western Europe under the Papacy and the Holy Roman Empire. In the sixteenth, seventeenth, and eighteenth centuries nationalism and nation states, the latter under absolute monarchs, became the prevailing pattern in the European political scene and affected other facets, including the religious, of the life of the area. National consciousness and particularism were augmented by the rise of literatures in the vernacular and the decline in the use of Latin as the language common to the educated.

In the sixteenth century outstanding among the nation states was Spain. Portugal, England, France, Sweden, and Russia were also prominent. Nationalism was present in Germany and Italy, but it was not sufficiently potent to bring about the political unification of these countries. Instead, each was divided into many units and remained so until the nineteenth century and was a prey to its more nearly consolidated neighbours. By the seventeenth century Spain and Portugal were waning and France was forging to the fore. Under Louis XIV, who came to the throne in 1643, assumed full charge in 1661, and reigned until his death in 1715, France was the strongest power in Western

Europe. Austria under the Hapsburgs was also prominent, partly as the heir of whatever prestige still clung to the fading ghost of the Holy Roman Empire. England was growing in importance, but chiefly on the seas and in colonial possessions. In the seventeenth century Russia recovered from her "Time of Trouble" and under the leadership of the Romanovs, one of whom, Michael, was elected Tsar in 1613, began to expand its territories. Late in the seventeenth century Peter the Great ascended the throne and not only enhanced the authority of the Tsar and continued the expansion of the realm, but also gave the land a Western European orientation. In the seventeenth and eighteenth centuries the Hohenzollerns made their possessions, under the name of Brandenburg and then of Prussia, a major Western European power.

In each of these states, and also in several of lesser might, the monarchs sought, with varying degrees of success, to control the Church. In some this entailed separation from Rome. In others communion with Rome was maintained but the administrative functions of the Papacy were markedly reduced. In all it meant an attempt to harness Christianity to the state and to render it ancillary to government and the purposes of the monarch. This, it is almost needless to say, was a major threat, for if successful it would pervert or stifle the true genius of the Gospel. Moreover, the nation states were chronically at war with one another and war was destructive not only of the unity among its adherents which was the essence of Christianity, but also of many of the other values for which the faith stood. Could the "power" overcome these handicaps and make itself effective in this new age?

Another group of developments which followed the passing of Western Europe from its Middle Ages into a fresh stage of culture was the striking enlargement of the world of the men of that area. In a very real sense this was an outgrowth of the Renaissance and humanism. It arose in connexion with that confidence of man in his powers which characterized these movements. Like them, it seems to have been in some degree an outgrowth of the trust in the orderliness and dependability of nature and the discipline given the spirit and mind of Western Europeans through the Christian faith.

The amazing development of scientific theory and method and through it the extension of knowledge, chiefly of the physical universe, can here be only high-lighted. Gradually there spread the realization, associated with the name of the Polish cathedral canon, canon lawyer, and physician, Koppernigk (1473–1543), better known by its Latinized form, Copernicus, that the earth is not the centre of the universe, but, with other planets, revolves around the sun. Kepler (1571–1630), trained for the Christian ministry, turned reluctantly to astronomy and, accepting the Copernican view of the solar system, did much to ascertain the orbits of the planets and contributed significantly to mathematics, including infinitesimal mathematics. Not far from the same time Galileo Galilei (1564-1642), educated at first in a monastery, eventually made major contributions to physical science in the discovery of the isochronism of the pendulum, the hydrostatic balance, the first principles of dynamics, and the fact that the path of a projectile is a parabola. He acquired notoriety by his pioneer use of the telescope in astronomy and his espousal of the Copernican theory. Francis Bacon (1561-1626), a contemporary of Kepler and Galileo, did much to shape the procedures of later natural science by stressing the importance of the observation of facts as the basis for conclusions.

A little later Thomas Hobbes (1588-1679), son of an Anglican clergyman, an Oxford graduate, a warm admirer of Galileo, and an amanuensis of Bacon, while outwardly conforming to the Church of England, revolted against scholastic philosophy. He was deeply interested in mathematics and physical science, but made no major contribution to them. Yet his philosophy tended to base knowledge upon what we learn through natural science. Popularly regarded as an atheist, he held that man can form no idea of God and that the state must decide religious issues. He stimulated thought on ethics and the study of society and government.

The somewhat younger Descartes (1596-1650), a devout Roman Catholic, in his intellectual processes methodically doubted everything. To him doubt entailed thought and thought implied a thinker. Accordingly he arrived at his basic conviction, *Cogito, ergo sum*—"I think, therefore I am." Beginning on that foundation, he argued for the existence of God as the supremely perfect Being. Contending that God would not deceive the beings whom He created, he held that our senses give us true insights into the world about us. His method and basic principles had a profound effect upon later Western philosophy. He was also a mathematician of note and was a pioneer in analytical and algebraic geometry. Slightly later than Descartes was John Locke (1632-1704). He regarded himself a Christian, but was the founder of English empiricism. His *Essay on the Human Understanding* was influential in stimulating thought and discussion on the certainty and adequacy of human knowledge and his *Treatises on Government* were important in political science.

Isaac Newton (1642-1727), deeply religious, made major contributions in mathematics, in his formulation of the "law" of gravitation, and in his "laws" of motion. Newton's contemporary, Leibnitz (1646-1716), philosopher and mathematician, elaborated differential calculus, a field in which Newton also claimed to have been an originator. Pascal (1623-1662), older than either Newton or Leibnitz but living on into their youth, will appear later in our pages because of his earnest Christian faith. A distinguished and original mathematician, he markedly furthered the development of calculus and, partly through novel experimentation, was one of the founders of hydrodynamics.

Through these and others man's horizons were enormously enlarged. The knowledge so acquired and the thought so formulated were spread by the growing use of the printing press. On many the effect was intoxicating and man seemed competent to achieve full understanding of the unimaginably vast universe in which he found himself and to bend that knowledge to his own use.

This growth of science and through it man's knowledge and mastery of his physical environment, then only in their incipient stages, were to attain colossal dimensions in the nineteenth and twentieth centuries. Although they were to no small degree the outgrowth of the Christian faith and were in large part the work of devout Christians, they brought a major threat to Christianity. The threat was that men might regard Christianity as untenable or irrelevant— untenable because it appeared to be contrary to reason or unsupported by it, and irrelevant because what men esteemed as the chief goods, namely, food, clothing, shelter, knowledge, and æsthetic enjoyment, were, so they thought, to be acquired through other channels.

Here was not only threat, but also challenge. Could Christians bring all of these new tools to the service of their faith? Could they, in seeking "first the kingdom of God and His righteousness," render the expanding knowledge and the material wealth which came through them ancillary to the "kingdom of God" and contributory to the welfare of man as the Gospel set it forth?

Closely connected with the expanding vistas into the universe which characterized the new age into which the major part of "Christendom" was entering were breath-taking geographic discoveries and conquests by peoples bearing the Christian name. The Americas were disclosed to Europeans and in part reduced to subjection. The coasts of Africa were traversed, the Philippines were conquered, and trading posts were established on the southern and eastern shores of Asia and in the East Indies. The Russians moved across northern Asia to the Pacific. Colonial empires were carved out by European peoples. The largest of these were held by Spain, Portugal, Russia, and, in the latter part of the period, by England, France, and the Netherlands. Never before had so much of the earth's surface been penetrated and controlled by any one group of mankind.

Here again a major contributory factor was the Christian faith. One of the declared motives of Columbus was the conversion of the peoples whom he might discover and he recorded that it was his faith in God which enabled him to persevere on his first trip across the Atlantic when his men would have turned back. Prince Henry the Navigator, who was the directing mind and will of expeditions which after his death carried the Portuguese around the

Cape of Good Hope to India, was an ardently religious man, Grand Master of the Order of Christ, who had a passion for the spread of the Christian faith as well as a desire for trade and allies against the hereditary foe, the Moslem. Magellan, who led the first expedition to circumnavigate the globe, had a marked zeal for propagating Christianity.

As in the growth of science, here were both threat and challenge. Here was threat because the professed Christians who carried through the explorations, commerce, and settlements were tempted to succumb to the lure of wealth and to exploit for their selfish ends the peoples with whom they came in contact. Indeed, most of them were obsessed with the passion for gain and brought in thrall many of the native peoples. The African slave trade was stimulated by the demand for cheap labour for the mines and plantations of the New World. It inflicted untold suffering upon millions, both in Africa and the Americas, and brutalized the masters. Yet Christians were challenged to bring their faith to the vast regions which were opened by them and to devise measures to eliminate the exploitation of non-Europeans and make the coming of the European a blessing and not a curse.

Due partly to the geographic discoveries, commerce, wealth, and cities continued to grow in Western Europe. The guilds by which industry and commerce had been organized declined, chartered joint stock companies came into being as a growing means for the conduct of business, and capitalism increased. Larger vessels were built and bulkier cargoes were carried. The growth of commerce and cities brought into prominence the *bourgeoisie,* a distinct and class-conscious group. The *bourgeoisie* often combined with the king to curb the power of the landed nobility. They were increasingly influential, and their distinctive mentality and customs modified the total social structure. Could Christianity permeate the economic life and the kind of society which were emerging?

Political changes in the largest bodies of population made more difficult the access of the Christian faith to the majority of mankind. The Ottoman Empire, dominant throughout this period in the Balkans, Greece, much of Southern Russia, all of Western Asia, and most of the north shore of Africa, effectively blocked efforts to win the peoples of these areas. China was under the rule of dynasties, first the Ming and then the Manchus under the official name of Ch'ing, which disdained or feared foreigners and made extensive Christian missionary effort all but impossible. In India the sixteenth century witnessed the founding of a regime by the Moslem Moguls which eventually extended over much of the country and which was not favourable to Christian missions. By the early part of the seventeenth century the rulers of Japan closed their country against Europeans with the express purpose of preventing the growth of the Christian communities which missionaries had brought into existence on the islands. Almost all the thickly populated portions of Asia were more nearly sealed against the spread of Christianity than they had been in the centuries before 1350 and some were more nearly barred than they had been before the sixteenth century.

In spite of all the threats and the obstacles, in the sixteenth and succeeding centuries Christians had the opportunity to influence with their faith a larger proportion of the earth's surface than at any previous time. The Americas and Siberia were relatively empty and in them were begun settlements which in succeeding generations were to grow until populations of European stock were to be dominant numerically and culturally. Here was the possibility of building new communities which would be Christian. Moreover, in the nineteenth and twentieth centuries Occidental civilization was to be carried to all quarters of the globe and all peoples were to seek to adopt the fruits and with them the methods of the science of the Occident. In other words, a civilization in the shaping of which Christianity had had a large part was now beginning to spread across the planet. Of that spread as well as of that civilization Christianity was in part the responsible cause. Would Christianity be sufficiently vigorous to continue to mould that civilization? Would it have the vitality to hold the allegiance and deepen the understanding commitment of those who went from "Christendom" to these new outposts of the Occident and to win the peoples who were now brought in contact with it, many of them for the first time? Could it convey the Gospel so persuasively that all men would respond? Or, if not all men, would minorities in every people and nation accept the Christian faith, begin to display evidences of the working of "the exceeding greatness of his power," and become effective centres of contagion among their fellows?

At the outset of the sixteenth century the prospects for the triumphant course of Christianity in face of this opportunity appeared to be far from encouraging. Christians were more divided than they had been for centuries and therefore less able to act in consort to meet the challenge. The churches in the East, the Christian communities nearest geographically to the vast aggregations of the civilized peoples of Asia who constituted the large majority of mankind, were subjects of the Moslems and were either dwindling or were on the defensive and only barely holding their own. In North-eastern Europe Russian Christianity had still to win many of the peoples and was only beginning to emerge from the Moslem Mongol yoke and to give evidence that it was possessed of a vigour which was not dependent upon the traditional connexion with Constantinople. In Western Europe the ecclesiastical structure of the Roman Catholic Church and the monasteries and orders from which heretofore had come most of the missionaries were, with striking exceptions, at a low spiritual and moral ebb.

The informed and thoughtful Christian might well be appalled and discouraged as he looked into the near and far future. The faith which he professed had never succeeded in bringing fully to its standards any people or, indeed, any individual. Even Paul had confessed that he had not yet attained and across the centuries even those who were regarded as saints, when measured by "the high calling of God in Christ Jesus," quite obviously were far from perfect. Great losses had been recently experienced in Asia where minorities scattered across the reaches of that continent, potential centres for the spread of the faith in that area of the most populous regions and seemingly highest civilizations of mankind, had either disappeared or had become encysted, effectively estopped from expanding. In Western Europe, where was to be found the largest body of Christians, the leadership of the Church was predominantly selfish and the attempt at reform through general councils had failed. Now Christianity, especially the Christianity of Western Europe, was confronted with a new age and problems which were complicated by fresh movements, some of them indifferent or even covertly hostile to the faith, and by the beginnings of a geographic expansion which challenged Christians with new vistas and ever more complex situations while they seemed to be losing out at home. Always on the south-eastern horizon, moreover, was the aggressive Turk, champion of the religion which had wrested more territory from Christianity than had any other, with an empire stronger than any of the diminutive kingdoms which supported the Christian cause, and against which a hopelessly divided and chronically warring Europe was unable to unite. The problems confronting Christians were more complex and had assumed larger dimensions than ever before. They seemed quite to dwarf the feeble men who had to face them.

However, there was ground for encouragement. Indications of vitality in Christianity were by no means lacking. These were numerous and widespread, especially in Western Europe, the area in which the most striking developments were taking place, and from which most of the geographic explorations were being made and the majority of the colonial empires were being constructed. We noted them earlier (Chapter 28) and saw that they were a kind of ground swell.

From this ground swell, as we have hinted, was to issue a high tide in the course of Christianity. Great awakenings were to emerge from the vitality inherent in the Christian faith. They were to transform hundreds of thousands of individual lives, place their stamp on civilization, and inspire a geographic expansion of the faith which for extent was unequalled in the previous history of mankind. To these awakenings we now turn.

Chapter 31

THE GREAT AWAKENINGS OF THE SIXTEENTH AND SEVENTEENTH CENTURIES: INCLUSIVE GENERALIZATIONS

The next tide of the pulsing life in Christianity reached its height in the sixteenth and seventeenth centuries. The dates 1500 and 1750 are somewhat arbitrary. As we have seen, the ground swell which issued in it began well before 1500. In places the tide had passed its flood before 1750 and in at least one country, England, was moving forward again before that peak. Yet these round numbers approximately mark respectively the beginning of the onward surge and the time when its retreat became marked.

In the main the tide had three major aspects, two of them in Western Europe and one in Russia. The two in Western Europe were closely connected and, indeed, were related although seemingly contradictory forms of the same movement. They were the Protestant Reformation and the Catholic Reformation. That in Russia was almost entirely independent of the other two.

It is significant that all three phases were in areas under ostensibly Christian governments and politically independent of non-Christian rulers. They were in territories which had not been submerged by the Moslem wave which had reached a fresh crest in the fourteenth and fifteenth centuries.

Moreover, they were in the regions from which the discoveries, growth in commerce, and colonial empire-building were to come during the same era. With some striking exceptions, they were to be most marked in the lands which were to lead in this advance and roughly synchronized with the peak in other forms of creative vigour in those countries. Thus Spain was the earliest to feel the full impact of the Catholic Reformation, and the height of the Spanish reformation coincided with the period when that realm was the foremost European state in military might and in territorial expansion in the New World and had her chief painters, authors, and scholars. So, too, in France the

Catholic Reformation reached its crest about the time when French hegemony was attained in Western Europe, in England the Protestant Reformation roughly paralleled advances in commerce, the beginnings of overseas colonization, and unprecedented activity in thought and literature, and in Russia the most stirring religious movements were when that country was recovering from its Time of Trouble, was experiencing the rise of the monarchy which was to rule it until the second decade of the twentieth century, and was pressing across Siberia to the Pacific. How far the connexion was causal we cannot know. That the different aspects of national life partly stimulated one another is certain. But to what extent if at all one was the cause of the others or to what degree all are traceable to a common outburst of vitality whose source we can only conjecture we cannot be sure.

We will first describe the course of events in Western Europe and from there move on to Russia, adding brief comments on the other Eastern Churches. We will then summarize the story of the spread of Christianity beyond the borders of Europe and say something of the effect of Christianity on the world of that day.

Before we embark upon an account of the Protestant Reformation and the Catholic Reformation there are inclusive generalizations and contrasts which are of major importance and which might escape us were we to allow ourselves to be submerged in details.

One of these we have already mentioned, but it is of such importance that we must again call attention to it. The Protestant and the Catholic Reformation were two phases of one movement. Both sought to cleanse the Church and to bring it to a closer approximation to the Christian ideal.

A second generalization, closely related to the first, is that they differed as to the fashion in which this was to be accomplished. The Catholic Reformation insisted that it be done within the existing patterns of the Roman Catholic Church. It strove for the thorough and basic moral transformation of both clergy and laity. It endeavoured to bring all Christians to a more intelligent appreciation of the essential Christian teachings, to foster the life of prayer, to encourage service to others, and to carry the Gospel to all men. However, in doing this it would avoid any changes in doctrine, and would merely make more precise what Catholics believed that the Church had always taught. It saw in communion with the Church of Rome and its bishop, the Pope, the assurance of the maintenance of the faith as given by Christ and transmitted through his apostles. While the rising nationalism markedly curtailed the administrative control of the Pope over the Roman Catholic Church, there was no separation from him on matters of dogma. The historic hierarchy was preserved and strengthened. The sacraments were treasured as they had been defined and administered through the Catholic Church of the West. Monasticism was prized as a road to the Christian ideal. Old monastic orders were recalled to their pristine standards and new ones came into being. Some of the latter assumed novel forms, but they were clearly in the monastic tradition.

In contrast, in varying degrees Protestants broke with the Church of Rome. All rejected the authority of the Pope, although some would have been willing to accept him as *primus inter pares* among the bishops. Many preserved the hierarchy without the Pope. Even more held to the Apostles' and Nicene Creeds. All esteemed the Scriptures authoritative, but none would concede to the Pope the right to give interpretations to the Scriptures which would be binding on all Christians. Almost all observed baptism and the Lord's Supper, but few or none kept all the seven sacraments. Although in the nineteenth century it was to be revived in the Anglican Communion, at the outset all rejected monasticism.

A third generalization is that the geographic line of demarcation between those who adhered respectively to the Protestant and Catholic Reformation in part coincided with the boundaries of the Roman Empire. In the main, with important exceptions which we are to note in a moment, those lands which had been assimilated to Latin culture before the sixth century remained loyal to the Church of Rome. This was true of Italy, Spain, Portugal, and to a large degree, although not so overwhelmingly, of France and Austria. In regions which had been on the borders of the Roman Empire, as in the Low Countries, the Rhine Valley, Switzerland, and the upper reaches of the Danube, and where conformity to Latin culture had not proceeded as far as in these other lands, both Protestantism and Roman Catholicism were represented. It seems significant that in the Low Countries the southern sections, where Latin culture had penetrated, remained Roman Catholic, while in the northern portions, where the rule of the Roman Empire had sat lightly if at all, Protestantism prevailed.

The island of Great Britain might appear not to bear out this generalization, for England had been within the Roman Empire for more than four centuries. But the exception appears to prove the rule. The region had never been thoroughly assimilated to Latin culture and the barbarian invasions of the fifth and subsequent centuries had fairly well erased whatever there was of it.

Other lands which seem to invalidate this identification of the post-Reformation Roman Catholic Church with Latin Europe immediately come to mind. Ireland, Poland, and Lithuania had never been within the Roman boundaries. Bohemia had been only on the border, and whatever of Latin culture it may have had presumably had disappeared in the welter of the Slav occupation. Yet all these countries came through the era of the Protestant Reformation predominantly Roman Catholic. In each, special reasons accounted for that fact. In Ireland, since the English overlords were Protestant, their Irish subjects clung to the Roman Catholic Church as a faith and institution which was distinctly their own, a badge and tie of their national particularism. In Poland contributory factors seem to have been opposition to the Germans, who on the Polish borders were Protestant; the efforts of the king, who, in his attempt to make his power effective against the nobility, among whom Protestantism was strong, found it to his advantage to espouse the Roman Catholic Church; skilful Papal diplomacy which, among other moves, was willing to concede to the king the authority to nominate the bishops; the zeal of the Jesuits; and weakening divisions among the Protestants. Then, too, Protestantism was not indigenous but imported and had not made much headway among the peasantry before other adverse factors rendered it impotent. Lithuania had close Polish ties and had so recently been brought into the Christian fold that the faith had not been deeply enough rooted to develop a reform movement. In the fore part of the seventeenth century Bohemia was predominantly Protestant, but the political vicissitudes of the Thirty Years' War and an alien Roman Catholic ruler reinforced by the missionary zeal of the Jesuits almost entirely eliminated Protestantism.

However, in none of these non-Latin lands did the Roman Catholic form of the faith display the creativity that it did in the regions that had been assimilated to Roman culture. In no one of them did there emerge a major new monastic order or a theological thinker of the first water. They accepted what was given them from Latin Europe.

In a sense the emergence of Protestantism was the reaction of Teutonic peoples against religious control from the Latin South. It was a revolt directed against the attempt of Rome to dominate those who had been won to the Christian faith in North-western Europe after the seventh century. These folk had accepted uncritically what had come to them. Now they were becoming self-conscious and were restive under the efforts of a corrupt Papacy to exploit them to its selfish advantage. The causes leading to the rebellion of North-western Europe against the Papacy were multiform and complex, but here seems to have been one of them.

It may be further evidence of the close relation of the division of Western Europe between the Church of Rome and Protestantism and the degree of assimilation to Latin culture, that the Holy Roman Empire, which professed to continue the tradition of the political empire which was once ruled from Rome, and which in practice had embraced Germany and Italy, thus including Latinized and non-Latinized peoples and which was already sadly weakened, was dealt a fatal blow by the divisions between Protestants and

Roman Catholics in Germany. It seems also significant that the rulers who claimed the title of Holy Roman Emperor, as they did until early in the nineteenth century, all maintained their communion with the Church of Rome. What continued to insist that it was the Catholic Church had become more and more clearly the Roman Catholic Church and increasingly was narrowed to Latin Europe and the overseas colonies of Latin Europe. Before the sixteenth century, except for small minorities, mostly Uniates, the ties which had held it to the non-Latinized Christians of the East had been severed. Now, again with the exception of minorities, those by which it had bound to it the Christians of the non-Latinized North-western portions of Europe were also broken.

We must note that Protestants did not think of themselves as innovators. They regarded themselves as reformers, as seeking to purge the Church of the corruptions which they ascribed to the Church of Rome and its Bishop and to return to the pure Christian faith.

A fourth generalization and one which also carries with it a contrast between the Protestant and the Catholic Reformation is that the first sprang chiefly from the lower social strata and the latter from the aristocracy. As we are to see, most of the outstanding creators of Protestantism were of peasant or very humble birth. Luther and Zwingli were born and reared in peasant families, although families which were modestly prosperous and not disposed to rebel against the existing order. Calvin was reared in an aristocratic environment, but his maternal grandfather was a manual labourer. Melanchthon was of artisan ancestry. Cranmer, who left a profound stamp upon the Church of England, was of humble farming stock. John Knox, who more than any other one man shaped the Protestantism of Scotland, was of lowly birth. In contrast, almost all the leaders of the Catholic Reformation were from the nobility. Ignatius Loyola, the founder of the Society of Jesus, the most influential of the new orders which arose out of the Catholic Reformation, was of the aristocracy. So were the creators of two others of the new orders, the Barnabites and Theatines. As we proceed with our story we shall note that this was true of many others.

To be sure, the class lines between the two wings of the reform movement were not tightly drawn. Many princes espoused the Protestant cause and used it for their own ends. One of the new groups in the Roman Catholic fold, the Capuchins, a fresh offshoot of the Franciscans, had as a founder one of very humble birth. In both Protestant and Roman Catholic lands, except for minorities, all classes held to the official faith. Yet in the main the pioneers of Protestantism were of humble origin, while most of the leaders in the Catholic Reformation were from the aristocracy. This may be because the aristocracy is usually more conservative and with some rebellious exceptions holds to the order in which it has been reared and by which it has profited, while the revolutionaries are generally from the groups which do not have so strong a stake in the preservation of the existing structure of society.

As we move on to the story of the great awakening in Western Europe we will deal first with Protestantism. This is not because it began first, for, as we have seen, the initial waves of the Catholic reform had appeared in the fifteenth century. It is, rather, because the Catholic Reformation was in part the Counter Reformation, directed consciously against the Protestants. It can, therefore, be better understood if the emergence and shaping of Protestantism be treated first.

In describing the rise of Protestantism we will take up separately each of the chief branches of that movement. First we will sketch the origins of Lutheranism, then of the Reformed Churches, next of the Anabaptists, then of the Socinians, and finally tell of the Church of England and the English Protestant bodies which dissented from it. We must remember, however, that in actuality these were largely contemporary with one another and with the Catholic Reformation. They interacted upon one another. The separation in our narrative is in part arbitrary and for the purposes of a somewhat artificial clarity.

Selected Bibliography

R. H. Bainton, *The Reformation of the Sixteenth Century* (Boston, The Beacon Press, 1952, pp. xi, 276). An admirable popular summary by an outstanding specialist.

The Cambridge Modern History. Volume II, The Reformation (Cambridge University Press, 1903). By various authors.

P. Janelle, *The Catholic Reformation* (Milwaukee, The Bruce Publishing Co., 1949, pp. xiv, 397). A Roman Catholic summary.

B. J. Kidd, editor, *Documents Illustrative of the Continental Reformation* (Oxford, The Clarendon Press, 1911, pp. xix, 742). A useful collection.

T. M. Lindsay, *A History of the Reformation* (New York, Charles Scribner's Sons, 2 vols., 1906). A standard work.

P. Smith, *The Age of the Reformation* (New York, Henry Holt and Co., 1920, pp. xii, 861). An excellent summary of the Protestant and Catholic Reformations and the general European setting.

W. Walker, *The Reformation* (New York, Charles Scribner's Sons, 1901, pp. vii, 478). A well-written summary by a specialist.

J. P. Whitney, *The History of the Reformation* (London, Society for Promoting Christian Knowledge, new edition, 1940, pp. xv, 527). A posthumous revised edition of a standard work.

Chapter 32

LUTHER AND THE RISE AND SPREAD OF LUTHERANISM

Martin Luther is usually, and rightly, regarded as the chief pioneer of what we call Protestantism. Protestantism was and is multiform. It had several sources. It sprang up almost simultaneously in several countries. Some of its earliest formulators were contemporaries. To it contributions came from such diverse factors as Augustine, the Bible, including especially the New Testament and notably Paul, nationalism, humanism, the rise of the *bourgeoisie* or middle class, the zeal for moral reform, mystical disciplines, and such dissenting pre-Reformation movements as the Lollards, the Hussites, and the Waldensees. Yet Luther was the first outstanding leader. He became the dominant distinctive personality in the origin and shaping of Lutheranism, one of the numerically largest forms of Protestantism, and his influence was more or less potent in almost all other expressions of that movement.

LUTHER AS BOY AND STUDENT

Martin Luther was the product of the Roman Catholic Christianity of the Middle Ages. He was born in Eisleben, November 10, 1483, the eldest of seven children. His parents were of free self-respecting peasant stock and were thrifty and hard-working. By the time Martin reached adolescence his father had become modestly prosperous through leasing several iron pits and furnaces. The atmosphere of the home was religious, but probably no more so than that of many peasant homes of the Germany of that day. Nor does it seem to have differed from the conventional views and practices of that class. The young Martin grew up to fear God, to believe in the reality of heaven, hell, angels, saints, the Devil, and demons. He stood in terror of Christ as judge, but he also believed in the efficacy of the intercession of the Virgin Mary, the apostles, and the saints. He was taught the Lord's Prayer, the Ten Commandments, and the Creed. He conformed unquestioningly to the Catholic Church as he knew it. He learned the popular hymns and could cry on occasion to St. Anne, the patron saint of the miners. His manners and speech were those of the peasant and throughout his life continued to bear the marks of that rearing.

In his seventh year Luther was sent to school and he continued, in various centres, through the university. During part of the time he had for teachers some of the Brethren of the Common Life. He was sturdy physically, quick of mind, diligent, and made an excellent record. The subjects in which he was drilled were the customary ones of the late Middle Ages. Apparently he had little or no introduction to humanism. He went to the most famous of the German universities of the time, Erfurt, and was trained in scholasticism of the Ockhamist kind that was then current as the "modern" philosophy. As we have seen (Chapter 21), Ockham had taught that the truths of Christianity could not be demonstrated by reason but must be accepted by faith on the authority of the Church and the Bible. How much this had to do with the emphasis of Luther upon justification by faith is not clear. Since he later differed from Ockham in theology, the influence, if present, may have been in his sub-conscious mind. In his student days Luther was companionable and enjoyed singing and playing the lute, but seems not to have shared in the vices which were common in student circles. All of his education was in towns where ecclesiastical influences were strong, attendance at mass and other services of the Church was customary, and religious processions, festivals, pilgrimages, relics, and the other outward expressions of Catholic life were part of the accepted environment. After completing his Master of Arts, to his father's satisfaction in May, 1505, when he was twenty-one, Luther began the study of law and was presumably headed for a successful career in that profession.

LUTHER BECOMES A MONK

Luther had scarcely embarked on that course when, suddenly, in July, 1505, he pledged himself to enter a monastery. While he was out walking, on a sultry summer day, a bolt of lightning felled him and, in terror of death, he called on St. Anne for help and made a vow to become a monk. Although the step appears to have been quite unpremeditated, it arose from the beliefs in which he had been nurtured and from his temperament. He had been reared in the fear of God and in the vivid certainty of judgement, heaven, and hell. In his student days at Erfurt he had known fits of deep depression, *Anfechtungen* he called them. What psychological or physiological basis they may have had we can only conjecture. It was inevitable that the threat of imminent death from the thunder clap brought terror of death and hell. It was natural that as the way of escape he bethought him at once of the monastic life, for it was by this road that the beliefs in which he had been reared held that hell could surely be avoided and heaven could be securely won. Luther had no liking for the way of the monk. Moreover, his father was bitterly disappointed and was made intensely indignant by the sudden step, for it robbed him of one of his dearest hopes, an eminent career for this able son and the security which that son could give to his sire's old age. Yet Luther had made his vow, believed himself to have been divinely summoned to the uncongenial road, and carried through with his plighted course. Within less than a month from that eventful hour he had entered in Erfurt one of those Observant Augustinian houses which, as we have seen (Chapter 28), had arisen from a reform movement of the previous century. Having embarked on a monastic career, Luther was not content with easy-going compromise, but chose an order which would enforce rigorous discipline and so assure him the salvation which was his compelling goal.

The Inner Struggle for Assurance

The monastery did not at once bring to Luther the assurance for which he longed. Indeed, for several years he was a disappointed, tortured soul. The time of his novitiate appears to have been one of inner peace. He was becoming accustomed to the routine of the monastic life. At the command of Staupitz, the Vicar-General of the Saxon province of his order, he studied theology. In 1507 he was ordained priest and on May second of that year celebrated his first mass. That initial mass brought him terror, terror at the thought that he, a sinner, was presuming to address himself to the living, eternal, and true God. So nearly overcome was he that he could scarcely finish the prescribed ritual. Now followed months of anguish. He sought by the means set forth by the Church and the monastic tradition to make himself acceptable to God and to earn the salvation of his soul. He mortified his body. He fasted, sometimes for days on end and without a morsel of food. He gave himself to prayers and vigils beyond those required by the rule of his order. He went to confession, often daily and for hours at a time. Yet assurance of God's favour and inward peace did not come and the periods of depression were acute. He visited Rome on business for his order and what he saw there of the carelessness and corruption of the clergy distressed him.

Only gradually did the light break. In obedience to his superiors Luther went further with the study of theology. Here he at first applied himself to such masters as Ockham and d'Ailly, and especially to Gabriel Biel. Biel was a fifteenth century nominalist of the Ockhamist tradition, who was a leader of the Brethren of the Common Life and a loyal Catholic whose works were widely influential in the Germany of the day. Luther read Augustine, Bernard of Clairvaux, and Thomas Aquinas, and next to Augustine valued Gerson. The doctrine of predestination brought him much distress. He accepted it, but to him it made God seem capricious. This view of the unpredictability and arbitrariness of God was heightened by the theology in which he was trained, for it held that God is not bound by law but may do what He pleases, even though from man's standpoint that may seem to be unjust. At times Luther almost hated God. At other times there would be a rebound of mystical exaltation. His condition was not helped by the burdens placed on him by his order. He was given heavy administrative duties. He also was assigned to teach theology in the University of Wittenberg, newly founded (1502) by the Elector Frederick III, "the Wise," of Saxony. It was from Wittenberg that he took his degree of Doctor of Theology. It was in the course of his lecturing at Wittenberg that assurance began to come. Staupitz, his confessor and spiritual director, had instructed him to study for his degree and undertake preaching and teaching. Presumably he hoped that thus, by seeking to help others, Luther would be delivered from his introspection and would find the way to peace. Moreover, Staupitz gave sage counsel born of his own struggles which helped Luther to growing insight.

The Light Breaks

Although light began to dawn by slow degrees as the prelude to dawn, Luther later looked back to a particular occasion when, like the sudden appearance of the sun, it broke upon him. He had been lecturing on the Psalms in the summer of 1513. In the autumn of 1515 he lectured on Paul's *Letter to the Romans*. In 1516–1517 his subject was the *Letter to the Galatians*. Somewhere along the way, at what precise hour we cannot tell, the phrase in the *Letter to the Romans* (1:17), "the just shall live by faith," brought him the illumination by which he was thereafter to live. "Justification by faith" became, through him, a distinctive principle of Protestantism.

Luther had been taught in his boyhood to believe that Christ is judge. Yet by his cry on the cross, "My God, my God, why hast thou forsaken me," Christ had shown that he, too, had experienced the anguish which Luther knew of separation from God and so had suffered with those whom he condemns. In the cross, moreover, Luther saw God reconciling the world to Himself, and as not only a consuming fire but also as burning that He may purge and heal. This, so Luther felt, was beyond reason, but is to be accepted by faith. Through faith the sinner knows Christ as his Saviour and sees into the fatherly heart of God. God is judge and condemns, but He longs to save the sinner and in Christ has provided a means by which that can be accomplished.

To Luther faith was not primarily intellectual assent, as it had been for most of the school men. It was, rather, the grateful whole-hearted response of one's entire being to the love of God in Christ: it was full confidence in God.

Indeed, Luther believed that justification was by faith *alone* (*sola fide*). In emphasizing *alone*, he was conscious that he was adding a word which did not appear in the Scriptures. Yet he believed that it was in accord with the Scriptures and that Ambrose and Augustine had said it before him. Experience and study had led him to the conviction that man could never earn God's favour by good works of any kind, whether these were morality or fidelity in the sacraments. He did not discount good works, but to his mind they do not earn justification but are the fruits of faith, the response in gratitude and love to the love of God in Christ which is appropriated by faith, evidences of the new birth which follows faith as described in the Scriptures.

Reading Anselm, especially his *Cur Deus Homo,* deepened Luther's conviction. Bernard of Clairvaux helped him and he found added illumination in the *Theologia Germanica* and the sermons of Tauler. To the end of his days Luther was to be troubled with *Anfechtungen,* but he had been given a basic insight which kept him from being powerless before them and he gradually learned how to deal with them.

Such relief had the light brought and so compelling was it that Luther could not but seek to transmit it to others. This he did in his lectures to students in the University of Wittenberg and in his sermons in the parish church. Because of his experience he rejected the scholastic nominalistic philosophy in which he had been nurtured. He was incredibly busy with preaching, preparing a commentary on the Psalms, overseeing eleven monasteries, and writing letters, but the inner illumination had come in the light of which he was to walk to the end of the journey.

The Outer Conflict Begins

Without intending it and to his surprise, Luther's religious pilgrimage and his releasing experience of justification by faith soon made him a person of importance in Germany and then in all Western Europe. In preaching he urged the moral reform of the Church, as did many another priest of the day. This, however, was comparatively innocuous. It was over the issue of indulgences that the spot-light was focused on him and that he became a centre of controversy. Through the controversy he was led, by steps which were inherent in his experience and convictions but which he did not anticipate, far beyond the demand for moral reform to a complete break with the Roman Catholic Church and to an attack upon basic teachings of that church which, to his mind, were a betrayal of the Gospel.

We have seen (Chapter 22) the rise of the issuance of indulgences in the eleventh and twelfth centuries and the belief that through them the Pope could draw on the treasury of the saints to remit the temporal penalties for sin not only for the living but also for the souls in purgatory. As time had gone on, the use of indulgences had increased and their sale had become an important source of revenue to the Pope and to those whom he favoured. The question was brought home to Luther by the granting of indulgences by the Pope to those who viewed on a specified day a famous collection of relics which the Elector Frederick had assembled at Wittenberg, provided they also made the required contributions. In sermons in 1516, to the uneasiness of the Elector, Luther questioned the efficacy of indulgences and declared that the Pope had no power to release souls from purgatory.

In 1517 indulgences were being hawked through parts of Germany by clever promotional methods by one Tetzel, a Dominican. Tetzel later defended his claim that as soon as the money fell into the coffer a soul was released from purgatory. It was announced that the proceeds were to aid the building of the new St. Peter's which the Popes were erecting at Rome. Actually half of them were to go to pay a debt which Albert of Brandenburg, of the aristocratic Hohenzollern family, had acquired in purchasing the Archbishopric of Mainz, a post which made him the ranking ecclesiastic of Germany.

This aroused Luther and on October 31, 1517, a date that is often called the birthday of the Protestant Reformation, he posted on the door of the castle church in Wittenberg, a kind of university bulletin board, ninety-five theses which he was prepared to debate. In academic circles this was a normal procedure for obtaining discussion. In crisp, vigorous language Luther challenged the indulgences. He protested against despoiling Germans to pay for the construction of St. Peter's, saying that few Germans could worship there, that the Pope was rich enough to do the building with his own money, and that he would do better to appoint one good pastor to a church than to give indulgences to them all. Luther said that indulgences did not remove guilt and that the Pope could remit only those penalties which he himself had imposed on earth and that he had no jurisdiction over purgatory. He denied that the saints had accumulated surplus credits. He held that indulgences bred a false sense of security and so were positively harmful.

To Luther's surprise, the ninety-five theses created an immense sensation. Within a few months they were printed in the Latin original and in a vernacular translation and were being read across Germany. That they had this effect was due in part to the skill and forthrightness with which Luther drafted them. It was even more because of an underlying restlessness which hailed them as saying what many were happy to have said. As a result, Luther was drawn into controversy. Although at the outset he had no thought of breaking with the Pope or the Church of Rome, he was not one to draw back, and prudence and guarded speech were alien to his nature. In the course of the debate he was led on step by step until he had declared that both Popes and general councils of the Church could err, that only the Scriptures are authoritative, and that he would concede that he was in error only if convinced that what he held was contrary to the Bible and to sound reason. In effect he was insisting upon the right and the duty of individual judgement which must not be surrendered, even to the Catholic Church.

Into the details of the stages by which Luther was driven to this position we must not take the space to go. We can only give them in rough outline. As was natural, Tetzel replied to Luther, but proved a somewhat stupid opponent whom Luther did not deign to refute. Luther had sent a copy of his theses to Archbishop Albert of Mainz and the latter sent it to the Pope. The then occupant of the Papal throne was that Giovanni de' Medici who through family pressure had been made a cardinal at the age of thirteen. Now, as Leo X, he was too deeply embroiled in Italian and European politics to take more than casual notice of what he regarded as a relatively unimportant debate among monks. He commanded the head of the Augustinians to quiet this member of his order, but instead the Augustinians tended to glory in him, perhaps because the leaders of the attack were their rivals, the Dominicans. At a chapter of the Augustinians Luther won followers, the most important of whom was Martin Bucer (or Butzer) (1491–1551) of whom we are to hear more.

In the summer of 1518 the Pope summoned Luther to Rome to answer to the charge of heresy and contumacy. Through the good offices of the Elector Frederick the hearing was transferred to Germany in connexion with a meeting of the imperial Diet (or Reichstag) at Augsburg. There the Pope was represented by Thomas Vio, better known, from his birthplace, as Cardinal Cajetan. The Diet was critical of the Church of Rome and of the fashion in which it took good German money beyond the Alps and through its absentee appointees left Germans without pastors. It declined to raise money for a crusade against the Turk. The atmosphere was not favourable to the Cardinal. To that dignitary's demand that he retract, Luther returned a refusal and appealed to the judgement of the universities and to the Pope "better informed." Fearing arrest, he appealed from the Pope to a general council.

Earlier that month a Papal bull clarified the position of Rome on indulgences, saying that they could only reduce the temporal penalties on earth and in purgatory, that they could not release a soul from hell, and that they could be applied only when guilt had been removed through the sacrament of penance. While affirming that the Pope could remit the penalties on earth it said that for those of purgatory he could only petition God, presenting the surplus merits of Christ and the saints.

Wishing the goodwill of the Elector Frederick in German politics, the Pope took a conciliatory attitude, for that prince was disposed not to deal with Luther in summary fashion. A Papal representative disowned Tetzel, who soon died of chagrin, and obtained from Luther a promise that he would refrain from debate if his opponents would do likewise.

THE CONFLICT DEEPENS

However, debate continued, for Luther's critics did not keep silent and outstanding members of the staff of the University of Wittenberg rallied to Luther's defence. One of these was Philip Melanchthon (1497–1560). Melanchthon, Luther's junior by nearly fifteen years, a grandnephew and protégé of the humanist Reuchlin, though unimpressive physically, was a competent scholar, especially in Greek, and had a facile pen which was later to be of outstanding service to Luther's cause. Newly installed as professor of Greek, he became convinced of the soundness of Luther's position and to some extent was an echo, although by no means merely an echo, of the older man.

The debate was joined at Leipzig, before a large and notable audience, between Luther and some of his colleagues on the one hand, and on the other hand Eck, a former friend, a humanist, and a professor at the University of Ingolstadt. Luther, affable, vivacious, and gay in company, but at times caustic in public speech, was led by the adroit Eck to admit that some of Hus's views were "Christian and evangelical," that general councils had erred and might err, that they had sometimes contradicted one another, and that articles of faith must come from Scripture and could not be established by Pope or Church. Soon Luther was to say that he and his supporters were "all Hussites without knowing it." He had broken with the authority of the Roman Catholic Church and against it had placed the Bible interpreted by the individual.

LUTHER ADVANCES TO THE ATTACK

The issue was now squarely joined. Luther was never one to hold back. In 1520 he boldly stated his position in five tracts which are often regarded as the primary expositions of his distinctive convictions. His *Sermon on Good Works* was completed in May, *The Papacy at Rome* in June, *The Address to the German Nobility* in August, *The Babylonian Captivity of the Church* in September, and *The Freedom of the Christian Man* in November. These were put in trenchant German vernacular and had a wide circulation.

In the first of the tracts Luther declared that the "noblest of all good works is to believe in Christ." He protested against limiting "good works" to praying in church, fasting, and giving alms, and held that they could also include "labouring at one's trade, coming and going, eating, drinking, and sleeping, and all the other acts that help nourish the body or are generally useful." He held that "the Christian who lives in confidence towards God knows what things he should do, and does all gladly and freely, not with a view to accumulating merit and good works, but because it is his great joy to please God and to serve Him without thought of reward." He held that seeking to amass good works by going on pilgrimages, fasting, confessing, and calling on the saints was evidence of a feeling of insecurity and of lack of oneness with God. Here, obviously, he was speaking out of his own bitter experience.

In the tract whose full title may be translated as *To the Christian Nobility of the German Nation Respecting the Reformation of the Christian Estate,* Luther held that the Roman Church had built up three walls in its defense from which Christendom had suffered. These he attacked. The first, the superiority of Popes, bishops, priests, and monks over the laity—princes, lords, artisans, and peasants—he declared invalid on the ground that all Christians are consecrated priests by baptism, and that the only difference among Christians is one of office. He held that the temporal power is ordained by God for the punishment of the bad and the protection of the good and should do its duty throughout the whole Christian body and without respect of persons, whether they be Popes, bishops, priests, monks, or nuns. He thus sought to sweep aside the principle which exempted the clergy from the jurisdiction of the civil authorities.

The second wall he described as the Papal claim to have the exclusive right to interpret the Scriptures. He proceeded to overthrow it by saying that many Popes had been in fact unbelievers and had therefore been incapable of understanding the Scriptures, but that every true believer, being by that fact a priest, was competent to discern what is right in matters of faith.

The third wall, Luther said, was the claim that only the Pope could summon a council and confirm its acts. He pointed out that the most famous of all the councils, that of Nicæa, had been called, not by the Pope but by the Emperor Constantine, and that after him "many other Emperors" had done the same. He held that when a Pope is a cause of offense to Christendom, temporal rulers should summon a council to deal with him. He attacked the pomp and luxury of the Pope and cardinals, and declared that Italy had been sucked dry to support it and that Germany was now going the same way. He challenged princes, nobles, and cities to forbid the payment of annates to the Pope, to abolish the practice of Papal reservations, commendam, and the like, and to show that the "drunken Germans," as the Italians derisively called them, were not to be mulcted forever but had also become Christians. He would have imperial law abolish the confirmation of any ecclesiastical appointment by Rome, the submission of temporal matters to Rome, the reservation of certain causes to the Papal curia, the appropriation of German benefices by the Pope, and the oaths of allegiance which bishops were required to swear to the Roman Pontiff. He would leave priests free to marry, and would have each town elect a "pious learned citizen from the congregation and charge him with the office of minister" and have him supported by the congregation and assisted by several priests and deacons. He advocated the abolishment, or at least the reduction, of the numbers of processions, annual festivals, and masses for the dead, the complete erasure of all saints' days, keeping only Sunday, the elimination of begging and the care by each town of its own poor, the expulsion of Papal legates from Germany, the reform of the universities, the exaltation of the teaching of the Bible in the schools, and advancing to thirty years the age at which one could enter a monastery.

Slightly longer was *The Babylonian Captivity of the Church*. In this Luther consciously went far beyond his earlier criticisms of the use of indulgences and freely acknowledged that his critics, whom he handled in caustic fashion, had assisted him to think more basically and to see more clearly the issues involved. To his mind the Papacy was the Kingdom of Babylon which had carried the Church into captivity. Here he dealt with the sacraments and in doing so emphatically departed from the teaching of the Roman Catholic Church.

One form of the captivity into which Rome had carried the Church, so Luther said, was the denial of the cup to the laity. From several passages of Scripture he argued against those who defended that practice and endeavoured to show that the weight of the Bible is on giving the communion to the laity in both the bread and the wine. He maintained that this sacrament belongs to all, not merely to the priests, and that the latter should give it in both kinds to those who sought it and as often as they sought it.

A second bondage Luther declared to be transubstantiation. He held that on the altar are real bread and real wine, not merely the "accidents," as the Pope had said, and that in them are the "real flesh and the real blood of Christ." Yet he would allow Christians to hold either for transubstantiation or with him. His own view is usually called, somewhat inaccurately, consubstantiation.

The third aspect of the captivity Luther described as teaching that the mass is a good work and a sacrifice. He maintained that the mass "is a promise of the remission of sins made to us by God and . . . has been confirmed by the death of the Son of God." Therefore it cannot be approached by works, strength, or merit, but by faith alone, and nothing is required for a worthy reception of the mass but faith, resting in confidence in the promise of Christ, and believing that Christ's body is given and his blood shed for the recipient. Luther maintained that although we are sinners and utterly unworthy of the gift of eternal life, God's incomprehensible mercy is such that we can cast ourselves upon Him in perfect trust and love Him above all things. The mass is not a sacrifice, an offering to God, and is therefore not a good work by which God's favour is earned, Luther said, but is a gift of God to be received with faith and thanksgiving.

Luther valued baptism and did not deny it to infants. He held that it is done, not by man, but by the Trinity through a man. But he also wrote that unless a man has faith, it profits him nothing. Baptism in itself, he declared, does not justify, but faith in the word of promise to which baptism is added. Baptism, in which the minister dips the child in the water, is a symbol of death and resurrection, and Luther therefore preferred total immersion. Through their entire lives, Luther held, Christians should carry out their baptism by dying to sin and living by faith in Christ. He maintained that the Popes caused Christians to forget their baptism and its meaning by requiring fastings, prayers, and almsgiving. Although when baptized the infants are not able to exercise faith, Luther said that they are aided by the faith of those who bring them to baptism and that through the prayers of the Church which brings the child in faith, the infant is changed, cleansed, and renewed by the faith infused in it. Here, as we are to see, Luther and those who were called Anabaptists parted company.

Luther insisted that no ground exists in the Scriptures for the other five of the seven sacraments. In some of these he found useful features, but he held that they had been corrupted by Rome. Thus in penance he believed that secret confession of sins is good and even necessary, but that it need not be to a specially ordained priest. Since Christ has bestowed the power of absolution upon every believer in him, it can be made to any brother Christian. He warned against regarding contrition for one's sins as a good work. He pointed out, probably with a vivid recollection of his own experience with confession, that "we can know only a small part of our sins," and said that it is enough to sorrow for those sins of which we are aware. He declared that while a contrite heart is of great moment, it can proceed only from a prior faith in the threats and promises of God. While he was prepared to acknowledge confirmation as a ceremony of the Church, Luther argued that the Scriptures give no ground for regarding it as a sacrament. He valued matrimony, abhorred divorce, and even preferred bigamy to it. But he inveighed against some of the regulations by which he believed the Pope had perverted matrimony and said that he could find no ground in the Bible for making it a sacrament.

Luther held that ordination had been invented by the Church of Rome. He admitted that as a rite practised for many ages it was not to be condemned, but he reiterated as one of his basic convictions that all Christians are priests, that what is called priesthood is merely a ministry entrusted to those who exercise it with the consent of other Christians, and that ordination is a ceremony for choosing preachers in the Church. As imposed by Rome, he said, the sacrament of ordination made for a separation of clergy and laity and the tyranny of the former over the latter which had wrought incredible injury to baptism and the communion. The Church, so he affirmed, can distinguish the word of God from the words of men and can do this—and here he seems to have reflected his Ockhamist training—by the illumination of the Spirit which she cannot demonstrate but which she holds as most sure. But he also said that the word of God is incomparably above the Church, and that she cannot ordain anything. Although not condemning extreme unction, Luther regarded its efficacy as depending upon the faith of the recipient and held that it is not warranted by the texts in *The Epistle of James* and *The Gospel according to Mark* to which the Church of Rome appealed as authority for it.

While not altogether sweeping aside or deprecating vows, Luther found no ground in Scripture for those of perpetual poverty, chastity, and obedience which are taken by monks and nuns, and advised growing youths and young men to keep aloof from them. This was partly because he could discover no precedent for them in the Bible and partly because they bred pride and contempt for the ordinary Christian life. He maintained that the works of priests and members of the religious orders are not a whit more sacred in the sight of God than those of a farmer in his fields or of a woman in her household duties.

The Freedom of the Christian Man, addressed to the Pope, contained the affirmation: "A Christian man is the most free lord of all, and subject to none; a Christian man is the most dutiful servant of all, and subject to everyone." By this Luther meant that, since justification is by faith alone and cannot be earned by good works, he who has this faith is freed from the bondage to the law and from seeking to earn his salvation by works. Here again are reflected the agony and seeming futility of Luther's struggle to win justification before God by the methods prescribed by the Roman Catholic Church and the monastic discipline. In the sense of release which had come to him Luther wrote: "One thing and one thing alone is necessary for life, justification, and Christian liberty; and that is the most holy word of God, the Gospel of Christ." Even here Luther was not bound by the literal word of Scripture, but declared that the word is "the Gospel of God, concerning His son, incarnate, suffering, risen, and glorified through the Spirit, the Sanctifier. To preach Christ is to feed the soul, to justify it, to set it free, and to save it, if it believes the preaching. For faith alone, and the efficacious use of the word of God bring salvation."

Yet, so Luther held, the Christian is the servant of all because he is bound by the faith which works through love to labour for the advantage of his neighbour. Faith does not permit immorality, for while good works do not make a good man, a good man does good works. "It is not from works that we are set free by the faith of Christ, but . . . from foolishly presuming to seek justification through works." A Christian man will fast, watch, and labour to keep down "the wantonness and concupiscence of the body," but with no thought of being justified by that discipline.

Through the rapidly multiplying printing presses, these and some of Luther's other writings were given a wide circulation. They were read not only in Germany but also in other countries. They created an enormous excitement, especially in Germany. Their burning conviction, obvious scholarship, and terse, bold expression quickly won them an extensive hearing. Thousands eagerly welcomed them, and for a wide variety of reasons. German patriots greeted them as giving leadership to the widespread resentment against what they considered the financial exploitation by aliens. Humanists heard in them a voice denouncing what they regarded as the superstitions and puerilities of much of the official religion. The cautious Erasmus was at best only moderately friendly, was soon to criticize Luther for the violence of his speech, and was later to break with him, but the fiery Ulrich von Hutten was outspokenly for him, largely on patriotic grounds. Many reformers saw here a heartening assurance of action against some of the abuses which had long been ineffectually decried.

In these tracts were set forth the convictions which became distinctive features of Protestantism—justification by faith alone, the priesthood of all believers, the authority of the word of God as contained in the Scriptures, and the right and duty of each Christian to interpret the Scriptures. Some of these convictions had been foreshadowed in groups which had been cast out of the Catholic Church in the centuries before Luther. Yet as compared with them the emphasis was new, especially the basic affirmation, justification by faith. Luther and his fellow-Protestants maintained that they were simply reasserting historic Christianity as it had been before its corruption by Rome.

As we are to see later, what is called Protestantism has been and is extraordinarily multiform. By no means all its manifestations have placed equal stress upon the principles which Luther enunciated. Some have given little weight to them. Others have made more of other convictions. Still others have carried them more nearly to their logical conclusions than did Luther. Yet among almost all the many kinds of Protestantism there is a family likeness. This, Protestants maintain, is due to their loyalty to the Gospel. They thought, and still think of themselves as Evangelicals, as holding to the Evangel, that is, the Gospel. However, to a greater or less degree, even when they were or are not aware of it, they were and are influenced by Luther. His basic views were set forth in these products of his pen thrown out at white heat in 1520.

For many the excitement caused by these publications was one not of approval but of outrage. They regarded them as heresy. In June, 1520, before the completion of some of the pamphlets, the Pope came out with the bull *Exsurge Domine,* which began "Arise, Lord, and judge Thy cause. A wild boar has invaded Thy vineyard." Forty-one alleged errors of Luther were condemned, the books containing them were ordered burned, and Luther himself was given sixty days to submit.

Efforts of two Papal nuncios and inquisitors commissioned to publish the bull in Germany met a varied reception. A few bishops found ways of evading or postponing formal publication. Luther issued a blast against the bull and on December 10, 1520, before an assembly of the students, teachers, and populace of Wittenberg, cast into the fire the bull, the works of his opponents, and some of the writings which traditionally had supported the Papal claims.

Since the sixty days had expired and Luther, far from recanting, had defied him, on January 3, 1521, the Pope issued the threatened bull of excommunication.

Luther Before the Emperor and the Diet

The Papal decrees made acute the question of what action would be taken by the Holy Roman Empire, the realm of which Luther was a subject. Would it harbour a heretic condemned by the Church, or would it extirpate him? In principle the Holy Roman Empire was the political aspect of the Christian community. Heresy was held to be a major peril to that community, for it might mislead Christians and bring them to hell instead of heaven. Now that the head of the Church had cut Luther off from its communion as a wild boar, would the state stand idly by or would it implement that action and burn the unrepentant offender?

At first thought there seemed to be only one answer. The newly elected Holy Roman Emperor was Charles V, the grandson of Ferdinand and Isabella, and not only shared his grandmother's desire for a moral reform of the Church but also her adherence to the doctrines of which the Pope was the guardian. He was under pressure from the Papal nuncio to rid the realm of this archenemy of the Roman Catholic faith.

However, the situation was by no means so simple. The Pope was not happy over the election of Charles to the imperial office for, with reason, he feared his influence in Italian politics. Moreover, German public opinion was largely with Luther, some of the German princes were for him, and his immediate superior, the Elector Frederick, while discreet in not as yet coming out firmly on his side, had taken no action against him and urged that he be given a fair trial. In Germany Charles was an alien, for he had been reared in the Low Countries. He had to rule as a constitutional monarch and it behooved him to walk warily.

Eventually, after much hesitation, the Elector agreed that Luther should answer to the Diet. In April, 1521, Luther appeared at Worms before that body and the Emperor. In his first hearing he admitted the books piled before the court to be his, but to the question whether he would stand by them all or would repudiate some of the views expressed in them, he asked time for reflection, saying that it affected the salvation of souls. At a hearing the next day he again acknowledged his authorship but refused to repudiate what he had said in them unless he were convinced of error from the prophets and the Gospel. On a further question he repeated that his conscience was captive to the word of God and that unless he were convicted by Scripture and plain reason, for he did not accept the authority of Popes and councils since they had contradicted one another, he would not recant anything. To do so would be neither right nor safe. He added, "God help me. Amen." Another version of his closing words, which may be accurate, has him say: "Here I stand. I cannot do otherwise." He spoke in German and, on being asked, repeated his statement in Latin.

It was a dramatic hour. A humble monk and university professor of peasant stock dared to set himself against the weight of constituted authority in Church and state. As at Augsburg, he did so at the risk of his life. Although the Emperor had guaranteed him safe conduct, the precedent of John Hus, who had come to his death in spite of a similar promise by an earlier Emperor, was by no means reassuring.

The scene was also highly significant. A single individual was pitting his reason and his integrity against established institutions which were the bulwark of society. To be sure, this was not new. Hus had taken a similar stand. Other less famous men who had been adjudged heretics had done the same. Yet the temper of the time was such that the deed stirred response in many hearts, some of ardent sympathy and some of uncompromising hostility. Here was what on the surface resembled the individualism of the contemporary humanists and that individualism which was to be a growing feature of Western civilization in the following centuries. However, unlike much of the latter, it was not selfish and irresponsible. It arose from a deep sense of divine compulsion. It was significant because it was characteristic of Protestantism. Yet it was also significant because the individualism which was not conscious of any such urge, which did not acknowledge responsibility, and which proved a disintegrating menace, probably arose in part from a distortion of the conception represented by Luther.

The scene was not only dramatic and significant. It was also tragic. It symbolized another breach in that unity among Christians which was part of the essence of their faith and which outwardly had been preserved among the majority in Western Europe. Now, from a variety of motives, but in part from profound and conscientiously held convictions on both sides, it was being broken and Western Christendom was being rent in twain. On the one hand were those who maintained that the individual must submit to the judgement of the collective Christian body. On the other were those who held that if he were true to God, the individual must pit his own judgement, when inspired as he believed by God, against that of the majority and the visible Church. Both positions were taken in the name of God and the Gospel. The result was disruption.

The Emperor Charles now frankly confessed his own Catholic faith, said that this monk in daring to set himself against the Christianity of a thousand years must be wrong, and declared his purpose to proceed against him. Shortly afterward, in May, 1521, with the consent of such members of the Diet as remained in Worms, Charles V adjudged Luther to be "a limb cut off from the Church of God, an obstinate schismatic and manifest heretic," and commanded all his subjects to refuse Luther hospitality, lodging, food, or drink, to take him prisoner and turn him over to the Emperor, and to deal similarly with all Luther's friends and adherents, confiscating their property. The decree also prohibited the printing, buying, or selling of Luther's works. To the end of his days Luther remained under the shadow of this edict.

The Wartburg and the Bible

The edict against Luther was never enforced. Before it had been issued many of the Diet had left, among them the powerful Electors Frederick of Saxony and Ludwig of the Palatinate. Luther had too many German sympathizers, among them his own prince, and the Emperor became too deeply engrossed in European politics to permit vigorous action against him.

Yet for a time the peril seemed great. Some days before the formal enactment of the edict Luther had left Worms. On his way home, at the command of the Elector Frederick, who thus sought to shield him, he was seized by friendly hands and taken to the nearly untenanted Wartburg castle. There, with the exception of a brief visit to Wittenberg in December, 1521, he remained, in the disguise of a knight and under an assumed name, until early in March, 1522.

For Luther the months were difficult. Living nearly in solitude, away from his friends, without the spur of action and battle to sustain him, he suffered from constipation, insomnia, and melancholia. To him the Devil was very real and his *Anfechtungen* returned in force. He was partially relieved by medical treatment and by rambles and rides.

Yet he was not idle. Indeed, unremitting intellectual toil probably contributed to his distress. In the nine months he wrote nearly a dozen books and translated the entire New Testament from Greek into German. In later years he also translated the Old Testament into his mother tongue and until his death he continued to revise what he had done to bring it more nearly to perfection.

Here was one of Luther's major achievements. His was by no means the first translation from the Bible into German. However, none other either before or later equalled it in dignity and felicity of expression. He endeavoured to make the apostles and prophets speak to the Germans as though they had been natives of the country. His version became the cherished possession of the nation and did much to standardize the literary language. It had an even more profound effect upon German than did the King James version of the Scriptures upon English. This emphasis upon the Bible and the influence of the book were typical of Protestants. To be sure, the Roman Catholic Church had cherished the Scriptures, but its fear of unauthorized interpretation had made it hesitant in circulating it widely among the laity. Luther, and with him other Protestants, stressed the primacy of the word of God as contained in the Scriptures and, holding to the priesthood of all believers, insisted not only that all Christians read the Bible but also on their competence, guided by the Holy Spirit, to understand it aright.

REVOLUTION GOES ON APACE

During the months that Luther was in laborious and suffering seclusion in the Wartburg the movement which he had spear-headed went on apace. As was to be expected, it centered at Wittenberg, but it was very widespread. It took radical forms. One of Luther's fellow-Augustinians denounced the mass and the use of images and urged the repudiation of clerical vows. In defiance of a command of the Elector Frederick, Carlstadt, a colleague of Luther on the faculty of the university, celebrated mass in abbreviated form without priestly garments or the elevation of the host, employed German in part of the service, and gave to the laity both the bread and the wine. Led by one of the reforming priests, some of the populace overturned altars and mutilated images and pictures of the saints. Carlstadt and others of the monks and clergy took wives. In his radical application of the principle of the priesthood of all believers, Carlstadt dressed like a peasant and wished to be addressed not as

Doctor but as Brother Andreas. There was denunciation of the use of music and musical instruments in church services. Auricular confession and fasts were falling into disuse. The town council took matters in hand, regulated public worship, and with provision for the sermon and words of consecration in German, permission to the communicants to take the bread and the cup in their own hands, and the gradual elimination of altars. Religious associations were abolished and their incomes together with other ecclesiastical revenues were placed in a common fund for the care of the unemployed and the orphans and the education of poor children. Begging and prostitution were forbidden and monks were required to earn their living by working. Radical preachers arrived from Zwickau, and, claiming direct divine inspiration, prophesied the early end of the world and denounced infant baptism.

Quite understandably the Elector Frederick was deeply disturbed by these measures and sought, not without some success, to restrain them.

LUTHER RETURNS AND OPENLY RESUMES LEADERSHIP

It was on March 6, 1522, that Luther finally returned to Wittenberg and openly resumed leadership of the movement which he had started. He did this at the invitation of the town council of Wittenberg and in part to hasten the publication of his writings and out of alarm at the radical measures of some of his followers. He did so at grave risk to himself, for the Elector Frederick had advised against it, the imperial edict condemning him still stood, and he could be by no means sure of Frederick's protection. The Elector's attitude towards the Reformation has been in debate. It is not agreed whether he acted more from political expediency or religious conviction. Perhaps he himself did not know. Certainly both factors seem to have been present.

Back in Wittenberg, Luther at once took charge of the situation. In a series of eight sermons he came out on the side of moderation, urging love and advocating freedom of choice on controversial issues. While not repudiating the monastic life or advocating the marriage of priests and nuns, he would leave that to the individual conscience. He would have the abolition of the mass carried through, but in orderly fashion, with the consent of the government, namely, the Elector.

LUTHER TURNS ORGANIZER

Luther felt constrained to exert a leadership far beyond the walls of Wittenberg. The Reformation spread rapidly and in many places congregations which sought to embody it were springing up. Not all of them yielded to Luther's authority, even when he might have been disposed to exert it. However, as the outstanding figure in the movement he felt in duty bound to offer guidance and to present a positive programme. He did this piecemeal as occasion seemed to demand and while continuing his duties in Wittenberg in the university and the town. Wittenberg became a centre to which eager students came to drink of the Reformation at its source. Many of them returned to their homes carrying with them what they had imbibed.

Luther was both radical and conservative. His basic principle was religious, justification by faith, and arose from his own experience. He gave primacy to the word of God and wished it to be presented in all its purity as he understood it. He held to the priesthood of all believers. He would have faith govern the entire conduct of all Christians and, since he contended that the distinction between sacred and secular was contrary to the Gospel, he wished them to carry on their occupations as vocations, callings of God. He would go back to the New Testament and the practice and faith of the early Christians, purging the Church of what he deemed the corrupting innovations of Rome. Yet he did not regard all the accretions of the centuries as evil. Holding that "what is not contrary to Scripture is for Scripture and Scripture for it," he preserved much from the post-apostolic past. He regarded confession before communion as desirable, but did not wish it to be obligatory. He favoured the use of candles, the crucifix, and pictures, although the latter were not to be specially revered.

For guidance to the clergy and congregations he prepared an *Ordering of Worship*, a *Formula Missae* ("Formula of the Mass"), and a booklet on baptism with a baptismal service in German. In the *Formula Missae* Luther omitted the portion of the liturgy called the canon of the mass, because it described the Eucharist as a sacrifice, and to him this smacked of earning something from God by good works, and so as contrary to justification by faith alone. In the Eucharist he stressed worship, fellowship, and thanksgiving to God. In 1526 he came out with a German mass.

Luther made much of music. One of the striking features of the Reformation, both Protestant and Catholic, was the fashion in which it found expression through hymns. Indeed, that seems to have been true of most and perhaps all of the great forward surges of the Christian tide. Luther seems to have been responsible for the musical settings of some of his hymns. Because of the high value that he placed on the Bible and its study by the ordinary believer, he was eager that the music in public worship should enable the words of Scripture to be clearly understood by the congregation. He prized and used polyphonic chorales, including those of Roman Catholic origin, and furthered the training of choirs. Congregational singing was one of his great joys and he took the initiative in encouraging it and giving it a large part in the liturgy and other services. Here was a corollary of his priesthood of all believers, and his own zest for singing, going back to his boyhood, reinforced it. He issued a hymnal and himself wrote some of the hymns. The most notable of the latter, *Ein feste Burg ist unser Gott* ("A Mighty Fortress is our God"), perhaps composed in 1527 or 1528 when Charles V was seeking to suppress the Reformation, was to inspire successive generations of Germans and in translation was to become a sturdy favourite in several other lands and branches of the Church.

To Luther the sermon was of first rate importance. He believed in it as the proclamation of the word of God. He himself preached regularly, often, and with great power. As with so much else, to no small degree although by no means entirely, Protestantism owed to him the prominence given to preaching.

Education was one of Luther's major concerns. This again was a logical outgrowth of his belief in the priesthood of all believers. He wished compulsory education under the direction of the state in which the Scriptures would be given prominence. He stimulated the production of religious literature for children. In doing so he blazed new trails. While Erasmus and the Bohemian Brethren had made a beginning in this direction, it was Luther who gave it a major creative impetus. He encouraged others to write and himself composed a Small Catechism for children. He also furthered adult education, for he wished the entire body of Christian believers to be intelligent in their faith. As one means towards this end he wrote his Large Catechism.

Luther emphasized the family. He helped arrange marriages for nuns who left the cloistered life and himself married one of them, Katherine von Bora. His was a happy home. Into it several children were born and at its table were numbers of his students who, admiringly, recorded his "Table Talk." Here was a precedent for the kind of parsonage which became characteristic of Protestantism.

The geographic spread of the Reformation confronted Luther with the problem of the structure and government of the Church. He declared that the true Church could never be identical with any visible institution, for it was comprised only of the redeemed and God alone knew who were and who were not of this number. Probably he would have preferred to assemble in groups those who had made the full commitment of faith. Yet he held to the territorial church into which all the inhabitants of a state are admitted by baptism. As we have seen, he advocated the retention of the baptism of infants. As the Reformation spread, great diversity was seen in practice and liturgy. Disorder appeared and chaos seemed threatened. Luther saw that some one must preserve order. Since the old ecclesiastical structure was dissolving before his eyes, he turned to the lay princes. In Saxony the Elector appointed visitors in 1527 and 1528 to report on the state of the parishes, much as bishops had formerly done. The Elector's domains were divided into districts and over each were superintendents responsible to the prince. They were to have administrative authority over the parish clergy with power to remove unworthy ministers and to bring some kind of uniformity into worship.

To Luther a repetition of the Inquisition with the execution of dissidents would have been abhorrent. From profound conviction he maintained that no compulsion should be used to induce individuals to believe as he did. Yet he desired orderliness in worship and held that in this the prince could help. He would not make the prince the head of the church in the latter's realms and he would not acquiesce in any attempt of the prince to constrain any one's conscience. But he believed that the convictions of the majority should determine the form of worship and religious instruction. Those who differed might go to a state where those of their beliefs outnumbered the others. Since Germany was divided into many states, large and small, this seemed a feasible method of dealing with differences.

Partly under the influence of Luther, *Landeskirchen,* or territorial churches, arose. Some parts of Germany remained Roman Catholic. In others the principles of the Reformation prevailed. Presumably this would have happened without the encouragement of Luther. As we have seen, nationalism and state consciousness were increasing in Western Europe. In Roman Catholic lands princes were insisting upon the administrative control of the Church within their borders. As Protestantism spread, whether of the Lutheran or some other form, each state where it became dominant gave preference to one or more kinds of it, putting the others under disabilities or suppressing them. In Germany great variety was seen among the *Landeskirchen* in ritual and organization.

LUTHER LOSES MANY HUMANISTS, PEASANTS, AND REFORMERS

Outstanding though he was as the first great leader of the Reformation, Luther did not long carry all those with him who wished change. Probably no one could have done so. So vital a movement inevitably had many expressions. Since they all had in common the repudiation of the authority of Rome, they were without an administrative centre to enforce outward unity. Luther would not have done so even had he possessed the power. Before many years numbers who at the outset were more or less sympathetic separated from him.

One of the early breaks was with the leading humanist, Erasmus. This was unavoidable. Humanism and Luther were incompatible. Humanism tended to take an optimistic view of human nature and to regard man as competent to work out his own salvation. His religious experience and the impress left upon him by his study of Augustine had been such that Luther completely rejected this view. He held man to be a sinner whose noblest deeds are corrupted by pride and selfishness. Man, therefore, can earn nothing from God and if he is to be saved it must be by the grace, the undeserved favour, of God. As we have seen, while in some ways sympathizing with Luther and for several years refusing to denounce him, Erasmus was early made uneasy by the former's outspoken and uncompromising denunciation of Rome. While the two were so much alike that there were those who attributed some of Luther's works to Erasmus, the latter was essentially a man of peace, a moderate, who wished the moral reform of the Church but dreaded violence and a breach in its outward unity.

As might have been expected, the issue between the two men was most sharply drawn over the question of predestination and the freedom of man's will. In 1524 Erasmus wrote a tract *On the Freedom of the Will* which he well knew would widen the breach. He held that God would be unjust and immoral if He were so to order the universe that man could not of himself fulfil the conditions which He had ordained for salvation and then were arbitrarily to choose some to be saved and by doing so condemn others to hell. Luther admitted that natural reason was offended by the doctrine of man's helplessness in sin and by a conception of God which, while holding Him to be good, taught that by His mere will He hardens and damns men whom He has not chosen to save. He confessed that at one time the apparent contradiction had so driven him to the abyss of despair that he wished that he had never been born. Luther stood in awe of the majesty and inscrutable justice of God. God, he maintained, is inaccessible to human reason. To Luther there was a paradox even in the self-revelation of God in Christ, that the Eternal and Omnipotent should be seen in a stable and on a cross. Man, so Luther held, does not have free will. Man's will is like a beast of burden. It is ridden either by God or by the Devil and does whatever the one who is in the saddle directs. In the heat of controversy Luther went beyond what he held in calmer moments, but his position was consistent with his basic conviction that none of a man's works avails.

Luther and Erasmus parted company. The latter never broke with the Roman Catholic Church and near the end of his life was wooed by the Pope with the tempting offer of an important post. Yet it was symbolic of his longing that the unity of the Church should not be broken that he died in Basel (July 11, 1536), by that time a Protestant city, and was buried in its cathedral.

Most but not all of the other humanists left Luther. Melanchthon remained loyal and some others of lesser note. Yet the breach with the majority was significant and important.

Luther also lost many of the class from which he had sprung, the peasants. In 1524 and 1525 there broke out the Peasants' War, the *Bundschuh*. The causes of the uprising were complex and were not primarily religious. Peasants' revolts had not been uncommon in medieval Europe and were against the economic and social disabilities under which that class suffered. The rebellion of 1524–1525 in Germany opposed rising taxes, deflation which made the taxes more burdensome, and curtailment of free access to woods, streams, and meadows. It was directed against the nobles, including the bishops and abbots, for they were, rightly, regarded as the exploiters. At the outset Luther looked with friendly eye upon the peasants' demands and some of the Roman Catholics charged him with the revolt. In Saxony a radical reformer, Thomas Müntzer, who had gone far beyond Luther, urged the peasants on and roused them to slaughter their oppressors. This was too much for Luther. He issued a fiery pamphlet *Against the Murderous and Thieving Hordes of Peasants* in which he urged the princes first to offer to come to terms with them and then, if they refused, to smite, slay, and stab them as rebels who were like mad dogs and were outside the law of God. Already the nobles were putting down the revolt and were butchering thousands. They needed no exhortation from Luther. Indeed, he issued another pamphlet in which he asked for mercy to captives. Yet the harm was done. The peasants in South Germany, where the uprising had centered, regarded him as a traitor. Here was one of the factors which lost much of the population of that region to Protestantism. Moreover, Luther was led to a deep distrust of the common man, to a fear of chaos, and to rely increasingly on the princes.

Luther also severed all connexion with the more radical reformers. They were increasing and held to diverse views. Some of them we are to meet again when we describe the Anabaptists. They rejected infant baptism and, repudiating the territorial church into which all in a given area were baptized, they would gather the true believers into congregations separated from the world. They wished, too, to return to the Christianity of the first century and thus free it from what they deemed the corruptions of later centuries. Luther had no use for those who advocated such measures and called them *Schwärmer,* fanatics. Luther had especially to deal with his former colleague, Andreas Carlstadt, and with Thomas Müntzer. Carlstadt denied the real presence of Christ in the mass and regarded the Lord's Supper simply as a memorial. He had no use for graven images or infant baptism and wished lay ministers who in no way would be distinguished from their fellow-believers. While holding to the priesthood of all believers, Luther insisted upon a specialized, trained ministry who would keep the rank and file from falling into ignorance of their faith. Wishing to be assured of the word of God, Müntzer believed that it continued to come, as it had to those who wrote the Bible, through prophets inspired by the Spirit. He sought to gather the elect into churches and to set them to slaughtering the ungodly and those who honoured images. Luther, appalled, urged the princes of Saxony to prevent such a use of the sword. He acquiesced in the banishment of both Carlstadt and Müntzer from Saxony.

Less radical, but still going beyond Luther were Zwingli and the reformers of Strassburg, whom we are to meet in the next chapter. Zwingli tended to regard the Lord's Supper simply as a memorial and the men of Strassburg took a position somewhat intermediate between that of Luther and that of Zwingli. In the interests of the common defense against the Roman Catholics, Philip, landgrave of Hesse, a leader among the princes who adhered to the Reformation, urged the outstanding representatives of the differing views to come together in an effort to reach agreement. This they did at Philip's castle at Marburg in October, 1529. Luther, Zwingli, Bucer, and Melanchthon were among those present. In a colloquy extending over several days, for a brief time it seemed that agreement might be reached. Zwingli was willing to concede that Christ is spiritually present in the Lord's Supper and Luther granted that no matter what the nature of Christ's presence only faith can make it of benefit to the Christian. Intercommunion might have been attained had not Melanchthon objected on the ground that for Luther to yield might make reconciliation with the Roman Catholics impossible. The differences between Luther and his followers on the one hand and those whom we are to call the Reformed on the other widened into a gulf.

The Appeal to Battle

Armed conflict between the Roman Catholics and the reformers could scarcely be avoided. The imperial decree against Luther and his followers issued at Worms in 1521 still stood. The Emperor did not forget it, but until 1529 he was so occupied with wars against France and in Italy and the threat of the Turk had been so serious that no determined attempt had been made to enforce it. In the meantime the princes and cities of Germany had been ranging themselves on one or the other side. In the main the South remained loyal to Rome. In 1524 a Papal legate succeeded in bringing into a league the Roman Catholic princes in that area. The North was moving towards Luther. The princes of Brandenburg, Mecklenburg, and Mansfeld were sympathetic. City after city, including some in the South, came over, among them Magdeburg, Augsburg, Strassburg, Nuremberg, and Ulm. Albert, one of the Hohenzollerns, Grand Master of the Teutonic Knights, that crusading order which had ruled in Prussia, attached himself to Luther, married, and, although deposed from his office with the Knights, became Duke of East Prussia and carried that region with him. Livonia turned Lutheran.

Hostilities did not at once break out. When, in 1526, the Diet convened at

Speier, in spite of the demand of the Emperor that the edict of Worms be enforced, it decreed that pending a "council or a national assembly" each of the princes was "so to live, govern, and carry himself as he hopes and trusts to answer it to God and his imperial majesty." This was interpreted as giving the Lutheran princes and cities authority to regulate their religious affairs as they pleased. When, in 1529, the Diet again met at Speier, it had a Roman Catholic majority. It ordered that no further change in religion be made, that in Roman Catholic territories liberty of worship should not be granted to Lutherans but that in Lutheran territories toleration should be accorded to Roman Catholics. Against this the Lutherans in the Diet entered a formal protest. This was the origin of the term Protestant as applied to those who dissented from the Roman Catholic Church. At first limited to Lutherans, the designation was eventually applied to all those movements which broke with that Church in Western Europe in the sixteenth century.

In 1530, Charles V, returning from Rome from his coronation as Emperor, called a meeting of the Diet at Augsburg and sought by a conciliatory attitude to restore religious unity. He asked the Protestants to put forth their beliefs and point out wherein they differed from the Roman Catholic Church. Melanchthon was given the assignment and he carried it through after consultation with Luther (who, being under the imperial ban, was not at Augsburg) and with others. The result was the Augsburg Confession, a lengthy document which was henceforth to be regarded as an official statement of the Lutheran position. Melanchthon endeavoured to make it as irenic as possible, but this did not deter him from frankly presenting the Lutheran case. The first part of the document set forth the positive convictions of the Lutherans and attempted to show that these were in accord with those of the Universal Church, and even with those of the Church of Rome "so far as that church is known in the writings of the fathers." The second part enumerated what the Lutherans regarded as the abuses which had crept into the Church. Luther heartily approved it and it was endorsed by Lutheran princes and cities. The Swiss, largely following the Zwinglian tradition, and the Strassburgers refused to sign it and each presented their positions in a separate document. The Roman Catholic theologians replied, attempts by the Emperor to reach agreement through committee conferences failed, the Diet, dominated by its Roman Catholic majority, held that the Protestants had been refuted, and Charles gave the latter until April, 1531, to submit.

Unwilling to yield, the Protestant princes met in Schmalkalden and formed a defensive league which is usually called by the name of that town. Strassburg was induced to accede to the Augsburg Confession and join.

Pressed by the necessity of defense against a Turkish invasion, in July, 1532, the Emperor and the Schmalkaldic League agreed upon a truce. In the years which followed Protestantism continued to spread. Until 1541 the Emperor was out of Germany. Conferences of Protestants and Roman Catholics held at his instance in 1540 and 1541 failed to bring accord.

The Emperor now undertook to rid the realm of Protestantism. His grand strategy included the convening of a general council by the Pope as a gesture and possibly as a means of conciliation, fomenting dissensions among the Protestant forces, and a final appeal to war. As we are to see in a later chapter, the Pope called what is known as the Council of Trent, but far from effecting reconciliation it deepened the gulf between Roman Catholics and Protestants.

Charles V succeeded in dividing the Protestants. In this he was aided by what became a notorious affair in which Philip of Hesse, a leader in the Schmalkaldic League, and Luther were both unhappily involved. At the early age of nineteen Philip, for political reasons, had been married to the daughter of one of the German princes. Although he had seven children by her, he engaged in the promiscuity which was common to men of his rank and day, including Charles V himself. After his conversion to Lutheranism his conscience troubled him so badly that only once in thirteen years did he take of the communion, for he found himself powerless to desist from his adulteries. He felt that a second marriage might help him to continence. With the consent of his first wife and of the girl's mother and also of Bucer, Melanchthon, and Luther, he contracted a bigamous marriage with a seventeen-year-old maid. Luther opposed divorce and held monogamy to be the form of marriage endorsed by Christ, but cited the polygamy of the Old Testament patriarchs as a precedent. He advised that the second marriage be kept secret, for being bigamous it was against the law of the land. The marriage was performed by a court preacher, and when the news leaked out Luther advised "a good, strong lie." To this Philip would not agree, especially since the bride's mother would not consent to having her daughter regarded as a concubine. Both Roman Catholic and Protestant princes professed themselves shocked and Charles took the opportunity to exact promises from Philip which led to a rift in the Protestant ranks. Charles also bought off one of the other Protestant princes by an offer of territory.

Thus prepared, the Emperor declared under the ban two of the leading Protestant princes, Philip of Hesse and the Elector John Frederick of Saxony, nephew and successor of that Elector Frederick "the Wise" who had so long befriended Luther. In the ensuing war the two were defeated and imprisoned. Politically Protestantism seemed crushed. This was in 1547, thirty years after the fateful posting of the ninety-five theses on the church door at Wittenberg.

Yet Protestantism was far from being eradicated. In large areas the populace were for it and resisted a compromise creed, the *Augsburg Interim,* which Charles attempted to force on them. The war broke out afresh. This time the Protestant princes were aided by the King of France. In return he was to have the border cities of Metz, Toul, and Verdun, which more than once across the centuries were to have a tragic role in relations between France and Germany. The Emperor was defeated and almost captured (1552).

THE PEACE OF AUGSBURG DIVIDES GERMANY AND BRINGS A LONG TRUCE

By treaty, the settlement was referred to the Diet. This met at Augsburg three years later, in 1555. After months of debate what was known as the Peace of Augsburg was formulated (September 25, 1555). It was a compromise. By it those princes who adhered to the Augsburg Confession, namely, the Lutherans, were to be allowed to do so and those princes who held to the "old religion," namely, Roman Catholicism, were not to be disturbed. Neither group of princes was to molest the other. Each lay prince was, therefore, to determine the kind of religion which was to prevail in his territories. This principle, *cujus regio, ejus religio,* was henceforth to govern the religious geography of Germany. No forms of Protestantism other than Lutheranism were to be tolerated. If on religious grounds either Roman Catholics or Lutherans wished to migrate they were to be allowed to do so and were to be permitted to sell their property. Protestant princes were to retain ecclesiastical properties confiscated by them before 1552. If, however, any Roman Catholic bishop, archbishop, or prelate became a Lutheran, he was to give up the properties and incomes belonging to his office. In other words, a spiritual prince could not turn Protestant and retain as a secular lord the lands or revenues which he had by virtue of his ecclesiastical post. The Protestant princes declared that they would not be bound by this provision. In the imperial free cities both Lutheranism and Roman Catholicism were permitted. The Lutherans demanded toleration for those of their faith living in the territories of Roman Catholic princes, but, while the new Emperor-elect promised that this would be done, it was not written into the treaty.

THE DEATH OF LUTHER

In the meanwhile, on February 18, 1546, more than nine years before the Peace of Augsburg, Luther had died. Fittingly the end came at Eisleben, his birth-place, and while on his return journey from a successful effort to arbitrate a dispute between two counts of Mansfeld. His later years had been marked by a complication of various physical illnesses, presumably aggravated by the strains and labours of a tempestuous life. This may in part account for his frequent irascibility and occasional outbursts of wrath and coarse vituperation

Although earlier he had opposed the burning of Anabaptists by Lutherans, eventually he reluctantly approved the death penalty for them on the ground that they were guilty of sedition and blasphemy. They had, indeed, proved very irritating, and, as we are to see, in the 1530's fanatics among them had undertaken at the city of Münster a kind of society which shocked their contemporaries and which Roman Catholics and Protestants had joined in suppressing by the sword. He also came out with a blast against the Jews, not on racial grounds, but because of their refusal to accept Christ, and urged that either they be deported to Palestine, or their synagogues be burned, their books be taken away from them, and they be forbidden money-lending and be compelled to earn their livelihood by tilling the soil. He also railed against the Pope. Yet to the end he was preaching, teaching, and revising his translation of the Bible. Some of his best writing and most moving religious insights were in the closing period of his life.

LUTHERANISM IN GERMANY IN THE SECOND HALF OF THE SIXTEENTH CENTURY

The second half of the sixteenth century saw a partial ebbing of the Lutheran tide. This was both in territory and in spiritual dynamic.

Territorially Protestantism reached its greatest extent in Germany about the year 1566. It then began to lose ground. There were those among both Roman Catholics and Protestants who wished to find a middle way which would effect a reconciliation. Indeed, some Lutheran services were deliberately very much like those of the Roman Catholics and in one area a Lutheran breviary was long in use which resembled that of the old church. There were Roman Catholics who were willing to go far towards meeting Protestant convictions on justification, the mass, and clerical celibacy. However, these attempts, always by minorities, failed to bring accord. Revived by an inner reformation, the "old religion" began to regain areas which it had lost. In this it was aided by the Jesuits, of whom we are to hear much in later chapters.

Protestants suffered from inner divisions. These were partly between Lutherans and that wing which by the end of the sixteenth century began to be called the Reformed and among whom the influence of Zwingli and Calvin was strong. As we are to see in the next chapter, by the beginning of the seventeenth century the Reformed Churches had made striking advances, largely in South Germany and at the expense of Lutheranism.

Among the Lutherans themselves serious dissensions broke out. Human nature being what it is, these were to be expected. They arose partly from personal rivalries between princes and partly from differences among theologians. We must not take time to go into the weary details. In some of the disputes Philip Melanchthon, who lived until April 19, 1560, a little over fourteen years after the death of Luther, was deeply involved. Rather reluctantly he consented to the reintroduction by the Elector Maurice (Moritz) of Saxony of some Roman Catholic practices and forms of organization in an attempt to mollify Charles V. Melanchthon regarded them as *adiaphora* or indifferent and so tolerated them. Some Lutherans, however, looked upon them with horror, especially since they were in force in Wittenberg, where Luther had made his home. From this arose the Adiaphoristic Controversy. Melanchthon was also attacked for his view of the Lord's Supper, as too near to that of the Reformed, and so a "crypto-Calvinism," and for his teaching that good works, while not earning salvation, are essential evidence of it. Associated with the latter view was synergism, that man works together with God to effect his salvation. Those who sided with Melanchthon were known as the Philippists and his distinctive views as Philippism. To the distress both of Melanchthon and of some of the latter's critics, Osiander (1498–1552) held that justification is not by the imputed righteousness of Christ through his death but that in those who are justified a positive righteousness arises from the continual inpouring of Christ's divine nature. In the heat of debate, one of Melanchthon's opponents declared that, far from being essential proofs of justification, good works are an obstacle to the Christian life. There were those who, going far beyond Luther, who never maintained that God's image had been obliterated by sin, insisted that man had no more freedom of will than a stone or a corpse.

In an attempt to effect agreement among the Lutherans, there was prepared, through long negotiations and the efforts of some of the theologians, what was known as the Formula of Concord. This was published in 1580, half a century after the Augsburg Confession. Signed by princes, cities, and thousands of ministers, it represented the convictions of the large majority of German Lutherans. Yet some of the princes and cities would not subscribe to it. Then, as later, Lutheranism did not present a solid front to the world.

In Lutheran circles increasing emphasis was given to dogma. The trend was towards making faith consist in intellectual assent to creedal statements. Theological discussion, a kind of Protestant scholasticism, tended to take the place of what faith meant to Luther, a commitment of the entire man, of which the intellect was a part but only a part. In the seventeenth century there came, as we shall see, a reaction in the form of Pietism. It stressed emotion, the commitment of the will, and conversion, and, while usually assenting to the historic confessions, made little of them.

Lutheran Hymns and Chorales

The absorption in dogma did not prevent a development, that in hymns and music, in which the Lutheran movement initiated and carried through a remarkable expression of religious faith. As we have seen, Luther himself wrote hymns and composed the music for some of them. Two of his contemporaries, John Walther (1496–1570) and Ludwig Senfl (1480–1555) did much to promote singing in which the entire congregation took part. Walther prepared a hymnbook which was published in 1524 and which took folk-songs or melodies after the manner of folk-songs and put them in forms in which all could join. Senfl developed chorales which prepared the way for the finished products of John Sebastian Bach (1685–1750). Late in the sixteenth century harmonies were simplified and popularized and in the seventeenth century additional chorales were composed.

The Northward Spread of Lutheranism: Scandinavia

From Germany Lutheranism spread northward into Scandinavia, Iceland, and Finland, and, in contrast with its homeland, became the religion of the entire region. Roman Catholics all but disappeared, and non-Lutheran forms of Protestantism made little or no headway.

The dominance of Lutheranism in Scandinavia is significant in view of the fact that Protestantism was not indigenous to that area. Catholic Christianity had also come in from the outside. As we have seen, it was introduced largely under royal auspices and at royal initiative, and at the outset was propagated chiefly by missionaries from England. German missionary effort had been discouraged, apparently because, coming from what was then a politically strong and expanding Holy Roman Empire, it had political implications and might be a precursor to incorporation in that realm. Again a change of religion was engineered by kings. It was accomplished more rapidly and encountered even less resistance than had the earlier one. This time the content of the religion adopted was from Germany. However, there was no danger that the reception of the new faith would be followed by political control from that land. Even had the Holy Roman Emperors been strong enough to attempt it, they were Roman Catholics and not Protestants, and would not have used Lutheranism to extend their authority northward.

Religiously, under Lutheranism as under Roman Catholicism, Scandinavia was long passive. It received what came to it from abroad without making major innovations. In its Roman Catholic centuries it had not produced a new monastic order which enlisted more than a minority of those of its sons and daughters who gave themselves to that way of life. To be sure, the Brigittines, of Swedish origin, spread widely, but compared with the Cistercians, Franciscans, or Dominicans, they were inconsiderable. Nor in its Roman Catholic days had Scandinavia given birth to a theologian of the first rank. Much the same was true after Scandinavia went over to Protestantism. There was marked vitality. We are to meet some men of great spiritual depth and zeal, such as Hauge, and of originality, such as Swedenborg and Kierkegaard, and of organizing vision, among them Söderblom, who were to have an influence which reached far beyond the borders of the North. However, they were late in appearing. It was long before Christianity had become sufficiently rooted in Scandinavia to stir any within that region to outstanding original creative thought and action.

At the beginning of the sixteenth century Denmark, Norway, and Sweden were ruled by the monarchs of Denmark under the Union of Calmar (or Kalmar), which had been formulated in 1397. However, while they had much in common, they differed in history and traditions and were really three nations. The tie between Norway and Denmark was much closer than that between these two lands and Sweden. In the second half of the fifteenth century the latter country was moving towards independence, and in a stormy fashion. German influence, especially through the merchants of the Hanseatic League, was strong in much of Scandinavia, but was resented, and was being weakened.

In the first half of the sixteenth century the Reformation came to the Scandinavian countries and was superficially accomplished in all of them.

LUTHERANISM TRIUMPHS IN DENMARK

In Denmark the Church was powerful and wealthy. It is said that on the eve of the Reformation in one or another way it owned a third of the land. The Pope claimed the right to make all ecclesiastical appointments, but the king made some of the nominations and the nobles, wishing to fill lucrative posts with their younger sons and resenting the diversion of Danish revenues to the creatures of Rome, demanded that bishops must be from their families and that other important church offices be filled either from their sons or by doctors of theology. Under these circumstances there was much corruption and worldliness.

Shortly before 1500 new life began to stir. In 1478 a university with a professor of theology was set up in Copenhagen. Early in the sixteenth century Paul Helgesen (or Eliae or Eliaeason) urged reform, especially in the sale of indulgences. In some circles the writings of Erasmus began to be read. From December, 1520, to March of the following year, Martin Reinhard, a German priest who had studied at Wittenberg, preached in Copenhagen as court chaplain and, to the distress of Helgesen, brought in some of Luther's views. King Christian II attempted a reform of discipline in the Church but was driven into exile (1523) before he could make it effective. Early in the 1520's Hans Tausen, who had been appointed professor of theology in Copenhagen and who had heard Luther preach in Wittenberg, began giving sermons which aroused popular enthusiasm. There were other preachers of the new views. Two Danish translations of the New Testament were circulated widely. Frederick I, who reigned from 1523 to 1533, moved in the direction of Lutheranism. A daughter and a son were married to German Lutherans. In spite of the opposition of the bishops, he permitted Tausen and others to teach Lutheranism and also declined to take action against priests and monks who were marrying Lutheranism won adherents among teachers and students in the University of Copenhagen.

In 1534 a son of Frederick, a convinced Lutheran, who seems to have been won by the impression made on him as a lad of eighteen by the great reformer at the Diet of Worms, came to the throne as Christian III and reigned until 1559. Under him Denmark became fully Lutheran. He had been elected king over the opposition of the bishops. Soon after he had defeated an attempt to restore Christian II, he had the bishops arrested and, with the approval of the lay members of the *Rigsraad* and of a national assembly (*Rigsdag* or *Thing*) confiscated the episcopal properties. Christian III asked Luther for help in carrying through the reorganization and the latter sent him John Bugenhagen, who had already performed a similar mission in Pomerania. Bugenhagen crowned the king and his queen. The king appointed seven superintendents who later were called bishops, and, although only a presbyter, Bugenhagen laid his hands on them in consecration. From the Catholic standpoint, therefore, they and those who followed them were not in the apostolic succession. An administrative structure for the Church was devised which had the approval of Luther. A liturgy was compiled, the Bible was translated into Danish, and eventually the Augsburg Confession, with modifications, was adopted. The translation of the Bible was the work of Christiern Pedersen, and was a literary masterpiece which by some has been deemed worthy of comparison with Luther's German version. Pedersen also translated various Lutheran works. He is said to have been the first writer of importance to use Danish and to have been the pioneer of a kind of Dane who wished his nation to combine Christian faith, popular education, and a knowledge of Danish history. The monasteries were not immediately abolished, but eventually they disappeared and their properties passed to the crown. Some Roman Catholic beliefs and practices persisted for a time, but the kingdom eventually became solidly Lutheran with a national church which had the monarch as its executive head.

In this adoption of Lutheranism Christian III seems to have been moved by genuinely religious motives. However, through it he greatly strengthened the power of the crown. The confiscation of church property gave the king large financial resources. His position as administrative head of the church in his realm enhanced his prestige and authority. Under him and his immediate successors Denmark entered upon an era of prosperity. Learning flourished as never before. Great care was taken to provide the kingdom with teachers, preachers, and schools.

LUTHERANISM IS IMPOSED ON NORWAY

In Norway the progress of the Reformation was not as happy as in Denmark. There appears to have been no popular demand for it. Under Frederick I, who was king in both countries, a Lutheran preacher arrived in the port of Bergen but seems to have had little influence outside the German community He was followed by two others who appear to have had letters of protection from Frederick. Before 1532, under the direction of royal officials, several churches in Bergen, including the cathedral, were destroyed. Lutherans came into possession of others of the churches. After the death of Frederick, the Archbishop of Trondhjem led the opposition to Christian III. However, as the country went over to the king the archbishop fled and remained a voluntary exile, thus depriving the Roman Catholics of their natural leader. Christian III made it his purpose to deprive Norway of its status as a separate kingdom united with Denmark by the personal tie of a common monarch, and to reduce it to a permanent dependency of the southern kingdom. All but two of the bishops were turned out. These two became Lutherans and retained their sees. However, religiously Norway was neglected. Only a few Lutheran pastors came, and some of them were embroiled in disputes over tithes and did not speak the Norse language which still prevailed in rural areas. The staffing of bishoprics was neglected. Many of the old priests remained until death and then there was delay in providing successors. At the outset some of these were of unworthy character. It was not until the beginning of the seventeenth century that conditions began markedly to improve.

LUTHERANISM WINS ICELAND

The early part of the fifteenth century had been one of hardship for Iceland and its church. The Black Death, arriving late, swept the island, severe winters added to the distress, population declined, and some of the bishops were foreigners who were far from worthy of their posts. The end of the century saw improvement. Native bishops of better character and education revived learning, and there was something of a religious awakening. By 1540 Lutheranism was penetrating Iceland through German merchants and youths who had travelled or studied in Norway, Denmark, or Germany. The New Testament was translated into Icelandic and published. Iceland was ruled from Denmark, and officials of Christian III, following the policy of that monarch, deposed the bishops and seized their property. In part of the island a native bishop resisted, using armed force, was supported by popular nationalistic resentment against the Danish innovations, was captured, and he and two of his sons were beheaded. Lutheranism made progress by more peaceable means, especially under Gudbrand Thorlaksson, the son of a priest, who, appointed by the king, was bishop from 1570 to his death in 1627, at the advanced age of eighty-three. He prepared a hymnal and published a translation of the Bible, both in Icelandic. Thanks in part to him, the old Norse tongue persisted and did not, as in Norway, give place to Danish. He had catechisms and other Lutheran literature produced and distributed, and it was in no small degree through him that Lutheranism prevailed. Yet many of the old customs persisted, among them auricular confession and reverence for the national saints.

LUTHERANISM PREVAILS IN SWEDEN

In Sweden Lutheranism was adopted in connexion with a political revolution. In 1520, in an effort to make himself supreme in Sweden, Christian II of Denmark had treacherously and dramatically executed some of the foremost men in the country in what was remembered as "the Stockholm blood bath." Executions were extended to other parts of Sweden and to Finland in an effort to root out all those of prominence who might resist his rule. The banner of revolt was raised by a young nobleman, Gustavus Ericksson, usually known as Gustavus Vasa, from the *vasa,* or sheaf, which was on his coat of arms. He was already among the opposition, for having as a hostage been carried captive to Denmark he had, before his escape, conceived a lasting distrust and hatred of Danish power. The deaths of his father and brother-in-law in the Stockholm massacre and of his mother and two sisters in prison in Denmark confirmed his hostility. He recruited his forces from the peasants, was elected king in 1523, drove the Danes out of Sweden, and was crowned in 1528. He then had the even more difficult task of consolidating his authority and bringing internal order in his realm.

As did monarchs elsewhere in Europe in that century, whether Roman Catholic or Protestant, Gustavus Vasa sought to bring the Church in his realms under the control of the crown. The Church had been both powerful and wealthy. Yet at the time that he fought his way to the crown it had been weakened by a loss of leadership. Two of its bishops had been victims of the "blood bath" and the primate, Gustav Trolle, Archbishop of Uppsala, a partisan of Christian II and from a family that was in chronic rivalry and enmity with the Sture, from which Gustavus Vasa sprang, had been deposed and had fled the country. Only one regularly consecrated bishop remained, and he went abroad when the ecclesiastical changes were well under way. The king was in desperate need of additional financial resources. These he found, as did Christian III of Denmark, in the appropriation of the possessions and revenues of the Church.

Ecclesiastical alterations went hand in hand with a great surge of national vigour which expressed itself creatively in several ways, and the Church of Sweden became the religious facet of that life. In it the Swedish people were bound together in a self-conscious community. State and Church were two aspects of one whole.

The Reformation had begun to penetrate Sweden only about the time that Gustavus Vasa was fighting his way to the throne. Its chief preacher was Olavus (or Olaus) Petri (Olaf Petersson) (1493–1552). The son of a smith, he studied at the recently founded University of Uppsala and then in several other places on the Continent. He took a master's degree at Wittenberg in 1518. He was, therefore, in that first home of the Reformation when Luther nailed his ninety-five theses on the church door. However, he had left Wittenberg before the movement there had reached its more radical stages and while Luther had as yet no thought of breaking with the Roman Catholic Church. Returning to Sweden, Olavus Petri began teaching in the cathedral school at Strängnäs. While his views reflected what he had heard at Wittenberg, they were for moderate reform and not for thoroughgoing changes. The archdeacon, Laurentius Andreas, was friendly. In 1523 Gustavus Vasa met these two men at Strängnäs. Impressed by them, the next year he asked Olavus Petri to Stockholm to serve as preacher. He also made Laurentius Andreae (Lars Andersson) (1480–1552) his chancellor. Thus the Reformation was given his endorsement.

A break soon came with Rome, but over Papal administrative authority rather than doctrine. The Pope supported the deposed Archbishop Gustav Trolle and appointed one of his own creatures, an Italian, to a Swedish bishopric. This angered the king. Recently he had written to the Pope asking authority for the Archbishop-elect of Uppsala to reform the Church, requesting confirmation of four bishops-elect, and saying that because of the poverty of the land the customary annates would not be paid to Rome. Now he said that if confirmation of the bishops was denied, he would have that given them by "Christ the only and highest pontiff." With this (November, 1523) the tie with Rome was severed, for neither king nor Pope would yield. Eventually consecration of the new bishops was obtained through two bishops who protested their loyalty to Rome and one of whom had been ordained at Rome. Thus the post-

Reformation Swedish episcopate was regarded as being in the apostolic succession. While the Church of Sweden put little emphasis upon this fact, at least some Roman Catholic opinion accepted it as probable, but deplored the variance of the ceremonies of ordination of priests from those of Rome and the emphasis in Sweden upon the preaching functions rather than the sacramental powers of the priests. In 1527 the Västerås Recess and the *Västerås Ordinantie* confiscated the bulk of the property of the Church, gave the king large powers over the Church, abolished compulsory confession, and made other innovations.

Changes in the Church of Sweden proceeded apace but did not lead to as wide a departure from those of the Roman Catholic Church as in much of Lutheran Germany. The incomes and powers of the bishops were greatly reduced. Marriage of priests, monks, and nuns was permitted. Preaching of the word of God was enjoined on the clergy. The Bible was translated into Swedish. In all this Laurentius Andreae, Olavus Petri, and the latter's brother, Laurentius Petri (Lars Petersson) (1499–1573), as Archbishop of Uppsala, had a large part. Olavus Petri especially had an important place in the creation of literature. He shared in the translation of the Bible, wrote voluminously, prepared hymnals in Swedish for the use of congregations, and brought out a Swedish mass. This last, with modifications, was long to remain standard in the Church of Sweden. It owed much to the *Canon Missae* of the Roman Catholic Church, but was not a slavish translation. Olavus Petri held that the words of institution were unalterable and that at each celebration the Gospel must be proclaimed, but that with these exceptions variations in the service were permissible. Olavus Petri attacked monasticism and clerical celibacy. Both disappeared, although not necessarily or primarily because of his onslaughts.

In these changes Olavus Petri and his associates were strongly influenced by Luther and were his warm admirers, but they did not follow him in every detail. Nor were the disputes between the various factions in German Lutheranism reproduced. Echoes of them were heard, but only faintly. In Sweden the Reformation took a course peculiar to that land. In some respects it held more closely to the old ways than it did in most of the Lutheran sections of Germany. The *kyrkoordning* ("church manual") prepared by Laurentius Petri and given official sanction in 1571 was distinctly Swedish and also retained some of the old customs, such as confession, excommunication, and public penance. Many of the parish priests continued in their posts and married their housekeepers or concubines to legitimatize their children.

Gustavus Vasa wished fully to subordinate the Church to royal authority and was irritated by what he deemed the independence of the bishops and some of the other clergy. Moreover, he differed from them on the course which reform should take, and, quite understandably, wanted his own way. He repudiated prayers for the dead and confession. On his deathbed he turned a deaf ear to the clergy who urged him to confess his sins and seek absolution. He moved much further from the old church towards an extreme Protestant position than did most of the clergy. He broke with Olavus Petri and Laurentius Andreae and markedly reduced the power of the bishops. Indeed, at the time of his death (1560) episcopacy seemed on the way out. Yet Laurentius Petri survived him, through him the episcopal succession was continued, and the Church regained partial autonomy.

Efforts of Eric XIV, son and successor of Gustavus Vasa, to introduce Calvinism were thwarted. The attempts of Johan (John) III, another son of Gustavus Vasa and the second king after him, to effect a *rapprochement* with Rome came to nought. When in 1592 the crown passed to Sigismund, a devoted Roman Catholic, a meeting of the Church at Uppsala in 1593 decided to hold to the unmodified Augsburg Confession. Charles IX, still another son of Gustavus, followed Sigismund on the throne. He had Calvinist leanings, was deeply interested in theology, and wrote hymns and prayers. His attempts to promote Calvinism met with determined and successful opposition, especially by professors in the University of Uppsala and the Archbishop of Uppsala. Sweden remained staunchly Lutheran.

LUTHERANISM ON THE EAST COASTS OF THE BALTIC

For centuries much of Finland had been subject to Sweden. It was to be expected that the Reformation would be carried there by Swedes. Gustavus Vasa was chiefly responsible for introducing and furthering it. About a hundred years later Isaac Rothovius, Bishop of Åbo from 1627 to 1652, did much to raise the level of the Christianity of the land. Through him church attendance was enforced, the quality of the clergy was improved, education was advanced, a university founded, and a Finnish translation of the Bible was printed.

Here and there along the east shore of the Baltic south of Finland, Lutheran enclaves arose, largely among the German and Scandinavian elements of the population.

LUTHERANISM SPREADS TO CENTRAL EUROPE

Lutheranism spread eastward as well as northward. It enjoyed no great vogue in Poland. It won some adherents, but the Protestantism of the land was chiefly Calvinism and Socianianism.

In Bohemia and Moravia the movements of which Hus had been the outstanding figure persisted into the sixteenth century. Luther made sympathetic contacts with them. On some points, notably the fashion in which Christ is present in the Lord's Supper, he was at variance with them. However, Bohemian students came to Wittenberg and in time those groups who looked back to Hus as their great hero were more and more permeated by Lutheran views. They grew in numbers and it is said that by the end of the sixteenth century nine-tenths of the population of Bohemia was Protestant. In general, the German elements were Lutheran and the Slavic elements tended towards the Swiss type of Protestantism in which Calvin's thought became dominant. In face of a common danger from an aggressive Roman Catholic attempt to rewin the country under a ruler of that faith and spear-headed by the Jesuits, Lutherans and Calvinists drew together for defense and in 1575 formulated a common confession of faith.

In Hungary and Transylvania several factors facilitated the spread of Protestantism. Here as in so much of Europe, in the fifteenth century the Catholic Church was suffering from corruption in both clergy and laity. The Hussite movement found sympathizers, a Hungarian translation of the Bible was made by two priests who adhered to it, and there may have been traces of the Waldensees. Humanism found a following in aristocratic circles, and while some of it undercut Christian faith, from it also came demands for reform. In the overwhelming defeat of the Hungarians by the Turks at the battle of Mohács in 1526, five bishops, two archbishops, and the king lost their lives, thus depriving the Catholic Church of much of its leadership. A large part of the country was occupied by the Turks and they tended to favour Protestants as against Roman Catholics, presumably because the former were less likely to support attempts by princes of the West, Roman Catholics, to reconquer the region. Possibly, too, many in the population subject to the Turks sought a deeper religious faith to support them in their trials and believed that they found it in Protestantism.

Protestantism first came in the form of Lutheranism. It spread through the Germans who were numerous in the area, especially in Transylvania. Hungarians studied at Wittenberg and brought back with them the teachings of Luther and Melanchthon. Among them were Matthias Biró of Déva, also known as Devay, who, a great preacher, came to be known as the Hungarian Luther, and Stephen Kis of Szeged, a doctor of theology from that university, whose theological works went through many editions and who trained many of the Protestant ministers. Both these men later swung towards the Swiss form of the Reformation. Anabaptists and anti-Trinitarians also won followings. By the end of the sixteenth century Protestants were probably in the majority in Hungary and Transylvania. Then began the partial reconversion of the population to Roman Catholicism through the Jesuits.

In Hungary and Transylvania Protestants were divided, largely along racial lines. In general, Lutheranism was recruited from Germans and Slavs, while most Magyar Protestants were of the Reformed faith. West of the Danube, where Magyars had tended to mingle with Germans and Slavs, the Protestants among them were mainly Lutheran. In Transylvania in 1568 the prince granted equal rights to Catholics, Lutherans, Reformed, and Unitarians. In 1571 this was confirmed by the Transylvanian Diet.

The Wide Dissemination of Luther's Writings

It was not only in lands where his views stimulated the formation of continuing churches which embodied his teachings that Luther was influential. His writings spread widely in other countries in Western Europe and with more or less pronounced effects. In the Low Countries Lutheran communities came into being but, as we are to see, the Reformed Churches were much more prominent. Luther's writings were circulated in Great Britain. In several sections of Italy, notably Venice, they were read, although in limited circles. They were known in Spain, but there humanism and especially Erasmus and his type of reform were more popular.

Summary

In the early years of the sixteenth century the tide of new life which had been preceded by the ground swell of the fifteenth century came to its flood in the Protestant and Catholic Reformations. The Protestant phase of that tide first appeared almost simultaneously in several lands. However, its earliest manifestation was in Germany in Martin Luther. Moulded by a profound religious experience issuing from soul-shaking struggles to satisfy the demands of a righteous and holy God, this peasant-born monk, priest, and university professor unexpectedly found that a courageous attempt to protest against abuses connected with the sale of indulgences made him a European figure. By his insistence, the fruit of his spiritual pilgrimage, on the sufficiency of the Scriptures as the record of the word of God, justification by faith alone, and the priesthood of all believers, he was led first to challenge and then to break with the Roman Catholic Church. It was a kind of individualism which was to characterize Protestantism, that of the naked soul face to face with God, redeemed by Him, and, responsible to Him, convinced that without disloyalty to Him it cannot submit to other authority unless convinced by reason and the Scriptures. Luther knew that he was not yet perfect and that within this life he would always be a sinner. He continued to be visited by periods of depression and inner conflict which he called *Anfectungen*. He had come to the conviction that he could never earn God's favour, whether by moral acts, deeds of mercy, or the ceremonies of the Church. Yet he believed that God's grace in Christ is sufficient and, received in faith, makes the sinner acceptable with God.

Quite without planning or intending it, Luther became a catalyst, to use a chemical analogy. Elements of many kinds, nationalistic and religious, found in him something which brought them to a fresh and partially unified reaction. Or, to use another chemical term, he set off a chain reaction which issued in an explosion that tore away much of Western Europe from the Roman Catholic Church. He was not alone responsible. The ingredients for the explosion were already there. Had he not given the decisive impulse some one else would soon have done so. However, he contributed distinctive features to what followed. In most of Northern Germany, in all of Scandinavia, and among minorities in adjacent lands on the Baltic and in Central Europe, Christianity took on a form which has rightly been called Lutheranism. By the middle of the twentieth century, through missions and migrations of peoples, Lutheranism was to be carried to all the other continents and to scores of countries.

Luther and his convictions were to have repercussions of greater or less intensity upon other forms of Christianity. Justification by faith alone was found in many more strains of Protestantism than those which bore the Lutheran name. Indeed, it was so widespread as to be the most distinctive feature common to Protestantism. Even among Roman Catholics there were those who went far towards accepting it and in some other respects were not unfriendly to Luther. He undoubtedly quickened the reform movement which remained within the Roman Catholic Church. This was in part in heartening some who were painfully aware of the moral evils in that church. It was also in part in stimulating many to work for reform to counteract the appeal of Luther and thus to prevent more from going over fully to Lutheranism and, if possible, to win back those who had followed him out of the Roman fold. It is to the wing of Protestantism which owed much to Luther and yet differed enough from him to constitute another ecclesiastical family, that of the Reformed Churches, that we must next turn.

Selected Bibliography

GENERAL WORKS ON PROTESTANTISM WHICH HAVE MUCH ON LUTHERANISM

R. H. Bainton, *The Reformation of the Sixteenth Century* (Boston, The Beacon Press, 1952, pp. xi, 276). An admirable popular brief summary by an outstanding specialist.

B. J. Kidd, *Documents Illustrative of the Continental Reformation* (Oxford, The

Clarendon Press, 1911, pp. xix, 742). A very useful collection of texts, about half on Lutheranism, with introductory notes.

T. M. Lindsay, *A History of the Reformation* (New York, Charles Scribner's Sons, 2 vols., 1906). A standard work, but not without mistakes.

E. de Moreau, P. Jourdan, P. Janelle, *Le Crise Religieuse du XVIe Siècle* (Paris, Bloud & Gay, 1950, pp. 461). Vol. 16 of A. Fliche and E. Jarry, *Histoire de l'Église depuis les Origines jusqu'a Nos Jours*). A Roman Catholic treatment attempting, not unsuccessfully, to be objective.

P. Schaff, *The Creeds of Christendom. Volume III, The Evangelical Protestant Creeds, with Translations* (New York, Harper & Brothers, 1877, pp. vii, 920). A standard compilation.

P. Smith, *The Age of the Reformation* (New York, Henry Holt and Co., 1920, pp. xii, 861). An excellent summary of the Protestant and Catholic Reformations in their general European setting.

W. Walker, *The Reformation* (New York, Charles Scribner's Sons, 1901, pp. vii, 478). A well-written summary by a reliable specialist.

MARTIN LUTHER

R. H. Bainton, *Here I Stand. A Life of Martin Luther* (New York and Nashville, Abingdon-Cokesbury Press, 1950, pp. 422). A superb combination of accurate scholarship based upon a thorough knowledge of the sources and secondary works with insight, vivid, readable literary style, and reproductions of contemporary illustrations. It also contains so valuable a bibliography as to render needless an extended one in this chapter.

H. Boehmer, *Road to Reformation. Martin Luther to the Year 1521*. Translated from the German by J. W. Doberstein and T. G. Tappert (Philadelphia, The Muhlenberg Press, 1946, pp. xiii, 449). Well written, semi-popular, by an outstanding German specialist.

E. M. Carlson, *The Reinterpretation of Luther* (Philadelphia, The Westminster Press, 1948, pp. 256). A useful summary of recent Swedish studies of Luther.

H. Grisar, *Luther,* translated from the German by E. M. Lamond, edited by L. Cappadelta (St. Louis, B. Herder; London, Kegan Paul, Trench, Trübner & Co., 6 vols., 1913–1917). By a Jesuit, very critical of Luther. There is a later edition, adapted from the 2d German ed. by F. J. Eble, edited by A. Preuss (Westminster, Md., The Newman Bookshop, 1950, pp. x, 609).

D. Martin Luther's Werke. Kritische Gesammtausgabe (Weimar, H. Bohlau, 82 vols. in 93, 1883–1948). The standard edition.

Luther's Correspondence and Other Contemporary Letters, translated and edited by P. Smith (Philadelphia, The Lutheran Publication Society, 2 vols., 1913).

Luther's Primary Works together with His Shorter and Larger Catechisms, translated into English, edited, with theological and historical essays, by H. Wace and C. A. Buchheim (London, Hodder & Stoughton, 1896, pp. xvi, 492).

M. Luther, *Three Treatises* (Philadelphia, The Muhlenberg Press, 1947, pp. 290).

Contains his *Open Letter to the Christian Nobility of the German Nation, The Babylonian Captivity*, and *The Treatise on Christian Liberty*.

Works of Martin Luther, translated and edited by H. E. Jacobs *et al.* (Philadelphia, A. J. Holman Co., and the Castle Press, 1915–1932).

A. C. McGiffert, *Martin Luther, the Man and His Work* (New York, Appleton-Century-Crofts, 1911, pp. xi, 397). Semi-popular, by a distinguished American church historian.

J. Mackinnon, *Luther and the Reformation* (London, Longmans, Green & Co., 4 vols., 1925–1930). Carefully done, by a Scottish Presbyterian historian.

M. Reu, *Luther's German Bible. An Historical Presentation together with a Collection of Sources* (Columbus, Ohio, The Lutheran Book Concern, 1934, pp. xiv, 364, 226). A careful study with extensive notes. About one-third is source material.

E. G. Schwiebert, *Luther and His Times: The Reformation from a New Perspective* (St. Louis, Concordia Publishing House, 1950, pp. xxii, 892). Competent, the most comprehensive account in English, by a Lutheran.

MELANCHTHON

J. W. Richard, *Philip Melanchthon, the Protestant Preceptor of Germany 1497–1560* (New York, G. P. Putnam's Sons, 1898, pp. xv, 399). Semi-popular.

LUTHERANISM OUTSIDE OF GERMANY

C. Bergendoff, *Olavus Petri and the Ecclesiastical Transformation in Sweden (1521–1552). A Study in the Swedish Reformation* (New York, The Macmillan Co., 1928, pp. 264). Based upon extensive research.

G. K. Brown, *Italy and the Reformation to 1550* (Oxford, Basil Blackwell, 1933, pp. 324). Based upon both the sources and secondary studies.

C. M. Butler, *The Reformation in Sweden. Its Rise, Progress, and Crisis; and Its Triumph under Charles IX* (New York, Anson D. F. Randolph & Co., 1883, pp. iv, 259). A useful summary.

E. H. Dunkley, *The Reformation in Denmark* (London, Society for Promoting Christian Knowledge, 1948, pp. 188). A good summary, based largely on secondary studies in Danish.

J. C. F. Hood, *Icelandic Church Saga* (London, Society for Promoting Christian Knowledge, 1946, pp. 241). A survey of the church history of Iceland from the beginning through the nineteenth century.

E. Révész, J. S. Kováts, L. Ravasz, *Hungarian Protestantism. Its Past, Present, and Future* (Budapest, Bethlen Gabor Literary and Printing House Co., 1927, pp. xiv, 222).

W. Toth, *Highlights of the Hungarian Reformation* (*Church History*, Vol. IX, pp. 141–156).

T. B. Willson, *History of the Church and State in Norway from the Tenth to the Sixteenth Century* (London, Constable & Co., 1903, pp. xii, 382). Semi-popular.

J. Wordsworth, *The National Church of Sweden* (London, A. R. Mowbray & Co., 1911, pp. xix, 459). By an Anglican bishop.

Chapter 33

THE RISE AND SPREAD OF THE REFORMED AND PRESBYTERIAN CHURCHES

Parallel with Lutheranism another kind of Protestantism was emerging and developing. It usually goes by the name of Reformed. In it were varieties, including Presbyterianism in its several manifestations. Yet, like Lutheranism, it constituted a family of churches which in the nineteenth and twentieth centuries was to be drawn together in a loose, world-wide association. Luther had an effect upon it, but in its origin humanism was more influential than it was in Luther. No single leader placed so profound a stamp upon it as did Luther upon the churches which are often known by his name. John Calvin more nearly shaped it than did any other man, but some, notably Zwingli, Farel, and Bucer (or Butzer), were earlier connected with it than was he. In the sixteenth and seventeenth centuries its chief geographic spread was on the borders between the lands in the north-west of Europe which became fairly solidly Lutheran and the countries in the south-west of Europe which remained either predominantly or overwhelmingly Roman Catholic. Most of such Protestantism as survived in Latin Europe was Reformed. That, however, was in France, Switzerland, and the mountain valleys in North Italy. No Protestantism succeeded in maintaining itself in the deep south of Latin Europe. The Reformed Churches stretched in a somewhat interrupted belt from Transylvania and Hungary on the east, through Switzerland, down the Rhine Valley into Holland, and across the North Sea into Scotland and North Ireland. Eventually, through migrations and missions the Reformed Churches were to have a much wider extension. In the twentieth century they were to be found on all the continents and in many of the islands of the sea.

The significance of the original geographic distribution of the Reformed Churches and especially the underlying reasons for it are obscure. It may be more than a coincidence that the area is on the border between those regions which had been fully assimilated to Latin culture and those into which that culture had not penetrated until after their conversion to Christianity and then chiefly through the Church. As we have noted, the lands in which Latin culture had been well established before their conversion remained within the Roman Catholic fold and there in general the renewed currents of life which produced reform fitted into religious patterns which were already developed and fairly well fixed. In the lands of the North the awakening profoundly stirred individuals, especially Luther, for whom the existing patterns proved an intolerable strait jacket. Even when these were in part retained, the effort was made to subordinate them to the life which issued from a fresh experience of the faith as seen in the Scriptures. The Reformed Churches more nearly rejected the inheritance from the Roman Catholic Church than did those churches that arose through Luther.

At first sight this is contrary to what might have been expected from the fact that the Reformed Churches were on the borders of the Latin lands. It arose at least partly from the share which Christian humanism had in the emergence of these churches. The two chief early figures, Zwingli and Calvin, were much more influenced by humanism than was Luther. As we have seen, humanism arose in Latin lands which had long been under Christian influence from a revival of the pre-Christian Græco-Roman tradition which had entered so strongly into Latin culture. It had the effect of driving men back to the original sources—in Christianity to the earliest documents, namely, the Scriptures. It did not necessarily imply the rejection of all subsequent developments in the Church, but it insisted that these be subjected to the test of whether they could be supported from the Scriptures.

To be sure, in Lutheranism humanism was strongly represented, notably through Melanchthon. Yet the experience of Luther, which was so largely apart from humanism, was controlling. However, stronger though humanism was in the creation of the Reformed than of the Lutheran wing of Protestantism, it was not as potent as it was in a much more radical Protestantism whose chief exponents came from Italy and Spain, deep in the Latin South.

In another way the Reformed Churches may have reflected the Roman tradition, possibly from unconscious contagion from the Latin culture on the fringes of which they emerged. Luther and those who were moulded by his views tended to be pessimistic about the possibility of bringing human society or any of its segments into conformity with the will of God. The kingdom of God would not be realized on this earth. Man is a sinner and even when an individual has been justified by faith he continues to sin. God's grace in saving man through Christ is an unfathomable mystery, for man can do nothing to deserve it. God's gift in Christ is to be accepted in amazed, glad, humble gratitude. But although Christians, especially Christian princes, can do much to restrain evil, the kingdom of God can never be realized within history. So said

Luther and those who thought with him. In contrast, the Reformed Churches, while recognizing as keenly as the Lutherans the depravity of man and the wonder of God's grace, were more hopeful that through the labours of those who in faith had accepted the salvation offered by that grace God would effect within history an approximation to His kingdom. This was more nearly akin to the Roman imperial tradition of striving through good laws, morals, and government to create civilized society and resembled what the great Popes of the Middle Ages had dreamed of realizing through the Roman Catholic Church.

THE BEGINNINGS OF THE REFORMED CHURCHES: ZWINGLI

The movements which produced the Reformed Churches arose almost simultaneously with those which had come through Luther. While they quickly became aware of Luther, they largely went their own way.

The earliest outstanding leader was Huldreich Zwingli (1484–1531). Zwingli was born in Switzerland. That in itself was important. Although nominally a part of the Holy Roman Empire, in practice Switzerland was substantially autonomus. It was divided into several cantons, some of them predominantly rural in their Alpine valleys, and some with small cities, such as Basel, Zürich, and Bern, which had a well-to-do citizenry and where the Renaissance had been welcomed and humanism flourished. Swiss mercenaries were in high repute and fought in many of the battles of Europe. The independent spirit made revolt from Rome more natural than in some other regions. Here, too, was a trend towards democracy which had an effect upon the thought and organization of the Reformed Churches.

Zwingli was born January 1, 1484, and so was only a few weeks younger than Luther. Like the latter, he was from a prosperous peasant home. His father was the village bailiff and an uncle the village priest. Another uncle was an abbot. A bright lad, the family determined to give him an education and prepare him for the priesthood. In his student days he acquired Latin and Greek and read in the Latin and Greek Fathers. Like Luther and so many others in Western Europe, he was much impressed by Augustine. The writings of Christian humanists appealed to him, among them those of Pico della Mirandola and especially Erasmus. He found congenial the latter's passion for reform and the Greek New Testament of that master so enthralled him that he memorized much of its text.

Zwingli seems never to have had the kind of soul-shaking religious experience which moulded Luther. His had been a happy boyhood and he grew up with no great sense of sin. Indeed, like so many priests of his day and quite unlike Luther, he did not observe the clerical obligation of chastity. However, most of his contemporaries regarded that as a peccadillo and it did not keep him from having a genuine moral earnestness. Serving for a time as a chaplain with Swiss mercenaries in Italy, he returned with a deep dislike for the practice which led Swiss sons to sell their bodies and prostitute their souls in the service of alien princes. He opposed it and thereby so won the dislike of the French that he was forced to leave his parish of Glarus. He then became people's priest at the famous pilgrimage centre, Einsiedeln, in 1516, the year before Luther came forward with his ninety-five theses. There his fame as a preacher increased and in 1519 he became people's priest in the Great Minster at Zürich, a small city of perhaps 7,000, but wealthy and with political influence.

It was at Zürich that Zwingli became prominent as a reformer. Although he had received a Papal pension, when he reached that town he was already advocating some reforms. Independent, in good Swiss fashion, with little regard for ecclesiastical authority, he thought of his rôle as that of a preacher, not unlike that of an Old Testament prophet. He greeted Luther's early writings with joy and did much to further their circulation. Yet he later belittled their influence upon him. At first his preaching seems to have been directed partly to an exposition of *The Gospel according to Matthew* and against the practice of providing mercenary soldiers and receiving pensions. He himself surrendered his Papal pension in 1520.

Zwingli stressed the authority of the Scriptures and soon began denouncing whatever in the old faith was not expressly warranted in them. Under his leadership and in accord with this principle Zürich moved by rapid steps away from the Roman Catholic Church. In December, 1520, the civil rulers decreed that priests should preach in freedom conformably with what they received from the Scriptures. In 1522 the issue of Lenten fasting arose, and while Zwingli supported the practice, the civil authorities, by taking the initiative in ruling for them on the ground of good order, virtually rejected the jurisdiction of the Bishop of Constance, in whose diocese Zürich lay. In 1523 Zwingli came out against monastic vows, clerical celibacy, the intercession of the saints, the existence of purgatory, the sacrificial character of the mass, and the teaching that salvation can be earned by good works. He proclaimed the doctrine of salvation by faith. The civil government supported him. Priests and nuns married, and in 1524 Zwingli himself was formally wedded to a widow with whom he had had an irregular connexion. By Easter, 1525, images, relics, and organs had been eliminated from the churches, monastic establishments had been confiscated and their properties largely devoted to schools, and the mass had been discontinued. A simple church service in German was developed in which the sermon was central. In all of this Zwingli acted in close coöperation with the civil government and an even closer union of Church and state was achieved than in Luther's Saxony.

Zwingli broke with Luther. He differed from the latter in temperament and in his religious experience. His was largely the intellectual and, eventually, the moral approach. Luther was mentally fully as able and was more many-sided, but his tempestuous struggles for an assurance of justification before God had made on him an emotional and religious mark much deeper than any which Zwingli knew. Zwingli stressed conformity with the sovereign will of God as revealed in the Scriptures. Luther could never cease to marvel at the forgiving grace of God in Christ and to rejoice in the release and freedom which it brought. Open separation between Luther and Zwingli came over the significance of the Lord's Supper. To Luther the declaration of Christ as he broke the bread, "This is my body," was to be taken at its face value. To him, through the eye of faith, Christ was actually present in the consecrated elements, even though the manner of that presence defied a fully rational explanation. In the communion, he held, the believer partakes of Christ. To Zwingli, in the Lord's Supper the command, "Do this in memory of me," was controlling. Although he believed Christ to be present and to be discerned by faith, he regarded the rite primarily as a memorial through which the worshippers were bound together in an expression of loyalty to their Lord. It was the Eucharist, the common rejoicing of those who declare the death of Christ. To him Christ's words, "The flesh profiteth nothing," were determinative. Luther's view seemed to him to be an irrational persistence of Roman Catholic superstition.

Yet Luther and Zwingli both taught that salvation is by faith alone. Zwingli said that one is only free from sin when his "mind trusts itself unwaveringly to the death of Christ and finds rest there," that faith is born "only when a man begins to despair of himself and to see that he must trust in God alone," and that "it is perfected when a man wholly casts himself off and prostrates himself before the mercy of God alone, but in such fashion as to have entire trust in it because of Christ who was given for us."

Zwingli perished (October 11, 1531) in an inter-cantonal war which arose from the attempt of Zürich to force Protestant preaching upon neighbouring Roman Catholic cantons.

THE SPREAD OF THE REFORMED CHURCHES

Before death removed Zwingli from the scene, the Reformation was spreading to other Swiss centres and in it the views of Zwingli loomed large. Basel, Bern, and several other cities came over to the movement. At Basel, John Hussgen, Heusgen, or Hausshein, better known as Oecolampadius (1482–

1531), was outstanding. Some of the cities of South Germany tended to side with the Zwinglian views. They were led to this partly by their affinity with the Swiss and partly by their distrust and fear of the princes who were supporting Luther. Among them Strassburg, on the French side of the Rhine, was prominent.

Zwingli wished to draw together in a league the Protestant cities, and Philip of Hesse hoped to have a comprehensive alliance of Protestant princes and cities which would include those who held to Luther as well as those moulded by Zwingli. In spite of the conciliatory efforts of Bucer, now influential in Strassburg, Luther and Zwingli could not agree and the dream of Philip of Hesse was frustrated. Bucer tried to make peace. He had led in the triumph of the Reformation in Strassburg and through his writings and the preachers whom he sent out he was potent in much of Central Europe. In the moot question of the Lord's Supper he took a middle ground between Luther and Zwingli. However, although some of the cities of South Germany accepted his view, it failed to heal the breach between Zwingli and Luther. The First Helvetic Confession, drafted at Basel in 1536, while conciliatory, also did not succeed in winning the Lutherans. The Lutheran and the Reformed wings of Protestantism were parting company. The Reformed Churches presented a variety of views and were by no means fully agreed among themselves. However, most of Protestant Switzerland except Basel, while by no means uniform, was drawn together by the Second Helvetic Confession (1562–1566) and to this Basel gave its adherence eighty years later.

In Zürich the work of Zwingli was continued and consolidated by his pupil and friend, Henry Bullinger (1504–1575). Conciliatory, Bullinger came nearer to the Lutheran view of the Lord's Supper than had Zwingli and gave refuge to persecuted Lutherans. Yet he remained true to the Reformed tradition. His enormous correspondence and his writings had a profound effect in England.

In French-speaking Switzerland Guillaume Farel (1489–1565) was a fiery preacher of the Reformation. Scion of an aristocratic family in Dauphiné, as a student he came under the influence of Jacques Le Fèvre (c.1455–1536). Modest, scholarly, deeply religious, Le Fèvre was a humanist who wrote commentaries on the Scriptures and wished to reform the Catholic Church from within. He had as a friend Guillaume Briçonnet (1470–1534), who was abbot of the monastery in Paris where Le Fèvre resided and who later, as its bishop, made Meaux a rallying point of Catholic reformers. Although he was under suspicion and for a time took refuge in Strassburg, Le Fèvre was later tutor to the children of Francis I of France and died without formally separating from the Roman Catholic Church.

Farel, however, was too impetuous to remain within that communion. His outspoken utterances made it necessary for him to leave France. He went to Basel, but his attack on Roman Catholic doctrines brought down on him the wrath of Erasmus and he was temporarily in Strassburg. He passed like a whirlwind through several cantons and cities in French-speaking Switzerland, and, visiting the Waldensees in their Alpine valleys, won some of them to the Reformation. He inspired and trained young men as preachers, sending them out to spread the Gospel. Fearless, singularly free from self-seeking, chivalrous, devotedly nursing the sick, he is one of the most attractive figures of an heroic era.

In 1532 Farel was for a time in Geneva, where the Council of Two Hundred had ordered the "pure Gospel" preached in every church and cloister, but the bishop's vicar soon brought about his expulsion. In 1533, after pressure from Bern had obtained freedom of worship for the Protestants, he returned to Geneva and in 1535 the mass was suppressed and the monks and nuns were driven out of the city. The Genevan movement towards the Reformation seems to have been as much from political as from religious motives. A commercial centre, Geneva was attempting to achieve its independence of both its bishop and the Duke of Savoy. Its adoption of Protestantism aided it in the struggle.

At this juncture John Calvin appeared on the scene. Urged by Farel to remain and help in the reorganization of the religious life, he began the connexion with Geneva which, with one interruption, continued until his death and was to make that city the main centre of the kind of Protestantism which bore the designation Reformed. Indeed, so potent was his influence that eventually he had more to do with giving the Reformed Churches their distinctive characteristics than did any other individual. Calvin was by no means dominant in all the Reformed Churches, for, like the Lutheran bodies, they displayed variety. Yet to a greater or less degree they were all indebted to him.

THE CONTRIBUTION OF JOHN CALVIN TO THE REFORMATION: HIS EARLY LIFE

Although of humble ancestry (his forefathers had been barge men on the Oise), John Calvin was reared in aristocratic society and had the manners of that class. He was born on July 10, 1509, at Noyon in Picardy, about sixty miles north-east of Paris. His father was in comfortable circumstances. Although he was never ordained, the young John was designed by his father for the Church and was educated, as was the custom in those lax days, by the income from ecclesiastical benefices the duties of which he did not perform. As a lad of fourteen he went to the University of Paris. There he seems to have escaped the vices which corrupted many of the youths who came to that stormy seat of learning. Indeed, from boyhood he was deeply religious and critical of any laxity in morals. He won and kept friends among some of the more serious of the students. By a strange coincidence he was in the university when Francis Xavier and Ignatius Loyola matriculated, men who were to be outstanding in the Catholic Reformation, but he may not have met them. When nineteen, he left Paris to study law. His interests were those of the current humanism. He wrote in lucid, almost elegant Latin, he acquired a knowledge of Greek and Hebrew, and, in accord with these interests, his first book, published when he was twenty-three, was a commentary on Seneca's *De Clementia.*

Not far from this time Calvin had what he regarded as a sudden conversion, but we have no knowledge of its details. It is clear that he had come under the influence of an earnestly religious group in Paris from which issued several Protestants, and it is probable that he had become acquainted, directly or indirectly, with some of the writings of Erasmus and Luther and that they had impressed him. In 1534, when he was about twenty-five, he left Paris, surrendered his ecclesiastical revenues, was imprisoned, freed, and found a haven in Basel, then recently become a strong Protestant centre.

CALVIN'S INSTITUTES

It was at Basel, at the age of twenty-six, that Calvin finished and had published what was probably the most influential single book of the Protestant Reformation, his *Institutio Christianæ Religionis* (early translated as *The Institution of the Christian Religion,* but more usually later as *The Institutes of the Christian Religion*). He addressed it to Francis I, who, unstable and inconstant, had for a time shown favour to the reformers. Written in Latin, he soon put it into French. Indeed, he is said to have done more than any other one man to make that language a vehicle for philosophical and theological discussion. Worked over again and again and enlarged, Calvin gave it the fourth and final revision in 1559, only a few years before his death.

The *Institutes* did not owe their prominence to the originality of the ideas which they contained, for Calvin was intent upon demonstrating that the Christianity which he set forth was not novel, but was simply what had been taught in the Church before what he regarded as the changes—to his mind the innovating corruptions—made by the Roman Catholic Church. They won their way because of their clarity, the orderly arrangement of their thought, and their comprehensiveness. They were the most inclusive and systematic presentation of the Christian faith as held by Protestants which had thus far appeared. They set forth the entire cosmic drama of creation, sin, and redemption under the sovereign will of God as Calvin believed that it was taught in the Scriptures. He prized the Scriptures as the authoritative record of God's dealings with the universe and man.

In the final edition of the *Institutes* there were four books. They were intended to conform to the order in the Apostles' Creed, for Calvin was intent upon holding to that early and generally accepted summary of the Christian faith. The first dealt with God the Father as creator, preserver, and governor of the universe, for God was primary in Calvin's thought. The second outlined the redemption wrought by God in Christ, the third had to do with the Holy Spirit, and the fourth with the Church and the relation to it of civil governments. Calvin showed himself familiar with much of the literature of pre-Christian Græco-Roman antiquity and with many of the outstanding Christian thinkers across the centuries, but he laid especial stress upon the Scriptures and Augustine. He was not so much concerned with refuting what he believed to be the errors of the Roman Catholic Church and of Protestants with whom he was in disagreement as he was in stating positively and giving the reasons for what he maintained was true Christianity. Here was a comprehensive statement of what Calvin believed about God, Christ, the nature of man, immortality, sin, redemption, the manner in which God's grace works in the lives of men, the Church, and the relations of Church and state. Calvin stressed the sovereignty of God and submission to His will.

Calvin held that although the essence of God transcends all human thought, something of a knowledge of God is to be had on the one hand through observation and study of the orderliness of the universe which He has created, both the stars and the symmetry, beauty, and use of the human body, and on the other hand through the Scriptures. He came out boldly for the Trinitarian understanding of God, using Augustinian language. He held God to be the creator and sustainer of the universe and to be sovereign in it. He declared God to be omnipotent and that "governing heaven and earth by His providence, He so overrules all things that nothing happens in it without His counsel." By God's providence Calvin meant not an idle Deity Who sits by and watches what takes place under the operation of the general laws which He has ordained, but One Who concerns Himself with every individual, Who holds the helm and overrules all events, so that not even a sparrow falls to the ground apart from His will. Calvin boldly faced the problem of whether, if nothing occurs without the direct will of God, God is responsible for evil and why, if wicked men do evil by the decree of God, as the Scriptures in many instances maintain, even in the crucifixion of Christ, God should hold them responsible. Here, as in so many places, he cited Augustine. He held that God is completely free from any taint of injustice or wrong and that, while He has ordained the evil deeds which men do, the latter are fully to blame. Calvin does not resolve the mystery of the paradox but exhorts to a meek acceptance of what is taught in the Bible.

Calvin dealt with the creation of man. He declared that of all of the works of God man is the noblest, most admirable specimen of His justice, wisdom, and goodness. He held that man is both body and soul, that he was created in the image of God, that the image is in the soul, that the soul is endowed by God with intellect, the power to discern good from evil, justice from injustice, and that it is immortal. Calvin described the sin of the first man, Adam, and said that its essence was revolt against the authority of God, and that this entailed pride, ambition, and ingratitude. Through that offense of the primal man corruption, "original sin," warped all his descendants. By it the image of God was not effaced but was distorted, and with results which in some respects were worse than if it had been completely erased. The pride which sprang from the likeness to God and the distortion of that likeness which is inseparable from sin penetrated to the inmost soul of man. Total depravity followed. Man's will was so impaired that he could do no good works unless he was assisted by grace, the special grace which God has given to the elect, those whom He has chosen and received through regeneration. Apart from grace every man is under the deserved wrath of God. Man's salvation is entirely from the initiative of God.

To effect man's redemption, Calvin went on to say, God of His great love and mercy gave the law to keep alive the hope of salvation until Christ should come. From the beginning of the world this had been in the plan of God. Although God hated the sin in man, He found in man that which claimed His love. To be the redeemer and the mediator it was necessary that Christ should be fully God and fully man. Here Calvin was clearly on the side of what had been expressed by the Catholic Church at Chalcedon and as in so much else he was in positive accord with what had been held by the majority of Christians in both East and West. Christ, so he said, fulfilled the expectation recorded in the Old Testament and was prophet, priest, and king. By freely giving himself in sacrifice, and by suffering not merely physical death, but also the torments of one irretrievably lost, the horror of spiritual death, the descent into hell, which, so Calvin held, had been appropriately added to the Apostles' Creed, Christ as man had fully satisfied the righteous judgement of God, had removed the curse laid on man for his sin, and had destroyed the spiritual death which is the punishment for sin. By his resurrection, so Calvin taught, Christ appeared as the conqueror of death. Therefore it is upon his resurrection that our faith chiefly rests. Christ's ascent into heaven marked the beginning of his kingly reign. At the last day he will appear as judge of all and as redeemer of the elect.

The Holy Spirit, so Calvin proceeded to say, moves the sinner to the faith which accepts what has been done for him in Christ. To Calvin, as to Luther, justification, or salvation, is by faith. Faith can come only as the result of the work of the Holy Spirit. It is more than intellectual assent to truth. It is "a knowledge of the divine benevolence towards us" and if it is to be valid that which the mind has grasped must "be transfused into the heart." Faith and repentance are indissolubly connected, as Calvin saw them, but repentance is a consequence of faith. By repentance is meant forsaking ourselves and turning to God and laying aside our mind and assuming a new one. It is "a true conversion of our life to God, proceeding from a sincere and serious fear of God, and consisting in the mortification of our flesh and of the old man, and in the vivification of the Spirit." The fruits of repentance are love towards God and charity towards men, with sanctity and purity in our whole life.

The evidence that one has entered into the new life of faith is that he does works pleasing to God. "We are justified not without, and yet not by works." Calvin placed great emphasis upon character. We are not saved by character, but salvation issues in character. We never become perfect in this life, but we are always to strive to advance "in the way of the Lord." We are not to "despair on account of the smallness of our success," but are "to press forward to the goal." We are to present our bodies "a living sacrifice, holy, acceptable unto God," "depart from ourselves that we may apply all the vigour of our faculties to the service of the Lord," and resign ourselves "wholly to the direction of the Divine Spirit."

With Luther, Calvin believed in the divine calling. He held that God had appointed "to all their particular duties in different spheres of life," and that the Christian is not "to attempt more than is compatible with his calling," whether that be obscure or prominent, seemingly sordid or respectable.

Like Luther, Calvin affirmed the liberty of the Christian. That liberty is seen in being reminded by the law of one's duty, yet being lifted above the law, yielding a voluntary obedience to the will of God, and being freed from an obligation before God in external things, for these can sometimes be used and at other times omitted.

Calvin stressed prayer and described it as entering into conversation with God. He wrote that since no one of us is worthy to present himself before God, the heavenly Father has given us Christ as our advocate and mediator with him.

Calvin came out plumply for election. He held it to be a "comfortable doctrine," for to him it meant that nothing can be out of the control of God. He asserted what is often called double predestination. By that is meant that God has chosen some to be saved and some to be lost—election and reprobation. The reconciliation of God's love with His choosing some for eternal damnation does not seem to have caused Calvin the anguish that it did Luther. He held it to be a mystery and, agreeing with Augustine, declared that we must not "set up the standard of human justice as the standard by which to measure the justice of God." Nor would he have a man constantly anxious whether he is among the elect. While, if we were absolutely sure in this life that we are among the chosen of God for salvation, we would be tempted to complacency and pride, there are marks which are evidence that we are presumably of the elect. If we have them, we are to stop our worrying. The tests are a profession of faith, an upright life, and participation in the sacraments. Men were not to make their salvation the major aim, but are to put first the glory and honour of God.

Finally, Calvin's *Institutes* dealt with the Church. The Church, so he maintained, is not identical with any visible institution, but includes all the elect, the dead as well as the living. As the creed declares, the Church is Catholic, that is, universal. It cannot be divided, for this would mean that Christ is divided, and that is impossible. Its head is Christ, and through him all the elect grow up together as one body. The Catholic Church is invisible and is known only to God. Calvin also believed that there is a visible Church, which, though composed of particular churches in different towns and villages, yet embraces all the living throughout the world "who consent to the same truth of divine doctrine and are united by the bond of the same religion." In it are many hypocrites who have nothing of Christ but the name, yet it exists "wherever we find the word of God purely preached and heard, and the sacraments administered according to the institution of Christ," and we should acknowledge as its members "all those who by a confession of faith, an exemplary life, and a participation of the sacraments profess the same God and Christ as ourselves." All Christians should associate themselves with the external communion of the Church, even though the Church be imperfect. Moreover, so Calvin confidently and hopefully declared, while the Church has not yet arrived at perfection, it is daily improving. None of the elect is perfect, and they stand daily in need of the forgiving grace of God, but in the creed there is the affirmation of faith not only in the communion of saints but also in the forgiveness of sins. Calvin recognized two sacraments, baptism and the Lord's Supper.

As to the structure of the visible Church, Calvin held that it should ensure that everything be done decorously and in order. It should have judiciaries appointed to censure vice and to excommunicate. For officers of the Church, Calvin, quoting Paul, held that they were originally apostles, prophets, evangelists, pastors, and teachers. The first three, he declared, are raised up only for special occasions, while the pastors and teachers are constant. He held that the terms bishop, elder, pastor, and minister have the same meaning. There are also deacons, who administer the alms and care for the poor. Ministers have the inner call of God and are to be chosen with the consent and approbation of the people at elections over which other ministers preside. Here is democracy, although not equalitarianism, with orderly procedure. Calvin recommended ordination by the laying on of hands.

To Calvin the holy community should have in it both Church and state. The state, so he said, should help to obtain food and drink for its citizens. It should also prevent sacrilege against God and other offenses against religion, preserve the public peace, protect the property of the individual, enable business to be transacted without fraud or injustice, ensure a public form of religion among Christians, and maintain a civilized society. He favoured an elective aristocracy and shrank from anything that savoured of revolution. He sanctioned capital punishment by the magistrate in executing the judgement of God and said that some wars are lawful. Nations need not be bound by the law given to Moses, but are to be free to enact such legislation as seems to them expedient, provided that it is in accordance with the law of love.

CALVIN MAKES GENEVA AN EXAMPLE AND CENTRE OF THE REFORMED RELIGION

It was this Calvin, then in his late twenties, the youthful author of the *Institutes*, who was induced by Farel to help him with the Reformation in Geneva. The two worked closely together and sought to make of the little city a model community, organized in such fashion that Church and state worked together in harmony. After a little less than two years, in April, 1538, they were banished for refusing compliance with what they regarded as improper interference of the civil authorities in the Church's sphere. Their dream seemed to have come to naught.

Calvin found refuge in Strassburg and there was befriended by Bucer. Now followed a little over three years which were happier and more peaceful than any which he was again to know. He became pastor to the French refugees and built up a congregation organized and disciplined in accordance with his principles and with a liturgy which, an adaptation of one already in use in German churches and with later modifications made after his return to Geneva, became a model for public worship in Reformed Churches elsewhere. At Strassburg he also showed his skill as a teacher. In spite of chronic ill health, he added literary labours to his other duties and brought out an enlarged revision of the *Institutes*. It was at Strassburg that he married. In spite of the early death of their only child and his wife's invalidism, the union was happy. From Strassburg, too, he went to conferences with other reformers, among them Germans, and formed a warm friendship with Melanchthon.

Meanwhile, a shift in the political situation in Geneva brought into power the party friendly to Calvin. Its leaders besought him to return. Pressed by Farel and from a deep sense of duty he reluctantly complied. From his arrival in September, 1541, until his death nearly a quarter of a century later, May 27, 1564, he was the dominant figure in the city. This was in spite of the fact that he often faced opposition, held no other office than that of one of the ministers, and in the earlier years was not even formally a citizen. Under his leadership, close coöperation between Church and state was carried through. A form of church organization was set up through the *Ordonnances,* a catechism was prepared, and a liturgy was introduced based on that which he had developed at Strassburg. He had the discipline of community morals and the sumptuary legislation enforced which in theory had long been advocated by the Roman Catholic Church. He did much to develop commerce and the weaving indus-try. This made for a prosperous community. He encouraged the lending of money, but only at what he believed to be a fair interest. He thus contributed to a new industrial and commercial economy. Here he was in contrast with Luther, for the latter held to medieval concepts which condemned interest and advocated a just price, and would have welcomed a return to a rural economy. Calvin encouraged education and founded what eventually became the University of Geneva. Indeed, he emphasized schools, for he believed in the necessity of learned ministers who could set forth the true faith, and of an educated laity who could understand them. He maintained that religious education is especially important. He preached, taught, wrote, carried on an enormous correspondence, and advised in matters of legislation, law enforcement, and administration. His commentaries covered most of the Bible.

Under Calvin Geneva became a haven for oppressed Protestants from many lands. In it men were trained who went back to their native countries to further the Reformation. While they did not always slavishly reproduce what they had seen there, through them and his writings Calvin became the most powerful single factor in shaping the distinctive features of the Reformed Churches.

In the early years after his return, Calvin's position was by no means unchallenged. Some were restive under the strictness of the discipline for which he stood. Many of the native stock resented the influx of strangers and sought to prevent them from having a voice in the city's affairs. There were those who vigorously and volubly dissented from Calvin on matters of doctrine. Among the latter was Sebastien Castellio (1515–1563), of Savoy, a humanist scholar who had become a Protestant, and for a time was a protégé of Calvin. Castellio aspired to the pastorate, but Calvin blocked him, largely on questions of doctrine, for Castellio questioned the inspiration of the Song of Songs and Calvin's interpretation of the phrase in the Apostles' Creed about Christ's "descent into hell." He failed of appointment, was dismissed from his teaching post, and, embittered against Calvin, went to Basel. He continued to engage in controversy, in part directed against Calvin, but he was now out of Geneva.

More serious was the test given by Michael Servetus (1511–1553). Servetus was a Spaniard, a scholar, a physician and scientist of originality and note, who by the time he was twenty had become a radical reformer. Deeply religious and devoted to Christ, wishing to restore what he believed to be true Christianity, he would not conform with the accepted doctrine of the Trinity. He also denounced predestination and infant baptism and believed that the millennial reign of Christ was about to begin. Temperamentally a controversialist, his was a stormy career. He and Calvin had already violently disagreed when, in 1553, fleeing from condemnation for heresy in Roman Catholic Vienne and passing through Geneva, he was recognized and arrested, certainly at Calvin's instance. In his trial for heresy Calvin's enemies rallied to his support. Had he been acquitted, Calvin's power in Geneva would have been threatened. Indeed, Servetus demanded that Calvin be arrested as a false accuser and a heretic, be driven out of the city, and his goods be given to him, Servetus. Servetus was condemned by the civil authorities on the charge that he had denied the Trinity and rejected baptism, offenses punishable by death under the Justinian Code. In spite of Calvin's plea for a more merciful form of execution, Servetus was burned at the stake (October 27, 1553), crying through the flames: "O Jesus, thou Son of the eternal God, have pity on me."

The condemnation of Servetus was a major defeat for Calvin's opponents. Henceforward his position in Geneva was not to be seriously contested. Abstemiousness in food, drink, and sleep, prodigious labours, the stress of controversies, and distressing moral delinquencies in his immediate family undermined an already frail health. Calvin died May 27, 1564, in the arms of Theodore Beza. His last letter had been to Farel. Reserved, except among his intimates, he was loyal to his friends. Few were close to him, but these few had for him an unshakable affection.

Like Luther, through his writings Calvin had an influence which extended over much of Western Europe. The two men were very different. Luther, deeply emotional, was moulded by his soul-shaking experience. He gave little or no thought or effort towards achieving an ideal social order here and now. Calvin, intellectual, clear, logical, seemed to put a minimum of emotion in his preaching and writing. He sought to bring to actuality ideal Christian communities. Although recognizing the imperfections in the Church and among Christians, he believed that progress could be made towards this goal. Efforts for social improvement arose within both the Lutheran and Reformed Churches, but they were more characteristic of the latter. However, the similarities between Luther and Calvin were fully as marked as their differences. Both were impressed with the majesty and sovereignty of God, both held to the historic creeds of the Catholic Church, both revered the Scriptures as authoritative, and both believed in predestination and salvation by faith. Although they did not fully agree as to the nature of the presence of Christ in the Lord's Supper, Calvin was nearer to Luther than was Zwingli.

After the death of Calvin Geneva was still a major centre towards which the Reformed Churches continued to look. Calvin's mantle fell on the shoulders of Theodore Beza (1519–1605). Ten years younger than Calvin, Beza was born in Vézelay, in Burgundy, about 150 miles south-east of Paris. He was of aristocratic stock and was reared with the nobility. A precocious lad, he was put to school in the household of Melchior Wolmar, who was also a teacher of Calvin. There he was given a thorough grounding in the humanistic studies of the day and acquired facility in the use of Greek and especially of Latin. Wolmar was deeply religious and became so committed to the views of Luther that he had to flee to Germany. Beza was designed by his family for the law. When he was twenty he went to Paris, wishing to be a poet, and there, supported by the income from benefices, was following a life of literary leisure when, in his late twenties, illness struck him low. He rose from his sick bed a changed man, cast in his lot with the Reformers, and went to Geneva. Soon he was established as a professor in the academy at Lausanne. There he became famous as a scholar and teacher and from there he went on trips into Germany to seek aid for the persecuted Waldensees and to attempt to draw Lutherans and Reformed together. In 1559 he was appointed rector of the School of Theology of the newly founded Academy in Geneva, the precursor of the later University of Geneva. He had a leading part in the constitution of the Reformed Church in France. Elected as Calvin's successor, he continued to make Geneva a refuge centre for Protestants. He wrote prodigiously and was the leading Reformed theologian in the generation after Calvin.

One of the developments in which Beza was of great assistance was in Reformed psalmody. Zwingli had opposed music in public worship and it was a century or so after his death before the Reformed Churches in which his influence was strong departed from that precedent. Calvin did not go as far as Zwingli, but confined the use of music to congregational singing in unison of metrical versions of the Psalms and Canticles. In 1539 at Strassburg and in 1542 and 1551 a Psalter was issued and in 1562 this was followed by what became the definitive edition of what was known as the *Geneva Psalter*. The musical portions were largely the work of Louis Bourgeois, master of the choristers in Geneva. Although the precise origin of that tune is debated, it is to him that the familiar *Old Hundred* (or *Old Hundredth*) is ascribed. A metrical version in French of about a third of the Psalms had been made by

Clement Marot, who died in 1544. It was Beza who completed the task of putting the Psalter into French poetic form. Marot and Beza's Psalter speedily achieved popularity and passed through many editions. Put to music, much of it popular ballad tunes, its Psalms were sung on the streets and in services of public worship. With alterations, Marot and Beza's Psalter long remained standard for French Protestantism. For use in the Reformed Churches, there were several versions of the Psalms in German and Dutch. As we are to see a little later, paraphrases of the Psalms in English were to be widely sung in the English-speaking churches of the Reformed tradition.

Swiss Reformed Churches Drawn Together

During Calvin's lifetime the Reformed Churches of Switzerland began drawing together. The process was not automatic. In addition to cantonal and civic particularism and to linguistic and cultural differences between French and Germans, those who followed Zwingli tended to look askance at Calvin's views of the Lord's Supper. Basel was not inclined to favour Calvin's convictions on predestination, and Bern disliked the independence of the Church from domination by the state which was part of his programme. However, in 1549 Calvin and Bullinger reached an accord on the sacraments which eventually was adopted in other Swiss centres. While the Germans did not approve of the rigid discipline of Geneva and variations remained, French and German Reformed Churches increasingly recognized their kinship.

The Waldensees Join the Reform Movement

The Waldensian remnants became associated with the Reformed Churches. This was natural. They had taken refuge in valleys of Piedmont and so were adjacent to the Swiss. The ideas of the Swiss reforms were carried to them in the 1530's, partly by Farel, and partly by a deputation of their pastors which visited Strasburg, Basel, and Bern. They seem to have greeted the new movement with enthusiasm and through it to have experienced a revival. Their Confession of 1655 was Calvinistic. They suffered severe persecution from Roman Catholic princes but a sturdy nucleus survived.

The Reformed Churches in Central Europe

We have already seen (Chapter 32) something of the rise of Reformed Churches to the east of Switzerland. We have noted that in Bohemia Slavonic Protestantism and in Hungary Magyar Protestantism tended to find expression through them, while German Protestants held to Lutheranism. In the sixteenth century Bohemia and Hungary seemed about to be swept fully into Protestantism, but in the seventeenth century reverses left only a minority of that faith. In Transylvania, on the extreme eastern fringe of Hungary, the German communities which had been there since the Middle Ages adopted Lutheranism, the Magyars constituted the main constituency of the Reformed Churches, the Socinians, of whom we are to hear later (Chapter 35), won a following among the Szeklers (a racial group which was probably closely related to the Magyars), some of the upper classes remained Roman Catholic, and much of the peasantry was Orthodox. Before the end of the sixteenth century the first four forms of Christianity were accorded official status by the state and were given an equal legal basis. Lutherans, Reformed, Anabaptists and Socinians all won adherents in Poland. Indeed, as we are to see (Chapter 38), the divisions among Protestants were a major cause of the triumphant resurgence of the Roman Catholic Church in that country. Many of the Bohemian Brethren, expelled from Bohemia in 1548, sought refuge in Poland. In 1555 they and the Reformed Churches in that land united in a permanent union.

The Reformed Churches in Germany

The Reformed Churches multiplied in Germany. Through Bucer and the temporary residence of Calvin, Strassburg was early inclined in that direction. The mediating influence of Melanchthon also made for that trend. In the controversies which arose after the death of the great reformer, those who held to a stiff Lutheranism, especially on the nature of the presence of Christ in the Lord's Supper, alienated many who were not prepared to go to such extremes. Accordingly, the latter moved in the direction of the Reformed Churches. Even before his death, the views of Calvin had begun to gain ground on German soil. Frederick III, the "Pious" (1515–1576), who became Elector Palatine in 1559, came out stoutly on the side of Calvinism, made it the established faith in the Palatinate, and persecuted both Roman Catholics and Lutherans. In 1563 the Heidelberg Catechism was issued. Written by younger friends of Calvin and Bullinger, one of whom had also been a student and friend of Melanchthon, it was less polemic and more based on Christian experience than were some of the other documents of the Reformation. It was widely adopted among the Reformed Churches, was used in Scotland, and became standard in the Netherlands and in the Dutch and German Reformed Churches in America. In the latter half of the sixteenth century the Reformed Churches also gained headway in Nassau, Bremen, Hesse, and Brandenburg.

The Reformed Churches in the Netherlands

The Reformation made great strides in the Netherlands and was intimately associated with a notable struggle for political independence. When Luther began the Reformation, Charles V was consolidating his rule in the Low Countries. The region had been more a geographic expression, the lowlands at the mouths of great rivers, than a political entity. It contained important and thriving commercial cities and prosperous farms, but it was divided linguistically and racially. Its chief elements were Dutch in the north, Flemings in the centre, and French-speaking Walloons in the south. Charles V, who had received the region by inheritance and had been reared there, attempted to weld the country together and build in it an absolute and unified monarchy after the manner of other states which were then emerging in Western Europe. Part of his programme was the creation of territorial episcopal sees which would make for more efficient discipline.

The writings of Luther early found an eager response in the Netherlands. The way for them had been prepared by movements in the previous century which we have already recorded, among them the Brethren of the Common Life, Christian mysticism, and Christian humanism. Here *The Imitation of Christ* had been composed and here Erasmus had been born and reared. Between 1513 and 1531 more than a score of translations of the Bible or the New Testament were produced in Dutch, Flemish, or French. Charles V undertook strenuous measures to stamp out Lutheranism, but in spite of them it prospered. Anabaptists were numerous and were severely dealt with. However, although there were martyrs among both Lutherans and Anabaptists, the successive regents who ruled for Charles, his aunt and his sister, were much more tolerant than he.

By the fourth quarter of the sixteenth century Calvinism was largely supplanting Lutheranism, especially among the Dutch, and in 1561 a Walloon who had studied at Geneva, Guy de Bray, prepared the Belgic Confession, a strongly Calvinistic document, which with some modifications long remained standard in the Dutch Reformed Church. The first general synod of that church was held in 1571.

In 1555, on the abdication of Charles V, his son Philip II took over the reins of government. Philip attempted to complete the work begun by his father of consolidating the region under royal rule. Part of the plan was carrying through the project for dividing much of the land among new dioceses. In 1559 Philip left the Netherlands, never to return, but he continued to govern it from a distance through his illegitimate half-sister Margaret and a Council of State. Local opposition soon arose, directed against the presence of Spanish troops, the stringent measures for the repression of heresy, the new bishoprics, and the disregard for the local charters and privileges which Philip had sworn to maintain.

In 1566 several scores of young nobles led by a Lutheran, a Roman Catholic, and a Calvinist demanded a change of policy and the suppression of the Inquisition. They called themselves "beggars," a name at first given them contemptuously. Their emblem, a beggar's sack, was adopted by thousands, both high and low. The numbers of the Reformed grew apace through services conducted by excommunicated ministers. Some of the more fanatical demolished images, pictures, and shrines in churches, chapels, and at least one cathedral. Philip II responded by sending additional Spanish troops under the Duke of Alva and set up a tribunal to stamp out opposition. Thereupon armed revolt broke out. It was led by William, Prince of Orange, also known as William the Silent. Although born of Protestant parents, he was a Roman Catholic. It was upon his arm that Charles V had leaned at the ceremony of abdication.

Into the details of the war which followed we need not go. Resistance to the Spanish forces was most effective by sailors and fishermen. Famous was the siege of Leiden which was relieved when, the dykes having been cut, the Sea Beggars, as the patriotic naval forces were called, sailed across the flooded fields to the aid of the beleaguered city. The University of Leiden, founded as a reward for the resisting townsmen, became a leading centre of the Reformed faith. Further fighting followed, the Duke of Parma proving an able general for Philip. Attempts to bring together permanently the Protestant North and the Roman Catholic South in an effective league against the Spaniards did not succeed. The Protestant North formed itself into the United Provinces, led by William of Orange, who in 1573 from deep conviction joined the Reformed Church. In 1581 the United Provinces renounced allegiance to Philip and declared themselves an independent republic. Religiously tolerant in an age and region where passions rose high, William failed to hold Protestants and Catholics together, but with patience, resourcefulness, and courage he led in what for years seemed a hopeless struggle for the achievement of the autonomy so boldly claimed. Assassinated in 1584 at the age of fifty-one, for Philip had placed a price upon his life, William did not see full independence. Not until 1609 did hostilities stop. The United Netherlands (as the United Provinces came to be called) had won their freedom.

While the struggle was still in progress, the Dutch Reformed Church was taking shape. Successive synods, some of them held at Dort (Dordrecht), helped to give it form. It adopted a Presbyterian government, the Heidelberg Catechism, and the Belgic Confession. The closeness of the tie with the state varied from province to province. In the exigencies of the struggle against Philip II and Spain, only in part religious as it was, to present a common front the United Provinces found it necessary to grant a degree of freedom to others than Calvinists. Anabaptists were protected and Roman Catholics were conceded the right of residence and employment, although not of public worship or office-holding.

After the political fighting had ended, a momentous struggle over doctrine broke out within the Dutch Reformed Church. Theologians were divided between supralapsarians and infralapsarians, namely between those who held that before He created the world God had decreed who should be saved and who should be damned, and those who maintained that in view of man's fall in Adam's sin, but not until after that catastrophe, God had decreed that certain men should be lost and others saved. Against both these views some, who came to be known as Remonstrants, protested. The chief figure among them was Jacob Arminius, a pupil of Beza and professor of theology in the University of Leiden, who, setting out to refute them, became convinced by them. Accordingly the Remonstrant position has been known as Arminianism. Rejecting supralapsarianism and infralapsarianism, limited atonement (namely, the teaching that Christ died only for the elect), irresistible grace, and the perseverance of the elect, it held that Christ died for all men, that salvation is by faith alone, that those who believe are saved, that those who reject God's grace are lost, and that God does not elect particular individuals for either outcome. Feeling ran high. Remonstrants were chiefly from the wealthy and favoured states rights. Their opponents were nationalists who wished a general synod to deal with the issue. At a synod held at Dort in 1618 and 1619 delegates came from Switzerland, Bremen, Hesse, the Palatinate, and England. In other words, it was widely representative of the Reformed Churches. It condemned Arminianism in strongly Calvinistic canons, and reaffirmed the Heidelberg Confession and the Belgic Confession. One of the leading Remonstrants was beheaded a few days after the synod adjourned. Another, Hugo Grotius, to become famous from his treatise *De Jure Belli et Pacis,* was imprisoned but escaped. Arminianism was by no means crushed. The Remonstrants continued in Holland as a distinct church and again and again where Calvinism was taught Arminianism raised its head.

The Reformed Churches in France: the Huguenots and Their Fate

As in the Netherlands, so in France, Protestantism had a stormy history. In both lands, compounded with other factors, it contributed to protracted wars. In contrast with the Netherlands, however, in France no permanent territorial division ensued. Here, rather, Protestants constituted a minority which won a special, tolerated status in the midst of a predominantly Roman Catholic population. Eventually, partly for the purpose of extending the monolithic power of the absolute monarchy and partly under the guise of stamping out heresy and obtaining religious uniformity, that status was abrogated, persecution was instituted, and a notable exodus followed.

In France the Protestant Reformation came from several sources. It had strong humanistic roots. We have already met Jacques Le Fèvre and Guillaume Briçonnet. As Bishop of Meaux the latter made his episcopal family a centre of reform. He was the spiritual director of Margaret (1492–1549), sister of King Francis I and by her second marriage Queen of Navarre and the grandmother of Henry of Navarre who, as we shall see in a moment, a fighting champion of Protestantism, eventually brought a semblance of unity to France by adopting Roman Catholicism and reigning as Henry IV. Margaret was intensely interested in humanistic studies, was deeply religious, was strongly impressed by Luther and Calvin, was a mystic of the Christian Platonist type, but, while dissenting from much in the Roman Catholic Church, never became a Protestant. The attitude of Francis I towards Protestants varied with his shifting international policy. At times he found it expedient to persecute them and there were executions. When he wished the friendship of the Protestant princes of Germany he smiled upon them.

A chief centre of vigorous opposition to the Reformers was the Sorbonne. Founded in the thirteenth century by Robert de Sorbon as a college within the University of Paris, it had become a faculty of theology and was regarded by the Roman Catholic world as an outstanding authority on questions concerning the Christian faith. The Sorbonne came out with a statement of the doctrines of the Catholic Church in refutation of Calvin's *Institutes* and compiled a list of prohibited books on which were the works of Luther, Calvin, Melanchthon, and Marot. Parlement issued proscriptions of Protestantism, the majority of the villages of the Waldensees were destroyed, and numbers of the Meaux group were burned at the stake.

Henry II, the son and successor of Francis I, was unrelenting in his attempts to extirpate the Reformation. However, the movement continued to spread. Monks and priests were converted to it. Schools and colleges became hotbeds. It was natural that it should follow the patterns of the Reformed Churches already in existence in the adjacent French-speaking parts of Switzerland. French youths, trained as missionaries in Geneva, Lausanne, and Strassburg, traversed the country, selling literature and meeting groups of converts. The writings of Calvin, a Frenchman, made an appeal to his fellow-countrymen. In 1559, five years before the death of Calvin, a national synod was convened in Paris. It framed a confession of faith based upon one drawn up by him. It also adopted a form of organization which was to have a marked effect upon churches of the Reformed family in Holland, Scotland, and America. French Protestants came to be known as Huguenots. They were strongest in the cities.

They had their chief spread among artisans, tradesmen, and farmers, but they also won converts from the aristocracy. Among the latter were Gaspard de Coligny, Admiral of France, the titular King of Navarre, and his brother, the Prince of Condé.

Henry II died in 1559 and was followed by his fifteen-year-old son, the feeble Francis II, son of Catherine de' Medici and husband of Mary "Queen of Scots." Francis died the following year. During his brief reign he was under the control of his uncles, the Cardinal of Lorraine and the Duke of Guise. These two were for extirpating Protestantism. Sprung from Lorraine, the Guises were regarded as foreigners and upstarts by such nobles as the Prince of Condé, descended as he was from Louis IX, the Saint, and their dominance was resented.

Francis II was succeeded by his younger brother, the ten-year-old Charles IX, and his mother, Catherine de' Medici, became Regent. An attempt at reconciliation between Catholics and Huguenots was made by the government in a colloquy in which Beza was among the representatives of the Protestants. No agreement was reached, but the Protestants were accorded a limited toleration.

In 1562 what were known as the Wars of Religion broke out. They were waged intermittently until 1594. Into the complicated and wearisome details we need not go. The most famous incident was what was remembered as the Massacre of St. Bartholomew, in August, 1572. Huguenot leaders had gathered in Paris for the marriage of Henry of Navarre, a Protestant, to Marguerite, daughter of Catherine de' Medici. By orders from Catherine, many among the Huguenots were killed. The massacre spread to other parts of France. War was resumed. As in its earlier stages, although the ostensible cause, religion was by no means the only factor. Personal and family rivalries and ambitions entered. On the Catholic side the Guises were prominent. In the later phases of the struggle the leader of the Protestants was Henry of Navarre. Since Henry III, the brother and successor of Charles IX, had no son, by right of descent from St. Louis Henry of Navarre was the heir presumptive. At first he declined to give up his faith and the war went on, even after the death of Henry III. The Protestants were a minority. As a means of uniting the realm Henry of Navarre, now legitimately Henry IV of France, decided to become a Roman Catholic. With characteristic wit he is said to have remarked: "Paris was well worth a mass." His conversion and coronation (1594) and his promise of protection to the Huguenots brought peace.

The Huguenots required more than this royal promise from one whom they regarded as an apostate. As a result, in 1598 the Edict of Nantes was promulgated. It guaranteed them freedom of public worship in several scores of specified towns, in two places in each of certain kinds of administrative divisions of the kingdom, and in more than three thousand castles. Although Paris was not among the cities where public Huguenot worship was permitted, private services might be held there in the apartments of high officials. Protestants were assured full civic rights and the privilege of admission to all public offices and to universities, schools, and hospitals. Protestant clergy were granted the same exemptions from military service and other charges as the Catholic clergy enjoyed. Huguenots could freely hold their church assemblies. As a safeguard, until 1607, later extended five years, they were to have complete control of two hundred towns, including La Rochelle and Montpellier, and the state was to pay the garrisons and governors of these strongholds.

The Edict of Nantes did not bring permanent peace. Causes of friction remained, partly religious and partly political. Roman Catholics and Protestants found it difficult to live amicably side by side in the same town. The Jesuits, of whom we are to hear more in later chapters, were active in seeking to win Protestants and to establish themselves in Protestant centres. In a realm where the king and his ministers, notably the great Richelieu, were endeavouring to extend the authority of the crown, the semi-independent status of the Huguenots was an irritant, especially since, in seeking to maintain themselves, the latter allied themselves with some of the nobility who were challenging the growing centralization of power under the king and sought foreign aid. Under Henry IV's son, Louis XIII, three domestic wars were fought in which the Huguenots and their cause were major factors. They culminated in the siege of their stronghold, La Rochelle, and its capitulation (October 29, 1628).

There then ensued three decades of comparative peace and prosperity. The Peace of Alais (June 27, 1629), which followed the fall of La Rochelle, while specifying the destruction of the fortifications of the towns held by the Huguenots, promised the restoration of most of the privileges which had been granted by the Edict of Nantes. So long as this was observed the Huguenots flourished. They seem never to have been more than a ninth of the total population, but they were especially strong in the South and South-west, possibly in part because of a tradition of revolt against the Catholic Church from the days of the Cathari. In some towns and cities they were in the majority. They stressed schools for their youth and were much better educated than the rank and file of their Catholic neighbours. Thrifty, prominent in the professions and business, they were more influential in national and community life than their numbers would have led one to expect.

Then, in the reign of Louis XIV, the "Grand Monarch" who followed Louis XIII, progressively severe restrictions were imposed. They culminated in the destruction of churches, the compulsory removal (1681) of Protestant children from their parents to be reared as Catholics, and, in 1685, the formal revocation of the Edict of Nantes. Louis was moved to these steps by his heightened devotion to the Catholic faith which came in middle age under the influence of his wife, Madame de Maintenon, and by his settled purpose to be supreme in his realm. This latter desire had been hampered by what remained of the privileged position of the Huguenot community.

To escape the persecutions which preceded, accompanied, and followed the abrogation of the edict, tens of thousands of Huguenots left the country and found refuge in other lands—in Prussia, Holland, England, Ireland, the English colonies in America, and even in remote South Africa. Some who remained conformed to the Catholic Church. Protestantism in France declined in numbers but did not disappear. It persisted and was to have a notable record in the nineteenth and twentieth centuries.

The Reformed Faith Becomes That of the Church of Scotland

In the sixteenth century Protestantism made its way into Scotland. There it was to become the faith of the overwhelming majority of the population and the official religion of the state and the community. The form of Protestantism which prevailed was Presbyterianism, a Presbyterianism which owed a profound debt to Geneva and Calvin but which did not fully conform to either. This development was to have a wide influence on the future history of Christianity. Although Scotland is a small country and in the sixteenth and seventeenth centuries it was sparsely settled and economically poor, in later centuries its Presbyterianism was to have an expansion which carried it into many lands. This was partly through its effect on English Puritanism, partly through extensive migrations to Ireland, North America, Australia, New Zealand, and South Africa, and partly through far-flung missions. To the story of the winning of Scotland we must now turn. As usual, we must content ourselves with the briefest possible summary.

At the dawn of the sixteenth century the Catholic Church in Scotland was in dire need of reform. Lawlessness was rife, the nobility were turbulent, unwilling to submit to royal authority, and divided into warring factions, some episcopal sees were vacant, where they were filled their incumbents were embroiled in the political strife of the realm, and many ecclesiastical posts were given to sons of the nobles who enjoyed the revenues but, absentees, did not perform the associated duties. The country was torn between those who wished closer relations with the hereditary foe, the English, and those who stood for the traditional anti-English tie with France.

Precursors of the later religious revolution were beginning to be seen. Through contact with England, Lollardy had some influence. Several of

Luther's writings were being read. Here and there preachers were boldly advocating the new views. In 1528 Patrick Hamilton was burned at the stake in St. Andrews, the ecclesiastical capital of the country. Of gentle birth, he had taken a degree at the University of Paris, had studied at Wittenberg, and, returning, before his arrest and condemnation had been allowed to present his views in the University of St. Andrews. In the next few years edicts against heresy were issued and several other advocates of the Reformation were put to death. One of these, George Wishart, was sent to the stake in 1546. Cardinal Beaton, Archbishop of St. Andrews, who had brought about his death, was murdered a few weeks later, partly in revenge and partly from opposition to his pro-French policy. The assassins fortified themselves in a castle on the coast, expecting aid from England, but were overwhelmed by forces sent on a French fleet.

The outstanding leader in the Scottish Reformation was John Knox. Born between 1505 and 1515 in or near Haddington, east of Edinburgh, of humble parentage, Knox studied in one of the Scottish universities and was ordained to the priesthood. He himself tells how he attended upon Wishart when the latter preached in Haddington and would have followed him had Wishart not dissuaded him. After Wishart's death and Cardinal Beaton's murder he and some of his "bairns" (presumably his students) joined the group in the St. Andrews castle and there preached Protestant views. He was captured, taken to France, for nineteen months was a galley prisoner, and then, released (early in 1549), went to England, where the Reformation was at full tide under Edward VI. He was one of the chaplains of the king, refused a bishopric, fled to the Continent when the Catholic reaction came under Edward VI's sister and successor, Mary, and was in a number of places, including Frankfort and especially Geneva. In Geneva he became an ardent disciple of Calvin. He married Margaret Bowes, from Northumberland, to whom he had been betrothed while in England.

While Knox was abroad, the Reformation was making progress in Scotland. In it national loyalty and religious fervour were combining. The child monarch, Mary "Queen of Scots" (1542–1587), born a few days before the death of her father, James V, was affianced to the Dauphin and was sent to France at the age of five. In 1558 she was married to the Dauphin, who was soon to be Francis II. In Scotland her mother, Mary of Lorraine, served as regent in her place. The regent was unpopular, partly because she was French and the Scots feared, with good reason, that this and the marriage of their Queen to a French king would lead to an attempt to annex their country. A possible English tie through the earlier proposed marriage of Mary to the future Edward VI was fully as abhorrent.

During several months in Scotland in 1555 and 1556 Knox gave a marked impetus to the Reformation. He preached extensively in the south of the country and had an attentive hearing. Partly as a result, on December 3, 1557, some of the nobility who were anti-French entered into a covenant to "establish the most blessed word of God and his Congregation." They were, accordingly, called the Lords of the Congregation.

It was in 1560 and 1561 that Scotland officially went over to the Reformation. In 1559 the regent forbade Reformed preaching. Civil war followed, with French troops supporting the regent, and English forces, sent by Queen Elizabeth of that country, aiding the Protestant party. The regent died and the French troops sailed for home. In August, 1560, the Scottish Parliament adopted a confession of faith which had been drafted by Knox and some others. It was more Calvinistic than Lutheran or Zwinglian. That month the same body declared that the Pope no longer had jurisdiction in Scotland and forbade the mass. Like Luther, Calvin, and many others of the reformers, Knox had turned to the civil authorities to effect the changes which he desired.

No detailed provision was made by Parliament for the organization and administration of the Church. Knox and his associates accordingly drew up what was known as the *First Book of Discipline*. It provided for the dedication of the wealth of the Church, including the continuation of the tithes, to the support of the ministry, education, and the relief of the poor. Parish ministers were to be nominated by the people, examined by the learned, and publicly admitted to their offices. There were to be superintendents who roughly corresponded to the old bishops, but they were to be of no higher rank than parish ministers and their functions were to be purely administrative, such as planting churches and placing clergy. A comprehensive system of schools was projected, culminating in universities, an expression of an emphasis on education which was already present in Scotland and which the Reformation was greatly to accentuate.

Not all the nobles assented to the document. This was partly because some had appropriated ecclesiastical lands and revenues. Although enough subscribed to it to give it standing, the failure of official approval by Parliament was an indication of the partial independence of Church from state which, in contrast with England, was to characterize the course of the Reformed faith in Scotland. Moreover, in the completed ecclesiastical structure which was here given its preliminary and partial formulation, the laity and the people were accorded a voice which monarchs were rightly to regard as a threat to their claims to absolute power. Provision was made on the parish level for the lay elder, and in the General Assembly which acted for the entire Church of Scotland the rank and file had a much larger voice than in Parliament. By declaring that "before God there is no respect of persons," *The Book of Discipline* furthered in the Scots a sturdy independence and democratic spirit.

The Book of Common Order, often known as *Knox's Liturgy,* adopted by the General Assembly in 1564, governed public worship. It showed the influence of the form employed in the English congregation in Frankfort, of Calvin, Farel, Strassburg, and Geneva. It was to be standard until 1645.

In August, 1560, a few months after the actions of Parliament in abolishing the mass and adopting a Reformed confession of faith, the weak Francis II of France breathed his last and in August, 1561, Mary, widowed, returned to Scotland. Reared a loyal Roman Catholic, she had mass said in her chapel in Holyrood Palace. Charming, determined, and intelligent, she could prove a formidable foe to the religious innovations. Although she made no immediate effort to upset them, she certainly was not their friend. Knox, a formidable preacher and now in the pulpit of St. Giles, the cathedral of Edinburgh up the street from Holyrood, thundered against this revival of the mass. He inveighed against the frivolities at the court and his audiences with Mary did not relieve the tension.

For a time, the tide seemed to be running against the Reformation. Knox temporarily lost the support of some of the more powerful of the Lords of the Congregation. Mary married her cousin, Darnley, a Roman Catholic. In complex politics which involved relations with England and Mary's ambition to win the succession to the English throne after the childless Elizabeth, a succession to which her Tudor blood gave her claim as the next of kin, the Protestant nobles were temporarily worsted.

However, Mary badly misplayed her hand. Her unwise matrimonial ventures and the intrigues, murders, and civil strife which were associated with them eventually drove her to seek refuge in England (1568). After years of detention in that land she was executed (1587) on the charge of complicity in a plot to assassinate Elizabeth. Her son, James VI (1566–1625, to become James I of England after the death of Elizabeth, in 1603), who came to the throne after the compulsory abdication of his mother (1567), was reared in the Reformed faith and Knox preached at the infant's coronation. Knox lived to see his cause apparently triumphant. A war horse to the end, he died November 24, 1572, after having earlier in the month inducted his successor to the pulpit of St. Giles.

Knox's work was carried forward by others. Outstanding among them was Andrew Melville (1545–1622), distinguished scholar, friend of Beza, teacher, reorganizer of the Universities of Glasgow and Aberdeen, and Rector of the University of St. Andrews. He led in giving to the Church of Scotland a thorough-going Presbyterian organization. This was embodied in the *Second*

Book of Discipline, adopted by the General Assembly in 1577, which was authoritative whenever the Church was left free by the state to follow it. In it, the terms pastor, bishop, and minister were employed to designate the same office. A few years later (1580–1581) the administrative powers which the *First Book of Discipline* had conferred on superintendents were transferred to presbyteries, ecclesiastical courts which were to exercise many of the functions of bishops.

For hymns the Scottish Presbyterians used versifications of the Psalms. In 1564, with the authorization of the General Assembly, a Psalter was issued. In 1635 the Great Scottish Psalter appeared, with tunes of various origins, some of them native and most of the others French and German. The Westminister Assembly of 1643 supervised the preparation of a drastic revision. As a result, in 1650 the Scottish Psalter was published which long remained standard.

The Presbyterian system and the Reformed faith continued to have a stormy course. James VI (James I of England) sought to foist episcopacy on the Church of Scotland, for to him it was essential to the royal prerogative. "No bishop, no king," was his conviction. Because of his firm Presbyterianism, Melville was forced into exile. Yet James left the presbyteries largely undisturbed. Moreover, he sent representatives to the Synod of Dort, and although none of these could speak officially for the Church of Scotland, the latter accepted the decrees of that gathering. James VI's son Charles I attempted not only to make the Church of Scotland episcopal but also to bring its services into conformity with the Book of Common Prayer of the Church of England. It was Scottish abhorrence of these measures which led to the resistance of the great body of Scots through the National Covenant (1638) and paved the way for the civil war which cost Charles the English and Scottish thrones and which culminated in his execution. In the course of the civil war, the Scots entered into the Solemn League and Covenant with the English Parliament which brought a Scottish army to the aid of that body against Charles and which was responsible for convening the Westminster Assembly of English churchmen and Scottish commissioners (the latter without vote) that drew up a system of Presbyterian church government, the Westminster Confession, and the Westminster Directory of Public Worship. In an effort to achieve religious uniformity in the two realms, the Scottish General Assembly and Parliament adopted the latter two documents.

When, with Charles II, the Stuarts were restored to power, that monarch reimposed bishops on the Church of Scotland and lay appointment to the parish pastorates was revived. Vigorous resistance greeted these acts, many ministers were ejected from their churches, and the disaffected met in secret conventicles.

Extreme Covenanters resorted to armed rebellion, a step of which moderate Presbyterians disapproved and which the government met with force and penal laws. In his effort for toleration of his fellow Roman Catholics, the successor of Charles II, James VII (James II of England), took measures similar to the ones which he adopted in England, and gave toleration to dissenters from the state church.

When James was forced to leave Britain, Scotland joined England in accepting William and Mary (1689). In 1690 an act was passed which established the Church of Scotland as it was to remain for generations, the laws favouring episcopacy were repealed, and the Westminster Confession was recognized. That year the General Assembly met for the first time since 1653. Queen Anne, who succeeded William and Mary, took oath to preserve the Presbyterian form of church government and the confession of faith.

Dissenters from the established church remained. Some were Episcopalians who had their own bishops. For many years Episcopalianism was especially strong in the North-east and centered in Aberdeen. There the combination of episcopalianism with the presbytery and synod long persisted and few representatives were sent to the General Assembly. Some, notably in the Highlands, were Roman Catholics. Numbers were Presbyterians who for one reason or another had broken with the Church of Scotland. However, the Church of Scotland embraced a larger proportion of the population of the country than did the Church of England in England. Like the latter and several of the Lutheran state churches, it was a continuation of the church of pre-Reformation days. Like them it had broken with Rome and had freed itself from what it deemed the corruptions that it associated with the Papacy. Yet it was in unbroken succession with the Christianity which had been planted by Columba and other early missionaries. Its leaders thought of it as being an integral part of the Catholic Church.

SUMMARY

On the Reformed Churches the impress of no one man was as marked as was that of Luther on the family of churches which are usually known by his name. Indeed, in the Reformed Churches the contributions made by Luther shared in importance with those features which were more specifically identified with them. In important ways, such as their conception of the manner in which Christ is present in the Lord's Supper, the relation of Church and state, and the degree of departure from what had come through the Catholic Church of previous centuries, they differed from Luther. They were more inclined to the independence of Church from state, more hopeful of realizing a Christian society, and less intent on perpetuating what had been inherited in ritual and organization. Yet they held to Luther's central distinctive affirmation, salvation by faith. They were clearly Protestants. Their outstanding figure, John Calvin, was to have an influence in Protestantism second only to that of Luther. Like the latter, it was to be felt far beyond the borders of the churches with which his system was most closely associated.

SELECTED BIBLIOGRAPHY

GENERAL WORKS ON PROTESTANTISM WHICH HAVE TO DO WITH THE
REFORMED CHURCHES

R. H. Bainton, *The Reformation of the Sixteenth Century* (Boston, The Beacon Press, 1952, pp. xi, 276). An admirable popular brief summary by an outstanding specialist.

The Cambridge Modern History. Volume III, The Reformation (Cambridge University Press, 1903).

B. J. Kidd, *Documents Illustrative of the Continental Reformation* (Oxford, The Clarendon Press, 1911, pp. xix, 742). A very useful collection, about half on the Reformed Churches.

T. M. Lindsay, *A History of the Reformation* (New York, Charles Scribner's Sons, 2 vols., 1906). A standard work.

E. de Moreau, P. Jourda, and P. Janelle, *La Crise Religieuse du XVI*e *Siècle* (Paris, Bloud & Gay, 1950, pp. 461. Vol. 16 of A. Fliche and E. Jarry, *Histoire de l'Église depuis les Origines jusqu'a Nos Jours*). A Roman Catholic treatment, which attempts to be objective.

P. Schaff, *The Creeds of Christendom. Volume III, The Evangelical Protestant Creeds, with Translations* (New York, Harper & Brothers, 1877, pp. vii, 920).

P. Schaff, *History of the Christian Church. Volume VII. The Swiss Reformation* (2d ed., revised, New York, Charles Scribner's Sons, 1894, pp. xvii, 890). A standard work, sympathetic with the Reformed tradition.

P. Smith, *The Age of the Reformation* (New York, Henry Holt and Co., 1920, pp. xii, 861). An excellent summary of the Protestant and Catholic Reformations in their general European setting.

HULDREICH ZWINGLI

S. Simpson, *Life of Ulrich Zwingli, the Swiss Patriot and Reformer* (New York, The Baker & Taylor Co., 1902, pp. 297). Semi-popular, based on extensive research, contains an excellent bibliography.

U. Zwingli, *Sämtliche Werke* in *Corpus Reformatorum*, II Ser., Vol. 88–100 (Berlin, C. A. Schwetschke und Sohn, and Leipzig, M. Heinsius Nachfolger, 1905–1944).

The Latin Works and Correspondence of Huldreich Zwingli Together with Selections from His German Works, translated by various scholars, inaugurated by W. J. Hinke (3 vols., 1912–1929. Vol. I published by G. P. Putnam's Sons, New York; Vols. 2, 3 by the Heidelberg Press, Philadelphia).

JOHN CALVIN

T. Beza, *The Life of John Calvin,* translated by H. Beveridge (Philadelphia, The Westminster Press, 1909, pp. 115). By an admiring, intimate friend.

Q. Breen, *John Calvin: a Study in French Humanism* (Grand Rapids, Mich., Wm. B. Eerdmans Publishing Co., 1931, pp. ix, 174). A doctoral dissertation of the University of Chicago.

J. Calvin, *Institutes of the Christian Religion,* translated from the Latin and collated with the author's last edition in French by J. Allen. Seventh American edition, by B. B. Warfield (Philadelphia, Presbyterian Board of Christian Education, 2 vols., no date).

Calvin, *Opera supersunt omnia* in *Corpus Reformatorum,* II Ser., Vols. 29–85 (Brunswick, C. A. Schwetschke et filium, 1863–1897).

H. G. Reyburn, *John Calvin, His Life, Letters and Work* (London, Hodder & Stoughton, 1914, pp. viii, 376). Carefully based on the sources.

W. Walker, *John Calvin, the Organizer of Reformed Protestantism 1509–1564* (New York, G. P. Putnam's Sons, 1906, pp. xviii, 456). A standard biography by a specialist.

MARTIN BUCER

H. Eells, *Martin Bucer* (Yale University Press, 1931, pp. xii, 539). Carefully done with extensive references to the sources and secondary works.

THEODORE BEZA

H. M. Baird, *Theodore Beza, the Counsellor of the French Reformation* (New York, G. P. Putnam's Sons, 1899, pp. xxi, 376). Semi-popular.

THE REFORMED CHURCHES IN THE NETHERLANDS

J. L. Motley, *The Rise of the Dutch Republic* (New York, E. P. Dutton & Co., 3 vols., 1906). The *Everyman's Library* edition of a standard work, warmly sympathetic with William of Orange, first published in 1855.

THE HUGUENOTS

H. M. Baird, *History of the Rise of the Huguenots of France* (New York, Charles Scribner's Sons, 2 vols., 1879). Warmly sympathetic with the Huguenots.

H. M. Baird, *The Huguenots and Henry of Navarre* (London, Kegan Paul, Trench, Trübner & Co., 2 vols., 1886). Well written, based upon extensive research.

H. M. Baird, *The Huguenots and the Revocation of the Edict of Nantes* (New York, Charles Scribner's Sons, 2 vols., 1895). Like the other two works by Baird, well written, sympathetic with the Huguenots, and based upon extensive research.

THE CHURCH OF SCOTLAND

J. Cunningham, *The Church History of Scotland* (Edinburgh, James Thin, 2d ed., 2 vols., 1882). A solid piece of work.

G. D. Henderson, *Religious Life in Seventeenth-Century Scotland* (Cambridge University Press, 1937, pp. 311). Based upon a careful study of the sources.

The Works of John Knox, collected and edited by D. Laing (Edinburgh, The Wodrow Society, 6 vols., Johnstone and Hunter, Thomas George Stevenson, 1846–1864).

John Knox's History of the Reformation in Scotland, edited by W. G. Dickenson (London, Thomas Nelson & Sons, 2 vols., 1949). Contains a valuable introduction, a useful bibliography, and excellent notes.

A. Lang, *John Knox and the Reformation* (London, Longmans, Green & Co., 1905, pp. xiv, 281). Carefully done.

H. M. Luckock, *The Church in Scotland* (London, Well Gardner, Darton & Co., 1893). A useful historical survey.

A. R. Macewen, *A History of the Church of Scotland* (New York, Hodder & Stoughton, 2 vols., 1913, 1918). A careful study from the beginning to 1560, terminated by the author's death.

T. M'Crie, *Life of Andrew Melville* (Edinburgh, William Blackwood, 2 vols., 2d ed., 1824).

M. Patrick, *Four Centuries of Scottish Psalmody* (Oxford University Press, 1950, pp. xxiii, 234).

Lord Eustace Percy, *John Knox* (London, Hodder & Stoughton, 1937, pp. 438). Very well done.

H. Watt, *John Knox in Controversy* (New York, Philosophical Library, 1950, pp. ix, 109). By an outstanding expert.

Chapter 34

THE RADICAL REFORMERS:
THE ANABAPTISTS

Thus far in recounting the Protestant Reformation we have dealt with two of its more conservative wings, Lutheranism and the Reformed and Presbyterian Churches. Both were in many ways a continuation of the Catholic Church in their respective lands. In principle Lutheranism rejected only those features of the Catholic Church which seemed to it expressly forbidden in the Scriptures. The Reformed Churches went further and retained from the Catholic Church only what they believed to have warrant in the Scriptures. Each sought to be the church of the entire community. In this they succeeded in several lands. Both continued infant baptism and by it endeavoured to bring into the visible church all who were born in the community. To be sure, Luther was not entirely happy over this procedure, for it did not fully accord with his basic principle of salvation by faith. Calvin taught that many so baptized were not among the elect and did not belong to that invisible church whose membership was known to God alone. Yet each wished the visible church to include all in a given area. Although they recognized it as imperfect and sinful, both maintained close relations with the state, believing it to be ordained of God. Calvin and the Reformed in general went further in standing for the independence of the Church from the state than did Luther. Yet both coöperated with it.

Contemporaneously with Lutheranism and Calvinism there was another kind of Protestantism, much more radical than either. It took many forms and was more remote from a common definition of the Christian faith than were these others. Yet those who adhered to it had much in common. In general they looked to the Scriptures and especially the New Testament as their authority and tended to discard all that they could not find expressly stated in that basic collection of sources. They wished to return to the primitive Christianity of the first century. They thus rejected much more which had come through the Catholic Church than did Lutherans and the Reformed. They believed in "gathered" churches, not identical with the community at large, but composed of those who had had the experience of the new birth. Rejecting infant baptism as contrary to the Scriptures, they regarded only that baptism valid which was administered to conscious believers. They were therefore nick-named Ana-baptists those who baptized a second time, but to them that designation was false, for they held infant baptism not to be baptism. The form of baptism seems in their eyes to have been of secondary importance. For many, perhaps for most, it was not by immersion but by what is known as affusion.

Many Anabaptists had as little as possible to do with the state. Some entirely refused coöperation with it. Large numbers were convinced that the Christian should never participate in war. They tended to withdraw from society and constitute communities of their own which would be uncontaminated by the world about them. Their forms of worship were marked by simplicity. In its heyday the movement gave rise to many hymns. Some looked for the early end of history and the imminent visible return of Christ to set up his millennial reign. Many believed that in them prophecy had been revived and that the Holy Spirit continued to guide and to speak. Some denied the divinity of Christ and regarded him simply as a leader and example. Many were ardently missionary, seeking to win not only professed Christians to their views but also dreaming of carrying the Gospel to all mankind. They tended to austerity in morals and simplicity in food, dress, and speech.

Anabaptists maintained a high standard of morality. Indeed, theirs was an ethical as well as a religious urge. They did not believe in salvation by works, but they taught that if salvation were genuine it would issue in good works. They expelled from their fellowship those who slipped from their standards. Even among their severe critics were those who admitted that they were honest, peaceable, temperate in eating and drinking, eschewed profanity and harsh language, and were upright, meek, and free from covetousness and pride. Many were total abstainers from all alcoholic beverages. They endeavoured fully to live up to the ethical demands of the Sermon on the Mount. The Catholic way of striving for Christian perfection was that of the monastery, communities of celibates apart from the world. The Anabaptists were akin to the monks in seeking perfection in communities separate from the world, but, unlike the monks, they married.

Usually Anabaptists were bitterly persecuted by other Protestants and Roman Catholics, for to both they seemed to be dangerous revolutionaries, upsetting the established order. Some may have had a continuity from groups which had been regarded as heretics in pre-Reformation centuries. Violence all but stamped them out on the Continent. Yet some survived. Moreover, they contributed to the emergence or development of movements in Britain, chiefly the Independents, Baptists, and Quakers. Through these, especially the first two, they were to have a profound and growing influence on the Christianity of the eighteenth and notably of the nineteenth and twentieth centuries.

EARLY ANABAPTISTS

Precisely when the Anabaptists began we do not know. As we have suggested, some of their communities may have sprung from heretical pre-sixteenth century movements. There have been those, indeed, who have asserted for them unbroken continuity from the Christians of the first century, a kind of apostolic succession different from that claimed by the Catholics. This, however, has not been incontestably proved. If continuity existed there was great diversity in its manifestations.

We would expect that in a time of religious ferment and of rebellion against the Roman Catholic Church such as was seen in the sixteenth century, when the Bible was being widely read in the vernacular and salvation by faith and the priesthood of all believers were being preached, Anabaptists would emerge independently and without collusion in several places and would display marked variety. This, indeed, was what happened. Some groups interacted on one another.

One early centre of the Anabaptists was Zürich. Here, in the city where Zwingli contributed so largely to the Reformed Churches, Conrad Grebel (c.1498–1526) and Felix Manz, young scions of prominent families, led in a radical movement which went far beyond Zwingli. In his student days Grebel was in Basel, Vienna, and Paris, and there imbibed the humanism which was popular in that day. Back in Zürich, he came in contact with Zwingli. His conversion occurred in 1522–1523, but of the details we know little or nothing. At the outset he was a warm friend and earnest follower of the reformer. In the autumn of 1523 he began to part from Zwingli. The latter would move no faster in abolishing the mass and the use of images than the city council, while Grebel believed that the civil authorities should not control the Church. Around Grebel there gathered what were known as the Swiss Brethren. They wished a more thoroughgoing reformation of the Church than Zwingli was prepared to advocate. They made contact with Carlstadt, who, it will be recalled, was one of the radicals who moved beyond Luther. They sought, apparently in vain, to get in touch with the much more violent Thomas Müntzer. Grebel wrote Luther, urging him to apply the Scriptures with less compromise than he was doing. In many places in Switzerland and South-west Germany the Scriptural basis for the baptism of infants was being questioned. By the autumn of 1524 Grebel and his associates had rejected infant baptism and, although they were also opposed to tithes being collected by the state for the support of ministers and to "usury," it was over baptism that they came into conflict with the

Zürich authorities. In January, 1525, the city council decided to stand by infant baptism and ordered Grebel and the Brethren to discontinue their movement. In spite of the city council, Grebel and his associates gave baptism to those believers who wished it. The Brethren also observed the Lord's Supper with very simple rites.

With missionary zeal, Grebel moved on to other cities. At Schaffhausen, a few miles north of Zürich, he met at first with favour. At the nearby Waldshut Balthasar Hübmaier was of kindred mind. In other centres, notably in St. Gall, Grebel and his colleagues had an enthusiastic popular reception. However, Grebel, Manz, and others were arrested, tried by the civil authorities in Zürich, and condemned to life imprisonment for not abiding by the city council's commands. After some months they escaped. Manz, recaptured, was executed by drowning (January 25, 1527), apparently the first martyr to the Anabaptist cause. Grebel had died a few months earlier.

Balthasar Hübmaier, a university graduate, a priest, a former pupil of that Eck whom we have met in his Leipzig debate with Luther, and a distinguished preacher, by 1523 had become a convert to the Reformation. He carried with him many of his parish in Waldshut. At first friendly with Zwingli and his colleagues, by 1525 he had rejected infant baptism. In that year he was baptized and at Easter in that year he baptized about three hundred and followed this with other baptisms, the Lord's Supper, and foot-washing. For a time he was in Zürich and there was imprisoned and tortured. Released, he went to Nikolsburg in Moravia and preached with such effect that thousands were baptized. He was arrested by order of the Archduke Ferdinand of Austria, was taken to Vienna, tried, condemned, and burned (March 10, 1528).

In the 1520's Anabaptist views spread rapidly and widely in much of German-speaking Switzerland, Austria, and South-east Germany. Strassburg was early an important centre and in the North-west Anabaptist views made rapid headway in the Low Countries. In places the way was prepared for Anabaptist convictions by the Friends of God and other fifteenth century mystics, and possibly by such communities as those of the beghards and beguines.

The missionaries of the movement were numerous. Melchior Hoffmann (c.1498–c.1543), a Swabian-born furrier of Livonia, wandered widely along the Baltic, in Scandinavia, the Low Countries, and Strassburg, preaching as he went and in some places winning converts and gathering communities. Even the fairly tolerant Strassburg found him impossible and he died in prison in that city. Hans Denck (1495–1527), a humanist scholar, a graduate of the University of Ingolstadt, for a time one of the Erasmian circle in Basel, influenced by Tauler, proficient in Greek and Hebrew, wishing an inner reformation by heeding the voice of the Spirit within us, the indwelling Christ, and the Scripture, and eschewing violence, was in several cities, among them Nuremberg, St. Gall, Strassburg, Worms, and Augsburg, and in his early thirties died of the plague in Basel. Denck's friend, for a time also a friend of Zwingli, the Swiss Ludwig Hetzer (1500–1529), who had been educated in humanist studies and who had drunk deeply from such mystical writings as the *Theologia Germanica,* was banished from Zürich for his Anabaptist teachings. For a few months in 1525 he headed the radicals in Augsburg, was for a time in Basel in the home of Oecolampadius, then was in Strassburg as a guest of Wolfgang Capito, a Zwinglian with Anabaptist leanings, joined with Denck in translating into German the prophetical books of the Old Testament, with Denck was forced to flee from Worms, and early in 1529 was tried and executed in Constance on the charge, probably false, of adultery. These were only some of the better known among those who propagated Anabaptist convictions.

As we have suggested, the Anabaptists presented a great variety. They were recruited mainly from the lowlier elements of the population, but they also included some men of learning. They were chiefly in the towns and cities, but were not grouped around any one centre or leader. Some advocated community of goods among the faithful. For many the rejection of infant baptism and insistence on the baptism of believers was only incidental. Some opposed all use of force, even in resistance to persecution. Others wished to employ force. Several, among them Hans Hetz, who disturbed Hübmaier in Nickelsburg, proclaimed that the day of the Lord was near and that the saints were the chosen people who, as had the children of Israel in conquering Palestine, were to root out the wicked before the visible reign of Christ was set up on the earth. Michael Sattler, a former monk who, after having been flayed and having his tongue torn out, was burned in May, 1527, had led, in February of that year, in drawing up articles of faith for Anabaptists. These regarded the Church as made up of local units of those who had been baptized as believers. Each of the local units was to choose its own officers and to be bound together through the Lord's Supper. The articles of faith rejected the Roman, Lutheran, and Zwinglian worship as "servitude of the flesh."

However, by no means all Anabaptists conformed to that statement.

ANABAPTISTS ARE PERSECUTED BY ROMAN CATHOLICS, LUTHERANS, AND REFORMED

As we have seen, Roman Catholics, Lutherans, and Zwinglians regarded Anabaptists as dangerous radicals, threatening to bring in anarchy in Church and state. Among all three there were those who sought to stamp them out by force. Late in the 1520's and early in the 1530's hundreds of Anabaptists were killed, some by drowning, some by beheading, and others by burning.

Persecution of the Anabaptists was intensified by the belief that they shared in responsibility for the peasant uprising of 1524–1525. Indeed, there was plausible ground for the accusation. Thomas Müntzer was the major fomenter of the revolt in Saxony. He is usually classed with the Anabaptists, and, while he did not make as much of it as did most of them, he rejected infant baptism and therefore, if the term were sufficiently inclusive, could be grouped with them. Certainly those concerned for the maintenance of public order were the more savage against the Anabaptists because of the fear that, coming as most of them did from the underprivileged classes, they would breed rebellion.

THE MÜNSTER EPISODE CONFIRMS THE FEARS OF THE OPPONENTS OF THE ANABAPTISTS

The worst fears of the critics of the Anabaptists were reinforced by events in Münster in 1533–1535. Münster, a city in Westphalia, not far from the Dutch border, in the Middle Ages a prominent member of the Hanseatic League, was the seat of a bishop. There about 1529 a young humanist chaplain, Bernhard Rothmann, began preaching justification by faith. He attracted many among the masses who were already restless under the exploitation of ecclesiastical rulers. In spite of the opposition of successive bishops and neighbouring nobles, the city was declared to be Protestant and was enrolled in the Schmalkaldic League. Yet Rothmann seems never to have been a Lutheran but to have been closer to the Anabaptists. By 1533 he had become convinced that infant baptism was wrong. Since he refused to baptize infants, some of the leading citizens, Lutherans, attempted to depose him from his pulpit, but were estopped because of his popularity with the masses. In a public disputation with a Lutheran and a Roman Catholic, the populace deemed Rothmann to have been the victor.

The news spread that Münster had become Anabaptist and to it flocked many of the followers of Melchior Hoffmann. Hoffmann had predicted that after his imprisonment and death he would return, in 1533, with Christ in the clouds of heaven, that the wicked would be judged, and the New Jerusalem be set up in Strassburg. The year 1533 passed, Hoffmann was still in prison, and the end of the age had not come. Outstanding among the immigrant Anabaptists was Jan Matthys, a baker from Haarlem, in Holland, who believed himself a prophet and who was convinced that Münster, not Strassburg, was to be the site of the New Jerusalem where the saints would reign. Another was Jan Beukelssen, a tailor of Leiden. The Anabaptists obtained control of Münster and there attempted to organize what they believed to be a Christian society. The Bishop laid siege. Aided by Lutherans and Catholics he took the city (June 24, 1535). Matthys had already perished in a sortie. The surviving leaders, including Jan of Leiden, were tortured and killed, and the authority of the bishop was reëstablished.

The effect of the Münster episode was to confirm the bad odour attached to the name of Anabaptist. Reports circulated of the extremes to which Anabaptist fanaticism had gone during the months of stress in community of property, polygamy, and the ruthless suppression of opposition. As is the manner of such reports, they grew as they were told and retold and departed further and further from the facts. Actually private property had not been abolished and, while some of the leaders had contracted polygamous marriages, severe laws were enacted against adultery and fornication. Although only a minority of the Anabaptists were involved, and these chiefly from one strain of the movement, that associated with Hoffmann, it was popularly believed, especially among the governing and respectable classes, that all Anabaptists made for chaos in government, society, morals, and religion.

MENNO SIMONS AND THE MENNONITES

The largest body of Anabaptists which survived the persecutions on the Continent was the Mennonites. They took their name from Menno Simons (1496–1561). Menno Simons was born in the Low Countries, was educated for the priesthood, along the way acquired an excellent knowledge of Latin and some acquaintance with Greek, and was consecrated priest in 1524. At first he seems to have been the worldly type of cleric so common in that age. Yet reform was in the air, and before he had been ordained Luther had become a familiar name. Within a year of his ordination Menno Simons had doubts about the efficacy of the mass. He had begun a careful study of the Bible when the execution of an Anabaptist in his native West Friesland deeply shocked him. Although still serving as a priest in the Roman Catholic Church, he came to the conclusion that that church and Luther, Zwingli, and Calvin were wrong in practising infant baptism and that only believer's baptism had Scriptural authority. Yet he disapproved of the Anabaptists of Münster and believed that they and the followers of Hoffmann were in error in appealing to the sword in self-defense. However, their heroism under persecution smote his conscience for his acceptance of ease and security in his priestly post. January 30, 1536, he publicly renounced his Roman Catholic connexion and not long afterwards was baptized by Obbe Phillips, an Anabaptist who had been influenced by Hoffmann but who had no lot with the Münsterites, was deeply disturbed by the claim of Matthys and others among them of the gift of prophecy, and held closely to the Scriptures. Menno Simons knew that this step, with its separation from the world, would entail persecution.

Menno Simons' expectation of persecution was amply fulfilled. He was ordained as an Anabaptist minister, became an itinerant missionary of the cause, and for years lived in the Netherlands as a fugitive and an outlaw under condemnation of death. Yet he married and had children. In 1543 he extended his missionary labours into Germany, almost always with persecution facing him from Roman Catholics and Lutherans. Eventually he found a refuge on the estates of a nobleman in Holstein, in Denmark, who, impressed by the courage of Anabaptists whom he had seen martyred, believed them to be harmless and protected them. There Menno Simons made his home for the remainder of his days, but still continued to venture forth on travels in the Netherlands and Germany. By the time of his death, through his extensive writings, his preaching, his organizing of congregations, and his journeys, he had become the outstanding leader of the Anabaptists in the Netherlands and North Germany.

Mennonites were very numerous in the Netherlands. Indeed, before the spread of the Reformed Churches, they probably there constituted the majority of Protestants. They also multiplied in various parts of Germany. They found it difficult to agree in doctrine, and various confessions of faith were drawn up. We hear of ones dating from 1577, 1579, 1582, 1591, 1600, and 1627. The Dortrecht Confession, 1632, was an attempt to bring about a union of the various bodies and was widely used in Flemish, Friesian, and Alsatian congregations. The differences were chiefly over the degree to which members should shun those who had been excommunicated. Mennonites were deeply concerned to maintain a high level of Christian living and to that end employed excommunication of those who were guilty of offenses.

Continuing Varieties of Anabaptists

Anabaptists continued to be divided. The Mennonites were the most numerous, but even they were not bound together in a single fellowship and differed among themselves. One branch, the Amish, taking their name from Jacob Ammann, of the latter part of the seventeenth century, endeavoured to return to a stricter discipline. The Hutterites, or Hutterian Brethren, from Jacob Hutter, who was tortured and burned in 1536, for several generations practised community of goods. Especially strong in Moravia, they suffered severely in the Thirty Years' War (1618–1648). Remnants took refuge in Hungary. Late in the eighteenth century many of them settled in South Russia, where they were welcomed because of their industry and thrift.

Driven by persecution and refusing to resist by force of arms, the Mennonites scattered widely. In the seventeenth century many of the Swiss Mennonites, constrained by persecution, especially in Bern and Zürich, found homes in the

Palatinate. Late in the eighteenth century under the religiously sceptical Catherine the Great many of them moved to South Russia, attracted by the promise of free land and exemption from taxation for a period of years. Numbers were also to make their homes in North and South America, especially in the United States.

A group having Anabaptist principles but with a distinct and relatively late origin was the Church of the Brethren or Taufers. Their founder was Alexander Mack and their inception may be dated in 1708 when eight men and women, stirred by the Pietist movement, of which we are to hear more later, and wishing to take the New Testament as their only rule and guide, were immersed in the River Eder. Their early centres were Schwarzenau, the Palatinate, and Marienborn. By 1750 several groups, moved by persecution, had taken refuge in religiously tolerant Pennsylvania.

In the course of their history the Mennonites and other descendants of the Anabaptists became ingrowing. Originally vigorously missionary, persecution caused them largely to withdraw within themselves and to perpetuate themselves by birth rather than conversion. In some places, especially the Netherlands, they became prosperous and gave up pacifism. In some other lands they held tenaciously to their historic convictions and practices.

Summary

Anabaptists were manifestations of a continuing strain in Christianity which had been present from the very beginning and which before and since the Reformation has expressed itself in many forms. It was seen in the Christians of the first century who, impressed by the wickedness of the world, sought so far as possible to withdraw from it and live in it as distinct communities but not to be of it. Montanists, Marcionites, and Novatians were in the tradition. Monasticism in its myriad forms arose from similar convictions. The Paulicians seem to have been originally from a corresponding impulse. The Waldensees, the Lollards, and many another movement of the thirteenth, fourteenth, and fifteenth centuries both inside and outside the Catholic Church were of that kin. We shall meet Christians of similar convictions again and again in the eighteenth, nineteenth, and twentieth centuries. There is that in the Christian Gospel which stirs the consciences of men to be ill content with anything short of full conformity with the ethical standards set forth in the teachings of Jesus and which awakens the hope and the faith that, seemingly impossible of attainment though they are, progress towards them can be made and that they must be sought in communities of those who have committed themselves fully to the Christian ideal.

SELECTED BIBLIOGRAPHY

R. H. Bainton, *The Travail of Religious Liberty. Nine Biographical Studies* (Philadelphia, The Westminster Press, 1951, pp. 272). Well written, by an outstanding specialist.

E. B. Bax, *Rise and Fall of the Anabaptists* (New York, The Macmillan Co., 1903, pp. 407). Chiefly an account of the Münster episode.

H. S. Bender, *Conrad Grebel, c.1498–1526, the Founder of the Swiss Brethren Sometimes Called Anabaptists* (Goshen, Ind., The Mennonite Historical Society, 1950, pp. xvi, 326). Thoroughly scholarly.

H. S. Bender, *Menno Simon's Life and Writings. A Quadricentennial Tribute 1536–1936* (Scottdale, Pa., Mennonite Publishing House, 1936, pp. viii, 110). A semi-popular biography by an expert.

A. Coutts, *Hans Denck, 1495–1527, Humanist and Heretic* (Edinburgh, Macniven & Wallace, 1927, pp. 262). Carefully done.

H. E. Dosker, *The Dutch Anabaptists* (Philadelphia, The Westminster Press, 1921, pp. 310). Carefully done.

R. Friedmann, *Mennonite Piety Through the Centuries, Its Genius and Literature* (Goshen, Ind., The Mennonite Historical Society, 1949, pp. xv, 287). Based upon extensive research.

J. Horsch, *Menno Simons, His Life, Labors, and Teachings* (Scottdale, Pa., Mennonite Publishing House, 1916, pp. 324). The fruit of careful research.

J. Horsch, *Mennonites in Europe* (Scottdale, Pa., Mennonite Publishing House, 1942, pp. xiii, 425). Embodying extensive research.

R. J. Smithson, *The Anabaptists: Their Contribution to Our Protestant Heritage* (London, James Clarke & Co., foreword, 1935, pp. 228). A competent popular survey incorporating wide reading.

H. C. Vedder, *Balthazar Hübmaier, The Leader of the Anabaptists* (New York, G. P. Putnam's Sons, 1905, pp. xxiv, 333). A semi-popular account by a careful scholar.

F. L. Weis, *The Life and Teachings of Ludwig Hetzer, a Leader and Martyr of the Anabaptists, 1500–1529* (Dorchester, Mass., Underhill Press, 1930, pp. 239). A doctoral dissertation.

J. C. Wenger, *Glimpses of Mennonite History and Doctrine* (Scottdale, Pa., Herald Press, 2d ed., 1947, pp. 258). Especially valuable for its bibliographies and translations from the sources.

Chapter 35

THE RADICAL REFORMERS: MEN OF THE INNER LIGHT AND RATIONALISTIC HUMANISTS

The vast and sweeping religious movement which was the Reformation had a multitude of manifestations. It stirred countless individuals to their depths and made of them quite unusual men and women. Many of these, as we are to see, remained within the Roman Catholic Church, working for moral and spiritual improvement, joining old religious orders, or organizing new ones. Others fitted in with what became standard forms of Protestantism—the Lutheran, Reformed, Presbyterian, and Anglican bodies. Even the Anabaptists, diverse as they were, conformed in the main to one or another of the patterns developed by their outstanding leaders. However, many individuals found any large community difficult. Some of them gathered small groups about them. Their number was legion. They remind one of the hermits and small communities which arose in connexion with monasticism, especially in its early days. But, unlike these, they owned no allegiance, even as tenuous as was that of many of the monks, to any ecclesiastical authority. Because they broke away from the Roman Catholic Church, they are usually regarded as Protestants. Yet many of them were not accepted by other Protestants. In general, they fell into two categories. One was made up of those who were either mystics or close kin to mystics and believed themselves to be guided by the Spirit through inward illumination, an illumination possibly aided and interpreted by Scripture. The other, for the most part arising from humanism, stressed the use of reason. The line of division between the two categories was by no means sharp. Many individuals could be classified under either or both. Some, especially among the mystics, tended towards pantheism. Others, usually humanists, made much of the rational approach to Christianity, emphasized the ethical aspect of New Testament teaching, and were inclined to be anti-Trinitarian and to regard Christ as an example and a leader to be followed rather than the divine-human redeemer.

Here is not the place for a detailed account or even a full catalogue of the individuals and the movements stemming from them which might be dealt with in this chapter. We must content ourselves with brief mention of a very few of the more outstanding. Some were popularly supposed to be Anabaptists and so may follow in close succession our treatment of that multiform expression of the Reformation.

MYSTICS OF THE INNER LIGHT

One of the more prominent of these individuals, a contemporary of Luther, was Sebastian Franck (1499–c.1542). A German, educated under strong humanist influences, for a time a Roman Catholic priest, about 1525 he left the old church, became a preacher of the reformed faith, and was accused of Anabaptist tendencies. Although himself a prolific author, he rebelled against what he deemed excessive emphasis upon the written word. He also denounced external observances, machinery, and organization. He was convinced that there is in each man a divine element which is the source of all spiritual life. The spirit of Christ, he held, makes men religious and all who have received the grace of God are members of the Church. He believed in the eternal Christ, the ever-living, ever-present self-revelation of God, but he was not limited to Jesus. He gloried in the heretics throughout the ages, and included among them all great souls "who had dared to strike out for the Church herself new paths to truth," naming among them Jesus, Paul, and Augustine. He was a pacifist and regarded persecution as a crime.

A friend of Franck was Caspar Schwenkfeld (1487–1541). Of noble blood and rearing, he was awakened by Luther and for a time was a zealous supporter of the Wittenberg reformer. However, he differed from the latter on the Lord's Supper and wished the Church to enforce a stricter discipline on its members than was customary in Lutheran circles. A mystic, he was unhappy over the attempt to confine the Christian faith by precise dogmas and stressed the inner experience of the grace of God. That grace needs neither sacrament nor formal institutions. The fact of its presence, so he held, would be demonstrated by its fruits in righteousness of life. He was looked at askance by Catholics, Lutherans, and Reformed. Opposed to coercion of conscience, because of his religious convictions he was perforce a wanderer. His followers formed societies in Silesia of the "Confessors of the Glory of Christ," but were usually known as Schwenkfelders. In the eighteenth century persecution forced some of them to seek refuge in the religiously free air of Pennsylvania.

Some of those attracted by Schwenkfeld found spiritual kinship with the devotees of the writings of Jacob Boehme (1575–1624). Boehme, the son of a peasant, reared in a Lutheran environment, was a mystic of the first water.

What to him were visions and revelations and the illumination which came with them led him to views of God, Christ, and man which differed radically from Lutheran orthodoxy and brought persecution. Yet his works long continued to be cherished.

INDIVIDUALISTS AND PILGRIMS

In Spain and Italy the new tides of life led, as we have more than once hinted and are to see at more length a little later (Chapter XXXVIII), to a cleansing of the Roman Catholic Church but were contained in it. They also created reformers who, while they remained within the Roman Catholic Church, had strong spiritual kinship with the Protestants. In addition they gave rise to striking individuals who, repudiating the Roman Catholic Church, were never comfortable within any of the existing patterns of Protestantism but were pilgrims and strangers. Most of them bore the humanistic stamp and directly or indirectly were indebted to that great Christian humanist and individualist, Erasmus.

For a time in the sixteenth century the influence of Erasmus was strong in Spain. That was partly because of the connexion between Spain and the Low Countries which resulted from the fact that Charles V, reared in the latter, also became King of Spain. In his train were scholars who were enamoured of their fellow-Netherlander, the great humanist. It was from this vintage that Servetus drank the heady wine which led to his rejection by the Catholics and to the stake in Calvin's Geneva.

From Spain, too, came Juan de Valdés (c.1500–1541). Of noble blood, he was shaped by a combination of the Catholic heritage, Erasmus, and the mystics of the North. Seeking reform in the Church in his native land, he fell under the suspicion of the Inquisition and took refuge in Naples, then with the same rulers as Spain. Here in his villa on an island in the Bay of Naples he gave himself to Biblical studies and the way of the mystic and became the centre of a coterie of devout souls. Some of these, like himself, died in the communion of the Church of Rome. Others broke with it.

One of the circle of Valdés who left the Roman Catholic Church was Pietro Martire Vermigli (1500–1562), often known as Peter Martyr. A native of Florence, son of a warm admirer of Savonarola, he was highly educated and for a time was abbot of an Augustinian monastery and a friend of Reginald Pole, whom we are to meet in the next chapter. As prior of a house of his order in Naples, he came under the spell of Valdés and his group. He also became acquainted with some of the writings of Bucer and Zwingli. Falling under the suspicion of the ecclesiastical authorities both outside and within his order, he fled to Zürich, went on to Basel and Strassburg, and in Strassburg, befriended by Bucer, married and became professor of theology. On invitation from Cranmer, then working the reformation of the Church of England, he went to that country and became regius professor of divinity at Oxford. On the accession of Mary and the restoration by her of the Roman Catholic faith, he again fled, and died as professor of Hebrew in Zürich.

Even more spectacular was the career of Bernardino Ochino (1487–1564). A native of Siena, Ochino early joined the Franciscans of the Observance. Even the strictness of that branch of the Brothers Minor did not satisfy his zeal and he became a member of the Capuchins, a still more austere scion of the spiritual family of the Poverello of Assisi which had newly sprung from the Catholic Reformation. There he rose to be the head of that branch of the Order of Brothers Minor and was one of the outstanding preachers of the day. His fire, eloquence, and sincerity attracted thousands. He, too, came within the circle of Valdés. Given a dispensation by the Pope to read and refute the Protestant works which were filtering into Italy, instead of shattering their arguments he was convinced by them. At the age of fifty-six he fled from Italy. First he went to Geneva, where he seemed fully to subscribe to Calvin's system. There he married. He next moved to Basel, where Castellio and he formed a friendship. Then he made his home in Augsburg where, coming in touch with the Schwenkfelders, he found spiritual kinship with them and began to doubt Calvinism. The advance of Charles V's forces compelled him again to flight, first to Basel and then to England, where he helped in the reformation of the church of that kingdom. The advent of Mary sent him once more on his travels, eventually to Zürich. Differences in doctrine developed between him and the authorities in that heir of Zwingli, and, at the age of seventy-six, he resumed his pilgrimage, this time to Poland. Forced out of that realm, he found a refuge with the Hutterian Anabaptists in Moravia and there died.

Celio Secundo Curione (1503–1569), a native of Piedmont, a humanist and a university professor, at the age of twenty was already reading the books of Luther. He heard lectures by Vermigli. Leaving Italy to escape the heresy-hunters, he was in Zürich, Lausanne, Basel, and Poland, and died in Basel. He never fitted fully into any of the forms of Protestantism, and was a champion of religious toleration.

Pierpaolo Vergerio, a contemporary of Vermigli and Curione, Papal nuncio, was for a time bishop of his native city, Capodistria, not far from Trieste in North Italy. Longing for the purification of the Church, he became convinced of the truth of the Protestant position and began to preach it throughout his diocese and to strive for a reform not only of doctrine but also of morals. Summoned to Rome, he resisted, was deposed by the Inquisition, and fled across the Alps. He, too, never conformed completely with the northern Protestantism, was a wanderer and something of an enigmatic figure, and his death (1565) must have been a relief to many in the Reformed ranks.

ANTI-TRINITARIANS

The books of the Protestant reformers which were read south of the Alps contributed to the thinking of numbers of individuals and groups, especially in North Italy. Many were those who, in peril from the Roman Catholic authorities, took refuge north of the Alps. Protestant tendencies were especially strong in Venetian territories, for the writings of the reformers entered through the extensive commercial contacts with Germany and Switzerland, and the Venetian authorities, jealous for their independence, resisted attempts of Rome to extend its inquisitorial activities to their domains. Anabaptist as well as Lutheran views gained headway in Venetian lands, and some of the Italian Anabaptists began to develop anti-Trinitarian convictions. These seem to have been traceable to writings of Servetus. The anti-Trinitarian Anabaptists multiplied and had congregations and pastors. In 1550 they held a council in Venice which formulated a statement of belief. Among other points, it declared that Christ is not God, but man, born of Joseph and Mary, but filled with all the powers of God, and that the elect are justified, not by the merits, the blood, or the death of Christ, but by the eternal love of God, and that Christ died to show forth the sum of all the mercy and the goodness of God. Persecutions soon scattered the congregations and numbers sought refuge in Moravia or in the lands ruled by the Turks.

Another centre of anti-Trinitarian views was in the Grisons, at that time an independent and democratic republic between Italy and Switzerland. Zwinglian doctrines early found rootage and in 1526 the state granted liberty to both Catholics and Reformed. Here many Italians found refuge in their flight from the Inquisition. With them came anti-Trinitarian views. These made for dissensions and the churches which followed the Swiss Reformation attempted to impose a Trinitarian faith. In 1553 the Synod of the Grisons adopted the Rhaetian confession which incorporated the Apostles', Nicene, and Athanasian Creeds and required subscription by all pastors. By 1575 anti-Trinitarian ministers had been largely rooted out.

Some of the Italian humanists who found refuge at Geneva sympathized with Servetus and, to the distress of Calvin, tended towards anti-Trinitarianism. Similar trends disturbed the Reformed Churches in Bern and Zürich.

THE SOCINIANS

Anti-Trinitarianism had a marked development in Poland. There it became associated with the names of the Sozini, uncle and nephew, Italians, and was

given the appellation of Socinianism. Laelius Socinus (Lelio Sozini), the elder
of the two, was born in 1525 at Siena of a distinguished family of jurists. While
studying law at the University of Padua he became engrossed in the reading of
the Scriptures, gave himself to the reform movement, and sought refuge first
in the more liberal Venice and then in the Grisons. He travelled widely among
Protestant churches and leaders north of the Alps and in England, and had
friendly contacts with Calvin. Courtly in manner, modest, deeply religious, a
reverent sceptic, and of irreproachable morals, his spiritual pilgrimage never
led him to a formal break with the Swiss and Genevan reformers. However, he
deplored the burning of Servetus and some suspected him of unsound doctrines.
Yet he had the confidence of Bullinger and, after journeys in Poland and Italy,
died in Zürich in 1562, still in his thirties. In the humanist tradition, he brought
reason to bear on questions of faith and valued it as well as the Scriptures.

More famous than Lelio Sozini was his nephew, Faustus Socinus (Fausto
Sozini). Born in 1539, he was educated more in letters than the law. From
boyhood he had been inclined towards Protestantism, but outwardly conformed to the Roman Catholic Church and from 1563 to 1574 was a secretary
in the court of the Medici in Florence. Eventually he left Italy for Basel.
While there he wrote a treatise, *De Jesu Christo Salvatore,* in which he said
that Christ did not appease the wrath of a righteous God by suffering the
penalty that we deserve because of our sin, but that he becomes our saviour by
making known the way of eternal salvation and that we may reach that goal
by imitating him. For a time he was in Transylvania, where an anti-Trinitarian
form of Protestantism was making rapid progress. He then spent a quarter of
a century in Poland, dying in 1604. There he was the outstanding figure in a
branch of the Reformed Churches which was anti-Trinitarian.

The Reformation early penetrated Poland. Dissatisfaction with the wealth
and corruption of the Catholic Church facilitated its spread. It entered in
several forms. Lutherans, Anabaptists, Bohemian Brethren, and Reformed all
made their appearance and flourished. At first strong in the towns and cities,
it won many of the nobility and progressed among the peasants. It had an able
leader in Jan Laski, also known as John à Lasco (1499–1560), of a distinguished
Polish family, nephew of a primate of the Polish Church. A priest and with
the prospect of rapid advancement in the Church, Laski became a friend of
Erasmus, laboured for reform in Poland, then spent a number of years abroad
furthering the Reformation in several countries, and during the last four years
of his life was in his native land, preaching, holding synods, stimulating the
translation of the Bible into Polish, and seeking to bring the varieties of
Protestantism into one ecclesiastical structure. There was a brief period when
it seemed that Protestantism would sweep the country. Divisions in the

Protestant ranks, a Catholic monarch, and especially the missionary zeal of the Jesuits, brought the downfall of Reformation and issued in the reconversion of most of those who had left the Catholic Church.

Before that reconversion, anti-Trinitarian views developed in the Reformed Churches in Poland and led to a division in which the minority held to them. To this minority Faustus Socinus gave leadership. The standard formulation of the beliefs of these churches was the Racovian Catechism, bearing the name of Rakow, the headquarters of the Socinians and where it was first published. It was the work of Faustus Socinus and some of his friends and disciples. Although it became an object of attack by Lutheran and Reformed theologians, it was not as radical a departure from the main stream of historic Christianity as were the convictions of some of the other anti-Trinitarians. It sought to base its positions solidly on the Scriptures as the divine revelation of the way to eternal life. It held that the authenticity of the Christian religion was established by the miracles and the resurrection of Christ. The way to eternal life, it maintained, is through the knowledge of God and Christ. Christ was a real but not an ordinary man and showed us how to return to God. He is prophet, priest, and king. Baptism was regarded as not appropriate for infants, but as an outward act by which converts acknowledge Christ as their master. The Lord's Supper was celebrated, but purely as commemorative of the death of Christ. The Holy Spirit is a divine power in the hearts of men. The Church is the company of those who hold to saving doctrine. The Christian life is characterized by prayer, thanksgiving, joy, the renunciation of the world, and patient endurance. Christians are to obey lawful magistrates, are not to lay up wealth beyond what is required for the ordinary needs of life, are to use any surplus for the relief of the poor, and are not to ask more than a reasonable interest on loans.

The Polish Socinians were actively missionary. For a time they seemed to have an opportunity in Russia and gained a footing in Volkynia, in what was later known as the Ukraine. They established contacts with many of similar views, including the Remonstrants and some of the Mennonites in Holland. Complete accord was not reached with these others nor did they fully agree among themselves. Some were pacifists, forswearing all war, while others maintained that armed resistance to injustice is permissible. In general they did not regard the Racovian catechism as a permanently binding statement of Christian belief, and subsequent editions of that document contained substantial modifications of the original. The Socinians tended to make an increasing appeal to reason in support of the convictions which they set forth. They stood for religious liberty, asking to be allowed to hold to such views as seemed to them sound and not seeking to constrain others, whether of their own number or of other religious bodies, to conform to any one pattern of belief.

Persecution wrought ruin in Poland for the Socinians as to Protestantism in general. Late in the sixteenth century and early in the seventeenth century it became acute during the forty-five year reign of Sigismund III. Of the house of Vasa, but a devout Roman Catholic, Sigismund was strongly under the influence of the Jesuits. During the rule of Sigismund and his immediate successors wars with Sweden, Moscow, and Turkey, and rebellion spear-headed by the Cossacks added to the distresses of those who survived the persecutions. In 1658 and 1659 in the stormy reign of John Casimir, formerly a Jesuit, a priest, and a cardinal, the Socinians were banished from Poland by decree of the Diet. Some of them found refuge in Transylvania. Here anti-Trinitarians were already strong, especially among one of the racial groups, the Szeklers. Indeed, the name "Unitarian," a general later designation, seems to have been first officially applied to them in 1600 in a decree of the Transylvanian Diet. Here, in the second half of the sixteenth century, Lutherans, Reformed, Unitarians, and Roman Catholics were accorded equal recognition before the law and were in effect state churches. A few others of the Polish Socinians found a precarious asylum in East Prussia and the Rhenish Palatinate. More went to Holland where they had an influence among the Remonstrants and the Mennonites.

It seems to be more than a coincidence that anti-Trinitarianism, or Unitarianism, was chiefly of humanist origin and that it found its most congenial soil among churches of the Reformed tradition. Its chief gains on the Continent were not among the Lutherans but among the Reformed. In England it was Presbyterians from whom most of the Unitarians were drawn. In the United States Unitarianism developed from the Puritanism around Boston. This may have been because humanism, with its emphasis upon the competence of human reason, tended to rule out all that seemed to it irrational and because the chief shapers of the Reformed theology came to Protestantism through humanism and made much of the use of reason. This does not mean that Calvinism and other strains within the Reformed tradition necessarily led to Unitarianism. It indicates, however, that the rational approach so congenial to humanism could easily exalt the competence of the intellect, stress the human side of Christ, regard Jesus as simply the best of men, emphasize the ethical aspects of the Biblical teachings, and believe that man is able to attain to them with the aid of God but without the basic new birth of which the New Testament speaks and which the majority of Protestants, along with Augustine, contend comes only through grace, the quite unmerited favour of God which no man can earn.

SELECTED BIBLIOGRAPHY

R. H. Bainton, *The Travail of Religious Liberty* (Philadelphia, The Westminster Press, 1951). Sketches of individuals, popularly written, by a thorough scholar and expert.

J. Böhme, *The Incarnation of Jesus Christ,* translated from the German by J. R. Earle (London, Constable & Co., 1934, pp. viii, 284). One of the more significant works of Boehme.

G. K. Brown, *Italy and the Reformation to 1550* (Oxford, Basil Blackwell, 1933, pp. 324). Carefully done.

Concerning Heretics . . . an Anonymous Work Attributed to Sebastian Castellio Now first done into English together with excerpts from other works of Sebastian Castellio and David Joris on religious liberty, by R. H. Bainton (Columbia University Press, 1935, pp. xiv, 342). Extremely well done.

F. C. Church, *The Italian Reformers 1534–1564* (Columbia University Press, 1932, pp. xii, 428). Well documented.

R. M. Jones, *Spiritual Reformers in the 16th & 17th Centuries* (London, Macmillan & Co., 1928, pp. li, 362). Based upon careful research into Continental and English precursors of Quakerism, with special emphasis upon Jacob Böhme, by a distinguished American Quaker.

C. Schultz, *A Vindication of Caspar Schwenckfeld von Ossig. An Elucidation of his Doctrine and the Vicissitudes of his Followers,* translated from the German and edited E. S. Gerhard (Allentown, Pa., Edward Schlechter, 1942, pp. 347). The first German edition was in 1771.

E. M. Wilbur, *A History of Unitarianism: Socinianism and its Antecedents* (Harvard University Press, 1945, pp. xiii, 617). A sympathetic account, based upon extensive research, by an American Unitarian.

Chapter 36

THE ENGLISH REFORMATION

In our treatment of the Protestant Reformation we have saved to the last an account of its course in England and the English dependencies, Wales and Ireland. That is not because in England the Reformation was less important than on the Continent. It was fully as significant. Indeed, through the global spread of English-speaking peoples and their culture in the seventeenth, eighteenth, and especially the nineteenth and twentieth centuries, and the missions which emanated from the English churches, it was world-wide in its influence. If we are to understand the Christianity of later years and particularly of the era after 1815 we must know the developments in English Christianity in the sixteenth and seventeenth centuries. Nor was the Reformation in England later than that on the Continent. It was almost simultaneous with it. As we are to see in a moment, its roots go back before the sixteenth century. However, while it was largely indigenous, the English Reformation was profoundly influenced by what was taking place on the Continent. Into it eventually entered to a greater or less extent all the main strains which we have thus far described. Luther, Zwingli, Calvin, the Reformed Churches of the Rhine Valley and Holland, Anabaptists, some of the men of the inner light, and the Socinians all made contributions. Yet in taking them over, the English worked them into a texture which was essentially and characteristically English.

Preparation for the Reformation in England

The ground in England was made fallow for the Reformation by developments which reached back into the fifteenth century and earlier. As in most of Western Europe, fifteenth century English Christianity had in it much of corruption and decay. Many of the devout were saying that the monasteries had outlived their usefulness and that the monks were idle and ignorant. Hundreds of the clergy had concubines. Pluralism and absentee enjoyment of the revenues of benefices were common. Scholasticism and scholastic theology were beginning to be out of fashion in intellectual circles. Yet the revival of Augustinian studies with which Wyclif was associated and the influence of the late scholastics, both natives of British soil, John Duns Scotus and William of Ockham, must have helped positively to prepare the way for the subsequent movements.

The old social, political, and economic order with which the Church was associated was passing. Beginning with the first of the line, Henry VII, and followed more emphatically by his son, Henry VIII, the Tudor monarchs were insisting on being full masters in the realm and were building an English variation of the absolute royal power which was growing on the Continent. Cities and their thrifty, industrious middle classes were increasing in importance.

Most of the bishops, although many were engrossed in affairs of state to the frequent neglect of their dioceses, were upright and able, and the rank and file of the populace were so devout that visitors from the Continent remarked upon it. Lollardy had never completely died out. It persisted, chiefly among the poor and often in outward conformity with the Church. Translations of the Bible existed in English and were read, although not by any means as widely as after the invention of printing. The writings of the mystics whom we have met in earlier chapters were circulated. We have also noted the presence of earnestly religious humanists who desired the reform and renewal of the Church, among them Colet, who eventually occupied the post of Dean of St. Paul's in London, the witty, learned, and deeply devoted Thomas More, and Erasmus himself. Preachers, some of them wandering friars, were denouncing vices. The morality plays, given in churchyards and churches and drawing appreciative audiences, pilloried vice and exalted virtue. Satirists were arraigning current sins. Didactic literature was issuing from some of the earliest printing presses. Then, too, a sturdy nationalism was restive under interference in ecclesiastical affairs by a foreign Pope and hotly resented the fashion in which Papal appointees battened on English revenues in luxury-loving circles in Avignon and Rome. This patriotism could readily be invoked by monarchs who sought to identify themselves with it and use it for their own ends.

First Moves towards Reformation

In this fallow ground the writings of Luther would certainly find fruitage. They were not long in reaching Oxford and Cambridge. In Cambridge, especially, they awakened interest. Here was a circle whose members, aided by the Greek New Testament of Erasmus with its Latin translation, were earnestly studying the Scriptures. The leader, Thomas Bilney, after an inner struggle of soul had come to inward peace. He had also become acquainted with some of the writings of Luther. In 1531 he was burned in Norwich as a heretic, but before his death he had a profound influence upon a young priest and graduate of Cambridge, Hugh Latimer, who was later to loom prominently in the Reformation and was also to seal his witness at the stake.

Even more influential as a pioneer was William Tyndale (c.1494–1536). Born of a prosperous yeoman family not far from Gloucester, he took a degree at Oxford and then went to Cambridge. He was ordained, but when and where we do not know. Soon after leaving Cambridge, he formed the purpose of putting the New Testament into English, to make it accessible to those who could not easily read Latin. This he did, apparently without taking advantage of the Wyclif translation, but using the Greek text and the Latin translation of Erasmus, the Vulgate, and Luther's translation into German. Eventually he added to it a large part of the Old Testament, utilizing the Hebrew text, the Vulgate, the Septuagint, and Luther's Bible. He also revised his translation of the New Testament. Most of his work was done on the Continent, but in spite of efforts to suppress them, his translations, printed, circulated in England. They were of substantial assistance to the translators of that later, seventeenth century Authorized or King James' Version, which became standard in English-speaking lands and which did almost as much to give form to English literary style as did Luther's translation to German.

While on the Continent Tyndale moved further over to the Protestant position. In 1528 he issued *The Parable of the Wicked Mammon* in which he came out flatly for justification by faith, and took over most of the text of a sermon by Luther on the unjust steward. That same year another book by him appeared which denied that he preached rebellion against secular rulers and declared that civil authorities should be obeyed, and all rulers, whether parents, husbands, masters, or landlords. Arrested for heresy in the Low Countries, he was tried, condemned, degraded from the priesthood, and strangled, and his body was burned (1536).

HENRY VIII LEADS IN A BREACH WITH ROME

What course the Reformation would have taken in England had it not been for Henry VIII we cannot know. It was that monarch who broke with Rome, set the Church of England on its independent course, and helped to give it some of its distinctive features.

Henry VIII (1491–1547), younger son of Henry VII, was being prepared for ecclesiastical office when the death of his older brother, Arthur, in 1502, made him heir to the throne. Handsome, athletic, able, well educated, musical, having more than a cursory knowledge of theology, masterful, he was not quite eighteen when (1509) his father's death made him king.

It was over the question of marriage that the strain between Henry and Rome arose. In 1501 Arthur, aged fourteen, had been wedded to Catherine, aged sixteen, daughter of Ferdinand and Isabella of Spain. It was purely an affair of statecraft whereby Henry VII, the hold of his family on the throne still shaky, sought to ally himself with a powerful neighbour, and whereby that neighbour was glad of a tie with a kingdom which, while far inferior to Spain in power, might prove useful in the chronic struggle among the monarchs of Europe. Catherine's dowry, too, proved attractive to the avaricious and parsimonious Henry VII. When, less than six months later, Arthur died, the father-in-law, loath to be deprived of the financial and other advantages of the match, arranged to have Catherine betrothed to the future Henry VIII. Since it was against the law of the Church for a man to marry his deceased brother's widow, a Papal dispensation was needed. Doubt existed as to whether the Pope had the right to remove so serious an obstacle, but after some delay the permission was granted. This was in 1504, when the young Henry was only thirteen. It was not until 1509, a few weeks after the death of his father, that Henry VIII was willing to proceed to marriage. Although he had doubts about the validity of the union, Warham, the Archbishop of Canterbury, officiated at the ceremony. After the manner of the princes of his day, Henry was not faithful to his marriage vows, but at the outset he and Catherine seem to have been happy and in the course of the years she bore him several children. Of these only one survived infancy, and she was a daughter, Mary. Henry passionately longed for a male heir, for only through a son could he be confidently assured of the succession of his family on the throne. Only once, and that in the twelfth century, had a woman sought to reign in England, and then the realm had been thrown into civil strife. Henry, therefore, began to wonder whether he was not being visited with divine displeasure for having married his brother's wife. After a time his doubts were sharpened by the attractions of Anne Boleyn. Anne had a strange fascination for him and would accept none of his favours except as his queen.

Now began efforts on the part of Henry and his compliant ministers to obtain a divorce from Catherine. Into the tortuous intricacies of the prolonged proceedings we must not take the time to go. Thomas Wolsey, cardinal, Archbishop of York, and long the king's first minister, failed, was dismissed, and died of chagrin (1530). The Popes could scarcely comply with Henry's urgent desire, for by doing so they would offend Catherine's nephew, the Emperor Charles V, who was more powerful than the English monarch and a much more serious menace.

Shortly before Wolsey's death a fresh figure, Thomas Cranmer (1489–1556), emerged, who was speedily to become prominent and was to have a major

part in carrying out the Reformation in the Church of England. A younger
son of a farmer, Cranmer was designed for the priesthood. He went to Cambridge, graduated, was made a fellow of his college, before he could be ordained
was married, then, his wife dying in child-birth, he again became a fellow
(for marriage had deprived him of that position), and c.1523, a few years
after the posting of Luther's ninety-five theses, was ordained. Studious, learned,
modest, dignified, courteous, deeply religious, by nature conservative, he did
not become a member of the group led by Bilney. In 1529, in a casual conversation Cranmer suggested that the question of the legality of the marriage
of Catherine to Henry could be put to the universities. The universities, it will
be recalled, were regarded with respect when they spoke on matters of theology.
The suggestion having come to his ears, Henry took Cranmer into his service
and had him appointed a chaplain in the Boleyn household.

By successive steps Henry VIII reduced the clergy of the realm to submission and broke with Rome. In accordance with Cranmer's proposal, the question of the marriage was referred to the universities, and the majority of the
replies, thanks in part to more or less adroit pressure from the king, were in
accordance with his wishes. He had the clergy indicted for a breach of the
statute of *Praemunire* on the ground that they had accepted Wolsey as Papal
legate. That law, it will be remembered, had first been enacted in 1353 to prevent suits being carried outside the realm to Papal tribunals. In January, 1531,
Convocation, representing the clergy of the archdiocese of Canterbury, was
constrained to vote a large financial grant to the king *in lieu* of a fine and to
declare Henry to be "the singular protector, the only and supreme lord, and as
far as is permitted by the law of Christ, even the supreme head" of the Church
in England. In 1532, under constraint, Convocation also undertook not to enact
any canon affecting the laity without royal approval. That same year, at royal
initiative, Parliament abolished the payment to the Pope of annates. The year
1532 also saw the death of Warham, Archbishop of Canterbury, who had been
unhappy because of the course of events, and the appointment of Cranmer to
succeed him. The approval of the Pope was obtained and Cranmer was consecrated. In January, 1533, Henry and Anne were secretly married, for she was
pregnant (with the future Elizabeth) and Henry wished legitimacy for the
child. In March an obedient Parliament passed an act in restraint of appeals,
which affirmed that the Church of England was competent to decide its own
cases, that Papal dispensations were unnecessary, and that no Papal interference in the appointment of bishops would be tolerated. The case of the marriage of Henry to Catherine was thereupon brought into the court of Cranmer
as archbishop and the decision desired by the king was obtained, although
with the stipulation that Mary was legitimate, and the union of Henry and

Anne Boleyn was declared valid. Catherine, who had carried herself with dignity through the difficult years, refused to acknowledge the competence of the court. The Pope reaffirmed the validity of her marriage to Henry and excommunicated the king. In 1534 Parliament forbade the payment of Peter's Pence to Rome. Late in 1534 Parliament declared that the king "is and ought to be the supreme head of the Church." The following year, Henry announced himself as *"in terra supremum caput Anglicanæ ecclesiæ"* ("supreme head on earth of the English Church") and a royal proclamation erased the Pope's name from all the service books. The breach with Rome was complete.

There were those in England who protested or refused to acknowledge the royal supremacy over the Church and paid for their temerity with their lives. These included several Carthusians, the devout and upright John Fisher, cardinal, Bishop of Rochester, former chancellor of Cambridge University, friend of Erasmus, and confessor to Catherine, and Thomas More, whom we have already met, humanist, scholar, earnest Christian, and a former chancellor of the realm and intimate of Henry. These executions, especially of Fisher and More, sent a thrill of horror through Western Europe, but Henry was not to be deterred from making himself autocrat in both Church and state. In the chronic struggle between the Church and the monarch which in England as elsewhere in Europe had been going on for centuries, Henry had won. To a degree which would have been the envy and admiration of even his strongest predecessors, he had made himself master of both state and Church.

CHANGES IN THE CHURCH OF ENGLAND UNDER HENRY'S HEADSHIP

The separation of the Church of England from Rome did not necessarily mean that Protestantism was to prevail. Indeed, Henry was proud of his orthodoxy and was punctilious in his daily attendance at mass and his use of a confessor. He was careful to give the guise of legality to his many acts. Earlier he had affixed his name to a book which professed to refute Luther and had received from a flattering Pope the designation of Defender of the Faith, a title which he and his successors were to continue to bear. The question was still unanswered as to whether the currents in England and on the Continent which were making for reform would work significant changes in the Church of England, either in the direction of Protestantism or of the kind which were occurring within the Roman Catholic Church.

By the time that death removed Henry from the scene, significant innovations had been introduced, all with his consent and some on his initiative. Autocrat though he was, Henry was careful not to move until he was fairly confident of carrying the bulk of public opinion with him. Much of his strength lay in his popularity with the majority of his subjects and in his ability to sense the temper of the nation.

To act as his agent as head of the English Church, Henry appointed Thomas Cromwell as his vicar-general and vicegerent. Cromwell, of lowly parentage, had been in the service of Wolsey. He had Protestant leanings, although how sincere they were has been a matter of debate. Thoroughly committed to the royal supremacy, he presided at Convocation, taking precedence over the Archbishop of Canterbury. Under his direction a systematic visitation of the monasteries was begun. This was followed by the dissolution of the monasteries. First the smaller ones were disbanded and then the friars were suppressed. The larger monasteries held out slightly longer, but by 1540 they had gone the way of the smaller ones. Some voluntarily surrendered their property to the king. The heads of three prominent houses were executed. The chief shrines of the saints, famous goals of pilgrimages, including that of Cuthbert at Durham, and especially that of Thomas Becket at Canterbury, for whom Henry had a marked antipathy, presumably because of his resistance to royal authority, were dismantled and despoiled of their treasures. The Pope retaliated for the treatment of Becket's tomb by placing England under the interdict, but the time had passed when that act by a Roman Pontiff could bring a king of England to his knees. The proceeds of the confiscated properties were used in part to endow new dioceses, schools, professorships in the universities, and Trinity College in Cambridge, for pensions for dispossessed monks and nuns, and for coastal defenses. However, as in Denmark and Sweden, the larger part went into the royal coffers, for Henry was chronically short of funds, and to royal favorites. Many of the populace availed themselves of the opportunity for plunder, and some of the monks were not above disposing of the movables of their houses.

Various results followed. Those given monastic properties were bound to the king and could be counted on for support against a renewal of the tie with Rome. The power of the clergy in Parliament was curtailed, for in the House of Lords there were no longer abbots and priors, and of the Lords Spiritual only the bishops remained. The poor who had formerly been cared for by the monasteries were thrown on the public and beginnings were made of the later system whereby they became the charge of the parishes.

Apart from the separation from Rome, the suppression of the monasteries was the most drastic change made under Henry VIII in the religious life of England, for the monks, their houses, and the friars had long been a prominent and accepted part of the social, economic, and religious structure of the realm. However, the monasteries were already waning. It is said that in the fifteenth century only eight new houses had been founded. Some had earlier been dissolved. Only slight resistance was offered to the step. The most notable was the uprising in the North known as the Pilgrimage of Grace, and this had the changes in religion as only one of its causes and was speedily put down. Except for the brief and partial revival under Mary and a few feeble remnants, monasticism disappeared from England and was not again to appear until the nineteenth century.

Successive statements of doctrine for the Church of England were issued. In 1536, two years or so after the final break with Rome, Ten Articles, drafted by Henry with the help of Cranmer, were promulgated. They mentioned three sacraments, baptism, penance, and the Eucharist, stressed the importance of teaching the people the Bible and the Apostles', Nicene, and Athanasian Creeds, declared that justification is by faith and by confession, absolution, and good works, that Christ is physically present in the Eucharist, and that masses for the dead, the invocation of the saints, and the use of images are desirable. In 1537 the *Institution of a Christian Man*, popularly known as the Bishops' Book, came out, a manual on Christian doctrine for the rank and file. In 1543 a thorough revision, greatly altered, of this treatise was published over the king's name, *A Necessary Doctrine and Erudition for Any Christian Man*, generally called the King's Book. In 1539 what were known as the Six Articles were passed by Parliament in the presence and under the authority of Henry, and over the opposition of Cranmer. They were much closer to the Catholic position than were the Ten Articles, for they came out flatly for transubstantiation, against the necessity of communion in both kinds, for the celibacy of the clergy, for the observance of vows of chastity taken by men or women, for private masses, and for auricular confession.

In accordance with this zeal for doctrinal orthodoxy as defined in the Catholic tradition, a few Zwinglians and Lutherans were condemned and burned, and several others were burned for denying transubstantiation.

Yet steps which might look in a Protestant direction were taken. In 1536 Cromwell, as the king's vicar-general, ordered a Latin and an English Bible placed in every church to encourage its reading by the laity. Later in the 1530's priests were commanded to set up a large English Bible in such a manner that it might be read by all who wished. The circulation of Tyndale's Bible, especially the edition with his glosses, for they were regarded as heretical, stimulated the authorities to essay a translation of which they could approve. Miles Coverdale, a former Augustinian friar, a graduate of Cambridge and a member of the reforming circle of which the martyred Bilney had been a leader, had made a full translation of the entire Bible into English, not from the original Greek and Hebrew, but probably from the Vulgate, another Latin version, Luther's translation, and a Zürich version, and possibly utilizing Tyndale. As a work of scholarship it was of dubious value, but it possessed marked literary merit, and some of its phrases were later taken over by the King James Version. What was called the Great Bible, had the approval of Cranmer, and had been assisted by Cromwell, was to be placed in the churches. It was a revision, by Coverdale, of Matthew's Bible. This took its name from Thomas Matthew, probably an alias for John Rogers. Matthew's Bible was made up of Tyndale's Pentateuch and New Testament, most of Coverdale's Old Testament, and a translation of the Apocrypha by Rogers. The Great Bible went into several editions, some of them with a preface by Cranmer and accordingly called Cranmer's Bible.

While Henry was still alive, Cranmer had begun the preparation of forms of worship, including a litany. By the king's order, the litany was to be sung in English in the churches.

Henry was gathered to his fathers in 1547. Cranmer was with the dying king. Although he had dared to oppose more than one of his royal master's acts and to intercede with him for some of the latter's victims, Henry had trusted him and had supported him against his enemies.

THE REFORMATION UNDER EDWARD VI

Henry VIII was succeeded by the son, Edward VI, whom his third wife, Jane Seymour, had borne to him. He had married her after the execution of Anne Boleyn for infidelity and her failure to present him the desperately desired male heir. Edward was only nine years of age when he came to the throne and, always frail of body, died in 1553, when he was not yet sixteen. He was highly intelligent, was given a strenuous education of a humanist, Renaissance kind, had a mind of his own, and was deeply religious and strongly Protestant. But policies during his reign were largely determined by his seniors. First to rule was his mother's brother, Edward Seymour, Earl of Hertford and then Duke of Somerset, who was given the title of Lord Protector. Then, after about two-and-a-half years, he was followed by John Dudley, Earl of Warwick and then Duke of Northumberland.

In the six-and-a-half years of Edward's reign England was carried towards Protestantism. Somerset was Protestant in his sympathies, probably sincerely so. Northumberland moved even further in that direction, although presumably more from expediency than from religious conviction, for just prior to his execution under Mary he professed reconversion to Roman Catholicism.

The main steps towards Protestantism can be quickly summarized. Early in the reign a step which Henry had planned and initiated was taken: chantries, hospitals, and free chapels were dissolved and the capital thus released went largely to the depleted royal exchequer. The first Parliament of the new reign repealed the Six Articles, all restrictions on the printing and circulation of the

Scriptures, and the laws under which heretics had been tried. The reign was not many weeks old when the removal of images from the churches was ordered. In some places violent iconoclasm followed. Indeed, in many quarters enthusiasts were moving faster than the government and the latter took measures to restrain them. In 1548 an Order of Communion was printed for use in connexion with giving the communion to the laity. In it appeared a general confession, taking the place of private confession to the priest. Yet the Latin mass was continued. Leading Continental reformers were welcomed. Among them were Peter Martyr, Ochino, and Bucer, each of whom was given an important post. Disputes over the Eucharist and whether mass should be said waxed hot and in places led to fighting and riots. The marriage of priests was legalized. The influences from the Continent which helped to shape the English Reformation were more from humanism and the Reformed Churches than from Luther and Lutheranism.

Partly to restore and preserve order, in 1549 an Act of Uniformity was passed by Parliament which required the clergy to use a Book of Common Prayer which was drawn up by a commission headed by Cranmer. Cranmer wished to move much further in the direction of Zwingli than many in Parliament were prepared to go, and to reject not only transubstantiation but the real presence in the Eucharist, the elevation and adoration of the host, and the use of the word "oblation." However, conservatives in Parliament led him to modify the Book of Common Prayer in the direction of the Catholic tradition. Cranmer had a deep religious conviction, a sensitivity to the things of the spirit, a wide familiarity with liturgies both Catholic and Protestant, Roman and Greek, and a command of dignified and felicitous English. In the Book of Common Prayer he combined what had previously been in the missal, the breviary, and the pontifical, and levied toll from forms of worship which had been developed in various branches and ages of the Church. Advantage was taken of uses employed in England, especially the Sarum missal, breviary, and pontifical, but these were by no means slavishly followed. For instance, from the breviary the eight daily offices were reduced to two, matins and evensong, with the hope that they would be of aid to the laity as well as to the clergy.

The First Prayer Book of Edward VI was of major importance. With modifications it has endured and has been a bond which has held together the diverse elements in the Church of England and the several branches of the Anglican Communion which arose in subsequent centuries in other countries. It has also had a profound influence upon the devotional life of individuals and on other communions which employ the English language. Its collects eventually became the common property of almost all English-speaking Protestants.

Yet the Book of Common Prayer did not immediately win its way. Those with Catholic leanings believed that it went too far towards Protestantism and many Protestants held that it retained too much from the hated Roman tradition. The swing towards Protestantism contributed to uprisings in various parts of the realm. Some of the bishops with Catholic convictions opposed the Act of Uniformity, were deposed, and were replaced by appointees in sympathy with the Reformed Churches.

In 1552 a new Act of Uniformity was enacted and Parliament gave its sanction to a revised edition of the Book of Common Prayer, the Second Prayer Book of Edward VI. This moved much further in the direction of Protestantism. It was the work of Cranmer and Ridley with some help from Bucer and Peter Martyr. In it, among other changes, the "altar" was called a "table," and the "priest" a "minister," the minister's vestments were limited to the surplice, and exorcism and anointing were omitted. The new Act of Uniformity was more stringent than was the earlier one. The laity were enjoined to attend service on Sundays and holidays and severe penalties were specified for failure to comply. The use of the revised Book of Common Prayer was made compulsory.

It will be noted that Parliament, an organ of state, rather than Convocation, the body through which the Church spoke, took responsibility for the Book of Common Prayer and imposed it on the nation. This, together with the supremacy of the crown over the Church, was in accord with the trend in both Western and Eastern Europe, and in Protestant, Roman Catholic, and Orthodox circles.

In 1553 the Forty-two Articles of Religion, giving the doctrinal position of the Church of England, were issued under the authority of the king. Their formulation was largely the work of Cranmer.

It was during the reign of Edward VI that English paraphrases of the Psalms began to have wide currency. The chief pioneer was Thomas Sternhold, a groom of the robes to Henry VIII and Edward VI. He seems to have drawn his inspiration in large part from what was being done in Geneva.

Marked though its progress was, by no means all the English were committed to the Reformation. It had a much larger following in London and the South-east, areas in close commercial contact with the Continent, than in the North and West. In the latter areas the majority were probably still attached to the old forms, although not necessarily to Rome.

THE CATHOLIC REACTION UNDER MARY

From the movement towards Protestantism which was being pushed in the name of the crown during the reign of Edward VI a reaction was to be expected. The Catholic elements were still strong and the majority of the population were either indifferent or attached to the old ways. Reform had not sprung widely from the rank and file of the nation and with the exception of minorities had not really penetrated to them. However, the reaction was greatly intensified by the accession to the throne of Mary, daughter of Henry VIII and Catherine.

Mary reigned for a little over five years, from the summer of 1553 to her death, November 17, 1558. It was a foregone conclusion that she would attempt to bring England back into the Roman Catholic fold. The daughter of Henry VIII and Catherine, she was intensely loyal to her mother's memory. During much of her life she had suffered indignities because of her birth, and by the nullification of the marriage between her mother and her father serious doubt had been cast on her legitimacy. Although her father's will had declared her and Elizabeth to be bastards, it had provided that in case Edward VI died without issue they should succeed to the throne in the order of their birth. The attempt of the Duke of Northumberland to have Lady Jane Grey, a grand-niece of Henry VIII, succeed Edward VI quickly failed, but while Mary was magnanimous, it did not serve to make her less opposed to Protestantism. Physically unprepossessing, thirty-seven years of age, and far from well, Mary had courage and intelligence of a high order and an indomitable will, and was very well educated. She could be counted on to give vigorous leadership to the realm.

With all her determination and ability, not for some months was Mary able to restore the Papal authority in England. Yet the trend was quickly in that direction. Many Protestants, including foreigners who had been prominent under Edward, seeing the writing on the wall, sought refuge on the Continent. A few went to France, but most of them found haven in cities where the Reformed Churches were strong—Zürich, Basel, Geneva, Strassburg, Heidelberg, and Frankfort. Important results from contacts in these places of refuge were to follow in the next reign. Mary had mass said in her private chapel. Catholic bishops, notably Stephen Gardiner of Winchester, who had been dispossessed under Edward, were restored to their sees. Although refusing to renew the tie with Rome or to restore the alienated ecclesiastical properties, in October, 1553, Parliament repealed all the laws enacted under Edward which affected religion, thus banishing the Book of Common Prayer, removing the permission for clerical marriage, and withdrawing communion in both kinds. Church services were back where they were in the last years of Henry VIII.

However, in 1554 Mary had her way. By her own choice she was married, not to an English nobleman, as Parliament had wished, but to her cousin, Philip, soon (January, 1556) by the abdication of his father, Charles V, to become King Philip II of Spain. Possessors of church lands were given assurances that they would not be disturbed in their holdings. In November, 1554.

Reginald Pole, Cardinal and Papal legate, formally absolved the realm from its schism and disobedience and received it back into communion with the Church of Rome. Closely related to Henry VIII and so to Mary, as a younger son Pole had from childhood been trained for an ecclesiastical career. Sincerely religious, impeccable in his private life, a friend of Thomas More, he had refused to approve of Henry's efforts to be separated from Catherine, had frowned on his move to make himself head of the Church of England, and had lived abroad for years. There he had been made a cardinal and had been a member of a circle of Catholic ecclesiastics and laywomen who desired the reform of the Church. Indeed, he had been denounced to the Inquisition for harbouring heretical views. Yet he narrowly missed being elected Pope. He now (1556) became Archbishop of Canterbury. In that office he sought to reform the Church of England, to revive monasticism, to raise up good priests, and, as chancellor of both Oxford and Cambridge, to make those universities serve the revived Roman Catholicism.

The reign of Mary witnessed a number of beheadings and burnings, so much so, indeed, that her critics remembered her as "Bloody Mary." That was not because she, Pole, or her chancellor, Gardiner, were cruel or vindictive. Indeed, all were kindly in their personal relations and Pole by temperament and conviction preferred reason and lenience to harshness. Yet the brief reign was punctuated with rebellions and the spirit of the times regarded as normal the execution of the leaders. Moreover, to the Catholic, heresy was a major crime against God and society. The laws against heresy were revived and under them about three hundred went to the stake. About a third were clergymen and about a fifth women. Two-thirds were in the stronghold of Protestantism, London and the South-east. By Continental standards the number was small, but it was much greater than the burnings of Lollards in a century and a quarter before 1529 or than the number of Catholics who suffered the death penalty in the long reign of Elizabeth. The most famous of the victims were Bishops Latimer, Ridley, and Cranmer, all of them burned at Oxford. The first two suffered together. Latimer is said to have encouraged his comrade at the stake with the words: "Be of good comfort, Master Ridley, we shall this day light such a candle by God's grace in England as, I trust, shall never be put out." Cranmer was in a hard dilemma. He had a profound conviction, on which he had acted under Henry and Edward, that the monarch was by right master of the religion of his realm and that his subjects must bow to his will in this as in other matters. Now the monarch was a Roman Catholic and demanded that England return to that faith. By disposition and long habit, Cranmer's mind moved slowly to new conclusions. It seems to have been at least in part for this reason that at first he submitted and made seven recantations. At the end, however, on the very day that he was given to the flames, he publicly, in St. Mary's, before a great throng, repudiated his recantations. At the stake he held in the flames the hand which had signed the documents he now bitterly regretted, that it might first be reduced to cinders.

THE ELIZABETHAN SETTLEMENT

Mary died an unhappy woman, for Philip was with her infrequently, she remained childless, and she had alienated the affections of many of her subjects. She was succeeded by her half-sister, Elizabeth, daughter of Henry VIII and Anne Boleyn.

Elizabeth reigned for nearly half a century, from 1558 to 1603. Her name is associated with one of the most glorious eras in English history, remembered for its literature, its commerce and growth in wealth, and its exploits on the seas, especially the defeat of the formidable armada by which Philip II of Spain thought to prepare the way for the invasion and conquest of the country. Disciplined by the adversities of a difficult youth in which a misstep might have meant her death, Elizabeth was astute in gaining and keeping power and popularity. Identifying the welfare of England with her own, she sought to bring unity to a divided nation and so far as possible to keep it out of weakening embroilment in foreign wars. She knew much about Christianity, but probably had little religious conviction. She loved pomp and ceremony and approved of them in church services. Although, for an adequate return, the Pope might have found a way to alter her status, from the Roman Catholic standpoint she was illegitimate and therefore was prejudiced against the recently reëstablished tie with Rome. Presumably, too, she wished, like her father and many another strong monarch, to have full control of the Church within her borders. She was not above despoiling it of some of its wealth. She kept some of the bishoprics unfilled for years and appropriated their revenues. Several ecclesiastical posts were paid for by their appointees by alienating portions of their endowments. Yet she wished such an ordering of the Church of England as would satisfy as many of her subjects as possible. Therefore, she sought to make it include both Catholic and Protestant elements. She could not hope to please both Roman Catholics and extreme Protestants, but she could and did achieve a settlement which proved acceptable to the vast majority of the Englishmen of her day and which, without basic alterations, was to characterize the Church of England from then onward.

The main features of the Elizabethan settlement of the ecclesiastical issues were shaped in the early months of her reign. In April, 1559, by what was generally known as the Act of Supremacy, the authority of the Pope and all payments and appeals to him were forbidden. In it she was called not the

"Supreme Head," but the "Supreme Governor of this realm, and of all other her highness's dominions and countries, as well in all spiritual or ecclesiastical things or causes as temporal," and members of the clergy and civil officials were required to acknowledge her as such and to renounce the jurisdiction of any foreign prince or prelate within the kingdom. Parliament also passed an Act of Uniformity restoring, with some alterations, the Second Prayer Book of Edward VI, and commanding it to be used in all cathedrals and parish churches for matins, evensong, and the administration of the sacraments. All inhabitants of the queen's dominions were to endeavour to be present at service on every Sunday and holyday or else be fined. To enforce the Act of Uniformity, royal visitors were commissioned and for their guidance what were known as injunctions were issued, modifications of those under the name of Edward VI, which regulated the clergy, public worship, and the care of the poor through the parishes. They permitted the marriage of the clergy but ordered that in each instance it should be by consent of the bishop, two justices of the peace, and the bride's parents. They commanded the destruction of shrines and all "monuments of feigned miracles, pilgrimages, idolatry, and superstition," in pictures, paintings, and glass windows. They provided for a censorship of books and for a holy table for the Lord's Supper in churches from which the altars had been removed. Simony was forbidden.

Most of the parish clergy subscribed to the Act of Supremacy. Many of them had continued from Henry through the reigns of Edward and Mary and were willing to conform to the monarch's wishes. Only about two hundred lost their posts. However, the episcopacy was sadly depleted, for Mary's bishops had died or would not accept the Act of Supremacy. Those who refused were deprived of their sees. Pole, mortally ill, had died twelve hours after Mary breathed her weary last and a new Archbishop of Canterbury was required. For this office Matthew Parker, the queen's instructor, was appointed. He was consecrated by four who had been bishops under Henry VIII and Edward VI but had been ousted under Mary. In due course other bishops were chosen and consecrated. Customarily, as in all subsequent reigns, the crown appointed the bishops but used the legal device of permitting the dean and chapter of the cathedral of the diocese formally to elect the person named. The spokesmen for the Church of England have insisted that, in spite of the separation from Rome and the deposition of the Marian bishops, the apostolic succession of the episcopate was preserved. This many Roman Catholics denied, partly because the forms used did not clearly state the conception of the priesthood held by their church. However, it was not until 1896 that the Pope, after careful investigation, formally declared the orders of the Church of England invalid.

Further to define the faith held by the Church of England, the Thirty-nine

Articles of Religion were issued. They were a modification of the Forty-two Articles of the reign of Edward. They were finally promulgated in 1571. That same year subscription to them was made compulsory for all priests and ministers.

Scholars were not wanting to give a reasoned defense for the Church of England as constituted under the Elizabethan settlement. John Jewel (1522–1571), a pupil of Peter Martyr who died as Bishop of Salisbury, wrote *Apologia Ecclesiæ Anglicanæ* (1562) in which he maintained the position of the Church of England against that of the Church of Rome. More notable was Richard Hooker's *Laws of Ecclesiastical Polity,* a massive work left uncompleted by the author's death (1600). This was a positive argument for Anglicanism against the attacks of the Puritan Presbyterians on the one hand and against the Roman Catholics on the other. Directly or by implication it included much more than the structure of the Church and the sacraments. In the midst of bitterly contending bodies of Christians, Hooker tried to make for peace by seeking a common ground in the rational principles which permeate the universe, which man, being rational, can apprehend, and which accord with the teachings of Scripture. The rational principles are seen, so Hooker said, in the eternal law by which God governs the universe. Human laws by which states and the Church are ordered should be in accord with this law of reason. They should be adapted to meet the needs of particular historical situations. With that as a basis, Hooker argued that the episcopal form of government was best for the Church of England, and that Church and state were two aspects of the same commonwealth, a commonwealth in which both were rightly under the monarch.

Although Elizabeth and her counsellors arrived at a structure, a form of worship, and a statement of belief of the Church which satisfied the large majority of Englishmen and which guarded the realm against the kind of civil strife complicated by religion which was so violent in France and Germany and which in the next century was to distress England, it was by no means acceptable to all. On the one extreme were those who held to Rome. On the other were those who were convinced that the Reformation should go much further. They were made up of various kinds of Puritans and, near the far extreme, of Independents and Separatists.

THE ROMAN CATHOLIC REVIVAL

During the reign of Elizabeth, in spite of persecution, Roman Catholicism had something of a revival in England. Through the reigns of Henry VIII, Edward VI, and, of course, Mary, there were those who held to Rome. The death of Mary and Pole and the popularity of Elizabeth and the Elizabethan settlement made impossible for the majority the renewal of the tie with Rome. However, not far from 1568, after Elizabeth had been on the throne for a decade, a marked renewal of Roman Catholic activity began. It arose in part from the rising tide of the Catholic Reformation on the Continent. The outstanding leader was William Allen (1532–1594), eventually cardinal. A graduate of Oxford and principal of one of its halls, he refused to take the oath of supremacy under Elizabeth, after a few years went to Rome, and was chiefly responsible for the founding (1568) of a Seminary in Douai, in Spanish Flanders, easily accessible to England and under Roman Catholic rulers, for the training of English missionaries to their mother country. In 1578, because of political troubles, the seminary was moved to Rheims. It was there that a translation of the Bible into English was made which is usually called the Douai Version. At Rome, partly at the suggestion of Allen, the hospice formerly used by the English was transformed into a college for the training of English priests. Jesuits and men prepared in these centres made their way into England, ministering to the faithful, strengthening the doubtful, and seeking to win converts. They dreamed of the time when England would again come into the Roman fold. To that end there was also a network of political intrigue, much of it pinning its hopes on Mary Stuart, "Queen of Scots," who by right of blood had a claim to the throne. It was this which led to the execution of Mary. Yet the intrigues and the fear of foreign intervention tended to augment the loyalty of the majority of the population to Elizabeth and the national church.

Slightly later, but part of the Catholic revival, was the work of Mary Ward (1585–1645). Of a Roman Catholic Yorkshire family, Mary Ward began in 1609 a religious community of women at St. Omer for the active, not the cloistered life. She met opposition, was dubbed the Jesuitess, and in 1630 the community was suppressed, for the Papacy looked askance at the suggestion of non-cloistered nuns. However, a few of her circle persisted and in 1703 their rule obtained Papal approval. The community was known as the Institute of Mary and more informally as the English Ladies and the Loretto Nuns. It spread widely.

The Growth of Puritanism

Much more numerous and influential than the Roman Catholics were those who were known as Puritans. They wished to "purify" the Church of England from all traces of what they held to be the remains of the corruption which survived from the Roman connexion. Many of them had been refugees on the Continent during the reign of Mary and there had had intimate contacts with Protestants. These were much more with Basel, Strassburg, and various other cities in the Rhine Valley than with Geneva. Moreover, Puritanism antedated the Marian interlude and, largely indigenous, was deeply rooted in England's own past.

Puritans differed among themselves as to the extent to which they would depart from the Elizabethan settlement. Some focused their attack on the vestments prescribed for the clergy, holding that they tended to perpetuate the conception that, contrary to the priesthood of all believers, the clergy are distinct from the laity and with special powers. This led to the Vestiarian Controversy. Some opposed kneeling to receive the bread and wine at the Lord's Supper as adoration of the bodily presence of the Christ. They emphasized the memorial aspects of the Lord's Supper, but in neither the Lutheran nor the Zwinglian sense. Some wished a Presbyterian form of church government, with the election of pastors by their people, and placing bishops, presbyters, and pastors on an equality.

In general, Puritans held to a covenant or federalist theology. This maintained that God had made promises to man but that they were conditioned upon man's obedience to His laws. God's laws, so this conception had it, are seen in the Scriptures. It was to enable men to read the Bible and to know these laws that Tyndale undertook his vast labour of translation. The covenant theory had a long history and went back to the Middle Ages and even earlier. By this theology there were eventually meant two covenants of a somewhat different nature—a covenant of grace between God and His elect and a covenant of works between God and Adam as the representative of all mankind. As developed in the Rhineland the covenant of works stressed man's obligation to God.

The covenant of works laid a theological foundation for an obligation binding on all men, elect and non-elect, and gave support to the political theory which held that the state and all society came into being as a contract, an expression of natural law. While this had been talked of at Heidelberg, its political applications were more extensively worked out in England. It was used to limit the power of the monarch and in an extreme form held both state and Church to be associations or contracts entered into voluntarily by those who constituted these units and therefore subject to modification or even revolution as the members of these units might agree.

Prominent among the exponents of Presbyterian Puritanism under Elizabeth was Thomas Cartwright, appointed in 1569 Lady Margaret Professor of Divinity at Cambridge. John Whitgift, as vice-chancellor of the university, deprived him of his chair (1570) and as master of Trinity College had him dismissed (1571) from his fellowship. Thereafter Cartwright led a persecuted and wandering life, much of it on the Continent. In several places some of the Puritans organized a classis or presbytery, but still within the Church of England. In 1572 and 1573 they issued two Admonitions to Parliament, the second by Cartwright, denouncing government by bishops and demanding that it be by presbyters. Some Puritan ministers ceased to use the Book of Common Prayer either entirely or in part.

To all this Whitgift was opposed, and as Archbishop of Canterbury from 1583 to his death in 1604 he stood for the sturdy enforcement of Elizabeth's policy of uniformity. To accomplish this he had created a Commission for Causes Ecclesiastical, popularly known as the High Commission. It became an agency for repressing the Puritans. In protest there came out under the pseudonym of Martin Marprelate a succession of tracts denouncing Whitgift and the bishops with witty and coarse epithets. Under pressure from Elizabeth and Whitgift Parliament passed (1593) acts directed at the Puritans under the guise of "seditious sectaries and disloyal persons" and ordering all those who would not conform to the laws by "coming to church to hear divine service" to leave the realm.

THE SEPARATISTS OR INDEPENDENTS

Even more radical were the Separatists or Independents. The Puritans wished to remain within the Church of England and to have it, cleansed according to their patterns, as the religious wing of the nation's life to which all the queen's subjects would belong. In contrast, the Separatists or Independents, like the Anabaptists on the Continent, believed in "gathered" churches, not made up of all the inhabitants of a particular area, but only of those who were consciously Christian. They were to be united with one another and with Christ in a covenant. Each congregation so united, with Christ as its head, was a self-governing church which elected its own pastor and other officers after what was believed to be the pattern discernible in the New Testament. No church was to have authority over any other and in each church every member was responsible for the welfare of the whole and of his fellow-members. In theory and to a large extent in practice, such churches were pure democracies. They were the spiritual ancestors of the later Congregationalists. They were Separatists in that they withdrew from the Church of England and were Independents in that they believed in the full autonomy of each local church. They were not Anabaptists.

An outstanding pioneer was Robert Browne (died 1633), a graduate of Cambridge and originally a Puritan. Indeed, he may never have given over the idea of a church embracing all the nation. Politically, he wished magistrates to hold office only by the choice of the people. He had a varied and stormy career, part of it in prison for his views and part in exile. Then at last he submitted to the Archbishop of Canterbury. Although at times the early Independents were called Brownists, it has been questioned whether he ever really was one of them.

With the death of Elizabeth (1603), the fears of Henry VIII were realized, and none of his descendants was left to claim the throne. The crown passed to James, the son of Mary Stuart "Queen of Scots," and greatgrandson of Margaret, daughter of Henry VII.

As we have seen (Chapter 33), James, reared a Presbyterian but favouring episcopacy on the principle of "no bishop no king," was King of Scotland as well as of England. The tie was purely personal and involved no union of the two realms. James was on the throne of England from 1603 to 1625, or for a little over two decades. The years were marked by growing prosperity, partly because James managed to keep the realm from being deeply embroiled in foreign wars, and by a rising tension between king and Parliament. James was determined to rule as an autocrat by divine right and the trend of national sentiment made that much more difficult than under the Tudors.

In the religious life of the nation, Roman Catholicism was being discredited and Puritanism was growing. The extreme Protestants outside the Church of England, although still a small minority, were increasing in numbers. Dissent from the state church, it may be noted, was expressing itself quite differently in England than in the neighbouring Scotland. While influenced by Continental movements, it took on peculiarly English forms.

At the outset of his reign, James seemed to be veering towards the Roman Catholics. However, he soon changed his attitude. In February, 1604, he ordered priests banished, and soon Parliament confirmed the Elizabethan laws against them. This led to what was known as the Gunpowder Plot associated with the name of Guy Fawkes. Its purpose was to store a cellar under the Parliament buildings with barrels of gunpowder and blow up both houses, along with James and his eldest son. The plot was discovered and the chief conspirators were shot or executed. This aroused much anti-Roman Catholic feeling and led Parliament to enact even more stringent acts against those of that faith.

On his way to London in 1603 Puritans presented James with what was known as the Millenary Petition, so called because it was supposed to bear a thousand signatures. It set forth some of their desires, on the whole fairly moderate, for changes in the Church of England. There followed, in January, 1604, a conference of bishops and Puritans at Hampton Court. The one tangible result of consequence, and that of first-class importance, was the initiation of a fresh translation of the Bible.

This was needed. Two new versions had been issued during the preceding reign. One, known as the Bishops' Bible, had followed in general Tyndale's translation, was of large size, and was used chiefly in the churches. The other, the Geneva Bible, had Tyndale's New Testament as its basis but contained a new translation of the Old Testament and was later than the Bishops' Bible. Especially in its marginal notes it had a strong Calvinist and Puritan tinge. Embodying thorough scholarship, it also had an English style which delighted the rank and file of readers, was printed in Roman rather than black letters and in convenient style, and enjoyed a wide circulation. A version was called for which would embody the best in the existing versions and which could be read both in the public services of the Church and in homes and by private individuals.

To produce the translation James appointed fifty-four scholars (of whom we have the names of forty-seven), presumably after consultation. They were divided into six companies of seven or eight men each, who worked individually and in conference. Then the whole text was gone over by a committee of twelve and two prepared the product for the press. They utilized the original languages in the best texts available, but also took advantage of previous translations. Indeed, the end product was essentially a revision of the earlier versions. Work was begun about 1607 and the Bible was published in 1611. Although it was called the "Authorized Version," no record exists to prove that it was ever submitted to the Privy Council or that it had the formal approval of the king. It did not bear the stamp of the genius of any one man as distinctively as did the German translation by Luther. It was, rather, the product of many hands and minds. Although other versions appeared, especially late in the nineteenth and in the twentieth century, it remained standard in the English-speaking world.

During the reign of James I Puritans were increasingly active. In many parishes they were establishing "lectureships" for Sunday afternoon preaching of a kind which favoured their convictions. They stressed the observance of Sunday and made much use of the metrical versions of the Psalms and of the music to which they were set. They emphasized Bible reading, had services in their homes, and, in the midst of an age of loose living and looser speech, endeavoured to be uncorrupted in morals by the world about them. They repeatedly clashed with James, partly on political issues, for they were a growing force in Parliament, partly over the royal encouragement of sports on Sundays, such as dancing, May games, athletics, and May poles, on which the king had made a formal declaration in 1618, and partly over forms of worship. James sought (1622) to restrict preachers to topics which seemed to him non-controversial and forbade them to deal with predestination or matters of state or to rail at "either Papists or Puritans," an obvious attempt to curb both Puritans and their opponents.

Separatists and Independents continued and grew, although still small minorities. Persecuted, some sought refuge on the Continent, especially in Protestant Holland, but many remained in England. They displayed a great variety of views. That was true even of those who were later called Congregationalists. There were the Seekers, who held that Antichrist had ruled so long that no true churches or valid office-holders existed and could not until God sent apostles to establish and ordain new ones. Baptists now appeared and spread. They differed from the Congregationalists chiefly in their repudiation of infant baptism and their insistence that the rite be given only to believers. The first English Baptist church arose in Amsterdam from among the Separatists and centred about John Smyth (died 1612, of tuberculosis, before he was forty-five), a graduate of Cambridge. It held what are usually termed Arminian views and was the spiritual ancestor of the General Baptists of Britain. Some of Smyth's followers united with the Mennonites. Thomas Helwys, one of Smyth's intimates who later broke with him but remained "Arminian," founded (1612) what seems to have been the first Baptist church on English soil, outside the walls of London, and took pains to disassociate himself from the Mennonites. A few years later, in the next reign, what were known as Particular Baptists arose, so designated because they held to a restricted or particular atonement which was only for the elect. They began as a secession from the (Congregational) Separatists. The two strains of Baptist churches, General and Particular, Arminian and Calvinist, continued apart until late in the nineteenth century.

Warm religious life was not confined to Puritans and Independents. It was also present among those in the Church of England who held to the Catholic tradition. Such a one was Lancelot Andrewes (1555–1626), a graduate of Cambridge, successively Bishop of Chichester, Ely, and Winchester, a trusted counsellor under Elizabeth, James I, and Charles I, and one of those who prepared the King James Version of the Bible. Scholarly, a noted and erudite preacher, presenting reasoned arguments against Roman Catholic views but not a Puritan, he may be longest remembered for his *Devotions,* composed in Greek for his private use, but published after his death.

CHARLES I AND THE PURITAN REVOLUTION

James I was succeeded in 1625 by his son, Charles I. Although he was handsome, dignified, athletic, pure in his private life in the midst of a corrupt court, courageous, a lover of beauty, and deeply religious, Charles increasingly alienated a large proportion of his subjects, both in England and Scotland. He held sincerely to the conviction that as king he ruled by divine right and that while seeking their welfare he must not in any way be controlled by his subjects. Nor did he believe that he need keep his promises, even when solemnly given, if they curbed his prerogatives. Increasing tension developed which culminated in civil war and the defeat and execution of Charles (1649). On the one side were the king, most of the nobility, and those who held to the established order and Catholic tradition in the Church of England. On the other side were Parliament, the growing urban middle classes, many of the lesser country gentry, the great body of Puritans, and the extreme Protestants, including the Independents and Separatists. Charles attempted to see as little of Parliament as possible, for each time that it met it was critical. Yet he was compelled to call it to obtain financial grants. From 1629 to 1640 he managed to rule without it. However, his attempt to force episcopacy and the English Book of Common Prayer upon Scotland led, as we have seen (Chapter 33), to an uprising in that country which brought added expense and forced him to summon Parliament to seek more taxes. First came a short and stormy session in the spring of 1640 and then what was called the Long Parliament which assembled in November, 1640, and with which Charles was eventually in open war.

Into the intricacies of the prolonged and complicated struggle we must not go. In it religion was only one factor. However, religion was prominent. Both the king and many of his opponents professed, quite honestly, to be acting from what they deemed Christian motives. The triumph of the king's enemies brought with it the rule of the Puritans and the extreme Protestants. While reaction eventually swept them out of power, these children of Protestantism left an indelible mark upon the political and religious life and structure of England.

In the earlier years of the reign, before the Puritans gained control, the Catholic element was in the ascendant in the Church of England. Charles was a loyal Anglican. To him as to his father the royal power was associated with the episcopacy and he appreciated the form and pageantry of elaborate church services. His queen, Henrietta Maria, daughter of Henry IV of France, was a Roman Catholic, but in spite of accusations to the contrary, he had no intention of carrying the Church of England back to Rome. Yet he favoured those who stood staunchly for episcopacy and against the Puritans.

In his ecclesiastical policies, Charles found an able ally in William Laud (1573-1645). A graduate of Oxford, as chancellor of the university Laud did much to improve its intellectual and moral discipline, enriched it with benefactions, and made it a stronghold of Anglican, anti-Puritan orthodoxy. Successively Bishop of St. David's, Bath and Wells, and the strongly Puritan London (1628–1633), and then Archbishop of Canterbury (1633–1645), he was a firm supporter of what later was known as the Anglo-Catholic tradition. He believed that the Roman Catholic Church was a true church and not as apostate as Puritans viewed it. However, he held that the Church of England, much more than Rome, preserved the Catholic faith and tradition in its purity. He transformed communion tables into altars, moving them back to the east end of the churches. He opposed Calvinistic theology and stood for "Arminianism." Wherever possible he suppressed Puritan lectureships. He discouraged the Puritan observance of Sunday and moved Charles to renew the encouragement to Sunday sports and amusements that had been given by James. A prodigiously hard worker, courageous, conscientious, he laboured to root out evils in the Church, fought corruption and irreverence, restored church fabrics, cleared tradesmen and lawyers out of St. Paul's in London, and sought to enforce uniformity against the Roman Catholics on the one hand and the Puritans on the other. While he had none of his opponents burned, he sponsored harsh penalties. He was very unpopular with the Puritans and became to them a kind of symbol of all that they hated in the ecclesiastical policies of Charles. The Long Parliament impeached him for high treason and imprisoned him in the Tower of London (March, 1641). After a delay he was tried, but was not found guilty. Thereupon a bill of attainder was passed and under it he was decapitated (January 10, 1645).

The Long Parliament took advantage of its power to work revolutionary changes in the Church of England. For months it intermittently debated various proposals which were urged on it. There was general conviction that the Catholic features introduced by Laud must go, such as making the communion tables into altars, the use of images and candles, and communion rails. On other points sharp differences of opinion developed. It was necessary to have the help of the Scots in the struggle with the king. Parliament accordingly agreed (1643) to accept the Solemn League and Covenant. In February, 1644, it was imposed upon all Englishmen over eighteen years of age. It stood for the preservation of the Reformed religion in the Church of Scotland, sought to make uniform with it religion in England and Ireland, and agreed to extirpate "popery" and "prelacy," meaning by the latter church government by archbishops, bishops, archdeacons, deans, and chapters. In accordance with this undertaking Parliament abolished the use of the Book of Common Prayer, substituted for it a directory for worship framed by the Westminster Assembly and without set forms of prayer, and ordered (June, 1646) the establishment of the Presbyterian form of church government. This last was never fully enforced.

The Westminster Assembly, called to advise Parliament on religious questions and composed of clergy and laity, mostly Puritans with a sprinkling of Episcopalians and Independents, and with Scottish commissioners without vote, convened in July, 1643. In addition to the *Directory for the Public Worship of God* it drew up what is usually called the Westminster Confession of Faith. This required several months and was completed in November, 1646. It was methodically considered and debated in Parliament, was ordered printed, but was never formally authorized by that body. To it the Westminster Assembly added a longer and a shorter catechism, the former for exposition in the pulpit and the latter for the instruction of children. All three had extensive use in Presbyterian churches both in Great Britain and America. They were formally adopted by the Church of Scotland. Setting forth the Reformed system of theology and church government, they were shaped much less by Calvin than by the Augustinian and federalist or covenant theology. They were influenced by earlier similar statements framed on the Continent but especially by the Irish Articles of 1615 which are usually supposed to have been the work of Archbishop James Usher (1581–1656), of the Church of Ireland, who is best remembered for compiling a long accepted Biblical chronology and who had refused to come to the Westminster Assembly.

THE PROTESTANT RADICALS IN THE SADDLE: CROMWELLIAN ENGLAND (1649–1660)

The civil war ended in the triumph of the Parliamentary armies. These were under the command of Oliver Cromwell. Quite without premeditation but through the inexorable course of events, by the defeat and execution of the king Cromwell found himself the ruler of the British Isles. The discrediting and death of Charles had created a political vacuum. Parliament and the army would not tolerate the continuation of the Stuart monarchy, Parliament was incompetent as an administrative body, and there were radicals who combined religious zeal with sweeping programmes for social and political reorganization and who, although minorities, wished to bring the country to their mind.

Chief among the extremists were the Levellers, the Diggers, the Fifth Monarchy Men, and the Quakers. The Levellers, with John Lilburne as their outstanding leader, were recruited in part from discontented London tradesmen. Lilburne had been won by the Baptists and was an ardent student of the Bible and of various works on law and political theory. Vain, quarrelsome, stubborn, he yet attracted followers. He held that there is a natural law to which all laws of man and the structure of state and society should conform, that it is written in the hearts and consciences of men, that sovereignty resides in the nation at large, that Parliaments should be elected by universal manhood suffrage, that they should have only limited administrative and police powers, and that no one should sit in two successive Parliaments. The Diggers protested against private ownership of land. The Fifth Monarchy Men maintained that according to Biblical prophecy Christ was soon to return to establish on earth the "Fifth Monarchy" in succession to the Assyrian, Persian, Greek, and Roman empires, and that he would reign, with his saints, for a thousand years. They differed greatly among themselves. Some wished to use force to establish the Fifth Monarchy, while others would await quietly the coming of Christ.

The Quakers, to use the nickname given them, or Society of Friends, to give them the title which they preferred, were to have a much longer existence than these others and were to play a more prominent role. Their founder was George Fox (1624-1691). Of humble birth, from boyhood he had heard Puritan preaching and had acquired an intimate familiarity with the text of the English Bible. At the age of nineteen, shocked by the contrast between the profession and practice of nominal Christians, he left home and entered upon a religious quest which led him to consult clergymen of the Church of England and of the dissenting groups. For four years he suffered severe spiritual depression induced by the spectacle of human suffering, especially in the civil war which was then raging, and by the doctrine of predestination which he heard expounded from Puritan pulpits. By temperament a mystic, he was eager for direct and unhindered access to God. None of the many priests and preachers from whom he sought help brought him relief and he came to have an impatient disdain for them. Eventually (1647) the light broke. He came to feel that Christ could speak to "his condition," his heart leaped for joy, and to him "the whole earth had a new smell." He believed that God is love and truth and that it is possible for all men so to open their lives to Him as to live victoriously in that power "that is a-top" of all evil and "that is over all." He would follow and have others follow the Inner Light. He renounced oaths, insisted on honesty and truth-speaking, practised simplicity in dress, food, and speech, opposed any participation in war, protested against all shams and formalism in religion and worship, pioneered in the care of the insane, demanded just treatment for the American Indians, held that governments exist for the benefit of the people as a whole and are bound by the moral law, advocated an extreme democracy which would put men and women on an equality, permitted women to preach, refused to doff his hat to any man, used the singular pronoun in addressing members of all classes, thus seeking to denounce special class privilege, came out for universal religious toleration, and wished to bring the Gospel to all. Completely fearless, he was often imprisoned for proclaiming his convictions.

Fox's appeal found a response in many hearts, for he was proclaiming what in one way or another many believed. He travelled widely in England, Ireland, Wales, the Continent, and America. Large numbers of the Seekers became his followers. Societies of Friends sprang up and hundreds of missionaries became "publishers of Truth." The Quakers provoked much opposition and met persecution, but during the remainder of the century their numbers multiplied.

Faced with these many radical movements, Cromwell strove to prevent chaos, to maintain order, and to help to make of England a genuinely Christian nation. He had not sought to rule the country, but as head of the Parliamentary army he found himself forced step by step to the headship of the government and to what in effect was a dictatorship. Yet he refused the suggestion that he become king and took instead the title of Lord Protector. The government was called the Commonwealth and was a kind of republic.

Himself deeply religious, inclined towards the Independents, and wishing to act always according to the will of God, in the midst of the strife of tongues Cromwell desired and in part obtained a large degree of religious toleration. He stood for a national church, endowed and supported by the state. It was not to have bishops and the Book of Common Prayer was not to be used in its services. Yet the Word must be preached and to this end the clergy must be carefully chosen and must be supported by tithes and by a central fund to supplement the income of the poorer parishes. All Protestants except Quakers were to be tolerated. The clergy might be Presbyterian, Independent, or Baptist, dissenters might form "gathered churches" of their own, Episcopalians might meet for worship if they did so quietly, and even Roman Catholics were left alone if they did not disturb the public peace. Episcopalians, Roman Catholics, Levellers, Fifth Monarchy Men, and Quakers were unfriendly or even hostile to him, but Cromwell gave to England a nearer approach to religious liberty than it had thus far known. He also laboured for the reform of morals, sunk to a low ebb during the civil wars, and worked for the improvement of education.

THE RESTORATION OF THE STUART MONARCHY AND THE REVIVAL OF EPISCOPACY

The Commonwealth could not last. It was rule by a minority and when once death had removed the strong hand of the Lord Protector it speedily came to an end. Oliver Cromwell died in 1658 and was succeeded by his son Richard. Although of pure life and popular as a man, Richard did not have the force of character, the experience, or the control of the army which were needed in the emergency. George Monck, the strongest of the generals, marched to London, and the son of the executed Charles I returned from exile as Charles II (1660).

Witty, charming, utterly unscrupulous, completely selfish, immoral in his private life, committed to the divine right of kings, Charles II did not wish to go again on his travels and was sufficiently clever to maintain himself on the throne. Parliament was restored much as it had been before the civil war, but was far from being inclined to servile compliance with the royal wishes. Privately preferring Roman Catholicism as the "religion for gentlemen," Charles hated the Presbyterians and extreme Protestants but outwardly conformed to the Church of England of which he was nominally the head.

Episcopacy was restored and through bishops dispossessed under the Commonwealth was enabled to continue the apostolic succession. The Book of Common Prayer, revised in a manner peculiarly distasteful to Puritans, was accepted by Parliament and through an Act of Uniformity was ordered read in all the churches. Non-episcopally ordained clergy were removed from their benefices. By the Conventicle Act, 1664, passed over the opposition of the king, meetings for worship of more than five persons were forbidden unless they used the Prayer Book. The Five Mile Act, enacted in 1665, ordered that no non-conforming minister come within five miles of a city or incorporated town or teach in any school unless he promised that he would not "at any time endeavour the alteration of government in Church and state." Since Puritans and other dissenting Protestants were strongest in the towns, the Five Mile Act bore especially heavily upon them. A second Conventicle Act was passed in 1670. When, in 1672, Charles II, with the purpose of aiding Roman Catholics and winning the goodwill of Protestant dissenters, issued the Declaration of Indulgence permitting public worship to both, Parliament forced its withdrawal (1673) and passed the Test Act which provided that all civil or military officers must take the oath of supremacy and allegiance and receive the Lord's Supper according to the usages of the Church of England.

In spite of these stringent measures and the laxity of morals of much of the population, dissenting congregations persisted and men and women of outstanding Christian character appeared in both the Church of England and non-conforming Protestantism. In the state church Jeremy Taylor (1613–1667), after the Restoration a bishop in Ireland, wrote extensively, but is best remembered for *The Rule and Exercises of Holy Living* (1650) and *The Rule and Exercises of Holy Dying* (1651), both composed during the Commonwealth. The Puritan Richard Baxter (1615–1691) had a noted record as a pastor during the Commonwealth in reforming morals and religion within his parish, refused a bishopric under the Restoration, was forbidden to preach, and was fined and imprisoned. He was a voluminous author, but it is significant that with him, as with Taylor, his best remembered work was one on Christian life and prayer, *Saints' Everlasting Rest.* Even more famous was John Bunyan

(1628–1688), Baptist preacher of Bedford. He had come into a warm Christian faith after a prolonged struggle and deep depression of which he later told in a moving spiritual autobiography, *Grace Abounding to the Chief of Sinners*. Imprisoned for years for preaching in violation of the Conventicle Act, while in jail he began to write *The Pilgrim's Progress,* an allegory of conversion and the Christian life which was to become one of the most widely read books in the English language and was to be translated into many other tongues. We do well also to remember that the Puritan, John Milton, closely identified with the Commonwealth and Latin secretary to Oliver Cromwell, escaped the scaffold at the Restoration and completed *Paradise Lost,* presenting the human drama as conceived by Christians.

It was during the Commonwealth and especially during the Stuart Restoration that there flourished the Cambridge Platonists, so-called because most of them were Cambridge graduates. They were against the views represented by Laud on the one hand, some of the extreme Protestant sects on the other, and extreme scepticism on still another front, and sought to reconcile science and religion. Chief among them was Ralph Cudworth (1617–1688), fellow of Emmanuel College and master of Christ's College, Cambridge. They stressed Plotinus rather than Plato and thought of love as the chief manifestation of God in human life.

These men were mountain peaks. There were many of lesser stature and fame who were evidence of the richness of the life which issued from the Reformation.

Charles II died in 1685, in his last hours was received into the Roman Catholic Church, and was succeeded by his brother, James II, an avowed member of that communion. James II favoured those of his faith and by a Declaration of Indulgence sought toleration for both Roman Catholics and those Protestants who dissented from the Church of England. It was widespread resentment against this policy, culminating in the popular support of seven bishops who were tried for refusing to read the Declaration from the pulpit and alarm at the birth of a son which seemed to mean a Roman Catholic successor that led to the "Glorious Revolution" of 1688. James was driven from the country and his Protestant daughter, Mary, and her consort, William of Orange, came to the throne.

THE HALF CENTURY AFTER THE "GLORIOUS REVOLUTION" OF 1688

The flight of James II and the coming of William and Mary were followed by the final victory of Protestantism and the permanence of many of the fruits of the Puritan revolution. The Bill of Rights, enacted in 1689, declared illegal many of the measures of James II and stipulated that no Roman Catholic should ever wear the crown. That same year, thanks largely to William who, although reared a Calvinist, was broad in his sympathies, the Toleration Act was passed. It suspended the laws against Protestant dissenters who did not attend services in the Church of England on condition that they took the oath of allegiance and supremacy and subscribed to a statement against transubstantiation. Roman Catholics and those who did not believe in the Trinity were excluded from the benefits of the measure. Dissenters were still under some disabilities and were taxed to support the Church of England. Yet such persecution as had been known under Laud and Charles II was a thing of the past. Two political parties developed, the Tories, reinforced by squires and country parsons and opposed to toleration of dissenters, and the Whigs, composed largely of the town clergy, most of the bishops, dissenters, merchants, and the Protestant elements in the Church of England. Under a Tory ministry, in 1711, it was made more difficult for dissenters to evade the Test Act, and in 1714 the Schism Act was passed which provided that no one could teach in a school unless he was a communicant of the Church of England. This latter would have made it impossible for dissenters to educate their children. However, four years later the Schism Act was repealed. Nonconformity and the Church of England went on side by side and in the latter there were still those who held to the Catholic tradition and those who leaned towards Protestantism. Henceforth no monarch dared seriously to challenge the supremacy of the voice of the nation expressed through Parliament or to attempt to rule without that body.

John Locke (1632–1704), reared in a staunchly Puritan home, would probably have gone into the ministry but for the intolerant attitude in the Church of England after the Restoration and continued to be interested in theology. Famous for his *Essay Concerning Human Understanding* (1690), in which he pointed out the limits to human knowledge, and condemned by some of the strictly orthodox for not subscribing to all that they deemed basic in the Christian faith, he would exclude atheists and Roman Catholics from the religious toleration which he advocated. His *Treatises on Government* reflected the political principles of popular sovereignty which had arisen largely through the Puritans and had found expression in the Puritan revolution and the Commonwealth, and were to go far toward shaping the democracy of the later England and the United States.

The Reformation had by no means completely purified the religious life of the country or the Church. Many of the clergy had little intellectual or spiritual interest and carried on the services of the Church in routine fashion. Some were viewed contemptuously by the upper classes and some were younger sons of the aristocracy for whom the Church was a way to a secure and easy living.

There was still pluralism and numbers of the higher ecclesiastics drew the revenues from more than one post. As we are to see, the rationalism which found expression in the Deism and religious scepticism that came to a climax in those years had begun to appear and to be formulated late in the seventeenth and in the fore part of the eighteenth century.

However, while the intense religious ferment which had marked the sixteenth century and which had boiled over in the seventeenth century seemed to have subsided, there was much of vigorous life, both within the Church of England and among the Protestant dissenters. As we are to see again later, George Berkeley (1685–1753), Bishop of Cloyne, formulated a philosophical defense of Christianity, criticizing the "natural religion" of the opponents of revealed religion and holding that the whole of the natural order is a conversation between God and man. Joseph Butler (1692–1752), whom we are to meet again, in his *Analogy of Religion, Natural and Revealed, to the Course and Constitution of Nature,* produced another apology for the Christian faith which was to be widely read in the eighteenth and nineteenth centuries. William Law (1686–1761), a mystic, profoundly influenced by Jacob Boehme, with high church convictions, in addition to controversial works, wrote much on the devotional life and, among others, produced two books, *A Treatise on Christian Perfection* (1726) and *A Serious Call to a Holy and Devout Life* (1728), which were to make important contributions to the Evangelical Revival which began in the second quarter of the eighteenth century and of which we are to hear much after 1750.

The earnest and buoyant religious life of the time was finding expression in hymns, especially among the Protestant dissenters. Notable were Isaac Watts (1674–1748) and Philip Doddridge (1702–1751), both nonconformists. Watts gave many hymns to the Church, among them "Oh God our help in ages past," "Joy to the world, the Lord has come," "When I survey the wondrous cross on which the prince of glory died," and "Jesus shall reign where'er the sun doth his successive journeys run." In addition to hymns which had prolonged and wide usage, such as "O God of Bethel by whose hand thy people still are led," "Awake my soul, stretch every nerve and press with vigour on," and "How gentle God's commands," Doddridge also wrote the extensively read devotional work *The Rise and Progress of Religion in the Soul.* It was late in this period, in 1738, that John Wesley had the stirring experience which is generally regarded as the beginning of the Evangelical Revival. In the 1720's and 1730's, moreover, there began the Great Awakening in the English colonies in America which was the precursor of the mass movements which revitalized the Protestant churches and brought into them an increasing proportion of the partially de-Christianized population. In the first half of the eighteenth century

England presented a striking contrast between much practical paganism and religious illiteracy on the one hand, with low moral conditions, and on the other a vital religious life which was to have world-wide repercussions in the nineteenth and twentieth centuries.

The Welsh Variety of the Reformation

Of the mountainous principality of Wales we can take time in this comprehensive survey for only three short paragraphs.

Under Henry VIII a formal act of union (1536) and a further act of 1542 incorporated Wales with England and sought to bring its people into administrative and political equality with the English. Welsh members sat in the Parliament at Westminster and English was made the language of all legal proceedings. Welshmen were to be found at court and in the universities. Among them were some who laboured for the reform of the Church and religion. Separation from Rome and the dissolution of the monasteries came by the same steps which accomplished them in England. This was followed by a decline in the quality and numbers of clergy and deterioration in the Church buildings. Richard Davies, Bishop of St. Davids, and a colleague put into Welsh the New Testament and the liturgy from the Book of Common Prayer. In 1588 the complete Bible in Welsh was published, the work of William Morgan, vicar and eventually bishop. Later this was supplanted by a Welsh translation of the King James Version done by a Welsh bishop. These translations did much to fix the form of literary Welsh. Late in the sixteenth and in the fore part of the seventeenth century marked improvement took place in the religious life of Wales. Many of the clergy were educated in Oxford and Cambridge, notably in Jesus College, Oxford, founded for the Welsh.

Puritanism was slow in penetrating Wales, but began to do so before the coming of the Commonwealth. By then, moreover, at least one Independent congregation had been formed. Wales was loyal to Charles I. After his execution, Parliament ejected most of the clergy of the established church and sought to replace them by preachers acceptable to the new regime, and that in spite of the protest by high churchmen and moderate Puritans. This brought new confusion. After the Stuart Restoration most of such of the old clergy as survived were reinstated and Puritan incumbents who refused to comply with the Act of Uniformity were dismissed. Thereafter the bishops were largely of the Catholic wing of the established church and sympathized with the Stuarts. The state church ceased to attract the masses and the latter knew little or no English and had few books in their own tongue. There was much pluralism, most of the clergy were of poor quality, and many parsonages were falling into ruin.

In the first half of the eighteenth century Griffith Jones, a clergyman, began what were known as "circulating charity schools" which taught thousands to read the Bible in their own tongue and raised the level of the religious life and education. The Society for Promoting Christian Knowledge, founded in 1699 by members of the Church of England, although having Wales as only one of its fields of effort, aided in the improvement of religious conditions. The way was being prepared for the great revivals of the latter part of the eighteenth and the nineteenth century.

The Long Agony of Ireland

Much more complex was the course of the Reformation in Ireland. Centuries before, that island, it will be recalled, had been the centre of a vigorous religious life when, relatively free from the incursions of the barbarians who were dealing serious blows to civilization and Christianity on the Continent and Britain, it was the scene of a distinctive monasticism which enriched both Britain and much of Western Europe.

Then came wave after wave of invasion and settlement, first by pagan Scandinavians and later by the Anglo-Normans. In the twelfth and thirteenth centuries the latter conquered most of the island and sought to bring it into conformity with English law and institutions. The Church, moreover, was drawn into a closer relationship with that of England and with Rome. Yet the Gaelic Irish were restless. In the fourteenth century they threw off the English yoke in much of the island and the conquerors were partly assimilated in language, law, and blood. In the fifteenth century the Gaelic Irish and the descendants of the older English settlers were almost independent of England.

The first Tudors, Henry VII and Henry VIII, attempted, with partial success, to revive the authority of the English crown in Ireland. In accordance with the procedure in England, Henry VIII was declared the head of the Church of Ireland and the dissolution of the monasteries was ordered. However, there was little or no indigenous movement for reform, the bishops were slow to accept the royal supremacy, and many monasteries persisted into the seventeenth century. Great resentment was felt against the attempted imposition of Protestantism under Edward VI. Although Elizabeth insisted upon the Acts of Supremacy and Uniformity, the established church which was loyal to her had few adherents outside of Dublin, the capital. Both the Gaelic population and the older English stock held to the Roman Catholic faith, partly from conservatism and partly in opposition to rule from England. While only a minority could be called practicing Catholics, so far as the majority had a religious allegiance it was to Rome. The Roman Catholic Church was becoming a symbol and a bond of Irish nationalism. Especially was that true of the Gaelic stock. During Elizabeth's time rebellions broke out, provoked partly by the grant of Irish lands to English adventurers.

During the reign of James I an extensive English and Scottish colonization of Ulster in the north of the island was begun, largely at the instance of the royal government. The immigrants were Protestant—Anglicans and Presbyterians. The Scottish Presbyterians were especially strong. Similar Protestant colonies were planted in some other sections. Rebellion broke out in 1641 and in Ulster thousands of the colonists were killed. The uprising was soon complicated by the civil war in England.

The Irish had no use for the Puritans and after the execution of Charles I the supporters of his son, Charles II, controlled most of the island. To meet the crisis, Parliament sent Cromwell as commander-in-chief of its armies. Within a few months he had subdued the east of the island, partly through the terror which he inspired by the slaughter of the garrison after his capture of Drogheda. By the end of 1652 the rest of the island had been overrun, but with a fearful toll of life. Fighting, famine, and pestilence are said to have reduced the population by a third. The Roman Catholic religion was ordered suppressed and extensive land grants were made to members of the conquering army and to those who had supported the Commonwealth forces by contributions of money. In theory the dispossessed Irish proprietors were given compensation in the form of lands in the western part of the island, but these were of poorer quality. As in England, the state church was in the hands of the extreme Protestants.

The Stuart restoration (1660) brought only partial relief to the Roman Catholics. Charles II was not disposed to jeopardize his rule by throwing the Protestants overboard. While about a third of the lands which had been given to the Cromwellians were returned to the Roman Catholics, the government was almost entirely in the hands of Protestants, and of Episcopalians rather than Presbyterians. The Presbyterians were at a decided disadvantage. During his brief reign James II favoured his co-religionists and after his flight from England (1688) he sought (1689) to regain the throne by way of Ireland. During the fifteen or sixteen months that he was in the island he set up a predominantly Roman Catholic government. In the ensuing war James and his forces were defeated by the "Orange men," the supporters of William of Orange.

While William stood for moderation, the Protestants in Ireland would have none of it. By the extension of the Test Act of 1691 to Ireland, Roman Catholics were excluded from the Irish Parliament. Roman Catholics were debarred from the legal profession, were kept out of the trades and from juries, could not vote, and were forbidden to teach publicly or to bear arms. Only a small proportion of the land was owned by them. The overwhelming majority of the Roman Catholics were tenants of Protestant landlords. Drastic penal laws made the lot of the Roman Catholics even harder and Roman Catholic prelates were banished. The outstanding leaders of the Irish either perished or fled the country. The Church of Ireland, sister to the Church of England and established by law, was in the ascendant and in close association with the state. Presbyterians as well as Roman Catholics were discriminated against. Laws restraining the commerce of the island added to the distress. Many of the poorer Presbyterians, the "Scotch-Irish," sought relief by migration to the American colonies, thereby laying the foundations of much of the Presbyterianism of the future United States.

While after the coming of the Hanoverian dynasty to England (1714) freedom of worship was granted Roman Catholics and the right to hold minor offices, and some relief was given the Presbyterians, tithes continued to be exacted for the support of the Church of Ireland, the English and Anglican minority were in control, and the poverty and distress of the masses were acute. The majority of the population were Roman Catholics and even more than before their church was for them the tie and symbol of Gaelic Ireland. The fear of Irish revolt hardened the attitude of the English. A legacy of bitterness augmented by religious differences was transmitted to later generations.

Selected Bibliography

GENERAL

L. Elliott Binns, *The Reformation in England* (London, Duckworth, pp. 224). A useful introduction carrying the story through the Elizabethan settlement.

J. Gairdner, *The English Church in the Sixteenth Century from the Accession of Henry VIII to the Death of Mary* (London, Macmillan & Co., 1902, pp. vii, 430). A standard work.

H. Gee and W. J. Hardy, *Documents Illustrative of English Church History compiled from Original Sources* (London, Macmillan & Co., 1896, pp. xii, 670). Very useful.

P. Hughes, *The Reformation in England* (London, Hollis & Carter, Vol. I, 1952, pp. xxi, 404). Very well written. Based on careful research.

PREPARATION FOR THE REFORMATION

J. Gairdner, *Lollardy and the Reformation in England. An Historical Survey* (London, Macmillan & Co., 3 vols., 1908–1911). Chiefly an account of the English Reformation through the reign of Edward VI, stressing the indigenous character of the movement. Based upon careful research.

H. M. Smith, *Pre-Reformation England* (London, Macmillan & Co., 1938, pp. xv, 556). Begins with the accession of Henry VII. Very well done, with extensive excerpts from the sources.

THE REIGN OF HENRY VIII

G. Baskerville, *English Monks and the Suppression of the Monasteries* (Yale University Press, 1937, pp. 312). Based upon extensive research.

G. Constant, *The Reformation in England. I. The English Schism: Henry VIII (1509–1547)*, translated by R. E. Scantlebury (New York, Sheed & Ward, 1934, pp. xxi, 531). An able, fairly objective Roman Catholic work.

The King's Book or a Necessary Doctrine and Erudition for any Christian Man, 1543, with an introduction by T. A. Lacey (London, Society for Promoting Christian Knowledge, 1932, pp. xx, 165).

H. E. Jacobs, *The Lutheran Movement in England during the Reigns of Henry VIII and Edward VI, and Its Literary Monuments* (Philadelphia, General Council Publication House, rev. ed., 1916, pp. xv, 376). Carefully done, by a Lutheran.

H. M. Smith, *Henry VIII and the Reformation* (London, Macmillan & Co., 1948, pp. xv, 480). Very well done.

THOMAS CRANMER

A. F. Pollard, *Thomas Cranmer and the English Reformation 1489–1556* (London, G. P. Putnam's Sons, 1905, pp. xv, 384). A standard account, favourable to Cranmer.

WILLIAM TYNDALE

S. L. Greenslade, *The Work of William Tindale* (London, Blackie & Son, 1938, pp. vi, 222). Important chiefly for selections from Tyndale's works.

J. P. Mozley, *William Tyndale* (New York, The Macmillan Co., 1937, pp. ix, 364). Contains extensive excerpts from Tyndale's writings.

EDWARD VI

G. Constant, *The Reformation in England. II. Introduction of the Reformation into England: Edward VI (1547–1553)*, translated by E. I. Watkin (New York, Sheed & Ward, 1942, pp. ix, 370). Based on extensive research, fairly objective, by a Roman Catholic.

C. H. Smyth, *Cranmer & the Reformation under Edward VI* (Cambridge University Press, 1926, pp. x, 315).

MARY

R. Demaus, *Hugh Latimer, a Biography* (London, Dalls, Lamar & Barton, no date. First published in 1869 by the Religious Tract Society, pp. 568).

C. H. Hallowell, *The Marian Exiles. A Study in the Origins of Elizabethan Puritanism* (Cambridge University Press, 1938, pp. ix, 388). Especially valuable for brief biographies of nearly five hundred exiles.

J. F. Mozley, *John Foxe and His Book* (London, Society for Promoting Christian Knowledge, 1940, pp. xi, 254). An account of Foxe's life and of his famous *Book of Martyrs*. That book went through many editions, supplemented by many hands. It is warmly sympathetic with the martyrs. In its original form it is chiefly valuable for its accounts of those who were killed under Mary.

J. A. Muller, *Stephen Gardiner and the Tudor Reaction* (New York, The Macmillan Co., 1926, pp. xiv, 429). Carefully and sympathetically done.

W. Schenk, *Reginald Pole, Cardinal of England* (New York, Longmans, Green & Co., 1950, pp. xvi, 176). Sympathetic, judicious, based upon careful research.

ELIZABETH

H. W. Clark, *History of English Nonconformity from Wyclif to the Close of the Nineteenth Century. Vol. I, From Wyclif to the Restoration* (London, Chapman & Hall, 1911, pp. xvii, 439). Well documented.

W. H. Frere and C. E. Douglas, editors, *Puritan Manifestoes, a Study in the Origin of the Puritan Revolt. With a Reprint of the Admonition to Parliament and Kindred Documents, 1572* (London, Society for Promoting Christian Knowledge, 1907, pp. xxxi, 155).

M. M. Knappen, *Tudor Puritanism. A Chapter in the History of Idealism* (University of Chicago Press, 1939, pp. xii, 555). Admirably done.

D. J. McGinn, *The Admonition Controversy* (Rutgers University Press, 1949, pp. xii, 589). Contains extensive excerpts from the sources.

W. Pierce, *An Historical Introduction to the Marprelate Tracts* (London, Constable & Co., 1908, pp. xvii, 350).

J. H. Pollen, *The English Catholics in the Reign of Queen Elizabeth: A Study of Their Politics Civil Life and Government* (London, Longmans, Green & Co., 1920). Sympathetic, based upon careful research, by a Jesuit.

JAMES I AND CHARLES I

C. Burrage, *The Early English Dissenters in the Light of Recent Research (1550–1641)* (Cambridge University Press, 2 vols., 1912). More than half is made up of original documents.

C. C. Butterworth, *The Literary Lineage of the King James Bible 1340–1611* (University of Pennsylvania Press, 1941, pp. xi, 394). Carefully done.

H. R. Trevor-Roper, *Archbishop Laud 1573–1645* (London, Macmillan & Co., 1940, pp. ix, 464). Soberly written, based solidly on careful research.

A. C. Underwood, *A History of the English Baptists* (London, The Baptist Union Publication Dept., 1947, pp. 286). Sympathetic, but objective.

B. F. Westcott, *A General View of the History of the English Bible*. Third edition, revised by W. A. Wright (New York, The Macmillan Co., 1927, pp. xx, 356). By a distinguished scholar.

THE COMMONWEALTH

W. C. Braithwaite, *The Beginnings of Quakerism* (London, Macmillan & Co., 1923, pp. xliv, 542). Based upon extensive research.

J. Buchan, *Oliver Cromwell* (Boston, Houghton Mifflin Co., 1934, pp. xi, 458). A standard life, very well written.

W. Haller and G. Davies, editors, *The Leveller Tracts 1647–1653* (Columbia University Press, 1944, pp. vi, 481).

H. Davies, *The Worship of the English Puritans* (Westminster, Dacre Press, 1948, pp. xi, 304). Represents careful work in the sources.

E. Russell, *The History of Quakerism* (New York, The Macmillan Co., 1942, pp. xxv, 586). A standard work, by a Quaker.

W. A. Shaw, *A History of the English Church during the Civil Wars and under the Commonwealth 1640–1660* (London, Longmans, Green & Co., 2 vols., 1900). Contains extensive excerpts from the sources.

FROM THE RESTORATION TO 1750

H. W. Clark, *History of English Nonconformity. Vol. II, From the Restoration to the Close of the Nineteenth Century* (London, Chapman & Hall, 1913, pp. xx, 458).

S. Hobhouse, *Selected Mystical Writings of William Law, Edited with Notes and Twenty-four Studies in the Mystical Theology of William Law and Jacob Boehme* (London, C. W. Daniel Co., 1938, pp. xv, 395). By a warm admirer.

N. Sykes, *Church and State in England in the XVIIIth Century* (Cambridge University Press, 1934, pp. xi, 455). A thorough and highly competent description of some phases of the Church of England, especially the clergy, in the eighteenth century. Gives a more favourable view than is sometimes done.

C. E. Whiting, *Studies in English Puritanism from the Restoration to the Revolution 1660–1688* (London, Society for Promoting Christian Knowledge, 1931, pp. xvi, 584). Comprehensive, scholarly.

B. Willey, *The Seventeenth Century Background. Studies in the Thought of the Age in Relation to Poetry and Religion* (London, Chatto & Windus, 1934, pp. vii, 315). Covers a wide range.

B. Willey, *The Eighteenth Century Background. Studies on the Idea of Nature in the Thought of the Period* (London, Chatto & Windus, 1940, pp. viii, 302). A semi-popular survey of religious and philosophical thought in the British Isles in the eighteenth century, especially of rationalism.

T. Wright, *Isaac Watts and Contemporary Hymn-Writers* (London, C. J. Farncombe & Sons, 1914, pp. xii, 280). Popularly written, but with research back of it.

WALES

A. G. Edwards, *Landmarks in the History of the Welsh Church* (London, John Murray, 1912, pp. vi, 317). By a Bishop of St. Asaph, friendly to the established church.

W. Hughes, *A History of the Church of the Cymry from the Earliest Period to the Present Time* (London, Elliot Stock, 1916, pp. xv, 412). By a clergyman of the established church. Contains a large assemblage of information.

IRELAND

J. C. Beckett, *Protestant Dissent in Ireland 1687–1780* (London, Faber & Faber, 1948, pp. 161). Well documented.

R. D. Edwards, *Church and State in Tudor Ireland. A History of Penal Laws against Irish Catholics 1534–1603* (New York, Longmans, Green & Co., 1935, pp. xliii, 352). Based upon an extensive use of the sources.

W. A. Phillips, editor, *History of the Church of Ireland from the Earliest Times* (Oxford University Press, 3 vols., 1933). A standard work, by several authors, from the introduction of Christianity through the nineteenth century.

Chapter 37

PROTESTANTISM: A PAUSE FOR
PERSPECTIVE

Before we move on to describe the reform within the Roman Catholic Church and to trace the somewhat parallel but quite distinct course of events in the Russian Orthodox Church, we will do well to pause for a moment to look at the emergence of Protestantism as a whole. Here was a vast movement which issued in churches which were to continue. Unlike the groups of the Middle Ages in Western Europe which dissented from the Roman Catholic Church, they did not disappear. Indeed, not only did they persist, but they also grew, and in the nineteenth and twentieth centuries displayed a far greater proportionate and numerical geographic expansion than did the rapidly spreading Roman Catholic Church. From them, moreover, came a succession of quite novel organizational and functional expressions of the Christian faith. Although seemingly the most divided of all the forms of Christianity, in the nineteenth and twentieth centuries Protestants increasingly found new ways of coming together which eventually drew in not only the majority of their own ranks, but also many from the Roman Catholic and Orthodox Churches. In several ways the Protestant era was not the sixteenth and seventeenth but the nineteenth and twentieth centuries. In the middle of the twentieth century Protestantism was still expanding, giving rise to fresh movements, and finding ways of drawing Christians together across ecclesiastical barriers. It was proving to be extremely flexible without surrendering the basic beliefs about God and the purpose, nature, and meaning of His revelation in Christ which the majority of Christians had formulated in the first five centuries of Christian history.

At first sight Protestantism seemed a confused medley of sects which warred with one another and the Roman Catholic Church. Moreover, its sources were not purely religious. They included political, national, social, and personal factors. Peoples and monarchs shared, somewhat confusedly, a common desire to be freed from the administrative control of the Papacy and from the diversion of their revenues to the support of the Holy See and of those who, basking in its favour, as absentees battened off benefices to the exclusion of native sons. In some of the cities many from the growing middle class found Protestantism congenial. Extreme forms, such as Anabaptism, flourished among the proletariat.

Yet the core of Protestantism was a strong religious impulse expressing itself in convictions which were common and central in all the varied forms. Protestantism sprang up in many different places and countries, seemingly almost independently, and had numerous creative leaders. However, common to all its forms, but not always equally stressed, was what had been emphasized by Luther, salvation by faith. As a corollary, even when not acknowledged in practice, was a principle, also formulated by Luther, the priesthood of all believers. Since salvation by faith meant the faith of the individual, by implication Protestantism entailed the right and the duty of the individual to judge for himself on religious issues. This was vividly demonstrated in Luther's dramatic refusal at the Diet of Worms to regard Pope or general council as infallible. Yet, so Luther and other Protestants held, this did not mean ungoverned, rampant individualism. To them the Christian was bound by his allegiance to God. Protestants acknowledged authority, the authority of the word of God as recorded in the Scriptures. The Scriptures must be interpreted by reason, the reason of the individual. On that memorable occasion Luther had declared, and in this he was enunciating a basic characteristic of Protestantism, that he would not renounce any of his beliefs unless "convicted by Scripture and plain reason." He had said: "My conscience is captive to the Word of God. I cannot and I will not recant anything, for to go against conscience is neither right nor safe." In this, whether they knew or did not know of Luther and his words, Protestants of otherwise diverse views were to share. This was true of Cranmer, the ranking bishop in the Church of England, who, holding to much of the Catholic tradition, slowly worked his way to clarity of insight and in his last hours repudiated the authority of the crown which he had regarded as set over him by God and went to the stake. At the other extreme was George Fox, who rejected all sacraments and inherited ecclesiastical traditions and forms.

Their distinctive convictions, Protestants declared, were of the essence of the Gospel and therefore were not new. They insisted that theirs was the primitive and therefore the true Christianity and that it was not they, but the Roman Catholics who were innovators and heretics. They had much in common with some of the pre-Reformation movements which the Catholic Church had denounced. Hus, as we have seen, had been burned because he was convinced that to bow to Pope or council was to be disloyal to Christ, and the remnants of the Waldensees had found the Reformed Churches sufficiently congenial to associate themselves with them. Yet in its emphasis upon salvation by faith alone, *sola fide,* Protestantism was distinct from other movements which had been cast out of the Catholic Church.

Salvation by faith alone and the attendant insistence of the individual that his conscience must not be surrendered to the authority of state or Church seemed to violate the sense of community so prominent in the Scriptures which the Protestants professed to revere and appeared to lead to anarchy. It is true that here was a sharp contrast between Protestants and Catholics and especially between Protestants and Roman Catholics. In principle Catholics submitted their consciences to the authority of the Church. They were not yet agreed on where that authority was finally lodged, whether in general councils or the Bishop of Rome, but "holy obedience" to ecclesiastical superiors was demanded of monks and clergy and in questions spiritual and moral the laity were under the direction of the clergy. Were salvation by faith alone and the priesthood of all believers to be carried to what seemed their logical conclusion, endless division and eventual rejection of beliefs inherited from previous generations of Christians would seem to follow. This, indeed, Roman Catholics have declared to be inevitable. At times their prediction has appeared to be proved by the event. Organizationally Protestantism, especially among those who sought to carry out its principles in thoroughgoing fashion, became more and more divided. Minorities went over to a rationalistic Unitarianism and, moving still further, ceased to believe in God, at least in any such sense as most Christians had conceived Him.

However, the vast majority of Protestants retained a sense of community. Their individualism was not irresponsible but submitted itself to the divine sovereignty. Luther, Zwingli, and Calvin and those who followed them were profoundly impressed with the majesty of God. It was that which was to a large degree the sustaining element in their individualism. They held themselves to be accountable to God and believed that to submit their conscience to Pope or council was to put another authority above Him. They remembered that Christ had made love to one's neighbour a corollary to the primary command of love to God. Luther had expressed it in the seeming paradox: "A Christian man is the most free lord of all, and subject to none; a Christian man is the most dutiful servant of all, and subject to everyone." The fashion in which, in increasing measure, in the nineteenth and twentieth centuries Protestants devised fresh ways of giving organizational forms to a sense of community reaching out to all who called themselves Christians was evidence that they were not atomistic.

It was no accident, moreover, that out of Protestantism arose democratic movements in Church and state. Such extreme Protestant groups as the Independents and Baptists were in theory pure democracies, with each member of the local church on an equality with every other. Luther, conservative in many ways, had stopped short of pushing the priesthood of all believers to its extreme implications. However, Calvin and others in the Reformed Churches moved in that direction. Puritans, Independents, and others on the far edge of Protestantism reinforced the principle that there is a body of law which the king must obey, and used as an instrument Parliament, inherited from the pre-Protestant Middle Ages, to curb the power of the monarch and to give a major impetus to the kind of democracy which was seen in the United States and in the nineteenth and twentieth century Britain.

In Protestantism the "exceeding greatness of the power" found fresh expression. Although mixed with alien and even contradictory elements, it gave rise to currents of life which were increasingly to mould human culture in art, literature, thought, government, economics, morals, and religion.

Chapter 38

THE CATHOLIC REFORMATION

The burst of life in Christianity which expressed itself through the various phases of the Protestant Reformation also issued in a reform movement which was contained within the Roman Catholic Church. As we have already noted (Chapter 31), this had begun before Luther and was proceeding simultaneously with the emergence of several varieties of Protestantism. It had its heart in Latin Europe, notably at the outset in Spain and Italy. However, eventually it made itself felt as well in most of Western and Central Europe, and through the extensive missions to which it gave rise it won back to the Roman Catholic Church large portions of Europe which had been lost to Protestantism and helped to plant the faith in wide territories in Asia, Africa, North and South America, and the islands which fringed the south and east coasts of Asia.

The Catholic Reformation is sometimes called the Counter-Reformation, but that designation can be misleading. It is accurate if by it is meant that it was in part a reaction against Protestant criticisms and secessions and that through it the Roman Catholic Church regained some of the ground which it had lost to Protestantism. It is inaccurate if it is intended to convey the impression that but for Protestantism the Catholic Reformation would not have come.

One effect of Protestantism was that the Roman Catholic Church became less inclusive. Heretofore it had permitted diversity of views on some of the issues raised by Protestants. Now it felt itself constrained to state its convictions more precisely. The definitions of dogma framed by the Council of Trent, to which we are to come a little later, were consciously directed against Protestant teachings. They ruled out opinions held by some who had remained within the Roman Communion. Those who cherished these opinions had either to surrender them and conform or to leave the fellowship of the Church of Rome. The inclusiveness for which many had hoped and which might have held thousands within the Roman Catholic fold was rejected. In this the Roman

Catholic Church was consistent. It could not have retained all or even the majority of Protestants without disavowing its genius and departing in drastic fashion from a course which it had been pursuing for centuries, perhaps from its very beginning. Yet if by sect it meant a division in the Christian Church, the Roman Communion had ceased to be catholic in the sense of embracing all Christians, if, indeed, it had ever been that, and had become a sect. Within a hundred and fifty years it had finally and irrevocably lost on the one hand the vast majority of what had once been the Eastern wing of the Catholic Church and on the other about half of Western Europe. It had clearly ceased to be universal and, although it was to achieve a wider geographic extension than it had yet known, it was to be more obviously centered in Latin Europe and especially in Italy. This was made vivid by the fact that after 1500, with one exception, all the Popes were Italians. Previously, while the large majority had been from that land, some had been drawn from beyond the Alps.

It is more than a coincidence that the Protestant and the Catholic Reformation ran concurrently. They were different expressions of a common fresh burst of life in Christianity. It is significant, moreover, that they paralleled the amazing vigour in other aspects of the culture of Western Europe—in geographic explorations, commerce, colonization, art, literature, political theory, and education. These movements interacted on one another, but, as we must again and again remind ourselves, we cannot be clear that they all arose from common causes, nor can we know precisely to what extent if at all the "exceeding greatness of the power" inherent in Christianity was the underlying factor.

In outlining the course of the Catholic Reformation we will follow the procedure of tracing it by major regions and countries. First we will describe it in Spain, then in Italy, and finally in France. We will also recount the efforts to win back Protestant Europe. We must not forget, however, that movements were taking place concurrently in several lands and that the geographic treatment is in part artificial. In the next chapter we will sketch the titanic series of struggles which is known collectively, but somewhat inaccurately, as the Thirty Years' War and the stabilization of the geographic boundaries in Europe between the Protestant Churches on the one hand and the Roman Catholic Church on the other.

The Catholic Reformation in Spain

We turn, then, to Spain. We do this because here the Catholic Reformation early had extensive developments. We have already seen (Chapter 28) how with the encouragement of Isabella, Ximénes de Cisneros had carried through measures for the improvement of monastic life and the better education of the clergy. Incidentally, he died at an advanced age in the very year in which Luther posted his epoch-making theses on the church door in Witten-berg. We have noted, too, the establishment of the Inquisition with its purpose of rooting out heresy, and the expulsion of all Jews and Moslems who refused to accept baptism.

In the sixteenth century the course of Christianity in Spain was one of a zealous orthodoxy which gave rise to strange contrasts. In accordance with the prevailing practice in Europe, the Spanish monarchs curtailed the administra-tive power of the Popes within the country and insisted upon dominating the Church, yet they encouraged the Inquisition to root out all dissent from the Roman Catholic faith. Charles V, who ruled during most of the first half of the century, laboured to restore religious unity in Western Europe and bled Spain to support his wars. His son, Philip II, who reigned from 1556 to 1598, was enormously hard-working, conscientious, hated heresy with a bitter hatred, and sought to use the strength of Spain to extirpate Protestantism in Europe, but in doing so brought great misery on the land. The Inquisition was better organized and more ruthless than anywhere else, but in spite of it thousands of professed Christians of Jewish and Moslem ancestry continued some of the religious observances of their pre-Christian forefathers, and many of the higher and lower clergy were morally corrupt. Zeal for a faith whose primary com-mandment is love contributed to extreme cruelty, through the Inquisition, in the chronic treatment of the Marranos, nominally Christian converts from Judaism, and in harshness towards the Moriscos, proselytes from Islam. An uprising of Moriscos provoked by drastic measures against them was sup-pressed with revolting barbarity and in 1609 the unhappy people were ordered expelled from the country. The hostility towards Marranos and Moriscos was aggravated by racial antipathy and jealousy of their economic prosperity, but far from allaying it devotion to the Catholic faith intensified it. From this Spanish Christianity there also arose in the sixteenth century the Society of Jesus, the largest and most powerful new religious order since the birth of the Franciscans and Dominicans, and as great mystics as the Church has ever seen. From this Spanish Christianity there also emerged as noteworthy champions of exploited peoples as the world has ever known, Bartolomé de Las Casas and Pedro Claver, and one of the pioneers in the struggle to place the rela-tions between nations on the basis of law rather than brute force, Francisco de Vitoria.

This Spanish Christianity, given added vitality by the reform movement, and with such stark inner contrasts, had a more extensive geographic spread than the Christianity of any other country in the period between 1500 and 1750. It was to prevail in large sections of the Western Hemisphere and the Philip-pines and, through the Society of Jesus, became the chief driving force in countering Protestantism in Europe and winning back to the Roman Catholic Church thousands who had departed from that form of the faith.

IGNATIUS LOYOLA AND THE SOCIETY OF JESUS

The Spaniard who was to have a wider and more enduring influence than any other of his fellow-countrymen of the sixteenth century was Ignatius Loyola (c.1491–1556). He can scarcely be called a product of the Catholic Reformation, for the decisive stages of his spiritual pilgrimage were little influenced by the new currents of life which were already running strong in his native land. However, no one else contributed as potently to that movement. A younger contemporary of Martin Luther, in his youth he experienced an intense spiritual conflict which reminds one of the agony through which the great German passed on his way to inward assurance. The soul struggles had similar yet strikingly different outcomes. Through them there came the two outstanding leaders of the Reformation. For Luther the path led to revolt from Rome and to the Protestant Reformation. For Loyola there came an enhanced devotion to the Papacy and a discipline and an organization which were the major new force in effecting and shaping the Catholic Reformation.

Ignatius Loyola was a younger son of a noble family of some antiquity in Guipuzcoa, one of the mountainous Basque provinces only slightly south of the Bay of Biscay on the Spanish side of what is now the French border. The family was conventionally and loyally Catholic and an older brother of Ignatius was a priest. The precise date of the birth of Ignatius is debated, but it was probably no earlier than 1491 and no later than 1495. He was baptized under the name of Iñigo López, but eventually he took the more familiar name Ignacio, or in its Latin form Ignatius. Although in his early youth he may have been given the tonsure, he grew up to a military career and may have shared in some of the vices common to men in that way of life.

The great change in the young aristocrat, what he rightly looked back on as his conversion, came in his late twenties as an outcome of what at first looked like disaster. In 1521, while engaged in the unsuccessful defense of the citadel of Pamplona against a French invasion, he was severely wounded. A cannon ball broke his leg and long weeks of suffering followed. They were prolonged because the leg had to be rebroken and reset. Then, since his pride balked at a protuberance which remained, he insisted on a fresh operation to remove the lump and had the leg stretched by means of a weight to keep it from being shorter than the other. The surgery was only partly effective, for always thereafter he walked with a limp. During the tedious convalescence, Loyola relieved the monotony by reading. Since none of the books on chivalry in which he delighted were at hand, he turned to the only literature available, a life of Christ by a Saxon Carthusian and a volume of the lives of the saints. These and his meditations led him to give himself fully to the way of the saint. He went to a Benedictine monastery on Montserrat, west of Barcelona, there made a comprehensive confession of his past life, gave away his fine clothes to a beggar, took the vows of chastity and poverty, and, hanging up his arms in a chapel of the Virgin Mary, kept a night's vigil before them. Thus, after the manner of the knight, he dedicated himself as a soldier of Christ.

From Montserrat the newly committed devotee of Christ set off on foot to the nearby town of Manresa. There he undertook the way of the ascetic which he believed to be entailed by his self-dedication. He fasted, prayed, begged his food from door to door, tended the sick, went to services in the Dominican priory where he made his home, and read works of devotion, among them *The Imitation of Christ,* a book which had a profound effect upon him. Like Luther, after the first joy and release of self-surrender, he went through grievous struggles of the soul and found the Devil a very present enemy. As did Luther, he followed assiduously the way commended by the "athletes of God," of confession, subduing the body by rigorous austerities, and prayer, but for a time found only anguish. Often he was tempted to commit suicide. Peace came, but not as to Luther by the way of salvation by faith which took the Saxon monk out of the Roman Catholic Church. It arrived, rather, through visions, trances, and ecstasies which kept within the confines of the church of his nativity and confined his ardent loyalty to it. In some of these visions Ignatius believed that he saw the "Trinity under the form of three keys to an organ" and was shown "how God created the world."

At Manresa, from his own experience Ignatius worked out the earliest form of the *Spiritual Exercises* which were to be one of his major contributions to the world. These were for the examination of conscience and to serve as a guide for meditation, contemplation, and prayer. Normally they were to require about four weeks and were to be taken under the supervision of a spiritual director. They were to enable the one who used them to conquer himself, to regulate life, and to avoid coming to a decision from any inordinate affection.

After about a year at Manresa, Ignatius went on a pilgrimage to Palestine. He planned to spend his life in Jerusalem, seeking to convert the Moslems. He reached the holy city and visited the sacred places, but the Franciscans in charge forbade him to carry out his missionary purpose. An obedient son of the Church, he acquiesced and returned to Europe, but not before he had had a vision of Christ on his way back from the Mount of Olives. Moreover, his sense of vocation to be a missionary did not die, but eventually matured, greatly broadened in its geographic horizons.

Once more in Spain, Ignatius spent some time in Barcelona in seeking the education with which his soldier youth had not equipped him. Although then about thirty years of age, he attended school with young boys and acquired Latin. He became acquainted with one of the writings of Erasmus, but was repelled by it. From Barcelona he went to the University of Alcalá, that institution which had recently been founded by Ximénes de Cisneros as a centre for Catholic reform. As had become his custom, he helped others in the religious life and put them through the regimen of his developing *Spiritual Exercises*. He preached informally in homes and hospitals, catechized children, talked with devout women, gathered about him a little group of like-minded young men, and sought to reach artisans and peasants with the Gospel. But he fell under suspicion from the dreaded Inquisition, he and his companions were commanded not to wear a common garb, for a time he was in jail, and he was released with the command not to teach or to hold meetings for three years and even then not without express permission from the proper diocesan authority. He and his companions went from Alcalá to the University of Salamanca, but he was there only two months, was clapped into prison, and, while he was soon released, restrictions were placed on what he could teach until he had studied four years more. The Church was taking no chances with a zealous free lance who might, in his ignorance, mislead souls.

From Salamanca Ignatius went to the University of Paris, to continue his studies in the most famous centre of Christian theological learning of the day. If the ecclesiastical authorities required further education, he would not be content with limiting himself to the mere letter of the law. It was a momentous step. Ignatius was in Paris for seven years, from 1528 to 1535, studied theology, and took a Master of Arts degree. More important still, he gathered about him the nucleus of what was to become the Society of Jesus. He refrained from the street preaching which he had done in Spain, but he formed intimate friendships with students and younger teachers, sought to win them to complete dedication to Christ, and gave to a few his *Spiritual Exercises*. One of the men with whom he roomed, Francis Xavier (1506–1552), was slow to yield, but proved to be a prize worth the effort. An aristocrat from Spanish Navarre and so, like Ignatius, of the Basque region, but several years younger, he was charming, able, and ambitious. He was, as we are to see, to become one of the greatest missionaries of all time. On August 15, 1534, Ignatius and six others took the customary three-fold monastic vows of poverty, chastity, and obedience, and were given the communion by the only one of their number who was a priest. This was the humble beginning of the Society of Jesus, which was to be the most potent expression and instrument of the Catholic Reformation.

A few months before, in November, 1533, Cop, the rector of the University of Paris, had delivered an inaugural address in which, advocating reform in language taken in part from Erasmus and Luther, he had given rise to great excitement. Moreover, it was only recently that another in that university circle, John Calvin, had had the sudden conversion which made him a leader in the Protestant Reformation. It was in the very year in which, stimulated by Ignatius, the immortal seven took their vows that Calvin renounced his benefices and fled to Protestant Basel, there to begin the composition of his *Institutes,* a book which was to have as wide and deep an effect as the *Spiritual Exercises.*

It may be unfair to both to contrast the two, for one was frankly a work in theology and the other a guide to private prayer and devotion. Different though they were, a basic assumption in each was the sovereignty of God, the redemption wrought by Him through Christ, and the conviction that human beings find the meaning and the fullness of life only through Christ and through dedicating themselves to the will and glory of God. Both saw in the beatific vision and enjoyment of God the goal of human life and of God's purpose for man. To both the Protestant and the Catholic Reformation the University of Paris, founded for the study of Christian theology—man's knowledge of God through Christ—made major contributions. Although emphatically opposed to each other, Calvin and Loyola were much alike in their deepest convictions.

In spite of the fact that many of its students and teachers were disgustingly corrupt morally, from the University of Paris issued springs which did much to swell that religious revival which had two such different forms as the Protestant and Catholic Reformations. In conflict though they were, the two had a great deal in common. In the University of Paris was seen in miniature something of the manner of the operation of Christianity in human history and of the interaction of the Gospel and human nature.

In 1535 Ignatius left the little band, for a digestive trouble which had long plagued him and which was aggravated by his austerities led his physicians to advise him to return to Spain. He spent a few months in his native province, teaching, catechizing, and preaching. He also visited the families of the Spanish members of his group to bring them news of the absent. Thence he made his way to Venice and a year or so later was joined by the other members of the company, now augmented by a few recruits. There he met Giovanni Pietro Caraffa, the future Pope Paul IV, a zealous, ardent, haughty reformer, one of the founders of the Theatines, an order of which we are to hear more a little later. While at Venice several of the group gave themselves to the care of the sick.

On Palm Sunday, 1537, the band arrived at Rome, there to seek of the Pope permission to make a pilgrimage to Jerusalem and license for ordination for such as were not yet priests. They obtained their wish and returned to Venice to wait for a ship to the Holy Land. It was in Venice that Ignatius and several of the others were ordained. Since, after a year, no opportunity developed to go to Palestine, Ignatius and two others went to Rome to place the services of the nascent order at the disposal of the Pope.

When nearing Rome, Ignatius, who, that he might better prepare for it, had allowed a year and a half to lapse between his ordination and the celebration of his first mass, had a vision of God the Father and God the Son, the latter carrying the heavy cross, in which Christ, at the request of the Father, accepted him as his servant.

It was in Rome that the companions took a step which they had not previously contemplated. After much prayer and consultation they came to the conclusion that they should seek permission to constitute themselves into an order. After some delay, due chiefly to the opposition of a cardinal who was against the multiplication of such organizations, in 1539 the Pope gave his oral approval and followed this, in September, 1540, with a formal bull of authorization. The new order was to be known as the Society (originally the Company) of Jesus. The name may have been suggested by the vision which had come to Ignatius as he was about to enter Rome.

The Society of Jesus was to be in the nature of an army whose members were soldiers of God. They were to fight under the direction of the Pope and to this end, to the perfect mortification of their wills, they took a special vow to do whatever the Pope commanded "for the good of souls, and the propagation of the faith in whatever countries he" might wish to send them, "whether to the Turks, or other infidels, or to the regions called India, or to the lands of heretics, schismatics, or of faithful Christians." All were to take a vow to obey the head, or General, of the society "in all things that appertain to keeping this rule," and were to "acknowledge and reverence him, as is befitting, as they would Christ, if He were present in person." Particularly were they to give themselves to "the instruction of children and the uneducated in Christian doctrine, teaching the Ten Commandments and the principles of faith." But they were also "to advance souls on the way of Christian life and doctrine, to propagate the faith by public preaching and expounding Holy Scripture, to give the *Spiritual Exercises,* to do works of charity . . . and, finally, to try to bring spiritual consolation to the faithful by hearing confession." They were to take the vows of chastity and poverty, and were not to own permanent property collectively, except for the colleges and universities which they might possess. Ignatius was unanimously chosen the first General. He protested and acquiesced only after prolonged prayer and the express command of his confessor, a Franciscan of the Observance. Having accepted, he lived up to the demands of the office. Small physically, slightly less than five feet two inches tall, he was every inch the commander. Resourceful, calm, confident, considerate of the welfare of each member, he would brook no disobedience.

Here was the Catholic faith giving birth to a new order, like yet unlike its monastic predecessors. It was like them in its three vows of chastity, poverty, and obedience, and in its practice of austerity and prayer. It resembled the mendicants in its emphasis upon preaching, teaching, and humble personal service to others. It was unlike all that went before it in its military-like organization, its intense discipline through the *Spiritual Exercises,* and its stress on obedience to the Pope and the General. Its members wore no special garb, but adapted their dress to circumstances. While given much to prayer, they were activists, seeking to influence the work-a-day world. Since the original group were university men, trained in theology, the Jesuits made much of education and insisted upon a prolonged training in philosophy and theology for their priests. They produced many notable scholars.

The Society of Jesus had a phenomenal growth. By the time of his death, only sixteen years after the Papal bull authorizing its formation, Ignatius had seen the Society grow to about a thousand members. They were in Italy, Portugal, Spain, and France, labouring for spiritual and moral reform in the nominally Roman Catholic populations. They were in Germany, combatting Protestantism, and in Ireland, seeking to strengthen the Roman Catholic Church. They stiffened the backbone of the reforming Council of Trent in its intransigence towards Protestants and its bowing to Papal direction. Francis Xavier had planted it in India, Malacca, the East Indies, and Japan, and had died seeking entrance into China.

Singularly adapted to the mission of the Roman Catholic Church of these centuries, the Society of Jesus continued its phenomenal growth after death had removed its founder. It attracted some of the ablest youth of the day and became the chief spearhead of the Catholic Reformation. Among its early members was Peter Canisius (1521–1597), a native of Holland, who was the great apostle of the Catholic Reformation to Germany. He became a Jesuit in 1543, was trained in Rome under the personal direction of Ignatius, was an eloquent preacher, taught in universities, established Jesuit colleges in Cologne, Ingolstadt, and Prague, composed catechisms which were used extensively in giving instruction in the Roman Catholic form of the Christian faith, and had marked influence at the Council of Trent. Robert Bellarmine (1542–1621), later cardinal, the nephew of a Pope, was from a noble Tuscan family, studied in a Jesuit college, joined the Society in his late twenties, became a scholar of extraordinary and varied erudition, aided in a revival of the study of Thomas

Aquinas which had begun at the University of Salamanca, for years taught controversial theology at Rome, and wrote what was probably the ablest literary defense of the Roman Catholic faith against Protestants to be composed during the sixteenth and seventeenth centuries. Aloysius Gonzaga (1568–1591), of a princely Italian family, created a sensation through much of Latin Europe by joining the Society. Before he could be ordained priest he died of the plague while nursing sufferers from an epidemic. Eventually he was made the patron saint of youth. Spectacular evidence of the changes being wrought by the Catholic Reformation and the Society of Jesus was the career of Francis Borgia (1510–1572), Duke of Gandia and great-grandson of the notorious Pope Alexander VI. Deeply religious from his boyhood, Francis Borgia early encouraged the Society and after the death of his wife joined it, was ordained priest, and at the command of Ignatius became an itinerant preacher in Spain. Elected the third General of the Society, he brought to the post marked administrative genius and is often spoken of as its second founder. He revised its rule, encouraged mental prayer, edited the *Spritual Exercises,* strengthened the training of the novices, and furthered the Society's missions, especially on the expanding frontiers of the Spanish empire in the Americas.

The Jesuits addressed themselves to youth. They developed a system of education under what was known as the *Ratio Studiorum,* first drafted in 1585 and given its definitive form in 1599. They sought to produce strong moral character and to train their pupils to think for themselves. For a time they were among the most progressive schoolmasters in Europe.

The Society of Jesus vied with the spiritual sons of Francis of Assisi in producing more missionaries than any other order of the Roman Catholic Church. Its members were the chief agents in pressing back the Protestant tide and rewinning some areas, notably Bohemia, Moravia, and Poland, to the Roman Catholic Church. They ranged over much of North and South America, had enterprises in Africa, and were the outstanding sixteenth and seventeenth century pioneers of the faith in India, Annam, China, and Japan.

So widespread and active an organization could not fail to arouse opposition. Indeed, it faced this from the first. It was distrusted and feared by both Roman Catholics and Protestants. Some critics objected to its appropriation of the name of Jesus. Others denounced what they believed to be the attempts of its members to attain its purposes through political intrigue and asserted that the vow of obedience to the General took precedence over the individual's own judgement of right and wrong and so made the members skilful and ruthless tools of their superiors. Some asserted that through their casuistry the Jesuits confused truth with falsehood. A Grand Inquisitor clapped several of their superiors into prison. Bishops disliked their independence of episcopal control.

Many from other religious orders were antagonistic, partly out of jealousy. Numbers of Jesuits, including Bellarmine, were adherents of a theology called Molinism, from one of their sixteenth century members, Luis de Molina (1535–1600). Molinism wrestled with the problem, which also concerned Protestants, of how to reconcile grace and the unchangeable decree of predestination with free will. Here they differed sharply from the solution offered by Thomas Aquinas and held to by a large proportion of non-Jesuits. As we shall see, after 1750 the Jesuits were expelled from the French and Spanish domains and then, for about a generation, were suppressed by the Pope.

GREAT SPANISH MYSTICS

The Society of Jesus was the most influential but not the only new movement which arose from the Catholic Reformation in Spain. The sixteenth and seventeenth centuries were marked by many evidences of Spanish vitality. Spaniards were building a vast empire in the Americas and the Philippines. For part of the time their armies were regarded as the mightiest in Western Europe. Mountain peaks in art and literature appeared—notably Velasquez, Murillo, Cervantes, Lopez de Vega, and Calderon. Simultaneously religious geniuses appeared, some of them, like many in other ages, combining mysticism with practical achievement. To what extent these varied expressions of vitality had a common cause and to what degree Christianity was responsible for each we do not know. Presumably, as in so many other periods of marked creativity, here was more than a coincidence. Whatever else may be said, it is clear that Christianity was by no means the only contributory common factor. It is also certain that to Christianity must be ascribed a major share in the impulse which shaped the mystics.

Mysticism characterized thousands of Spaniards and gave rise to scores of writers and a vast literature. It was not confined to any one religious group but was found in several of the existing orders and now and again produced a new one. Like the Spanish phase of the Catholic Reformation it became noticeable late in the fifteenth century, reached a climax in the sixteenth century, began to decline in the seventeenth century, and by the middle of the eighteenth century had largely faded out. Its course paralleled the rise and decline in other aspects of Spanish greatness, some of them apparently only slightly related to Christianity. The Spanish mystics were not, as a rule, philosophical or even speculative. They were, rather, intent on the practical means of nourishing the life of the spirit and had uncanny insight into what would now be called psychology, with an analysis of the state of the soul.

Fittingly, the first outstanding pioneer of the classic era of Spanish mysticism was Francisco García Ximénes de Cisneros (1455–1510), cousin of the Ximénes de Cisneros who led in the reform of the Spanish church. Moreover, he it was who, only a few years before Ignatius Loyola came there for guidance in the early stages of his spiritual quest, had purified and reinvigorated the Benedictine monastery on Montserrat. How far if at all his *Book of Exercises for the Spiritual Life,* which appeared in 1500, influenced the more famous *Spiritual Exercises* of Ignatius has been hotly debated, but without clear proof of any conscious copying.

Ignatius Loyola must be given a place in the list, although we need not repeat what we have already said about him, but only point out that he is easily among the first three or four in eminence and probably first in wide-ranging influence.

It is usually and rightly said that the leading Spanish mystic was Teresa (or Theresa) of Avila (1515–1582). She is sometimes regarded as the outstanding woman of all Spanish history. We are fortunate in having a singularly candid autobiography, devoting especial attention to her spiritual development. Like the *Confessions* of Augustine, it ranks with the more important documents of the Christian faith.

Of aristocratic birth, one of a large family of children, six of whose seven sons became soldiers, Teresa was reared in an earnestly religious home. From infancy she had a deep strain of piety. When still a child, she and her favourite brother, inspired by reading the lives of the saints, set out, as she later recorded, for "the country of the Moors," begging their way "for the love of God," "and to be beheaded there." They had scarcely crossed the bridge outside the city gate of Avila when an uncle overtook them and brought them back to their mother.

Against home opposition, in 1536, when twenty-one years of age Teresa entered a Carmelite convent in Avila as a novice. For many years she remained an obscure nun. Troubled by chronic ill health, at one time in her twenties she fell into a kind of trance which left her helpless and seemingly paralyzed for more than eight months. For years the paralysis recurred intermittently. In her early forties she began to hear interior voices, see visions, and experience what to her were revelations. As she looked back upon her life she believed that during the first nearly twenty years of her monastic career she had almost constant inner conflict and knew "neither any joy in God nor any pleasure in the world." She thought of herself as a great sinner. Yet usually she spent many hours a day in prayer. Then came improvement, but in no single hour. She was helped by the sight of an image of Christ, "sorely wounded," and by the *Confessions* of Augustine. She began to find deep satisfaction in long and uninterrupted periods of communion with God and knew the "prayer of quiet." There came also union and rapture. To her these were gifts for which to be profoundly grateful.

When in her mid-forties Teresa came to believe that a stricter way of life was demanded than that practised in her convent. The older rule had been mitigated. Instead of having perpetual solitude, nuns were allowed visitors and might even go out into the town. The Lenten fasts were not kept as at first enjoined. In the face of opposition, but with her bishop's reluctant permission, in 1562 she founded in Avila what proved to be the initial convent of Reformed (or Discalced) Carmelite nuns. She began in a small way, with only four novices, but in the early years of the new community she had the most peaceful days of her life. Then, in 1567, with the consent of the general of her order, she began to travel up and down the land, inaugurating new houses of the reform. She enlisted two monks, one of them best remembered as John of the Cross, and through them established reformed Carmelite houses for men. The journeys entailed physical hardships of heat, springless carts, bad roads, worse inns, and unbridged rivers. As was to be expected, her successful efforts at reform aroused opposition within the order. After a few years, in 1580–1581, the Discalced Carmelites were allowed to form a distinct province and elect their own superior. Stricken with paralysis about the time that this was accomplished, Teresa was a sufferer the rest of her days. Yet she continued to be an itinerant and died while on a trip to start a new house. In her own person she had founded thirty-two houses.

Within her lifetime Teresa was revered as a saint. Her official canonization came only forty years after her death, simultaneously with that of Ignatius Loyola and Francis Xavier, both of whom had to wait longer than she for that recognition. Organizer, efficient administrator, careful of details as well as concerned with the wider sweep of her plans, repeatedly ill with fever, ague, quinsy, abscesses and tumours, in addition to paralysis and disorders which might be classified as primarily nervous, at times despondent, keenly aware of her sinfulness, she was first of all and always a mystic, given to prayer and with a growing faith, increasing inward calm, and a sense of the marvellous and quite unmerited mercy and love of God. None other of their saints has quite so gripped and held the affection of the Spanish people. Here is evidence both of the quality of her life and of a strain in the Spanish soul which responded to it.

Only slightly less famous than Teresa of Avila was her close friend, John of the Cross (1542–1605). Younger than she by a quarter of a century, he was profoundly influenced by her. Born and christened as Juan de Yepes, he was the son of an aristocrat who had been disinherited for marrying below his station. Reared in poverty by his early-widowed mother, he obtained his education partly in return for serving in a hospital and partly in a school established by the Jesuits. Before he was twenty he felt the call to the monastic life. Early in his twenties he entered the ranks of the Carmelites and for several years was a student in Salamanca. Frail and short of stature, he subjected his diminutive body to severe austerities. When he was twenty-five he attracted the attention of Teresa and became to her almost a spiritual son. As we have seen, she chose him to help initiate men's houses of her reform movement. Imprisoned for some months by fellow-Carmelites who opposed the reform, he wrote some of his choicest poetry and had some of his most vivid visions while in a noisome cell. Escaping, he went from monastery to monastery, strengthening his brethren, founding houses, serving as a prior of one and for a time as vicar-provincial. In his last months, internal dissensions among the Discalced Carmelites stripped him of his offices but freed him for intense and uninterrupted communion with God.

John of the Cross believed profoundly that to be filled with God the soul must empty itself. He treated of this and the road to this goal in his exquisite lyrics and in his three chief prose works, the *Ascent of Mount Carmel, The Dark Night*, and the *Living Flame of Love.* The road was difficult, and, with keen insight into human nature, he forewarned those who would undertake it of the perils along the way. Only the few could attain the higher reaches of which he wrote. Yet he had a profound influence, was canonized in 1726, and two hundred years later was proclaimed a doctor of the Church.

Space fails even to name all the other Spanish mystics, lesser peaks below these higher ones. There was Francisco de Osuna (c.1497–c.1542), the Franciscan whose *Third Spiritual Alphabet* aided Teresa of Avila in one stage of her pilgrimage. Luis de Granada (1504–1588), a Dominican, prior, provincial of his order for Portugal, famous as a preacher, wrote voluminously, but is best remembered for his *Sinners' Guide,* of use to the ordinary Christian in his prayers and devotions. The Franciscan Juan de los Angeles (c.1536–1609), in spite of his duties as provincial of his order, found time to write guides to the mystic life, among them *Triumphs of the Love of God, Spiritual Strife, Dialogues of the Conquest of the Spiritual and Secret Kingdom of God,* and a continuation of this last, *Manual of the Perfect Life.* Peter of Alcántara, eventually canonized, was counsellor to Teresa of Avila both in things material and things spiritual.

Much later and of a quite different kind was Miguel de Molinos (1640–1697). A mystic, he taught interior annihilation as the means to purity of soul, perfect contemplation, and inner peace. Here was a form of quietism. Yet it contained features which sanctioned gross immorality, for it held impure carnal acts to be excusable since only the lower, sensual man was concerned in them and they need not taint the soul. He had a wide influence in several countries, but in 1687, while in Rome, was condemned as a heretic and sentenced to life imprisonment in the garb of a penitent.

REFORM IN PORTUGAL

In Portugal there were no indigenous movements for reform at all comparable in vigour and magnitude with those in Spain. Portugal gave birth to no new order which approached the influence of the Jesuits or the Discalced Carmelites. It knew no such flowering of mysticism as did its larger neighbour. This does not mean that the Catholic Reformation did not touch it. The Jesuits early extended their operations to Portugal and it was through the Portuguese that Francis Xavier carried out his amazing mission in India, the East Indies, and the Far East. Portugal had zealous monks and eloquent preaching. Yet most of the reinvigoration of Portuguese Christianity came by contagion from other lands.

This lack of a major native reform movement in Portugal had significance for wide areas of the globe. In the sixteenth century Portugal built a colonial empire which was second in extent only to that of Spain. Portuguese established themselves in Brazil, along the coasts of Africa, in India, Ceylon, Southeast Asia, the East Indies, Japan, and China. Everywhere they went Catholic missions arose under their ægis. Yet in general these never had the vitality of the Spanish enterprises. The difference was reflected in the future course of Christianity in Brazil and much of Africa and Asia.

THE CATHOLIC REFORMATION IN ITALY

While the Catholic Reformation was proceeding in Spain, what was taking place in Italy? Here was the centre of the Roman Catholic Church. From Italy had come some of the greatest theologians, notably Anselm and Thomas Aquinas. Here had arisen several of the largest orders, especially the Franciscans. Here, more recently, had been such saints as Catherine of Siena, and here Savonarola had only recently perished in his attempt to make Florence fully Christian. In Italy, too, some of the most notorious corruption in the Church was found. Here was the home of the Renaissance, with its paganizing tendencies. Here, in spite of notable attempts to effect a viable reconciliation with Christianity, humanism was displaying de-Christianizing trends. The Papacy and the Papal curia had succumbed to the evils which we have earlier described (Chapter 28) and attempts to cleanse the Augean stables had thus far proved unsuccessful. How effective was the fresh pulsation of life?

As in Spain, so in Italy, the era was one of creativity in culture. Although divided and weak politically, Italy, as the original centre of the Renaissance and humanism, was producing magnificent art and exquisite literature. The flowering came somewhat earlier than in Spain and before 1600 had passed its peak. Leonardo da Vinci died in 1519, Raphael in 1520, the Titanic and long-lived Michelangelo in 1564, and Titian in 1576. Palestrina (1526–1594), who set a new standard for the music of the Church, was a sixteenth century figure, in part the product of the Catholic Reformation, as was the unhappy, mad Tasso (1544–1595), with his master epic, *Jerusalem Delivered*. Machiavelli died in 1527 and Ariosto in 1533. The Catholic Reformation was slightly later in getting well under way, but, as in Spain, it reached its peak before the close of the sixteenth century.

A major precursor and instrument of the Catholic Reformation in Italy was the Oratory of Divine Love. A confraternity, a type of fellowship which had long been common in the Catholic Church, it may go back to a group which came into being as early as 1497. The centre of the Oratory of Divine Love was in Rome and it counted among its members men of deep devotion and outstanding ability who wished the moral reform of the Church. Prominent among them was Giovanni Pietro Caraffa (1476–1559), later, as we have seen, to be Pope Paul IV. Its members, highly placed though they were, showed their zeal by visiting hospitals and prisons. Branches arose in several Italian cities.

Partly in association with the Oratory of Divine Love, there came into being the Theatines, the earliest of a new kind of monastic order. Their purpose was the reform of the secular clergy, the rank and file of the priests who ministered to the nominally Christian population. The founders of the Theatines were aristocrats. The chief mover was Gaetano dei Conti di Tiene (also known as Cajetan, but not to be confused with his contemporary, Cardinal Cajetan, whom we met in connexion with Luther). He was one of the Oratory of Divine Love and consecrated the order to the cross of Christ. He was eventually canonized. The first head of the Theatines was Caraffa, who, with Papal permission, divested himself of his various benefices to assume the post. Since he had been Bishop of Chieti (in Latin Theate), the popular designation of the order, Theatines, was from that see. Papal approval of the Theatines was given in 1524. They multiplied rapidly, soon spread to Spain and France, and also conducted foreign missions.

Somewhat similar to the Theatines were the Regular Clerics of St. Paul, better known as the Barnabites, from the Church of St. Barnabas in Milan, with which they were closely associated in their early days. They were founded in 1530 by three Italians of noble family. In addition to the customary vows of poverty, chastity, and obedience, their members solemnly promised not to seek any office. They catechized, heard confessions, and conducted missions, but as means to their chief end, the revival among the clergy of a zeal for souls.

The Somaschi, so-called from the site of their mother house, were begun (1532) by Jerome Emiliani (1481–1537), who gave himself so devotedly to the founding of hospitals, orphanages, and a home for fallen women, and to personal ministrations to the physically wretched that he was later canonized. The chief work of the Somaschi, like that of the founder, was the care of the sick and the poor.

Resembling the Somaschi, but eventually having a much wider extension, were the Brothers Hospitallers of St. John of God. Their founder, John of God (1495–1550), was Portuguese by birth but was reared in Spain and spent most of his life there. His was a striking spiritual pilgrimage which at one stage led him to go through the streets of Granada, scourging himself in such fashion that many thought him mad. John of God was a designation which he believed had been given him in a vision by the infant Jesus. In Granada he began devoting himself to the sick. Eventually an order arose which was accorded Papal approval in 1572 and which was to follow the rule of Augustine. The order spread to Rome in 1584 and there what was regarded as its mother house was established. Other hospitals were soon inaugurated in Italy and France.

A movement, that of the Oratory, which was to be the means of deepening the Christian faith and life of many thousands was begun in Rome by Philip Neri (1515–1595). Philip Neri was a native of Florence and had some of his early instruction from the Dominicans of San Marco, the house intimately connected with Savonarola. When he was eighteen he went to Rome and there laboured for the sick and the poor and through informal conversations sought to lead chance acquaintances in many different walks of life to more earnest Christian living. He founded a confraternity to minister to the pilgrims who thronged the city. In 1556 he began an institute, the Oratory, for religious meetings of a novel kind. They were held in the evening and consisted of prayers, readings from the Scriptures and the fathers, and lectures or sermons of an informal and unconventional kind calculated to reach those not usually moved by the formal services of the Church. Hymns and music were prominent in the meetings, and Palestrina did much of the composing for them. Musical settings for scenes from sacred history were written. Known as the oratorio, this novel use of music gained wide circulation. For a time Philip Neri met bitter opposition, but in 1575, when he was sixty years of age, Papal permission was given for a community of secular priests known as the Congregation of the Oratory. Its members were bound by obedience but by no vows. Each house was independent of the others. The movement spread in

Italy, Spain, and France, and with modifications the various units followed the rule of the founder. The successor of Neri as superior of the Roman Oratory, Cæsar Baronius (1538–1607), was especially distinguished as the author of a voluminous church history, *Annales Ecclesiastici,* which carried the story down to 1198 and was in part an answer to the Protestant *Centuriæ.*

What was to become the most extensive of the sixteenth century religious orders of Italian origin was the Capuchins. Like the Jesuits, they were evidence of the new tides of life which were beginning to run strong and were a stimulus to them. They were also proof of the attraction of the ideals of Francis of Assisi in times when men were seeking to follow Christ without compromise or reservation. They arose from the Observants, the branch of the order of Brothers Minor who in principle more nearly held to the rule of Francis than did the Conventuals. Yet the Observants had also become lax. One of their number, Matteo di Bassi (or da Bascio), believed that he had heard a voice which repeatedly commanded him to observe the rule "to the letter." He obeyed and in such meticulous fashion that he insisted on wearing what he believed to be the primitive Franciscan habit. Part of this was a pointed hood, a *cappa* or *capuche,* which became a kind of symbol of the reform. Hence came the designation Capuchin. Matteo di Bassi did not at first intend to separate from the Observants but sought, rather, to win them to a return to what tradition declared was the pristine way of the *Poverello.* As he might have expected, he encountered opposition. In 1526 a Papal brief permitted the Capuchins to separate in part from the Observants and to follow, as they wished, the way of the hermit. In 1528 they were made a distinct family within the Franciscans. Much emphasis was placed, as it had been by Francis of Assisi, on preaching. Similar movements sprang up elsewhere among the Observants and swelled the ranks of the Capuchins.

For a time the Capuchins were under the suspicion of heresy. These fears seemed to be confirmed when one of their early heads, Ochino, whom we have earlier met, became a Protestant. The Pope gave serious consideration to suppressing them and for two years forbade them to preach.

Other counsels prevailed, partly because some of the new recruits proved to be staunchly orthodox and zealous. In 1619 the Capuchins became a separate order with their own minister general. They multiplied rapidly and were effective preachers of the Catholic Reformation in both Roman Catholic and Protestant areas. This was partly because they mingled with the ordinary life of the masses, serving the sick and the poor and giving themselves with noteworthy devotion to the sufferers from epidemics. While they did not do as Matteo di Bassi had wished, observe the primitive rule of Francis "to the letter," but relaxed some of its austerities, they were a revival of the zeal of the early Brothers Minor and were missionaries to much of Europe and on the new geographic frontiers opened by the explorations of the sixteenth and seventeenth centuries.

The creative vitality in the Catholic Reformation is also shown in the coming into being of the Ursulines, an order of women of a quite new kind. They were begun by Angela de Merici (1474–1540). From childhood deeply religious, at about the age of twenty she believed that a great need of her time was the better instruction of girls in the rudiments of the Christian faith. She turned her home, in Desenzano, into a school and later moved it to Brescia. She chose other virgins to multiply her work. They lived with their families and met at stated intervals for conference and prayer. In 1535 twelve of them formed a community named for St. Ursula. The idea caught fire and similar groups quickly arose in Italy, Germany, and France. A constitution was adopted in 1540 and in 1544 Papal approval was received. The rule was that of Augustine. The functions of the order were primarily teaching. Several congregations sprang up, each calling itself Ursuline, and with varying garbs and customs. The foundress was canonized in 1807.

Among the furtherers of the Catholic Reformation in Italy were some of the bishops. A pioneer was Giberti, who in his personal and public life was an example of the progress of the reform and did much to encourage it in his diocese, Verona. His beginnings were quite unpromising. The illegitimate son of a Genoese admiral, he owed his rapid advancement in the Church to the Medici who was later Pope Clement VII. Although naturally religious and in his youth wishing to become a monk, he allowed himself to be drawn into administrative duties, made his home in Rome a hospitable centre of the humanists, and accepted appointment as non-resident Bishop of Verona. However, he was brought into the circle of the Oratory of Divine Love, was a friend of Caraffa, aided in the formation of the Theatines, and about 1528, when in his mid-thirties, he took up his residence in his see, resigned all his other benefices to which the cure of souls was attached, began a strictly ascetic way of life, and devoted himself to the diocese. He went from village to village, examining the priests, reconciling enemies, caring for the poor, and insisting that the clergy perform their duties and maintain a worthy way of life. He improved the services in the parish churches, enjoined on his priests weekly confession, had a bell rung at the elevation of the host, and had the sacrament reserved in a tabernacle on the high altar. He reformed both the secular and the regular clergy, encouraged confraternities for the care of the poor, and had prepared and published a catechism and a manual for preachers. Several other prelates followed Giberti's example.

Outstanding among the reforming bishops was Charles Borromeo (1538–

1584). Of aristocratic birth in a deeply religious family, he was a nephew of Pope Pius IV. His uncle gave him rapid ecclesiastical promotion and when he was twenty-two made him a cardinal and entrusted him with important administrative duties. To these responsibilities was soon added the Archbishopric of Milan, one of the most important sees in the Church. For some years Borromeo seemed to be one of the prelates who were unhappily very common even after the Catholic Reformation was well under way, drawing the incomes from many benefices, pushed forward by influential relatives, living in splendour, and a handicap rather than an aid to the professed purpose of the Church. Yet he was never guilty of the gross vices which were widespread in Rome and his religious life deepened. The death of a beloved brother is said to have done much to promote his spiritual growth. After the death of Pius IV and the election of a worthy successor, partly with his support, Borromeo took up his residence in Milan and gave himself unsparingly to carry through a thorough transformation of the archdiocese. He founded seminaries to train priests, reformed monasteries, inaugurated schools for the nobility, furthered elementary education for the masses, encouraged the Ursulines, sought to relieve the poor, provided advocates to help them in their lawsuits, set himself against usury, established homes for beggars, worked for conciliation in labour disputes, and in a **great epidemic reduced his own table, sold his** plate to aid in the relief of the sufferers, and had his tapestries made into clothing for the destitute. He emphasized frequent communion and set the example in fasting and pilgrimages. It is not surprising that he wore himself out and died in his middle forties. It speaks for the new temper of the Roman Catholic Church that he was canonized in 1610, less than a generation after his death.

THE REFORMATION CAPTURES THE PAPACY

A time lag existed between the forward surge of the wave of reform in the Roman Catholic Church and the permanent commitment of the Papacy to it. Reform was already well under way in Spain when the Spaniard, Alexander VI, was bringing the Papacy to the lowest point of moral degradation since the tenth century. It had made substantial progress in Italy before it was securely entrenched in Rome. In this the record was not unlike that in the earlier and more serious recession, from A.D. 500 to A.D. 950. Then, it will be recalled, the reform associated with the name of Cluny had made substantial progress elsewhere before it seated its advocates on the throne of Peter.

A brief review of the Popes of the sixteenth century may illustrate this generalization and will also shed light on some of the other problems faced by the Holy See.

As we enter upon this survey we do well to recall something of the complexity and magnitude of the problems with which the Popes had to deal. There was the tradition, reinforced by the dreams and actions of the reforming Pontiffs of the Middle Ages, that the Papacy should be not only the exponent and guardian of doctrinal orthodoxy but also, for the achievement of a fully Christian society, the administrative head of Christendom. This entailed both authority over the entire ecclesiastical structure and active participation and even dictatorial powers in all aspects, including especially the political, of the life of Christendom. To implement these claims, the Popes had built up a centralized bureaucracy and to support it had been driven to financial expedients which had aroused much opposition, especially in distant countries, and which had furthered corruption in the curia. The corruption was of sufficient magnitude to tax the ability and resolution of any Pope who would seek to curb it. In addition, the Popes of the sixteenth century were confronted by the chronic menace of the Ottoman Turks who might at any time engulf Western Europe. As the traditional leaders of Christendom against the Moslems they strove desperately, but in vain, to unite against them a hopelessly divided Europe. They were faced with a rising tide of nationalism headed by monarchs who were building for total control in their respective realms. This nationalism and these monarchs, even when emphatically Catholic in doctrine, were intent upon limiting the administrative and taxing functions of the Papacy within their borders. Catholic monarchs insisted upon controlling appointment to bishoprics and other important ecclesiastical posts in their realms. The more prominent sought to dominate the Papacy and to use it as a pawn in the unremitting struggle of power politics. Spanish, French, and Italian cliques among the cardinals had to be reckoned with in Papal elections. Militarily weak, the Popes attempted to play off one monarch against another. On one memorable occasion, in 1527, the unruly troops of the Emperor Charles V, orthodox Catholic though he was, seized Rome, forced the Pope to take refuge in the castle of St. Angelo, and for months held and pillaged the city. Charles was presumably not unwilling to see the Pope thus dealt with, for the latter had been siding with France. To many the emotional shock was even greater than the physical destruction. Some careless devotees of the Renaissance believed the disaster to be divine retribution for the wickedness of the city and the curia and were led to repentance. Even more serious for the Papacy was the defection of the major part of North-western Europe and Great Britain to Protestantism. Distracted by other pressing crises, Rome was never entirely free to deal with that movement.

It is not surprising that under these circumstances the Papacy was slow in being fully committed to reform or that reforming Popes, when elected, found the obstacles to improvement mountainous.

The succession of Popes reveals much of the story. Alexander VI was followed (1503) by Pius III, a man of ability and blameless life, who reigned for only a few months. Next came Giuliano della Rovere who as Julius II held the post from 1503 to 1513. Sixty years of age when elected and troubled by gout, he nevertheless proved himself a man of energy and determination. Impetuous, he was more like an emperor than a bishop and much of his ten years in office was devoted to restoring, consolidating, and extending the territorial domains of the Papacy and rendering the Holy See independent of any temporal prince by its possession of a strong state under its direct rule. Yet he wished reform, repudiated the nepotism which characterized so many of his fifteenth century predecessors, condemned simony in Papal elections, laid the foundation stone of the new St. Peter's, was a patron of art, and encouraged missions in America, India, and Africa.

Next on the Papal throne was Giovanni de' Medici (1475–1521), son of Lorenzo the Magnificent, whom we have already met (Chapter 28) as having been loaded with benefices since childhood and as having been named cardinal-deacon in his early teens. When elected he was not yet a priest. As Leo X he was Pope from 1513 to 1521. Although he was punctilious in his religious observances, promoted art, and, elegant in his manners, made Rome a growing centre of culture, he was a lover of luxury and the chase, was intent upon the aggrandizement of his family, and, engrossed in the political and diplomatic intrigues of the time, employed in them the kind of deceit and shrewdness associated with the name of Machiavelli. No reform could be hoped for from him, and under him corruption increased. Something of the moral condition of the Papacy and its entourage can be visualized from a plot in 1517 (the year of the ninety-five theses of Luther) to rid the post of Leo by poisoning him. In retaliation Leo had the leader, a twenty-two-year-old, dissolute cardinal, tortured and executed, imposed heavy fines upon other cardinals who had been implicated, and then ensured his control of the sacred college by creating thirty-one new members. Leo sought to replenish his coffers and obtain funds to build St. Peter's by the promotion of the sale of indulgences. He was not the man to sense the significance of Luther or of the movement which the great German spear-headed.

After death had removed Leo X, for a brief time, 1522–1523, reform seemed to have come to its rightful own. To break a deadlock in the college of cardinals over the election, a native of Utrecht of lowly birth, a boyhood tutor and trusted official of the Emperor Charles V, was elected and took the title of Adrian VI. Scholarly, ascetic, deeply religious, an experienced administrator, he set himself to the herculean task of reform. But he aroused bitter opposition, especially by his attempts at urgently needed financial retrenchment, was confronted by the advancing Turks, rising Protestantism, and feuds among the Christian princes, and died after less than two years in office. Incidentally, he was the last non-Italian Pope.

Following Adrian VI came another of the Medici, who under the title of Clement VII wore the tiara from 1523 to 1534. They were crucial years in the rise of Protestantism, in the relations of Henry VIII of England with Rome, and in the growth of the reform movement in the Catholic Church. Of illegitimate birth, the future Clement VII had been declared legitimate by his cousin, Leo X, and had been raised by him to the purple. Although neither extravagant nor pleasure-loving as had been Leo X, hard-working, upright in his private life, and a patron of the arts, he was given to procrastination, indecision, timidity, and inconstancy of purpose. He made some steps towards reform, but his interests were predominantly political and he was caught in the Maelstrom of Italian and European intrigue and diplomacy. His appointments to high ecclesiastical office were largely from political or personal considerations and few of the cardinals created by him had at heart the real interests of the Church. One of them was his nephew, a Medici who at the time of his elevation had only entered his eighteenth year. It was during his reign that the sack of Rome occurred to which we have already referred. Yet around him, even in groups in Rome, although still minorities, the reform wave was rising. It was he who gave the needed Papal approval to the Theatines, and the Oratory of Divine Love had its headquarters in the city.

With the coming to the chair of Peter of Alessandro Farnese (as Paul III, Pope from 1534 to 1549), the Catholic Reformation may be said to have made significant strides towards capturing the Papacy. The early life of the later future Paul III gave no hint that here would be an active furtherer of reform. Of an ancient and noble lineage, Alessandro Farnese had been reared in the circle of the Medici and owed his cardinal's hat to Alexander VI who, before he became Pope, had had a liaison with his sister. He himself had sired illegitimate children. In common with many ecclesiastics of his age he accumulated benefices. A skilful diplomat, able, and prudent, he had succeeded in winning the favour of successive Pontiffs, but by instinct and experience he was more a secular prince than a priest and bishop. However, after he was ordained priest (1519) his private life seems to have been above reproach. As Pope, although he used the post to advance members of his family, including his grandsons, he turned his great abilities to the physical improvement and adornment of Rome and to the reform of the Church. He curbed some of the worst abuses connected with the sale of indulgences, ordered absentee bishops to go to their sees and attend to their episcopal duties, appointed outstanding re-formers to the cardinalate, among them Pole and Caraffa, reorganized the Inquisition with headquarters in Rome, appointed a commission which out-lined a notable programme for reform, gave Papal approval to the Society of Jesus, forbade the enslavement of the Indians in the New World, and (1545) brought about the assembling of the Council of Trent, of which we are to hear more in a moment.

It was during the reign of Paul III that Luther died. The rising tide of Catholic reform was about to surge against the Protestant tide which he had evoked.

Julius III, Pope from 1550 to 1555, came to the post with an excellent record, for he had been a member of the commission on reform appointed by Paul III, had served as Papal representative at the Council of Trent, had apparently been zealous for the improvement of the Church, and had conscientiously per-formed his part in religious ceremonies. In supreme authority he was a dis-appointment. Lacking in steadfastness and firmness, easily dispirited, coarse in his jokes, a lover of pomp, worldly, popular in Rome because he encouraged the amusements connected with the carnival, fond of the chase, gambling with his intimates for large sums, enjoying jesters and unseemly theatrical perform-ances, given to nepotism, elevating a quite unworthy seventeen-year-old favourite to the cardinalate, he was a belated and unhappy relapse into the pre-reform days. Yet the Catholic Reformation had gathered such momentum that Julius III could not have stopped it even had he wished to do so. Indeed, officially he took measures to further it. He commanded bishops to reside in their sees, encouraged the reform commission, and at the time of his death was preparing a bull to further comprehensive changes for the improvement of the secular and regular clergy.

After the three weeks' reign of Marcellus III, the reform party won a com-plete victory and put in the Papacy one of its most zealous members, Caraffa, a member of the Oratory of Divine Love and the first head of the Theatines. Although nearly seventy-nine years of age when elected, his physical energy was unabated and during the four years of his pontificate (as Paul IV, 1555–1559) he gave vigorous leadership. Learned, incorruptible, deeply religious, ascetic, uncompromising, forthright, often hasty of speech and temper, he had ideals for the Papacy such as Hildebrand and Innocent III cherished and held that as vicar of Christ he should have all princes at his feet. He carried through reforms with a high hand, stiffened the Inquisition, had the index of forbidden books revised, was implacable towards those suspected of heresy, and had one of the most eminent of the cardinals, Morone, a zealous reformer, thrown into prison and tried before the Inquisition. Yet he was guilty of using his high office to bestow favours on members of his family. He was intensely unpopular with the Roman populace and on his death they rioted, mutilated his statue, freed the prisoners of the Inquisition, and destroyed its records.

Pius IV, the next to wear the tiara (1559–1565), continued the reform, reconvened the Council of Trent, had it complete its work, and confirmed its decrees. He had two Caraffa cardinals, nephews of his predecessor, accused of high crimes, and caused one of them to be convicted and executed, thus showing his power as against the Sacred College. He was a patron of the arts and in his later months scandalized some of the reformers by his pleasures.

Pius V (1566–1572) was outstanding. The fact that he was the latest of the Popes to be canonized (although in 1951 Pius X, reigned 1903–1914, was beatified) and the first to be accorded that recognition since Gregory X, who reigned in the latter half of the thirteenth century, is indication of the esteem with which he was regarded. A Dominican, a teacher of theology and philosophy, an inquisitor, humble, keeping the rule of poverty, he was the candidate of the reformers. He continued in the Vatican his ascetic way of life, made the Papal court a model in morals, sought to enforce the observance of Sunday, and discouraged profanity, animal baiting, and prostitution. He set his face against nepotism, disciplined some members of his own family, refused to show special favour to his order, and stiffened the Inquisition. Under him a new catechism and a revised breviary and missal were issued. He laboured for the improvement of the secular and regular clergy. Pius V was evidence that the Catholic Reform was now in full charge of the Papacy. It was not again really to lose control.

In his youth he had had an illegitimate child, but in his maturity he who was to be Gregory XIII (1572–1585) had led a blameless life. Best remembered for the reform of the calendar accomplished during his pontificate, he encouraged the Jesuits and sought to win back some of the ground lost to Protestants. A gifted organizer, he enforced the decrees of the Council of Trent and refused to confirm the nominations by secular princes to bishoprics until he was convinced of the worthy character of the candidates. He struggled to curb the control of the Spanish monarchs over the Church in their domains, not hesitating to challenge even the mighty Philip II.

Although he reigned for only five years, 1585–1590, Sixtus V, a Franciscan, a former inquisitor-general in Venice, a noted preacher, ardent in his devotions, proved to be one of the ablest of the Popes, carried through extensive building enterprises in Rome, reorganized the Papal curia, and furthered the Catholic Reformation in Germany, Poland, Switzerland, and the Netherlands. Yet in his effort to put Papal finances on a sound basis he sold offices right and left and increased the taxation in the Papal states.

In spite of the fact that he was given to nepotism, Clement VIII (1592–1605) promoted some excellent men to the cardinalate. He granted absolution to Henry IV of France, and so helped to end the wars of religion and to ensure the triumph of the Roman Catholic faith in that troubled land. He obtained the readmission of the Jesuits to France. Aspiring to restore Papal sovereignty over the rulers of Europe, he helped to make peace in the chronic feud between Spain and France. He saw to a revision of the breviary, missal, and pontifical and the completion of the revision of the Vulgate which had been begun under Sixtus V.

Paul V (1605–1621), a canon lawyer, cherished exalted conceptions of the prerogatives of his office, sternly sought to enforce what he believed to be the rights of the Church in several of the Italian states, opposed Gallicanism, the attempt to render the Church in France administratively independent of Rome, and encouraged missions. Like so many of his predecessors, he used his authority to further the interests of the members of his family.

Urban VIII (1623–1644), holding office as he did during more than half of the Thirty Years' War (1618–1648), wished to make the Papacy the arbiter in the international scenes, but without success.

And so we might continue through the list of the Popes of the seventeenth and eighteenth centuries. Some aided their relatives to acquire wealth, but for the most part they were virtuous in their private lives, several laboured at the perennial problem of improving the morals of the clergy, and not a few of them encouraged the missions which, as we are to see, were planting the Catholic faith among many peoples in both hemispheres.

None of the Popes of the sixteenth, seventeenth, and eighteenth centuries ranked with such predecessors as Leo the Great, Gregory the Great, Gregory VII, or Innocent III. They seem not to have had the ability of these men. Nor were the times propitious for the exercise of such gifts. After 1648 the Roman Catholic Church made very few counter advances against Protestantism. In that respect the Catholic Reformation had spent its force. The more powerful Catholic states insisted upon controlling the Church within their borders: the struggle between Church and state which had punctuated so much of the course of Christianity in Western Europe during the Middle Ages had been resolved in favour of the state. Now and again the Popes had an important part in negotiations between Catholic monarchs and they were chronically involved in Italian politics. Some contributed to victories against the Ottoman Turks. Yet none exerted as much power as had many of the pre-fourteenth century Pontiffs. The fact that the Church canonized only one after the thirteenth century is apparently an indication that none of the others attained to the spiritual and moral stature of their sainted predecessors of earlier ages.

The Council of Trent Furthers Reform and
Deepens the Breach with Protestantism

Again and again in the troubled years when the Roman Catholic Church was palpably suffering from moral corruption and large segments of Europe were leaving it and becoming Protestant, the cry went up for a general council. In spite of the failure of the councils of the fifteenth century to effect substantial reform, many continued to look longingly towards that device as a means of curing the Church's ills. Charles V urged it and on several occasions the cardinals sought to exact from candidates for the Papacy the promise to convoke one. That was probably in part because of the tradition begun at Nicæa in 325 for seeking the common mind of the Church through a general or ecumenical council, and partly because the Popes had thus far not reformed even their immediate entourage, the Roman curia.

It was Paul III who at long last brought a general council together. It held its first session in Trent in December, 1545. In 1547 the Italian members obtained its transfer to Bologna, farther from the North. In May, 1551, it was once more at Trent. Less than a year later, in May, 1552, it adjourned, and did not again convene for nearly a decade, in January, 1562. It finally completed its work in December, 1563. The Roman Catholics count it as the nineteenth ecumenical council.

The council was called by the Pope and not, as had been that of Nicæa and several of its successors, by the Emperor. Powerful though he was and Holy Roman Emperor, Charles V did not presume to convene it. Moreover, the Popes dominated it. Many, including Charles V, had hoped that the council would heal the breach between the Lutherans and other Protestants on the one hand and the Church of Rome on the other. In this, however, they were to be disappointed.

In the council itself there were many elements and numbers of currents and cross currents. Some members, including eminent Spanish prelates, resented any effort by the Pope to control the gathering and stood for the independence of the bishops within the framework of the Catholic Church. The Spanish and northern bishops, especially the French, were particularly emphatic that while they were prepared to admit that the Bishop of Rome was *primus,* he was only *primus inter pares* and that, as Cyprian had long ago insisted, each bishop drew his authority directly from Christ through apostolic succession and not through Rome. Some, and in general this was the viewpoint of Charles V, wished the moral reform of the Church but feared discussions of debatable doctrinal issues as jeopardizing efforts to win the Protestants. They held that if the Church were morally what she should be, Protestants and those who differed from them might come together and discuss amicably the issues which divided them. Charles V and the German Roman Catholics wished permission to give the cup to the laity, the marriage of priests, the singing of vernacular hymns in public worship, the use of some of the ecclesiastical revenues for schools for the poor, and the reduction of the power of the Pope. Reginald Pole, one of the earlier delegates, was from a group of Catholic reformers of whom Gasparo Contarini (1483–1542) was the leader. A Venetian, and, like Pole, of distinguished aristocratic lineage, Contarini was inclined to find common ground with Protestants on the issue of justification by faith. Marcello Cervini represented reformers of whom Caraffa, the later Paul IV, was the outstanding spokesman. While zealous for moral cleansing, they distrusted Pole and Contarini as verging on heresy and stood for a stiff formulation of dogma which would make it emphatic that the Church of Rome could have no part or lot with Protestants. There were those who opposed any meddling with the existing state of affairs and were suspicious of those who in the name of moral reform would disturb the perquisites of the hierarchy and of members of the Papal curia. Some, perpetuating the conciliar ideal of the preceding century, were fearful of Papal interference with the work of the gathering. Others, notably the Jesuits, stood for the authority of the Pope.

Into the complicated details of the history of the Council we need not go. Much of the work was done in committees. The physical surroundings were uncomfortable and proved trying to elderly prelates accustomed to luxury. Because of the long life of the council, more protracted than any other in the series that claimed the title ecumenical, and the interruptions, one of them for many years, the personnel was far from continuous. Yet in its achievements the Council of Trent proved to be one of the most important and significant in the history of the Church. It gave definitive formulation to the principles of the Catholic Reformation, cut off all possibility of reconciliation with the Protestants, and reinforced the forward surge of the Roman Catholic Church, revived and in part cleansed, into territories lost to Protestantism and into lands opened to the faith by the explorations, conquests, and commerce of the fifteenth and sixteenth centuries.

In general it was the views represented by the Jesuits and the group centering around Caraffa which triumphed. Roman Catholic dogma was explicitly stated on the distinctive convictions of Protestantism and in such fashion as to make it clear that the latter were regarded as no longer debatable but were heresies. So far as legislation could accomplish it, thoroughgoing moral reform was enacted and concrete measures devised and enjoined for enforcing it. Moreover, the council in part rebuilt the hierarchical structure, making provision for the better training and support of the parish clergy, extending the powers of the bishops within their dioceses, untangling conflicting jurisdictions, and enhancing the authority of the Pope.

Among the decisions on dogma reached by the Council of Trent the following stand out. The council declared the Old Testament (which was made to include what Protestants call the Apocrypha), the New Testament, and the unwritten traditions believed to have been received by the apostles from the mouth of Christ and preserved in the Catholic Church to have been dictated by the Holy Spirit and to have God as their author. It held that of all the Latin editions of the Scriptures, the Old Vulgate was to be regarded as authentic. It ordered that no one should presume to interpret the Bible contrary to the sense authorized by the Church. It affirmed the transmission of Adam's sin to all his posterity, that this original sin is taken away only by the merit of one mediator, Jesus Christ, that this merit is applied both to adults and infants by the sacrament of baptism administered in the form used by the Church, and that infants are baptized for the remission of original sin. Although, so the council declared, Christ died for all, only those receive the benefit of his death to whom the merit of Christ's passion is communicated. Justification can be given only through the new birth which is wrought through baptism or the desire for it, for "unless a man be born again of water and the Spirit he cannot enter into the kingdom of God." Reaffirming the modified Augustinianism substantially as expressed by the Council of Orange in 529, the Council of Trent held that while by his grace God moves men to turn to Him and that one cannot of his own free will, without God's grace, take the initiative towards being just in God's sight, men are free to reject God's grace and are also free to coöperate with it. Thus, by implication, the council rejected irresistible grace. While stating that we are justified by faith and grace and not by works, the Council declared that it could not be asserted that anyone is justified by faith alone, since heretics and schismatics boast in "vain confidence" that they are thus justified, and "no one can know with certainty of faith, which cannot be subject of error, that he has obtained the grace of God." The council held that Christians can advance and be still further justified by observing the commandments of God and of the Church, "faith coöperating with good works," and that it is possible for one who is justified to keep the commandments of God.

Striking at Protestants, the council anathematized those who taught that since Adam's sin the free-will of man is extinguished, that all works done before justification are sins and merit the hatred of God, that justification is by faith alone, by confidence in the divine mercy which remits sins for Christ's sake, that justification is only attained by those who are predestined to life and that all others are predestined to evil, and that the just ought not for their good works done in God to expect an eternal reward from God. The council came out plumply for purgatory and for merits earned by good works.

Again with Protestants in mind, the council put itself on record for the seven sacraments, declared that they are necessary for salvation, and that through them grace is conferred by the act performed (*ex opere operato*). The council denounced the beliefs held by some Protestants about the sacraments, such as the power of all Christians to administer the word and all the sacraments, in other words, the priesthood of all believers, and the denial of the validity of infant baptism. The council reaffirmed transubstantiation, came out for the reservation of the sacrament, denied "consubstantiation," and held that the whole Christ is in both the bread and the wine, thus making it unnecessary to give the cup to the laity. It declared that only bishops and priests have the power to pronounce the forgiveness or the retention of sins. It came out emphatically for the invocation of the saints, for the veneration of the relics of the saints, for sacred images and paintings, and for indulgences.

To aid pastors in teaching the Catholic faith the council entrusted to a commission the preparation of a catechism. This, bearing the name of the council, was compiled and accorded Papal approval.

Measures for the reform of the Church and of the laity were numerous and were closely associated with those for an improved preparation of the clergy and a better ordered hierarchical structure. Duelling was forbidden on pain of excommunication. The celebration of the mass was closely regulated to ensure that it should be done with reverence. In it only such music was permitted as would contribute to dignity and true worship. The sale of indulgences was controlled and some of the worst abuses were eliminated. Magical properties popularly ascribed to images were disavowed. Earlier decrees against non-residence of bishops in their sees were renewed. Similarly, the absence from their charges of those having the care of souls (*cura animarum*), while not proscribed, was carefully restricted. The holding of several cathedral churches by any one incumbent was forbidden and the guilty were required to resign all but one of them. Those who, contrary to earlier canon law, enjoyed the incomes of several benefices were to be deprived of them. Provision was made for the repair of church buildings and the adequate supervision and management of hospitals. As to ordination, no one was to be promoted to the diaconate before his twenty-third year or to the priesthood before his twenty-fifth year. Much attention was paid to education in preparation for the priesthood. This was not new, but was now extended and provided for more adequately. Every cathedral and metropolitan church was to have near it a college or seminary for training boys for the clergy and specific measures were taken to ensure adequate financial support. All in holy orders were to be appointed to definite posts, so that the wandering, impoverished cleric might disappear. The ancient custom of provincial synods was reinforced, and it was directed that they be held at least every third year. Similarly, the traditional visitation, by travel, of his entire diocese by the bishop or those delegated by him to the task, was reaffirmed and was commanded to be made completely at least once in two years. Bishops and parish priests were to preach and were to explain the sacraments to their congregations in the vernacular. Private confession to priests was continued, but, unless commuted by the bishop, in the case of public sin the rebuke was to be public. Bishops were admonished to live frugally and not to use the property of the Church to enrich their relatives. The prohibition of clerical concubinage was renewed.

The authority of bishops within their dioceses was strengthened and some of the limitations which had gradually weakened it were annulled. None, whether regular or secular, could preach in a diocese without the bishop's license, a decree directed especially against the friars, who had wandered about, preaching as they wished, often without even nominal regard for episcopal jurisdiction. Similarly, within his diocese only the bishop had the right to confer ordinations. Candidates for benefices within the dioceses, even if presented by a Papal nuncio, were not to be admitted unless they were examined by the bishop and found worthy. To correct the trend which had made cathedral chapters largely independent of the bishops with what amounted to episcopal powers, the bishops were now clearly supreme.

The custom which had grown across the centuries of placing monasteries under the immediate protection of the Pope had made for a lamentable lack of discipline and was sharply curtailed. All monasteries were now either to be under the jurisdiction of the bishop or were to be organized into diocesan or provincial orders with their own visitors or general chapters. The heads of orders were commanded to visit their monasteries.

Thus the administrative machinery of the Roman Catholic Church was overhauled and tightened. Territorially, as of old, the area ruled by the Church was governed through dioceses. Now the effective power of each bishop within his diocese was augmented. The system of taxation and administration which had been developed in the Middle Ages by the reformers to enable the Popes to purify the Church and which, beginning with Avignon Popes, had become a source of corruption and scandal was curtailed. The demands of the bishops were so far met as to restore much of the authority that had been taken from them by the Papal curia.

Yet, in principle, and this also, at least in theory, made for administrative efficiency, the authority of the Papacy was stressed. The Pope was expressly declared to be the vicar upon earth of God and Jesus Christ, and all patriarchs, primates, archbishops, and bishops were to promise obedience to him. To the Pope the council left the confirmation of its decrees. In carrying out this mandate, the Pope made clear his position that the council had acted only with his permission, and reaffirmed his authority by commanding all prelates to observe the decrees, by admonishing the Emperor-elect and all Christian kings and princes to assist in their enforcement, and by reserving to his See all right of interpretation.

The Council of Trent marks an epoch in the history of the Roman Catholic Church. The centuries since it met are rightly called post-Tridentine. Through it, as far as any ecclesiastical assembly could bring that about, the Roman Catholic Church put its house in order and girded itself for combat with the Protestants and for the pursuance of its world mission. It so defined its dogmas that no room was left for such distinctive Protestant convictions as salvation by faith alone and the priesthood of all believers. It cleared the ground for dealing with the moral corruption of which its own sons as well as Protestants had complained. It made its structure more effective. In doing so it scrapped much of the machinery that had mushroomed from the measures of the reforming Popes of the Middle Ages. It so far yielded to the demands of the episcopate of Spain, France, and Germany that it revived and augmented the authority of the bishops in their dioceses. While, by a close vote, the council seemed to come out against the claim that each bishop rules directly by divine right and not by authority delegated by the Pope, the Pope did not press the point. Yet on paper the authority which the Popes had long claimed was recognized. While not expressly disavowed, the theory urged in the preceding century which would have subordinated the Popes to ecumenical councils was in practice repudiated. No recognition was given to the claims of secular princes, including the kings of Spain, Portugal, and France, to control the Church and its hierarchy within their domains.

The way was cleared to put the Roman Catholic Church in fighting trim. While still containing a majority of those who bore the Christian name, it embraced only a small minority of the peoples of the earth. As the centuries passed, it was even more tightly integrated under the Pope. It continued to be a minority, but a minority whose leaders were intent upon the spiritual conquest of mankind. However, it had become more emphatically the Roman Catholic Church and its heart-land was more clearly Latin Europe, that region which had been assimilated to imperial Rome.

The Further Progress of the Catholic Reformation

The reforming decrees of the Council of Trent were not permitted to become empty words. The leaders of the Catholic Reformation who were responsible for them regarded them as mandatory. Given direction and added momentum by them, to no small degree the Catholic Reformation put them into effect and swept on into lands which thus far had been but little affected by it. Many of the old evils were chronic, as they had been for centuries, and were never completely eliminated. Successive Popes found it necessary to inveigh against them. Moreover, Papal administrative control of the Church was largely blocked by the crown and national particularism in Spain, Portugal, France, and their colonial possessions, as well as in some lesser states. Philip II published the decrees, but with the reservation that he was doing so "without prejudice to his royal rights". There were long delays in gaining acceptance of them in France, and in Germany only the Catholic princes acceded to them. In the course of the seventeenth century the reforming impulse began to wane in Spain and Portugal. Yet, viewing Europe as a whole, the Catholic Reformation continued, made itself felt in new territories, and in some countries, notably France, did not reach its peak until late in the seventeenth and early in the eighteenth century. While in the eighteenth century the Roman Catholic Church was faced by a mounting series of new threats, never again did it suffer so severely as it had before the sixteenth century from the kind of corruption against which the Catholic Reformation had been a reaction.

Some of the ways in which the decrees of the Council of Trent were carried out we have already noted. The index of books prohibited to Catholics was modified. A catechism was compiled, partly on the model of the one drawn up by Peter Canisius, and was translated into several vernaculars. The missal and breviary were reworked. The latter was given a drastic revision. Many of the lives of the saints formerly in it were excised and more readings from the Scriptures were added. A corrected edition of the Vulgate was prepared and published. All these had Papal authority. Worship in the churches was improved. Substantial progress was achieved in the education of the secular clergy. Notable was the founding in Rome of colleges for the training of priests from a number of countries and special groups. The last quarter of the sixteenth century saw the inauguration in that city of a German college, a Hungarian college, an English college, and a Greek college. There were also a college for the Armenians, one for the Maronites, and one for converts from Judaism and Islam. All these were largely under the direction of the Jesuits. For them a central teaching institution, the Roman College, later the Gregorian University, was founded, and in it Bellarmine and other distinguished Jesuits lectured.

Further Vitality in Italy

In Italy the Roman Catholic Church continued to give evidence of vigour in the emergence of additional religious orders. In 1732 Alphonsus Maria Liguori founded the Redemptorists (officially the Congregation of the Most Holy Redeemer). This was at Amalfi. The purpose was "to preach the word of God to the poor." The order conducted missions and retreats and eventually had a wide spread. In 1720 Paul Francis Danei, better known as Paul of the Cross (1694–1775), a native of the Genoese Republic, drew the rule for the Passionists, an order which received Papal approval in 1741. It was especially devoted to the passion of Christ, and combined the contemplative life of the Carthusians with the active missionary life of the Jesuits.

The Catholic Reformation in Germany, Switzerland, Poland, and Hungary

As we have suggested, the Catholic Reformation was given a marked impulse in Germany by one of the early Jesuits, Peter Canisius. His work was reinforced and continued by other members of his Society. They established colleges and residences in several centres. Clergy trained by them in Germany and Rome spread through the Empire, bringing improvement in morals and enhancing zeal. In 1564 Duke Albert V of Bavaria (1550–1579) and several prelates decided to observe the decrees of the Council of Trent. Fresh schools were begun and entrusted to Jesuits and youths were forbidden to attend Protestant universities. Although from a Protestant family, Balthazar von Dernbach, the prince-abbot of the territory which included the ancient foundation of Fulda, associated with the name of the great English missionary to the Germans, Boniface, aided by Jesuits and those trained by him and in spite of opposition which fought him for three decades, largely purged his domains of Protestantism and enforced discipline in the various monastic houses. Assisted by the Abbot of Fulda, and encouraged by the Trentine decrees, numbers of the Benedictine abbeys in Germany came together in a union for the better observance of discipline. A similar movement centered around the Benedictine abbey of Melk or Melek in the diocese of Passau. In Austria Peter Canisius was a pioneer in reinvigourating the Roman Catholic Church and combatting Protestantism. The movement was aided by the Hapsburg Emperors, Ferdinand I, Maximilian II, and Rudolf II.

In Switzerland the Jesuits and Capuchins headed the Catholic Reformation and held large sections to the Roman Catholic Church. On the Italian side of the Alps Borromeo, while Archbishop of Milan, made extensive and arduous journeys into the mountain valleys, combatted Protestantism, and improved the quality of Catholic life.

In Poland, Stanislas Hosius, who had studied in Italy with the future Gregory XIII and in 1549 became Bishop of Chelmno, was a pioneer in the Catholic Reformation. The king, Sigismund II, promptly enforced the Trentine decrees. They were confirmed by a synod in 1574. The Jesuits were in the fore front of the Catholic revival. Peter Canisius was there for a time in 1558. The first Polish Jesuit college was founded in 1565 and this was followed rapidly by the inauguration of others. The rising tide of Protestantism which had threatened to overwhelm the land was swept back and Poland became one of the bulwarks of the Roman Catholic Church.

For a time it had seemed that Hungary might go over to Protestantism. In part because of the Jesuits, Protestants were reduced to minorities and the Roman Catholic Church was purified and strengthened.

THE CATHOLIC REFORMATION IN FRANCE

The Catholic revival was slower to gain substantial headway in France than in Spain or Italy. As we have seen, early in the sixteenth century there were stirrings of reform, some of them in high ecclesiastical and aristocratic circles and in the University of Paris. Moreover, it was at the University of Paris that the nucleus of the Society of Jesus came into being, although not through Frenchmen. However, what are usually known as the wars of religion racked the land. They did not end until the 1590's. While the kingdom was in such turmoil, Catholic Reform was retarded.

Yet in France the Catholic Reformation had a luxuriant even if somewhat belated fruitage. It began in the sixteenth century and came to a climax in France's heyday as the dominant power in Western Europe, during the reign of the *Grand Monarque,* Louis XIV (1643–1715). As in Spain, the peak of vigour in the Church roughly paralleled that in literature, art, and prominence in the international scene.

The Society of Jesus spread rapidly. About 1550 Jesuits among the students in the University of Paris were gathered into the Paris residence of the Bishops of Clermont and there began what was known as the Collège de Clermont, which soon developed into a school. They met bitter opposition from the faculty of theology of the university, the Sorbonne, for the latter were champions of Gallicanism and the conciliar tradition and were critical of the support given by the Jesuits to Papal authority. The Sorbonne also deemed the immaculate conception of the Virgin Mary to be a matter of faith, a dogma to which the Jesuits were not yet prepared to agree. Moreover, the Sorbonne denounced the teaching of a leading Jesuit that the pains of purgatory might not be of more than ten years' duration. In spite of opposition, before the end of the seventeenth century numbers of Jesuit colleges had been established in France, a Jesuit university had been begun, and Jesuit preachers were attracting large congregations. The attempted assassination (1594) of Henry IV by a former student in the Collège de Clermont precipitated an anti-Jesuit storm and led to the expulsion of the Society from Paris and several other cities. Yet in 1603 they were restored by an edict of Henry IV, and a Jesuit became the confessor of that king and tutor of his successor, Louis XIII. Between 1606 and 1640 forty-seven new Jesuit colleges were begun in France.

The Catholic Reformation was early stimulated by other new monastic movements, some of them from abroad and some of them indigenous. In the 1570's Italian Capuchins came, established houses, and quickly gained popularity and recruits. Early among the latter was one of the highly placed men of the court. Before 1600 the Cistercians were brought back to their primitive rule and the Benedictines complied with the decree of the Council of Trent which called for the grouping of their houses in assemblies that could help enforce discipline. Not far from 1593 the Congregation of Christian Doctrine was founded at Avignon. It was composed of secular priests who were to give themselves to teaching the catechism to the rank and file of Catholics, thus raising the level of intelligent Christian living. One branch of the new movement eventually became an order of regulars and another modelled itself on the Roman Oratory of Pierre de Bérulle.

Pierre de Bérulle (1575–1629), in later life a cardinal, was the pioneer of what was known as the French School of mysticism. Reacting against the current humanism with its optimism about man and strongly influenced by Augustine, he stressed the sovereignty of God, the depravity of fallen human nature, the complete dependence of man on God, and the wonder of the incarnation. Indeed, when he was only seventeen years of age, while assisting at Christmas matins and mass, he had a vision which brought him vivid insight into the significance of the birth of Christ. This was repeated after his ordination as priest, when he was making a retreat with the Jesuits. A diligent student of Paul's epistles and *The Gospel according to John,* he sought to subject himself fully to the Word made flesh and to the Virgin Mary, "the Mother of God."

Following Bérulle, the French School stressed devotion to the Word made flesh, the Augustinian conception of grace, dedication to Jesus Christ both in his humanity and in his divinity, and to the Virgin Mary. To have no other being or life but in Jesus, the French School said, the Christian must be rid of all that is of himself and of the fallen Adam within him.

A warm admirer of Augustine and Thomas Aquinas, Bérulle found especial spiritual kinship with his older contemporaries, Teresa of Avila and Philip Neri, and introduced to France both the Discalced Carmelites and the Oratory. He was also active in political affairs.

Bérulle had a widespread and expanding influence. Many Jesuits were partly shaped by him. Even more striking was his contribution through his disciple, the second Superior of the French Oratory, Charles de Condren (1588–1641).

Attracted at an early age to the priesthood, Condren studied at the Sorbonne and in 1614 was ordained priest. He wrote little or nothing, abstaining, so he said, "from the love of Jesus Christ," but gave himself to the mission of "illuminating souls." He stressed the necessity of annihilating within us our evil inclinations and even ourselves that we may acknowledge our nothingness before God. One outcome of his teaching and that of Bérulle was devotion to the Child Jesus and to the Sacred Heart of Jesus, a devotion which was to have a growing popular clientele.

One of Condren's followers and a member of the Oratory was Jean-Jacques Olier (1608–1657). In his student days Olier had shared in the dissipations in Paris common to that class. However, he was converted and was ordained priest (1633). He taught that the Christian should unite himself to Jesus by clinging to him. Olier also learned much from Francis de Sales and Vincent de Paul, of whom we are to hear more in a moment.

Intimately associated with the French Oratory were efforts to provide better training for the priesthood; obviously, it would be through priests, especially the seculars who served in the parishes, that the rank and file of the population would be reached by the awakening. These efforts were reinforced by the Council of Trent, for that body, as we have seen, stressed the foundation of seminaries. The French Oratory founded numbers of colleges in which philosophy and theology were taught and which were to rival the schools of the Jesuits. Olier was one of a group of Oratorians who began a seminary near Paris. He himself founded a seminary in the parish of St. Sulpice in Paris of which he was the priest, and laboured for the conversion of one of the worst quarters of that city. He inaugurated seminaries in the provinces and to serve them created the Society of St. Sulpice.

Even more famous than Olier was Vincent de Paul (1576 or 1580–1660). He not only founded seminaries but was also the initiator of other enterprises, including the Congregation of the Priests of the Mission. Unlike most of the leaders of the Catholic Reformation, for generally they were of aristocratic stock, Vincent de Paul was the son of peasants. Spiritually he was deeply indebted to Bérulle and Condren and must be counted among their disciples. Ordained in 1600, five years later he was captured by Turkish pirates and sold as a slave. However, he converted his master, an apostate from the Christian faith, and in 1607 escaped with him. Ever after he had a compassionate heart for galley slaves and for Christians who, captured by Barbary corsairs, were in servitude in North Africa. He did what he could to relieve the physical and spiritual sufferings of the former and to ransom the latter.

Deeply concerned for the spiritual nurture of the Catholic masses and the conversion of Protestants, Vincent de Paul founded (1625) the Congregation of Priests of the Mission. It was an association of seculars, but eventually took on some of the aspects of an order. Beginning in a small way with the approval of the Archbishop of Paris (1626), within the more than thirty years that Vincent de Paul led it, it grew to large dimensions. Before long its headquarters were established at the house of St. Lazare on the outskirts of Paris, and its members were, accordingly, often called Lazarists. Commonly, too, they were alternately known as Vincentians. Not only did the Lazarists carry on missions among the masses. They also conducted retreats for candidates for holy orders and conferences for clergymen, better to equip them for the cure of souls. From this arose seminaries for the preparation of priests, and when in 1789 the storm of the Revolution broke over France, about a third of the seminaries in the kingdom were conducted by the spiritual sons of Vincent de Paul. Within the lifetime of their founder, Lazarists were going as missionaries to other lands.

Not content with these wide-ranging and arduous labours, Vincent de Paul founded (1633) the Sisters (or Daughters) of Charity, also known as Servants of the Sick. As the latter designation indicates, they dedicated themselves to nursing. He called into being the Ladies of Charity, recruited from the nobility, for the care of the ill. He founded in Paris a home for the aged and a general hospital. He organized relief for sufferers from the Thirty Years' War (1618–1648) and from the civil war known as the Fronde (1648–1652). He stimulated reform movements in several of the older religious orders of France. He also mingled in international politics.

Like many other mystics, of abounding energy and superb organizing and administrative gifts, Vincent de Paul was inspired and sustained in his colossal labours by the love of God, devotion to Christ, and unhurried meditation and prayer. His great passion was the "illumination of souls."

Vincent de Paul was indebted not only to Bérulle and Condren but also to his older contemporary, Francis de Sales (1567–1622). Of the aristocracy of Savoy, Francis de Sales had the title of Bishop of Geneva. By the time he was given the post, Geneva was in the hands of the Reformed, for he was also contemporary with Beza, Calvin's successor in that city. Although he visited Geneva and attempted to win Beza to the Roman Catholic Church, Francis de Sales had to make his headquarters elsewhere. Within such of his diocese as was accessible to him, he inspired priests and laboured personally to raise the level of Christian living and to convert Protestants. He founded the Institute of the Visitation, made up of women. However, he is best remembered for his discourses and writings on the life of the spirit. Here he blazed a trail which was distinctly his own. He stressed the love of God and loving fidelity to His will. Issuing from a heart overflowing with the love of God and men, his writings have nurtured both Catholics and Protestants. He has been classed among the devout humanists.

Of the Berullian school of mysticism and devotion and for a time a member of the Oratory was John Eudes (1601–1680). At fourteen he took the vow of chastity. In his youth he was distressed by the indifference of the clergy, the neglect of church structures, and the slovenliness of church services. In 1623, in his early twenties, he joined the Oratory, and hoped to improve conditions by founding seminaries and so furthering the training of a better corps of clergy. An eloquent preacher, he held missions for the masses, sometimes out of doors, conducted religious services with pomp and dignity, organized leagues to fight blasphemy and duelling, and presided at the burning of immoral books and pictures. He was the creator of the Congregation of the Good Shepherd for the care of fallen women. When its superior general refused to permit him to found seminaries, he left the Oratory and (1643) initiated what were popularly known as the Eudists. The Eudists were made up of secular priests, postulants, and lay brothers, who did not take the stringent vows of most religious orders, but were organized into a society under the joint names of Jesus and Mary. They began and conducted seminaries for the preparation for the priesthood and, like the founder, conducted missions. True to the tradition of Bérulle and Condren, to whom he owed much, John Eudes furthered the mystical life by interior devotion to Jesus and Mary. He is credited with having inaugurated the liturgical worship of the Sacred Hearts of Jesus and Mary which was to spread widely in succeeding generations.

The devotion to the Sacred Heart of Jesus was especially connected with the name of Margaret Mary Alacoque (1647–1690). To her came what she profoundly believed to be visions of Christ, especially in 1675, in which he allowed her to rest her head on his heart and commanded her to propagate that devotion, a recognition of his incarnate love by gratitude, penitence, and frequent communion.

In 1713 Louis-Marie Grignion de Montfort founded the Missionaries of the Company of Mary. Recruited from secular priests, they promoted the recital of the rosary and held missions and retreats under the protection of the Virgin Mary.

The list of those who were at once the products and the stimulators and shapers of the Catholic Reformation in France could be greatly lengthened. It would include a number of Benedictine abbesses who revived the religious life for women. High on it would be the name of John Baptist de la Salle (1651–1719) who, impressed with the paucity of schools and the need of teachers, resigned his comfortable post as canon in the Cathedral of Rheims, begged funds to found schools, opened (1684) a normal school, developed an educational method which earned him the title of "father of modern pedagogy," a designation, incidentally, which could be accorded to several men who were inspired by either the Protestant or the Catholic Reformation, and founded the Institute of the Brothers of the Christian Schools. On the list would also go the name of the nobleman Francis le Clerc du Tremblay (1577–1638), known by his name in religion as Father Joseph. A brilliant scholar, in his early twenties he joined the Capuchins, thus committing himself to humility, asceticism, and the life of the spirit. He shared in the reform of the Benedictines, assisted the Bernardines, a reformed branch of the Cistercians, established numerous houses of the Capuchins, was a zealous spiritual director, and wrote an *Introduction to the Spiritual Life by an Easy Method of Prayer* which was an adaptation of Loyola's *Spiritual Exercises.* He is also remembered for his activity in politics. He helped to put an end to a civil war in 1616 and laboured long though without success to unite Western Europe in a crusade against the Turks. As a trusted counsellor of Richelieu (1585–1642), who was dominant in the state during much of the reign of Louis XIII, he strengthened the chief minister's resolution to curb the Huguenots and persevere in the Thirty Years' War.

A development from the Catholic Reformation in France which was to culminate in bitter controversy and schism was associated with the name of Cornelius Jansen (1585–1638), Bishop of Ypres. As a student Jansen had been in the University of Louvain, where a dispute was raging between the Jesuits and those who held to a strict Augustinianism. Through life he continued to be at verbal sword's points with the sons of Loyola. Eventually he was professor of theology at Louvain, where the Society of Jesus had a rival theological faculty. Towards the end of his life he produced a book, *Augustinus,* intended to be a digest of Augustine's teaching and setting forth his own views. It was only two years before his death that he was made Bishop of Ypres.

In important respects Jansen seemed to be a Calvinist, for he stressed the divine predestination of those who were to be saved, but he insisted that he was no Protestant. He was against a moralism more akin to Stoicism than Christianity which he believed that he saw about him. He emphasized personal religious experience, the direct relation of the individual soul to its Maker which might come by a sudden conversion. Yet he rejected justification by faith as the Protestants understood it and held that the full Christian life was possible only through the Roman Catholic Church.

Jansen's views won an extensive following. One of his disciples, Antoine Arnauld, wrote a book on *Frequent Communion* which evoked a storm of criticism. Another leader of the school, Pasquier Quesnel, wrote *Réflexions morales sur le Nouveau Testament,* which had a wide circulation as an aid to devotion but which was also denounced. A convent at Port Royal became a Jansenist centre. Notable among the Jansenists was Blaise Pascal (1623–1662), a mathematical genius who had a sudden conversion through contact with them and especially through a sister who became a member of the Port Royal community. In his *Provincial Letters* Pascal came out with a brilliant defense of Arnauld against the Jesuits.

Eventually Jansen was condemned by the Roman Catholic Church. In 1653 Pope Innocent X declared heretical several propositions from the *Augustinus*. In 1661 the general assembly of the clergy endorsed an anti-Jansenist formula which all the clergy were required to sign. Four years later a similar formula was issued by the Pope. Under it four bishops were tried, but since several other bishops rallied to their support a compromise was reached under which Jansenism continued. Under pressure from the Jesuits Louis XIV asked the Pope to leave no doubt about the status of Jansenism. In 1713 the Pope responded in the bull *Unigenitus,* which ruled out Jansenist teachings. The quarrel continued, for many regarded Papal intervention as a violation of the liberty of the Church in France. Even the Cardinal Archbishop of Paris protested and appealed to a general council. Some of the Jansenists found refuge in the Netherlands where many Roman Catholics had long been in sympathy with their views. There, early in the eighteenth century, partly because of Jansenist convictions and partly out of antagonism to the Jesuits, several thousand of the laity and clergy broke with Rome and formed what is known as an Old Catholic Church with its Archbishop of Utrecht as its ranking ecclesiastic.

Famous also was a controversy arising from the mysticism of a remarkable woman and an equally remarkable man. Madame Guyon (1648–1717), a highly neurotic woman of great energy and charm, had an unhappy married life from which she was released by her husband's death before she was thirty. Partly under a Barnabite spiritual director she developed a type of mysticism which attracted many, among them the high-born Fénelon (1651–1715), Archbishop of Cambrai and tutor to the heir apparent. Fénelon modified Madame Guyon's ideas after his own pattern. In it Neoplatonism mingled with the Christian faith. He became a spiritual counsellor to many. The famous preacher, Bossuet (1627–1704), one of whose main dreams, incidentally, was the conversion of Protestants, vigorously criticized both Madame Guyon and Fénelon. The former was imprisoned and then was released on the condition that she would henceforth live on her son's estate under careful episcopal supervision. Bossuet declared dangerous some features of Fénelon's writings. Fénelon appealed to Rome. Feeling ran high in France, for both Bossuet and Fénelon had their ardent partisans. Louis XIV urged the Pope to act. The result was the Papal condemnation of several of Fénelon's views. Fénelon at once submitted, was exiled by the king to his diocese, and there lived until his death, faithfully performing his episcopal duties.

SUMMARY AND PROSPECT

Through the great reformation which swept across it in the two and a half centuries between the latter part of the fifteenth century and the second quarter of the eighteenth century, the Roman Catholic Church was reinvigorated and was cleansed of some of the worst of the evils which had threatened its existence. Moral abuses remained to challenge the zeal of earnest spirits and in many places much of formalism and lassitude persisted. By the end of the seventeenth century the fresh burst of energy began to show signs of having passed its peak. Yet the sixteenth and seventeenth centuries were ones of extraordinary vitality. Out of it came the prodigious geographic expansion of which we are to hear more in a later chapter.

What would happen as this revived and expanding Roman Catholic Church met an aggressive and expanding Protestantism? We have already seen that, largely through the Society of Jesus, the Roman Catholic Church won the victory in some lands which were wavering, but where Protestants were still in the minority. This was especially true in Bavaria, some other sections of Germany, and Poland. In the first half of the seventeenth century the struggle between the Roman Catholic Church and Protestantism contributed to one of the most exhausting armed conflicts in the history of Europe. Waged intermittently between 1618 and 1648, it is known as the Thirty Years' War. Through it the Roman Catholic Church achieved some gains, but after it the territorial boundaries in Europe between that church and Protestantism remained substantially unchanged. The western part of the continent was permanently divided between these two wings of the Christianity of the Occident.

It is a strange and tragic fact that the greatest revival which had thus far been experienced in the religion which has at its very heart the kind of sacrificial and self-giving love seen in the humility of the incarnation and the non-resistant suffering on the cross and whose primary commands are love for God and neighbour, was a major factor in bringing on an exhausting war and intensified the resolution, the bitterness, and the hatred with which the war was waged. Here is high-lighted one of the paradoxes with which the course of Christianity has been marked. Men fired with what they believe to be devotion to the will of God as seen in Christ have been nerved to prolonged and mortal combat, not only with non-Christians, but also with one another. In the Thirty Years' War other factors, of palpably un-Christian and even anti-Christian origin, were mixed and became more prominent as the struggle dragged out its weary length to an only partially decisive conclusion.

Yet out of the tragedy of these years there emerged, largely from regions which had been most badly laid waste and from minorities of passive sufferers, movements which were to prepare the way for even greater awakenings than the Reformation and which were to issue in enterprises world-wide in ambition and eventually in extent for the alleviation or elimination of many of the chronic ills of mankind.

To that story we now turn. Only the Thirty Years' War and its early aftermath to about the year 1750 will be covered in the succeeding chapter. To the far outreach in the two centuries which followed that year reference will be made from time to time in later stages of our narrative.

Selected Bibliography

THE ROMAN CATHOLIC REFORMATION IN GENERAL

P. Janelle, *The Catholic Reformation* (Milwaukee, The Bruce Publishing Co., 1941, pp. xiv, 397). An excellent comprehensive account from a Roman Catholic viewpoint, slanted favourably towards the Jesuits.

IGNATIUS LOYOLA AND THE SOCIETY OF JESUS

P. Dudon, *St. Ignatius of Loyola,* translated by W. J. Young (Milwaukee, The Bruce Publishing Co., 1949, pp. xiv, 484). By a Jesuit, based upon extensive and prolonged research.

M. P. Harney, *The Jesuits in History. The Society of Jesus through Four Centuries* (New York, The America Press, 1941, pp. xvi, 513). A useful, but somewhat uncritical review by a Jesuit.

H. D. Sedgwick, *Ignatius Loyola* (New York, The Macmillan Co., 1923, pp. xiii, 399). Well written, based on extensive research, sympathetically objective, by a non-Roman Catholic.

THE SPANISH MYSTICS

Saint John of the Cross, Doctor of the Church. The Complete Works, translated and edited by E. A. Peers from the critical edition of P. Silverio de Santa Teresa (London, Burns, Oates & Washbourne, 3 vols., 1947).

E. A. Peers, *Spanish Mysticism, a Preliminary Survey* (London, Methuen & Co., 1924, pp. xi, 277). By the outstanding English specialist: contains extensive excerpts from the works of the mystics.

E. A. Peers, *Studies of the Spanish Mystics* (London, The Sheldon Press, 2 vols., 1927, 1930). The best survey in English.

The Complete Works of Saint Teresa of Jesus, translated from the critical edition of P. Silverio de Santa Teresa and edited by E. A. Peers (New York, Sheed & Ward, 3 vols., 1946).

THE ROMAN CATHOLIC REFORMATION IN ITALY

C. Orsenigo, *Life of St. Charles Borromeo,* translated by R. Kraw (St. Louis, B. Herder & Co., 1943, pp. lx, 390). A semi-popular, laudatory biography.

L. Pastor, *The History of the Popes from the Close of the Middle Ages,* Vols. VI–XXXV (St. Louis, B. Herder & Co., 1902, and London, Kegan Paul, Trench, Trübner & Co., 1902–1949). These volumes, by an eminent Roman Catholic scholar, cover the years embraced in this chapter.

THE COUNCIL OF TRENT

H. J. Schroeder, *Canons and Decrees of the Council of Trent: Original Text with English Translation* (St. Louis, B. Herder & Co., 1941, pp. xxxiii, 608). A useful reference volume.

THE ROMAN CATHOLIC REFORMATION IN GERMANY

J. Brodrick, *Saint Peter Canisius, S.J., 1521–1597* (London, Sheed & Ward, 1939, pp. xiii, 859). Sympathetically written by a Jesuit.

THE ROMAN CATHOLIC REFORMATION IN FRANCE

H. Bremond, *A Literary History of Religious Thought in France,* translated by K. L. Montgomery (London, Society for Promoting Christian Knowledge, 3 vols., 1928–1936). Confined almost entirely to the seventeenth century, based on extensive research and with copious quotations from the sources.

P. Pourrat, *Christian Spirituality. Later Developments. Part I. From the Renaissance to Jansenism,* translated by W. H. Mitchell (Vol. III of the larger work. New York, P. J. Kenedy and Sons, 1927, pp. xii, 405). A standard work by a Roman Catholic; well documented.

L. Rea, *The Enthusiasts of Port-Royal* (New York, Charles Scribner's Sons, 1912, pp. xiv, 354). Sympathetic, scholarly.

E. K. Sanders, *S. François de Sales 1567–1622* (New York, The Macmillan Co., 1928, pp. x, 304). A sympathetic biographical account, based on the sources.

W. J. Sparrow Simpson, *A Study of Bossuet* (London, Society for Promoting Christian Knowledge, 1937, pp. viii, 222). Thoughtful and vigorous.

Chapter 39

THE CONFUSED ARBITRAMENT OF ARMS
AND THE AFTERMATH

The Roman Catholic Church, reformed and resurgent, pressed forward to reclaim the territories which it had lost to Protestantism. One result was the Thirty Years' War. In this confused and titanic struggle, as we have just now suggested, the religious conflict was only one factor. Rivalries between ambitious monarchs, generals, and adventurers, reinforced by burgeoning national loyalties, entered and may have been more important. Had the religious element not been present, they alone might have produced the war. Yet the contest between Roman Catholics and Protestants was prominent. In general the Roman Catholics won. They regained some ground which was either about to turn Protestant or already had become such. However, they did not succeed in erasing Protestantism. Unlike the movements of the Middle Ages which the Roman Catholic Church branded as heretical, Protestant Christianity persisted. Indeed, from areas and groups which suffered most from the war and the Roman Catholic advance, tides of life issued which in the eighteenth, nineteenth, and twentieth centuries were to be of major importance in the world-wide extension of Protestantism.

The Setting of the Thirty Years' War

As we saw in the previous chapter, Luther had been dead only about twenty years and Calvin's body was scarcely cold in its grave when the Roman Catholics began to rewin much of the debatable ground which they had lost in Germany and its dependent regions. In Bavaria, in the territories ruled by the Abbot of Fulda, the Archbishop of Mainz, and the Archbishop of Trier, the Catholic princes were eliminating the Protestants. The principle of *cujus regio, ejus religio* embodied in the Peace of Augsburg (1555) gave legality to their measures, for by it each prince was to determine the faith of his subjects. An aggressive Roman Catholic regime was also bringing distress to Protestants in

Austria. The princes were aided by the Jesuits and the progress of the Catholic Reformation in renewing the vigour of the old church. In the territory under the Archbishop of Cologne, in 1582 the incumbent, Gebhard von Truchsess, adopted the Reformed faith, wished to marry, and proposed to continue to rule and to take his subjects with him. One of the seven electors of the Holy Roman Empire, he was an important personage. Had he succeeded, the Roman Catholic cause would have been given a serious blow. However, he was acting in defiance of the Peace of Augsburg, he was placed under the ban of the Empire, a rebellion broke out in his domains, aid came to it from Bavaria, most of the Protestant princes stood idly by, partly because they were Lutheran and he was Reformed, and he was defeated and driven from his see. In 1608, at the imperial Diet Catholics demanded that the terms of the Peace of Augsburg be strictly observed and that ecclesiastical properties which had become Protestant after 1552 be restored to the old faith. Enforcement would mean heavy losses to Protestantism. In 1607 Maximilian, Duke of Bavaria, was given an imperial mandate to deal with the free city, Donauwörth. Overwhelmingly Protestant, it contained Catholic monasteries and smouldering antagonism had broken into flames when in 1606 a Catholic religious procession had been stoned. Maximilian kept Donauwörth under his rule and, in violation of the Peace of Augsburg, suppressed Protestant worship.

The Roman Catholic gains had been chiefly in South Germany and in the Rhine Valley. Here, in contrast with the nearly solidly Lutheran North, the Reformed Churches were strong. The Peace of Augsburg had given no recognition to the latter, but only to Roman Catholics and Lutherans. The division between Reformed and Lutherans weakened the Protestant forces.

The Donauwörth episode helped to draw together several of the Protestant princes. In 1608, headed by the Elector Palatine, Frederick IV, who was of the Reformed wing, they organized themselves into the Evangelical Union. Roman Catholics, led by Maximilian, aligned themselves in what was eventually known as the Catholic League.

The situation was complicated by economic distress, by heightened sensitiveness among both Catholics and Protestants which vented itself on supposed witches, and by the intrigues of the French rulers, who were quite willing to take advantage of the divisions among the German princes to extend their borders into what was still the Holy Roman Empire.

The Outbreak and Course of the Thirty Years' War

Hostility broke out into open war in Bohemia in 1618. There Protestantism was strong and was resentful of the rule of the Catholic Hapsburgs. In May, 1618, a group of Protestant nobles flung two Hapsburg regents from a high window in Prague and began open rebellion. In 1619, after the death of his cousin, Ferdinand, Archduke of Styria, became head of the Hapsburgs, Holy Roman Emperor-elect, and King of Bohemia. He had been educated by the Jesuits, was an ardent Roman Catholic, and on dynastic and religious grounds was determined to make himself master of Bohemia and eliminate Protestantism. The revolting Bohemians chose as their king the Elector Palatine, Frederick V, son of Frederick IV and of the daughter of William of Orange, "the Silent," son-in-law of James I of England, and an adherent of the Reformed faith. The Lutheran princes were not minded to come to the support of the Reformed Elector Palatine. James I wished not to become embroiled and did not go further than permit English "volunteers" to participate. Ferdinand was aided by Maximilian of Bavaria and Spanish troops under the Walloon General, Tilly. The hapless Frederick was driven from Bohemia, Protestant properties were confiscated, and the vigorous and ruthless eradication of Protestantism was begun. Spanish troops overran Frederick's hereditary possession, the Palatinate, the title of elector and much of the territory were given to the staunchly Catholic Maximilian, and Catholicism was restored and enforced. Concurrently, the eradication of Protestantism was proceeding in Austria. One stage of the war was ended (late in 1622 and early in 1623) and the Roman Catholic cause was in the ascendant.

The next stage of the conflict involved North-west Germany and Denmark. In North-west Germany, in violation of a provision of the Peace of Augsburg to which many Protestant princes had declined to assent, much ecclesiastical property had become Protestant, including several bishoprics and many monasteries. Some of the Protestant princes drew together in defense against anticipated attack. The year 1623 saw the defeat of a leading Protestant prince by Tilly. In 1625 King Christian IV of Denmark and Norway entered the fray. This was after prolonged and complicated diplomatic negotiations in which, among others, England and France were involved. The Emperor Ferdinand called to his aid a remarkable adventurer, Wallenstein. Born a Protestant, Wallenstein had nominally become a Catholic and had profited by the acquisition of confiscated Protestant estates in Bohemia. Utterly upscrupulous, he had no deep religious convictions. In 1626 Christian IV was defeated by Tilly and in the following two years, partly through Wallenstein, Catholic forces overran much of Protestant North Germany.

Now, in March, 1629, the triumphant Catholics, insisting upon the enforcement of the Peace of Augsburg, obtained an imperial "Edict of Restitution" which ordered that all ecclesiastical property which had been alienated by Protestants since 1552 once more become Catholic. This led to the return to Catholics of several bishoprics, scores of monasteries, and hundreds of parish churches. The Edict of Restitution also approved of the exclusion of Protestants from the territories of Catholic rulers and gave no countenance to Protestants who did not adhere to the Augsburg Confession. Thus the Reformed as well as other non-Lutheran Protestants were denied toleration.

This triumph of the anti-Protestant forces was frustrated by two developments. The victorious Catholics were divided by internal dissensions which resulted, among other things, in the dismissal of Wallenstein, and Gustavus Adolphus intervened. Gustavus Adolphus, grandson of Gustavus Vasa, staunchly Lutheran, highly educated, and ambitious, was intent upon making the Baltic a Swedish lake and saw in the Hapsburg advance in the North a threat to this dream. In June, 1630, he landed with an army and drove the Hapsburgs out of Pomerania. In his German enterprise he was aided by the chief minister of France, Richelieu. Catholic though he was, Richelieu was more intent upon the aggrandizement of France than upon the defeat of Protestantism and mixed in the troubled sea of German affairs to gain, if possible, territory and prestige for his king. The leading German Protestant princes did not at first support the Swedish monarch. However, skilful diplomacy and the fear inspired by the capture by Tilly of Protestant Magdeburg (1631) and its sack through horrible atrocities brought the powerful Brandenburg and Saxony to his side. The tide of battle now turned. Gustavus Adolphus defeated Tilly and marched to the Rhine. The Saxons captured Prague. Terrified, the Emperor recalled Wallenstein and that doughty warrior soon defeated the Saxons. Wallenstein, in turn, was soundly beaten by Gustavus Adolphus at Lützen, near Leipzig (November 16, 1632), but in that battle the latter lost his life.

The war, already long, now bogged down into a kind of stalemate. The death of Gustavus Adolphus was a staggering blow to the Protestant cause. The Swedes continued the war, but were overcome by a combination of Spanish and imperial armies (September, 1634). In the meantime (February, 1634) Wallenstein had been removed by assassination by some of his own officers. It had become clear that the Roman Catholics could not regain the overwhelmingly Protestant North Germany and that the Protestants could not hope to become dominant in the prevailing Roman Catholic South Germany. In 1635 peace was made between the Emperor and Saxony. Most of Germany assented to it.

It was Richelieu who further dragged out the war. Eager for French gains at the expense of the Hapsburgs who, ruling in Spain and Austria, menaced French ambitions from both south and north, he sought to take advantage of the divisions in Germany to gain territory. Spain and Sweden also continued to be embroiled. Sweden wished to assure her position on the Baltic. More and more the religious issue faded. Roman Catholic France was in association with Lutheran Sweden. The struggle was a sordid one for power. Germany, divided, was the battle ground. Armies ranged across it devastating large areas of a land that had already been wasted by years of fighting.

THE PEACE OF WESTPHALIA AND THE FIXING OF RELIGIOUS BOUNDARIES

The Peace of Westphalia, October 27, 1648, eventually marked the terminus of the seemingly interminable struggle. Negotiations had long been in progress and a congress of representatives of the interested powers had been at work since 1645. It is significant that the Papacy, while represented, played no such important part in the negotiations as it had in the Middle Ages or even in the preceding century. The time had passed when it could dictate to Western Christendom.

With the territorial aspects of the Peace of Westphalia we are not greatly concerned except as they affected religious boundaries. France was confirmed in her possession of the bishoprics of Metz, Toul, and Verdun, and, at the expense of the Hapsburgs, was given much of Alsace. In Alsace, divided religiously, France was placed under obligation to maintain Catholic worship wherever it had been carried on under the Hapsburgs and was to restore it wherever it had been interrupted by the war. Sweden was given a continuing slice of German territory and a voice in the affairs of the Holy Roman Empire. This, however, did not seriously affect the religious aspects of German life. The branch of the Hohenzollern family which ruled in Brandenburg was awarded additional territory, notably the Bishoprics of Minden and Halberstadt and the Archbishopric of Magdeburg. Since Brandenburg was Protestant, its growth strengthened the Protestant cause. What remained of the Holy Roman Empire of the German Nation was substantially weakened, for its princes were permitted to make alliances with foreign powers and not only Sweden but also France now had a voice in it. However, the prestige of the Hapsburgs who ruled in Austria was such that the title of Holy Roman Emperor in effect became hereditary in that house. Since the Hapsburgs were resolutely Roman Catholic, the office never passed into the possession of Protestants. In connexion with the general European settlement, Spain formally recognized (1648) the independence of Holland, and the Protestant cause was thus reinforced. The Peace of Westphalia gave formal legality to what also had long been tacitly accepted fact, the independence of Switzerland.

What most interests us are the specifically religious phases of the Peace of Westphalia. A settlement was effected which fixed the boundaries between Catholics and Protestants as, with slight modifications, they were to remain. While the terms had to do only with Germany, they were an indication that through Europe the two forms of the faith had reached comparatively stable boundaries. Henceforward in that continent neither made substantial gains at the expense of the other.

In general, the Peace of Westphalia was more favourable to the Protestants than conditions a few years earlier would have warranted. The Catholic counter-advance had reached its height and had slightly retreated. The Reformed were now officially tolerated along with the Lutherans. The Edict of Restitution was in effect annulled, with its attempt to restore to Catholics the ecclesiastical properties which had become Protestant. January 1, 1624, not 1552, was fixed as the date beyond which no ecclesiastical property was to be alienated to Protestants. This left many former Catholic bishoprics, monasteries, and churches in Protestant hands. Yet further Protestant advance was also halted and the debatable West and South-west remained largely Roman Catholic.

While the principle of *cujus regio ejus religio* still had some validity, Catholic princes were required to permit Protestant worship in their realms where it had existed in 1624, and Protestant princes were to do likewise with Catholic worship in their domains. Subjects who were of another faith than that of their ruler were to be permitted to conduct private worship and to educate their children in the religion of the parents. The same provision for reciprocal toleration applied as between Lutherans and Reformed in territories where the ruler was of the opposite form of Protestantism. In a few places Catholics and Protestants worshipped in the same church building, but at different hours.

The major exception to this toleration was in the regions ruled by the Austrian Hapsburgs. Save for the prevailingly Protestant duchies in Silesia, the city of Breslau, and the nobility of Lower Austria, in the domains of the Hapsburgs no Protestants enjoyed the free exercise of their religion.

The year 1624 was also set as determinative for the status of religion in the free cities of the Empire. Those that were then Catholic were to remain so, and those Protestant were to hold to that form of the faith. Cities where Protestantism and Catholicism were about equal in that year were to continue to be mixed religiously.

A curb was placed on Roman Catholic missions among Protestants by the provision that no religious order founded since the Reformation was to be introduced. Obviously, although not by name, directed against the Jesuits, it proved a brake on the activity of the Society to which much of the counter-gains of the Roman Catholic Church had been due.

The religious settlement was not completely satisfactory to either Protestants or Roman Catholics. The Pope condemned it. Yet it proved to be a viable compromise.

ATTEMPTS TO OBTAIN RELIGIOUS UNITY

Could the Christians of Western Europe achieve unity under these new conditions? To many it seemed that whatever of unity had existed had been irretrievably shattered by the Protestant revolt. As we have earlier noted, the true unity among Christians, that of love, had never been realized. Behind the façade of the visible structural unity achieved through the Catholic Church bitter dissensions had been chronic. However, even that façade had now been broken. Not only were Protestants separated from Roman Catholics, but among themselves Protestants were deeply divided. Could inclusive fellowship be achieved, perhaps in some new way, and if not between Roman Catholics and Protestants, at least among the many varieties of Protestantism?

Efforts were not wanting to attain that goal. Roman Catholics continued, but largely in vain, to seek to win Protestants. Some Protestants were adventuring, mainly in new directions, for unity among themselves and a few dreamed and laboured for a reunion of Protestants and Roman Catholics which would be without the sacrifice by either of cherished central convictions.

The outstanding leaders of the Protestant Reformation did not surrender the hope of comprehensive Christian fellowship. Luther and Calvin longed for it. Luther held to the Apostles', Nicene, and Athanasian Creeds as *tria symbola catholica sive ecumenica,* "three catholic or ecumenical symbols," thus stressing a universal church inclusive of all Christians. He affirmed the "communion of saints."

While maintaining that councils of the universal church might err, Luther did not abandon the hope that general councils might be assembled, later ones correcting earlier ones if and when necessary. Calvin believed in both a visible and an invisible Church, the latter made up of all whom God had predestined to eternal life and the former found wherever the Word was purely preached and reverently heard and the sacraments "administered according to the institution of Christ." The Augsburg Confession, the formulation of the faith to which more Lutherans adhered than to any other, declared "that one Holy Church is to continue for ever. Moreover, the Church is the congregation of saints in which the Gospel is rightly taught and the sacraments are rightly administered. And unto the true unity of the Church, it is sufficient to agree concerning the doctrine of the Gospel and the administration of the Sacraments." Similarly among the Reformed Churches, the First Helvetic Confession declared that there is "one holy universal Church, the society and assembly of all the saints, the spotless bride of Christ," and the Second Helvetic Confession said "that there is but one Church which we call Catholic for the reason that it is universal and is spread out through all parts of the world and extends to all times."

We have noted that before the Council of Trent stiffened the official Roman Catholic attitude and made impossible the healing of the breach, there were those among both Roman Catholics and Protestants who laboured to close it. Among them were humanists, including Erasmus, and some of the German rulers, notably the Emperors Charles V, Ferdinand I, and Maximilian II.

In the first generation of Protestant Reformers there were several who worked for solidarity among those who broke with Rome. Discussions were held between the Bohemian Brethren and Luther. Bucer endeavoured to bring Zwingli and the Lutherans together. For a time it looked as if Bullinger and Luther might agree. The large majority of the Waldensees were drawn into fellowship with the Reformed. Although differing on the sacraments and especially upon the fashion in which Christ is present in the Lord's Supper, Calvin and Bullinger reached accord and with them most of the Reformed Churches in Switzerland. Calvin, Farel, and Beza hoped and strove for coöperation with the Lutherans, especially in behalf of the persecuted Protestants in France. Cranmer attempted to induce Melanchthon to come to England, and, as we have seen, several of the Continental reformers of varying views found haven in that realm when, under Edward VI, important changes were being made in the Church of England. Jan Laski (John à Lasco), influential in shaping Protestantism in Poland, was an irenic soul who exerted himself in behalf of accord among Protestants.

Late in the sixteenth and early in the seventeeth century there were efforts for the union of Protestants. The national synods of the French Reformed Church sent emissaries to England, Switzerland, Germany, Denmark, and the Netherlands to see whether steps could be taken towards accomplishing it. In the Netherlands Jacob Arminius suggested a general council as a way of bringing Christians together. David Pareus (1548–1622), a Reformed theologian of Heidelberg, in his *Irenicum* proposed that Protestants seek union against the Roman Catholics through "a regular and free council." Pressure in that direction was often exerted by princes, but more from political expediency than deep religious conviction. Most of it had as its object religious uniformity within their respective realms, but sometimes monarchs and their ministers strove through diplomacy to unite some or all of their fellow-Protestant rulers in a common front against the Roman Catholic menace.

During and after the Thirty Years' War numbers of Protestants sought to bring together their fellow-Protestants and some even dreamed of the union of Protestants and Roman Catholics. Thus John Valentine Andreae (1586–1654) in his picture of an ideal society in his *Christianopolis* maintained that unity in learning and in society could be given by Christianity which "unites men together" and made his confession of faith accord with the creeds on which Roman Catholics and most Protestants were agreed. The Lutheran George Calixtus (1586–1656) whose father had studied under Melanchthon and who himself taught theology at Helmstadt for nearly a third of a century, wished union, even with a reformed Roman Catholic Church, on the basis of the formula put forward by Vincent of Lerins in the fifth century, *"quod semper, quod ubique, quod ab omnibus creditum sum"* ("what has been believed always, everywhere, and by all"). He advocated councils as a means of reaching agreement. We must note, however, that he was far from carrying all of his fellow-Lutherans with him, and that his views provoked a controversy which continued after his death. John Amos Comenius (1592–1670), bishop of the Bohemian Brethren (*Unitas Fratrum*), an exile and refugee from the terrors of the Thirty Years' War which all but extinguished his church, uncrushed by the seeming disaster, a friend of Pareus and Andreae, hoped for the union of all Christians and the integration of all civilization under the leadership of religion. To this end he urged that Christian missions be supported. Hugo Grotius (1583–1645), an Arminian, best remembered for his pioneer treatise on international law, *De Jure Belli et Pacis,* wished the elimination of divisions among Christians and brought out a book on *The Way of Ecclesiastical Peace,* and that in spite of the fact that he was embroiled in theological controversy. The Scot John Durie (Dury) (1596–1680) spent more than half a century of his long life working for the union of Protestants. He accepted reordination from Archbishop Laud, was a member of the Westminster Assembly, wrote pamphlets, carried on an extensive correspondence, travelled widely on the Continent, had the support of Gustavus Adolphus, and was the agent of Oliver Cromwell in seeking to bring together the Protestants on the Continent. In his last work he wished union to embrace the Roman Catholics.

In the closing quarter of the seventeenth century a Spanish Franciscan, Spinola, Bishop of Neustadt, for part of the time with Papal consent, negotiated with Protestants for reunion through a council to which Protestants would be admitted as "visible members of the Catholic Church." He had conferences with Lutherans, especially with G. W. Molanus (1633–1722), a pupil of Calixtus, who prepared an irenic proposal which was viewed with some favour in Rome. G. W. Leibnitz (1646–1716), Protestant by rearing, son of a professor of moral philosophy at Leipzig, wide-ranging in his intellectual interests, and distinguished as scientist, mathematician, and philosopher, as a youth had read extensively in theological literature of the Roman Catholic and several Protestant churches. He worked for the union of the Lutherans and Reformed of Prussia and carried on an amicable correspondence with the great

French Roman Catholic preacher, Bossuet, on the possibility of the union of all Christians. He looked to general councils as a means towards this end, but would not regard their decisions as final.

Similarly in the fore part of the eighteenth century there were those in Western Europe who dreamed of unity and worked for it, at least among Protestants. The Lutheran Christoph Mathew Pfaff (1686–1760) of Tübingen, in his *Pacific Address* to the Protestants (1720), held that all the Protestant communions are basically one. Count Nicolaus Ludwig von Zinzendorf, of whom we are to hear more in a moment, saw the Catholic Church in all the churches and carried on a friendly correspondence with a French cardinal. Three Swiss whose major work was in the first half of the eighteenth century sought to make the Reformed Churches of their native land more appreciative of other Protestants and laboured for union among Protestants.

Seventeenth and eighteenth century Great Britain and Ireland also had those who strove for unity both among the Christians of the British Isles and with those, especially Protestants, on the Continent. Archbishop James Usher (or Ussher) (1581–1656), Anglican primate of Ireland, noted as a scholar, held that bishop and presbyter differed merely in rank and not in order, advocated union with the Presbyterians, and regarded the latters' ordinations as valid. Oliver Cromwell seems to have favoured a central council for all Protestants. Richard Baxter, a Presbyterian, whom we have already met, was an ardent proponent of Christian unity, wrote extensively on it, and with others proposed to Charles II a plan of union like that of Usher. Edward Stillingfleet (1635–1699), an Anglican, in his *Irenicum* (1661), held that while they might be useful, neither the episcopal nor the presbyterian form of church government rested upon divine right, that neither was unalterable, and that from the Anglican standpoint presbyterian ordination was not invalid. William III, brought to power by the "glorious revolution" of 1688, reared in the Reformed tradition and now an Anglican by virtue of his office, wished all his Protestant subjects to be united and a bill to bring this about failed of passage in the House of Commons only by a narrow margin. John Robert Tillotson, Archbishop of Canterbury from 1691 to his death in 1694, sought, unsuccessfully, to persuade his fellow bishops to agree to concessions to the Protestant Nonconformists. Archbishop William Wake carried on a friendly correspondence with a French Catholic who stressed the rights of the Church of France as against the Church of Rome and also with several leaders of the Reformed churches.

How much of these efforts for unity carried over into the nineteenth and twentieth centuries and contributed to what eventually came to be called the Ecumenical Movement we cannot certainly know. That some connexion existed is clear.

Awakening out of Tragedy

The Thirty Years' War was a major tragedy. By it much of Germany was laid waste. Prosperous cities and villages were decimated or destroyed and even greater damage was suffered in the coarsening and lowering of morals. As the chief victim, Germany would have seemed to be the last place in Western Europe to which to look for fresh stirrings of Christian life. Yet here, in part from the tragedy itself, came vital currents which, swelling from small beginnings to significant proportions, persisted into the nineteenth and twentieth centuries and even in the eighteenth century contributed powerfully to the awakenings elsewhere in Protestantism that after 1750 made that form of the faith the most vigorous and rapidly growing branch of Christianity.

Why this was true of Protestantism rather than of the Roman Catholic Church we cannot say. Both Protestant and Catholic portions of Germany shared in the devastation. While in the later stages of the conflict some of its earlier gains were lost, territorially the Roman Catholic Church came out of the war better off than when it entered it, and at the expense of Protestantism. Yet it was within Protestantism, and notably from one of its churches, the Bohemian Brethren or *Unitas Fratrum* which had been the major victim, that the new tides of life chiefly issued.

Even during the long agony of the war there were evidences of vigour. It was in 1612, on the eve of its outbreak, that the first book appeared of Jakob Böhme (1575–1624), whom we have already met. Shoemaker and mystic of Upper Lusatia, across the mountains from that Bohemia which was soon to be the scene of the first stages of the struggle, he lived to see the initial years of the disaster. His thought, which scarcely belongs in what may be called orthodox Christianity, had wide repercussions in Germany, the Netherlands, Russia, and England, and among others influenced Isaac Newton and the much read Anglican, William Law, whose *Serious Call to a Devout and Holy Life* made a profound impression on John Wesley. Paul Gerhardt (1607–1676), whose youth and early manhood spanned the years of the war, was one of the greatest of Lutheran hymn-writers. Some of his hymns were translated into English by John Wesley, among them "Jesus, thy boundless love to me" and "Give to the winds thy fears, trust and be not dismayed," and were used widely.

The most striking phase of the religious awakening which followed the Thirty Years' War was Pietism. It had its roots far in the pre-war past. To it contributions came from the mysticism which we met in pre-Reformation Germany, from Luther, from English Puritanism, and possibly from the Anabaptists. Profoundly influential was the *Wahres Christenthum* ("True Christianity") of the Lutheran John Arndt (1555–1621), a work which appeared in the first decade of the seventeenth century, was translated into several European languages, and carried far the *unio mystica* side of Luther's teachings. It was a chief means of awakening Philip Jacob Spener (1635–1705), who is regarded as the immediate source of Pietism.

A Lutheran, as a student in Strassburg and Geneva Spener had become familiar with practices of the Reformed Churches which seemed to him admirable. In 1663 he became a pastor in Strassburg and then (1666) in Frankfort. While in Frankfort, a commercial city which had been dealt severe blows by the war but which was making a rapid recovery, he sought to nourish a deeper Christian life in his flock. Perhaps because of what he had seen at Strassburg, he took seriously catechetical instruction. More important, he gathered in his own home a group for the cultivation of the Christian life through the discussion of the Sunday sermons, prayer, and the study of the Bible. The movement spread and the groups became known as *collegia pietatis,* from which came the designation Pietism which clung to the movement.

Spener was intent upon a moral and spiritual reformation. He was grieved by controversy over doctrine, sometimes bitter as it was and often arid and having little direct bearing upon everyday living. Much of the contemporary preaching was of that kind. The lives of many of the clergy were unworthy and among the laity, partly as an aftermath of the long war, there were drunkenness and immorality. Church services tended to be formal and sterile. The state, he felt, interfered overmuch in the affairs of the Church. What he stressed was genuine conversion and the cultivation of the Christian life. To this end he discounted doctrinal sermons, preached the necessity of the new birth, a personal, warm, Christian experience, and the cultivation of Christian virtues. He gathered the serious-minded into small groups, *ecclesiolæ in ecclesia*—"little churches in the Church"—he called them, for the reading of the Scriptures and for mutual assistance in spiritual growth. As did the Catholic Church in the Middle Ages and many of the Calvinist and Puritan traditions, he inculcated a self discipline which included abstinence from cards, dancing, and the theatre and moderation in food, drink, and dress. Much of this he set forth in his *Pia Desideria,* published in 1675.

Almost inevitably, Spener and his methods aroused a storm of criticism. He was accused of being untrue to Lutheran doctrines. In this his opponents were not altogether incorrect. While he did not attack Lutheran orthodoxy, Spener held that if one had been really converted and had a right heart, doctrinal differences were relatively unimportant. In Frankfort opposition developed among the civil authorities, partly because some of those who came to his groups did not attend public worship and absented themselves from the Lord's Supper. In 1686 he went to Dresden as court preacher, but there met with hostility from the Saxon universities, Leipzig and Wittenberg, and eventually from the prince, whom he reproved for his drunkenness. In 1691 he accepted the invitation of the Elector of Brandenburg, later to become the King of Prussia, to Berlin. There, with growing influence, he remained until his death.

Prominent in the Pietist movement was a younger contemporary of Spener, August Hermann Francke (1663–1727). While teaching in the University of Leipzig, Francke and some of his friends inaugurated what they called a *collegium philobiblicum* for the study of the Scriptures. A few months later, when in his mid-twenties, Francke experienced what he believed to be the new birth. Then followed some weeks with Spener and the hearty acceptance of Pietism. As might have been expected, opposition developed at Leipzig. Francke was forced out of the university, especially because his meetings aroused much excitement among the students, and then out of a post in Erfurt. Through Spener's influence he was appointed to the University of Halle, at that time being founded by the Elector of Brandenburg, and to a pastorate in a neighbouring village.

Largely through Francke Halle became a chief centre of Pietism. Of prodigious energy, enthusiasm, and organizing ability, he was the dominant figure on the theological faculty and in the training of young men for the ministry. A faithful pastor in his own parish, he brought to his lecture room not only theory but also practical experience. At Halle he founded schools which became popular because of new educational programmes carried on in an atmosphere saturated with Pietism. He inaugurated an orphanage. The maintenance of these institutions was made possible by gifts which Francke profoundly believed came in response to prayer. From Halle missionaries went forth, some of them to India, some, from an institute founded for that purpose, to the Jews, and at least one, Muhlenberg, to the German colonists in America. Incidentally, but by no means of slight importance, the Halle schools had a part in shaping the future educational system of Prussia.

Pietism proved contagious. It had numerous and varied expressions. While many, perhaps the majority, were indifferent or even hostile, it spread rapidly through the Lutheran Churches. For example, it had a following in the Scandinavian countries. Arndt's works were widely read. In Norway, where, as we have seen, the Reformation had been largely imposed from without, Pietism stirred the masses. There Erik Pontoppidan, a Pietiest, drew up an explanation of Luther's catechism which with the Bible and hymnbook became a part of almost every Norwegian's library and was called "the dogmatics of the common people of Norway." Hans Adolph Bronson (1694–1764) wrote hymns which sang the Pietist awakening into the hearts of the rank and file. In 1736, largely as a result of the Pietist movement, confirmation was made compulsory in Norway. Pietism became especially vigorous and widespread in Württemberg. Here it became part of the warp and woof of parish life. This was due largely to Johann Albrecht Bengel (1687–1752), scholar and notable Bible commentator, who was high in the ecclesiastical structure of that state.

Closely linked with Pietism and combining it with the heritage of Hus and the *Unitas Fratrum* was the Moravian movement. Beginning in 1722, a few refugees from the persecutions of Protestants in Bohemia and Moravia settled on the estates of Nicolaus Ludwig, Count of Zinzendorf (1700–1760), near Berthelsdorf, about seventy miles from Dresden. Sensitive, able, with a global, encompassing imagination, this young nobleman had been reared in a strongly Pietist atmosphere and had been educated at Halle. His Pietism took the form of an ardent devotion to Jesus, so that he said of him: "I have one passion, 'tis he." He also had an intense desire to spread the Christian faith throughout the world. In the handful of persecuted refugees he saw the means of fulfilling that vision. They founded the village of Herrnhut on his property, he identified himself with them and became a bishop of their church, and through him missionaries from among them went out to various parts of the world. Zinzendorf wished them to become members of the state church of Saxony, but in 1745, while being a section of that church, they were formally organized with their own bishops, in the succession of those of the *Unitas Fratrum,* and with their distinct services, liturgy, and hymnology. As we are to see in a later chapter, contact with the Moravians contributed significantly to the profound experience of John Wesley which made him the outstanding leader of the Evangelical Awakening and the founder of Methodism. From Zinzendorf and other Pietists, as usual from awakenings in Christianity, many fresh hymns issued.

SUMMARY

The Roman Catholic Church did not succeed in eliminating Protestantism as, except for a few remnants, it had the earlier movements in Western Europe which it deemed heretical. That was probably partly because Protestantism proved to have much greater inner vitality than did these others. It was also, and quite certainly, in large measure because of the political situation and emergent nationalism. The peoples of North-western Europe and Great Britain were restive under Roman domination and their princes, many of them joining in the resentment and seeing in it means of augmenting their authority, acquiesced in it and sometimes gave it leadership. Confronted by nationalism and absolute monarchs in its historic stronghold, South-western Europe, embroiled in Italian politics, and at first weakened by internal corruption and inefficiency, Rome could not enforce its will as it had at the height of the Middle

Ages. Although internal reform and reorganization eventually enabled it to win back some of the lost ground, that was chiefly on the border between Latin and non-Latin Europe. Most of North-western Europe and Great Britain became and remained overwhelmingly Protestant.

Arising in part from the efforts of Roman Catholics to regain Bohemia, Moravia, and Germany but complicated by other non-religious factors, the Thirty Years' War drew in most of Western Europe. After its end few changes were made in the boundaries between Protestants and Roman Catholics. What had been the Catholic Church of Western Europe now became unmistakably the Roman Catholic Church, with its heart-land henceforward clearly Latin Europe. Most of the Christianity of the non-Latin North had torn away and, displaying great inner vitality, was to have an amazing growth, both in territory covered and in new movements. Indeed, the precursors of that expansion and of some of those movements were to become apparent within two generations after the war which laid waste much of the orginal home of Protestantism. Protestants were badly divided, but efforts were not wanting to bring them together. In the following centuries the fresh currents which began to be apparent in Pietism were to go far towards a basic and visible unity. However, in spite of efforts on both sides, the gulf which separated Protestants and Roman Catholics remained and seemed permanent.

Selected Bibliography

The Cambridge Modern History. Volume IV, The Thirty Years' War (Cambridge University Press, 1906).

H. E. F. Guerike, *The Life of Augustus Herman Franke,* translated from the German by S. Jackson (London, R. B. Seeley and W. Burnside, 1837, pp. viii, 296).

J. T. McNeill, *Unitive Protestantism. A Study in Our Religious Resources* (New York and Nashville, Abingdon-Cokesbury Press, 1930, pp. 264). A study of Protestant efforts at union, chiefly in the sixteenth, seventeenth, and eighteenth centuries. Admirably done.

H. Römer, *Nicolaus Ludwig Graf von Zinzendorf* (2d ed., Gnadau, Unitäts-Buchhandlung, 1900, pp. 193).

Chapter 40

STAGNATION AND ADVANCE: THE
EASTERN CHURCHES, A.D. 1500 - A.D. 1750

While the great burst of life was making itself felt in the Christianity of Western Europe through the Protestant and Catholic Reformations, what was happening in the Christianity of the East? Did the adversities which had overtaken it between 1350 and 1500 continue, or did they ease their impact?

The story is a mixture of stagnation and advance. The older churches centering around the historic patriarchal sees of Jerusalem, Antioch, Alexandria, and Constantinople, whether Monophysite or Orthodox, continued to suffer from the political dominance of Moslem masters. The same was true of the Nestorians and, for the most part, of the Armenians. The Roman Catholic Church still reached out to the East, seeking to bring its Christians under the control of the Papacy, largely through Uniate bodies, and its fresh access of life augmented those efforts. In one region, Russia, the Christianity of the East exhibited great vitality. This had little connexion with the awakenings in Western Europe and expressed itself in forms peculiar to its genius. Yet in its own way it was as remarkable as the larger and more varied movements in Western Christianity. Moreover, as we are to see in the next chapter, the Christianity of the West, predominantly Roman Catholicism, was carried to the South and East of Asia and to the islands which there fringed that continent and gave rise to continuing Christian communities which were more numerous and spread over a larger area than any which that part of the world had yet known.

THE OLDER EASTERN PATRIARCHATES

The stagnation of the Christianity connected with the historic patriarchates of the East was to be expected. The capture of Constantinople in 1453 was not the highwater-mark of the advance of the Crescent under the Ottoman Turks. In the sixteenth century those doughty empire-builders enlarged their conquests. Syria and Egypt came under their rule, their borders were extended northward not only to include almost all the Balkan Peninsula, but also into Hungary, and such Christian outposts in the Mediterranean fell to them as Rhodes (the stronghold of the Knights [Hospitallers] of St. John), Crete, and Cyprus. Since the Turks were sturdy Moslems and under them conversions from Islam to Christianity were all but impossible, the Christian communities could at best hold their own, reproducing themselves by birth but losing by leakage to Islam.

As before 1500, the Turkish rulers treated the Christian churches as social and legal entities, governing them through their clergy and especially their patriarchs. The Orthodox Patriarch of Constantinople was particularly important because of the prominence of his see in the past and the size of the Christian community over which he was the titular head. The Turkish authorities were careful that those who held the post were subservient to them. The office was usually bought from them, for the approval of the sultan was required. Changes in it were frequent, intrigues were chronic, and some of the occupants came to violent ends. The character of the Patriarchs was reflected in that of the bishops. Like the former, according to the tradition of the Eastern Churches, they were monks. They, too, often, perhaps usually, held their offices through purchase. The Phanariots, inhabitants of the Phanar quarter in Constantinople, largely controlled appointments to the higher posts in the Greek Orthodox Church. The Orthodox Patriarchates of Antioch and Alexandria, ruling as they did over small minorities, seem not to have been deemed sufficiently important by the Turkish rulers to warrant much attention. They appear, therefore, to have been filled through the customary forms of election without interference by the civil authorities.

An outstanding exception to the dubious character of the higher clergy of the Greek Orthodox Church was Cyril Lucar (1572–1637). Born in Crete while that island was under Venetian rule, he was reared in the Orthodox Church. Part of his education was in Italy, but he seems early to have acquired a strong dislike for the Roman Catholic Church, although later for a brief time he may have leaned in its direction. He travelled in Western Europe and came in touch with the Protestant Reformation, especially with the Reformed Churches. For a period he was in Poland as a representative of the Patriarch of Constantinople among the Orthodox. In 1602 he was elected Patriarch of Alexandria and in 1621 he became Patriarch of Constantinople. In these high offices he worked for the moral and spiritual improvement of the Orthodox Church. To this end he sent young men to study in the Protestant churches in Europe. He entered into correspondence with church leaders in non-Roman Catholic Western Europe, among them Archbishop Laud. His tenure of the Patriarchate of Constantinople was stormy, and he was several times deposed and as many times reinstated, not without the payment of money. He had implacable foes among the Jesuits, for they were seeking to bring about the submission of the Orthodox Church to the Pope and he was known to be intimate with the Dutch and English ambassadors and to have Protestant leanings. Indeed, a confession of faith which is attributed to him (and which he seems at least to have endorsed) but the authorship of which has been hotly debated has in it Protestant elements, including salvation by faith and predestination. Eventually he was strangled by order of the Sultan. In 1638 a synod of the Orthodox Church anathematized both Cyril and the confession attributed to him. In 1642 another synod condemned the confession and Calvinism, but without mentioning Cyril.

Many conversions from Christianity to Islam occurred, especially during the years of the forward surge of the Ottoman Turks. Some of the clergy went over, and throngs from the lower and middle classes. In 1620 a sultan ordered all churches turned into mosques and all Christians to become Moslems. Only with difficulty did a Patriarch dissuade him. Later two other sultans nearly carried out a similar project. In Crete after the Turkish conquest several thousand children of Christians were forcibly taken from their parents, circumcized, and reared as Moslems. In the seventeenth century many Serbs became Moslems and in Bosnia numbers of Bogomils took the same step. In that same century a ruler in Georgia, reared a Moslem in Persia, attempted to force Islam on his realm. Early in the preceding century a Moslem conqueror compelled many Christians in Abyssinia to apostatize—although several years later, when Moslem rule was overthrown, hundreds of the unwilling converts returned to their ancestral faith.

In Armenia, in spite of adverse political conditions, something of an awakening was seen. That mountainous country lying between powerful neighbours was, as earlier, debatable ground and was a chronic battle field. In these centuries Persians and Ottoman Turks were the antagonists. This meant that civilization and the Church suffered severely. However, in the seventeenth century an awakening began. Zealous monks, inspired partly by what they had seen in Jerusalem, set about the renewal of monasticism. Using the ancient foundation of the monastery of Datev as a centre, they began the Order of Siunik. As was customery in fresh monastic movements, whether in the East or the West, a strict discipline was adopted. Here it included renunciation of all private property, complete obedience to the abbot, stringent fasting, confession of sins each morning and evening, and meditation with the use of helpful books.

The revival was not confined to the monasteries. Some of the monks who had caught the contagion went out among the rank and file of the population preaching, founding schools, and seeking to improve morals, reconcile enemies, and discourage superstition. Outstanding among them was Moses of Datev. He began his work as an itinerant preacher about 1618. Later he was consecrated bishop and eventually (1629) Catholicos or Patriarch, thus bringing the reform movement into the supreme leadership of the Church of Armenia. Another centre of the revival of religion and learning was a monastery in Bitlis.

Among the Armenian churches of the dispersion these centuries also saw life, some of it in Constantinople and some in Persia. At New Julfa in Persia there was an Armenian community from which merchants went out into many parts of Europe and Asia. It was a centre of religious devotion and learning, but in 1721 an Afghan invasion wrought great damage. In 1652 a synod was held in Jerusalem which passed decrees designed to promote reform and to allay friction. In the seventeenth century the printing press made possible the wider distribution of religious literature, including an Armenian version of the Bible.

A constant feature in the history of the Eastern Churches, especially after reform had begun to take effect in the Roman Catholic Church, was the effort of zealous missionaries to bring all the Christians of the East to submit to the Pope and to enter into communion with the Church of Rome. As we have seen, Uniate Churches, namely those from the Eastern bodies who acknowledged the Pope and brought their creeds into conformity with Rome but who preserved their ecclesiastical languages and many of their peculiar rites and customs, had come into being before 1500. After 1500 Jesuits, Capuchins, Discalced Carmelites, and Theatines, products of the Catholic Reformation, as well as Dominicans and Franciscans, orders much longer in the area, ranged through much of the East, seeking to strengthen the Uniate bodies and eventually to bring about the full reunion of the several branches of the Catholic Church under the leadership of the Pope.

We must not take the time or the space to tell of all these Uniate bodies and their growth. We may, however, pause to notice a few of them. They included the Ruthenians, largely of Russian stock, formerly Orthodox. One was in domains under Polish and therefore Roman Catholic political control and came formally into being from a congress at Brest in 1596. In 1652 large groups of White and Little Russians living south of the Carpathians entered into communion with Rome and were known as the Podcarpathian Ruthenians. In 1701 about two hundred thousand Rumanians submitted to Rome, along with some of their clergy. There were Uniates in Egypt under a Patriarch of Alexandria. In Syria, Palestine, and Egypt those of the Byzantine rite who were in fellowship with Rome were known as Melchites, a term which had also been used to designate the Greek Orthodox in these areas. They had their own Patriarchs distinct from those who ruled the Greek Orthodox who kept aloof from Rome. In the sixteenth century, supported by Portuguese who came in to help the Ethiopians against the Turks, Jesuits brought numbers of the Abyssinians into communion with Rome. In 1555 Pope Julius III appointed a Jesuit as Patriarch of the Church in that country. Early in the seventeenth century another Jesuit was named for the post and for a time a ruler sympathetic with the Jesuits seemed to bring most if not all of the Ethiopian Church into accord with Rome. However, a nationalistic reaction drove out the missionaries and severed the Roman connexion. Roman Catholic missionaries were active in Constantinople, seeking to draw both the Greek Orthodox and the Armenians into fellowship with Rome. The ensuing friction looms large in the annals of these bodies. Numbers of the Jacobites, in Syria, were won to fellowship with Rome and in time had a Patriarch of their own. In the sixteenth century an aspirant for the headship of the Nestorians made his submission to Rome and carried many with him. Thus came into being the Chaldean Christians, Nestorian Uniates, and a continuing division in that ancient church. In that same century Jesuit missionaries succeeded in bringing over to Rome the Syrian Christians of India, who had been closely associated with the Nestorians in Mesopotamia. Indeed, in 1599 the Synod of Diamper seemed to have accomplished that union. However, in the following century unrest arose and the majority, led by their clergy, severed the Roman tie, leaving only a minority in communion with the Pope. Zealous though Roman Catholic missionaries were, they were unable to win more than a minority of the Eastern Christians to fellowship with Rome. Only the Maronites, largely in the Lebanon, remnants of the Monothelite controversy, came over fully to the Pope. The connexion had been made during the Crusades, and after 1516 became uninterrupted.

THE CHURCH IN RUSSIA

In Russia one of the Eastern Churches, the Orthodox, had a striking territorial expansion and in it and from it issued fresh movements of remarkable power. This vitality was closely associated with the development of the monarchy, the beginning of which we have noted in the preceding period, and which had Moscow as its capital. The rulers were professedly Christian and identified themselves and their authority with the Orthodox Church. It was that fact which favoured the spread of the faith in and near the territories governed from Moscow and which did much to shape the course of Christianity in Russia.

THE STRANGE STORY OF IVAN "THE TERRIBLE"

In an earlier chapter (27) we have noted that on the north-eastern frontier, around Moscow, there was arising a state which, achieving its independence of the Mongols, took over something of the autocratic idea which it had seen in them. Its rulers were descendants of that Vladimir through whom Kiev had been converted late in the tenth century and who is usually regarded as the founder of Christianity in Russia. In the sixteenth century this state was greatly expanded under one of the most remarkable men in Russian history, Ivan (John) IV, "the Terrible" (1530–1584), grandson of Ivan III. He was little more than an infant when, in 1533, his father's death brought him nominally to power, so that his reign extended over more than half a century.

At the time of his accession the state over which Ivan IV ruled occupied an area much smaller than the later Russia. The Mongols still had territory in Europe. The Cossacks, sturdy frontiersmen who in the fifteenth century had arisen in the southern part of Russia, largely between the Mongol and the Muscovite domains, were organized in a democratic fashion and were formidable warriors. To the west the Poles and Lithuanians held lands which were chiefly peopled by Russians, members of the Orthodox Church.

Ivan IV extended his domains over Kazan towards the east (1552) and southward to the Caspian, and exercised some authority east of the Urals. On the west he fought, not always successfully, with the Poles, Lithuanians, and Swedes. The menace of his arms helped to force the Poles and Lithuanians together under Polish leadership and made the two peoples an even greater menace to Moscow.

Ivan IV augmented his office. He reduced the power of the ancient nobility and created a new court nobility, largely dependent on himself. He also did much to curtail the freedom of the peasants by fixing them to the soil in the condition of serfdom in which they were to remain until the nineteenth century. When he was seventeen (1547) and assumed full charge of the government, Ivan IV had himself crowned as Tsar (Cæsar) and thus professed himself to be Emperor in the succession of the Christian Emperors of Constantinople, since that city was now in the hands of the Moslem Ottoman Turks.

In character Ivan IV was a combination of contradictions. He was highly sensitive and after a fashion deeply religious. Yet his childhood rearing had accustomed him to licentiousness and to impulsive lack of control. He was undoubtedly able, as the record of his achievements shows. But, especially in his later years, his contradictions seem to have developed into insanity. Extravagant orgies would be followed by periods of equally extravagant remorse and penance. He would destroy monasteries and then found new ones. Murders multiplied at his command, and he would send the list of his victims to monasteries commanding prayers for their souls.

Moscow "The Third Rome"

During the reign of Ivan IV important developments took place in Russian Christianity. In the Russian Orthodox Church the Josephites (Chapter 27) were dominant. Early in the sixteenth century, as we have seen, the Non-possessors had been decisively defeated. The Josephites, it will be recalled, believed in the possession of property by the monasteries and the Church. They were ascetic, approved works of charity, and stressed ritual, with elaborate services, large choirs, and ornate churches and vestments. Intensely patriotic, they held Moscow to be the third Rome, the successor of the first Rome, which had succumbed to the heresies of the Latins, and of Constantinople, the second Rome, which had fallen victim of the Moslems. Moscow, therefore, they regarded as the guardian of the Gospel in all its purity. The Josephites believed in the maintenance of a close tie between Church and state.

A leader of the Josephites was Makary, Metropolitan of Moscow during the early years when Ivan IV assumed full control of the state. A high-minded and able churchman, Makary had much influence with the young monarch. In 1551 he called a council, known as the Stoglav, or "Hundred Chapters," because of its resolutions which came to that total, which endeavoured to correct many of the evils in the Church. Its decisions had mainly to do with the liturgy and public worship, but it also sought reforms in ecclesiastical government, in clerical life, in the monasteries, and in the life of the laity.

Since Ivan IV had raised his office to that of tsar, Makary held that the head of the Church in Russia should have the title of Patriarch, thus placing crown and altar on an equal footing and giving visible recognition to Moscow's claim to be the third Rome. Long negotiations were required to gain formal consent to this step by the other members of the family of Orthodox Churches. These were not completed until after the death of Makary, but in 1589 the Patriarch of Constantinople agreed to the creation of a Russian Patriarchate and in 1590 a council of the other Orthodox Patriarchs in Constantinople confirmed the decision. The Patriarchate of Moscow was formally admitted to the list which included Constantinople, Alexandria, Antioch, and Jerusalem. Presumably it was to take the place of the Patriarchate which Rome was deemed to have forfeited. After Moscow became the seat of a Patriarch, four Russian sees were raised to the rank of metropolitan, several bishoprics became archbishoprics, and a number of new dioceses were created, partly by the subdivision of old ones, and partly by the extension of the Church into areas newly conquered by Moscow.

INTERNAL DISSENSIONS

Shortly before Ivan IV there began an interesting stage of an important controversy which lasted not only into his lifetime but which in the following century was to lead to a major disruption in the Church in Russia. It had to do with what to many outsiders seemed absurdities, matters of form in the services of the Church and the correctness of the translations of the texts which were used in them. As early as the fifteenth century a dispute had arisen as to whether in the public use of the Psalms the *Alleluia* should be recited twice before the *Gloria* as was the Greek custom, or thrice, as had been the Russian manner. The contender for the Greek form was deemed to have denied the Trinity and was branded as a heretic. In 1551, the Stoglav decided in favour of the double rather than the triple repetition.

In 1518 Maxim, a monk, an Albanian who had studied in Italy, had been a member of a monastery on Mt. Athos, and was learned in Greek and Latin, was invited to Moscow by one of the princes and was asked by the Metropolitan to revise the translations of some of the service books. In these many variations and errors were found, partly because of the mistakes of the original translators, partly because of the several sources through which they had come to Russia, and partly through the errors of copyists. Some changes had been made by the Judaizers (Chapter 27) who had regarded Christ as merely a created man and said of him that he had died an eternal death. So great a storm was aroused among the conservatives by the corrections made by Maxim (and he was also guilty of mistakes of his own) that the luckless foreigner was clapped into a monastic prison, was kept there for several years, was transferred to another monastery for confinement, and only after a long interval, perhaps at the instance of Makary, was released. His tragedy was complicated and the enmity against him intensified by his endorsement of the stand of the Non-possessors as against the dominant Josephites.

TERRITORIAL EXPANSION OF THE RUSSIAN CHURCH

While these developments were taking place within the church which centered around Moscow, the area occupied by that church was also expanding. This was partly in connexion with territorial conquests by the state and partly through the northward advance of the monks and the population of which we have earlier spoken (Chapter 27). Thus in the sixteenth century, after the annexation by Ivan IV of Kazan and the region around it, Kazan was made the seat of an archbishop. The first incumbent, Gurius, a man of noble birth, laboured indefatigably for the conversion of the non-Christians, especially the Cheremis (also called Tcheremis and Marii), a people speaking a Finnish tongue. On the middle reaches of the Volga the Mordvs, with a Finnish-Ugrian language, were subdued by Ivan IV. Ivan charged the nobles among whom he divided the land to prepare the inhabitants for baptism and monks were active in seeking to make the conversion effective. As late as the eighteenth century, as among the Cheremis, conversion was still far from being fully accomplished and special exemption from taxation, forced labour, and military service was offered by the state to those who accepted baptism. In 1602 a bishopric was erected at Astrakhan, a short distance above the mouth of the Volga. In the opposite direction, in the extreme North the borders of Christianity were being pushed forward. During the reign of Ivan IV and partly through his encouragement, zealous monks were founding monasteries and winning converts among the Lapps. By the end of the sixteenth century what we may now call the Russian Orthodox Church had extended its borders southward to the Caspian Sea, northward to the White Sea and the coasts of the Arctic, and eastward to and even beyond the Urals.

The Uniate Secession

While these territorial gains were being made in Eastern and Northern Europe, the Orthodox Church was losing ground on its western borders to the Roman Catholic Church. This was because of a combination of Polish rule and the missionary activity arising from the Catholic Reformation, chiefly through the Jesuits. We have seen that the Poles and the Lithuanians had long been extending their rule over Russians who held to the Orthodox Church. Since the Poles and the Lithuanians were Roman Catholics, this quite naturally tended to bring the Orthodox under the control of Rome. The impact of the Catholic Reformation roughly coincided with the reigns of Stephen Batory (1575–1586), who as one of Poland's ablest kings markedly strengthened Polish rule eastward, and of Sigismund III (1586–1632) who, although a descendant of that Gustavus Vasa who had been largely responsible for the transfer of Sweden to Lutheranism, was ardently Roman Catholic. Both monarchs supported the Jesuits.

Under these circumstances the sections of the Orthodox Church which looked for leadership to Kiev, the historic centre of early Russian Christianity, were hard pressed. A Jesuit college which had been opened at Vilna in 1570 attracted the sons of the Orthodox nobility. The Polish kings took a hand in the choice of bishops for their Orthodox subjects and favoured men who would cooperate with them. Many of these bishops were scions of the nobility who regarded their posts as opportunities for comfortable living, some were married and quite secular and had little either of education or character. Numbers of the nobles who had remained Orthodox and of the Orthodox laity in the middle classes in the cities rallied to the support of their faith and formed brotherhoods on its behalf. Among other activities they subsidized the printing of Orthodox books. In 1588 the Patriarch of Constantinople visited the region, sought to stem the tide towards Rome, deposed the Metropolitan of Kiev, and replaced him with another man. Several of the Orthodox bishops had their Rome-ward proclivities strengthened by irritation at the activity of the laity. Some of them met at Brest in 1591 and complained to the king and by the end of 1594 several bishops expressed their desire for union with Rome.

The decisive step was taken in 1596. Sigismund III had issued a manifesto announcing the union of the Orthodox with Rome and called a council at Brest. When the gathering assembled, it was found to be divided. The Orthodox party included Cyril Lucar, then in his mid-twenties and representing the Patriarch of Alexandria, and also a spokesman for the Patriarch of Constantinople. It broke away from the council, met separately, and adhered to its traditional faith. The elements favouring union with Rome passed resolutions endorsing it. Sigismund and the Polish and Lithuanian governments regarded these as authoritative and sought to enforce them. A large proportion of the Orthodox acceded and became Uniates. Pressure was brought by Jesuits to bring the Uniates into closer conformity with Roman customs, but the Uniates resisted and, while in communion with Rome, maintained much of their distinctive rites and procedures. Among them arose (1604), with its mother house at Vilna, partly on the model of Roman Catholic monasticism, what was known as the Basilian Order, a name which suggested an Eastern precedent. It spread rapidly and did much for the intellectual and moral advancement of the Uniates. It also entered actively into the controversy with the Orthodox.

The Orthodox did not all become Uniates. The lay brotherhoods which had been loyal continued. They engaged in controversy with the Uniates and a substantial output of books and pamphlets followed. They carried on schools which, in contrast with those of the Jesuits, were Orthodox and often had Greek teachers. Some Orthodox monasteries survived and new ones were organized, and that in spite of the confiscation by the government of many of their properties for the benefit of the Uniate Basilians. Indeed, something of a religious awakening occurred.

The persistence of the Orthodox branch of the Church was not on purely religious grounds. Much of it was from nobles who resisted the extension of the authority of the king. Part of it was racial and an incipient nationalism which looked upon the Uniate movement as a surrender to the hated Poles and Lithuanians. The Cossacks who were spreading in the region held to the

Orthodox Church as a badge of independence from the foreigner. On one occasion a mob, resenting his efforts to suppress Orthodox worship, fell upon a Uniate bishop, beat him to death, and flung his body in the river.

The Orthodox eventually scored signal victories. Their Patriarch of Jerusalem visited the region in 1620 and consecrated a metropolitan and six bishops. After the death (1632) of the ardently Roman Catholic Sigismund III, the Diet which elected to the throne his son and successor, Vladislav (Ladislaus) IV, also granted the Orthodox the right to have a hierarchy consisting of a metropolitan (at Kiev) and four suffragan sees. As metropolitan it appointed Peter Mogila. Mogila, of noble stock, had been well educated in the schools of the Orthodox brotherhoods and abroad. At Kiev he made important innovations, largely in the field of education. He inaugurated schools which took over much of the newer methods that were appearing in Western Europe, made Latin a medium of instruction, raised standards, and founded an academy which he wished to equal the best of the education that was being given by the Jesuits. He wrote voluminously. He attacked Lucar's confession of faith and partly as a rejoinder compiled a catechism in which he set forth what he believed to be the Orthodox faith. Although he was looked upon with suspicion by conservatives as bringing in Latin influence, he made Kiev an outstanding centre of Orthodox theological activity which was to have marked fruits in wider ranges of the Russian Orthodox Church. He did much to put Kiev in touch with the thought of the Roman Catholic Church and one of his many writings, his *Orthodox Confession of Faith,* was eventually accepted as an authoritative statement of the beliefs of Russian Orthodoxy.

The Russian Orthodox Church a Stabilizing Centre in the "Time of Trouble"

For a few years at the end of the sixteenth and the beginning of the seventeenth century Russia went through a period of disorder which is technically known as the "Time of Trouble." In 1598, with the death of Tsar Fedor (Theodore), the childless son of Ivan IV, the dynasty which had had Vladimir as one of its distinguished early monarchs came to an end. There were uprisings due to social unrest. A disputed succession augmented the civil strife. Dmitri who believed, mistakenly, that he was the youngest son of Ivan IV had the support of the Poles and the Jesuits. With Polish aid he organized an army which took Moscow and for the moment it looked as though the Jesuit dream might be fulfilled and the Russian Church submit to Rome. Dmitri was killed, but other aspirants for the throne were put forward, among them a second false Dmitri, and the land fell into a sad state of anarchy. The Poles occupied Moscow and Smolensk and the Swedes held Novgorod.

Under these trying circumstances the Orthodox Church provided leadership and a rallying centre for the Russian spirit against the foreigner and Rome. The Patriarch Hermogen headed the resistance and was supported by the monasteries. He was cast into prison by the Poles and died there, presumably of starvation. A combination of patriotic forces took Moscow, expelled the Poles, and called a representative assembly to put the country in order. This assembly, or *Zemsky Sobor,* elected (1613) as tsar a sixteen-year-old noble, Michael Romanov, of a family related by marriage to the former imperial house, thus founding a dynasty which was to last until 1917. The "Time of Trouble" was at an end and Orthodoxy and nationalism, aiding each other, had triumphed. Philaret, the father of Michael Romanov, who earlier had been forced by a political enemy to enter a monastery and his wife to become a nun, became Patriarch of Moscow. For twenty-four years father and son as Patriarch and tsar coöperated in restoring order and strengthening the power of the Romanovs.

After the disorders of the preceding years morality and religion were at a low ebb. The Christianity of Russia had sufficient vigour to produce men who sought to reform the Church and raise the level of Christian living. Reform took at least two roads. One was conservative, partly of the Josephite tradition, endeavouring to revive the Church by a stricter observance of the old Russian ways. The other welcomed contact with the outside world, especially with the Greeks, and strove to bring improvement by adopting the usages of the mother church, the Greek Orthodox, from which the Russian Church had sprung.

The Patriarch Nikon and the Great Division in the Orthodox Church of Russia

We now come to one of the most momentous series of events in the history of Christianity in Russia. It resulted in a secession from the state church which for persistence, although not for magnitude, can be compared with the emergence of Protestantism from the Roman Catholic Church in Western Europe more than a century earlier. There was no connexion between the two movements. Each was purely indigenous and had features peculiar to itself. Both had social aspects. The rise of Protestantism was aided by nationalism and in some places, as in England, by the growth of the urban middle class. In Russia the secession was associated with the unrest of the common people and the parish clergy against the wealth and dictation of the higher clergy. Each had profoundly religious aspects. Protestantism was an effort at the moral reform of the Church and to go back of the changes associated with Rome to the original Christian faith. In Russia the revolt was in part a desire to reform the monasteries and adherence to the liturgical books through which the masses received their faith against an effort at the thoroughgoing correction of those books to make them conform more nearly to the Greek originals. That effort at correction was led by the Patriarch, so that in a sense the Russian dissent was akin to Protestantism in that it was a reaction against innovations by the administrative centre of the Church.

Yet Protestantism and seventeenth century Russian dissent, although having much which seemed in common, were quite different. In the latter there was nothing akin to salvation by faith and the priesthood of all believers. While Protestantism was eventually to be strikingly missionary and was to have a phenomenal growth, Russian dissent had few if any converts from non-Christians. However, as Protestantism was the source of much of the later democracy in Western Europe, the Russian seventeenth century dissent is said to have laid the foundations for liberty and revolution in that land.

This attempt at a parallelism with Protestantism is not altogether happy. There was more resemblance between the Russian dissent and that of Western Europe of the Middle Ages. Yet here, too, the differences were greater than the similarities.

The great seventeenth century secession from the Russian Orthodox Church was closely connected with one of the most remarkable men in Russian history, the Patriarch Nikon. Nikon (1605–1681) was of peasant, possibly Finnish stock, and was earlier known as Nicetas or Nikita Minin. As a lad he was noted both for his asceticism and for his rapid progress in learning. He wished to be a monk and, indeed, undertook a monastic novitiate. However, his relatives urged him to marry and become a parish priest. He yielded, was ordained, and served in Moscow. Before he was thirty his children died. Perhaps seeing in this divine judgement or direction, he persuaded his wife to take the veil (she eventually became an abbess) and he became a monk and went north. Before many years he was prior of a monastery on the western shore of the White Sea. In connexion with the duties of that office he journeyed to Moscow to attend a council. There the Tsar Alexis noticed him, was impressed by him, put him in a position of prominence in a monastery near the capital, gave him public duties, and frequently consulted him. It speaks well for Nikon that he used his influence with Alexis to intercede for widows and orphans who had not been able to obtain their rights in the courts. Soon (1649) he was made Metropolitan of Novgorod. In that post he showed initiative, marked ability, and reforming zeal, and helped to put down a revolt. Then, in 1652, he was appointed Patriarch. He was very reluctant to take the post, but the tsar insisted, and he finally consented, but only on his own terms, and with the approval of the synod, clergy, and people. He stipulated that his convictions of the high place of the Patriarchate should be observed, and that the tsar and the Church *Sobor,* or assembly, obey him in everything as "shepherd and father." He took the title of Great Sovereign.

As Patriarch, Nikon inherited many problems. Not many years earlier, some of the laity and nobles, desiring to regulate the monasteries, many of which were rich and badly managed, and the Church, enormously wealthy and with privileges which hampered civil administration, had a code enacted for the regulation of the civil side of the Church and set up a civil department, the "Monastic Office" (*Monastyrskii Prikaz*). As a result many privileges of the clergy and monasteries were curtailed. The bureau also reached out into highly debatable ground and dealt with the spiritual functions of the Church. Many of the clergy were bitterly opposed to it and sharp dissensions arose. After the great tradition established for the Patriarchate by Hermogen and Philaret, in which that office had overshadowed the tsar, recent Patriarchs had been weak. Nikon had a lofty conception of the Patriarchate and was determined to make it a reality. That way lay trouble. Moreover, he inherited the thorny problem of the revision of the translations of the sacred books, to bring them more nearly in accord with the Greek originals.

The issue of the service books and ritual had not been finally settled by the decision of the *Stoglav* and the death of the luckless Maxim. It arose from time to time and early in the seventeenth century became acute over the section in the Epiphany rite of the benediction of the waters, where in copies long in use the prayer was offered that the water might be sanctified "by the Holy Spirit and by fire." In seeking a correct text for this passage Archimandrite Dionysius of the influential Trinity-Sergius Monastery, together with his collaborators, could find the phrase "and by fire" in only two old Slav copies and in no Greek copy. Accordingly he omitted it. This aroused intense opposition, for it was held to be a denial that the Holy Spirit is composed of fire, an ancient and widely held belief. Dionysius and his associates were haled before the Patriarchal court, tortured, and imprisoned. However, after his accession, the Patriarch Philaret pardoned them and in 1625, following opinions of the Patriarchs of Alexandria and Jerusalem, had the debated words "and by fire" excised from the ritual. The work of editing the texts of the books used by the Church was carried on under the direction of Philaret and of the Patriarchs who immediately preceded Nikon. This was done in connexion with the preparation of editions for the press, for printing was being increasingly employed. Much of the scholarship was faulty and the confusion became worse confounded. Yet some of the revisers were competent. Among them were Greek scholars imported for that purpose. Here was a knotty problem to which a prelate of Nikon's vigour would be fairly certain to address himself.

In making innovations any Patriarch would find himself confronted by the conservatism associated with large elements of the Josephite tradition and also by the nationalistic and anti-Roman Catholic sentiment which had been aggravated by the unhappy events of the "Time of Trouble." As an example of this attitude, a synod declared that since Roman Catholics were guilty of many heresies, their baptism was not valid and that any of them seeking membership in the Russian Orthodox Church must be rebaptized. The synod also declared that the only valid baptism was by immersion, and that Orthodox coming from the Kievan jurisdiction or elsewhere who had had the rite through sprinkling must be rebaptized through the correct form.

Nikon was not one to hesitate before difficulties. During his first few years as Patriarch he had the unqualified support of Alexis. The tsar consulted him on matters of state and while he was away on his wars Nikon was dominant in the civil as well as the ecclesiastical phase of the empire's administration. Nikon addressed himself vigorously to Church affairs. He insisted upon rigid discipline for the clergy, a policy much needed in an age which had not yet recovered from the license of the last years of Ivan IV and the "Time of Trouble." He encouraged preaching. He made it clear that he believed that the Church should not be subject to the state and curbed the activities of the Monastic Office. He held that the tsar should not control synods, the appointment of bishops, ordinations, or ecclesiastical courts.

Nikon continued the revision of the books in use in the Church. To that end he established contacts with Kiev, where, as we have seen, marked advances had been made in education and scholarship. He sought to discover Greek usage and in part to adopt it, and to help him brought in Greek scholars. Some of this may have been out of a desire to bring the Russian Church into close contact and full fellowship with other units of the Orthodox Church. Nikon's purpose, too, seems to have been to induce the Orthodox in the South-west who looked to Kiev, including Kiev itself, to accept the jurisdiction of Moscow. He insisted upon the use of three fingers instead of two in crossing oneself or giving the blessing. He had a synod (1656) condemn the rebaptism of Roman Catholics and gave recognition to the baptism and orders of the Roman Catholics and Orthodox in South Russia. He made official the revised copies of the service books and required their use throughout his jurisdiction.

Nikon sought to crush opposition, especially to his service books. He suppressed most of it and had one of its leaders, Avvakum (Habbakuk), exiled to Siberia. Avvakum belonged to a group of priests in the circle of the Archpriest Stephen Vonifatievich, the spiritual father of the Tsar Alexis. They were seeking reform by the older Russian ways of observance of the ecclesiastical rules of prayer, fasting, and strict morals. They stressed preaching and confession.

Much of the resistance arose not only from conservatism but also from the conviction that the section of the Orthodox Church headed by Moscow, the third Rome, could not be in error and from the suspicion of influences stemming from the first Rome, now become heretical, and from the Greeks who after the fall of the second Rome, Constantinople, so it was believed, had fallen into errors. Criticism also arose from what was interpreted as the Patriarch's oppression of the parish clergy and their flocks. Nikon enforced the tithes on cities and towns and on the deacons and priests. He was accused of strengthening the grip of the higher grades of the hierarchy on the lower grades and on the masses. He widened the gulf between the parish priests, married as they were, and the bishops who by the Eastern tradition were monks and celibate. In seeking to make the Church independent of the civil authorities, Nikon withdrew the parish priests from the jurisdiction of the village elders and placed them more directly under the bishops and the archpriests. Resistance from the lower clergy was, accordingly, especially marked.

Here was leadership such as the Russian Orthodox Church had not previously known. More nearly than any other figure in the history of Russia Nikon resembled the great Popes of Rome. His was the dream of making the Russian Church, led by the Patriarch, dominant in the life of the nation. Yet it ended in tragedy for Nikon personally and for the Church.

Nikon's power lasted only about six years. Then came his downfall. He had alienated a large proportion of the nobles, the clergy, and the monks, but so long as the tsar backed him he was relatively secure. In 1658 it became clear that he was out of favour with the tsar. Alexis seems to have resented the fashion in which Nikon dominated him and determined to break the spell which the Patriarch had exerted over him. Finally, when the tsar purposely absented himself from services where Nikon was officiating, the latter withdrew from Moscow in protest and ceased to perform his patriarchal duties. He retired to a monastery, first one near by and then one on the White Sea. Yet he still regarded himself as Patriarch.

Nikon's absence was followed by confusion, for his post was not filled and the removal of his strong hand gave the seething discontent opportunity for expression. Those who opposed his changes won the ear of the tsar. Avvakum was recalled from his Siberian exile and Alexis went out of his way to ask his blessing. Some among the Moscow populace besought the tsar to restore the old ways and hailed Avvakum as a hero. Numbers of the clergy returned to the use of the unrevised service books and the ways of singing in the services which Nikon had proscribed. As the year 1666 approached, many connected it with 666, the number of the beast in *The Revelation of John,* and charged

Nikon with being associated with it, if not actually being that monster itself, and with the prophesied apostasy through the worship of the beast.

Efforts were made to force Nikon out of office. In 1660 a synod met at imperial command, with the purpose of deposing him. The Patriarch was charged with arrogance, ambition, maladministration, and encroaching on the civil authority. Yet objectors declared that a Patriarch could be deposed only with the concurrence of the other Patriarchs and the administration of the office was entrusted to a *locum tenens*. The other Patriarchs were approached. Pressure was put on Nikon to resign or to come before a civil court, but he declined to do either. In December, 1664, Nikon returned to Moscow. He appeared dramatically in patriarchal state at a service in the cathedral and, according to custom, called on the tsar to attend. This the tsar declined to do and ordered Nikon back to a monastery to await the verdict of the other Patriarchs.

Eventually Nikon's enemies prevailed. In November, 1666, a synod assembled in Moscow which was attended by the Patriarchs of Alexandria and Antioch and a throng of bishops and other prelates. It gave Nikon a formal trial, condemned him, deposed him, and sent him into exile. The chief grounds urged for the action were that he had cursed bishops without trial, that he had deserted his throne and left the Church defenseless, that he had slandered the tsar and the Church, that he had used improper language against his opponents, that he had not treated his judges with proper respect, and that his administration had been cruel and arbitrary. The synod avoided what was to Nikon, in addition to his personal grievances, the central issue, the control of the Church by the state, and the interference of the tsar with functions properly reserved to the Church, such as ordinations, the decisions of ecclesiastical courts, the appointment of bishops, and synods.

Nikon was never rehabilitated. For a time he and Alexis resumed contact by letter, but on the coming of the next tsar, Nikon's enemies, implacable, had him sent into deeper obscurity and he died while on the way (August 17, 1681).

Nikon's work was not completely undone. Before his death the Monastic Office to which he had objected was abolished. Synods enacted discipline and monastic reforms in the direction which he had envisaged, and some restraint was placed on lay interference with ecclesiastical jurisdiction. Even more significant was the action of the synod (1666–1667) which deposed Nikon in accepting much that he had accomplished in the revision of the service books. The books as corrected under his direction were approved and also the use of the three fingers in giving the blessing. The recalcitrants who held to the old ways were ordered to repent. Some did so. Others refused and for their obstinacy numbers among them were excommunicated and sent to prison.

The action of the synod of 1666–1667 hardened the resistance. Those who refused to conform were known as the Old Ritualists, the Old Believers, or Raskolniks. The last designation, from *Raskol,* or division, schism, is a general term which may be applied to all who had withdrawn from the Russian Orthodox Church. The Old Believers held that the official church had become apostate by following the errors of the Greeks. The first Rome, they contended, had become heretical, the second Rome, Constantinople, had also departed from the true faith, and now the third Rome, Moscow, by adopting the errors of the later Greeks, had followed in the way of the first two. Many of the Old Believers were convinced that the end of the world was at hand and lived in expectation of it.

The Old Believers were in part rebels against the upper ranks of the hierarchy. No bishops joined them and while some among the higher classes held to them they were chiefly recruited from the monks, the parish priests, and the common people. In at least one monastery the abbot refused to join in the use of the old books and the body of the monks persisted in spite of him. The movement was, then, in large measure a revolt of the underprivileged. In that respect it was not unlike several of the dissident movements in Western Europe during the Middle Ages and some aspects of Protestantism.

The state viewed the Old Believers as seditious and took vigorous action. In 1685 an imperial decree was issued against them. If they did not give up their Raskol ways they were to be tortured and if obdurate they were to be burned alive. Those who repented were to be sent to an ecclesiastical prison for reëducation. Death was the penalty for Raskol rebaptism, both for him who administered it and for the unrepentant recipient.

While the edict was seemingly concerned with the religious aspects of the movement, the government may have been quite as much alarmed by the social and political implications. Thus in 1682 there broke out an uprising among the *Streltzy,* the Moscow garrison of infantry, the organization of which went back to Ivan IV. The *Streltzy* had the sympathy of many of the populace of the capital. One of their officers succeeded in injecting the religious issue into the movement and induced the *Streltzy* to champion the cause of the Old Believers and to demand the restoration of the old service books. It was Sophia, elder sister of Ivan, co-tsar with Peter, of whom we are to hear as the Great, who was responsible for the edict of 1685. A woman of marked force of character, she was regent, for Ivan was weak and Peter was in his early teens. Obviously she wished to suppress a movement which was closely tied with what she deemed insubordination and a dangerous threat to the authority of the tsar.

The authorities were not content with words but engaged in active persecution. The Old Believers were hounded down. For example, Avvakum was confined to a subterranean prison and in 1682, in the year following the death of

Nikon, to whom he was the great opponent, he was burned at the stake. Both men had been rejected by the official church and the state. Thousands of Old Believers were put to death, some by hanging and others by burning. To escape death at the hands of their persecutors or from despair at the state of the world, many of the Old Believers burned themselves alive. Thousands are said to have perished in this fashion. Others starved themselves to death.

Yet the Old Believers persisted. Some hid themselves. Others fled from the vicinity of Moscow, where the central authorities could reach them, to regions where the power of tsar and Patriarch was weak. Numbers found this refuge in the northern forests. Some went south, some to Poland, and others into Swedish territory.

The Old Believers had no one central organization and varied greatly among themselves. Since no bishops had come out with them from the state church, they had no episcopacy and did not ordain priests. They would not accept the ministrations of the state church, because from their standpoint it was apostate. Among them were former priests of the state church. The latter's services were, accordingly, acceptable. In the course of time the Old Believers divided into those who had priests, the *Popovsty,* and those who did not have them, the priestless, *Bezpopovsty.*

Those who had priests at first depended upon the clergy who had seceded with them. Later they accepted priests who had been ordained in the state church but who for one reason or another threw in their lot with them. These priests were required by their flocks to use the service books which were free from the changes brought in by Nikon. At first they were rebaptized, some of them fully garbed in their clerical vestments. Lay converts coming over from the state church were also rebaptized. Eventually some of the *Popovsty* dropped the requirement of rebaptism. Usually, however, they at least anointed with oil the priests who joined them. In the first half of the eighteenth century a bishop of the state church joined them, but died after a few months. Some priests were obtained with the consent of the bishops of the state church. Others were accepted from the Uniates. In the nineteenth century a branch obtained a bishop from the Greek Orthodox Church and through him had bishops in the apostolic succession and who could ordain clergy.

The priestless among the Old Believers divided into many groups. They agreed that the true priesthood had ended with the death of those who had been ordained before the time of Nikon. On many other issues they were not in accord. Some of them held that for baptism, confession, and burial a priest was not necessary and a layman or an unordained monk could officiate. None had the Eucharist. Many held that, since marriage required a priest, they would live strictly as celibates. Some others tolerated concubinage without marriage.

Others were for marriage by the priests of the state church. Some declined to pray for the tsar since, from their standpoint, he was unbaptized. Others offered prayers for him. Many held that Antichrist had appeared or was about to appear and some identified Peter the Great with him. Numbers entirely repudiated baptism, contending that no layman could administer it. Some practised communal living. Others were wanderers. The varieties of the priest-less multiplied with the years.

Some of the Old Believers sought to win converts from the Orthodox. Others lived in what were in effect closed communities, refusing to marry outside their group and having as little as possible to do with those not of their particular sect.

Here, then, in the Old Believers was a movement, or, rather, a number of movements, peculiarly Russian, evidences of vitality in Orthodox Christianity. They attracted many of the more independently minded and those searching for a way of satisfying their religious hunger. The majority were peasants. A minority were merchants with a sturdiness of character which won them success in business.

OTHER DISSIDENT MOVEMENTS

The Old Believers were not the only Russians who departed from the state religion. There were also the Khlysty, who called themselves the People of God. Their origin is obscure. We do not know the date of their origin or whether here was a purely indigenous movement or one which sprang from foreign contacts, possibly with the Bogomils. They themselves dated their beginnings from the seventeenth century, but they may have been much older. They regarded their founder as a peasant, Daniel Filippov, who is said to have been one of the priestless Old Believers. Khlysty tradition had it that the God Sabaoth descended from the clouds and took possession of Daniel, who thus became the living God. It is said that Daniel began preaching, saying that he had come to save men's souls and that none other teaching than his was true. His followers were to abstain from intoxicating liquors and marriage. If married, husbands and wives were to separate. Stealing and foul words were to be shunned, hospitality and charity were to be practised, with prayer, and keeping the commandments of God. Daniel had a spiritual son, Suslov, who was declared to be a Christ. The Khlysty held that there were many incarnations, or Christs, of whom Jesus Christ was merely one, and that all could be saved by their own good works. They kept their membership secret and outwardly conformed to the state church. Their secret meetings included dances which induced ecstasy and speaking with tongues. Discovered, they were persecuted. They were not exterminated but merely driven underground.

It may be that the Dukhobors and Molokans, of whom we are to hear more later (Chapter XLIII), were in existence at this time.

The Russian Orthodox Church Is Influenced by the Roman Catholic Church but Rejects It

While the Old Believers were hiving off from the state church, influences from the Roman Catholic Church were being felt in that body. They entered largely through Kiev but partly through the Jesuits in the regions under Polish influence and in the Austrian embassy in Moscow. The innovations at Kiev which were mainly the work of Peter Mogila had admirers in Moscow. In the 1680's an academy for theological study was begun in that city. It was inspired by the one in Kiev. A struggle ensued for the control of the institution between those sympathetic with Rome and those of the Orthodox tradition. The latter won, and the assignment of inaugurating the Moscow Academy was given to two brothers, Greek monks who had studied in Venice and Padua but who had kept their Orthodox convictions. A controversy also arose over the Eucharist, whether, according to the Roman Catholic view, the consecration of the bread and wine was through the words of Christ recited by the priest or, as the Orthodox maintained, by the invocation of the Holy Spirit at a later point in the prayer of consecration. In 1690 a council condemned the Roman Catholic position. The reaction against any influence from the West became so strong that the academy, even though it was safely in Orthodox hands, was allowed to fall into a sad state of neglect.

While it was rejecting anything that smacked of Rome, the Russian Orthodox Church was expanding westward into territory which was threatened by the Roman Catholic Church. In the middle of the sixteenth century the Cossacks of the Ukraine broke away from Poland and became incorporated with Russia. In 1685 a further shrinkage of Polish political influence was accompanied by the extension over Kiev of the ecclesiastical authority of Moscow.

The Striking Changes under Peter the Great

The defeat of Nikon in his efforts to free the Church from the domination of the state and to make the Patriarch more important than the tsar was not merely the frustration of one individual. The great Patriarch's body was scarcely cold in its grave when there came to power a tsar who brought the Church into more extensive subjection to the throne than it had yet been and who caused the Patriarchate to lapse for about two centuries. Nikon died, banished, in 1681. Eight years later, in 1689, at the age of seventeen, Peter, who had come to the throne as a child in 1682, the year after the death of Nikon, dismissed his sister Sophia, the regent, and took full charge. The most vigorous

tsar since Ivan IV, he was the dominant figure in Russia for nearly a generation, until his death (1725).

Into the dramatic and often repeated story of those three and a half decades
we need not go, except in the briefest summary. It included the subjugation of
the rebellious *Streltzy,* Peter's sojourn in Western Europe, his Westward
orientation of Russia, symbolized by the founding of St. Petersburg and the
transfer of the capital from Moscow to that city with its Baltic and Western
confrontation, his reorganization of the state on the models of Western administration and absolute monarchies—for he was a contemporary of Louis
XIV of France—and his wars and extensive conquests.

We are here concerned with what Peter did to the Russian Orthodox Church
and through it to the Christianity of Russia. Peter was not irreligious, but
while outwardly he conformed, his faith was not by any means in full accord
with that of the Orthodox Church. As he was bringing all the state and society
under the control of the throne and disregarding old traditions and precedents,
so he insisted that the Church be subordinate to the crown. He had seen
Protestantism in Western Europe with its principle of *cujus regio ejus religio*
and the domination of territorial and national churches by the princes. It may
be, too, that Peter was influenced by the experience of his father, Alexis, in his
conflict with Nikon and had been convinced by it that as tsar he must not be
embarassed by the rival power of the Church.

Peter made the Church distinctly subordinate to the state. When, in 1700, the
Patriarch died no one was appointed to succeed him. The office was not formally
discontinued, but it was not filled. Since the Patriarch's court was in abeyance,
many cases were taken from the tribunals of the Church to those of the state.
Questions of doctrine and ecclesiastical discipline were left to the Church, for
the experiment of putting the clergy under the civil courts was soon abandoned.
The Monastic Office was reëstablished and to it was given the management of
the huge properties of the Church and the monasteries. Some of the revenues
from them were diverted to education, charity, and purely secular objects. In
1721 a substitute for the Patriarchate was inaugurated. Instead of an individual,
a body, a Spiritual College, later called the Holy Synod, was put in charge of
the Church. This body was entrusted with the reform of superstitious customs,
the direction of education, both secular and religious, for the two were combined in the same schools, the supervision of the religious duties of the laity,
the censorship of writings, the investigation of miracles and of charges of
heresy, the examination of those proposed for the episcopate, the trial of
bishops, and the supervision of the finances of the Church. The duties of the
collegium, then, were to be administrative, legislative, and judicial.

Peter took other actions which affected the Russian Orthodox Church. He restricted the number of the clergy, regulated the interior life of the monasteries, and commanded the laity to make at least an annual confession and to attend church every Sunday and feast day. At first Peter was inclined to be lenient towards the Old Believers. Later, however, he enforced the existing legislation against them and treated them with great harshness. He tended to make the parish clergy an hereditary class. He stressed the education of the priesthood and of the sons of the clergy. By his insistence that the Church keep out of civil affairs he strengthened a trend which was already present, that of emphasis upon worship and the liturgy as the chief concern of the Church.

With his desire to give Russia a Western outlook, Peter favoured those among the clergy who had been trained with that viewpoint. Some of them he called from Kiev, where, as we have seen, Western influence was stronger than in Moscow. Some, while Orthodox, had a Roman Catholic orientation. Others were inclined towards Protestantism, especially since through his residence in the West Peter had imbibed sympathy for that form of the faith. Numbers of Russians became acquainted with Western theologians, including Augustine, others of the Roman Catholics, and several of the Protestants.

After Peter a partial reaction occurred. His changes aroused opposition among the conservatives. Under the brief reign of Peter II (1727–1730) it was marked. Then came a decade of German influence under Ann of Courland (1730–1740) a niece of Peter the Great and Ivan VI (1740–1742), grandnephew of Ann. Under Peter the Great's daughter Elizabeth (1742–1762) reaction was again in full swing, with the unpopularity of things Western and the attempt to restore what was purely Russian. Yet many of the changes of Peter persisted.

SUMMARY

In contrast with Western Europe it was a fairly sombre picture that the East presented in the two hundred and fifty years after 1500. In contrast with the abounding vitality in the West which expressed itself in the Protestant and Catholic Reformations, in most places in Western Asia and South-eastern Europe the churches which represented Christianity either only barely held their own or lost ground. The one exception was Russia. Here was geographic expansion and here were currents of life which cut themselves channels which were peculiar to that country. One would like to know more of the Christianity of the masses, especially in Russia. Monasticism continued and in Russia, although we hear little of it, the kenotic tradition persisted.

Although not making striking gains or breaking out in new ways as did the Christianity of the West, the Eastern Churches believed themselves to be preserving the Christian faith in its purity as it had come from the apostles. That was true of all of them, but it was especially the conviction of the Orthodox

Churches, both Greek and Russian. They knew that they were on the defensive as against the politically dominant Islam, but they believed themselves to be the guardians of a sacred treasure.

SELECTED BIBLIOGRAPHY

W. F. Adeney, *The Greek and Eastern Churches* (New York, Charles Scribner's Sons, 1908, pp. xiv, 634). A useful summary.

L. Arpee, *A History of Armenian Christianity* (New York, The Armenian Missionary Association of America, 1946, pp. xii, 386). Warmly sympathetic, by an Armenian Protestant.

S. Bolshakoff, *Russian Nonconformity* (Philadelphia, The Westminster Press, 1950, pp. 192). A useful, comprehensive summary.

F. C. Conybeare, *Russian Dissenters* (Harvard University Press, 1921, pp. x, 370). A useful collection of material from Russian accounts.

G. P. Fedotov, *A Treasury of Russian Spirituality* (New York, Sheed & Ward, 1948, pp. xvi, 501). Valuable for this chapter for its autobiography of Avvakum, pp. 137–181.

A. Fortescue, *The Orthodox Eastern Church* (London, Catholic Truth Society, 1929, pp. xxxiii, 451). By a Roman Catholic, based upon wide reading.

A. Fortescue, *The Uniate Eastern Churches. The Byzantine Rite in Italy, Sicily, Syria, and Egypt* (London, Burns, Oates & Washbourne, 1923, pp. xiii, 244). A posthumous work, by a Roman Catholic.

W. H. Frere, *Some Links in the Chain of Russian Church History* (London, Faith Press, 1918, pp. xvi, 200). A comprehensive survey by an eminent Anglo-Catholic scholar, making extensive use of Russian materials.

A. H. Hore, *Eighteen Centuries of the Greek Orthodox Church* (London, James Parker & Co., 1899, pp. vi, 706). Semi-popular, not always critical.

G. Vernadsky, *A History of Russia* (Yale University Press, rev. ed., 1930, pp. xix, 413). A comprehensive survey by a distinguished specialist.

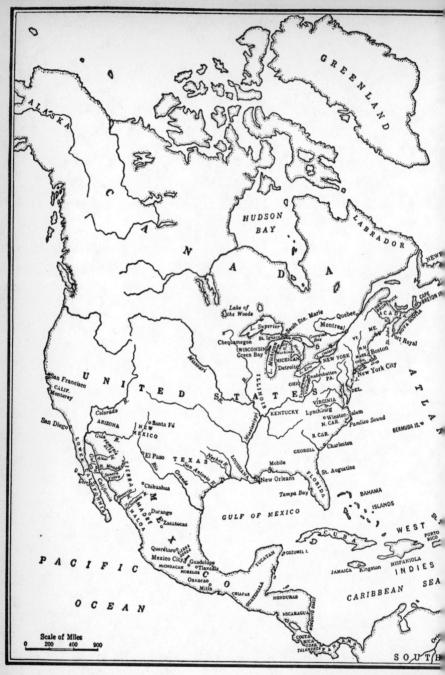

NORTH AND CENTRAL AM

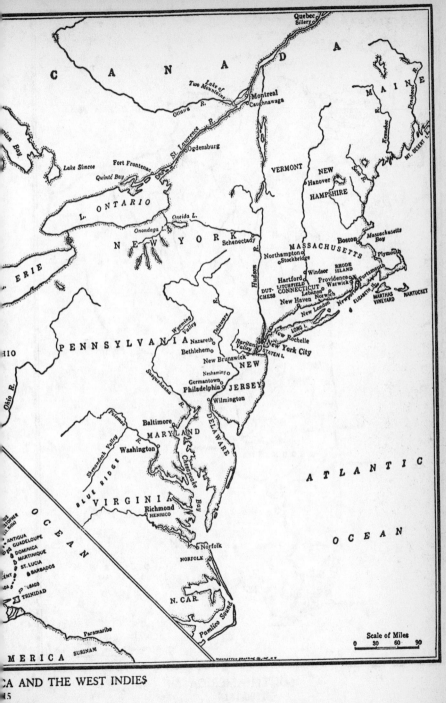

SOUTH AMERICA
1500-1815

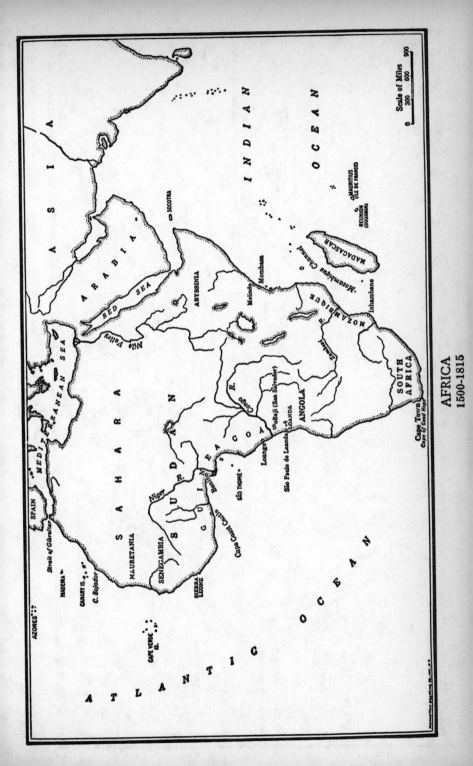

AFRICA
1500-1815

Scale of Miles
0   300   600   900

ASIA

ARABIA

RED SEA

SOCOTRA

ABYSSINIA

INDIAN

OCEAN

MAURITIUS
(ÎLE DE FRANCE)

REUNION
(BOURBON)

COMORO

MADAGASCAR

Mozambique Channel

Melinda

Mombasa

MOZAMBIQUE

Inhambane

Zambezi

SOUTH
AFRICA

Cape Town
Cape of Good Hope

Nile Valley

MEDITERRANEAN SEA

SPAIN

Strait of Gibraltar

AZORES

MADEIRA

CANARY IS.

C. Bojador

MAURETANIA

SAHARA

SUDAN

Niger R.

SENEGAMBIA

SIERRA
LEONE

GUINEA COAST

Cape Coast Castle

Benin R.

SÃO THOMÉ

Loango

Congo R.

S. Paji (San Salvador)

São Paulo de Loanda

LOANDA

ANGOLA

CAPE VERDE IS.

ATLANTIC OCEAN

ATLANTIC OCEAN

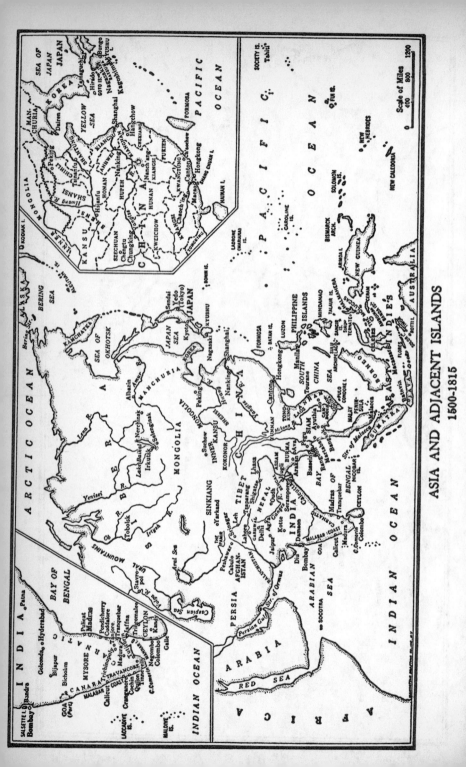

ASIA AND ADJACENT ISLANDS

1500-1815

Chapter 41

CHRISTIANITY RESUMES ITS WORLD-WIDE SPREAD

One of the most striking features of the two hundred and fifty years between 1500 and 1750 was the resumption of the world-wide spread of Christianity. As we have seen, the century and a half between 1350 and 1500 saw a marked loss of territory. During the preceding four centuries the faith had been carried across Eurasia, even to Greenland, and probably to North America. It was also found as far south as the Sudan, Ethiopia, and South India. Yet by the end of the fifteenth century its outer boundaries had shrunk. It had died out in China and in most of Central Asia, in Western Asia it was slowly losing ground, it was retreating in Egypt and the Sudan, with the extinction of the feeble Scandinavian settlements it had vanished from Greenland, and any footing in North America had been ephemeral. Beginning with the closing years of the fifteenth century Christianity renewed its geographic expansion. By the middle of the eighteenth century Christian communities were on all five continents and on many of the islands that fringed these continents. It had been replanted in China and had a larger following there than ever before. It had been introduced to Japan, had won the majority of the population of the Philippine Islands, had been carried across Siberia to the north-eastern shores of Eurasia, had taken root in South-eastern Asia and the East Indies, had established a substantial foothold in Ceylon, and had become more widely extended in India. It was represented by scattered communities along the coast of Africa south of the Sahara. It had been reintroduced to Greenland and had become the prevailing religion in the West Indies and the more thickly settled portions of North and South America. With a pause and slight recessions for a generation or more after 1750, its forward march continued in the nineteenth and twentieth centuries. By 1750 it was more widely spread than it or any other religion had ever been. Three other faiths, Hinduism, Buddhism, and Confucianism, although within narrower geographic boundaries, may have outnumbered its professed adherents and Islam was still a formidable rival with a constituency not far from its size. Two centuries later, in the 1950's, in spite of serious recent losses, Christianity was still spreading and had clearly outstripped every other religion, not only in the area covered but also in numbers of professed adherents and in influence upon mankind.

This phenomenal spread of Christianity accompanied an equally remarkable expansion of European peoples and culture. Both were chiefly from Western Europe. Viewed superficially, the spread of Christianity in the four and a half centuries after 1500 was an integral, secondary, and inevitable phase of the world-wide extension of Europeans and their influence. That extension was partly by exploration, partly by conquest, partly by vast migrations, and partly by commerce. Since Christianity was the professed faith of Western Europeans and the Russians, it was to be expected that they would carry it with them.

Yet the spread of the Christian faith was not an inevitable accompaniment of the expansion of Europe. In important respects the latter hampered it. A large proportion, probably a majority of the Europeans through whom it was accomplished, although nominally Christian, denied it by their conduct. There were cruel exploitation and here and there extermination of non-Europeans. Withdrawn from the environment in which they had been reared, which, though by no means fully Christian, gave at least lip service to Christian standards, many Europeans deteriorated morally. Coming from societies where baptism and confirmation were practically universal and attendance at Christian instruction and public worship a social convention, in migrating to another region thousands and eventually millions tended to drift away from the Church and their children and grandchildren to lose what little of Christian tradition remained and to become quite de-Christianized.

The spread of Christianity in connexion with the expansion of Europe was chiefly through minorities, sometimes small minorities, who, committing themselves fully to it, became expressions of the abounding vitality inherent in the Gospel. That commitment was largely through awakenings in Christianity. In the years between 1500 and 1750 these were what we have described as the Protestant Reformation, the Catholic Reformation, and the movements, much less powerful, in Russia. It was these minorities, especially from the first two, who laboured to make the coming of the European a blessing and not a curse to non-Europeans, who strove to hold to the faith the migrating Europeans and their descendants, and to see that Christianity became an effective leaven in the new nations that arose from the migrations.

ROMAN CATHOLIC PREPONDERANCE

Between 1500 and 1750 the geographic spread of Christianity was mainly through Roman Catholics. This was for three reasons. It was first and chiefly because in the fore part of that period the expansion of Europe was predominantly by Spain and Portugal, countries which were almost solidly Roman Catholic. The majority of the first voyages of exploration were through them and it was they who established the largest colonial empires. Spain ruled most of the West Indies, the southern coasts of North America, Mexico, most of Central America, the western and much of the southern and northern coasts of South America, and the Philippines. Portugal held Brazil, established posts along the shores of Africa, obtained footholds in India, conquered much of Ceylon, and had outposts on the Malay Peninsula and in the East Indies and China. Somewhat tardily Roman Catholic France entered into the race for colonies and at one time staked out a claim to the heart of North America, the region of the Great Lakes and the Mississippi Valley. Protestant powers were late in entering the race for commerce and colonies. In the seventeenth century Great Britain and Holland became active, but until after 1750 their colonial possessions, while far-flung, had only a small fraction of the population and the territorial extent of those of the Roman Catholic powers. In contrast with the Roman Catholics, the areas which contained the majority of the Protestants, Germany, Scandinavia, and Switzerland, before the nineteenth century had very little share in the expansion of Europe. While spreading over a huge area which stretched across all the northern reaches of Asia and after 1750 extended down the west coast of North America, Russian expansion was in regions which were thinly populated and did not count as much in the world scene as did those occupied by Western Europeans.

In the second place, the fact that the Roman Catholics had the leading place in the spread of Christianity between 1500 and 1750 was because the Catholic Reformation coincided with the explorations, conquests, commerce, and settlements of the Roman Catholic powers. The Catholic Reformation began in Spain on the eve of the discoveries of Columbus and the daring achievements of the *conquistadores*. It was an order begun by a Spaniard, the Society of Jesus, which carried on the most extensive missions of the era. The great days of the French colonial empire in North America followed soon after the height of the Catholic Reformation in France. Most of the Roman Catholic missions, whether by Spaniards, French, Portuguese, Italians, or from areas under the control of Spain in Italy and the Low Countries, were through orders which either came out of the Catholic Reformation, such as the Jesuits, Capuchins, Theatines, and Lazarists, or had been reinvigorated by that awakening, notably the Franciscans, Dominicans, and Augustinians.

A third but less important reason for the predominant role of Roman Catholics in the spread of Christianity during this period was that in the great monastic orders they had both the tradition and the instruments for spreading the faith, while at the outset the Protestants had neither. There had been a long standing precedent for the support and even the inauguration of missions by Roman Catholic princes. The missionaries had generally been monks, and such orders as the Franciscans, Dominicans, and Jesuits had missions as a major objective, whether among nominal Christians or non-Christians. Moreover, in the seventeenth century Rome devised a new instrument for the furthering and supervision of missions. This was the *Sacra Congregatio de Propaganda Fide*, usually known as the Propaganda. Begun in 1622, under it was placed a college, founded in 1627, for the training of missionaries. Eventually it was to become the major Papal agency for the coordination and direction of missions in non-Christian and non-Roman Catholic lands.

In contrast, by abandoning monasticism Protestants had deprived themselves of that instrument and most of their princes were so intent upon gaining the control of the Church in their domains by promoting Protestantism and were so engrossed in the struggles which engaged Protestantism in its early years that they could give little attention to missions, even had they desired to do so. Some of the Protestant reformers were frankly not interested in missions to non-Christians. It is significant, however, that as soon as explorations, commerce, and migrations put Protestants in close touch with non-Christians, among Protestants there were those who saw in the contacts both an opportunity and a duty and quickly devised means for propagating their faith.

As we recount the expansion of Christianity in the two and a half centuries after 1500, we can do it with less confusion if we trace its course region by region. We will begin with Africa south of the Sahara, then move to India, South-east Asia, the East Indies, the Philippines, Japan, China, and Siberia, and from there journey to the Western Hemisphere, ending our survey with the Thirteen Colonies which were soon to become the United States and, in point of numbers and influence, eventually to be the most important region in which Christianity was freshly planted in this period.

Africa South of the Sahara

The planting of Christianity on the islands which fringe the west and east coasts of Africa and on the shores of Africa itself was mainly by Portuguese and so by Roman Catholics under their auspices. It was the Portuguese who led Europe in the discovery of the route to the East by way of the Cape of Good Hope. It was chiefly they who spotted the shores of Africa with trading posts. The pioneer in the undertaking, Prince Henry the Navigator, was, as we have more than once reminded ourselves, Grand Master of the Order of Christ, a military monastic body which in Portugal succeeded to the property of the Knights Templars. In his direction of the enterprise he seems to have been moved in part, or at least so a Papal bull declared, by the desire to unite with the Christians of India against the Moslems and pagans of that land and to spread the Christian faith.

The chief commodity derived from Africa was Negro slaves for the plantations of the New World. Here, as we have suggested, was a major exploitation of one race by another, an exploitation with a record of untold suffering and brutality. It is thought-provoking for those who would enquire into the effect of Christianity that explorations commenced partly for the purpose of propagating the Christian faith and carried through by those who bore the Christian name had as one of their effects a traffic brutalizing both to those who constituted its wares and to those who conducted it. As we are to see later, those fully committed to Christ did much to mitigate it and eventually it was those moved by the Christian faith who brought to an end both the traffic and the slavery which fed on it. Yet here is a sobering paradox.

Beginning in the fifteenth century Portuguese colonized the Azores, the Madeiras, and the Cape Verde Islands. Under Portuguese auspices and in part by missionaries from Portugal, the colonists were given spiritual care and churches were built.

At several points on the African coast Christian communities arose from the conversion of the Negroes. In the area just south of the Congo in what was known as the Kingdom of the Congo a native chief was baptized near the end of the fifteenth century. His son who succeeded him seems to have been earnestly Christian and under him a large proportion of his subjects were baptized. A son of this second generation Christian was consecrated bishop. So far as we know he was the first Negro to be raised to that dignity. Several other Negroes were ordained to the priesthood. Schools were begun, and what gave promise of becoming a permanent and thriving African Christian community came into being. Jesuits from Portugal were there through much of the sixteenth century and near the end of that century Franciscans arrived. There were also Capuchins and Discalced Carmelites. Yet in time Christianity died out, leaving only a few physical relics and possibly some traces in folklore. There were also important missions farther south, in Angola, and on the east coast at Mombasa and Mozambique.

In the sixteenth and seventeenth centuries several efforts were made by Portuguese to propagate Christianity in the island of Madagascar, but without continuing success.

Protestant Christianity came late to Africa. Its chief centre was on the southern tip of the continent. Here, in 1652, the Dutch began a continuing settlement as a way station to their trading posts in India, Ceylon, Malacca, and the East Indies, and a community arose made up of the Dutch and their descendants, of Huguenot refugees, of Malays and others brought from the East, and of local Hottentots. Within a few years a resident clergyman arrived and services and religious instruction were carried on according to the faith of the Reformed Church. In 1737 a Moravian missionary came who for six years laboured among the Hottentots. The Dutch ministers also baptized some of the non-Christians and a church was built in Capetown for the converts. In this fashion began what in the nineteenth and twentieth centuries was to be a major stronghold of Protestant Christianity.

FRANCIS XAVIER, THE GREAT PIONEER IN SOUTH AND EAST ASIA

In the half century after the first of their number rounded the Cape of Good Hope and arrived in India, the Portuguese established commerce and trading posts from the west coast of that land to Japan. In several of these centres there were priests, and efforts were made to hold the Portuguese to the faith, to baptize the children which sprang from their unions with the women of the region, and to win the non-Christians.

The great pioneer in the missions in South and East Asia and the fringing islands was one of the children of the Catholic Reformation and an initial member of the Society of Jesus, Francis Xavier. Xavier had only a decade in the East, from 1542 to 1552, but in that brief time he laboured in several lands, introduced the faith to Japan, and died while trying to make his way into China. A flaming spirit, few missionaries of any religion have made so notable a record.

Francis Xavier was born in 1506, of Basque stock and of a noble family in the Spanish part of Navarre, not far from the Pyrenees. Although lithe and athletic, he was fond of books, had no desire for a military career, and, the youngest son, chose to prepare for service in the Church. When less than twenty he went to the University of Paris to obtain the necessary training and was there eleven years. He seems to have been uncontaminated by the vices which were common among the student body and younger teachers, but for a time in that early flush of the Reformation before lines were tightly drawn he was on the fringes of a group with Protestant tendencies. However, as we have noted, he came in touch with Ignatius Loyola. Loyola, a fellow-countryman and about fifteen years his senior, set out to win the charming, brilliant Basque, and with success. Xavier was one of the Paris group who made their dedication with Loyola and journeyed to Italy.

While in Rome, Loyola received a request from King John III of Portugal for four missionaries for that monarch's possessions in the Indies. Loyola felt that he could not spare so many from his small company, for his vision was even farther-ranging than all the East. However, he agreed to send two. One of the two fell ill and, giving him only a day's notice, Loyola commanded Xavier to fill the vacancy. Xavier unhesitatingly obeyed, the more readily since he had already dreamed of going to India. He and his companion went to Lisbon and while waiting for passage were missionaries among the nominal Christians in that capital. The other was detained in Portugal to continue that mission, and Xavier sailed (1541) for India without him. On the long, tedious voyage he gave himself unstintedly to his fellow-passengers, surrendering to the sick his own privileged quarters.

Landing in India, Xavier was not content to remain long in any one spot. His was the vision of the pioneer and he ranged over most of the vast area covered by Portuguese commerce, blazing new trails for the faith and for the Society of Jesus. A devoted friend, intensely interested in individuals, seeking by love, gayety, and a timely word to win them to the Christian faith or to a deeper Christian life, Xavier also had an imagination which covered whole countries and peoples. He sought to raise the level of Christian living of the Portuguese adventurers and their nominally Christian mixed-blooded children. He recruited members for his Society, asked for more missionaries from Europe, and made provision for training for the service of the Church converts from among the peoples of the East.

The geographic range of Xavier's travels was prodigious. In Goa, the head-quarters of the Portuguese in India and the Far East, Xavier cared for the sick and the prisoners, preached, heard confessions, taught the children, and founded a college to prepare youth of several races and nations as possible missionaries. After a few months he went to South-east India to the Paravas, a low-caste pearl-fishing folk about twenty thousand of whom, to obtain Portuguese help against their hereditary enemies, the Moslem Arabs, had recently accepted baptism. Without priests, the sacraments, or Christian instruction, they attracted Xavier. He was with them about two years and learned enough of their language to impart to them in their vernacular the Apostles' Creed, the Ten Commandments, and some of the prayers, including the Lord's Prayer. He concentrated his attention on the children, encouraging them to teach their elders and to destroy idols and other symbols of their former religions. He baptized whole villages and trained and appointed catechists. It is interesting to record that the Paravas remained Christians, rose in economic status, and in the twentieth century were still bulwarks of the Roman Catholic Church. From the Paravas Xavier went to Travancore where, aided by Indian priests, he won several thousand converts from fishermen of a still lower social level. He was in Ceylon, then at Malacca, and then in the Moluccas. Back in India he strengthened the Goa college, observed that the Parava mission was advancing, and founded a college in Cochin, on the west coast south of Goa. In 1549 he went to Japan, where the Portuguese had begun commerce a few years earlier. There he inaugurated what was to be one of the most successful and tragic missions of the period. Having seen that enterprise begun and in responsible hands, his imagination was fired with the hope of starting a mission among the Chinese, the most numerous and most highly civilized people in the Far East. Before making that attempt and in part to prepare for it, he was once more in Goa. Then he went to an island off the coast of South China, where the Portuguese had a commercial rendezvous, hoping to gain access to the mainland. Failing but still hoping, he remained after all the Portuguese ships except his own had left. There he fell ill and died, late in 1552. As we are to see in a moment, his fellow Jesuits followed his lead and in several areas, notably India, Japan, and China, partly fulfilled his dream.

The Spread of Christianity in India

It will be remembered that the Portuguese were not the first to bring Christianity to India. Legend, unfortunately not fully dependable, has it that the faith was introduced by Thomas, one of the original apostles. There were almost certainly Christians in India before the fourth century. When the Portuguese arrived they found a large body of Christians on the south coast having Syriac as their ecclesiastical language and with ties with the Nestorians in Mesopotamia.

Partly under Portuguese auspices and partly independently of them, in the sixteenth, seventeenth, and eighteenth centuries Roman Catholic missions were widely spread in India. Early in the eighteenth century Protestant missions were begun.

In the course of time the overwhelming majority of the population of the areas in India under Portuguese political control adopted the Christian name. These areas were not large and had ports, chiefly Goa, as their nuclei. Not far from 1700 the number of Christians in the Portuguese possessions is said to have been half a million. Later the French established themselves in India, with their main centre at Pondicherry, on the south-east coast. There, too, a Christian community arose. However, French territories were much less extensive than those of the Portuguese.

Roman Catholic missions were by no means confined to the Portuguese and French enclaves. They were scattered over much of India. They were begun and maintained by the Franciscans, Dominicans, Carmelites, and Augustinians, and the orders which arose out of the Catholic Reformation, such as the Jesuits, Capuchins, and Theatines.

The Jesuits long maintained a mission in the centres of Mogul power in the North. The Moguls were descendants of the Mongols. They established themselves in the North in the first half of the sixteenth century and built an empire which eventually stretched over much of India. They were Moslems, but one of the line, Akbar, who reigned from 1556 to 1605, conceived the idea of devising one religion for his subjects which would combine the qualities of several and would thus help to unify his realm, divided as that was by deep cleavages between various religious communities. In his attempt to work out such a religion he asked Jesuits to his court and questioned them about their faith. With interruptions, the Jesuit enterprise continued under Akbar's successors into the latter part of the seventeenth century. Not many converts were made, but a few were gathered in Agra, Lahore, and Delhi.

More fruitful and in some ways more interesting was a Jesuit mission with headquarters at Madura, in the South, inaugurated by Robert de Nobili (1577–1656). Nobili was of a distinguished Italian family, nephew of Bellarmine, Jesuit theologian and cardinal, and related to Pope Julius III. On reaching India he found that Catholics were from the lowest social levels and were regarded as Portuguese. The term *prangui* was given to both. He was assigned to Madura to care for Paravas who resided there. Noting the contempt in which they were held by the majority of Indians, he realized that if Christianity were to have a wider appeal, a fresh approach must be devised. He found that the Brahmins were the highest caste and believed that by winning leaders from among them much of the rest of the population would be attracted. He therefore announced that he was not a *prangui,* built a hut in the Brahmin quarter of the city, declared himself to be a Roman rajah and ascetic, adopted a manner of life and dress much like that of the Brahmin teachers, made himself familiar with the local vernaculars and the Sanskrit in which the sacred classics of Hinduism were written, and prepared an extensive Christian literature in Indian languages. He excluded Parava Christians from the church which he built and permitted his Brahmin converts to dress in a manner not unlike their pre-Christian garb. His methods soon aroused a storm of criticism among some of his fellow-missionaries, for they charged him with compromising the Christian faith. However, his archbishop supported him and in 1623 Rome pronounced in his favour. In the course of time an extensive enterprise arose in Madura and the vicinity which followed his procedure and amplified it. Only a minority of the converts were from among the Brahmins, but by 1703 the total Christian community was said to number two hundred thousand. In that year a Capuchin complained to Rome that in several ways the Jesuits were allowing their flocks to retain pagan customs. Controversy followed which disturbed the missions in South India and in 1744 was ended by a Papal bull which specifically condemned the questionable practices—the Malabar rites as they were called.

An Indian clergy was recruited and trained and we hear of bishops of Brahmin stock. Not a few of the clergy were said to be of inferior moral quality, but some of them were zealous and courageous missionaries.

The Portuguese connexion proved both an asset and a liability to Catholic missions in India. It was an asset, for Portuguese protection, especially in Goa and other Portuguese possessions, assisted in the process of conversion and in other ways the civilian authorities aided the Church. It was a handicap, partly because of the scandalous lives of many Portuguese who were far from ideal exemplars of the Christian faith. It also proved an obstacle because the Portuguese claimed the right to control missions throughout the country, as, indeed, they did in much of South Asia and the Far East. Papal decrees had given the King of Portugal what was called the *padroado,* or patronage, over ecclesiastical affairs. This included the naming by the crown of bishops and other forms of control. It was a phase of the domination of the Church by the crown which was, as we have seen, widely prevalent in Roman Catholic as well as Protestant lands. In India, Rome insisted that the *padroado* applied only to territory actually under Portuguese rule, while the Portuguese held that it covered all the land. Rome sought to dodge the issue and ease the friction by appointing to supervise the Church in non-Portuguese areas not bishops, but vicars apostolic. Since Portugal claimed the right to name the bishops, and this Rome conceded, vicars apostolic were given the titles of bishops of extinct sees, usually in Western Asia, and exercised their episcopal powers not in their own names but as direct representatives of the Pope. However, this device only slightly eased the tension. The Portuguese often placed obstacles in the way of missionaries sent out under the authority of Rome in disregard of the *padroado.* The issue troubled Catholic missions in India well down into the twentieth century.

We have already noted the attempt, in part successful, to bring into submission to Rome the Syrian Christians, and have seen that later the majority severed their Roman connexion. The Syrian Christians had in effect become a closed community, like an Indian caste, and made no effort to spread their faith among non-Christians.

Protestantism was late in coming to India. In the seventeenth century it arrived in the persons of Dutch, British, and Danish traders. Each of these groups had chaplains who ministered to the Europeans and their servants. However, while here and there were those who proposed to seize the opportunity to spread the Protestant faith among the Indians, nothing of consequence was done until early in the eighteenth century. The mission then begun sprang from Pietism. The first two missionaries, Ziegenbalg and Plütschau, had been students at the Pietist centre, Halle, and in 1706 arrived at Tranquebar, a Danish trading post on the south-east coast. They came at the instance of the Danish king. They were not welcomed by the local Danish authorities, but persevered, learned Tamil, and won converts from Hinduism and Roman Catholicism. Recruits came from Pietist circles in Germany, financial aid was given by Anglicans and Danes, and a Lutheran community arose which grew and persisted into the twentieth century.

CEYLON

On Ceylon, predominantly Buddhist in religion, a substantial Roman Catholic community arose in connexion with the Portuguese conquest of part of the island. That conquest began early in the sixteenth century. The missions were chiefly by the Franciscans. Some of the conversions were by force. Others were of native chiefs or kings and their followers from the hope of obtaining Portuguese support. Some groups accepted baptism in the expectation of Portuguese protection and of freedom from galling social, legal, and financial restrictions and exactions. In a few sections early in the seventeenth century Christians were in the majority.

In the seventeenth century the Dutch drove the Portuguese out of Ceylon. In 1658 they captured the last of the Portuguese strongholds. They sought to eliminate Roman Catholicism and substitute for it the Reformed faith. Roman Catholic clergy were expelled and in 1658 the death penalty was decreed for any who harboured a Roman Catholic priest. Many Roman Catholic church buildings were converted to Protestant uses and public and private meetings of Roman Catholics were forbidden. Non-Protestants, both Roman Catholics and non-Christians, were declared ineligible for office or employment under the Dutch and we hear in one temple of the suppression of Buddhist worship. We also read of the imposition of fines for non-attendance at church services and of the confiscation of a third of the property of some who refused to be baptized. Dutch clergy were sent out from Holland and an ecclesiastical structure was set up. In 1722 the number of Protestant Christians in Ceylon was said to be 424,392. However, the faith of most must have been very superficial, both because of the manner in which conversions were effected and of the lack of clergy. In 1747 it was reported that in all the island there were only five ministers and that of these only one understood the language.

In spite of the Dutch prohibition, thousands of Roman Catholics held to their faith. Indian priests, chiefly from Goa, ministered to them, often working in secret. They not only instructed Christians and gave the sacraments to them. They also won some non-Christians.

South-east Asia

In the sixteenth, seventeenth, and eighteenth centuries Roman Catholic Christianity was planted in Burma, the Malay Peninsula, Siam, Cambodia, Cochinchina, Annam, and Tonkin.

In Burma no extensive Christian communities were gathered, but Jesuits, Dominicans, and Barnabites, especially the last, were active and made converts.

The Malay Peninsula was fairly solidly Moslem. From 1511 to 1641 the Portuguese were in possession of Malacca and there had churches and clergy. In 1641 they were driven out by the Dutch and the latter either turned the church buildings into Protestant houses of worship or diverted them to secular uses.

Roman Catholic missionaries came to Siam in connexion with the Portuguese and their commerce. As in Ceylon and Burma, the population was predominantly Buddhist. Unlike Ceylon, but like Burma, Christianity made little appeal, possibly because Europeans did not rule any of the land, and only a small Christian community was gathered.

In the region later known as Indochina, composed of Cambodia, Cochinchina, Annam, Tonkin, and the thinly settled Laos, extensive missions were carried on, chiefly by Jesuits, Dominicans, Franciscans, and the Paris Society of Foreign Missions. This last organization arose out of the appeal of a Jesuit who had laboured in Cochinchina and had become convinced that among the missionaries there should be secular priests who would not only seek to win non-Christians but also raise up and train a secular native clergy to care for the converts. In Paris he found a group of young men, fruits of the Catholic Reformation, who gave him an eager response. The result was the organization of the Society of Foreign Missions, formally founded in 1663. Eventually it had missions in much of South-east and East Asia. By the middle of the eighteenth century Indochina had Christian communities which totaled several tens of thousands.

The East Indies

South and east of Asia there stretches a vast congeries of islands which Europeans have known as the East Indies or the Malay Archipelago. It presents a mixture of races, languages, and religions. The Malay stock in its various divisions predominates racially and linguistically. Animism, Hinduism, Buddhism, and Islam had been present before the coming of Christianity and all these except Buddhism had followings when the first Christian missionaries landed. Islam was the most recent arrival and by the beginning of the sixteenth century had won the large majority of the population and was still spreading.

Christianity was introduced by the Portuguese, Spaniards, and Dutch. The first two brought the Roman Catholic form of the faith and the third propagated the Reformed variety of Protestantism. All three, but especially the Portuguese and the Dutch, were attracted by the spices of the islands, for these were much in demand in Europe. The Portuguese were the first to appear. Members of several religious orders took advantage of their trading posts to begin missions. In 1569 the Jesuits were said to be in charge of eighty thousand Christians. As we are to see in a moment, the Spanish strength was in the northernmost extension of the archipelago, the Philippines, but some of their missionaries reached southward, and an Italian Theatine from Palermo, then under Spanish rule, was called the apostle to Borneo and became the first vicar apostolic on that island.

The Dutch arrived late in the sixteenth century. Before many years they drove the Portuguese out of most of the archipelago and established their headquarters at Batavia, on the island of Java. The Roman Catholic communities dwindled or disappeared in the areas under Dutch control and persisted mainly on what remained to the Portuguese, chiefly part of the island of Timor. Dutch interests were in the hands of their East India Company. The Company supported pastors of the Reformed Church and in some of the islands gave active assistance to efforts at conversion. Many of the Malays accepted baptism, probably usually from the desire to stand well with the Dutch. Translations of the Bible were made into Malay and the New Testament in Malay was the main textbook in the schools. The Christianity of the majority was largely formal, but a state Protestant church came into being which continued into the twentieth century and then, disestablished, proved to have sufficient vitality to survive the adverse vicissitudes of World War II and its aftermath.

The Philippine Islands

As we have suggested, the Philippine Islands are actually the northernmost of the East Indies. They owe their name and their distinctive culture to the Spanish conquest which began in the sixteenth century. Their inhabitants are predominantly of Malay stock. At the dawn of the sixteenth century they were mostly animists in religion and in the primitive stages of culture. Islam was entering and had won some of the peoples in the South, Moros, as they were called by the Spaniards, not because of any racial difference but because of the Moslem faith and culture.

Sailing under commission from the Emperor Charles V, Magellan was the first European to reveal the islands to Western Europeans. He there lost his life (1521), and it was not until the third quarter of the sixteenth century that the effective Spanish conquest was begun. The Spaniards came by way of Mexico, a vast distance. Their occupation had little commercial significance, for only a limited trade was carried on by way of Manila and Mexico. It was primarily missionary and was accompanied and followed by the conversion to the Roman Catholic faith of the large majority of the population. The Philippines became the first nation in the Far East in which the majority bore the Christian name and into the twentieth century continued to be the only one to have that distinction.

Conversion and religious instruction were encouraged by the Spanish rulers and were through the members of religious orders, first the Augustinians, then the Franciscans, the Dominicans, the Jesuits, and a reformed branch of the Augustinians, the Augustinian Recollects. A few seculars came and some members of the hospital order of St. John of God. To avoid friction and duplication of effort, the civil authorities forbade more than one order to labour in any one province. Expenses were met chiefly from the royal purse, from tithes collected from the Filipinos, and by the Spanish landowners. By the end of the sixteenth century more than four hundred and fifty regulars had embarked for the islands. Very little armed force was employed. The Filipinos, docile and with neither a high culture nor an advanced religion to offer resistance, quickly conformed to the wishes of their masters. It is said that by 1586 four hundred thousand had been baptized. In 1612 there were reported to be 322,400 Christians on the one island of Luzon alone and in 1735 a total of 837,182 Christians was given for all the islands. In 1750 there were said to be over a million Christians if children were included.

The islands were divided into dioceses and a native clergy was recruited and trained. However, the control of the Church continued in the hands of the Spaniards, for from them came the bishops and they made up the membership of the religious orders. Friction was chronic between the civil and ecclesiastical authorities, between the regulars and the seculars, and between the bishops and the regulars, for the latter resisted episcopal supervision.

Much of the Christianity was superficial and was mixed with remnants of pre-Christian beliefs. Yet the missionaries strove to purify the morals of their flocks, did much to improve agriculture, cultivated a love of music, maintained hospitals, and founded schools, including two universities.

THE STRANGE AND THRILLING STORY OF JAPAN

When in 1549 Francis Xavier introduced Christianity to Japan, that land was emerging from a long period of disunion and civil strife. Union was being accomplished by Oda Nobunaga, Toyotomi Hideyoshi, and Tokugawa Ieyasu. Nobunaga was then in power. The country had received most of its civilization from China, including Buddhism, its leading religion. Upon that culture as it was imported the Japanese had placed their own stamp and to it had made additions of their own. In spite of the efforts of Nobunaga, the land was still divided into a number of feudal states, each of which was governed by an hereditary lord known as a *daimyo*. The Portuguese had reached Japan about 1542 and their commerce was proving profitable to them and to those *daimyo* with whose domains they traded. These were chiefly on the island of Kyushu, and the port which eventually enjoyed more of the Portuguese trade than any other was Nagasaki.

Xavier was in Japan only about two years, but he found the country so promising a mission field that other Jesuits quickly followed him. They had immediate and startling success. In 1582 churches were said to number about two hundred and Christians about 150,000. The growth seems to have been due to a number of factors. Nobunaga was friendly, partly because he was being opposed by some of the powerful Buddhist monasteries and hoped in the Christians to have a counter-poise to them. The *daimyo* who found the Portuguese commerce lucrative favoured the missionaries, for they saw that the latter were honoured by their fellow-countrymen and thought in this wise to obtain a greater share of the trade. Having learned eagerly from the Chinese, the Japanese were predisposed to be taught by another foreign people. The head of the Jesuits in the Far East deemed the Japanese the ablest of those whom he had known in that region and made efforts to raise up a clergy among them and to admit some of them to the Society of Jesus.

The death of Nobunaga (1582) and the advent of Hideyoshi to power did not immediately alter the situation. To be sure, in 1587 Hideyoshi issued an edict against Christianity, but a nephew of his wife became a Christian and one of the two commanders in the invasion which he launched against China by way of Korea was also of that faith. In 1588 Rome made Japan a bishopric. Although in 1585 Rome had specifically reserved Japan to the Society of Jesus, in the 1580's and especially the 1590's, to the great annoyance of the latter, Franciscans and Dominicans made their way to that country and won converts, but from lower social strata than those touched by the Jesuits.

In 1596 Hideyoshi began active persecution, but for specifically what reason is not entirely clear. Several missionaries and Japanese Christians were crucified, *daimyo* were forbidden to become Christians, numbers of churches were destroyed, and missionaries were ordered assembled at Nagasaki preparatory to deportation. The early death of Hideyoshi (1598) brought a pause to these measures.

Ieyasu, who soon became the effective power in Japan, eliminated Hideyoshi's son and placed his own family, the Tokugawa, so firmly in control that as

Shoguns they gave Japan its real rulers, although in the name of the *faineant* Emperors, until the 1860's. At first he was friendly to the missionaries. That seems to have been because he wished to develop foreign commerce. Missionaries flocked to Japan, not only Jesuits, Franciscans, and Dominicans, but also Augustinians. Ieyasu received the bishop with honour and gave financial aid to the Church. Christians rapidly increased. How many there were we do not know. Soon after 1600 they are variously estimated as between two hundred thousand and seven hundred and fifty thousand. Certainly they were a larger proportion of the population than they were to be in the nineteenth or the first half of the twentieth century. They were especially numerous in the South. In Nagasaki the majority seem to have been of that faith.

Then came the renewal of persecution, first under Ieyasu and even more drastically under his successors. The reason seems to have been primarily political. Ieyasu and the other Tokugawa Shoguns feared Christianity as a threat to the unity and the dominance of their family which they had so painfully established. It might be, so they thought, a precursor to Portuguese or Spanish invasion or the occasion for rebellion. The fears of those who followed Ieyasu were heightened by the pertinacity of missionaries in seeking entrance to the country, by the contumacy of the Japanese Christians in holding to their faith in the face of anti-Christian edicts, and, in 1637 and 1638, by a rebellion in which many Christians joined. Christians were visited with excruciating tortures and many of those who held to their faith were killed. To keep out missionaries, commerce was cut off with the Portuguese and Spaniards, and Japanese were forbidden to leave the country. At first English and Dutch traders were permitted in the ports, for they showed no disposition to spread their faith and were Protestants, not Roman Catholics. However, when for a time the English discontinued their trade they were not allowed to resume it. Only the Dutch were admitted and they were confined to an island in the harbour of Nagasaki and required to submit to other galling restrictions. Edict boards were posted throughout the realm proscribing Christianity.

Yet Christianity persisted. Several thousand Christians, most of them in the hills back of Nagasaki, held to their faith. Outwardly they were Buddhists, but they kept up baptism and Christian prayers, transmitting them to their children and the latter in turn to theirs. It was not until the second half of the nineteenth century that they were revealed to a startled Europe and to hostile Japanese political authorities.

THE REPLANTING OF CHRISTIANITY IN CHINA

Twice, in the seventh and then in the thirteenth century, Christianity had been introduced to China. Both times its constituency seems to have been prevailingly foreign and neither time does it appear to have won many converts from among the Chinese themselves. Twice it had died out, and so completely that we do not know precisely when or how.

Now, in the sixteenth century Christianity was brought again to China. It was through Roman Catholics and was planted so firmly that in spite of persecution it persisted and grew.

The reintroduction of Christianity was in connexion with Portuguese trade. As we have seen, Xavier had attempted it and had perished (1552) while seeking to enter the empire. Within less than a generation after his death the Portuguese acquired a permanent foothold at Macao, not far from Canton. In 1576 Macao was made the seat of a bishop and the King of Portugal agreed to provide financial aid for him and his cathedral staff. It was largely through Macao, as a small key hole; that Christianity reëntered China.

The situation was not propitious. Under the ruling dynasty, the Ming, the Chinese did not care for intimate contacts with the outside world. They considered themselves as givers not recipients of culture. Confucianism was dominant. Officialdom was made up of those who had been recruited through a highly competitive system of civil service examinations which were based on the Confucian classics. The state, the family, and ethics were governed by Confucian ideals and precepts. Every *hsien,* or local administrative unit, had a temple to Confucius and the other worthies of his school in which ceremonies were periodically held which all scholars were supposed to attend. Unless in some way Christianity could make its peace with Confucianism, it would find the going very hard.

Although it was through Macao that many of the missionaries came, it was chiefly by those from other countries than Portugal that the planting of Christianity was achieved. The Jesuits led, but several other orders and groups were active.

After Xavier the leading pioneer was Matteo (Matthew) Ricci (1552–1610). Born in the very year that Xavier died, apparently frustrated, Ricci, a Jesuit and well educated in mathematics and astronomy, arrived in Macao in 1582. By his knowledge of geography, mathematics, and astronomy, he won the somewhat grudging respect of a number of Chinese scholars and officials. He set himself to the diligent study of Chinese and the Confucian classics and became expert in them. He believed that Christianity could so be presented to the scholars and the masses as to win them without requiring them to make a complete break with Confucianism. For translating the word God he employed terms which he found in the Confucian classics, *Shang Ti* and especially *T'ien,* thus seeking to present Christianity as something not entirely new and to say, as Paul had long before said at Athens: "Whom ye ignorantly worship, him declare I unto you." He believed that the ceremonies in honour of ancestors which constituted an integral part of family life and those celebrated in the Confucian temples did not possess a religious significance in the sense that would make participation in them compromising for Christians. Thus a Chinese might become a Christian while still remaining a loyal member of his family, an official, and a Confucian scholar. Thanks to his friendship with scholars and officials, Ricci succeeded in establishing a residence for himself and his fellow-Jesuits in the capital, Peking. Before his death he had seen the conversion of a number of important persons, including an imperial prince.

The mission inaugurated in Peking by Ricci had a long but chequered history. Soon after his death the Jesuits were given charge of a revision of the Chinese calendar and of the bureau of astronomy which was closely connected with it. They thus had official position and status. From time to time they faced persecution, largely instigated by those who accused them of plotting for the overthrow of the dynasty or by jealous rivals for their position in the astronomical bureau. Yet the change of dynasty from the Ming brought by the Manchu conquest in the middle of the seventeenth century did not displace them. Under the greatest of the Manchu rulers, best known under the designation K'ang Hsi, who reigned from 1661 to 1722, and who was therefore a contemporary of Louis XIV of France and Peter the Great of Russia, they long enjoyed imperial favour. In 1692 what was in effect an edict of toleration was issued.

Reinforcements came. Some of these were to the Jesuits, among them a contingent from France, men who by their scholarly attainments won the friendship of K'ang Hsi, for that Emperor had an eager and inquiring mind. Other orders and societies also established themselves in China. They included Dominicans, Franciscans, and Augustinians from Spain by way of the Philippines, Italian Franciscans sent by the Propaganda, and members of the Paris Society of Foreign Missions.

By the beginning of the eighteenth century Christianity was making marked progress. Christians were found in almost all the provinces, perhaps in them all. They numbered between two hundred thousand and three hundred thousand. To give the nascent Church a structure, bishops and vicars apostolic were appointed, one of them a Chinese. Chinese were recruited and trained for the priesthood. In spite of occasional persecutions the prospects were encouraging.

Shortly after the beginning of the eighteenth century misfortunes began to beset the course of Christianity. They arose from a number of causes. The Portuguese insistence upon extending the *padroado* over all China proved a handicap. The waning of Spain and Portugal reduced the support of missions from those lands. More serious was a prolonged and bitter division among the missionaries known as the rites controversy. It centred about the methods which had been adopted by Ricci. Even some of the Jesuits were not at first convinced that these were not compromising the faith. Members of other missionary bodies, especially Dominicans and the Society of Foreign Missions of Paris, perhaps not uncontaminated by jealousy of the Jesuits, were emphatic that to follow the course pursued by Ricci would denature Christianity. They appealed to Rome. The struggle lasted for almost a century, from the first appeal to Rome, in 1643, to the final Papal bull, in 1742. The Jesuits insisted that nothing in the rites in honour of the ancestors and of Confucius as they permitted them were idolatrous and that to forbid them would convince the Chinese, already suspicious, that Christianity was subversive to Chinese morals and culture. The opponents of the Jesuits insisted that the rites were idolatrous. In an effort to adjust the difficulty two Papal embassies were sent to China. The first angered K'ang Hsi and fell afoul of the Portuguese *padroado* by seeking to by-pass it. Much of scholarly Europe became interested and a flood of argument poured from the presses. K'ang Hsi became involved and eventually insisted that if they were to remain in China missionaries must have official permits and that these would be given only to those who agreed to the attitude of Ricci. Since the Pope had come out against the methods of Ricci, the missionaries were posed with the unhappy choice of either leaving China or disobeying Rome. Some of them left. Others remained, hoping that on further representations Rome would alter its opinion. Rome was adamant and required all missionaries going to China to promise obedience to its decree against the rites. Yet that decree was provisional and contained the saving words: "Until it is decided otherwise." In the twentieth century the attitude of Rome towards the rites in honour of ancestors was reversed. Further disasters overtook missions in China in the second half of the eighteenth century, but of these we are to speak in a later chapter. In 1750 Christians still numbered about two hundred thousand.

The Spread Across Northern Asia

Christianity was carried across Northern Asia by the Russians. Russian trans-Asian expansion commenced shortly before 1500, but it was not until the sixteenth century that the region began to be politically subject to Moscow. By the middle of the seventeenth century Russian adventurers—Cossacks, fur-traders, and trappers—had made their way across the continent to Bering Strait. Russian Orthodox Christianity accompanied or followed that expansion. It was supported by the state, notably by Peter the Great and more for political than religious purposes. The missionaries were priests and monks. The population was sparse. Some of it was made up of Russians from west of the

Urals. For obvious reasons these were most numerous in the areas nearest Europe. They were held to a nominal allegiance to the faith. Much of the population was indigenous. Among them missions were conducted. They reached as far east as Kamchatka and by 1750 most of the peoples of that distant peninsula were reported to be Christian. There were also many conversions nearer Europe. A Russian mission was established in Peking, but it was more diplomatic than religious and confined its religious efforts chiefly to caring for a small contingent who had been taken captive by the Manchus in a border war and brought permanently to Peking.

In Asia, then, by 1750 Christianity was more widely spread than it had ever been. It had not recovered the ground lost in the central and western parts of the continent, but on the southern, eastern, and northern shores it was more widely represented than ever before.

The Spread of Christianity in the Western Hemisphere

It was not in Africa or Asia but in the Western Hemisphere that Christianity was to have its major spread between 1500 and 1750. In the first two continents and their fringing islands, except the Philippines, only minorities were won. In the major centres of civilization, Western Asia, India, Japan, and China, the minorities were only small fractions of the population and with some exceptions were under constant threat of persecution. Save for some of the islands, the thinly peopled northern reaches of Asia, and small enclaves in Africa, India, Malaya, and China, Europeans had no political control and effected no continuing settlements. In contrast, in the Western hemisphere by 1750 Europeans had made themselves masters of the more thickly peopled and civilized areas, had extended their control over almost all the coasts of South America and Central America, over the southern and eastern shores and much of the eastern interior of North America, and over most of the fringing islands. They had won to the Christian faith the majority of the pre-Columbian populations, including those highest in the scale of civilization, and had formed extensive settlements which in wide reaches, notably in the West Indies and the east coast of North America, by the middle of the eighteenth century constituted the overwhelming majority of the population. So far as they had religious loyalties, these settlements were professedly Christian. However, that faith sat more lightly upon some of them than it did on the countries from which they came. Here lay one of the challenges to Christianity. That faith was also challenged by the thousands of Negroes, most of them non-Christians, who were brought as slaves from Africa to work on the farms and plantations of the white men.

A major reason for the contrast between the course of Christianity in Africa and Asia on the one hand and the Western Hemisphere on the other was that the Eastern Hemisphere was well peopled and the home of high civilizations while in the Western Hemisphere man was relatively a new comer, for the most part had only sparsely occupied the wide reaches, and in only a few places, on the uplands of Mexico, Central America, and the northern cordillera of South America, had developed civilizations. These civilizations could not offer effective resistance to those of Europe. The more nearly primitive cultures of the other pre-Columbian peoples were even more yielding when once close contact was had with the white man.

Before 1750 European conquests, settlements, and the spread of Christianity were chiefly through the Spaniards, the Portuguese, the French, and the British, with lesser contributions from the Dutch, the Swedes, the Danes, and the Germans. It is convenient, therefore, to tell of the planting of Christianity by national categories and the areas occupied by each.

The Planting of Christianity in Spanish America

It was under Spanish auspices that Columbus made his momentous voyages of discovery. It was the Spaniards who occupied more territory than did any other European people before the middle of the eighteenth century. It was through them that the earliest major spread of Christianity was accomplished in the New World.

Spanish America included most of the major islands of the West Indies, Mexico, almost all Central America, Florida, part of the northern and southeastern, and nearly all the western coast of South America. The Spaniards were also reaching north from Mexico into what was later much of the southern border of the United States. In the West Indies the native populations died out within a few years after the advent of the Europeans. The cruelty, the exploitation, and the diseases of the white man accomplished their destruction before the Christian conscience could stir the home authorities to effective action. The populations which replaced them were white or Negro or a mixture of the two. In most of the mainland of Spanish America the white men were in the minority. They were the ruling minority. Under them were the Indians, generally the large majority, with here and there enclaves of Negroes. Wherever the white men could do it, they compelled the Indians to labour for them in mines and on plantations. The main centres of Spanish power and the largest populations were in Mexico and Peru. Here had been the most numerous peoples and the highest civilizations at the time of the Spanish conquest and from here most of the wealth, especially in the precious metals, was obtained for export.

We can take time for only the briefest summary of the spread of Christianity in Spanish America and must content ourselves with a few broad generalizations, some of them illustrated by concrete examples.

First of all we must note that the Church and the spread of Christianity were under the direction of the crown. This was exercised from Spain but was carried out by officials appointed from Spain who were mostly Spanish-born rather than American-born whites. This minute and absolute control by the crown was part of the general colonial policy and was seen in all aspects of Spanish American life, whether economic, political, or religious.

A second generalization is closely associated with the first. Most of the missions to the Indians were staffed from the Old World and not from the whites in the New World.

A third generalization follows almost inevitably from the first two. The Christianity of Spanish America was largely parasitic and passive. Depending as it was constrained to do by royal colonial policy upon the Old World for its missionaries and bishops, it showed little inclination to be missionary or to act for itself. Increasingly priests and monks were recruited from the American-born whites and here and there from Indians and mestizos. By the end of the eighteenth century the majority of the bishops were natives of America. However, the tradition had been established that leadership must come from Europe. Here in time arose one of the largest bodies of professing Roman Catholics in the world. Yet even in the nineteenth and twentieth centuries it did not produce enough clergy to fill its own needs and contributed very little in personnel and money to the spread of the faith beyond its borders. Roman Catholics of Europe and later of the United States sent clergy to care for the nominally Christian population as well as to reach out to the non-Christian Indians.

A fourth generalization is that the Papacy had practically no voice in Spanish America. The crown appointed the bishops and no Papal decree could be published in the Spanish colonial possessions without royal consent. Doctrinally the Spanish American church conformed to Rome. No serious schisms or heretical groups arose. The Inquisition and royal authority would have crushed them even had the Christianity of the region possessed sufficient vitality to produce them. Yet administratively Rome had almost no authority.

A fifth generalization is that in the main centres of pre-Columbian population and civilization, Mexico and Peru, accession to the Christian faith was by mass conversions. In Mexico in 1523 a royal letter to Cortés, the leader in the conquest, declared that the conversion of the Indians was the king's chief interest in that enterprise. In 1523 Cortés ordered that those who had been given *repartimientos,* or bodies of Indians to work on their lands, must see that idols were done away and that provision be made for the instruction of their charges in the Christian faith. Scores of Franciscans, mostly of the strict branch called the Observants, arrived to carry through the work of conversion. Dominicans and Augustinians soon followed. Then came Jesuits, Discalced Carmelites, and a member of the order of St. John of God. Benedictines and a few seculars also entered. The Indians, accustomed to docility under their former rulers, were quite willing to follow the wishes of their new masters. It was said that in 1531, only twelve years after the first landing of Cortés, the Franciscans alone had baptized more than a million persons. In 1536 a missionary estimated the number of baptized at between four and nine millions. One of the most famous of the early missionaries was a Franciscan, Peter of Ghent. A relative of Charles V, while a courtier he had been won to the religious life by two confessors of the Emperor and had declined a bishopric to remain a humble lay brother. In 1529 he wrote that he and a colleague often baptized fourteen thousand in one day and that together they had administered the rite to more than two hundred thousand. Instruction was given to the neophytes much more slowly, but various devices were employed to impart it, so that the change of faith would be more than purely formal. By the end of the sixteenth century the pre-Christian pagan cults had disappeared in the more thickly settled portions of Mexico.

After the initial enthusiasm of the converts passed and when the first generation of missionaries was followed by new arrivals, complaints began to be heard. The clergy were too few, the dioceses were too large, and many of the priests were accused by even the first Archbishop of Mexico of being ignorant, immoral, and corrupt. The old faiths were said to persist in attitudes and in rites in connexion with supposedly Christian worship.

In Peru the story was very similar. The second Archbishop of Lima, Toribio Alfonso de Mogrovejo y Robles, later canonized, of a noble family, highly educated, came to the New World in his late forties, acquired an Indian language, and is said to have administered confirmation to about eight hundred thousand. He built roads, schools, chapels, and hospitals, introduced the reforming decrees of the Council of Trent, and stood up for the rights of the Indians and the Negroes. Francis Solanus (1549–1610), also canonized, a Franciscan of the Observance, acquired a command of several Indian tongues, journeyed widely, barefoot, crucifix in hand, preaching, and teaching his hearers to join with him in chanting Psalms to the accompaniment of his violin.

A sixth generalization is that in Spanish America after the first wave of conquest the mission was the characteristic pioneer institution. It was through missionaries that the frontier was usually pushed forward into territories hitherto unoccupied by the whites. As a rule little or no force was employed. An armed guard might be sent with the missionaries to afford them protection, but it was by other means that the missionaries persuaded the Indians to receive instruction. Offers of food and clothing were employed to induce the Indians to settle around the mission. In time the Indians were drawn into a community of which the church was the centre and where they were taught agriculture and simple industries and had their entire lives supervised by the missionaries.

These frontier missions were broadly scattered. Eventually they were found in places as widely separated as California, Texas, Florida, Central America, Venezuela, the upper reaches of the Amazon and its tributaries, and Paraguay.

One of the most famous of the frontier missions was that of Jesuits in Paraguay. Various attempts to establish continuing stations had been made in the sixteenth century, but not until the first decade of the seventeenth century was the enterprise really inaugurated. Its purpose was the conversion of the Indians and their protection against the vices and exploitation of the colonists. The Indians were gathered into villages under the supervision of the missionaries. Here they were given Christian instruction, were taught to work, and were organized into a closely regulated communal pattern. Each village had a church on which wealth and devotion were lavished and where much was made of music, choirs, and religious dances. Cattle-raising and agriculture were nurtured and the Indians were trained in various handicrafts. Armed forces were organized to guard against raids by slave-traders. At one time about one hundred and fifty thousand Indians are said to have been under the Jesuits and in more than two score villages in much of the vast interior of the later Patagonia, Paraguay, Uruguay, and Southern Brazil.

A seventh and final generalization is that Christianity made for the softening of the impact of the Spaniards on the Indians. In its first few years the Spanish occupation was marked by extreme cruelty. Nor did exploitation ever cease. The Spaniards were a minority and most of them had come to America to improve their fortunes. If they were to do this, they must have labour for their mines and plantations. They were unwilling to undertake the kind of work demanded and could not obtain enough labourers from Europe. They partly made up the deficiency with Negroes, but it was chiefly to the Indians that they had recourse. Yet, moved by the Christian conscience, there were Spaniards who appealed to the monarchs and obtained legislation on behalf of the Indians.

Queen Isabella charged Bobadilla, who followed Columbus in the governorship of the Indies, to respect the liberty of the Indians. Allotments (*repartimientos*) of Indians were made to grantees (*encomenderos*) to enable them to work plantations and mines, but Isabella stipulated that the *encomendero* was to see that his Indians entered voluntarily into the relationship, were treated as free, were paid for their labour with wages adequate to support themselves and their families, that the work was non-hazardous and in proportion to the strength of the labourer, and that Christian instruction was given to all. These provisions were so frequently ignored in practice that the system became one of the chief targets of the reformers.

As conquest and colonization progressed, additions were made to what were called the *Laws of the Indies* which had the protection and the temporal and spiritual welfare of the Indians at heart. Officials were appointed to see that they were observed. Selfishness and economic considerations tended to make the code a dead letter, but from time to time men arose who sought to have it enlarged and obeyed. Some of these were in Spain. Francisco de Vitoria, a Dominican, a leading theologian of the sixteenth century and a pioneer in international law, championed the rights of the Indians, to his personal hurt, and there were many others.

Outstanding among those who laboured for the Indians was Bartolomé de Las Casas (1474–1566). It is symbolic of the effect of Christianity that he seems to have been the first in the New World to be ordained a Christian priest. His father was one of the companions of Columbus on the latter's second voyage to America. Bartolomé came as a youth after having received the conventional education of his time. He was slow to awake to his mission. On the island of Hispaniola where he first made his home he shared in the raids on the Indians and had some of the captives assigned to him for his plantation. In his middle thirties he was ordained to the priesthood and not far from that time had his conscience troubled by the preaching of a Dominican. He did not at once break with the system and shared in the conquest of Cuba. Before long, however, in a sermon before the governor and leading settlers he denounced the cruelties that he saw about him. Since the crown exercised a minute direction over the colonies, Las Casas went to Spain, for it was from there that effective action must begin. After vexatious delays he won the ear and the good will of the powerful Cardinal Ximénes. He was appointed Protector-general of the Indians and in 1516 returned to the New World in that capacity. He found himself blocked and went again to Spain to renew his suit. Faced with the argument that to adopt his method would deprive the settlements of labour and so work their ruin, he attempted a colony to prove that the Indians could be won by kindly treatment and without force and brought with him whites to be labourers. That experiment, made west of one of the mouths of the Orinoco, proved a failure. Baffled, he retired for some years to Hispaniola and joined the Dominicans.

Eventually Las Casas was again on his travels. Once more he voyaged to Spain to seek royal decrees on behalf of the Indians in Peru, for that region was then being conquered. He was soon back in America with the desired orders and went to Peru to obtain their publication. In Nicaragua he had a part in a mission which seemed to him to demonstrate his contention that Indians could be won to the Christian faith through friendship and to assent to Spanish authority without the use of armed force. He was ordered to Hispaniola to deal with an Indian revolt and induced a chief who had long terrorized the colonists to lay down his arms and persuaded his followers to accept baptism. For several years he was a missionary among the Indians of Guatemala, seeking further to prove the truth of his theory that force should not be used against the Indians and that coercion was quite powerless to effect the changes demanded by true Christian conversion.

In the 1530's he was again in Spain and probably had large influence on the New Laws which were framed in 1542. He was offered the see of Cuzco, in some respects the most important in the New World, but instead chose that of Chiapa, in Mexico, one of the poorest. He was consecrated and at the age of seventy again set out for America. There he met bitter opposition, for the colonists held him responsible for the New Laws, legislation which they believed meant their ruin. In 1547 he returned for the last time to Spain and there, until an advanced old age, continued to argue the case for the Indians.

Las Casas was by no means alone. Many, some of them laymen and others clergy, took a similar position. Several missionaries lost their lives in the attempt to win warlike tribes without asking for the protection of armed forces. Others persisted and proved successful. It was an heroic record. It seems almost invidious to single out one among many. Fairly typical, however, was Domingo de Salazar (1513–1594), a Dominican, a student of Vitoria and a follower of Las Casas, who, over twenty-five years in Mexico, made himself fluent in Indian languages to preach in them, and as the first Bishop of Manila championed the cause of the Filipinos.

There were also those who gave themselves to serving the Negroes who had been so cruelly wrenched from Africa into slavery in the Americas. Famous among them was the Jesuit, Pedro Claver (1581–1654). A Catalonian and of noble lineage, like many of the high born youth of his day he was early caught up into the devotion and enthusiasm of the Society of Jesus. He was sent to Cartagena, long the chief port of entry of the slave ships from Africa. There for nearly forty years he spent himself in behalf of the poor wretches whom greed had torn from their homes in Africa. On their arrival he visited the slave-ships, foul with the stench of crowded and ill-tended humanity, and carried food, fruit, wine, and tobacco to their black cargoes. He baptized the infants, cared for the ill, gave instruction in religion and morals, and trained catechists to supplement his labours. He made long journeys to visit the blacks in the mines and plantations. He braved the enmity of slave-dealers and slave-owners. Against vigorous opposition he insisted that Negroes be admitted to the church where he served on full equality with the whites. He is said to have baptized more than three hundred thousand. That he became the patron saint of missions to the Negroes is proof that there were those who appreciated him and followed his example.

As a result of the labours of many, lay and clerical, the overwhelming proportion of the population in Spanish America were nominally Christian. It is true that this Christianity was to a large degree passive, parasitically dependent upon continued fresh blood from Europe in the form of clergy and missionaries. It is also true that in 1750 and later millions of pagan Indians remained untouched on the fringes of the Spanish settlements. Yet an ecclesiastical structure covered most of the vast area, with parishes, dioceses, and archdioceses. Education was fostered, universities were founded and maintained, and gradually, even though in insufficient numbers and often of inferior quality, clergy were recruited and trained from the Indians, mestizos, and American-born whites.

The Planting of Christianity in Portuguese America

In some ways the course of Christianity in Portuguese America was like that in Spanish America. Here, in Brazil, which embraced the Portuguese possessions, was an area, not as populous as that of Spanish America and with no high pre-Columbian civilizations, but still enormous in extent. Here, too, were the problems of holding the European immigrants to the Christian faith and of winning the Indians and the imported Negro slaves. As in Spanish America, the crown directed the Church, the state, and the economic life. As elsewhere in these years, the missionaries were largely from those orders which were the fruits of the Catholic Reformation—among them Jesuits, Capuchins, and Observant Franciscans. Here, too, heroic individuals were stirred and emboldened by the Christian faith to plead the cause of the exploited, to obtain legislation on their behalf, and to strive to see that it was enforced.

Among the latter was Mem de Sá, a governor who came out in 1558, who forbade any Indian from one of the Christian communities being sold as a slave, and prohibited, except on explicit authorization by himself, the restoration to their masters of slaves who had taken refuge with missionaries. Another was the Jesuit, Antonio Vieira. Having served as a youth among the Indians and Negroes of Brazil, he returned to Portugal and became one of the most famous preachers of the day. But he insisted on going again to Brazil. Once there, he was appalled by the neglect of the sacraments and Christian morals by the Portuguese settlers, by the low quality of many of the clergy, by the enslavement and progressive extermination of the Indians, and by the inadequacy of episcopal ministrations. Sailing for Portugal to press reform measures on the king, he obtained a decree (1655) which was designed to remedy the worst of the abuses. He then went to Brazil to aid in the enforcement of the edict and to resume his labours as a missionary. The decree aroused great resentment among the colonists and Vieira and several of his fellow-Jesuits were deported. Yet the law wrought some improvement. Eventually Vieira made his way back to Brazil and died there at an extreme old age.

In spite of the efforts of Vieira and men like him, Christianity in Brazil remained distinctly behind that in Spanish America, far from ideal as was the latter. Educationally the colony was backward. Apart from the missions maintained by the regulars, the religious care of the whites, the mixed population, and the Christian Indians was woefully inadequate. Stipends for the seculars were niggardly, few from the better classes entered the priesthood, and outside the main cities there were not many resident pastors. The low state of the Roman Catholic Church in Brazil in the nineteenth and twentieth centuries had its roots in the early days of the colony.

Roman Catholic Christianity in French America

For more than a century the French seemed to be building a colonial empire in the Americas which in geographic extent rivalled those of Spain and Portugal. In the West Indies, on the northern coast of South America, along the Atlantic seaboard of North America north of the British possessions, in the vast valleys of the St. Lawrence River, the Great Lakes, and the Mississippi and its tributaries the French staked out and partly occupied a region which might have made them dominant in much of the Western Hemisphere. In the eighteenth century they lost nearly all of it, largely in conjunction with European wars and notably in the course of the Seven Years' War (1756-1763).

Before they were driven off of North America the French made lasting contributions to the Christianity of that continent. Most of it was through colonists. Few at first, the latter multiplied by a wide margin between births and deaths and laid the basis of a French-speaking element in the white population which under English rule identified its faith with its French nationality and remained conservatively and loyally Roman Catholic. Eventually it spread over much of Canada and southward into the New England portion of the United States.

There were also wide-flung missions to the Indians. However, the aboriginal population was small, scattered, and lived largely by hunting, trapping, and an unthrifty agriculture. Numerical success was slight.

As in so much of the rest of the world, the missions in French America were by the orders which sprang from the Catholic Reformation—Jesuits, Recollects (Franciscans), Capuchins, Sulpicians, and Ursulines. Montreal, in the nineteenth and twentieth centuries the second city in size in Canada, was founded as an idealistic Christian community from which secular priests would go out as missionaries to the Indians and to the colonists. Famous was the Jesuit mission to the Hurons, cut short by attacks from other Indian tribes. Missionaries of various orders ranged over most of the area claimed by France and here and there made converts.

The Planting of Protestant Christianity Outside the Thirteen Colonies of the British

Compared with Roman Catholicism, Protestantism was late in establishing a continuing foothold in the Americas. However, long before 1750 it had been planted by white settlements and by missions among Eskimos, Negroes, and Indians. In 1721 there went to Greenland Hans Egede, a Norwegian Lutheran pastor who wished to make contact with the Scandinavian population which he believed might have survived on that island from the colonies of earlier centuries but which had not been heard from within the memory of living man. He found that all the Europeans had long since perished, but he remained, learned the Eskimo tongue, and began a mission which after several generations won most of that people to the Christian faith. The Danish-Norwegian mission was supplemented by Moravians who arrived in 1733. Shortly after 1750 the Moravians extended their operations to Labrador. Through the initiative of Zinzendorf, in 1732 Moravians began a mission to the Negroes in the Danish West Indies and in 1735 in the Dutch possessions on the north coast of South America.

Numerically more impressive was Protestantism in the British West Indies. Here, until after 1750, it was introduced and nourished chiefly by the Church of England. In Bermuda, Barbados, the Leeward Islands, the Bahamas, and especially in the largest of the British West Indies, Jamaica, churches were erected for the white settlers and missions were carried on among the African slaves. In 1680 Barbados had eleven churches. In 1701 the Society for the Propagation of the Gospel in Foreign Parts was begun with the British colonies as its original scope. It had representatives among both the white population and the Negroes. The settlers from the British Isles also included Presbyterians, Independents, Baptists, and Quakers.

Christianity in the Thirteen Colonies

Far more important for the future course of Christianity than the Protestantism in Greenland, Labrador, and the West Indies was what was taking place in the Thirteen Colonies which soon after 1750 became the United States of America. In the nineteenth and especially in the twentieth century, the

Christianity of the United States had a much larger share in the total life and world outreach of that faith than did that in Spanish, Portuguese, or French America, or, indeed, than all the rest of the Christian communities in the Western Hemisphere taken together. This was not so much in numbers, although in this respect the Christianity of the United States was impressive, as it was in vitality as seen in new movements, in the fashion in which it initiated and maintained missions in the United States and in much of the rest of the world, and in its effect upon the United States and mankind as a whole. Because of the significance of Christianity in the Thirteen Colonies for later history we must give more space to it than we would if we were considering only its numerical strength before 1750 or if we were confining our attention to the world scene between 1500 and 1750. Judged from the situation the world around in those two and a half centuries what was taking place in the Thirteen Colonies was of minor moment. Like the other phases of their life, the Christianity of the Thirteen Colonies was merely a projection of Western Europe and chiefly of portions of the British Isles among a few hundred thousand people scattered along a part of the eastern seaboard of North America.

In our brief summary of the history of Christianity in the Thirteen Colonies we must speak first and chiefly of the white population and then, much more quickly, of the Indians and Negroes.

For the white population we must content ourselves with brief but important generalizations, here and there amplified by specific incidents, individuals, and movements.

The white population of the Thirteen Colonies was predominantly from the British Isles. That British element was mostly from England, but before 1750 a large contingent had entered of what were known as Scotch-Irish, namely, those of Scotch descent who had their homes in Ireland and who came to the New World because of adverse conditions in that island. They were distributed quite widely from north to south and were Presbyterians by heredity. In addition there were many Germans, mostly in Pennsylvania, some Swedes from a short-lived Swedish colonial enterprise on the Delaware, a substantial contingent of Dutch who survived from the Dutch enterprise in New Amsterdam, after its transfer to the English known as New York, Huguenot refugees, found at intervals all the way from South Carolina to Massachusetts, and a few Roman Catholic Irish.

So far as the white inhabitants of the Thirteen Colonies had a church connexion, it was overwhelmingly Protestant. Roman Catholics constituted only a very small fraction of the population. One of the Thirteen Colonies, Maryland, was founded by English Roman Catholics, George and Cecil Calvert, successively Lords Baltimore, but it was upon the basis of religious liberty, the large majority of the settlers were Protestants, and within a generation the Church of England was established by law.

Religion was very important in the inauguration of some of the colonies. That was especially true in New England and Pennsylvania, but was by no means confined to these areas. It was Separatists who, coming on the *Mayflower*, in 1620 founded Plymouth. In the 1620's and 1630's Puritans, seeking to escape Charles I and Archbishop Laud, made extensive settlements around Massachusetts Bay. A group from Massachusetts Bay guided by their pastor, Thomas Hooker, founded Hartford (1636) and Connecticut. In 1638 another band of Puritans, led by Theophilus Eaton and John Davenport, began New Haven, later to be united with Connecticut. The Puritans and the Separatists merged and formed churches of a Congregational pattern. In principle New England was made up of Christian commonwealths where Christians controlled both the Church and the state and where all society was governed by Christian standards. Although in New England they were supported by public taxation and were intimately tied with the state, the churches were "gathered." Their membership was not composed of all the inhabitants, as was the theory in the state churches in Europe, but only of those who could narrate a conscious Christian experience. They were bound together by a covenant with one another and with Christ, as the head of the Church.

At first the Congregationalists in Massachusetts sought to force conformity with their conceptions of the Church. Quakers especially fared badly at their hands. For a time pastor at Salem, but banished from Massachusetts as an irritating non-conformist, Roger Williams founded Providence as "a shelter for persons distressed in conscience." Later this united with other settlements as the colony of Rhode Island on the basis of complete religious liberty and full civic democracy. With the counsel of George Fox and William Penn, Quakers founded West Jersey and East Jersey. William Penn himself, a leading Quaker, inaugurated Pennsylvania as a "holy experiment" with Philadelphia, the City of Brotherly Love, as its capital, and operating under a *Frame of Government* which, like Massachusetts and Connecticut, sought to lay the foundations of a society built on Christian principles and governed by Christian ideals. The *Frame of Government* granted religious liberty, but limited the franchise and office-holding to "such as profess faith in Jesus Christ."

It must also be noted that it was radical Protestantism which was prominent in these beginnings in the Thirteen Colonies. While in several of the colonies, notably the oldest, Virginia, the Church of England was established, in the majority it was not. Everywhere in the Thirteen Colonies it suffered from having no resident bishop. The colonies were under the Bishop of London, and he was represented by ecclesiastical officials called "commissaries," but without a bishop confirmation was not administered and aspirants for ordination had to make the long, expensive, and sometimes dangerous journey to England for that rite. The Anglican churches were chiefly dependent for clergymen upon those who came from England.

Radical Protestantism was relatively more prominent than in the British Isles or anywhere on the Continent of Europe. In 1750 the most compact and the most numerous and influential group of churches was not the Church of England but New England Congregationalism.

In general, the radical Protestants were of the Reformed tradition. Whether Puritans, Independents, Separatists, Baptists, or Quakers, they were either distinctly of it or had been profoundly influenced by it, even when, like the Quakers, they had rebelled against it. New Englanders had a large share in founding Presbyterianism in the Thirteen Colonies. They were closely allied in spirit and in some instances in personnel with the more widely spread Presbyterianism. The New England churches held to the Westminster Confession as standard. Usually those who moved away from New England to other colonies organized themselves into Presbyterian churches. The Reformed strain from England was reinforced by Reformed from Holland and Germany and by Scotch-Irish Presbyterians.

In the Thirteen Colonies Christianity presented a much greater variety than in any country east of the Atlantic. In addition to the several kinds of Protestantism from the British Isles, it had German and Swedish Lutherans, German Reformed, Dutch Reformed, and, as we have said, a few Roman Catholics. In this it foreshadowed the even richer variety which was to characterize the United States.

In spite of the part which Christianity had in initiating and shaping the Thirteen Colonies, in 1750 the large majority of the white population were without a formal church connexion. It has been estimated, although this may be excessively low, that in 1750 only about five out of a hundred were members of churches. The overwhelming proportion of the settlers came to the colonies for economic or social rather than religious motives. They were mostly from the underprivileged and by migrating to the New World sought to better their financial or their social standing. They were from countries where baptism and confirmation or its equivalent were social conventions which in some places were required not only by custom but also by law and where attendance at church was expected or made a legal obligation. In the Thirteen Colonies these rules, if they existed at all, usually were not rigidly enforced. In the absence of a bishop, those affiliated with the Church of England could be baptized, but were not confirmed, and many did not partake of the communion. In consequence, away from the patterns of the Old World, most of the population were in danger of being largely de-Christianized. From heredity and to some degree, particularly in New England, by local custom, remnants of Christianity survived among the unchurched in ethical standards and religious ideas. However, there was a decided trend towards allowing them to fade out. That was especially the case in the newer settlements away from the coast, on the westward-moving frontier. Here the traditional institutions and habits of Europe were even less in evidence than on the seaboard and in the fluid society of these newer regions tended not to be reproduced.

In New England the situation was partly remedied by what was known as the Half-Way Covenant, a designation given it by its critics. Even before the first generation of immigrants had died, complaints began to be heard of waning zeal. In the initial contingents there were many who were not in full sympathy with the high purposes of those who wished to build an ideal Christian society. In at least one of the New England colonies at the outset only a minority were church members. As time passed, those who could qualify for church membership by offering evidence of a spiritual rebirth were few. In consequence, the custom gradually spread of permitting those who as children of church members had been baptized and were regarded as sharing in the covenant to present their children for baptism. Usually only full church members could partake of the communion, but eventually in some churches all the baptized were allowed to do so. The Half-Way Covenant was the occasion for much controversy. Its opponents regarded it as an ungodly compromise, but in 1662 a synod sanctioned it and its use spread rapidly. Yet it tended to make baptism a mere form.

Efforts were not lacking to win the unchurched. These were partly from the other side of the Atlantic but were chiefly from the inherent vitality of the Christianity of the Colonies.

From the other side of the Atlantic the concern for the religious welfare of the colonists was mainly in the Church of England. As we have seen, the Bishop of London, as head of the Church of England in the chief seaport, was given ecclesiastical jurisdiction over the English colonies and was represented in the Thirteen Colonies by commissaries. One of the latter, Thomas Bray (1656–1730), although only a few months in America, made two outstanding contributions, the organization of the Society for Promoting Christian Knowledge (1699—1698 old style) and of the Society for the Propagation of the Gospel in Foreign Parts (1701). Bray was eager that clergymen going to America have books. Accordingly he founded libraries in the chief ports in England from which they sailed and in a number of colonial parishes. The Society for Promoting Christian Knowledge was created by him to perpetuate this activity. With the purpose of publishing and distributing books, it eventually extended its operations to many countries. The Society for the Propagation of the Gospel in Foreign Parts, for which Bray obtained a charter, was primarily for sending to the colonies and supporting clergymen and schoolmasters of the Church of England. It is said that when it was founded, in all the Thirteen Colonies there were only fifty clergymen of the Church of England and that most of these were in Virginia and Maryland, and that seventy-five years later, when the colonies declared their independence, the churches numbered about three hundred and the clergymen about two hundred and fifty. Most of the increase was due to the Society for the Propagation of the Gospel in Foreign Parts. Its missionaries were mainly among the whites, but some spent their years among the Indians and a few gave attention to the Negroes.

Missionaries were sent not only from England but also from the Continent. A few of them were Roman Catholics, and went chiefly to Maryland. In that colony, founded by men of their faith, there were both Jesuits and seculars and Jesuits went from there to the neighbouring Delaware, New Jersey, and Pennsylvania, to care for their co-religionists. They did not have a resident bishop until after the formation of the United States of America. A Swedish colony was founded on the Delaware in 1638, largely at the instance of Gustavus Adolphus, who had in mind not only commerce but also the conversion of the Indians and the dominance of Protestantism in the New World. Although in 1655 the Dutch eliminated Swedish rule, a Swedish population remained and to it until 1791 the Church of Sweden continued to send clergymen and financial aid. The Swedish Lutheran churches, some of them prosperous, eventually became Episcopalian. Because of the strength of the common Catholic tradition, the transition was easy.

The Germans were much more numerous than the Swedes. Thousands of them, mostly Protestants, came to the Thirteen Colonies. Some fled from the Palatinate when it was being ravaged by the armies of Louis XIV and settled in New York, the Carolinas, and Pennsylvania. Others were from the Archdiocese of Salzburg, which the archbishop who came to the post in 1728 was attempting to purge of all Protestants. William Penn had travelled in Germany and had induced some Germans to come to his colony. With its religious liberty, Pennsylvania proved peculiarly attractive to small, persecuted groups, such as the Mennonites and the Church of the Brethren (Dunkers). The Moravians inaugurated a colony which had headquarters at Bethlehem, Pennsylvania, with Spangenberg as its chief leader, and were visited by Zinzendorf. Zinzendorf found the Germans more than half of the population of Pennsylvania, but largely without clergy and schools. They were of varying forms of Protestantism, but mostly Lutheran and Reformed. He wished to bring them all together in one Protestant Church.

Moved partly by apprehension that the Germans would go over to Zinzendorf's plan of union, but chiefly by the fear that they would drift entirely away from Christianity, the Pietists of Halle sent money and missionaries. Of the latter the chief was Henry Melchior Muhlenberg (1711–1787). He arrived in Philadelphia in 1742. With the motto *Ecclesia plantanda,* "the Church must be planted," he became a pastor of Lutheran churches in Philadelphia, travelled widely, in 1748 brought together the first Lutheran synod in the colonies, and became the outstanding organizer and overseer of Lutheranism. The Germans were not confined to Pennsylvania but were found in others of the colonies, especially in the South. To them also came ministers and missionaries, some of them from Halle.

For the Germans of the Reformed church, Michael Schlatter (1716–1790) was the outstanding missionary and organizer. A native of Switzerland, he was sent to America by the Dutch synods. There he organized a *coetus* or synod, helped to bring order into the congregations, and induced ministers to come from Europe. He also stimulated the formation in England of a society to maintain schools among Germans of all denominations.

Even more far-reaching in effect than the missionaries from the other side of the Atlantic were movements from within the churches in the colonies themselves. The chief of these was what was known as the Great Awakening. It arose in New England and in Presbyterian circles closely associated with New England and swept through most of the Thirteen Colonies.

Revivals or awakenings were not new in those of the Separatist tradition in the colonies. The conception of the "gathered" church which was integral in New England Congregationalism contributed to them, especially since so large a proportion of the population were not members of churches. A "gathered" church meant that each of the members, as a prerequisite for admission, must be able to narrate an experience of the new birth without which no one could enter the kingdom of God. The alternative to the eternal life begun by the new birth was being eternally lost. In communities where, as in the Thirteen Colonies, the large majority of the population were unregenerate, the regenerate, especially among the clergy, were deeply concerned. Among many of the unregenerate they would find those prepared to listen to them, for such knowledge of Christian belief as had been spread abroad bred convictions or at least an uneasiness which would respond to the preacher who pled with the unconverted and urged them to repent and turn in faith to God. The doctrine of election, out of the Augustinian heritage which was dominant in the churches of the Reformed tradition and which except for those influenced by Arminianism was generally accepted in New England and the Presbyterian churches, would seem to have discouraged any appeal to the unregenerate. If one were among the elect, so the belief ran, God's grace would prove irresistible and would reach all those whom He had chosen for salvation. If, on the other hand, one were not among the elect no amount of preaching could change his status. Yet it was mainly in the circles of British ancestry which were most committed to what was usually called Calvinism and its doctrine of election that the Great Awakening began and made its chief appeal.

Part of the appeal was due to an alteration in traditional Calvinism which prevailed in New England as an early importation from England. Calvin had held that the evidences that an individual was among the elect were adherence to correct doctrine, a worthy life, and faithful attendance on the sacraments. In New England it was maintained that the evidences were adherence to correct doctrine, a worthy life, and an experience of salvation. This last was akin to Pietism. Since experience was essential, and that experience had in it much of emotion, seasons were to be expected when a community was aroused and tides swept through it changing many individuals. There were those, especially among the clergy, who prayed for such seasons and sought to encourage them.

The Great Awakening was an early stage in a mass conversion of the partially de-Christianized population which characterized the religious history of the Thirteen Colonies on the eve of independence and then of the United States. That mass conversion, in part by "revivals" and "evangelistic" preaching for reaching the "unconverted" or "unsaved," was one of the distinguishing features of the Christianity of the United States, and especially of those elements of the population of Protestant, particularly Anglo-Saxon heredity.

The beginnings of the Great Awakening were in New Jersey. Frelinghuysen, a German, educated under Pietist influence, pastor of Dutch Reformed churches in the Raritan Valley, in the 1720's began proclaiming with impassioned conviction the necessity of a deep inward transformation rather than the mere outward performance of religious ceremonies. He also introduced private prayer meetings. His preaching provoked criticism from other ministers of the Dutch churches, but won a wide following. Freylinghuysen contributed to the shaping of Gilbert Tennent, minister of a Presbyterian church in New Brunswick, also in the Raritan Valley. Gilbert Tennent was the son of William Tennent, an Irish minister who had come to America in 1716, had become a Presbyterian, and had trained for the ministry his sons and other young men in what was somewhat scornfully called the "log college," a building which he erected opposite his manse in Neshaminy, Pennsylvania. Through Gilbert Tennent and others prepared in the "log college" the revival spread among the Scotch-Irish. Graduates of the "log college" founded other "log colleges," largely for the education of ministers, and from them young men went out to preach the urgency of conversion.

In 1734–1735 the Great Awakening broke out in Northampton, Massachusetts, under the preaching of Jonathan Edwards. Jonathan Edwards (1703–1758) was one of the outstanding figures in the history of the Thirteen Colonies. The son of a Congregational pastor and through his mother a grandson of Solomon Stoddard, the dominant personality in the Connecticut Valley, Edwards combined a precocious and brilliant mind with a deep Christian devotion. A graduate of the infant Yale, after brief pastorates he taught there for a time and then, in 1727, succeeded Solomon Stoddard as minister of the Congregational church in Northampton. Edwards was acquainted with the writings of Locke, Newton, and the Cambridge Platonists, especially Cudworth (Chapter 36). He had a keen, penetrating intellect, there was something of the mystic in his temperament, and he responded to both these predispositions. He combined Calvinism with Neoplatonism. At Northampton he denounced the tendency towards Arminianism by which many in New England were in actuality departing from the Westminster Confession while they still adhered to it in theory. Speaking slowly, distinctly, and with great solemnity, he made vivid the loathsomeness of sin. In the winter and spring of 1734–1735 a wave of conviction swept over the community and hundreds professed conversion.

The Great Awakening was powerfully reinforced by George Whitefield (1714–1770). Born at Gloucester, England, the son of an inn-keeper and reared in poverty, Whitefield had entered Oxford in 1733, was closely associated with the Wesleys, and had gone through a religious crisis from which he emerged with great joy in the love of God. Of him as of the Wesleys we are to hear more later (Chapter 44). Having a voice which could reach thousands in the open air, expressive, dramatic, and with intense feeling, he could sway audiences as few men have ever done. He moved even so practical and religiously unorthodox a man as Benjamin Franklin. He came to Georgia in 1738 at the suggestion of John Wesley and made six other visits to America. In 1739–1741, then in his mid-twenties, he had his first preaching tour of the Colonies. He landed in Delaware and spoke in many centres. In Boston it is said that thirty thousand heard him at one time on the common. He found congenial those who were already preaching the revival and had more of a following among the Presbyterians and Congregationalists than among his fellow-Anglicans.

The Great Awakening spread through the Colonies, mostly through Presbyterians and Congregationalists. After 1750 it was to give rise to many Baptist preachers who, mostly men of little education, could speak the language of the lowliest and won an increasing following among the humblest of the unchurched.

Much excitement and many emotional disturbances accompanied the revival. Although the expressions were different, one is reminded of the Flagellants whom we have met in Roman Catholic circles. There were screaming, laughing, trances, visions, and convulsions. Some of the preachers and lay exhorters deliberately stimulated these phenomena.

Divisions in the churches accompanied and followed the Great Awakening. The more ardent preachers of the revival had sharp words for those ministers whom they deemed unconverted. Whitefield occasionally spoke caustically of those who did not follow him. Others were even more vehement. On the other side were many, both clergy and laity, who were alienated by the emotional excesses, were angered by the denunciations of the more ardent itinerant preachers, and held to the cold, rational approach to religion which was becoming characteristic of what was dubbed the Age of Reason. "New Lights" and "Old Lights" in Presbyterian and Congregational churches often separated into distinct units. The "Old Lights" were critical of what they deemed the lack of education of the "New Light" clergy, trained as many of the latter were in the "log colleges." Jonathan Edwards was forced out of his parish in Northampton (1750).

The Baptists began the rapid growth which was later to be so marked. Holding that infant baptism was not true baptism and stressing a regenerate church membership to which entrance was had through the baptism of conscious believers, usually by immersion, they attracted many.

The Great Awakening was evidence of vigour inherent in the Protestantism of the Thirteen Colonies. Here was a vitality which through succeeding decades was to reach a growing proportion of the partially de-Christianized population, was fairly steadily to augment the percentage of church members, and was to continue the mass conversion of which the Great Awakening was the beginning. Out of the Great Awakening came a large increase in churches, of young men entering the ministry, of earnestness among the rank and file of professing Christians, and of missions. The Great Awakening emphasized the importance of individual decision, tended to nurture the belief that the Christian should be able to tell the day and the hour of his conversion, and to encourage each Christian to seek to win his non-Christian or only nominally Christian fellows. It also fostered education and gave rise not only to "log colleges" but also to some institutions of a more permanent character, including, before 1750, the College of New Jersey, the later Princeton University, and the University of Pennsylvania. Others were to emerge after 1750.

Partly stimulated by the Great Awakening there were currents in theology which were increasingly prominent after the Thirteen Colonies became the United States of America. Jonathan Edwards was the first great formative figure in what has often been called New England Theology. His powerful mind expressing itself through widely read writings stimulated and helped to shape a modification of the Reformed faith which, while not denying the doctrine of the sovereignty of God, and, indeed, stressing it, or of election to salvation by divine decree, made more room for the action of the sinner in accepting the divine forgiveness. It was at once the outgrowth of, and helped to encourage the preaching central in the Great Awakening and the subsequent revivals which urged the hearers to repent. There were still the "Old Calvinists," holding to pre-Edwardsian views, but in New England they tended to give way to Edwards and his successors. Partly as a reaction against the revivals, an already existing tendency was strengthened which soon was to reject Calvinism with its doctrine of the total depravity of man and the arbitrary choice by God of some for salvation. It was strongest in and around Boston, where in the comfortable and well-to-do merchant and professional groups a more optimistic view of man was congenial. It was reinforced by contacts with similar movements in England and late in the eighteenth and early in the nineteenth century was frankly to become Unitarian.

It was later said of the Pilgrim fathers that they fell first on their knees and then on the aborigines. This had enough truth in it to give it sting, but it was so far from the whole truth that it was not even a caricature. In every one of the Thirteen Colonies there were missions to the Indians. In New England they were very extensive. Especially outstanding was John Eliot who, a graduate of that nursery of Puritans, Cambridge, came to America in 1631 and became pastor of a church on the outskirts of Boston. Through a long life he preached to the Indians in the neighbourhood of Boston, gathered them into churches, and translated the entire Bible into their tongue. Roger Williams and the Quakers established friendly relations with the Indians and insisted that lands be not taken from them by violence but be acquired through voluntary sale. For nearly two generations, or so long as they were in control of the colony, the Quakers kept peace with the Indians in Pennsylvania. From the earliest settlements in Virginia, clergy of the Church of England sought to win the Indians to the Christian faith. After its organization the Society for the Propagation of the Gospel in Foreign Parts took over most of the Anglican effort for the Indians and numbers of its missionaries specialized on them, notably on the borders of British influence in upper New York. Famous among the missionaries to the Indians were Moravians. The Great Awakening stimulated many missions to the Indians. Prominent among them was a prospective son-in-law of Jonathan Edwards, David Brainerd, who died before his marriage and whose journals marked by deep and sensitive devotion were widely read and had a profound influence on many youths both in America and in Britain. The Indian population was sparse, found adaptation to the agricultural economy of the white man difficult, and suffered from the diseases and the strong liquors introduced by the whites. However, in most of the Colonies Indian churches were gathered and through them adjustment to the new cultural environment was aided.

Nor were the Negroes entirely neglected. During the colonial period the mass conversion which we are to follow after 1750 had scarcely begun. Yet there were those who were seeking to win the Negro slaves who were increasingly providing the labour for the plantations of the South and who, some of them free, were in cities in the North. The Great Awakening spread among the Negroes. Before 1750 agitation for emancipation had scarcely commenced. However, among both Mennonites and Quakers there were those who believed slavery and the slave trade to be wrong and were beginning to protest against them.

As a result of the factors which we have briefly mentioned, there was arising in the Thirteen Colonies a distinctive Christianity. Predominantly Protestant and having its roots in the Old World, in the New World it was being modified. In it the extreme forms of Protestantism were relatively more prominent than anywhere on the other side of the Atlantic. Because of the varied sources from which the immigrants came—English, Scotch-Irish, German, Dutch, French, and Swedish—Christianity presented a greater variety than in any one country in Europe. Partly for this reason and partly out of profound conviction, especially in Pennsylvania and Rhode Island, there was more religious liberty than in Europe. It was by no means complete. In more than half of the Thirteen Colonies one or another church was either fully established or given special preference, but even in them enforcement of that status was more difficult than in most countries in Europe and by 1750 was weakening. The separation of Church and state was foreshadowed. This also meant the principle of voluntarism, the support of the Church not by public taxation levied on all, as was the practice in Europe, but by free will offerings by the membership. In several of the colonies the European procedure was followed, but in them it was beginning to break down. This Protestant Christianity was much less passive and less dependent on the Old World than was the Roman Catholicism of Spanish, Portuguese, and French America. Some help, mostly in the form of clerical personnel, continued to come from the other side of the Atlantic. Yet increasingly the churches were producing their own leadership. Confronted with a majority in the white population which, uprooted from its

European environment where affiliation with the Church was required, was drifting towards pure secularism, they rose to the emergency. Through the Great Awakening they were reaching out to the unchurched. Here and there, notably in Jonathan Edwards, independence of thought was appearing in the American-born whites. In general, perhaps because of its predominantly Reformed rootage, American Protestantism was activistic. Especially in New England and in the Quaker colonies, it was seeking to build here and now an ideal Christian society.

This extreme Protestantism with its strong Reformed strain was helping to shape the nascent nation. Even though those with a formal church membership constituted only a small fraction of the population, ideals and institutions were being moulded by their faith. Moral standards were set by it. It was resisting sexual irregularities, profanity, faithlessness to promises, drunkenness, quarreling, and gambling. It was easing the impact of the whites upon the Indians and the Negroes. It was responsible for most of such formal education as existed. All the colleges founded before 1750 had their beginnings in the zeal of earnest Christians and most of them were closely connected with the churches. The Protestantism of the Thirteen Colonies was laying the foundations for the democracy which found expression in the American Revolution and the United States. For example, in New England the clergy were preaching the rights which come from nature and nature's God, the theory that all men are born free, the duty of resistance to encroachments on those rights, and the popular element in government. While many of the clergy looked askance at pure democracy, the radical Protestantism which predominated in the churches in the Thirteen Colonies, seeking as it was to carry through the distinctive principles of the Reformation, salvation by the faith of the individual and the priesthood of all believers, underlay and permeated the democracy which characterized the United States.

SUMMARY

The two and a half centuries which followed 1500 witnessed a phenomenal spread of Christianity. This accompanied the equally phenomenal expansion of European peoples which marked these years. For that expansion of European peoples Christianity was to some degree responsible. The exact measure of that responsibility we do not know, for other factors entered. Yet the Christian faith did not automatically accompany that expansion. Indeed, some features of the expansion were flagrantly contrary to it and hampered it. The lives of many, probably most of the nominal Christians who represented the impact of Europe upon the rest of mankind were a denial of the faith. The greed, the sexual irregularities, the violence, the exploitation of subject peoples, the arrogance, and the truculence of the large majority of Europeans were accentuated in the contacts of exploration, conquest, and settlement. However, the great access of vigour in Christianity which was seen in the Catholic and Protestant Reformations produced a missionary activity which for geographic extent had never been equalled by any other religion. While surpassed by Christianity itself in the nineteenth and twentieth centuries, it was greater than anything which that faith had displayed up to that time. Christianity was now planted along the fringes of Africa south of the Sahara, in India and China attracted a larger constituency than before, and was introduced for the first time to much of South-east Asia, the East Indies, the Philippines, Japan, and the northern reaches of Asia. In the Western Hemisphere it won the majority of the Indian population and was firmly established among the settlements made by Europeans.

In this spread of Christianity Roman Catholics had the chief part, and the heroic lives and achievements of its great missionaries are among the most stirring in the history of mankind. But it was through Protestantism that the most vigorous churches were planted, those in the British colonies on the Atlantic seaboard of North America which were soon to become the United States.

Selected Bibliography

GENERAL SURVEY

K. S. Latourette, *A History of the Expansion of Christianity. Volume III, Three Centuries of Advance* (New York, Harper & Brothers, 1939, pp. ix, 503).

FRANCIS XAVIER

A. Brou, *Saint François Xavier 1506-1548* (Paris, Gabriel Beauchesne & Cie, 2 vols., 1912). A standard life, containing footnote references to the pertinent sources and literature.

H. J. Coleridge, *The Life and Letters of St. Francis Xavier* (London, Burns, Oates & Washbourne, 2 vols., 1872). Fairly good, by a Jesuit.

E. A. Robertson, *Francis Xavier* (London, Student Christian Movement Press, 1930, pp. 207). Brief, popularly written.

INDIA

A. Jann, *Die katholischen Missionen in Indien, China und Japan. Ihre Organization und das portugiesische Patronat vom 15 bis ins 18 Jahrhundert* (Paderborn, Ferdinand Schöningh, 1915, pp. xxviii, 540). Scholarly, by a Capuchin.

E. Maclagan, *The Jesuits and the Great Mogul* (London, Burns, Oates & Washbourne, 1932, pp. xxxi, 434). A scholarly study based on the sources.

J. Richter, *Indische Missionsgeschichte* (Gütersloh, C. Bertelsmann, 2d ed., 1930, pp. 294). The standard history of Protestant missions in India. It also contains a brief sketch of the Roman Catholic missions of the sixteenth, seventeenth, and eighteenth centuries. There is an English translation of an earlier edition.

CEYLON

S. G. Prakasar, *A History of the Catholic Church in Ceylon. I. Period of Beginnings, 1505-1602* (Colombo, Literature Committee for the Catholic Union of Ceylon, 1924, pp. xiv, 283). In general objective, based upon wide reading, by an Oblate.

Fernão de Queroz, *The Temporal and Spiritual Conquest of Ceylon,* translated by S. G. Perara (Colombo, A. C. Richards, Acting Government Printer, 1930, pp. 28, xxviii, 1274). Written 1671-1686, by a Jesuit, and based in part upon original sources. Seeks to animate Portugal to recover Ceylon.

J. E. Tennent, *Christianity in Ceylon: Its Introduction and Progress under the Portuguese, the Dutch, the British, and American Missions; with an Historical Sketch of the Brahmanical and Buddhist Superstitions* (London, John Murray, 1850, pp. xv, 345).

THE EAST INDIES

C. W. T. van Boetzelaer van Dubbeldam, *De Gereformeerde Kerken in Nederland en de Zending in Oost-Indië in de dagen der Oost-Indische Compagnié* (Utrecht, P. Den Boer, 1906, pp. viii, 358). A doctoral dissertation.

THE PHILIPPINES

E. A. Blair and J. A. Robertson, *The Philippine Islands 1493-1803. Explorations of Early Navigators, Descriptions of the Islands and their Peoples, Their History and Records of the Catholic Missions, as Related in Contemporary Books and Manuscripts, Showing the Political, Economic, Commercial and Religious Conditions of Those Islands from their Earliest Relations with European Nations to the Beginning of the Nineteenth Century* (Cleveland, The Arthur H. Clark Co., 55 vols., 1903-1907). A standard collection.

JAPAN

C. R. Boxer, *The Christian Century in Japan 1549-1650* (University of California Press, 1951, pp. xv, 535). Scholarly, readable, the best survey of the subject.

CHINA

K. S. Latourette, *A History of Christian Missions in China* (New York, The Macmillan Co., 1929, pp. xii, 930).

A. H. Rowbotham, *Missionary and Mandarin* (University of California Press, 1942, pp. xi, 374). A careful, scholarly survey.

SPANISH AMERICA

C. S. Braden, *Religious Aspects of the Conquest of Mexico* (Duke University

Press, 1930, pp. xi, 344). By a Protestant, objective, in large part from printed first-hand sources.

M. Brion, *Bartholomé de las Casas, "Father of the Indians,"* translated from the French by C. B. Taylor (New York, E. P. Dutton & Co., 1929, pp. xvii, 314). Popularly written, favourable to Las Casas, based partly upon Las Casas's writings.

L. Hanke, *The Spanish Struggle for Justice in the Conquest of America* (University of Pennsylvania Press, 1949, pp. xi, 217). Scholarly. Deals chiefly but by no means entirely with Las Casas. Carries the story down to 1600.

J. M. van der Kroef, *Francisco de Vitoria and the Nature of Colonial Policy* (*The Catholic Historical Review,* July, 1949, Vol. XXXV, pp. 129–162).

J. F. Rippy and J. T. Nelson, *Crusaders of the Jungle* (The University of North Carolina Press, 1936, pp. x, 401). The story of missions in tropical South America during the colonial period. Scholarly, semi-popular in style.

E. Ryan, *The Church in the South American Republics* (New York, The Bruce Publishing Co., 1932, pp. viii, 119). By a Roman Catholic priest; popular in style, scholarly.

FRENCH AMERICA

F. Parkman, *The Jesuits in North America in the Seventeenth Century* (Boston, Little, Brown & Co., 1903, pp. xvii, 586). Based chiefly on the *Jesuit Relations.*

R. G. Thwaites, *The Jesuit Relations and Allied Documents: Travels and Explorations of the Jesuit Missionaries in New France 1610–1791. The Original French, Latin, and Italian Texts, with English Translations and Notes; Illustrated by Portraits, Maps, and Facsimiles* (Cleveland, The Burrows Brothers, 73 vols., 1896–1901).

THE THIRTEEN COLONIES

P. Miller, *Jonathan Edwards* (New York, William Sloane Associates, 1949, pp. xv, 348). Well written, based upon careful research.

W. W. Sweet, *Religion in Colonial America* (New York, Charles Scribner's Sons, 1942, pp. xiii, 367). A standard survey.

L. J. Trinterud, *The Forming of an American Tradition. A Re-examination of Colonial Presbyterianism* (Philadelphia, The Westminster Press, 1949, pp. 352). Very well done. Especially valuable for the Great Awakening.

L. A. Weigle, *American Idealism* (Yale University Press, 1928, pp. 356). About a third of this highly competent survey of the religious history of the United States is on the colonial period.

Chapter 42

THE EXPANDING EFFECT OF CHRISTIANITY

In the two and a half centuries between 1500 and 1750 Christianity was having effects over more of the surface of the globe than in any earlier era. It continued to be the professed faith of the majority of the population of Europe and of minorities in Western Asia and North-eastern Africa. As we have seen in the preceding two chapters, through the Russians it was making itself felt in parts of Eastern Europe which previously had known it only slightly if at all and for the first time it was being represented, even though by little minorities, across the northern reaches of Asia. It was now, also for the first time, touching the coastal fringes of Africa south of the Sahara, was making its initial penetration of South-east Asia, of the islands which fringed that area, and of Japan. Although still excluded by Islam from Central Asia where it had once been, it was probably touching more of the peoples of India and of China than at any former time. The majority of the population of the Americas had given it their nominal allegiance.

Did this wider geographic spread mean an enhanced influence upon mankind as a whole? If so, what was the quality of that influence? Judged by the standards of the New Testament, was it for good or for ill?

It may seem surprising and even impertinent to suggest that it may have been for ill. Yet there is much in the records of these years which could be adduced to support that thesis. The geographic explorations and conquests which marked the period were by professedly Christian peoples, most of whom had been under the influence of Christianity for many generations. Some of the explorers and conquerors avowed themselves to be moved by the Christian faith. But, as we have seen, grievous exploitation of non-European peoples followed, including the African slave trade, Negro slavery in the Americas, and the near enslavement and even the extermination of a large proportion of the American Indians. In Europe itself, as we have also noted, especially in Western Europe, where Christianity had done much to shape civilization, forces were at work which were actual or practical denials of the faith. Some of them were accentuated by Christianity and others had their roots partly in Christianity. Wars were not new in Europe. For several of them, notably the Crusades, loyalty to Christianity had been the declared motive. Crusades were dying out, although successive Popes sought in vain by invoking them to unite Western Europe against the Turks. Now, however, the division of Western Europe between Roman Catholics and Protestants was either causing wars or making them more bitter. Such were the wars of religion in France and the Thirty Years' War. In England and Germany civil strife was either brought on or heightened by the appeal to rival conceptions of the Christian faith. What seemed like a secularization of Europe was in progress and this was in part from forces set in motion by Christianity. The Renaissance and some aspects of the humanism which was associated with it and followed it were in part, as we have said, fruits of Christianity. Yet they made for pride and attempts at human self-sufficiency which tended to rule out the Christian faith. The Papacy had less and less influence in the relation between states and with occasional exceptions, such as Richelieu and Mazarin, members of the clergy had a much smaller part in the affairs of their respective governments than a few centuries earlier. The intellectual life centered less around the Christian faith than in the Middle Ages. Theology was no longer regarded as the "queen of the sciences" in the sense of being the central subject of study. Some thinkers were challenging the truth of Christianity, a trend which was to assume larger proportions after 1750. Literature and art were more concerned with secular subjects and less devoted to specifically Christian themes. If these aspects of the story were all, the impartial observer might be pardoned if he came to the conclusion that Western Europe was outgrowing the faith which had done much to guide and shape its infancy and that what survived of that faith was being perverted to man's hurt and was destroying such remnants of itself as persisted.

However, this is only one side of the picture. Christianity was also producing the positive fruits which were to be expected from it, and these were more widely evident than in the centuries which had gone before. It is at least an arguable explanation of the seeming contrast that as the Gospel is longer in the world and makes its way more widely across the earth, God entrusts men with more knowledge and more mastery of their environment. He does this fully aware of the risk that He is taking, realizing that some will pervert His gifts, but also confident that others will be so gripped by the Gospel that they will be stirred and empowered not only to counteract the evil but also to produce fruits far greater than if the possibilities for the abuse of God's gifts had not been present. It is conceivable that this is God's way of dealing with men, that He is seeking to produce men of character, not automatons, and that this can be done only by giving men freedom of choice either to their infinite hurt or to their infinite good, but that He is also sovereign and will not permit evil to get completely out of hand, but will overrule it for His own purposes of love. It may be that something of this is hinted at in such passages of Scripture as "where sin abounded, grace did much more abound," "God is faithful, who will not suffer you to be tempted above that ye are able," and "My thoughts are not your thoughts, neither are your ways my ways, saith the Lord. . . . My word . . . shall not return unto me void, but it shall accomplish that which I please. . . . Ye shall go out with joy and be led forth with peace. . . . Instead of the thorn shall come up the fir tree and instead of the brier shall come up the myrtle tree, and it shall be to the Lord . . . for an everlasting sign that shall not be cut off."

The Effect Outside of Europe

In the preceding chapter we have seen many instances of the fashion in which Christianity not only stirred men to counteract the evils brought by the impact of Europeans upon non-Europeans but also to make of that impact a positive blessing. Thus Las Casas and less famous advocates of the cause of the Indians brought about legislation to protect the aborigines and then laboured as missionaries to bring the Gospel to them and through it to open to them a larger life. Protestants seized the opportunity given by the discovery of America to plant settlements through which the Gospel could be more nearly realized in human society than in the Old World. In doing so they laid the foundations for a new nation many of whose ideals were to be shaped by Christianity, especially by Protestantism of the Reformed tradition. In later chapters we shall see, as we sketch the course of Christianity in the United States, how profoundly that country was moulded by Christianity and how that faith was the source of many movements for social and moral reform and for the embodiment of the teachings of the New Testament.

The Effect on Europe

We must now seek to enquire how far and in what ways Europe, especially Western Europe, was affected by Christianity during these two hundred and fifty years. Here the faith had longer enjoyed a nearer approach to free course than anywhere else. Unlike the Eastern Churches, while threatened, except recently and in limited areas, it was not engulfed by the aggressive Islam. Here Christianity was the official religion of the several states and of the community. In South-western Europe it had occupied that position for a thousand years or more and in most of North-western and Central Europe by 1500 it had held it for at least five centuries. In much of Eastern Europe its adoption was much more recent and there were still unassimilated pagans and Moslems in its midst or on its fringes.

The Effect on Religion

First of all, we turn, as is natural, to the area of life which we call religious. In a very real sense this is a narrowing of the scope of religion which is contrary to fact, for religious convictions permeate all phases of life. However, there is a degree of validity in focusing attention on the ecclesiastical structures, the formal acceptance of beliefs, the worship, public and private, and the movements, new and old, which are clearly religious. When we define religion in this fashion, it is demonstrable that Christianity was shaping this aspect of the life of Europe more profoundly than at any earlier time. This was seen in a variety of ways.

To a greater degree than ever before, unless it may have been in the first two or three centuries, in the years between 1500 and 1750 Christianity gave rise to new and potent religious movements. This was seen in both the Protestant and the Catholic Reformation. The emergence of Protestantism came from a powerful thrust of the vigour inherent in Christianity. Although, as we have seen, factors extraneous and even hostile to Christianity, such as nationalism, the ambitions of monarchs, and the growth of an urban middle class, must be counted among the causes of the Protestant Reformation, they were distinctly secondary. They helped to make possible the survival of Protestantism as against the Catholic Church and did much to shape the forms which Protestantism assumed, but in themselves, either singly or collectively, they could not have produced Protestantism. Without them, although it might not have flourished and survived, Protestantism would have come into being. It was to the dynamic which is of the essence of Christianity that Protestantism owed its origin. It was that dynamic which chiefly accounted for the variety exhibited by Protestantism. The "denominations," "confessions," and "communions" of Protestantism roughly corresponded to the monastic orders in the Catholic Church. Like the latter, they arose basically from a fresh surge of conviction and devotion. They owed their forms partly to the political and social environment in which they emerged, but they were primarily the creation of individuals who had been gripped by the Christian Gospel. These individuals would have remained individuals were it not for the fact that there were others, sometimes only a few scores or hundreds, at other times thousands, similarly moved, to whom they gave leadership.

In the Roman Catholic Church, as we have seen, the fresh access of life in Christianity made for the revivification of old monastic orders and brought about the rise of new ones. Several of these, like the Society of Jesus, seeking to meet the needs of the times, took forms somewhat different from those of their predecessors. In the main they were more missionary and activistic.

In the Russian Orthodox Church the new burst of life was not as marked as in Western Europe, but it was largely indigenous, and although somewhat affected by what was taking place in the Christianity of Western Europe had expressions which were quite native to Russia.

The religious awakenings of the age touched every class. In this they were in partial contrast to their predecessors in the Middle Ages and were evidence that Christianity was penetrating all levels of society and becoming their conscious property. It will be recalled that in the tenth, eleventh, and twelfth centuries the new monastic movements had their creators and leaders chiefly from the aristocracy. In the thirteenth century some of the new movements, notably the Franciscans and several of those which the Catholic Church branded as heretical, were strongest in the growing urban population. Now all classes were stirred. Loyola and most of the founders of new monastic orders in the Roman Catholic Church were from the nobility. Luther, Zwingli, and a number of other Protestant pioneers were of peasant stock. Cranmer was of sturdy but humble farming parentage. Not many generations back, Calvin's paternal ancestors had been boatmen. George Fox was the son of a weaver. Many of the Anabaptists were in the towns and cities. Numbers of intellectuals were prominent in both the Protestant and the Catholic Reformation. Christianity was less and less passively accepted from social convention, as had been the case in the conversion of Europe, and was increasingly moving all classes of society.

Even the conscious departure from Christianity which was being fore-shadowed in this period and was to assume much larger proportions in succeeding centuries was evidence that men were no longer willing to conform to the faith uncritically, but were insisting upon investigating it for themselves. This very freedom was in part the fruit of Christianity.

The new life was accompanied by an improvement in the education and morals of the clergy. In the Middle Ages the majority of the clergy, whether in Western Europe or Russia, had little education. In Europe, both Western and Eastern, with notable exceptions, the parish clergy, those who set the level for the masses, were badly tarnished exemplars of Christian living. As the recurring efforts of reformers show, they were notorious for their avarice, sexual laxity, and ignorance. The higher clergy were little better. On the average they had an education which was superior to the rank and file of those who served the parishes, and among them were some of worthy character, even saints, but in involvement in secular affairs and in lust for power and wealth many set a corrupting example for their subordinates.

Perfection did not come with the Reformation, whether in Protestantism or in the Roman Catholic Church. Not all the clergy, either Protestant or Roman Catholic, were well educated or were of high moral character. Pluralism, that is, holding more than one office in the Church and drawing the revenues without performing the functions, continued. For example, it was notorious in the Church of England.

Yet the Reformation wrought distinct improvement, both in the areas served by Protestants and in the Roman Catholic fold. In general, the clergy of both wings of the Church in Western Europe exhibited a higher level of morality and better educational preparation than had been characteristic of the Church in that area during the Middle Ages.

For the rank and file of the laity the level of intelligent comprehension of the Christian faith was lifted by both the Protestant and the Catholic Reformation. The widespread discussion of religious issues was promoted by the controversies which accompanied the rise of Protestantism and its separation from the Roman Catholic Church. Printing made books and pamphlets accessible to a larger proportion of the population and much that issued from the presses dealt with religion. For the instruction of church members catechisms for their respective constituencies were prepared by both Protestants and Roman Catholics. Among Protestants the circulation of the Bible in vernacular translations markedly increased. Among Roman Catholics education in the tenets of the faith was promoted by such organizations as the Congregation of the Priests of the Mission. The emphasis upon preaching made for a similar advance among Protestant constituencies.

Whether equivalent gains were made in approximation to Christian moral standards would be difficult either to prove or to disprove. It is clear that both Protestant and Roman Catholic leaders sought to inculcate morality among the membership of their churches. In Protestantism the "gathered" churches, such as the Independents and the Anabaptists, especially stressed a high standard of morals among all their members. The Reformed tradition, notably in Puritanism, operated in the same direction. So also did Pietism in the Lutheran Churches.

Most and perhaps all awakenings within Christianity have given rise to hymns and singing. The Reformation was no exception. We have noted them in Protestantism. In that branch of Protestantism which is designated by his name, Luther was only the first in a long succession. The Reformed Churches favoured paraphrases of the Psalms, and of these there were many. German Pietism and English dissent gave birth to hundreds of hymns. With its emphasis upon the active participation of those assembled in public worship, Protestantism was particularly productive of hymns and metrical versions of the Psalms and Canticles which could be sung by congregations, but hymns for less formal use as well as great music for the mass emerged from the Roman Catholic Reformation.

Whether Protestant or Roman Catholic, the Reformation stimulated the life of the spirit and issued in a fresh surge of mysticism. By mysticism is meant, as it has throughout our narrative, the sense of the presence of God. In some degree, although for the majority very slight, this is common to most of those for whom the Christian faith is more than a nominal acquiescence in beliefs and customs shared by the community. From time to time there emerge from the mediocre level of the rank and file those who can be called great mystics, by whom the sense of the immediacy of the Divine presence is sought with intense desire and in whom it is realized. Their numbers are an indication of the temperature of the Church. In times of quickening, when devotion is warm, they multiply. We would expect that they would be numerous in this period. In this, as we have seen, we are not disappointed. They were found among both Protestants and Roman Catholics. Some were retiring contemplatives. Others were activists, their deeds in organization and leadership intensified and multiplied through the vision and strength which came from prayer and meditation. Among the common run of Christians there may have been more of private and group prayer than in the preceding periods. Certainly printing was utilized to give wide circulation to books of devotion. We read that in Scotland early in the eighteenth century most country houses and even flats in Edinburgh had closets for private prayer to which members of the family were supposed to retire daily. For respectable Scottish families Sundays were marked by abstinence from work and play and were given to family prayers and attendance at church services. Presumably there were other areas than Scotland in which the equivalents of these customs were maintained.

Whether religious liberty is evidence of the growing influence of the Gospel can be and has been hotly debated. It is certain that during this period there were Protestants who stood for religious liberty and did so on grounds which they believed were rooted in the Gospel. They constituted a minority and were mostly in or near the radical wing of Protestantism. Some were in the Reformed tradition. Only rarely and then chiefly in a few of the Thirteen Colonies, was there within Christendom a near approach to religious liberty. In some countries in Europe, notably the Netherlands and England, a limited religious toleration existed, but toleration differs from freedom. Toleration was usually more from political expediency or necessity than from religious conviction.

Extra-religious Areas in General

In other areas of life than the strictly religious the effect of Christianity continued to be marked. Indeed, it had fresh manifestations, evidence that it was not a dwindling survival of what are often, but mistakenly, called the Ages of Faith.

At first sight this statement will be surprising and may provoke dissent. The traditional Christendom, the *corpus Christianum*, appeared to be in process of secularization. The dream of a Christian society cherished by many in the Middle Ages seemed to be shattered. Not only Popes and lesser ecclesiastics, but also some among the laity had pictured the ideal society as one in which the Church would be regnant. Pope and Holy Roman Emperor were to be the joint rulers, the one of the spiritual and the other of the temporal aspect of the human community. Many had asserted that the Pope must be superior to the Emperor. The struggle between Church and state had been chronic, and some of the outstanding saints, among them Anselm, Becket, and Hildebrand, were famous for resistance to what they deemed the encroachments of the state. After 1500 the state had seemingly triumphed. On the eve of the sixteenth century the breach between the Eastern and Western wings of the Catholic Church had become final. In the sixteenth century what the Catholics called the Protestant revolt shattered what remained of Catholic unity in Western Europe. In the course of the fifteenth, sixteenth, and seventeenth centuries the severed fragments of the Church became subject to monarchs who sought absolute power over their subjects. In much of the East that power was not even nominally Christian, but was exercised by Moslem rulers, chiefly the Ottoman Turks. Where the rulers were professedly Christian, whether Protestant, Roman Catholic, or Orthodox, they were dominant. In Lutheran lands and England this was supported by many of the leaders of the Church on grounds of principle. The principle was called Erastianism, from Thomas Erastus (1524–1583), a German-Swiss physician, a Zwinglian, accused of Socinianism, who held that the sins of Christians should be punished by civil, not ecclesiastical authorities. The doctrine which wrongly goes by his name maintains that the Church is of right dependent on the state and is to be controlled by it. In the more powerful Roman Catholic states, as we have seen, the monarchs, while professing to be orthodox in belief, some of them zealously and even militantly so, insisted upon administrative direction of the Church in their realms. In Russia efforts of Nikon to make the Patriarchate preëminent failed and within a generation after his death Peter the Great allowed the office to remain unfilled and substituted for it the Holy Synod, completely a creature of the tsar. What is called Cæsaropapism was a fact.

CHRISTIANITY AND POLITICAL LIFE AND STRUCTURE

In spite of the control of the Church by the state, the influence of Christianity on the political life of Europe was striking and was exhibited in both old and new ways. With the exception of the Turks, the monarchs professed to be Christian. Claiming absolute power, they did so on the theory of divine right. Hence in principle they held themselves accountable to God. This was old.

Here and there after 1500 ecclesiastics held high political office and exerted a striking influence over governments. As in the Middle Ages when the chief ministers of monarchs were often bishops, this did not necessarily mean that Christianity was potent in determining their actions. Indeed, as in earlier centuries, in political office clergy were usually as un-Christian in their advice and action as though they had been frankly pagans. Outstanding in this period were Wolsey in England, Richelieu, Mazarin, and Fleury in France, and Alberoni in Spain. All cardinals of the Roman Catholic Church, they were as avid for power and as little governed by Christian principles in their policies of state as though they had not borne the Christian name. It is doubtful whether even Nikon in the days when he controlled the tsar was an exception to this generalization.

Some of the lay rulers were as intent upon exercising their power as Christians as had been any of the monarchs of the Middle Ages. Examples can be found among both Roman Catholics and Protestants. To mention only a few, they include Philip II of Spain, Mary of England, Gustavus Vasa and Gustavus Adolphus of Sweden, William the Silent of the Netherlands, and Oliver Cromwell of England.

Partly old and partly new were the efforts to bring order into what threatened to be destructive chaos in the relations between the nation-states ruled by absolute monarchs into which Europe was divided. War among them was chronic. The power of the Papacy over their relations had been declining since the thirteenth century and, except for Italy, had virtually disappeared.

The Christian faith and conscience inspired and constrained Christians to formulate principles for regulating the relations between states. What came to be known as international law was developed. Some of its basic ideas went back to pre-Christian philosophy, but the courage to give them actuality came chiefly from the Christian Gospel. The family of nations envisaged by international law was at the outset made up of professedly Christian states.

This is not the place for a full account of the rise and growth of international law. We must, however, pause to note a few outstanding figures. Francisco de Vitoria, a Basque by birth, a Dominican, Professor of Theology at the

University of Salamanca, whom we have already met as a champion of the cause of the American Indians, in the first half of the sixteenth century in *De Indis Noviter Inventis* and *De Jure Belli* set forth a conception of a community of nations which was broader than Christendom and coextensive with the human race. He declared that no attempt to right a wrong to a particular state should be undertaken if it involved a greater injury to the entire world community. He maintained that differences in religion, the glory of a prince, and the extension of an empire were not just causes for war and that if the subjects of a prince were convinced that a war was unjust they should not serve in it. Both Emperor and Pope were offended by his plain speaking. In the next generation a Jesuit, Francisco Suarez (1548–1617), who had been educated at Salamanca, helped further to develop the theory of international law. A contemporary of Suarez, Alberico Gentili (1552–1608), who for his Protestant convictions left his native Italy and became Professor of Civil Law at Oxford, gave to the world a book, *De Jure Belli,* which was another landmark in the growth of international law. Most famous of all the pioneers was the Dutch Protestant, Hugo Grotius or Huig van Groot (1583–1645). From his youth he had been deeply interested in theological issues. He was an Arminian and suffered persecution for espousing the cause of the Remonstrants. A layman and a lawyer, the spectacle of professedly Christian nations disregarding divine and human law in their conduct of war led him to write *De Jure Belli et Pacis,* a treatise which was long a classic for its formulation of principles. Significantly, it was published in 1625, while the Thirty Years' War was being waged. Although treating with respect what was called the law of nature, Grotius maintained that the New Testament is more authoritative and gave it preëminence.

A small minority of Christians were impelled by their faith to denounce all war and some went further and declined to participate in it in any fashion. Erasmus declared that all war is un-Christian. Dean Colet of St. Paul's Cathedral in London aroused the displeasure of Henry VIII by asserting in a sermon preached in his presence that wars are seldom undertaken except from hatred and that a Christian prince would do well to seek to imitate, not Cæsar or Alexander, but Christ. Several of the radical Protestant groups kept aloof from any active share in war. These included the early Mennonites, others of the Anabaptists, and the Friends. Something of the same attitude had been taken by most Christians in the first two centuries and in the Middle Ages by several of the groups adjudged heretical by the Catholic Church. Now as then it had little if any effect upon the policies of governments. Those who held it were not as influential as had been those who had laboured for the Peace of God and the Truce of God or as were those who sought to place the relations between states on the basis of law, whether in peace or war. Yet their witness was evidence that there were those whom the Christian faith impelled to be unreconciled to what to them were compromise and half-way measures.

The Christian faith inspired a few to suggest structures which would obviate war and ensure peace. In 1623, a monk, Émeric Crucé, put forward a plan for establishing perpetual peace and freedom of commerce throughout the world. This entailed an assembly of representatives of the monarchs of the world to adjus⁺ differences which might lead to war. William Penn, the Quaker, in his *Essay toward the Present and Future Peace of Europe* suggested a European diet or parliament in which disputes could be settled by vote. In 1710 a devout Quaker and a friend of Penn, John Bellers, proposed an organization for Europe which would curtail armaments and ensure peace. Soon after the close of the War of the Spanish Succession (1713), Charles Irénée de Saint-Pierre, a French priest who had been a secretary in the negotiations which ended that costly struggle, developed a plan for permanent peace which included non-Christian as well as Christian states.

In these projects and in the development of international law, Christian faith was inspiring thoughtful men to meet constructively a changed situation. In the Middle Ages Christian idealists built their hopes for world order on the achievement of a universal state with two heads, the Pope and the Holy Roman Emperor. The attainment of that dream had clearly become impossible. Europe was now divided among numbers of nation-states, each of which was seeking to be sovereign and fully independent. Undiscouraged, Christians were now daring to propose and make actual a society of nations which would be governed by law.

Christianity also had important effects upon the political theories which governed individual states. As we have suggested, it was called upon to reinforce the absolute monarchies which characterized the period. Generally monarchs were believed to hold their office by divine appointment. They were usually crowned with a ceremony which was a religious service designed to symbolize their dedication to their high office as Christians responsible to God.

When carried to its logical conclusion, Protestantism made for democracy. Its basic principles, salvation by faith and the priesthood of all believers, issued in governments in which each citizen had a voice and possessed rights and responsibilities equal with those of all his fellows. The majority of Protestants did not go as far as this. Most Lutheran states were monarchies. The Reformed Churches moved further towards democracy. Calvin disliked monarchies, but held that if God ordains governments we must obey them. He was not an egalitarian or a leveller. He taught liberty and fraternity but not equality. He shrank from revolution and desired an elective aristocracy. Yet under his leadership Geneva became a firmly established republic. The organization of the Reformed Churches had in it much of democracy. That was especially true of the Presbyterians. Still more democratic were the "gathered" churches, including the Independents, the Baptists, and the Quakers. The seventeenth century struggle in England in which Puritanism and the Independents were prominent and even more radical groups had a voice, contributed immeasurably to the democratic trend in the government of that country.

In the Thirteen Colonies the aristocratic patterns of the mother country were weakened and the radical groups—Puritans, Congregationalists, and Quakers—were much stronger than in England. Because of that fact, democracy flourished earlier and more vigorously in the Thirteen Colonies than in the British Isles. Sometimes the democracy of the United States is attributed to the westward-moving frontier, for it is said that conditions on it made for individual initiative and for the belief that one man is as good as another and that any one, regardless of birth, is competent to occupy any post. Yet the frontier was a constant factor in the Spanish, Portuguese, and French possessions in America and in none of them did democracy and the democratic dream develop in the form prized in the United States. The difference seems in large part to have been due to contrasts in religion. In the Spanish, Portuguese, and French colonies Roman Catholicism was the only religion permitted. In the Thirteen Colonies, so far as the population adhered to any religion, it was to one form or another of Protestantism, and in that Protestantism the Reformed and radical wings were in the majority. In the Thirteen Colonies John Locke (1632–1704) had more immediate influence than in England. From a Puritan home and educated in a Puritan atmosphere, Locke was widely read and quoted by those who, after 1750, shaped the nascent United States. In Locke, for example, was the assertion that men are "by nature, all free, equal, and independent. No man can be put out of his estate without his full consent." This was to be echoed, partly in the identical words, in the Declaration of Independence of the Thirteen Colonies.

In contrast, the Roman Catholic Church did not make for democracy as the Anglo-Saxon world understood that term. In France, reinforced by that church in his effort to make the crown supreme, Louis XIV sought to crush out the Protestant minority. That minority, it will be recalled, was of the family of Reformed Churches, from which issued much of Anglo-Saxon democracy. Bossuet, the most famous preacher of France in the age of Louis XIV, supported with his eloquence the power of the crown and inveighed against the theory propounded by such Protestants as Hugo Grotius that there is a law higher than the state and which the king must obey. As we are to see (Chapter 44), those who created French democracy drew their inspiration partly from Christian sources, but in doing so denounced the Christian faith, identified as that was for them with the Roman Catholic Church.

THE EFFECT ON ECONOMIC THEORY AND PRACTICE

What effect, if any, did Christianity have upon the economic life of Europe? That the economic aspects of Western Europe were passing through a revolution is one of the commonplaces of history. The surviving traces of feudalism were fading. Commerce was mounting. The guilds through which industry and trade had been conducted in the Middle Ages were disappearing. There was more of individual initiative, foreshadowing the *laissez faire* which was to characterize much of the eighteenth and nineteenth centuries. *Laissez faire* was in large part a reaction against the close control of all commerce by states dominated by absolute monarchs. Stock companies were being organized and capitalism was developing. In what fashion, if at all, was Christianity connected with the economic changes, whether as cause, deterrent, or regulator?

It has been argued brilliantly and with much erudition that Protestantism and especially Calvinism were a major source of capitalism. The thesis is propounded in the following manner. The Reformed faith made incumbent upon all its adherents a kind of asceticism. It taught that every Christian, and not alone clergymen, should regard his occupation a vocation which he should pursue in response to the "call" of God. In it he should work conscientiously as in the sight of God. He was to seek to produce what would be useful for the community. He was not to be idle nor was he to spend in selfish or luxurious fashion the fruits of his labours. He was to make all he could, spend only what was necessary, and save the surplus, although giving part of it for worthy causes. This led to the accumulation of private wealth and so made capitalism possible. Moreover, while Luther followed the precedent of the Church of the Middle Ages and forbade the taking of interest, Calvin permitted it. This also furthered capitalism. The acquisition and use of capital could be a virtue. Thus Protestantism encouraged the growth of the *bourgeoisie,* the urban middle class, which thrived on capitalism. In support of this generalization it is pointed out that the Netherlands, committed to the Reformed faith, became a great commercial power and that in England Puritanism had its chief strongholds in the middle class in the cities which were thriving on the expanding industry and trade of the realm.

This thesis has been vigorously attacked. In criticism it is said that the hypothesis quite misunderstands the Protestant teaching of "calling." The Puritans used it to rebuke covetousness and ambition, both qualities associated with capitalism. More cogently, it is pointed out that capitalism has its roots far back in the Middle Ages, long before the emergence of Protestantism, that the earliest European bankers were not Protestants but Catholics, that the urban middle class is a phenomenon of both Roman Catholic and Protestant countries, that in some countries Protestantism is quite as much rural as urban, and that this is true of the Reformed phase of Protestantism (as in Scotland, Switzerland, the Netherlands, and France), the phase which has been charged with primary responsibility for capitalism. In light of these considerations, so it is said, it cannot even be proved that Calvinism gave a decisive impulse to the development of capitalism, much less that it was the primary cause of it.

The Effect on Various Aspects of Social Life

On wide ranges of social life Christianity was having effects. Some of these were a continuation of what we have noted in earlier centuries. Others were new. They were more marked in Western Europe than in the East. What is often called activism, the attempt to better social conditions, was far more prominent in the Christianity of Western Europe, whether Roman Catholic or Protestant, than in the Christianity of the East. This seems to have arisen from several causes. One was the fact that in the West the practical spirit had been inherited from the pre-Christian Roman tradition. Another was the collapse of the Roman Empire in most of the West in the dark period after the fifth century and the assumption by the Church of some of the functions previously performed by the state, especially in the protection of the weak. In the East, in contrast, the Roman Empire persisted, gradually becoming the Byzantine Empire, and the populace could look to it for the social services which the Church undertook in the West. After the seventh century, the control by Moslem states of an increasing proportion of the area of the Eastern Churches worked against the undertaking by the latter of extensive care for the poor, the helpless, and the sick. Whatever the reasons, in the West the power inherent in the Christian faith gave rise to many efforts on behalf of the underprivileged and for social reform.

Among the social services traditional with Christians in the West was care for the sick and the poor. In the Roman Catholic Church this was continued, partly in the accustomed ways and partly through new organizations, some of them formed specifically for that purpose. The latter included bodies which we have already noted, such as the Brothers Hospitallers of St. John of God and the Sisters (or Daughters) of Charity, also known as Servants of the Sick. Only partially new, but greatly expanded, was the ransoming of those taken captive by Moslems, especially by the corsairs from North Africa who infested the Mediterranean. Also both old and new was the provision for the reclaiming of prostitutes.

Protestants were slow to do as much for the poor, the sick, and the orphans as were the Roman Catholics. This was partly because, stressing salvation by faith alone, they decried efforts to win merit by doing good works. It was chiefly because, from conviction, they had no monastic orders, and these were the chief instruments through which Roman Catholics cared for those members of society. Yet eventually Protestants developed means of performing these functions. They did it partly through the parish, as in England and Scotland, and partly through new types of institutions, such as the orphanage which the Pietists created at Halle.

From both Roman Catholics and Protestants there were the beginnings of prison reform which in the nineteenth century was to assume major proportions. Thus a leader of the Reformation in Sweden, Olavus Petri, denounced the use of torture as a means of compelling criminals to confess. James Oglethorpe, the Anglican, had as one of his motives in furthering the settlement of Georgia enabling convicts to make a new start and urged in Parliament projects for prison reform. Almost at its very beginning the Society for Promoting Christian Knowledge was discussing plans for bettering conditions in prisons in London. Late in the seventeenth century the Benedictine Mabillion advocated more humane treatment of prisoners.

Both Roman Catholics and Protestants did much for women. Societies and orders made up of women now became more prominent in the Roman Catholic Church. In extreme forms of Protestantism, notably the Quakers, women were placed either on a near equality or a complete equality with men.

The married clergy of the Protestants marked a distinct change in family life in the West and gave new honour to the wife. No longer was marriage unlawful for the clergy and concubinage of the clergy condoned as a lesser evil than clerical promiscuity. Nor, even as in the East, where the lower clergy were married and the bishops were required to be monks, was celibacy esteemed the higher way for the Christian. So far from regarding the unmarried state as nearer to the Christian ideal, Protestants repudiated monasticism and the overwhelming majority of their clergy, including bishops, were married. This added dignity to marriage, to the home, and to the wife.

Before 1750 there were to appear convictions of the perfectibility of man and of human society which were to be widely influential in the eighteenth and nineteenth centuries. Some of them were cherished in earnestly Christian circles. They were found in England in several of the churches and religious movements. For instance, George Fox and other Quakers insisted that every man who comes into the world is illumined by an inner light which is Christ. Many, and not alone the Friends, believed that a better age was dawning. This conviction led to active efforts to improve mankind. There was much of optimism. A familiar expression of it was in the hymn of Isaac Watts:

Jesus shall reign where'er the sun
Does his successive journeys run.
His kingdom spread from shore to shore
Till moons shall wax and wane no more.

THE EFFECTS ON INTELLECTUAL LIFE

At first sight, a survey of the intellectual life of Christendom between 1500 and 1750 would seem to indicate progressive de-Christianization. To be sure, the acute paganism of early stages of the Renaissance and its attendant humanism was partly dulled. The humanism of the North had more nearly held to Christian faith and morals than had that of the South. Both the Protestantism of the North and the Catholic Reformation in the South to some degree counteracted the paganizing tendency. The vast majority of intellectuals continued to pay at least lip service to the Church and Christianity and many, perhaps most, were sincere in their profession.

Yet some of the new learning, especially in the realm of natural science, was in seeming conflict with what many Christians had held to be essential in their faith. This was notable in the Copernican theory which taught that the earth revolves around the sun and not the sun around the earth. As popularized by Galileo Galilei (1564–1642) it was opposed by elements in the Roman Catholic Church. But others who accepted it and developed it were devout Christians.

Moreover, principles developed by convinced Christians were later to undercut the Christian faith of many. Thus, as we have seen, a younger contemporary of Galileo, René Descartes (1596–1650), often hailed as the father of modern philosophy, as a basic instrument of enquiry doubted everything. He believed that after all had been questioned one irrefragable truth remained, his own existence as a thinker. This was stated in the famous proposition, *cogito ergo sum* ("I think, therefore I am"). With that as a starting point, he was persuaded that he could believe in God as absolutely perfect being and continue to be a Roman Catholic.

Others, however, using the method of Descartes, did not reach that conclusion. The insistence of Descartes that all must be doubted until proved and that proof must be as logical as mathematical demonstration, led many away from the Christian faith. Nicolas Malebranche (1638–1715), born in Paris, trained in theology at the Sorbonne, and at one time a member of the Oratory, devoted to patristics and church history, had the course of his life changed by reading Descartes. He elaborated a system of philosophy which, while having a place for God, brought on him attacks from orthodox Catholics. Spinoza (1632–1677), of Jewish parentage, a native of Amsterdam, beginning with the *cogito ergo sum* of Descartes, departed from the latter's sharp distinction between matter and spirit and became a pantheist. He believed in God, but God as he conceived Him was not God as Christians believed Him to be. To Spinoza, God and nature are identical. All is determined and no room is left for creation, divine purpose, or miracle. Yet he regarded Jesus as the greatest of the prophets, in whom the wisdom of God assumed human nature.

Gottfried Wilhelm Leibnitz (1646–1716), for forty years a librarian at Hanover, was a man of enormous erudition in many fields. As we have noted, he sought ways of achieving unity among Christians—between Roman Catholics and Protestants, and between Lutherans and Reformed. He was a Lutheran. Yet whether his view of God can be called Christian is questionable. He held that the essential to all substance is active force. Substances are individual. Each is an atom or monad, an indivisible centre of force. Monads differ qualitatively, but all proceed as "fulgurations" or radiations from God, Who is the perfect, primary, and supreme monad.

John Locke (1632–1704), of Puritan rearing, trained at Oxford, we have already met more than once. He regarded himself as a Christian. Throughout his life he was deeply interested in religion and in his last years gave much of his time to the study of the Scriptures. In his *Reasonableness of Christianity* (1695), while holding that the Bible contains truths which unaided human reason could not discover and which are there attested by miracles, he maintained that nothing in the central message of the Scriptures is contrary to reason and that miracles are not unreasonable. He acknowledged Jesus as the Messiah and regarded as binding his moral teachings. These he held are in accord with reason. By stressing the ethics of Jesus and the consonance of Christianity with reason, Locke hoped to by-pass theological disputes, and by emphasizing what he believed to be essential Christianity to bring Christians together and to allay the strife of tongues among the many divisions of the Church. He was an advocate of religious toleration. Yet the most famous and widely read of his works, translated as it was into several languages, his *Essay Concerning Human Understanding,* while not intended to do so, led some of its readers to a complete scepticism.

A pupil of Locke, the third Earl of Shaftesbury (1671–1713), grandson of Locke's great friend and patron, wrote extensively. While himself believing in God, instead of basing morality, as had Locke, upon the command of God, he held that it is dependent upon an inner "moral sense" and so made possible ethical systems which have no place for God.

Isaac Newton (1642–1727), born the year in which Galileo died, did much more for astronomy and natural science than had the latter. While he himself was deeply interested in theology, his scientific findings were used by some as a means of disregarding or even denying Christianity.

Further from Christianity than these was Thomas Hobbes (1588–1679). Vigorous to an extreme old age, he wrote extensively. In philosophy a materialist, believing only in the existence of matter, he was violently attacked by some of the churchmen of his day. In political theory he upheld absolute monarchy as the way of preventing chaos in society.

A contemporary and friend of Hobbes, Edward Herbert, Baron Herbert of Cherbury (1583–1648), laid foundations for Deism, a view which was to be popular in the eighteenth century. While many who continued to call themselves Christians were profoundly influenced by it, some of its advocates openly repudiated Christianity. Herbert held that there is a natural religion which was that of primitive man. Its main tenets are that God exists and is to be worshipped, that He is served by virtuous lives, that man must and can repent of his sins, and after death there are reward for the virtuous and punishment for the wrong-doer.

Before the middle of the eighteenth century several had further developed Deism. Among them was John Toland (1670–1722) who, reared a Roman Catholic, in adolescence became a Protestant. In 1696 there appeared his *Christianity not Mysterious* in which he held that anything in the Bible which seems beyond the reach of reason will, on further investigation, prove to be quite understandable by the mind of man. He held that God never acts in a suprarational manner, but always in such fashion that man can comprehend. God is not aloof, so Toland held in his later years, but is universally present. Some Deists attacked the reliability of the Bible and in general denied miracles.

Most of the early Deists were English. This may have been in part because of the multiplicity of the forms of Christianity in England. Underneath them all men were looking for the common denominator. That led some to seek not only for what all Christians believed but for what was universal in all religion. In the eighteenth century, especially after 1750, Deism was to have a wide vogue not only in the British Isles, but also on the Continent.

Deism had many variations, but in general it held that there is a universal religion which is in accord with reason. All that is best in Christianity, so the Deists were prone to say, is older than Christianity and is completely in accord with reason. This universal, rational religion includes belief in God as the great Architect of the universe. He created the world, planted reason in man, gave him the moral law, and governs the universe by laws which are in accord with reason. God is to be revered and is to be honoured by a life which observes the moral law. Religious beliefs and practices which cannot be justified by reason, so the Deists went on to say, are superstitious and, being irrational, are to be rejected. Irrational superstitions have been imposed by priests of various religions. These include what Deists deemed irrational elements in the

Christian relevation. The law of nature, God's law, can be discerned by reason and is to be obeyed. To follow reason is to be loosed from the shackles of superstition. Therefore man must be a "free thinker," namely, he must insist on his right to bring all beliefs to the bar of reason, and must be liberated from inhibitions which would curb the use of his intellect. Obviously consistent Deists had no place for such central Christian convictions as the incarnation and grace. Deism tended to be optimistic. Man, so its adherents held, was on the eve of full emancipation from the superstitions which had hampered him in the past and was now moving into a better, grander age in which he was to govern himself by pure reason.

In view of these trends it might easily be believed that Christianity was fading out of the intellectual life of Western Europe.

However, here, as in so many other aspects of the course of history in Europe, is only one side of the picture. The truth is far more complex. In this phase of European culture, as in others, there was striking evidence of the "exceeding greatness of the power."

We must remind ourselves first of all of the large place which Christianity had in stimulating fresh approaches to education and with them in broadening the base and scope of learning and devising new methods to quicken and train the human mind and spirit. We have already noted something of the fashion in which both the Protestant and the Catholic Reformation and the later awakenings in Protestantism gave rise to novel movements in education and thought. Indeed, this seems to be characteristic of Christianity. We have seen that in the first five centuries, in a culture which was thinking and saying little that was new, Christianity was inspiring the creation of great systems of theology. In Western Europe in the twelfth, thirteenth, and fourteenth centuries, it was the chief impetus which gave rise to scholastic philosophy and theology, to the cathedral and monastic schools, and then to the universities. Now, in the sixteenth, seventeenth, and eighteenth centuries, Lutheranism worked a marked improvement in educational methods in Germany. Melanchthon and another friend of Luther, John Bugenhagen, brought the *volksschule* into existence and reconstructed the university curriculum. It was Hecker, a pupil of the Pietist Francke, who created the prototype of the *realschule* which had a large part in later German education. John Amos Comenius (1592–1670), a bishop of the *Unitas Fratrum*, made a refugee by the Thirty Years' War, was a pioneer in an educational theory which was to exert a wide influence, especially in its understanding handling of the child as a child. In Scotland John Knox had high ideals for a comprehensive system of education for the entire country. Although this was not fully carried out, it was not forgotten and contributed to the characteristic Scottish hunger for learning.

Out of the Catholic Reformation came many new movements for education. We have noted the *Ratio Studiorum* of the Jesuits and the extensive development of schools by the Society under its pattern. In the sixteenth, seventeenth, and eighteenth centuries several congregations of women arose with the education of the masses as their aim. Some of these we have met, among them one of the earliest, the Ursulines. In the latter part of the seventeenth century John Baptist de la Salle founded the Brothers of Christian Schools largely for the purpose of instructing the children in the rural districts. In the seventeenth and the fore part of the eighteenth century several teaching brotherhoods came into being with the education of the children as their objective. In Ireland the "hedge schools," with lay teachers and encouraged by the priests, were a major agency in giving what education was had by the poverty-stricken Roman Catholic peasantry. The Jansenist Gentlemen of Port Royal began a number of schools which stressed the use of the vernacular, paid considerable attention to science, and emphasized love for the child and close personal contacts between pupils and teachers.

Moreover, from Christianity came impulses to creative thought which did not issue in departure from the faith but, rather, sought to reinforce it. Such were the theological systems of the Protestant reformers, including Calvin's *Institutes*. Joseph Butler (1692–1752), whom we have already mentioned, was reared a Nonconformist but in his youth joined the Church of England and died as Bishop of Durham. He intended his *Analogy of Religion Natural and Revealed, to the Constitution and Course of Nature* (1736) as an answer to the Deist criticism of the Christian revelation. The result of prolonged and profound reflection but written in an English style which was quite lacking in grace, it was widely read and in some circles was long considered the standard intellectual support of the Christian faith. It maintained that since the objections raised to the Christian revelation can also be directed against the structure of the universe and the course of nature, the probabilities are that both Christianity and the universe have God as their author. So, too, the resemblances of the Christian revelation and the course of nature warrant the same conviction. We know too little of nature to deny the probability of revelation, and the truth of revelation is confirmed by miracles and the fulfilment of prophecy.

A contemporary of Butler was George Berkeley (1685–1753), whom we have also already named. A native of Ireland and educated in Trinity College, Dublin, an Anglican institution, in his later years Berkeley was Bishop of Cloyne, of the established church of that island. A man who won the respect of many who knew him for a singularly pure and unselfish character, and persuaded, to use his own words, that "westward the star of empire takes its way, the four first acts already past, a fifth shall close the drama with the day, time's noblest offspring is the last," he dreamed of founding in Bermuda an institution for training clergy for the care of the colonists and missionaries to the Indians. To that end he spent some time in Rhode Island, but the funds promised to carry through the enterprise were not provided and he returned to England. He is best remembered for his philosophy. To him, only mind and ideas have real existence. What we call matter is not outside the mind but within it and is imposed on the mind by the power of God. We must believe in God, for ideas are universal and constant and must arise from an eternally active mind, which is God. Since, from this viewpoint, matter does not exist, the materialist conception of the universe must be false. It would then follow that the Deist philosophy is untenable, for it maintains that the universe is a vast mechanism set running once for all by God and governed by His immutable laws.

Berkeley's philosophy had a profound influence on many minds in several countries, both in the eighteenth century and later. However, numbers of those who agreed with some of its premises about the primacy of mind did not accept his conclusions about the existence and operation of God. They were either sceptical about the truth of Christianity or completely abandoned the Christian faith.

We must remind ourselves that many of the scientific discoveries and much of the closely related developments in mathematics were by men of Christian faith. At once there come to mind such names as Kepler, Isaac Newton, and Pascal. Others less widely known could be added. Among them was John Flamsteed (1646–1719), a clergyman of the Church of England, founder of the royal observatory at Greenwich, compiler of an early catalogue of the fixed stars, and famous in his day for his observations of the moon.

There was that in Christianity which stimulated minds to activity. Many of them dissented from Christianity but others, among them some of the finest which Europe knew, were sincerely committed to it. Not all of the latter were fully orthodox, either from the standpoint of the Roman Catholic Church or of any of the major Protestant communions. Yet they regarded themselves as Christians and were deeply interested in the problems which that faith presented to the human intellect.

Not only in philosophy but also in literature in general the effects of Christianity were mixed. Some literature was pagan. Some, even when the work of those who were professionally committed to Christianity and drew their support from the Church, was of dubious Christian content. In this group belonged Rabelais, for a time a Franciscan and then a Benedictine, and Jonathan Swift, priest and dean in the established church in Ireland. Several, notably the many-sided Shakespeare, while having spots which could not be made to square with Christian morals, had passages which revealed profound insight into the Christian faith and warm sympathy with it. Some of the most notable literature of the time, as we have suggested, was devoted to Christian themes and was clearly inspired by the Christian faith. Such were Milton's *Paradise Lost* and Tasso's *Jerusalem Delivered*. There were also many lesser poets who were deeply gripped by the Christian faith. Among them were, in Italy, Luigi Tansillo (1510–1565) and Erasmo de Valvasone, pioneers in poems of remorse, centering largely on the tears of Peter and of Mary Magdalen, which enjoyed a wide vogue in circles affected by the Catholic Reformation. Writing in English were the Anglicans George Herbert (1593–1633), younger brother of Lord Herbert of Cherbury, deeply religious, by choice a clergyman, who put his dream of what that calling should mean in *The Country Parson,* and Henry Vaughan (1622–1695), much influenced by Herbert. Richard Crashaw (c.1613–1649), son of an Anglican clergyman and a convert to Roman Catholicism, wrote lyrics on the raptures of the saints and martyrs.

Effects upon Art and Music

As in scholarship and literature, so in art and music, a contrast was seen. No longer were Christian themes as dominant as in the Middle Ages. Yet Christianity had a marked influence. It inspired some of the greatest painting, sculpture, architecture, and music ever produced.

In painting some of the most treasured examples of art with Christian themes are from this period. It was in 1498, on the eve of the Catholic Reformation, that the extraordinarily versatile Leonardo da Vinci completed his memorable mural of the Last Supper in the refectory of a monastery in Milan. As we have reminded ourselves, Raphael and Michelangelo made their contributions in the sixteenth century. Spending most of his life in the opulent surroundings of commercial and worldly Venice, from which, significantly, came no great religious movement, Titian devoted much of his genius to quite secular and even pagan subjects. Yet Christian themes also appealed to his genius. Velásquez (1599–1660) gave most of his attention to other than religious subjects, but the crucifixion moved him to one of his most notable pictures. His younger contemporary, Murillo, was a member of an austere brotherhood whose members devoted themselves to the burial of the bodies of the drowned and the murdered and to the spiritual care of the last hours of those condemned to death. Murillo's themes were Christian, especially memorable being his treatment of the immaculate conception.

The construction of Christian churches continued to call forth the genius of architects. Notable was St. Peter's in Rome, in part the creation of Michelangelo. In their early days the Jesuits did much to produce a new style of church building. While, like St. Peter's, making pre-Christian classical style serve Christian purposes, they designed their churches so that the worshipping congregation could see the celebration of the mass, thus more appreciatively participating in it, and removed the screen which in many earlier churches had separated the altar from the nave. With the increased emphasis on preaching as a result of the Catholic Reformation, more prominence was given to the pulpit and greater care was devoted to so building the churches that the sermon could be heard.

If this was true in Roman Catholic church architecture, even more were Protestant churches so planned that the sermon might be easily heard. Reacting against what they deemed the idolatry in the use of images, sculptures, paintings, and stained glass windows in Roman Catholic churches, many Protestants made their churches severely plain. Yet among them, too, the Christian impulse inspired architecture which adapted pre-Christian classical forms to Christian worship. Outstanding were the structures which Christopher Wren (1632–1723), son of an Anglican clergyman, designed for the Church of England and those built, often by unremembered architects, in the Thirteen Colonies.

The Reformation, both Catholic and Protestant, called forth superb music. Giovanni Pierluigi (1524–1594), better known as Palestrina from his birthplace, successively choir master in three of Rome's largest churches, wrote more than ninety masses as well as scores of other musical settings for public worship. As we have seen, the Oratory gave rise to a new form, centering about Christian themes. Some of the greatest music ever written was by Johann Sebastian Bach (1685–1750), a Lutheran, who devoted most of his genius to the service of the Church. George Frederick Handel (1685–1759), born the same year as Bach but surviving him by nearly a decade, had his earliest musical training in Pietist Halle. He wrote much secular music, including operas, but he is best remembered for his oratorios and anthems, above all for his *Messiah*.

THE EFFECT ON INDIVIDUAL LIVES

It is not only by its impress upon various aspects of civilization and the collective life of mankind that the effect of Christianity is to be appraised. It is also, and primarily, by what it does to individuals. While Jesus had much to say of the kingdom of God and taught men in masses, he gave himself to men and women one by one. Some of his most moving parables had to do with single persons—the man who fell among thieves and the Samaritan who rescued him, the prodigal younger son and his older brother—and he warned his disciples not to despise even a single child. Obviously individuals are profoundly moulded by others and the society and culture in which they are immersed. They also leave their impress on their social environment, some of them so markedly that great masses of men are different because they have lived.

That Christianity placed its stamp on individuals in the two and a half centuries which followed the year 1500 must be apparent. This is one of the most obvious conclusions from the preceding chapters. It is clear that it affected individuals over a larger proportion of the earth's surface than at any earlier time.

A moment's reflection will bring the conclusion that the impact of Christianity was followed by more kinds of responses by individuals than in any previous period. This was partly because Christianity had more different expressions than in any preceding age, not even excepting the first three centuries when it proliferated into the many kinds of Gnosticism, the Ebionites, the Marcionites, the Montanists, and the Novatians—to mention only the best remembered. After 1500 there were not only the several Eastern Churches, the Roman Catholics, and the Protestants, but in most of these there were varieties. We have seen them in the Russian Orthodox Church, in the new expressions of the monastic tradition in the Roman Catholic Church, and in the many kinds of Protestantism. Moreover, as Christianity moved beyond Europe and Western Asia into East and South-east Asia, Africa south of the Sahara, and the Americas, individuals and groups from many different cultures were brought within the scope of the Christian impact and reacted to it far from uniformly.

Even from as cursory a summary as we have made in the preceding chapters, there can be no doubt that within all of its many variations in many individuals Christianity was producing distinctive and characteristic fruits—love, joy, peace, longsuffering, gentleness, goodness, faith, meekness, and self-control. We can be certain that for each of those individuals whom we have named in which these qualities were being displayed there were thousands in whom they were seen.

It is equally indubitable that in none of the men and women whom we have described were these fruits perfectly realized. All displayed qualities which contradicted them. At the very outset of Christianity this had been obvious. It was seen in the original apostles. Paul spoke of the Christians whom he knew as "being saved," implying that they were not yet fully saved, and frankly said of himself that he was not perfect and had not attained, but was pressing on to the "high calling of God in Christ Jesus." So in the period from 1500 to 1750 in some who called themselves Christians traits contrary to the Christian virtues were accentuated. For instance, out of what they believed to be zeal for the Christian faith many became bigoted, hard, unloving, and tortured or killed others, among them those who also regarded themselves as followers of Christ.

Whether the individuals who were being brought into conformation to the Christian ideal were fewer or more numerous than in the preceding eras we cannot know. Probably, in view of the wider geographic spread of the faith and the dynamic shown in the Protestant and Catholic Reformations, there were more of them, more who in the New Testament use of that term could be called saints, than in any other previous period of equal length.

SUMMARY

How shall we summarize the effect of Christianity in the two and a half centuries which we have just now surveyed? If, as we must, we seek to answer that question from the standpoint of mankind as a whole, it is clear that more of the earth's surface and a larger proportion of mankind had been touched than at any earlier time. With the advance of the Ottoman Turks in the East, the main centre of Christianity was more and more in Western Europe, with a secondary major centre in Russia. Western European peoples were rapidly extending their domains and their commerce, especially in the Americas. Roughly parallel with the growth of the colonial and commercial empires of European peoples went the spread of Christianity. Each aided the other, but the association was not inevitable. The missionaries were from the fresh burst of life within Christianity. Sometimes they preceded and sometimes they followed their non-missionary fellow-countrymen. The latter never went where the missionaries did not eventually come, but the missionaries went to many areas where merchants, conquerors, and settlers did not make their way until after 1750. How far the non-missionary expansion of Europeans was due to Christianity we cannot determine. That it was often accompanied and followed by ruthless and quite un-Christian exploitation is obvious. It is also clear that the Christian conscience softened the impact and at times made it of advantage to individuals and groups.

In "Christian" Europe itself contradictory movements were seen. On the one hand there was much tacit and a little patent denial of the faith. Although taking some new forms, the ruthless competition for power and prestige among monarchs, usually masked by the profession of righteous motives, but issuing in chronic war, was no more marked than in earlier centuries. Yet it was contrary to Christian precepts. So, too, was the struggle for wealth by individuals and groups. Much more of art and literature was secular than in the Middle Ages. Rather more of the philosophy which engaged the intellectuals denied or would seek to make unnecessary distinctive Christian tenets than did that of the Middle Ages. However, before we declare that a progressive de-Christianization of thought was setting in, we must recall the popularity of Averroes and Maimonides in the high Middle Ages, the persistent reverence for Plato, and the vogue enjoyed by Aristotle, all with non-Christian implications.

As against these features of Western Europe which seemed to argue the waning of Christianity, we must remember the profound effect on religion, probably making that phase of life a closer approximation to Christian standards than ever. We must also remind ourselves of the fashion in which Christian faith and conscience dealt with the relations between states and with political theory, of the Christian family aided by the Protestant Reformation, of the results in new educational systems and principles, and of the literature, art, and music which were inspired by Christianity. We must remember that much of the science which by many was deemed destructive to the Christian faith was the achievement of men committed to that faith and at least to some degree inspired by it to courageous search. Even the philosophy that denied or ignored central Christian convictions was to no small degree stimulated by the vigour of the Christian position.

In view of these facts, we must not lightly say that the world was becoming more Christian, or, on the other hand, bewail the departure of the Ages of Faith and declare that Christianity was a declining force. The picture is far too complex to permit sweeping generalizations. The geographic impact of Christianity had undoubtedly widened and a larger proportion of mankind was affected than ever before. But whether the world was more or less conforming to Christian standards it would be hard to determine.

Selected Bibliography

E. D. Bebb, *Nonconformity and Social and Economic Life 1660–1800. Some Problems of the Present as They Appeared in the Past* (London, The Epworth Press, 1935, pp. 198). Carefully done.

C. C. Conrad, *The Papacy and World-Affairs as Reflected in the Secularization of Politics* (University of Chicago Press, 1937, pp. xiv, 310).

C. Dawson, *Progress and Religion: An Historical Inquiry* (London, Longmans, Green & Co., 1929, pp. xvii, 254). A thoughtful study by a Roman Catholic layman.

P. J. Dowling, *The Hedge Schools of Ireland* (London, Longmans, Green & Co., 1935, pp. xvii, 182).

J. N. Figgis, *Studies in Political Thought from Gerson to Grotius 1414–1625* (Cambridge University Press, 2d ed., 1931, pp. vii, 224). A standard survey.

G. P. Gooch, *English Democratic Ideas in the Seventeenth Century. Second Edition, with Supplementary Notes and Appendices,* by H. J. Laski (Cambridge University Press, 1927, pp. x, 315). A standard work.

H. G. Graham, *The Social Life of Scotland in the Eighteenth Century* (London, A. & C. Black, 1937, pp. xi, 545). Well documented; full of detailed information.

P. Janelle, *The Catholic Reformation* (Milwaukee, The Bruce Publishing Co., 1948, pp. xiv, 397). Sympathetic, by a Jesuit.

C. M. Kennedy, *The Influence of Christianity on International Law* (London, Macmillan & Co., 1856, pp. xvi, 158). A Hulsean prize essay in the University of Cambridge.

W. S. M. Knight, *The Life and Times of Hugo Grotius* (London, Sweet & Maxwell, 1925, pp. xiv, 304). Carefully done and well documented.

L. Lallemand, *Histoire de la Charité* (Paris, Alphonse Picard et Fils, 4 vols., 1902–1912). Well documented, favourable to the Church.

K. S. Latourette, *A History of the Expansion of Christianity. Volume III, Three Centuries of Advance* (New York, Harper & Brothers, 1939, pp. ix, 503). Chapter XVI deals with the subject of this chapter.

A. Lincoln, *Some Political and Social Ideas of English Dissent 1763–1800* (Cambridge University Press, 1938, pp. 292). Well documented.

A. C. McGiffert, *Protestant Thought before Kant* (New York, Charles Scribner's Sons, 1911, pp. 261).

J. T. McNeill, *Christian Hope for World Society* (New York, Harper & Brothers, 1937, pp. vii, 278). A thoughtful series of lectures by a church historian.

J. ter Meulen, *Der Gedanke der Internationalen Organization in seiner Entwicklung* (Haag, Martinus Nijhoff, 2 vols., 1917–1929). Well documented.

P. Monroe, *A Text-book in the History of Education* (New York, The Macmillan Co., 1914, pp. xxiii, 772). By an outstanding expert.

H. R. Niebuhr, *The Kingdom of God in America* (New York, Harper & Brothers, 1937, pp. xvii, 215). A brilliant interpretation of the religious history of the United States.

H. M. Robertson, *Aspects of the Rise of Economic Individualism: A Criticism of Max Weber and his School* (Cambridge University Press, 1933, pp. xvi, 223).

J. B. Scott, *The Spanish Origin of International Law. Francisco de Vitoria and His Law of Nations* (Oxford, The Clarendon Press, 1934, pp. 19a, 288, clviii). Scholarly.

W. R. Sorley, *A History of English Philosophy* (New York, G. P. Putnam's Sons, 1921, pp. xv, 371). By an outstanding specialist.

F. H. Stead, *The Story of Social Christianity* (London, James Clarke & Co., 2 vols., no date). Laudatory of the social changes wrought by Christianity throughout the course of its history.

L. Stephen, *History of English Thought in the Eighteenth Century* (New York, G. P. Putnam's Sons, 2 vols., 1876).

R. H. Tawney, *Religion and the Rise of Capitalism* (London, John Murray, 1926, pp. xiii, 339).

E. Troeltsch, *The Social Teachings of the Christian Churches,* translated by Olive Wyon (New York, The Macmillan Co., 1931, pp. 1019). A standard work.

M. Weber, *The Protestant Ethic and the Spirit of Capitalism,* translated from the German by T. Parsons (London, George Allen & Unwin, 1930, pp. xi, 292). A study which provoked a warm discussion.

B. Willey, *The Seventeenth Century Background. Studies in the Thought of the Age in Relation to Poetry and Religion* (London, Chatto & Windus, 1934, pp. viii, 315). A competent survey.

B. Willey, *The Eighteenth Century Background. Studies on the Idea of Nature in the Thought of the Period* (London, Chatto & Windus, 1940, pp. viii, 302).

Chapter 43

RETROSPECT AND PROSPECT

At the dawn of the sixteenth century the outlook for Christianity was decidedly grim. The old order with which Christianity had been associated was passing. In the East the once flourishing minorities in Central Asia either had disappeared or were disappearing. Constantinople, long a bulwark against Islam, had fallen to the Turk. All the historic patriarchates except Rome were under Moslem rule. In Russia a professedly Christian state was emerging from Mongol domination, but its church, while vital, appeared to give little hope for the future now that the Greeks, to whom it had traditionally looked, were mostly Turkish subjects. Western Europe, although politically independent of non-Christian princes and nominally holding to Christianity, appeared to be outgrowing that faith. The Renaissance and humanism had brought a thinly veiled recrudescence of paganism. The Papacy was morally decadent and emerging nation states under absolute monarchs were extending their control over the Church in their realms and were seeking to make it ancillary to their purposes. As time passed, the expanding intellectual horizons, with the growth of natural science and the attendant enlargement of knowledge of astronomy, physics, and mathematics, although due in no small degree to Christianity, shook the confidence of many in the Christian faith. Geographic explorations and conquests led to an exploitation of non-European peoples in ways which were a negation of Christian ethics. Christianity appeared impotent to deal with the new age which it had helped to call into being.

Yet within the Church movements and individuals witnessed to continued vitality, to a ground swell which issued in a fresh tide of life. There followed the greatest forward surge which Christianity had known since its first centuries. Here and there this showed itself in the Eastern Churches, notably in Russia, largely but not entirely independently of what was taking place in Western Europe.

The forward surge was most prominent in Western Europe. This was partly because Western Europe was more nearly free from the Moslems and the invasions which from time to time had poured into the East from the heartland of Eurasia and partly because, beginning with Augustine and Benedict of Nursia in the fifth and sixth centuries, the Christianity of the West had given rise to more creative movements than had that of the East.

In Western Europe the forward surge of the tide took two main forms. One was a complete separation from the Church of Rome which came to be known collectively, although with dubious accuracy, as Protestantism. The numerically largest expressions of Protestantism were Lutheranism, the Reformed Churches, and the Church of England, but there were several others. Varied though Protestantism was, and more varied still though it later became, it had common characteristics. Negatively, it repudiated the jurisdiction of the Pope and what it deemed the corruptions for which the Pope stood. Among the latter were the invocation of the saints, the cult of the Virgin Mary, the treasury of the Church, and indulgences. It also would have none of monasticism or of the obligatory celibacy of the clergy. Positively it made much of the Bible as the authoritative record of God's revelation of Himself and His redemption of man through Christ, it declared that salvation is by faith alone in the quite unmerited love of God in Christ and not by works that men do in an attempt to acquire merit, and it maintained the priesthood of all believers. Protestants had a specialized ministry. Insisting as they did upon God's call, or vocation, to various specialized occupations, all of them made sacred by God, they held that the ministry was one of these callings. Yet it was not dominant as was the hierarchy in the Roman Catholic Church, but shared with the laity the control of the churches. The large majority adhered to the formulations of the faith which the Catholic Church, both East and West, regarded as standard, especially what were known as the Apostles' and Nicene Creeds. However, a minority either rejected these or, endeavoring to go back to the primitive church and its beliefs and practices as pictured in the New Testament, declined to be bound by creeds. They deemed them later developments, even though they might assent to much or all of what was expressed in them. Protestantism was not a purely religious movement. It was associated with nationalism, the aspirations of absolute monarchs to control all phases of the life of their realms, including the churches, and here and there with the growing urban middle class. Yet it was primarily religious.

The other form taken by the forward surge in the Christianity of Western Europe was in the Roman Catholic Church. It purified old monastic orders, called new ones into being, brought about an improvement in the morals of laity and clergy, revised the organization in such fashion as to make for better discipline, and so defined the beliefs of that branch of the Church that they became more explicit as against Protestantism. In practice the Pope had slighter influence in the politics of Europe and less administrative control over the Roman Catholic Church than in the Middle Ages. Moreover, while maintaining even more emphatically than ever that it was the guardian of the Christian faith and the Catholic Church, the one founded by Christ and the apostles, in fact the Roman Catholic Church was only one of a number of churches, several of which made similar claims. The ties which had bound it with the Orthodox Church of the East had been finally severed and most of Great Britain and North-western Europe had been lost to it.

Although it had become a sect in the Catholic Church, to use that term to designate the Church Universal, the "blessed company of all faithful people," "all who profess and call themselves Christians," the Roman Catholic Church was making territorial gains which appeared to justify its claim to be *the* Catholic Church. By the middle of the seventeenth century it had won back some of the territory which it had lost to Protestants. By the middle of the eighteenth century it had gained the allegiance of minorities within all the Eastern Churches. Taking advantage of the colonial expansion of Spain, Portugal, and France, sturdy adherents to the faith of Rome although jealously limiting its administrative power, it was the chief channel for a phenomenal geographic spread of the Christian faith. By 1750 the Roman Catholic Church had adherents on all five continents and in many of the islands which fringed them. The same was true of Protestantism, but it had not nearly as large a share in the spread of Christianity as had the Roman Catholic Church. The only one of the Eastern Churches which was winning fresh converts was that of Russia, and these were limited to Eastern and North-eastern Europe and to the northern, sparsely settled reaches of Asia. In light of these facts, Roman Catholics might well view Protestantism as a congeries of heresies, doomed to disappear as the once numerous Gnostics, Marcionites, Novatians, Donatists, and Arians had done, and to look forward to the time when the severed Eastern Churches would be reunited under the Pope.

In the latter part of the eighteenth century great changes were to gain headway which were to go far towards altering this picture. A combination of movements and events was to deal severe blows to Christianity and to usher in another recession in the Christian tide. This recession was not to last as long or to be as severe as its two great predecessors, those from A.D. 500 to A.D. 950 and from A.D 1350 to A.D. 1500. As we are to see, it differed from both in presenting a paradox. On the one hand there was a growing and what looked like a permanent de-Christianization of large elements in the traditionally Christian peoples of Europe and, at the same time, on the other hand, there were marked renewals of life in the Christianity of these very peoples and what

was to become a geographic expansion of the faith of unprecedented proportions. At the outset these blows affected the Roman Catholic Church much
more than Protestantism and the renewal of life began in Protestantism much
earlier than in the Roman Catholic Church. It was not until after 1815 that
revival became marked in the latter. Throughout the eighteenth century and
nineteenth centuries, and through as much of the twentieth century as has thus
far elapsed, the tides of life ran more vigorously through Protestantism than
through any of the other branches of Christianity, not even excepting the
Roman Catholic Church, and proportionately the geographic expansion of
Christianity was more through Protestantism than through any of the others.
It is to an early stage of that story, from 1750 to 1815, that we must now turn.

REPUDIATION AND REVIVAL
A.D. 1750 — A.D. 1815

Chapter 44

REPUDIATION AND REVIVAL,
A.D. 1750 - A.D. 1815

Not far from 1750 there came another recession in that pulsation of advance, retreat, and advance which has characterized the history of Christianity. The initial date, like the others, is only a round number. An earlier or a later year might be given. Some of the movements and events which made the period a recession and which also marked it as one of revival began before that year. Others began after it. The year 1815 is a more precise date, for it registered the end of the Napoleonic Wars and the beginning of a century of relative peace and was quickly followed by another forward surge of the Christian tide.

This particular recession was not as prolonged or as severe as its predecessors. However, as we suggested at the close of the last chapter, it differed strikingly from the others in what were possibly highly significant ways. The others had been marked by the decay or collapse of cultures with which Christianity had become intimately associated, by extensive losses of territory due largely to invasions of non-Christian peoples, mainly Moslems, and by a decline of morale in the churches. This recession was due to a more complex set of factors, it saw no major losses of territory, nor was it accompanied by any such corruption of morals within the Church as had been the case in the earlier recessions. It was, rather, characterized by the open or tacit repudiation of Christianity by growing elements within what had been known as Christendom, a repudiation which was to continue, especially in Europe, after 1815. But it was paralleled by a remarkable revival, primarily in Protestantism, which was also to continue and to swell to large proportions after 1815, which was largely to reshape that branch of Christianity and which, joined with other factors, was to lift it from the position of a narrowly regional faith and make it world-wide.

FACTORS ADVERSE TO CHRISTIANITY

The factors adverse to Christianity were varied, but, as we have suggested, bore most severely on the Roman Catholic Church. They permit of no logical order, but must be arranged in almost haphazard fashion.

A major movement militating against Christianity was the decline of Spain and Portugal, especially of Spain. It was in Spain that the Catholic Reformation had had its rise. It was from Spain that the Society of Jesus had sprung, that chief organized agency of the Catholic Reformation and the major instrument in rewinning territories lost to Protestants and in pushing forward the frontiers of Christianity into previously non-Christian territories. Through Spain and Portugal most of the territorial expansion of Christianity between 1500 and 1750 had been effected. By 1750 both countries were palpably in decline. The reasons for that decline are in part conjectural and we must not take the space to go into a discussion or even an enumeration of those which have been suggested. The decline had been apparent as early as the seventeenth century and continued in the eighteenth century at an accelerated pace. Although nominally it was not terminated until after 1815, actually control by Spain of most of its possessions in the New World came to an end between 1750 and 1815 as a result of the occupation of the mother country by the Napoleonic armies. Slight territorial advances were made by Spanish missions after 1750. For example, some new ones were opened in Texas, partly to hold that area against the French, for until 1762, when they transferred Louisiana to Spain, the former had been extending their control in the valley of the Mississippi. Another expansion was accomplished in California. There the Spanish authorities were occupying the country to counter the advance of Russia southward from Alaska. Between 1750 and 1800 at least eighteen missions were begun in that region by the Franciscans. Yet these were efforts of a waning power which was soon to be expelled from the mainland of the Americas.

Another blow to Christianity, with particularly grave repercussions on its geographic frontiers, was the dissolution of the Society of Jesus. The Jesuits had long been viewed with suspicion and rising antagonism, not only in Protestant but also in Roman Catholic quarters. For this, as we have suggested, there were several reasons. Their tight organization combined with their numerical strength led many to fear them. Members of other religious orders and of the secular clergy were jealous of them. They were accused of mixing in politics and of being untruthful if that served the purposes of their superiors. They engaged extensively in commerce. Statesmen who were committed to the rationalism of the day regarded them as bulwarks of obscurantism. In 1759 they were expelled from the Portuguese domains, both in Europe and overseas. In 1764 they were suppressed in France and French colonies. In 1767 Spain and Naples took similar action, effective throughout all the vast Spanish colonial possessions. In 1773, under pressure, the Pope dissolved the Society. On the plea that the Papal brief could not be published in Russia, the Jesuits continued a precarious existence in that realm. They also persisted in Protestant Prussia, and, partially disguised under other names, in Belgium, Italy, and France. In 1801 their reconstitution in Russia received Papal approval, in 1804 they were restored in Naples, and in 1814 the Pope authorized their full legal existence throughout the world. However, the lapse, lasting as it did for a generation or more and in a period when the Roman Catholic Church was suffering from an accumulation of other reverses, brought severe losses, from some of which there was no recovery. The extensive missions which the Jesuits had initiated in Asia, the Americas, and Africa were entrusted to other orders, in China to the Lazarists, in parts of India to the Society of Foreign Missions of Paris, and in much of the Americas to the Franciscans. Yet in the transition there was inevitable loss of headway, and in few if any of the missions did those who substituted send enough experienced personnel to compensate for what the Jesuits had supplied.

We must also note some quite unrelated circumstances which in these years combined to hamper the spread of Christianity on its geographic frontiers. Japan was all but hermetically sealed against the outside world, a step, it will be recalled, which had been taken in an effort to stamp out Christianity. Christians still were in that country, but only in secret. In China severe persecutions were directed against Christians, in striking contrast with the toleration of the 1690's and the early 1700's. In the 1780's Christianity was introduced to Korea but after a brief period of prosperity was visited with resolute efforts at extermination.

While by no means anti-Christian, Freemasonry, which flourished in this period, tended to adopt Deist views. It spread from Great Britain to the Continent and there for many became a centre of opposition to the Roman Catholic Church.

A set of movements which militated against Christianity was in the climate of opinion. Intellectual currents, some of which antedated 1750, were circulating which were adverse to the faith. They reached a climax in these years. They affected the Russian Orthodox Church and Protestantism, but they proved especially embarrassing to the Roman Catholic Church.

One of these currents we have already noted (Chapter 42). The eighteenth century is often called the age of reason. What seemed to be the prevailing belief in Western Europe was confidence in man's mind. Man, so it was held, had heretofore been bound by ignorance and superstition. Now, by the use of reason he was achieving emancipation and there was nothing that, with this tool, he could not hope to accomplish. In view of the advances in the natural sciences and mathematics, this attitude is quite understandable. It gave rise to what in German was known as the *Aufklärung* and in English as the Enlightenment. Religiously it found its chief expression in Deism. As we have seen (Chapter 42), Deism held to what was called natural religion. This was said to be universal, discernible by all men everywhere through their reason, quite apart from special revelation. It believed in God and revered Him as the great Architect of the universe. God was to be worshipped. Virtue was his true service. After death virtue was to be rewarded and sin punished. But Deism held that God governed all through immutable law which He had created. It left no room for miracle, the incarnation, or the Trinity. In the new age in which they were living, so it was maintained, men were being enlightened by the use of their reason and were moving away from superstition.

Those affected by this view were legion. One of its most popular advocates was he who chose to call himself Voltaire (1694–1778). His voluminous writings, clever and daring in style, had a wide reading. Much as Erasmus had been the outstanding popularizer of sixteenth century humanism, Voltaire was the most widely known and read author of the Enlightenment. It is significant, however, that in contrast with Erasmus, who was earnestly Christian, Voltaire openly attacked that faith. Here seemed to be evidence to support the thesis that in the movement which began with the Renaissance, Christendom was moving away from Christianity.

Some thinkers went beyond Deism in their departure from Christianity. Thus in Scotland David Hume (1711–1776), whose first significant book, *Treatise of Human Nature,* appeared in 1739, followed in 1748 by *Philosophical Essays,* in 1751 by *Inquiry into the Principles of Morals,* and in 1757 by the *Natural History of Religion,* was a thoroughgoing sceptic. Starting from Locke, he went far beyond that thinker in challenging accepted beliefs. Declaring that cause and effect are figments of our mental processes, arising from our noting the association of our experiences, he believed the argument for the existence of God as the primal cause to be invalid. He thus undercut not only Christianity but also Deism. He challenged the Deist contention that the primitive universal religion of mankind was monotheism and maintained that polytheism preceded monotheism. He also attacked the belief in miracles, in his day put forward as one of the chief evidences for the truth of Christianity. Pure in his own conduct, he held to a frankly utilitarian ethics. He had a wide influence, both in staunchly Presbyterian Scotland, where the Church looked on him with disfavour, and far beyond the borders of his native land. Edward Gibbon (1737–1794), reared in a deeply religious home in England and for a brief time a convert to Roman Catholicism, in his famous *Decline and Fall of the Roman Empire* described that event as the triumph of barbarism and religion—and by religion he meant Christianity.

Rationalism and Deism had repercussions on the several churches. In Russia a large proportion of the upper classes, while keeping a formal connexion with the state church, were committed to the rationalism which was the vogue in Western Europe, for since the days of Peter the Great it had been fashionable to look towards the West.

Most branches of Protestantism were also affected. Many, even among the clergy, sought to present that faith as rational and to decry emotion. The trend was vividly seen in Halle, that major centre of Pietism. Here taught Christian Wolff (1679–1754), a rationalist, akin to the Deists in his religious beliefs. Here rationalism cooled the missionary zeal of many and undercut the enterprises which had drawn recruits from it. Hermann Samuel Reimarus (1694–1768), professor of Oriental languages at Hamburg, who acquired Deist views while in England in early life, in posthumously published writings expressed belief in a wise Creator, morality, and immortality, but decried special revelation and miracle and declared that the authors of the various books of the Bible were selfish and dishonest. The critic and dramatist Gotthold Ephraim Lessing (1729–1781), who saw to the publication of the works of Reimarus, spread the impression that Christianity belonged to a stage in civilization which the human race, in its advance, was now leaving. In England anti-Trinitarian views attracted a following among some of the intellectuals. The Presbyterian churches in that country, small in numbers, largely became Unitarian. Some of the General Baptists also moved in that direction. Prominent among the Unitarians was Joseph Priestley (1733–1804), originally a minister of dissenting congregations, and the discoverer of oxygen. A few of the Anglican clergy were inclined towards anti-Trinitarianism or actually moved out of the Church of England. Theophilus Lindsey (1723–1808) was one of these and organized a Unitarian congregation. Some of the bishops in England and Ireland were close to Unitarianism. Even the defenders of Christianity were affected. William Paley (1743–1805), whose *View of the Evidences of Christianity,* published in 1794, and *Natural Theology,* issued in 1802, while widely acclaimed by Christians, showed the effect of Deism and of rationalism.

The Roman Catholic Church particularly suffered, for rebellion against Christianity was especially marked in its constituency. Voltaire had his early education in a Jesuit school and, as we are to see in a moment, it was in strongly Roman Catholic France that a revolution broke out which largely incorporated the rationalism that had been one of its complex sources.

Another intellectual current which in some of its aspects undercut Christianity was romanticism. Romanticism is a term which is used to cover an attitude in feeling and thought which has been found in many peoples and ages. In the eighteenth century it was in large part a reaction against rationalism and the closely associated conventional classicism. It was not necessarily anti-Christian. Indeed, some of its leading exponents were earnestly Christian. Several, however, could not be put in that category. Prominent among the latter was Jean Jacques Rousseau (1712–1778), whose writings enjoyed wide popularity. Also to be classed here was the more profound Goethe (1749–1832). While in much of romanticism there was a warm and even deep religious feeling, for many it could not be contained within historic Christian patterns but took forms at variance with it, at times a pantheistic mysticism.

These intellectual currents contributed to movements which attempted to bring in reforms and in doing so treated the Church cavalierly, whether Russian Orthodox, Protestant, or Roman Catholic. The second half of the eighteenth century has been called the age of enlightened despots. Monarchs, endeavouring to follow the dictates of reason, sought to improve conditions in their realms. Among them were Frederick II of Prussia, a Deist, and Catherine II of Russia, who made presents to Voltaire and discussed the possibility of emancipating the serfs. In Spain Charles III (1759–1788) encouraged manufactures and agriculture, curbed the Inquisition, and suppressed the Jesuits. Joseph II of Austria (1765–1790), although a Roman Catholic, was much influenced by Rousseau, confiscated many church lands, abolished some religious orders, put the training of priests under state control, altered religious ceremonies, nominated the bishops, and forbade the publication of Papal bulls in his domains without his permission. His ecclesiastical policy was known as Josephism. In Tuscany a brother of Joseph attempted to restrict the power of the Pope. What was known as Febronianism, from its author, a bishop who wrote under the pen name of Febronius, had much influence. It advocated that the secular rulers control the Church in their domains and that general councils be superior to the Pope.

These intellectual currents came to a flood in revolutions which swept away much of the old order. The first was in the Thirteen Colonies and gave birth to the United States of America. The American Revolution was by no means anti-Christian. Some of its basic ideals were from John Locke and the way for it had been prepared by the Reformed faith and the sermons of the clergy, especially in New England. As we have suggested (Chapters XLI, XLII), the democracy of the United States was largely from Christian rootage. However, the American Revolution brought a pause in the Great Awakening, for the absorption of the population in agitation for and against independence and in war, and the moral disintegration attendant on war worked against serious attention to the Christian message. Some of the outstanding builders of the new nation, while not antagonistic to Christianity, were more Deist than Christian. Prominent among them were Thomas Jefferson, the framer of the Declaration of Independence, the third President of the United States, and the chief creator of what is known, from him, as Jeffersonian Democracy. Here, too, must be classed Benjamin Franklin. In some intellectual circles, with a strong appeal to youth, there were much more outspoken critics of Christianity than these two men. For instance, Thomas Paine (1737–1809), a warm advocate of American independence and whose pamphlets *Common Sense* and *Crisis* gave impetus to that movement, was an ardent Deist and in his *The Age of Reason* was as much opposed to Christianity as he was to atheism. In the latter part of the eighteenth century a militant rationalism and Deism had something of a vogue in the United States.

Much more serious from the standpoint of Christianity were the French Revolution, the repercussions of that revolution in Western Europe, and the wars which issued from it, culminating in Napoleon Bonaparte. The French Revolution broke out in 1789. It arose from criticism of an incompetent government which had brought the state to the verge of bankruptcy, from seething discontent with basic social and economic conditions to which objection came from the rising middle classes in the cities and the humble folk, including especially the peasants, and from ideas which had been given form by such men as Locke, Voltaire, Rousseau, Montesquieu, and others of lesser fame.

Some of these ideas were of Christian origin. They could be traced to both Roman Catholics and Protestants. Centuries earlier, Augustine had declared that man should not have dominion over man, for man is a rational creature, made in God's image. The Jesuit cardinal, Bellarmine, had said that it depended on the consent of the people whether kings, consuls, or other magistrates were to be established in authority over them, and that if there was legitimate cause the people should change a kingdom into an aristocracy, or an aristocracy into a democracy. In England, largely through the efforts of radical Protestants, more effective control of the nation over the king had been established. In the newly constituted United States, mainly through ideas formulated and propagated by Protestants, progress had recently been achieved towards a democracy. Out of a desire to weaken her ancient foe, Great Britain, France aided the Thirteen Colonies to obtain their independence, and the ideals expressed in their Declaration of Independence had a marked effect on the French. Most of the recent French thinkers and pamphleteers who had laid the ideological foundations for the revolution in their land were children of the Enlightenment, rationalists or romanticists, more Deist than Christian. Yet many of their convictions were from Christian sources and their hope of creating an ideal human society had more than an accidental likeness to the hope which had inspired the *De Civitate Dei* of Augustine and the dreams of Christians of Western Europe across the centuries to create a society embodying Christian principles. The French Revolution was to a large extent a secularized version of the heavenly city as conceived by Christians.

The French Revolution was of major importance for the world. That was partly because it quickly had repercussions throughout most of Christendom, both in Europe and America. Paris, where the Revolution centered, was the most populous city of Western Europe and for a century or more France had been the most powerful realm in that region. So sweeping a series of changes could not fail to have effects of primary importance in the rest of Western civilization. Of even more consequence was the fact that the French Revolution was an early and potent stage in a succession of similar movements which were to spread across the earth and which by the middle of the twentieth century were to alter profoundly the life of all mankind. The series began with the English Civil War, the Commonwealth and "Glorious Revolution" of the seventeenth century, continued in the American Revolution of the 1770's and 1780's, came to an even more explosive phase in the French Revolution, went on with ever expanding geographic scope in Europe and the Americas in the nineteenth century, in the latter half of the nineteenth and in the twentieth century swept into Japan, China, and India, and through the Russian Revolution and its aftermath profoundly moulded much of mankind.

It is highly significant that this series of revolutions had its beginning and its early course in Christendom and that the ideas which inspired and shaped them had their birth and initial formulations in lands and among peoples which for centuries had been under the influence of Christianity. Many of the revolutionary programmes repudiated that faith, but most and perhaps all of them embodied ideals and conceptions which had come through it. They took only part of what had been given by Christianity and to a lesser or greater extent distorted what they took, but even when they did not recognize or acknowledge their source, they were deeply indebted to it.

We must hasten to say that this generalization is not framed as an attempt to claim for Christianity whatever of good may be in these movements. If Christianity is to any degree the source of what, from its standpoint, is admirable, it may also be charged with at least some responsibility for what, by its criteria, is evil.

Here, rather, we are seeking to point out what we have more than once had occasion to note and what we must remark even more frequently as our narrative proceeds. This is the part which Christianity has had in shaping the most dynamic civilization which mankind has thus far known, that of Western European peoples. The precise extent of that part we may not be able to determine. We know, however, that it was present and that Western civilization reached and changed all mankind. Much in that civilization and its effects bore a family likeness to Christianity and was in the direction of what is intrinsic in that faith. Much, on the other hand, was in tacit or open contradiction of Christianity. The contrast between these two aspects of Western civilization and its fruits in mankind as a whole became increasingly striking as the nineteenth and twentieth centuries progressed. To the possible meaning of the contrast we must recur again and again.

The purpose of our story does not require even an outline of the course of the French Revolution. We need only point out the immediate effects upon Christianity. These effects were especially serious for the Roman Catholic Church. They dealt it severe blows. As we are to see in later chapters, the blows were not to end with 1815 but were to continue through the nineteenth and into the twentieth century.

Some of the earliest stages of the French Revolution brought actions which struck at the privileges and status of the Roman Catholic Church. To meet the grave financial situation which confronted his government, Louis XVI called the Estates General. This met in May, 1789. Late in the following month it resolved itself into the National Assembly and began drastic changes in the life and structure of the nation. Among them were some which were momentous for the Roman Catholic Church. On August 4, 1789, tithes were abolished, thus at once relieving the peasants of a burden which had taken about a twentieth of their produce and depriving the Church of one of its chief sources of revenue. That same year all the land of the Church, which then comprised about a fifth of the area of France, was confiscated and became the property of the state. In 1790 the monasteries were ordered dissolved. In July, 1790, what was called the Civil Constitution of the Clergy was enacted by the National Assembly. By it parish priests and bishops were to be chosen by elections in which all citizens, Protestants and Jews as well as Roman Catholics, were to vote and were to have their salaries paid by the government. The Pope might still define its doctrines, but he could no longer have any administrative control of the Church in France. The old diocesan boundaries were erased and each civil division, or "department," was to be a diocese. Most of the clergy refused to accept the new arrangement and the Pope strengthened their resolution by forbidding them to assent to it. The National Assembly retaliated by requiring the bishops and clergy to swear to abide by it. About a third of the parish priests and seven of the bishops complied, but the large majority did not and thus set themselves against the Revolution. The constitution of 1791 gave complete religious freedom to all citizens, thus fulfilling the dreams of such men as Voltaire, but cutting further into the privileges of the Roman Catholic

Church. From then into the twentieth century many Roman Catholics, laity and clergy, were opposed to the principles of the Revolution.

From 1792 to 1795 the Revolution mounted. Neighbouring governments took alarm at it as a threat to their own positions. Urged on by emigré nobles and clergy, they attempted to suppress it by armed force. Revolutionary France resisted, and the wars began which were to culminate in Napoleon Bonaparte and his empire. The threat from abroad threw the Revolution into the hands of the radicals. In 1792 a new assembly was elected, known as the National Convention. The National Convention successfully defended the country against the foreign invaders, conquered Belgium and Holland, and declared that the French armies would come to the relief of any people who wished liberation from the tyranny of kings and nobles. It also transformed France into a republic with "liberty, equality, and fraternity" as its slogan, and executed Louis XVI and his queen, Marie Antoinette. The threat of foreign invasion and domestic insurrection stimulated the "Reign of Terror," in 1793 and 1794. Hundreds were executed on the charge of being "partisans of tyranny . . . or enemies of liberty."

On June 8, 1794, on the eve of the height of the Terror, a new religion was formally inaugurated. In Deist fashion, the National Convention decreed that the people of France recognized the existence of a Supreme Being and the immortality of the soul. Atheism, vice, and folly were decried and the triumph of wisdom celebrated. Christianity was denounced as superstition, a new calendar was adopted to begin its reckoning with the establishment of the republic, and instead of the seven day week each month was divided into three periods of ten days each. The worship of the new religion would be festivals in honour of the great events of the Revolution.

After the Terror came a conservative reaction and in 1795 a new constitution placed the state under the government of a Directory. Religious freedom was proclaimed, but the Directory and its regime were anti-Christian. In 1798 the armies of the Directory created a republic in Rome and the Pope (Pius VI, reigned 1775–1799), who had been hostile to the Revolution, was carried to France, a prisoner, and within a few months was dead.

It was under the Directory that Napoleon Bonaparte (1769–1821) came to power. The most successful general that revolutionary France had known, in 1799 he did away with the Directory, by this time proved to be incompetent and corrupt, and had himself chosen as the first of three consuls to govern the state. In 1802 he had himself made consul for life and in 1804, with the outward consent of the overwhelming majority of the French people, he terminated the republic and turned France into an empire with himself as the first of a line of supposedly hereditary emperors. He held this position until his enforced abdication in 1814 and then again briefly in 1815 until, defeated at Waterloo, he was exiled to the island of St. Helena.

The attitude of Napoleon towards the Church was masterful. He was himself a nominal Roman Catholic, but had very little religious faith. Yet he saw that a large proportion of his subjects were loyal Roman Catholics and he regarded that Church as an institution which must be recognized and used for his purposes. At his orders, the vacancy in the Papacy left by the death of Pius VI was not immediately filled. However, in 1800 a conclave was held in Venice which elected a Benedictine monk, Chiaramonti, who took the title of Pius VII and reigned through striking vicissitudes until 1823. Napoleon restored Rome to the Pope, but by no means all the Papal States. After long negotiations, in 1801 a concordat for France was concluded between the Pope and Napoleon. Such of its confiscated lands as were in the possession of the state were to be restored to the Church, bishops were to be appointed by the Pope on nomination by the state, and while the lower clergy were appointed by the bishops, the government could veto the episcopal choices. The clergy were to be paid by the state. To this concordat Napoleon added (1802) the Organic Articles, but against the protest of the Pope. By them no Papal decrees were to be published or synods held in France without the permission of the state. At the same time Protestants were given religious freedom and their ministers were to be paid by the government.

When he assumed the title of emperor, harking back to the precedent of Charlemagne, Napoleon had the Pope share in the coronation (1804). However, he treated that dignitary far more cavalierly than Charlemagne had the Pontiffs of his day. Napoleon brought Pius VII to Paris for the ceremony, was anointed by him, and then placed the crowns on his own head and the head of his empress.

Pius VII and Napoleon had a complete break. The latter attempted to induce the Pontiff to abandon his neutrality in the life and death struggle with England and to join in the blockade against that power. The Pope refused. In 1808 Napoleon's troops occupied Rome and in 1809 the Papal States were merged in the French Empire. Napoleon contemplated making Rome his second capital. Pius VII retaliated by excommunicating Napoleon as "robber of the patrimony of Peter." Napoleon countered by having him imprisoned, eventually at Fontainebleau. In 1813 Napoleon published the Concordat of Fontainebleau. The Pope at first assented to the document but later repudiated it. In Rome Napoleon drastically suppressed monasteries.

After the fall of Napoleon Pius VII returned to Rome (1814) amid great popular acclaim. However, he fled during the hundred days of Napoleon's brief return to power. When Napoleon was finally defeated (1815) and the Congress of Vienna met to undo what had been accomplished by the French Revolution and the emperor, all the Papal territories were restored to the Pontiff except Avignon, another bit of land in France, and a section on the left bank of the Po.

Elsewhere in Europe the Napoleonic storm shook the Roman Catholic Church. For instance, in Germany, in 1801, the ecclesiastical states, some of them dating back to the tenth century and the policy of Otto I, were divided among secular princes. In Spain a reform cortes which met in 1810 suppressed the Inquisition and reduced the privileges of the clergy.

The French Revolution and Napoleon also brought grave embarrassment to Roman Catholic missions. Added to the other factors which we have mentioned, especially the decline of Portugal and Spain and the dissolution of the Society of Jesus, they led to sharp decline on some of the geographic frontiers of the faith. From 1789 to 1815 few new missionaries were sent from Europe and it was difficult to give financial aid to those already abroad. For a time the Society of Foreign Missions of Paris was forced to seek headquarters outside of France. Later Napoleon wished to combine it with two other missionary bodies and make it a tool of his imperialism. Even more serious were the vicissitudes of the Congregation for the Propagation of the Faith, the bureau through which the Papacy supervised missions abroad. In 1798 it was driven out of Rome and from 1810 to 1814 Napoleon sought to reduce it to an instrument of his ambition. In consequence there was a marked falling off in numbers and morale of the Roman Catholic community in India. In China adverse domestic conditions added to the handicaps in Europe and threatened the extinction of the Church in that land. Missions in Latin America suffered, especially after the occupation of Spain by Napoleonic armies and the attack on Portugal.

As we have hinted, conditions in Russia were also adverse. From 1762 to 1796 that country was ruled by Catherine II, sometimes called the Great. A German, owing her position to the fact that she had been the consort of the feeble Tsar Peter III, who reigned for only a few months, she was a woman of great force and ability, and intellectually a child of the Enlightenment. Under her the vast holdings of the monasteries in lands and serfs were expropriated by the state and support of these institutions came from grants from the government. In consequence the numbers of monks markedly fell off. In court and aristocratic circles religious scepticism was common. The masses, but little affected by currents from the West, held to the historic Church or were members of the non-conforming sects which had flourished since the days of the revolt against the changes made by Nikon or even earlier and of which we are to say more. The state regarded the Church as an instrument for the moral education of the masses. Catherine's successor, Paul, declared that "the tsar is the head of the Church." It was under Paul that, in 1797, by imperial ukase, the parishes lost the right of electing their clergy, a function which they had held even under Peter the Great. Appointments to parishes were made by the state. This meant that the parish priests were government quite as much as Church officials.

BEGINNINGS OF REVIVAL

Grievous as were the losses suffered by Christianity in the latter part of the eighteenth century and in the first fifteen years of the nineteenth century, there was ample evidence that the faith was by no means moribund. Indications of vitality, some of them old, others of them new, were seen. After 1815 they were to swell to major proportions. They were found among Roman Catholics, in some of the Eastern Churches, and in Protestantism. To them we now turn.

THE BEGINNINGS OF REVIVAL IN THE ROMAN CATHOLIC CHURCH

During the storm of the Napoleonic Wars a revival began in the Roman Catholic Church. As we have seen, although he dealt rudely with the Roman Catholic Church, Napoleon did not treat it as drastically as had his precursors of the high tide of the Revolution. Nor was he, as had been some of them, openly anti-Christian. This was a gain, even though cold comfort. Some aspects of the romantic movement were distinctly friendly to the Roman Catholic Church. Many caught up in it conceived a warm admiration for the Middle Ages and for that Church as an integral part of medieval culture. In 1802 there appeared *Génie du Christianisme, ou Beautés de la Religion Chrétienne,* by Chateaubriand. It helped to make Roman Catholicism intellectually respectable and emotionally attractive. Although his first work was placed on the index of books denounced by that Church, Louis Claude de Saint-Martin (1743–1803) always remained attached to the Roman Catholic faith. A mystic, he was much influenced by Jacob Boehme.

Here and there new monastic orders, congregations, and societies began to appear, always a sign of life. In 1800 Madeleine-Sophie Barat founded the Society of the Sacred Heart of Jesus, a congregation of women devoted to education. In that same year Coudrin, a priest who had laboured in secret in France during some of the most anti-Christian years of the Revolution, took monastic vows and began what was known as the Congregation of Picpus, officially called the Congregation of the Sacred Hearts of Jesus and Mary and of the Perpetual Adoration of the Blessed Sacrament. It grew and obtained formal Papal approval in 1817. Its members gave themselves to missions and to prayer. In 1802 Edmund Ignatius Rice founded the Christian Brothers of Ireland.

In Germany the conversion to Roman Catholicism of two men of Protestant rearing, the poet Friedrich Leopold Stolberg (1800) and Friedrich von Schlegel (1808), a poet and a critic of the romantic school, was an indication of a trend to the Roman Catholic Church, still limited, but which might become important.

In the United States before 1815 the Roman Catholic Church began the policies and the growth which were to give it prominence in that country and in the world-wide life of that communion. In 1789 Roman Catholics in the United States numbered only about thirty-five thousand, because of the founding of that colony by a peer of that faith fully half of them in Maryland and about a fourth in religiously tolerant Philadelphia. They had been under the ecclesiastical jurisdiction of the Vicar Apostolic of London. In 1784 John Carroll (1735–1815) of a prominent Maryland Roman Catholic family, a former Jesuit, was made Prefect Apostolic and in 1789, at the request of the American clergy, was appointed Bishop of Baltimore. He proved an able and devoted leader, travelled extensively in his huge diocese, and strove to weld into one church the various nationalities, resisting the attempts, especially of the Germans, to have separate national bodies. He also successfully fought "trusteeism," an effort of the lay trustees of the property of various parishes to choose and dismiss their pastors without reference to the bishop. For the training of an American clergy he founded a college at Georgetown (1789) adjoining the national capital. In 1808 he was made archbishop with four suffragan sees. One of these was in Kentucky, on the westward moving frontier. The others were strategically located in the chief cities, Philadelphia, New York, and Boston. In 1809 Elizabeth Ann Seton, a convert, inaugurated a religious community which took the name Sisters of Charity. In spite of strong prejudices against Roman Catholics and provisions in some of the state constitutions excluding men of that faith from some or all offices, in its first amendment the Constitution of the United States assured religious liberty. By 1815 the Roman Catholic Church was prepared to take advantage of its opportunity in the new republic.

SIGNS OF LIFE IN THE EASTERN CHURCHES

Here and there were indications of vigour in the Christianity of Western Asia and Eastern Europe. Some of these arose from changes in the political situation, but the latter would have had no effect had there not been sufficient life in Christianity to take advantage of them.

In these years the Russian Empire advanced southward at the expense of Moslem rulers. The Turkish Empire was waning and its Christian subjects were beginning to hope that the Cross might not always be ruled by the Crescent. Russia, officially Christian, enlarged its holdings on the Black Sea. For a brief time the Russians occupied the predominantly Christian Wallachia and Moldavia, the later Rumania, and while by the treaty which ended the war (1774) these provinces were restored to Turkey, by that document Russia was accorded a protectorate over the Orthodox Christians in the Turkish domains.

Armenian Christianity seemed to be making advances. In the Armenian community in Constantinople numbers of church buildings were erected and several parochial schools were begun. In Armenia itself gains in education were achieved and the training of the clergy was improved.

In Russia, in spite of the deadening effects of the Enlightenment, especially among the upper classes, and the blows dealt monasticism by Catherine the Great, in several ways Christianity was showing signs of life and was making territorial gains.

Influences were entering from the West and were stimulating the native faith. Freemasonry had been introduced and now, partly in Russian guise, was having a positive religious effect of a mystical kind. A press in Halle was set up especially for the purpose of preparing Pietist literature in Russian. Arndt's *On the True Christianity* passed through several Russian editions. Works of the mystics Jacob Boehme and Saint-Simon were translated into Russian. In some circles the Latin fathers, including Augustine, were being read. In the theological seminaries which existed in most dioceses for the training of priests, text-books by Roman Catholics and Protestants adapted to the Russian Orthodox Church were widely used and much of the teaching was in Latin. Typical of these influences was Tikhon of Zadonsky (1724–1783), originally known as Timofey Sokolov, who was to became a favorite saint of nineteenth century Russia. For six and a half years a zealous and effective diocesan bishop, by his own choice he retired to a monastery and there spent the rest of his life. His spiritual counsel was sought by many. He knew deep inner conflict, depression, and ecstasy. He combined the traditional Russian kenoticism with meditations on the sufferings of the crucified Christ, a devotional practice derived from the West, some of it from Roman Catholicism and some probably from Pietism. He also fused theological conviction and adherence to dogma with study of the Bible, especially the New Testament, and a living faith in Jesus Christ.

In this period, too, was formed the spiritual life of Seraphim of Sarov (1759–1833) who after 1815 was to become a religious guide to many laymen. The son of a building contractor, from boyhood he was deeply religious and at the age of eighteen decided to become a monk. He spent years alone in austerities and prayer, seeking self-mastery. It is said that for a thousand days and nights he stood on a stone in the woods, repeating in essence the prayer of the publican, "God be merciful to me a sinner." For years he maintained the rule of silence. When he finally emerged from it, many miracles of healing were attributed to him. He became spiritual adviser to a convent of nuns.

In some monasteries there was a revival of the methods of the hesychasts.

There were also notable ecclesiastics. Prominent among them was he who was known as Platon (1732–1812), successively head of the famous Trinity monastery near Moscow, a member of the Holy Synod, Bishop of Tver, tutor to the future Tsar Paul, and Archbishop and then Metropolitan of Moscow. He was famous as a preacher, wrote what became standard text-books on the doctrine of the Russian Orthodox Church in the form of manuals of instruction, and promoted the study of the history of the Russian Church. It was he who drew up rules which (1800) sought to formulate a compromise by which the Old Believers and some other dissenters would be admitted to the communion of the state church while being permitted to retain their distinctive rites.

Soon after 1800 a revival in the state church gained momentum. Plans were set on foot for the development of church schools. Through Pietist contacts Golitsyn, Procurator (head) of the Holy Synod, had been converted from indifference to a warm religious interest and became the first president of a newly organized (1813) Russian Bible Society. The Napoleonic invasion led to a revulsion against rationalistic French influence and to something of a religious awakening. Philaret, a protegee of Platon, became head of the Academy of St. Petersburg and encouraged the circulation of the Bible in translations into the vernacular. The tsar himself, Alexander I, had a profound experience through several channels, among them the writings of Swedenborg, of whom we are to hear more later in this chapter, and contact with Madame Krüdener of the Livonian nobility, who had been converted under Moravian and Pietist influence. He became earnestly Christian, with results which were to be even more apparent after 1815. Swedenborg helped to shape not only Alexander I but also some who eventually held high office in the Russian Orthodox Church.

As Russia expanded its territories, larger areas were brought within the sphere of the Orthodox Church. When, through the partition of Poland in the 1790's, a large slice of that country was assigned to the tsar, Ruthenians who had become Uniates under Polish Roman Catholic rule returned to the Orthodox faith of their fathers. It is said that by 1796 over two million had taken that step. At the other geographic extreme of the empire, in the second half of the eighteenth century Russian authority was extended over the Aleutians and Alaska. Missionaries accompanied or followed this advance and baptized many of the aborigines.

Dissent from the Russian Orthodox Church continued to flourish, and that in spite of persecution by the state. The Old Believers persisted and in the

North had a following which in some places may have numbered as much as half the population. The Khlysty went on. From them came the Skopsty. The Skopsty had as their chief originator Selivanov, whose real name was Andrei Ivanov. He found that some of the Khlysty failed in their efforts to maintain their principles of strict sexual abstinence. To make that effective, he emasculated himself and induced others to do likewise. Exiled to Siberia, Selivanov professed to be the Tsar Peter III, who had been assassinated. Brought back to the capital, he attracted a wide following, among whom were some of the army and the clergy. In 1820 he was confined to a monastery, but even after his death a decade or more later the Skopsty persisted and spread, largely among artisans and merchants.

The Dukhobors emerged to prominence in the second half of the eighteenth century and gained adherents over wide reaches of the empire. They appealed especially to the humble, the peasants and the labourers. Their origin is obscure and they may have begun long before the eighteenth century. They repudiated the Russian Orthodox Church, but were noted for their excellent moral lives, temperance, and industry. Among their tenets was the belief that God dwells in all men, but especially in some, and that each generation possesses its Christ. In their meetings they sang Psalms and commented on a collection of extracts from the Bible. They had no priests. One of their main precepts was mutual love and in following it they practised community of goods. They were hospitable to travellers and refrained so far as possible from killing animals. In formulating their creed they were aided by Gregory Skovoroda (1722–1794), a Ukrainian mystic and philosopher who had travelled widely in Western Europe. They regarded Jesus as a man who was inspired by the word of God much as were the saints and taught that the Father, Son, and Holy Spirit are merely aspects of the one God. They held that in the Old Testament the Son of God revealed himself as divine wisdom and that the New Testament inaugurated the age of the Holy Spirit. They believed that souls who fell with the angels enter human bodies when these reach years of discretion and that each is saved by his own efforts. They insisted that there is one church of God, invisible, transcending all races and religions, and that they, the visible Church, were the core of the invisible Church. They rejected baptism by water. Like some other dissenting groups, they divided into several sects.

Molokan was a nickname given to a movement the members of which thought of themselves as Spiritual Christians. Molokan is from the Russian word for milk and was applied to the sect because, contrary to the custom of the Russian Orthodox Church, its adherents drank milk during Lent. The beginnings of the Molokans, like that of the Dukhobors, are not clear. Some trace them to a leader who was martyred under Ivan the Terrible. Others assign them to Simeon Uklein, of the latter part of the eighteenth century, who broke from the Dukhobors. It is certain that the Molokans were in existence before 1815. They made more of the Bible than did the Dukhobors. They refused to take human life and therefore would not do military service. Icons were repugnant to them, they had no buildings especially consecrated for worship, and they did not have the historic sacraments. Their religious services generally consisted of the recital of passages from the Scriptures and of prayers. They had love feasts and on the anniversary of the institution of the Last Supper they met and broke bread in memory of Christ but did not regard that act as a sacrament. They were industrious, thrifty, and cleanly, and abstained from luxuries and condemned gambling and drink. Eventually, like the Dukhobors, they split into sects.

Into Russia in the latter part of the eighteenth century there came colonies of Mennonites. They were attracted by special concessions offered them by Catherine the Great, for she saw in their industry and thrift a means of promoting the economic progress of her realms.

The Revival among Protestants: General Features

It was in Protestantism rather than the Roman Catholic Church or the Eastern Churches that after 1750 awakening was most marked. Here, by 1815 movements were under way which in the nineteenth century were to swell to major proportions. In connexion with them and largely as a result of them Protestantism was to exhibit a rapid expansion. By the middle of the twentieth century it was to be spread far more widely than were the Eastern Churches. While, so far as statistics went, it still was not as strong numerically as was the Roman Catholic Church, it was in as many countries as the latter and in proportion to its adherents in 1750 it had grown far more rapidly.

The awakening was not confined to any one branch of Protestantism. It cut across existing denominational and confessional lines. It began with the Pietist movement in Germany in the seventeenth century and at first was most marked in Lutheranism. Mainly because of the leadership of Zinzendorf, it had a striking manifestation in the rise of the Moravians and their spread from Herrnhut. Almost simultaneously it was seen in the Great Awakening in the Thirteen Colonies and in Great Britain in the Evangelical Awakening in which the Wesleys and Whitefield were outstanding. In the Thirteen Colonies its chief channels were the churches of the Reformed tradition. In Great Britain it was initially most prominent in the Church of England, but it was also manifest in the Church of Scotland and in bodies which dissented from both, mostly Methodists, Congregationalists, and Baptists. Later it spread to the Reformed Churches on the Continent of Europe.

In whatever country or branch of Protestantism it appeared, the awakening had distinctive features. It was characteristically Protestant and stressed the authority of the Scriptures, salvation by faith alone, and the priesthood of all believers. It made much of a personal religious experience, of a new birth through trust in Christ, commitment to him, and faith in what God had done through him in the incarnation, the cross, and the resurrection. Indeed, some beliefs were so widely held by most of those touched by the awakening that the faith held by all came to be known technically as "Evangelical." The awakening was intensely missionary. To employ technical terms, it was "evangelistic" and emphasized "evangelism." It sought to win to an acceptance of the Gospel the nominal Christians and the de-Christianized in Christendom and non-Christians throughout the world. It endeavoured hopefully, in the words of the New Testament command, to "preach the Gospel to every creature." A youth organization which sprang from it late in the nineteenth century, the Student Volunteer Movement for Foreign Missions, took as its "watchword": "The evangelization of the world in this generation."

The awakening gave rise to efforts to relieve suffering and to remedy collective evils. Many of those touched by it, while believing that it was not in accord with the Scriptures to work and hope for the transformation of society as a whole, were active in promoting such institutions as orphanages and hospitals and in such enterprises as nursing the sick and relieving famine. Others, taking seriously a form of the "great commission" more sweeping than "preach the Gospel to every creature," namely, "make disciples of all the nations, baptizing them in the name of the Father, and of the Son, and of the Holy Ghost: teaching them to observe all things whatsoever I have commanded you," laboured to bring all mankind to obedience to Christ in all aspects of its life.

The fact that the awakening spread across denominational and national boundaries and had common characteristics and beliefs tended to draw together all who were committed to it. It brought them into coöperation for common objectives, such as religious education in Sunday Schools, efforts for youth and for students, and movements for the abolition of slavery, for international peace, for temperance in the use of alcoholic beverages or the complete prohibition of the manufacture and sale of such beverages, and for giving the Gospel to particular countries or classes or to the entire world. In the nineteenth century the numbers of these enterprises multiplied. In the nineteenth century, too, there arose what was eventually known as the Ecumenical Movement. While beginning with Evangelicals, namely those who were the products of the awakenings, in the twentieth century it reached out far beyond them and in one or another of its expressions drew in the majority of Protestants, some of the Eastern and other non-Protestant bodies, and even individuals who retained their membership in the Roman Catholic Church.

Although the awakening drew Christians together regardless of their denominational affiliations, it also either gave rise to new denominations or greatly strengthened existing ones. Among these were the several branches of Methodists, Baptists, Congregationalists, fellowships known as Christians and Disciples of Christ, and scores of smaller bodies. They were not territorial, as were most of the Lutheran and Reformed Churches, and as was the Church of England. Seldom did they win the allegiance of all or even the majority of the inhabitants of a particular geographic area. They were more nearly akin to the many religious orders within the Roman Catholic Church. Like them they were consciously within one branch of Christianity, in this case Protestantism. As were the Roman Catholic orders, each was bound together in a common organization. Like that of the Benedictines, this might be very loose, giving much autonomy to the local congregation. Or, like the Jesuits, it might be closely knit. Increasingly, moreover, branches of Protestantism which were at the outset territorial tended to conform to this denominational pattern. As Lutherans, Reformed, Presbyterians, and Anglicans migrated to the Americas or Australasia, or as they founded missions among non-Western peoples, they ceased to be dominant in a particular country and became minorities, one of several branches of Protestantism.

The awakening greatly strengthened what might be called the extreme fringe of Protestantism. It brought new vigour to Lutheran, Reformed, and Anglican bodies. But it especially stimulated the growth of denominations further removed from the Catholic tradition, such as Congregationalists, Baptists, and Methodists. Within those churches which had retained more that had been developed in the Catholic form of the faith it brought into being groups which tended to discard much of the Catholic heritage. The trend was to go back to Christianity as described in the New Testament, regarding as at best dubious what had been added by the Catholic Church, whether Roman or Orthodox.

Akin to this last modification of Protestantism by the awakening was another. The lay element became prominent. This was to be expected from the Protestant principle of the priesthood of all believers, but what had been held in theory now became more of a reality in practice. In some of the major new movements, such as the societies for distributing the Bible and the Sunday Schools, the laymen were outstanding. In the nineteenth and twentieth centuries the laity were increasingly to the fore. Women had a growing place and laymen had more and more initiative and participation. This was in striking contrast with the Roman Catholic Church, where the clergy were emphatically in control. The Orthodox Churches accorded a larger place to laymen than did the Roman Catholic Church, but the Protestantism which arose from the revivals of the eighteenth and nineteenth centuries had far more of lay leadership than did they.

While the impact of the awakening was felt in all lands where there were Protestants, it was especially potent in the British Isles, the United States, and the newer countries of English speech, Canada, Australia, and New Zealand. This is significant because in the nineteenth and the fore part of the twentieth century it was these lands which had the largest growth in territory and wealth and, proportionately, in population. As Spain and Portugal, Roman Catholic lands, had led in the expansion of Europe between 1500 and 1750, after 1750 it was through peoples that are often called Anglo-Saxon that this expansion was chiefly accomplished. Here again, as so often, the question arises of the connexion between marked vitality in a particular form of Christianity and creativity in other aspects of life. The two were contemporary. Was this pure coincidence or was the relationship causal? If causal, was Christianity the source of the other features of the cultural activity? Or were the causes in neither but common to them both? We do not know. However, we are certain that each acted on the other. Anglo-Saxon Christianity in part reflected the abounding vigour in other ranges of British and North American achievement, and its forms were to some extent determined and its expansion made possible by them. In turn, the other phases of Anglo-American civilization were moulded, several of them profoundly, by the revived Christianity.

While Anglo-Saxon peoples were exhibiting a phenomenal growth which was being accompanied by striking vitality in the Protestantism within their ranks, significant movements were afoot in the Protestantism of the Continent of Europe, chiefly in Germany and Scandinavia. Some of them were in the Pietist tradition, some a reaction from rationalism towards conservative Lutheranism, and others, following up the rationalist tradition but not entirely dominated by it, gave rise to currents of thought and scholarship which put Germany in the forefront of Biblical and theological study in the nineteenth and the early part of the twentieth century.

From what we have outlined it may be gathered that through the revival Protestantism was exhibiting striking modifications. It was still true to the main principles of the Protestant Reformation. Indeed, the developments which were taking place were largely the outgrowth of these principles. Here was more and more emerging a form of Christianity which was not sectional, chiefly confined to North-western Europe and the British Isles, as Protestantism had been down to 1750, but which, under the impulse of the awakening, in the nineteenth and twentieth centuries was to have a world-wide spread and from which was to issue a new kind of inclusive fellowship embracing Christians from all divisions of Christianity. From it were to spring many movements, numbers of them quite without precedent, and in it were to take place fresh developments in thought and institutions. If the vitality of a religion is measured by its ability to give rise to new expressions, then the Protestantism which emerged from the revival was one of the most potent forms of religion that mankind has known. Although in the nineteenth century the Roman Catholic Church and Russian Christianity displayed a somewhat similar vigour, in neither did it have as manifold and novel manifestations as in Protestantism. To this the developments between 1750 and 1815 were preliminary.

Revival among Protestants in the British Isles

It was in the British Isles and especially in England that between 1750 and 1815 the awakening in Protestantism was particularly marked. It commenced before 1750 and was to swell to much larger proportions after 1815. However, in the years between 1750 and 1815 it began to develop forms which were to characterize it in the nineteenth and twentieth centuries.

The revival was by no means all from one source nor did it centre about any single individual. The Great Awakening in the Thirteen Colonies had repercussions in the British Isles, notably in Scotland and England. The writings of Jonathan Edwards describing that revival had a wide circulation in Great Britain. New England Congregationalism and Scottish Presbyterianism were closely akin. Both, for example, regarded the Westminster Confession as a standard statement of the Christian faith. It was natural, therefore, that the Great Awakening, largely channelled as it was through Congregationalism and the Reformed Churches, should be followed with peculiar interest in Scotland and that Edwards should be in frequent correspondence with Scottish friends. After he was ousted from his church in Northampton he was invited to come to Scotland. Although he declined, the tie with Scotland continued to be close. There were also men in England and Scotland who were little influenced by Edwards or that more prominent leader of the revival, John Wesley, who contributed to the Evangelical movement. Prominent among them were the Haldane brothers, Robert and James Alexander, who had a profound effect in Scotland and on the Continent of Europe, and, through Thomas and Alexander Campbell, in the United States. Moreover, late in the seventeenth century and early in the eighteenth century a large number of informal societies had sprung into being, mainly but not entirely among members of the Church of England. They were for reading the Bible, prayer, frequent communion, and service to prisoners, the poor, soldiers, and sailors.

THE REVIVAL IN THE BRITISH ISLES: THE BIRTH OF METHODISM

The most famous leader and creator of the Evangelical movement was John Wesley (1703–1791). Prominent with him were his brother Charles (1707–1788) and their friend George Whitefield (1714–1770). John and Charles had for father Samuel Wesley (1662–1735) who, the son of a Nonconforming clergyman, had become a priest of the Church of England and was long in charge of the rural parish of Epworth. The wife of Samuel Wesley was Susanna, whose father, Samuel Annesley, was a nephew of the first Earl of Anglesea and, a clergyman, had also been among the Nonconformists. Samuel and Susanna Wesley had nineteen children, of whom eight died in infancy. John and Charles owed much to both parents. Their father, hard-working, had organized one of the religious societies then in vogue. Their mother, a woman of great force of character, exercised a methodical discipline over her large brood, setting the elder to care for the younger children and exacting regularity and obedience. In 1709, when both John and Charles were still very young, the parental home was burned and they so narrowly escaped perishing with it that John came to regard himself as "a brand snatched from the burning." John went to the Charterhouse School in London and thence to Christ Church, Oxford. Although not profoundly philosophical, he was a diligent and able student. Throughout his life he read widely. Eventually he became adept in several languages, ancient and modern. He loved riding and walking and was an expert swimmer. Deeply religious, he early treasured Thomas à Kempis and Jeremy Taylor. He was ordained deacon (1725) and priest (1728) in the Church of England. He was a fellow of Lincoln College, Oxford. At intervals for a few years after he was given the appointment he had leave from its duties to help his father in the latter's parish.

While John was away, Charles came to Oxford, also as a member of Christ Church, and formed with two others (1729) a little club to aid one another in their studies, to read helpful books, and to participate in frequent communion. When, in November, 1729, he returned to Oxford, John became the leader of the group. They attracted other students, but probably not more than twenty-five. John later considered this as the first rise of Methodism. The group was called the Holy Club and for its disciplined ways was given the nickname of Methodist, a term which had been in use in the seventeenth century. It was that name which stuck and became the official designation of what was eventually a world-wide movement. The members tended to be Catholic and were influenced by the ideals of an older Cambridge contemporary, William Law, who in turn had been much impressed with Jacob Boehme and whose *Serious Call to a Holy and Devout Life* was published in the very year in which the group was formed.

In this stage of his Oxford career, John Wesley gave himself to an intensive reading of the Greek New Testament, fasted on Wednesdays and Fridays, received the communion weekly, which, according to the practice of the time was deemed frequent, and laboured among the prisoners in the local jail. It was in 1735, while still at Oxford that he preached a sermon on "the circumcision of the heart" which he later declared to have contained all the principles which he taught in after years, among them salvation from all sin and loving God with an undivided heart. However, these had not yet become emotionally his possession.

It was in 1735 that George Whitefield, then only twenty years of age, joined the group. He had entered Oxford in 1733 and a severe illness in the spring of 1735 brought a depth that was reflected in his amazing career as a preacher on which he launched soon after his ordination, in 1736.

In 1735 there began another important stage in the career of John and Charles Wesley. They sailed for Georgia as missionaries of the Society for the Propagation of the Gospel in Foreign Parts. Georgia had been founded two years before by the philanthropist James Oglethorpe as a refuge for debtors and for persecuted Protestants from Germany. On the voyage to Georgia the Wesleys made the acquaintance of Moravians who were on the same ship and John was impressed and humiliated to find that in the midst of storm and the imminence of death they had a quiet fearlessness which his religion had not given him. Arriving in Savannah, he met the Moravian leader Spangenberg. The latter pointedly asked him: "Do you know Jesus Christ?" John could only reply: "I know he is the saviour of the world." Whereupon Spangenberg countered: "True, but do you know that he has saved *you?*" In spite of their lack of the inner assurance of which the Moravian had spoken, the Wesleys laboured earnestly in the young colony. They had intended to be missionaries to the Indians but confined their efforts chiefly to the whites. Ill, Charles returned to England in 1736. John remained and in 1736 gathered a small society of serious Christians, on which he later looked back as the second rise of Methodism. Yet he felt himself frustrated. A stiff high-churchman, he irritated some of the colonists by his requirements. He had an unfortunate love affair and, refusing to give the communion to the young lady involved who, after he had not pursued his courtship, had married another man, he aroused further resentment. Suits were started against him. Disheartened, he returned to England.

It was soon after he arrived in London that John Wesley had the profound experience which sent him out as preacher and organizer of the Methodist movement. Impressed as they had been by the Moravians while on the Georgia mission, he and Charles sought counsel with one of that church who was in London on his way to Georgia. He spoke to them of self-surrender, instantaneous conversion, and joy in conscious salvation. On May 21, 1738, quiet confidence and inner peace came to Charles. Three days later, on May 24, 1738, they found John. After attending evening prayer in St. Paul's Cathedral, John went to a meeting of an informal Anglican society on Aldersgate, not far away. While Luther's preface to the *Commentary on Romans* was being read, there suddenly broke upon him something similar to what that epistle had brought to the tortured soul of the great German. As Wesley recorded it in his journal: "About a quarter before nine, while he [Luther] was describing the change which God works in the heart through faith in Christ, I felt my heart strangely warmed. I felt I did trust in Christ, Christ alone, for salvation; and an assurance was given me that he had taken away my sins, even mine, and saved me from the law of sin and death." Thus did the experience so central in Protestantism, of salvation by faith alone, grip the seeking high Anglican. It sent him out to start what was to be in all its various branches one of the largest of the Protestant denominations, Methodism. But that did not come at once.

After that Aldersgate night, John Wesley not unnaturally sought to learn more from the Moravians, for it was they who had been decisive in his quest. He was an original member of the Fetter Lane Society which a Moravian had gathered in London, but that was not enough. He went to Germany, met Zinzendorf, and had several days at Herrnhut. Although he was critical of some features of what he saw there, he adopted and adapted more than one of the Moravian methods.

Back in England, John Wesley preached extensively, as did his brother Charles. At first this was only in religious societies and churches. In many of the latter his message provoked such opposition that he would record in his journal that he was not to preach there again. His main themes were conscious acceptance with God and daily growth in holiness. He held that a Christian could have as his dominant motives the love of God and of his neighbour and that these could free him from sin. However, he recognized that perfection was seldom attained in this life.

In 1739 Whitefield, whose sermons in Bristol were arousing great excitement, began preaching in the open air to the miners and saw the tears make channels down their coal-begrimed faces. He urged John Wesley to try that method. John went to Bristol, his high-churchly prejudices were melted by what he saw, and he himself began proclaiming his message in the fields. He travelled widely, speaking wherever he could gain a hearing, in churches or out of doors. According to the regulations of the Church of England he was not to preach within the boundaries of a parish until the clergyman in charge gave his consent. When a clergyman refused permission, Wesley preached without it, declaring: "The world is my parish." This phrase was to become a Methodist slogan.

In the initial years of his itinerary Wesley faced persecution. The emotion which his message aroused brought criticism, not only in church circles and among the upper classes where, under the influence of the current vogue of reason, any enthusiasm was looked at askance, but also among the masses. Sometimes Wesley was met by mobs and violence. Yet he never quailed nor was he deterred from his mission.

The preaching of John Wesley, like that of Whitefield, attracted chiefly the lower and middle classes. In spite of widespread vulgarity, drunkenness, obscenity, and calloused cruelty in eighteenth century Britain, and a large degree of religious illiteracy and scepticism, there was a general, even if superficial knowledge of the main tenets of Christian teaching about morals and faith. In many, although a minority, there was a hunger left unsatisfied by the formal services in most of the churches. Among them the preaching of Wesley, Whitefield, and others of similar stripe awakened a response. Wesley did not have the kind of eloquence for which Whitefield was noted. Nor did he have a commanding physical presence. In cold print his sermons seem doctrinal, practical, and even prosaic. Yet, as with those of Whitefield and as in the Great Awakening in the Thirteen Colonies and some of the later revivals in the United States, they often released striking emotions. Men and women screamed, were physically convulsed, or fell insensible.

Although John Wesley believed the physical accompaniments of his preaching were due either to the resistance of the Devil or to the Holy Spirit, he did not allow himself to be diverted by them. He was intensely practical, an extraordinarily able organizer and administrator, and had an unusual capacity to accept suggestions and to adopt and adapt methods from various quarters. He himself realized that this gift for organization was his "peculiar talent." He gathered his converts into "societies," in part after the pattern of the ones in which he had shared in Oxford, organized in Georgia, and had had his heart-warming experience, and of that which the Moravian had brought together in Fetter Lane. One of the earliest of the Methodist societies was in Bristol and another in an old foundry in London. After the Moravian pattern, the societies were at first divided into "bands" to aid their members in the nourishment of the Christian life. Early, in addition, they were divided into "classes," each with its "class leader." Originally mainly a device for raising money, for each member was to give a penny a week and the leader was to collect it, the classes became primarily a means of intimate fellowship for spiritual and moral growth under the direction of a mature Christian. "Love feasts" were early introduced, again a Moravian custom. Members of the societies were at first received on trial and, after testing, were issued tickets to show that they were in full standing. When some laymen began preaching, Wesley demurred. However, his mother admonished him that in doing so he might be thwarting the Holy Spirit. He yielded and lay preachers became an outstanding feature of Methodism. Other devices which Wesley learned from others were watch-night services, covenant services, and stewards to care for the property of the societies.

Within John Wesley's long lifetime the societies multiplied and were knit into an inclusive organization. In 1790, on the eve of his death, they were said to have 71,668 members in Great Britain. For a time Wesley himself visited each of the societies to supervise them and enforce discipline. As they increased this became impossible and he assembled his preachers in "annual conferences." As societies and preachers further grew in numbers, he established "circuits" with travelling preachers and soon, as an assistant to himself, a "superintendent" was placed in charge of each circuit. He himself kept an autocratic control of the whole.

Wesley travelled almost incessantly. In spite of the physical difficulties of poor roads, he averaged about five thousand miles a year, much of them on horseback, and fifteen sermons a week. He not only covered England but also visited Ireland and Scotland again and again. In his later years he was greeted with acclaim and his journeys became triumphal progresses. The short, slight figure, with its clean-shaven ruddy face, its bright eyes, and its snowy locks, evoked something akin to veneration.

Wesley was distinctively an activist. Not only was he an organizer and administrator. Himself an inveterate reader, he encouraged the taste for literature and to this end saw to the publication and sale of inexpensive editions of good books. He also wrote extensively. From a substantial income from the sale of his books he aided what he deemed good causes. He furthered the care of deserving poor and the creation of lending funds to assist struggling business men.

John Wesley devoted himself to his mission with singleness of purpose. He did not marry until he was in his late forties. Then it was to a widow, the marriage proved unhappy, and he and his wife parted.

In common with many of the fresh outbursts of the Christian faith, from the outset Methodism gave rise to song. John Wesley contributed notable translations of German hymns. His brother Charles composed hundreds of hymns. Many of the hymns of the Wesleys gained wide circulation far outside the boundaries of Methodism. Among the more famous of Charles Wesley's hymns were "Jesus lover of my soul," "Love divine, all loves excelling," "O for a thousand tongues to sing," "Christ the Lord is risen today," "Rejoice the Lord is King," and "Ye servants of God your master proclaim."

By degrees Methodists separated from the Church of England. John Wesley thought of himself as remaining within the church of his birth. He tried to bind his societies to the Church of England and to encourage their members to receive the sacraments through it. Doctrinally he did not wish to be an innovator, but desired simply "to spread Scriptural holiness over the land." However, the Methodist movement had not been many years under way when he became convinced that in the New Testament presbyters and bishops were the same order. He believed that, as a presbyter, he had as much right to administer ordination as had any bishop. Moreover, the problem arose of finding enough priests of the Church of England to give the sacraments to the members of his societies. This first became acute in the United States. There, as we are to see in a moment, Methodism spread rapidly. Yet there the Church of England was weak numerically and the number of priests of that communion in the country declined sharply as a result of the rift with the mother country. Moreover, not until late in the 1780's were bishops consecrated for the remnant and a national organization achieved by the Anglicans. Accordingly, in 1784, the year after the formal recognition by Great Britain of the independence of the United States, John Wesley and Thomas Coke, the latter also a priest (presbyter) of the Church of England, ordained two as presbyters ("elders") for the United States and, assisted by other ministers, Wesley set apart Coke as "superintendent" for America and appointed Francis Asbury, already in the United States, to a similar office. Later he ordained other presbyters for Scotland, where the Anglican communion was weak, and eventually ordained some for England. His brother Charles, it may be added, disapproved of this procedure.

It was in 1784 that by a Deed of Declaration John Wesley, now in his eighties, provided for the continuation of the organization after his death by naming a "conference" of one hundred ministers to hold the property and to assume the direction of the movement. Upon his death, in 1791, the Wesleyan Methodist Church was formally constituted. Before the decade was out the Methodist New Connexion hived off in protest against what it called the priestcraft of the other body.

As we are to note, Methodism, thus inaugurated by John Wesley, had a growth which made it the largest group of Nonconforming Protestants in England, next to the Baptists the largest body of Protestants in the United States, along with the Church of England and the Presbyterians one of the three largest Protestant denominations in the British overseas dominions of Canada, Australia, and New Zealand, and through its missions prominent on the Continent of Europe, and in Asia, Africa, Latin America, and many of the islands of the sea. It divided into several churches, partly by nations. Yet everywhere it preserved common characteristics which went back to John Wesley—zeal in preaching, especially to the middle and lower classes, tightly knit organization, and emphasis upon education and social service.

The Revival in the British Isles: Outside of Wesleyan Methodism

The eighteenth century awakening in Christianity in the British Isles was by no means confined to the societies which were associated in the Wesleyan Methodist Church and the Methodist New Connexion. As we have suggested, it was also in the Church of Scotland and among Presbyterians in Scotland who dissented from that body. It was seen as well among the Congregationalists and Baptists in England. It spread to Wales and Ireland. It made itself felt in circles in the Church of England which did not follow Wesley or Whitefield.

Whitefield and the Wesleys drew apart. The cause was doctrinal. John Wesley was Arminian. Whitefield believed in predestination. At first the break was with bitterness. Although reconciliation was effected and friendship was restored, the difference in theology persisted and the paths remained distinct. Whitefield was supported by Selina, Countess of Huntingdon (1707–1791). Wealthy, widowed in her late thirties (1746), and a woman of forceful character, before her husband's death the Countess of Huntingdon had been an early member of the Methodist society of Fetter Lane. Too independent to be happy under the autocratic control of John Wesley, and a Calvinist rather than an Arminian, she formed what came to be known first as the Countess of Huntingdon's Connexion and later as the Calvinistic Methodists. She built chapels and appointed to them men whom she designated as her chaplains. Whitefield was one of them. In 1779 she and those associated with her separated from the Church of England. Until her death she dominated the movement. Unlike Wesley, Whitefield did not have the gift of organization and administration. Yet from him arose a distinct body, the Welsh Calvinistic Methodists.

Strong for the doctrine of election was Augustus Montague Toplady (1740–1778). A clergyman of the Church of England, he vigorously attacked John Wesley for the latter's Arminianism. However, he is best remembered for his hymn, "Rock of Ages."

The attacks by the predestinarians tended to confirm Wesley and his followers in their Arminianism. A stout defender of Wesley was the Swiss Jean

Guillaume de la Fléchère, better known as Fletcher of Maddeley (1729–1785), who, having come to England, had a parish in the established church.

Within the Church of England the revival strengthened the Protestant element that had been there since the Reformation. Those who were committed to it were known as Evangelicals. In general they were Calvinistic in theology. They stressed conversion, strict morals, a life of active service to others, and simplicity in worship. Prominent among them was John Newton (1725–1807) who, self-educated, after an adventurous life at sea, part of the time as captain of a ship engaged in the African slave trade, was ordained, served in Olney, in Buckinghamshire, and then as rector of a church in London. A friend of Wesley and Whitefield, he was a notable preacher and was the author of widely popular hymns, among them "How sweet the name of Jesus sounds" and "One there is above all others." Newton was a close friend of William Cowper (1731–1800), whose life was saddened by periods of melancholic insanity, but who in long lucid intervals wrote verse and hymns, some of them notable. The Milner brothers, Joseph (1744–1797) and Isaac (1751–1820), both graduates of Cambridge, the latter senior wrangler and later professor of experimental philosophy and master of Queen's College in that university, were strong Evangelicals. Isaac Milner was a close friend of William Wilberforce (1759–1833), was instrumental in the conversion of that charming scion of a wealthy home, and did much to make Cambridge a centre of Evangelicalism. The tradition was reinforced and continued by Charles Simeon (1759–1836) who, born in the same year as Wilberforce, was a member of King's College, Cambridge, and for more than fifty years was in Trinity Church in that city and as preacher and pastor had a profound influence in the university. A notable succession was Henry Venn (1725–1797), a graduate of Cambridge and a distinguished Evangelical clergyman, a son, John Venn (1759–1813), one of the founders of the Church Missionary Society, and a grandson, Henry Venn (1796–1873) for nearly a third of a century honorary secretary of that society. Hannah More (1745–1833) moved in the literary and artistic circles of the England of her day, had a warm Evangelical piety, and was a prolific author whose writings, largely of a religious and moral nature, enjoyed an enormous circulation. The list of prominent Evangelicals might be greatly lengthened. Evangelicals were a minority in the Church of England, but their influence was striking.

Although they were loyal to the Church of England, Evangelicals in general were willing to coöperate with Nonconformists of Evangelical views. Indeed, they often encouraged the latter. Since new parishes could be created only by act of Parliament, to provide better facilities for the masses Evangelicals built numbers of chapels in existing parishes, placed in them Nonconforming ministers, and supported a school to train incumbents.

THE OUTREACH OF THE BRITISH REVIVAL

The eighteenth century revival in British Protestant Christianity had repercussions which touched life at many angles, both in the British Isles and in many other parts of the world. They did not attain their largest proportions until after 1815, but by that year some of their characteristic manifestations were seen. The emphasis of the revivals was upon the transformation of the individual through faith in Christ and his sacrifice on the cross, through complete dedication to God, and through the work of the Holy Spirit. Those so committed were ardently missionary and sought to win others to a similar experience. They also strove to alleviate or abolish social conditions which warped or destroyed human lives. The movement begat radiant hope and inspired many to intense and unremitting activity.

It was a time when Britain was growing in wealth and empire. The loss of the Thirteen Colonies proved an asset, for Britain was relieved of the cost of their defense and after a period of adjustment the United States continued to be a major outlet for British manufactures and capital. Britain engaged in a life and death struggle with Napoleon, but won, and in so doing achieved and confirmed a mastery of the seas. The industrial revolution was beginning, with its early home primarily in Great Britain, and a sense of boundless opportunity was in the air. In this many of those touched by the religious awakening shared. They dreamed and laboured to take advantage of the new day to reduce the evils inherited from the past or brought by the new conditions and to make of British trade and empire a blessing and not a curse. Their efforts were legion. For them the year 1815 is an artificial date, for the end of the Napoleonic Wars did not bring them to a pause but, if anything, gave them an added impetus. We can take the space merely to mention a few of the more outstanding.

Some of the efforts at improvement at the outset were primarily for the British Isles but ultimately were not confined to meeting domestic problems. In 1780 an Evangelical layman of the Church of England, Robert Raikes (1735–1811), began a Sunday School in his home city, Gloucester. A lover of children, he designed it to give moral and religious instruction to the very poor on the day of the week when most of them were not working. This involved teaching many of the pupils to read. The idea was not new. Somewhat similar procedures had been known at least as early as the seventeenth century. However, through Raikes it was given a decisive impetus, partly through the *Gloucester Journal* which his father and then he owned. In 1785 there was formed in London the Sunday School Society for extending the movement throughout the British Empire. Among her other activities, Hannah More organized schools among the neglected miners and colliers of the Mendip Hills. Joseph Lancaster (1778–1838), a Quaker, inaugurated a method of teaching the underprivileged which for some years enjoyed a wide vogue.

John Howard (1726–1790), a warm friend and admirer of John Wesley, a worshipper in Nonconformist congregations, used the leisure made possible by inherited wealth to labour indefatigably for the reform of the appalling conditions in the prisons. He did this first as high-sheriff of Bedfordshire, then as the inspirer of acts of Parliament to improve prison conditions throughout the realm, and later by prolonged journeys to study prison conditions in Great Britain, Ireland, and Europe. Characteristically, he lost his life while in Russia, travelling to find ways of preventing the spread of the plague. Evangelicals were active in promoting a stricter observance of Sunday and in seeking to curb the gambling, duelling, and cruel sports which were then prevalent. They also strove to regulate child labour in the newly emerging factories and to protect the boys employed as chimney sweeps. They promoted the education of the masses. They objected to the immoral character of current eighteenth century fiction.

At Clapham, a suburb of London, several wealthy Evangelicals made their home. Known derisively as the Clapham Sect, they worked, sometimes together and at other times individually, for a wide variety of religious and philanthropic projects. One of their number, Granville Sharp, was chiefly responsible for the founding, in 1787, of Sierra Leone, for freed Negroes. Another, Zachary Macaulay, father of Lord Macaulay, the historian, was also active in fighting slavery. Even more famous for his prolonged and successful struggle against Negro slavery, another resident of Clapham, William Wilberforce, led in Parliament the campaign which in 1807 put on the statute books an act abolishing the slave trade in the British Empire and lived to see the assurance of the abolishment of slavery (1833) in the British domains. For this end also laboured Thomas Clarkson (1760–1846), son of a clergyman of the Church of England, who gave up his plans to follow his father's profession to devote himself to the anti-slavery cause.

It was in these years that the revival brought about the formation of a number of missionary societies. Although the seventeenth and the opening years of the eighteenth century had witnessed the founding of several such bodies, including some Dutch undertakings, the Society for the Propagation of the Gospel in New England, the Society for Promoting Christian Knowledge, the Society for the Propagation of the Gospel in Foreign Parts, the (Scottish) Society for Propagating Christian Knowledge, and the Moravian efforts, the

1790's and the opening years of the nineteenth century have generally been counted as seeing the beginning of the Protestant foreign missionary enterprise. We shall find this issuing both from the United States and from the Continent of Europe. However, it was in Great Britain, mainly England, and from impulses given by the awakening, that most of the societies of this period were begun. In 1792 the Baptist Missionary Society was organized, primarily as the result of the efforts of William Carey (1761–1834), self-educated, teacher, shoemaker, and pastor. Three years later, in 1795, what was at first called the Missionary Society, later the London Missionary Society, was inaugurated. It was intended to enlist the support of those of "Evangelical" sentiments, regardless of denomination, but it drew its funds and personnel chiefly from the Congregationalists. In 1796 the Scottish Missionary Society and the Glasgow Missionary Society were begun. In 1799 Evangelicals within the Church of England, prominent among them some from the Clapham group, started what was eventually called the Church Missionary Society. That same year the Religious Tract Society was organized, to enlist both Anglicans and Nonconformists in the spread of Christian literature. In 1804, partly through the efforts of Thomas Charles, a Calvinistic Methodist pastor in Wales, and with the endorsement of several of the Clapham circle, the British and Foreign Bible Society was founded for the purpose, as its name indicates, of printing and distributing the Bible at home and abroad. It was not until 1817–1818 that the Wesleyan Methodist Missionary Society was organized, but long before then Methodists had been active in proclaiming the Gospel outside the British Isles. For that purpose Thomas Coke travelled extensively in the United States and the West Indies and died (1814) on a journey to establish a mission in the East. Beginning in 1790 the Wesleyan Conference made organizational provision to assist him, and in 1813 auxiliary societies were formed.

By 1815 these various societies and efforts independent of them were spreading Christianity in several parts of the rapidly growing British Empire and were reaching beyond into vast areas hitherto untouched by Protestant Christianity. In 1793 William Carey and a colleague sailed for India, there to initiate the first undertaking of the Baptist Missionary Society. Since the East India Company, which then enjoyed a monopoly of British territory and trade in India, was hostile to missions, Carey eventually settled in Serampore, a Danish possession near Calcutta. There he, Marshman, and Ward, the "Serampore Trio," translated and printed part or all of the Bible into several of the languages of India and the East of Asia, including Chinese, and founded a school for the training of Indian Christians. David Brown, a protégé of Charles Simeon of Cambridge, conducted an orphanage in Calcutta. Another protégé of Simeon, Henry Martyn (1781–1812), senior wrangler at Cambridge and fellow of St. John's College, arrived in India in 1806 as a chaplain of the East India Company, exclaiming in his diary: "Now let me burn out for God." He did just that, adding to the faithful performance of his duties to the troops of the Company schools for Indians, preaching to Hindus and Moslems, and translations of the New Testament into three different languages. When in his early thirties he died in Asia Minor on his way to England. By 1815 the London Missionary Society had begun enterprises in several parts of India. In 1813, due largely to efforts of Evangelicals, among them Wilberforce, the charter of the East India Company was so altered by Parliament that missions became possible within the Company's territories and an episcopal establishment of a bishop and three archdeacons was set up in India for the Anglican Communion.

East of India, before 1815 English Baptists had begun, through Carey's sons, missions in Burma and the East Indies. By 1815 the London Missionary Society, the English Baptists, and the English Methodists had inaugurated missions on Ceylon, for during the years of the French Revolution and Napoleon the Dutch had been driven from that island by the English. In 1807 the first Protestant missionary to China, Robert Morrison, sent by the London Missionary Society, reached Canton.

The pioneer undertaking of the London Missionary Society was not in Asia, but in the South Pacific. In 1796 a party sent by that society sailed on *The Duff* and landed its missionaries on three widely separated island groups. The majority were placed on Tahiti and, after a few discouraging years, shortly after 1815 most of the population of that island and a smaller neighbour had become at least nominally Christian.

The earliest continuing white settlement on Australia was by convicts transported by the British Government. In 1787, with the first contingent, went a chaplain of the Church of England, an Evangelical. He was soon (1793) given a colleague, Samuel Marsden, also an Evangelical, who served until his death (1838) and did much to plant Christianity not only in Australia but also in New Zealand and some of the other islands of the Pacific. It was he who persuaded the Church Missionary Society to appoint men to the Maoris of New Zealand. The first contingent landed in New Zealand in 1814. In 1795 during the wars of the period the British took over the Dutch possessions in South Africa. The London Missionary Society sent representatives, most of whom gave themselves to the Africans, but at least one of whom served the Dutch churches.

In the British West Indies Anglicans, Methodists, and Baptists spread the Christian faith among the Negroes who formed the larger part of the population of most of the islands. Except for a few small islands off the coast, in 1763 France lost to England all of such territory as remained to her in what in the next century became the Dominion of Canada. English and Scottish settlers and some New Englanders, all predominantly Protestant by ancestry, moved into what were later the Maritime Provinces and the provinces of Quebec and Ontario. Numbers of those who were loyal to Britain when the Thirteen Colonies revolted migrated into these regions. Here, with some help from the British Isles, and, in the case of the Methodists, from the United States, the largest Protestant communions became the Church of England, the Presbyterians, the Methodists, and the Baptists. By 1815 all these were strongly represented.

THE REVIVAL IN THE UNITED STATES

As we have suggested, the immediate effect of the war for independence was adverse to Christianity in the United States. The political agitation and the fighting distracted attention from religion and in some quarters led to a decline in morals. Independence had barely been attained (1783), a constitution for the United States adopted, and a government under it set up (1789) when the French Revolution broke out. That upheaval and the rationalism and Deism associated with it had ardent sympathizers, especially among youth.

However, well before 1815 recovery was more than achieved, the mass conversion of the partially de-Christianized population which had been furthered by the Great Awakening was resumed, and the faith continued to make progress among Indians and Negroes.

Soon after independence some of the churches set up national organizations. In 1789 the Presbyterians formed a General Assembly as the capstone of their judicial and administrative structure and as a country-wide cohesive agency. In 1792 the (Dutch) Reformed Church and the following year the (German) Reformed Church ceased their dependence on the Continent of Europe and became fully self-governing.

In the 1780's the Anglicans drew together in what became the Protestant Episcopal Church. As we have said, the Church of England suffered greatly from the Revolution and independence. Many of the clergy, loyal to the king, left, never to return. Nearly all the missionaries of the Society for the Propagation of the Gospel in Foreign Parts were forced to retire and the society itself, formed as it had been for work in the British Empire, withdrew. There was no bishop and with independence such episcopal supervision as had been given by the Bishop of London and his commissaries ceased. Disestablishment came in such states, notably Virginia, as had given the Church of England the support of the government. Moreover, not all the Anglicans were of one mind.

In the North, and especially in New England where they were a dissenting minority from the "Standing Order," the dominant Congregationalism, they tended to be high church, stressing the Catholic features of their inheritance. In the South, where they had been socially and politically in control, they were usually low church, emphasizing the Protestant tradition. There was much objection to bringing all into a national church. Yet there was vitality in what had been the Church of England. Some of its more prominent clergy had supported the Colonies in their struggle for independence and many of those who led in creating the new United States of America were among its members.

Largely due to the tireless efforts of the irenic William White, rector of Christ Church, Philadelphia, in 1789 all parties met in a General Convention and formed the Protestant Episcopal Church. As early as 1780 a conference of clergy and laity in Maryland had suggested the name Protestant Episcopal, for the designation "Church of England" would scarcely be acceptable in a country which had so recently become independent of the mother country. In 1782 White sketched a plan for a national organization, in 1784 a gathering representing eight states assembled in New York, and in 1785 a General Convention adopted a constitution which was largely the work of White and asked the English bishops to ordain bishops for the United States. Samuel Seabury, chosen by the Connecticut constituency, was consecrated by bishops of the Scottish Episcopal Church in 1784. An act of Parliament was obtained authorizing the consecration of bishops through the Church of England, and in 1787 two, one of them White, were given that rite. At the General Convention of 1789, therefore, the Protestant Episcopal Church could be formally constituted. Both laity and clergy were represented and the Book of Common Prayer, modified to meet American needs, was adopted.

The Protestant Episcopal Church early received additions from the Swedish and German Lutherans. In 1791 the tie of the Delaware Swedish Lutherans with the mother country was severed, thus enabling them to move towards the Episcopal Church. Some of the English-speaking Lutherans of German descent were repelled by an effort to maintain the German language in the Lutheran congregations and went over to that church.

The revivals first represented by the Great Awakening broke out afresh with augmented fervour and swept various parts of the country.

In the South they had never really ceased. Preaching largely to those with low incomes and scanty or no education, the Baptists grew rapidly, notably in North Carolina, Virginia, and Kentucky. In Virginia they were at first persecuted, for the Church of England was established by law. In 1776 the principle of religious liberty was put into the Virginia bill of rights, and in 1785 it was made effective by appropriate legislation. This facilitated the further growth of the Baptists. In 1785 a revival began in Virginia which added thousands to the Baptist churches and many to other denominations.

In the 1790's what was known as the Second Awakening stirred the Congregational and some other churches in New England. Less marked by intense emotional manifestations than the movement earlier in the century, it stimulated the rise of missionary societies and the founding of academies, colleges, and theological seminaries.

Late in the 1790's and early in the 1800's a revival swept across Kentucky, then on the frontier. It seems to have begun in 1797 through the preaching of a Presbyterian clergyman. It broke out afresh in 1799. In 1800 came what was sometimes regarded as the first of the "camp-meetings." In preparation for the Lord's Supper hundreds gathered from miles around to listen to preaching. Several clergymen solemnly exhorted to searchings of conscience before coming to the communion table. Intense excitement followed. The custom of camp-meetings spread and persisted. Hundreds, sometimes thousands, flocked to a camp ground, many from curiosity or as a social gathering in a new country where opportunities for large concourses of people were rare. The meetings lasted for days and several preachers might be exhorting the hearers simultaneously in various parts of the grounds. The emotional and physical accompaniments were often extreme and bizarre. Yet some of the preachers sought to restrain them.

Several denominations shared in the revivals, but those which made the largest numerical gains were the Baptists, the Methodists, and new movements variously called Christians or Disciples of Christ. All emphasized the importance of conscious conversion.

The Baptists had a peculiar appeal to the masses. Their preachers, usually with very slight education, knew their audiences and how to address them in language which would hold their attention and bring conviction. They tended to be highly emotional. Their churches, simple democracies, fitted into the temper of the rural communities and isolated farmsteads in which most of the population lived. The informality of the services and of the singing and the simple language and music of the hymns were congenial to the rank and file. Baptists multiplied in many parts of the country, but especially in the South. In the nineteenth and twentieth centuries they constituted the large majority of all the Baptists in the world.

There were several different kinds of Baptists. Some were strict predestinarians, Particular Baptists, believing that Christ died only for the elect. Others were Arminian, like the General Baptists of England, holding that Christ died for all. A group of the latter, organized as a separate denomination and known as the Free Will Baptists, owed their origin to Benjamin Randall. A New

Englander by birth and rearing, Randall was converted through Whitefield—although after the latter's death. He preached widely, had marked gifts of organization, and at his own death (1808) the churches which he had called into existence numbered one hundred and thirty, with about six thousand members.

Methodists were not far behind the Baptists in their nation-wide spread. They far outnumbered the Methodists in any other country and next to the Baptists became the single largest Protestant denominational family in the United States.

Methodism seems not to have reached the Thirteen Colonies until after 1750. Some Methodists arrived in New York in 1760 and what appears to have been the first Methodist society in the Colonies was organized in that city in 1766. Other societies were soon formed in Maryland. In 1769 John Wesley sent two missionaries, one to New York and the other to Philadelphia. In the 1770's in Virginia a revival followed the preaching of an Anglican clergyman, Devereux Jarratt, and it was aided by one of Wesley's missionaries. By 1777 there were six Methodist circuits in Virginia and one in North Carolina with a membership of over four thousand, nearly two-thirds of the entire Methodist enrollment in the Colonies at that time. Jarratt gave the sacraments to these Virginia and North Carolina Methodists.

At first the Revolution seemed to be dealing Methodism a mortal blow. John Wesley issued a public appeal to the Colonies urging submission to the king. All but one of the missionaries whom Wesley had sent left, and for a time native-born Methodist preachers were persecuted. However, Methodists continued to increase. They are said to have multiplied from five hundred in 1771 to fifteen thousand in 1784.

Because of this growth, the opportunity in the new land, and the lack of Anglican priests to give the communion, drastic measures were necessary. Wesley and the Methodists of the United States had the courage to take them. As we have seen, in 1784 Wesley appointed Coke as "superintendent" of the Methodist societies in the United States and named Asbury to be his colleague in that office. Knowing the temper of the new country, Asbury refused to accept the post unless he was freely elected to it by his fellow preachers. In 1784 a conference of these preachers met in Baltimore, approved Wesley's plan of organization, formed the Methodist Episcopal Church, and chose Asbury and Coke as superintendents, a title soon to be changed to bishop. The autocratic Wesley was not happy over this refusal to continue under his direction, but, while respectful to him, the American preachers were firm.

Francis Asbury (1745–1816) was the organizer, the dominant figure, and the driving power in the formation and early growth of the Methodist

Episcopal Church. Born in England of humble and devout parents, himself deeply religious from boyhood, he was early caught up in the Methodist movement, became a lay preacher, and offered and was accepted by Wesley for service in America. Arriving in the Colonies in 1771, he went through the difficult days of the Revolution and eventually won the confidence of the country by braving Wesley's possible displeasure and coming out boldly for independence. At the Baltimore conference he was unanimously chosen as superintendent and was ordained deacon, elder, and superintendent on successive days. Since Coke was not content to remain in one country but travelled across much of the face of the world furthering Methodism, the burden of leadership fell on Asbury. Deliberately remaining unmarried the better to give himself to his mission, Asbury was incessantly on the road. Frail and often ill, from Maine to Georgia and from the Atlantic seaboard to the newest settlements on the far frontier in Kentucky, Tennessee, and Ohio he ranged. Dauntless, the crude accommodations and the cruder roads and trails and even the pathless wilderness did not deter him. Like Wesley, but under much more difficult physical conditions and over a much wider area, he was almost always on the road. Although, unlike Wesley, he was not a university graduate, like him he was well read and believed in education. As did Wesley, he went both preaching and organizing. By the time of his death the Methodists of the United States had grown from the fifteen thousand who greeted him on his election as superintendent to about two hundred thousand.

The growth of Methodism in the United States, even more striking than that in England, was due to a variety of factors. Here was a largely de-Christianized population, but with remnants of Christian belief to which appeal could be made. The country was new, virile, and hopeful, and the western frontier was being rapidly settled. It was predominantly rural. Like the Baptists, the Methodist preachers were usually men from the people, with slight education, and, speaking the language of ordinary folk, were able to reach them. Moreover, Arminian in theology and not holding to the doctrine of election as did Presbyterians, Congregationalists, and many Baptists, the Methodists proclaimed the love of God for all and that all might repent and be saved.

Methodist growth was predominantly in the rural sections and on the frontier, both North and South. This was in part because of the Methodist organization. The circuit plan which Wesley had devised for England proved singularly adapted to the rural and frontier areas of the United States. Under Asbury and the bishops who were later given him as colleagues were district superintendents. Under the district superintendents were circuit riders. As the name indicates, the latter were assigned areas to cover. Over some of these the route might be as much as five hundred miles. It had to be traversed by whatever conveyance was possible—on horseback, by canoe, or, where these failed, on foot. The circuit riders spoke wherever they could gain a hearing—in log cabins, court houses, school houses, taverns, or in the open air. Asbury wished them, like himself, to remain celibate, and while they took no vows, and some married, for the most part in effect theirs were the three obligations of the Roman Catholic monastic orders, poverty, chastity, and obedience. There was that about them which strongly resembled the Franciscans in the initial days of that movement. Like the latter they preached and sang the love of God in Christ. Even more than the latter they desired above all things conversions. In addition to the circuit riders there were local preachers, exhorters, quarterly meetings which gathered the members from farms and villages for fellowship, and camp-meetings. The system of classes and class leaders provided the pastoral function.

Methodists, like Baptists, were found all over the United States, but in general Baptists became more numerous in the South and Methodists in the North. The reason for this distinction is by no means clear.

From Methodism issued other bodies in addition to the Methodist Episcopal Church. The latter had only barely been launched when what was called the Republican Methodist Church arose in protest against the extensive powers granted to Asbury. The United Brethren in Christ had as their chief creator Philip William Otterbein (1726–1813). Born in Germany of a family of clergymen and coming to America in 1753 as a minister of the Reformed Church, in Pennsylvania Otterbein had a profound religious experience which made him an earnest and compelling preacher of the new life. As an associate he had Martin Boehm (1725–1812), of Pennsylvania Mennonite stock who, after a marked conversion, also began preaching in a heart-stirring manner. From the labours of these two men and of lay preachers of their fellowship there arose a new denomination which at the outset preached only in German and which was consciously modelled after the Methodist Episcopal Church, both in spirit and organization. Its constitution was adopted in 1799 and its first annual conference was held in 1800. Smaller than the United Brethren but, like it, patterned after the Methodist Episcopal Church and ministering to the German-speaking population, was the Evangelical Association. Its founder was Jacob Albright (1759–1808), a Pennsylvania German Lutheran who, out of the anguish which followed the death of several of his children, came into a joyous faith and joined the Methodists. A layman of little formal education, he began preaching among his fellow-German-Americans with marked success. In 1803 a council of his followers ordained him and in 1807 an annual conference assembled which elected him bishop.

Quite new movements arose from the revivals and after 1815 the majority of them coalesced into new denominations. In the freedom of the New World with the sense of emancipation from the confining institutions of the Old World across the Atlantic and of adventuring as pioneers in building a new and better order which characterized the United States in its youth, many, especially converts and preachers of the revivals, became dissatisfied with inherited denominational divisions. They sought to transcend them by simply calling themselves Christians or Disciples of Christ and going back to the New Testament to find the initial Gospel in its purity and the organization, forms, worship, and ceremonies of the pristine churches, which they idealized, before what they deemed corruptions and divisions had been added by later generations. Independently of one another, these groups sprang up in several different parts of the country, but chiefly on the frontier. What became the two main movements, movements which fused in 1832, were led by Barton W. Stone and Thomas and Alexander Campbell.

Barton W. Stone (1772–1844) was born in Maryland and was reared in the backwoods of Virginia. Hungry for education, in a pioneer academy he had as good training as the frontier could offer. After a heart-searching struggle he came into a Christian faith which had as its central tenet the conviction that God is love. With reservations openly expressed, he was ordained a Presbyterian clergyman, became a pastor in Kentucky, and was caught up in the revivals and camp-meetings which were then in their early heyday in that frontier state. Becoming increasingly dissatisfied with the doctrines of total depravity and unconditional election which he found in the Westminster Confession, he and a few others of like mind began preaching that God loved the whole world and had sent His Son to save all men if they would but believe, and that sinners were capable of fulfilling that condition. They urged sinners to believe immediately. This led to the expulsion from their synod of Stone and his friends. Accordingly they formed themselves into an independent presbytery. In 1804, distressed by the controversy produced by this action, they dissolved their presbytery, desiring it, so they said, to "sink into union with the Body of Christ at large." They called themselves simply Christians, foreswore the right of ordination, passing it back to "the Church of Christ," asked that the Bible be taken "as the only sure guide to heaven," and pled "that preachers and people cultivate a spirit of mutual forbearance, pray more, and dispute less." They also came to the conviction that the baptism of infants was wrong and baptized one another by immersion.

Thomas Campbell, of Scottish lineage and education, had been a Presbyterian pastor in Ireland. He had contact with one of the Haldanes. In 1807, in search of health, he came to Western Pennsylvania. Long disturbed by the sectarian strife among Christians, he admitted Presbyterians of various beliefs to the Lord's Supper. Censured for this by his presbytery, he withdrew. He and his followers formed "The Christian Association of Washington" (Pennsylvania), adopting as a slogan "where the Scriptures speak, we speak; where the Scriptures are silent, we are silent," and declared that "division among the Christians is a horrid evil. . . . It is anti-Christian." In 1809 Thomas Campbell was joined by his son, Alexander Campbell (1788–1866). The latter had remained in the British Isles after his father had come to America. There he had had a deep religious experience induced by a shipwreck and had come in touch with the ideas of the Haldanes and with the Sandemanians, a small group founded by John Glas (1695–1773), originally a Scottish Presbyterian clergyman. It took its name from Glas's son-in-law, Robert Sandeman, and had reached some of the conclusions arrived at by the "Christians" in the United States. On joining his father, Alexander found himself in accord with the latter's views. The more forceful, and a willing and able debater, he soon took over the leadership. In 1812 infant baptism was repudiated and the baptism by immersion of believers was adopted. For a time, beginning in 1813, fellowship was found with the Baptists, but after a few years (1827–1830) separation came over differences in doctrine and practice. The following of the Campbells grew rapidly, under the name of Reformers or Disciples.

Stone and Alexander Campbell met, found their views to be very much alike, and adjusted such differences as they discovered. Eventually about half those associated with Stone joined with the followers of Campbell.

The revivals produced a further rupture in Presbyterianism, the Cumberland Presbyterian Church. In the Cumberland region of Tennessee, partly as a result of the rapid growth which issued from the revivals, a presbytery was formed in 1802. Its members came to believe that the high educational standards required by the Presbyterian Church for training for the ministry were unsuited to the frontier and also dissented from the doctrine of predestination as held by that church. This led the Synod of Kentucky to order the presbytery dissolved. Appeal was taken to the General Assembly, but in vain, and in 1810 three members of the Cumberland Presbytery constituted themselves an independent body. Numbers grew rapidly and methods were adopted, including that of circuit riders, suited to the needs of the frontier.

The revivals combined with other movements to bring changes in Congregationalism. As we have seen, Congregationalism was the prevailing form of Christianity in New England. Confined almost entirely to that region, with some overflow into Presbyterianism in New York and New Jersey, in 1776 it had more than a third of all the ministers and congregations of the nascent nation, far outdistancing any of the others. By long tradition believing in gathered churches made up of members who could relate an experience of conversion, Congregationalists were deeply stirred by the Great Awakening and the renewal of that awakening which began in the 1790's. They stressed an educated clergy and some of the clergy as well as the laity were affected by the Arminianism, Socinianism, and rationalism which enjoyed a vogue across the Atlantic. Subscribing officially as they did to the Westminster Confession and to doctrines contained in it, including that of predestination and election, Congregationalists committed to the revivals were forced to seek to reconcile their doctrines with the preaching which urged men to repent. These currents and counter-currents led to divisions and changes in theology.

In and around Boston, partly in opposition to the theory and methods of the revivals, partly from contacts with movements in England, there was a trend towards Arminianism and Socinianism. Charles Chauncy (1705–1787), pastor of the influential and staid First Church of Boston, and Jonathan Mayhew (1720–1766) were among its leaders. In the 1780's King's Chapel, Boston, the oldest congregation of the Church of England in New England, officially abandoned belief in the Trinity. In 1800 a schism over "liberalism" took place in the church in Plymouth. In 1805 a man of known anti-Trinitarian views was chosen to the professorship of divinity in Harvard. In protest, those who held to Trinitarian convictions founded (1808) Andover Theological Seminary for the training of ministers. In his pulpit in Boston and in his writings, William Ellery Channing (1780–1842), out of deep, painful struggle of soul, became a saintly, persuasive exponent of Arian or Socinian views. In 1815 he accepted the name Unitarian for the movement. It was in 1818 that the main division began in the Congregational churches. In most cases the Unitarians won possession of the church property and the Trinitarians withdrew and formed new churches. In 1825 the American Unitarian Association was organized. Unitarians never constituted more than a minority of the population, but because of their ability, wealth, and education they exercised an influence far out of proportion to their numbers.

In the second half of the eighteenth century those who repudiated the doctrine of election and believed that God would find a way ultimately to save all began to raise their voices, especially in New England and in part as a result of the revivals. The most influential leader was Hosea Ballou (1771–1852), long a pastor in Boston and of Arian views. In 1790 the Universalists, as he and those of like mind were called, held a convention in Philadelphia and in 1793 organized a convention in New England which in 1803 adopted a creed that long remained the basis of the Universalist churches of the United States.

As we have suggested, those committed to the revivals were constrained to seek so to rethink their inherited belief in predestination as to make room for their preaching. Jonathan Edwards, to whom we have already referred, led the way. Others followed. Among them were Joseph Bellamy (1719–1790), Samuel Hopkins (1721–1803), Jonathan Edwards the younger (1745–1801), and a nephew of the latter and a grandson of the elder Jonathan Edwards, Timothy Dwight (1752–1817), President of Yale. Especially influential were Timothy Dwight, who by his force of character and preaching moulded several student generations at Yale and made that institution a centre from which issued clergymen who carried the views for which he stood to many parts of the country and of the world, and his older contemporary, Samuel Hopkins, whose writings set the standard for what was known as Hopkinsianism. Hopkinsianism was particularly potent in the Second Awakening. These men did not completely agree among themselves. Yet they all believed in conversion. In general they taught that this side of the grave no one could be sure that he was among the elect. They declared that all should submit unconditionally to the will of God, even to the extent of being reconciled to being among those whom God had not chosen for salvation. Hopkins made much of the phrase "disinterested benevolence," by which was meant living and labouring for the love of God and men with no thought of reward, no concern as to whether this would bring happiness to oneself in this world or the world to come. Indeed, one was to be willing to be damned, should that in His inscrutable wisdom be held by God to make for His glory. Under the influence of this theology, candidates for the Congregational ministry were often asked as a test of their fitness: "Are you willing to be damned for the glory of God?" Common to many was also what was known as the "governmental" theory of the atonement, that Christ's death was a satisfaction of "general justice" rather than of the specific sins of a particular individual. In general they agreed with the elder Jonathan Edwards that while all men have the natural ability to repent and turn to God in faith, they do not have the moral ability to do so. Some reacted vigorously against these views. For instance, William Ellery Channing was reared under the preaching of Hopkins and Universalism had its main stronghold in New England.

We must pause to note that the Friends, who had had a large share in the settlement of Pennsylvania, New Jersey, and Rhode Island, continued. Always a minority, they remained so. Out of them came notable contributions. Famous as a work of devotion, valued not only among the Quakers, was the *Journal* of John Woolman (1720–1772), begun in 1756 and interrupted only by his death.

THE ACCENTUATION OF THE DISTINCTIVE CHARACTER OF THE CHRISTIANITY OF THE UNITED STATES

The developments between 1750 and 1815 helped to strengthen features present in the colonial period and to add others which made the Christianity of the United States different from that of the Old World of Europe and from anything which had thus far appeared elsewhere, even in the Americas. It was clearly continuous with historic Christianity, but it was also distinctive. It was of major importance because of the increasing place which it was to have in the total Christianity of the world, both in its numerical strength and in its growing part in the spread of Christianity.

In 1815 the Christianity of the United States, like that of the Thirteen Colonies, was still overwhelmingly Protestant. The great Roman Catholic immigration of the nineteenth century had not yet begun. Even more than in the Thirteen Colonies, it was showing a marked variety. To the denominations brought from Europe, several were being added. Some were divisions from the old and others were quite new. Still more than in colonial days, the Christianity of the United States represented the extreme wing of Protestantism. To the Congregationalists, the largest body in 1750, and the Quakers were added the rapid growth of the Baptists, a body only feebly represented in that year, the Methodists, now fully separated from the Church of England, and the several kinds of Christians or Disciples of Christ.

The trend, already present in a few of the Colonies, towards placing all churches in a position of legal equality and not giving financial support to any through taxation, was continued. The first amendment to the Constitution of the United States, adopted in 1791, forbade Congress to make any "law respecting an establishment of religion or prohibiting the free exercise thereof." There was no prohibition of such action by individual states, but the traces of that privileged position which existed in 1750 disappeared fairly rapidly. This did not mean that the government, either of the nation or of individual states, was anti-Christian or purely secular. The armed forces and both houses of Congress had chaplains. In many of the schools maintained by the state the reading of Scripture and the Lord's Prayer were required. Presidents took the oath of office on the Bible. Although feeling against Roman Catholics was strong, no one church was given a favoured position. This was quite different from the situation in any country in Europe in 1750. By 1815, under the influence of the French Revolution, a somewhat similar situation was beginning to appear across the Atlantic, but due far more to a religiously sceptical spirit than in the United States. In the nineteenth and twentieth centuries, as we are to see, the pattern was to spread to much of the world.

Another feature, present before 1750 but now accentuated, was upon "evangelism," the seeking to win every individual to allegiance to Christ. From the standpoint of the churches this was especially important in view of the fact that there was no legal requirement of membership and that a large majority of the population were not formally connected with any church and were in danger of being de-Christianized. In such bodies as the Congregationalists, Baptists, Methodists, and most Presbyterians, in other words those comprising the large majority of the church members of the country, personal conversion was stressed. This was not so general among Episcopalians and Lutherans, but except in some communities these churches were in the small minority.

The emphasis on individual decision and conversion led to a modification of the Augustinian, Reformed theology which usually went by the name of Calvinism and which was the heritage of most of the churches and was contained in the official statements of the faith of several of them. Some churches quite abandoned as much of that theology as taught the divine election of specific individuals to salvation. In practice, most but not all of the others tended to ignore it.

There was also a trend in some denominations, in part the heritage from the Quakers and the founders of New England, to seek to make all society conform to Christian standards. After 1815 this was to issue in many reform movements. Some of these, indeed, notably against Negro slavery and for temperance in the use of alcoholic beverages, began before that year.

In several denominations modifications were made in what had been inherited from Europe. Thus in the Protestant Episcopal Church the name itself was significant, stressing the Protestant element and ignoring the national character of the Church of England: the lay element was given prominence and there were no archbishops, only a presiding bishop. In the Lutheran bodies, under the influence of Muhlenberg, who lived on well into this period (he reached Philadelphia in 1742 and died in 1787), a congregational form of government was adopted in which officers were chosen by the local congregation and the ministers were organized into synods.

THE BEGINNING OF THE WORLD OUTREACH OF THE PROTESTANTISM OF THE UNITED STATES

By 1815 the Protestantism of the United States was reaching outside the borders of the country and propagating its faith in other lands. This began slightly later than in the British Isles and did not soon reach the dimensions that it attained in the mother country. Late in the nineteenth and in the twentieth century, however, it was to supply the majority of the funds and the personnel of Protestant foreign missions.

The revivals of the eighteenth century stimulated a marked accentuation of missionary activity. This showed itself in increased efforts to win the Indians to the Christian faith. In a few states missionary societies were formed, partly for missions among the Indians. In 1801 the Congregationalists of Connecticut began a plan of union with the Presbyterian General Assembly which spread to other Congregational churches for joint effort in planting Christianity on the westward-moving frontier. In some circles there was much interest in what was being done in Britain through the Baptist Missionary Society and the London Missionary Society. The Moravians were active in missions to the Indians and in 1787 reorganized their Society for Propagating the Gospel among the Heathen.

The most notable pioneer undertaking was the American Board of Commissioners for Foreign Missions. It was organized in 1810 by the Congregationalists of New England in response to an appeal by students of the recently founded Andover Theological Seminary. The leader of the student group was Samuel John Mills (1783–1818), spiritually a child of the Second Awakening. While an undergraduate in Williams College he had taken the initiative in the formation of the Society of the Brethren, whose purpose it was "to effect in the persons of its members a mission or missions to the heathen." The American Board of Commissioners for Foreign Missions long attracted the support not only of Congregationalists but also of Christians of other denominations, especially the Presbyterians. In 1812 it appointed its first contingent of missionaries, with Asia as their goal. After they left the United States three of the appointees, Adoniram Judson and his wife and Luther Rice, felt constrained by their consciences to become Baptists, resigned from the society which sent them, and asked support of the American Baptists. The latter rose to the occasion and so began their enterprise abroad. The Judsons inaugurated a continuing mission in Burma and those who remained with the parent society obtained access to India. Rice returned to the United States to arouse the Baptist churches to rally to the Judsons and to missions. This he did with marked success.

The Protestant Revival on the Continent of Europe

The awakening in Protestantism was chiefly in the British Isles and the United States but it was by no means confined to these countries. It was also marked on the Continent of Europe. There it was a continuation of Pietism and the Moravians and was reinforced with repercussions from the awakenings in Great Britain. It was in large part a reaction against the cold rationalism of the Enlightenment which had gripped a large proportion of the pulpits. As in the British Isles and the United States, it gave rise to undertakings to bring about the conversion of nominal Christians within Christendom and to spread the Gospel throughout the world. We can take the time to point out only a few of its outstanding examples.

In 1797 there was organized in the Netherlands, partly on the model of the London Missionary Society, the Netherlands Missionary Society (Nederlandsche Zendelinggenootschap). It had its immediate rise through John Theodore Vanderkemp who by a devious and tragic route had come from the life of a dissolute army officer to a warm Christian experience. In 1800 Johann Jänicke, a pastor in Berlin of Moravian descent and with Moravian and Pietist contacts, founded a school to train youths for service as missionaries. He received financial aid from England and like-minded circles in Germany. Most of those whom he prepared were German Pietists and served under the London Missionary Society, the Church Missionary Society, and the Netherlands Missionary Society. In the second half of the eighteenth century several groups arose in Germany and Switzerland largely from Pietist sources to pray and labour for a revival. One of their fruits was the founding of a school at Basel (1815) which trained missionaries. As with the products of Jänicke's institution, most of the early Basel graduates served under British societies. Not until 1822 did Basel develop an organization to send out and support its men. In Germany a mounting tide of Pietism profoundly affected that and other countries and after 1815 gave rise to several movements and societies to win other Germans and to carry the Gospel to other lands.

In a poverty-stricken community in the Vosges Mountains John Frederic Oberlin (1740–1826) devoted himself through a long ministry to the spiritual, moral, and material transformation of his parish. He built roads, founded what are said to have been the first of the "infant schools," and pioneered in the application of scientific agriculture. He became famous for that combination of individual and group transformation which is found along much of the course of the history of Christianity.

Norway was the scene of the beginning of a notable awakening which had as its initial leader Hans Nielsen Hauge (1771–1824). From a deeply religious family, Hauge was led by a serious accident when a boy and by much reading of the Bible to undertake preaching. Although unordained, in six years he travelled about ten thousand miles, preaching nearly every day, proclaiming the need and the possibility of a warm personal Christian experience. This was in contrast with the cold rationalism which prevailed among most of the clergy, for here as elsewhere in Scandinavia the Lutheran state church, from which there was almost no dissent, was strongly impregnated with currents from the Germany of the *Aufklärung*. He denounced the dead orthodoxy and inconsistent lives of the pastors, wrote hundreds of books and tracts, and taught his followers to be preachers and to build mills and factories to help them to a better economic status. In 1804, after less than a decade, Hauge was arrested for preaching as a layman. For about ten years, until 1814, he was incarcerated. When at last, through the importunities of his friends, he was released, he was a broken man. However, the movement which he had encouraged continued in groups and individuals called by his name. They did not break with the state church, but they had lay preachers, stressed conversion, and were known as *Leser* because of their diligence in teaching and reading the Scriptures. They were mostly from the farmers and represented a revolt against the aristocracy, a class which included the pastors.

A figure which emerged in Scandinavia from Protestantism but which was much further removed than Hauge from the usual forms of Christianity was Emanuel Swedenborg (1688–1772). The son of a professor of theology and bishop in the Church of Sweden who had been suspected of heresy for stressing faith, love, and communion with God above dogma, he travelled widely in Western Europe and had a broad range of learning and a mind of marked originality, especially in the natural sciences and engineering. He wrote voluminously. Late in middle life he gave himself fully to religion and to an intensive study of the Scriptures. He had visions and dreams through which he was convinced that fresh revelations had come to him from Christ. Although he did not attempt to organize a religious body, he believed himself commissioned to teach of the New Church and from his writings there arose a widely spread but numerically small body, the Church of the New Jerusalem. His writings had an influence on such diverse men as Kant, Goethe, and Russian churchmen.

INTELLECTUAL CURRENTS IN PROTESTANTISM IN GERMANY

While these awakenings, largely Evangelical and of what in the broad sense of the term could be called Pietistic were occurring among minorities across the length and breadth of Protestantism, another set of movements was in progress. They were present in several countries but were most marked in Germany. They were largely intellectual. They were not confined to religion but were seen in a wide range of cultural activity, in Germany notably in philosophy, literature, and music. Becoming entrenched in the universities of Germany and growing in the nineteenth century, they were to make of these institutions centres to which students were to flock from much of the Occident, especially from Scandinavia, Great Britain, and the United States.

By 1815 these movements were only in their beginnings, but already they were showing the direction which they were to take in their heyday. They were to have a profound effect upon Christianity, particularly upon Protestantism, and in every land where Protestantism was found. In general Evangelicals and Pietists were to regard them and their effect upon Christianity with suspicion and even hostility, but like the Evangelical movement they were to overpass existing denominational and ecclesiastical boundaries and were to have wide repercussions which were not confined to Protestantism but which were to have a greater or less effect upon most of the other branches of the faith. In the end they were to be rejected by the Roman Catholic Church and did not make major inroads on it or on the Eastern Churches. Yet they constituted one of the most potent combinations of movements which Christianity had thus far known. They embodied what was called the scientific and rationalistic approach to the study of the Scriptures and the history of Christianity and applied to theology the results both of these studies and of current philosophy. Arising largely from the currents out of which issued Deism and the Enlightenment, they were not confined to them.

We can here do little more than list the names of a few of the outstanding scholars who shared in these movements before 1815, with some slight indication of the contributions of each. Johann Lorentz von Mosheim (1694–1755), successively professor at Helmstädt and Göttingen, in his *Institutiones Historiæ Ecclesiasticæ* (1726, revised edition 1755) wrote a comprehensive history of the Christian Church in which he attempted to be purely objective and factual rather than controversial. He thus inaugurated a new era in the study of the history of Christianity. Jean Astruc (1684–1766), professor of medicine at Paris, and Johann Gottfried Eichhorn (1752–1827), professor of Oriental languages at Jena and Göttingen, who wrote extensively on the Old and New Testaments and has been called the founder of Old Testament criticism, held that there are distinct documents in Genesis, a view which was later accepted as axiomatic by scholars who applied to the Bible the methods of historical criticism. Jean le Clerc (1657–1736), reared in Geneva, later an Arminian in Amsterdam, endeavoured to find the actual meaning of the words and passages of the Bible rather than to seek in the Scriptures texts to prove preconceived doctrines. Somewhat similarly Johann Albrecht Bengel (1687–1752), a Pietist of Württemberg whose commentary, *Gnomon Novi Testamenti* (1742), was used by John Wesley in preparing his *Notes on the New Testament* (1755), worked on the conviction that in attempts to understand the Bible nothing should either be omitted from or read into the Biblical text, but that the meaning should be sought through the strict application of grammatical principles. His contemporary, Johann Jakob Wettstein (1693–1754), out of a lifetime of study produced a work giving the various readings of the text of the New Testament, thus furthering the effort to establish the original forms of the writings of that fundamental document of the Christian faith. Johann August Ernesti (1707–1781) of Leipzig, eventually professor of theology in that university, vigorously anti-Roman Catholic, a distinguished student of the Greek and Latin classics, approached the New Testament with the same criteria that he applied to non-Christian writings. Reimarus, whom we have already met, brought to the New Testament records of the life of Christ the principles which he would employ in the study of the biography of any historical figure. In doing so he ruled out the supernatural and miraculous, for, like all historians, he could not achieve complete objectivity but came to his task with either conscious or unconscious presuppositions, but he stimulated further studies of Jesus. Johann Salomo Semler (1725–1791), educated in Halle and for nearly forty years professor of theology there, was a leader in the rationalistic trend which cooled the ardour of that centre of Pietism. He believed in revelation and held that it is to be found in the Bible, but that not everything in the Bible is revelation, that not all parts of the Scriptures are of equal value, and that while the Bible contains permanent truths, they are conditioned by the circumstances in which the various books were written. He declared that a difference existed between the Pauline and Jewish types of Christianity and prepared the way for the kind of study of the Scriptures and theology which in the nineteenth century had a major development at Tübingen. Johann Gottfried von Herder (1744–1803), preacher, writer, child and stimulator of the romantic movement, and friend of Goethe, maintained that the various books of the Bible can be understood only in the light of the views and feelings of the environment and times in which they were written.

Why rationalism and romanticism should have acquired these particular religious aspects in the Protestant areas of Germany is not entirely clear. It may have been for reasons akin to those which about three centuries earlier had directed humanism in Germany into religious channels. It is clear that the German soul and mind had been ploughed deep by the Reformation and that when confronted by the new movements of the mind and the spirit represented by rationalism and romanticism, many Germans sought to relate them to their inherited religious faith. By no means all German Protestants, then or later, accepted the methods or the conclusions of these new trends. Yet the latter were strong in the universities in which the intellectuals, including many of the clergy, were trained.

A figure who must have two or three paragraphs to himself is Immanuel Kant (1724–1804). While he was a philosopher rather than a theologian, Kant had so profound an influence on theology as well as philosophy, and especially on Protestant theology, that he must be given special attention. He was born and spent his life in Königsberg, a strong Pietist centre in East Prussia. At first he seemed designed for the ministry and is said to have preached a few times. But it was to philosophy and to teaching and writing that he gave his life. Refusing offers to go elsewhere, he remained in his native city and eventually, when he was in his middle fifties, a professorship in the local university was given him. He had a wide range of intellectual interests. Early he majored in the Greek and Roman classics, then in mathematics and physics, and his chair was one of logic and metaphysics. With some areas of knowledge he was not particularly concerned, but he read widely, keeping abreast of new books. In philosophy he was not much impressed by Descartes and those who followed him, but Locke and Leibnitz influenced him and he knew and was critical of the work of his older contemporary, Wolff. Frail, short of stature, slight, with a concave chest and a deformed right shoulder, he held to a rigid physical discipline and until his later years did not know serious illness. He never married. He matured slowly and it was not until 1781, when he was in his later fifties, that the first work which brought him fame was published, *The Critique of Pure Reason,* and its second and enlarged edition did not appear until 1787, when he was in his early sixties. The book quickly attracted excited attention in the German universities and eventually won a wide hearing in other countries. Dealing drastically as it did with the scope and limitations of reason, in which the intellectuals of eighteenth century Western Europe placed their confidence, it was very timely. Kant's other important works were his *Critique of Practical Reason* and his *Critique of Judgement.*

Kant's views aroused a storm of criticism in conservative Protestant circles. They, and the fear that he might be on the side of the French Revolution, led the government of Prussia to exact a promise from him, in the 1790's, that he would not lecture or write on religion. With this he complied, but regarded the death of King Frederick William II (1797) as releasing him from that obligation. By that time his mental and physical powers were beginning to show symptoms of the decay that enfeebled his later years. Although of high moral character, exemplifying the exacting standards which he set forth in his treatment of ethics, he disturbed the orthodox by his religious convictions and their implications.

Yet Kant was by no means anti-Christian. To be sure, his *Critique of Pure Reason* undercut the grounds which Deists, notably the then popular Wolff, gave for a belief in the existence of God. Kant maintained that the knowledge which comes to us through our minds and reason is compounded of two elements, what enters from without, through our senses, and the interpretation given by our minds. That interpretation is governed by the laws of our intellect. This means that we cannot know things in themselves, but only what our minds transmit to us from without. If this is true, through reason alone, or "pure reason," we can never, as Wolff and other Deists who depended on it claimed, demonstrate the exact nature of the universe or of God as they actually are. Kant dealt ruthlessly with the traditional arguments for the existence of God.

However, in his *Critique of the Practical Reason* Kant declared that in addition to his reason man is aware of a feeling of moral obligation and is confronted by the "categorical imperative," an unconditional and unqualified command. This awareness of moral obligation, so Kant maintained, is the highest quality of man. If he obeys the categorical imperative, Kant said, each man will live in such fashion that the principles on which he acts can become those on which all men should act. It followed, Kant was convinced, that man can obey the categorical imperative and is, therefore, free; that man must be immortal, for only thus can he live long enough fully to respond to the categorical imperative; and that God must exist, for only He can make happiness the outcome of virtue. In his *Religion within the Limits of Unaided Reason,* which appeared in 1793, six years after his *Critique of Pure Reason,* Kant went on to say that any man governed by obedience to the categorical imperative is pleasing to God and is a son of God. He believed Jesus Christ to have been the highest example of that obedience and therefore of that sonship, that the visible Church should be a fellowship for mutual stimulus to that obedience, and that there is an invisible Church made up of all the obedient.

While his effect was great during his lifetime, since he was late in maturing and died in 1804 it was not until after 1815 that Kant had his greatest influence upon Christian thought.

SUMMARY

In the brief but important period between 1750 and 1815 the situation in respect to Christianity became increasingly complex and more patently paradoxical.

Always the course of Christianity had been marked by seeming contradictions. At the very outset there had been the apparent impotence of a Nazarene carpenter-preacher-healer pitted against the established order in the Jewish combination of Pharisees and Sadducees and in the Roman state, to the casual observer a powerlessness confirmed by what looked like its end in futility on a cross. The proclamation by Jesus of the kingdom of God and of the impossibly high standards of members of that kingdom seemed to be the most fantastic of dreams. Yet within five centuries the overwhelming majority of the population of the Roman Empire had given at least nominal allegiance to that Nazarene as the unique Son of God. For the majority that professed adherence was contradicted by lives at variance with the ideals set forth by Jesus. But, on the other hand, at least a minority were haunted by those ideals and were giving evidence of the new life of which Jesus had spoken. In a civilization which had ceased to do or to say much that was new they had created the Christian Church, Christian worship, and Christian theology, the latter daring and universe-embracing in its affirmations.

There followed almost five centuries in which it seemed that Christianity was dying. Christianity failed to save the Roman Empire and about half of what had been Christendom was overrun by the followers of a later, more warlike, and seemingly more practical prophet. Then Christianity surged forward, having held about half the area which had been the Roman Empire, won the avowed loyalty of the pagan barbarians who from the North and East had seized upon that part of the Empire, and pressed out into Central and Eastern Asia.

The life of the Christendom of what we call the Middle Ages, sometimes in retrospect viewed nostalgically by later generations as the age of faith, also presented striking contrasts. All but a very few in that Christendom called themselves Christians. But the perfidy and self-seeking of the Byzantines, the chronic wars of the Byzantine realm and of Western Europeans, the pride, the sexual irregularities, the lust for power, and the callous cruelty, even in the Church, practical denials of the faith, were all the more starkly set forth because of the continuing challenge of Christ and the fashion in which a minority responded to it in monastic and other movements, in art, literature, and thought, and in attempts to lift society to "the high calling of God in Christ Jesus."

There followed, after 1350, a thinly veiled recrudescence of paganism, partly stimulated by the very success of Christianity and paying lip-service to it. This was paralleled by fresh advances of the followers of the Arab prophet and corruption in the strongest of the churches which posed as the guardian of the Christian heritage.

When the night was at its blackest streaks of a coming dawn were visible which heralded a new day in what was called the Reformation. Yet in the centuries of the Reformation there was much which contradicted the Christian faith in the individual and group performance of its professed adherents and by 1750 the revived paganism of the Renaissance had been followed by what was a more nearly open repudiation of the faith by intellectuals and the ruling classes than had yet been seen in lands which bore the Christian name.

In the second half of the eighteenth century a culmination of movements appeared to be sounding the death knell of the faith. The Spaniards and Portuguese, recently the most active in the geographic propagation of the faith, were declining, the climate of opinion favoured Deism, which ruled out as irrational some of the distinctive convictions of Christianity, a scarcely less Christ-denying romanticism was making headway, and the revolutions spearheaded by that of France, committed to Deism and on its extreme front blatantly anti-Christian, seemed to be the wave of the future. Naked power in the form of Napoleon sought to tie the Church to its chariot wheels. There were intelligent and apparently well informed men who seriously believed that Christianity would not outlast another century. Yet in the very years of what looked like the triumph of these forces, life was breaking out again in Christianity. It was still among minorities, but these were in peoples who in the following century were to show the most spectacular growth and were to shape much of mankind.

After 1815 contradictions were to be intensified. On the one hand were movements which appeared to make certain the demise of Christianity. On the other were pulsing tides of life which planted Christian communities over practically all the inhabited globe and which made themselves felt in all cultures. From one angle, never had the prospect for Christianity seemed so grim. From another, never had the faith been so widely spread or exerted such extensive effects on mankind.

SELECTED BIBLIOGRAPHY

GENERAL SURVEY

H. Hermelink, *Das Christentum in der Menschheitsgeschichte von der französischen Revolution bis zur Gegenwart.* Vol. I, 1789–1835 (Tübingen and Stuttgart, J. B. Metztersche Verlagsbuchhandlung and Hermann Leins, 1951, pp. xix, 528). Chiefly on Germany and France.

MOVEMENTS ADVERSE TO CHRISTIANITY

A. Aulard, *Christianity and the French Revolution,* translated by Lady Frazer (London, Ernest Benn, 1927, pp. 164). Carries the story through 1802.

C. L. Becker, *The Heavenly City of the Eighteenth-Century Philosophers* (Yale University Press, 1932, pp. 168). By a thorough-going sceptic, but showing the contribution of Christianity to the conceptions of the intellectuals whose ideas shaped the French Revolution.

H. N. Brailsford, *Voltaire* (New York, Henry Holt and Co., 1935, pp. 256). In the *Home University Library.*

The Cambridge Modern History, Vol. VIII, *The French Revolution,* Vol. IX, *Napoleon* (Cambridge University Press, 1904, 1906). A standard work by various authors.

J. Y. T. Greig, *David Hume* (Oxford University Press, preface 1931, pp. 436). By an expert.

W. H. Jervis, *The Gallican Church and the Revolution* (London, Kegan Paul, Trench, Trübner & Co., 1882, pp. xxiii, 524). Carefully done, by an Anglican; carries the story through Napoleon; favourable to the Pope.

J. Leflom, *La Crise Révolutionnaire, 1789–1846* (Paris, Bloud & Gay, 1949, pp. 524). By a Roman Catholic scholar.

H. M. Morais, *Deism in Eighteenth Century America* (Columbia University Press, 1934, pp. 203). A competent survey.

John Viscount Morley, *Rousseau and His Era* (London, Macmillan & Co., 2 vols., 1923. First published 1873, revised by the author 1921).

John Viscount Morley, *Voltaire* (London, Macmillan & Co., 1923, pp. xiii, 365. First published 1872, revised 1921).

J. W. Oman, *The Problem of Faith and Freedom in the Last Two Centuries* (New York, A. C. Armstrong and Son, 1906, pp. xxiv, 443). Less than half on the pre-nineteenth century period.

J. Orr, *English Deism, Its Roots and Its Fruits* (Grand Rapids, Wm. B. Eerdmans Publishing Co., 1934, pp. 289). A comprehensive survey.

The Confessions of Jean Jacques Rousseau (New York, Random House, 1945, pp. xviii, 683).

L. Stephen, *History of English Thought in the Eighteenth Century* (New York, J. P. Putnam's Sons, 2 vols., 1876). Long a standard work.

N. Sykes, *Church and State in England in the XVIIIth Century* (Cambridge University Press, 1934, pp. xi, 455). Thorough and competent. Gives a more favourable view of the Church of England than is sometimes done.

N. L. Torrey, *Voltaire and the English Deists* (Yale University Press, 1930, pp. x, 224).

B. Willey, *The Eighteenth Century Background. Studies in the Idea of Nature in the Thought of the Period* (London, Chatto & Windus, 1940, pp. viii, 302). An excellent survey, confined to British thought.

THE BEGINNINGS OF REVIVAL IN THE ROMAN CATHOLIC CHURCH

P. Guilday, *The Life and Times of John Carroll Archbishop of Baltimore (1735–1815)* (New York, The Encyclopedia Press, 1922, pp. xiv, 864). A standard biography.

T. Maynard, *The Story of American Catholicism* (New York, The Macmillan Co., 1941, pp. xv, 694). Sympathetic, readable, by a Roman Catholic.

C. S. Phillips, *The Church in France, 1789–1848: A Study in Revival* (London, A. R. Mowbray & Co., 1929, pp. viii, 315). Sympathetic.

SIGNS OF LIFE IN THE EASTERN CHURCHES

S. Bolshakoff, *Russian Nonconformity* (Philadelphia, The Westminster Press, 1950, pp. 192). A comprehensive survey.

F. C. Conybeare, *Russian Dissenters* (Harvard University Press, 1921, pp. x, 370). Based on standard Russian secondary accounts.

W. H. Frere, *Some Links in the Chain of Russian Church History* (London, Faith Press, 1918, pp. xvii, 200). By a competent scholar, a high Anglican.

N. Gorodetzky, *Saint Tikhon Zadonsky, Inspirer of Dostoevsky* (London, Society for Promoting Christian Knowledge, 1951, pp. xii, 249). Based upon extensive research. Well done.

E. J. Knapton, *The Lady of the Holy Alliance. The Life of Julie de Krüdener* (Columbia University Press, 1939, pp. xiii, 262). Well written, based on extensive research.

THE RISE OF METHODISM

A. D. Belden, *George Whitefield—the Awakener. A Modern Study of the Evangelical Revival* (New York and Nashville, Abingdon-Cokesbury Press, 1930, pp. xvii, 302). Warmly sympathetic, based on earlier biographies.

J. W. Bready, *England: Before and After Wesley: The Evangelical Revival and Social Reform* (London, Hodder & Stoughton, 1938, pp. 463). Based on solid research, stressing the change wrought by Wesley.

W. A. Candler, *Life of Thomas Coke* (New York and Nashville, Abingdon-Cokesbury Press, 1923, pp. vi, 408). Very favourable to Coke.

L. F. Church, *The Early Methodist People* (London, The Epworth Press, 1948, pp, viii, 286). Sympathetic, based on careful research.

L. F. Church, *More about the Early Methodist People* (London, The Epworth Press, 1949, pp. xviii, 324).

The Journal of the Rev. John Wesley, A.M., edited by N. Curnock (London, The Epworth Press, 8 vols., 1938). The standard edition.

The Letters of the Rev. John Wesley, A.M., edited by J. Telford (London, The Epworth Press, 8 vols., 1931). The standard edition.

F. J. McConnell, *John Wesley* (New York and Nashville, Abingdon-Cokesbury Press, 1939, pp. 355). A brilliant and remarkably objective appraisal by a distinguished Methodist bishop.

THE BRITISH REVIVAL OUTSIDE OF METHODISM

Memoirs of the Life of the Rev. Charles Simeon, M.A., . . . with a Selection from His Writings and Correspondence, edited by W. Carus (London, J. Hatchard & Son, 2d ed., 1847, pp. xxx, 848).

THE OUTREACH OF THE BRITISH REVIVAL

W. Canton, *A History of the British and Foreign Bible Society* (London, John Murray, 5 vols., 1904–1910). An official history.

S. P. Carey, *William Carey, D.D., Fellow of Linnæan Society* (New York, George H. Doran Co., preface 1923, pp. xvi, 428). By a great-grandson; a standard biography.

R. Coupland, *Wilberforce, A Narrative* (Oxford, The Clarendon Press, 1923, pp. vi, 528).

J. Field, *The Life of John Howard* (London, Longmans, Green & Co., 1850, pp. xvi, 495).

R. Lovett, *The History of the London Missionary Society, 1795–1895* (London, Henry Frowde, 2 vols., 1899).

E. Stock, *The History of the Church Missionary Society* (London, Church Missionary Society, 4 vols., 1899–1916). An official history.

THE REVIVAL IN THE UNITED STATES

J. H. Allen and R. Eddy, *A History of the Unitarians and the Universalists* (New York, The Christian Literature Co., 1894, pp. ix, 506). One of the *American Church History Series.*

The Heart of Asbury's Journal, edited by E. S. Tipple (New York, Eaton and Mains, 1904, pp. xii, 712).

G. N. Boardman, *A History of New England Theology* (New York, A. D. F. Randolph Co., 1899, pp. 314). A comprehensive survey.

J. M. Buckley, *A History of Methodists in the United States* (New York, Charles Scribner's Sons, 1903, pp. xix, 714).

J. W. Chadwick, *William Ellery Channing, Minister of Religion* (Boston, Houghton Mifflin Co., 1903, pp. xiv, 463). A sympathetic biography.

C. C. Cleveland, *The Great Revival in the West, 1797–1805* (The University of Chicago Press, 1916, pp. xii, 215). Carefully done.

F. H. Foster, *A Genetic History of New England Theology* (The University of Chicago Press, 1907, pp. xv, 568). Critical, but in places sympathetic.

R. V. Foster, *A Sketch of the History of the Cumberland Presbyterian Church* (New York, The Christian Literature Co., 1894, pp. 258–509). In *The American Church History Series.*

W. E. Garrison, *Religion Follows the Frontier. A History of the Disciples of Christ* (New York, Harper & Brothers, 1931, pp. xvi, 317). Readable, scholarly.

W. M. Gewehr, *The Great Awakening in Virginia, 1740–1790* (Duke University Press, 1930, pp. viii, 292). Scholarly, well documented.

E. F. Humphrey, *Nationalism and Religion in America, 1774–1789* (Boston, Chipman Law Publishing Co., 1924, pp. viii, 536). Competent, comprehensive.

C. R. Keller, *The Second Great Awakening in Connecticut* (Yale University Press, 1942, pp. ix, 275). Scholarly.

W. W. Manross, *A History of the American Episcopal Church* (New York, Morehouse-Gorham, Inc., 1935, pp. xvi, 404). A competent comprehensive survey.

B. W. Stone, *The Biography of Eld. Barton Warren Stone, Written by Himself: with Additions and Reflections by Elder John Rogers* (Cincinnati, J. A. and U. P. James, 1847, pp. ix, 404).

L. J. Trinterud, *The Forming of an American Tradition. A Re-examination of Colonial Presbyterianism* (Philadelphia, The Westminster Press, 1949, pp. 352). About half of this excellent book is on the post-1750 years.

R. G. Torbet, *A History of the Baptists* (Philadelphia, The Judson Press, 1950, pp. 538). A comprehensive, competent survey, with valuable footnotes and bibliographical references to the literature and the sources.

C. W. Ware, *Barton Warren Stone, Pathfinder of Christian Union. A Story of*

His Life and Times (St. Louis, The Bethany Press, 1932, pp. xiv, 357). Based largely upon printed sources.

L. A. Weigle, *American Idealism* (Yale University Press, 1928, pp. 356). A competent survey, with running commentaries on pertinent illustrations, of the religious history of the United States.

THE BEGINNING OF THE WORLD OUTREACH OF THE PROTESTANTISM OF THE UNITED STATES

T. C. Richards, *Samuel J. Mills* (Boston, The Pilgrim Press, 1906, pp. 275).

S. Warburton, *Eastward! The Story of Adoniram Judson* (New York, Round Table Press, 1937, pp. xi, 240). Very carefully done.

THE PROTESTANT REVIVAL ON THE CONTINENT OF EUROPE

M. Dawson, *Oberlin. A Protestant Saint* (New York, Harper & Brothers, 1934, pp. ix, 166).

W. Schlatter, *Geschichte der Basler Mission, 1815–1915* (Basel, Basler Missionsbuchhandlung, 3 vols., 1916). Based especially on unpublished sources.

Swedenborg's Works, Rutch edition (Boston, Houghton Mifflin Co., 32 vols., no date).

G. Warneck, *Abriss einer Geschichte den protestantischen Missionen von den Reformation bis auf die Gegenwart mit einem Anhang über die katholischen Missionen* (Berlin, Martin Warneck, 10th ed., 1913, pp. x, 624). A standard survey.

INTELLECTUAL CURRENTS IN PROTESTANTISM IN GERMANY

E. Caird, *The Critical Philosophy of Immanuel Kant* (Glasgow, James Maclehose and Sons, 2d ed., 2 vols., 1909). A comprehensive treatment of Kant by an eminent British philosopher.

Immanuel Kant's Critique of Pure Reason, translated by F. M. Müller (New York, The Macmillan Co., 2d ed., 1907, pp. lxxix, 808).

Immanuel Kant, *Critique of Practical Reason and Other Writings on Moral Philosophy,* translated by L. W. Beck (The University of Chicago Press, 1949, pp. xv, 370).

Kant's *Critique of Judgment,* translated by J. H. Bernard (London, Macmillan & Co., 1931, pp. xlviii, 429).

THE GREAT CENTURY:
GROWING REPUDIATION PARALLELED
BY ABOUNDING VITALITY
AND UNPRECEDENTED EXPANSION
A.D. 1815 — A.D. 1914

Chapter 45

GENERAL CONDITIONS WHICH
CONFRONTED CHRISTIANITY: THE
CHALLENGE OF DISAFFECTION,
REPUDIATION, AND OPPORTUNITY,
A.D. 1815 - A.D. 1914

The ninety-nine years from 1815 to 1914 formed a distinct period in the history of mankind and of Christianity. They, rather than the conventional 1800 to 1900, were the nineteenth century. Because of a combination of geographic expansion, inner vitality, and the effect upon mankind as a whole, they constituted the greatest century which Christianity had thus far known. This achievement of Christianity was associated with a prodigious burst of creativity in Western European peoples, the traditional Christendom. It was paralleled by movements which seemed to threaten the very existence of the faith and by challenges which called forth all its inner resources.

MOVEMENTS WHICH CONSTITUTED THE SETTING FOR CHRISTIANITY

Following the final defeat and exile of Napoleon in 1815, the Western world entered nearly a century of relative peace and mounting prosperity which persisted until the outbreak of a succession of world wars in 1914. Never over so prolonged a period had Christendom been as nearly free from war. Wars there were, notably that centering about Crimea, in 1854–1856, in which Turkey, Russia, Great Britain, France, and Sardinia were engaged, the Franco-German War of 1870–1871, and, most destructive and prolonged of all, the Civil War in the United States, 1861–1865. Wars were waged on the widening fringes of the expansion of European peoples—with the Indians in the United States, in India, in Burma, in Indochina, in China, with the Maoris in New Zealand, between the British and the Boers in South Africa, and between the Russians and Japanese. None of these, however, were of major dimensions in the number of lives lost. In China an uprising, that with the name of T'ai P'ing, which was due partly to ideas derived from contacts with Christianity, cost hundreds of thousands of lives. Yet contrasted with the eighteenth and the twentieth centuries there was no war which involved all of Christendom or which approached the dimensions of a world conflict. Seldom if ever had mankind been so nearly free from the scourge of war for so long a period. It is not surprising that many were hopeful that the human race was outgrowing war and that beginnings of international organization were made and still more extensive plans proposed for putting the intercourse between peoples on the basis of law.

The century was also marked by the rapidly mounting exploration by man of his physical environment. Through the scientific approach and at an exhilarating pace men pushed out the boundaries of their knowledge of the world about them and within them. Through daring hypothesis, observation, and experiment they delved into the constitution of matter, became more and more aware of electricity, peered into the stellar spaces, and began to unravel the story of the geologic past of the planet which was their habitation. By conjectures associated with the name of Charles Darwin scientists sought to understand the course of life on the planet. By methods to which the name "psychology" was given they endeavoured to disclose the workings of their own and others' minds. Anthropology and sociology were labels placed on efforts to comprehend men as animals and the manner in which the societies in which they associated operated. Through what was called economics scholars probed into the fashion in which wealth was produced and distributed.

This increasing knowledge was utilized to effect progress in the mastery by men of their environment. Steam was harnessed, at first in manufactures and then in transportation by boats and railways. Through the telegraph, the telephone, and the trolley men made electricity their servant in speeding up communication. They constrained electricity to light their homes and their streets. Through antisepsis and anesthesia surgery was robbed of some of its terrors. By the discovery of germs and of ways to control or eliminate them disease and the death rate were reduced and the span of life was prolonged. Men found new ways of fighting the pests which assailed their crops and domestic animals and of supplying more nourishment to their plants. By better seed selection and by improved methods of breeding they augmented their supply of food.

The additions to the knowledge and mastery of the physical environment contributed to great and transforming changes in the life of mankind. They made possible the industrial revolution. This began in the eighteenth century but mounted in the nineteenth century. Wealth grew by leaps and bounds. As throughout history, great extremes existed in the possession or absence of wealth. Huge fortunes were accumulated by the few, moderate comfort was achieved by a large minority, but for another minority, in some places a majority, the new industrial processes meant grinding toil, sordid poverty, and moral and physical degradation. Populations multiplied. Cities mushroomed. The largest of them attained unprecedented dimensions. A new kind of urban life arose. It was the age of the urban middle class, the *bourgeoisie*. Capitalism, private enterprise, open competition, *laissez-faire,* the reduction of control by the state to a minimum, were the vogue and were believed by many to be indispensable to the rising prosperity.

These developments had their origin and were most marked among Western European peoples, whether in the Old World or the New. They were accompanied by a general atmosphere of optimism. To be sure, there were many who were sensitive to the evils of the new order and were pessimistic. However, the prevailing temper was hopeful and expectant. Belief in progress, apparent in the eighteenth century and even earlier, became widespread among peoples of Western European stock. Man was held to be moving upward and onward towards the conquest of the evils, collective and individual, which had historically beset him, to an inconceivably happy future. He was to do this by the use of his reason and his will. The eighteenth century is often thought of as the age of reason. Yet the coming of the nineteenth century did not mean that Western man had lost confidence in his intellect. He still trusted it as a tool to ever greater achievements.

The nineteenth century also witnessed either the development or the initial appearance of revolutionary theories for the social organization of mankind and the extensive application of some of them. We have seen that beginning at least as early as the Middle Ages schemes had been propounded for the organization of society. They had multiplied in the sixteenth, seventeenth, and eighteenth centuries. They were largely, perhaps chiefly, the effects, direct or indirect, of Christianity. The ideals which had triumphed in the French Revolution were in part divorced from Christianity and were even antagonistic to it. Yet to no small degree they had their roots in it. In the nineteenth century the hopes which had shaped the Revolution continued to operate in France and in most of the rest of Europe. For a time after 1815 the old order was in part restored. The Bourbon monarchy was renewed in France with the ancient union of crown and altar, and there and elsewhere what was known as the age of Metternich, from the statesman who controlled Austria, appeared to prevail. However, the revolutionary tide ebbed only temporarily. It surged forward afresh in the 1830's and especially in 1848. In the latter year Metternich was swept out of office and into exile and the tide was once more at the flood. Democracy pulsed forward on the Continent of Europe, in the British

Isles, in the Americas, and in the British colonial territories in Canada, Australia, New Zealand, and South Africa. Under the word "democracy" several conceptions were gathered. Some of them were compatible with the prevailing *laissez-faire,* but others were antagonistic to it.

Most of the theories which reacted against *laissez-faire* were known as socialism. Socialism was varied. In general it stood for equality of economic opportunity as well as for the political egalitarianism which was associated with democracy. Some socialists, prominent among them Robert Owen (1771–1858), sought to establish communities in which there would be no poverty, vice, intemperance, or strife. In France Fourier (1772–1837) proposed the organization of industrial communities of eighteen hundred persons each in which there would be a distribution of the earnings among capitalists, workmen, and talent according to a fixed proportion. Comte Henri de Saint-Simon (1760–1825) advocated a form of socialism in which men of science rather than the Church would be the spiritual directors and in which the organization would be by productive labour. It was in France that the journalist Louis Blanc urged that the state establish "social workshops" in which the workmen would elect the managers and divide the profits.

Outstanding among the socialists was Karl Marx (1818–1883). The son of a middle class Jew who for prudential reasons had formally accepted the Christian faith for himself and his family, Karl Marx, baptized as a child, had been reared as a Christian. He attended German universities, and in Berlin came under the influence of Hegel, of whom we are to hear more later. Although he eventually repudiated the latter's philosophy of history, Marx was profoundly shaped by it. Caught up in the politically liberal movements of his youth, his enthusiastic advocacy brought him under the suspicion of the authorities and so kept him from fulfilling his ambition to become a university professor. He became more and more radical, formed an enduring friendship with Friedrich Engels (1820–1895), the son and heir of a German Jew who was a cotton manufacturer in Manchester, England, and from 1849 to his death lived in London, eking out a precarious livelihood by writing. In 1848 he and Engels issued the *Communist Manifesto,* a pamphlet which, almost ignored for the moment, was later regarded as the birth-cry of modern socialism. Marx's major work, *Das Kapital,* the first volume of which appeared in 1867 and the second, third, and fourth volumes of which, edited by Engels, were published posthumously, became the standard for the kind of socialism which was to be known by his name. In the twentieth century, as we are to see, that form of socialism was to sweep across much of the world.

Stirred by the squalor of the urban proletariat in the mines and the new manufacturing and commercial cities and the contrast with the comfort of the dominant middle classes, Marx was filled with burning indignation and hate for the institutions and the classes, especially the "capitalists," which seemed to him to be battening off the misery of the majority. He denounced the Church and believed that the course of history would eliminate the *bourgeoisie* and religion and bring the proletariat to power. He held that history was controlled by economic factors, that the society of his day had developed out of class struggles in the past, and that capitalistic society would inevitably give way to another structure. The process could be accelerated, so he contended, by political measures. He climaxed the *Manifesto* with the challenge: "The proletarians have nothing to lose but their chains. They have the world to win. Workingmen of the world, unite."

For the attainment of his aims, in the 1860's Marx led in forming the International Working Men's Association, known as the "International" or the "First International," with units in various lands. It came to an end in the 1870's. It was followed, in 1889, by the "Second International," a loosely knit assembly of workers' organizations of many shades of opinion. This in turn disintegrated, but not until after 1914.

In the meantime socialist parties were formed. In the second half of the nineteenth century they became prominent in the politics of several European countries. That in Germany which had the name of Social Democratic was especially strong.

Socialists by no means agreed among themselves. They held some principles in common, but they differed sharply, particularly as to method—whether their goals should be achieved by revolutionary tactics, with resort to war, or by slower, peaceful steps. The advocates of the latter were often known as the "reformists," "revisionists," or "possibilists."

Other social programmes were put forward. One of them was anarchism. A pioneer in formulating and advocating it was William Godwin (1756–1836), an Englishman who had been educated for the Nonconformist ministry. More prominent, and the one who coined the word "anarchist," was Pierre Joseph Proudhon (1809–1865), a Frenchman. Reacting against the growing wealth of the owners of factories through what seemed to him the exploitation of the labourers, Proudhon declared that "property is theft," rejected it and all forms of government, and held that if they lived together by compacts entered into voluntarily and not under the compulsion of the state, the innate goodness of human nature would lead men to observe their contractual obligations. He decried violence and believed that by gradual education men could make progress towards perfection. It was a Russian, Bakunin (1814–1876), who advocated "direct action" through terrorism and "general strikes" of workingmen as the means of annihilating the state and existing classes and traditions.

Bakunin's form of anarchism found a congenial home in Russia as a protest against the repressive autocracy of that realm and was known as nihilism.

These programmes for the reorganization of society were not merely doctrinaire, nor were they entirely the product of visionaries who had completely lost touch with reality. They were symptomatic of a vast restlessness, a passionate desire, especially among the urban proletariat of the industrial and commercial cities, for more of the good things of life. The majority of their formulators were not from the proletariat, but from the middle class. They attracted an extensive following because they offered a rationale and proposed concrete action for the largely inarticulate and imperfectly formulated longings and demands of the masses.

Not necessarily espousing any of these programmes, labour unions sprang up and multiplied. They sought through collective action to better the lot of their members. In many places the state attempted to suppress them or control them, but they became increasingly prominent and influential.

Another movement which was widespread in the Occident was nationalism. Nationalism was not entirely new. From at least the fourteenth century it had contributed to the growth of nation states. However, in the nineteenth century it attained such dimensions that it seemed a new phenomenon. It was a major factor in the achievement of the independence from the Turkish yoke of Greece, Bulgaria, Rumania, and Serbia. It brought about the unification of Germany and Italy. It held the United States together against threatened disruption by sectionalism. There were no European countries in which it did not make itself felt.

The nineteenth century was also marked by the acceleration of the expansion of European peoples. This was partly by migration. On a scale hitherto unmatched by any segment of mankind, Europeans thronged across the Atlantic to the Americas, especially to the United States, but also to Canada and the southern sections of Latin America. Lesser numbers, but still totalling hundreds of thousands, founded new nations in Australia and New Zealand. The expansion was in part commercial. In search of raw materials for their factories and of markets for the output of industries augmented by the new machines, Europeans penetrated to all but the remotest corners of the globe. Much of the expansion was political. Several states built colonial empires, some large and some small.

In mechanical inventions, in the industrial revolution, in commercial and political expansion, and in the growth of wealth, the lead was taken by Great Britain and the United States. The British navy controlled the seas. Great Britain had the largest commercial fleet and the dominant share in overseas commerce. It became a cliché that hers was an empire on which the sun never set. It was found in all the continents and in islands in all the major oceans.

As the pioneer in the industrial revolution Great Britain for a time held a near monopoly of its processes and of the commerce which arose from it. London became the largest city and the banking centre of the world. The United States was not far behind, although in a somewhat different way. The new republic rapidly reached across North America, annexing vast sparsely peopled areas fabulously rich in soil, forests, and minerals. Its population increased by leaps and bounds, partly by an immigration from Europe which immediately before 1914 was more than a million a year and partly by a birth rate far in excess of the death rate. That population swelled the cities, manned the multiplying factories, and poured westward, before 1914 eliminating the frontier. In both Great Britain and the United States wealth mounted at a dizzying pace and fortunes, large and small, multiplied.

Several other nations shared in the expansion of European peoples, although not as markedly as Great Britain and the United States. France built a new colonial empire in Africa and Asia. Emerging late as a united nation, Germany acquired colonial territories in areas not occupied by the British and the French. By 1914 it was more and more industrialized and in shipping and commerce was threatening British supremacy. Italy, also tardily united, picked up African territories of dubious value. Russia strengthened her hold on the northern reaches of Asia and encroached on the Chinese Empire. Portugal expanded its footholds in Africa. The Netherlands annexed more land in the East Indies, and its neighbour, Belgium, acquired possession of a huge slice of Equatorial Africa.

The Spanish Empire broke up and by 1914 had almost entirely disappeared, but from its fragments new nations of European culture emerged and increased in wealth and population. Portugal lost her major overseas possession, Brazil, but this meant the appearance of another new and growing nation of the cultural family of Europe.

The impact of Europeans and their cultures brought the beginnings of vast revolutions among non-European peoples. After 1914 these were to assume gigantic proportions, but even before that year they were spreading. The so-called primitive cultures were the first to disintegrate, notably those of the American Indians and of the peoples of the islands of the Pacific. But even so advanced a civilization as that of China was crumbling, and, without sacrificing the essentials of their inherited culture, outwardly the Japanese were becoming Westernized.

THE CHALLENGE OF THREAT

Much in the new situation threatened the very existence of Christianity. As more than once in the past, Europe was moving into a new age. In contrast with its earlier periods of rapid change, the entire human race was now involved. Until now cultural revolutions had been localized. Even the tremendous transition between 1500 and 1750 and the drastic movements which from 1750 to 1815 radiated from the United States and France did not reach all mankind. They had repercussions far outside of Europe, but the majority of the world's population, embraced as it was in China, Japan, and India, was either completely untouched or was as yet but slightly affected. After 1815, however, the currents which were ushering European peoples into a fresh era increasingly, through the expansion of Europe, produced cultural and political revolutions the world around.

By its very success Christianity might seem to have prepared the way for its own downfall. That faith had been woven into the warp and woof of the civilization of Europe: most of that continent had become Christendom. As the old order with which it had appeared to have become identified faded away or was violently swept aside, the casual and even the thoughtful observer might well expect Christianity to wane and, if it survived, to do so only in areas, largely rural, as yet unpenetrated or but little altered by the new currents. Thus weakened, presumably Christianity would be in no condition to move effectively into the areas opened by the expansion of Europe and to enter into the new cultures which would emerge from the revolutions induced by the impact of the Occident. Unless he were biased by identification with them, in the fore part of the nineteenth century the student of the contemporary scene would scarcely believe that the awakenings in Protestantism and the Roman Catholic Church, confined as they were as yet to small minorities, would prove sufficiently potent to offset the adverse forces. Throughout the nineteenth century even the convinced Christian, if he were really aware of the forces which were shaping European peoples and through them the rest of the world, could not but question whether he and his fellow-believers would rise to the challenge. He would reluctantly harbour the sobering fear that he and they were fighting a rear guard and delaying action in a losing campaign.

The forces arrayed against Christianity were undeniably potent. To many, both among the intellectuals and the masses, science, in its multiplying ramifications and amazing discoveries, appeared to be making Christianity untenable to the honest and informed mind. The evolutionary hypothesis associated with the name of Charles Robert Darwin (1809–1882) seemed to render obsolete the story of the creation of living things, including man, in the first chapters of Genesis and thus to cast doubt upon the reliability of the Bible. Stretching out as they did the history of the universe and of the earth to time dimensions which numbed the imagination, astronomy and geology discredited the chronology which the learned Archbishop Usher (1581–1656) had worked out in the middle of the seventeenth century on the basis of what he believed that he found in the Bible and which placed the creation of the world at 4004 B.C. Since this had been printed in the margin of the King James or Authorized Version of the English Bible, it seemed to many readers to be part of the Scriptures and in the minds of some of them the latter suffered in credibility. While the roll of distinguished scientists included the names of devout Christians, many others on that roster either repudiated the faith or held it to be irrelevant.

Even to list the names of all the widely read thinkers of the nineteenth century who either denounced Christianity or were lukewarm to it would prolong this chapter unduly. We can take the space to mention only a few outstanding examples. In Germany Arthur Schopenhauer (1788–1860), distinguished as a philosopher, was outspoken in his criticism of theism and Christianity, denied the priority of reason, sought to show the limitations of science, and accorded primary place to the will. Another German philosopher, Ludwig Andreas Feuerbach (1804–1872), declared belief in personal immortality to be untenable, held that Christianity had in actuality long since "vanished from the life of mankind," maintained that God did not have a separate existence, and made of Him simply a projection of men's conscience or unconscious inner needs.

Both the father and the grandfather of Friedrich Wilhelm Nietzsche (1844–1900) were Protestant clergymen and his mother and his father's mother were daughters of clergymen. Nietzsche entered the university as a student of theology but, persuaded by Schopenhauer and to the great grief of his family, abandoned his inherited faith. For a time he was under the influence of Wilhelm Richard Wagner (1813–1883), the famous writer of opera, but he later broke with him and with Schopenhauer. Through painful inner struggle he worked his way to his own philosophy. That philosophy rejected as illusory and as a handicap to life what he deemed the ruling values in Western civilization—the good, the true, and the beautiful—and stressed the will to power. The will to power through which each individual seeks to affirm and promote his own life should use, so he held, the true, the good, and the beautiful, but merely as means to that end. He declared that it was from the Jews, a chronically subject people, that there had arisen the moral standards which through religion and ethics had shaped the modern world. The Jews, so he said, possessed the will to live, but their mentality and moral ideals were those of slaves, for they exalted humility, cleverness, pacifism, mendacity, and adaptability and decried as evil self-respect, strength, hardness, energy, and exuberance. Through Jesus of Nazareth, so Nietzsche went on to maintain, the Jews had bequeathed this slave morality to Christianity. Christianity had accentuated it, proclaiming salvation to the sick, the sinful, and the poor. From it had come the movements which were dominant in the nineteenth century— pacifism, the emancipation of women, democracy, socialism, and the casting off of the yoke of the ruling classes. Nietzsche looked forward to the time when Europe would be rid of what he deemed the handicaps of the Jewish-Christian heritage and when through wars and revolutions a new ruling caste would emerge and from it would come Superman.

Ernst Heinrich Haeckel (1834–1919), an eminent German biologist who gave the weight of his great name to promoting in Germany the acceptance of Darwinian evolution, applied his findings to religion, held to a materialist determinism, and denied the freedom of the will, the immortality of the soul, and the existence of a personal God.

In France Auguste Comte (1798–1857) was the creator of Positivism, which for many intellectuals, especially in Latin Europe and Latin America, became a substitute for Christianity. He wished to apply scientific principles to the study of society and to bring all the sciences to serve the welfare of mankind. Deeply religious after his own fashion and with the *Imitatio Christi* and Dante as close companions, he elaborated a cult in which humanity conceived as the Great Being took the place of God, which had as its object the progressive welfare of mankind, and which was to possess a priesthood and forms of worship.

In Great Britain there were distinguished and influential intellectuals who either repudiated Christianity or promulgated views which shook the faith of many. Thomas Carlyle (1795–1881) began preparing for the ministry of the Church of Scotland. However, while still a young man he felt himself constrained to give up Christianity, and while he believed profoundly in God as inspiring human effort and revealed by all nature, he emphatically rejected the accepted Christian dogmas. Charles Darwin's *On the Origin of Species* (published in 1859), setting forth the evolutionary hypothesis, aroused a storm of criticism from many Christians and seemed to others to make their faith untenable. Although he did not accept all of Darwin's views, Thomas Henry Huxley (1825–1895), distinguished as a scientist, especially in biology, insisted upon observed fact as the basis of knowledge and discarded Christianity on the ground that "the exact nature of the teachings and the convictions of Jesus is extremely uncertain" and that there is no proof for the existence of the God of the theologians. Yet he was not an atheist, but rather an agnostic, declaring the evidence to be insufficient for either the affirmation or the denial of the central Christian convictions. Moreover, he advocated the teaching of the Bible in the London schools both for its literary qualities and for its usefulness in inculcating morality. Darwin himself, who had been designed by his father for the clergy and who studied in Cambridge with that purpose, was eventually an agnostic religiously. John Stuart Mill (1806–1873), in childhood and youth subjected to a severe mental discipline by his able father, James Mill (1773–1836), a thinker of distinction, helped to give vogue to a utilitarian ethics which seemed to leave little room for Christianity. However, in an essay on theism written late in life he declared that the balance of evidence favoured creation by intelligence, said that science does not refute immortality, and applauded Christ as the ideal guide of humanity.

Herbert Spencer (1820–1903), who in his extensive writings had a wide influence, believed profoundly in progress and in evolution and coined the phrase "survival of the fittest." He held that religion began with the worship of the ghosts of ancestors—ghost fear—and that it dealt with the realms of the mysterious which transcend the kind of knowledge acquired by the scientific method. In the United States William Graham Sumner of Yale, in his youth an Episcopalian pastor, followed Spencer and did much to shape the early forms of sociological thinking in that country.

Leslie Stephen (1832–1904), of Evangelical stock, on his mother's side with the background of the Clapham circle and in his early manhood a clergyman of the Church of England, became an agnostic. He declared that most men of intellect had really ceased to be Christians, even though some still called themselves such and either did not have the courage to deny the central affirmation of that religion, the divinity of Christ, treated it and other Christian dogmas as irrelevant, or hesitated to think through their faith and to part with what still seemed to them the good which it contained. He believed theology to deal with realms which are beyond human intelligence, and that Christ, far from being an incarnation of God, was merely a man and that attainment of character such as Christ's was within the range of the possible for other men.

The widely read Matthew Arnold (1822–1888), son of a distinguished clergyman of the Church of England who had attempted to fuse the new knowledge with Christianity, regretted the waning of the beliefs which he had held in boyhood. Yet to him religion was all that mattered. While he could not hold to orthodoxy, he wished England to remain religious and hoped that Christianity would be rethought in terms of the new knowledge.

The popular and respected novelist who wrote under the pen name of George Eliot, Mary Ann Evans, later Mrs. J. W. Cross (1819–1880), reared in a devout home of the Evangelical type, in her early twenties departed from orthodox Christianity and rejected a belief in God and immortality. But she kept a high moral sense and a deep and not unsympathetic understanding of Evangelical convictions and experience.

In lowlier social circles there were those who pointed out what seemed to them inconsistencies in the Bible and declared that they could not believe in God. Many of them propagated their views through public lectures and the press. They met determined opposition and some of them were haled before the courts for violations of laws which sought to protect religion. In the course of time changes in legislation permitted freedom of speech and of publication, including attacks on the Christian faith. Among the many who struggled for that freedom through repeated lawsuits and much obloquy was Charles Bradlaugh (1833–1891). It must also be said that some of these religious radicals were originally earnestly Christian in belief and had been driven to a repudiation of their early faith by those who in the name of Christianity denounced honest doubts as wicked or presented lives which were palpably contrary to Christian standards. Often the revolt against Christianity was associated with indignation against the injustices of the existing order and the connexion of the Church and the clergy with it.

In the United States, as in Britain, Thomas Paine's *Age of Reason* had a continuing and wide reading. Robert Green Ingersoll (1833–1899), son of a Congregational clergyman, a lawyer and politician of some distinction, was best known for his lectures directed against the Bible and Christianity and was heard by audiences in many parts of the country. On a quite different level was Ralph Waldo Emerson (1803–1882), from a long line of New England ministers, himself a Unitarian minister and for a time a pastor. Without attacking the historic Christian faith he departed from some of its central affirmations. Famous as a lecturer and an essayist, regarded as a spokesman for Transcendentalism, a rôle which he disclaimed, but a movement, also remote from historic Christianity, which owed much to him, he had an influence which was nation-wide and which expressed and shaped much of the self-reliant, optimistic idealism of the youthful United States. Near the end of the century and carrying over beyond 1914 in mounting effect was the non-Christian instrumentalist philosophy of which John Dewey (1859–1952) was the chief formulator and spokesman. While he distinctly disavowed atheism, Dewey gave a meaning to the word God which was far from having a Christian content. His views became the more menacing to Christianity because, issuing from his professorial chair in the University of Chicago and then in Columbia University, both institutions begun on Christian foundations, they dominated the field of education from the primary schools through the universities and thus touched most of the population.

As may be gathered from what was said of them a few pages above, many of the most popular movements for the reorganization of society were either tacitly or frankly anti-Christian. That was notably true of the kind of socialism which was associated with the name of Marx. Marx held that the proletariat needed courage, self-confidence, pride, and a sense of personal dignity and independence, but that Christianity inculcated self-contempt, abasement, submission, and humility, and thus was an enemy. By no means all socialists were anti-Christian. Some were frankly Christian. Yet in the main, even when it did not attack Christianity, socialism tended either to ignore it or to drift away from any Christian moorings which it once had. This last was especially seen in the labour movement and the later Labour Party in Great Britain. Largely socialist in its trend, in its early stages some of its outstanding organizers were earnest Christians, men who owed their skill in public speech to their training and experience as Methodist lay preachers. Yet as the years passed that element became less prominent.

Also threatening to the persistence of Christianity were the vast movements of population which were one of the features of the nineteenth century and the conditions to which the industrial revolution subjected great masses of mankind. Millions left Europe for the Americas, Australia, and New Zealand. For the most part they came from lands where churches were established by law and drew much or all of their support from public taxation and where baptism, confirmation, and church attendance had been part of the pattern of life. They went to lands where the establishment was non-existent or fading, where society was in flux, and where the Old World habits of life were not binding. In the United States they found themselves in a country where church members were in the minority. Other millions moved from rural sections where the Church was firmly integrated with the life of the community to rapidly growing cities where the erection of churches lagged behind the growth of population and where the routine and conditions of life, especially for those in the factories and in transportation, made parish life in its traditional forms difficult or impossible. The Church found the going less arduous in the middle classes, but the urban proletariat often regarded it with indifference or hostility as part of the order which was exploiting them.

Nationalism and the growing power and expanding functions of the nation state added to the threat. In the long struggle between Church and state which was as old as Christianity the Church seemed to be losing. Education, for centuries under the auspices and control of the Church, now was being made a function of the state. That meant that youth was being trained primarily for the service of the state and was being indoctrinated with the ideology to which the state was committed rather than reared in the Christian faith. To be sure, in some lands, both in the Old and the New World, the Church still controlled education and in several others, where the state was in full charge of education, religious instruction was given. Increasingly, however, the schools tended to be purely secular, not necessarily combatting Christianity but indifferent to it or ignoring it. This trend was early marked in the United States, where the absence of a state church and the inability of the several churches to agree on the form and content prevented any religious instruction from being given, except that in some places the reading of the Bible without comment and the formal repetition of the Lord's Prayer were maintained. In several countries, notably in France, the elements in control of the state looked upon the Church as an enemy and sought to debar members of religious orders from teaching. The mounting trend was to render marriage a civil ceremony, thus ushering the Church out from another important stage in life which had long been under its control. The tendency was towards making the state supreme and harnessing Christianity and the Church to its purposes rather than subordinating the state to the Christian conscience.

Moreover, Church and state were being separated. The trend was against the traditional relationship which had regarded them as coördinate expressions of the faith of an officially Christian nation. This was due to two quite different movements. The one arose from conviction within the churches themselves, partly from a desire for religious liberty for all branches of organized Christianity and partly from the belief that the Church should be freed from control by the state. The other was a symptom of de-Christianization. It was moved by enmity against the Church and its faith and was often called anti-clericalism. The former was strongest in predominantly Protestant countries and the latter was most prevalent in traditionally Roman Catholic lands. Whatever the cause, the effect was towards cancelling the position which Christianity had long held of being the faith professed by all members of a particular people. Christendom could no longer be described by that name. In what had once been avowedly Christian nations convinced Christians were becoming a minority.

That these movements menaced the very existence of Christianity is clear. They also constituted a challenge. Did Christianity possess sufficient vitality to rise to them? Would it be stirred by them to fresh creative manifestations of vigour? In earlier ages some of the challenges had proved too great. That had been notably true of the one posed by Islam. Only in the Iberian Peninsula and Sicily had Christianity regained ground lost to that religion. Some other threats had been the occasion for fresh advances. That was the case in Western Europe after the break-up of the Roman Empire and the barbarian invasions from the North. It was seen again after the low ebb which followed the disintegration of the Carolingians. It had been vividly displayed in the response through the Protestant and Catholic Reformations to the menace presented by the passing of the medieval order, by the Renaissance, and by the fifteenth, sixteenth, and seventeenth century expansion of Europe. Yet in some respects the danger was now greater than at any time since the great recession between the close of the fifth and the middle of the tenth century.

Fully as sobering was the fact that to no small degree the threats to Christianity arose from Christianity itself. Nietzsche was hitting close to the truth when he declared that democracy and the various forms of socialism were sprung from the Christian faith. As we have more than once indicated, science owed its origin and development to Christianity, albeit to an undetermined degree. Man's increased knowledge and mastery of his physical environment must, therefore, in part be attributed to Christianity. In many instances the professed repudiation of the faith was to some extent due to impulses which issued from Christianity, such as an honesty which refused to hold to accepted views without careful investigation, and moral indignation against social injustices which were ignored or condoned by those who bore the Christian name, including spokesmen for the churches. Even in the abbreviated list of those who led the procession away from Christianity which we gave a few moments ago, it is evident that numbers of those who repudiated the faith had been reared as Christians and were not led to their stand by ignorance of it. Was Christianity to be the source of its own dissolution?

Here, then, was a combination of threats which constituted a test of the viability of Christianity. Would Christianity fade out of the human scene or did it possess the power of self-renewal which would prove equal to the occasion?

THE CHALLENGE OF OPPORTUNITY

Christianity was challenged not only by the threats to its continuing existence. It was also challenged by an unprecedented opportunity. Western civilization was in rapid flux and if Christianity were sufficiently dynamic to enter creatively into its reshaping it could be more profoundly influenced by that faith than at any earlier stage in its history. The impact of the Occident was producing revolutions in all the other cultures under which men lived. Here was an opportunity to help mould the future of non-Occidental mankind. Coming as it did in association with the culture which was producing the revolutions which were disturbing the human race, Christianity met an opposition which arose from resentment against Occidentals as its supposed adherents. But it also was accorded a wider hearing than if it had not derived prestige from that association. The dominance by Occidental peoples broke down political and cultural barriers which had stood in the way of the spread of Christianity. The reduction of time-distances and the improved methods of transportation and communication made possible the development and maintenance of a world-wide missionary enterprise. The growing wealth of European peoples supplied Christians with the material means for the support of that enterprise on an unprecedented scale. Here was an opportunity greater than Christianity had ever faced to carry its message to all mankind and to make itself felt by every human being.

Preview of the Response

In an amazing fashion Christianity rose to the challenge of threat and opportunity. It did not fully meet it. The de-Christianization of much of Christendom continued. As we have hinted and shall see again and again, Christians were becoming a minority in what had once been called Christendom. Even in the United States, where the mass conversion of a partially de-Christianized population was in progress, in 1914 the members of churches were less than half the whole. Christianity did not fully keep pace with the expansion of Europe. A major effect of that expansion and of the accompanying revolutions in non-Occidental cultures was the progressive secularization of mankind. Other religions suffered from the impact of the Occident and the currents of the new age, most of them much more than did Christianity. An outstanding Chinese intellectual declared shortly after 1914 that mankind was outgrowing religion and that the Chinese were to be the first to complete that process. Yet all the major branches of Christianity experienced revivals. These were seen in the Orthodox Churches, notably the largest, that of Russia, in the Roman Catholic Church, and in Protestantism. They were much more marked in the Roman Catholic Church than in the Orthodox Churches and they were even more striking in Protestantism. That was all the more significant in view of the fact that the abounding life in Protestantism was especially prominent in Great Britain and the United States, lands which led in the industrial revolution, in the rapid growth in wealth, and in the increase in territory and population. For the first time in its history Christianity made actual its inherent genius and became world-wide. In this it surpassed the achievement of every other religion. Mankind was far from conforming fully to Christian standards. In most lands not only were professed Christians merely a minority: in the major population masses in Asia and Africa even by the year 1914 after a century of growth they were still but a small fraction of the population. Yet by 1914 nearly every culture felt to a greater or less extent the influence of Christianity.

This growth of Christianity in spite of the adverse conditions in the lands of its historic strength is the more remarkable when it is contrasted with the course of other religions. The latter were suffering from the impact of movements which had their origin in the historic home of Christianity and which were strongest in the traditional Christendom. Presumably, Christianity would have been more nearly shattered by them than were these others, for more than they it bore the full brunt of the onslaught. Yet far more than any of the others it rose to the challenge, put forth fresh life, and spread. It is to this story that we now turn.

Selected Bibliography

In a field so extensive as that covered in this brief chapter it is almost impossible to give a bibliography which will at once be not too long and at the same time cover the field with something approaching satisfaction. The following list by no means achieves this ideal. For instance, only two of the works of the many writers cited are given. Yet it may prove of some assistance.

J. Baillie, *The Belief in Progress* (Oxford University Press, 1950, pp. viii, 240). A history of the belief and some affirmations by a competent Christian theologian.

J. B. Bury, *The Idea of Progress. An Inquiry into Its Origin and Growth*. Introduction by C. A. Beard (New York, The Macmillan Co., 1932, pp. xl, 357). An American edition of a well-known work by a distinguished historian.

The Cambridge Modern History (Vols. X, XI, XII, XIII, Cambridge University Press, 1909–1911). A standard survey, primarily political, by several authors.

J. E. Courtney, *Freethinkers of the Nineteenth Century* (London, Chapman & Hall, 1920, pp. 260). A sympathetic, well-written account of several English intellectuals.

J. Dewey, *A Common Faith* (Yale University Press, 1934, pp. 87). The religious position of Dewey comprehensively stated by himself.

F. J. C. Hearnshaw, *The Social & Political Ideas of Some Representative Thinkers of the Age of Reaction and Reconstruction 1815–1865* (London, George G. Harrap & Co., 1932, pp. 220). Essays by several writers.

F. J. C. Hearnshaw, editor, *The Social & Political Ideas of Some Representative Thinkers of the Victorian Age* (New York, Barnes & Noble, 1930, pp. 271). A series of lectures by several authors.

R. N. Carew Hunt, *The Theory and Practice of Communism. An Introduction* (New York, The Macmillan Co., 1951, pp. 231). An excellent, penetrating survey, both historical and critical.

Karl Marx, *Capital. A Critique of Political Economy*. Translated from the third German edition by S. Moore and E. Aveling, edited by Frederick Engels, revised and amplified according to the fourth German edition by E. Untermann (New York, The Modern Library, 1906, pp. 869).

J. M. Robertson, *A History of Freethought in the Nineteenth Century* (New York, G. P. Putnam's Sons, 2 vols., 1930). Warmly sympathetic.

H. C. Sheldon, *Unbelief in the Nineteenth Century. A Critical Survey* (New York, Eaton & Mains, 1907, pp. vii, 399). From the viewpoint of a Christian scholar.

B. Willey, *Nineteenth Century Studies: Coleridge to Matthew Arnold* (London, Chatto & Windus, 1949, pp. v, 287). A very important survey and interpretation of religious thought.

EUROPE IN THE
NINETEENTH CENTURY
(Political Boundaries of 1914)

Scale of Miles

0   100   200   300   400   500

Chapter 46

THE ROMAN CATHOLIC CHURCH ON
THE CONTINENT OF EUROPE,
A.D. 1815 - A.D. 1914

The Roman Catholic Church suffered more from the inroads of the adverse conditions of the nineteenth century than did Protestantism. It was more intransigent than was the latter. It found itself less flexible, less able to adapt itself to the age. Yet it also displayed remarkable vigour. It put forth many new movements. Although it lost ground in Europe and Latin America, lands where it had had its chief strength, it achieved an amazing geographic spread in Asia, Africa, the islands of the Pacific, Australia, Canada, and the United States. More than at any time since the conversion of Constantine, it was a self-conscious minority. Much more than ever before it was tightly knit, under the increasingly close direction of a central authority, the Papacy.

THE ROMAN CATHOLIC REVIVAL

After the fall of Napoleon the Roman Catholic Church experienced a striking revival. As we have seen (Chapter 44), it had suffered severely from the upheaval of the French Revolution, the accompanying movements elsewhere in Europe, and the Napoleonic measures. Much of its property had been confiscated, many of its monasteries had disappeared, and its clergy had declined in numbers. However, by 1815 the tide had begun to turn and in the ensuing century a marked revival was seen.

The revival was due to a number of factors. It was partly because of the reaction against the Revolution, the desire to restore conditions as nearly as possible to what they had been before 1789. The Bourbons returned to the thrones of France, Spain, and Naples, and the King of Portugal from his refuge in Brazil. Metternich, the symbol and leader of the effort to revive the *status quo,* was all powerful in Austria and in much of Central Europe. Austria controlled large portions of Italy. All of these lands were predominantly Roman Catholic and the attempted return to "legitimacy," the pre-revolutionary order, included the renewal, so far as feasible, of the former privileges and institutions of the Church. Rome and the larger part of the Papal states were restored to the Pope. In 1814 the Pope formally revived the Society of Jesus, but without censuring the action of his predecessor in dissolving it or clearing it of the charges which had been given as the grounds for that action. The Jesuits were readmitted to France and Spain. In Spain the Inquisition was reëstablished. In France penalties against sacrilege and blasphemy were strengthened.

However, we must note that while for the moment political and emotional reaction seemed to favour the Roman Catholic Church, all was not well. That Church by no means fully regained its former position. The Congress of Vienna which effected the post-Napoleonic settlement of Europe did not return to it all its former properties. Some of the Papal lands were left in the hands of secular princes. In Germany the confiscated ecclesiastical territories were not restored. In Austria Josephism continued. More serious was the association of the Church with reaction. The revolutionary movements had merely paused. They soon again swept forward. Not unnaturally, their leaders looked upon the Roman Catholic Church as an enemy.

Another cause of the revival was the desire for security in a rapidly changing world. To many the Roman Catholic Church seemed to stand for a timeless stability, the one solid institution in an age of storm.

Still another factor was romanticism. Although among many it weakened the authority of the Church, it led others back to it. As we have suggested, some phases of the romantic movement were accompanied by a nostalgic admiration for the Middle Ages. Since the Roman Catholic Church had been an integral and prominent part of medieval life, it profited by this enthusiasm.

A much more potent cause of the Roman Catholic revival was the vitality inherent in the Church. Without it the other factors would have been ineffective.

The Roman Catholic Church was a minority, but probably more than at any time since the mass conversions which began in the third century a substantial portion of that minority made their faith and the Church a major concern.

To this there were striking exceptions. For reasons which we shall describe at the appropriate place, in Latin America, nominally Roman Catholic, the overwhelming majority were even more spiritually parasitic than they had been before the nineteenth century, dependent on Europe for many of their clergy and leaving missionaries from Europe to bear the main burden of missions to the non-Christian Indians on the fringes of white settlement. Yet in most countries which by tradition were predominantly Roman Catholic the challenge of adverse conditions, while bringing many defections, tended to make those who remained loyal more active in the expression, the support, and the propagation of their faith.

The Renewal of Monastic Life and the Multiplication of Orders and Congregations of Men and Women

One manifestation of the Roman Catholic revival was the strengthening of the monastic life. As we have repeatedly seen, an invariable expression of a forward surge of the Roman Catholic Church had been a revitalization of monasticism. It had been through this channel that Roman Catholics had normally sought to give themselves fully to the call of Christ. This had meant the reinvigoration of older orders and congregations and the emergence of new ones. Between 1815 and 1914 this experience was repeated. Numbers of the monastic houses, orders, and congregations that had suffered from the lethargy of the eighteenth century and the onslaught of the Revolution were restored or renewed. Many new ones came into being. None of the latter attained the dimensions of the Franciscans, Dominicans, or Jesuits. However, more of them appeared than in any other single century. Here was evidence of abounding vitality.

Even to list all the new bodies of a monastic character which sprang up in the course of the century would unduly prolong this chapter. Here we can merely mention and briefly describe a few of them. It appears to be significant that most of them continued a trend which had been evident in the Roman Catholic Church for several centuries. They were concerned primarily not for the salvation of their own souls but for service to others. Some were for teaching, some for ministering to the poor and the sick, and many were for missions, either at home or abroad or both. Even the contemplatives who devoted themselves to prayer gave a large place to intercession for others and for the spread of the faith. The many orders and congregations and the numerous societies, less tightly knit than the former and making fewer demands on their members, constituted a kind of spiritual army and increasingly made of the Roman Catholic Church a force for world-wide extension.

In 1815 three priests founded the Society of the Missionaries of France, with the purpose of reviving the religious life in the parishes. In that same year William de Chaminade inaugurated the Marianists, who directed schools, workshops, and boarding schools in the south of France. In 1816 Charles Joseph Eugene de Mazenod (1782–1861) began the Oblates of the Immaculate Virgin Mary. Mazenod was of the French nobility. A priest, he deplored the fashion in which the Revolution had drawn so many thousands away from the faith. The Oblates had their rise in Provence, and Mazenod designed them to be missionaries among the de-Christianized population. They received Papal approval in 1826. Their founder died as head of the See of Marseilles.

The year that saw the beginning of the Oblates of the Immaculate Virgin Mary was also that of the birth, likewise in France, of the Society of Mary (the Marist Brothers, or Little Brothers of Mary). The Society of Mary was begun by a group of students in a theological seminary of whom the retiring and modest Jean Claude Marie Colin (1790–1875) was the leader. It adopted a simple rule, like the long familiar one of Augustine. Its members carried on missions among the de-Christianized or partially de-Christianized masses. Their bishop wished to confine it to his diocese, but Colin had wider dreams, obtained for it Papal approval (1836), and as its first superior general expanded its operations not only in France but also to the islands of the Pacific. Like Mazenod, he reacted against the traditional Gallicanism of the French Church and emphasized obedience to the Holy See.

The Congregation of the Most Precious Blood, inaugurated in 1815, owed its existence in part to the desire of Pope Pius VII to revive the quality of Christian living in the Papal States. Returning to Rome after the fall of Napoleon, he was distressed by the deterioration of the faith in his domains. The actual founder was Gaspare del Bufalo (1786–1837). A native of Rome and of humble birth, deeply religious from childhood, while yet in his teens as a catechetical instructor he was called "the little apostle of Rome." He inaugurated the congregation, made up of secular priests, to conduct missions and to spread devotion to the Most Precious Blood. He himself was a convincing itinerant preacher. Pius VII saw in the congregation a means of improving the religious life of his subjects and gave it his official recognition and encouragement. The congregation spread in Italy and North America. With it were associated the Sisters of the Precious Blood, who undertook the instruction of youth and works of charity.

It was in the Rome of the restoration of Papal power that there lived Vincent Mary Pallotti (1798–1850), the founder of what was officially known as the Pious Society of Missions, but whose members were usually called Pallottines. Pallotti, of a noble Roman family and educated in the Eternal City, was ordained priest in 1820. Although possessing high academic degrees, he gave himself with selfless devotion to the physical and spiritual care of the poor and the sick. He won the respect of aristocrats, bishops, and the Pope. In 1835 he began what he at first called the Catholic Apostolate, a name soon changed to the Pious Society of Missions. Its members included laymen, priests, and sisters. Its purpose was to preserve and nurture the faith of Catholics, especially emigrants. Strictly speaking, it was not an order, for its priests were seculars. It spread through Italy and into England, Germany, the Americas, and Africa.

The Society of the Holy Ghost had its origin early in the eighteenth century, but it was reconstituted, in Paris, in 1816. Its rules obtained Papal approval in 1824. It was to find its chief fields in the French colonies. Eventually (1848) there was merged with it the Congregation of the Immaculate Heart of Mary. The latter's founder was a Jew, Jacob Libermann. The son of a rabbi and himself preparing for that profession, Libermann became a Christian while trying to win back to Judaism a brother who had been converted by reading the New Testament. Baptized as Franz Maria Paul (1826), he studied theology in the seminary of St. Sulpice, was ordained priest, and in 1841 inaugurated the Congregation of the Immaculate Heart of Mary with missions among the Negroes of Africa and America as its objective.

Two other converts from Judaism, Maria Theodore Ratisbonne (1802–1884) and his brother, Maria Alphonse Ratisbonne (1814–1884), had an important part in the beginnings of new congregations. The former inaugurated the Sisterhood of Our Lady of Sion, which had as its purpose the Christian education of Jewish youth. The latter, won to the faith while on a visit to Rome by what he believed to have been a vision of the Virgin Mary, shared in the founding of the Fathers of Sion, whose aim was the conversion of Jews and Moslems.

John Bosco (1815–1888) was responsible for the formation of what were called the Salesians of Don Bosco. The name Salesian was from Francis de Sales, for whom Bosco had great admiration. A priest, Bosco gave himself to the underprivileged boys in the rapidly growing industrial city of Turin. The society which he founded was intended to extend and continue his work. It spread widely on both sides of the Atlantic. In coöperation with Bosco, Domenica Mazzarello (1837–1881) inaugurated the Sisters of Maria Conciliatrix.

THE REVIVAL AND ENLARGEMENT OF FOREIGN MISSIONS

Several orders and congregations were founded for the spread of the faith outside Christendom. They multiplied as the century wore on. What were known as the White Fathers, officially the Society of Missionaries of Our Lady of Africa, were begun in 1868 by Charles Martial Allemand Lavigerie (1825–1892). Lavigerie, Archbishop of Carthage and primate of Africa and eventually cardinal, was a leader in the renewal of the Roman Catholic Church in North Africa. The White Fathers had their popular designation from their garb, designed to resemble that of the Moslems of North Africa whom they were at first intended to serve. However, they early extended their operations south of the Sahara into Equatorial Africa.

In the 1860's Theophile Verbist founded in Belgium the Congregation of the Immaculate Heart of Mary, with headquarters at Scheutveld, near Brussels. Its first mission was in Inner Mongolia. Verbist went with the initial contingent and died before the enterprise was well established. However, the Congregation persisted, and in time had extensive missions in Inner Mongolia, the Belgian Congo, and other parts of the world.

The Society of the Divine Word was a German order, inaugurated in 1875 by Arnold Janssen. It had its headquarters at Steyl, in Holland, not far from the German border. Its purpose was to create an institution for training and sending Germans to non-Christians. Its first mission was in China, but it later spread to other lands. It also recruited and trained missionaries, largely of German ancestry, in the United States.

In England, out of the nineteenth century revival of the Roman Catholic Church, came St. Joseph's Society of Mill Hill, founded by Herbert Vaughan, later head of the British hierarchy and cardinal. It drew its students chiefly from Holland.

Several institutions for the preparation and support of secular priests as missionaries were begun somewhat on the pattern of the Society of Foreign Missions of Paris which, as we have seen, dated from the seventeenth century and had had a large part in missions in the Far East. One, at Milan, dated from 1850. Another was in Rome.

Scores of communities of women were instituted for foreign missions. The largest was the Franciscan Missionaries of Mary, founded by Helene Marie Philippine de Chappotin (1839–1904), better known by her religious name, Mary of the Passion. In 1866 Mary of the Passion went to India under the newly inaugurated Society of Marie-Réparatrice and rose to become head of three houses of that congregation. Differences developed between her and her superiors in Europe and with some of the sisters. She withdrew from the society and, with Papal permission, began a fresh organization. After a period of intense opposition, it flourished prodigiously, and its houses multiplied in several countries.

Numbers of brotherhoods and sisterhoods were created with the primary purpose of teaching. Among them were the Brothers of Christian Instruction, begun in France in 1817 by Jean Marie de Lammenais, whom we are to meet again a little later.

Societies were formed to enlist lay activity for the care of the sick and the poor. Famous was the Society of St. Vincent de Paul. This was organized in 1833 in France by Antoine Frédéric Ozanam (1813–1853). Stung by the taunt of the socialist critics of the faith that Christianity had lost the power to stir its adherents to service of the underprivileged, Ozanam instituted a society to recruit laymen for that purpose. It spread rapidly and widely, not only in France but also in other lands.

Novel kinds of bodies sprang up to mobilize the prayers and the financial support of the laity for Roman Catholic missions. Before the nineteenth century, missions to non-Christians had very little active assistance from the rank and file of Christians. They were aided by the state, and the personnel and the financial undergirding were mostly from monastic orders. In the nineteenth century vigorous and successful efforts were made to widen the base of missions and to enroll in their behalf men and women in the ordinary occupations of life. That they were marked by growing success was evidence of mounting loyalty among the Roman Catholic constituency. That constituency might be dwindling percentage-wise in historic Christendom, but it was increasingly and actively committed to the Church.

What became the most widespread of the movements on behalf of missions was the Society for the Propagation of the Faith. It arose out of the revival of the Roman Catholic Church in France. It had its origin in 1822 in Lyons, a growing industrial centre, and in part from the efforts of Pauline-Marie Jaricot (1799–1862). In her early twenties Mademoiselle Jaricot began collecting from a circle of her friends weekly contributions of a centime a week. As the society developed, it adopted the principle of recruiting members who would pray daily for missions and give at least a centime weekly. It sent out no missionaries, but subsidized orders, societies, and congregations which did so. Its growth was little short of spectacular. Until after 1914 it had its headquarters in France, but by then it had spread to several other lands.

A sister organization was the Association of the Holy Infancy. Pauline-Marie Jaricot is said to have aided its inauguration, but its main founder was Charles de Forbin-Janson, Bishop of Nancy, and its first council was assembled in 1843. It sought to enlist children to pray daily for missions and to give a centime a week to aid work for infants and children. Like the older society, it did not send out missionaries but gave subventions to organizations that were doing so. Also like that society, it was long French in its leadership but gained support from other countries as well.

Similar to these in purpose and methods were the Leopoldinen-Stiftung, or Leopold Association, begun in 1829 and with its seat in Austria, and the Ludwig-Missionsverein, of Bavaria, dating from 1828 but not formally organized until 1838. Both arose originally from an appeal of Frederic Rese, Vicar General of the see of Cincinnati, for assistance in holding the German immigrants to their hereditary faith.

The Revival of Education and Scholarship

The Roman Catholic revival also found expression in the creation of schools, including universities, which would be frankly of that faith. Instead of succumbing to the drift towards secularism, as had many of the older universities, including that historic citadel of theological orthodoxy, the University of Paris, they were intended to be radiating centres of sound scholarship under the control of the Church and under the inspiration of the Christian faith. After their restoration, the Jesuits, following their tradition, multiplied their schools under a revised *Ratio Studiorum,* issued in 1832. The many teaching brotherhoods and sisterhoods inaugurated and conducted schools. A notable university was begun at Louvain, in Belgium, in 1834. After 1875 five Roman Catholic universities were founded in France. As we are to see in a later chapter, in the United States the Roman Catholic Church developed an extensive system of schools from the primary grades through several universities.

Roman Catholic scholarship again became vigorous. The century was not one of creative theological activity. Roman Catholic savants gave themselves, rather, to apologetics, some of the sciences, and historical studies. Numerous learned journals were published, notable books were written, and enormous collections of sources were compiled in a diversity of fields, including philosophy, archeology, history, and several of the natural sciences. Scholastic philosophy and theology were stressed. In 1879 Pope Leo XIII came out with an emphatic endorsement of Aquinas, declared him standard for theology, and thus gave marked impetus to the study of his works. Congresses drawing together theologians from many countries helped to make theology international rather than provincial or national.

The Deepening of the Religious Life of the Rank and File

The religious life of laity and clergy displayed a growing earnestness. There was a rising tide of devotion to the Virgin Mary. A vision of Mary which Catherine Labouré, a Parisian Sister of Charity, believed that she had in 1830, emphasizing the immaculate conception of the Virgin, led to the striking of the Miraculous Medal and the spread of that medal to many lands. The increase of devotion to Mary was encouraged by successive Popes and in 1854 Pope Pius IX formally declared the immaculate conception to be a dogma of the Church. By this was meant that from the first moment of her existence Mary was "immune from all taint of original sin." This gave added impetus to the cult of the Virgin. It seems to have been in this atmosphere that in 1858 a peasant girl, Bernadette Subirous, believed that the Virgin appeared to her eighteen times in a grotto near Lourdes, in France, and that at the Feast of the Annunciation she had heard her say: "I am the immaculate conception." Pilgrims thronged to the place, miracles of healing were reported, and within half a century the shrine of Our Lady of Lourdes is said to have attracted more than five million visitors. Devotion to the Heart of Mary also became widespread.

It may have been because of the devotion to Mary that added honours were paid to her consort, Joseph. Pope Pius IX proclaimed him patron of the entire Church and in 1889 Pope Leo XIII issued an encyclical enumerating the virtues of Joseph and emphasizing his position as patron.

Parallel with added reverence for the Virgin Mary went increased devotion to the Sacred Heart of Jesus. We have seen this in France in the seventeenth century in connexion with the Catholic Reformation and a fresh stage of mysticism. It was much older than the seventeenth century, but it was then given especial emphasis, partly through John Eudes and partly through the visions of Margaret Mary Alacoque. In the nineteenth century it spread through the entire Roman Catholic Church. It emphasized the sacrificial love of Christ in his incarnation and his suffering. The physical heart of Jesus was its sacramental symbol. It stressed consecration to Christ, reparation for his sufferings, and frequent communion. In the course of the nineteenth century groups, societies, and congregations, especially of women, dedicated themselves to the Sacred Heart of Jesus. Several of them bore that designation. Pictures and scapulars of the Sacred Heart multiplied. There were also such movements as the Apostleship of Prayer, the Month of the Sacred Heart, confraternities of the Sacred Heart, and the Confraternity of Prayer and Penance.

In numbers of orders and congregations perpetual adoration of the Blessed Sacrament was practised. It was by no means a new custom. It seems to have developed first in the Middle Ages, but then it was not common. It became much more frequent in the sixteenth and seventeenth centuries, in association with the Catholic Reformation. In the nineteenth century it spread very widely. Not only monastic congregations and orders, but also confraternities of lay folk observed it. Its purpose was in part to seek to make reparation for the lack of regard by the majority of mankind for the incarnation and the sufferings of Christ. Its popularity in the nineteenth century may have been furthered by the realization that multitudes whose ancestors had professed to be Christians were drifting away from the faith. It was certainly one aspect of the intensification of the faith of what was becoming the self-conscious Roman Catholic minority.

The popularity of devotion to the Sacred Heart of Jesus was by progressive stages. In 1856 the Pope extended to the entire Roman Catholic Church the feast of the Sacred Heart. In the next few decades the adoration spread and at least one state, Ecuador, was formally dedicated to the Sacred Heart. In the 1870's over five hundred bishops petitioned the Pope to consecrate the entire Roman Catholic Church to the Sacred Heart. Late in the 1890's the Pope formally consecrated all of mankind to the Sacred Heart.

Partly associated with the adoration of the Sacred Heart of Jesus was added emphasis upon the Eucharist and frequent communion. In 1905 Pope Pius X invited all Roman Catholics to daily communion. To combat the drift away from the Church in France, beginning in 1881 Roman Catholics of that country from time to time held Eucharistic congresses. These spread to other lands and eventually were convened on a world-wide scale. The custom of paying visits to the reserved sacrament for prayer and adoration increased.

In the nineteenth century there arose what was known as the liturgical movement. It is said to have received its first major impetus from Guéranger, Abbot of Solesmes, who died in 1875. One aspect of it was the discontinuation of the Gallican and local German rites and the substitution for them of the Roman rite. This phase was part of ultramontanism, the enhancement of the power of the Pope, of which we are to say more in a moment. Another and quite as significant feature was the promotion of intelligent and earnest worship, especially by the laity, and thus the nurture of the spiritual life of the rank and file of Roman Catholics, both clergy and laity. It was to swell to much larger proportions after 1914.

Associated with the liturgical movement was more attention to the music of the Church. In 1903 Pope Pius X issued *motu proprio* on church music. In it, in the interest of public worship, he set forth what he believed to be the characteristics of sacred music and commanded that these should be observed throughout the Church but with variations to suit conditions in particular countries. He declared that the Gregorian form, going back traditionally to Pope Gregory the Great, although not necessarily his creation, should be standard. He ordered that so far as possible the Gregorian chant be restored.

The Enlistment of the Laity Through Catholic Action

In the second half of the nineteenth century stress began to be placed on what was called Catholic Action. Catholic Action seems to have had its origin in Bologna in 1868 in an effort to band youth together for the defense of the Church through the *Gioventu Cattolica Italiana,* under the motto, "Prayer, action, sacrifice." Beginning in 1874 national congresses of the Catholics of Italy were held annually. Under the leadership of a Venetian lawyer, Count Giambattista Paganuzzi, Catholic Action became very influential in Italy.

Like the liturgical movement, Catholic Action was to assume larger proportions after 1914. Subsequent to that year it was to receive the Papal definition of "the participation of the laity in the hierarchic apostolate of the Church." It was under the direction of the bishops and its expressions varied from diocese to diocese. In general it was by groups of the laity in the service of the bishop and trained to extend Catholic life. It was to seek the development of the spiritual life of the individual, the family, and society. It was an attempt to bring the rank and file of Roman Catholics to a higher plane of Christian living and to make Christian principles effective in society. Catholic Action might express itself in endeavouring to win individuals to the Roman Catholic faith, in promoting Roman Catholic schools, in political activity, or in one of several other channels. It was another facet of the movement which tended to make Roman Catholics an intelligent, loyal, disciplined community under the direction of a tightly knit hierarchy headed by the Pope, striving to win the world.

The Appearance of Saints

The nineteenth century witnessed the appearance of several who were adjudged by the Roman Catholic Church to be ideal Christians and who, even before the 1950's, had been officially so recognized by solemn beatification or canonization. Two of them were John Bosco and Bernadette Soubirous, whom we have already mentioned. Among the others was Jean Baptiste Marie Vianney (1786–1859), better known as the Curé of Ars. He spent most of his life as a priest in charge of the parish of Ars, a village near Lyons. There he established what he called "The Providence" for the care of girls, and with such success that it served as a model for similar institutions in other parts of France. He became especially famous for his skill and power in the direction of souls. High and low, bishops, priests, and laity, poor and rich, flocked to him. In the last ten years of his life he is said to have spent from sixteen to eighteen hours a day in the confessional. Strictly ascetic in his eating and drinking, humble, cheerful, patient, radiating faith and the love of God, he had a singular ability to read character and to see the sins and weaknesses of those who came to him in the confessional even when the penitent would not or could not fully disclose them to him. His good judgement and his spiritual insight and faith brought to him thousands of the sick of soul or body and of those bewildered by the rapidly moving times in which they lived. We shall find parallels to him in both the Protestant and the Russian Orthodox branches of the Church.

It seems to have been significant that the age produced the only Pope for many generations who was deemed to have a character and quality of life which deserved formal beatification. This was Giuseppe Sarto (1835–1914), who as Pius X reigned from 1903 to 1914. Born of humble parents, he rose to high office after years as a parish priest, and was known as the "peasant Pope." He was declared blessed in 1951.

NUMERICAL GAINS

Although the Roman Catholic Church lost substantial numbers to a non-religious secularism, in at least three countries of Europe, predominantly Protestant, as we are to see slightly more at length later, it registered gains. These were the Netherlands, Scotland, and England. In the Netherlands the increase was due to the excess of births over deaths. Protestants did not have so high a birth rate and watched with some trepidation the growth of the Roman Catholic minority. In Scotland, overwhelmingly Presbyterian by long allegiance, immigration from Ireland, mainly of labourers, to the manufacturing city of Glasgow, produced a substantial Roman Catholic element. England saw a few conversions to the Roman Catholic Church, chiefly through the Oxford or Tractarian movement of which we are to hear in a subsequent chapter. However, here as in Scotland the increase was mostly by the influx of Irish labourers to industrial and commercial centres.

THE INCREASING AUTHORITY OF THE POPE

The nineteenth century witnessed the growing administrative authority of the Pope and with it the tightening of the hierarchical structure of the Roman Catholic Church under his direction. More than at any earlier time in its long history the Roman Catholic Church became a world-wide organization under one administrative centre operating through the territorial episcopate. Minority though it was, embattled against the new and old forces which were sweeping the world and especially Europe, suffering numerical losses in lands where it had once held the nominal allegiance of almost all the population, losses which were to mount as the century wore on, the Roman Catholic Church was more and more knit into a global community guided by a single head working through loyal subordinates, bishops, priests, monastic orders and congregations, and a devoted laity.

Perfection in this structure was by no means achieved. Hundreds of thousands of professed Roman Catholics were still only nominally of the faith and over them the hierarchy had little control. In some lands the clergy were too few, notably in Latin America, and their quality in morals and intelligence left much to be desired. With the Church in several countries, strikingly in Spain, Portugal, and Latin America, the Pope had to walk warily. The tradition of independence of Papal administrative control did not quickly die. Yet in the main the movement was in the direction which we have indicated.

The reasons for the growth of Papal power were several. One was the persistence of the spirit and actions of the Council of Trent. That gathering, it will be recalled, had been marked by the enhanced power of the Papacy and by administrative changes which enlarged the effective power of the bishops within their dioceses. Another cause was the movement towards the separation of Church and state. In predominantly Roman Catholic countries this came from anti-clericalism, namely, hostility to the Church and its influence in the government. It was especially marked in France, as we are to see in a moment, but to a lesser degree was found in other Latin lands and was also vigorous in Germany. One effect of anti-clericalism was to curtail or end the control of the state over the Church within its borders, including the appointment of bishops, and to render the bishops more dependent upon the Pope. Roman Catholics, with the tide setting against them, were inclined to ultramontanism, to look "beyond the mountains," the Alps, for support from Rome. Thus the Gallicanism which had long been characteristic of the Church in France was decidedly weakened. Still another cause was the geographic expansion of the Church. The Vatican exercised more direct control over the Roman Catholic Church in lands where it was weak or newly planted than in countries where it was better established. The Congregation for the Propagation of the Faith had suffered severely at the hands of Napoleon and in 1808 had been discontinued. However, in 1814 it was revived and much of its property was restored. It was the instrument through which the Papacy supervised and directed missions in lands where the Roman Catholic Church was non-existent or in the minority. Some of the nineteenth century Popes made much of it. Through it they exercised greater authority over the ecclesiastical structure in those lands than they could in Europe where traditions of semi-autonomy, even though weakened, persisted. This was the situation in most of Asia and Africa, in the Pacific, and in the rapidly expanding Roman Catholic Church in the United States.

The administrative authority of the Pope was augmented by increased acquiescence in his claim to have the right to define dogma. Thus, without seeking the concurrence of an ecumenical council, Pius IX pronounced that the immaculate conception of the Virgin Mary was to be held by all the faithful as true. There had long been division of opinion as to the validity of that doctrine. Now the Pope removed it from the category of the debatable and in doing so encountered no serious opposition.

More important was the action of the Vatican Council, counted by Roman Catholics as the twentieth in the ecumenical succession, in coming out flatly for Papal supreme administrative power and doctrinal infallibility. No general council of the Roman Catholic Church had been held since the adjournment of that of Trent, in 1563. Thus a period of slightly over three hundred years had elapsed without such a gathering, the longest gap in the series since the first had been convened at Nicæa in 325. In summoning it the Pope took the initiative. This in itself was an assertion of authority. He invited not only all Roman Catholic bishops, abbots having episcopal jurisdiction, and heads of orders, but also Orthodox bishops and Protestants. It was made clear that if the Orthodox and Protestants accepted, they would by that act be acknowledging the supremacy of the Pope. Obviously none of them came. In contrast with earlier councils, no secular princes were asked. This was at least partly because some of them had broken their concordats with Rome. The council assembled late in 1869 and continued into 1870.

The chief issue before the council was Papal infallibility. There were some who wished the formal approval of the dogma of the bodily assumption of the Virgin, but this was not to be given until 1950, and then by Papal, not by conciliar action. The bishops were by no means unanimous. Some held what was often called the Gallican position, namely, that only the body of bishops, and no particular bishop, not even the Bishop of Rome, could make infallible judgements on matters of dogma. With this, in one or another form, stood some of the French, Austrian, and German episcopate. On the other extreme were those who wished the enactment of the complete authority of the Pope over the bishops.

The council approved a "dogmatic constitution on the Catholic faith" to be proclaimed by the Pope. In this, because of the many departures from that faith through, so it said, Protestantism, rationalism, and nationalism, the main tenets of the Catholic faith were reaffirmed, including the relation of reason and faith in ascertaining and accepting truth. In the same fashion, the "first constitution on the Church of Christ" known, by its opening words, as *Pastor æternus,* was promulgated by the Pope "with the approval" of the council. It affirmed that "the primacy of jurisdiction over the universal Church of God was immediately and directly promised and given to Blessed Peter the Apostle by Christ the Lord"; that Peter's successors are "the Bishops of the Holy See of Rome"; that they therefore "by the institution of Christ himself obtain the primacy of Peter over the whole Church"; and that "it has at all times been necessary that every Church—that is to say, the faithful throughout the world—should agree with the Roman Church." The *Pastor æternus* went on to declare that to the "jurisdiction of the Roman Pontiff . . . all, of whatever right and dignity, both pastors and faithful, both individually and collectively, are bound . . . to submit, not only in matters which belong to faith and morals, but also in those which appertain to the discipline and government of the Church throughout the world." This, however, was said not to weaken the power of the bishops, but to strengthen and protect it. Hitting directly at the fashion in which some Catholic monarchs had insisted that all communications between the Pope and the Church in their realms be permitted only with the consent of the crown, the *Pastor æternus* held that free communication between the Pope on the one hand and the bishops and their flocks on the other could not lawfully be impeded and that it should not be subject to the will of the secular power. It also expressly declared that no appeal could be taken from the Roman Pontiffs to an ecumenical council, thus asserting the superiority of the Pope over the latter. The Pope was emphatically pronounced to have the office not "merely of inspection and direction" but also "full and supreme power of jurisdiction over the Universal Church." This power was to be exercised not indirectly, but directly and without an intermediate authority.

The climax of the *Pastor æternus* was the solemn declaration that "it is a dogma divinely revealed that the Roman Pontiff, when he speaks *ex cathedra,* that is, when in the discharge of the office of pastor and doctor of all Christians, by virtue of his supreme apostolic authority he defines a doctrine regarding faith or morals to be held by the universal Church, by the divine assistance promised to him in blessed Peter, is possessed of that infallibility with which the divine Redeemer willed that His Church should be endowed for defining doctrine regarding faith or morals: and that therefore such definitions of the Roman Pontiff are irreformable of themselves, and not from the consent of the Church." This authority was held not that the Popes might make known new doctrine, but that by the aid of the Holy Spirit "they might inviolably keep and faithfully expound the revelation or deposit of faith delivered through the apostles" and "that the whole flock of Christ, kept away by them from the poisonous food of error, might be nourished with the pasture of heavenly doctrine; that the occasion of schism being removed, the whole Church might be kept one, and, resting on its foundation, might stand firm against the gates of hell."

By this action the council, professing to speak for the entire Church, came out plumply for the supreme authority of the Pope, both as the administrative head of the Church and as the custodian of the Christian faith. This was asserted against the state, other bishops, and ecumenical councils.

Papal Intransigence Widens the Gulf Between the Roman Catholic Church and Other Churches and the State, but Except for a Small Minority Wins General Acquiescence in the Roman Catholic Church

The action of the Vatican Council widened the gulf, already great, between the Roman Catholic Church and other Christian churches. The claims set forth for that church were not new, but their reiteration in clear and emphatic form accentuated the impossibility of reconciliation with the Eastern Churches and the Protestant bodies except through acceptance of the authority of the Papacy both in administration and in doctrine.

Pastor æternus also placed the Roman Catholic Church unequivocally against the kind of control exercised in the past by several governments which were professedly loyal to the Catholic faith. It made more acute the historic conflict between Church and state, a conflict already sharpened by the trends of the nineteenth century.

Within the Roman Catholic Church there had by no means been unanimity. While in the final formal vote the council's approval was by an overwhelming majority, only a little over two-thirds of the bishops of the church were there at the time. When the vote was taken, four-fifths of those present were Italian bishops, cardinals, officials of the church, and vicars apostolic, the last named being bishops who were the direct agents of the Papacy. Even then, one of the dissenting votes was by an Italian bishop. Several of the bishops who were opposed left before the final action. Some felt that having voted in the negative at an earlier session they had fulfilled their duty. Most of the dissidents submitted.

However, some prominent Roman Catholics refused to conform, and from them came what were known as the Old Catholics. The Old Catholics had their centre in Germany, Austria, Bohemia, and the German portions of Switzerland. Their leaders were scholars, mostly members of the teaching staffs of universities. Outstanding was Johann Joseph Ignaz von Döllinger (1799–1890), of Bavaria, who had been a vocal and determined critic of Papal infallibility. For a time the governments of Bavaria and Prussia were sympathetic and the tradition of national churches in communion with Rome but largely independent of its administrative control, known variously as Gallicanism and Febronianism, favoured the movement. Febronianism had its origin on the border between France and Germany and was especially influential in the Roman Catholic part of Germany. It took its name from Justinus Febronius, the pseudonym of Johann Nikolaus von Hontheim, auxiliary bishop of Trier. In a book, *De Statu Ecclesiæ Præsenti et de Legitima Potestate Romani Pontificis,* published in 1763, with the professed purpose of facilitating the union of the churches, he had attacked the more extreme claims of the Papacy. He held that while the Pope was necessary to unity, his legitimate place was only that of *primus inter pares* among the bishops and that he should be subordinate to the Church as a whole. The book won a wide hearing. Some of the Old Catholic leaders were hopeful that union could be achieved with the Eastern Churches and the Church of England on the basis of the historic episcopate and creeds freed from Papal domination. In the 1870's the Old Catholic Church was organized. Although he had been excommunicated by his archbishop and gave it counsel, Döllinger refused to join it. No Roman

Catholic bishop adhered to it. Episcopal succession was obtained through the small church which had left the Roman Catholic fold partly over the issue of Jansenism and which had its headquarters at Utrecht. Only a few thousand adherents were attracted, but the Old Catholic Church persisted as a distinct body.

The net result of the Vatican Council and of the development of which it was a major stage was, as we have suggested, to render the Roman Catholic Church a still more tightly coördinated body under the direction of one man exercising absolute administrative and religious authority. In principle this had long been the ideal of the Papacy. That ideal was now made an actuality. More than before, although that had long been the trend, especially after the Council of Trent, the Roman Catholic Church had become a sect, that is, a hard and fast division within the total body of organized Christianity. It was the largest of the sects. It was probably represented in more countries than was any other of them. Like several of them it claimed to be the only one which had held firmly to what had been taught by the original apostles and regarded the other churches as having wandered from that faith. Its attitude precluded compromise on what it deemed the essentials of the Christian faith and made impossible in the foreseeable future an inclusive unity of all who bore the Christian name. Because of the rapid growth of Protestantism in the nineteenth and twentieth centuries, both in numbers and geographic outreach, a growth which made that branch of Christianity as world-wide as the Roman Catholic Church, in 1914 and even more a generation later, the Roman Catholic Church embraced a smaller proportion of Christians than it had in 1500, 1750, or 1815. Moreover, there was much less prospect of its attracting what was fast becoming the majority of Christians, those who were not in communion with it, than there had been in 1500 or even in 1815. Although it made some gains from the Eastern Churches, and a few slight ones from Protestantism, by 1914 it was losing heavily to Protestantism in Latin America and the Philippines, lands in which it had had its major territorial gains between 1500 and 1750.

In the meantime, as we are to see, there was emerging from Protestantism a fresh approach to Christian unity. In one way or another by the middle of the twentieth century it drew in not only the majority of Protestants but also several of the Eastern Churches and even many individuals of Roman Catholic allegiance.

THE ROMAN CATHOLIC CHURCH SETS ITSELF FIRMLY AGAINST THE TREND OF THE AGE

The Roman Catholic Church, increasingly closely knit, set itself consciously against some of the dominant trends of the age. Probably it would have done this no matter who the individuals were who occupied the chair of Peter. However, the attitude was made more emphatic because of the convictions and policies of the Popes who reigned during the larger part of the century. Leo XII, Pope from 1823 to 1829, frail, stern, hard-working, openly opposed some of the movements of his day. He denounced liberty of faith and conscience, condemned the Bible societies for circulating the Scriptures in the vernacular tongues as furthering interpretations deemed erroneous by the Roman Catholic Church, restored the Inquisition, struggled against the Freemasons and the revolutionary *Carbonari* in the Papal states, and supported monarchs against efforts of liberals. Skilful diplomacy, largely due to the policies of the able Consalvi in the preceding reign, obtained favourable concordats with several states. The brief rule of Pius VIII (1829–1830) was marked by efforts to restrict mixed marriages between Protestants and Roman Catholics in the Rhineland. Pius VIII was followed by Bartolommeo Alberto Cappellari (1765–1846) who reigned from 1831 to 1846 under the title of Gregory XVI. A Camaldulese monk, a scholar, head of the Propaganda, and a cardinal, he was in his middle sixties at the time of his election. Conservative by temperament and conviction, he opposed the revolutions which were sweeping through Italy and did nothing to reform the inept and unpopular administration of the Papal states.

When in his mid-fifties and at the height of his powers, Giovanni Maria Mastai-Ferretti (1792–1878), a scion of a noble family, came to the Papal throne (1846) as Pius IX. He ruled the Church for almost a third of a century. Those decades witnessed momentous changes in Italy and Europe. They saw a triumph of nationalism in the political unification of Germany and Italy. They covered the period of revolt against the age of Metternich and the victories of the resurgent Revolution in the constitutional monarchy in Italy, the coming of the Second and Third Republics in France, and liberal movements in much of the rest of Europe, with emphasis upon the secular state. They spanned the appearance of Darwin's *On the Origin of Species* and *Descent of Man* and the spread of the evolutionary theory with its challenge to the conception of creation held by the majority of Christians.

At the outset Pius IX was hailed as a liberal. In the first few months of his reign he instituted reform measures, including a constitution for Rome, greater freedom of the press, permission to build railways in his domains, and the appointment of laymen to office in the Papal states. In protesting against the Austrian occupation of Ferrara he seemed to be placing himself at the head of the movement for a united Italy freed from foreign intervention.

However, the apparently liberal phase of the reign was of short duration. Pius IX was essentially a conservative. Alarmed by what he deemed the excesses of the revolutions which broke out in 1848 and which swept across Western Europe, including Italy, he set his face against the new forces. It was during his pontificate that the Papal states were incorporated into the new Kingdom of Italy and that Rome was made the capital of that state. Unreconciled, he refused to acquiesce, declined the proffered financial compensation for the confiscated territories, and became the protesting "prisoner of the Vatican." Moreover, he issued momentous decrees in which he strengthened the power of his office over the Roman Catholic Church and blasted at the prevailing trends of the age.

It was Pius IX who proclaimed as dogma the immaculate conception of the Virgin Mary, who called the Vatican Council, and who affirmed, with the manipulated consent of that body, the supremacy of the Pope over the Roman Catholic Church and Papal infallibility.

The most famous of the pronouncements of Pius IX on the movements of the times was contained in what is usually known as the *Syllabus of Errors*. Issued in December, 1864, as a supplement to the encyclical, *Quanta cura,* it was addressed to the bishops of the Roman Catholic Church. It had been in preparation for some time and its subjects had been discussed with theologians and bishops. The *Syllabus* listed under eighty headings what the Pope deemed the errors of the day. Its denunciations were collected from his "allocutions, encyclicals, and other apostolical letters."

Among what were labelled as errors were the belief that God is not distinct from the universe, but is nature; that human reason, without regard for God, is the sole judge of truth and falsehood; that all the truths of religion are derived from human reason; that divine revelation is imperfect and is therefore subject to continual and indefinite progress; that Christian faith contradicts human reason; that the prophecies and miracles recorded in the Scriptures are the fictions of poets; that Jesus Christ is a mythical invention; that theology is to be treated by reason in the same manner as philosophy; that the dogmas of the Christian religion are of such a nature that human reason, by its own strength, can arrive at a true knowledge of them; and that the Church ought never to stand in judgement on philosophy.

The *Syllabus* went on to condemn the current belief that the decrees of Rome fettered the progress of science; that the principles and methods of the school men were not congruous with the needs of the age or the progress of science; that every man is free to adopt whatever religion he deems in accord with the light of reason; that in any religion men may find the way to eternal life; that there is a well-founded hope for the eternal salvation of those who are not in the true Church of Christ; and that Protestantism is another form of the Christian religion in which it is as possible to be pleasing to God as in the Roman Catholic Church.

The *Syllabus* also strongly dissented from the views that socialism, communism, secret societies, Bible societies, and clerico-liberal societies were to be permitted rather than regarded as pests condemned by repeated Papal pronouncements; that the civil power might define the rights and limits within which the Church could exercise authority; and that the obligation which binds Catholic teachers and writers extends only to such matters as are set forth for universal belief as dogmas of the faith by the infallible judgement of the Church.

The *Syllabus* dealt with the relations of Church and state and in so doing rejected as error the assertions that Roman Pontiffs and ecumenical councils had usurped the rights of princes and had committed errors in defining matters of faith and morals; that the Church might not use force or direct or indirect temporal power; that ministers of the Church and the Roman Pontiff should be excluded from all charge and control over temporal affairs; that bishops could not promulgate their own apostolic letters without the consent of the state; that ecclesiastical courts should be abolished; that the immunity of the clergy from military service should be discontinued; that the teaching of theological subjects is not exclusively a prerogative of the Church; that national churches could be separated from the authority of the Pope; that definitions made by national councils are final and not subject to further discussion; that the state is the source of all rights and that its right is unlimited; that the civil power, even when exercised by an unbelieving ruler, has a veto in spiritual affairs; that the civil power may interfere in matters which pertain to religion, morals, and spiritual rule; that the civil power should have full control of the public schools for the education of youth in Christian states; that public schools should be freed from all ecclesiastical authority; that the secular authority can present bishops and require of them that they take office before having been formally confirmed by the Holy See; that the secular power can depose bishops; that the state can suppress religious orders, churches, and benefices, and make what disposition it pleases of their properties and revenues; that in disputed questions of jurisdiction kings and princes are not under the jurisdiction of the Church but are superior to it; that Church and state should be separated; that philosophy and morals and civil laws should be freed from divine and ecclesiastical authority; that authority is nothing but the sum of numerical superiority and material strength; that it is permissible to refuse obedience to legitimate princes and to rise in rebellion against them; that the violation of a solemn oath is not only permissible but praiseworthy when done for the love of country; that divorce may be pronounced by the civil authority; that marriage is not a sacrament and that civil contract constitutes true marriage among Christians; that the state has jurisdiction over marriage; that the abolition of the temporal power of the Holy See would contribute to the freedom and prosperity of the Church; that it is no longer expedient that the Catholic religion should be the only religion of the state to the exclusion of other forms of worship; and that the Pope should become reconciled to progress, liberalism, and modern civilization.

From this long list of what he deemed errors, it is clear that Pius IX was holding to the position which the Roman Catholic Church had been taking for centuries in its conflict with the state, in its claim to be the sole custodian of saving truth, in its struggle against what it regarded as heresies, and in its efforts to shape youth and to direct the lives of Christians. The area of conflict had broadened. The state was now entering into areas which in Western Europe since the disintegration of the Roman Empire had been the domain of the Church, the education of youth and the control of marriage. Here the Roman Catholic Church found itself fighting what was largely a delaying battle in a slow retreat. Similarly, in its efforts to hold men to the faith the Roman Catholic Church was setting itself against the kind of use of reason which was increasingly becoming the accepted, almost the axiomatic mode of thought among the majority of intellectuals in the Occident.

THE ROMAN CATHOLIC CHURCH PARTIALLY ACCOMMODATES ITSELF TO SOME OF THE CURRENTS OF THE DAY

Under Leo XIII, the successor of Pius IX, the Roman Catholic Church sought to accommodate itself to some of the currents of the day and to control and direct them into channels which it regarded as in accord with Christian principles. This it did primarily in the new conditions of labour and politics. That accommodation was by no means complete. Basically Leo XIII did not depart from the principles of his predecessor. Indeed, he reinforced some of the latter's policies. However, he was more diplomatic, less negative, and instead of merely setting himself against the tide sought to guide some of its manifestations.

Gioacchino Pecci (1810–1903), who as Leo XIII was Pope from 1878 to 1903, was of a Sienese family and was educated by the Jesuits. He early displayed skill in diplomacy, and for thirty-two years was Archbishop in Perugia. In that see he built many churches, laboured to raise the intellectual and spiritual level the clergy, and was zealous for social reform and learning. Although he was lukewarm towards the *Syllabus of Errors,* he was made a cardinal by Pius IX. He openly opposed the termination of the temporal power of the Pope, would not welcome the King of Italy to his diocese, protested against the confiscation by the state of the property of the religious orders, and denounced the enactment of the Italian law of civil marriage.

During his quarter of a century on the Papal throne Leo XIII issued many encyclicals. In general these did not surrender the ground claimed by his predecessor. In stressing the education of the clergy, notably in the encyclical *Æterni patris* (1879), he based it largely upon the theology of Thomas Aquinas, thus being in accord with the loyalty of Pius IX to the school men. His emphasis upon the right of private property, his condemnation of socialism and of the control of marriage and the permission of divorce by civil law, his criticism of the theory of the sovereignty of the people and of the assertion that society arises from a social contract arrived at by the consent of its members, his opposition to the attitude of the state which placed all religions on an equality, regarding them as equally good, his denunciation of the belief that public education is a duty of the state and of the freedom of the press, and his insistence that the state recognize its duty to God and religion and to protect the Church were in the same direction as the pronouncements of Pius IX. He held to the decree *Non expedit* of the preceding reign which forbade Roman Catholics to vote or hold office under the Kingdom of Italy, thus showing his adamant displeasure at the absorption of the Papal states by that realm. He maintained unflinchingly that the features in the political and intellectual life of Europe which he deplored were the fruitage of the Protestant Reformation.

However, in other ways Leo XIII was more positive and conciliatory. While holding it to be unlawful to place various forms of Divine worship on the same level, he said that under some circumstances religious toleration by the state was permissible. He declared that the Roman Catholic Church did not repudiate the discoveries of modern scientific research and he himself added to the equipment of the Vatican observatory.

Leo XIII might have adduced as evidence for the friendliness of the Roman Catholic faith to science the fact that what became generally accepted as laws of heredity were worked out by an Augustinian monk, Gregor Johann Mendel (1822–1884), later abbot, in his monastic garden, and that Louis Pasteur (1822–1895), whose investigations greatly promoted the knowledge of germs, antisepsis in surgery, and the protection of men and animals against bacilli, was a devout believer.

In the encyclical *Libertas præstantissimum* (1888), Leo XIII held that the Church is not hostile to liberty and that Catholic governments are not bound to crusade against liberals. In the encyclical *Sapientiae Christianæ* (1890), while insisting that all Catholic political organizations give full obedience to the Church and the Pope, he said that Catholics might participate in politics, even in states not based on Catholic principles, although looking forward to the time when these governments would be thus organized. He sought to induce French Catholics to support the Third Republic, a regime which regarded the Roman

Catholic Church as a major enemy. While coming out (1896) against the validity of the orders of the Church of England, he took kindly notice of the jubilee of Queen Victoria's accession to the throne. He established friendly relations with Russia, Switzerland, and the German Empire, and so won the confidence of Bismarck after the latter's war against the Roman Catholic Church, of which we are to hear a little later, that the Iron Chancellor asked him to arbitrate a dispute between Germany and Spain over the Caroline Islands.

Abstemious in his private life almost to the point of asceticism, Leo XIII was generous in his charities. By his character and his deeds he greatly enhanced the prestige of the Holy See.

One of the most memorable pronouncements of Leo XIII, and which gained for him the popular designation of "the workingman's Pope," was his encyclical *Rerum novarum* (1891). In this he distinctly put himself on the side of labour in the mounting industrialism. Condemning socialism as a false remedy for the evil conditions under which workingmen suffered, supporting private property, rejecting the theory of the inevitability of class warfare which was postulated by Marxian socialism, and declaring that religion enjoined workingmen to fulfill contractual obligations freely assumed and to refrain from violence in pressing their claims, he also insisted that religion taught that the employer must not tax his employees beyond their strength, must not assign to them work unsuited to their age and strength, nor deprive them of their wages. The employer was commanded to see that his workmen received just wages, had time for the duties of piety, were encouraged in their family life, and were guarded against corrupting influences. Leo XIII came out for the right of both employers and workmen to organize, and therefore for labour unions. He held that it was the duty of the state to see that labour was properly housed, clothed, and fed. He said that laws should be enacted to prevent strikes by removing the causes of conflict between employers and employees. He declared that work should cease on Sundays and certain festival days, and that these days were not to be used for idleness or dissipation, but for the observances of religion. He maintained that hours of labour should be regulated, that proper provision should be made for rest, and that the labour of women and children should be so safeguarded that conditions under which it was carried on would not injure the health or the morals of either. Associations of labouring men, so he insisted, must look first and foremost to God, must provide for the religious instruction of their members, and must encourage the latter to reverence and love the Church and frequent its sacraments.

Even before Leo XIII, some leaders in the Roman Catholic Church had inaugurated measures which looked in this direction. Thus Wilhelm Emmanuel von Ketteler (1811–1877), Archbishop of Mainz, had encouraged the formation of labour unions and had advocated laws for the regulation or the prohibition of the labour of women and children, the limitation of working hours, and the provision in factories of satisfactory sanitary and moral conditions. In 1868, at the instance of a priest, Joseph Schlimps, the Roman Catholic social organizations in Germany banded together and in 1878 published a programme for social reform.

Leo XIII established in Italy what was known as the Work of the Conferences which brought together on a national scale Roman Catholic associations, including the press, popular conferences, circles, and parochial committees. In some other countries Catholic labour organizations came into being.

THE STIFFENING OF THE ATTITUDE OF THE PAPACY UNDER PIUS X

The "peasant Pope," Pius X (1903–1914), held in high honour and eventually beatified, was more pronounced in his opposition to current trends than had been his predecessor. Positively he set himself to reform some of the abuses which had crept in during the later years of Leo XIII, for that Pontiff had lived to be past ninety years of age and during his last days did not have the vigour which had once characterized his reign. Pius X tightened the discipline of the clergy, suppressed numbers of inefficient schools and seminaries, and, as we have seen, encouraged frequent communion of Catholics the world around.

However, Pius X refused to be reconciled to some of the trends in France and probably made conditions more difficult for the Church in that land.

Most notably of all, he took emphatic measures against what was known as "modernism." There had arisen in the Roman Catholic Church a minority, small to be sure, but including some very able priests and laymen, who sought to accommodate Christian scholarship and methods to the age. To the movement had contributed the widely read *Life of Jesus* (1863) by Ernest Renan (1823–1892), once a theological student but who had left the Church and who painted Jesus in glowing colours as a man, but not as God. The "modernists" applied current methods of historical criticism to the study of the Scriptures and the history of the Church. Among them were Hermann Schell in Germany, Alfred Loisy in France, the Jesuit, George Tyrrell, a convert to Roman Catholicism, in England, and the devout and learned layman, Baron von Hügel, who spent much of his life in Britain. In 1907 Pius X issued the decree, *Lamentabili,* and the encyclical, *Pascendi,* in which he commanded the bishops to "purge their clergy of modernistic infection." A number of books were banned as departing from orthodoxy, some priests were excommunicated, and several teachers were dismissed. The kind of critical scholarship which was being increasingly applied by Protestant scholars to the Bible and church history was condemned. In 1910 Pius X required all clergy having the cure of souls or engaged in teaching to take a drastic anti-modernist oath.

In 1910 Pius X issued an encyclical proscribing a kind of "social modernism," especially the programme advocated by the periodical *Le Sillon*, which advocated social action in coöperation with Protestants or those of any or no faith. In 1912 he followed this with restrictions on a practice found in Germany of admitting to Catholic syndicates all men of good will, regardless of their religion. He said that this should be done only with modifications and held (1911) that all Catholic organizations must be subject to the control of the bishops.

The Struggle in Various Countries between the Roman Catholic Church and the Newer Trends

The struggle between the Roman Catholic Church and the major currents in Western civilization of the nineteenth century was not confined to the Papacy. It was to be found in every country in Western Europe. In some it was more severe than in others. The outcome varied, but in most lands the Church suffered confiscation of much of its property, was placed under restrictions, and lost some of its former control of education and marriage.

The conflict bore most heavily on the Roman Catholic Church in France. The Revolution which had begun in 1789 continued, with varying success, throughout the nineteenth century. It seemed to be thwarted by the restoration of the Bourbons after the fall of Napoleon I, but it broke out afresh again and again, notably in 1830, in 1848, and, after the fall of the Second Empire and Napoleon III, in 1870 in the Third Republic. In general the conviction prevailed that the Roman Catholic Church and the Revolution were incompatible and that each was the enemy of the other. Thus after the return of the Bourbons Count Joseph Marie de Maistre (1754–1821) contemplated with horror the sovereignty of the people, believed that the greatest crime of the Revolution was that it sought to make men free, maintained that king and Pope were both ordained by God with absolute authority, and held that the Pope is above kings. Another of the prophets of the Restoration, Vicomte Louis Gabriel Ambroise de Bonald (1754–1840), regarded the spirit of the Revolution as "satanic," taught that the king could not be deposed under any circumstances, and was convinced that Roman Catholicism meant order and Protestantism disorder.

There were, to be sure, outstanding Roman Catholics who believed that their faith and political democracy were not reciprocally contradictory, but they were frowned upon by the Papacy. Prominent among them were Lamennais, Lacordaire, and Montalembert. Hugues Félicité Robert de Lamennais (1782–1854), a priest, sensitive and subject to periods of deep gloom, early acquired fame by his *Essai sur l'indifférence en matière de religion* in which he argued that the right of private judgement ended in atheism and that Europe could be regenerated only by accepting ecclesiastical authority. He was ultramontane and against the Gallican liberties of the Church in France. Later he came out against monarchy and advocated a theocratic democracy. He wished the Church to be freed from all civil domination. He began the periodical *L'Avenir* with the motto "God and liberty." But Rome condemned his programme and he broke with the Church and became an ardent advocate of the principles of the Revolution. Jean Baptiste Henri Lacordaire (1802–1861), led to enter the priesthood by the *Essai* of Lamennais, sought to show that Roman Catholicism was consistent with the slogans of the Revolution—liberty, equality, and fraternity—and that popular sovereignty in civil government could be reconciled with Papal supremacy in religion. He became a Dominican, hoping to rewin France to Christianity by the preaching and teaching of that order. He openly declared himself a republican. Charles Forbes René de Montalembert (1810–1870), a layman, a friend of Lamennais and Lacordaire, a political liberal, while emphatically opposed to the *Syllabus of Errors,* did not break with the Church. The ultramontanes were his enemies and some of his teachings were condemned by the Pope.

In the Revolution of 1848 which ended the July Monarchy and sent Louis Philippe into exile, the old antagonism between the Roman Catholic Church and the French Revolution seemed to have died. Partly because of the influence of Lamennais and his disciples, democracy and the Catholic faith were held to be interdependent. The bishops praised the Revolution and the Second Republic which it inaugurated. The initial National Assembly included in its membership several priests and three bishops. Under Louis Napoleon the Second Republic and the Second Empire maintained the Pope in Rome by the support of French arms as against the recently inaugurated Kingdom of Italy.

When, after 1870, the Second Empire was followed by the Third Republic, most leading Roman Catholics, both clergy and laity, were opposed to the latter and wished the restoration of the monarchy. This made the government anticlerical, and clericalism was declared to be its enemy. Restrictions on Roman Catholic influence and teaching in the schools were enacted. Priests were forbidden to share in asylums and charitable institutions, all chaplaincies in the army and the normal schools were suppressed, divorce was legalized, and Sunday labour was authorized.

Thanks in part to the conciliatory tactics of Leo XIII and in part to the desire of the leaders of the government for peace, for a time the tension between the Church and the French state was eased. In 1879 the Papal legate advised Roman Catholics to accept the fact that the monarchy would not be restored and in 1892 in a Papal encyclical urged that the faithful accept the republic.

Then, in the 1890's, in the famous Dreyfus case which shook all France for years, Roman Catholic opinion in general was against Dreyfus and the eventual exoneration of that unhappy victim of the miscarriage of justice tended to discredit the Church. In 1901 the Associations Act was passed which forbade any religious order to exist in France without governmental authorization. Authorization proved difficult to obtain and hundreds of members of orders were driven out of the country. In 1902 and 1903 several thousand Catholic schools were closed. This was followed, in 1905, by the abrogation by the French Government of the Concordat of 1801 which since that year had been the basis of the relations of Church and state. This meant the disestablishment of the Roman Catholic Church and giving it no more favoured place than other cults. Pope Pius X condemned the act and forbade Catholics to form the associations which the law required for the use of buildings for public worship. In 1907 a new law eased the situation, but did not restore the establishment of the Church.

The antagonism of the Roman Catholic Church and the Third Republic accelerated the progressive de-Christianization of France. In general the Church remained strong in the rural districts, where pre-nineteenth century conditions more nearly persisted, and was weakest in the cities, where the new currents were potent.

In striking contrast with the drift away from Christianity was the vitality in the Roman Catholic Church in France. Among other manifestations, this showed itself in new foreign missionary movements, such as the creation and rapid growth of the Society for the Propagation of the Faith, and in the leadership which French Catholics took in the overseas missions of their Church in the nineteenth century. Here the Catholics of France out-distanced those of every other country.

In Germany the Roman Catholic Church was more successful than in France in its struggle with the state. In South Germany Febronianism persisted into the nineteenth century, but then faded. In the 1830's and 1840's a contest between Prussia and Rome in the Rhine provinces over the question of mixed marriages issued in concessions by the state.

The major conflict in Germany is usually known as the *Kulturkampf* ("struggle for civilization"). It began in South Germany in the support accorded by the governments in that area to the Old Catholics in their protest against the doctrine of Papal infallibility. Those loyal to Rome found a rallying point in the Centre Party, but it was not until 1890 that they were sufficiently strong in Bavaria to obtain the repeal of the concessions granted to the Old Catholics.

In the *Kulturkampf* the main opponent of the Roman Catholic Church was Bismarck. It was largely by Bismarck that German nationalism was utilized to bring unity to that long divided country. This was accomplished by making the prevailingly Protestant Kingdom of Prussia the dominant nucleus, first in the North German Confederation, formed in 1867, and then in the German Empire, the constitution of which was adopted in 1871. Since Austria was not in the Empire, the latter had a Protestant majority, but with a strong Roman Catholic minority. For several reasons, Bismarck was antagonistic to the Roman Catholic Church. He was a Protestant. Ultramontanism culminating in the recent promulgation of Papal infallibility appeared to him to threaten with the interference of a foreign power the German unity which had been so painfully achieved. The Centre Party stood for the rights of the South German states as against Prussia and so tended to perpetuate the weakening divisions which Bismarck was determined to overcome. Bismarck was irritated by the pressure from German Roman Catholics to intervene to restore the temporal power of the Pope, for it was disturbing the friendly relations between Germany and Italy.

In 1872 Bismarck embarked on measures designed to weaken the power of the Roman Catholic Church in Germany and especially in Prussia. Diplomatic relations between the Vatican and Germany were severed. The Jesuits, the Redemptorists, and some other religious orders were expelled. In Prussia laws were passed requiring all who held office in the Roman Catholic Church to be Germans who had received the larger part of their education in German institutions and placing theological seminaries under the control of the state. When some of the bishops refused to comply, governmental financial aid to the Church was discontinued in their dioceses and additional punitive measures were taken.

The opposition proved so great that Bismarck found it wise to retreat. In 1880 diplomatic relations with the Vatican were resumed and in 1886 most of the laws against which Roman Catholics had complained were repealed.

The net result was that the Centre Party, led by Ludwig Windthorst, the former Hanoverian minister, was greatly strengthened. It championed the cause of religious liberty, won the votes of Roman Catholic workingmen by promises to support social legislation in their favour, and flirted with the Socialists. The Roman Catholic cause, far from being weakened by the *Kulturkampf,* was enhanced.

In Austria the Papacy registered gains, but gains which were partly offset by reverses. Through the concordat of 1855 between Austria and the Holy See the last remnants of Josephism were removed. Among other concessions to Rome were the freedom of communication between the bishops and the Vatican, the control of the elementary schools, the education of the clergy by the Jesuits, the surrender by the state of all share in the administration of ecclesiastical property, and the increase of clerical authority in questions connected with marriage. Yet in 1861 an edict of toleration was issued which eased the restrictions on those who were not in the Roman Catholic Church. Moreover, in Hungary, a partner in the dual Hapsburg monarchy, in 1894, against the opposition of Roman Catholics, civil marriage was made compulsory. Late in the nineteenth century Bohemia, then also under Hapsburg rule, was the scene of a movement away from Rome.

In Belgium and the Netherlands the Roman Catholic Church made advances. In 1830, Belgium, united to the Netherlands by the Congress of Vienna which had made the post-Napoleonic settlement, declared its independence and succeeded in maintaining it. It was overwhelmingly Roman Catholic by religion. It also became highly industrialized, and the supposition would have been that, in common with industrialized areas elsewhere, it would drift towards de-Christianization. As in other Roman Catholic countries a struggle between clericals and anti-clericals ensued. With some modifications, the former won. From 1847 to 1884, the Liberals, anti-clerical, were generally in control and abolished religious instruction in the public schools. This aroused intense opposition among the more ardent Roman Catholics and for a time the Belgian ambassador was recalled from the Vatican. However, in 1884 the elections gave the government to the clericals and from then until after 1914 the Catholic party was in power. Partly to undercut the Liberals and the Socialists, it enacted legislation which promoted democracy, brought in a factory code to protect labour, recognized trade unions, began a system of old-age pensions, and promoted better housing. Education was fostered to such good effect that literacy was markedly advanced. Religious instruction was restored in most of the schools. Strong Roman Catholic labour organizations were formed which had a large part in the political, industrial, and social life of the land. In the predominantly Protestant Netherlands Roman Catholics mounted in numbers, chiefly, as we have said, because of the excess of births over deaths, and in 1853 the Vatican created a hierarchy for the country.

In Scandinavia, nearly solidly Lutheran since the sixteenth century, religious toleration gave opportunity for the growth of Roman Catholics. In Norway toleration was enacted in 1845, in 1892 a bishop was consecrated, and in 1897 most of the remaining legal disabilities of Roman Catholics were removed. In Denmark religious freedom was granted in 1849 and the first vicar apostolic was appointed in 1892. It was not until 1873 that a Swedish law permitted departure from the state church, and then only for those over eighteen years of age.

The Roman Catholic Church faced official opposition in Russia, committed as was that realm to the Orthodox Church. Especially stringent measures were taken in those portions of Poland which were under Russian rule, for there the

Roman Catholic Church, historically very strong, was regarded with suspicion as a possible rallying centre of Polish nationalism. Revolts in 1831 and 1863 accentuated Russian apprehensions. After the rebellion of 1863, in which some of the clergy were active, religious orders were suppressed and diplomatic relations between Russia and the Vatican were discontinued. In 1839 what is said to have been a total of about two million Uniates who had been constrained by the Polish authorities to assume that status after the merger formally effected at Brest in 1596, resumed their connexion with the Orthodox Church. More followed in 1875. In connexion with the varied revolutionary movements in the Russian Empire which took advantage of the Russo-Japanese War to come to a head in 1905, a group of Poles who combined "modernistic" views with the veneration of Mary broke from the Roman Catholic Church and found fellowship with the Old Catholics.

In linguistically and religiously diverse Switzerland friction developed which in 1847 led to civil war. The Catholic *Sonderbund* was defeated. However, under the constitution of 1848, while religious orders, including the Jesuits, were not permitted in any canton, religious liberty was accorded all Christians, and many Roman Catholics and Protestants moved into cantons which had hitherto been restricted to the opposite form of the faith. The constitution of 1874 was deemed by Roman Catholics to have placed them at a serious disadvantage and relations between the Swiss Government and the Vatican became strained.

In Spain, Portugal, and Italy, where, with the exception of the small Waldensian minority in the last named country, the Roman Catholic faith had long been the only religion, the nineteenth century was peculiarly stormy for that Church. The liberalism which was the child of the movement that had produced the French Revolution often found the Roman Catholic Church a major opponent and through various organizations, including the Freemasons, had anti-clerical manifestations.

In Spain the record was especially violent and marked by sharp extremes. As we have seen, Ferdinand VII, the returning Bourbon who was restored by the British in 1814, revived the old order, including the Inquisition and the Jesuits. In 1820 opposition exploded in an insurrection. This led (1823) to the intervention of a French army in support of the king. Back in full control, Ferdinand VII was even more fanatical in his suppression of liberalism. Following his death (1833) civil war broke out between contenders for the throne. The liberals gave their support to Christina, the mother and regent of the youthful Isabella II, daughter of Ferdinand, while in general the clericals rallied to the support of Don Carlos, the brother of Ferdinand. The Pope endeavoured to remain neutral. The forces of Isabella were victorious and her government banished the Jesuits, suppressed almost all the monasteries, confiscated their property, and refused to appoint bishops acceptable to the Vatican. In 1841 the number of bishops in Spain had been reduced to six. Isabella's rule satisfied neither the liberals nor the Roman Catholics. In 1868 an insurrection sent the incompetent and immoral Isabella into a French exile and was the prelude to seven years of civil strife with vain attempts at union, first under an Italian prince and then, even more briefly, under a republic. During these chaotic years anti-clericalism was rampant. In 1875 the Bourbons were restored in the person of Alphonso XII, son of Isabella II, and on his death (1885) the throne passed to his posthumous son, Alphonso XIII. Under Alphonso XII anti-clericalism was checked and the Jesuits and other religious orders returned, flourished, and had charge of the schools in which more than half of such of the youth as were educated were enrolled. The Queen-mother, Maria Christina, who served as regent during the minority of Alphonso XIII, was loyal to the Church, but did not hesitate to call a liberal to be her premier. For a time in 1909–1910, after Alphonse XIII came of age (1902), anti-clericals were sufficiently strong to have Protestant worship legalized and to prohibit the founding of new religious houses without government consent. Diplomatic relations with the Vatican were temporarily broken off, but were renewed in 1912.

The majority of Spaniards remained Roman Catholics. Their Roman Catholicism was singularly rigid, true to the tradition which both had given rise to the Inquisition and had been enforced by it. Spanish foreign missions were continued, but they were pale and attenuated when compared with their predecessors in the sixteenth and seventeenth century heyday of Spanish power. Moreover, there were those who either broke with the Church or remained only loosely attached to it. Some thought vigorously and independently. Notable among them was Miguel de Unamuno y Jugo (1864–1936), a university professor, whose writings were widely read and were known far beyond the borders of Spain.

In Portugal the nineteenth century was marked, as in Spain, by political struggles in which anti-clericalism was a marked feature. The House of Braganza occupied the throne until 1910, when it was overthrown and a republic established. As in Spain, the population was overwhelmingly Roman Catholic, but, also as in Spain, Freemasonry became a rallying centre of anti-clericals and there were liberals, socialists, and republicans. Elective, representative institutions made headway. From 1831 to 1840 anti-clericalism held sway. The Jesuits were expelled, religious orders were dissolved and their properties confiscated, the clergy were not allowed to administer the sacraments without the permission of the civil authorities, the crown exercised the power to appoint to all ecclesiastical offices from the bishops to the parish priests, and some of the episcopate were consecrated without so much as notifying the Pope. While, after 1840, confiscated religious properties were returned and uneasy relations were renewed with the Vatican, the state continued to control theological education. In several dioceses the populace refused to accept the bishops appointed by the crown. The Concordat of 1886 permitted the Pope to appoint the bishops on the nomination of the crown. Some years later religious orders were allowed under certain restrictions. The republic was strongly anti-clerical. In 1911 the religious orders were expelled, their properties were taken over by the government, and the formal separation of Church and state was carried through. In 1913 relations with the Holy See were severed. Yet, as in Spain, so far as the masses had a religion it was Roman Catholicism. Secularism made headway, especially among the intellectuals and the upper classes, but Protestantism had few adherents. Overseas missions were continued, but feebly, and were confined almost entirely to the Portuguese colonial possessions.

In the first decades after 1815 many of the leaders of the nationalism which was sweeping across Italy advocated the political unification of that long-divided country under the presidency of the Pope. Indeed, in 1847 the colourful and popular patriot, Garibaldi, offered his services to the Pope. However, after his initial brief liberal period, Pius IX became an opponent of Italian unity and the effective leadership passed to the Kingdom of Sardinia and its ruling family, the House of Savoy (which had its chief territories in Piedmont), engineered by the extremely able premier, Cavour. Cavour (1810–1861), a liberal, was strongly anti-clerical. Under the slogan, "A free Church in a free state," he expelled the Jesuits and suppressed many of the monasteries. In 1860 much of North Italy came over to the House of Savoy and a revolution in the Kingdom of the Two Sicilies (Sicily and South Sicily, with the capital at Naples), led by Garibaldi, drove out the decrepit Bourbons and brought their realm into the Kingdom of Italy, formed under the House of Savoy. In 1866 Venetia was annexed. Supported by French bayonets, until 1870 the Pope precariously held on to Rome and a small area about it. Then the Franco-Prussian War led to the withdrawal of the troops of Napoleon III and in September an Italian army entered the city. In 1871 the Italian Government sought to mollify the Pope by the "law of Papal guarantees." It offered the Pope the status of a reigning sovereign with full authority over the two chief Papal properties in Rome, the Vatican and the Lateran, and the Papal summer resort, the villa of Castel Gandolfo, and, as an indemnity for the loss of the Papal states, a substantial annual pension. To this Pius IX refused to accede, holding that it was unilateral action by the Kingdom of Italy and had not been arrived at by a concordat as between equals. He appealed to Catholic princes to restore his temporal power and in 1868 (through the decree *non expedit*) forbade Roman Catholics to vote or hold office under the new regime. Yet, although it confiscated much of the property of the Church, reduced by several thousands the number of monasteries, made it difficult for some bishops to assume office, and put all works of charity under the state, the Italian Government continued to pay the salaries of the clergy, permitted religious instruction in the schools, did not require a civil ceremony before the religious ceremony of marriage, and did not offend Papal convictions by sanctioning divorce. However, although the large majority ignored the Papal prohibition, the abstention of the more loyal Roman Catholics from the government left the state in the hands of those lukewarm to the Church or hostile to it and thus heightened the division between Church and state, weakening them both.

The tension was gradually relaxed. King Victor Emmanuel, under whom Italian unification was achieved, on his death bed (1878) was reconciled to the Church. His successor and Leo XIII exchanged courtesies on the latter's accession (1878) and that same year the government deleted clauses which were offensive to the bishops in the documents which they were required to fill out when drawing their salaries from the state. From time to time Leo XIII permitted Catholics to vote in local elections. In 1905 Pius X made it possible for the faithful to vote in national elections. Almost all Italians remained nominally Roman Catholic and there were flourishing Italian foreign missions. Yet much of religious indifference existed.

SUMMARY

In Western Europe, the home and traditional centre of the Roman Catholic Church, the nineteenth century record was one of contrasts.

On the one hand, the currents which had been flowing strongly against the faith of that Church in the eighteenth century continued and were augmented by others which issued from the new political, economic, social, and intellectual movements of the day. Many liberals regarded the Church as an enemy. In countries which had been the main strongholds of the Roman Catholic faith thousands of monastic houses were dissolved and their properties confiscated, and the education of youth was in part taken out of the hands of the Church. In several marriage was put under the control of the state, and in France Church and state were formally separated. The Popes were deprived of the territories upon which they had depended to make them politically independent. The Popes set themselves resolutely against these currents, and, condemning them, sought to stem them. Thus the distinction between the Church and the world was made sharper than at any time since the conversion of Constantine. In some respects the Roman Catholic Church lost ground. The de-Christianization of large elements of the population proceeded apace.

On the other hand, after the storm of the French Revolution and the cavalier treatment by Napoleon Bonaparte, the Roman Catholic Church made a striking recovery. Religious orders which had suffered severely were revived in part or in whole. New religious orders arose. Between 1815 and 1914 more seem to have come into being than in any previous hundred years. In general the devotion of the rank and file of the laity who remained faithful was increased. Fresh agencies for Catholic action by the laity began to be developed. Notably in Germany and Belgium, Catholic labour unions were organized, partly offsetting the secular labour organizations, and Catholic political parties appeared. A larger proportion of the laity were stirred to give financial support to the world-wide extension of the faith than ever before. Roman Catholic missions attained a geographic and numerical extent never before equalled. Papal administrative authority in the Roman Catholic Church was greatly augmented, and Papal infallibility in questions of faith and morals was formally affirmed. The Roman Catholic Church more and more took on the aspect of a militant minority, represented in more and more lands, and knit together and directed by the central authority in Rome. None of the Popes of the century was corrupt. The earlier ones were rigidly intransigent and of only moderate ability. The two later ones were of outstanding character. The next to the last, Leo XIII, was a man of first-class ability and brought the prestige of the office to a higher point than it had reached since the Reformation. The last, Pius X, was the first in several hundred years to be deemed worthy of beatification with the prospect of canonization.

Selected Bibliography

J. B. Bury, *History of the Papacy in the 19th Century* (*1864–1878*) (London, Macmillan & Co., 1930, pp. lx, 175). By a distinguished historian, covering the *Syllabus of Errors* and the Vatican Council.

C. Butler, *The Vatican Council. The Story Told from the Inside in Bishop Ullathorne's Letters* (New York, Longmans, Green & Co., 2 vols., 1930). By a Roman Catholic monk.

C. C. Eckhart, *The Papacy and World-Affairs as Reflected in the Secularization of Politics* (The University of Chicago Press, 1937, pp. xiv, 309). Mostly on the pre-nineteenth centuries.

M. Heimbucher, *Die Orden und Congregationen der katholischen Kirche* (Paderborn, Ferdinand Schöningh, 2 vols., 1897). A useful compendium.

H. Hermelink, *Das Christentum in der Menschheitsgeschichte von der Französischen Revolution bis zur Gegenwart, Vol. I, 1789–1835* (Stuttgart and Tübingen, J. B. Metzlersche Buchhandlung and Herman Leins, pp. xix, 528).

F. R. Hoare, *The Papacy and the Modern State. An Essay on the Political History*

of the Catholic Church (London, Burns, Oates & Washbourne, 1940, pp. xiv, 413).
By a Roman Catholic, mainly on the nineteenth century.

E. Hoçedez, *Histoire de la Théologie au XIX Siècle* (Paris, Desclée de Brouwer,
3 vols., 1947, 1948). The standard survey of Roman Catholic theology in the nineteenth century, by a Jesuit.

H. L. Hughes, *The Catholic Revival in Italy (1815–1915)* (London, Burns, Oates
& Washbourne, 1935, pp. xii, 177). Sympathetic with the Roman Catholic Church.

P. Hughes, *The Popes' New Order. A Systematic Summary of the Social Encyclicals and Addresses from Leo XIII to Pius XII* (London, Burns, Oates & Washbourne, 1943, pp. viii, 232). Useful as a summary, but usually not giving the precise
texts.

J. Husslein, *Social Wellsprings. Fourteen Documents by Pope Leo XIII* (Milwaukee, The Bruce Publishing Co., 1940). A useful compilation, by a Jesuit.

J. Husslein, *The Christian Manifesto. An Interpretative Study of the Encyclicals
Rerum Novarum and Quadragesimo Anno of Pope Leo XIII and Pope Pius XI*
(Milwaukee, The Bruce Publishing Co., 1931, pp. xxiv, 329). By a Jesuit.

C. K. Murphy, *The Spirit of Catholic Action* (London, Longmans, Green & Co.,
1943, pp. xi, 197). Describes Catholic Action in simple terms, chiefly for Catholics.

J. H. Nichols, *Democracy and the Churches* (Philadelphia, The Westminster
Press, 1951, pp. 298). By a Protestant scholar, dealing with both Protestantism and
Roman Catholicism, chiefly in the nineteenth and twentieth centuries, critical of the
Roman Catholic Church.

F. Nielsen, *The History of the Papacy in the XIXth Century,* translated under the
direction of A. J. Mason (London, John Murray, 2 vols., 1906). Objective, through
the reign of Pius IX.

F. Nippold, *The Papacy in the 19th Century,* translated by L. H. Schwab (New
York, G. P. Putnam's Sons, 1900, pp. iv, 372). Critical of the Papacy.

C. S. Phillips, *The Church in France 1789–1848: A Study in Revival* (London,
A. R. Mowbray & Co., 1929, pp. viii, 315). Scholarly.

C. S. Phillips, *The Church in France 1848–1907* (London, Society for Promoting
Christian Knowledge, 1936, pp. 341). Carefully done.

C. Poulet, *A History of the Catholic Church,* translated and adapted by S. A.
Raemers (St. Louis, B. Herder Book Co., Vol. II, 1948, pp. xxi, 735). A useful handbook, by a Roman Catholic.

P. Schaff, *The Creeds of Christendom, with a History and Critical Notes* (New
York, Harper & Brothers, Vol. II, 1877, pp. vii, 607). Valuable for the Latin text
and English translation of the *Syllabus of Errors* of Pius IX and the encyclical *Im-
mortale Dei* of Leo XIII.

J. Schmidlin, *Papstgeschicte der neuesten Zeit* (Munich, Josef Kosel & Friedrich
Pustet, 3 vols., 1933–1936). Covers the period from 1800 to 1922. A continuation of
the famous work of Pastor, by a competent Roman Catholic scholar. Based largely
upon the archives.

W. J. S. Simpson, *Roman Catholic Opposition to Papal Infallibility* (London, John Murray, 1909, pp. xv, 374). Sympathetic with the opposition.

E. Soderino, *Leo XIII Italy and France* (London, Burns, Oates & Washbourne, 1935, pp. viii, 280). Sympathetic with Leo XIII, based upon careful research.

Miguel de Unamuno y Jugo, *The Tragic Sense of Life,* translated by J. E. C. Flitch (London, Macmillan & Co., 1921, pp. xxxv, 332).

Chapter 47

PROTESTANTISM ON THE CONTINENT OF EUROPE, A.D. 1815 - A.D. 1914

As we have suggested, the Protestant wing of Christianity was not as adversely affected by the dominant currents in the Occident of the nineteenth century as was the Roman Catholic wing. In proportion to its geographical distribution and its numerical strength at the outset of the century, it had a much greater expansion than did the Roman Catholic Church. It displayed much more creativity than did the latter. From it issued far more novel movements, both in visible organizations and in thought. The Roman Catholic Church, as we saw in the last chapter, exhibited amazing vitality. In it there arose many expressions of a pulsing vigour. Yet most of these, whether monastic congregations or forms and objects of worship, largely fitted into existing patterns. Here and there were quite fresh creations, among them Catholic Action, Catholic labour unions, Catholic political parties, and new ways of enlisting the support of the laity for missions. By and large, however, the vitality of the Roman Catholic Church found vent in familiar stereotypes inherited from earlier ages. Led by the Popes, the Roman Catholic Church expressly disavowed an evolutionary growth in doctrines. In contrast, Protestantism, while in general holding to the historic convictions which it shared with the Roman Catholic Church and the Orthodox Churches, gave birth to an astonishing number of fresh movements, many of which we shall see as we pursue our narrative. Among them were new denominations, the Young Men's and Young Women's Christian Associations, scores of missionary societies, a rich and varied outpouring of hymns, original methods of presenting the Christian faith to non-Christians, a mounting number of organizations and associations for coöperation across confessional and denominational boundaries, and new approaches to the study of the Bible, theology, and the history of Christianity.

To be sure, many of the trends in Western civilization worked adversely to Protestantism, as they did to other forms of the faith. Some of the programmes for the reorganization of society, such as anarchism and Marxist socialism, were frankly anti-Christian. The drift of intellectuals away from the faith was seen in traditionally Protestant peoples as well as those of Roman Catholic and Orthodox background. The forms of community life which arose from the industrial revolution, such as factories and the manufacturing and mining towns and cities, and the passing of the older, agricultural order, presented problems to Protestantism as well as to the Roman Catholic Church. In Protestant as in Roman Catholic and Orthodox lands the de-Christianization of some elements of the population was occurring. Yet Protestantism did not suffer as striking or as extensive losses as did the Roman Catholic Church.

The reasons for the greater success of Protestantism in the nineteenth century were complex. Some of them are in part conjectural or at least debatable. One of them obviously was the fact, to which we have already called attention, that it was the predominantly Protestant Great Britain and United States which had the largest increase in wealth, population, and territory. Probably another was that Protestantism was more congenial than Roman Catholicism to the kind of liberal democracy which was having the widest spread of any of the political and social programmes of the age. That form of democracy had its main origin and chief expression in Great Britain and the United States, was intimately associated with Protestantism, and was to no small degree the fruit of the more radical wing of that branch of Christianity. Closely related to this last was still another. As Pius IX rightly discerned, an historic connexion existed between Protestantism and the rationalistic humanism which was potent in the intellectual and social movements of the day. The two were by no means identical, but more convinced Protestants than devout Roman Catholics were willing to bring to the tenets and documents of their faith the assumptions, findings, and procedures of the science and philosophy of the age. This led to the greatest ferment in theology that had been seen since the thirteenth and sixteenth centuries. It was possibly more daring and creative than anything in theology since the fourth century. A factor, and one which is so palpable as not to be debatable, was the vitality inherent in Protestantism and which was already apparent in the surge of life that before 1815 was beginning to find expression in Pietism, the Evangelical Awakening in the British Isles, and the revivals in the United States. Increasing in the nineteenth century, that surge of life cut across denominational and confessional lines and in one or another form was seen in all the main and many of the minor branches of Protestantism.

In this chapter we will describe Protestantism on the Continent of Europe. In the next chapter we shall see it in the British Isles. Later chapters will trace its course, along with that of Roman Catholicism, in the United States and other countries.

On the Continent of Europe, as elsewhere, any attempt at a comprehensive, accurate picture must face a complex action and interaction of movements. Individually, in groups, and in churches, Christians were played upon by diverse and often contradictory forces. Some were from the general environment and some from within the several Christian bodies. In addition to the factors external to the churches which we have mentioned, there were many currents within these organizations. Much of the rationalism associated with the eighteenth century and the "Enlightenment" continued. Numbers of Christian intellectuals, repelled by this rationalism, moved towards romanticism. Others repudiated both. Kant was a pervasive influence. Theologies were formulated which showed the effects of several preceding systems but went on to partially fresh approaches and conclusions. The older orthodoxy, holding to the historic confessions and creeds, had a striking revival, rejecting both the rationalism of the *Aufklärung* and some of the newer philosophical and theological speculations and methods of Biblical study. Pietism persisted and spread, reinforced and paralleled by somewhat similar movements in the British Isles and the United States. Many new efforts for welfare issued from men and women of Christian faith. Here was a prolific ferment which was evidence of abounding vitality.

Here was also great peril. The very flexibility and diversity of Protestantism might mean the abandonment by that branch of Christianity of historic and distinctive Christian convictions. Many Roman Catholics believed that this was taking place. In some of the extreme expressions of Protestantism it was undoubtedly occurring. It was the risk which Protestants took, whether consciously or unconsciously. Yet the "exceeding greatness of the power" inherent in Christianity was very much in evidence, probably more so than in any other branch of the faith.

PROTESTANTISM IN GERMANY

On the Continent it is fitting that we should first address ourselves to Germany, for it was in that country that Protestantism had its rise, it was there that the oldest form of Protestantism, Lutheranism, had its chief stronghold, and there the Reformed Churches, while a minority, were vigorous. In the German universities in the nineteenth century theological thought and a kind of study of the Bible and of the history of Christianity flourished which gained wide circulation in the Protestant world. In Germany, indeed, most of the trends and currents which we noted in the last paragraphs had expressions, many of them with repercussions far beyond that land.

The religious developments of nineteenth century Germany were intertwined with other aspects of that country's life. Germany experienced a remarkable awakening and showed a creativity which had many facets. Politically, as we saw in the last chapter, a wave of nationalism which was in part a reaction against the conquests and drastic measures of Napoleon and also in part a fruit of the French Revolution brought the large majority of Germans into a new empire. In this unification Prussia, predominantly Protestant, took the lead. A strong liberal movement came to a climax in the revolutionary year of 1848, but it suffered defeat and it was through the conservatives, led by Bismarck, and through "blood and iron" that the consolidation of Germany was achieved. In that consolidation Austria, prevailingly Roman Catholic, was left out. It was through Protestant, largely conservative Protestant Prussia, that it was attained. Literature and music had a flowering which was the admiration of the Occident. The universities became centres of intellectual activity in philosophy, the natural sciences, and historical, literary, and social study which attracted students from most of the Western world, and particularly from those lands in which Protestantism was strong—Scandinavia, the Netherlands, Switzerland, Great Britain, and the United States. Towards the end of the century industry mounted. Germany became highly industrialized and won a rapidly growing share in the world's commerce. Rather late, in the 1880's, it began to build a colonial empire and entered into competition with Great Britain and France, the major colonial powers of the century.

This abounding and varied vitality was paralleled by religious awakenings. These were seen, as we have hinted, in the Roman Catholic Church. They were even more prominent in Protestantism. The deadening influence of eighteenth century rationalism was passing. In a variety of ways German Protestantism was blossoming forth in what promised a rich harvest.

Fully as much as in any other country there was diversity. Rationalism, romanticism, the newer philosophies, including notably those of Kant and Hegel, the older creedal or confessional orthodoxy, Pietism, and new currents from British and American Protestantism, all had their effect. Also of importance were the official churches, the *Landeskirchen,* by which German Protestantism was organized. The division of Germany into many states and cities, large and small, in 1815 largely independent of one another, combined with the principle of *cuius regio, eius religio* inherited from the Reformation and post-Reformation struggles, made for variety. The political unification of Germany in the third quarter of the nineteenth century did not completely erase it. It was to be reckoned with even beyond 1914.

PROTESTANT SCHOLARSHIP IN NINETEENTH CENTURY GERMANY

It was most strikingly in Germany that the challenge was daringly accepted by Protestants: could the intellectual forces first released by the Renaissance, themselves in part the product of Christianity, be reconciled with the faith and be used to enrich its insights into the meaning of what Christians believed had been revealed and wrought by God in Jesus Christ? To this question the Roman Catholic Church had given an emphatic no. Some Protestants were to do the same, and, like the Roman Catholic Church, to hold tenaciously to inherited beliefs. In wrestling with the issue some other Protestants felt constrained to give up the faith. Still others were convinced that they had met the challenge and that in doing so had come to a deeper understanding of the Gospel. However, it is significant that in general those Protestants who were most active in propagating the faith were the least reconciled to the interpretations given by the German theologians and Biblical scholars of the "modern" schools. The labours of the latter, honest and earnest though they were, took from those Christians who followed them something of conviction and urge to share the faith with others. This might be an indication that they had not met the challenge with entire success.

Even to sketch the entire outline of German Protestant theology and Biblical and historical scholarship in the nineteenth century would extend these pages far beyond their proper length. We must content ourselves with singling out only the main figures, and them only briefly. We turn first of all to theology.

In theology the outstanding thinker of the first part of the century was Friedrich Daniel Ernst Schleiermacher (1768–1834). He exerted a prolonged and wide influence both in Germany and in several other countries. His father was an army chaplain and his mother, earnestly religious, was from a family high in the Reformed Church. His father had been profoundly moved by the Moravians. It was to them that he entrusted the education of his son and to them and their Pietism the latter was indebted to the end of his days. In later years he declared himself to be still one of them, "only of a higher order," and his theology was based upon what he called *Gefühl,* roughly but not with entire accuracy translated as "feeling," perhaps better, but somewhat paraphrased, as "religious experience." In the Moravian school in which his father had placed him the discipline was supposed to induce the experience of the risen Christ. This did not come to him. While emotionally he remained a Moravian, he had a marked critical faculty. It was first stirred by Kant. In the Moravian school in which young Schleiermacher was enrolled, Kant's writings, then in their first heyday, were forbidden. He obtained a copy, read it with his roommate behind drawn curtains, and was thrilled. He went to the University of Halle, where Kant was being studied, there to gain more familiarity with him. While still in his youth he became acquainted with other philosophers, ancient and modern, among them Plato, Spinoza, Leibnitz, Fichte, and Schelling, but Kant remained a profoundly moulding influence.

Ordained, in his late twenties and early thirties Schleiermacher was chaplain in a hospital in Berlin and there became a member of a fashionable circle of young intellectuals, some of them rationalists and some of them romanticists who had reacted against both orthodox theology and the rationalism and moralism of the Enlightenment. It was primarily to them that he addressed his first work, *Reden über die Religion, an die Gebildeten unter ihren Verächtern* ("Discourses on Religion to the Cultured among Its Despisers"). In it he argued that what his friends believed that they were rejecting was not really religion, for religion is not primarily a set of dogmas to be accepted by the reason nor a system of ethics, but arises from *Gefühl* and is based upon it. The book made a profound impression.

For a time Schleiermacher was a pastor in Pomerania and next was professor of theology and philosophy at the University of Halle. For the last twenty-seven years of his life he lived in Berlin, where he was minister in Holy Trinity Church and professor of theology in the newly organized University of Berlin. While holding his professorial post he continued to preach and to carry on his duties as pastor. As a preacher he was not emotional but was clear, forceful, and attracted large congregations. Patriotic, he worked earnestly for the recovery of independence from Napoleon, reinforced the national spirit, shared in the reorganization of the Prussian church, and, although he did not wish it to be imposed by the state, laboured for the union of the Lutheran and Reformed. He lectured on a wide variety of subjects, philosophical, ethical, and theological. His major work, *Der christliche Glaube nach den Grundsätzen der evangelische Kirche in Zusammenhange dargestellt* ("The Christian Faith According to the Fundamentals of the Evangelical Church Systematically Set Forth"), first appeared in 1821–1822 and then, in a thoroughly revised edition, early in the 1830's. By some it was hailed as the most important formulation of Protestant theology since Calvin's *Institutes*. Others regarded it as a major threat to Christianity. Among their criticisms was that to them its view of God was pantheistic. Singularly pure, high-minded, with a deep love for people, Schleiermacher made a profound impression, and his death was regarded as a public calamity.

To Schleiermacher religion was "the feeling of absolute dependence." As he conceived it, true Christianity is not primarily a set of intellectual propositions, a system of dogma to which the would-be believer must give assent. It is, rather, an inner experience, the experience not merely of the individual, but also of the Christian community, of the Church as he believed that term should be used. Out of that experience, he maintained, verbal formulations of the faith had and would come, but they were secondary and derivative. They had changed and would change again. His death bed remark was characteristic:

"I feel constrained to think the profoundest speculative thoughts and they are to me identical with the deepest religious feelings." He believed that the feeling of dependence is common to all religions and that the object of the latter is to bring men into harmony with God. Religions, he maintained, vary in the degree to which they attain this end, and of all religions Christianity is, so he declared, the highest.

Schleiermacher held that we have no objective knowledge of God, but that we know Him in relation to ourselves, in our feeling of absolute dependence on Him, and in His relation to the universe. God is eternal, omnipresent, almighty, in the sense that He can do whatever He wills, is the Creator, and is all-knowing. The world and man as created by God were originally good, so Schleiermacher maintained. He believed that sin is man's claim to self-sufficiency and is in seeking to find satisfaction elsewhere than in God. Sin, he taught, is original in that it is not simply the act of an individual but is an inescapable trend in all men. The world about man has so far lost its pristine perfection that from it continually come promptings to sin. Were men rightly related to God these promptings would not prove temptations, but, because of sinful tendencies in man, they induce men to sin. Through sin men are alienated from God and therefore fear Him as judge, knowing that they deserve His wrath.

There comes, however, the experience of redemption. This, so Schleiermacher said, had been the purpose of God as an integral part of His plan of creation. In redemption are seen both the love and the wisdom of God, love in seeking to bring men into union with Himself, and wisdom in the skill with which God makes all things serve His loving purpose. He maintained that redemption is by grace through Christ and that in Jesus Christ human nature reached perfection. Jesus Christ was a man, but a man who was entirely unique in that he was dominated by the consciousness of God as no man had been before him and no man has since been. Here was a miracle, quite unpredictable. Christ's perfection could be only because of the presence of God in him. Jesus Christ, therefore, was both human and divine. Redemption works through a dynamic without which men could not attain the goal which God has for them, but through which, because Jesus Christ is perfect man, men are enabled to have fellowship with Him and sin in them is overcome by the consciousness of God working in them. The experience of redemption by the individual involves a response in faith and love which is regeneration, justification, and sanctification. This means the birth and the growth in believers of the experience of God which comes through Jesus Christ. What Christians have called the Holy Spirit, so Schleiermacher explained, was the consciousness of God in Jesus Christ operating through the community of believers which is the Christian Church. That Church is made up of all those in whom the consciousness of God is dominant. It is also visible institutions, institutions which are shaped by being involved in history. Within them true believers constitute the invisible core. The Church is the custodian of the means of grace and of the Scriptures. The Scriptures are the record of those who had the word of God. They are reports of experience. Schleiermacher recognized that the world in which the Church is set is hostile, but he hoped that it would ultimately be completely transformed and that the whole created world would be saved.

Much of this, it will be seen, was historic Christianity as Protestants had understood it. The novelty in Schleiermacher was his method of approach. He began, not with the Bible, a creed, or revelation, but with personal experience, with what happens to the individual and to the community.

The earnestness and the freshness with which Schleiermacher presented Christianity had a profound and eventually a wide influence. He contributed powerfully to the religious awakening in German Protestantism in the nineteenth century and aided it in other lands. To many he seemed to make the Christian faith compatible with the thought forms of the day and therefore acceptable to honest minds. Many theologians, both in Germany and in other lands, owed him a great debt. In Germany some followed philosophical and psychological paths, others reinforced loyalty to existing confessions, and some tried to find common ground for Lutherans and Reformed by minimizing creeds and stressing the identity of the religious experience which was found in both.

Contemporary with Schleiermacher both in years and as a professor in the University of Berlin and far more famous and influential in the general history of thought than he was Georg Wilhelm Friedrich Hegel (1770–1831). In his late teens Hegel entered the University of Tübingen as a student of theology and five years later received a theological certificate from that institution. After leaving the university, for several years he was a private tutor in Switzerland and then in Germany. In his leisure he gave much time and thought to the study of Christianity, and especially of Jesus. He wrote a life of Jesus, regarding him as the son of Joseph and Mary, and seeking to discover what it was in his teachings and conduct that had given him so unique a place in history. Hegel developed slowly. He taught at Jena, Nüremberg, Heidelberg, and eventually (1818–1831) in the University of Berlin. There fame came to him and hundreds of students flocked to his lectures. Hegel thought that he saw in the universe, as a clue to understanding it, a dialectical process. The dialectical process consists of a thesis interlocking with an antithesis, followed by a transition to a synthesis. The synthesis incorporates everything both in the thesis and the antithesis. The synthesis immediately becomes a new thesis. This involves an antithesis and the process is repeated.

Hegel held that religion arose in the tension between the individual and his world. He believed religions to advance from natural religion to moral religion and then to spiritual religion. He maintained that Christianity is the highest of all religions, the only one which can be called absolute. He declared that through myths Christianity had already presented truths which philosophy could fully define. Among these myths were the incarnation, the atonement, and the Trinity. He was convinced that the meanings which he gave to these terms were those intended by the Early Church Fathers. In some ways his understanding of Christianity resembled that of the Gnostics. Like them he conceived Christianity to be a philosophy stated in the form of myths. With them he made history subordinate to what he deemed universal and eternal truths.

While not primarily a theologian, Hegel influenced theologians, both those who regarded him as shedding fresh light on Christian truths and thus reinforcing them, and those who radically disagreed with him.

After Schleiermacher, the most prominent German Protestant theologian of the nineteenth century was Albrecht Ritschl (1822–1889). The son of a Lutheran bishop, he studied in several universities, and at Halle came under the influence of Hegelianism. He reacted against the Pietism which he had known, with its assurance based exclusively upon an inner experience. He had no use for mysticism. Eventually he repudiated Hegelianism. For a while he was won to the Tübingen school of Biblical studies of which we are to read in a moment, and by one of its outstanding representatives, Baur, but in time he rejected it. He was successively professor of theology at Bonn and Göttingen. His major work was *Die christliche Lehre von der Rechtfertigung und Versöhnung* ("The Christian Doctrine of Justification and Reconciliation"). Ritschl professed to believe that metaphysics and philosophy are a hindrance rather than a help to theology and must be excluded from it. He rejected ecclesiastical dogma. Yet he was not always consistent. He took much from the theory of knowledge of a contemporary German philosopher, Rudolf Hermann Lotze (1817–1881), who, while agreeing with Kant that things cannot be known in themselves, maintained that they could be known in their attributes or activities. Ritschl held that we pass "value judgements" on these attributes and activities as they affect us, namely, as they give us pleasure or pain, and that religious knowledge is from these value judgements. He maintained that we can know God not through philosophy or "natural religion," but only through Christ, and only if we belong to the company of believers. God revealed through Christ is love.

Christianity, as Ritschl saw it, is not a circle described from a single centre, but an ellipse around two foci, the one the relation of the individual to God as a son of God and the other the kingdom of God. Christianity, he declared, "is the monotheistic, completely spiritual, and ethical religion, which, based on the life of its Author as Redeemer and as Founder of the kingdom of God, consists in the freedom of the children of God, involves the impulse to conduct from the motive of love, aims at the moral organization of mankind, and grounds blessedness on the relation of sonship to God, as well as on the kingdom of God." Ritschl held that Christ is central in Christianity and is unique because he first realized in himself and then reproduced in others the perfect religion and revelation. This uniqueness is expressed in the value judgement which appraises him as divine. The Christian life is seen in the Church, the worshipping community, and the kingdom of God, or the moral community. The Church and the kingdom of God are interdependent. The one cannot really exist without the other.

Ritschl influenced many. Some of them emphasized one phase of his teaching and some another. In general, he made for a joyous faith, based on the Gospel of Jesus Christ and stressing the ethical and the practical. Himself deeply religious, humorous, wholesome, unafraid of controversy, he radiated confidence and brought light and hope to many a perplexed soul. Men were moved to trust in God's love and to labour to make all human society the kingdom of God, where God's will as seen in Christ would be perfectly done. Much that Ritschl taught was congenial to the activistic, optimistic temper which was prevalent in the Western world in the nineteenth century, and especially in the second half of that century. Young men from Great Britain and the United States, coming in touch with Ritschlianism in their student days in German universities carried it back with them. In the United States it contributed to what we are later to see described as the "social gospel."

One of the outstanding Ritschlian theologians was Wilhelm Herrmann (1846–1922). The son of a clergyman, at Halle in his student days he was urged to make philosophy his life work. However, from deep conviction he chose theology and from 1879 to his death taught it in Marburg. Like Ritschl's, his was a warm religious faith. Also like Ritschl, he exerted an influence, although not as wide as that of his master, in Great Britain and the United States.

In Biblical and historical studies of Christianity nineteenth century German universities were also the scene of a ferment of daring thought and conflicting convictions. Indeed, theological, Biblical, and historical studies interacted, each stimulating and modifying the others. This Biblical and historical scholarship was a flowering of what had been begun in the eighteenth century. It applied to the Bible and to the history of Christianity the methods of research and analysis which were being developed by historians, especially German historians, to determine the dates, authorship, and reliability of the documents upon which they depended in their efforts to understand and reconstruct the past. It was also moulded by the current philosophies and theologies.

No other documents were subjected to as prolonged and minute study by as many inquiring minds as were those which constituted the Bible. Uniformity in findings was far from being completely attained and substantial agreement appeared to be reached only to be challenged. The methods and the results spread through much of Protestantism and, although eventually condemned, as we have seen, by the Pope, through small minorities in the Roman Catholic Church.

Here again, as in theology, we can take the space to mention only some of the more prominent figures.

It was inevitable that scholars who combined a religious interest with confidence in reason as expressed in eighteenth century rationalism should address themselves to the Bible and especially to the Gospels. Thus H. E. G. Paulus (1761–1851), after 1811 professor in Heidelberg, sought to rule out the miraculous from the Gospels and to offer explanations which would make such events accord with human experience. For example, he suggested that when Jesus was reported to be walking on the sea he was actually walking on the shore by the sea, and that the feeding of the five thousand was made possible by the generosity with which Jesus shared his meagre store and which stirred others to follow his example. He held that Jesus had only swooned on the cross and that his seeming resurrection was due to an earthquake which revived him and released him from his tomb.

Much more epoch-making was the work of what was known as the Tübingen school. Its pioneer was Ferdinand Christian Baur (1792–1860). Educated in Tübingen, in 1826 he became professor of theology in that university. Captivated by the philosophy of Hegel, he applied it to the New Testament and the history of Christianity, particularly of early Christianity. He maintained that Christianity as taught by the original intimates of Jesus, especially Peter, was a messianic Judaism. In this he saw the Hegelian thesis. The antithesis he believed to be in Paul, who, he maintained, first made Christianity a universal religion. The synthesis he found in the combination of the two in the Catholic Church which emerged in the second century. He attempted to date the books of the New Testament by the fashion in which they gave evidence of the struggle and believed that most of them were written in the second century. He later began a five-volume survey of Church history which, finished by other hands, carried the story from the beginning into his own day.

More sensational was the *Leben Jesu* ("Life of Jesus"), by one of Baur's students, David Friedrich Strauss (1808–1874). Educated in a Protestant seminary and in Tübingen and Berlin, Strauss became familiar with the thought of both Hegel and Schleiermacher. To his *Leben Jesu* he devoted years of study and writing. In his preface he said that the Christian faith was quite independent of any criticism that he might make, that "the supernatural birth of Christ, his miracles, his resurrection, and ascension, remain eternal truths, whatever doubts may be cast on their reality as historical facts," and that "the dogmatic significance of the life of Jesus remains inviolate." Yet he held that while not all the history of Jesus as given in the New Testament is mythical, in it there is an admixture of the mythical. He cast doubt on the historicity of much in the Gospels, including the virgin birth of Jesus, the details of the accounts of the crucifixion, the resurrection, and the post-resurrection appearances of Jesus, and questioned the accuracy of the reports of the sayings and deeds of Jesus. In spite of his initial avowal, he also doubted the basic Christian dogmas built upon the New Testament accounts of the life of Jesus. He summed up the queries which had thus far been raised about the historicity of the picture given by the Gospels, introduced some of his own, and left the impression of a lack of dependable knowledge of Jesus as an historical character. He attacked the positions of both the rationalists and the orthodox. The book created an enormous stir and awakened a mixture of hearty agreement, partial endorsement, and vigorous and often emotional rebuttal. Its repercussions continued to be felt at least as late as the middle of the twentieth century. In his *Christliche Glaubenslehre,* published in 1841 and 1842, Strauss undermined confidence in Christian doctrines by tracing their history in such fashion as to cast doubt on their validity. At the outset a Christian, Strauss, unable to find employment as teacher in a theological faculty and embittered by the intense criticism directed against him, eventually broke completely with his early faith and died a materialist and a pessimist.

Strauss added stimulus to the application to the New Testament of nineteenth century historical methodology with its attempt to determine "what actually happened," as Ranke, one of the greatest of the German historians of the period, put it. Scores of names of distinguished scholars were added to the list of those who devoted themselves to the problem, and a voluminous literature poured from the presses.

Much the same intensive study was devoted to the Old Testament and here also the names of earnest students were legion. Prominent and provocative was Julius Wellhausen (1844–1918). Beginning in theology and for a time professor of that subject, before he was forty his conscience compelled him to resign from a position where he could no longer teach what was expected, and, devoting himself to oriental languages, he spent most of his professional life at Göttingen. Although he wrote on the New Testament, it was to the Old Testament that he gave his chief attention. Here his conclusion both brought on him attacks from those holding the older accepted views and spurred others to go further along the trails which he had broken.

In the history of religions and of Christianity one of the most stimulating scholars was Ernest Troeltsch (1865–1923). Indeed, Troeltsch was the outstanding representative of a distinctive approach to the study of Christianity as a phase of the history of religion. A teacher of theology and philosophy, first in Heidelberg and then in Berlin, he was deeply concerned with the philosophy of history and especially of the history of religion. In a sense he was in the succession of Schleiermacher. To him religion was the direct sense of the presence of God. Enormously learned and familiar with much of the thought of his time, he sought to work out the kind of theology which was required by the age. Yet he believed that religion could never be really reconciled with culture and held that a tension must always exist between Christianity and the thought world in which it is set. He was familiar with Hegel but did not fully follow him. He was also influenced by Ritschl, so much so that with the latter he maintained that religion is not philosophy, but is quite different from it. Yet he could not fully subscribe to Ritschl's sharp distinction between faith and reason. In philosophy an idealist, he believed that the cosmic process is the effect in space and time of a Reality which cannot be grasped by our senses.

History, Troeltsch held, is permeated by the self revelation of God. Yet he was not willing to say that in Christ mankind has the conclusive revelation of God. He viewed Christianity as one of many religions. To him religions, including Christianity, are the outgrowth of religious feeling. Even though not reconcilable with culture, they are affected and their distinctive forms are in part determined by the cultures of which they are a part. Holding that the Christian Gospel "is the loftiest and most spiritual revelation we know," he described it as "a profound inner experience." That experience is "the criterion of validity, but . . . only of its validity *for us*. It is God's countenance revealed to us; it is the way in which, being what we are, we receive and react to the revelation of God." Christianity, as Troeltsch viewed it, is not necessarily final. Like other religions, it is relative, associated with a particular culture. Being inseparably linked to a civilization which may, like other civilizations, pass away, it too may eventually be left behind in the stream of time. In a later stage of history, so his view would lead him to say, men might become conscious of needs which the Christian Gospel does not meet. In that event, presumably, the Divine Reason, the Divine Life (and there was something akin to pantheism in Troeltsch's view of God), would manifest itself afresh in a new way, which, valid for the men of that age and culture, would in turn pass and be superseded by another manifestation.

A historian of Christianity who was very much in the Ritschlian tradition was Adolf von Harnack (1851–1930). The son of a professor of pastoral theology, most of his mature years were spent as professor in the University of Berlin. His writings had a wide circulation, both in German and in translation. Especially famous was his account of the history of Christian doctrine. In general his thesis was that Christian beliefs were early so moulded by the Greek thought in which they took shape as to introduce permanently into the teachings of the Church much that was not of the true essence of the faith. He would, accordingly, have Protestants reëxamine what had come from the past and seek to recover the original Gospel. He connected the Gospel inseparably with Jesus and described it as "the knowledge and recognition of God as the Father, the certainty of redemption, humility and joy in God, energy, and brotherly love." He believed that in spite of the fashion in which it had been compromised and obscured by the churches and by the cultural environments and heritages through which it had been transmitted, it had persisted, "still traceable, like a red thread in the centre of the web," and was sure to "emerge afresh and free itself from its entangling connexions."

Most of the scholars whom we have thus far mentioned in this extraordinary ferment of thought centering around theology and the Bible departed more or less widely from what had been inherited from the Christian past, including the beliefs cherished by the Lutheran and Reformed churches which constituted the prevailing forms of German Protestantism. Varied and often reciprocally contradictory as their views were, not all of them could be accepted by any one person or group. No one of the men whom we have listed was followed unquestionably by more than a small minority. The effect, rather, was to stimulate further thought which often issued in conclusions which differed, sometimes widely, from those which had provoked them.

Among the responses to the radical departures from accepted views were vigorous reassertions of the historic doctrines contained in the confessions of the Lutheran and Reformed churches. In Lutheranism confessional conservatism was often closely associated with political conservatism and, like the latter, was strengthened by a reaction against the liberalism that had been prominent in the revolutionary year of 1848. As were those of radical tendencies, the conservatives by no means fully agreed with one another. Much of this confessional orthodoxy was opposed not only to rationalism but also to Pietism.

Sometimes called "New Lutheranism," much of the confessional orthodoxy tended to emphasize the sacraments, including the sacrament of ordination, and to make of the ministry of the Church a distinct clerical priesthood. Here again we can take the time to do no more than note a few of the outstanding figures.

Prominent among the staunch "New Lutherans" was Friedrich Julius Stahl (1802–1861). Of Jewish parentage, in his late teens he joined the Lutheran Church under the influence of Schelling, the brilliant romanticist and philosopher. For years he was in Berlin. There he departed from the philosophy which he had imbibed from Schelling and became a vigorous exponent of Lutheran confessionalism. Denouncing revolution and rationalism as the great menaces of the day, leading to revolt against the authority of the state and the Church and to the attempted rejection by man of his creatureliness and obedience to God, he stoutly maintained that kings rule by divine right, insisted that the policies of the state must be governed by Christian principles, held to the close union of Church and state, and believed episcopacy to be the ideal form of Church government. Eloquent and persuasive, he became the leader and the spokesman of the conservatives in Prussian politics, especially of the landed gentry and aristocracy and the Lutheran pastors who made common cause with them.

Others of this "New Lutheran" school of thought held that purity of doctrine is the sign of the true Church, that there can be only one true Church, and that the Lutheran Church has in its confessions of faith the full truth and therefore is that Church. Like Stahl, they tended to identify the kingdom of God with the Church. For example, Theodor Kliefoth (1810–1895), for nearly a generation the leader of the *Landeskirche* of Mecklenburg, in conscious opposition to Pietism held that the object of salvation is not so much the individual as all humanity, and that the saving grace of God is not transmitted through individuals to the world, but rather through peoples and their institutions to individuals. In the sacramental emphasis of the "New Lutherans," one writer placed the sacraments above the word of God, holding that since the latter, transmitted through the mouth of man, is subject to alteration, the sacraments, requiring passivity on the part of him who ministers and of them who receive them, are much more an act of God.

The "New Lutherans" were not all of one mind. For example, Johann Christian Konrad von Hoffmann (1810–1877) put forward a view of the atonement which he believed was that of the Bible but which brought down on him the charge of heresy from others of that school.

In some of the *Landeskirchen* the "New Lutherans" with their strong confessionalism were in control and in several others they were very influential. In Prussia, for instance, in the reaction after the revolution of 1848 they had much power in the schools and universities, saw to it that the head body of the church was given an influential role in the appointment of professors of theology, and weakened the union of the Lutheran and Reformed of which we are to hear more in a moment.

Parallel with the "New Lutheranism," but distinct from it, was an orthodoxy, some of it in the Reformed but much of it in the Lutheran churches, which had a strong Pietist strain. There was, indeed, a revival of Pietism which had similarities to the evangelical awakenings in the British Isles and the United States. Some of it made common cause with the latter in foreign missions and other enterprises. True to the Pietist tradition, it stressed personal commitment. This orthodoxy, some of it called "Old Lutheranism," like the "New Lutheranism," varied, and, also like it, denounced the rationalism inherited from the eighteenth century, rejected the methods and the conclusions of the current radical historical study of the Scriptures, held to the inerrancy of the Bible, and looked askance or with open hostility at the radical theologians. Pietism had especially strong centres in Württemberg and Basel, but was to be found as well in other places.

One of the leaders in the revival of orthodoxy was Klaus Harms (1778–1855). A native of Holstein and of peasant stock, he early passed from rationalism to Schleiermacher and then to Lutheran orthodoxy. He supported absolute monarchy. As pastor and writer he exerted a marked influence.

Another prominent figure in sturdy orthodoxy, but for a time with a much stronger Pietist strain, was Ernst Wilhelm Hengstenberg (1802–1869). At the outset inclined to rationalism, in his early twenties he entered the missionary training school at Basel, a stronghold of Pietism, and became thoroughly committed to that religious movement. In 1824 he became the head of the Pietist group in Berlin. As such, beginning with 1826, he was a professor in the University of Berlin. He stood stoutly for the infallibility of the Bible and gave to its passages allegorical interpretations. He believed that the millennial reign of Christ had begun with Charlemagne in 800 and had been concluded in 1800 and that the end of the world and the final judgement were at hand. As the founder and editor of the *Evangelische Kirchenzeitung* he denounced rationalism, democracy, and France, and, in late youth (1840) breaking with Pietism, he became a champion of the Lutheranism of the sixteenth century confessions and the orthodoxy of the seventeenth century and denounced as heretics all who departed from it.

In all this theological strife there were not wanting those who sought to mediate, to combine the best from each of the major views, and to make for peace and Christian unity. They were in part the products of the religious awakenings of the day. Among them was he who is best known as Johann August Wilhelm Neander (1789–1850). Of Jewish parentage and in his boyhood known as David Mendel, he was led to the Christian faith by reading

Schleiermacher and at seventeen was baptized and took the name of Neander to signify that he had become a new man in Christ. A pupil and warm friend of Schleiermacher and beginning with 1812 his colleague on the faculty of the University of Berlin, he was by no means a slavish imitator of the older man. He disliked theological polemics and for that reason severed his connexion with Hengstenberg's *Evangelische Kirchenzeitung* when it attacked two rationalistic professors of Halle. Warmly and deeply religious, with a childlike Christian trust, he won the affection of hundreds of students and sought to lead them into an earnest and joyous Christian experience. In scholarship his great contribution was his *Allgemeine Geschichte der christlichen Religion und Kirche* ("History of the Christian Religion and Church") which he did not live to complete. Based upon an exhaustive examination of the sources, it saw the history of Christianity as the permeation of human life by the divine life and stressed the place of individuals rather than the community or institutions.

Another who is usually said to belong to the conciliators was Friedrich August Gottreu Tholuck (1799–1877). While a student in Berlin he came under the influence of Pietism and Neander. In 1826, when in his late twenties, he was appointed professor of theology at Halle with the hope that he would combat the rationalism which had captured that earlier radiating centre of Pietism. He sought to combine the Pietist heritage with what seemed to him best in the methods and findings of rationalism. Full of vigour, transparently good, an eloquent preacher, insisting upon a personal religious experience, holding that to love Christ is preferable to scholarship, warm in his personal friendships with students, a prolific writer, the author of many books, including several collections of sermons and works of devotion, he did much to shape the Pietism of the nineteenth century.

Similarly of the mediating school was Isaac August Dorner (1809–1884). Moved in his youth by the controversy aroused by Strauss's *Leben Jesu,* he deplored the bitterness of the attack on that book and, while not accepting its conclusions, sought to use it as a stimulus to a further understanding of Christ. This he attempted in his *Entwicklungsgeschichte der Lehre von der Person Christi* ("History of the Development of the Doctrine of the Person of Christ"). He added other books, chief among them *System der christlichen Glaubenslehre* ("System of Christian Doctrine") and *System der christlichen Ethik* ("System of Christian Ethics"). He believed that much in the modern views could be accepted without discarding the historic doctrines and attempted to demonstrate how this could be accomplished. He held that to the enlightened Christian mind its faith and experience are in harmony with what is seen in the Scriptures and in the historic faith of the Church. He believed that the core of Christianity is the revelation in Christ of what God is and what man may become. To his mind the Son, the perfect image of God, is also the ideal man. Translated into English, his books had a wide influence in the British Isles and the United States.

ATTEMPTS AT UNION

A movement which entered largely into the life of German Protestantism and which, seeking harmony, both produced it and provoked strife was the union of the Lutheran and Reformed churches. As we have seen (Chapters 32, 33), unsuccessful efforts at union had been made near the outset of Protestantism. It had since been attempted more than once, but had fallen short of the goal. Eighteenth century rationalism, dulling the sharpness of historic convictions which had separated the two main forms of German Protestantism, had prepared the way. Actual union came in part as a result of the weakening of the old patterns by the Napoleonic conquests. Between 1815 and 1830, after the defeat of Napoleon and the opportunity for a new beginning, unions of the two confessions were achieved in several German states.

The chief union, that in Prussia, which did much by example to bring the others into being, was mainly the work of Friedrich Wilhelm III, who reigned from 1797 to 1840. Although not a particularly strong monarch, Friedrich Wilhelm III was deeply religious and took an active interest in the Church. His purpose in seeking to accomplish the union was in part the desire to have religious uniformity in his domains, so that with one state there would be one church. In 1817, the tercentenary of the Protestant Reformation, the union was declared. The royal attempts to enforce the use of a uniform liturgy met with stubborn opposition. For years the king persisted and by dint of force seemed to have some success. However, numbers of the Lutheran pastors and their flocks, denominated "Old Lutherans," continued to resist. When, under the next reign, that of Friedrich Wilhelm IV (1840–1861), constraint was relaxed, many of the Lutheran congregations drew together (1841) and in a general synod constituted the Evangelical Lutheran Church in Prussia. In 1845 this was accorded royal recognition.

Resistance to the union developed in several other *Landeskirchen* in the 1850's and 1860's. This arose in part from the conservative reaction after the revolutionary year of 1848. It also sprang from hostility to the growing political strength of Prussia.

PARTY STRIFE

To the strife over the attempt to bring about the union of the Lutherans and the Reformed was added that among the adherents of the several main strains of theology. The contestants grouped themselves by organized parties.

For a time in the 1830's and 1840's some of the minority among the pastors who held to rationalism, irked by the rising tide of orthodoxy and its power in the *Landeskirchen,* formed separate congregations. They drew together in what were known as the *Lichtfreunde* ("Friends of Light") or the *protestantischen Freunde* ("the Protestant Friends"), but in the conservative reaction after 1848 the movement lost ground.

In 1849 the Prussian Lutherans formed an association. In 1868 the Lutherans in Prussia and in the territories newly annexed by Prussia organized the *Allgemeine lutherische Konferens* ("The General Lutheran Conference") and began publishing a periodical.

In 1857 the more conservative friends of the Lutheran-Reformed Union associated themselves with the Evangelical Alliance.

In the 1860's theological liberals formed the *Protestantenverein* ("the Protestant Union"). It stood for the reconciliation of religion and modern culture, resistance to compulsory conformity with doctrine, and Lutheran-Reformed Union.

Between these various groups there was distrust which often broke out into open and bitter conflict.

It is sobering to observe that while the leaders of the churches had much of their energy absorbed in internecine strife, a large proportion of the laity were drifting away from the faith. They were still bringing their children to be baptized and confirmed, religious instruction was given in the schools, and taxes were collected for the support of the churches. However, many of the intellectuals were reading Strauss, Feuerbach, Renan, and Schopenhauer and were having their faith shaken by them, thousands of the labourers in the new industries were moving away from contacts with the churches, and the revival of orthodoxy and its alignment with political conservatism were alienating numbers of political and social liberals. Especially in the cities the churches were losing ground. Their strength was chiefly in the rural districts where the old social and economic order more nearly persisted.

ORGANIZED EFFORTS TO PREVENT DE-CHRISTIANIZATION AND TO REACH THE DE-CHRISTIANIZED

Party strife and the progressive de-Christianization of large elements in the population were only one side of the picture. Protestants were reaching out in fresh ways to serve the needy and to win back those who were rejecting the faith or were drifting away from it.

The examples of this vitality in Protestantism were numerous. Bible and tract societies were formed, partly stimulated by similar earlier organizations in England. They had been begun even as early as 1811 and 1814. In the second decade of the century several individuals, moved by Christian charity, took steps to care for the children orphaned by the Napoleonic Wars. In 1833 Johann Hinrich Wichern (1808–1881), who had been nourished in Pietism, founded a home for underprivileged and delinquent children near the rapidly growing Hamburg. In 1849, the year after the far-reaching revolutionary disturbances, and partly stimulated by them, Wichern instituted what was known as the Inner Mission. It sought, partly through sisterhoods and lay brotherhoods, to reach the masses, and to serve seamen, the unemployed, prisoners, and needy children. Its programme included Sunday Schools, city missions, colporteurs to distribute Christian literature, and Christian lodging houses. Local units were formed to further the Inner Mission and a national organization for it was instituted. It was associated with the *Kirchentag* which drew throngs and met annually in some large city and which had for its purpose the spiritual rebirth of the German nation. In 1849 Konrad Wilhelm Loehe (1808–1872), a pastor in Neuendettelsau in Bavaria, founded a Lutheran society for the Inner Mission and four years later inaugurated a union of deaconesses.

Efforts were made towards improved pastoral care for the masses in the growing cities. The larger parishes were sub-divided, new church structures were erected, and more clergy were provided. Reforms in liturgy and the wider use of hymn books helped to enrich the services and make them more attractive. Discussion evenings were held for labourers to give them more contact with the Church and the faith. Better methods of preparing for confirmation were devised, with an improvement in the confirmation vows. Women were accorded a larger place in the churches. The Young Men's Christian Association movement, which had been begun in England, found kinship in similar groups in Germany and brought into its fellowship Christian young men, largely in the cities.

The use of deaconesses had a marked spread. In 1833 Theodore Fliedner, a pastor at Kaiserswerth, a destitute parish, began the use of deaconesses to assist him. He founded a training school for them. They nursed the sick as well as cared for the spiritually destitute. Partly stimulated by this precedent, in 1894 in Germany nearly eight thousand deaconesses were serving in hospitals, poor-houses, orphanages, and schools, and as parish-helpers. Partly through contact with Elizabeth Fry, Fliedner also, and earlier, organized (1826) the Prisoners Society of Germany and he and his wife inaugurated a home for discharged women convicts.

In general, the quality of the Protestant clergy improved in the nineteenth century. At the outset it was low and a marked difference existed between those in the cities and those in the rural districts. The former were much better educated and better paid than were the latter. Gradually the gap was narrowed as the preparation and status of the rural clergy rose.

Increasing Autonomy in the Landeskirchen of Germany

Parallel with the political unification of Germany and in part as a sequel to it, the *Landeskirchen* developed forms of government which promoted their autonomy as against the state. Characteristic, but with variations from state to state, was an ascending structure beginning with a representative body in each congregation, going on to regional synods, and culminating in a general synod for the entire state. The members in each higher body were chosen by the bodies below it. The synodical organization facilitated legislation by the churches. The tie with the state was maintained and included support through taxation. However, the churches had more control over their own affairs than formerly.

The progress towards ecclesiastical autonomy, while by no means entirely ascribable to it, was facilitated by the reduction of the powers of the states as they were drawn into the newly formed North German Confederation (1867) and its successor the German Empire (1871). Some of the states lost their separate existence through annexation by Prussia, but even in these the *Landeskirchen* persisted and maintained their identity. Presumably under the new order the states and their princes were in a less favourable position to control the churches in their realms. It may well have been, moreover, that something of the spirit of local particularism which had flourished in the days before the union when each German state was practically independent of every other found refuge in reinforcing the autonomy of the churches, continuing as they did the earlier territorial divisions.

In general the *Landeskirchen* were controlled by the conservatives. The liberals and radicals were usually small minorities in the synods by which the churches were governed.

The Growth of Free Churches

Not all Protestants were in the state churches. As the nineteenth century wore on, "free churches" appeared and grew, independent of the established ones.

Several of these were of purely German origin. As we have seen, some were constituted by the liberals. Others were by conservatives who were of the strict confessional Lutheranism. Those in Prussia were aided by a law of 1908 which made it easier for members of the *Landeskirche* to join them. The Evangelical Free Church of Hanover was formed (1878) by Theodor Harms in connexion with the Hermannsburg training school for missionaries which had been founded in 1849 by his brother, Ludwig Harms.

Others of the free churches arose from contacts with other countries. Methodism entered from Great Britain and the United States, chiefly through missionaries from the latter country. Baptist churches came through a German who had been in touch with the revival movement in Scotland and through assistance from the United States. It was from the United States that Seventh Day Adventists were represented. In 1914 none of these churches numbered more than 50,000 members.

THE OUTREACH OF GERMAN PROTESTANTISM TO OTHER LANDS

If British and American forms of Protestantism found footholds in Germany, even more did German Protestantism make itself felt in other lands. This was partly, as we have suggested, through the writings of German Protestant scholars. It was also through the extensive emigration of Germans, chiefly to the Americas. We will say something of it when, in our geographic pilgrimage, we come to these regions and will note how missionaries from the Fatherland helped to hold the settlers to their ancestral faith and to shape the forms which it took.

Much of the overseas expansion of German Protestantism was through missions to non-Christian peoples. The vitality of nineteenth century German Protestantism was vividly seen in the number and extent of the societies which were created as a means of stimulating and carrying on these missions. Unlike most of the missionary societies in the United States, the majority had no organic connexion with the official ecclesiastical bodies: few churches as such conducted missions. The missionary societies were, rather, the creation of individuals and groups and depended for their support not on the general funds of a church but upon the gifts of friends. In 1914 there were at least thirty-two societies which sent missionaries, all but two of them organized after 1815, six societies exclusively for the collection of funds, twenty-three missionary conferences (provincial unions composed principally of clergymen and for the purpose of cultivating interest in missions), and more than a dozen organizations for the support of medical missions. German missionaries were in all the continents and some of the islands of the Pacific. They were predominantly from Pietist and confessionally conservative constituencies. A partial list of the major societies will give some indication of the extent and nature of the movements.

The pioneers in German foreign missions were the Moravians. Early and continuously prominent was the Basel Evangelical Missionary Society. Although officially Swiss, it drew much of its financial support and many of its missionaries from Germany. Organized in 1815 as an institution for training missionaries, until 1822 its graduates went out under British societies, but in that year it began sending them under its own auspices. Also prominent were the Berlin Missionary Society, begun in 1824, the Rhenish Missionary Society, founded in 1828, the Leipzig Evangelical Lutheran Mission, stemming from the Basel Mission and dating from 1836, the North German Missionary Society, formed in 1836 by the union of several societies which had been affiliated with Basel, and the Bethel Mission, inaugurated in 1886, with headquarters at Bielefeld, where it also had an extensive institution for the care of unfortunates.

Creative Danish Protestantism

From Germany we turn naturally northward to Scandinavia, for that region was overwhelmingly Lutheran by faith and many of the religious movements in German Lutheranism had repercussions in it. As in Germany, Pietism was strong, although only among minorities, and the years which followed 1815 saw marked awakenings and a revulsion against the rationalism of the Enlightenment. We come first to Denmark, as the only one of the Scandinavian lands with a common boundary with Germany.

Denmark emerged from the Napoleonic Wars in a parlous condition. It had lost its fleet, Norway, long joined to it, had become independent, it was deeply in debt, and bankruptcies were common. In the 1860's Denmark had a disastrous war with Prussia and Austria which cost it the partly German provinces of Schleswig and Holstein. Yet following 1815 the country became prosperous, and there were significant achievements in literature and education.

Religiously, the years after 1815 saw a remarkable revival. The nineteenth century was the most creative in the history of the Church in Denmark. Not only was Danish Christianity vigorous. It also took on distinctive forms within the general framework of Lutheranism and in one of its sons, Søren Aaby Kierkegaard, made a contribution which in the twentieth century had wide and deep effects, far beyond the borders of the country.

In Denmark the religious awakening took a number of forms. One feature of the revival was the strengthening of Pietism. In Denmark in the nineteenth century, instead of being opposed by the official church, as it was in the Hauge movement in Norway, it was given hospitality by that church, permeated it, and had a marked effect upon its life.

Closely connected with Pietism was the Inner Mission. Distinctively Danish and not a copy of the German Inner Mission, it had as its purpose the deepening and enrichment of the religious life of the nation. It stressed personal conversion and drew together those who had experienced it into circles for the cultivation of the spiritual life. It was utterly opposed to the kind of critical study of the Bible that flourished in German universities and contributed little to hymnody, but it made much of preaching. It grew in the course of the century and eventually had several hundred mission houses and nearly a thousand lay preachers. About a third of the pastors of the country were intimately connected with it.

In Denmark, as in much of Protestantism, there was a strong reaction against eighteenth century rationalism. One of its chief exponents was J. P. Mynster (1775–1854). A university graduate, in his early days as a pastor he was profoundly influenced by Kant and showed a strong pantheistic trend. Before he was thirty he had a heart-warming and transforming Christian experience. Later as court preacher, teacher in a theological seminary closely connected with the university, bishop, and primate of the Church of Denmark, he had an effect upon the entire nation. Although he was frankly opposed to rationalism, he sought to be positive rather than negative and to emphasize the heart of the Gospel and the work of Christ for man and in man as interpreted by historic Lutheranism.

Even more distinctive and influential was Nicolai Frederick Severin Grundtvig (1783–1872). The son of a clergyman, himself also a clergyman, late in life Grundtvig was made a bishop of the Church of Denmark. He believed in an indissoluble connexion between the Christian life and the national life and wished the latter to be permeated and transformed by Christian faith and action. Stressing baptism and the Lord's Supper as means to a living faith, he fought both rationalism and an arid and dogmatic adherence to the historic Lutheran dogmas. He sought to promote a singing church. He wrote more than fourteen hundred hymns, of which about two hundred found their way into the hymnal of the Church of Denmark. His was a joyous faith and he wished Christians always to be joyful for God's grace and to God's honour in the name of Jesus Christ. In politics he was a liberal. He inaugurated "folk schools" which stressed training in practical subjects and which became widely popular not only in Denmark but also in the other Scandinavian lands. He encouraged the coöperative movement in agriculture. Through what he did for education and through coöperatives he contributed notably to the prosperity of the country. "Grundtvigism" became a potent and characteristic strain in Danish life. It and the Inner Mission were sharply opposed to each other and the conflict issued in party strife in the Church.

As we have suggested, it was Søren Aaby Kierkegaard (1813–1855) who was eventually the most widely known and read of Danish Protestants. Said to have been the most original thinker in Danish history, Kierkegaard was a tortured soul who after prolonged struggle progressed from dread to faith. He was reared by a profoundly gloomy father who made him an intimate. When a poor peasant lad his father had at one time in bitterness at his hard lot deliberately cursed God. Later, although he became prosperous, he believed that by this act he had committed the unpardonable sin. To this he had added a secret sin which he later confided to his son, thus intensifying the latter's sense of guilt. Yet the father was also deeply religious and, placing great dependence upon Mynster and his sermons, reared his son on them. For a time in his student days Søren was dissipated and idle. Brilliant in conversation he could also be caustic and cynical. In his mid-twenties there came an emotional shock which made him believe that the entire family had the curse of God resting on it and was to disappear, wiped out by the hand of God. He studied theology and took a degree in philosophy. He became affianced to a girl whom he never ceased to love, but broke off the engagement because he felt that he must not burden her with his melancholy, the secret sin of his father, and the sins of his own youth. In his thirties and early forties, with one interruption of about two years, he wrote prodigiously. In his last months there came a measure of peace and he died at the age of forty-two.

Kierkegaard's works dealt with both philosophy and religion. He denounced the trend in thought represented by Hegel, with its serene confidence in human reason, its calm objectivity, detached from struggle, and its optimism. He held it to be quite irreconcilable with the Gospel. Idealist philosophers such as Hegel, he maintained, assumed the attitude of spectators of the drama of life, refusing to take sides. They reduced the Gospel to ideas and were blind to the gulf between the Creator and the creature. To such men the incarnation was unnecessary and the cross a scandal. Kierkegaard insisted that true Christianity demands decision and action, a commitment which abandons the rôle of the spectator. He looked upon Christianity as entailing a dialectic, but, unlike that of Hegel, which was one of thesis and antithesis resolved in a synthesis, it was composed of opposites which could not be reconciled and which negated each other, such as time and eternity, holiness and love, grace and responsibility. He saw in Christianity what for men are paradoxes, but paradoxes which for God are transcended. Christianity, so he believed, confronts man with God and the necessity of decision. Before God man is always a sinner and his best as well as his worst stands under the judgement of God and needs divine pardon. We are born as sinners and by our deeds add to our sins. Between God, Who is sinless, and sinful man a vast abyss yawns. Yet what to human reason is impossible is done by God. The Son of God becomes incarnate. He appears incognito, in weakness and obscurity. In himself Christ unites two elements which repel each other, man and God, and the Eternal enters time. Here is at once an affront to human reason and an object of saving faith. The cross of Christ offends man's reason and his moral sense. In the leap of faith we sacrifice our intellects and accept what is to us the great paradox, that God and man are opposites and yet in Christ have become one. To Kierkegaard to follow Christ entails suffering, suffering which must be borne without the benefit of human companionship. One must stand solitary before God in pure pain, with his soul naked under the divine eye which knows our every sin and its infinite guilt. In being reconciled to God we must absorb the agony and humiliation of Christ as our own.

In all this can be discerned the significance of a term which is closely associated with Kierkegaard, "existential." By it "existence" is contrasted with mere "life." "Existence" is reached by the inner decisions of the individual. To think "existentially" is to abandon the pose of a spectator on the ultimate issues and to act.

Even from this brief summary it can be seen that Kierkegaard was driven to adopt an attitude which became prominent in the last years of his brief life, the condemnation of what he saw about him which was called Christianity and which was accepted as such by the masses. To him it was exemplified by one who had been his father's spiritual guide and his own friend, Mynster. In an address preceding his funeral Mynster was acclaimed as one of the genuine witnesses to the truth. This provoked Kierkegaard to pronounce as false to the Christianity of the New Testament what Mynster had preached. Kierkegaard's denunciation included the established church as "an impudent indecency," with its paid ministers, half-Christian, half-worldly civil servants, who on Sundays proclaimed what they contradicted by their actions on Mondays. He declared that official Christianity resembled the Christianity of the New Testament no more than enjoyment resembles suffering, or being at home in the world resembles being a pilgrim and a stranger. Consistently, on his death bed Kierkegaard refused to accept the sacrament from the "king's officials."

In his life time Kierkegaard was little noticed. This was because he wrote in Danish, a language known by few outside that country and Norway. It was only later that his works were translated into more generally read languages. It was also because he ran counter to the prevailing temper of his time.

After 1914 Kierkegaard had a profound influence in widening and varied circles. This was in large part because he spoke to the condition of an age which knew two world wars and was sobered by what it believed to be the fatal illness of Western civilization. In his denunciation of the confidence in reason which characterized the Occident he seemed to have laid bare a basic weakness of Occidental culture. His emphasis upon human sinfulness appealed to many who were impressed with the tragedy which mankind was bringing on itself. His stress on the utter contrast between the holiness of God and the sinfulness of man and on the un-Christian character of the official churches struck a responsive note in the hearts of many disillusioned Christians who had been nurtured on the theological liberalism of the nineteenth century, a liberalism which with its optimism and its confidence in reason had now seemed to end in futility. "Existentialism" became a pass-word in many intellectual circles. It was adopted by Christian theologians and by non-theistic, even atheistic philosophers. Protestant theology was deeply affected and some Roman Catholics were interested. Long almost unknown, Kierkegaard was acclaimed by some as the "greatest Christian thinker of the nineteenth century."

Denmark continued to be overwhelmingly Lutheran. However, in the course of the nineteenth century a few other churches constituted growing although small minorities. They were aided by the grant of religious liberty in 1849. In 1907 Roman Catholics numbered about 12,000. There were also Methodists, Baptists, Disciples of Christ, and the Church of the Brethren, all of them springing chiefly from contacts, mainly through missionaries, with the United States.

Danish Lutheranism spread far beyond the confines of Denmark. This was partly through emigration, mainly to the United States. It was also by missions to non-Christian peoples. Here was evidence of the mounting life in Danish Christianity. The eighteenth century Danish missions in India had been staffed by Germans and latterly had been aided financially from England. Between 1815 and 1914 several missionary societies came into being in Denmark, chief among them the Danish Missionary Society, formed in 1821, and eventually operating in Greenland, India, and Manchuria. They were manned and supported from Denmark.

Christianity did not have its full way in Denmark. Here, as elsewhere, scepticism and secularism were at work. A symbol and a furtherer of a non-Christian naturalism was the eminent critic and literary historian, Georg Morris Cohen Brandes (1842–1927). Born in Copenhagen, the son of a Jewish merchant, widely travelled in Europe, he was a radical whose extensive and influential writings were contrary to the religious strains which had been dominant in Danish life.

CHRISTIANITY IN NORWAY IN THE NINETEENTH CENTURY

The course of Christianity in Norway in the nineteenth century was far from being a pale reproduction of that in Denmark, the land with which there had been a close political bond. By the post-Napoleonic settlement at Vienna in 1815 Norway was transferred from Denmark to Sweden. However, the tie with Sweden was purely through the crown. The two realms had one monarch and under him foreign affairs were conducted and military matters managed, but Norway was declared to be "a free, independent, and indivisible kingdom." It preserved its own constitution and in domestic affairs was autonomous. Predominantly agricultural and commercial, with a large merchant marine, it was a nation of sturdy farmers and sailors. The Norwegian constitution, adopted in 1814, was strongly democratic and placed the supreme authority in a parliament elected indirectly by male tax-payers.

In the nineteenth century Norway developed a vigorous national and cultural life. Out of it came at least two writers of European fame, Bjornstjerne Björnson (1832–1910), poet, dramatist, and novelist, and Henrik Johan Ibsen (1826–1906), poet and dramatist. Both men were critical of the Church, but both bore to no small degree the impress of Christianity, even when they reacted against it. Björnson was the son of a pastor. Ibsen was widely read in theology, and while he waged war on the conventional religion about him, he did so in behalf of a more intense Christianity and was a mystic to whom the final wrong was the denial of love.

Nineteenth century Norwegian Christianity had in it many elements, several of them from without, some of them indigenous, and all of them having in the Norwegian environment a distinctive vitality.

That Christianity was inherited from a long past. It could not forget Olaf Haraldsson who, as patron saint, represented the era of conversion and what had survived from the Middle Ages. It bore deeply the impress of the Reformation. It was prevailingly Lutheran and the state church was of that confession.

The severing of the political tie with Denmark brought to the Church a sense of freedom. However, influences continued to flow in from Denmark and other countries. Eighteenth century rationalism survived for a time. Grundtvig's ideas had their followers. Pietism was strong. The Moravians were active. The revival of Lutheran orthodoxy in Germany and Denmark found congenial soil and Hengstenberg was potent. The example of the Inner Mission movement in these two lands helped to stimulate a similar one in Norway. Ideas entered from Sweden. The repeal in 1842 of the conventicle act of 1741 made easier the lot of dissenters from the state church. In 1845 legal restrictions on dissent were further relaxed. This helped to make possible the growth of Methodists and Baptists, stimulated by missionaries from the United States, and of the Plymouth Brethren through contacts with England. In the latter part of the century the radical theologies and Biblical study which flourished in Germany won something of a following.

At the same time there were Norwegians who were in the forefront of religious awakenings and in shaping the religious life of the nation. Although he did not die until 1824, Hans Nielsen Hauge had done his main work before 1815. Yet what he had begun grew. As a lay movement it was potent in a land where democratic tendencies were strong and where there was a large element of sturdy farmers who owned the soil that they tilled. It was in part nationalistic, directed against the half-Danish clergy. It gained momentum after the repeal of the conventicle act. Gisle Johnson (1822–1894), lecturer beginning in 1849 and from 1860 to his death (1894) professor of theology in the University of Christiana (Oslo), attempted to domesticate the lay revival in the state church. In 1868 he inaugurated a society named after Luther to send out Bible colporteurs and to prepare and distribute literature to educate the masses in Lutheran beliefs. Johnson had a close friend and colleague in C. P. Caspari (1814–1892), of German origin and training. The movement stimulated by Johnson and Caspari was in part due to the resurgence of Lutheran confessionalism in Germany and one of its effects was to lessen the influence of Grundtvigianism. It had affinities with Pietism and attracted some of the Haugeans. A revival in Western Norway, not content with the clergy-controlled movement of Johnson, gave rise to a lay organization which, without leaving the state church, built its own "prayer houses," and called its units Inner Mission Unions. Increasingly laymen won a voice in the Church's affairs. Beginning with 1888 they could speak in the Church. Pastors possessed less and less exclusive authority. The declining proportion of clergy to the population and their insufficient number contributed to a greater dependence upon lay preachers. Those reached by the religious awakening were largely contained in the official Church through voluntary organizations within it. A synodical organization developed. The conservative reaction after the revolutionary year of 1848 strengthened the Pietist and theologically conservative trend. The hymnal and the liturgy were revised to give expression to the new life. G. A. Lammers (1802–1878), a pastor in the state church, was profoundly changed by contact with the Moravians, preached repentance and conversion, for a time left the establishment, and led in a free church movement.

The vigorous life in Norwegian Christianity stimulated the formation of numbers of missionary societies, some for special enterprises for Norwegians, such as the large seafaring class, and others for non-Christian peoples. Norwegian Lutheranism was also carried overseas by the large emigration, notably to the United States.

CHRISTIANITY IN SWEDEN IN THE NINETEENTH CENTURY

In Sweden, as in so many other countries after 1815, there came a revival of historic Christianity and a reaction in the Church against the rationalism of the eighteenth century. As in some of the others, the reaction may have been furthered by the sufferings and humiliations of the Napoleonic Wars. Sweden had lost Finland to its hereditary foe, Russia, and was also forced to surrender

Pomerania to Denmark, although the injury to its pride had been partly assuaged by having the close tie established with Norway. The dynasty founded by Gustavus Vasa and associated with the days of the country's military glory had proved incompetent and had died out, and an alien, Bernadotte, one of Napoleon's marshals, had been elected monarch. Sobered by these changes, many felt the rationalism of the *Aufklärung* to be shallow and unable to meet the needs of the day. The reaction in part took the form of romanticism, but romanticism united with deep religious feeling. The influence of Pietism and the Moravians persisted and had fresh expressions.

Here, as elsewhere, the revival had a variety of aspects. It was seen in a new church hymnal, completed in 1819, largely the work of J. O. Wallin, who, a poet and a preacher, died as Archbishop of Uppsala (1839). It had an early leader in Henrik Schartau (1757–1825), pastor in the university town of Lund, who was strong as a preacher but was particularly earnest and skilled in spiritual counsel to individuals. He was critical of the sentimentality often associated with Pietism and stressed the sacraments of the Church. Eric Gustaf Geijer (1783–1847), a layman, a distinguished historian and professor at Uppsala, regarded history as a continuous manifestation of God and exerted a profound influence on a whole generation of intellectuals in leading them to a deeper religious life. Within the state church two theological trends, both in the nature of a strengthening of Christianity, issued from the universities, Uppsala and Lund. Uppsala stressed subjective experience and a philosophic view of Christianity and made little of the Church. Lund exalted the Church, was influenced by Kliefoth, whom we have already met in Germany, and became the radiating centre of a high-church tendency.

There were movements which either maintained only a loose connexion with the state church or completely broke with it. In the eighteenth century the North had been the scene of a revival, due in part to contact with Pietism and the Moravians. It stressed free grace through the blood of Christ, the conversion of the individual, lay preaching, and informal conventicles outside the churches. Its adherents were called "readers," because of their use of the Bible and other Christian literature. Some of the "readers" administered the sacraments. The "reader" movement found kinship with one which had as its chief stimulus George Scott, an English Methodist, who came to Stockholm in 1830 as chaplain to a group of English labourers employed by an English manufacturer. Scott's preaching attracted crowds of Swedes and did much to further the distribution of Bibles and tracts, foreign missions, Sunday Schools, and total abstinence from alcoholic beverages. Scott was joined by two young students from the North, C. O. Rosenius and Anders Wiberg. When, in 1842, Scott was forced out of the country by the authorities, Rosenius took over the leadership and, although the tie became tenuous, kept most of the former's followers within the communion of the state church. Rosenius was followed by Paul Peter Waldenström (1838–1917). Waldenström eventually severed fellowship with the disciples of Rosenius over the question of the atonement, putting forward a subjective view in contrast with the one which spoke of the expiatory death of Christ being "for all," for he held that the latter was being made an excuse for immorality. In 1878 he brought together most of the free church movement into what was called the Swedish Mission Covenant. The strain with the state church was heightened by the refusal of the authorities to permit Waldenström and those associated with him to have a free celebration of the Lord's Supper and liberty to preach. Although the Swedish Mission Covenant technically remained within the state church, it built scores of chapels throughout the kingdom and maintained its own foreign mission society.

To the Swedish Mission Covenant were added other dissenting groups. Among them were the Baptists, who arose from contacts with the United States and had Anders Wiberg, who had resigned from his pastorate in the state church, as an outstanding leader. There were also Methodists, although they were only about a third as numerous as Baptists. The Mormons attracted several thousand to Utah but a few hundred of their converts remained in Sweden. By 1914 Seventh Day Adventists, also of American origin, had nearly a hundred churches. The way was made easier for dissenters by the removal (1858) of the act against conventicles and further legislation in 1860 and 1873 in the direction of religious liberty.

The rising tide of life within Swedish Christianity expressed itself in many other ways. The Church of Sweden acquired a larger voice in the control of its own affairs. Although the king was still the highest earthly ruler of the church and the Riksdag, or Parliament, passed, repealed, or altered church laws, the monarch exercised his power only on the counsel of a minister of church affairs and of the Council of State. Moreover, a national ecclesiastical council, the Kyrko-möte, authorized in 1863, holding its first meeting in 1868, made up equally of laymen and clergy, representative of each of the dioceses and of the two universities and in part elected, had an important voice in crucial decisions. Deaconesses were trained. More lay initiative and lay organizations were seen in the congregations of the Church of Sweden. As Stockholm grew, additional church buildings were erected, partly by voluntary contributions. Christian youth movements came into being, some of them among students, and the latter were brought into touch with similar movements outside of Sweden through the World's Student Christian Federation, which was organized in 1895 in Sweden and partly by Swedes. More than a dozen missionary societies were created to spread the Gospel overseas. They represented either various theological convictions in the Church of Sweden or the different free churches. Among them was the *Evangeliska Fosterlands-stiftelse* ("Evangelical National Institute"), founded in 1856, and originally for work in Sweden by lay evangelists in connexion with the state church, but later extending its operation to seamen and to other lands. The large Swedish emigration, notably to the United States, was in general held to distinctively Swedish churches, some of them springing from the establishment and others, notably the Swedish Mission Covenant and the Baptists, from dissenting bodies. As in several other countries, out of Protestantism arose a vigorous movement to combat the use of alcoholic beverages. It was provoked in Sweden by a widespread addiction to brandy and other liquors of heavy alcoholic content. Outstanding as an advocate of total abstinence was Peter Wieselgren (1800–1877), scholar and clergyman. Efforts were made to reach the labourers, especially the youth in the growing factories. A Christian social settlement arose in Stockholm. Some pastors were active in the social democratic movement and at least two represented it in the Riksdag.

Swedish Christianity could not hope to remain unaffected by the multiform movements which were shaping the Occident of the nineteenth century. In the more strictly religious realm the currents, such as Ritschlianism, the critical study of the Bible, and the historical approach to religions which were potent in Germany quickly reached Sweden, for many Swedes studied in German universities. Here, as elsewhere, they provoked controversy. In general, the University of Uppsala was hospitable to them. Waldenström and others of similar convictions viewed them with suspicion or hostility. Frankly anti-Christian ideologies and philosophies also entered, among them Marxist materialism. Many of the labourers in the growing industries tended to drift away from the faith. Numbers of the educated, while retaining their formal connexion with the Church, were indifferent or sceptical.

As a whole, however, in Sweden, as in Germany, Denmark, and Norway, Protestantism was much more vigorous in 1914 than it had been in 1815.

Protestantism in Finland

Separated from Sweden and placed under Russia by the outcome of the Napoleonic Wars, Finland was permitted to preserve its constitution and its distinctive institutions and culture. The attempt of the tsar in 1899 to assimilate Finland to Russia and to "Russify" the country broke down within a few years. Because of the long connexion with Sweden, the Finns were overwhelmingly Protestant and Lutheran. The Lutheran Church was the established Church of Finland. Less than 2 per cent. of the population were Russian Orthodox and even by 1914 a still smaller per cent. were Methodists, Baptists, and Roman Catholics.

Nineteenth century developments in the religious life of Finland must be sketched only in summary fashion. In the eighteenth century both Pietism and the rationalism of the *Aufklärung* made themselves felt. As in Scandinavia, after 1815 Pietism continued, but, unlike most of Scandinavia, the reaction against rationalism was late in coming. The rationalism of the Enlightenment remained dominant in the Church until the middle of the nineteenth century. During the first years of Russian overlordship the Church of Finland was fortunate in having extraordinarily able leadership in its primate, Jacob Tengström, Archbishop of Åbo (Turku) from 1803 to 1832. He aided in the formation of a Bible society and a tract society and encouraged the formation of voluntary organizations to reinforce the official church. Yet he and his successor represented the spirit of the *Aufklärung*. Ostensibly the traditional orthodoxy remained, but it was largely sterile. Partly influenced by the Russian pattern, the clergy tended to be a bureaucracy emphasizing the administrative side of their functions.

Late in the eighteenth century a religious awakening began, chiefly among the laity, especially the farmers. It developed lay preachers. It spread to the students and the younger clergy and had its major centre in the new capital, Helsinki. Although opposed by the leadership of the state church, the revival reached a peak in the 1840's. It was closely associated with a rising tide of nationalism. The state church became the religious bond and symbol of Finnish patriotism. Mainly as a result of the revival, it acquired, through legislation in 1869, a large degree of independence from the state and was brought together and given a central organization under a national synod. In the second half of the nineteenth century a revision was made in the liturgy, a revised catechism was issued, and a new hymnal was compiled. All reflected the fresh life brought by the revivals. While in the 1880's many of the educated, affected by the secularism and the anti-Christian or agnostic strains in Western thought, were alienated from the Church, new revivals broke forth, partly under Finnish leadership and partly through contacts with Britain and the United States. As a result, some dissenting bodies arose. Sunday Schools, the Young Men's and Young Women's Christian Associations, and the Student Christian Movement entered and flourished. Missionary societies were founded and were concerned with both Finland and other countries. They sent representatives to China, Africa, Palestine, Japan, and the Finnish tribes in Russia.

PROTESTANTISM IN THE NETHERLANDS

What was the state of Protestantism in the nineteenth century in the Netherlands, the country where the struggle for independence had been so inextricably associated with that form of the faith?

Here, even after the separation of the predominantly Roman Catholic Belgium (1830) from the unnatural union which had been forced on the two countries by the Congress of Vienna (1815), a large Roman Catholic minority remained. By 1914, due chiefly to its birth rate, higher than that of Protestants, it constituted slightly more than a third of the population. A significant movement away from all formal connexion with any religion began and in 1909 those in that classification numbered nearly 5 per cent. of all the inhabitants, a proportion which trebled in the next two decades. In 1914 Protestants constituted about three-fifths of the population.

The Netherlands Reformed Church (*De Nederlandsch Hervormde Kerk*), long closely associated with the state, remained the largest of the Protestant bodies. When, during the Revolution, the French "liberators" had set up the Batavian Republic, the tie between the Reformed Church and the state was severed (1798) and was never again fully restored. For a time the effect upon the Reformed Church was serious and loosened the bond which held it together. After the downfall of Napoleon the House of Orange returned and one of the early acts of King William I (January 7, 1816) was to promulgate an order which gave to the Reformed Church a structure which it was to keep until after 1914. This was almost entirely administrative and accorded a degree of self-government through local and synodical bodies. Yet it also curbed the full independence of the local congregation and in 1819 church property was put under the control of the crown. Subsidies from the state continued in lieu of expropriated ecclesiastical lands. In 1852 and 1866 the crown returned to the church the control of the latter's finances.

Partly as a result of its loose organization and partly because of the complexity of the forces which played upon most churches in the nineteenth century, many parties, groups, and tendencies developed in the Netherlands Reformed Church. There was an early awakening, a repudiation both of eighteenth century rationalism and the orthodoxy of Dort. Its leaders were the poet W. Bilderdijk (died 1831) and Isaac de Costa (died 1860), a converted Jew. The main alignment was between orthodox and liberals, but there were many sub-divisions. Some of the liberals were much influenced by Hegel, had a pantheistic trend, and made little of sin, grace, and Christ. Others stressed the Jesus of the Gospels, regarded him as divine but hesitated to call him God, viewed as secondary the epistles and their theology, and had no use for the vicarious atonement. German theology had marked repercussions, especially in the universities, and some of the professors of theology were more radical than were the Germans who shaped their thinking. The Tübingen school of Biblical criticism won acceptance from many. The trend which regarded Christianity as a phase of the general development of religion was represented. There was also a movement which, stressing the ethical side of Christianity, rejected the conclusions of the critical study of the Gospels and emphasized the authority of the Bible, especially the New Testament. Some from most of these groups coöperated in missions, the care of orphans, and social efforts with those, of whom there were many, who held to the older orthodoxy. In general, liberal views prevailed among those who taught Biblical and theological subjects in the universities.

Liberalism became dominant in the Netherlands Reformed Church. Under its influence the tie with the state was made more and more tenuous, the teaching of the Reformed confession in the state schools was discontinued (1856), and the doctrinal subscription of candidates for ordination was relaxed, until, in 1883, all that was required was a promise to "further the interests of God's Kingdom."

The nineteenth century saw two major secessions from the Netherlands Reformed Church. One was in 1834 by those who in 1869 took the name of the Christian Reformed Church (*De Christelijke Gereformeerde Kerk*). Its original leader was Hendrik de Cock. It was a protest against the prevailing rationalism in the Netherlands Reformed Church and held strictly to the findings of the famous Synod of Dort of 1619. The majority united in 1892 with the Reformed Churches in the Netherlands, the other of the chief secessions, but a minority maintained its separate existence, holding to infralapsarianism rather than supralapsarianism as did the other.

The Reformed Churches in the Netherlands (*De Gereformeerde Kerken in Nederland*), the largest of the Protestant bodies outside the Netherlands Reformed Church, in 1909 had attained about a fifth the size of the former body. Its chief early figure was Abraham Kuyper (died 1920) and the major break with the Netherlands Reformed Church occurred in December, 1886. The movement was a protest against the liberalism of the Netherlands Reformed Church. It crystallized a discontent which had long been simmering, a discontent which had given rise to private schools in which the historic confessions of the Reformed Churches were made the basis of religious instruction and to the founding, by Kuyper, of the Free University of Amsterdam. Beginning with 1887 the dissenting congregations began the development of a national ecclesiastical structure. Kuyper was a vigorous leader, carried his principles into politics, and from 1901 to 1905 as premier was the real executive head of the state.

Other Protestant bodies were represented in the Netherlands. The most prominent among them were Lutherans, Mennonites, and a small remnant of the Remonstrants, a church going back to the Arminian controversy in the seventeenth century.

We must also note that towards the end of the century movements for reaching youth through voluntary organizations mounted. Through contacts with Great Britain, in 1896 the Netherlands Student Christian Union was formed. In addition there were Christian youth organizations which by 1914 enrolled several scores of thousands. In the Netherlands, as in Protestant circles in neighbouring lands, an Inner Mission was active.

In spite of these many divisions and the drift towards secularism of a large part of the population, Dutch Protestantism gave birth to a varied and growing missionary enterprise. Indeed, the divisions were evidence of vitality, of conviction which was not content with standing on the defensive but which sought to propagate the faith in other lands. Most of the missionary effort was directed towards the Netherlands East Indies, that vast area with its teeming and growing population where the Dutch were building a colonial empire and which absorbed much of the energy and provided a large proportion of the livelihood of the Dutch people.

Christian principles had a large part in Dutch politics, for there were many who sought to make them effective in the affairs of state and in the nation's colonial policies. Not only was there a Roman Catholic party, but there was also a Christian national party which was Protestant and interconfessional which drew chiefly from the farmers and the middle classes.

Protestantism in Switzerland

In Switzerland, as in Western Europe in general, rationalism pervaded the Protestant churches in the decades which immediately preceded 1815. Not far from that year a revival began which was either directly from Pietism or was closely akin to it. It stressed individual conversion. To it contributed several foreign visitors and residents, prominent among them being Robert Haldane from Scotland and Madame Krüdener. The awakenings took many forms and issued in several quite different expressions. Prominent were the Basel Evangelical Missionary Society which, as we have seen, was begun in 1815, depending largely on a Pietist constituency, and the Pilgrim Mission of St. Chrischona, on the outskirts of Basel, begun in 1840, for the training of evangelists for work at home and abroad.

The awakening met with resistance in the state churches—for it will be remembered that each of the cantons into which Switzerland was divided had an established church. In several cantons this led to the formation of free churches. Prominent among them was one in Lausanne, where the step was taken in 1845, led by Alexander Vinet (1797–1847), sometimes called the Schleiermacher of French Protestantism, and who had long been advocating on religious grounds the separation of Church and state.

The relations of Church and state were long a vital issue. They became such in the revolutionary period of 1830 and 1831, when, as in much of Western Europe, there was a swing towards democracy from the aristocratic post-1815 reaction. The constitution of 1848 which transformed Switzerland from a league of states into a federal republic permitted public worship of any recognized Christian confession in all the cantons. Amendments to the constitution in the 1870's strengthened the control of the Church by the state, forbade the creation of new Roman Catholic bishoprics without the consent of the state, made civil marriage compulsory, guaranteed liberty of belief and conscience, forbade the restriction of civil or political rights on the grounds of religious belief, and said that no one need pay taxes for the support of a religious body to which he did not belong. For the most part the loosening of the ties between Church and state, especially in predominantly Protestant cantons, did not arise from anti-clericalism. The situation varied from canton to canton, but in general each of the state churches was left free to manage its affairs and only a financial connexion remained. The chief authority in church administration was in the individual congregations and in some of these women as well as men were given a voice.

Protestants outnumbered Roman Catholics. They constituted about three-fifths of the population, but a slightly smaller percentage in 1914 than in 1815. Before the end of the century both branches of Christianity were found in each canton, but the proportionate strength varied greatly, some cantons being overwhelmingly Protestant and others predominantly Roman Catholic.

The free churches included the Baptists and Methodists. They arose through contacts with Great Britain and the United States.

Protestantism in Central Europe

In the Central European countries—Poland, Bohemia, Slovakia, Austria, and Hungary—Protestants were minorities. The nineteenth century witnessed the loosening of the restrictions placed on them by governments in which Roman Catholic influence had been potent.

Throughout the century Poland remained divided between Russia, Prussia, and Austria. Thousands of Germans, among them many Protestants, moved into the zones controlled by Prussia and Austria and thus greatly strengthened the Protestant minority which since the Catholic Reformation had been subject to persecution. There were also Protestants in the Russian zone. The Protestants were divided among Lutherans, Reformed, Moravians, and the church which represented the union of Lutherans and Reformed. There were smaller groups of Baptists and of what was known as the Christian communion.

In Bohemia and Slovakia where under Hapsburg rule and the Catholic

Reformation Protestantism had suffered chronic persecution and had been reduced to small minorities, an edict of toleration of 1781 brought some relief. In the course of the nineteenth century, especially after the revolutionary year of 1848, further progress was made towards religious liberty and relaxing control by the Roman Catholic Church.

Similarly in predominantly Roman Catholic Austria the century witnessed increasing freedom for Protestants. An imperial edict of 1861 gave them full civil rights and legal equality with Roman Catholics and permitted them to choose their own clergy. Within the next few years both Lutherans and Reformed achieved national organizations. Beginning with 1898 a movement away from Rome brought several thousand converts from the Roman Catholic Church.

In Hungary the position of Protestantism became less unfavourable. Lutheran, Reformed, and Unitarians had been present since the Reformation. Here as elsewhere in the Hapsburg domains the edict of 1781 eased earlier restrictions. In the first half of the nineteenth century Protestants were accorded equal civil rights with Roman Catholics. In the latter half of the century the awakenings which were stirring Protestantism in Western Europe, Great Britain, and the United States began to be felt and to infuse new life into churches which had been largely formal and rationalistic.

PROTESTANTISM IN LATIN EUROPE

In Latin Europe, predominantly Roman Catholic, the nineteenth century brought the Protestant minorities varying degrees of relaxation of adverse pressure.

In Spain and Portugal Protestantism in 1815 was non-existent. In the course of the nineteenth century missionaries entered, chiefly from Great Britain and the United States. Through their efforts small Protestant bodies came into being.

Italy had an indigenous Protestantism, the Waldensees. In the nineteenth century some of the Waldensees moved from their ancestral Alpine valleys into the cities. They were aided by financial grants from fellow-Protestants in Great Britain and the United States and by measures looking towards religious liberty taken under the Kingdom of Italy. Missionaries also came from several British and American denominations.

Belgium had a few small Protestant congregations in the midst of an overwhelmingly Roman Catholic population. In the 1830's, after the achievement of Belgian independence, these drew together in two national unions.

France contained more Protestants than did any other Latin country. They were partly Lutheran, chiefly in the border province of Alsace, and partly Reformed, the descendants of the Huguenots who had suffered severe persecution across the years. Napoleon I had granted them toleration and the position of state churches. This status was respected by the successive regimes which controlled the state in the nineteenth century. For Protestants as for Roman Catholics, the separation of Church and state came in 1905 and for a time brought financial embarrassment.

As with Protestantism elsewhere, so in France, the nineteenth century witnessed a revival of a Pietist nature (due in part to the efforts of Haldane) and a liberalism which arose from the attempt to accommodate the faith to the intellectual temper of the age. In the French Reformed Church these contrasting currents brought on a conflict which led to division (1849). The orthodox, with a warm personal faith, had the Monods, Adolphe and Frédéric, as leaders, left the Reformed Synod, thus renouncing all endowments, and depended on voluntary gifts for support. They constituted themselves as the Union of Evangelical Free Churches.

The annexation (1871) of Alsace and Lorraine by Germany led to a sharp diminution of the numbers of Protestants, especially Lutherans, under the French flag. In place of the theological faculty of Strassburg, lost by the cession, a Protestant theological school was founded in Paris in which both Reformed and Lutherans joined. The Reformed also had missions to the Roman Catholics and the unchurched. The McCall Mission, begun in 1872 and supported from Great Britain and the United States, endeavoured, with the cordial concurrence of French Protestants, to reach the labourers in the cities who were being de-Christianized by the forces of the age. Missionaries, mostly Methodists and Baptists from the British Isles and the United States, gathered converts, but these never exceeded more than a few thousand.

SUMMARY

From what has unavoidably been a somewhat bewildering array of details several generalizations emerge which characterize the Protestantism of Continental Europe in the nineteenth century.

First of all is extreme complexity. In spite of an attempt to reduce the narrative to a minimum and the omission of many important names and movements which would have to be given a place in a complete story, the perusal of this chapter must leave even the most courageous and painstaking reader somewhat bewildered.

As a second generalization there is an impression of abounding vitality. The multiplicity of details may arise in part from our nearness to the period and a consequent lack of perspective which would enable us to sort out the more significant. However, it is primarily due to the extraordinary vigour of nine-teenth century Protestantism. Although it was faced by hostile forces which threatened the existence of Christianity and which were progressively de-Christianizing large elements of the population, Protestantism was experienc-ing a marked revival, was inspiring many of the intellectuals to re-think their faith in terms of the new methods and knowledge of the age, was moving others to seek to bring their faith to bear upon the social and political forces of the day, was working in millions a transforming experience, and was giving birth to societies which were spreading the Gospel in all the continents and in many of the islands of the sea. That vitality was mounting. Continental Euro-pean Protestantism came to 1914 more vigorous than in 1815 and, by immigra-tion and missions, more widely spread than at any earlier time.

A third generalization is that there was in progress a separation of Church and state. Unlike the similar dissociation which was affecting the Roman Catholic Church, it had in it little of hostility to the Church. It arose partly from the democratic secular liberalism which was prominent in politics and partly from the desire of the churches for freedom from control by the state. It was accompanied by growing autonomy in the churches, an autonomy which was at once an evidence and a contributory cause of enhanced vigour.

A fourth generalization is the rise of fresh tensions and divisions in Protes-tantism. They cut across denominational, confessional, and national boundaries. In general they fell into three classifications. One was the emphasis upon his-toric creeds, confessions, and forms of worship. Another stressed a personal religious experience and tended to exalt the Bible as the inspired word of God to men. The third endeavoured to accommodate the faith to current philosophies and the scientific approach. The three interacted on one another, but the conflicts were often sharp.

A fifth generalization is the leading place held by Germany in Continental Protestantism. Through Pietism in its varied forms, through its historic con-fessions, and through its new formulations of theology and its Biblical studies German Protestantism, especially German Lutheranism, was dominant. The reasons are not entirely clear. They are to be found partly in the fact that Ger-many was the original home of Protestantism, partly in the size of the country, and partly in the surge of nationalism which was uniting the country politi-cally. Yet these seem not to have been all. There may be other reasons which defy the methods and the insights of the historian.

A sixth generalization which can be only dimly discerned from what has been said in the preceding pages was the growing unity of Protestantism, a unity which after 1914 was to mount by leaps and bounds. In spite of the many frictions and the new divisions added to the old, Protestantism was not a congeries of relatively isolated movements. The multiform aspects of Protestantism were affecting one another, often profoundly. Currents in one land or branch of Protestantism were flowing into other lands and into other branches of that wing of the faith. The Protestantism of the Continent was influencing that of the British Isles and America. In turn, British and American Protestantism was making itself felt on the Continent. As we are to see in later chapters, as never before Protestants were beginning to find ways of coöperating interconfessionally on a world-wide scale. Here was a new kind of Christian unity, as yet very imperfect, but growing.

SELECTED BIBLIOGRAPHY

R. B. Brandt, *The Philosophy of Schleiermacher. The Development of His Theory of Scientific and Religious Knowledge* (New York, Harper & Brothers, 1941, pp. viii, 350). Useful.

T. K. Cheyne, *Founders of Old Testament Criticism. Biographical, Descriptive, and Critical Studies* (New York, Charles Scribner's Sons, 1893, pp. ix, 372). Judiciously sympathetic.

G. Cross, *The Theology of Schleiermacher. A Condensed Presentation of His Chief Work "The Christian Faith"* (The University of Chicago Press, 1911, pp. lx, 344). Sympathetic.

A. L. Drummond, *German Protestantism since Luther* (London, The Epworth Press, 1951, pp. x, 282). Contains much useful material. Especially valuable for the nineteenth and twentieth centuries.

A. E. Garvie, *The Ritschlian Theology, Critical and Constructive. An Exposition and an Estimate* (Edinburgh, T. & T. Clark, 1899, pp. xxvii, 400). A useful and sympathetic summary by a competent Scottish theologian.

M. Gerhardt, *Ein Jahrhundert Innere Mission. Die Geschichte des Central-Ausschuss für die Innere Mission der Deutschen Evangelische Kirche* (Gütersloh, C. Bertelsmann Verlag, 2 vols., 1948). Excellent not only for the Inner Mission but also on the German Church in general and on the relations of Church and state.

J. I. Good, *History of the Swiss Reformed Church Since the Reformation* (Philadelphia, Publication and Sunday School Board of the Reformed Church in the United States, 1913, pp. xii, 504). Sympathetic, especially with the free churches.

W. Herrmann, *Systematic Theology (Dogmatik)*, translated by N. Micklem and K. A. Saunders (New York, The Macmillan Co., 1927, pp. 152). A brief posthumous summary of his views.

F. Kattenbusch, *Die deutsche evangelische Theologie seit Schleiermacher. Ihre Leistungen and ihre Schäden* (Giessen, Alfred Topelmann, 5th ed., 1926, pp. vi, 160).

Kierkegaard's Attack upon "Christendom" 1854–1855, translated with an introduction by W. Lowrie (Princeton University Press, 1944, pp. xviii, 303).

S. Kierkegaard, *The Gospel of Suffering and the Lilies of the Field,* translated by D. F. Swenson and L. M. Swenson (Minneapolis, Augsburg Publishing Co., 1948, pp. 239).

[S. Kierkegaard] Johannes Climacus, *Philosophical Fragments or A Fragment of Philosophy,* translated by D. F. Swenson (Princeton University Press, 1936, pp. xxx, 105).

H. Koch, *Grundtvig,* translated by L. Jones (Yellow Springs, Ohio, Antioch Press, 1952). A standard work.

F. Lichtenberger, *History of German Theology in the Nineteenth Century,* translated by W. Hastie (Edinburgh, T. & T. Clark, 1889, pp. xxxix, 629). A comprehensive sketch.

H. R. Mackintosh, *Types of Modern Theology Schleiermacher to Barth* (New York, Charles Scribner's Sons, 1937, pp. vii, 333). By a competent Scottish theologian.

K. D. Macmillan, *Protestantism in Germany* (Princeton University Press, 1917, pp. viii, 282). A semi-popular and sketchy historical survey.

E. C. Moore, *An Outline of the History of Christian Thought Since Kant* (New York, Charles Scribner's Sons, 1912, pp. x, 249). A useful, popular, critical summary survey of Protestant thought in Europe and America.

J. W. Oman, *The Problem of Faith and Freedom in the Last Two Centuries* (New York, A. C. Armstrong and Son, 1906, pp. xxiv, 443). Mainly on Continental Protestant thought in the nineteenth century. By a competent scholar.

J. Orr, *Ritschlianism. Expository and Critical Essays* (London, Hodder & Stoughton, 1903, pp. xii, 283). The author believes Ritschlian theology to be basically unsound.

O. Pfleiderer, *The Development of Theology in Germany since Kant, and Its Progress in Great Britain since 1825,* translated by J. F. Smith (London, Swan Sonnenschein & Co., 1890, pp. xii, 403).

E. Révész, J. S. Kováts, L. Ravasz, *Hungarian Protestantism, Its Past, Present and Future* (Budapest, Bethlen Gábor Literary and Printing House, 1927, pp. xiv, 222).

A. Ritschl, *A Critical History of the Christian Doctrine of Justification and Reconciliation,* translated by J. S. Black (Edinburgh, Edmonston and Douglas, 1872, pp. xvi, 605).

A. Ritschl, *The Christian Doctrine of Justification and Reconciliation. The Positive Development of the Doctrine.* English translation edited by H. R. Mackintosh and A. B. Macaulay (New York, Charles Scribner's Sons, 1900, pp. xii, 673).

F. E. D. Schleiermacher, *Schleiermacher's Werke* (Leipzig, Felix Meiner, 3 vols., 1927).

F. Schleiermacher, *The Christian Faith,* translated from the second German edition by H. R. Mackintosh and J. S. Stewart (Edinburgh, T. & T. Clark, 1928, pp. xii, 760).

W. B. Selbie, *Schleiermacher, A Critical and Historical Study* (New York, E. P. Dutton & Co., 1913, pp. ix, 272). By a competent British theologian.

The Life of Schleiermacher as Unfolded in His Autobiography and Letters, translated by F. Rowan (London, Smith, Elder & Co., 2 vols., 1860).

F. Siegmund-Schultze, editor, *Ekklesia. Eine Sammlung von Selbstdarstellungen der Christlichen Kirchen:*

II. *Die Skandinavischen Länder. Die Kirche in Schweden* (Gotha, Leopold Klotz, 1935, pp. 180).

II. *Die Skandinavischen Länder. Die Kirche von Norwegen* (Gotha, Leopold Klotz, 1936, pp. 207).

II. *Die Skandinavischen Länder. Die Kirche in Dänemark. Die Kirche in Island* (Leipzig, Leopold Klotz, 1937, pp. 195, 35).

II. *Die Skandinavischen Länder. Die Kirche in Finnland* (Leipzig, Leopold Klotz, 1938, pp. 203).

III. *Die Mitteleuropäischen Länder. 9. Die Evangelischen Kirchen der Niederlande* (Gotha, Leopold Klotz, 1934, pp. 176).

III. *Die Mitteleuropäischen Länder. 10. Die Evangelischen Kirchen der Schweitz* (Gotha, Leopold Klotz, 1935, pp. 254).

V. *Die Osteuropäischen Länder. Die Kirchen der Tschechoslowakei* (Leipzig, Leopold Klotz, 1937, pp. 250).

V. *Die Osteuropäischen Länder. Die Evangelischen Kirchen in Polen* (Leipzig, Leopold Klotz, 1938, pp. 274).

This very useful series is composed of carefully written articles, historical and descriptive, but chiefly historical, by specialists in the respective countries.

P. Stiansen, *History of the Baptists in Norway* (Chicago, The Blessing Press, pp. xi, 175). Carefully and sympathetically done.

D. F. Strauss, *The Life of Jesus Critically Examined,* translated from the fourth German edition by M. Evans (New York, Calvin Blanchard, 2 vols., 1860).

A. T. Swing, *The Theology of Albrecht Ritschl, Together with Introduction in the Christian Religion by A. Ritschl,* translated by A. T. Swing (New York, Longmans, Green & Co., 1901, pp. xiv, 296).

J. Wordsworth, *The National Church of Sweden* (London, A. R. Mowbray & Co., 1911, pp. xix, 459). An historical survey by an Anglican bishop.

Agnes von Zahn-Harnack, *Adolf von Harnack* (Berlin, Walter de Gruyter & Co., 1951, pp. xiii, 453).

Chapter 48

CHRISTIANITY IN THE BRITISH ISLES,
A.D. 1815 - A.D. 1914

In the history of Christianity in the nineteenth century the British Isles were peculiarly important. They were dominant in the commerce and banking of the world of that day. They led in the phenomenal expansion of Western European power and culture that was bringing the world-wide revolutions which, affecting all mankind, were mounting, especially in the latter part of the century, and which after 1914 were to display ever-increasing acceleration. They built an empire on which, so it was proudly said, the sun never set. Largely through emigration from them new nations arose in Canada, Australia, and New Zealand. That emigration also contributed notably to the growth and character of the United States and South Africa. Near to the Continent of Europe and intimately related to its life and problems, and yet partially detached by the North Sea and the English Channel, the British Isles influenced the Continent and were influenced by it, and also had a distinct development. In this rôle of the British Isles in the nineteenth century course of mankind the Christianity of the islands had a very important part. As we pursue our geographic survey of the globe of these days we shall find it again and again. For this reason as well as for its place in the islands themselves, we must seek to understand it.

GENERAL FACTORS AFFECTING THE NINETEENTH CENTURY COURSE OF CHRISTIANITY IN THE BRITISH ISLES

At the outset of our attempt to trace the history of the Christianity of the British Isles in the nineteenth century we must note a number of factors which to a greater or less degree had a part in shaping it. They were very diverse and not all of them were interrelated, but we must bear them in mind, even when, absorbed in the details of our narrative, we do not specifically call attention to them. They do not fall into any logically arranged order. We can simply mention them one by one.

Prominent both in the general life of the islands and in its challenge to Christianity was rapid and progressive industrialization. Great Britain was the pioneer in the industrial revolution. During much of the nineteenth century it held what was almost a natural monopoly of the new industrial processes. This entailed vast changes in the life of Great Britain and, to a less extent, of its sister island, Ireland. It contributed to a striking increase in population which challenged the resources of the churches. Even more significantly, it led to enormous shifts of population and the phenomenal growth of cities. The churches' structure had been adapted to a rural economy and small cities. Now proportionately farming was declining, new cities were springing up, and existing cities, such as London and Glasgow, were becoming larger than any one would have once believed possible. Could the churches build enough physical plants to care for the expanding urban populations?

Still more challenging and perplexing were the altered social conditions produced by the industrial revolution. Not only were the majority of the people now in cities. In the towns and cities the environment which shaped the lives of their inhabitants was changing. Mining, especially coal mining on which industry and commerce depended, gave rise to communities in which life was drab and working conditions grim. Factories brought larger and smaller aggregations of labour, usually in overcrowded tenements. At the outset they were characterized by long hours, no protection to women and children, a lack of safeguards against disease and accident, and insecurity of employment. The port cities were no better. Poverty and squalor were not strangers in the British Isles. However, in the slums of mining, industrial, and commercial towns and cities they now attained unprecedented dimensions. They were the frightful price that Britain paid for her collective power and wealth. Could Christianity win and retain and hold a place in such a society? Still more, could it ameliorate the lot of those who were caught in its toils?

A concomitant of industrialization was the rising power of the middle classes and the declining place of the landed gentry and aristocracy. This was to contribute to a change in the religious complexion of the country. Especially did it make for the growth of Nonconformity in England, for it was among the middle classes that the "free" churches had their chief strength.

Intimately connected with the mounting industrialization were movements, some of them revolutionary, in politics and social organization. Democracy gained headway. The Reform Bill of 1832 gave a larger voice in the House of Commons to the towns and cities, especially the newer ones, and to the middle class. The year 1848 which witnessed sweeping changes on the Continent was paralleled in England by the culmination of the Chartist movement. Chartism gained rapid headway among the industrial workers and made demands which were eventually granted. The Reform Act of 1867 accorded additional seats in the House of Commons to the cities and broadened the franchise, largely among the urban working classes. The adoption of the secret ballot (1872) furthered democracy, and in 1884 and 1885 the privilege of voting was extended to almost all adult males. In 1911 the power of the House of Lords as against the House of Commons was drastically restricted. Labour organized into unions. In 1800 these had been forbidden, but in 1824 that action was repealed, and in 1825 legislation was enacted which permitted workmen to organize "to determine the scale of wages and the hours of labour." Unions increased in numbers and power. A Labour Party was organized and in 1914 it controlled forty seats in the House of Commons. There was also an Independent Labour Party which was frankly socialist. In the course of the century much humanitarian legislation was put on the statute books for mitigating the criminal laws and regulating the hours and conditions of labour.

Here again was a challenge. Could Christianity shape these movements towards Christian ends? Many of those who pioneered in the march towards democracy, for the organization of trade unions and the Labour Party, and for laws to improve the conditions of the masses were earnest Christians, products of religious awakenings and acting from Christian motives. However, some of the leadership was agnostic or even anti-Christian. Much of labour was hostile to the Church, and especially to the Church of England, for the latter was regarded as a bulwark of entrenched privilege and the exploiting classes. Moreover, it was in London that Marx did much of the formulation of the socialism which is associated with his name and he was bitter against the Church and its faith.

Closely related to the industrialization of the British Isles was a vast and multiform emigration. As we have hinted, most of it went to North America, Australasia, and South Africa. Much of it was from England, Scotland, and Wales. Much, too, was from the Roman Catholic elements of the population of Ireland. In the first half of the nineteenth century an increase in population, the evils of landlordism, and, in the 1840's, a blight that ruined the potato crop which was a main source of food and which was followed by famine, brought about a vast migration from Ireland. This was especially to the United States and the British colonies, but it was also to the manufacturing towns and cities of Great Britain. It did much to shape the Christianity of the lands to which it went.

The intellectual currents which were noted in Chapter 45 and which challenged Christianity operated in the British Isles as well as on the Continent. Here, as on the Continent, many believed that science and its findings had made Christian faith impossible for an intelligent, honest mind and turned either atheist or agnostic. The task of reconciling science and Christianity became one of the major concerns of Christian scholars.

Not only did the Christianity of the British Isles influence that in many other portions of the world. It was also in part shaped by what came to it from current movements in several other lands. In theology and Biblical studies it showed the effect of what was taking place on the Continent, especially in Germany. There was little or no slavish acceptance of Continental thought. Much of the latter was rejected outright, much was taken over in modified form, and much proved a stimulus to fresh approaches and conclusions. The Christianity of the United States was potent. That was partly because of the common heritage in language and religious life. The effect of the United States was seen chiefly in a reinforcement of the continuation of the Evangelical Awakening and of the movements which issued from it. Numbers of American "evangelists," itinerant preachers who sought the conversion of non-Christians and the deeper commitment of Christians, toured the British Isles. Prominent among them in the first half of the century was Charles G. Finney (1792–1875), who had two preaching missions to the British Isles and whose writings, notably his *Lectures on Revivals of Religion,* had an extensive sale. In the second part of the century Dwight Lyman Moody (1837–1899) and the singer who accompanied him, Ira David Sankey (1840–1908), made three extended visits to the British Isles, in 1873–1875, 1881–1884, and 1891–1892, with effects comparable with those of Wesley and Whitefield in the eighteenth century. No new denomination arose as a result of their meetings. Rather, most of the existing denominations were stirred to deeper life. Their *Gospel Hymns,* with simple and moving melodies and words, became the common property of thousands. Partly from the Moody movement came two other Americans, John Raleigh Mott (1865——) and Robert Parmelee Wilder (1863–1938), of both of whom, especially the former, we are to hear more later, and who addressed themselves primarily to students. Mott held evangelistic meetings in universities. Wilder introduced the Student Volunteer Movement for Foreign Missions, which had begun at a summer student conference under Moody's leadership in 1886 and had swept with great power through the colleges, universities, and theological seminaries of the United States. Out of the Student Volunteer Movement sprang the Student Christian Movement of Great Britain and Ireland, soon to be the major agency for volunteer student Christian activity in the colleges and universities of the British Isles.

We have designedly named this chapter "Christianity in the British Isles A.D. 1815–A.D. 1914," for we must seek to cover both of the main branches of the faith that were represented there, namely Protestant and Roman Catholic. As we are to see shortly, the Roman Catholic Church was important, especially in Ireland. However, it was Protestantism that predominated. There was a memorable revival of the Catholic tradition in the Church of England, but it was Protestantism which was chiefly notable for abounding vitality.

British Protestantism continued to be invigorated by the Evangelical movement. This movement persisted through the century. To a greater or less extent it affected all the churches except the Roman Catholic. From time to time it reached a crescendo. Especially striking was a revival in the late 1850's which stirred Anglo-Saxon Protestantism on both sides of the Atlantic.

Most of the nineteenth century was embraced by the reign of Queen Victoria (1837–1901). While, because of the declining power of the British monarchs before the growing authority of Parliament, Victoria did not leave as deep an impress on the country as had Elizabeth, it was no accident which named the latter half of the century the Victorian era. The queen both symbolized and reinforced much that characterized the period. Especially was that true of religion. She was genuinely devout and took an active interest in the Church of England. In her personal and family life she was in striking contrast with the monarchs who immediately preceded her and was an indication of the improvement which the mounting momentum of the religious awakening was making in the faith and morals of large elements in the population.

Although under one rule, the British Isles contained four nations, England, Wales, Scotland, and Ireland, each with a somewhat distinct culture and religious life. We must, therefore, pursue our way through them one by one rather than attempt to treat them as a unit. Yet they interacted on one another and clearly belong together. We first turn to England as the largest, richest, and most populous of the four lands.

England: The Established Church

In England we naturally begin with the Church of England, for of the several Christian communions it was the largest, the only one established by law, and in theory represented the religious facet of the nation, paralleled by the government which stood for the political phase of the people's life.

Taken as a whole, in 1815 the Church of England was far from healthy. It was rich in its endowments and its revenues, but it was closely bound to the existing order and its leaders were fearful of any change that would jeopardize their position. In a manner reminiscent of pre-Reformation abuses, pluralism, non-residence, and carelessness in the observance of the services and sacraments abounded. Even some of the higher ecclesiastics drew the revenues from more than one post and entrusted the performance of their duties to substitutes. In 1831 it was said, apparently on the basis of official statistics, that more than half the clergy did not reside in their benefices. Among the bishops were those who were distrustful of enthusiasm, worldly, indolent, luxurious, and attached to the perquisites of their office. Confirmation was often administered in a slovenly manner and with notable exceptions services were performed carelessly and in a routine fashion or were even neglected. Many cathedrals were in disrepair and were far from being centres of orderly worship and spiritual life. The bulk of the parish clergy, especially in the rural districts, were decent men who were interested in the physical welfare of their flocks, but they shared in the manner of life and the prejudices of the country gentry. They were better educated and probably more moral than their predecessors of fifteenth century, pre-Reformation days, but they left much to be desired. The prevailing system of pew rents tended to shut out the poor and to identify the Church of England with a class.

There was a happier side of the picture. The Evangelicals, although a small minority, were active. Outside their ranks worthy bishops and clergy were also found. However, in general the Church of England entered the nineteenth century in poor condition to meet the threats and the challenges which that age presented to Christianity. The bulwark and refuge of privilege, it is not strange that it was viewed with dislike and even hostility by many who longed and worked for the betterment of the conditions of the masses and by multitudes of those on whom the new industrialization bore heavily.

The nineteenth century witnessed a striking awakening and transformation within the Church of England. In a sense the real reformation of that church was then rather than in the sixteenth and seventeenth centuries. This came both from without and from within.

The forces which, working from without, made for improvement in the Church of England were in part those which brought modernization in the political structure of the state, were a phase of the onward march of democracy, and operated through the government. Aided by some churchmen, they found expression in acts of Parliament in the 1830's, after the Reform Bill of 1832 which based the House of Commons on a wider and more representative electorate. They were designed to correct the more flagrant abuses and to enable the Church of England better to meet the conditions of the new day. A permanent body was set up called the Ecclesiastical Commissioners for England, which was to see that the new laws were carried out and was to manage the property entrusted to it. Several of the larger sees were reduced to a more manageable size and new sees were created. The revenues of the archbishoprics and of some of the wealthier bishoprics were so managed that the incomes of the incumbents were reduced and the savings used to augment the stipends of the poorer sees. Several sinecure benefices were suppressed and the number of resident canons attached to cathedrals was curtailed and the sums thus freed were assigned to needy livings. Pluralism was all but abolished and non-residency was proscribed. Parish boundaries were altered to make them more nearly coincide with current needs. The tithe, a form of revenue for the Church which had come down from the Middle Ages and which had largely been paid in the produce of the soil, was increasingly irritating and was commuted to a rental to be paid in cash. In 1868 as a result of agitation which began at least as far back as the 1830's and which was pushed by Dissenters, the compulsory payment of local parish rates for the maintenance of the church fabric was abolished and was made purely voluntary.

Many movements worked from within the Church of England. One of these was for the erection of new church buildings to care for the growing urban population and for the repair and restoration of older church fabrics. Several societies were formed for this purpose. To them came gifts from private individuals. In 1818 and 1828 they were augmented by substantial grants by the government. In 1836 the Pastoral Aid Society was organized to increase the number of clergy.

Another movement was the continuation of the Evangelical strain within the Church of England. At the outset of the nineteenth century the Evangelicals, although a minority, were the most active and zealous in that church. They preached the necessity of conversion, stressed family prayers and the observance of Sunday, endeavoured to live their lives "in the great Taskmaster's eye," were ardent students of the Bible, produced a religious literature which was widely read, brought more of the singing of hymns into the church services, elevated marriage, were self-sacrificing in their gifts to charity, and were zealous in promoting social reform. Although often derided, even by clergymen of the Church of England, they contributed in large measure to the improvement in the language and morals of the land which became noticeable in the fore part of the nineteenth century. They were not especially active in speculative theological thought. Indeed, they had little interest in the philosophy of religion or of history, nor did they stress scholarship. Distrustful of the nineteenth century critical study of the Bible, they were content to regard the Scriptures as the authoritative word of God. They believed firmly in the incarnation, in the substitutionary death of Christ, in justification by faith, in the salvation of the individual, and in the present operation of the Holy Spirit. They were willing to coöperate with those of like views in other communions and were active in home and foreign missions.

From the Evangelicals and those sympathetic with them issued a wealth of hymns. The tradition in the Church of England, supported by the weight of Cranmer, had been to employ only the metrical versions of the Psalms in public worship. Now, thanks in part to the Evangelicals but also to other influences, hymns of "human" composition came into use. Among Evangelical hymn writers were Henry Alford (1810–1871), eventually Dean of Canterbury Cathedral, whose best remembered productions were "Come ye thankful people, come" (1844), "Ten thousand times ten thousand" (1867), and "Forward be our watchword" (1871); Anna Laetitia Waring (1820–1910), whose "In heavenly love abiding" (1850) had a long and wide use; George Croly (1780–1860), Irish by birth and rearing, a magnetic preacher in London, and the author of "Spirit of God, descend upon my heart"; Edward Henry Bickersteth (1825–1906), in later life Bishop of Exeter, compiler of the hymnal *Christian Psalmody,* and author of "Oh God the Rock of Ages" (1860); Arabella Katherine Hankey (1834–1889), whose father was a member of the "Clapham sect" and who wrote "I love to tell the story" (1866); and especially Francis Ridley Havergal (1836–1878), daughter of an Anglican clergyman who did much to improve church music, herself highly educated, a talented musician, an earnest and happy evangelist, the writer of many hymns, among them "Lord, speak to me that I may speak" (1872) and "Take my life and let it be consecrated, Lord, to Thee" (1874).

It is said that in the first half of the century the Evangelicals began to be popular, especially among the well-to-do, and to have become conventional. However, Evangelicalism was revitalized by the revivals in the latter part of the century, especially those which accompanied the visits of Moody and Sankey. Conferences were held for the deepening of the spiritual life at which not only Anglicans but also Nonconformists were welcome. A famous centre for them was at Mildmay, where William Pennefather was vicar, and where in 1870 a hall to seat 2,500 was built. It was Pennefather who first asked Moody to England. Another centre, begun in 1875 at Keswick, in the Lake District, in Cumberland, by T. D. Harford-Battersby, a clergyman of the Church of England, persisted annually into the twentieth century. At first looked upon with suspicion by some Evangelicals of the old school, eventually it became a radiating focus of spiritual power among Evangelicals and those among dissenters who held kindred convictions. Evangelicals also began schools for the training of deaconesses, among them one founded at Mildmay by Pennefather, partly suggested by the one at Kaiserswerth, in Germany.

Another current making for revival in the Church of England was what is sometimes known as the Tractarian movement but more often as the Oxford movement. It contributed powerfully to the Anglo-Catholic movement. Like the Evangelical Awakening, it was from within the Church, but in several respects the contrast between the two was striking. While loyal to the Book of Common Prayer and to the ecclesiastical structure, the Evangelicals, stressing, as we have seen, individual conversion, holy living, missions, and moral and social reform and improvement, had little sense of the historic Church and the Catholic tradition, willingly coöperated with Christians of similar convictions outside their communion, and, as we have said, had few profound scholars and were not much interested in speculative theology. On the other hand, the Oxford movement was deeply concerned for the historic Church, looked back nostalgically to the Catholic Church as it was in the early centuries before it had been torn apart through the stresses of regionalism, nationalism, and conflicting dogmas, and longed for what it called "reunion." It saw in the apostolic succession of the episcopate an essential characteristic of the Catholic Church, prized the sacraments, holding them to be valid only when administered by clergy ordained by bishops in the apostolic succession, valued the writings of the Early Church Fathers, made much of theological scholarship, and distrusted or completely rejected the contemporary intellectual currents which undermined Christian faith as expressed in the creeds of the Catholic Church. It stressed worship, both private and public, and, insisting that the latter be conducted with dignity and beauty, brought back from the Catholic practice such appurtenances as vestments, candles, and incense. While tolerating the connexion between Church and state and holding that the Church was the instrument appointed by God to guide the nation in the path of truth, the Oxford movement wished the Church to be free from the state in issues which concerned its inner life, such as creeds and forms of worship.

The Oxford movement had affinities with several other trends, both past and contemporary, yet it was not identical with any of them. It was in part a fresh expression of one which had been present in the Church of England ever since the breach with Rome, namely, that which cherished the Catholic heritage rather than the Protestant changes. It found in the Church of England a high church wing which emphasized the connexion with the state and had kinship with an orthodox wing which gave much weight to the historic creeds and the theology inherited from the Catholic tradition. Romanticism, strong in England in the first half of the century as on the Continent, with its nostalgic admiration for the Middle Ages, contributed to a climate of opinion and feeling congenial to the movement. There were similarities to the reaction against the French Revolution which on the Continent contributed to the revival of the Roman Catholic Church and to orthodox Protestant confessionalism and kinship with the loosening of the control of the Church by the state and the return to much in Catholic practice which was seen in some Lutheran circles in Germany and Scandinavia. Yet affinities and similarities did not mean identity. Here was a vital movement, based upon profound thought, deep conviction, and intense religious feeling and commitment which was the channel for a fresh burst of life in the Church of England.

The Oxford movement is usually dated from a sermon, "National Apostasy," preached in the university pulpit at Oxford on July 14, 1833. The sermon was a protest against the act of Parliament which had reduced the number of bishoprics of the (Anglican) Church of Ireland. To the preacher this seemed an infringement of civil authority on prerogatives which by divine appointment belonged solely to the Church. The preacher, John Keble (1792–1866), the son of a clergyman, had had an extraordinarily brilliant student career at Oxford. Inflexible in his conservatism, antagonistic to liberalism, he was moved by a profound conviction of the divine origin and authority of the Church. His *Christian Year* had already been published (1827). It was a devotional book made up of poems fitted to each Sunday and festival and saint's day observed by the Church of England. It had an enormous circulation and in less than fifty years went into over 150 editions. Early associated with Keble were Richard Hurrell Froude (1803–1836) and John Henry Newman (1801–1890). Froude, brother of the more famous and ultimately sceptical historian, James Anthony Froude (1818–1894), died young, leaving behind him a spiritual diary, his *Remains,* which revealed an unusually, almost morbidly sensitive conscience. With this he combined fierceness of attack on those who differed from his convictions. Newman had been reared an Evangelical and from this background derived assurance of personal salvation, a deep direct awareness of God, and a conviction of personal guidance by God. Possessed of a subtle and powerful intellect he was for some time the chief figure in the movement.

The Oxford movement was spear-headed by *Tracts for the Times.* Of these ninety were published between 1833 and 1841, when they were abruptly terminated. Newman reinforced them by his sermons from the pulpit of St. Mary's, the university church in Oxford, of which he was the vicar.

The group early had a powerful recruit in Edward Bouverie Pusey (1800–1882) who, with Keble and Newman, was a fellow of Oriel College. In 1828 he was made regius professor of Hebrew and canon of Christ Church, Oxford, but it was not until 1835 and 1836 that he became fully associated with the movement. Deeply religious, implacable in controversy, humble and generous in his charities, he was later regarded as the outstanding leader. Indeed, the movement was often called Puseyism.

The *Tracts for the Times* and the other writings and the preaching of those associated with the Oxford movement provoked excited opposition. In England Protestantism was strong and the antagonism to Rome pronounced. The latter had been accentuated by the removal, in 1829, of the restrictions which had debarred Roman Catholics from public office and membership in Parliament. Criticism reached a high pitch when, in 1841, the ninetieth *Tract,* which had Newman as its author, was published. In this Newman declared that the

Thirty-nine Articles which officially stated the position of the Church of England were not contrary to Catholic doctrine and practice but simply condemned some of the abuses which had arisen in connexion with them. He recognized other sacraments than baptism and the Lord's Supper, came out for the real presence of Christ in the Eucharist, made room for purgatory and the invocation of the saints, qualified the Protestant doctrine of salvation by faith alone, and in other respects attempted to show how those who held to the faith of the Catholic Church could subscribe to the Thirty-nine Articles. The *Tract* caused such a commotion that the Bishop of Oxford commanded the termination of the series.

The fears of the critics were confirmed and their opposition heightened when numbers affected by the Oxford movement, mostly from the clergy and largely younger men, left the Church of England and were admitted to the Roman Catholic Church. Of these the most notable were Newman himself, who made his submission to Rome in 1845, and Henry Edward Manning (1808–1892), an ascetic, devoted, able Oxford graduate and priest. Manning was received into the Roman Catholic Church in 1851, in 1865 was made Archbishop of Westminster and head of the English hierarchy, was strongly ultramontane, worked zealously for the acceptance of the dogma of Papal infallibility, was indefatigable in labours to better the conditions of the poor, and died a cardinal. Newman was created a cardinal late in life, but was regarded with suspicion in stricter Roman Catholic circles. He had intellectual kinship with some of the modernism which was officially condemned a few years after his death, for he believed that the doctrine of the Church had developed. Yet, distrusting reason, he held that an infallible authority was required to control the course of that development and he regarded Rome as that authority. He joined the Oratory, founded, it will be remembered, by Philip Neri during the Catholic Reformation, and inaugurated a community of the order in Birmingham. There he henceforth made his home.

The large majority of those committed to the Anglo-Catholic movement remained within the Church of England. Through them many changes were introduced in the practices of that church. More elaborate ritual was developed, with eucharistic vestments, genuflexions, and incense. Private confession to the priest was revived. Monasticism reappeared, with communities and orders of men and women living by rule. Frequent communion was encouraged.

Much of this continued to be met with criticism which at times and in a few places became riotous. Not only were the Anglican Evangelicals among the opponents. Nonconformists were also critical and the adoption of Catholic practices drove them further from the Church of England. Here was one of the sources of the formation of the Evangelical Alliance. Inaugurated in 1846, its purpose was partly negative, but was also and primarily positive. It sought to draw together the great body of Evangelicals of all denominations for fellowship and prayer.

The Anglo-Catholic movement was not simply intent upon strengthening the sense of the corporate Church and the Catholic tradition in doctrine, sacraments, and worship. It was a revival of Christian devotion which showed itself in many other ways. Its clergy and sisterhoods often gave themselves unstintedly to the service of the poor who abounded in the cities of industrialized England. There was a fresh outburst of hymn writing. Newman's "Lead kindly Light" dated from his Anglican days. Especially prominent was John Mason Neale (1818–1866), noted for putting some of the hymns of the Latin and Greek Catholic past into exquisite and compelling English verse. Numbers of hymns written by former Anglicans after they made their peace with Rome won their way into Anglican and Protestant hymnals. Among them were Frederick William Faber's "Faith of our fathers, living still," "Hark, hark my soul, angelic songs are swelling," and "There's a wideness in God's mercy"; Matthew Bridges' "Crown him with many crowns"; and Adelaide Anne Proctor's "My God I thank Thee Who hast made the earth so fair."

The Anglo-Catholic movement had effects beyond the circles that were committed to it. It contributed to the growing improvement in worship which generally characterized the Church of England in the nineteenth century. It gave an impetus to a corporate sense in the Church of England which encouraged the renewal or inauguration of institutions and devices through which that body could express its voice and not be as completely subservient to the state as in the past. Thus in the 1850's the convocations of the two provinces of Canterbury and York, which had held only brief and formal meetings since 1717, began to be more active. Eventually they were enlarged by the addition of laymen. Diocesan synods were also revived. Here was a parallel to what was taking place on the Continent, where the Protestant state churches acquired organs for a nearer approach to independent action and for a consciousness of a corporate life.

How far could the Church of England make its peace with the new currents of thought and the programmes for the organization of the state and society which were sweeping across Europe and the British Isles? We have seen (Chapter 45) that numbers of men and women rejected Christianity, some gladly, others reluctantly. Some held to Christian ethics while surrendering the religious convictions upon which they rested. There were others, among them men of prominence and influence in the Church, who held that reconciliation was impossible and regarded any peace as a compromise of essential Christian truth. At the most they would consent only to a truce. Still others were prepared to adopt at least some of the conclusions of the contemporary critical historical study of the Bible and the methods, findings, and even the hypotheses of the scientists of their day, including Darwin, and to seek to find a way at the same time to hold without contradiction to the historic beliefs of the Church. Many were vividly aware of the social evils for which the several varieties of socialism offered remedies and strove to remove them, some through legislation, others through personal ministry and private initiative through voluntary societies, and still others through a socialism which endeavoured to embody Christian hopes and principles. Some who sought one or another of these solutions were Evangelicals, others were Anglo-Catholics, and still others belonged with neither. Many of these last were classified as Broad churchmen. Indeed, as the nineteenth century wore on, there were said to be three parties in the Church of England, Evangelical, Anglo-Catholic, and Broad. The lines which separated them were not sharp and there were numbers who could not rightly be placed plumply in any of the three.

To list even the more important names of those who in one way or another attempted to adjust the Church of England to the currents and demands of the day would issue in what to the uninitiated would be a dreary catalogue. We must select a few men and groups and say something about each, but at the same time be painfully aware that others of equal or nearly equal importance have been omitted. It is evidence of the abounding life of the nineteenth century Church of England that in it were so many able and devoted men and women who displayed such a variety of convictions and activity.

One of the men who must be mentioned was Samuel Taylor Coleridge (1772–1834). He had a spiritual pilgrimage which began in a vicarage under a father whose memory he revered and which included an uncompleted course at Cambridge, a brief period in the army, enthusiasm for the French Revolution, friendships with Southey and Wordsworth, a few years when he planned to become a Unitarian minister, a residence in Germany, pantheism, disillusion as to the Revolution and Napoleon, a long and tragic struggle with addiction to opium, and a return to the Church of England, so that for the last twenty years of his life he was a practising churchman. Brilliant and charming in conversation, poet, and writer of prose, Coleridge exerted a profound influence upon a younger generation. The religious convictions of his Christian maturity are seen in his *Aids to Reflection* and his *Confessions of an Inquiring Spirit*. In them he maintained that "Christian faith is the perfection of human intelligence" and that "the scheme of Christianity, though not discoverable by reason, is yet in accordance with it—that link follows link by necessary consequence—that religion passes out of the ken of reason only where the eye of reason has reached its own horizon, and that faith is then but its continuation."

He did not believe in what is usually called the verbal inspiration of the Scriptures, but he declared that "whatever finds me bears witness to itself that it has proceeded from the Holy Ghost. In the Bible there is more that finds me than in all other books which I have read."

Coleridge gave his own definition to "reason," distinguishing it from "understanding." Reason he believed to be the organ of the supersensuous, an "inward beholding," the eye of the spirit by which we directly perceive religious truths, the knowledge of the law of the whole considered as one. To him understanding was the faculty by which we generalize and arrange the phenomena of perception. It is not strange that he is sometimes called the English Schleiermacher. Yet it was from different backgrounds that the two developed the quality which gave them similarity. Both showed the effects of the current romanticism, but romanticism was by no means the sole cause of the resemblance.

One of the younger men who felt the influence of Coleridge was Thomas Arnold (1795–1842). A graduate of Oxford and a clergyman of the Church of England, deeply religious with a life "rooted in God," and of noble moral character, he was chiefly remembered for the fashion in which, as headmaster of Rugby, he set a standard which largely made over, for the good, the public schools of England. He was neither an Evangelical nor an Anglo-Catholic, but frankly differed from both schools. He deeply desired to realize a fully Christian society in which the entire life would conform to Christian ideals and wished to make Rugby such a society in microcosm. He aroused opposition among several of the conservatives by his view of the Bible. Aware of some of the contemporary German critical study of the Scriptures and partly approving it, he held that the Bible must be viewed in the light of the times in which it was written. Yet, with Coleridge, he maintained that it had in it divine truth which finds us.

Another of the younger men who owed a debt to Coleridge but one who was by no means solely the product of his influence was John Frederick Denison Maurice (1805–1872). The son of a politically liberal Unitarian clergyman and school teacher who came out of a long line of English Presbyterian dissent, Maurice had been designed by his father for the Unitarian ministry. In the course of the years, which included Cambridge and Oxford, from profound conviction he entered the Church of England and was ordained. For many years he was in London, part of the time holding professorships in King's College from which he was removed (1853) for alleged departure from orthodoxy. Yet he continued as chaplain of Lincoln's Inn and as priest in a parish church. In 1866 he was made professor of moral philosophy at Cambridge. A man of singularly pure life, integrity of mind, sensitive spirit, and high purpose, he attracted some and repelled others. The controversies in which he was engaged arose partly but not entirely from the fresh way in which in his efforts to make them accord with current knowledge he stated the historic Christian convictions and from the misunderstandings to which it gave rise. He also rejoiced in paradoxical language which proved provocative. He held that God is love, that Christ is the head of all humanity, and that man is not only depraved but also has a natural righteousness because of the indwelling of Christ, the Son of God. To him revelation is the unveiling of the knowledge of God and aids the intuitive knowledge of God which may exist in every human soul. The atonement is not the offering of a vicarious sacrifice of the innocent for the guilty to satisfy the requirements of a just God, but the fulfilment of the law of righteousness by sharing the sufferings of mankind, of which Christ is the head, and by the perfect obedience of the Son of God whose will is one with the Father's. Eternal death has nothing to do with time, but is alienation from God because of unrepented sin. All that men need do to be reconciled is to recognize their sonship, repent, and give God the love which is the natural relation of a son to the Father. Presumably God's love will ultimately triumph and all men be led to repent and turn to God in trust and love.

Maurice has sometimes been classified with the Broad wing of the Church of England. He himself would have repudiated that identification, for he was grieved by party strife, his longing for the unity of all Christians was one of the reasons why he left what he regarded as a sect, and by his attitude towards the Scriptures he antagonized some of those who could with a nearer approach to accuracy be placed with that group.

Partly because of his boyhood background, for his father was a social liberal and took him to anti-slavery meetings, and partly because of his theological convictions, Maurice laboured indefatigably to improve the lot of the under-privileged. In a day when higher education for women was a generally distrusted novelty he founded Queen's College for them (1848). The revolutionary year of 1848 and the Chartist movement spurred some Christians to seek to bring Christianity to bear upon the construction of a better order. What was known as Christian Socialism arose. Maurice was the spiritual leader of the group and incurred added opprobrium from those to whom the word "socialism" stood for destructive revolution. While the movement accomplished little immediately beyond the passage of an act of Parliament giving legal status to coöperatives, the ideal which inspired it did not die. Moreover, the better to prepare the masses for intelligent participation in the new age brought by the industrial revolution, Maurice headed the Workingmen's College in

London, furthered similar projects in other cities, and thus was a pioneer in the adult education which later attained substantial proportions.

A younger contemporary of Maurice was Frederick William Robertson (1816–1853). Highly sensitive, reared in a strongly Evangelical environment, intense, somewhat lacking in the sense of humour which might have softened some of his inner suffering, by deep conviction he turned aside from a career in the army to become a clergyman. Honest, unwilling to accept traditional views without examining them for himself, by the hard road of agonizing struggle he came to a clear faith, but it was not one which fitted him into any of the existing groups in the Church of England. For six years, 1847–1853, he filled the pulpit in Trinity Chapel, Brighton. One of the greatest preachers in English history, he attracted throngs from all classes. Speaking to revolutionary years, and believing that Christianity has a message for daily living, for the nations, and for the world, he aroused fear and criticism among the conservative, but attracted ardent support from many of the thoughtful. Through lectures in a workingmen's centre which he helped to establish he won a hearing among the servants and labourers. He burnt himself out physically at the early age of thirty-seven, but his published sermons had a wide circulation in the English-speaking world and profoundly influenced more than one generation of preachers.

Along with Maurice and Robertson there should be mentioned Charles Kingsley (1819–1875). A graduate of Cambridge, a clergyman classed theologically with the Broad churchmen, he is best remembered as a novelist. To his contemporaries he was also known as a Christian socialist and as one whose sympathies were with the Chartists. Yet in many ways he was conservative and orthodox, more so as the years passed.

Biblical studies akin in method to those in vogue in German universities, but usually less drastic in their conclusions, made headway among scholars of the Church of England. Famous were the three friends, Brooke Foss Westcott (1825–1901), Joseph Barber Lightfoot (1828–1889), and Fenton John Anthony Hort (1828–1892). All three were graduates of Cambridge and at one time and another all occupied professorships in that university. All were experts in the critical study of ancient texts, especially of the New Testament, and were skilled in methods of discovering the original reading and meaning. Lightfoot and Westcott occupied successively the ancient and influential see of Durham. Both wrote commentaries on books of the Bible and were theologians of distinction. Westcott and Hort's reconstructed text of the New Testament became a standard. Oxford had Thomas Kelly Cheyne (1841–1915), William Sanday (1843–1920), and Samuel Rolles Driver (1846–1914). Cheyne and Driver were especially noted for their work on the Old Testament, and Sanday for his studies in the life of Christ.

The newer views did not immediately gain assent. While by 1914 most of the clergy and numbers of the laity had accepted many of the more moderate findings of nineteenth century Protestant Biblical scholarship and of those theologians who were attempting to think through inherited beliefs in light of current scientific and philosophical views, acquiescence in them was by no means universal. So far as it had been reached, it had come only through debate, much of it acrimonious.

A few of the landmarks of that struggle centered about a volume entitled *Essays and Reviews,* another book, *Ecce Homo,* a work on the Pentateuch by Colenso, and a volume of essays called *Lux Mundi.*

Essays and Reviews, published in 1860, the year following the appearance of *The Origin of Species,* was made up of contributions from seven liberals, lay and clerical, mostly from Oxford, who included Frederick Temple (1821–1902), later Archbishop of Canterbury, and the redoubtable Benjamin Jowett (1817–1893), professor of Greek and later master of Balliol College, Oxford. Most if not all of the views put forward would not have been considered especially radical or dangerous fifty years later, but at the time they provoked a storm of protest.

Ecce Homo, issued anonymously in 1866 and with John Robert Seeley (1834–1895), later professor of modern history at Cambridge, as author, while marked by religious fervour and portraying Christ as king of the spiritual realm, stressed the human side of Christ, contained the phrase "enthusiasm for humanity," and was regarded in some quarters as highly dangerous.

John William Colenso (1814–1883) was the object of violent attack. A graduate of Cambridge, a mathematician, and the first Bishop of Natal, he had already been accused of laxity in dealing with polygamy among his African flock, when, in 1862–1863, a work by him, *The Pentateuch and Book of Joshua Critically Examined,* was published. Among other startling statements it declared that little if any of the Pentateuch was written in the Mosaic age, that Moses may never have lived, that Joshua is a purely mythical figure, that the Books of Chronicles are fictitious, and that Christ's knowledge of history in speaking of Moses was not more than that of any educated Jew of his day and might be faulty. Forty-one bishops advised Colenso to resign. He did not do so and was deposed by the Bishop of Cape Town, who claimed jurisdiction as metropolitan in South Africa. An unhappy, involved, and prolonged struggle followed, in which the original issues faded into the background and Colenso stood by his claim to hold office under patent from the crown and the Bishop of Cape Town denied the authority of the crown in purely ecclesiastical matters.

The question became one of the degree to which the Church was subject to the state. Not until after the death of Colenso was it resolved.

Lux Mundi, published in 1889, was the work of a group of Oxford Anglo-Catholics and one Cambridge man, and was edited by Charles Gore (1853–1932), later successively Bishop of Worcester, Birmingham, and Oxford. It sought to put "the Catholic faith in its right relation to modern intellectual and moral problems" and thus to commend "the faith to the acceptance of others." Some of the older Anglo-Catholics believed that it went too far towards liberal views, especially in its attitude on the critical study of the Bible. It nearly caused a split in that wing of the Church of England.

The controversies did not stop the growth in vigour of the Church of England. Indeed, they were evidence of life. As the century advanced that church displayed increasing vitality. While still controlled by the state, subject to Parliament, its bishops and other leading officers appointed by the crown, it was more nearly autonomous than it had ever been. An unofficial series of gatherings, the Church Congress, which first met in 1861 and which afforded an opportunity for hearing and discussing papers, but which passed no resolutions, became a flourishing institution. The parish clergy and the bishops showed decided improvement. Among them were so many devoted and extraordinarily able men that simply to list them would require a small volume. From time to time new dioceses were created the better to meet the growth of population and its city-ward shift. In the cities hundreds of new churches were erected. Increasingly the clergy interested themselves in the social problems posed by industrialization and urbanization. Movements were initiated for furthering better housing. Christian social settlements were founded. In 1889 the Christian Social Union was formed. Confined to members of the Church of England and with Westcott as its first president, it sought "to claim for the Christian law the ultimate authority to rule social practice," "to apply the moral truths of Christianity to the social and economic difficulties" of the age, and "to present Christ in practical life as the Living Master and King."

The Church of England also spread widely overseas. As we have suggested, this was partly by migration and partly by missions among non-Christian peoples. The missionary societies organized before 1815, notably the Society for the Propagation of the Gospel in Foreign Parts and the Church Missionary Society, greatly expanded their staffs and the areas covered. To them were added others, among them the Colonial and Continental Church Society, begun in 1823, especially, as its name implied, for English settlers and merchants in other lands. The family of autonomous Anglican Churches markedly increased in numbers, membership, and geographic extent. To tie it together the Lambeth Conferences were begun, so called because they convened in the London residence of the Archbishop of Canterbury. To the Lambeth Conferences all bishops of the Anglican Communion were invited. The first assembled in 1867. They were held approximately every ten years thereafter. They met on the invitation of the Archbishop of Canterbury, for while he had no authority outside England and some of the colonies, he was looked up to as the ranking ecclesiastic, *primus inter pares.* The Lambeth Conferences could not legislate for their respective churches. However, they gave opportunity for something more important, the knitting together of the bishops of a world-wide communion in fellowship and in prayer, the discussion of common problems, and the formation, where possible, of a common mind.

In the latter part of the nineteenth century the Church of England was more vigorous than in any earlier period of its history and it came to 1914 on a mounting tide. To be sure, the bishops were less prominent in the House of Lords and in civil administration than they had been in the eighteenth century. The lay element in that body had been augmented while the number of bishops in it had not increased. The proportion of the population who attended the services of the church seems to have declined in the second half of the century, especially in the large cities. Yet the average quality of the clergy in learning and devotion was higher than at any previous time. The Church of England was more nearly in control of its own life than in any period since the separation from Rome. It had in large part made its adjustment to the new learning. It displayed marked variety, from extreme Evangelicalism to a Catholicism which held a high view of the Church, its ministry, and its sacraments. It had given rise to a revival of monasticism. For the first time the Anglican communion had become world-wide. It still constituted only a small minority of the total number of Christians, but the ability of its leadership combined with the prestige of the British Empire to accord it a large voice in the Church universal.

THE GROWING VIGOUR OF ENGLISH PROTESTANT NONCONFORMITY

The nineteenth century witnessed a growth of English Protestant Nonconformity which was fully as striking as that of the Anglican Communion. Even in 1815 organized Christian dissent from the established church was stronger than in any other country on the Continent of Europe or the British Isles, with the exception of Ireland, where Roman Catholics were a majority, Wales, where Protestant dissent was strong, and possibly Russia, where the Old Believers and some of the other movements which we noted in Chapter XLIV were potent. On Sunday, March 30, 1851, a census was taken of those attending church. About 40 per cent. of the population were in church on that day. Of them about 52 per cent. were of the Church of England, about 44.3 per cent. of Protestant Nonconforming churches, and about 3.5 per cent. Roman Catholics.

In proportion to its situation in 1815, in the nineteenth century in its growth in England and in its world-wide spread English Protestant Nonconformity outstripped any other congeries of religious movements in Europe.

To this phenomenal record several factors contributed. One was the position of Nonconformity at the outset of the century. Ever since the prodigious vitality, the civil war, and the Commonwealth of the seventeenth century it had had a larger place in the life of the country than had Protestant dissent anywhere else east of the Atlantic. It had been reinforced by the revivals of the eighteenth century and especially by the emergence of Methodism from the established church. It came to 1815 on a rising tide. In the nineteenth century it was further augmented by the continuation of what in its broadest sense may be called the Evangelical movement. It experienced an almost continuous awakening, an awakening which was largely indigenous but which was repeatedly aided by visitors from the United States, particularly Moody. Moreover, Nonconformity had its strength chiefly in the classes which were prospering and multiplying in the nineteenth century. It numbered relatively few from the landed aristocracy and gentry, an element in the population which was losing its dominance in government and in economic life. It drew chiefly from the lower and the upper middle classes, the thrifty and self-respecting among the farmers and the labourers in the cities, the artisans, the clerks, the small shopkeepers, and the manufacturers and merchants. It was these classes which were coming to the fore in England. As they became wealthy, many from them moved out of Nonconformity into the Church of England, but the majority remained true to the religious groups in which they had been nurtured. Then, too, Nonconformity was favoured by the progressive removal of the legal disabilities from which it had suffered. That emancipation was due in large part to the liberalism which marked the nineteenth century Occident and which had somewhat similar effects in several countries in Europe and in lands outside that continent dominated by peoples of European descent and culture. Finally, and chiefly, the cause must be found in the vitality inherent in the Nonconforming churches and the faith of which they were an expression.

It was by a series of measures scattered over many years that Protestant Nonconformists were accorded legal equality with members of the Church of England. The year 1813 saw the removal of the statutes enacting penalties for those denying the Trinity and thus brought relief to Unitarians. In 1828 the Test and Corporation Acts were repealed which had made as a prerequisite for office-holding taking the communion in the Church of England. These had long been circumvented by annual Acts of Indemnity which safeguarded Dissenters, but the laws themselves, a chronic irritant, were now removed. Beginning with 1836 marriages were permitted in Nonconformist places of worship and a generation later, in 1880, burial services by dissenters were allowed in churchyards. In 1868 the payment of church rates for the maintenance of the fabrics of the parish churches was made voluntary. The religious tests for degrees in Oxford, Cambridge, and Durham which had debarred Nonconformists were abolished by acts of Parliament in 1871, except for theology.

Some Nonconformists laboured for still more drastic measures. In 1844, led by a Congregational pastor, Edward Miall, they formed the British Anti-State-Church Association, after 1853 called the Society for the Liberation of Religion from State Patronage and Control. Nonconformists fought vigorously and long against state financial aid to denominational schools, holding that it would work against them and for the Church of England. They did not win, and the education acts of 1870 left religious instruction in the schools and in 1902 legislation assisted denominational schools by public taxation.

At the outset of the century the largest Nonconforming Protestant bodies were the Congregationalists, Baptists, and Methodists. Much smaller but influential were the Friends (Quakers) and the Unitarians. The Unitarians were chiefly the descendants, physically or spiritually, of the Presbyterians, for the latter, thrown out of the Church of England by the Stuart Restoration in the seventeenth century, had objected to creedal or confessional tests and under the influence of the rationalism of the eighteenth century had moved increasingly towards a non-Trinitarian faith. In general the Unitarians were from the upper income classes and highly educated. In economic level and education the Congregationalists ranked next to them. The General Baptists were on the whole from a higher level of culture than the Particular Baptists. The latter were largely humble folk.

In the course of the nineteenth century Congregationalists, Baptists, and Methodists increased greatly, but the Methodists had the largest growth. Quakers and Unitarians persisted, still small minorities. Presbyterianism of the Scottish type reappeared, by migration from Scotland. Some other denominations and movements were added. In general, it was what in the Church of England was known as Evangelicalism which prevailed. Among the Nonconformists there was, naturally, almost nothing corresponding to the Oxford movement. The liberalism in theology and Biblical studies which was current in the Church of England, in Scotland, and on the Continent made itself felt and here and there produced controversy. Enough community of conviction existed to make possible a degree of coöperation. This showed itself in many ways, including the formation of a Free Church Council, and in 1892 it took a further step in the meeting of the Free Church Congress out of which came the National Free Church Council (the National Council of the Evangelical Free Churches). With it the majority of the Nonconformists were associated. We must say something about each of the major denominations, both old and new, but it must be tantalizingly brief.

Congregationalism entered the nineteenth century on the rising tide brought by the Evangelical revival. The Congregationalists were the spiritual descendants of the Independents of the seventeenth and eighteenth centuries. In the middle of the eighteenth century they suffered somewhat from the spiritual lethargy of the age. However, they preserved the sobriety, the deep interest in theology and politics, the loyalty to the Westminster Confession, the austerity in morals, the delight in intellectual pursuits, and the Sunday observance which had long characterized the movement. The Evangelical Awakening wrought marked changes. Many former Presbyterians, distressed by the drift towards unitarianism in their own churches, became Congregationalists. Thousands, stirred by Congregational revival preaching, flocked in from the Church of England or from the religiously indifferent multitudes. Under the revival preaching the inherited Calvinism was weakened, with its doctrine that only the elect could repent. Mid-week prayer meetings became common. Lay preaching increased. New academies and colleges came into being to prepare men for the pastorates of the rapidly multiplying churches. In 1832 a national organization was formed. It was eventually known as the Congregational Union of England and Wales and was a federation of Congregational churches. In 1833 that body adopted a Declaration of Faith and Order which, in contrast with the Savoy Declaration of 1658, long a standard for the Independents, was only mildly and vaguely Calvinistic. In addition to the London Missionary Society which, it will be recalled, was formed in 1795 and depended chiefly upon Congregational churches for its support and personnel, various societies were organized to aid Congregationalism in Great Britain and Ireland and the colonies. While in Britain hundreds of new chapels were built, especially in the growing cities, in the colonies Congregationalism was weak as compared with its strength in England and Wales. Congregationalism produced outstanding ministers and laymen. Prominent among the former was Robert William Dale (1829–1895), for more than forty years minister in Carr's Lane Church in the rapidly growing industrial city of Birmingham. There he was not only a great preacher, but he also took an active part, on the progressive side, in municipal and national politics.

The Baptists entered the nineteenth century far from united. The division persisted between Particular and General Baptists, the one holding what are usually called Calvinist views and the latter what is generally termed Arminianism. It went back to the separate origins in the seventeenth century.

Other divisions had entered, one in the General Baptists late in the eighteenth century in protest against a trend towards unitarianism and universalism which resulted in the New Connexion General Baptists, and others over the question of the standards for admission to the Lord's Supper. There were some Seventh-Day Baptists, partly descended from the Fifth Monarchists of the seventeenth century, observing Saturday rather than Sunday. No national or even local organization bridged the gulf. General Baptist churches were more inclined to draw together in regional associations and a national union than were the Particular Baptists. Both General and Particular Baptists felt the invigorating impact of the Evangelical Awakening. It was among Particular Baptists of moderate Calvinistic convictions that the Baptist Missionary Society was organized in response to the appeal of William Carey. Although they were slow to meet the challenge of the shift of population to the cities, Particular Baptists formed various societies for specific purposes, some of them home missionary. They grew in numbers and eventually organized new churches in the cities.

The most famous English Baptist preacher of the nineteenth century was Charles Haddon Spurgeon (1834–1892). Reared a Congregationalist, in his teens he joined the Baptists. At nineteen he became pastor of an old church in London and before he was thirty his preaching had attracted such throngs that (1861) the Metropolitan Tabernacle was erected, seating over five thousand. A moderate Calvinist, warmly evangelistic, a Liberal in politics and a friend of Gladstone, he was an indefatigable worker, the founder of orphanages and of a school for training ministers, the editor of a monthly magazine, and the author of many books.

Formed in the 1890's, the Baptist Union of Great Britain and Ireland drew together both Particular and General Baptists and embraced the majority of the Baptists of the British Isles. A leader in that merger, John Clifford (1836–1923), a General Baptist London pastor, was also prominent in the founding of the Baptist World Alliance (1905) and in the National Free Church Council.

Of the Nonconforming bodies it was the Methodists who attained the largest dimensions. The zeal, long life, and organizing ability of John Wesley had inspired Methodism, had given it a structure, and had attracted to it and channeled through it much of the Evangelical Awakening. After Wesley's death the first outstanding leader was Thomas Coke (1747–1814) whom we have already met and who had a major share in the spread of the movement overseas as well as in the British Isles. In the nearly half a century following Coke the most influential man in British Methodism was Jabez Bunting (1779–1858). An organizer, administrator, and forceful and persuasive preacher, he held many offices and for years to an unusual degree displayed the ability to embody, express, and put into effect the will of the majority of the Methodist constituency.

As was inevitable, Bunting was accused of being autocratic. Restlessness developed and after his strong hand was removed open division came. Even before he had become well established in power, and not as an opposition movement to him, the Bible Christians (1815) arose under the leadership of William O'Bryan, who, a flaming evangelist, rebelled against control by the tightly knit Methodist organization. Between 1827 and 1857 the United Methodist Free Churches were formed out of a union which attracted successive secessions from the main body of Wesleyan Methodists. First were the Methodist Protestants (1827), then the Wesleyan Methodist Association (1835), then the Wesleyan Reformers (beginning in 1849), and finally the formation (1857) of the United Methodist Free Churches. In 1907 the Bible Christians, the Methodist New Connexion, founded in 1797 by Alexander Kilham (1762–1798) and those who sympathized with him, and the United Methodist Free Churches came together in the United Methodist Church.

The majority of Methodists remained within the Wesleyan Methodist Church. In the latter part of the nineteenth century its outstanding figure, called by some the most notable Methodist since Wesley, was John Scott Lidgett (1854——). Inspired by a great predecessor, Hugh Price Hughes, he was outstanding as a theologian, a preacher, a social reformer, and a leader in the Liberal party.

Taken together in all its various branches Methodism had outstanding characteristics. It was warmly evangelistic and grew rapidly and fairly steadily. It drew largely from the middle classes and the sturdier, more reliable labourers. It developed great preachers. Many of these were ordained. Many were laymen. Lay preaching, indeed, was very prominent. Women were recruited and trained as deaconesses: Methodism as well as the Church of England and some of the Continental Protestant churches was finding a way to utilize the full-time service of women which roughly paralleled the sisterhoods of the Roman Catholic Church. Methodism proved adaptable to the rising cities. In addition to its familiar chapels, it instituted mission centers in the low income areas and great "central halls" in strategic locations for preaching and social work. It stressed education. From Methodism came leaders in the early stages of the trades union movement and in inaugurating coöperatives. Methodist chapels were friendly social centres for colliers and other labouring folk. Methodism was ardently missionary. It spread rapidly in the colonies among the settlers and their children and there attained larger dimensions than any other denomination except the Church of England, the Presbyterians, and the Roman Catholics. It multiplied missions in Asia, Africa, and the islands of the sea. As we are to see, it had an even more phenomenal growth in the United States.

In spite of its divisions, Methodism maintained and developed a sense of community throughout the world. In 1881 it held the first of the conferences which took the name ecumenical. There followed at fairly regular intervals similar gatherings which drew together for fellowship Methodists from many lands.

On the smaller pre-nineteenth century Protestant denominations in England we can pause for only fragmentary notice. The Unitarians had as an outstanding figure James Martineau (1805–1900). Of Huguenot ancestry, a man of noble and independent character, as preacher, author, and teacher he exerted a wide influence. The Friends (Quakers) had an effect far greater than their numbers would have given ground for anticipating. Thus Stephen Grellet (1773–1855) and Elizabeth Fry (1780–1845), the latter in spite of her responsibilities as the mother of a large family of children, had a share in the initiation of the urgently needed prison reform in Britain and the Continent second only to that of Howard. On the outskirts of Birmingham the Cadbury family, which made a fortune in the manufacture of chocolate, developed around their factories a community which was a model in housing, education, and parks, and encouraged the Selly Oak Colleges for the training of religious workers and teachers of several denominations. The Sandemanians, really springing from John Glas of Scotland, but taking their name from Robert Sandeman, had their beginning in the middle of the eighteenth century and contributed to the rise of the Christian denomination in America and Britain. From another small group, the Moravians, came one of the greatest hymn writers of the nineteenth century, James Montgomery (1771–1854). Montgomery, who never married, was the son of a Moravian clergyman and in middle life made a public profession of faith, returning to the church of his boyhood. He wrote about four hundred hymns, of which many made their way into the use of numbers of Protestant denominations. Among them were "Angels from the realms of glory, wing your flight o'er all the earth"; "Hail to the Lord's anointed, great David's greater Son"; "Prayer is the soul's sincere desire, uttered or unexpressed"; and "In the hour of trial, Jesus pray for me."

The swelling tide of life gave birth to new denominations and groups which were akin to denominations. Of these we can take the space for brief mention of only three. One was the Catholic Apostolic Church, sometimes known as the Irvingites, because of the part which Edward Irving (1792–1834) had in its inception. Irving, a Scot, a Presbyterian clergyman, was profoundly influenced by Coleridge. A compelling preacher in a Presbyterian church in London, he came to believe that the second coming of Christ was near at hand and held that the early apostolic gifts of prophesying, speaking with tongues, and healing by faith were being revived. He was ejected from the Presbyterian Church for heresy, but his views found expression in the Catholic Apostolic Church (begun in 1832) which had an elaborate organization of apostles, prophets, evangelists, and pastors, and a liturgy based upon Eastern rites.

More numerous were what were popularly known as the Darbyites, or Plymouth Brethren, but who called themselves simply the Brethren, Christians, or Christian Brethren. The outstanding early leader was John Nelson Darby (1800–1882), a clergyman of the (Anglican) Church of Ireland. They began in Dublin but soon had a second centre at Plymouth. At first they were largely an upper class movement, recruited from those who were dissatisfied with what seemed to them the worldliness and spiritual dryness of the existing churches, especially the Church of England. Eventually they drew chiefly from middle class and humble folk. They endeavoured to take the Bible literally and to gather themselves together on the model of the New Testament. Students of the Biblical prophecies, many of them believed the second coming of Christ to be imminent. They held that in preparation for Christ's coming they were to live separate from the world in righteousness and holiness, eschewing the amusements and whatever else in the world might be contaminating. They looked with distrust upon the existing churches, for they believed them to have compromised with the world. They gathered in meetings but had no central organization. They rejected creeds and maintained that the Holy Spirit guides true Christians and binds them together in faith and worship. They believed in conversion. Holding that social reform is useless, they taught that the mission of Christians is saving men and women out of the world. They had believer's baptism by immersion, and the breaking of bread (the Lord's Supper) every Sunday. They did not have ordination, but had lay evangelists. They early were divided, partly on the issue of the degree to which it was permissible to mix with other Christians. Prominent among them was George Müller (1805–1898). A native of Prussia, at about the age of twenty he was converted in a Pietist circle in Halle. In 1829 he went to England as a missionary to the Jews. Influenced by the example of A. H. Francke and the latter's orphanage at Halle, he began and maintained orphanages at Bristol, relying entirely on faith and prayer for the necessary material means. The Brethren were zealous missionaries and developed what they called Christian Missions in Many Lands, and eventually were on all the continents.

More conspicuous than the Brethren and devoted to serving and saving the dregs of the industrial urban civilization was the Salvation Army. The Salvation Army was the creation of William Booth (1829–1912). Born in humble circumstances, at fifteen Booth was converted and became a preacher. For about nine years he was with the Methodist New Connexion, but he broke with it and became an independent evangelist. Hating the dirt, squalor, and vice of the cities and believing profoundly in the power of the Gospel to transform even the most degraded lives, in 1864 Booth went to London, where the most extensive slums were found, and there, in one of the worst districts, began the Christian Mission. In 1878 this became the Salvation Army. The latter was organized in military fashion, with uniforms, military titles for its officers, and with Booth as its general. It sought to enlist its converts in efforts to win others to the Christian life and to minister physically as well as spiritually to the lowest of the underprivileged. Its methods were unconventional, with open-air meetings on the streets and with drums and other musical instruments. At first the Salvation Army aroused ridicule and violent opposition, and its members were even arrested as disturbers of the peace. After a few years criticism either diminished or entirely ceased. Booth's *In Darkest England and the Way Out* (1890) described the desperate economic, social, and moral conditions in the slums and proposed concrete measures for relief and cure, among them a farm colony, emigration overseas, rescue homes for prostitutes, preventive homes for girls, a poor man's bank, and model suburban villages. He and his subordinates laboured to make at least some features of the programme a reality. In all this Booth was helped by his wife, especially in reaching and caring for women. The Salvation Army spread rapidly, chiefly in the United States, the British colonies, and India. In its tightly knit organization, its selfless devotion, its zeal for the spiritual and physical care of the unfortunate, and its internal dissensions, it had much in common with some of the orders of the Roman Catholic Church, notably the Franciscans in their early days.

Movements Which Crossed Denominational Borders

Nineteenth century England saw either the origin or the extensive development of numbers of societies and movements which transcended denominational lines. They were recruited chiefly from those who shared the convictions and the experience of the Evangelical Awakening and who sought and found fellowship with those of similar mind on the Continent, in other countries of the British Isles, and in the United States and the British colonies. They were very numerous, and from them only three can here be singled out for specific mention.

Sunday Schools, as we have seen (Chapter 44), had their rise late in the eighteenth century. Originally intended to give religious and moral instruction to the very poor and including teaching the illiterate to read and write, they proved adaptable to the children of other classes and spread to various denominations as a means of religious education. At least one of their early

London promoters dreamed of them as an instrument for teaching every one in the world to read the Bible. They flourished especially among Protestants in the English-speaking world and of British tradition, and most notably in the United States. They were used by missionaries in Asia, Africa, and the Americas. In 1889 the first of a series of World's Sunday School Conventions assembled in London, and at the seventh of these, in Rome in 1907, the World's Sunday School Association was constituted. Although having strong support from the clergy, the Sunday School movement was largely a lay enterprise, depending chiefly on laymen and women for its teachers, a voluntary unsalaried service.

Another movement, somewhat different, was the Young Men's Christian Association. The first Young Men's Christian Association was begun by George Williams (1821–1905). George Williams was of yeoman ancestry. Born and reared on a farm in Somerset County, in his early teens he sought his fortune as an apprentice in a draper's shop in the nearby town of Bridgwater. In Bridgwater he committed himself as a Christian and joined a Congregational Church. He was profoundly influenced by the books of Charles G. Finney, the American evangelist. At nineteen he finished his apprenticeship and then went to London and at the age of twenty was a clerk in a large draper's house. There he was both faithful in business and active in religious work. He sought to win his fellow-clerks to the Christian life and began a prayer meeting. In June, 1844, twelve young men, all but one of them fellow-employees in the same firm with himself, met in his room and formed a society to win other young men to the Christian faith. The idea of a Young Men's Christian Association, as the group called itself, was contagious, for it came on a rising tide of the Evangelical movement. Other similar groups quickly sprang up in the British Isles. Within less than a decade they had begun to be seen in the United States and Canada. Similar societies, some of them older, were appearing on the Continent. In 1855, only eleven years after the first Association had been formed in Williams' room, the World's Alliance of the Young Men's Christian Associations was constituted in Paris by representatives from both sides of the Atlantic. George Williams lived to see the Young Men's Christian Associations spread to many other lands. He himself became wealthy and was knighted. To the end of his days he was active in his support of missions and in his devotion to various religious and philanthropic enterprises, mainly those of Evangelical origin and connexions.

The Young Men's Christian Association appealed chiefly to those of the lower income levels of the white collar class, not unlike those among whom it had its origin. Born in evangelism, prayer meetings, and Bible study, it added educational, social, and athletic facilities to promote the wholesome life of young men and boys. In the United States and Canada in the latter part of the century it was the chief channel and promoter of voluntary religious activities among students. It had its greatest growth in the United States and there in time built many physical plants, some of them large. Primarily a lay movement, it reminds one of some of the Roman Catholic confraternities, except that, unlike them, it was not under the control of the hierarchy and drew members from many denominations. In its origin Protestant and always predominantly such, it attracted many who continued their affiliation with the Roman Catholic and Eastern Churches. At least one of its national movements was predominantly Roman Catholic and another Greek Orthodox in membership. It far overspread confessional boundaries.

The sister organization, slightly younger, the Young Women's Christian Association, first arose in the 1850's in Germany and Great Britain, and, like the Young Men's Christian Association, had its largest development in the United States. In 1894 the World's Young Women's Christian Association was organized.

THE ROMAN CATHOLIC REVIVAL

It was in the nineteenth century that the Roman Catholic Church again raised its head in England, began to gain in numbers, and revived its hierarchy and its monastic orders. In 1815 Roman Catholics were under serious political disabilities. To be sure, in 1778 and 1791 some of the most severe of the penal laws against them had been repealed, but they still could not hold public office. Yet Roman Catholics were to be found, mostly in Lancashire and Yorkshire, and had the support of some of the landed gentry who had clung to their ancestral faith. The number of Roman Catholics had been augmented by refugees from the French Revolution. In 1829, largely as a result of agitation in Ireland, what was known as the Roman Catholic Emancipation Act was passed and took effect throughout the United Kingdom of Great Britain and Ireland. Roman Catholics might now hold office and sit in Parliament, but all who occupied these posts, whether Protestant or Roman Catholic, were required to disavow the temporal sovereignty of the Pope within the kingdom and to promise support to the Protestant settlement of Church and state. Roman Catholics were still debarred from the throne, from the Lord Chancellorship of England and Ireland, and from the Lord Lieutenancy in Ireland.

In 1850, by a step which because of the historic fear of Roman Catholicism provoked a great furor in England, the Pope reëstablished the English hierarchy. Nicholas Patrick Stephen Wiseman (1802–1865), of Anglo-Irish ancestry, was created cardinal and Archbishop of Westminster, thus, from the Roman Catholic standpoint, renewing the succession of the Archbishops of

Canterbury which had been broken in the reign of Henry VIII and, revived briefly under Mary, had again been interrupted under Elizabeth.

Not far from 1850 the numbers of Roman Catholics rapidly mounted through the immigration of Irish who were fleeing from the famine brought by the blight on the potato crop, their chief source of food. The Irish, poverty stricken, sought employment as unskilled labourers, chiefly in the rapidly growing industrial, commercial, and mining towns and cities. Henceforward they and their descendants constituted the major element in the Roman Catholic Church in England, Wales, and Scotland. There were added immigrants from Italy. As we have seen, some, a large proportion of them clergymen, came over from the Church of England as a result of the Oxford movement. Difficulty was experienced in bridging the gulfs which separated the various new elements from one another and from the old native Roman Catholic communities. The contrast was enhanced by the fact that the former were predominantly urban and the latter mainly rural.

In spite of the initial extreme poverty of the immigrants, striking progress was made by the Roman Catholic Church. As in the United States at the same time, this was not by conversions, for, except through marriage, these were relatively few, but by creating and developing the physical and institutional expressions and facilities of Roman Catholic life. Churches were erected, hundreds of parochial schools were built and maintained, some higher schools were founded, provision was made for the care of the poor, a priesthood was recruited and trained, and religious communities of men and women were brought into being. This last was chiefly by renewing or introducing the familiar monastic orders, but was also through the inauguration of new ones.

THE ADVANCE OF CHRISTIANITY IN NINETEENTH CENTURY WALES

At the outset of the nineteenth century the religious life in Wales had only begun to recover from the sad state into which it had fallen after the Stuart Restoration in the second half of the seventeenth century. The Evangelical Awakening was making itself felt and improvements in education had been initiated by earnest Christians. However, the established church was in poor condition. Its bishops were political appointees, Englishmen most of whom did not know or take the trouble to learn the Welsh tongue, its clergy were too few and most of them were desperately poor, and it was viewed by some of the English as a means of assimilating the Welsh to the English language and culture and was, accordingly, separated from the rank and file.

In the nineteenth century awakenings came which brought the religious life of the country to the highest level that it had ever known. These were in large part through revivals which swelled the Nonconformist Churches. In the re-

vivals and Nonconformist Churches the preaching and the services were
mainly in the Welsh language and thus reached the masses, many of whom
knew no English and the majority of whom knew Welsh and English but
with English as a second tongue. The revivals were enriched and furthered by
vernacular hymns: Welsh Christians became famous for their deeply moving
congregational singing. The revivals continued at intervals through the century. The denominations which had the major growth through them were the
Calvinistic Methodists, the Independents (Congregationalists), the Wesleyan
Methodists, and the Baptists.

The (Anglican) Church of Wales shared in the religious awakening and
helped to further it. The organization of the church was modified and improved. In 1835 clergy serving Welsh-using parishes were commanded by act
of Parliament to have an adequate knowledge of the language. Residential
canons were added to the cathedrals. Increasingly Welshmen were appointed
to the episcopal sees. Scores of new churches were built, and better provision
was made for preparing the clergy. In contrast with any of the other bodies
the established church had a diocesan and parochial organization which covered
the entire country and in some parishes possessed the only facilities for public
worship. In 1915 an act of Parliament was passed which disestablished the
Church of Wales. Because of World War I it was not put into force immediately, but in 1920 it came into effect.

REVIVAL, DIVISION, AND ADVANCE IN SCOTLAND

Scotland shared with England in the processes and fruits of the industrial
revolution. Coal mines were developed. Manufacturing communities arose.
Commerce flourished. Glasgow became the second city in size on the island of
Great Britain, ranking immediately after London. Rural populations tended
to be depleted by the drift to the towns. The nineteenth century currents of
thought made themselves felt. All this worked vast changes in the setting in
which the Church operated. In face of the changing conditions, as in England,
Christianity, far from waning, displayed a striking revival. Partly as a result
of that revival, a major division split the Church of Scotland. Following the
division even greater vigour was seen in Scottish Christianity. This vitality
showed itself in part in measures to meet the altered situation in Scotland and
partly in phenomenal geographic expansion. Some of the expansion was by
missions among non-Christian peoples. More of it was through migration.
Scots vied with the English and the Irish in the rapid settlement of the British
colonies, especially in Canada, Australia, New Zealand, and South Africa.
Presbyterianism, their inherited faith, was sufficiently vital to inspire them to
build strong Presbyterian Churches in these regions and to make that branch

of the faith, along with the Church of England, Methodism, and the Roman Catholic Church, characteristic of the life of these emerging nations.

Presbyterianism was even more dominant in the Christianity of Scotland than was the Anglican Communion in that of England. It is, therefore, on that form of the faith that in this rapid survey we must centre our attention. At the outset of the nineteenth century the overwhelming majority of the Presbyterians were in the state church, the Church of Scotland. There were Presbyterian minorities who had broken away from that church, not primarily on matters of doctrine but because of what they believed to be a compromise of Christian standards and of too great subservience of the Church to the state.

The religious awakening which had begun in Scotland before 1815 continued to mount after that year. As we have seen (Chapter 44), it had come partly from indigenous vitality, partly from contact with the Great Awakening in America, especially through the writings of Jonathan Edwards, and partly through Wesley and other leaders of the Evangelical movement in England. As elsewhere, its exponents were unhappy over the fashion in which eighteenth century rationalism had penetrated the Church and had weakened conviction and warmth.

Outstanding in the awakening in the years which immediately followed 1815 was Thomas Chalmers (1780–1847). Coming from a large family of children, with enormous physical vitality, merry, lively, impetuous, quick-tempered, and with a wide range of intellectual interests and an extensive knowledge of mathematics and science, he was early ordained into the ministry of the Church of Scotland. He was already winning fame as a preacher and a scholar when, at about the age of thirty, partly through family sorrows and problems and aided by reading Wilberforce, he had a religious experience which made him a leader in the Evangelical revivals. From 1815 to 1823 he was minister successively in two parishes in Glasgow. There he distinguished himself not only as a preacher but also for his work among the poor of that growing metropolis. Through a system of organized visitation, care of the poor, and education he wrought a striking improvement in the physical, moral, and spiritual condition of his parishioners. In his forties he occupied chairs first in St. Andrews and then in Edinburgh. In his teachings and writings he did much to reconcile the newly emerging science with the Christian faith. At Edinburgh especially he became a national figure, deferred to and consulted by the more influential in Church and state. He was outstanding in a movement which added scores of church buildings and ministers to enable the Church of Scotland to keep pace with the growth and shifts in population. In the year 1831–1832 as Moderator he held the highest office in his church. He believed profoundly in the principle of a national, established church as the best way of covering comprehensively the entire population of a country, but he maintained that such a church should not be subservient to the state but should have Christ as its one and only head and should be unfettered by king, magistrate, or legislature in her "sacred and spiritual jurisdiction." This conviction of the necessity of the autonomy of the Church made Chalmers an outstanding leader in a major event in the religious history of Scotland, the Disruption, which in 1843 rent the Church of Scotland and led to the formation of the Free Church of Scotland.

Although, when it came, the Disruption seemed sudden, it was the climax of a long movement. Repeatedly since the Reformation there had been those who were conscientiously opposed to any subordination of the Church to the secular arm. Indeed, from the Reformation onward the Church of Scotland had been far less acquiescent in the attempts at control by the state than had the Church of England. Much as in the Middle Ages in many places in Western Europe there were those who believed that appointment to ecclesiastical office by lay lords and princes corrupted the Church and was an unholy compromise of the latter's divine commission, so in Scotland the issue had been chiefly although not solely joined over the power of the lay proprietors to determine the choice of ministers for the parishes. In the eighteenth century there had been several secessions from the established church. There were the Cameronians, largely a lay movement, who refused adherence to the settlement after the Revolution of 1688 which brought in William and Mary, on the ground that, being uncovenanted, the regime was not a lawful government. In 1743 it constituted itself into a Reformed Presbytery. In 1733 Ebenezer Erksine led what was known as the Secession, which, believing that the union of 1707 which made the Parliament at Westminster the only one for Great Britain and the ensuing Act of Patronage of 1712 were infringements on pledges given at the time of the Revolution and had been followed by the inroads of rationalism in the ministry, broke with the established church. The Seceders divided between what were known as the Burghers and the anti-Burghers over the issue of whether a Christian could take the oath of the burgess, but in 1820 the two wings came together in the United Secession Church. In 1761 Thomas Gillespie founded the Relief body, from a protest against forcing on unwilling congregations patrons' nominees of moderate, namely, rationalistic views.

As the Evangelicals, products of the rising tide of spiritual life, grew in numbers, they became increasingly restive over any hint of subservience to the state and the lay proprietors. In 1820 they carried through the General Assembly an action refusing to recognize as binding the orders of the Privy Council commanding prayers for the new king, George IV. They did this on the ground that they were an infringement on the right of the Church of Scotland to determine its own modes of worship. In 1834, by what was known as the Veto Act, the General Assembly declared "that no pastor shall be intruded on any congregation contrary to the will of the people." A test case soon arose in which, against the wish of the overwhelming majority of the congregation, the Earl of Kinnoull made an appointment to a parish. The question, carried to the highest court, the House of Lords, was decided against the Church, thus saying in effect that the Church was a creature of the state and subordinate to it. In the next few years the issue came up in several more appointments in which a presbytery either refused to ordain and install a candidate appointed in contradiction to the Veto Act, or, in violation of that Act, complied.

The final breach came in 1843. The Church of Scotland and with it most of Scotland were deeply stirred. On the one hand were those who insisted that the Church must not be under the state. For the most part they were Evangelicals, committed to the new tides of revival. On the other were those, largely moderates not moved by the revival, who believed in submission to the state. The decision was precipitated by the action of the House of Lords in 1842 in requiring a presbytery to ordain a candidate presented by a patron to an unwilling congregation and imposing a fine on the presbytery for recalcitrance. The controversy was brought to the House of Commons through the presentation of what was called the Claim of Rights. Predominantly English as it was, and not really comprehending why Scotland should be so excited, the House decided against the Evangelicals. Seeing that protest was of no avail, in a dramatic scene those standing for the full independence of the Church walked out of the General Assembly, formed themselves into the Free Church of Scotland, and elected Chalmers as their first Moderator. More than a third of the ministers of the Church of Scotland went with them.

The action was heroic, for it meant that the ministers of the Free Church had surrendered all claim to support by the ancient endowments and that the congregations had lost the buildings in which they and their ancestors had worshipped. The foreign missions of the Church of Scotland were also lost. With great enthusiasm and much sacrifice the laity of the Free Church erected new buildings, supported their ministers, and organized for the initiation and support of foreign missions. The way had been prepared by the generosity of the voluntary gifts which had aided the earlier remarkable building of new churches that had been promoted by Chalmers.

The formation of the Free Church of Scotland was not an isolated movement. It grew out of the Evangelical revival which was strong in much of Protestantism in Europe and America. It was reinforced by the contemporary swing towards democracy in Europe, the British Isles, and America. It had similarities with the Oxford movement, for, while by no means, as did the latter, seeing the life of the Church in the historic Catholic ecclesiastical structure and sacraments, like it the Free Church of Scotland stressed the Church as a distinct community with its own life. Indeed, it was partly because of the similarity and the unpopularity of the Tractarian movement that the House of Commons rejected the Claim of Rights. Here, too, was one phase of the trend towards the separation of Church and state which, for several and often conflicting reasons, was fairly general in the contemporary Roman Catholic and Protestant world. Fully accomplished in only a few lands in Europe, it prevailed in the United States and the British colonies.

In Scotland the majority of the Presbyterians outside the Church of Scotland gradually drew together. In 1847 the Secession and Relief churches became one in the United Presbyterian Church. In 1852 those known as the Original Seceders joined the Free Church. In 1900 the Free Church and the United Presbyterian Church formed the United Free Church of Scotland. Fresh sacrifice seemed to be entailed by the refusal of a minority of the Free Church, the "Wee Frees" as they were derisively called, to go into the merger and the action of the courts in awarding them as the legal Free Church the properties of that body. However, an act of Parliament removed that menace.

The established church survived the shock of the withdrawal of the Free Church and displayed marked vigour. It endowed new parishes and constructed additional church buildings. It inaugurated young men's and young women's guilds and recruited and trained deaconesses.

The established church drew progressively nearer to the Free Church and its successor, the United Free Church. At the Disruption it had retained the majority of the clergy and the laity. In 1874 Parliament abolished lay patronage, thus giving to the congregations the right to choose their own ministers which had been the crux of the original dissension. A movement for disestablishment made some headway. In 1898 the churches adopted a common hymnal, *The Church Hymnary*. But not until after 1914, namely, in 1929, was reunion consummated.

These controversies by no means constituted the entire history of Christianity or even of Presbyterianism in Scotland. Indeed, only from time to time did they come to the fore. The churches were channels and expressions of a pulsing life which showed itself in many ways. Some of this was in preaching, for much emphasis was placed on it in the Scotch churches. Several very great preachers appeared. Even to list them would unduly lengthen this section. Here, as in so many other places in nineteenth century Protestantism, hymn writers emerged and their contributions were used to vary the metrical versions of the Psalms which until the nineteenth century had prevailed in public worship. Outstanding among them was Horatio Bonar (1808–1889), a pupil of Thomas Chalmers who went with the Free Church at the Disruption and who for nearly a quarter of a century was pastor of the Chalmers Memorial Church in Edinburgh. A prolific author of evangelistic tracts and devotional books, he also wrote hundreds of hymns. Among them were "Go, labour on: spend and be spent, thy joy to do thy Father's will" and "I heard the voice of Jesus say." Elizabeth Cecilia Douglas Celephane (1830–1869), who in spite of physical frailty ministered to the sick and poor near her home, wrote at least two hymns which came into wide use, "Beneath the cross of Jesus I fain would take my stand" and "There were ninety and nine that safely lay in the shelter of the fold." The latter gained currency through Moody and Sankey. The brilliant blind preacher and pastor, George Matheson (1842–1906), both scholar and mystic, contributed, among other hymns, "O love that will not let me go."

The interest in scholarship, philosophy, and theology which was a strong strain in the Scotch mind flowered in notable literature. Some of this was highly provocative. William Robertson Smith (1846–1894) was a pioneer in introducing the type of Biblical criticism which was flourishing in Germany. As professor of Oriental Languages and Old Testament in the Free Church college in Aberdeen and as the author of articles on Biblical subjects in the ninth edition of the *Encyclopædia Britannica,* he distressed some of the conservatives. In the 1870's he was tried for heresy by the General Assembly of the Free Church, and while the indictment was dropped, a vote of lack of confidence was passed and he was deprived of his chair. Yet he was soon appointed to a professorship at Cambridge. In general the Scottish scholars were moderate, open-minded to new views, willing to accept those which seemed to them sound, but not inclined to go to extremes. Thus George Adam Smith (1856–1942), who, as a specialist on the Old Testament, combined deep religious insight with a knowledge of German scholarship acquired at Tübingen and Leipzig and through continuing studies, commanded the confidence of both scholars and the popular evangelist, Dwight L. Moody, and in his later years had a term as Moderator of the United Free Church. A slightly older contemporary, whose biography he wrote, Henry Drummond (1851–1897), was notable for aiding many to fit the findings of modern science, especially the belief in evolution, then a relatively fresh challenge, into a rational scheme with the Christian faith. Through lectures and writing, especially *Natural Law in the Spiritual World* and *The Ascent of Man,* two works which enjoyed an enormous circulation, Drummond answered the questions of thousands. As an evangelist to students and other intellectuals and as a friend of Moody he had a wide hearing in the British Isles, Germany, America, and Australia and gave a great impetus to growing student Christian movements. In the New Testament, Marcus Dods (1834–1909), of the Free Church, professor and principal of that church's theological school in Edinburgh, New College, and the author of books which had an extensive circulation, was exonerated of the charge of heresy by the General Assembly. J. McLeod Campbell's *Atonement* (1856) presented the reconciling work of Christ as purely through love and was regarded by some friendly critics as the greatest work in theology in English in the first six decades of the century.

Developments in public worship were seen, with the introduction of organs and the use of liturgical forms, some of them drawn from the ancient and modern practices of other churches. A prolific devotional literature appeared.

Action was taken through the Church to further various social reforms, among them better housing, the reduction of drunkenness, and the simplification of the transfer of land.

The minority of Christians in Scotland outside the several Presbyterian churches were divided among several bodies. There was the Episcopal Church, a member of the Anglican Communion. It knew some of the controversies which were troubling its larger neighbour south of the border and in general tended to move in a high churchly direction. The Independents or Congregationalists and the somewhat similar body, the Evangelical Union, merged in 1897. In 1869, Baptists, long lacking cohesion and presenting a wide variety, came together in a union. The Methodists were not numerous and were chiefly in the cities. A few thousand Roman Catholics, mostly in the Highlands and islands, had preserved their faith uninterruptedly since pre-Reformation times. In the nineteenth century they were augmented and swamped by a huge Roman Catholic immigration from Ireland, predominantly in the cities, especially Glasgow, and by 1914 the total membership of that church was approximately a half million. Religious orders reappeared and in 1878 the Pope restored the hierarchy, with two archbishops and two suffragan bishops.

THE IRISH STORY: ROMAN CATHOLIC EMANCIPATION AND THE
DISESTABLISHMENT OF THE (ANGLICAN) CHURCH OF IRELAND

While these developments, with their marked increase in the vigour of the churches, were taking place in Great Britain, what was happening on that island, Ireland, which across the centuries had suffered so much from its large neighbour, England?

The problem which the past had bequeathed to the nineteenth century was grim. The Anglo-Irish minority, largely identified with the Church of Ireland, sister to the Church of England, had long been in control. They were the landlords, the officials, the well-to-do farmers, the clergy of the Church of Ireland, and the elements associated with them. The Scotch-Irish, in Ulster in the North and predominantly Presbyterian, business men and farmers, had suffered from discrimination and had often been disaffected. The large majority of the population was Roman Catholic and most of it, peasants and labourers, was poverty-stricken and ignorant. To Protestant England, Roman Catholic Ireland had been a threat, for it might rise in support of the Roman Catholic claimants to the throne of England of the House of Stuart. During the wars of the French Revolution and Napoleon, for England a life and death struggle, there was the chronic danger that Ireland might go over to the enemy, and at times open rebellion broke out. In 1800 a parliamentary union was effected and the Irish Parliament was abolished. Henceforward representatives from the island were to sit in the Parliament at Westminster. However, the majority of the Irish, Roman Catholics, were under legal disabilities. In the years immediately succeeding 1815 the fiscal union of the governments of the two islands was completed.

The nineteenth century story was one of mingled tragedy and achievement. As we have more than once noted, the blight which destroyed the potato crop in 1846 and 1847 precipitated famine. This was aggravated by a striking increase in population, from about 1,250,000 in 1700 to about 4,500,000 in 1800, and to 8,175,124 in 1841. Famine relief by the government and the emigration of more than 1,500,000 in the ten years after 1847 partly mitigated the misery. In 1861 the census showed a population of about 5,800,000, a substantial decline in two decades. A combination of necessity, agitation in Ireland, prudential self-interest, and conscience led Parliament to improve conditions. In 1829 what was known as Catholic emancipation removed most of the legal disabilities under which those of that faith had laboured. In the 1880's and the 1890's land reform measures first gave relief to tenants, then assisted tenants in the purchase of their holdings, and later reduced the rentals of such lands as were still tilled by tenants. In 1869 the (Anglican) Church of Ireland was disestablished. The local government act of 1898 transferred the control from the landlords to elected county councils and in these the rising Roman Catholic middle class was strong. It was in this setting that developments in the Christianity of Ireland took place.

Improvement in the condition of the Roman Catholic majority was achieved. In addition to the removal of legal disabilities, in 1831 a system of primary schools was inaugurated which worked especially for the benefit of the previously underprivileged Roman Catholics. In 1879 an act which subsidized intermediate education aided them. The national university begun in 1908 was predominantly Roman Catholic. The economic condition of Roman Catholics was mitigated. Better provision was made for the preparation of Irish clergy. Until the French Revolution many of the priests had been educated in France.

The hostility of the Revolution to the Church made that impossible and in 1795 by act of the Protestant government a college for the training of priests was authorized. The institution was placed at Maynooth and was assisted by a grant of funds for the erection of buildings and by annual subsidies. In the first half of the century, due in part to active missions and in part to the economic and social benefits which accrued from the step, several thousand Roman Catholics became Protestants. Rome took alarm, a prelate of ultramontane convictions was appointed to one of the archiepiscopal sees, in 1850 a national synod was convened, the first in many years, and discipline was tightened on clergy and laity. To hold the children to the faith, Roman Catholic schools were emphasized and the work of the Christian Brothers in teaching them was stressed.

The Protestant Churches flourished. In mid-century Protestants constituted a little less than a fourth of the population. Slightly more than half of them were in the Church of Ireland and most of the remainder were Presbyterians, mainly in Ulster. The awakenings which characterized the churches in Great Britain also extended to Ireland. In the first half of the century the Evangelical movement brought a marked increase in vitality to the Church of Ireland. Voluntary societies arose for various purposes, at least two for missions among the Roman Catholics which were followed by many conversions. In the course of time bishops were appointed who concerned themselves more with the spiritual welfare of their flocks than had their predecessors. The Oxford movement had repercussions which brought new life. More churches were built, largely by private gifts, some of them proprietary chapels and many in the rapidly growing cities, especially Belfast. More facilities were provided for the preparation of the clergy. Disestablishment required readjustments, but the constituency rose to the challenge. The Presbyterians also were quickened. Revivals, notably that of 1859, felt on both sides of the Atlantic, brought an access of vigour. In 1840 the General Assembly of the Presbyterian Church of Ireland was formed, uniting the Synod of Ulster and the Secession Synod, and thus added strength. Better provision was made for the education of the priesthood. Foreign missions were undertaken. Next to the Church of Ireland and the Presbyterians the Methodists were the largest Protestant body. They grew rapidly, but were only a small minority of the whole.

The Christianity of Ireland entered the twentieth century much stronger than it had been a hundred years earlier.

THE PART OF CHRISTIANITY IN SHAPING THE LIFE OF THE BRITISH ISLES IN THE NINETEENTH CENTURY

What did Christianity do to shape the life of the British Isles in the nineteenth century? In that age of abounding vitality and of rapid change, when the British built the most extensive and populous empire that the world had ever seen and were the leaders in industry, commerce, and banking, in that period when the land presented the contrast between great wealth on the one hand, with a prosperous middle class, and abject squalor on the other, when it was stirred by urgent movements to better the lot of the underprivileged, what part did Christianity have? From the preceding pages it is obvious that the churches were more vigorous at the close than at the outset of the century. To what extent and in what ways did the Christianity of which they were the partial expression and the vehicle modify or mould the scene about them? No brief or simple answer can be given. Only a few facts can be summarized which would have to be given prominence in any fully-rounded picture.

From what has been said, it must be clear that in spite of the perplexities presented by the broadening horizons of human knowledge and widespread agnosticism and scepticism, among a larger proportion of the population in 1914 than in 1815 Christianity was a force in shaping the outlook and the purposes of life. In nominal allegiance there had been little change. In actuality, on the one hand, probably both among the workingmen and among the intellectuals, more were pronouncedly sceptical or antagonistic, and on the other hand more were zealously committed. Probably, too, in morals a larger number more nearly approximated to Christian standards in 1914 than in 1815.

A striking example of improvement was in the agitation to reduce drunkenness. Christians led the way in it, sometimes backed but sometimes unsupported by their churches. Protestants were notable in their leadership, but some Roman Catholics had a share. Outstanding was the Capuchin, Theobald Mathew (1790–1856), an Irish priest who first came to the public notice through his untiring devotion to the sufferers from a cholera epidemic in 1832 and who was won to the temperance cause by a Quaker. In Ireland it was he who is said to have been chiefly responsible for a striking reduction in the consumption of spirits. He extended his campaign to Britain and America.

In addition to the efforts of the Salvation Army, there were many other enterprises springing from Christian motives to better the lot of the underprivileged. Among them were the orphanages of George Müller, which we have already mentioned; Toynbee Hall, the precursor of many "settlements," named for one who made much of the *Imitation of Christ;* the homes begun by Thomas John Barnardo (1845–1905), who while in London preparing to be a medical missionary to China became interested in the waifs of the metropolis and founded institutions with the rule "no destitute child ever refused admission"; and various city mission societies.

Impelled by a Christian motive, Florence Nightingale (1820–1910), who went to Pastor Fliedner's school at Kaiserswerth in Germany for training, rose to fame for her organization of the nursing service to the fighting men in the

Crimean War, and was outstanding in promoting the development of the nursing profession.

Many names spring to mind of those who, inspired by their Christian faith, led in efforts for various aspects of social reform, some by legislation and others through private philanthropy. Thomas Fowell Buxton (1786–1845), reared a Quaker and married to a sister of Elizabeth Fry, succeeded the Evangelical William Wilberforce in the leadership of the anti-slavery movement which culminated in the act of Parliament (1833) that ended Negro slavery within the British Empire (1838). Anthony Ashley Cooper (1801–1885), heir to a great title, eventually the seventh Earl of Shaftesbury, who owed his sturdy Evangelical faith to a boyhood nurse, was for many years a champion in Parliament of legislative measures to improve the lot of the labourers in mines and factories. He was also president of numerous philanthropic and missionary societies, among them the Ragged School Union and the National Society for the Prevention of Cruelty to Children, and aided the Young Men's Christian Associations and workingmen's institutes. J. K. Hardie, socialist and pioneer in the formation of the Independent Labour Party, began his public career as a lay preacher in the Evangelical Union. Methodist local preachers led in the formation of several of the early labour unions.

That literature felt the effects of Christianity is obvious, especially when such poets as Alfred Tennyson and Robert Browning are recalled.

Some of the statesmen who moulded British domestic and foreign policy, particularly in the latter half of the century, sought to make Christian principles effective in the actions of the government. Outstanding was William Ewart Gladstone (1809–1898), who would have preferred to become a clergyman but, urged by his father, entered politics. Many years in Parliament and on the cabinet, and four times prime minister, he endeavoured always to act as a Christian. The high sense of public duty which characterized a large proportion of British civil servants and colonial administrators in the nineteenth century, which was in striking contrast to the prevalence of corruption and selfishness in the eighteenth century, must be in part ascribed to the mounting influence of Christianity.

Summary

One of the most striking parallels in history is the fact that a flood tide in the Christianity of the British Isles, and especially of the dominant partners, England and Scotland, went *pari passu* with enormous growth in wealth, power, population, and empire. This was in spite of intellectual and social currents which were running strongly against the faith. In this there seems to be something akin to the coincidence of the high peak of creative life in the

Middle Ages of Western Europe with the revivals in Christianity represented by the mendicant orders, great formulations of theology, and such "heretical" movements as the Waldensees and Cathari. Resembling it was likewise the fashion in which the Protestant and Catholic Reformations were contemporary with the many other vigorous movements in the sixteenth century. We have also remarked that the Catholic Reformation in Spain came at approximately the same time with the era of Spanish colonial empire building and the most notable contributions of Spanish artists.

That here is more than coincidence seems probable. As we have said before, it would be difficult to know which are causes and which are effects. We can be sure, however, that, whether cause or effect, in each of these periods the forward surge of Christianity profoundly influenced the other phases of the life and culture in the midst of which it occurred.

Selected Bibliography

J. Barr, *The United Free Church of Scotland* (London, Allenson & Co., 1934, pp. 302). A useful historical survey.

G. A. Beck, editor, *The English Catholics 1850–1950* (London, Burns, Oates & Washbourne, 1950, pp. xix, 640). By various authors, all friendly, and in general designed to show the advance of the Roman Catholic Church in the century after the reëstablishment of the hierarchy. Contains some very useful data.

K. Bliss, *The Service and Status of Women in the Churches* (London, Student Christian Movement Press, 1952, pp. 208).

W. Booth, *In Darkest England and the Way Out* (London, International Head-quarters of the Salvation Army, preface 1890, pp. 285, xxxi). The famous programme of General Booth.

[S. Brooks], *Life, Letters, Lectures, and Addresses of Fred'k W. Robertson* (New York, Harper & Brothers, no date, pp. xxiii, 840).

S. C. Carpenter, *Church and People, 1798–1889. A History of the Church of England from William Wilberforce to "Lux Mundi"* (London, Society for Promoting Christian Knowledge, 1933, pp. 598). In general, objective, comprehensive, and carefully done.

H. Cnattingius, *Bishops and Societies. A Study of Anglican Colonial and Missionary Expansion 1698–1850* (London, Society for Promoting Christian Knowledge, 1952, pp. viii, 248). Carefully done.

T. K. Cheyne, *Founders of Old Testament Criticism. Biographical, Descriptive, and Critical Studies* (New York, Charles Scribner's Sons, 1893, pp. ix, 372). By an expert.

H. W. Clark, *History of English Nonconformity. Vol. II. From the Restoration to the Close of the Nineteenth Century* (London, Chapman & Hall, 1913, pp. xx, 458). Sympathetic. Carefully done.

S. T. Coleridge, *Aids to Reflection with a Preliminary Essay by J. Marsh*. From the fourth London edition, edited by H. N. Coleridge (New York, Gould, Newman and Saxton, 1840, pp. 357).

F. W. Cornish, *The English Church in the Nineteenth Century* (London, Macmillan & Co., 2 Parts, 1910). A valuable survey by an Anglican.

A. W. Dale, *The Life of R. W. Dale of Birmingham* (London, Hodder & Stoughton, 1902, pp. x, 771). By his son.

R. W. Dale, *History of English Congregationalism* (London, Hodder & Stoughton, 1907, pp. xii, 787). Left unfinished by the death of its author, a distinguished Congregational clergyman.

J. E. de Hirsch-Davies, *A Popular History of the Church in Wales from the Beginning to the Present Day* (London, Sir Isaac Pitman & Sons, 1912, pp. xii, 356). By an Anglican.

L. L. Doggett, *History of the Young Men's Christian Association* (New York, Association Press, 1922, pp. 405). A competent survey.

L. E. Elliott-Binns, *Religion in the Victorian Era* (London, The Lutterworth Press, 1936, pp. 525). A standard survey, covering the entire range of Christianity in England during that period.

L. E. Elliott-Binns, *The Development of English Theology in the Later Nineteenth Century* (London, Longmans, Green & Co., 1952, pp. ix, 137). Brief, but comprehensive.

St. John Ervine, *God's Soldier. General William Booth* (London, William Heinemann, 2 vols., 1934). A full-length, sympathetic biography.

J. R. Fleming, *The Story of Church Union in Scotland, Its Origins and Progress, 1560–1929* (London, James Clarke & Co., pp. 176). A popular, sympathetic survey, by an expert.

J. R. Fleming, *A History of the Church in Scotland 1843–1874* (Edinburgh, T. & T. Clark, 1927, pp. x, 276). A standard survey.

J. R. Fleming, *A History of the Church in Scotland 1875–1929* (Edinburgh, T. & T. Clark, 1933). A continuation of the preceding book.

W. Y. Fullerton, *C. H. Spurgeon, A Biography* (London, Williams & Norgate, 1920, pp. xii, 358). Sympathetic, based upon careful research, well written, by a fellow Baptist.

D. Gwynn, *Cardinal Wiseman* (Dublin, Browne & Nolan, 1950, pp. x, 197). Admiring.

W. Hanna, *Memoirs of the Life and Writings of Thomas Chalmers, D.D., LL.D.* (New York, Harper & Brothers, 4 vols., 1851, 1852). By a son-in-law, valuable for its extensive inclusion of portions of Chalmers' journals and letters.

G. D. Henderson, *The Claims of the Church of Scotland* (London, Hodder & Stoughton, 1951, pp. vii, 251). An excellent survey, largely of history, from the Reformation. Especially good on the nineteenth century.

J. W. James, *A Church History of Wales* (London, Arthur H. Stockwell, 1945, pp. 190). A good summary with an Anglican emphasis.

W. D. Killen, *The Ecclesiastical History of Ireland from the Earliest Period to the Present Times* (London, Macmillan & Co., Vol. II, 1875, pp. xix, 592). By a Presbyterian, with an inclusive coverage, but stressing the Presbyterian phases of the story and with a strong Protestant bias.

W. F. Knapp, editor, *The History of the Brethren* (Denver, W. F. Knapp, 2 vols., 1936). Detailed, sympathetic, with many excerpts from the sources.

E. A. Knox, *The Tractarian Movement 1833–1845* (London, Putnam, 1933, pp. xix, 410). By a former Bishop of Manchester, frankly critical of the Oxford movement, yet attempting to be fair, and placing it in the general contemporary setting of the religious revival.

J. Scott Lidgett, *My Guided Life* (London, Methuen & Co., 1936, pp. 279). The autobiography of an outstanding British Methodist.

H. B. Marks, *The Rise and Growth of English Hymnody* (New York, Fleming H. Revell Co., 1937, pp. 288). By a long time student of the subject.

The Life of Frederick Denison Maurice, Chiefly Told by His Own Letters, edited by his son, F. Maurice (London, Macmillan & Co., 2 vols., 1884).

Autobiography of George Müller, compiled by G. F. Bergin (London, J. Nisbet and Co., 1905, pp. xiv, 735).

J. H. Newman, *Apologia pro Vita Sua, Being a History of His Religious Opinions* (New York, The Macmillan Co., 1931, pp. xxi, 380). Frankly in answer to criticism: one of the most famous of spiritual autobiographies.

W. A. Phillips, editor, *History of the Church of Ireland from the Earliest Times to the Present Day, Volume III, The Modern Church* (Oxford University Press, 1933, pp. 499). From an Anglican point of view.

C. E. Raven, *Christian Socialism, 1848–1854* (London, Macmillan & Co., 1920, pp. xii, 396).

T. Rees, *History of Protestant Nonconformity in Wales from Its Rise to the Present Time* (London, John Snow, 1861, pp. vii, 512). Sympathetic, based upon extensive use of the sources.

P. Rogers, *Father Theobald Mathew Apostle of Temperance* (Dublin, Browne and Nolan, 1943, pp. xxiii, 166). Sympathetic, based upon careful research.

G. A. Smith, *The Life of Henry Drummond* (New York, Doubleday & Company, 1898, pp. xiii, 541). Sympathetic, by a friend and distinguished scholar.

V. F. Storr, *The Development of English Theology in the Nineteenth Century 1800–1860* (London, Longmans, Green & Co., pp. viii, 486). A competent survey. The best on the years which it covers.

J. Stoughton, *Religion in England from 1800 to 1850. A History, with a Postscript of Subsequent Events* (London, Hodder & Stoughton, 2 vols., 1884). Comprehensive, temperate in spirit, with major emphasis upon Nonconformity.

W. J. Townsend, H. B. Workman, and G. Eayrs, editors, *A New History of Methodism* (London, Hodder & Stoughton, Vol. I, 1919, pp. xx, 598). By distinguished Methodist scholars, this volume deals with the history of Methodism in the British Isles.

J. Tulloch, *Movements of Religious Thought in Britain during the Nineteenth Century* (New York, Charles Scribner's Sons, 1886, pp. xi, 338).

D. O. Wagner, *The Church of England and Social Reform since 1854* (Columbia University Press, 1930, pp. 341). Sympathetic, a doctoral dissertation.

W. Ward, *The Life of John Henry Cardinal Newman Based on His Private Journals and Correspondence* (London, Longmans, Green & Co., 2 vols., 1912). Written with insight, with a combination of objectivity and sympathy.

R. F. Wearmouth, *Methodism and the Working-class Movement of England 1800–1850* (London, The Epworth Press, 1937, pp. 289). Based upon careful research.

C. C. J. Webb, *A Study of Religious Thought in England from 1850* (Oxford, The Clarendon Press, 1933, pp. viii, 192). A competent brief survey.

B. Willey, *Nineteenth Century Studies: Coleridge to Matthew Arnold* (London, Chatto & Windus, 1949, pp. v, 287). A very important survey and interpretation of religious thought.

W. T. Whitley, *A History of British Baptists* (London, The Kingsgate Press, 2d ed., 1932, pp. xii, 384). A comprehensive survey.

J. Whitney, *Elizabeth Fry Quaker Heroine* (Boston, Little, Brown & Co., 1937, pp. 337). Charmingly written, with many excerpts from the sources.

Chapter 49

THE CHRISTIANITY OF NORTH AFRICA, WESTERN ASIA, AND EASTERN EUROPE: REEMERGENCE, SUFFERINGS, COMPLEXITIES AND VITALITY, A.D. 1815 - A.D. 1914

The Eastern Churches, continuations of regional branches of the Catholic Church of the first three centuries, had a chequered course in the nineteenth century. As the Turkish tide retreated, some of them reëmerged and became autocephalous national bodies and rallying centres of nationalism. Others, remaining encircled, suffered further from the attrition which had been their lot since the Moslem-Arab conquest. The largest, the Russian Orthodox Church, displayed vitality in a variety of ways. Upon them all and upon all the regions which they occupied, the Christianity of the West, Roman Catholic and Protestant, impelled and empowered by the awakenings of the nineteenth century, had greater or less effect. To give some indication of what took place we will make a geographic pilgrimage, beginning on the southern shore of the Mediterranean, journeying eastward and northward, and ending with what because of their magnitude and their importance for the world as a whole were the most significant, the developments in Russia.

THE NORTHERN SHORES OF AFRICA AND THE NEAR EAST

On the north shore of Africa west of Egypt the Christian churches which had flourished in the early centuries had gradually disappeared under Moslem rule. At the dawn of the nineteenth century Christianity was represented only by Spanish footholds in Morocco, European merchants, and the captives of the corsairs.

Between 1815 and 1914 most of the north shore west of Egypt was occupied by Western European powers and this led to a striking increase in the numbers of Christians. Almost all the growth was by immigration from north of the Mediterranean. There were also missions, both Roman Catholic and Protestant, among the Moslems and Jews, although with very few converts. Most of the Christians were in Algeria, conquered by the French in the 1830's and 1840's, and in Tunisia, occupied by France in 1881. By the end of the century Algeria contained about half a million who were registered as Roman Catholics. The majority were French but there were substantial numbers of Italians, Spaniards, and Maltese. There were also several thousand in Tunisia. A Roman Catholic hierarchy was developed and in 1884 the Archbishopric of Carthage, made famous in the early centuries by a distinguished succession of prelates, chief among them Cyprian, was revived. The first to hold the renewed see and the outstanding nineteenth century bishop in North Africa was Charles Martial Allemand Lavigerie (1825–1892). Lavigerie was also cardinal and primate of Africa. Lavigerie was a man of sweeping vision, who wished the French holdings in North Africa to be the vantage from which the Roman Catholic faith would spread throughout the continent. As we have seen (Chapter 46), he was the founder of what were known as the White Fathers (1868), who extended their activities south of the Sahara. In spite of the coolness or outright hostility of French officials, due partly to fear that the revived Christianity would arouse resentment among the Moslems and partly to the anticlericalism of the Third Republic, other religious orders entered and dioceses and parishes multiplied. There were also some Protestant immigrants, mostly from France. Libya, occupied by Italy in 1911, contained a few thousand Roman Catholic immigrants of the nineteenth century.

In Egypt the story was somewhat different. Here were ancient churches which had never died out. The largest was Monophysite in faith, and, although the vernacular of its members was Arabic, it continued its services in the Coptic language which had been the speech of the most of the population before the Moslem-Arab conquest. Its numbers are said to have grown in the second half of the nineteenth century, but from an excess of births over deaths and not by conversions. The chief strength of the Coptic Church was in the cities and Upper Egypt. The Greek Orthodox Church had been present before the Arab occupation and had existed continuously ever since. It was under its own Patriarch of Alexandria. In the latter part of the nineteenth century its numbers were augmented by the immigration of Syrians and Greeks, and schools, hospitals, and other charitable institutions were carried on. Armenians and Syrian Monophysites were also in Egypt, but in smaller numbers. Roman Catholics had been present since the seventeenth century, but at the outset of the nineteenth century were very few. Like the other churches, they increased in the second half of the century. This was partly by immigration from Europe. It was chiefly by accessions from the Copts, the fruits of missions by several religious orders. These converts and their descendants were gathered into a

Coptic Uniate body which in 1895 was given a Patriarch of Alexandria and in 1904 was said to have 22,000 members. Protestantism was represented by several denominations. Among them were the Church Missionary Society which gathered a few converts from the Moslems and the Copts and the United Presbyterian Church of North America, which built up a community of several thousand, almost entirely from the Copts and chiefly in Upper Egypt.

Christianity reëntered the Sudan, in the upper part of the Nile Valley, south of Egypt. There, it will be recalled, it had been introduced in the sixth century and had been strong for many years, only to succumb to slow extinction by Islam. Shortly before the middle of the nineteenth century Roman Catholic missionaries gained a footing and in the second half of the century the British and Foreign Bible Society, the Church Missionary Society, and the United Presbyterians made their way into the region.

South-east of the Sudan, in the mountain fastnesses of Ethiopia (Abyssinia), an ancient church, the official faith of the realm, held out against the encroachments of Islam. It drew its head from one or another of the Coptic monasteries of Egypt and was Monophysite in creed. The country also contained pagans, Jews, and Moslems. In the nineteenth century Roman Catholics renewed the efforts to win the Ethiopian Church which had enjoyed a fleeting success in the sixteenth and seventeenth centuries. They gathered several thousand into a Uniate Ethiopian Church. Protestants, largely Germans, Swiss, and Swedes, entered. For a brief time in the 1880's there was an attempt to bring the Church of Ethiopia into union with the Russian Orthodox Church, but as much in an effort to offset the encroachments of French, British, and Italian imperialism as from religious motives.

Palestine, the "Holy Land," with Jerusalem as its chief city, presented a varied religious complexion which was enhanced in the nineteenth century. Jerusalem was regarded by Jews, Christians, and Moslems as especially hallowed. Although, as was most of the Near East, ruled by the Ottoman Turks, Moslems, during the larger part of the nineteenth century, it contained many Christians. In 1815 several ancient branches of the Catholic Church were represented, among them Orthodox, Armenians, and Roman Catholics. During the course of the century the Roman Catholics were reinforced and several kinds of Protestantism entered. To the Franciscans who had been the traditional representatives of the Roman Catholic Church were added other orders. In the latter part of the century much was made of the several Uniate Churches. An interesting phase of Protestantism was a bishopric in Jerusalem which was a joint enterprise of the Church of England and the Evangelical Church of Prussia. The incumbents were named alternately by the crowns of England

and Prussia. It was begun in 1840, but the Prussian Government withdrew in 1886.

Syria, to the north of Palestine, had a larger proportion of Christians than did Palestine. In it at the outset of the century the Christians were mostly Jacobites, Greek Orthodox, and Roman Catholics. The Roman Catholics were chiefly Maronites. Massacres of Maronites by the Druzes in 1860 were the occasion for French intervention. As a result, Syria became an autonomous province within the Turkish Empire and with a Christian governor. Under these conditions Roman Catholic missionaries increased. The two chief Uniate bodies, Maronite and Syrian, flourished. The latter was from the Jacobites and had its origin late in the eighteenth century. It was augmented from time to time by the accession of Jacobite bishops. Protestantism was introduced, chiefly by American missionaries.

Cyprus, administered by the British after 1878 but until 1914 nominally under Turkish suzerainty, was predominantly Greek Orthodox in religion and continued to be such. Here the Orthodox Church had been autocephalous since the fifth century, independent of any of the historic patriarchates.

To the Armenians the nineteenth century brought additional suffering. Russia moved southward across the Caucasus. In 1828, after a long war with Persia, she established her control over a considerable section of Armenia, including Echmiadzin, the seat of the Catholicos, and in 1878, after a war with Turkey, obtained from that power a large slice of Armenia on the west of the portion acquired in 1828. In 1836 Russia reorganized the Armenian Church in her domains, according the tsar authority over it through his representatives. In Turkey the chief Armenian official was the Patriarch who resided in Constantinople. Following the Crimean War, in the 1860's the Armenians in Turkey were given a constitution which governed both their civil and ecclesiastical affairs, for by the Ottoman regime each major religious body was regarded as a distinct *millet,* or nation. Under this arrangement the quality of the clergy and the life of the Church seem to have improved.

But the Armenians were caught in the intrigues of the great powers, especially Russia and Great Britain. By the Russo-Turkish Treaty of San Stefano, in 1878, Russia was awarded a kind of protectorate over the Armenians in Turkish territory. The British Government was disturbed by this and other provisions of the treaty and a congress of European powers at Berlin (1878), among other measures, substituted the joint guardianship of the powers for that of Russia. A secret convention between Great Britain and Turkey placed the Christians of Asia Minor under British protection. Partly from fear that Armenian nationalism, centering around the Church, might become a British tool, the Russians tightened their control, prohibited the use of the Armenian language in the schools, and in 1903 confiscated the properties of the Church. In the meantime, in the mid-1890's the Turks, from alarm at Armenian nationalist agitation and because of chronic animosity, launched massacres which took a toll of several thousand lives. By 1914, however, the Armenians were effecting a recovery.

The Armenian religious scene was complicated by other factors. There was a revival of an indigenous religious movement which was apparently either a continuation of the ancient Paulicianism or akin to it and which was labelled by the Armenian Church as heretical. The Roman Catholics augmented their missionary activity and won numbers to the Uniate body drawn from the Armenian Church. The Armenian Uniates were under the protection of France, for that power saw in this a means of extending its political influence in Western Asia. Thanks to French pressure, in 1830 the Turkish Government recognized the Uniates as a separate *millet*. The laity were restive under the restrictions by Rome of their participation in the affairs of their church and the course of the Uniates was troubled by their insistence on a larger voice. Protestants, mainly missionaries of the American Board of Commissioners for Foreign Missions, addressed themselves to the Armenians. At first they sought to stimulate fresh life in the Armenian Church rather than bring into being Protestant churches. To this end they translated the Bible into the vernacular and opened schools and theological seminaries. However, conservatives took alarm and in 1846 the Armenian Patriarch in Constantinople formally excommunicated those who followed the missionaries. As a result what were known as Evangelical churches were formed. Later friendly relations between Evangelicals and the old church were to some degree restored.

It may be noted that early in the nineteenth century the Georgian Church, in the Caucasus, Orthodox by long tradition, was subjected by the Russian conquerors to the Holy Synod of the Russian Orthodox Church and was forcibly assimilated to that body.

In the nineteenth century the Nestorians had their chief centre around Lake Urmia, in the mountainous north-west of Persia. They had sadly dwindled since the days, centuries earlier, when communities of them were to be found from Mesopotamia to the China Sea. They were sometimes known, not quite correctly, as Assyrian Christians, and also were called the Church of the East. Again and again, notably in the 1830's and 1840's, their numbers were reduced by massacres by their fierce neighbours, the Kurds. As early as the sixteenth century some of the Nestorians had become Uniates. Known as Chaldeans they persisted, and in the nineteenth century, thanks in part to Roman Catholic missionaries from Europe, their numbers increased. In the nineteenth century Protestants, chiefly Anglicans and Americans (the latter at first under the

American Board of Commissioners for Foreign Missions and then Presbyterians), established missions among them. They sought to infuse new life in them rather than produce separate communities, but, as among the Armenians, distinct churches came into being, in this instance Anglican and Presbyterian.

It must be added that while in the nineteenth century Roman Catholic and Protestant missions multiplied on the northern shores of Africa and in the Near East, they won very few except from the existing Christian bodies. Now and then a Jew was converted and occasionally a Moslem. However, Moslem law and custom made accessions from Islam almost impossible. Through personal contacts, literature, schools, and hospitals thousands of Moslems were brought under the influence of Christianity and here and there a Christian leaven penetrated some elements of Moslem society. But very few declared themselves Christians by receiving baptism.

THE REËMERGENCE OF ORTHODOX CHURCHES IN SOUTH-EASTERN EUROPE

The nineteenth century witnessed the rapid decline of the once mighty Ottoman Empire. Indeed, it became known as "the sick man of Europe." By 1914 it had surrendered all its possessions in Europe except Constantinople and a small area north and west of that city. It had also lost Crete and most of the islands in the Ægean. The retreat of the Turks was accomplished partly with the help of Russia but chiefly through the surging nationalism of the peoples of the Balkan Peninsula. Nationalism was closely associated with the Orthodox Churches. Indeed, they were the symbol and the rallying centres of the reëmerging nations. As a result, there came into being national, autocephalous churches which were independent of one another and of the Patriarch of Constantinople. That ecclesiastic, while enjoying the title of Ecumenical and having a priority of dignity, ceased to have the administrative control in the Balkan Peninsula which he had exercised under the Turks. His effective authority was limited to the Orthodox within the Turkish realm. In 1914 these were mainly the Greeks in Constantinople and in the coastal cities of Asia Minor.

The story of the achievement of the independence of the Balkan nations and with it the autonomy of the several Orthodox Churches is fairly complicated. Here we can take the space to give it only in the barest outline. As we have seen, the Ecumenical Patriarchs were under the control of the Turkish rulers. The latter gave them the administration of the Orthodox Church in their realms. In some areas this meant the appointment of Greek bishops and clergy who did not know the language of their flocks, who sought to exploit them for their own profit, and who were hated as aliens. Political independence was, accordingly, accompanied and at times preceded by the throwing off of the Patriarchal yoke and the achievement of ecclesiastical independence.

Before the year 1815 the Orthodox Church in Montenegro had been auto-cephalous. For most practical purposes its mountain people, Serbs, had long been independent, governed by a succession of prince bishops. In 1766 their archbishop was recognized as autonomous, but with a formal dependence on the Holy Synod of the Russian Orthodox Church.

In 1804 revolt against the Turk broke out among the Serbs. In 1817 what amounted to political autonomy was gained, although still under the nominal suzerainty of the Sultan of Turkey. As a result of the Russian invasion of Turkey in 1828–1829 and as one of the provisions of the Treaty of Adrianople (1829), this position was accorded international recognition. A national Ortho-dox Church was organized under a metropolitan with his seat at Belgrade. As a result of the defeat by Russia in 1877–1878 Turkey recognized the full in-dependence of Montenegro and Serbia. In consequence, in 1879 the Serbian Orthodox Church became completely free from the Ecumenical Patriarch. But from time to time it was in conflict with that prelate over the appointment of Greek bishops in Macedonia, where both claimed jurisdiction. The Congress of Berlin (1878) gave to Austria-Hungary the right to occupy and administer the adjacent Bosnia and Herzegovina and in that year the Austria-Hungarian Government entered into an agreement with the Ecumenical Patriarch by which the latter recognized the autonomy of the Orthodox Church in those provinces but retained a nominal oversight.

There were other Orthodox in the Austria-Hungarian realms. Late in the seventeenth and early in the eighteenth century several thousand Serbs took refuge from the Turks in the south of Hungary and there formed an auto-cephalous church which had its primate at Karlowitz. In 1848 the Austrian Emperor Francis Joseph gave to that ecclesiastic the title of Patriarch. In 1873 the Austria-Hungarian Government took from the See of Karlowitz two dioceses of Serbs and some Orthodox in Bukowina and grouped them under another autocephalous church with headquarters at Czernowitz in Bukowina.

In Greece in 1821 a movement for political independence broke out into an uprising. The war was fought with great ferocity and dragged on to 1829. Russian intervention (1828–1829) led to the virtual recognition of what soon became the Kingdom of Greece. In the struggle most of the clergy supported the insurgents. In 1833 the national assembly passed a resolution, signed by thirty bishops, which declared that the Church of Greece owned no head but Christ, and the king gave a charter to the autocephalous national Church of Greece. This was done without consultation with the Ecumenical Patriarch, presumably because the latter was still under the Turk. Not until 1850 did that prelate formally accede to the step and then only with reservations. These were designed to keep the Church of Greece in the same faith as the other Orthodox

Churches, with the Church in Constantinople as the centre to which all questions of dogma were to be referred and the Patriarch of Constantinople as the source of the holy oil which he consecrated for all the Orthodox Churches. As Greece extended its territories the Church of Greece brought more areas under its jurisdiction, thus restricting further the territory directly under the Ecumenical Patriarch.

In 1829, because of the defeat of Turkey by Russia, Wallachia and Moldavia had their autonomy confirmed under a Russian protectorate. In 1862 nationalism fused the two principalities into the state of Rumania. Under Turkish rule the Orthodox Church had been subjected to the administration of Greeks from the Phanar district in Constantinople. Greek was substituted for the traditional Slavonic as the liturgical language. However, by the end of the eighteenth century the use of the vernacular Rumanian had become general in church services. Under the first prince of the unified Rumania the Church was declared autonomous. The Ecumenical Patriarch protested, but in 1885 formally recognized the autocephalous status of the Church of Rumania. It is said that the quality of the parish clergy, poorly trained, poorly paid, and overworked though they were, tended to improve in the latter part of the century. In Transylvania, which in 1918 was to become part of Rumania, the Orthodox Church became autonomous in 1864.

Bulgarian nationalism led to ecclesiastical as well as political independence. When, in 1856, as a result of the Crimean War, the Turkish Government decreed the freedom and equality of the Christians in its realms, Bulgarians demanded reforms in the Orthodox Church in their midst. The Ecumenical Patriarch in part complied and appointed some bishops of Bulgar blood. However, in 1860 the Bulgarians were insisting upon full antonomy for their Church and in 1870 the Ottoman Government formally conceded it. The Ecumenical Patriarch was indignant, excommunicated the clergy and members of that Church, and in this was sustained by a synod (1872) in which more than a score of bishops, four ex-Patriarchs, and the Patriarchs of Alexandria and Antioch participated. They declared heretical the nationalism ("phyletism") which, from their standpoint, was dividing the Church of Christ. Not until 1945 was the Bulgarian Church received back into the communion of the Ecumenical Patriarch. In Macedonia the Greeks and Bulgars competed for control. Rival bishoprics were set up and the Greeks supported the Turks in the forcible suppression of the Bulgars.

In much of the Balkan Peninsula the ecclesiastical picture was further complicated by Roman Catholics and in some places by Protestants. On the eastern shores of the Adriatic there were, as had been true for centuries, Roman Catholics of the Latin rite. In the Balkans there were Uniates, mostly of the

Byzantine and, in Constantinople, also of the Armenian rite. These were augmented in the nineteenth century, partly as the result of missions among the Greeks and partly by Bulgarian restlessness under the Greek yoke of the Ecumenical Patriarch. Protestant missionaries, chiefly from the United States, were in Greece and Bulgaria, but they had only slight numerical success.

THE INCREASING COMPLEXITY OF THE RUSSIAN SCENE

In Russia, even more than in Western Europe, in the nineteenth century the religious life was marked by stark contrasts and increasing complexity. The domain of the tsars was expanding, partly to the southward at the expense of the decadent Turkish Empire but chiefly east of the Caspian and on the northeastern shores of Asia. This vast area, in square miles the largest continuous empire on the globe, contained a variety of peoples and religions. Even in Europe, in addition to the Christian majority, there were pagans, Moslems, and Jews, and in Asia there were pagans of many stripes, Buddhists, and Moslems. As we are to see, the government put forth strenuous efforts to weld together the diverse conglomeration through a programme of Russification which had as one of its features the incorporation of as much of the population as possible into the Orthodox Church. Yet this did not prevent a mounting diversity. On the one hand, as in Western Europe, there was an extensive de-Christianization of traditionally Christian elements, especially among the intellectuals. On the other hand, also as in Western Europe, but in somewhat different fashion, there was fresh access of vigour in the churches. Much, both of the de-Christianization and of the religious awakening, was through currents from Western Europe. There was also an indigenous and emphatically anti-Western trend. Russian Christianity did not show as great vitality as Protestantism or Roman Catholicism, but it displayed more variety than at any previous time and, far from being moribund, registered decided advances.

Important though they were, we cannot devote any considerable amount of space to the de-Christianizing and anti-Christian movements. We must, however, note several general facts about them. First is what we mentioned a moment ago: they were largely through contagion from the Occident. The science and philosophy of the new age were penetrating Russia and here as in Western Europe they furthered religious scepticism among many who were touched by them. Among others, Hegel and Comte were influential. The social theories of the West also entered. Liberal democracy had its advocates. Socialism, including that of Marx, won followers, and anarchism and nihilism had their devotees. Much of the social radicalism was anti-religious.

At the beginning of the century the Tsar Alexander I (reigned 1801–1825) moved towards liberalism, but in his later years he became fearful of it. His successor, Nicholas I (reigned 1825–1855) was staunchly conservative. In the first decade of the next reign, that of Alexander II (1855–1881), a number of liberal measures were put through, including the emancipation of the serfs (1861) and the institution of zemstvos (1864) to further local self government. For the last fifteen years of his reign Alexander II reversed his early policy and supported repressive measures. He met his death through the bombs of terrorists who had resorted to violence to sweep aside the old order. It is not surprising that the next tsar, Alexander III (reigned 1881–1894), was even more intent on curbing the political and social theories from Western Europe. Under his son and successor, the amiable but weak Nicholas II (reigned 1894–1917), and after the defeat of Russia in a disastrous war with Japan (1904–1905) had enfeebled the existing regime, the most potent revolution which modern Russia had thus far known broke out (1905) and wrought what at the time seemed to be drastic changes in the direction of a liberal government.

Under these circumstances, when through much of the century stern measures were being taken to suppress the political and social theories issuing from the Occident, the advocates of these programmes, driven underground, resorted to plots and counter-violence and, after the complete discrediting of the tsarist regime in World War I (1914–1918), they staged an explosive revolution (1917) which was captured by the extremists.

In this setting the Russian Orthodox Church had its life. It continued to be controlled by the state through the Holy Synod instituted by Peter the Great. It was played upon by various currents, some of them from the West and some from within Russia. From abroad came influences from Protestantism and Roman Catholicism. From within issued contributions from the past and from great souls nurtured in the Orthodox Church. Closely tied to the state as it was, the Russian Orthodox Church also reflected in part the shifts of attitude of the tsars towards the forces emanating from the West.

As we sketch the course of the Russian Orthodox Church in the nineteenth century we will first follow in rough chronological outline the successive stages. Then we will speak of some of the more notable men and movements in the Church.

We have seen (Chapter 44) that the Russian Orthodox Church came to the year 1815 on a rising tide. The Tsar Alexander I had experienced what was akin to a conversion. The Procurator of the Holy Synod, Golitsyn, had undergone a similar change and had given the support of his high position to the Russian Bible Society, formed (1813) under the inspiration of the British and Foreign Bible Society. Translations of the Bible into the vernaculars were prepared and distributed. They enjoyed a wide reading and created a religious ferment. In 1817 the Ministry of Religious Affairs and Public Education was created, Golitsyn was appointed to head it, and under it were placed the Holy Synod and the supervision of all forms of religion. Golitsyn laboured to promote education.

In the exaltation of his religious enthusiasm and partly under the influence of a Roman Catholic theologian who believed the salvation of Europe would be as a community ruled by a universal church, in 1815, the year which saw the end of the Napoleonic Wars, Alexander I, hoping that the world was being ushered into a new day, called on his fellow-monarchs to rule as Christians. At his instance the majority of the sovereigns of Europe subscribed to what was called the Holy Alliance, by which the signers undertook to base their reciprocal relations "on the sublime truths which the Holy Religion of our Saviour teaches" and declared that "the precepts of justice, Christian charity and peace . . . must have an immediate influence on the councils of princes and guide their steps."

As the zeal of Alexander I cooled, reaction set in. It was marked under the next tsar, Nicholas I. Attacks were made on the Bible Society, partly by the conservatives and partly through pressure from the Jesuits, for the latter were in favour with some in high places. Golitsyn fell (1824) and in 1826 the Russian Bible Society was suppressed. Earlier, in 1815, alarmed by the inroads which they were making among the nobility to the detriment of the Orthodox Church, Alexander I had banished the Jesuits from the capital and in 1819 had expelled them from the empire. The Holy Synod was removed from the jurisdiction of the Ministry of Religious Affairs, its Procurator was given the status of minister, and through him the control of the Church by the state was tightened. The formula Orthodoxy, autocracy, nationalism became the tsar's policy and entailed the reciprocal support of Church and state. To enable the clergy better to inculcate their flocks with greater loyalty to the tsar additional provision was made for their education. More theological seminaries were founded and from them the kind of training was banned which had been based on what had been learned from the Jesuits. The state paid the salaries of the clergy, thus giving them better financial support and tying them more closely to the government.

What were known as the Slavophiles became vocal. In opposition to those who admired the West, including those who looked with friendly eyes upon the Roman Catholic Church or Protestantism, they held that the Slavs had been divinely commissioned to preserve the Christian faith in its purity and that the Russian Orthodox Church and the Russian state were the guardians of true Christianity and the ideal society. They maintained that, in contrast, the West was marked by class conflict and that in it the Christian faith either had been corrupted and distorted by Papal tyranny and Protestant individualism or had been weakened by the misuse of reason. They believed, therefore, that Russia should free all Slavs from alien rule and induce all Christians to come into the Orthodox fold. Obviously they reinforced the belief that Moscow was the third Rome, the centre of true Christianity, and that Russia was Holy Russia. They did not win all Russians to their side, but from time to time their views prevailed in the policies of the state and the Holy Synod and were in part reëchoed by spokesmen of the Russian Orthodox Church under the Communist regime in the next century.

In the liberal period of Alexander II, some of the clergy hoped for a less iron-clad control of the Church by the state. Indeed, they asked the tsar that the Church might have a degree of self-government. The tsar put them off and before action was taken reaction set in.

In the latter part of the century the dominant figure in the administration of the Russian Orthodox Church was C. P. Pobiedonostsev, Procurator of the Holy Synod from 1880 to 1905. A layman, a lawyer, extraordinarily able, he was profoundly and sincerely committed to the Russian Orthodox Church and to the monarchy. He distrusted all that came from the West and was resolved to use his office to keep Russia so far as possible uncontaminated by the ideas from that region which, as he believed, would undermine the existing order in Church and state and weaken Christian civilization. He was against trial by jury, parliaments, newspapers, and secular schools. To safeguard Russia he furthered a strict censorship of the press. He wished to assimilate the diverse peoples of the empire to Russian culture. To this end he encouraged missions of the Orthodox Church among non-Christians, supported the repression of social radicals and revolutionaries, was sympathetic with the Slavophiles, and was against the Jews and Judaism. So far as he could, he put the Orthodox Church solidly on the side of the existing order with its secret police and its use of Siberia and Siberian prisons as places of exile for those convicted or suspected of endangering that order.

The Revolution of 1905 seemed to give promise of the emancipation of the Church from its servitude to the state. For some time there had been those who had been agitating for more self-government in the local parishes, for a council (*sobor*) which would be a voice for the Church and reform it, and for the restoration of the Patriarchate. However, while a few minor reforms were made and a council was promised, the latter was not called. A minority among the priests were active in the revolution, but the majority were on the side of the conservatives.

Under these circumstances it is not surprising that the quality of the clergy left much to be desired. Parish priests and diocesan bishops were state functionaries. A large proportion of the priests were regarded by their flocks with contempt or dislike. They tended to become an hereditary caste with no sense of vocation. Many of them had difficulty in making a living, some of them were regarded as grasping, not a few of them were drunkards, and numbers of the sons of priests were unemployed and discontented. Church periodicals which constituted much of their limited reading matter helped to make them supporters of autocracy.

In spite of the many adverse factors the Russian Orthodox Church gave evidence of internal vigour and in the course of the nineteenth century its vitality seems to have mounted. The evidence is in part notable personalities. One of these was Philaret Drozdov (1783–1867). The son of a priest, in his student days he displayed marked ability as a scholar. In 1808 he became a monk and in 1812 he was put at the head of the ecclesiastical academy in St. Petersburg. In 1819 he was made a member of the Holy Synod and in 1821 he was appointed Archbishop of Moscow. He was active in promoting the translation of the Scriptures into the vernacular. At the request of the Holy Synod he compiled a catechism in Russian rather than the ancient Slavonic. In spite of criticisms it became a standard. Although for a time his opponents had him put out of office, Nicholas I restored him to the Holy Synod and made him Metropolitan of Moscow. In 1842 his enemies finally forced him into retirement, but although the last ten years of his life were spent in strict monastic seclusion, for the quarter of a century between 1842 and his death (1867) Philaret exerted great influence. His counsel was sought by many of the outstanding leaders in Church and state and he is said to have drafted the proclamation of 1861 by which Alexander II emancipated the serfs. Well read in the mystical literature of several churches, he believed in prayer and practised it. Reticent about his inner life, he was intense in it. He had a marked effect upon theological thought and study, probably more than any other bishop of the nineteenth century.

Prominent in the religious life of nineteenth century Russia were *startzi* (elders), monks who through spiritual discipline developed characters which commanded reverential respect. To them many came for counsel. Especially famous as a nursery of the *startzi* was Optina Pustyn, a monastery in the province of Kaluga, south of Moscow. Typical of the *startzi* was one whom we have already mentioned (Chapter XLIV), Seraphim of Sarov (1759–1833), who was canonized in 1903.

The *startzi* represented a tradition which was remote from the nineteenth century Western world and perpetuated the monastic discipline and the mystical experience which went back to the early Christian centuries, to the solitaries and monastic communities of Egypt and Syria. In it was much of the Hesychast movement and of the kenoticism which we have repeatedly met in

Russia. The *startzi* were in part the fruits of a revival which began late in the eighteenth century through Païsius Velochkovsky. Païsius was a Russian monk who had been in monasteries in Rumania and on Mt. Athos and who had put into Slavonic a compilation of Greek mystical ascetic writings called the *Philocalia.*

Among the *startzi* who were outstanding in the nineteenth century was Bishop Feofan of Vysha (1815–1894). He rearranged the *Philocalia,* adding to it from other writings. He carried on a prodigious correspondence with those who wrote him for counsel in the life of the spirit, and his letters, posthumously published, were extensively read.

A philosopher who is classed as a Slavophil was Ivan Kireyevsky (1806–1856). Of noble birth, widely travelled, and familiar with the thought of the Western Europe of his day, he was a frequent visitor at Optina Pustyn and established close friendships with its *startzi,* especially with Makary (1758–1842), to whom another "elder," Philaret, a hermit of the Novospassky monastery, entrusted him and who was marked by humility and love for men. In his youth tending to drift from the Orthodox Church, Kireyevsky soon returned to it. While not rejecting Western philosophy, he believed that Russian Christianity and the Eastern fathers had a depth of spiritual life which was in contrast with the abstract rationalism which he regarded as characterizing Western theology.

Outstanding as a Slavophile philosopher was A. S. Khomiakov (1804–1860). Of the aristocracy, deeply religious from boyhood, and never swerving from his loyalty to the Russian Orthodox Church, he believed that the latter ideally displayed *sobornost,* or community. He regarded *sobornost* as combining unity and freedom derived from the love of God and as shown in the mutual love of those who love God. This he held was in contrast with the Roman Catholic Church which, so he maintained, had unity without freedom, and with Protestantism which he viewed as possessing freedom but not unity.

Here and there a parish priest stood out as a spiritual guide. This was rare. It is said that no secular priest of the Russian Orthodox Church has been canonized. In general, parish priests were not held in high esteem. However, a few exceptions made their appearance in the nineteenth century. Prominent among them was John Sergiev of Cronstadt (1829–1908). The son of a deacon, he was given as thorough an education for the priesthood as Russia could provide. For more than fifty years he was in charge of the parish of Cronstadt near St. Petersburg and never aspired to rise in the ecclesiastical hierarchy. Like other seculars, he was married. He was not an ascetic or a mystic of the contemplative kind. Apparently his growth in religious faith and experience was without intense struggle with doubt or a striking crisis. He believed profoundly in prayer, especially in prayer for others. For him officiating at the Holy Communion was a stirring emotional experience. He encouraged frequent communion and, since the Russian Orthodox Church required confession before communion and he could not hear individually all who came, he encouraged each to confess orally, publicly, and simultaneously with others in the congregation. Thousands, and from many ranks in society, asked for his prayers and many miracles of healing were believed to have been wrought through them. He was steeped in the Bible, preached many sermons, and his spiritual diary revealed the quality of his inner life. Large sums passed through his hands for the relief of the sick and the poor. He made journeys, some of them extensive, to assist those who sought his aid. He was called to the death bed of Alexander III to administer the last rites. A staunch supporter of the crown and the Church, in the revolutionary years that came in his old age he was denounced by liberals as an arch reactionary.

By no means all the earnest Christians in communion with the Russian Orthodox Church were Slavophiles, believing pure Christianity to be confined to that body. Famous as an outstanding intellectual and deeply religious soul who sought the unity of all Christians was Vladimir S. Soloviev (1853–1900). He has been described (although this is not a unanimous judgement) as the greatest of Russian systematic religious thinkers, at once a mystic, a philosopher, a theologian, a prophet, and a moral teacher. The grandson of a priest and the son of a distinguished historian and university professor, from childhood he was deeply religious and, an ardent student, acquired great erudition. Through most of his life he had visions, some of them of a mystical character. Disappointed in love, he never married, but lived a wandering life. He thought of becoming a monk, but was unwilling to undergo the loss of liberty which that would have entailed. For a somewhat similar reason he would not undertake the duties of a university professorship, but made a precarious living through writing. Generous to a fault, gay and charming in conversation, he had many friends among the lowly, the intelligentsia, and the highborn. After a period of doubt and inner struggle in his teens during much of which he was an atheist, a socialist, and a communist and read several of the Western contemporary philosophers, he came to a deep religious faith, holding that rational philosophy is darkness and that "God is everything." He made much of Sophia, God's Wisdom, which he conceived to be the eternal and perfect feminine. In him the Platonist, the gnostic, the theosophist, and the orthodox Christian were mixed. A member of the Russian Orthodox Church, he longed to see all Christians, Orthodox, Roman Catholics, and Protestants, brought together. It was said that he became a Roman Catholic, but this appears to be at least highly doubtful. The report seems to have arisen from his effort to achieve Christian unity in his own person by taking the communion, after a manner which left his own position ambiguous, in both the Orthodox and the Roman Catholic Church.

Soloviev sought to give the Christian faith a philosophical and theological basis for his day in such fashion that it would again become relevant to those who had discarded it and that thus the truth of Christ might regenerate humanity and reform the world. True knowledge, he maintained, comes through the right inter-connexion of the empirical, rational, and mystical ways. He held God to be the Absolute, Nothing, the Super-personal, transcending all form and content, but existing as three persons, bearers of the love which renounces self-assertion and which form a perfect unity through perfect love. He declared that God is love. As love He pervades the cosmos. God's love reveals itself through the Logos in the rationality of the universe. Through the incarnation the Logos descends into the stream of events in Jesus Christ and "from being the centre of eternity becomes the centre of history." Through the life, death, and resurrection of Jesus Christ, the God-man who combines the Logos and Sophia, what should be the relation between the divine and the human and has been disturbed by man's sin is restored and the redemption from evil is accomplished. Soloviev accepted evolution from lower to higher forms of life, but taught that evolution is not through materialistic means but through creative spirit. He maintained that nations should regulate their relations with one another on the basis of Christian principles. In his youthful hopefulness he believed in the possibility of all mankind becoming a redeemed society ruled by a theocracy through love. For a time he seemed to side with the Slavophiles, for he hoped that the Slavs and especially the Russians, because of what he deemed to be their proved ability to combine Western and Eastern principles, would lead mankind in the formation of a universal free theocracy.

In Soloviev's later years came disillusionment and despair, both for the Slavophiles and for the realization within history of the theocracy of which he had dreamed. He was made unhappy by the policy of forcible russification which was being pursued by the tsarist regime and regarded the Slavophiles as having succumbed to nationalist egoism. He maintained that the course of mankind on the planet would culminate in a world empire governed by an ascetic, philanthropic reformer, an intellectual genius, who would in reality be Antichrist, for he would be ruled by vanity rather than love and would tempt mankind with the promise of a social order which would ensure to every one "bread and circuses," the satisfaction of their material cravings. He believed that a small minority, remaining really Christian, would retire to a desert, achieve the union of the churches, and prepare for the second coming of Christ. The second advent would then bring the millennial reign of Christ.

Partly through the impact of the thought and writings of Soloviev, early in the twentieth century some intellectuals passed through a youthful Marxist stage and worked out, either independently or in collaboration, a Christian understanding of the universe and history. They were a minority and after the revolution of 1917 and the triumph of the Bolsheviks lived in exile. Their writings, especially those of N. A. Berdyaev (1874-1948) were to have an influence far wider than Russia and Russian communities. We are to meet them again in a later chapter.

Among the creative developments connected with the Russian Orthodox Church we must note music. A striking feature of public worship was the male choirs, singing without instrumental accompaniment. For them deeply moving music was written, much of it in the nineteenth century.

The Christian stream in nineteenth century Russia was by no means confined to the channels of the Russian Orthodox Church. Several of the nonconforming bodies which had existed before 1815 continued. At times they were persecuted, but in 1905 as a result of the revolution in that year, religious liberty was promised and they flourished. Among them were the Old Believers. These, it will be recalled, were divided between those who had priests, the *Popovsty,* and those who did not have priests, the *Bezpopovsty.* Both branches persisted. The *Popovsty* had difficulty in attracting priests from the state church, especially under the strict rule of Nicholas I, and they possessed no bishops who could ordain them. However, in the 1840's they obtained permission from the Austrian Government to import a foreign bishop into the Austrian domains and persuaded a Greek bishop to accept the post. Through him apostolic succession was acquired, eventually dioceses were set up in Russia, and the *Popovsty* ceased to be dependent upon the state church for priests. In the 1880's they were said to number three millions. The *Bezpopovsty* were divided into several sects and to them at least one was added in the nineteenth century. Some sects which held property in common were classed with the *Bezpopovsty.* The Khlysty, the Skoptsy, the Dukhobors, and the Molokans also perpetuated themselves.

During the religious ferment in the reign of Alexander I several movements arose, some of them remaining technically within the Orthodox Church and most of them ephemeral. Thus, in 1817, after a conversion which came partly through the Khlysty and the Skoptsy and partly through German Pietist writings and which led her into the Orthodox Church, Catherine Tatarinov, a widow in high social circles, began prayer meetings in her home which attracted some of the aristocracy and which gave rise to the Spiritual Union.

Still other sects were added in the nineteenth century. Several of them were proliferations of the *Bezpopovsty.* Some were from the Molokans. Others were of independent origin. Several were inspired by contacts with the Protestantism of Western Europe. One of the largest, itself of diverse origins and not fully united, was that of the Stundists and the Baptists. It arose partly through the influence of the Mennonites from Western Europe who had settled in Russia, partly from other German immigrants, and partly among the aristocracy through Lord Radstock of the Plymouth Brethren. The movement made many of its early accessions from the Molokans. In the 1870's and 1880's one of the converts of Lord Radstock, V. A. Pashkov, was an ardent missionary, especially through literature, and sought to unite the Stundists, Baptists, and Molokans. He did not succeed in his effort to bring these various groups together. The government dealt severely with them. Pashkov was banished and died in exile, and many of their leaders were deported to Siberia. Pobiedonostsev, as Procurator of the Holy Synod, was especially vigorous in his attempts at suppression. However, they continued. In general they fell into two camps, the Evangelicals and the Baptists, but they had many similar views.

Another movement, not so much a sect as a social and economic project which sought to build ideal communities on Christian principles, was the Religious Working Brotherhoods, founded in the latter part of the nineteenth century by N. Neplieuv, a man of wealth who set up as a basis for them factories and estates owned and operated communally by the workers.

One who did not form a new sect but who, while not fitting into the pattern of the Orthodox Church, exerted a profound religious influence both in Russia and in other countries, was Count Leo Nikolayevich Tolstoy (1828–1910). Tolstoy had already achieved fame as an author, had lived a varied life, and, happily married to a wife much younger than he, was prosperous as a farmer and from the sale of his books when, in middle life, profound religious disquiet seized him. For a time he sought an answer in science, but could not find it. Then he looked to the lives of those of his own class but returned disillusioned. He felt that the common folk were nearer to the truth and for a time he turned to the Orthodox Church and complied with its worship and its rites. Here, too, what he craved seemed to be lacking. Then, through a reading of the Gospels an answer came which satisfied him and instead of despair he knew happiness which no fear of death could obscure. He had been converted.

But Tolstoy's conversion was to his own variant of Christianity. It rejected the dogmas of the Church and the approval by the Church of persecutions, executions, and wars. It took as central Christ's teachings and found the key to them in the injunction: "Resist not him that is evil." He stressed the light that is in the human conscience. He believed that the Christian must abstain not only from war but also from all forms of violence. To Tolstoy property was the chief source of violence. He held that love must embrace all living things and will lead the Christian to abstain from eating the flesh of slaughtered animals. He eschewed the use of alcohol and tobacco. Only a relatively few of his fellow-countrymen followed Tolstoy's teachings. Yet his writings had a circulation which was almost world-wide.

The Russian Orthodox Church had missions, but these were not nearly as extensive as were those of Roman Catholics and Protestants and were mostly within the Russian Empire. The chief exception was one in Japan. There was also some slight missionary activity in China and Korea. Missions were maintained in Alaska, but they were begun while that region was in the empire. Migrations were the source of Russian Orthodox Churches in the United States and South America. For political purposes the Russian Government gave aid to the Orthodox in the Balkans and Western Asia. However, none of these enterprises outside the Russian Empire could compare in size with what was being done by Roman Catholics and Protestants. Within Russian territories the missions were endorsed and partly supported by the state and were closely related to the efforts at assimilating the non-Russian elements of the diverse population to Russian culture. Yet many missionaries seem to have been moved primarily not by nationalism but by their faith.

The main outlines of the chief missions in the Russian Empire can be quickly given. In 1870 the Orthodox Missionary Society was organized to raise funds for the support of missions. Endorsed by the Holy Synod it eventually had branches in fifty-five dioceses. A mission Sunday, with sermon and collection, was made obligatory on all parishes. Long before the Orthodox Missionary Society was formed, the Holy Synod was sending missionaries to Moslems between the Urals and the Volga and translations of the Bible were being made in the languages of non-Christian peoples. Outstanding in this effort was Nicolai Ivanovitch Ilminski (1822–1891). With his centre at Kazan and eventually with the hearty support of Pobiedonostsev, he led in translating the Bible and the liturgy into various tongues and in the utilization of the vernaculars by missionaries. Missions to non-Christian peoples under Russian rule in Asia and its fringing islands were carried on. They had existed before 1815. They were now increased. They were found not only in regions adjacent to European Russia, but also in the Altai region on the borders of Mongolia and in Kamchatka, the Aleutians, and the Kuriles. They were also in Alaska, for that region was under Russia during the first half of the century.

Summary

The Eastern Churches experienced no awakenings in the nineteenth century comparable in vigour and extent to those in the Roman Catholic Church and

Protestantism. Both these forms of the faith had repercussions on them. In Egypt and Western Asia they gathered communities from them. In Russia Protestantism stimulated the emergence of groups who separated from the Orthodox Church. Russian Christianity was by no means entirely dependent upon Roman Catholicism and Protestantism for its vitality. The Orthodox Church displayed movements which rose from its own past and the majority of Christians who dissented from that Church were in sects of purely Russian origin. In the nineteenth century Russian Christianity showed greater variety than at any previous time. Here was evidence of vitality, even though the Orthodox Church itself was tied hand and foot to the state.

SELECTED BIBLIOGRAPHY

W. F. Adeney, *The Greek and Eastern Churches* (New York, Charles Scribner's Sons, 1908, pp. xiv, 634). An excellent historical survey, but with only small sections on the nineteenth century.

L. Arpee, *The Armenian Awakening. A History of the Armenian Church, 1820–1860* (The University of Chicago Press, 1909, pp. xi, 235). By an Armenian Protestant.

L. Arpee, *A History of Armenian Christianity from the Beginning to Our Own Time* (New York, The Armenian Missionary Association, 1946, pp. xii, 386).

N. Arseniev, *Holy Moscow. Chapters in the Religious and Spiritual Life of Russia in the Nineteenth Century* (London, Society for Promoting Christian Knowledge, 1940, pp. vii, 184). A warmly sympathetic description of the religious life of the Russian Orthodox Church, especially in Moscow.

D. Attwater, *The Christian Churches of the East* (Milwaukee, The Bruce Publishing Co., rev. ed., 2 vols., 1947, 1948). By a Roman Catholic. The first volume is on the churches in communion with Rome and the second volume on the churches not in communion with Rome.

S. Bolshakoff, *Russian Nonconformity* (Philadelphia, The Westminster Press, 1950, pp. 192). A comprehensive historical survey.

F. C. Conybeare, *Russian Dissenters* (Harvard University Press, 1921, pp. x, 370). Contains much useful information from Russian secondary accounts.

J. S. Curtiss, *Church and State in Russia. The Last Years of the Empire 1900–1917* (Columbia University Press, 1940, pp. ix, 442). Based on careful research.

G. P. Fedotov, compiler and editor, *Treasury of Russian Spirituality* (New York, Sheed & Ward, 1948, pp. xvi, 501). Especially useful for its translations from the sources and its historical introductions to the translations.

A. Fortescue, *The Orthodox Eastern Church* (London, Catholic Truth Society, preface 1911, pp. xxxiii, 451). A careful historical survey with a description of current beliefs and practices, by a Roman Catholic.

A. Fortescue, *The Lesser Eastern Churches* (London, Catholic Truth Society, preface 1913, pp. xv, 468). A useful historical survey by a Roman Catholic.

W. H. Frere, *Some Links in the Chain of Russian Church History* (London, Faith Press, 1918, pp. xvi, 200). Only briefly deals with the nineteenth century.

N. O. Lossky, *History of Russian Philosophy* (New York, International Universities Press, 1951, pp. 416). By a Russian Christian philosopher. Deals mostly with the nineteenth and twentieth centuries. The best survey of that period in English. Stresses the religious aspects of philosophy.

H. Y. Reyburn, *The Story of the Russian Church* (London, Andrew Melrose, 1924, pp. vii, 323). About a third of the book is on the nineteenth and twentieth centuries.

E. Smirnoff, *A Short Account of the Historical Development and Present Position of Russian Orthodox Missions* (London, Rivingtons, 1903, pp. xii, 83). By the chaplain of the Russian Embassy in London, based on the reports of the Procurator of the Holy Synod and of the various missions.

A Solovyov Anthology, arranged by S. L. Frank, translated from the Russian by N. Duddington (New York, Charles Scribner's Sons, 1950, pp. 256).

L. Tolstoy, *A Confession and What I Believe,* translated, with an introduction, by A. Maude (Oxford University Press, 1921, pp. xii, 390).

L. N. Tolstoï, *What Is Religion and Other Articles and Letters,* translated by V. Tchertkoff and A. C. Fifield (New York, Thomas Y. Crowell & Co., 1902, pp. 177).

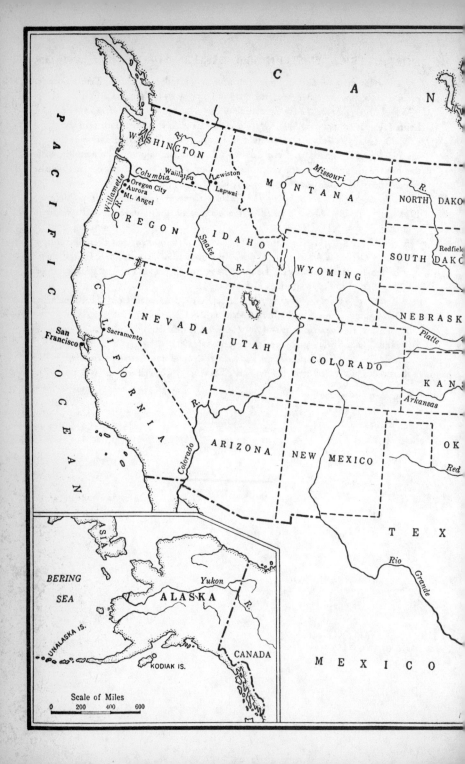

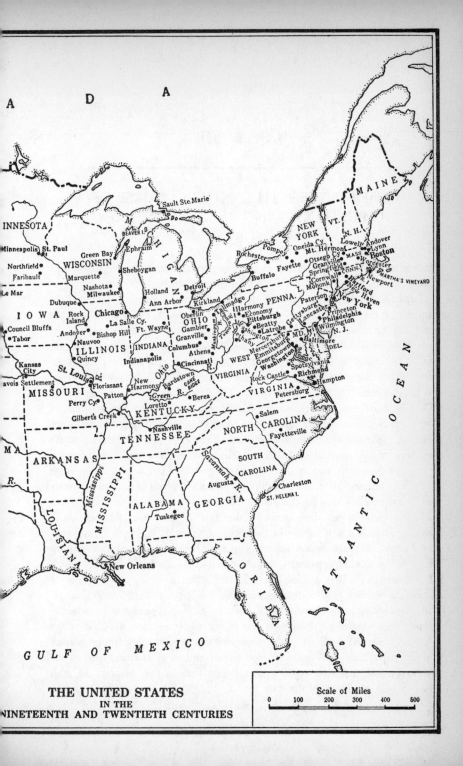

THE UNITED STATES
IN THE
NINETEENTH AND TWENTIETH CENTURIES

Chapter 50

THE NINETEENTH CENTURY COURSE OF CHRISTIANITY IN THE UNITED STATES

It was in the United States that in the nineteenth century Christianity had its greatest numerical growth and its most striking changes.

Superficially the Christianity of the United States seemed at most a mild variant of that of the Old World. It stemmed from that of Europe and the majority of those who had a formal connexion with the faith were in denominations which had had their origin on the other side of the Atlantic and which remained in communion with their respective mother churches. Moreover, many of the forces and movements which affected Christianity in Europe were also found in the United States. The United States was a part of the Occident and much more nearly than Russia its life was an extension of Western civilization. Here science had some of its most daring achievements, both in expanding the boundaries of man's knowledge and in extending man's mastery of his physical environment. Here the machine and the industrial processes eventually displayed their greatest growth. Here wealth mounted to dizzying heights. Here cities multiplied in numbers and in size to a greater degree than elsewhere on the planet. Here private enterprise and capitalism attained their largest dimensions. While most of the social theories which characterized Western culture in the nineteenth century had their formulation in Europe, they also found followers in the United States and that country became the chief representative and champion of the kind of democracy which had arisen in the British Isles. In the United States the threat and challenge of these movements to Christianity were fully as great as in Western Europe. In some respects the Christianity of Western Europe appeared to be in better condition to meet the threat and rise to the challenge than did that of the United States. At the dawn of the nineteenth century a much larger proportion of the population of Western Europe were members of churches than in the United States and, to a much greater degree than in that country, the faith had the official support of the state.

Yet, similar though the Christianity of the United States and the conditions which confronted it were to those of Europe, there were also striking differences. In many respects the Christianity of the United States was unique and proved bewildering and at times irritating to the Christians to the east of the Atlantic. Moreover, while in Western Europe a progressive de-Christianization of large elements in the population was taking place, and that in spite of the abounding and rising vitality in the churches, in the United States a mass conversion of large non-Christian elements and the re-conversion of partially de-Christianized elements was in progress. The Christianity of the United States and that of Europe interacted on each other. However, as time passed, movements indigenous to the United States added to the differences. Because of the rapidly mounting population and wealth of the United States and the vigour and missionary outreach of its churches, the Christianity of that land had a growing share in world-wide Christianity and the life of mankind. To that story we must now turn.

Conditions Confronting Christianity in the United States of the Nineteenth Century

We have already hinted at some of the conditions which confronted Christianity in the United States in the nineteenth century. If we are to have the entire picture before us we need again to summarize them and to add to them the others with which Christianity had to deal.

One of the conditions was the rapid and enormous growth in area. In 1783, when Great Britain formally recognized the independence of the United States, the Western boundary was the Mississippi River. Before 1815 the Louisiana Purchase had carried that boundary far beyond the Mississippi. In 1818 joint occupancy with Great Britain of the Oregon Country brought the United States to the Pacific. In 1819 Florida was purchased. In the 1840's Texas was brought in, the ensuing war with Mexico added a huge region in the Southwest, including California, New Mexico, and Arizona, and the end of joint occupancy gave the United States undivided possession of the territory later carved into the states of Oregon, Washington, and Idaho, and a part of Montana. The purchase of Alaska in 1867 substantially lengthened the Pacific littoral. Late in the 1890's Puerto Rico, Hawaii, and the Philippines were annexed.

Along with the growth in territory went an even greater one in population. In 1800 the census showed the total population to be 5,305,937. In 1820 it was 9,638,191; in 1840, 17,069,453; in 1860, 31,443,322; in 1880, 50,155,783; in 1900, 75,994,575; and in 1910, 91,972,266. From 1800 to 1900 the increase percentage-wise was eight times as great as that in the British Isles and nearly seven times that in Belgium, the country which held the record in Europe. Much of this growth, especially in the first part of the century, was due to the high birth rate of the native-born stock. Beginning in the 1830's, it was even more because of a vast flood of immigration, mostly from Europe, and the birth rate of the foreign-born elements.

The increase in territory and population was partly the cause and partly the result of an even more striking multiplication of wealth. The enormous natural resources of the new country in soil, forests, and minerals were tapped. The inventiveness of the American became proverbial in devising machines, in building factories and transportation systems, and in organizing and managing companies small and large to take full advantage of them. The fact that the wide expanse of the country was under one central government and without internal tariff barriers contributed to the utilization of these assets.

Industrialization was made possible by developments in mathematics and the scientific method. It was accompanied and facilitated by the wide extension of education. Primary education became almost universal and secondary and higher education, instead of being an aristocratic privilege, as in the rest of the world, was increasingly placed within the reach of all and with a growing emphasis in the curriculum upon science and the application of science to man's livelihood.

A concomitant of the rapidly mounting industrialization was the growth of cities and the decreasing proportion of the population engaged directly in agriculture. It is estimated that at the dawn of the century less than a twentieth were in cities of more than three thousand and that 90 per cent. lived on farms. In 1860 only two out of five engaged in gainful occupations were in agriculture and about a sixth of the population were in cities of eight thousand and over. In 1910 about two-fifths of the population was classified as urban and if towns and cities of twenty-five hundred and over be put in that category, in 1914 less than half of the population could be counted as rural.

United though it was, the nation was not without sectionalism and inter-sectional rivalries. The most distinct section was what was called the South. Embracing all the states south of the northern border of Maryland and of the Ohio River, and Missouri, Arkansas, and Texas, it was almost a separate nation with its own culture. The difference was largely due to the presence of the Negro and, until the 1860's, Negro slavery. To a large extent the South was rural and had a plantation economy, until the 1860's based upon slavery. After emancipation, the presence of the Negro and of agriculture which to a con-siderable extent depended on Negro labour continued to keep it apart. The attempt to withdraw from the rest of the country by forming the Confederate States of America was frustrated by the North in what, along with the roughly contemporary T'ai P'ing Rebellion in China, was the most costly war of the century in life and treasure. For the most part nineteenth century immigration avoided the South and the latter's white population remained more nearly representative of the older, pre-nineteenth century stock than was that of any other part of the United States.

Each of these factors brought a threat and a challenge to the Christian faith. Could Christianity keep pace with the rapidly westward moving population as it poured into the territories on the frontier, heretofore only sparsely occupied by Indian tribes? Could it hold to the faith the immigrants from Europe? Could it protect the Indians against exploitation by the whites and bring them into the fold of the Church? Could it win the Negroes, all of them non-Christian when brought to America, and the sprinkling of Chinese and Japanese who settled on the West coast? Could it counter the materialism encouraged by the pursuit and enjoyment of wealth? Would it follow successfully the movements of population from the farms to the cities and, after having adapted itself to a rural society, devise methods for dealing effectively with urban conditions and problems? Would it be able to demonstrate that it was not disproved by science but that its insights and imperatives were necessary to the fullest life?

In several respects Christianity seemed ill-prepared to meet the threat and the challenge. It has been estimated that in 1800 only 6.9 per cent. of the population had a church membership. Removed from Europe where Church and state, while often in conflict, were in close association, where the churches were generally supported by public taxation, and where baptism and confirmation or its equivalent were either required by law or were an established social convention, and in a country where churches were supported only by voluntary contributions and church membership was the exception rather than the rule, white elements in the population were in danger of complete de-Christianization. Moreover, the Church did not present a united front. Even in 1815 Christianity displayed a greater variety and was represented by more different ecclesiastical bodies than in any other country in its history. As the century advanced this was augmented, chiefly by the addition of more denominations from the Old World but also by some of indigenous creation. Instead of working unitedly, the churches were in competition which was often unseemly. Even small towns had several churches, most of them too feeble to be really effective and only slowly and imperfectly developing coöperation with one another. It was chiefly because the denominations could not agree on what form of the faith should be taught that in the public schools, namely, those supported and controlled by the state, either no religious instruction was given or only a bare minimum was to be had.

Not only did much religious indifference and scepticism exist. There was also some militant atheism. We have already noted (Chapter 45) the vogue of Thomas Paine's *Age of Reason* and the lectures of Robert G. Ingersoll. Probably more dangerous was the less obviously hostile humanism represented by such men as John Dewey. Possessing points of sympathetic similarity and to no small degree with historical roots in Christianity, it was basically a denial of the Christian faith. Capturing many intellectuals in positions of influence in education, it filtered into large elements of the population.

In spite of these adverse conditions, in an amazing fashion Christianity rose to the challenges and made progress towards solving the problems which confronted it. We have earlier seen (Chapter 44) that in the United States Christianity entered the nineteenth century on a rising tide. A mass conversion of the non-Christian and partially de-Christianized elements of population was under way. It was to continue through the nineteenth century and into the twentieth century. In 1910, as contrasted with the 6.9 per cent. in 1800, the percentage of the population having formal membership in some religious body was 43.5. This mass conversion was primarily through Protestantism, for at the outset such Christianity as existed was predominantly of that wing of the Church and it continued to spread. Roman Catholicism also displayed a remarkable growth and the Eastern Churches, although small minorities, were represented.

We will now turn to the several aspects of this mass conversion. Although they were proceeding simultaneously and in places and at times interacted on one another, for the sake of clarity we will take them up one by one.

ADVANCE OF THE FRONTIER

One aspect of the progressive mass conversion of the partially de-Christianized elements of the population was the spread of the faith in the new communities which sprang into being on the rapidly moving frontier. Frontier society was fluid. Many of the minority who had had a church connexion before coming West made no effort to reëstablish one in their new homes. There was a tendency to ignore Christian moral standards. Yet it was on the frontier that Christianity made some of its most striking advances.

The advances were by a variety of channels and agencies. Some were in existence before 1815. Others came into being after that year. In the variety may have been one of the reasons for the success.

We have already seen the channels and agencies that ante-dated 1815. Here and there a group organized a church before leaving their home in the older states and, settling together, already possessed a Christian nucleus. Much more numerous were laymen and women who took the initiative in the new communities in gathering others together in Sunday Schools and prayer meetings which grew into churches. Many clergymen moved West and, without support from the East, took up farms, worked on them six days a week for a livelihood for themselves and their families, and preached on Sundays. Eventually voluntary gifts from those to whom they ministered made it possible for numbers of these clergymen to give a larger proportion of their time to the Church. "Revivals" continued. They had been a feature of much of Protestantism in the new country even before political independence and had broken out spectacularly in the Great Awakening, the Second Awakening, and the camp-meetings. The "evangelism" which was already characteristic of American Protestantism and which had as its aim winning all the population to the Christian faith stressed revivals as a normal way of attaining this goal. Baptists, Methodists, and the Disciples of Christ, the last also known as Christians, who had demonstrated their appeal to the new communities, maintained their spectacular growth. State missionary societies were organized, chiefly by Congregationalists but also by some other bodies, partly with the frontier in mind.

After 1815 more agencies and channels were added. Churches in the older centres began missionary societies on a national basis. In 1826 the American Home Missionary Society was formed. Having as its foundation the United Domestic Missionary Society which had been organized four years earlier by Presbyterians and (Dutch) Reformed, it drew its chief support from Presbyterians and Congregationalists. As we have seen, at the outset of the century Congregationalism was the strongest of the denominations of the United States. Compact in its New England setting, where it was dominant, with able leaders, many of them highly trained, and earnestly evangelistic, with it were connected the three outstanding figures in the movements for mass conversion in the eighteenth and nineteenth centuries, namely Jonathan Edwards, Charles G. Finney, and Dwight L. Moody. Congregationalism was long in intimate coöperation with Presbyterianism. Theologically the two were akin. Beginning in the 1790's the state organizations of Congregationalists in New England exchanged delegates with the Presbyterian General Assembly. By the Plan of Union inaugurated in 1801 Congregationalists and Presbyterians joined in planting churches in the West. They worked together not only in the American Home Missionary Society but also in other organizations, among them the American Bible Society, begun in 1816 to unite the various local and state Bible Societies, the American Tract Society, inaugurated in 1825, and the American Sunday School Union, founded in 1824. As what was known as the New England theology moved further and further from the traditional Presbyterian theology, the majority of the Presbyterians, especially those of Scottish and Scotch-Irish antecedents, known as the "Old School men," and with their main centre of ministerial training at Princeton, repudiated the Plan of Union

(1837), severed their ties with the American Home Missionary Society and some of the other interdenominational bodies, and cut off from their fellowship four synods in which the New England theology prevailed. The expelled synods formed their own General Assembly and, known as the New School Presbyterians, continued their collaboration with the Congregationalists until 1861. In 1852 a national gathering of the Congregational churches abrogated the Plan of Union. In 1893, to recognize what had been fact since 1861, the American Home Missionary Society was renamed the Congregational Home Missionary Society. After 1815 several other denominations organized societies, either purely for home missions or for both home and foreign missions.

Out of thousands who served devotedly under these societies it seems almost invidious to choose any for special mention. Yet two can be mentioned as showing in an outstanding way what was done, although usually in lesser measure, by many others. George H. Atkinson (1819–1889) established Congregational churches in Oregon and Washington, had a major share in founding a college and in inaugurating the public school system of Oregon, and contributed to the development of wheat-growing in the Pacific North-west. Sheldon Jackson (1834–1909), from ancestry which had been prominent in the political life of the state of New York and dedicated from childhood by his parents to the Christian ministry, served as a Presbyterian missionary to the Indians in what was later Oklahoma and then helped to begin Presbyterian churches in Minnesota. For many years he was Presbyterian "Superintendent of Missions for Western Iowa, Nebraska, Dakota, Montana, Wyoming, and Utah." He travelled throughout that vast area planting churches, enlisted in the East young men to serve as their pastors, and extended his labours to Colorado, New Mexico, Arizona, and Nevada. He spent the last period of his life in Alaska, especially serving the Indians and introducing reindeer from Siberia to provide food for the Eskimos.

Three of the interdenominational societies which we have mentioned, the American Bible Society, the American Tract Society, and the American Sunday School Union, drew their support from others in addition to Congregationalists and Presbyterians. They covered both the frontier and the older sections of the country. Several times during the century, first in 1829, the American Bible Society attempted to put a copy of the Scriptures in every family in the United States, including both the cities and the frontier. In 1830 the American Sunday School Union framed a programme for organizing a Sunday School in every community west of the Alleghenies where one was needed, and doing it within two years. In 1832 the American Tract Society adopted a plan to place some of its literature in every religiously destitute family in the United States. In 1847 most of its 267 colporteurs were in the

Mississippi Valley, in much of which frontier conditions still prevailed.

Another channel through which Christianity spread on the frontier was educational institutions planted under the auspices of the several denominations. In time each of the major and some of the minor denominations had a chain of academies, colleges, and universities stretching across the country, most of them founded when frontier conditions existed in their respective regions. In them in their pioneer days men and women taught at great personal sacrifice to give an education to the laity and prospective clergy of churches in the new communities and to train under Christian auspices leaders for the future commonwealths.

To the denominations that rose or flourished on the frontier one more large one was added after 1815, the Church of Jesus Christ of Latter Day Saints, more generally known as the Mormons. Eventually, although not until after 1914, it had a membership of over a million. Its founder, Joseph Smith (1805–1844), was born in Vermont of old New England stock. He was from a family of the floating, semi-illiterate, poverty-stricken type which was frequently found on or near the frontier. As a boy he went with his parents to Western New York, then not far removed from pioneer conditions. The region had been swept by revivals preached by itinerant or semi-itinerant Baptists and Methodists and Smith was touched by them. Impatient with existing denominational differences and eager to know which was right, he believed that he had visions which told him that no existing ecclesiastical body represented the divine will and that God had chosen him to restore the true Church. He maintained that at the behest of the visions he dug in a hill, found a book written in strange characters, and translated it through miraculous assistance. This translation was published in 1830 as the *Book of Mormon*. It contained extensive excerpts from both the Old and New Testaments along with what purported to be a history of peoples descended from a family which, fleeing from Jerusalem before its fall to the Babylonians, had made its way to America. To the *Book of Mormon* was later added a *Book of Commandments,* soon called *Doctrine and Covenants,* which came out of the sermons and revelations of Smith.

The Church of Jesus Christ of Latter Day Saints was founded by Smith in 1830 in Seneca County, New York. Self-confident, tall, athletic, witty, of distinguished appearance, Smith attracted followers. They made their centre first in Ohio, then in Missouri, and eventually in Illinois. They were persecuted and in Illinois Smith was killed. The majority then followed one of Smith's early converts, Brigham Young (1801–1877), to Utah. There, beyond what was at that time the frontier, Young led them in forming an idealistic community. Young was an extraordinarily able organizer and administrator. Under him a closely knit economic-social-ecclesiastical community grew up. It increased rapidly, partly through a high birth rate to polygamous marriages which Young set the example of contracting and partly through converts who were won from the underprivileged partly in the United States but mostly in Europe by extensive and zealous missions. Polygamy was later discontinued, but the Church of Jesus Christ of Latter Day Saints continued to mount in numbers. A minority of Smith's disciples did not follow Brigham Young to Utah but, under Joseph Smith, Junior (1832–1914), moved to Iowa and then to Missouri. It did not practise polygamy and did not become nearly as large as the other wing.

The chief growth of Christianity on the frontier was not by the Mormons, numerous though they became, but, as we have suggested, by Baptists, Methodists, and the Disciples of Christ or Christians. They spoke the language of the common frontiersman and knew how to win him. Congregationalists, Presbyterians, and Episcopalians, with their highly educated ministry, as a rule could not effectively reach the rank and file but attracted mainly the better educated minority.

Holding or Winning the Immigrants: The Phenomenal Growth of the Roman Catholic Church

What of the nineteenth century immigration from abroad? How well was it held to its inherited forms of the faith or won by other branches of the Church? The flood that poured in was prodigious. Down to the 1880's it was mostly from the British Isles and North-western Europe. Between 1820 and 1865 nearly two million came from Ireland, most of them poverty-stricken, seeking escape from intolerable economic conditions rendered acute by the famine of the 1840's which followed the blight that killed the potatoes upon which much of the population depended for food. In that same period about a million and a half Germans entered and about three-quarters of a million from England. Hundreds of thousands also came from Scandinavia. In the last decades of the century the majority of the immigrants were from Italy, Central Europe, Russia, Greece, the Balkans, and the Near East. Several hundred thousand French Canadians moved south, principally into New England. Into the South-west filtered Mexicans, by 1914 about a quarter of a million. Except for Jews, the overwhelming majority of the immigrants were from Christian backgrounds. A few tens of thousands of Chinese and Japanese entered, almost all of them non-Christians, but legislation prevented either group from totalling more than 100,000. Numbers of the immigrants became farmers, many of them on the frontier in the Middle and Far West. However, the majority made their homes in the manufacturing and mining towns and cities of the North-east. There the first generation, usually poor, eked out a living as unskilled labourers in mines and factories or in building railroads.

We have hinted at the problem which the immigrants presented. Coming to a land where churches depended upon voluntary offerings, would they contribute out of their poverty to erect churches and parochial schools and to train and support teachers and clergy? Whether Roman Catholics, Protestants, or Orthodox, they did so to an amazing degree.

This was not always or even predominantly from religious motives. The Church formed the main tie with the old home. Its worship was familiar, its sermons were in the mother tongue, and in Protestant churches the services were in the old country vernacular. The churches were social centres where the immigrant could find those of his native speech and cultural background. Denominations tended to arrange themselves according to national origins. Although, as we shall see in a moment, the Roman Catholic Church brought all its adherents together under one hierarchical structure, individual parishes were often predominantly or entirely of one nation.

Whether Roman Catholic or Protestant, the success of the Church in holding the immigrants was not due entirely or even chiefly to sociological factors. Had there not been in it inner vitality, greater than that of any social institution which came out of the immigrants' background except the family, the Church would not have existed. The immigrants were attracted not merely because the Church provided social centres. They were drawn by the religious imperative.

To the Roman Catholic Church the immigrants were both a problem and an opportunity. At the outset of the nineteenth century Roman Catholics were only a small minority in the United States. So far as they had any religious attachment, the overwhelming majority of the population was Protestant. In contrast, in 1910 about seven and a half millions of the foreign born, approximately 60 per cent. of those in that category, were Roman Catholics in background. It was no easy task to make provision for the religious education and spiritual care of these millions. They were in danger either of drifting entirely away from the faith or of being assimilated to the prevailing Protestantism. Moreover, the Roman Catholic Church operated in the face of chronic Protestant opposition which from time to time broke out into active and even violent anti-Roman Catholic movements. In the 1830's and 1840's the Native American Association opposed the easy naturalization of foreigners, most of whom were Irish and Germans, and was anti-Roman Catholic. It was followed in the 1850's by the Know Nothing Party and in the latter part of the century by the American Protective Association.

To help meet the challenge personnel and money were contributed from

Roman Catholics of Canada and the Old World. From Canada came clergy and nuns to serve their fellow-countrymen. Some priests and sisters were sent from France, but since very few immigrants were from that country and other nationalities found them difficult, theirs was a minor role. Numbers of priests, especially regulars, were from Belgium. In 1857 there was founded at Louvain, in Belgium, an American College in which in the course of seventy-five years over a thousand young Americans were prepared for the priesthood. Many priests, lay brothers, and nuns were from Ireland, Germany, and Switzerland. Some money came from Europe. It was partly with the purpose of collecting it for the United States that the Society for the Propagation of the Faith was organized (1822). For years the United States was the chief beneficiary of the Ludwig-Missionsverein which was founded in Bavaria to raise money for missions. In 1871 the Raphaelsverein was begun under the leadership of Cahensly, a merchant, for the purpose of aiding German immigrants.

The Raphaelsverein was the chief source of what is usually known as the Cahensly movement. That movement declared that by ignoring their national origins the Roman Catholic Church was losing thousands of the immigrants. As a remedy it urged that separate parishes and missions be set up for the several nationalities, that each of them be entrusted to priests of the appropriate nation, that in the parochial schools instruction be given entirely in the language of the parents, that church societies be grouped by nationalities, and that in each diocese the bishop be appointed from whichever group was in the numerical ascendancy. This would have made for a church organized by trans-Atlantic national patterns. It was viewed with alarm by non-Roman Catholics as preventing assimilation to American life and as threatening disloyalty to the United States. The American hierarchy were opposed to the plan, for it was a menace to the unity of the Church and gave ground for the charge that the Roman Catholic Church was promoting un-American enclaves. Rome sided with the hierarchy and the movement died.

Extensive as was the aid which came from abroad to help the Roman Catholic Church hold its hereditary constituency to the faith, even more was from Roman Catholics in the United States. Theological seminaries for training youths for the priesthood were begun. By 1900 they numbered thirty-seven and in 1915 preparatory seminaries totaled thirty-four. An American College in Rome, founded in 1859, was supported by funds from many dioceses. In addition to the orders and congregations of Old World origin which more and more recruited their ranks from native-born youths, new ones sprang up in the United States. Especially was this true of sisterhoods, most of them with teaching as their purpose.

Most of the funds for the construction and maintenance of Roman Catholic churches and schools and for the support of clergy, monks, and nuns came, not from Europe but from the immigrants and their children. In 1910, for instance, nearly a million and a quarter pupils were in parochial schools. This achievement becomes all the more remarkable when we recall the poverty of the vast majority of the immigrants.

Roman Catholic priests, monks, and nuns were recruited chiefly from those of Irish and German birth or descent. This seems to have been partly because until past the middle of the century these two nationalities constituted the bulk of the Roman Catholic immigration and partly because in the mother country they were the more actively loyal. As we have seen, for the Irish the Roman Catholic Church had been the tie and the symbol of Irish nationalism as against the English overlords.

Several of the Uniate Churches were represented among the immigrants. Some provision was made to supply them with clergy of their own rites and thus to keep them from being lost to the Church. The Ruthenians constituted the largest of these bodies. They were mainly concentrated in the coal mining communities in Pennsylvania. By 1909 they had a bishop and more than a hundred churches and priests. From time to time groups of Ruthenians, dissatisfied with attempts to alter their traditions and bring them more nearly into conformity with the Roman pattern, went over to the Russian Orthodox Church.

Efforts were put forth by Protestants of the older American stock to win Roman Catholics. This was partly through interdenominational agencies but chiefly through denominational societies. Numerically these attempts had only slight success. Foreign language churches composed of former Roman Catholics were few and usually small. As time passed, especially after 1914, and the immigrants were more and more assimilated into the patterns of life of the United States, an increasing number of Roman Catholics joined Protestant churches. However, in doing so they went, not into churches which were especially designed for them, but into congregations which were prevailingly of the traditionally Protestant elements of the population. Some of this was by marriage to Protestants, some was because of residence in predominantly Protestant communities, some from the desire to be accepted socially, and some from profound religious conviction. Although accurate statistics are lacking, it seems probable that most of such Roman Catholics as abandoned their hereditary faith did not become Protestants but drifted away from all religion.

Roman Catholics also endeavoured to win Protestants. There were notable converts. One of them founded the Sisters of Charity of Emmitsburg, Maryland. Another, Isaac Thomas Hecker (1819–1888), a scion of German immigrant stock, was the chief mover in the formation of the Missionary Society of St. Paul the Apostle, whose members were better known as the Paulists. At first made up mostly of converts, it sought to adapt Roman Catholicism to the American environment and thus to attract Protestants. However, accessions through these direct methods were not numerous. They came mainly through marriages with Roman Catholics.

By the year 1914 the Roman Catholic Church, while having only a minority of the total church membership, was the largest of the Christian denominations in the United States. It counted between fifteen and seventeen millions as being in its fold. Its hierarchical structure covered the entire nation. Chiefly dependent as it was on the nineteenth century immigration, it was strongest in the places where this had settled—in the urban centres of the North-east, in many of the cities of the Middle West and West, and in some rural sections in the Middle West. Through the French and Spanish background of these areas, it had pockets of strength in Louisiana and the South-west. Because of the comparative absence of the nineteenth century immigration, with the exception of Louisiana it was weak in the Southern states east of the Mississippi.

The Roman Catholic Church in the United States was knit together as one ecclesiastical body loyal to Rome. In 1829 what was called the First Provincial Council was held in Baltimore and directly or by association was representative of all the hierarchy of the nation. Six other provincial councils of Baltimore followed. In 1852 the First Plenary Council met. It was a demonstration of the growth of the Roman Catholic Church and its hierarchy and sought to give unity to it in the United States. Other such gatherings convened. In the Roman Catholic Church in the United States there were many differences due partly to the diverse national sources from which it was drawn and partly to contrasts between outstanding members of the episcopate. Yet, with the exception of a few small minorities, the faithful had no thought of rebelling against Rome. Until 1908 the Holy See exercised control through the Congregation for the Propagation of the Faith. In that year the United States was removed from the jurisdiction of the Propaganda. The act was a formal recognition that the Roman Catholic Church in that country had come of age.

Before that step was taken it had become clear that the Roman Catholic Church in the United States could be trusted to hold to the faith and not to succumb to the predominantly Protestant environment by which it was encompassed or to the diverse national origins of its constituency. It had successfully overcome what at the time seemed major dangers. One was trusteeism, the effort of local congregations represented by trustees who were the legal owners of the property of a parish to choose and dismiss pastors without reference to the ecclesiastical superiors. This procedure had seemed to be in accord with American democratic principles, but it limited the authority of the bishop. Eventually a series of court decisions recognized the bishop as in control of the property of each congregation. A plan approved by the Holy See (1911) vested the property in a board of trustees composed of the bishop, the vicar general, the parish priest, and two laymen approved by the bishop. Another danger was one which we have already mentioned, that rivalries among the several national groups would tear the Church apart. Thus early in the century the appointment of French priests to predominantly Irish parishes and of French bishops to sees in which the Irish were numerous aroused deep resentment among the latter. In Charleston and Philadelphia open rebellion was followed by schisms and in New York there were quarrels over the issue. We have noted the Cahensly movement, a feature of the chronic friction between the Irish and the Germans.

Late in the century came agitation over what was known as Americanism. The storm centered around Hecker and especially around his methods as described in a French translation of his biography and in an enthusiastic introduction by the translator commending him as worthy of imitation by the French clergy. The founder of the Paulists, Hecker had been prominent and persuasive in presenting the Roman Catholic faith to non-Roman Catholics. To meet the widespread criticism that the Roman Catholic Church was from another culture and alien to the American tradition and way of life, he had insisted that as the Church divinely appointed for all mankind it was adaptable to the religious needs of every people and culture, including the United States. Many, especially in Europe, believed that by this Hecker meant that to gain converts missionaries should pass over or modify doctrines which gave offense and allow each individual in terms of American freedom, to follow his own judgement without reference to the Church and its hierarchy. A tempest arose in the Roman Catholic press, and in some circles in Europe the Roman Catholic Church in the United States was looked at askance as at least verging on heresy and perhaps as actually guilty of it. In 1899 the Pope sent a kind but firm formal letter, *Testem benevolentiæ,* to Cardinal Gibbons, the outstanding member of the hierarchy in the United States, condemning views which the critics had said characterized "Americanism" and setting forth the proper stand on the issues under discussion. The American bishops hastened to say that they were completely in accord with the letter and declared that the errors which it condemned were by no means widespread.

Although it did so without compromising its inherited faith, in important ways the Roman Catholic Church in the United States reflected its environment. This arose from the problems forced on it by the vast influx of immigrants who were of its fold. As we have seen, it had to give itself to an almost impossible programme of recruiting and training clergy, nuns, and lay brothers, of erecting thousands of churches, and of developing a system of schools from the elementary grades through theological seminaries and universities. In this it did what only a few Protestant denominations attempted. The majority of Protestant churches did not have elementary schools on the parish level. They maintained secondary schools, theological schools, colleges, and universities, but for the primary grades they depended on the schools financed and managed by the state, and for the religious instruction of their children they relied upon the home, the Sunday School, a large number of youth organizations closely or loosely related to the churches, catechetical classes, and the regular services of the Church. The Roman Catholic Church was not content to trust its children to the public schools. It had long insisted that training the child was its obligation. It held that religion must be fully integrated with the rest of education. As we have seen (Chapter 46), in the *Syllabus of Errors* Pius IX expressed the official attitude of Rome in condemning the growing practice of freeing schools from all ecclesiastical authority and of putting the civil power in full control of the public schools. Although in a country in which it was a minority the Roman Catholic Church might perforce acquiesce in something less than its ideal, it could do so only as a temporary expedient until such time as it was in the clear majority. In the meantime it must, where possible, set up schools of its own. The First Provincial Council (1829), representing the hierarchy of the country, decreed that wherever possible each parish should have a school. This was reiterated by the First Plenary Council. In 1875 the Third Plenary Council ordered the erection of a school near each church within two years, declared it to be the obligation of Roman Catholic parents to send their children to these schools unless they were otherwise adequately instructed, and recommended that pastors who were negligent in carrying out the programme be removed.

Leading Roman Catholic bishops advocated state aid to religious schools, but this aroused controversy and reduced the likelihood of its being given. An attempt was made at compromise, the so-called Faribault plan from the city in Minnesota where it was tried, by which the state leased the parish school buildings during school hours and paid nuns who taught in them. On this, however, the bishops were not united. In general the Church erected and maintained its own schools and staffed them with members of its sisterhoods, teaching brotherhoods, or monastic orders. The Catholic University of America was opened in the national capital in 1889 under the control of the hierarchy. It tended to be Irish, and, drawn into some of the controversies which were agitating the Church, including that between the Irish and the Germans, it grew slowly.

Numbers of religious orders and congregations, both of men and of women, entered the country, and for them physical plants had to be provided. Many hospitals and orphanages were founded and equipped.

All this building of churches, schools, monasteries, seminaries, colleges, universities, hospitals, and orphanages entailed raising money from a constituency most of whom were of the poor of the land. This meant that the clergy and especially the bishops were of necessity promoters, organizers, and administrators. They tended to be activists. Periodicals of various kinds were numerous, but scholarship was slow in developing. No great theologians emerged. Sanctity of the traditional kind was rare: by the middle of the twentieth century only one citizen of the United States had been canonized, and she was not native born, but was an Italian immigrant nun. Outstanding representatives of the life of prayer and mystics of the first water were either few or entirely lacking. The energies of the Church were too absorbed in caring for the immigrants to permit much share in the missions outside the United States.

With the dwindling of immigration to a trickle after 1914 these qualities distinctive of the Roman Catholic Church in the United States began to change, but not rapidly.

A Roman Catholic organization which was distinctly American was the Knights of Columbus. Organized in New Haven, Connecticut, in 1882, it eventually spread throughout the country. It was similar to the many fraternal bodies which flourished in the United States, such as the Masons and the Oddfellows, and had as one of its outstanding features a plan of life insurance for its members. It also engaged in various charitable undertakings and in attempts to present the Roman Catholic faith to non-Roman Catholics.

Moreover, in part reflecting the predominantly Protestant environment, the Roman Catholic Church in the United States did not display some of the features which marked it in prevailingly Roman Catholic lands. Public religious processions were less in evidence. Shrines of healing, such as that at Lourdes, were not as prominent. Much of the popular Roman Catholicism which to the Protestant appeared superstition was either absent or inconspicuous.

It was not strange that out of the struggle to care for the immigrant and build the Church some extraordinarily able Roman Catholic bishops emerged, with something of the breadth of vision which is often termed statesmanship. Even to enumerate them would unduly prolong these pages. The most eminent was James Gibbons (1834–1921). A native of Baltimore, he was ordained priest in 1861, rose rapidly, was the youngest bishop at the Vatican Council, in 1877 became Archbishop of Baltimore, and in 1886 was created cardinal, the second from the United States to attain that **dignity**. He wrote extensively but not profoundly. He was ardently American, approved the separation of Church and state, threw the weight of his position and skill on the side of giving the Roman Catholic Church in the United States a unified structure rather than letting it divide on national lines inherited from Europe, worked for the founding of the Catholic University of America as a national institution, and in the controversy over the Knights of Labour in the 1880's came out flatly for the right of labour to organize.

HOLDING THE IMMIGRANTS: THE EASTERN CHURCHES

Some thousands of the immigrants were members of one or another branch of the Orthodox Church. Before 1815 the Russian Orthodox Church had missions in Alaska. When, in 1867, Alaska was bought by the United States the Church continued, although without the financial support of the Russian Government. In 1872 the bishop transferred his residence to San Francisco. In 1904 the see was raised to an archiepiscopate, and in 1905 its headquarters were moved to New York City. Until after 1914 it had jurisdiction over all the Orthodox in the United States. The numbers of the Orthodox mounted rapidly in the latter part of the century. Greeks, Roumanians, Bulgars, Serbs, Syrians, and Albanians were among them. Armenians arrived, especially after the massacres of the 1890's in their home land. Jacobites and Nestorians were also among the immigrants. For all of these congregations were organized and clergy obtained.

HOLDING AND WINNING THE IMMIGRANTS: THE PROTESTANTS

The Protestant immigrants were partly from the British Isles and partly from the Continent of Europe. If they sought a church connexion, those from the British Isles, a minority of the whole, had little difficulty in fitting into the churches of the older American stock. Most of these churches were offshoots of British denominations, orders of service and hymns tended to be the same as in their British counterparts, and Americans were often familiar with current developments in theology and religious life in the British Isles. Communicants of the Church of England were easily at home in the Protestant Episcopal Church with its familiar Book of Common Prayer, vestments, and architecture. Presbyterians from Scotland and the North of Ireland did not feel the Presbyterianism of the United States entirely alien. Congregationalists, Baptists, and Methodists often found congenial the corresponding churches in the United States. Welsh Calvinistic Methodists and Welsh Congregationalists for a time formed distinct churches in which the Welsh language was used, but as the younger generation grew to maturity with English as their tongue the former merged with the Presbyterians (although not until 1920) and the latter went into the wider Congregational fellowship.

In somewhat similar fashion the majority of the immigrants of the Reformed faith from the Netherlands, large numbers of whom settled in Michigan, were absorbed into the Dutch Reformed Church, later called the Reformed Church in America. A minority, ultra-conservative, withdrew (1857) and formed what eventually (1904) was known as the Christian Reformed Church. So, too, from immigrants from Hungary of that faith there was organized (1904), with assistance from the homeland, the Hungarian Reformed Church in America.

A very large proportion of the Protestant immigration was German. Many had been largely de-Christianized by the rationalistic and politically radical movements of the day. Numbers of others were glad to be freed from the obligations to support the Landeskirchen of the homeland. Yet others were earnestly Christian and took the initiative in welcoming and even seeking pastors.

A small minority of the Germans were Mennonites, many of whom were from Russia. They had earlier sought haven in that empire and when conditions became adverse came to the United States, hoping for the religious liberty and freedom to abide by their pacifist principles the promise of which had lured them to the tsar's domains. They divided into several groups.

A considerable minority of the Germans were of the Reformed faith and were eventually served either by missionaries of that confession from Germany or by pastors from the German Reformed Church which had its stronghold in Pennsylvania. Others, also a minority, were from the Evangelical churches which had arisen in Prussia and some other German states from the union of Lutheran and Reformed.

The majority of the German Protestants were Lutheran by heredity. Indeed, that was true of Protestants in general from the Continent of Europe. In contrast with the Roman Catholics, no centre of administrative or doctrinal control existed for Lutherans, whether German or Scandinavian, either in Europe or in America. As we have seen, in Europe Lutheranism was divided, partly by territorial, partly by national, and partly by theological groupings. Pietism was also a pervasive influence and sometimes was a source of controversy. In the United States all these factors entered and were complicated by others of American origin. By 1914, next to the Roman Catholics, Baptists, and Methodists, the Lutherans constituted the largest family of churches in the United States. However, they were not an integrated family, but, as we shall see, were badly severed. For a variety of reasons, some linguistic, for they were slow to use English in their services, some doctrinal, and some from the fact that, being state churches in Europe they were inclined to look with disfavour and even contempt on other denominations, they tended to hold aloof from non-Lutheran

Protestants and were tardy in moving into the main stream of American religious life.

In general the Lutheran bodies in the United States were conservative. The Biblical scholarship and the theological ferment which were marked in German universities in the nineteenth century and which profoundly affected Continental European and British Protestantism and much of the Protestantism of the older American stock were, with a few exceptions, rejected. That kind of Christianity seemed not to have enough dynamic to inspire and sustain those who held to it to undertake the hard labour required to gather and nurture churches in the rough and often raw environment of a new country. It was Pietists and those who held staunchly to unmodified older Lutheranism who were mainly responsible for the founding and growth of Lutheran Churches in the United States. We have seen (Chapter 47) that in Germany these strains had enjoyed a revival in the fore part of the nineteenth century, partly as a reaction against the rationalism of the Enlightenment and the French Revolution.

It was the American Lutheranism of the eighteenth century which had been organized by Henry M. Muhlenberg (Chapter 41) which constituted the nucleus of what by the formation of the United Lutheran Church (1918) out of three other bodies, the General Synod, the General Council, and the United Synod, South, became the largest of the Lutheran bodies of the United States. The General Synod, the first Lutheran organization which aspired to be nation-wide, was constituted in 1820. Its early years were stormy but it was saved from dissolution by Samuel Simon Schmucker (1799–1873). Reared in a Pietist minister's family, the best educated clergyman of his church in his day, Schmucker became the initial professor in its first theological seminary, at Gettysburg. A leading advocate of Christian unity and of fraternal relations among the denominations, he also endeavoured to nourish in his own fellowship an intelligent loyalty to Lutheranism. Missionaries, many of them graduates of Gettysburg, went to the West and the General Synod extended its boundaries far beyond the older states. In Schmucker's later years, partly under the influence of the newer immigration, Lutheranism became more emphatically confessional and he was rejected as too liberal, too willing to conform to the American environment, and even as heretical. For a time the General Synod languished because of withdrawals. During the Civil War the Lutherans in the Southern states separated and formed what was eventually the United Synod of the South. In 1867 the General Council was constituted, partly by groups from the General Synod with additions of other synods and with Charles Porterfield Krauth (1823–1883) as its leading spirit. It was not until 1918, as we have said, that the three were fused in the United Lutheran Church.

In the West still more conservative Lutheranism arose. Its conservatism was accentuated by the desire to hold to the German language, dislike for the use of English which was creeping into the General Synod, and distrust of the tendencies in that body to depart from staunch Lutheranism. It was also in part a phase of the reaction against rationalism which was seen in some Lutheran circles in Germany and against the union of Lutherans and Reformed.

The largest of the conservative Lutheran bodies and one which eventually vied with the United Lutheran Church as the most numerous Lutheran group in the United States was officially called the German Evangelical Lutheran Synod of Missouri, Ohio, and other States, but was usually known as the Missouri Synod. It was constituted in 1847. The leader in its creation was Carl Ferdinand Wilhelm Walther (1811–1887). The son of a Saxon parsonage, a great lover of music, under pressure from his father Walther had enrolled in Leipzig, as a student of theology. There, poverty-stricken and troubled by doubts, he came in touch with a Pietist circle and rebelled against the prevailing rationalism of the university. He came to the United States in a company of about seven hundred led by a pastor, Martin Stephan, for whom he had a great admiration. They formed a colony near St. Louis. Stephan proved to be a libertine and a rascal and was deposed. This disillusioning experience might well have been followed by the disintegration of the colony. Walther rose to the emergency. Characterized by an extraordinary combination of organizing ability, a genius for friendship, magnetic charm with audiences large and small, generous hospitality, an enormous capacity for work, a mastery of the Lutheran theology of the sixteenth and seventeenth centuries and its literature, a skill in vigorous polemics, and a self denial which was content with frugal living and which turned the income from the sale of his writings into synodical channels, he enabled the Missouri Synod to achieve phenomenal dimensions. Through the periodicals which he founded and edited, a weekly, *Der Lutheraner,* and a monthly, *Lehre und Wehre,* he exerted a continuous and pervasive influence. In Concordia Seminary in St. Louis and its branches in other cities a growing leadership was raised up, shaped by the strict Lutheranism of the pre-rationalistic period. A network of parochial schools undergirded the whole. Lutheran pastors from Germany, also conservative theologically, were attracted, with their congregations. A system of inspection by district presidents helped to knit the synod together and to prevent departure from strict adherence to its doctrinal standards. Before his death Walther saw the Synod expand to fifteen hundred congregations and nearly a thousand pastors. He also became the first President of the Lutheran Synodical Conference of North America. Organized in 1872, it drew into association with the Missouri Synod several other synods on a plan which emphasized the autonomy of the congregation. After Walther's death the Missouri Synod continued to expand. It reached from the Pacific to the Atlantic and had strong foreign missions.

Other Lutheran synods arose out of the nineteenth century immigration of Germans. We must not take the space even to name all of them. One, centering in Buffalo, was in some ways even more conservative than the Missouri Synod and was charged by Walther with continuing too much of the Roman Catholic tradition. Another, the Evangelical Synod of Iowa and Other States, was largely the creation of missionaries sent from the Missions Institute of Neuendettelsau by Konrad Wilhelm Loehe, a leader in the Inner Mission who had become interested in the needs of the Germans in America. For a time the Neuendettelsau men worked with the Missouri Synod, but Walther and Loehe had differences as to the nature of the Church and its ministry which were not removed by a trip that Walther made to Germany for a conference with Loehe. The Synod of Iowa and Other States established churches in every state west of the Mississippi except Arizona and New Mexico. Into it eventually went the Lutheran Evangelical Synod of Texas which was the outgrowth of the labours of men from the Pilgrim Mission of St. Chrischona.

Missionaries who helped in more than one synod came from the missionary training institution at Basel, from a missionary society founded by Pastor Gossner of Berlin, from the Rhenish Missionary Society, and from Barmen.

Out of the German immigration there sprang what was at first known as the *Kirchenverein des Westens* and then as the Evangelical Synod of the West. In it Lutherans and Reformed united. Congregations of Germans in which Lutherans and Reformed combined early came into being in several centres in the West. When Germans of Lutheran and Reformed background first moved into a community in the West the bond of language and nationality often drew them together. This was facilitated by clergymen in whom Pietist convictions and a theology which embraced features common to both were stronger than the differences which separated the Lutherans and the Reformed. Moreover, many of the immigrants were from German states in which Lutherans and Reformed had fused into one Evangelical Church. While in the freedom of the New World some immigrants took the opportunity vigorously to repudiate that union and joined outspokenly Lutheran synods, others held to it. In its early years the *Kirchenverein des Westens* owed much to missionaries from Bremen, Strassburg, and the Rhenish Missionary Society. It was especially indebted to the men from Basel, for the latter, Pietists trained in a school which held both Lutherans and Reformed, found the union natural. The *Kirchenverein des Westens* spread widely in Missouri, Indiana, Illinois, Ohio, Iowa, and Wisconsin, and in 1877 its successor, the Evangelical Synod of the West, drew in other similar bodies to form the Evangelical Synod of North America.

In 1910 about a million and a quarter in the United States were of Scandinavian birth, the outcome of a vast movement in the latter part of the nineteenth century. A small sprinkling came from Iceland, about a sixth were from Denmark, about a third from Norway, and slightly more than a half from Sweden. Here also, because of geography and their Lutheran-Scandinavian culture, may be classed the Finns. In the United States the Scandinavians were widely scattered, but the majority settled in the block of territory made up of Northern Illinois, Iowa, Wisconsin, Minnesota, and the Dakotas. Since Lutheranism was the state religion in the Scandinavian countries and embraced the overwhelming majority of the population, almost all the immigrants were technically of that faith. While in the new environment some of them left it, either to drift entirely away from Christianity or to be enrolled in some non-Lutheran body, such as the Baptists or the Methodists, most of them were held to the Lutheran fold. The Scandinavian Lutherans grouped themselves ecclesiastically by languages and according to national origins.

The smaller groups can be quickly summarized. In 1885 those from Iceland formed themselves into a synod. The Danish Lutherans were of various ecclesiastical traditions. They were chiefly of the high church wing, of the Grundtvig tradition, or of the Inner Mission, with kinship to Pietism. Separate churches arose, but in 1906 the two largest united to form the United Danish Evangelical Lutheran Church in America, from which the word Danish was later deleted. By 1914 the Finns were in three distinct Lutheran churches.

In the Norwegian immigration several Lutheran traditions were represented which issued in distinct bodies. Among them were Haugeans, Grundtvigians with a high church background, and some who were opposed to coöperation with the Missouri Synod. In 1917 the majority came together to form the Norwegian Lutheran Church of America. Eventually the word Norwegian was omitted and the name became the Evangelical Lutheran Church of America.

Several thousand Swedes were gathered into the Augustana Synod. The Augustana Synod was clearly Lutheran and obviously had the Church of Sweden for its mother. However, it had in it so strong a Pietist strain, and under the influence of the American environment was so modified in the direction of Presbyterianism and Congregationalism, that its parent looked at it askance and did not formally recognize it until 1903. Only a minority of the Swedes were gathered into the Augustana Synod. Many were drawn into two synods and some independent congregations, fruits of revivals and in part inspired by the Swedish Mission Covenant Church of the mother country (Chapter 47) which in 1885 united to form the Swedish Evangelical Mission Covenant.

The Protestant denominations of the older American stock attracted a greater number from the immigrants of Protestant background than they did from the Roman Catholics and Orthodox. Much of this was a phase of the assimilation, so natural as to be almost unnoticed, of individuals and families to the dominant culture. Some was into churches which maintained the language of the mother country. Of these the largest were the Methodists and the Baptists. The Methodists had several German conferences, a Danish-Norwegian Conference, and Swedish churches. Partly with the assistance of the American Baptist Home Mission Society and Baptist state conventions, Danish Baptist churches, Norwegian Baptist churches, Swedish Baptist churches, and German Baptist churches came into being and grouped themselves into associations and conferences. The American Home Missionary Society gave assistance to German pastors without asking them to change their denomination, but in the 1880's German Congregational churches became sufficiently numerous to constitute themselves into a distinct conference.

Of the large Jewish immigration only a small minority became Christians. Some of the latter were Protestant and some Roman Catholic. Few were in purely Jewish-Christian congregations. Most converts joined predominantly non-Jewish congregations. It is said that many became Christian Scientists, but accurate statistics could not be had. Most of the Jews who either drifted away from the synagogue or openly repudiated it did not become Christian but abandoned all religion.

Christianity, mainly Protestantism, made headway among the Chinese and Japanese. These peoples were restricted by discriminatory measures to small minorities in the continental United States and were mainly on the West Coast. They constituted the largest element of the population of Hawaii.

The Rapid Spread of Christianity among the Indians

The Indians were a challenge to the Christian churches. They constituted only a small minority, for they seem never to have totalled as many as half a million. Yet they were found in every state. In 1815, in spite of missions among those nearest to the white settlements, the vast majority were non-Christian. In an utterly different stage of culture than the white man, their lands coveted by him, they were in constant danger of exploitation. The chronic friction broke out from time to time into open war, the inherited patterns of life disintegrated, and both morals and morale tended to deteriorate. Conscience prodded Christians to action. Some of this was by bringing pressure on the government to see that the Indians had fair treatment and an opportunity for the kind of education that would enable them to adjust successfully to the white man's world. Much was through missions which sought to win the Indians to the Christian faith.

A full account of Christian missions to the Indians would require several volumes. Since the Indians were divided into many tribes and languages and there were missions in almost every tribe, each with its own history and with varying degrees of success, the complete story has never been told. It would be a record of heroism, of mistakes and achievements, and of failures and successes spelled out in thousands of individual lives. Both Protestants and Roman Catholics would be included, for the two wings of Christianity won about equal numbers. There were also the much more restricted efforts of the Russian Orthodox in Alaska.

Extensive financial aid came from the United States Government, not with the purpose of furthering conversion but to schools conducted by missions, for these were a major means of education. As government schools increased the aid to mission schools was reduced. For some years after 1869, presumably to lift the Indian Service from the morass of incompetence and corruption into which it had fallen through political appointments, the nomination of government Indian agents was delegated to the several religious bodies.

A few of the more famous missions can be singled out for brief notice, not because they are typical, but as indications of the variety which characterized the record. One was among the Cherokees, a semi-civilized tribe which dwelt in the piedmont and mountains of the southern states from Virginia southward to Georgia and which in the fore part of the nineteenth century was imbibing much of the white man's culture. To them several Protestant bodies, especially the American Board of Commissioners for Foreign Missions, sent missionaries. Schools were started, churches were gathered, and able Cherokee youths were trained to lead the Christian community. Then the white peoples of the neighbouring regions, coveting their fertile lands, induced the United States Government to compel the Cherokees, along with other tribes, to move west of the Mississippi River, into what was eventually administered as Indian Territory, the later state of Oklahoma. Two of the missionaries of the American Board went to prison to test the legality of a law of Georgia which deprived the Indians of their lands and in other ways the American Board strove to prevent the deportation. When, mainly in the 1820's and 1830's in spite of protests, the Cherokees were forced to go West, missionaries went with them and sought to mitigate the hardships entailed and to aid the Indians in adjusting to their new homes.

Several missions arose out of an incident in the early part of the 1830's. In 1831 four Indians from beyond the Rocky Mountains came to St. Louis, then on the frontier of white settlement, seeking information about the pale-face's religion. Two of the four died while in St. Louis and while ill were baptized by Roman Catholics. The other two returned to their own people, but without the desired knowledge. The news of the Indians' quest made its way into the religious press. Both the Methodists and the American Board of Commissioners for Foreign Missions responded. The former soon began several missions in the Pacific North-west under the leadership of Jason Lee (1803–1845). Within the same decade the American Board inaugurated an enterprise in the Pacific North-west but farther inland. Its most famous figure was Marcus Whitman who, with his wife, was killed by the Indians in 1847. In the 1840's, partly under the stimulus of the Indian delegation to St. Louis and to a large degree through the initiative of a Jesuit, Pierre-Jean DeSmet (1801–1873), the Roman Catholics moved into a number of tribes in the Far West, including the Pacific North-west.

As a result of the efforts of Roman Catholics and Protestants, in 1914 about 120,000, approximately 45 per cent. of all the Indians, had a church connexion, slightly more than half of them as Protestants. This was a little larger than the percentage of church members in the white population. Beyond these bare statistics is a record of helping the Indians in various ways to make the painful adjustment to the engulfing culture of the white man. The adjustment was by no means fully successful, but that it was not less so was due in no small degree to the missionaries.

WINNING, FREEING, AND ADVANCING THE NEGROES

A challenge to Christianity of much larger dimensions than that presented by the Indians was that of the Negroes. In 1815 the Negroes constituted slightly less than a fifth of the total population. In 1910 they numbered 9,827,763, or a little over a tenth of the whole. In 1815 the vast majority were slaves in the Southern states and were pagans. Torn from their homes in Africa, scattered among the whites, and without their hereditary tribal organization, their ancestral culture and language quickly dropped from them. They acquired English and in additional ways began to adopt the ways of their masters. With this they tended to conform to the religion of their masters, especially since that was then spreading, chiefly by revivals and camp-meetings, among the partly de-Christianized white population. By the middle of the century emancipation had been achieved in the North. In the 1860's, largely under the pressure of the Christian conscience and through the tragic arbitrament of arms in the Civil War, emancipation was forced upon the South and so far as the Constitution of the United States could do it the Negroes were given civil rights and the franchise. This brought sudden and drastic changes to the Negroes and posed them and the nation with the problem of helping them and the white men to adjust themselves to the new status.

Before the Civil War considerable progress had been made in the conversion of the Negroes. In the South in 1859 Negro church members were said to number 468,000, of whom 215,000 were reported to be Methodists and 175,000 Baptists. The gain was partly through the efforts of white masters and mistresses, partly through white missionaries, especially Methodists, partly through the efforts of white pastors, and partly through Negro preachers. Some of the Negroes were members of white churches. More were in purely Negro churches. Two denominations, the African Methodist Church, later the African Methodist Episcopal Church, organized in 1816 in Philadelphia, and the African Methodist Episcopal Zion Church, which grew out of a congregation begun in 1800 in New York City and which in 1821 was formally organized, sprang up in the North. Some beginnings were made towards schools for the Negroes. By 1860 about 11.7 per cent. of the Negroes were church members, or about half the proportion of the whites who were then in churches. It is significant that most of the Negro Christians were of those denominations, the Methodists and Baptists, which flourished among the whites of lower income and educational levels. Moreover, few were Roman Catholics.

After emancipation the growth of Negro membership was rapid. In 1916 the total was reported as 4,602,805. This was about 44.2 per cent. of the total Negro population, a proportion which was almost exactly the same as that of whites in churches in that year. The overwhelming majority of the Negro membership was in denominations and congregations entirely under Negro control. Although with some encouragement by the whites, this was primarily by the choice of the Negroes themselves. Their churches were almost the only institutions in which they were fully independent of the white men. They were the Negroes' own. They were not only expressions of his religious life but were also social centres. Often insurance companies, burial societies, and banks were closely connected with them. The overwhelming majority of the Negro church members were still Baptists and Methodists. Whereas before emancipation Methodists had been more numerous than Baptists, by 1914 the reverse was the case. This seems significant, for in the South white Baptists outnumbered white Methodists and were on the average from a lower economic and educational level than were the latter. To this pattern the Negroes tended to conform. The Methodists and especially the Baptists ministered to the proletariat of the older American stock, white and black. There were Negro minorities in other churches. Some were in the Methodist Episcopal Church, the main Methodist organization of the North. A few were in the Protestant Episcopal Church. Others were Presbyterians. After emancipation several tens of thousands withdrew from the Roman Catholic Church in Louisiana, presumably to assert their independence. Roman Catholics had missions among them which multiplied in the latter part of the century, but without large numerical results.

In 1916 about nine-tenths of Negro church members were in five Baptist and Methodist bodies entirely controlled by them.

After emancipation, the assistance of white churches to the Negroes was chiefly in the realm of education. For years after the Civil War the white churches of the South, impoverished by that struggle, even when they had the desire did not have the financial resources to do much for the freedmen. In contrast the churches of the North felt an obligation to help and had the financial means to do so. They believed that they could be of most use by furthering the preparation of leaders. Several denominations were active, but the most extensive programme was that of the American Missionary Association. Founded in 1846, from its inception it had been unequivocally against slavery. In principle it was undenominational and members of several churches contributed funds and personnel. However, it depended primarily on the Congregationalists. At the outset it sought to establish schools of all grades, from the elementary level through college and university. It also maintained theological schools to provide an educated ministry. However, by 1872 the governments of the Southern states had made such strides in opening and conducting elementary schools that the American Missionary Association confined its attention to secondary and higher education. Some of this was in handicrafts and agriculture and some of the kind offered in liberal arts colleges for the whites. Outstanding among the institutions inaugurated by the American Missionary Association were Hampton Institute, Atlanta University, and Fisk University. Several private foundations, initiated from avowedly Christian motives, also substantially aided Negro education. Especially notable were the gifts of John D. Rockefeller, partly through Baptist home mission societies and partly through the General Education Board which, an outgrowth of the Baptist Education Society, was incorporated in 1903.

The Negroes did much for themselves in education, in no small degree through their churches. Thus Booker T. Washington, who received most of his training at Hampton, was the chief creator of an institution at Tuskegee, Alabama, which was one of the most progressive in fitting the Negro to share and improve the life of the community.

In general, the Christianity of the Negroes was a modification and adaptation of the patterns of the white churches, especially of the Baptists and Methodists. There were prayer meetings, Sunday Schools, "revivals," and "protracted meetings." The Negro "spirituals" which were a distinct contribution to the hymnody of the United States had white prototypes. Yet the Negro added something of his own. His religious gatherings often had a heightened emotionalism beyond what was seen among the whites. Even if as a class the "spirituals" were originally inspired by white originals, the majority were entirely original both in words and music.

The advance made by Negroes in the first half century after emancipation was phenomenal. It left much to be achieved, but when it is remembered from what a low level it began and what had been accomplished in a little over a generation for a body of people who by 1914 numbered about ten millions, the record is amazing. To no small degree it was due to the fact that the Negroes were immersed in the white man's culture and because many whites gave themselves unselfishly to the freedmen and their children. Much must be ascribed to the native ability of the Negroes themselves. Not a little, however, was because of the impulse which came through Christianity.

THE EFFORT TO WIN THE CITIES

Rapid though the growth of cities was in the Old World under the impetus and facilities of the industrial revolution, it was even greater in the United States. Millions flooded in from the rural districts and the majority of the immigrants from Europe chose for their homes not the country but the city, and this in spite of the fact that on the other side of the Atlantic most of them had been peasants. Could Christianity so adjust itself to the new urban conditions that it could not only hold those who before coming to the cities had had a church connexion but also win those who in their pre-urban days were among the de-Christianized elements of the population?

The Roman Catholic Church had remarkable success in meeting the challenge. For it the problem was probably less difficult than that presented by the cities on the Continent of Europe and was more nearly akin to that which it faced in the Irish in England and Scotland. As we have seen, the bulk of the nineteenth century Roman Catholic immigration went as unskilled labourers to the industrial, commercial, and mining towns and cities. There, because of its vitality and initiative, the Roman Catholic Church provided what were both religious and social centres which were the chief places where the immigrants, nostalgic and seeking fellowship with their own kind, found familiar ceremonies, an institution, the use of their native speech, and peoples which gave them a sense of being at home. They therefore rallied to them, much as did the Irish in a somewhat similar situation in the cities of Great Britain. In contrast, on the Continent of Europe, the urban industrial proletariat tended to be anti-clerical and to regard the Roman Catholic Church as a tool of exploiters. In the United States, however, the main strength of the Roman Catholic Church was in the hearts of the great cities.

Protestantism was not as successful in the centres of the cities as was the Roman Catholic Church. Its constituency was chiefly from the older American stock. This tended to move "uptown" and to the suburbs, for it prospered through the toil of the newer arrivals and found the physical and cultural environment more pleasant away from the older sections. In the latter the Protestants were usually either the very poor without much sense of community or cohesion, or, in their town houses, the very wealthy. In general the churches followed their constituencies. Protestant churches, some of them very strong, were numerous in the suburbs. Thus in time, so far as they retained a religious complexion, Boston and Manhattan Island were predominantly Roman Catholic, but Protestantism was vigorous on the fringing outskirts.

To this generalization there were many exceptions, some of them striking. Protestantism by no means abandoned the cities, not even the hearts of the largest of them. Nor did it entirely fail. In the cities of the United States the Young Men's and Young Women's Christian Associations had their greatest growth. Often erecting large buildings, they developed a varied programme, mainly for those in the lower income brackets of the middle class. In time the more strictly religious phases of their activities declined and stress was placed on the educational, social, and athletic aspects of their life. For the lowest income groups there were the Salvation Army and many "rescue missions."

As the years passed, itinerant "evangelists," those who gave themselves as missionaries to winning non-Christians and the de-Christianized, utilizing preaching, "personal work," and "revivals," devoted themselves increasingly to the cities. Their number was legion, but among them two stood out preëminently, Charles Grandison Finney (1792–1875) in the middle of the century and Dwight Lyman Moody (1837–1899) in the latter part of the century.

Born in New England, as a child Finney was taken to what was then the frontier in the west central part of New York. Handsome, musical, exuding energy, he was a leader among the youth, dissented from much of the preaching which he heard, and entered the legal profession. Then, still young, after intense struggle, he was converted and became a travelling preacher-missionary. He was the outstanding figure in the religious awakenings which swept across much of the North in the second quarter of the century. At the outset a Presbyterian, he eventually left that denomination, largely because, contrary to strict Calvinism, he taught that every individual had the ability to repent and in his preaching urged that all do so. At the height of his career as an evangelist he made New York City his headquarters, first as pastor of a Presbyterian Church and later in Broadway Tabernacle, erected especially for him, in which there grew up about him an independent Congregational church. He also had preaching tours in cities in the British Isles. From middle life until extreme old age he taught theology at Oberlin, an idealistic institution in Ohio which pioneered in the co-education of the sexes and in enrolling both Negroes and whites. There he was also pastor of the First Congregational Church and for fifteen years was president of the college.

In contrast with Finney, Moody was never ordained. He was born in Northfield, Massachusetts. His father died when he was a child and his formal education ended when he was thirteen. Baptized a Unitarian in the only church in his native town, when in his later teens he sought his fortune in Boston he came in contact with a Congregational church, was converted, and became active in its life. Then, still under twenty, he went to Chicago and quickly proved himself a successful salesman of shoes. However, he devoted an increasing proportion of his abounding vitality to voluntary religious work, organizing a Sunday School, prayer meetings, home visitation, and welfare activities, and promoting preaching and efforts to win individuals one by one. In 1860, in his early twenties, he gave up business and became an independent city missionary. He gathered an undenominational church and was a secretary and then president of the Young Men's Christian Association of Chicago. For about two years, 1873 to 1875, as we have seen, he held evangelistic meetings in the British Isles. There and through much of the rest of his life he had as an associate Ira David Sankey (1840–1908). Sankey was a singer who usually played his own accompaniments on a reed organ. With deep conviction and with emotional feeling he made popular "Gospel hymns" a means of stirring audiences, large and small. The Moody and Sankey tour of the British Isles culminated in meetings in London which attracted wide attention. Returning to the United States, Moody, often with Sankey, conducted similar meetings in many cities and with great effect. In 1881–1884 and 1891–1892 he made other prolonged tours in the British Isles. Although equipped with only an elementary education, he was increasingly acceptable among students, had missions in American and British universities, and, beginning in 1886, chaired student conferences at or near his home in Northfield. The profits from the sales of the *Gospel Hymns* went largely into a school for girls at Northfield and one for boys in the adjacent Mt. Hermon, both for those of limited means. Making no pretense of being a profound theologian, believing unquestioningly in the Bible as the word of God, Moody, stressing the love of God for all men, wished all men everywhere to know of that love and, repenting, to accept it. Irenic, possessed of excellent judgement, he worked happily with men of quite different religious convictions, enlisted the help of such scholars as George Adam Smith and Henry Drummond, and commanded the confidence of many different elements, including business men of large means. He had a wide and profound influence through the length and breadth of Protestantism in the English-speaking world, especially that of the Evangelical tradition, and through it upon much of mankind.

It was through the preaching not only of itinerant "evangelists" but also of resident pastors that Protestantism made its impression on the burgeoning cities of the United States. There were many ministers of urban churches who had a wide hearing, not only by huge audiences reached by the voice but also by much larger constituencies, often nation wide, who read their sermons and books. Two of the most outstanding were Henry Ward Beecher (1813–1887) and Phillips Brooks (1835–1893).

Henry Ward Beecher was one of a remarkable family of children which included Harriet Beecher Stowe whose novels, especially *Uncle Tom's Cabin,* had an enormous circulation. His father, Lyman Beecher (1775–1863), was one of the most distinguished preachers of "revivals" of the first half of the century. Lyman Beecher was himself an example of the effort to reach the cities, for beginning as pastor in rural communities, he later served churches in Boston and the rapidly growing Cincinnati. Henry Ward Beecher first attracted attention as pastor in the youthful Indianapolis but achieved fame during his forty years (1847–1887) as pastor of Plymouth (Congregational) Church on Brooklyn Heights, overlooking lower New York City. Not original or profound, hating theological controversy and reacting against the Calvinism in which he had been reared, he had a deep sense of the love of God, thought of Christ as ever near him to help and sustain him, sought to effect moral change in his hearers, and had great power over the heart.

Phillips Brooks, like Beecher, was of old New England stock. His maternal relatives had endowed two academies which bore the Phillips name and had been a main stay financially of Andover Theological Seminary. He was first an Episcopal rector in Philadelphia, then became widely known as rector and inspiring preacher of Trinity Church in Boston, and died as Bishop of Massachusetts. Strikingly handsome and impressive physically, of singular nobility and purity of character, influenced by Coleridge, Maurice, Robertson, and Bushnell (the American Congregationalist of whom we are to hear more in a moment), he was an interpreter of the theological trends represented by these men rather than a pioneer. He brought to his calling high vision, poetic insight, and deep earnestness.

Influential in helping Protestants to meet the problems of the cities were various movements directed towards youth. Outstanding were Sunday Schools and the Young People's Society of Christian Endeavour. The latter, initiated by a young New England Congregational pastor, Francis E. Clark, was followed by denominational organizations such as the Epworth League, the Luther League, and the Baptist Young People's Union. There were also the Daily Vacation Bible schools, begun in 1899 in New York City.

In one important phase of urban life Protestantism made little headway. It did not successfully reach many of the element in the population which was usually known as "labour," namely, that employed in the factories, mines, and forms of transportation which were multiplying as the century progressed. This, as we have seen, was true of Christianity, both Protestant and Roman Catholic, on the other side of the Atlantic. In the United States the record of the Roman Catholic Church was somewhat better than that of Protestantism, but nearly everywhere, whether in America or Europe, industrialization made for the de-Christianization of the masses of workers who were caught up in it.

The Intellectual Challenge

As in Europe, so in the United States, the intellectual currents of the nineteenth century constituted both a threat and a challenge. Many believed that science was outmoding Christianity. In the rapidly growing colleges and universities, including those begun through the churches and officially Christian, the trend, especially in the later years of the century, was away from Christianity. Yet Christians were far from abject surrender. Books, some of them notable and many for popular consumption, appeared in defense of the faith or to demonstrate, by restatement, that the faith and the new knowledge and methods were not incompatible. On the campuses voluntary student Christian movements sprang up and flourished. In the latter part of the century these were chiefly Young Men's and Young Women's Christian Associations. Through the Student Volunteer Movement for Foreign Missions, a Protestant organization which, as we have suggested, had its birth in 1886 at a student Christian conference under Dwight L. Moody at Mt. Hermon, Massachusetts, and which spread rapidly, thousands from the colleges, universities, and theological seminaries went to other lands to spread the faith and to plant and nourish churches.

It was through the Student Young Men's Christian Association and the Student Volunteer Movement for Foreign Missions, and largely through contacts, direct and indirect, with Moody, that there emerged John R. Mott (1865———). Coming from Iowa to Cornell, it was at that university that Mott was enlisted, largely through J. K. Studd, a Cambridge athlete who was one of the converts of the Moody movement. Soon after graduation Mott became a travelling secretary of the student department of the Young Men's Christian Associations. He was one of the original members of the Student Volunteer Movement and was long the chairman of its executive committee. A layman, he travelled widely across the world, first as an evangelist and an organizer among students and later as an outstanding leader in Protestant missions and what came to be known as the Ecumenical Movement. We shall meet him again more than once, especially after 1914. Combining a simple faith issuing from a complete commitment to Christ with a commanding platform presence, world-wide vision, skill in discerning and enlisting young men of ability, and the capacity to win the confidence of men of affairs, and reaching out across ecclesiastical barriers in the effort to unite Christians of many traditions in the endeavour to win all mankind to the faith, Mott became one of the outstanding leaders in the entire history of Christianity.

The Changing Character of the Christianity of the United States

At the outset of this chapter we noted that the Christianity of the United States was in many respects unique and different from that of Europe. That was true at the beginning of the century and was still true in 1914. Some of the developments of the century heightened the contrast. Changes came in the Christianity of the United States. Some of them accentuated characteristics which had been present in 1815. Others introduced new elements.

It will be remembered that we pointed out (Chapter 44) the distinctive marks of the Christianity of the United States at the dawn of the nineteenth century. These were that it was prevailingly Protestant and with the more radical Protestant denominations in the majority, that it showed great variety, that all churches tended to be legally equal with no one accorded a privileged position, that "evangelism" was stressed, the effort to win all to an allegiance to the Christian faith, that the attendant emphasis upon conversion was modifying the Augustinian, Reformed theology, usually called Calvinism, which was the common heritage of the denominations which enrolled the majority of the church members, and that there was among many Christians the ambitious purpose to bring all society into conformity with Christian standards. All of these features continued, even though modified.

In 1914, in spite of the phenomenal growth of the Roman Catholic Church through the immigrant flood of the preceding century, the United States was still prevailingly Protestant. The total membership of Protestant churches was larger than that of the Roman Catholic Church. The ideals of the country were those which the radical Protestantism of the older American stock had done much to shape. That radical Protestantism continued to be numerically in the ascendant. Baptists far outnumbered any other type of Protestants and the Methodists were second. Protestants of the denominations which went back to colonial days or those with that kind of background predominated in the national and most of the state governments, business, and the professions. In some of the cities Roman Catholics were in control, but no Roman Catholic had been elected President. Although the violence with which the opposition to the Roman Catholic Church was sometimes expressed was deplored by most Protestants, there was widespread recognition of the fact that the Roman Catholic

Church was alien to much that was basic in the principles on which the United States and its life were built and that if Roman Catholics were ever to be in control and were true to what had again and again been enunciated by the Popes, including those of the nineteenth century, they would work fundamental alterations in the life of the nation.

The variety presented by the Christianity of the United States was markedly increased. We have noted (Chapter 44) that in the interval between 1750 and 1815 the multiplicity of denominations resulting from immigration had been augmented by others of American origin. Methodists and Baptists, although owing their inception to impulses from abroad, were spreading rapidly. Denominations sharing Methodist convictions and having a Methodist ecclesiastical structure but not included in the Methodist Episcopal Church had sprung up, notably the United Brethren and the Evangelical Association. Groups calling themselves Christians or Disciples of Christ had come into being, centering chiefly around Barton W. Stone and Alexander Campbell. In New England the Unitarians and the Universalists were becoming distinct denominations. As we have seen in the present chapter, between 1815 and 1914 the number of denominations was swelled through the nineteenth century immigration. Roman Catholics multiplied. The Orthodox Churches were represented. Lutheranism rose to prominence and the number of Lutheran synods mounted, some of them so distinct from one another as to constitute separate churches. We have also noted the appearance of new Protestant churches on the frontier, notably the Church of Jesus Christ of Latter Day Saints.

From the fertile religious soil of the United States sprang additional Protestant denominations. Several of them either began in New England or had for founders men of New England stock. One was the Seventh Day Adventists. The Seventh Day Adventists arose from William Miller (1782–1849). Born in Western Massachusetts and coming to manhood in New York, a farmer, at first a Deist, after prolonged struggle with doubts and a painstaking study of the Bible, Miller was converted and joined a Baptist church. Meditation on the Bible prophecies convinced him that Christ was to return in 1843. Earnest disciples spread his views and a movement arose which attracted wide attention. When the first date passed without the expected Second Advent, a rechecking of the data set the day in 1844. Although this, too, came and the world still stood, Miller's followers, persecuted in the existing religious bodies, formed themselves into Adventist churches. Through contact with the Seventh Day Baptists the larger proportion of the Adventists adopted the seventh instead of the first day of the week for worship and abstention from labour. Although numbering only about 80,000 in 1916, they were well organized, actively missionary, and propagated their views through much of the world.

Of more strictly New England birth was the Church of Christ, Scientist, teaching what was called Christian Science. The founder was Mary Morse Baker Eddy (1821–1910). Reared in a devout home, a member of a Congregational church, as a young woman she was frail and suffered much from what appear to have been nervous disorders and hysteria. What seemed to her to be health came through a faith-healer, also a New Englander, a man of complete sincerity and beauty of character who believed in Christ but not in an orthodox way. From him and at least one other she acquired convictions which she elaborated in her own way and set forth in a volume, *Science and Health,* first published in 1875 and to which she subsequently gave many revisions. In 1879 the Church of Christ, Scientist, was chartered in Massachusetts and headquarters were eventually set up in Boston. Mrs. Eddy proved to be an able organizer and devised a structure for the movement which placed a large amount of authority at the centre. Although in her later years officially retired, she was long the directing spirit. The Christian Science churches had a rapid growth. They were chiefly urban and their appeal was mainly their assurance of physical healing.

A movement, not of New England origin, which began before 1914 and was to be widely spread after that year was what was known variously as Jehovah's Witnesses, the International Bible Students' Association, the Watch Tower, and the Russellites. It came into being through the teachings of Charles Taze Russell (1852–1916). On the basis of his study of the Bible Russell believed that Christ had come in invisible form in 1874 and that the millennium had begun. He denounced all existing churches as rejected by God. He travelled and preached widely and hundreds of congregations sprang up which theoretically had him as pastor.

A number of small denominations arose, some of them offshoots of Methodism and regarding the Methodist Episcopal Church as too lax. Several of them believed that freedom from sin is attainable. Some taught faith healing. There were also similar groups which in one combination or another had the word Holiness in their title and spoke of a "second blessing" beyond conversion and an ensuing perfection of life. There were various Pentecostal churches, believing in the outpouring of the Holy Spirit as at Pentecost with a resulting "speaking with tongues." The Church of the Nazarene spread fairly widely. The Christian and Missionary Alliance, at first undenominational, later a distinct ecclesiastical body, warmly evangelistic, sent missionaries to several parts of the world. The roster of these denominations was long and included both white and Negro bodies, but the total membership was but a small fraction of that of the larger, what might be called the "standard" churches.

A feature of the variegated denominational picture of the Christianity of the

United States was sectional division. Because of the strains brought by the issue of slavery and the Civil War, a cleavage took place in some of the larger Protestant denominations. Thus in 1845 the Southern Baptist Convention was organized by delegates from eight slave-holding states. That same year saw the coming into being of the Methodist Episcopal Church, South, precipitated by an action of the General Conference of the Methodist Episcopal Church in 1844 which asked a Southern bishop to suspend his episcopal duties until he had divested himself of some slaves which he had acquired through a second marriage. In 1861 the Old School Presbyterians in the South formed the Presbyterian Church in the Confederate States of America which after the defeat of the South became the Presbyterian Church in the United States. The body from which it withdrew retained the name the Presbyterian Church in the United States of America. The Lutherans also divided. During the Civil War the southern dioceses of the Protestant Episcopal Church organized a separate Confederate church, but the parent body did not officially acquiesce in the action and at the end of hostilities the Southern bishops were welcomed back into the General Convention. In contrast, the breach in the Baptist, Presbyterian, Methodist, and Lutheran ranks persisted. In the case of the last two it was healed after 1914.

In the social stratification of the churches still another element entered to multiply the variety. We have noticed it in the groupings according to the national and racial origins of the population. It also reflected the economic and educational status of the members. Thus Unitarians, Episcopalians, Presbyterians, and Congregationalists tended to be in the upper income brackets. Of the larger bodies the Methodists and Baptists were drawn predominantly from those of the older American stock who were of the lower income and educational levels. In general this was more true of Baptists than of Methodists.

As the years passed the theological complexion of the Christianity of the United States changed. Obviously it was rendered much more varied by the growth of the Roman Catholic Church, the coming of the Orthodox Churches, and the multiplication of the shades of Lutheranism which we have noted.

Alterations took place in the theologies of the Protestant churches which were drawn largely from the older American stock. As we have seen (Chapter XLIV), these had begun before 1815. Augustinian or Calvinistic theology had been that of the Congregational, Presbyterian, Reformed, and many of the Baptist churches. Before 1815 this had begun to be abandoned by the Unitarian wing of New England Congregationalism. On the extreme left of that movement, going far beyond his older contemporary, William Ellery Channing (1780–1842), the outstanding earlier formulator of Unitarianism, was the intellectually eager and extraordinarily learned Theodore Parker (1810–1860) who presented religion in terms of inner experience, "the felt and perceived presence of Absolute Being infusing itself" in the soul. Reared in Unitarianism, but eventually moving beyond it away from historic Christianity, was Ralph Waldo Emerson (1803–1882), whom we have already met and who by his lectures and writings exerted a widespread and enormous influence.

In the orthodox Congregational churches the inherited theology was being modified by the stream which issued from Jonathan Edwards. In the nineteenth century what was called New England theology departed further and further from the Augustinian tradition with its doctrines of original sin and divine election or predestination. Much of this, as we have noted, was from the purpose of making room for the preaching which urged men to repent and was a necessary accompaniment of the revivals which were then a feature of Congregationalism. It was also in part through influences from contemporary European Protestant thought. Some of it came from Nathaniel William Taylor (1786–1858) of Yale. Some was through Andover Theological Seminary.

These trends were countered by adherents to Augustinianism as represented in Calvin, the Westminster Confession, and the historic faith of the Reformed Churches. Outstanding was Charles Hodge (1797–1878) who, a graduate of Princeton, both the college and the theological seminary, through a long life taught in the latter institution and by his influence in the class room and his extensive writings in journals and books was a bulwark of the older orthodoxy both in Presbyterian circles and in the country at large. Hodge's voluminous *Systematic Theology* was at once a history of Christian doctrine and an orderly presentation of the standard Reformed faith, giving what was to Hodge the logical basis for that faith, answering objections to it, and pointing out the weaknesses in the rival positions. A man of deep emotional piety with the love of God in Christ at its heart, through his writings Hodge gave the impression of a massive intellectual structure erected on the foundation of the infallible Bible by means of uncompromising logic. Somewhat similar was the slightly later *Systematic Theology* by Augustus Hopkins Strong (1836–1921), a Baptist, professor and president in the Rochester Theological Seminary. It, too, had wide use both in and beyond the denomination of the author.

Radical in his departure from Augustinianism as traditionally represented in the Reformed Churches was Horace Bushnell (1802–1876). Reared in Connecticut, early joining a Congregational church, educated at Yale, he was familiar with the modified Calvinism of that environment. He rebelled against what seemed to him to be the hair-splitting logic of the vigorous and often acrimonious theological debate about him and the kind of revivalism which prevailed. Yet it was a revival at Yale while he was a young tutor there which took him out of the study of law and sent him to the Yale Divinity School.

Coleridge, and especially the latter's *Aids to Reflection*, had, so he said, a greater influence upon him than any writings outside the Bible. As a pastor in Hartford, Connecticut, from 1833 to 1858 and especially through his writings then and later he helped to shape the thought of many, particularly among the clergy and thoughtful laymen. A mystic, he believed that truth is apprehended by intuition. Reacting against revivalism with its insistence upon the conversion of the adolescent or adult as the only entrance to the Christian life, in his *Christian Nurture* he maintained that "the child is to grow up as a Christian and never know himself as being otherwise." He believed in miracles, but not as a suspension of natural law. To him nature and the supernatural were a single universe created and governed by God. He was a Trinitarian, but sought to rescue the doctrine from the danger of tritheism. He exalted Christ, but appreciated his humanity as well as his divinity. He was convinced of the efficacy of the death of Christ, but through what is often called its "moral influence." He was denounced by many of his fellow-clergymen in the Congregational churches, but for his singular nobility of character and the force of his thought he was held in honour by thousands.

In the latter part of the century there arose other formulators of what came to be called "liberal" theology. Among them were the Baptist, William Newton Clarke (1841–1912) whose *Outline of Christian Theology* (1898) had a wide circulation, and Henry Churchill King (1858–1934), a Congregationalist, for many years teacher and president at Oberlin. Borden Parker Bowne (1847–1910), earnestly religious, intensely critical of Herbert Spencer, long a teacher at Boston University, a Methodist institution, attacked mechanistic determinism, emphasized the freedom of the self and its relation to the Unseen, was near to the conservative position in his estimate of Christ, and formulated a philosophy known as Personalism which helped to shape much of contemporary Methodist theology.

Also in the latter half of the century there came into prominence in wide reaches of the Protestantism of the United States what was known as the "Social Gospel." It sought to inspire Christians to strive to bring all society as well as the individual into conformity with the teachings of Jesus. To no small degree it was an outgrowth of the dream which had brought the Independents, Puritans, Quakers, and many another Christian minority across the Atlantic, that of building in the New World an ideal Christian society. It was favoured by the optimism of the era, was given impetus by a poignant appreciation of the evils which attended the growing industrialization, and was encouraged by the Ritschlian theology which was entering from Germany and by the writings of Thomas Chalmers and Frederick Denison Maurice. Bushnell and some of the Unitarians helped to prepare the way for it.

The Social Gospel had many expressions and spokesmen. Among the more prominent was Washington Gladden (1836–1918), for thirty-six years a Congregational pastor in Columbus, Ohio. A champion of what he called "applied Christianity," he attacked *laissez faire* on the ground that it often meant "let ill enough alone," served on the city council, advocated municipal ownership of public-service utilities, and sought to ease the tension between employers and labour unions. The outstanding prophet of the Social Gospel was Walter Rauschenbusch (1861–1918). Of German ancestry, the seventh in an unbroken succession of clergymen in his family, he was born in the United States of parents who had taken refuge in that country after the defeat of liberalism in Germany in the outcome of the revolutionary year of 1848. A graduate of the University of Rochester and of Rochester Theological Seminary, Baptist institutions, after a period as a pastor in New York City in which he came to know the people and problems of a great city he returned to Rochester Theological Seminary as a teacher. His *Christianity and the Social Crisis,* published in 1907, brought him nation-wide recognition and was followed in quick succession by additional volumes of a similar tenor. Dynamic, gracious, winsome, and vividly humorous, he was much sought after as a speaker and lecturer.

The trends of which Bushnell and Rauschenbusch were outstanding expressions and spokesmen aroused alarmed opposition in much of the Protestantism of the United States. It was heightened by the efforts of scholars to reconcile science and religion and by the application to the Scriptures of the kind of historical method which was known as the "higher criticism." "Evolution" became to thousands a symbol of all in the scientific approach that seemed to them destructive of the Christian faith. The tension was aggravated by radical departures, in the name of Christianity, from many historic Christian convictions, notably by scholars connected with the Divinity School of the University of Chicago. That institution, under Baptist auspices, built on earlier beginnings, dated its founding from 1892 when through the first of a succession of princely gifts by John D. Rockefeller and the daring vision of its young President, William Rainey Harper (1856–1906) it entered upon a spectacular rise to prominence in the world of education. Here and there heresy trials punctuated the course of the struggle of conservatives against the new views. Not long before 1914 the opposition began to call themselves and to be called Fundamentalists, from their adherence to what they deemed the fundamentals of the Christian faith. After 1914 the contest was to be intensified.

A feature of the Christianity of the United States which became increasingly prominent in the Protestantism of the country as the century progressed was the share of laymen. As we have seen, the hierarchy of the Roman Catholic Church early defeated the efforts of the laity to take control of its parishes. In

Protestant circles laymen and women more and more came to the fore. They did this partly through their financial gifts to the churches and various religious organizations and institutions. Laymen's organizations sprang up, first in connexion with local churches, and then as denomination-wide fellowships. Many women's societies appeared, both in the individual parishes and on a national scale. By deliberate policy the American Bible Society was under lay control. The Young Men's and Young Women's Christian Associations were primarily lay institutions. The laity were prominent in the Sunday Schools. Some of the outstanding evangelists, notably Moody and Mott, were not ordained. This made for a kind of lay Christianity. For the most part it had little patience with what it regarded as theological subtleties. Largely from the Evangelical background of the revivals, it respected, studied, and taught the Bible, sought to win individuals to a personal Christian commitment, was activist, and was generous in giving time and money.

The lay element and the emphasis upon evangelism and revivalism with the consequent mass conversion were phases of a kind of popular Christianity. Among other expressions were hymns which had about them the quality of folk songs. Prominent among them were those which were born from the camp-meetings of the early part of the century. They were followed by what were often called Gospel hymns. We have already met them in connexion with Moody and Sankey, but they were by no means confined to these two men. Appealing by words and simple tunes they sang their way into the hearts of millions. They were numbered by the thousands and were published in inexpensive hymnals which together attained circulations of hundreds of thousands. Here was a singing faith which voiced and helped to shape the aspirations, prayers, and actions of multitudes. Probably nothing of this kind of similar dimensions had previously appeared in the history of Christianity or of any other religion. Prominent among the writers was Fanny Jane Crosby (1820–1915) who, blind from birth, is said to have composed at least eight thousand songs. Among them were "Jesus keep me near the cross," "Blessed assurance, Jesus is mine," and "Rescue the perishing, care for the dying."

The abounding religious life of the Protestantism of the United States gave rise to still other hymns, many of them of a more dignified kind, but also having a wide appeal. When taken together with the religious folk songs of the masses they constituted most impressive evidence of the vitality of the Protestantism of the country.

Some came from the Unitarians and Quakers, who, although small minorities, penned hymns which were in use in much larger denominations and on both sides of the Atlantic. Among the Unitarians were Samuel Johnson (1822–1882), memorable for "City of God, how broad and far outspread thy walls sublime" and "Life of ages, richly poured," and Samuel Longfellow (1819–1892), younger brother of the more famous Henry Wadsworth Longfellow and author of "I look to Thee in every need and never look in vain." The Quaker whose poems were most used as hymns was John Greenleaf Whittier (1807–1892). Among others he gave to the world "O brother man, fold to thy heart thy brother" and "Immortal love, forever full, forever flowing free."

Still more of the hymns issued from the larger denominations. A Congregational layman, Lowell Mason (1792–1872), promoted the multiplication of singing schools and the introduction of music in the public schools. Alone or in collaboration with others he compiled hymnals, some of which went through several editions. He himself composed many hymn tunes, some original and others adaptations of what he had acquired elsewhere. Mason's most important collaborator was likewise a layman, a Presbyterian, Thomas Hastings (1784–1872), who with him sought to raise the level of church music in the United States. Hastings also worked independently, did much for the church music of New York City, issued several hymn books, and composed many tunes and numbers of hymns, among the latter "Hail to the brightness of Zion's glad morning." Samuel Francis Smith (1808–1895), a Baptist clergyman, wrote hymns for Mason, among them "America," the most widely used of the patriotic songs of the United States. He was the author of "The morning light is breaking." Ray Palmer (1808–1887), a Congregational clergyman, contributed "My faith looks up to thee, thou lamb of Calvary," "Jesus, these eyes have never seen that radiant form of thine," and English paraphrases of Latin hymns, among them "Jesus, thou joy of loving hearts." Phillips Brooks gave to the world "O little town of Bethlehem, how still we see thee lie," written for the children of his Philadelphia parish for their Christmas service and set to music by his organist. George Washington Doane (1799–1859), from the age of thirty-three until his death bishop of the Protestant Episcopal Church in New Jersey, among other hymns composed "Softly now the light of day," "Thou art the way; to thee alone," and "Fling out the banner, let it float." Washington Gladden was best remembered not so much for his advocacy of the Social Gospel as for his hymn, "O Master, let me walk with thee in lowly paths of service free." The list might be greatly lengthened. Hundreds of hymnals were compiled, some for use in dignified services, others for meetings of a more informal character, and many for both kinds of services. American Protestantism was a singing religion.

The Protestant Christianity of the United States made much of assemblies in the open air and in camp grounds. In the fore part of the nineteenth century these were predominantly the camp-meetings of which we have spoken. In the latter part of the century sites with more enduring buildings were developed.

Some were by the ocean, some by the lake-side, some in mountains, and others by rivers. To them groups came for shorter or longer periods for recreation, fellowship, study, worship, and hearing lectures and sermons. Notable was the summer assembly begun on Lake Chautauqua, in New York, in 1874, by John H. Vincent (1832–1920), the first chairman of the International Sunday School Lesson Committee, for the training of Sunday School teachers. It grew into an institution for adult education, encouraged and aided home reading and study, and was copied in many places across the country. Numbers of other summer assemblies were restricted to specifically religious programmes.

Still another feature of the Christianity of the United States was a trend towards common patterns. This was most marked among the Protestant bodies which had been longest in the country, but it gradually became apparent in ones more recently arrived. It included forms of worship, hymns, and orders of service. Sunday Schools became characteristic of most Protestant churches, and through the International Sunday School Lessons, prepared by an inter-denominational committee, the same passages of Scripture and often the same materials for teachers and pupils were used simultaneously by several different denominations. Youth organizations multiplied, mid-week meetings for all members, usually under the name of prayer-meetings, were common, and mis-sionary societies became normal. This meant that a stranger going from church to church would find striking similarities, regardless of the denomination. In general, Roman Catholics and Eastern Orthodox stood outside the trend.

A closely associated feature of the Christianity of the United States, espe-cially of the Protestantism of the older American stock, was a growing co-operation across denominational lines. It was furthered by the fact that no denomination was accorded preference by the state and that all were on the basis of legal equality. Coöperation took many forms. It was seen in organiza-tions in which Christians of several denominations joined as individuals and not as official representatives of their respective churches. Such were the Ameri-can Bible Society, the Young Men's and Young Women's Christian Associa-tions, and the Young People's Societies of Christian Endeavour. In others more than one denomination coöperated, as in the Plan of Union of the Presby-terians and Congregationalists, the American Board of Commissioners for Foreign Missions, and the American Home Missionary Society. In 1838 S. S. Schmucker, whom we have already met as a creative figure in American Lutheranism, issued a *Fraternal Appeal to the American Churches, with a Plan for Catholic Union on Apostolic Principles*. In it he suggested a federation which would not abolish existing denominations or do violence to doctrines held by any one and believed by him to be true, but which would be based upon the Apostles' Creed and a *United Protestant Confession* stating the faith common to all orthodox Protestant bodies and among whose members there should be "free sacramental, ecclesiastical, and ministerial communion." In part in response to the *Appeal* a society for promoting Christian union was launched. In 1846, to some extent because of this movement, the Evangelical Alliance was begun in England. It brought together not churches but individuals and was international in its scope. A branch of the Alliance was organized in New York in 1867. In 1873 a notable meeting of the general conference of the Alliance with representatives from a number of countries was held in New York.

Prominent in the Alliance was Philip Schaff (1819–1893). Born in Switzerland, educated in Germany, at the sacrifice of a promising scholarly career in the latter country he came to the United States as a young man to teach in the theological seminary of the German Reformed Church in Mercersburg, Pennsylvania. In his later years he was professor in Union Theological Seminary in New York City. An outstanding church historian, author or editor of a prodigious number of volumes, he directed his energies, including those which found outlet in his prolific pen, to furthering unity among Christians.

In the 1890's and the opening years of the twentieth century several bodies for coöperation in which churches or denominational missionary societies officially coöperated came into being. Among them were state federations of churches, the Foreign Missions Conference of North America (1893), the Home Missions Council (1908), and the Federal Council of the Churches of Christ in America (1908). In a later chapter we are to see the amazing fashion in which after 1914 these organizations grew and similar organizations multiplied.

THE EFFECTS OF CHRISTIANITY IN THE UNITED STATES

It is hazardous, indeed almost preposterous, to attempt to estimate and still more so to attempt to summarize in a few paragraphs the effects of Christianity in the United States. Some of the most important elude statistics or concrete statements which can be compressed on the printed page. Who can accurately record the results in millions of individual lives, some slight, others transforming and issuing in radiant but usually obscure men and women who were noted and remembered only by their families and local communities? Yet, as in other countries and ages, it was such fruits which were the most significant.

However, it is possible to give some hint, even in a few pages, of what a fuller and more discerning account would include and from it to gain an inkling of the fashion in which Christianity entered into the shaping of the life of the United States in the nineteenth century.

We have already seen that the percentage of church members in the population increased more than six-fold. Whether this meant a decline or an increase in the average quality of the faith and life of church members we do not know. No statistics are available for church attendance, on the comprehension of the Christian faith, or on the degree of approximation to Christian ethical standards which would make possible an accurate comparison.

That Christianity had an important part in moulding the ideals of the country is certain. The American dream of realizing in the New World a better social order than that of the Old World was largely from Christian sources, predominantly from the extreme wing of Protestantism, especially since the latter attained much larger prominence in the United States than in Europe.

The hope of creating a model society expressed itself in many ways. The kind of democracy which was the purpose of the United States, although far from perfectly achieved, was predominantly from radical Protestantism. The same was true of the many reform movements which characterized the United States in the nineteenth century.

The Christian conscience and resolution were a factor, probably the major factor, in bringing about the abolition of Negro slavery. This was seen in many ways, notably in the great increase in the anti-slavery movement which issued from the Finney revivals. We have noted the manner in which those moved by the Christian faith aided the former slaves and their descendants to adjust themselves to emancipation and take a worthy and growing part in the life of the country, sharing its opportunities and its obligations.

Another outstanding effort for moral improvement was that directed against alcoholic beverages. In the fore part of the century liquors of high alcoholic content were in wide use. Whiskey was characteristic of the frontier and in the eighteenth century rum had popularity through the extensive trade with the West Indies. Before 1815 some churches, notably the Methodists, began to protest against the customs which made drunkenness common. Throughout the century the revivals had as one of their fruits temperance movements and campaigns to prohibit the sale of alcoholic drinks. In 1826 the American Temperance Society was organized, largely by clergymen. In the 1850's thirteen states, led by Maine and all but one in the North, forbade the manufacture and sale of intoxicating liquors except for industrial and medicinal purposes. A reaction followed, heightened by the lowering of morals which accompanied and followed the Civil War. However, the temperance movement revived. In 1869 a National Prohibition party was formed, with a clergyman as the first chairman of its executive committee. The Woman's Christian Temperance Union came into being in 1873 and soon became nation-wide. In 1895 the National Anti-Saloon League was organized, growing out of local movements.

Drawing its support largely from Protestant churches, mainly those of the radical wing and of the older American stock, it sought to enlist voters of all denominations. By 1900 more than thirty states allowed voters in a given area to decide by "local option" whether they would permit the sale of liquor. By 1916 nineteen states had entirely forbidden the sale of liquor, and in 1919 an amendment was ratified which wrote prohibition into the Constitution of the United States.

Organizations for the achievement of world peace flourished, mainly through the initiative and leadership of earnest Christians. In 1815 David Low Dodge, a New York merchant of New England birth and ancestry, the progenitor of a long line of Christian philanthropists, along with his father-in-law, a clergyman and convert of Whitefield, formed the New York Peace Society. That same year two clergymen led in constituting the Massachusetts Peace Society. In 1828, largely through the leadership of William Ladd, an earnest Congregationalist, the American Peace Society was created. The Mexican and Civil Wars dealt blows to the peace movement, but it revived. In 1914, shortly before the outbreak of World War I, the Church Peace Union came into being.

Other reforms which owed much to Christianity were that which opposed secret societies, the attempt, ultimately successful, to place women on an equality with men in legal status and in social, intellectual, and economic opportunity, the improved care of the insane, more enlightened treatment of criminals, and efforts to clean out the political corruption in the great cities. As an example of this last, it was a Presbyterian clergyman, Charles H. Parkhurst (1842–1933), who in the 1890's by his fearless preaching contributed to the defeat of the noisome Tammany Hall and the placing of a reform government in control in New York City.

Another of the results of Christianity was seen in the vast extent of private philanthropy. By the end of the century the voluntary gifts by both rich and poor totalled hundreds of millions of dollars annually. Hundreds of hospitals, large and small, were founded by Roman Catholics and Protestants. Many orphanages and homes for the aged were maintained under church auspices. Christians pioneered in care for the blind and the deaf. Numbers of the wealthy gave lavishly and often, perhaps usually, from Christian motives. In the first half of the century Arthur and Lewis Tappan, devout Christians, were well known for their generosity. Through more than a century members of the Dodge family, avowed Christians, were devoted in giving both time and money. John Davison Rockefeller (1839–1937), a Baptist layman, who accumulated the nucleus of his vast fortune through pioneering in developing and marketing the petroleum resources of the country, sought counsel in the initial stages of his philanthropies from friends among the Baptist clergy, and largely channelled his enormous giving through organizations which he either chose or set up on their advice. His son, John Davison Rockefeller, Jr., for years the teacher of a men's Bible class, continued in the paths marked out by his father, although without as much counsel from the clergy.

Literature felt the influence of Christianity. By no means all the outstanding authors were committed to it. Some were critical and even hostile. However, several of the most prominent writers were consciously and deeply indebted to it. Among them were Henry Wadsworth Longfellow, John G. Whittier, Harriet Beecher Stowe, James Russell Lowell, Ralph Waldo Emerson, Oliver Wendell Holmes, and Nathaniel Hawthorne.

Education was markedly furthered by Christianity. All the older colleges and universities owed their existence to it. The same was true of several of the newer universities and of a majority of the colleges which were begun in the nineteenth century. As we have seen, some denominations, notably the Roman Catholics, conducted elementary and secondary schools. Protestants pioneered in higher education for women and, as we have said, in primary, secondary, and higher education for Negroes. Acting from frankly Christian motives, in several states Protestant clergymen and laymen were chiefly responsible for the beginnings of the system of state public schools.

The Share of the Christians of the United States in the World-wide Spread of the Faith

We have already seen (Chapter 44) the fashion in which the Protestants of the United States, not content with confining their energies to winning the Indians, Negroes, and de-Christianized whites about them, shared with their fellow-Christians on the other side of the Atlantic in spreading the faith to other lands. As the nineteenth century progressed American Protestant foreign missions were augmented. This is not the place for a detailed account of what was done. However, we must pause to note that by 1914 foreign as well as home missions became part of the normal programme of all Protestant denominations. Although usually only a minority of the membership were actively interested, almost every denomination made foreign missions a part of its commitment. Protestant denominations new to the American scene for the most part conformed, even though slowly, as they did to Sunday Schools and other features of the religious life about them.

A great forward surge came to the Protestant missionary movement through the Student Volunteer Movement for Foreign Missions which, as we saw a moment ago, was born in 1886 at a summer conference held at Mt. Hermon, Massachusetts, under the direction of Moody. From it in subsequent years thousands went abroad, or, remaining at home, led mission boards or formed a convinced and sacrificial constituency for the support of the enterprise.

By 1914 more missionaries served from the United States in the overseas extension of Protestant Christianity and more money was given than from any other country. Americans served in every continent and in scores of lands and formed the large majority of the Protestant missionaries in Latin America, Japan, the Philippines, and Korea.

Roman Catholics of the United States, as we have said, were slower than Protestants in undertaking foreign missions. They were so absorbed in taking care of the vast immigration of those who by heredity were of their faith and in building churches and schools that they had little energy to spare for enterprises abroad. It was not until after 1914, when immigration dwindled to a trickle, that they began to take a substantial share in the missions of their church in other lands.

Summary

The nineteenth century course of Christianity in the United States was like and yet unlike that in Europe. Here was a new nation, fired by the spirit of hopeful adventure, essaying in what it called the New World to make a fresh beginning and, as its great seal declared, to build, under the eye of God and with His benevolent approval, an enduring structure in a new order of the ages. Its territory grew by leaps and bounds. Its population mounted even more rapidly. An immigration of unprecedented magnitude, drawn from all the countries of Europe and to some extent from Asia, added to one which was already diverse because of a composite of aboriginal Indian tribes, settlers from several nations in Western Europe, and slaves from Africa. The majority of the immigration was from Christendom and was Christian by heritage. It brought with it almost all the existing varieties of Christianity and made for a scene of greater ecclesiastical complexity than the world had ever known.

Yet, coming to a land where, except for a few remnants which early disappeared, no church enjoyed a privileged status given it by law, where only a small minority were members of churches, and where it was easy to drop Old World patterns of life, the immigrant population was in grave danger of de-Christianization. The peril was accentuated by the threats to Christianity in both Europe and America brought by the temper and currents of the new age which, arising in part from the distortion of impulses emanating from Christianity, seemed to threaten the very existence of the faith.

Under these apparently untoward conditions, Christianity achieved phenomenal gains. It won an increasing proportion of the older, partially de-Christianized white stock, both on the westward moving frontier and on the Atlantic seaboard. It held a majority of the nineteenth century nominally Christian immigration. It made striking advances among those of non-Christian ancestry—the Indians, the Negroes, the Chinese, and the Japanese—but not, significantly, among the Jews, and that in spite of the fact that this people was being rapidly secularized. Christianity was confronted by the mounting urbanization and industrialization of the nation's society. While not completely solving the problem, it was not defeated by it.

In the course of the century the Christianity of the United States became increasingly distinctive. It continued to be predominantly Protestant and the churches which embodied radical Protestantism enjoyed a striking growth. In endeavouring to bring about the mass conversion of the de-Christianized and non-Christian elements of the population the older Protestantism, especially of the radical wing, moved forward through revivalism. Out of the Protestantism of the older American stock there came new denominations, some of them far removed from traditional Christianity. The variety presented by Christianity was even more diversified by the addition of Protestant denominations of the newly arrived immigration grouping themselves according to national origins, by contingents from the Eastern Churches, and, even more prominently, by the rapid growth, through immigration, of the Roman Catholic Church. From being one of the smaller denominations in 1815, by 1914 the Roman Catholic Church was the largest. In the United States the Roman Catholic form of Christianity departed in no way from the accepted dogmas of its church or from obedience to the Pope: it was neither heretical nor schismatic. Yet it was inclined to be more activistic than in Europe. Much of the Protestantism of the older American stock tended to move away from the Augustinian theology which it had inherited from Europe through what is often called, with only partial accuracy, the Puritan strain. Through its revivalism and mass conversion it sought hopefully to win all men, disregarding in practice the doctrine of predestination which regarded some as elected by God to salvation and others left, irremediably, to the consequences of original sin. Impelled by what was termed the Social Gospel, many within it laboured for the transformation of society with the avowed goal of complete accord with Christian standards.

While the dream of the advocates of the Social Gospel was by no means fully realized, Christianity had a profound effect on many aspects of the life of the United States. It was responsible for some of the basic and most compelling ideals of the nation. It brought about the end of Negro slavery and aided the freedmen in their progress towards social, educational, and economic equality with their former masters. It fought the excessive use of alcoholic beverages and inspired better care of the sick, the insane, the criminals, the blind, the orphaned, and the aged. It contributed strikingly to education and intellectual advance.

Moreover, the Christianity of the United States took an increasing part in the world-wide extension of the faith and began to make significant contributions to coöperation among Christians of different denominations and towards new approaches to Christian unity.

Selected Bibliography

L. Abbott, *Henry Ward Beecher* (Boston, Houghton Mifflin Co., 1904, pp. xxviii, 457). By a friend and admirer.

J. T. Addison, *The Episcopal Church in the United States, 1789–1931* (New York, Charles Scribner's Sons, 1951, pp. xii, 500). Well done.

A. V. G. Allen, *Life and Letters of Phillips Brooks* (New York, E. P. Dutton and Co., 2 vols., 1900). The standard biography.

O. F. Ander, *T. N. Hasselquist. The Career and Influence of a Swedish-American Clergyman, Journalist, and Educator* (Rock Island, Ill., The Augustana Library Publications, 1931, pp. 260). Based in large part on manuscript sources and contemporary periodicals.

G. G. Atkins and F. L. Fagley, *History of American Congregationalism* (Boston, The Pilgrim Press, 1942, pp. ix, 432). A sympathetic, comprehensive account.

N. B. Atkinson, *Biography of Rev. G. H. Atkinson, D.D.* (Portland, Ore., F. W. Baltes and Co., 1893, pp. 508).

W. C. Barclay, *History of Methodist Missions. Part One. Early American Methodism 1769–1844* (New York, The Board of Missions and Church Extension of the Methodist Church, 2 parts, 1949, 1950). An official history based upon extensive research. To be further extended.

G. H. Barnes, *The Antislavery Impulse, 1830–1844* (New York, Appleton-Century-Crofts, 1933, pp. ix, 298). Based upon careful research.

Lyman Beecher, *Autobiography, Correspondence, etc.*, edited by Charles Beecher (New York, Harper & Brothers, 2 vols., 1864, 1865).

C. S. Braden, *These Also Believe* (New York, The Macmillan Co., 1949, pp. xv, 491). A careful study of various religious groups and movements in the United States on the fringes of Protestantism.

F. M. Brodie, *No Man Knows My History. The Life of Joseph Smith, Mormon Prophet* (New York, A. A. Knopf, 1945, pp. ix, 476, xix). Well written, critical of Smith.

J. A. Burns, *The Principles, Origin, and Establishment of the Catholic School System in the United States* (Cincinnati, Benziger Brothers, 1912, pp. 415). Based chiefly on well-known printed material, but in part upon manuscript sources.

J. A. Burns, *The Growth and Development of the Catholic School System in the*

United States (Cincinnati, Benziger Brothers, 1912, pp. 421). A continuation of the preceding book, covering the period from about 1840 onward.

H. Bushnell, *Christian Nurture* (New York, Charles Scribner's Sons, 1861, pp. vi, 407).

M. A. Cheney, *Life and Letters of Horace Bushnell* (New York, Harper & Brothers, 1880, pp. x, 579).

E. H. Cherrington, editor, *Standard Encyclopedia of the Alcohol Problem* (Westerville, Ohio, American Issue Publishing Co., 6 vols., 1925–1930). Compiled under forces working for prohibition, to aid in the fight against alcohol.

E. T. Clark, *The Small Sects of America* (New York and Nashville, Cokesbury Press, 1937, pp. 311). Based upon extensive research, often through personal visitation.

J. B. Clark, *Leavening the Nation. The Story of American Home Missions* (New York, The Baker & Taylor Co., 1903, pp. 362). An excellent survey.

W. R. Cross, *The Burned-Over District. The Social and Intellectual History of Enthusiastic Religion in Western New York, 1800–1850* (Cornell University Press, 1950, pp. xiii, 383). Extremely well done.

E. F. Dakin, *Mrs. Eddy. The Biography of a Virginal Mind* (New York, Charles Scribner's Sons, 1930, pp. x, 563). Based on solid research, critical of Mrs. Eddy.

Dictionary of American Biography (New York, Charles Scribner's Sons, 22 vols., 1928–1937). The standard work. A monument of careful research.

J. H. Dubbs, *History of the Reformed Church, German* (New York, Christian Literature Society, 1895, pp. 213–423).

W. E. B. DuBois, editor, *The Negro Church* (Atlanta, The Atlanta University Press, 1903, pp. viii, 212).

H. O. Dwight, *Centennial History of the American Bible Society* (New York, The Macmillan Co., 2 vols., 1916). By a secretary of the society.

W. Elliott, *The Life of Father Hecker* (New York, The Columbus Press, 1894, 2d ed., pp. xvii, 428). Warmly sympathetic.

H. W. Foote, *Three Centuries of American Hymnody* (Harvard University Press, 1940, pp. x, 418). A competent survey.

R. H. Gabriel, *The Course of American Democratic Thought. An Intellectual History Since 1815* (New York, The Ronald Press Co., 1940, pp. xi, 452). A standard survey.

C. B. Goodykoontz, *Home Missions on the American Frontier. With Particular Reference to the American Home Missionary Society* (Caldwell, Idaho, The Caxton Printers, 1939, pp. 460). Based upon extensive research.

P. Guilday, *The Life and Times of John Carroll, Archbishop of Baltimore (1735–1815)* (New York, The Encyclopedia Press, 1922, pp. xiv, 864). Well and sympathetically done.

Charles Hodge, *Systematic Theology* (New York, Charles Scribner's Sons, 3 vols., 1872, 1873).

C. H. Hopkins, *History of the Y.M.C.A. in North America* (New York, Association Press, 1951, pp. xii, 818). Based upon prolonged and competent research in the sources.

C. H. Hopkins, *The Rise of the Social Gospel in American Protestantism, 1865–1915* (Yale University Press, 1940, pp. xxii, 352). A standard work.

W. S. Kennedy, *The Plan of Union: or a History of the Presbyterian and Congregational Churches of the Western Reserve; with Biographical Sketches of the Early Missionaries* (Hudson, Ohio, Pentagon Steam Press, 1856, pp. iv, 262). Drawn from the original sources.

K. S. Latourette, *A History of the Expansion of Christianity. Volume IV, The Great Century, A.D. 1800–1914. Europe and the United States of America* (New York, Harper & Brothers, 1941, pp. viii, 516).

W. A. Linn, *The Story of the Mormons from the Date of their Origin to the year 1901* (New York, The Macmillan Co., 1902, pp. xxv, 637). Based on extensive research and antagonistic to the Mormons.

W. W. Manross, *A History of the American Episcopal Church* (New York, Morehouse-Gorham, Inc., 2d ed., 1950, pp. xiv, 415). Except for chaps. 1, 2, and 8, based upon original sources.

B. Mathews, *John R. Mott, World Citizen* (New York, Harper & Brothers, 1934, pp. xiii, 469). A warmly appreciative biography by a personal friend, based upon data provided by Mott.

H. F. May, *Protestant Churches in Industrial America* (New York, Harper & Brothers, 1949, pp. x, 297). Covers the period from 1828 to 1895.

T. Maynard, *The Story of American Catholicism* (New York, The Macmillan Co., 1941, pp. xviii, 694). With official ecclesiastical imprimatur.

W. R. Moody, *D. L. Moody* (New York, The Macmillan Co., 1930, pp. 556). By a son.

H. N. Morse, editor, *Home Missions Today and Tomorrow. A Review and Forecast* (New York, Home Missions Council, 1934, pp. xvi, 419). An official study by the Home Missions Council.

H. R. Niebuhr, *The Kingdom of God in America* (New York, Harper & Brothers, 1937, pp. xvii, 215). A discerning interpretation of the religious history of the United States.

H. R. Niebuhr, *The Social Sources of Denominationalism* (New York, Henry Holt and Co., 1929, pp. viii, 304). Brilliantly conceived and written.

O. M. Norlie, *History of the Norwegian People in America* (Minneapolis, Augsburg Publishing House, 1925, pp. 602). Packed with information, but without footnote references to the sources.

J. H. O'Donnell, *The Catholic Hierarchy of the United States* (Washington, The Catholic University of America, 1922, pp. xiv, 223). A doctoral dissertation. Contains brief biographies of the bishops and extensive bibliographies.

T. O'Gorman, *A History of the Roman Catholic Church in the United States* (New York, The Christian Literature Co., 1895, pp. xviii, 515).

W. Rauschenbusch, *Christianity and the Social Crisis* (New York, The Macmillan Co., 1907, pp. xv, 429).

B. H. Roberts, *A Comprehensive History of the Church of Jesus Christ of Latter Day Saints* (Salt Lake City, Deseret News Press, 6 vols., 1930). An official history.

I. D. Sankey, *Sankey's Story of the Gospel Hymns and Sacred Songs and Solos* (Philadelphia, The Sunday School Times Co., 1906, pp. vii, 272).

D. S. Schaff, *The Life of Philip Schaff, in Part Autobiographical* (New York, Charles Scribner's Sons, 1897, pp. xv, 526).

C. E. Schneider, *The German Church on the American Frontier. A Study of the Rise of Religion among the Germans of the West* (St. Louis, Eden Publishing House, 1939, pp. xx, 579). Detailed, scholarly, based upon extensive research.

G. Shaughnessy, *Has the Immigrant Kept the Faith? A Study of Immigration and Catholic Growth in the United States 1790–1920* (New York, The Macmillan Co., 1925, pp. 289). By a Roman Catholic, learned and optimistic.

C. P. Shedd, *Two Centuries of Student Christian Movements, Their Origin and Intercollegiate Life* (New York, Association Press, 1934, pp. xxii, 466). The standard account.

J. H. Snowden, *The Truth about Mormonism* (New York, George H. Doran Co., 1926, pp. xix, 369). A history of origins and developments, based on careful research, critically objective.

G. M. Stephenson, *The Religious Aspects of Swedish Immigration. A Study of Immigrant Churches* (University of Minnesota Press, 1932, pp. viii, 542). Competent.

G. M. Stephenson, *The Puritan Heritage* (New York, The Macmillan Co., 1952, pp. 282). A semi-popular account of Protestantism in the United States, mostly on the colonial period and the first half of the nineteenth century.

P. L. Stewart, *Sheldon Jackson* (New York, Fleming H. Revell Co., 2d ed., 1908, pp. 488).

A. P. Stokes, *Church and State in the United States* (New York, Harper & Brothers, 3 vols., 1950). The standard work in its field.

A. H. Strong, *Systematic Theology* (Rochester, N. Y., E. R. Andrews, 1886, pp. xxix, 758).

W. W. Sweet, *Religion on the American Frontier. The Baptists, 1783–1830. A Collection of Source Material* (New York, Henry Holt and Co., 1931, pp. ix, 652).

W. W. Sweet, *Religion on the American Frontier. Vol. II, The Presbyterians, 1783–1840, a Collection of Source Materials* (New York, Harper & Brothers, 1936, pp. xii, 939).

W. W. Sweet, *Religion on the American Frontier, 1783–1850, Vol. III, The Congregationalists. A Collection of Source Materials* (University of Chicago Press, 1939, pp. xi, 435).

W. W. Sweet, *The Story of Religion in America* (New York, Harper & Brothers, 2d rev. ed., 1950, pp. ix, 492). A useful survey.

D. G. Tewksbury, *The Founding of American Colleges and Universities before the Civil War. With Particular Reference to Religious Influences Bearing upon the*

College Movement (Teachers College, Columbia University, 1932, pp. x, 254). Based upon extensive reading in primary and secondary sources.

R. S. Walker, *Torchlights to the Cherokees. The Brainerd Mission* (New York, The Macmillan Co., 1931, pp. xii, 339).

L. A. Weigle, *American Idealism* (Yale University Press, 1928, pp. 356). An excellent survey of the religious history of the United States in the form of comments on pertinent illustrations.

A. B. Wentz, *The Lutheran Church in American History* (Philadelphia, The United Lutheran Publication House, 2d ed., 1933, pp. 465). An authoritative survey.

A. S. Will, *Life of Cardinal Gibbons, Archbishop of Baltimore* (New York, E. P. Dutton & Co., 2 vols., 1922). Based upon personal acquaintance and extensive research in the letters and journals of Gibbons.

C. G. Woodson, *The History of the Negro Church* (Washington, D. C., The Associated Publishers, 2d ed., 1921, pp. x, 330).

G. F. Wright, *Charles Grandison Finney* (Boston, Houghton Mifflin Co., 1893, pp. vi, 329).

G. J. Zeilinger, *A Missionary Church with a Mission. A Memoir of the Seventy-fifth Anniversary of the Evangelical Synod of Iowa and Other States* (Chicago, Wartburg Publishing House, 1929, pp. 115). Published under the authority of the Synod.

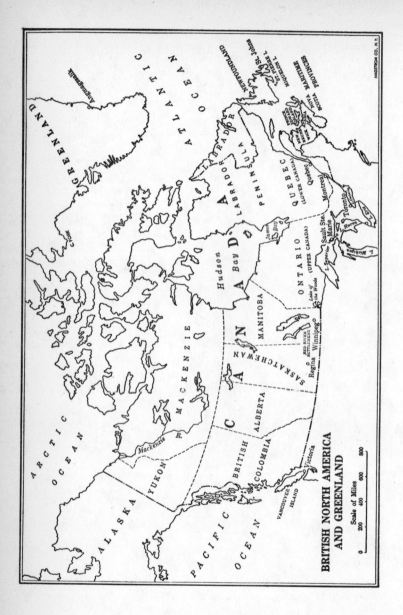

BRITISH NORTH AMERICA
AND GREENLAND

Scale of Miles

0   200   400   600   800

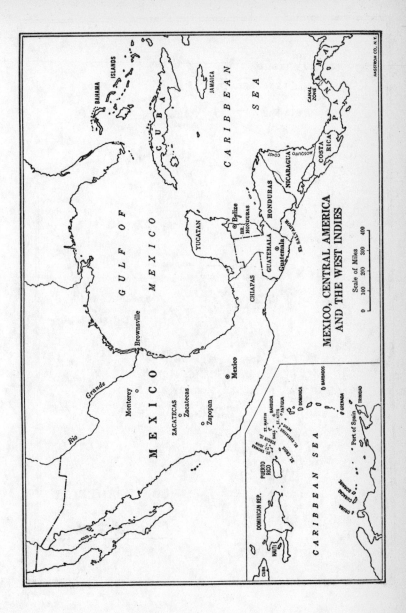

MEXICO, CENTRAL AMERICA
AND THE WEST INDIES

Scale of Miles

0   100   200   300   400

SOUTH AMERICA

Scale of Miles

0   200   400   600   800   1000

Chapter 51

CHRISTIANITY IN BRITISH AND LATIN AMERICA IN THE NINETEENTH CENTURY

Christianity in the Americas was by no means confined to the United States. It was also present in every other country in the Western Hemisphere. In none other was it exactly like that of the United States. In most it was very different. Yet in general the course of Christianity in the Western Hemisphere was characterized by the same problems. The population was predominantly from Western Europe, either of the pre-nineteenth century or the nineteenth century immigration. It faced some of the same forces making for de-Christianization. In almost every land there were representatives of the aboriginal Indian peoples whose inherited cultures had either disintegrated or were disintegrating under the impact of Western civilization. In several countries there were larger or smaller numbers of Negroes. Originally slaves, by the end of the nineteenth century legal emancipation had come to all of them, but they still were faced with problems arising from their earlier servile status. For the most part the Americas outside the United States fell into two categories, those portions where the political and dominant cultural connexions were with the British Isles, and those where they were with Latin Europe. For a variety of reasons, chiefly because it did not have so prominent a place in the world scene, we need not give as much space to the Christianity of these lands as we have to that of the United States. We must, however, trace its course, even though more briefly than we have that of the latter.

British North America

For those portions of North America which in the nineteenth century were part of the British Empire, the period opened, not in 1815 but in 1763 and 1783. By the peace of Paris, in 1763, which ended the Seven Years' War, the exclusion of France from North America which had been begun earlier was all but completed. Except for two small islands, St. Pierre and Miquelon, off the Newfoundland coast, and, from 1801 to 1803, a brief renewal of power in the vast region including and reaching northward from Louisiana, French rule was at an end. North of what soon became the United States, the British supplanted it. The secession of the Thirteen Colonies, formally acknowledged in 1783, removed from the British Empire the most populous portion of its North American possessions. However, in the course of the nineteenth century expansion to the north of the United States completed the incorporation into the Empire of an area which was slightly larger than that country. By the fourth quarter of the century all of it except Newfoundland and Labrador came together to form, under a federal form of government, the Dominion of Canada.

Largely because much of the territory was sub-arctic in climate, the population of Canada remained smaller than that of the United States. In 1914 the total for Canada and Newfoundland was about eight millions. Its growth was very rapid. Most of it was near the southern border. In 1914 its chief elements were French, descendants of settlers from the pre-British period, a large immigration from the British Isles, and thousands from the United States. That from the United States was made up, first, of those loyal to the Empire who would not or could not remain in the seceding Thirteen Colonies, and, second, of those who in the nineteenth century sought homes on the great prairies of the Canadian West. Immigration also came from the Continent of Europe, but by no means as large as that which poured into the United States. There were scattered minorities of Indians and, in the far North, of Eskimoes. Negroes were present but were by no means as prominent as in the great republic on the south.

Proportionately the Roman Catholic Church was stronger and more compact than in the United States. It constituted about two-fifths of the population. It was predominantly of French descent, but in it there were a substantial Irish contingent and smaller elements from Germany, Italy, Poland, Austria-Hungary, and Belgium. The bulk of the French were in the province of Quebec. Most of them were rural and they had large families and multiplied rapidly. In spite of the anti-Roman Catholic temper of Great Britain in the eighteenth and the fore part of the nineteenth century, from its outset British rule was tolerant of the Roman Catholic Church in Canada. To no small degree this was because of the desire to prevent the French from siding with the United States in its war of independence and in its second war with Great Britain. To the French Canadians the Roman Catholic Church was the symbol and bond of their nationalism as against the British. They looked with intense dislike upon the anti-Roman Catholic actions of the French Revolution and upon the anti-clericalism which characterized much of France in the nineteenth century. They deemed France apostate. Very few of them became Protestants or drifted into secularism. From an earlier Gallican attitude of administrative independence of the Holy See, in the course of the nineteenth century they became more and more ultramontane. In few countries did the Roman Catholic Church have so firm a hold on all phases of the lives of its members as it did on the French in Canada. The non-French elements, mainly Irish, were mostly outside the province of Quebec, the French stronghold, and did not mix easily with their French fellow-believers. Between the French and the Irish Roman Catholics, indeed, tensions existed, somewhat similar to those which were found in the Roman Catholic Church in the United States between the various national groups. There were Roman Catholic missions among the Indians and Roman Catholics shared in the settlement of the Western frontier.

Canada had very few from the Orthodox Churches. Several thousand Dukhobors came from Russia, seeking refuge from persecution, but they did not have a large place in the religious life of the country.

The Protestantism of Canada was both like and unlike that of the United States. Like the latter, it had denominations of British origin—Anglicans, Presbyterians, Methodists, Congregationalists, and Baptists. However, Congregationalists played no such large rôle as in the United States and, in contrast with the United States, where they were the largest denominational family, Baptists were a small minority. Methodism was prominent, but not as much so as in the great republic to the south. It entered partly through contacts with the United States and partly because of its rapid growth in contemporary England. The Church of England and Presbyterianism were much stronger in Canada than in the United States. This was due to the dominance of the English and Scottish elements in the nineteenth century immigration. De-Christianization made no such initial inroads as in the United States. In 1911 95 per cent. of the population of Canada professed to have a church connexion as against 43.5 per cent. in the United States in 1910. There was, accordingly, no mass conversion of a partially de-Christianized population and revivalism was not as prominent as in the latter country. As in the United States, by the end of the century no church was established by law. However, for many years financial aid was given the Church of England by the governments of Upper and Lower Canada, approximately the later provinces of Ontario and Quebec. This was in the form of government lands which were set aside as clergy reserves. Other denominations protested against what they deemed to be discriminatory preference. The Presbyterians were especially vocal, coming as most of them did from Scotland, where the state church was of their faith. Eventually portions of the clergy reserves were commuted for a permanent endowment.

Substantial aid in nurturing Protestantism among the white population and in missions to the Indians was given from the British Isles. The Society for the Propagation of the Gospel in Foreign Parts was represented by hundreds of missionaries, some to the whites and some to the Indians. The Society for Promoting Christian Knowledge assisted in the erection of Anglican churches and in establishing colleges and universities. The Church Missionary Society sent missionaries and substantial sums of money for both whites and Indians. Some societies were founded by Anglicans, especially for Canada or Newfoundland. Famous among the Anglican missionaries was Charles James Stewart (1775–1837). A younger son of the Earl of Galloway and a graduate of Oxford, he lived simply, devoted his private means and his stipend to nurturing the Church of England in Canada, travelled widely founding new churches, and in his later years was (Anglican) Bishop of Quebec. The Church of Scotland, the Free Church of Scotland, and the Irish Presbyterian Church aided Presbyterianism with funds and personnel. The London Missionary Society and the Colonial Missionary Society helped Canadian Congregationalism. In 1837 the Baptist Canadian Missionary Society was organized in England. One of the outstanding missionaries from the British Isles was Wilfred Grenfell (1865–1940). A physician and surgeon, greatly impressed by Moody and some of Moody's converts, he gave himself first to the fishermen of the North Sea and then, beginning in 1891, to the fishermen and other dwellers on the bleak coast of Labrador. Through hospital ships, schools, coöperatives, and other devices, and with assistance in money and personnel from Britain and the United States, he did much to transform wholesomely the life of a widely scattered and hard-pressed community.

As the century wore on Protestantism in Canada became sufficiently strong to assume more and more of the responsibility for the founding and support of churches, for recruiting and training the ministry for them, and for making itself felt in the new settlements on the western frontier. It also began to share in the world-wide missionary enterprise and to that end organized its own societies. Here was a vigorous Protestant Christianity which by the end of the century largely dispensed with help from abroad and began to reach out beyond the borders of the Dominion to other lands.

GREENLAND, THE BRITISH, DANISH, AND DUTCH WEST INDIES, BRITISH AND DUTCH GUIANA, AND BRITISH HONDURAS

In addition to British North America, there were several islands and island groups near to the Americas and three pieces of territory on the mainland of Central and South America which belonged to predominantly Protestant powers. In most of them, as was to be expected, Protestantism was the prevailing form of Christianity. In almost all it made substantial progress in the nineteenth century. Since the populations involved were not large, they must be dismissed with only passing mention.

On Greenland the Christianity which had been re-planted by Scandinavian Lutheran and German Moravian missionaries in the eighteenth century continued to gain and by 1914 had won all but a few of the scanty Eskimo, Danish, and mixed Danish and Eskimo inhabitants. Most of the Christians had been taught to read and write. The missionaries responsible for this achievement under the adverse climate were still Moravians and Danish Lutherans. In 1900 the Moravians deemed their mission accomplished and withdrew, leaving the Danish Lutheran state church in sole charge.

In most of the West Indies the peoples were predominantly Negroes. Long before the end of the nineteenth century emancipation had been accomplished. In the Dutch West Indies the majority of the Negroes were Roman Catholics and in the nineteenth century that form of the faith continued to gain. Protestantism was confined chiefly to the ruling Dutch minority. In contrast, the Danish West Indies, also predominantly Negro, were prevailingly Protestant, partly Moravian and partly Church of England.

Of the British West Indies the largest was the island of Jamaica and with a population at the end of the century of about 800,000, the large majority of them Negroes. From the British occupation (1655) until 1870 the Church of England was established and received financial support from the state. Several Anglican missionary societies were represented and after the emancipation of the slaves sought to help the freedmen to make the best use of their new status. Next to the Church of England, the Baptists and Methodists had the largest constituencies, but there were as well other denominations, not only Protestant but also the Roman Catholics. By 1914 almost all the population had a connexion with some church, although for many this was very tenuous.

The second largest of the British West Indian islands, Trinidad, did not come into British hands until late in the eighteenth century. It had previously belonged to Spain and, in consequence, the Roman Catholic Church was strong. Under British rule Protestant missionaries of several denominations entered, including notably the Church of England, which until 1870 had the support of the state.

In most of the others of the British West Indies the Church of England was dominant, but the Methodists usually also had constituencies gathered through earnest missionary efforts. In a few of the islands Roman Catholics were in the majority.

On the mainland, British Honduras, flanked as it was by Spanish America, with a culturally backward population of Negroes, Indians, and whites of Spanish or British blood was much more Roman Catholic than Protestant. By

1914, due to faithful missionary effort, largely by Jesuits, Roman Catholics constituted about two-thirds of the whole, a substantial growth in the nineteenth century. Thanks also to heroic missionaries, there were Anglicans, Methodists, and Baptists.

In Dutch Guiana (Surinam), predominantly Negro, but with Indian, Chinese, Javanese, and white minorities, Protestants were the most numerous of the religious groups. This was due chiefly to the Moravians who, entering in 1735 and persisting in spite of peculiarly difficult conditions, by 1914 had gathered a very considerable membership. British Guiana, taken from the Dutch during the Napoleonic Wars, was larger in both area and population than Surinam. In 1914 about two-fifths of its population were Negroes and another two-fifths were from India and Ceylon, largely Tamils, brought in as labourers on the plantations. Most of the Roman Catholic minority were Portuguese, originally labourers from Madeira. Several Protestant denominations sent missionaries. Of these the Anglicans, assisted by the state, attracted the largest numbers of converts.

Nineteenth Century Latin America: The General Setting

What was known collectively as Latin America embraced Mexico, almost all of Central and South America, and several islands in the West Indies, including the largest, Cuba and Haiti. In 1789, at the outbreak of the era of the French Revolution and the Wars of Napoleon, all of it was in a colonial status, governed from the Old World. By 1815 that position had begun to change. In the island of Haiti French rule was overthrown by an insurrection of the Negro majority. To escape the Napoleonic armies the Portuguese ruling house shifted its residence to Brazil. In Spanish America, during the French occupation of the mother country, local governments were set up, in part by American-born whites, the *creoles,* which professed to rule on behalf of the King of Spain.

By the year 1914 all of Latin America had become fully independent politically of Europe except French Guiana and some islands in the West Indies which remained in French hands. With the exception of Puerto Rico, which was ceded to the United States by Spain as a result of war in 1898, all of autonomous Latin America had republican forms of government. In the several countries this status had been reached at widely different times. In the largest of the lands, Brazil, Portuguese by language and inheritance, it was not attained until 1889. From the severing of the ties with Portugal in 1822 until that year Brazil had been governed as an empire under a branch of the Portuguese royal family. In Spanish America, except for Puerto Rico, Cuba, and adjacent islands, political independence from the mother country was achieved before 1850, partly through war and often through marked internal disorder.

Political independence did not mean political stability. Although the governments were nominally republics and democracies, many of them were in fact military dictatorships. As a rule, dictators were overthrown only by revolutions, and while few of these were costly in life, they brought recurrent disorder. In some lands upsurging movements of the submerged majority with demands for true democracy added to the revolutions.

In most Latin American lands independence of the mother countries did not immediately greatly alter the social and economic structure inherited from colonial days. To be sure, in Haiti it was accomplished by uprisings which brought the former Negro slaves into power, and in Mexico the desire of the Indian majority for release from exploitation by the whites and for more voice in the government and larger opportunity for the good things of life was a complicating factor. In general, however, the white minority remained in power. For the most part independence came as a revolt of American-born whites and mestizos against paternalistic rule from Europe under European-born officials. Modern industries were slow in arriving and the economy was still based upon agriculture, cattle-raising, fruit-growing, mining, and, latterly in some countries, petroleum. Exports were of fruits and foods of various kinds, coffee, and minerals and were exchanged for the products of the industries of Europe and the United States.

LATIN AMERICA: THE DIFFICULT SITUATION OF THE ROMAN CATHOLIC CHURCH

The new age brought grave difficulties for the Roman Catholic Church. Some of these were from the heritage of the past. We have seen (Chapter 41) the striking successes of Roman Catholic missions in Spanish and Portuguese America in the sixteenth, seventeenth, and eighteenth centuries. Through them the immigrants from Europe had been held to the faith, the vast majority of the Indians and a large proportion of the Negroes had been won to at least a formal acceptance, schools and universities had been created, and laws had been enacted and to some degree enforced to protect the Indians from selfish exploitation by the whites. A beginning had been made towards recruiting and training an indigenous clergy.

Yet the Spanish and Portuguese American churches were still parasitic. Like the civil governments, they were paternalistically controlled and directed from the mother countries. The bishops were appointed by the crown. Rome had little or no voice in the administration and, while the churches were emphatically orthodox in doctrine, Papal decrees could be promulgated only with the consent of the crown. Most of the missionaries and bishops were not American-born but were from the Old World. Moreover, the expulsion of the Jesuits from the Spanish and Portuguese domains in the second half of the eighteenth century had deprived the missions of numerous and able personnel. Although other orders, notably the Franciscans, took over their responsibilities, the transition had made for loss of momentum. At best, under the new conditions of political independence the Roman Catholic Church, accustomed to depend on the Old World, would have been seriously handicapped.

The struggle for political independence brought additional and grave problems. As we have seen, it was to no small degree a revolt of the native-born whites against European-born officials. In this European-born clergy were involved. Many of the latter perished or left the country, and the parishes, missions, and dioceses staffed by them suffered. Some of the schools in which missionaries were prepared were closed. In large areas missions and their flocks were taken from the regular and put in charge of the secular clergy. The transfer was usually followed by decline, especially since on the average the seculars were inferior in character to the regulars. Moreover, the Church became the victim of a contest between the Spanish crown and the new governments for control of the appointments to the episcopate. The Spanish crown insisted on exercising its traditional power of naming the bishops. In view of the historic administrative autonomy of the Church in Spain as against Rome and the rising tide of anti-clericalism in that land, the Vatican did not dare openly to dissent, or its authority in Spain and in the Church in that country might further suffer. The new governments insisted on assuming the authority formerly granted the crown and upon naming the bishops. This Rome was slow to concede. As a result, in 1826 only 10 of the 38 bishoprics in Spanish America were occupied and of these only 5 were being actively administered. In 1847 Venezuela, which had been a special sufferer, had about 200 fewer priests than at the end of the colonial period.

Added to these difficulties were anti-clerical and anti-Christian currents from Europe. As was to be expected, the cultural ties of Latin America were primarily with Latin Europe. France was especially influential. It was natural, therefore, that the anti-clericalism and the secular, rationalistic revolt against Christianity which were striking features of Latin Europe in the nineteenth century and particularly of France had repercussions in Latin America. The movement for political independence in Spanish America was profoundly shaped by the ideas and example of the French Revolution. It was inevitable that the religious aspects of that upheaval would have repercussions in America and that the continuation of the Revolution throughout the nineteenth century would also be a persistent factor in Spanish and Portuguese America.

Comte and his Positivism won many followers among the intellectuals. While outward conformity to the Church might be continued, for a large proportion of the upper classes the Roman Catholic faith and therefore Christianity were a waning influence. The more conservative among the wealthy who clung to their special privileges inherited from the old order often supported the Roman Catholic Church as a bulwark against change, but those wishing to improve the lot of the masses regarded it as an obstacle.

In almost every Latin American country the struggle between the clericals, who backed the Church, and the anti-clericals, who sought to subordinate it to the state, was chronic. First one would be in control and then the other. Thus from 1860 to 1875 Ecuador was dominated by García Moreno, a highly educated aristocrat who was convinced by what he saw of the fruits of liberalism in Europe that the only alternative to anarchy was the moral discipline and the national unity given by the Roman Catholic faith. He therefore accorded great power to the Church and Rome. His assassination (1875) was followed by an anti-clerical reaction. The pendulum then swung again towards the Church, but from 1897 to 1914 anti-clericals were in power. For the most part compromises were reached in the Latin American republics by which the Roman Catholic Church was the official religion of the state, but religious liberty was professedly granted, for each vacancy in the episcopate the state and Rome joined in naming the new incumbent, civil marriage as well as that by the Church was accorded recognition by the state (although in Brazil late in the century civil marriage was made compulsory), and the state increased its control and support of education as against the Church.

As a result of these various factors, in 1914 the Roman Catholic Church in Latin America was distinctly weaker than in 1815. Many of the upper classes and of the masses had drifted from it. It did not possess sufficient vitality to recruit enough priests from its indigenous constituency to give adequate pastoral care to its nominal children. New cults entered or sprang up, including spiritualism in one or another form. Among many of the Indians and the Negroes superstitions and pagan rites and customs persisted from the pre-Christian past. Throughout the masses there were ignorance, poverty, and deplorable distortions of the faith, and both among the educated and the masses Christian standards of morals, especially in sex relations, were widely ignored. The Latin American Church continued to be parasitic, depending in part on Europe for its clergy, taking almost no share in the world-wide propagation of the faith, doing little to reach the pagan Indians who existed in the mountain fastnesses and in the tropical jungles of its river valleys, and giving rise to no major new monastic orders or creative theological thinking. This was all the more serious in view of the fact that Latin America held the largest body of nominal Roman Catholics outside of Europe and that the emergence of this body through immigration and the conversion of the Indians and the Negroes had been the major achievement of the great forward surge of Roman Catholic missions which accompanied and followed the Catholic Reformation. Taken together with the losses in Europe, it seemed to bode ill for the future of that form of the Christian faith.

The problem was aggravated by fresh immigration from Europe, chiefly of Roman Catholics and mainly to Southern Brazil, Uruguay, Argentina, and Chile. Much of it was from Italy and, while nominally Roman Catholic, in contrast with the Irish and Germans of that faith in the United States, it showed little religious zeal.

Latin America: Attempts to Revive and Strengthen the Roman Catholic Church

Rome and the Roman Catholics of Europe did not supinely accept the grim condition of their Church in Latin America. They sought to come to the rescue. Partly as a result, by the year 1914 the Church registered some improvement. It reached its low point in the first half of the century and thereafter achieved gains.

The Papacy was able to exert more influence than had been permitted it by the Spanish and Portuguese governments before independence. It now had a voice, even if not complete control, in the naming of bishops. It had apostolic delegates in the region. In 1858, with the endorsement of Pope Pius IX, who had been apostolic delegate in Chile, the *Collegio Pio-Latino-Americano Pontificio* was opened in Rome for the education of clergy for Latin America. In 1899 a plenary council of the clergy of that area was held in the college.

To reinforce the Church in its ministry to nominal Roman Catholics and to staff its missions to non-Christians, clergy, mostly regulars, and lay brothers and sisters came to Latin America from Europe. They were of many orders and congregations and from several countries. There were Lazarists from Portugal and Spain, Capuchins from the Tyrol and Italy, Mercedarians from Italy, Franciscans from Italy, Germany, and the Netherlands, Dominicans from France, Redemptorists from Austria and the Netherlands, German Missionaries of the Holy Family, Barnabites, Salesians of Don Bosco, Pallottines, Benedictines, Missionaries of the Holy Ghost, and members of the Society of the Divine Word. Undiscouraged by their earlier expulsion from the Spanish and Portuguese domains, the Jesuits reëntered, coming from several countries. Barred from time to time from more than one of the republics, they usually contrived to gain readmission. In 1899 a college was founded at Burgos, Spain, to train clergy for Latin America. Sisters of several congregations came from

Canada and the United States. At least one teaching brotherhood conducted schools. Through the assistance from Europe not only were many existing parishes staffed, but also several missions to non-Christian Indians which had lapsed were renewed and new ones were founded. The geographic frontiers of Christianity were again pushed forward in the mountains of Mexico, in the Andes, in the Gran Chaco, in Patagonia, and in the vast and steaming valley of the Amazon and its tributaries. Clergy and teachers were provided for some of the nineteenth century immigration from Europe. The Pious Society of Missions, usually known as the Pallottines, founded in Italy in 1835 by Vincent Mary Pallotti to serve immigrants to America, staffed a number of enterprises. Some provision was made for reaching the large Japanese contingents in Brazil. Clerical ministration was given to thousands of Uniates who migrated to the southern portions of South America.

In spite of all the assistance from abroad and although some recovery had been achieved from the low point reached in the first half of the nineteenth century, in 1914 the Roman Catholic Church in Latin America was far from healthy. It was still parasitic, dependent upon continuing infusions of life from the Old World, and taking little more than a negative rôle in the world-wide extension of its branch of the Christian faith.

Latin America: The Coming of Protestantism

In view of its low vitality, it was not to be expected that any indigenous movement as vigorous as Protestantism would emerge from the Roman Catholic Church in Latin America. In the course of the nineteenth century Protestantism appeared, flourished, and put down such firm rootage that after 1914 much of its growth was without help from the outside. However, at the outset Protestantism was entirely from abroad. It came partly through immigration and partly through extensive missions, some from the British Isles but chiefly from the United States.

The Protestantism which entered through immigration was of varied origin. Some was from the British Isles. Through the world-wide extension of their trade and investments in the nineteenth century, British merchants established themselves in Latin American ports, notably in Buenos Aires, the largest city in South America, and thousands of British sailors had shore leave. To meet their needs Anglican chapels and chaplains were provided, at first with financial assistance from the British Government but later chiefly by the British residents. There were a few Presbyterian churches for the Scottish colonists and merchants. Contingents of Italian Waldensees entered Uruguay and Argentina and their clergy not only served their own congregations but also conducted missions for Roman Catholics. After the Civil War, settlers took refuge in

Brazil from the defeated South of the United States, among them Baptists, Methodists, and Presbyterians, and became nuclei for missions to their Roman Catholic neighbours. There were other Protestant immigrant churches, mostly small, among them Swedish Lutherans and Swiss, Boers, and Dutch of the Reformed faith. The largest Protestant immigration was from Germany. It began in the first half of the nineteenth century and settled chiefly in Brazil. German colonists also found homes in Uruguay, Argentina, and Chile. While, failing clerical ministrations from their faith, some of the German Protestants had their children baptized by Roman Catholics, the majority were gathered into Protestant churches. Here, as in the United States, during at least the first generation the services were in German and the congregations drew their strength from the fact that they were social as well as religious associations bound together by the common tie of nationality and language. At the outset in Brazil stipends for the pastors of the larger German communities were provided by the government. Missionaries and financial assistance came from Europe. Some of the former were from Basel and Barmen. The largest of the resulting denominations was one in which both Lutherans and Reformed joined, but several others were represented and in 1900 the Missouri Synod began an enterprise which ultimately gathered several thousands into its fellowship.

British Protestants early began missions, some among non-Christian Indians and others among Roman Catholics. The most extensive among non-Christians were by the South American Missionary Society, an Anglican enterprise which arose out of the efforts of Allen Francis Gardiner (1794–1851). Gardiner, a former commander in the British navy, selected Patagonia because it was difficult, and in an attempt to inaugurate a mission perished, with his companions, on bleak Tierra del Fuego. Partly because of the inspiration of his heroism, the society attracted recruits and funds and conducted missions, chiefly in Patagonia and the Chaco. There were other British missions, but less extensive, for non-Christian Indians in several parts of Latin America. The South American Missionary Society also had missions among Roman Catholics. Beginning in the 1820's the British and Foreign Bible Society entered Latin America, stimulated the formation of local Bible societies, and distributed Bibles in Spanish and Portuguese. Although most of the local societies were ephemeral, the mother society persisted in its programme and maintained scores of sub-depots for the circulation of the Scriptures. Several British missions, largely conservative theologically and of the Evangelical type, and including the Plymouth Brethren, were active in Latin American countries. In Brazil, partly as the outcome of one of them, Congregational churches arose akin to Baptists in practice, and early in their history became self-supporting and self-propagating.

It was through missions from the United States that the major spread of Protestantism in Latin America was achieved. The missions were directed mainly to the nominally Roman Catholic population, but to a lesser extent were also among non-Christian Indians. They began soon after 1815 but did not attain significant dimensions until the second half of the century. They then grew rapidly, came to 1914 on an ascending scale, and continued to mount after that year. Ultimately they were operating in each of the Latin American republics. They were mainly from the larger denominations of the older white stock—Methodists, Baptists, Presbyterians, Episcopalians, Congregationalists, and Disciples of Christ—but they also were from some of the younger, enthusiastic movements, notably the Seventh Day Adventists, the Christian and Missionary Alliance, the Church of the Nazarene, and the Central American Mission. The American Bible Society was active almost from its inception.

The numerical strength of Protestantism varied from country to country. Because of the proximity of the United States, it was marked in Mexico. It was greatest in Brazil. That was partly because Brazil was the largest of the Latin American countries, both in population and in area. To some degree it was because of the weakness of the Roman Catholic Church, in part it was because of the presence of large bodies of Protestant immigrants (although only a small minority of them sought to win their non-Protestant neighbours), and it was also through the weakening of the old patterns of life and the striking increase in wealth and population in the south of the country, the area in which Protestantism became strongest. It was especially in Brazil that Protestants drawn from former Roman Catholic constituencies early became self-propagating. In general, Latin American Protestants tended to be sharply critical of Roman Catholicism and conservative theologically. By 1914 Protestant communicants in Latin America totalled well over half a million. By the middle of the twentieth century they had more than doubled and what could be counted as the Protestant community was still larger. Protestantism was making more substantial gains from a nominally Roman Catholic population than anywhere else in the world. They were several times greater than those being made by the Roman Catholic Church from professedly Protestant constituencies the world around.

SUMMARY

In their formal profession the populations of British and Latin America were overwhelmingly Christian. The Christianity of Canada, both Roman Catholic and Protestant, was vigorous and by 1914 was beginning to reach out beyond the borders of the country and share in the world-wide spread of the faith. That of the British, Danish, and Dutch West Indies, mainly among Negroes who were not emancipated until the nineteenth century, left much to be desired. In Latin America, where at the outset of the century the large majority were professedly Roman Catholic but where the Church was drawing most of its leadership and missionaries from Europe and was only slowly developing its own clergy, independence and intellectual currents from Europe which were undermining Christianity made for a serious reverse. In the latter part of the century some recovery was accomplished, but this was chiefly by personnel from Europe. Latin American Roman Catholic Christianity was anemic and depended for its continuing life upon transfusions from abroad. Protestantism had been introduced and was making rapid strides, but in 1914 was still a minority movement.

Selected Bibliography

E. Braga and K. G. Grubb, *The Republic of Brazil. A Survey of the Religious Situation* (London, World Dominion Press, 1932, pp. 164). Competent, by Protestants.

W. H. Calcott, *Church and State in Mexico 1822–1857* (Duke University Press, 1926, pp. 327). Ably done.

W. H. Calcott, *Liberalism in Mexico, 1857–1929* (Stanford University Press, 1931, pp. xiii, 410). A careful piece of work.

G. B. Camargo and K. G. Grubb, *Religion in the Republic of Mexico* (London, World Dominion Press, 1935, pp. 166). A pro-Protestant able survey.

K. G. Grubb, *Religion in Central America* (London, World Dominion Press, 1937, pp. 147). By a Protestant, an expert in missionary surveys.

K. S. Latourette, *A History of the Expansion of Christianity. Volume V, The Great Century in the Americas, Australasia, and Africa, A.D. 1800–1914* (New York, Harper & Brothers, 1943, pp. ix, 526).

L. Lemmens, *Geschichte der Franziskannermissionen* (Münster i.W., Aschendorffschen Verlagsbuchhandlung, 1929, pp. 376). Carefully done, by a Franciscan.

C. Lindsey, *Rome in Canada. The Ultramontane Struggle for Supremacy over the Civil Authority* (Toronto, Lovell Brothers, 1877, pp. 398).

J. A. Mackay, *The Other Spanish Christ. A Study of the Spiritual History of Spain and South America* (London, Student Christian Movement Press, 1932, pp. xv, 288). By a scholarly Protestant, long a missionary in Peru.

J. L. Mecham, *Church and State in Latin America* (University of North Carolina Press, 1934, pp. viii, 550). Objective. Based largely on printed sources.

E. A. Peers, *Spain, the Church and the Orders* (London, Eyre & Spottiswoode,

1939, pp. xi, 219). By an Anglican, sympathetic, from long residence and much reading.

E. Ryan, *The Church in the South American Republics* (New York, The Bruce Publishing Co., 1932, pp. viii, 119). By a Roman Catholic priest, popular in style, but scholarly.

[E. Ryerson], *"The Story of My Life." By the Late Rev. Egerton Ryerson, D.D., LL.D. (Being Reminiscences of Sixty Years' Public Service in Canada)*, edited by J. G. Hodgins (Toronto, William Briggs, 1883, pp. 613).

A. Shortt and A. G. Doughty, editors, *Canada and Its Provinces* (Toronto, Glasgow, Brook and Co., 23 vols., 1914–1917). A standard work of reference.

C. W. Vernon, *The Old Church in the New Dominion. The Story of the Anglican Church in Canada* (London, Society for Promoting Christian Knowledge, 1929, pp. viii, 215). Semi-popular.

M. Watters, *The History of the Church in Venezuela, 1810–1930* (University of North Carolina Press, 1933, pp. ix, 260). Carefully done; based upon the sources.

R. Young, *From Cape Horn to Panama. A Narrative of Missionary Enterprise among the Neglected Races of South America, by the South American Missionary Society* (London, 2d ed., South American Missionary Society, 1905, pp. xii, 212).

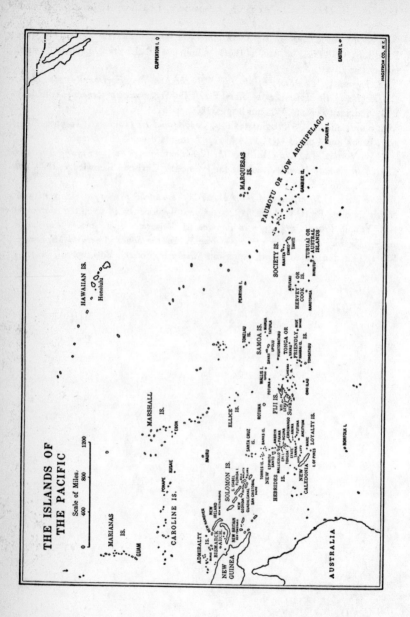

THE ISLANDS OF
THE PACIFIC

Scale of Miles,
0   400   800   1200

MARIANAS
IS.

GUAM

CAROLINE IS.

KUSAIE

PONAPE

ADMIRALTY
IS.

NEW HANOVER

BISMARCK
ARCH.

NEW IRELAND

NEW BRITAIN

NEW
GUINEA

SOLOMON IS.

N. GEORGIA

GUADALCANAL

SAN CRISTOBAL

SANTA CRUZ
IS.

BANKS IS.

TORRES IS.

NEW
HEBRIDES

NEW
CALEDONIA

LOYALTY IS.

I. OF PINES

AUSTRALIA

NORFOLK I.

NAURU

MARSHALL
IS.

EBON

ELLICE
IS.

ROTUMA

WALLIS I.

FUTUNA

FIJI IS.
VITI
SUVA

ONO ILAU

TONGATABU

FRIENDLY, OR
TONGA OR

SAMOA IS.
SAVAII
UPOLU

TOKELAU IS.

PENRHYN I.

HAWAIIAN IS.
Honolulu

HERVEY, OR
COOK IS.

RAROTONGA

AITUTAKI

SOCIETY IS.
RAIATEA
EIMEO
TAHITI

TUBUAI OR
AUSTRAL
ISLANDS

MARQUESAS
IS.

PAUMOTU OR LOW ARCHIPELAGO

GAMBIER IS.

PITCAIRN I.

CLIPPERTON I.

EASTER I.

HAGSTROM CO., N.Y.

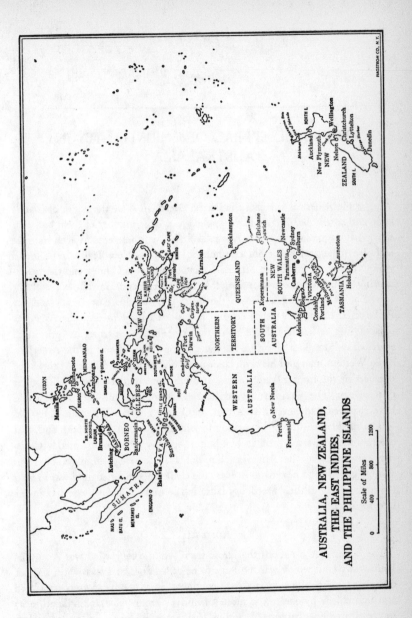

AUSTRALIA, NEW ZEALAND,
THE EAST INDIES,
AND THE PHILIPPINE ISLANDS

Scale of Miles

0   400   800   1200

Chapter 52

THE RAPID SPREAD OF CHRISTIANITY IN AUSTRALASIA

West of the Americas stretches the Pacific Ocean. In it are thousands of islands large and small. A collective name applied to a large number of them but with somewhat vague boundaries is Australasia. We will here employ it in its most inclusive sense and will embrace under it Australia, New Zealand, the island groups known as Polynesia, Melanesia (including New Guinea and the neighbouring islands on the east and south), Micronesia, and Hawaii. We will not regard it as extending as far to the north-west as the East Indies and the Philippines. In the nineteenth century it possessed similarities to the Americas of a slightly earlier day. Here, as in the Americas, were tribes in "primitive" stages of culture with animistic religions. Upon them, also as in the Americas, came Western man and his civilization with disintegrating effects. At times the pioneers of the impact were traders, at other times settlers, and at still others missionaries. The Occident would have come and the disintegration would have followed had never a Christian missionary arrived. What the latter did was to modify the impact by seeking to win the islanders to his faith and, that accomplished, to assist them in building a society which would embody Christian ideals. As in the Americas, but not as extensively, immigration from Europe gave rise to new nations. Here the challenge to Christianity was to hold the immigrants to their hereditary faith and to make that faith effective in the new societies.

AUSTRALIA

The larger of the nations that arose from white colonization was Australia. Here was a land which was too huge to be called an island and which did not quite rank unquestionably as a sixth continent. In 1815 only sparsely populated and that chiefly by one of the most "primitive" groups of mankind, and in its southern portions lying well within the temperate zone, in an age when

Western European peoples were flooding into the vacant spaces of the earth it constituted an invitation and a temptation to white settlement.

As we have seen (Chapter 44), that settlement had begun late in the eighteenth century and by the involuntary transportation of convicts from the British Isles. While the sending of convicts to Australia did not entirely cease until the 1860's, before the nineteenth century was well advanced free settlers were pouring into the land. In 1914 they and their descendants constituted the overwhelming majority of the population. They established their homes mainly on the south-east coast and in the neighbouring Tasmania and in distinct colonies which did not come together as states in a federal government until 1901. The new nation was prevailingly urban, and organized labour became powerful.

In Australia as in British North America where another self-governing dominion arose, also largely by nineteenth century immigration, Christianity was confronted with the challenge of holding the colonists and their descendants to their historic faith, and of doing so in the face of currents which seemed to be working against it. Among them were the weakening of Old World patterns of life in the fresh environment, the growth of cities and large bodies of labour in industry, absorption in acquiring the material goods of life in a new country, and the intellectual movements of the nineteenth century Occident which were adverse to the faith. In addition to these conditions, shared with other new commonwealths of the British Empire, in Australia in its earlier years Christianity faced the handicap of dealing with a convict population.

Although slightly less so than in Canada, in Australia Christianity was strikingly successful in weaving itself into the warp and woof of the new nation. In spite of the obstacles peculiar to the country, in 1914 the proportion of those professing a connexion with one or another of the churches was almost the same as in Canada. In this, as in Canada, Christianity was assisted by the rising tides of life in the British Isles.

More than in Canada and much more than in the United States, the white population was from the British Isles. There was not the problem, as in Canada, of a large non-British element which had gained rootage before the advent of British rule: Australia had no French enclave or anything corresponding to it. There was only slight immigration from the Continent of Europe, and the adamant policy of a "white Australia" kept out all but very small contingents from the islands which bordered the country on the east and north and from the teeming millions of Asia and its fringing islands. This meant that except for small Lutheran minorities of German ancestry the Christianity of Australia was overwhelmingly from the British Isles.

In proportion to the total church constituency of the country, the Roman Catholic Church was only about half as strong in Australia as in Canada and the United States. It was almost entirely from the Irish immigrants and their descendants. It was not until 1819 that uninterrupted services of the clergy began. In 1842 Australia was given a comprehensive hierarchy.

In 1914 the Church of England had twice as many constituents as the Roman Catholics. For years it received assistance from England in the form of clergy and funds through several missionary societies. For a time financial aid was given by the colonial governments, and before many years this was also accorded to some other churches. Eventually, for the most part in the 1860's and 1870's, it was discontinued, and the Church of England, along with the other denominations, became dependent upon voluntary contributions. Increasingly the initiative and support were from the Australians. The first clergy arrived before 1815, but it was not until 1836 that a Bishop of Australia was consecrated. He was William Grant Broughton. Able, energetic, sympathetic with the Oxford or Tractarian movement, he travelled widely in his vast see, recruited clergy, and obtained the creation of additional bishoprics. He became the first metropolitan of the ecclesiastical province of Australia, and died (1853) while in England attempting to gain greater freedom of the Church of England in Australia from state control under an autonomous ecclesiastical structure in which the clergy and laity would share.

The Presbyterians, with not quite an eighth of the population in 1914, were mainly of Scottish and Scotch-Irish origin. Several branches of Presbyterianism were represented, but eventually some of them coalesced. As was true of the Anglicans, for many years assistance in clergy and money came from the British Isles, but in time self-support was achieved. The outstanding pioneer was John Dunmore Lang. Of Scottish birth and education, he came to Australia in 1823 with the express purpose of promoting Presbyterianism. Of great physical and mental vigour, an ardent advocate of the financial independence of the Church from the state, he encouraged Protestant immigration, recruited clergy from the British Isles, and fostered education.

In 1914 Methodists had about the same numbers as the Presbyterians. The first class meeting was gathered in 1812 and the pioneer missionary reached the country in 1815. Aid came from British Methodism, but in 1855 the first Australian Conference assembled and formulated a plan for the Australian Wesleyan Connexion, partly independent of the mother church.

Baptists, Congregationalists, and some other British denominations gathered churches in Australia, but were much less numerous than Roman Catholics, Anglicans, Presbyterians, or Methodists.

The aborigines were not forgotten. Under the initial impact of the white man their numbers, estimated to have been about 250,000 or 300,000 in 1788, by the fore part of the twentieth century dwindled to about 50,000 pure bloods and

25,000 mixed bloods. By 1914 they were mostly in the western and northern portions of the country, regions where white population was small. They were served by several missions, some Roman Catholic and some Protestant, some from abroad and others maintained by Australian Christians.

Long before 1914 Australian Protestants began reaching out beyond their borders to propagate their faith. They regarded themselves as having peculiar obligations to the primitive peoples in the islands to the east and north and also sent missionaries to Asia.

Here was a vigorous Christianity which was holding the immigrant, was doing much to shape the ideals, morals, and education of the new nation, and was beginning to share in the world-wide spread of the faith.

New Zealand

Much smaller in area than Australia, the group of islands known collectively as New Zealand had in 1914 only about a million people, slightly over a fourth of that of the commonwealth on its north. At the outset of the nineteenth century the population was made up of Maoris, the descendants of Polynesians who had arrived a few hundred years earlier. White immigration did not begin on a large scale until the 1840's. It was then overwhelmingly from the British Isles, with a proportionately much smaller contingent from Ireland than in Australia.

Christianity first entered New Zealand in the form of Protestant missions to the Maoris. This was at the instance of Samuel Marsden whom we have already met (Chapter 44) as one of the earliest clergymen of the Church of England in Australia. The initial party of Anglican missionaries landed in 1814. Partly at the instance of Marsden, Methodists also came. Their pioneer station was opened in 1822. The first Roman Catholic mass in New Zealand was said by a French missionary in 1838. Christianity spread rapidly, mainly through the representatives of the Church Missionary Society. The first Anglican bishop, George Augustus Selwyn, arrived in 1842. Able, devoted, with an iron physical constitution, a high churchman, he had a large share in establishing his church among the Maoris and the white settlers and in inaugurating Anglican missions in several of the island groups to the north and east of Australia. In 1854 it was said that all but about 1 per cent. of the Maoris were at least nominally Christian.

The Church Missionary Society sought to prevent the coming of white colonists, for it believed, correctly as the event proved, that it would lead to the exploitation of the Maoris and to war. In spite of its opposition, in the 1840's whites began to pour in.

White settlement was to some extent from religious motives. Edward Gibbon

Wakefield, impressed with the way in which earnestly Christian minorities had contributed to the shaping of the Thirteen Colonies which later became the United States, sought to bring similar elements into the founding of what he dreamed of as the future nation of New Zealand. He himself appears to have had little interest in religion and to have valued it simply as a means to attracting colonists of a high type. Partly through the impulse given by him in the 1850's an Anglican colony was founded around Christchurch, on the South Island. Slightly earlier, in the 1840's a similar contingent of Scottish Presbyterians, hoping to create an ideal Christian community, established a centre which they called Dunedin, an old Celtic designation of Edinburgh, at Otago, also on the South Island.

The majority of the white colonists came from other than a religious impulse. Yet in 1914 all but a small fraction of them claimed a church connexion. More than two-fifths were Anglicans. The Church of England in New Zealand owed its organization chiefly to Selwyn. He called its first synod in 1844. In 1858 he was made metropolitan and had under him four bishoprics. In 1857 a constitution was framed for the Church and the first general synod assembled in 1859. Presbyterians constituted about a fourth of the population, nearly twice their proportion in Australia. Methodists were the third largest of the denominations, and Roman Catholics, mainly of Irish stock, ranked fourth. Baptists, Congregationalists, both small in numbers, and a few other denominations were represented.

THE OTHER ISLANDS OF THE PACIFIC

It is a temptation to go at length into the nineteenth century spread of Christianity among the aboriginal populations of the many islands and groups of islands that stud the Pacific east and north of New Zealand and Australia. On each island or island cluster it had a distinct history. Deeds of heroism abounded, mass conversions were common, and often within less than a generation almost the entire island or island group became professedly Christian. However, the population total, even of all the vast expanse, was not large, and we must content ourselves with a few generalizations and three concrete thumb-nail sketches.

The generalizations must be briefly given. The larger part of the mission were by Protestants, mostly Congregational, Anglican, Methodist, and Presbyterian from the British Isles, Australia, and New Zealand. Congregationalists from the United States were prominent in Hawaii and Micronesia. The Roman Catholics were chiefly from France. The usual but not the invariable course of Christianity was the arrival of the first missionaries, initial resistance, possibly prolonged and aggravated in the native mind by unhappy memories of cruelties and exploitation by white traders, next a few conversions, then the conversion of the chief, that event followed by a mass conversion of the island, and finally the slow process of instruction to make the nominal faith actual and to build a group life which would be somewhere nearly worthy of the designation Christian. In the process the language would be reduced to writing, part or all of the Bible translated into it, school books and other literature prepared, schools inaugurated and conducted, and, on some islands, simple handicrafts taught. Often, perhaps from the first generation of Christians, some went as missionaries to distant islands, facing the perils both of the sea and of a hostile reception. Long before 1914 most of Polynesia, the eastern fringe of islands stretching from Hawaii to New Zealand, all of Micronesia, and part of Melanesia had accepted the faith. Progress was being registered in some of the larger groups of Melanesia and on the fringes of formidable New Guinea.

It will be remembered that it was on Tahiti of the Society Islands that eighteen, the chief contingent of the initial enterprise of the London Missionary Society on *The Duff,* had landed in 1796. In 1798 eleven of the eighteen, discouraged, sought haven in Australia and two others, taking native wives, were cut off by the mission. In 1808 the paramount chief of Tahiti, while in close association with the missionaries on a neighbouring island from which he had taken refuge from a rebellion, asked for baptism. This was not at once granted him, but when, in 1815, he returned to Tahiti and reëstablished his power, he toured the island urging his subjects to accept the new faith. The population complied, a printing press was set up, the Bible was translated, schools were organized, and a code of laws based on Christian ideals was promulgated by the chieftain. The faith and its associated code of laws quickly spread to others of the Society Islands.

Some of *The Duff* party were landed on the Tonga or Friendly Islands. However, within about four years three were killed, one acquired a native wife and abandoned his faith, and the others fled to Australia. Partly through interest aroused by contacts with these last, British Methodists took up the enterprise, before 1840 mass conversions had brought most of the islands into the Christian fold, and the chief of one of the islands had proclaimed a code of laws based on Christian principles.

Hawaii had been frequented by white traders for about a generation before the first missionaries arrived. Because of that contact the population had declined by more than half, the disintegration of its culture was far advanced, and a chieftain, utilizing fire-arms obtained from the traders, had brought all the islands under his rule. Then, in 1820 there landed the first group of a succession of Congregational missionaries from New England. Within twenty years the language was reduced to writing, parts of the Bible were translated, thousands were enrolled in schools, laws were enacted by the native government against prostitution, gambling, drunkenness, and the profanation of Sunday, and a mass movement brought about a sixth of the population into the membership of the Church. In 1863 the American Board of Commissioners for Foreign Missions, under which the missionaries had come, deeming that its task had been accomplished and that the churches were ready for self-government, greatly reduced its aid. In the latter part of the century the scene was complicated by an extensive immigration, most of them labourers on the plantations, a minority of them Roman Catholic Spaniards, Portuguese, and Filipinos, and the majority non-Christian Japanese, Chinese, and Koreans. Some advance was made among the Asiatics by several denominations.

Summary

In the nineteenth century Christianity became the dominant religion in the Pacific. This was chiefly through the emergence of two new nations, Australia and New Zealand, by immigration from the British Isles and through success in holding it to its hereditary faith. It was also through the conversion of a large proportion, although as yet only a minority, of the indigenous peoples.

Selected Bibliography

R. Anderson, *History of the Sandwich Islands Mission* (Boston, Congregational Publishing Co., 1870, pp. xxiv, 408). By an official of the American Board of Commissioners for Foreign Missions.

H. N. Birt, *Benedictine Pioneers in Australia* (London, Herbert & Daniel, 2 vols., 1911).

J. W. Burton, *The Call of the Pacific* (London, Charles H. Kelley, 1912, pp. xiv, 286). A study book for the churches.

W. W. Burton, *The State of Religion and Education in New South Wales* (London, J. Cross and Simpkin and Marshall, 1840, pp. vii, 321, cxxxvi). By a judge with a strong Anglican bias.

J. Cameron, *Centenary History of the Presbyterian Church in New South Wales* (Sydney, Angus and Robertson, 1905, pp. xxii, 449). An official history based on documents.

R. A. Giles, *The Constitutional History of the Australian Church* (London, Skeffington & Son, 1929, pp. 320). Scholarly.

G. Goodman, *The Church in Victoria during the Episcopate of the Right Reverend Charles Perry, First Bishop of Melbourne* (London, Seeley & Co., 1892, pp. xxiv, 476). By a clergyman who served under Perry. Quotes extensively from documents.

R. Hamilton, *A Jubilee History of the Presbyterian Church in Victoria . . . from the Foundation of the Colony to 1888* (Melbourne, M. L. Hutchinson, 1888, pp. xx, 495, xxx). Based largely on church records.

H. Jacobs, *New Zealand. Containing the Dioceses of Auckland, Christchurch, Nelson, Waiapu, Wellington, and Melanesia* (London, Society for Promoting Christian Knowledge, 1887, pp. xvi, 480). Deals chiefly with the development of the structure of the Church of England in New Zealand.

K. S. Latourette, *A History of the Expansion of Christianity. Volume V, The Great Century* A.D. *1800–1914 in the Americas, Australasia and Africa* (New York, Harper & Brothers, 1943, pp. ix, 526).

D. MacDougall, *The Conversion of the Maoris* (Philadelphia, Presbyterian Board of Publication and Sabbath-School Work, 1899, pp. viii, 216).

J. S. Needham, *White and Black in Australia* (London, Society for Promoting Christian Knowledge, 1935, pp. 174). By a former missionary among the blacks.

D. M. Stewart, *The Presbyterian Church of Victoria . . . 1859–1899* (Melbourne, D. W. Paterson & Co., pp. vi, 129). An official history.

H. W. Tucker, *Memoir of the Life and Episcopate of George Augustus Selwyn* (London, William Wells Gardner, 2 vols., 1879). Based on original sources.

W. Ullathorne, *The Catholic Mission in Australasia* (London, Keating & Brown, 3d ed., pp. 58).

F. T. Whitington, *William Grant Broughton, Bishop of Australia* (Sydney, Angus & Robertson, 1936, pp. xiv, 300).

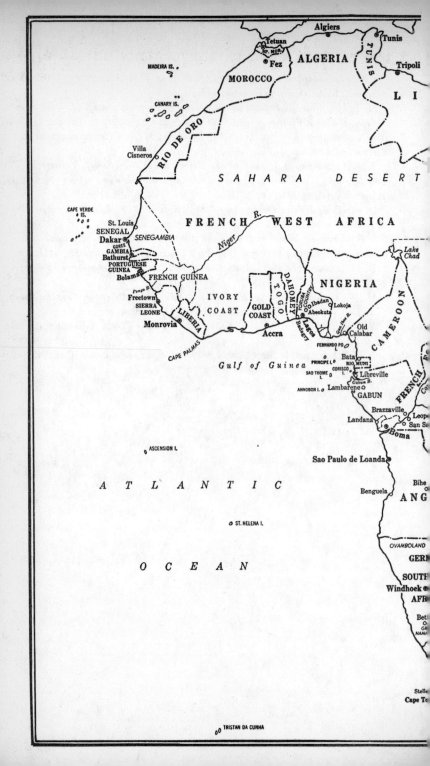

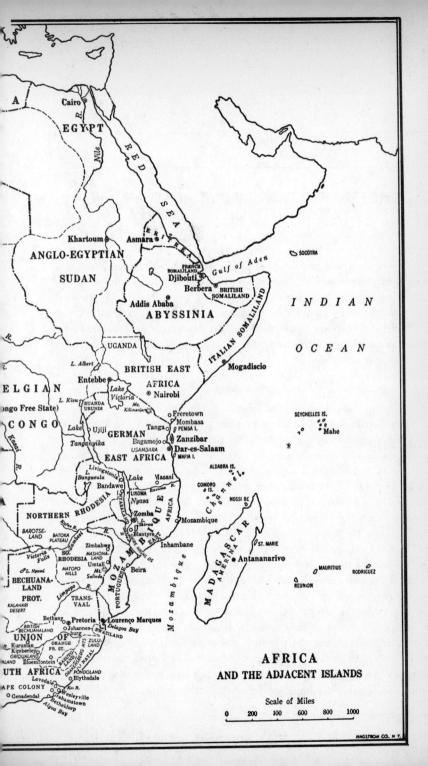

AFRICA
AND THE ADJACENT ISLANDS

Scale of Miles

0   200   400   600   800   1000

HAGSTROM CO., N.Y.

Chapter 53

THE PENETRATION OF MADAGASCAR AND AFRICA SOUTH OF THE SAHARA

From Australasia and the islands of the Pacific we move, appropriately, west-ward to Madagascar and Africa south of the Sahara. Here, too, the white man and his culture impinged upon "primitive" man; here, too, in the temperate zone extensive white immigration led to the emergence of a new nation; here, also, "primitive" cultures began to disintegrate through the infiltration of white civilization; and here Christianity had a striking advance which continued after 1914 at an accelerated pace.

MADAGASCAR

Madagascar, one of the largest islands of the world and separated from Africa by a strait which at its narrowest point is about 250 miles wide, ethnically was quite distinct from the neighbouring continent. In language and race its population, known collectively as the Malagasy, was more akin to the Malays, Polynesians, and Melanesians than to the Africans. The most active and most nearly dominant of its many tribes were the Hòva, with their home in the central plateau from 4,000 to 6,000 feet above sea level and so more conducive to vigour than the enervating tropical lowlands. At the dawn of the nine-teenth century the Malagasy and especially the Hòva were beyond the "primi-tive" stage of culture but were not yet highly civilized. Some time before 1800 the highlands had become politically united under the Hòva. In the first decade of the nineteenth century one of the Hòva chieftains began the acquisi-tion of fire-arms and through them extended his rule.

It was under this chieftain that Christianity was effectively introduced and entered on what was to be a dramatic course. It had first been brought by Roman Catholics during the sixteenth and seventeenth centuries but had not gained a firm foothold and had disappeared. The chieftain was eager to employ European methods and tools to enlarge his domains and render them more prosperous. To this end he made diplomatic and commercial overtures to the

British and encouraged the coming of teachers. He therefore showed favour to representatives of the London Missionary Society. Under him and his immediate successor the Bible and a hymn book were translated and printed, schools were opened, and a number of the Hòva were baptized. Then, from 1836 to 1861, an anti-foreign and anti-Christian reaction was led by the reigning chieftainess. The missionaries were ordered out and Christians were persecuted. Yet the faith spread and Roman Catholic missionaries entered. Late in the 1860's a new chieftainess and her leading aids were baptized, as Protestants, and Christianity began a rapid spread. Additional societies entered, some of them Protestant and some Roman Catholic. Most of the Protestants were British, with the London Missionary Society leading, and in 1868 the Madagascar Congregational Union came into being as a means towards an autonomous Malagasy church. Lutherans from Norway and the United States came. By 1890 Christians numbered about a third of a million. In 1895 France annexed the island. French officials were both anti-clerical and anti-British and for a time missions, especially those of British Protestants, found conditions adverse. French Protestants came to the rescue and took over numbers of the schools and hundreds of the congregations associated with the London Missionary Society. Additional Roman Catholic orders entered from France. By 1914 Protestants, both baptized and adherents, totalled about 400,000 and Roman Catholics over 200,000. Together the Protestant and Roman Catholic constituencies were between a fifth and a fourth of the population.

Africa South of the Sahara: The Penetration of the Interior by Europeans

In the nineteenth century Africa south of the Sahara contained the largest population of "primitive" cultures to be found anywhere on the planet. Except in a few places, largely on or near its northern borders, it had no continuing states or kingdoms. For the most part its organization was tribal. The vast majority were not only illiterate but also spoke languages which had never been given a written form. Religion was chiefly animism in one or another of its protean manifestations.

The nineteenth century witnessed the penetration of this congeries of "primitive" peoples by the white man, the partition of the land among European powers, and the beginning of a disintegration of the inherited patterns of life which was to proceed at an accelerated pace after 1914. In 1815 that penetration had only barely begun. Here and there on the coast were trading posts, most of them having the slave trade as a main cause of their existence. For three centuries vessels freighted with their tragic cargoes of involuntary emigrants had been sailing from them to provide labourers for the plantations of the New World. The "black ivory" had been obtained by the attack of one tribe on another and for every slave delivered to the white trader two or three dead were left somewhere along the tracks of the raiders. Exploration of the interior began in earnest late in the eighteenth century and was continued from the early years of the nineteenth century by numbers of intrepid adventurers. It was not completed until after 1900, but most of its startling disclosures were in the third quarter of the nineteenth century. In it several missionaries had a part. Indeed, the two most famous explorers were David Livingstone, of whom we must say more in a moment, and Henry M. Stanley who, although not a missionary, became involved in his African journeys through his successful effort to find Livingstone.

In the 1880's and 1890's earth-hungry European powers divided most of the Africa which had been revealed and by arrangement among themselves delimited the boundaries of the possessions thus acquired. At a conference in Berlin in 1884–1885 they agreed upon general principles and also set up the Congo Free State under the King of Belgium with the provision that it was to be "perpetually neutral." In the partition Great Britain, France, Portugal, and Germany obtained the major shares and in 1905 Belgium annexed the Congo Free State, thus formally making it what it had increasingly actually been, the Belgian Congo.

Exploration and the setting up of colonial regimes combined with the effects of foreign commerce and traders and the labours of missionaries to bring about the weakening of old customs and institutions. That weakening proceeded more rapidly in some areas than in others and, gathering momentum and accelerated by events after 1914, in the twentieth century became general.

Could Christianity minister to the millions of individuals thus become accessible? As the old society disappeared, partly because of the missionary impact, could Christianity help protect the Africans from the evils brought by the new day and assist in building a structure which would make for a richer life for the otherwise deracinated and often bewildered multitude?

In seeking to answer these questions we must not take the space to record in detail the spread of Christianity in Africa. That would lengthen this chapter to several volumes. All that we can attempt is to formulate a few generalizations and to deal rapidly with the course of the faith in a few sections of the continent.

THE SPREAD OF CHRISTIANITY IN AFRICA SOUTH OF THE SAHARA: INCLUSIVE GENERALIZATIONS

The main characteristics of the spread of Christianity in Africa south of the Sahara can be quickly summarized. It was seen in all the political units into which European powers had divided the region by the end of the nineteenth century, but it was more rapid in some than in others. It was more by Protestants than by Roman Catholics. In 1914 the former outnumbered the latter two to one, but by 1914 the latter were taking an increasing part and in some sections after that year were to forge ahead of the other. Both branches of the faith were represented in all the European possessions, but in general, as was to be expected, Protestants were stronger in the British territories and Roman Catholics in the French, Portuguese, and Belgian colonies. Missionaries fought slavery and the slave trade, reduced scores of languages to writing, in the tongues thus given a literary form began the preparation of Christian literature, including the translation of part or all of the Bible, inaugurated and maintained the vast majority of the schools which sought to prepare the Africans for the white man's world, were pioneers in bringing Occidental medicine to deal with the diseases of the African, sought to inculcate Christian standards of morals and, sometimes clumsily, sometimes skilfully, encouraged the Africans to adjust their inherited mores to them. Above all, they won Africans to the faith, brought them into churches, and began recruiting and training Africans to lead them, thus seeking to give Christianity permanent rootage.

THE COMPLEX STORY OF CHRISTIANITY IN SOUTH AFRICA

It was in South Africa that by 1914 Christianity made a more rapid and extensive advance than in any other part of the continent in the nineteenth century. There in that year, with the possible exception of Ethiopia (Abyssinia), Christians constituted a larger proportion of the population than in any other African country.

By 1914 there had emerged in the southern extremity of the continent, predominantly in the temperate zone, a new nation, the Union of South Africa, as a self-governing dominion within the British Empire. It presented an extraordinarily complex ethnic picture with multiple and intense cleavages and frictions along racial and national lines. The whites were the governing group, but they were in the minority, although a substantial minority, and were divided between the Boers or Afrikanders of mixed Dutch and French Huguenot ancestry and the British. Afrikander-British relations, long tense, had recently been further embittered by a war (1899-1902) after which the British, technically the victors, had sought to heal the sting and solve the problem by giving the region dominion status (1909-1910). Yet the two groups remained apart, distinct in language, religion, and, to some extent, in outlook and customs. The Africans were divided among the Bushmen, a dwindling minority, the Hottentots, also a minority, and the Bantus, consisting of many tribes and who, migrating from the North, had begun filtering into the area not far from the time of the first arrival of the whites. In addition there were what were known as the Coloured, a mixed stock, mostly at the Cape, descendants of slaves and convicts from the East, mostly Malays commingled with Hottentots and with some admixture of white blood. There was an Indian minority, chiefly in Natal. There were also several thousand Chinese.

The Afrikanders, largely rural, multiplying rapidly with their large families of children, speaking their own language, Afrikaans, from the inherited Dutch, tended to be clannish, much as were the French in another British dominion, Canada, and for the same reason. The vast majority were members of the Dutch Reformed Church in one or another of its several branches. As the French Canadians found in the Roman Catholic Church a symbol and tie of their nationality as against the ruling power and the immigrant British and abhorred the liberalism of revolutionary and post-revolutionary France, so the Afrikanders were loyal to the Dutch Reformed Church as a bond and a feature of their distinctive life and culture and that church was theologically very conservative.

Into the Dutch Reformed Church there entered a strong infusion of the Pietistic strain of the Evangelical awakening. This was chiefly through a Scot, Andrew Murray, who came to South Africa early in the nineteenth century in response to a plea, reinforced by the British governor, for clergy to meet the dearth of pastors for the Dutch churches. His sons, John and Andrew, Jr., after their education in Scotland, where they were in close touch with a revival movement, and in Utrecht, where they were members of a little circle which, reacting against eighteenth century rationalism, were symptoms of a rising tide of faith, returned to South Africa and became ministers in the Dutch Reformed Church. John Murray became prominent as a teacher in the leading theological seminary and Andrew Murray, Junior (1828–1917), became extremely influential as a pastor and as the author of devotional books which had a wide circulation not only in South Africa but also through much of that wing of world-wide Protestantism which was committed to revivals and the Evangelical movement.

The British elements entered after the occupation by their mother country during the Napoleonic Wars and the subsequent annexation. They were mainly English, Scotch, and Irish. Most of them seem to have held at least nominally to their hereditary faith. The Roman Catholics were predominantly Irish. Proportionately the Church of England was stronger among the British element than in Canada, Australia, or New Zealand, and the Presbyterians less so. As was to be expected after what we have found in the other dominions, Methodism was prominent and the Baptists and Congregationalists, the other large British denominations, were present but far behind these others in size.

The outstanding place held by the Anglicans was in part due to the leadership given by the first resident bishop, Robert Grey, who was appointed in 1847 to the See of Cape Town, was in sympathy with the Oxford movement, travelled indefatigably over his huge diocese, built churches, recruited and trained clergy, and initiated missions to non-Christians. When he died, in 1872, he was Metropolitan of the (ecclesiastical) Province of South Africa with other bishops under him.

Christianity spread rapidly among the non-Europeans of South Africa. By 1914 about 30 per cent. of that element were accounted as Christian. The proportion varied from section to section. It was highest in the Orange Free State, next highest in the Cape Province, where contact with the white man and the missionary had been longest, and lowest in Natal. The total mounted rapidly in the latter part of the century. The non-European Christians were overwhelmingly Protestant. The Dutch Reformed Church had a share in their conversion, especially after the impetus given by the younger Andrew Murray, but was not as active as the British and tended to treat them in a paternalistic fashion.

The leading pioneer in British missions to the non-Europeans was the London Missionary Society. As its first representative it sent the Dutchman, John Theodore Vanderkemp, whom we have met as the one chiefly responsible for the formation of the Netherlands Missionary Society. He died in 1811 and in 1820 there came to head the London Missionary Society's enterprise John Philip, who served until 1850. Vigorous, courageous, and characterized by marked initiative, Philip championed the cause of the Africans, fought slavery, furthered treaties with native chiefs to end the wars on the frontiers of white settlement, worked to have native states set up from which all whites except missionaries and those approved by missionaries would be excluded, and encouraged the entrance of other Protestant societies. British Methodist missionaries won more converts than the London Missionary Society, the Scottish Presbyterians specialized on Christian schools for the Africans, the Anglicans had extensive enterprises, and some other British missions came. French, Scandinavian, Swiss, and German Protestants shared in spreading the Christian faith. Americans arrived chiefly through the American Board of Commissioners for Foreign Missions and the African Methodist Episcopal Church. Roman Catholics were present but were a small minority. To these denominations of foreign origin were added a rapidly mounting number of African origin, mostly among the Bantus. Yet the multiplicity of the varieties of Christianity did not make for as much confusion as might have been expected. Some of the denominational missions were confined to particular areas. For example, the French Protestants centered their efforts on Basutoland and Barotseland, and the Hermannsburg Mission in a section of the Transvaal.

DAVID LIVINGSTONE AND WHAT ISSUED FROM HIS VISION AND LABOURS

The most famous missionary to Africa, David Livingstone (1813-1873), began his labours in South Africa but moved on to an even wider sphere and was a powerful stimulus and inspiration to the initiation of missions in several areas. A Scot of mixed Highland and Lowland descent, the son of humble and deeply religious parents, he was born in a tenement at Blantyre, a small factory community near Glasgow. He went to work in a cotton mill at the age of ten, but, avid for learning, he attended night school, read such books on science and travel as he could obtain, and, after a deep religious experience, decided to become a medical missionary to China and acquired an education in theology and medicine. With sympathies which could not be confined to any one denomination, he applied to the London Missionary Society, for its undenominational character appealed to him. Since war between Great Britain and China kept him from the land of his first choice, he went to South Africa, lured by the challenge of Robert Moffat, a missionary on the frontier in that country who said that from where he lived on any clear morning the smoke of a thousand villages could be seen where the name of Christ had never been heard. Livingstone joined Moffat and married his daughter. However, he could not long be content in any one place. The urge to travel and discovery which had been with him from boyhood, transmuted by his Christian faith, drove him to journey after journey to parts of the interior never before seen by a European. His purpose was to open the way for the Gospel, for the righting of wrongs, and the healing of social sores. He dreamed of the benefits which Western civilization could bring to Africa. He loved the Africans, dealt with them tactfully and selflessly, and won their confidence. Fearless and with an indomitable will, he drove his body, often racked and spent with fever and dysentery, to incredible exploits. A keen observer, he made voluminous records of what he saw. His Christian faith sustained him, kept him humble, and in the end mellowed the native asperity of his character. In his later years he severed his connexion with the London Missionary Society, not because he had changed his purpose, but because he believed that he could best fulfill it as an agent of the British Government.

The fame of Livingstone's journeys and his appeals led to the inauguration of a number of missions in the areas which he revealed to the European world. In a lecture at Cambridge (1857) his challenge: "Do you carry on the work which I have begun. I leave it with you," called forth (1858) the Universities'

Mission to Central Africa, an Anglican enterprise. It had as its initial goal Lake Nyasa and the valley of the river which drained it, the Shiré. What looked like disaster met its first efforts, but, establishing headquarters at Zanzibar, it gradually made its way to Lake Nyasa from the east rather than the south and expanded its activities to other areas as well. Stirred by the life and death of Livingstone, both the Free Church of Scotland and the Church of Scotland began missions in the neighbourhood of Lake Nyasa, the one with head-quarters at a station called Livingstonia and the other at a centre to which the name Blantyre was given. Through them languages were reduced to writing, numbers of schools opened, and thousands of converts gathered into churches.

Due to the impulse given by Livingstone, there arose a very important centre of Christianity in Uganda, in the highlands of equatorial Africa. Here dwelt a vigorous people, the Baganda, Bantus with an intermixture of Hamitic blood, under a ruling dynasty which may have been in power since the fifteenth century. They were first brought into effective contact with Christianity through Henry M. Stanley. Stanley, a newspaper correspondent sent by Bennett of *The New York Herald* to find Livingstone, from whom the outer world had not heard for some time, during their few days together was tremendously impressed by the intrepid traveller-missionary. After the death of Livingstone, alone in the interior to which he had given his life, Stanley felt constrained to take up the unfinished task of exploration. In 1874 he reëntered Africa on an expedition which brought him to Uganda. There he taught the principles of the Christian faith to the king of the Baganda, the half-pagan half-Moslem Mtesa, and translated part of the Bible for him. Convinced of the truth of the white man's religion by the superiority of the mechanical inventions of the Europeans and by the assertion (by that time substantially true) that, in con-trast with the Arabs, Christians did not enslave Africans, Mtesa professed him-self a Christian. Stanley gave publicity to what had transpired and called for missionaries to follow up what he had begun. To enter the opening there came, first representatives of the Church Missionary Society (1877), and then, in 1879, White Fathers despatched by their founder, Lavigerie. In spite of persecu-tion instigated by Mtesa's successor from fear that the acceptance of Christianity would be followed by annexation by some European power, both the Anglicans and the Roman Catholics had striking numerical success. In 1894, the year that Uganda became a British protectorate, a section of the country was assigned by Rome to an English society, the Mill Hill Fathers. By 1914 Christians totalled more than 200,000, about 40 per cent. of them Anglicans and about 60 per cent. Roman Catholics. Each church had an extensive system of schools and was recruiting and training an indigenous clergy.

Some Other Centres of Rapid Christian Expansion

The Congo Free State, by 1914 reconstituted as the Belgian Congo, was another area of the rapid growth of Christianity. Here, with the possible exception of Nigeria, was the largest African population of any political unit south of the Sahara. The majority were Bantus of many tribes. Into the Congo Free State, beginning in the 1870's, challenged by the information about the region given by Stanley, came many Protestant societies, some of them interdenominational "faith" missions and some denominational. They were mostly from Great Britain and the United States. Simultaneously there entered an increasing number of Roman Catholic orders. Some of these were French, such as the White Fathers, and some were German, but more and more they were Belgian. Belgian Roman Catholics, predominant in their native land, became progressively more active in missions and centered most of their attention upon this, their one colonial possession. Stressing the fact that they were Belgians as against the Protestants, who were non-Belgians, they asked, often successfully, for preferential treatment by the government. Both Protestants and Roman Catholics attracted large numbers of converts, but the latters' growth was peculiarly spectacular.

Nigeria, British-administered in the partition of Africa, appealed to the consciences of British Christians. In it, especially in the animistic South rather than in the North, for the latter was more distant from the sea and was penetrated by Islam, Presbyterians from Scotland, the Church Missionary Society, and Methodists, as well as some others from the British Isles were active. Here Samuel Adjai Crowther, rescued as a lad from a slave ship and later the first African to become an Anglican bishop, had his diocese. Southern Baptists from the United States were also represented and there were some Roman Catholics.

Summary

Long a victim of the greed of the white man, in the nineteenth century Africa south of the Sahara, penetrated partly from imperial ambition, partly from the spirit of adventure and insatiable curiosity, and partly from the motive of spreading the Christian faith, was covered, in places thinly, by a network of Christian missions. In the fore part of the century these were mostly Protestant. By the year 1914 Roman Catholics were rapidly increasing their participation. Missionaries were reducing languages to writing, translating and distributing the Bible, founding and conducting hundreds of schools, fighting the retreating remnants of slavery, and gathering Christian communities. Numerically Christianity was strongest in South Africa, where a new nation dominated by whites was emerging. There were other centres, notably Uganda, where Christians were becoming a considerable proportion of the population. The momentum given before 1914 mounted after that year and by the middle of the twentieth century a mass conversion was well under way.

Selected Bibliography

W. G. Blaikie, *The Personal Life of David Livingstone* (New York, Fleming H. Revell Co., preface 1880, pp. 508). The best popular biography.

J. Bouniol, editor, *The White Fathers and Their Missions* (London, Sands & Co., 1929, pp. 334). A popular account.

R. J. Campbell, *Livingstone* (New York, Dodd, Mead & Co., 1930, pp. x, 295). More critical than the biography by Blaikie.

J. Du Plessis, *The Evangelisation of Pagan Africa. A History of Christian Missions to the Pagan Tribes of Central Africa* (Cape Town and Johannesburg, J. C. Juta & Co., 1930, pp. xii, 408). By a competent scholar, but with few references to sources.

J. Du Plessis, *A History of Christian Missions in South Africa* (London, Longmans, Green & Co., 1911, pp. xx, 494). Well done, but with few references to the sources.

J. Du Plessis, *The Life of Andrew Murray of South Africa* (London, Marshall Brothers, 1919, pp. xvi, 553). Not only the standard biography, but also virtually a history of the Dutch Reformed Church in South Africa in the nineteenth and the early part of the twentieth century.

W. Ellis, *The Martyr Church: A Narrative of the Introduction, Progress, and Triumph of Christianity in Madagascar* (London, John Snow & Co., 1870, pp. x, 404). By one with first-hand knowledge of the events.

C. P. Groves, *The Planting of Christianity in Africa. Volume One, to 1840* (London, Lutterworth Press, 1948, pp. xiii, 330). Carefully done.

K. S. Latourette, *A History of the Expansion of Christianity. Volume V, The Great Century in the Americas, Australasia and Africa, A.D. 1800–1914* (New York, Harper & Brothers, 1943, pp. ix, 526).

J. Page, *The Black Bishop, Samuel Adjai Crowther* (New York, Fleming H. Revell Co., no date, pp. xv, 440).

J. Richter, *Geschichte der evangelischen Mission in Afrika* (Gütersloh, C. Bertelsmann, 1922, pp. 813). The standard comprehensive account of the history of Protestant missions in Africa, written with a German bias.

H. M. Stanley, *Through the Dark Continent* (New York, Harper & Brothers, 2 vols., 1878).

E. Stock, *The History of the Church Missionary Society: Its Environment, Its Men, and Its Work* (London, Church Missionary Society, 4 vols., 1899–1916). The standard history, by a secretary of the society.

A. E. Tucker, *Eighteen Years in Uganda & East Africa* (London, Edward Arnold, 2 vols., 1908). Autobiographical, by a distinguished Anglican bishop in that region.

F. D. Walker, *The Romance of the Black River. The Story of the C.M.S. Nigeria Mission* (London, Church Missionary Society, 1930, pp. xvi, 267). A popular account.

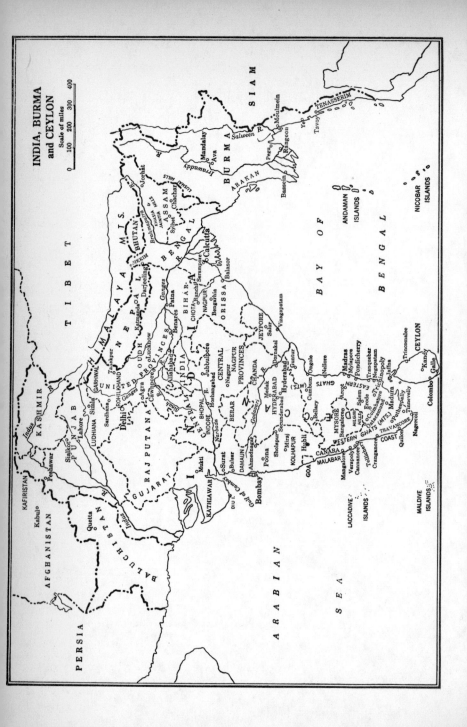

INDIA, BURMA
and CEYLON

Scale of miles

0   100 200 300 400

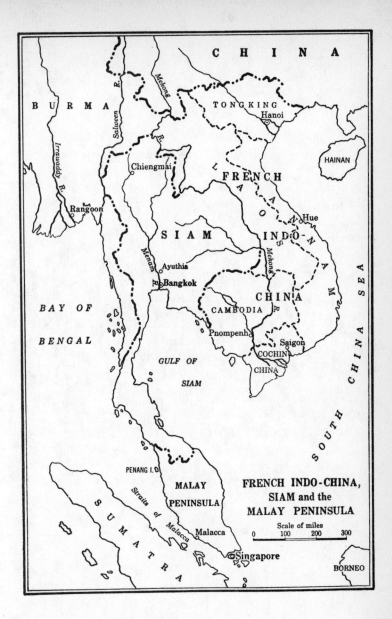

CHINA

BURMA

TONGKING

Hanoi

FRENCH

Chiengmai

HAINAN

Irrawaddy R.

Saluween R.

Mekong R.

Rangoon

Hue

SIAM

INDO-

L A O S

Menam R.

Ayuthia

Bangkok

CHINA

Mekong R.

BAY OF

CAMBODIA

Pnompenh

BENGAL

Saigon

COCHIN

GULF OF

CHINA

SIAM

SOUTH CHINA SEA

PENANG I.

MALAY

PENINSULA

FRENCH INDO-CHINA,
SIAM and the
MALAY PENINSULA

Straits of Malacca

Malacca

Scale of miles

0   100   200   300

SUMATRA

Singapore

BORNEO

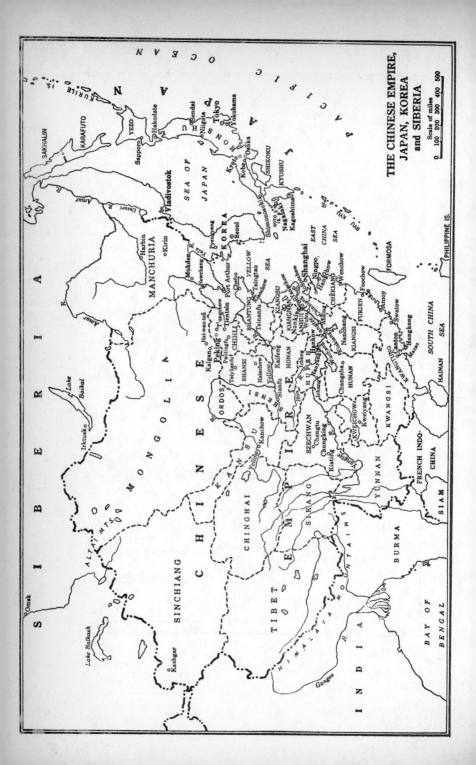

Chapter 54

THE NINETEENTH CENTURY SPREAD OF THE FAITH IN SOUTH, SOUTH-EAST, AND EAST ASIA AND THE FRINGING ISLANDS

As we move from the islands of the Pacific and Africa south of the Sahara to South, South-east, and East Asia and the fringing islands we come into a different world. We are no longer in an area of great, relatively unoccupied, salubrious lands into which peoples of European blood poured to found new nations as they did in the Americas, Australia, New Zealand, and South Africa. Nor are we where the pre-white population was prevailingly of "primitive" cultures, as in the Pacific islands which we have seen and in Africa south of the Sahara. We are, rather, in a region of teeming populations, where more than half of the earth's inhabitants were crowded into less than a fourth of the land surface of the globe and where the latter part of the nineteenth century saw the total mount rapidly and the pressure on subsistence become increasingly intense. Moreover, the region was one of ancient, high civilizations. There were also millions of "primitive" peoples, but they were in the minority and were usually dominated by their "civilized" neighbours. These civilizations were more resistant to the impact of the Occident than were the "primitive" cultures of the American Indians, the Pacific islanders, and the Africans south of the Sahara.

However, here as in these other regions the Europeans became dominant politically and their culture and their commerce effected a progressive penetration. Under the pressure cultural and political revolutions set in. They were slower in beginning than among the "primitives" with whom we have thus far had to do and for the most part were only well under way by 1914. They were to continue after that year, and with startling developments.

In these areas in the nineteenth century Christianity was almost everywhere present and the numbers of Christians were growing. Here were the large majority of the missionaries, both Roman Catholic and Protestant. However, the numerical gains were chiefly among those of "primitive" or near-"primitive" cultures. Only small minorities were gathered from the more highly civilized elements. Yet Christianity was having an increasing effect on the region and was making its impress upon the changing cultures.

Here, even more than in most of our chapters, we must be tantalizingly brief, not even mentioning some of the most radiant and heroic lives which issued from the Christian Gospel. Nor can we attempt to give to the region the space which the dimensions and importance of its populations would seem to demand. We must content ourselves with only such a condensed account as the size of the Christian communities seems to permit. We have earlier (Chapter 49) dealt with Western Asia to the borders of India and with the reaches of Asia under Russian rule. We will therefore now begin with India and move eastward.

CHRISTIANITY PENETRATES ALL INDIA

In India Christianity was confronted by what in extent and separate existence is a continent. In many ways it resembled Europe. Both India and Europe are peninsulas jutting out from the land mass of Eurasia. The great mountains which separate India from the rest of Eurasia are a much more formidable barrier than are the Urals, the range which is considered the landward border of Europe. Both regions are varied in language and race, India even more so than Europe. In both a dominant culture was associated with a religion, that of Europe with Christianity and that of India with Hinduism. Both had minority religions, but these were more numerous in India than in Europe, and in India Islam was more prominent than in Europe. Neither had ever been completely united politically under one rule, but each had seen empires which had had that as their goal.

The outstanding new feature of nineteenth century India was British rule. Beginning early in the seventeenth century through their purely commercial East India Company, as a means of protecting their persons and their trade the British had felt themselves forced to control some of the land surface of India. Having once begun to occupy territory, the British, to make secure what they held, believed themselves to be under the necessity of extending their rule to the natural borders of the country. The conquest is usually regarded as having begun in the 1750's and as having been completed in the 1850's with the suppression of what was remembered as the Mutiny, an attempt by Indian troops in the British armies to unseat their masters. With the post-Mutiny settlement Great Britain ceased to administer India through the East India Company and put the vast country directly under the crown.

The British brought in much of Western civilization. They criss-crossed the land with railways and telegraph lines, instituted a postal service, and developed a system of education in which English was the medium of instruction in the higher grades and the subjects studied were prevailingly Occidental. They built up a series of courts which administered impartial justice. They fought famine and disease and eliminated domestic war, giving India more than a generation of profound peace, the *pax Britannica.*

Yet even Great Britain did not bring all of India under one rule. In 1914 the Portuguese and French still had enclaves, albeit small ones, and a large minority of the population were governed indirectly through what were called native states, in which the historic princely families were permitted to reign under British supervision.

Some years before 1914 a movement began, chiefly under the Indian National Congress, which was to win independence for India less than a century after the completion of the British conquest.

At the dawn of the nineteenth century Christianity had been present in India continuously for many centuries. In 1815 it was represented by three main wings. There was the ancient Syrian Church, professiong to trace its origin to the Apostle Thomas, and with connexions with the Jacobites in Syria. The Roman Catholic Church had had communities in India since the closing years of the fifteenth century. The majority of the population in the Portuguese possessions, the chief of which was Goa, were of that faith, and Portugal claimed through its historic padroado, or right of patronage, the control over all Roman Catholic enterprise, including especially the naming of bishops, not only in its territories, but elsewhere in India. Many thousands of the Syrian community had long been joined to Rome as Uniates. There were some Roman Catholics outside the Portuguese territories, including those in the much less extensive French enclaves and in and around such centres of missionary activity as Madura. Protestants had been making converts in India since the beginning of the Danish-Halle mission early in the eighteenth century. However, they were much less numerous than either the Syrian Christians or the Roman Catholics.

The English East India Company had long opposed missions within its territories from the fear that by stirring up religious animosities among non-Christians they would make its rule more difficult and cut into its profits. Friends of missions had done much to relax the restrictions by writing favouring changes into the Company's charter, notably at the time of its renewal by Parliament in 1793 and 1813. Indeed, by the alterations in the latter year provision was made for the creation of an Anglican episcopate in India and what amounted to permission was obtained for missionaries to live and work in the Company's territories.

The vast majority of the Christians of all three wings of the faith were in South India. The North had scarcely been touched. Moreover, due to the adverse factors which affected Christianity in Europe in the second half of the eighteenth century, Roman Catholics were declining in morale and numbers. Their number was said to have fallen off more than half from the estimated 2,000,000 or 2,500,000 of 1700.

The nineteenth century witnessed an amazing growth of Christianity. This was achieved chiefly by the Roman Catholic Church and Protestantism. The Syrian Church did not experience much expansion, for it had long been what in effect was a caste, a closed community neither losing many to non-Christian faiths nor gaining many from them. Through revivifying contacts with Protestants, especially through the Church Missionary Society, in the nineteenth century a large minority, seeking to purify the Church, withdrew from the Syrian body and formed themselves into the Mar Thoma Church.

The Roman Catholic missionary body was greatly augmented. Some of this was by the restoration of the Jesuits and the coming of new orders and societies. Much was by the reinforcement of orders already represented. The Portuguese padroado was a chronic irritant and handicapped Rome both in providing needed episcopal jurisdiction in territories newly entered and in dealing with abuses in areas which were clearly Portuguese. Agreements between Portugal and the Holy See in the latter half of the century, while not entirely removing it, eased the tension and gave Rome a free hand in most of the country. In 1884 Rome appointed an apostolic delegate to represent it in India and in 1886 it created a hierarchy for the country. The land was divided into seven ecclesiastical provinces and various vicariates and prefectures apostolic were given the rank of bishoprics. More provision was made for the preparation of an Indian clergy. Here and there mass movements brought thousands into the Church. They were largely among hill tribes of "primitive" cultures and the depressed or outcaste classes, the lowest rung in the caste ladder. There were also conversions among the middle castes and even from the highest caste, the Brahmins. In some places missionaries undertook measures to raise the economic level of the chronically destitute Christians by coöperative stores, rice banks, industrial schools, cottage industries, and improved methods of agriculture. Tracts of land were obtained and on them Christian colonies were developed from outcaste or low caste groups. In the half century between 1861 and 1911 the total number of Roman Catholics is reported to have more than doubled, from slightly over a million to nearly two millions and a quarter.

Protestant Christianity had an even more striking increase. Its numbers were not as great. In 1914 it counted about one million baptized adherents. This, however, was an increase from only a few thousand in 1815. The advance was achieved through hundreds of missionaries. In 1914 the Protestant missionary staff totalled 5,465, which was more than that of the Roman Catholics. It came from many denominations and from the British Isles, the United States, and the Continent of Europe, especially Germany, Switzerland, and Scandinavia. The Serampore Trio, Carey, Marshman, and Ward, did some of their most notable translating of the Bible into Indian tongues after 1815, and Carey lived until 1834.

Partly with government sanction, the Anglican communion gradually developed a structure which embraced the large part of India. The foreign personnel was mostly provided and supported by organizations which depended upon members of the Church of England, among them the Church Missionary Society, the Society for the Propagation of the Gospel in Foreign Parts, the Church of England Zenana Missionary Society, and the Cambridge and Oxford Missions. Famous among its bishops was Reginald Heber (1783-1826), best remembered for such hymns as "Holy, Holy, Holy," "The Son of God Goes Forth to War," "From Greenland's Icy Mountains," and "Brightest and Best of the Sons of the Morning," and who died, deeply lamented, after less than three years in India. Notable also was the sturdy Evangelical, Daniel Wilson (1778-1858), who gave more than a quarter of a century to that country. Towards the end of the period, in 1912, an Indian, V. Z. Azariah (1874-1945), was consecrated bishop, the first of his countrymen to be given that rank by Anglicans. He proved to be an inspiring leader both in his own diocese and in world-wide Protestantism.

Next to the Roman Catholics and the Anglicans in numbers of missionaries and in the area covered was the Methodist Episcopal Church of the United States. Its outstanding pioneer in extending its lines not only in India but also to Burma and the Malay Peninsula was James Mills Thoburn (1836-1922). He was reinforced by the itinerant William Taylor (1821-1902), who through years in California soon after its annexation to the United States, then in Australia (from which he sent the eucalyptus seeds which introduced that tree to its extensive use in California) and New Zealand in the formative years of those countries, next in the British Isles, then in India, then on the west and east coasts of South America, and finally as missionary bishop in Africa, did more than any other one man to effect the broad geographic spread of American Methodism.

Most of the numerical gains of Protestantism, even more than of the Roman Catholic Church, were through mass conversions of the animistic tribes and the depressed or outcaste groups.

Protestantism's approach to India was varied. Much of it was through mass conversions, although at the outset these came almost unexpectedly. Some of it was through schools. In time these were assisted by grants-in-aid from the Government of India, not because they were Christian but because they helped the British programme of education. They ranged from village schools which to members of the depressed classes were doors of hope to a world of larger opportunity, through secondary schools, to colleges of university grade. A notable pioneer in Christian higher education was Alexander Duff (1806–1878) who, kindled by the Evangelical Awakening and Thomas Chalmers and coming to India in 1829 as the first foreign missionary of the Church of Scotland, sought to win the Brahmins and through them, presumably the natural leaders of the land, all India, by schools in which the best of Western learning, superbly taught, would be combined with an ardent Christian faith. At the Disruption he went with the Free Church of Scotland. His method became largely that of the Scottish Presbyterians and greatly influenced other Protestant missions. Protestant missions also furthered the education of women and girls. They did much for medicine, pioneered in some forms of agriculture, and cared for lepers.

Although the large majority of the Protestants were from the hill tribes and the depressed classes, numbers were won from the castes, including the Brahmins. Among the upper class converts were those who sought to acclimatize Christianity in India. Thus N. V. Tilak, a Brahmin, attempted to fuse the Christian message with the Hindu *bhakti,* religious devotion directed towards a particular deity, and composed Christian hymns after the Indian manner. Sundar Singh, from a wealthy Sikh family, a mystic, endeavoured to embody Christian ideals in the guise of a *sadhu,* or Indian holy man. There were others from the higher castes who were not so concerned to give Christianity an Indian garb, but who, each in his or her own way, were notable examples of Christian living. One of them was Pandita Ramabai (1858–1922). Of Brahmin parentage, educated by her father, a learned Hindu teacher, early orphaned and then widowed, she gave herself to her fellow-widows, became a Christian, and was led by her faith to a deeper devotion to widows, particularly those of low caste.

Christianity began to have effects outside the circles of the churches and their constituencies. Thus the Brahmo Samaj, organized in 1828 in an attempt to reform Hinduism, was clearly due to contacts with Protestant missionaries. The Ramakrishna Mission, also from within Hinduism, was founded on a Christmas Eve after the telling of the story of Jesus.

CHRISTIANITY MAKES READJUSTMENTS AND GROWS IN CEYLON UNDER BRITISH RULE

In Ceylon, separated from India by a shallow narrow strait, the dominant religion was Buddhism. The Portuguese rule of the sixteenth century had been accompanied by the planting and growth of the Roman Catholic Church. The displacing of the Portuguese by the Dutch in the seventeenth century brought Protestantism, and as we have seen, Dutch pressure led to defections from the Roman Catholic fold and the seeming prosperity of Protestantism. The British occupation during the Napoleonic Wars and the formal annexation by Great Britain were followed by the extension of British rule over the entire island. The expulsion of the Dutch and the religious toleration granted by the British led to the rapid decline of the Protestant communities. Thousands joined the Roman Catholics, presumably because of an hereditary attachment, and other thousands returned to their ancestral Buddhism and Hinduism.

Then were seen recovery and advance. Scores of missionaries from Europe furthered the Roman Catholic cause and in 1911 the census showed 339,300 of that faith as against a count of 66,830 in 1806. Protestant missionaries came, mostly British Baptists, Methodists, and Anglicans, but also a few American Congregationalists. Protestantism was not as strong numerically as in Dutch days, but it was in a much healthier condition. In 1911 the government census showed Christians to be more than one-tenth of the population of the island, a much larger proportion than in India and than in any country in South-east or East Asia or its fringing islands except the Philippines.

Burma

In Burma the dominant group, the Burmese proper, were solidly Buddhist. The country also contained several other peoples, largely animistic in religion. The numerically strongest of these were the Karens. British rule was extended over the country in three successive wars, in 1824–1826, 1852, and 1885. At the outset of the century there were almost no Christians, and such few as existed were Roman Catholics.

The nineteenth century saw a rapid growth of Christianity. Most of it was among the Karens and was chiefly through American Baptists, with Adoniram Judson (1788–1850), whom we have already met (Chapter 44), as the great pioneer. Some other Protestant groups were represented, and also Roman Catholics.

The Malay Peninsula and Singapore

Jutting out between Burma and Siam, athwart the sea lanes between India and the Far East, is the Malay Peninsula, its tip the southernmost point of Asia. Successive waves of seafarers from the West had seized points along its coast— the Arabs, from whom came the Islam which was dominant from the fifteenth century onward, then the Portuguese, who left a small deposit of Roman Catholicism, next the Dutch, and finally, during the Napoleonic Wars, the British. The British built Singapore and in the course of the nineteenth century extended their control over all the lower part of the peninsula. Chinese and Indians came, attracted by the economic opportunities. Eventually there were far more Chinese than Indians. It was among these two peoples that Christianity achieved such gains as it registered. Almost no converts were made from the Malays who constituted the majority of the population, for they were solidly Moslem. Both Roman Catholicism and Protestantism were propagated, the latter mainly by Anglicans and American Methodists, and substantial Christian minorities were gathered.

Siam (Thailand)

Siam, or Thailand, to give it its alternative name, maintained its political independence. It was more solidly Buddhist than the neighbouring Burma, with a much smaller percentage of animistic folk. It was probably for these reasons that Christianity made much less progress than in Burma. The Roman Catholic wing of the faith continued to be represented by the Society of Foreign Missions of Paris, as it had been since the seventeenh century, but in 1912, even after some accessions in the preceding century, it counted only about 36,000 adherents. Protestantism entered in the fore part of the nineteenth century and was spread mainly by American Presbyterians. Numerically it was weaker than Roman Catholicism.

Striking Growth in Indo-China

The story was far otherwise in what was collectively known as Indo-China, made up of Cambodia, Cochin-China, Tonkin, Annam, and Laos. Here the French gradually extended their rule, beginning with footholds in the South in 1787.

Before 1914 the spread of Christianity was almost entirely through the Roman Catholic Church. At the dawn of the nineteenth century this was chiefly by the Society of Foreign Missions of Paris, the Spanish Dominicans, and a large body of native priests. Christians then were said to number 310,000. The first two-thirds of the nineteenth century were punctuated by recurring persecutions, with the execution of hundreds of priests and catechists and of thousands of lay Christians. In spite of persecution the faith continued to thrive and in the intervals of peace had a rapid growth. France made the persecutions the excuse for extending her rule and with the completion of the conquest in the last quarter of the century they virtually stopped. Under these favouring conditions Christians multiplied and in 1914 totalled slightly less than a million. Many were gathered into villages which were purely of their faith and, thanks to the tutelage of the missionaries and the native clergy, were generally more prosperous than their non-Christian neighbours.

THE SPREAD OF THE FAITH IN THE EAST INDIES

South and east of Asia stretched the vast congeries of islands, large and small, known collectively to nineteenth century Europeans as the East Indies. As we have reminded ourselves (Chapter 41), the inhabitants were predominantly of one or another variety of Malay stock and language. In the course of the millenniums several waves of culture had flooded in, each leaving a deposit of religion. Hinduism and Buddhism had once been dominant and in the nineteenth and twentieth centuries one of the smaller islands, Bali, was still Hindu. Islam had arrived, borne by the Arabs, and had become the religion of the majority. As we have also noted (Chapter 41), in the sixteenth century the Portuguese had brought Roman Catholic Christianity. In the nineteenth century it persisted in the small areas which remained to that people in the Little Sunda Islands. In the seventeenth century Protestantism had been introduced by the Dutch. Under Dutch auspices a state church of the Reformed faith had arisen and had attracted substantial numbers, chiefly on the smaller islands. In 1815 it counted between 65,000 and 200,000 members.

In the nineteenth century the Dutch extended their rule over almost all the archipelago. The exceptions were the British territories on the north-eastern coasts of Borneo and the Portuguese section, now confined to the eastern part of Timor.

With the expansion of Dutch rule missionary activity increased. Most of it was Protestant and by Dutch societies. Some Protestant missions were German. The Dutch missions were the fruitage of the religious awakenings of the nineteenth century and of the sense of responsibility which issued from them for the welfare of the peoples of this largest of the Dutch colonial possessions. The state church, the so-called Protestant Church of the East Indies, also grew. Roman Catholic missions revived, in part from the Netherlands and in part from Germany, and by 1914 were mounting.

The main gains of Christianity were among the animists. They were chiefly in the island of Celebes, notably the northern peninsula, Minahassa, where a mass movement into the state church occurred, and from the Bataks, a vigorous folk in Sumatra among whom the Rhenish Missionary Society had an extensive enterprise. A few thousand Moslems were won, chiefly on the most populous of the islands, Java. By 1914 there were over a half million baptized Protestants in the Dutch portions of the East Indies. To these must be added those in the British portions of Borneo, the fruits of British missions, and the Roman Catholics.

The results of Christianity were striking, not only numerically, but also in other ways. Scores of languages were reduced to writing and the beginnings of a Christian literature were made in them. Hundreds of schools were begun. Medical care was given. The status of women was improved. Due to the pressure on the Dutch Government of the Christian conscience, organized into parties and led by Abraham Kuyper, whom we have previously met (Chapter 47), much of the earlier exploitation of the inhabitants through what was known as the "culture" system was reduced and what was called the "ethical policy" was adopted. More significant still, churches were growing with an increasing number of indigenous leaders.

Drastic Changes in the Philippines

As we have seen, in the Philippines under Spanish rule the majority of the population became Roman Catholics. The non-Christians consisted of animists, mostly in the mountains, the immigrant Chinese minorities, and the large Moslem contingent, the Moros, in the South. Until the coming of the Americans the islands were, in general, tranquilly somnolent, only slightly disturbed by outside currents until the eve of the American conquest.

Occupation by the United States (1898) was quickly followed by marked changes. The American educational system was introduced and beginnings were made in training the Filipinos in the kind of democratic political life and institutions which were standard in the United States.

Marked stirrings of religious life were seen. Protestantism was introduced by missionaries from the United States and made rapid strides, chiefly among the nominally Roman Catholic elements. As a phase of the nationalist movement which had arisen in the 1890's, the Independent Catholic Church of the Philippines, or the Filipino Independent Church, came into being as a secession from the Roman Catholic Church. All the Roman Catholic bishops and most of the leading Roman Catholic clergy had been Spaniards. Many Filipinos wished Rome to appoint Filipino bishops. Since Rome would not assent, hundreds of thousands broke away. A Roman Catholic Filipino priest, Aglipay, was elected archbishop and several other Filipino priests were elected bishops. Through the influence of a Filipino who had been in touch with liberal thought in Europe, the new church sought fellowship with the Unitarians. However, the civil courts denied it the possession of the church buildings which it had sought to take over from the Roman Catholics and it experienced difficulty in obtaining an able, educated clergy.

Faced with Protestantism, the Aglipay secession, and disestablishment, the Vatican took drastic measures. Numbers of priests came from the United States, American Archbishops of Manila were appointed, several Filipino priests were raised to the episcopate, hundreds of the more obnoxious Spanish friars who had battened off the land left, not to return, and the effort was made to provide better training for candidates for the priesthood. Some of the irritation against the landlordism of the friars was removed by the purchase by the civil government of over 400,000 acres of the land held by the orders. Several non-Spanish European orders sent missionaries. Fresh reinforcements arrived from Spain. Existing Roman Catholic schools altered their courses of study to meet the new conditions and new schools were begun.

By these several measures the Christianity of what was still the only predominantly Christian people in the Far East was reinvigorated.

The Renewed Penetration of China by Christianity

In the year 1815 the outlook for Christianity in the Chinese Empire seemed very bleak. That realm, the most populous of any on the globe, was all but hermetically sealed against the foreigner. The Portuguese retained a slight toe-hold at Macao, near Canton. The Russians were permitted a tenuous semi-political, semi-ecclesiastical mission in Peking. Western merchants were allowed a strictly limited commerce through one port, Canton, and in that port were confined to a narrow strip of land, the "Thirteen Factories," along the river. Diplomatic and even consular relations on terms of equality were not permitted, nor was travel within the empire possible for foreigners. A few Roman Catholic communities continued, the fruits of heroic missions of earlier, less adverse days. Roman Catholics may have totalled 200,000, and were widely scattered. They were served surreptitiously by a few Chinese and still fewer foreign priests. In Canton the sole Protestant missionary, Robert Morrison, maintained a precarious residence as a translator for the East India Company, devoting himself chiefly to the preparation of Christian literature. The one colleague sent him before 1815 was compelled to leave China and sought contacts with the Chinese through their overseas emigrants in the British-owned Malacca.

China's doors were forced open by the Western world, led at first by the major commercial power of the nineteenth century, Great Britain. However, not until late in the century did Chinese culture really begin to crumble. Then the revolution set in which continued to mount and in the middle of the twentieth century seemed to be still far from completed. The main successive stages of the impact can be quickly described, together with such of their features as made for the spread of Christianity.

First was a war from 1839 to 1842 through which the British sought to obtain larger commercial privileges and consular relations based upon equal status with the Chinese officials. Unfortunately for the good name of Great Britain it was precipitated by British resistance to the efforts of the Chinese Government to prevent the importation of opium, the chief commodity in British sales to China. By the ensuing treaty, a treaty which was supplemented by ones with the United States and some other Western powers, five ports were opened to foreign residence, the island of Hongkong was ceded to Britain, foreigners were accorded extraterritorial status, a fixed tariff was scheduled, and official intercourse was based on the principle of equality. Following these treaties, in the 1840's the Chinese Government granted toleration to Christianity, but forbade missionaries to propagate it outside the five treaty ports. The Chinese viewed the treaties as conceding too much, the foreigners as granting too little.

An uneasy truce was succeeded, in 1856–1860, by a second war in which the French joined the British. The treaties which followed, most of them signed in 1858, opened additional ports to foreign trade and residence, provided for the establishment of legations of the powers in the capital, Peking, permitted foreigners to travel anywhere in the Empire, assured missionaries the right to propagate their faith, and promised protection to both missionaries and Chinese Christians in the practice of their faith. Then came nearly a generation of penetration by missionaries and other foreigners but with no basic changes in the inherited structure of Chinese life.

In 1894–1895 a war with Japan in which China was defeated and forced to cede Formosa to the victor and to acknowledge the independence of Korea was followed in the late 1890's by the acquisition of leaseholds, spheres of influence, and concessions for the building of railways which seemed to presage the partition of China among Western powers; by attempts, in 1898, at reforms and changes which would enable China to escape her doom; by the Boxer movement in 1900 which sought to expel the foreigner and which was suppressed by foreign troops and climaxed by punitive measures and the stationing of foreign troops in Peking and Tientsin to guard the legations; and by a war between Russia and Japan in 1904–1905 which, to the humiliation of the Chinese, was mostly fought on their soil while they stood by, helpless.

As a result, in an attempt to preserve their political independence the Chinese sacrificed their cultural independence. In 1905 the civil service examinations were abolished which had been based upon the Confucian Classics and through which the civil bureaucracy had been recruited. Simultaneously drastic changes were made in the educational system which demoted Confucian literature from its historic supremacy and introduced Western subjects. In 1911–1912 the Confucian monarchy was swept aside and China entered upon the experiment of a republic made perilous by her complete lack of experience with it and by the vast dimensions of the country. Confucianism, long the basis of Chinese life, was fatally weakened and a fundamental revolution in Chinese life and institutions began.

Under these circumstances, could Christianity be so effectively presented that it would be built into the warp and woof of the new China which was emerging? By the year 1914 great strides were made by both Roman Catholic and Protestant Christianity and it seemed that the answer would be in the affirmative.

The body of Roman Catholic missionaries was progressively augmented. The staffs of orders and societies already present were greatly enlarged and new orders and congregations entered. They were almost entirely from the Continent of Europe. The French led, especially through the Society of Foreign Missions of Paris, but Germans, Italians, Spaniards, and some others were also represented. In 1914 the total foreign staff was not far from 2,500. Roman Catholic missionaries placed their chief emphasis upon winning converts and building the Church. In this they persisted in spite of chronic persecutions and a tragic loss of life through the Boxer madness. In 1912 the total number of Roman Catholics was reported to be 1,431,258, approximately a seven-fold increase in a hundred years. That the Church was taking root was seen in the growing numbers of Chinese who were entering the priesthood or becoming lay brothers or sisters, and the many organizations of Chinese Christians which were springing up. In addition to building the Church, the Roman Catholics had schools, although not as many in the middle and higher grades as Protestants, they engaged in famine relief, maintained many orphanages and homes for the aged, and in Inner Mongolia had Christian colonies on lands owned by the mission.

Protestants increased their missionary staffs even more rapidly. In 1914 the total was said to be 5,462. The missionaries were from scores of societies and many denominations. In 1895 about two-thirds were from the British Isles, approximately one-third were from the United States, and between two and three per cent. were from the Continent of Europe. In 1914 about half were from the United States, about two-fifths from the British Isles, and nearly one-tenth from the Continent of Europe. The organization having the largest number of missionaries was the China Inland Mission. It was begun in 1865 by J. Hudson Taylor. Conservative theologically after the Evangelical pattern, it accepted "willing, skilful workers" regardless of their denominational affiliation. As its name indicates, it sought to reach the regions untouched by other Protestant missions. It promised no fixed salaries but distributed among its members what came in. It was adamantly opposed to going into debt and it never directly solicited gifts. It depended on prayer for recruits and funds, and such Biblical words as *Ebenezer* and *Jehovah Jireh,* carrying the assurance, "hitherto hath the Lord helped us" and "the Lord will provide," were prominent. In 1914 it had over 1,000 missionaries on its rolls.

Protestant converts rapidly increased. In 1914 communicants totalled over

250,000 and the baptized more than a third of a million. While these figures were much less than those of Roman Catholics, they represented a larger proportional increase.

Protestants adopted a wide variety of methods and sought to make the Gospel effective in many different although not unrelated ways. As did the Roman Catholics, they endeavoured to found and nourish churches. In contrast with the Roman Catholic Church, these were not knit into one ecclesiastical structure, but until after 1914 even the Roman Catholics had little sense of cohesion except through distant Rome, and, as we are to see in the next chapter, in China as in some other areas where Protestantism was being newly planted, coöperation among Protestants was increasing. Protestants also had as an aim familiarizing all Chinese with the Gospel. That was the major purpose of the China Inland Mission and it was shared by other groups. Towards it contributed not only personal contacts and preaching in streets and in halls open to the street, but also the preparation and widespread distribution of literature, especially of translations of the Bible. Millions of copies of portions of the Scriptures were circulated. Protestants founded most of the best secondary and higher schools through which before 1914 the Western learning desired by the Chinese in the two decades before that year could be obtained without leaving the country. They pioneered in the introduction of Western medicine, in public health education, and in the creation of medical and nursing professions which would apply the rapidly advancing medical skills of the Occident. They led in the care of the insane and the blind. They engaged in famine relief. They sought to prevent famines by introducing or developing improved methods of agriculture and forestry, ways of fighting plant and animal diseases, and increasing the yields of grains and fruits. Largely under the leadership of Timothy Richard (1832-1919) through the Christian Literature Society, in the 1890's and the early 1900's they provided literature by which the Chinese could learn of the history and institutions of the Occident. In other words, through many channels they were striving to prepare the Chinese for the vast changes which were inevitable and to make the impact of the Occident a blessing and not a curse to the millions of that great realm.

In its early days in China Protestantism shared in the responsibility for a tragic uprising. It centered around a leader who had received Christian instruction through Protestant literature and a Protestant missionary. It took over some features of Christianity, but its resemblance was only superficial. It sought to displace the reigning dynasty with its own, which it designated hopefully T'ai P'ing, "Great Peace." It was also a revolt of the underprivileged masses and in some respects was the abortive first stage of the revolution which in the twentieth century swept away the old order. It first clashed with the existing government in 1848 and was not finally suppressed until 1865. In the intervening years it laid waste much of the lower Yangtze Valley.

CHRISTIANITY IN HELPLESS AND UNHAPPY KOREA

By geographic position Korea was foredoomed to the unhappy role of being a bone of contention among powerful neighbours. A peninsula commanding the sea approaches to North China, Manchuria, much of Japan, and Eastern Siberia, China, Japan, and latterly Russia sought either to dominate it or to prevent it from falling into the hands of one of the others. From time to time across the centuries China had controlled part or all of Korea. Japan had intermittently possessed footholds in the South and on one occasion had overrun all the country. At the dawn of the nineteenth century Korea was tributary to China and had drawn much of its culture from that empire. In the 1870's Japan began to take a renewed interest in the peninsula. In the 1880's Korea reluctantly opened its doors to the Occident and entered into treaty relations with Western powers. In 1894 China and Japan went to war over the question of the control of the country. China was defeated and eliminated. Then Russia entered the scene as the chief rival of Japan. The result was the Russo-Japanese War of 1904–1905, the defeat of Russia, and the annexation of Korea by Japan (1910).

Christianity appears first to have been introduced to Korea in the 1590's in connexion with the Japanese invasion, carried by Christians in the Japanese army. It seems to have made no converts among the Koreans and to have vanished with the evacuation of the Japanese forces.

It was not until 1784 that Christianity began a continuing life in the land. Late in 1783 a Korean in the annual embassy to Peking, one of a circle who since the preceding decade had been studying Christian books prepared by Roman Catholic missionaries in China, sought out Roman Catholic missionaries in the Chinese capital. He asked baptism and was given it. Returning to Korea in the spring of 1784, he won converts, largely in scholarly and official circles. Persecution soon followed. In the course of the next ninety years several priests, Chinese and Europeans, made their way into the country, but they were either executed or driven out. Yet the faith persisted, and that in spite of recurring persecutions, the last severe one in 1866, which took toll of thousands of lives.

After treaty relations were established with Western powers serious persecution ceased for over a generation. Roman Catholic missionaries increased, all of them from the Continent of Europe and most of them from France. Converts multiplied and candidates for the priesthood were recruited and trained.

It was in the 1870's that Protestant missionaries began to have some touch with Koreans through Manchuria, but it was not until the 1880's that they established continuous residence in the country. The first to do so were Presbyterians and Methodists from the United States and it was through these American denominations that Protestantism had its chief growth. By 1914 Protestants outnumbered Roman Catholics, both in missionary staffs and in converts. The increase of converts was striking after 1894 and particularly so between 1906 and 1910. Among the reasons for the Protestant growth was the early adoption of the principles of insisting on early self-support, of encouraging each Christian to seek to win his neighbours, of setting aside some Christians, as the churches were prepared to support them, for spreading the faith, and of church structures in Korean style built only as the Koreans paid for them. Many Bible classes were developed to train the laity to share in the propagation of the faith.

THE RE-INTRODUCTION OF CHRISTIANITY TO JAPAN

We have seen (Chapter 41) how Christianity was introduced to Japan in the sixteenth century, made rapid headway, and then, early in the seventeenth century, was proscribed and driven underground. We have also noted that, to keep the empire uncontaminated by Christianity, Japan's rulers closed the country against all contacts with the Western world except for a strictly limited and tightly regulated trade with the Dutch through one port, Nagasaki. Edict boards denouncing Christianity were posted throughout the realm, but several thousand Christians, mostly in the island of Kyushu, transmitted their faith in secret from generation to generation, maintained baptism, the one sacrament which could be administered by lay folk, and, without priests, continued their prayers.

Until the 1850's Japan remained all but hermetically sealed against the Western world and rebuffed several attempts to induce her to alter her policy. After the beginning of the opening of China and the rapid increase of Occidental commerce and shipping in the Pacific, Japan could scarcely expect to maintain her isolation. It was in 1853 that at the insistent invitation of the United States through Commodore Perry her doors became slightly ajar. Later in that decade she entered into her first commercial treaties, the initial one with the United States. In the 1860's there began the rapid adoption of much of Occidental institutions, culture, and industrial methods. It continued at a mounting pace throughout the rest of the century.

Some of the basic traditions and institutions of the past were strengthened rather than weakened, notably the reverence paid to the emperor, the nourishing of patriotism through the state cult, Shinto, and the prominence of the military. Buddhism persisted, more vigorous than in China or Korea, and many Shinto cults flourished.

Yet great innovations were made. The prevailing feudalism was abolished, telegraph lines, railways, and a commercial marine were built, industrialism was begun, an army and navy were created on Western models, codes of law and law courts inspired by the Occident were brought into being, a constitution with a diet or parliament and a cabinet was framed and put into force, and an educational system of a Western type was developed based upon universal, compulsory primary education and culminating in universities. Population was mounting and the standard of living was rising. Hard work, intelligence, and intense national pride and ambition were outstanding characteristics. By 1914 Japan was on the way to becoming one of the major world powers.

It was into this changing yet conservative Japan that, in the late 1850's, Christianity was re-introduced. It came, almost simultaneously, through the Roman Catholic Church, the Russian Orthodox Church, and various forms of Protestantism. At the outset progress was slow, for the old distrust and hostility survived, and it was only in 1873 that the anti-Christian edict boards throughout the realm were ordered removed. Fairly rapid increase in the Christian communities was seen in the 1870's, and in the 1880's the growth was so startling that some among the missionaries and their supporters were hoping that a mass conversion would soon sweep the nation into the Christian fold. In the 1890's a reaction occurred and gains were much slower. They again became marked after 1900, but not as much so as in the 1880's.

The Roman Catholic missionaries were mostly from France, Spain, and Germany and were of several orders and societies, including those, the Jesuits, Dominicans, and Franciscans, which had had the major part in planting the faith in the sixteenth and seventeenth centuries. In the 1860's the hidden surviving Christian communities were uncovered. The government renewed its persecution, although not in so severe a form as in the seventeenth century, and discontinued it only because of pressure from the Western powers. Many of the hidden Christians resumed their ancestral connexion with the Roman Catholic Church. Several thousand did not do so but, cherishing the variations which had developed during the centuries, maintained an existence separate from any form of Christianity from the West. In 1912 Roman Catholics are said to have totalled 66,134, most of them from the humbler walks of life.

The Russian Orthodox Church came in as a phase of the eastward movement of the Russian Empire, for in the latter part of the nineteenth century the tsars were extending their domains on and near the Pacific at the expense of the Chinese Empire and were threatening Japan. However, the planting and growth of the Russian mission were due primarily to one man, Ivan Kasatkin, better known as Nicolai. Coming in 1861 as a chaplain to the Russian consulate at Hakodate in the northern island, Hokkaido, at first he only slowly won converts. As they increased, he moved his headquarters to Tokyo. He received substantial financial aid and some personnel from Russia. He was made successively bishop and archbishop and at the time of his death, 1912, more than 30,000 were of his faith. Here was numerically the most successful mission of the Russian Orthodox Church among non-Christians outside the Russian Empire.

Of the three main branches of Christianity it was Protestantism that had the most extensive growth in Japan and which exerted the greatest influence. In 1913 the membership of Protestant churches was 102,790, or more than that of the combined totals of the Roman Catholics and Russian Orthodox. Nor was that figure a true measure of the extent of Protestantism. There were an undetermined number who thought of themselves as Christians and had become such through Protestants, but who had no formal church connexion. Many of them arose from the lectures, Bible-teaching, and writings of Kanso Uchimura (1861-1930) who, earnestly Christian, out of conviction did not associate himself with any ecclesiastical body. The Protestant missionaries were overwhelmingly although not entirely from the United States. Many denominations were represented, but the largest were the Congregationalists, Presbyterians, Methodists, and Anglicans. Protestantism was mostly urban. It was recruited mainly from the professional and middle classes and numbers of its leaders were from the *samurai,* what might be called the knightly class or minor aristocracy of the feudal hierarchy which had controlled the country before the formal abolition of feudalism in the 1870's. Many Japanese Protestants early wished their churches to be independent financially and administratively of the foreigners. For instance, he who is best known as Joseph Hardy Neesima (1843-1890), a radiant, devoted spirit of *samurai* stock, educated in America, had as his major achievement the founding of the Doshisha, a Christian university in the ancient capital, Kyoto, a stronghold of conservatism, and while welcoming in it foreign funds and personnel, insisted that it be controlled by Japanese. Protestantism approached Japan from several angles, but it stressed education and most of its more prominent leaders came into the faith through contacts with teachers, either in mission or government schools.

Rapid though the growth of Christianity was, in 1914 missionaries had been continuously in the country only slightly more than a half century. While Christians, and especially Protestant Christians, were more influential in the nation's life than their numbers would have led the casual observer to expect, in 1914 less than one in two hundred were of that faith.

Summary

By the year 1914 Christianity had come full circle about the globe. By moving westward it had been firmly planted on the west coast of the Americas and in some of the islands of the Pacific. Carried chiefly from the British Isles and Western Europe, it had been equally well established in Australia, New Zealand, and South Africa. Entering from both directions, namely, from the British Isles and Western Europe on the one hand and from the Americas on the other, it had expanded its existing footholds and established new ones in the islands of the Pacific, Africa south of the Sahara, and the south and east of Asia and the fringing islands. This was almost entirely through Roman Catholics and Protestants, in proportion to the situation at the outset of the century more by the latter than the former. In most of Asia and Africa Christianity was only beginning to take root and was dependent on personnel and funds from the Occident. Moreover, in South, South-east, and East Asia and the fringing islands, with the exception of Ceylon, Indo-China, some of the East Indies, and the Philippines, Christians were still very small minorities, constituting not more than 1 per cent. of the population and usually less. In several lands even these gains had been made chiefly not from the ruling groups, but from the lowest rungs of the social scale, from those of animistic or near-animistic faith. Striking though the advances had been, most of them were very recent, mainly in the second half of the century. In 1914 they were on the momentum of a rising tide, but it was not yet clear whether they would be permanent. Christianity was much stronger in Africa south of the Sahara, South, South-east, and East Asia and the neighbouring islands than it had ever been, but the historian remembered that it had twice before vanished from the most populous of these lands, China, and had all but been extinguished in Japan. He might well find himself wondering whether it would again disappear. That was one of the questions which he was to pose to the twentieth century. As we are soon to see, the gains continued in that century and in every land the faith put down deeper roots and more and more had indigenous leadership. However, as old adversaries weakened, new ones emerged and in the middle of the twentieth century in most lands the position of Christianity was still precarious. Yet we need to remind ourselves that this had been the condition of the faith since its beginning, from the days of the lowly birth in a manger in Bethlehem and the crucifixion in Jerusalem.

SELECTED BIBLIOGRAPHY

M. Broomhall, *The Jubilee Story of the China Inland Mission* (London, Morgan & Scott, 1915, pp. xvi, 386). An official history, well written.

The Capuchin Mission Unit, Cumberland, Maryland, *India and Its Missions* (New York, The Macmillan Co., 1923, pp. xxi, 315). A useful survey of Roman Catholic missions in India, for the most part based on excellent authorities.

O. Cary, *A History of Christianity in Japan* (New York, Fleming H. Revell Co.,

2 vols., 1907). The standard account in English, especially of Protestant missions. The first volume is on Roman Catholic and Russian Orthodox missions, the second on Protestant missions. The author, a Protestant, attempts to be objective.

E. R. Clough, *Social Christianity in the Orient. The Story of a Man, a Mission and a Movement* (New York, The Macmillan Co., 1914, pp. xiii, 409). Important for the light shed on one of the early mass movements to Christianity in India.

J. N. Farquhar, *Modern Religious Movements in India* (New York, The Macmillan Co., 1915, pp. xv, 471). A standard work, valuable for what it says of the influence of Christianity on other faiths.

G. G. Findlay and W. W. Holdsworth, *The History of the Wesleyan Methodist Missionary Society* (London, The Epworth Press, 5 vols., 1921–1924). An official history, based largely on the manuscript records of the society.

W. J. Hail, *Tsêng Kuo-fan and the Taiping Rebellion* (Yale University Press, 1927, pp. xvii, 422). A standard account, carefully done.

M. H. Harper, *The Methodist Episcopal Church in India. A Study of Ecclesiastical Organization and Administration* (Lucknow, The Lucknow Publishing House, 1936, pp. vii, 222). A doctoral dissertation at the University of Chicago, by a Methodist missionary.

R. L. Howard, *Baptists in Burma* (Philadelphia, The Judson Press, 1931, pp. 168). By a former missionary in Burma.

D. J. B. Kuruppu, *The Catholic Church in Ceylon. A Brief Account of Its History and Progress* (Colombo, "The Messenger" Press, 1923, pp. 24).

K. S. Latourette, *A History of Christian Missions in China* (New York, The Macmillan Co., 1929, pp. xii, 930). Comprehensive.

K. S. Latourette, *A History of the Expansion of Christianity. Volume VI, The Great Century in Northern Africa and Asia, A.D. 1800–1914* (New York, Harper & Brothers, 1944, pp. vii, 502).

A. Launay, *Histoire Générale de la Société des Missions-Étrangères* (Paris, Pierre Tequi, 3 vols., 1894). By a member of the society. Based on the archives.

G. B. McFarland, editor, *Historical Sketch of Protestant Missions in Siam 1828–1928* (Bangkok Times Press, 1928, pp. xvii, 386).

F. Marnas, *La "Religion de Jésus" (Iaso Ja-kyō) Ressuscitée au Japon dans la Seconde Moitié de XIX e Siècle* (Paris, Delhomme et Briquet, 2 vols., c.1897).

L. G. Paik, *The History of Protestant Missions in Korea 1832–1910* (Pyeng Yang, Union Christian College Press, 1929, pp. v, 438, xiii). A Yale doctoral dissertation, carefully documented.

J. W. Pickett, *Christian Mass Movements in India. A Study with Recommendations* (New York and Nashville, Abingdon-Cokesbury Press, 1933, pp. 382). Based upon prolonged, objective study.

J. Rauws, H. Kraemer, F. J. F. Van Hasselt, and N. A. C. Slotemaker de Bruine, *The Netherlands Indies* (London, World Dominion Press, 1935, pp. 186). A survey and study of missions in the Netherlands Indies, by experts.

J. Richter, *Indische Missionsgeschichte* (Gütersloh, C. Bertelsmann, 2d ed., 1924, pp. vi, 570). The standard history of Protestant missions in India. There is an English translation of an earlier edition.

J. Richter, *Die evangelische Mission in Fern- und Südost-Asien, Australien, Amerika* (Gütersloh, C. Bertelsmann, 1932, pp. xii, 488). Readable. Few references to sources, but occasional bibliographies.

J. Richter, *Die evangelische Mission in Niederländisch-Indien* (Gütersloh, C. Bertelsmann, 1931, pp. 167). The only general history, except in Dutch, of missions in the Netherlands Indies.

J. Richter, *Das Werden der christlichen Kirche in China* (Gütersloh, C. Bertelsmann, 1928, pp. xvi, 584). A readable and comprehensive account, chiefly of Protestantism.

J. Schmidlin, translated from the German, with additions and modifications by M. Braun, *Catholic Mission History* (Techny, Ill., Mission Press, 1933, pp. xiv, 862). A standard survey.

F. Schwager, *Die katholische Heidenmission der Gegenwart in Zuzammenhang mit ihrer grossen Vergangenheit* (Steyl, Missionsdruckerei, 1907, pp. 446). A standard work.

J. M. Thoburn, *My Missionary Apprenticeship* (New York, Phillips and Hunt, 1887, pp. 425).

H. St. G. Tucker, *The History of the Episcopal Church in Japan* (New York, Charles Scribner's Sons, 1938, pp. 228). By a bishop of that church who served in Japan.

H. G. Underwood, *The Call of Korea. Political-Social-Religious* (New York, Fleming H. Revell Co., 3d ed., 1908, pp. 204). By a distinguished Protestant missionary to Korea.

S. R. Warburton, *Eastward: The Story of Adoniram Judson* (New York, Round Table Press, 1937, pp. xi, 240). The standard life.

A. W. Wasson, *Church Growth in Korea* (New York, International Missionary Council, 1934, pp. xii, 175). A scholarly study, chiefly of the part of the Korean Church related to the Methodist Episcopal Church, South.

Chapter 55

THE EXCEEDING GREATNESS OF THE POWER: WHERE SIN ABOUNDED GRACE MUCH MORE ABOUNDED

As we look back across this survey of Christianity in the nineteenth century, what can be said of the effect of the faith upon the human scene? To answer that question we must view the world as a whole and not confine our attention to any one segment of it. If, as Christian faith affirms, God was in Christ reconciling the world unto Himself, if He sent His son into the world that the world might be saved through him, was that purpose nearer to accomplishment in 1914 than in 1815? Here is essentially a global question and it requires a global answer.

In the preceding ten chapters (Chapters 45–54, especially Chapter 45) we have repeatedly seen something of the challenge with which Christianity was confronted. Vast movements were in progress in the historic Christendom, where the faith had longest been supposedly dominant, which threatened the very existence of Christianity. It was sobering that most of these were in part the fruits of Christianity, some more, some less. The scientific approach, the utilization of science and man's ingenuity in such fashion that the nineteenth and twentieth centuries became the age of the machine, forms of philosophy which either repudiated the faith outright or seemed to supersede it, the application of historical methods to the Bible with the result that that collection of documents which had been revered as inspired was declared to be imperfect and abounding in errors of fact and opinion, the rise of social theories and programmes which, while owing much to Christianity, either ignored or rejected it, the pressure of supposedly Christian peoples upon non-Christian peoples the world over with the danger, real or latent, of wholesale exploitation of the latter in the presumed interest of the former—these and many other trends and movements were a menace to Christianity. Some were perverting to man's hurt what had come through Christianity. Sin, collective and individual, was abounding on a vast scale. Could Christianity rise to the occasion? Was it the channel of a power so "exceeding great" that grace would much more abound?

Something of the answer to these questions must have been sensed in the narrative in the preceding chapters. All that we need take the space to do here is to summarize what has been given piecemeal and to add some facts and movements that have not thus far been mentioned.

In the first place it must be clear that in the nineteenth century Christianity became more widely spread geographically than it or any other faith had ever been. This spread was in connexion with the expansion of European peoples. Although Christianity was in part the cause of that expansion, it by no means followed automatically that it would be propagated with it. Only an abounding vigour could have held to their ancestral faith so large portions of the European emigrants who created the new nations and could have won contingents from most of the peoples who heretofore had been touched slightly or not at all.

Among non-European peoples the Christianity thus planted had a much more extensive influence than the size of the churches which were called into being would have led one to expect. These churches were of first-class importance. Presumably it was primarily upon them that the perpetuation and continued spread of the faith among their respective peoples would depend. In them, moreover, were lives in which were seen the characteristic "fruits of the Spirit" which Paul described in the first century of the Christian faith. In addition, usually but not always more or less closely related to them, were other contributions through the missionaries who spread the Christian faith. Hundreds of languages were for the first time given a written form, the Bible was translated into them in whole or in part, other Christian literature was prepared, and schools of a Western type were opened, often the pioneers of the kind of education which was to prevail as governments, either colonial or indigenous and independent, undertook an educational system for the new day. Orphanages were conducted in which thousands of children were cared for who would otherwise have perished. Famine relief was undertaken and attempts were made to introduce improvements in agriculture and forestry which would reduce or eliminate famine. Hospitals were founded and steps were taken to initiate medical and nursing professions trained in the science and techniques which were making rapid strides in the Occident. Public health education was inaugurated. Efforts were made to raise the status of women. All this, and more, was accomplished through a body of missionaries, men and women, which never numbered more than a quarter of a million and which was usually much less and which was not concentrated in one country but was distributed thinly over more than half the land surface of the globe and among much more than half the earth's population.

In addition the Christian conscience fought the selfish exploitation of non-white peoples by the dominant white race. Sometimes it found expression in missionaries. Even more often it stirred to action Christians who were not missionaries. It brought about the abolition of Negro slavery. It sought to curb the production and sale of opium and opium derivatives. It opposed any form of forced labour. The empire which ruled over the most people and the widest area was that of Great Britain. In the nineteenth century the quality of the British colonial official showed a marked improvement over the eighteenth century. The official might still regard himself as belonging to a superior race and culture and speak contemptuously of those whom he ruled as "lesser breeds without the law" and as "half devil and half child," but towards them he felt an obligation to give devoted and honest service, to bear what in the latter part of the century a poet who grew up in that atmosphere called "the white man's burden." This improvement seems to have been due, at least in part, to the Evangelical Awakening, the revivals which followed it, and the general rise in the level of Christian living which were their products.

Among the traditionally Christian peoples in Europe, the Americas, and Australasia, the faith also had striking effects. We have noted the fashion in which it was the stimulus and the sustaining impulse in the successful struggles for prison reform, for better care of the insane, and for legislative measures shortening the hours of labour, safeguarding the health of labourers, protecting women and children in mines and industry, and obtaining improved housing. This was especially important in an age and countries in which the industrial revolution was bringing together aggregations of labour, some of them vast, in the mining and factory towns and cities which were springing up almost over-night. Moved by their faith, Christians devised new methods and programmes for the education of the masses. They brought into being hundreds of colleges and universities, even though some of these later departed from the Christian principles of their founders. Christians also were the initiators and supporters of measures and movements to reduce the sufferings attendant on wars and to eliminate war by devising and operating institutions and measures for the peaceful adjustment of friction between nations and for international coöpera-tion for the welfare of mankind. By its symbol and name the Red Cross bore witness of its Christian origin. It came into being through the efforts of a Protestant layman of Geneva, Henri Dunant.

The hundreds of hospitals begun and maintained by various religious orders and churches were evidence of the continuing care for the sick which had been a feature of Christianity since its beginning. The new nursing profession which arose in the nineteenth century, largely from Protestant sources, further attested to the power of their faith to impel Christians to give themselves to the care of the sick and the wounded which had earlier again and again been displayed in orders, congregations, and confraternities in the Roman Catholic Church and which continued to find expression through them. The devout Roman Catholic, Louis Pasteur (1822–1895), by his research contributed immeasurably to advances in man's age-old struggle against disease.

Christianity helped to mould philosophy, even philosophies which did not acknowledge it or which rejected it.

Christianity's contributions to literature were so multiform and so numerous that to single out a few authors as examples seems invidious. Among the many thousands who showed its impress in accepting it, in struggling with the issues which it raised, or in paying tribute to it by repudiating it were the Russians N. V. Gogol (1809–1852) and T. M. Dostoievski (1821–1881), the Norwegian Ibsen, the German Goethe, the French Victor Hugo (1802–1885), the Scottish Thomas Carlyle, the English George Eliot, Alfred Tennyson, and Robert Browning, and the Americans Nathaniel Hawthorne, H. W. Longfellow, and J. R. Lowell.

Christian faith moulded and sustained such statesmen and shapers of nations as Abraham Lincoln and W. E. Gladstone.

Increasingly the churches and their benevolences were maintained by the voluntary contributions of their members rather than by compulsory taxation, thus attesting the loyalty of the rank and file of their constituencies. Gifts to a multitude of services for the public good, most of them moved by a sense of responsibility springing from the Christian faith, were an outstanding feature of the century, especially in the British Isles and the United States. Of this the large number of philanthropic agencies supported by private subscriptions were striking evidence. Some of the giving was on a princely scale. Most of it was in modest sums from millions with only moderate incomes.

Fully as important as any of these effects was the direct operation of the faith in millions of men and women. Many were lifted from moral defeat and degradation to enduring victory. Others, nurtured in the faith from childhood, either with or without some inner crisis grew into radiant spirits. Millions, notably in the partially de-Christianized elements of the population of the United States, were brought into a vital religious experience. Still others, nominally Christian, found that to them the faith became alive and thrilling. We must always remember, moreover, that Christian conviction holds that what follows beyond the gate of death and in the realm which the historian cannot penetrate is of even more importance than what is within the scope of the historian's craft.

To most of these effects we have already called attention. It was clear that Christianity came to 1914 and entered the twentieth century on a rising tide.

Another set of movements, an outcome of the Christian faith which partly began and partly was given an added impulse in the nineteenth century and which mounted rapidly after that year, was that by which Christians were coming together across denominational barriers and were achieving unity in ways which were essentially novel. It was significant that these movements issued from the most divided branch of Christianity, Protestantism, and at the outset from extreme forms of Protestantism, namely, those springing from the Evangelical awakening, which by pushing towards their full implications the distinctive Protestant convictions of salvation by faith and the priesthood of all believers seemed to make for unmitigated individualism and endless fissiparousness. It is also significant that they were mounting in a day when because of improved means of transportation and communication which had their origin in Christendom the inhabited world was rapidly shrinking in time-distances and all men were geographically becoming neighbours. The world was a neighbourhood, but it was a neighbourhood which suffered from frictions and tensions which threatened to make it a shambles. Could it be transformed into a coöperative brotherhood? If so it must be by spiritual and moral more than material forces. Christianity, rapidly becoming world-wide, more so than any other religion, by its professed major emphasis upon love of God and love of neighbour would seem to be the source to which men would most hopefully look for such a unifying tie. Yet the Christian Church was divided, apparently hopelessly so. Attempts at unity had been followed by fresh divisions. Especially after the rise and growth of Protestantism, even the largest of the Christian bodies, the Roman Catholic Church, drew into its fold a decreasing proportion of those who bore the Christian name. Although that church stoutly maintained that unity could rightly be found only by submitting to its head and entering its fellowship, an increasing proportion of Christians were refusing to respond to the repeated Papal invitations to conform. Now a fresh approach was being made, and with growing although still far from complete success. Here was a manifestation of the exceeding greatness of the power, so that where sin, collective, national, and individual, threatened the human race with added woes, grace was manifesting itself through fresh and unexpected channels.

The growing unity emanating from Protestant Christianity expressed itself in a number of ways, all interrelated and each contributing to the others. Eventually it came to be known as the Ecumenical Movement.

Among the earliest methods of attaining unity and one which persisted and had increasing manifestations and ramifications was coöperation in planning and action across denominational lines by individuals and groups but without the official participation of ecclesiastical bodies. Originally the organizations and conferences of this kind were drawn primarily from those committed to the Evangelical Awakening and kindred circles, such as the Pietists on the Continent of Europe and those in the United States in sympathy with the revivals. Eventually some of the movements drew in individuals from other traditions, including Anglo-Catholics, Roman Catholics, and communicants of the Orthodox and other Eastern Churches.

Coöperation by individuals rather than officially by ecclesiastical bodies had so many expressions that we must content ourselves with only a few examples. Among the first were the London Missionary Society, formed, it will be remembered, in 1795, the Religious Tract Society, begun in 1799, the British and Foreign Bible Society, founded in 1804, and the American Bible Society, organized in 1816. The Sunday Schools were another such movement. After various world gatherings, as we have noted, in 1907 the World's Sunday School Association was formally organized. The Young Men's Christian Associations belonged in this category. As we have seen, from their humble beginning in 1844 they multiplied rapidly and in 1855 the World's Alliance of the Young Men's Christian Associations was organized. Eventually the Associations, while remaining predominantly Protestant, also attracted members of the Roman Catholic Church and of some of the Eastern Churches who remained in full communion in their denominations. Similar were the Young Women's Christion Associations. In 1894 their various national coördinating bodies joined in forming the World's Young Women's Christian Association. The Young People's Society of Christian Endeavour, inaugurated in a Congregational Church in New England, proved contagious, and in 1895 the World's Christian Endeavour Union was launched. Partly out of the Young Men's and Young Women's Christian Associations and the Student Volunteer Movement for Foreign Missions came, in 1895, the World's Student Christian Federation, made up of various national movements which recruited students from many different denominations while encouraging them to remain loyal to their respective churches. Outstanding in its formation and early leadership was John R. Mott, whom we have already met and are to meet again and again in connexion with various expressions of the Ecumenical Movement.

What was known as the Evangelical Alliance made important contributions to the movement towards Christian unity. It had its origin partly in 1845 in a collective effort of clergy of several denominations to counteract the Tractarian or Oxford movement and to strengthen Protestantism. It was followed by a gathering in London in 1846 of over eight hundred from several countries of Europe and America. At the London meeting the Evangelical Alliance was founded. It had as its purpose "the advancement of Evangelical Protestantism

. . . and the counteraction of infidelity, Popery, and other forms of superstition, error, and profaneness, especially the desecration of the Lord's Day." It confessed the reality of the one Church, recognized what it deemed the essential unity of the Church, deplored the divisions, and sought to join in cultivating brotherly love. It adopted a doctrinal basis which was that of most Evangelicals of the day, regardless of denomination. Branches were formed in several countries and from time to time world meetings were held. Among the latter was one in Berlin in 1857 at the invitation of the King of Prussia and which bishops of the Church of England, including the Archbishop of Canterbury, and English Nonconformists joined in endorsing. Another was held in Geneva in 1861, and still another in Amsterdam in 1867. As we have seen, the most notable of the series of world gatherings of the Evangelical Alliance convened in New York in 1873, largely through the initiative and driving energy of Philip Schaff, and in it the trend was more towards the union of Evangelicals than opposition to Catholicism. Later world meetings were held, but with the emergence of other forms of coöperation, some of them partly from the stimulus given by the Evangelical Alliance, they gradually ceased to attract wide attention. Yet in its heyday the Evangelical Alliance had marked repercussions. From 1886 to 1898 the Congregational clergyman Josiah Strong (1847–1916) was the general secretary of the American branch. One of the leaders in the Social Gospel movement, he urged that the churches coöperate in helping to Christianize the social order and to bring to realization the kingdom of God on earth. However, in general the Evangelical Alliance did not follow him.

Another approach to Christian unity was through proposals for the federation or actual union of churches. Here pioneer documents were the *Fraternal Appeal to the American Churches* (1838) by S. S. Schmucker, the Lutheran whom we have already met (Chapter 50), which offered a *Plan for Protestant Union,* followed in 1845 by the *Overture for Christian Union* drafted by Schmucker and signed by fifty clergymen from several denominations. The *Overture* proposed a concrete procedure and structure for the formation by the churches of what was called the Apostolic Protestant Union. The suggested programme was not adopted by the churches, but it helped to prepare the way for later coöperation.

Anglicans were active in approaching the Eastern Churches, the Roman Catholic Church, and Protestant Churches in efforts to encourage fellowship and to explore bases of union. Successive Lambeth Conferences of the bishops of the Anglican Communion devoted much attention to that subject. The Conference of 1888 adopted as a basis the proposal made in 1886 by the General Convention of the Protestant Episcopal Church and which came to be known as the Lambeth Quadrilateral. In the form given it in 1888 it read:

The Holy Scriptures of the Old and New Testament as containing all things necessary to salvation, and as being the rule and ultimate standard of faith.

The Apostles' Creed as the baptismal symbol; and the Nicene Creed as the sufficient statement of the Christian faith.

The two Sacraments ordained by Christ himself—Baptism and the Supper of the Lord—ministered with the unfailing use of Christ's words of institution and the elements ordained by Him.

The historic episcopate, locally adapted in the method of its administration to the varying needs of the nations and peoples called of God into the unity of His Church.

Approaches made by Anglicans to other communions before and after the formulation of the Lambeth Quadrilateral did not lead to union. Indeed, conversations with Rome were given a note of finality when in 1896 Pope Leo XIII declared Anglican orders invalid.

Nor, except in the case of some closely related churches of the same denominational family, did the nineteenth century see the fusion of two or more denominations. That was to wait until after 1914. What may be regarded as a possible exception was the South India United Church, formed in 1908 by congregations connected with the United Free Church of Scotland, the Reformed Church in America, the London Missionary Society, and the American Board of Commissioners for Foreign Missions, but these were bodies which in theology came out of the Reformed tradition and had long regarded themselves as akin.

Several denominational families devised ways of furthering fellowship among their several branches. Such were the Lambeth Conferences for the Anglicans, the World Alliance of the Reformed Churches holding the Presbyterian System, organized in London in 1875, the International Congregational Council, which had its initial meeting in London in 1891, the Ecumenical Methodist Conferences, the first of which convened in London in 1901, and the Baptist World Alliance, organized in 1905.

Although no striking "organic union" of churches was achieved, coöperation among ecclesiastical bodies mounted as the century progressed. We have noted the Plan of Union through which in the fore part of the century the Congregationalists and the Presbyterians joined in planting the faith on the Western frontier of the United States. We have also seen that in its earlier years churches of several denominations contributed to the American Board of Commissioners for Foreign Missions. Similarly, from its formation in 1826 until the withdrawal of the New School Presbyterians in 1861, the American Home Missionary Society, predominantly Congregational, drew its support from more than one denomination. From 1840 until 1886 the Church of England and the Prussian Church shared in a Protestant episcopate at Jerusalem.

In the latter part of the century coöperation embracing a larger number of denominations began to appear. Several state councils and federations of churches came into being. Various movements, among them the National Federation of Churches and Christian Workers, officially formed in 1901, culminated in 1908 in the organization of the Federal Council of the Churches of Christ in America, by twenty-nine national denominational bodies, with the purpose of expressing "the fellowship and catholic unity of the Christian Church" and of exerting "a larger combined influence for the Churches of Christ in all matters affecting the moral and social conditions of the people." While made up of official representatives of its member churches, the Federal Council of Churches was forbidden to have any authority over its constituent bodies. It could simply offer counsel and recommend courses of action on matters of common interest. From the beginning, partly because of the influential place which Josiah Strong had in its formation, it gave much attention to encouraging joint action by the churches in bringing Christian principles to bear upon various aspects of human society. In 1892 a Free Church Congress met at Manchester, in England, and there followed, also in the 1890's, the National Council of the Evangelical Free Churches. Numbers of local councils of churches also sprang up in the British Isles.

Important developments, in some ways the major developments towards effecting Christian unity through Protestantism, came through the missionary outreach of the churches. This is not surprising. In regions to which Christianity was being introduced the divisions perpetuated from the lands where the faith had been longer planted often seemed anachronistic, irrelevant, and a handicap to the spread of the Gospel. In the new environment the impulse to a united approach, while often meeting obstacles, was strong. Moreover, in the countries and sections from which missionaries were sent, joint consultation appeared imperative.

Early in the nineteenth century conferences of missionaries in particular areas and countries across denominational barriers began to be held. As the century progressed they multiplied in numbers and size. Thus in 1825 the Bombay Missionary Union was formed by members of four societies and included Anglicans, Congregationalists, and Presbyterians. In the 1850's regional conferences of missionaries in North and South India were seen. In 1873 there convened the first of a series of decennial all-India missionary conferences. They increased in the numbers of societies represented. Indians were also included. In 1902 the Fourth Decennial Conference, following the precedent of the South India missionary conference of 1900, was made up, not of all individuals who cared to come, but of delegates officially appointed by their respective bodies. In Japan conferences of Protestant missionaries from the entire country began in 1872 and the third in the series, that of 1900, appointed a continuing standing committee which brought into being the Conference of Federated Missions in Japan which met annually beginning in 1907. The 1900 gathering also gave an impetus to what was later the Federation of Churches in Japan. In China missionaries joined in translating the Bible as early as 1843, but the first general missionary conference was not until 1877. It was followed by others in 1890 and 1907, each larger than its predecessor. The 1907 gathering gave much attention to the promotion of continuing and visible unity. Other national or regional missionary conferences were convened, beginning in Mexico in the 1880's and in the first decades of the twentieth century in South Africa and for the Moslem world.

In the lands from which missionaries were sent, regular and continuing consultation and coöperation were devised early. In 1819 the secretaries of foreign mission boards with headquarters in London formed an association for "mutual counsel and fellowship." Beginning in 1863 delegates from several Scandinavian missionary societies met in Northern Lutheran Missions Conferences. In 1866 the first of a series of Continental Missions Conferences was held with representatives of several societies. In 1885 what was known as *Der Ausschuss der deutschen evangelischen Missionen* was constituted, a standing committee of all the Protestant missionary societies of Germany. It grew in its scope and work. A general Dutch missionary conference met in 1887 and became an annual event. What was eventually called the Foreign Missions Conference of North America convened for the first time in 1895. It met annually thereafter, chiefly as a gathering where officials and board members of the several Protestant missionary societies exchanged views. In 1907 it arranged for more nearly continuous consultation by the appointment of a smaller Committee of Reference and Counsel.

Meetings on a world scale on behalf of Protestant missions also developed. Precursors with attendance from only one nation were held in New York and London in 1854. What is usually regarded as the first of the series convened at Liverpool in 1860, drawing almost entirely from the British Isles. There followed others in London in 1878 and 1888, both international, and then the Ecumenical Missionary Conference in New York in 1900, with attendance from the United States, the British Isles, and the Continent of Europe. Each was larger than its predecessor. The 1900 gathering was especially outstanding with delegates from 162 mission boards and huge public meetings which by their programmes gave impressive demonstration to the variety and extent of foreign missions.

The most notable in the succession of the international, inter-denominational assemblies was the World Missionary Conference, held in Edinburgh in 1910.

It became a landmark in the history of the Ecumenical Movement, for it influenced profoundly some of the most important developments of the next forty or more years. In several ways it was in contrast with its predecessors and was an advance beyond them. First, it was more strictly a delegated body, made up of official representatives of the missionary societies. Second, it was a deliberative body, seeking to formulate policy for the years ahead. While it possessed no legislative authority, it could suggest, and because it was composed of leaders of the various societies there was reason to hope that its recommendations would be followed by action. In the third place, as a preliminary to the deliberations prolonged and extensive studies were made of the several aspects of the missionary enterprise and in their preparation hundreds of correspondents were enlisted in many different parts of the world, thus stimulating widespread thought. In the fourth place, the gathering was more comprehensive ecclesiastically than its predecessors. The latter had, in general, enlisted only Evangelicals. At Edinburgh several Anglo-Catholics were present and took part. Moreover, members of what later came to be called "the younger churches," namely, those founded by eighteenth and nineteenth century Protestant missions, while few, were prominent. Of first-class importance, in the fifth place, was the fact that provision was made for carrying forward the work of the gathering. A Continuation Committee was appointed. Through it conferences were held in 1912 and 1913 in various centres in Asia preparatory to more permanent coöperative bodies, a comprehensive scholarly journal, *The International Review of Missions,* was inaugurated, and, after 1914, as we are to see later, the International Missionary Council emerged. In the sixth place, the Edinburgh gathering also was in part responsible for the two organizations, the World Conference on Faith and Order and the Universal Christian Council for Life and Work, the two bodies which, after 1914, merged to form the World Council of Churches.

A seventh feature of major significance was the fashion in which "Edinburgh 1910" either brought to the fore or enlisted men who were to have an outstanding part in the growth of the Ecumenical Movement. John R. Mott was active in the preparations for the conference, presided at most of its sessions, and became the chairman of the Continuation Committee and then of the International Missionary Council. Joseph Houldsworth Oldham (1874———), born in Scotland, the first full-time secretary of the Student Christian Movement of Great Britain and Ireland, was chiefly responsible for the preparations for Edinburgh, became the first secretary of the International Missionary Council, and had a large part in the development of the Universal Christian Council for Life and Work. Charles H. Brent (1862–1929), a bishop of the Protestant Episcopal Church, there caught the vision which made him one of the chief initiators of World Conference on Faith and Order. William Temple, present as a "steward" or "usher," was later a vice-chairman of the International Missionary Council and the first chairman of the provisional committee which brought into being the World Council of Churches. V. S. Azariah, whom we have already met as the first Indian Anglican bishop, and a Chinese, Chêng Ching-yi (1881–1940), had leading parts in the Ecumenical Movement. There were also present some other men whose names later became household words in the Ecumenical Movement.

By deliberate choice, the Edinburgh conference confined its attention to missions to non-Christians and therefore did not include Protestant missions among the Roman Catholics in Latin America. As an eighth result of the gathering, some who believed that this huge area should be covered in coöperative fashion in 1913 had the Foreign Missions Conference of North America call a meeting from which emerged the Committee on Coöperation in Latin America, a body which was to have a notable history.

SUMMARY

Christianity came to the year 1914 on a rising tide and with mounting momentum. In spite of the many adversaries which it encountered and which seemed to threaten its existence, in 1914 it was more widely spread geographically than at any previous time, it had given rise to men and movements which were as outstanding as any in the history of the faith, and it was making its impress upon more of mankind than ever before. The chief channel of this vitality was Protestantism. In addition to its striking geographic spread, proportionately much greater than that of any other wing of Christianity, to the fresh and novel movements which issued from it, and to its creative thought and scholarship, Protestantism also devised ways of drawing Christians together which were beginning to meet with marked success.

SELECTED BIBLIOGRAPHY

W. R. Hogg, *Ecumenical Foundations. A History of the International Missionary Council and Its Nineteenth-Century Background* (New York, Harper & Brothers, 1952, pp. xi, 466). The indispensable and definitive study of the subject.

K. S. Latourette, *A History of the Expansion of Christianity. Volumes IV, V, VI, The Great Century* (New York, Harper & Brothers, 1941–1944).

G. J. Slosser, *Christian Unity. Its History and Challenge in All Communions, in All Lands* (New York, E. P. Dutton & Co., 1929, pp. xix, 425). Comprehensive, detailed.

VIGOUR AMIDST STORM: BEGINNING IN A.D. 1914

Chapter 56

AN AGE OF STORM: THE GENERAL SETTING, THE CHALLENGE TO CHRISTIANITY, AND THE VIGOUR OF THE CHRISTIAN RESPONSE

The summer of 1914 ushered the entire world and with it Christianity into a new and tumultuous age.

We have seen that for what was still regarded as Christendom the century between 1815 and 1914 was one of comparative peace, of amazing increases in population and wealth, and of even more astounding geographic expansion. By 1914 all the inhabited world had been penetrated and for the most part mastered by peoples who had been traditionally known as Christian. In other cultures the impact of the "Christian" Occident and its culture had begun to bring either profound changes or complete disintegration.

In spite of rising threats in the Occident to its historic faith and increasing open dissent and departure from it on the part of many, Christianity came to 1914 on a rising tide, gathering momentum as it spread across the face of the planet. Vigour and geographic expansion characterized all three of the major forms of Christianity. While showing less of them than any of the others, the Orthodox, especially the Russian Orthodox, clearly displayed them. The Roman Catholic Church, which had suffered severely both in the period from 1750 to 1815 and from the secularizing currents of the nineteenth century, had been knit together more closely under the Pope, had put forth many fresh movements, and had spread more widely geographically than ever before. But it was Protestantism which had been the vehicle of the greatest vitality. From it had issued many movements, some of them novel and evidence of quite astounding creativity. From being confined almost entirely to North-western Europe and the British Isles and a narrow strip on the eastern seaboard of North America, it had become world-wide and the dominant faith of burgeoning new nations in both the Southern and the Northern Hemisphere. By its very genius seemingly endlessly divisive and dividing, it was beginning to draw together, grop-ing in fresh institutional ways towards the unity which all Christians in prin-ciple believed should characterize the followers of Christ. The main stream of the faith was beginning to surge through the channels of Protestantism.

Now came, apparently abruptly, an age which from some of its aspects seemed an ominous ebb in the Christian tide. Indeed, there were those who spoke of the age as the "post-Christian era." From what had once been de-nominated Christendom issued wars and revolutions which threw the entire world into disorder and set all humanity on the march. That march appeared to many to be moving mankind away from Christianity. If only one set of facts were taken into consideration here seemed to be another of the major reces-sions which had punctuated the course of the faith. Indeed, so serious did it appear to be that pessimists and critics might proclaim it as the last of the reces-sions, certain to end in the disappearance of Christianity, or, if not its complete disappearance, its decline to an inconspicuous and unimportant rôle in the life of the race.

Two facets of the age differentiated the period from the earlier ones which were indubitably recessions. One of these was the fact that the threats to the faith arose in large part from Christianity and were a menace because they were perversions of the gifts which had come to man through it. They seemed to be spelling the doom of Christianity—as though Christianity itself had given birth to enemies which were to destroy it.

In ages of retreat the enemies had come in some degree from distortions of Christian contributions. Indeed, that had been progressively more prominent with each of the successive recessions. In the first, that from A.D. 500 to A.D. 950, the chief initial causes had been the internal decay of the Roman Empire and the irruption of barbarians from the North. For neither of these was Christianity a significant cause. The major later factor was the Arab invasion from the South-east, given added dynamic and unity by Islam. It was Islam which by A.D. 950 had become dominant in about half of what had been Christendom, and Islam was indebted both to Judaism and Christianity, although more to the former than the latter.

The second major recession, that from 1350 to 1500, arose in part from the break-up of the Mongol Empire, for which Christianity was not responsible, and from the blows dealt by the Black Death, or bubonic plague, of which Christianity could not be counted as a source. More potent was the fresh surge of Islam, born by Mongols and Turks. Presumably the exploits of Tamerlane and the Ottoman Turks were not due as much to the fact that they were Moslems as had been those of the Arabs in the earlier recession. Proportionately to the geographic extent of Christianity the gains of Islam at its expense were not as great as in the eighth and ninth centuries. But in so far as Islam was a factor, Christianity, as one of the formative although minor contributors to the birth of Islam, was a cause. More serious threats to Christianity in the period between 1350 and 1500 were from within Christendom. They arose partly from the failure of the Catholic Church, whether of the East or of the West, to purge itself of corruption and to allow itself to be a sufficiently effective channel for the "exceeding greatness of the power" of the Gospel. They were also from the passing of the medieval civilization of Western Europe which Christianity had done much to produce and with which it was intricately associated. The waning of that civilization was chargeable to a complex variety of developments. Not all of them are fully discernible, but to some Christianity contributed. One was the Renaissance and another the humanism which was closely associated with the Renaissance. Both could be ascribed in some degree to Christianity. Another was the rising prosperity with the growth of cities and the decay of feudalism, a process which Christianity had assisted by helping to discipline the rude barbarians who had overwhelmed much of South-western Europe and by making for an inclusive order in that region.

The fact that the period from 1750 to 1815 had brought serious crises for Christianity and in some areas was a recession was due almost entirely to forces at work within Western Christendom and for which Christianity was to some degree responsible. Such were the rationalism and the Deism of the era and the political ideas which inspired and largely shaped the French Revolution. They were in part from Christianity, even though only distorted expressions or perversions of it.

The age which began in the summer of 1914 was made distinct by movements all of which either issued from Western Europe or were profoundly influenced by contact with Western Europe. Whether Western Europe should still be called a part of Christendom was questionable, but it was there that Christianity had shown its chief vitality from the tenth into the nineteenth century, or for only a little less than a millennium. Moreover, most if not all of the features peculiar to the era bore the impress of Christianity, even when they were perversions of it and menaced its existence.

One of the most obvious of the features of the age was war. Within a little less than forty years two world wars devastated much of the earth's surface and several lesser ones were waged. Never before had so much of mankind been engaged simultaneously in war, war which might be called internecine because it was really a civil war within the totality of the human race. Never before had mankind massed such large armies or produced weapons which worked wholesale destruction on so gigantic a scale. The first of the two world wars originated in Western Europe and there took its greatest toll in life and property. The second had its first rumblings in the Far East in the "Mukden incident" between China and Japan in September, 1931, and in the large scale invasion of China by Japan in July, 1937, but it attained global proportions in the late summer of 1939 through Western Europe. Everywhere it was fought with the kind of organization and equipment which had first been developed by Western European peoples and it dealt even more severe blows to Western Europe than had World War I.

It was sobering to recall that the intense nationalism which was a major cause of the two wars was historically closely associated with the self-consciousness of the masses which could be traced in part to Christianity with its emphasis upon the dignity and worth of every individual. It was also provocative of thought that the science which made possible the weapons with which the wars were fought was indebted to Christianity through its emphasis upon an orderly and dependable universe and the initiative and courage which it had inspired in Western man since the heyday of the Middle Ages.

Another of the outstanding characteristics of the post-1914 world was revolution. Ancient monarchies were swept away. Outstanding in their collapse were those of China, Russia, Germany, and Italy. It was not simply that the ruling house toppled, discredited by lack of success in dealing with foreign foes, although this is a phase of the change. More important was the disappearance of the entire monarchical structure, centuries old, in China going back more than two thousand years, and the substitution of what were called republics. Usually a determined minority seized control and, asserting that it was acting on behalf of the masses, attempted to erect a new framework inspired and maintained by a body of ideas.

The ideologies varied from country to country. Some were democratic in the sense in which Anglo-Saxons and Western Europeans understood that term. One took the name of national socialism, another was fascism, and what vied in its dynamic force with the Anglo-Saxon type of liberal democracy was communism, the Marxist form of socialism. In some other countries, notably in India, Burma, and Indonesia, a Western regime founded on imperialistic expansion was discarded and a republic was substituted for it. Under whatever name or ideology, these regimes appealed to the masses, masses restless under age-long oppression and official exploitation and corruption and roused to a great hope, a hope of a better day for themselves and their children.

It was highly significant that all the ideologies that gained the mastery, with the possible exception of that which dominated Japan in the 1930's and the fore part of the 1940's and here and there a resurgent Islam, were originally formulated in Western Europe and, even when they were hostile to it, were to some degree indebted to Christianity. From time to time we have noted that debt (especially in Chapter 45). It was particularly marked in the two most widely spread of the ideologies, democracy of the Anglo-Saxon and French types and the Marxist communism which was professed by the party which mastered Russia and which, spreading from Russia by a combination of physical force and extraordinarily skilful intrigue, political manipulation, and propaganda, by 1953 was dominant in most of Central Europe, Western Germany, Central Asia, North Korea, and China. Communism was a secularized version of the Christian understanding of history. Under the influence of Judaism and Christianity it believed that history moves to a climax. However, it declared that the climax is not to be reached by the power and under the direction of God, as the Jewish and Christian faiths held, but is to be from the inevitable course of nature, and the goal is not to be the perfected kingdom of God, but a classless society in which the nation state will fade away and each individual will contribute according to his ability and each is to have according to his need. In contrast with the Christian Gospel, based upon self-giving love, it inculcated hate, stimulated class conflict, and utilized lies in its propaganda when lies seemed to serve its ends. Here was a vast, some called it a demonic, perversion of Christianity which was frankly anti-Christian and which many regarded the most serious threat to Christianity since the rise of Islam.

It is also significant that the hopes and aspirations which these ideologies promised to fulfill were roused by contact with the West and to no small extent were due to the Christian elements in Occidental culture. Some of the outstanding men and movements that called them forth were either professedly Christian or were frank to admit that they were influenced by Christ. Thus much of the post-1914 restlessness among Africans south of the Sahara was fed and given hope by the Watch Tower Movement, another name for Jehovah's Witnesses. He who did most to shape the ideals of revolutionary China between 1911 and the late 1940's was Sun Yat-sen, an avowed Christian who owed most of his formal education to Christian schools. The chief architect of the foundations of the Republic of India and the main leader in seeking to erase the caste barriers which kept the depressed classes in hereditary squalor was M. K. Gandhi, who, while not a Christian, gladly affirmed the impress which Christ had made on him.

Still another feature of the era which began in 1914 was the decline of Western Europe in the total world scene. With an interruption in the fourteenth and the fore part of the fifteenth century, from as far back as the first of the Crusades Western European peoples had been expanding. In the nineteenth century they had grown strikingly in wealth and numbers and by the year 1914 they and their culture dominated the globe. Seen against the background of the total span of human history that hegemony was brief. In 1914 it began a rapid decline. The culture which had its rise in Western Europe continued to spread. Nations chiefly of Western European stock, notably the United States, loomed ever more prominently in the affairs of mankind. In spite of wars the population of Western Europe showed an increase. Yet Western European nations were not as masterful as they had been. Peoples whom they had governed rose in revolt and cast off their rule even when, as latterly had been true of several of the powers, especially Great Britain and the Netherlands, that rule had been benevolent and had prepared its subjects for autonomy. Many in Western Europe believed and loudly proclaimed that the region and its culture were victims of fatal illnesses. The optimism which had prevailed in the nineteenth century gave way to profound pessimism. The obvious causes of the decline and the pessimism were the two world wars and the subsequent revolutions which swept across Western Europe, but the conviction was held that these, while undoubtedly important, were symptoms of a much more basic malady. The fear and the pessimism were shared, although by no means as deeply, by nations which had arisen chiefly from the migrations of Western European peoples, including the United States, and that in spite of the fact that by the middle of the twentieth century the latter country was the wealthiest and the most powerful on the planet.

The decline, sickness, and pessimism of Western Europe took on added significance in view of the fact that the area was the heart of what had been "Christian" civilization. Here for nearly a thousand years most of the creative movements in Christianity had had their rise—the revivals in the Roman Catholic Church which had found expression in new monastic orders, the main ferment of creative theological thought, and various awakenings which had broken with the Roman Catholic Church, the chief of them Protestantism. Here the two forms of Christianity which had spread most vigorously since the fifteenth century, Roman Catholicism and Protestantism, had their historic centres. Was Christianity responsible for the illness of Western Europe, whether by contributing to the applied science and the ideologies which were working its doom or from inability to prevent or counteract the perversions of its good gifts which were at the root of the disease?

The situation was made the more grave by the contrast between the apprehensive gloom which covered what had been the heart of Christendom and the aggressive confidence which, at least outwardly, characterized communism and communists, an openly anti-Christian fruit of Western "Christian" civilization and to which Christianity had contributed. Was Christianity, as communists and many of its other critics declared, a waning force, to be left behind by the onward course of history? A somewhat similar hopefulness characterized the peoples of India and Pakistan after their achievement of independence from British rule in the latter part of the 1940's.

As if to confirm the dire prophecies of the demise of Christianity was the fact that the Christian churches were suffering numerical losses in Europe, and this in contrast with the mounting tide on which they had reached 1914. As we are to see somewhat more in detail later, the de-Christianization of great masses in Western Europe which had been begun at least as early as the eighteenth century and which had been partly obscured by the vigour displayed by that faith in the nineteenth century was making rapid strides.

The de-Christianization was all the more serious because it was most marked in what some of the contemporaries called "modern mass society," the urban centres which continued to grow as a result of industrialization. Christianity remained strongest in the rural districts, the small towns, and some of the suburbs where the older social patterns more nearly persisted and which by its earlier successes Christianity had permeated even when it had not transformed them. Christianity was finding it difficult to maintain footholds among the labourers in the mines and factories and among the shifting masses of population, some displaced by war, some by movements from country and small town to city, some in the new housing developments, and some by migration, often seasonal, from one occupation to another. It was sobering to reflect that the industrialization which brought this challenge and these losses was in part, as we have more than once reminded ourselves, a fruit of the science to which Christianity had contributed.

Disturbing also were the vast increases in population which continued in the twentieth century. These meant that in spite of the phenomenal geographic spread of Christianity, there were more non-Christians in the middle of the twentieth century than in 1815 or even in 1914. They also carried with them growing pressure upon subsistence, added physical suffering, and mounting dissatisfaction and restlessness which could easily become the seeds of new revolutions and more gigantic wars.

Over the entire human race hung the threat of wars to which the first two world holocausts of the century would be only preliminary. By mid-century the human race was being gathered into two camps around rival colossi. On the one hand, with the advantage of the possession of the heart-land of the largest of the continents, Eurasia, were Russia and her satellites and allies, inspired by a confident communism. On the other hand was the United States, the centre of a less closely bound congeries of states scattered over much of the rest of the globe. The two colossi were feverishly arming and, utilizing the science which had originated in the erstwhile Christendom, were developing ever more destructive weapons. The outlook seemed grim, both for the human race and for Christianity. There were many, even among intelligent and informed Christians, who could see only this side of the picture.

Yet there was another side, a second facet. It made the years which followed 1914 one of the greatest eras in the history of Christianity. Christians who knew the world scene as a whole were conscious that they and their fellow-believers were a minority set in a hostile world, but they were not content to be on the defensive. For them the figure of speech still held true with which at the outset Christ had described his Church. That Church was like a besieging army against a foe who was on the defensive, ensconced in a beleaguered city, and they believed the promise that the gates of hell which the Church was attacking would not prevail against it. They were mindful of their Lord's parting commission to the apostles to make disciples of all nations, baptizing them and teaching them to observe all that he had commanded them, assured of his continuing presence to whom all authority had been given. In the face of the many threats and challenges, after 1914 Christianity was putting forth fresh movements, was becoming more widely spread, more deeply rooted among more peoples, and more nearly united on a world scale, and was having growing constructive effects which were at least partly offsetting the perils. In the succeeding chapters we are to see this somewhat more in detail, although even then necessarily only in cursory fashion.

In Europe, long the traditional stronghold of the faith, the proportion of those who called themselves Christians declined, and the percentage of those who regularly attended church services seems to have fallen off even more. Yet fresh and vigorous new movements issued from Christianity in worship, thought, and action. In the United States, in contrast, the mass conversion of the non-Christian and partially de-Christianized elements of the population continued. For instance, in the twenty-four years between 1926 and 1950 the membership of all religious bodies, including the Jewish congregations, increased 59.9 per cent. as against a growth of 28.6 per cent. in the population. The percentage increase of Protestants was 63.7, of Roman Catholics 53.9, and of Judaism 22.5. In other words, Judaism was losing, and if the totals of membership had included only Christians the gains would have been above 60 per cent. In the rest of the Americas and in Australasia the percentage of church membership did not greatly alter, except that in Latin America, particularly in Brazil, Protestantism mounted rapidly in numbers and vitality. In North Africa and Western Asia the shrinkage of the ancient churches persisted and was accelerated as against the nineteenth century, but in Africa south of the Sahara the mass conversion proceeded, in some areas spectacularly. In India and Indonesia and to a lesser extent in most of the lands of South-east Asia the proportion of Christians in the population multiplied. In China and Japan, in

spite of foreign wars, invasions, and domestic stress, the numerical strength of
the Church grew, although not as markedly as in India. While still represented
by small minorities in Asia, at the mid-century mark Christians were more
nearly evenly distributed the world around than in 1914. The growth was by
both Roman Catholics and Protestants.

Even more significant of the mounting strength of Christianity in the entire
human scene was the fashion in which Christianity was taking root and on its
newer geographic frontiers in Asia and Africa was becoming less dependent
on missionaries from the Occident. Both Roman Catholics and Protestants
stressed the recruiting and training of indigenous leaders and were transferring
administrative responsibility to them. An increasing proportion of Roman
Catholic nuns, priests, and bishops were of native stock and the same was true
of the corresponding personnel in Protestant churches and institutions. In time
of stress, when Occidental missionaries were compelled to withdraw or were
interned, many although not all of the indigenous bodies displayed the ability
not only to survive but also to grow. Indigenous forms of Christian art and
music were appearing.

The movement towards Christian unity which was issuing from Protestantism and expressing itself through novel channels and which we noted as beginning before 1914 gained in momentum. By mid-century it had not drawn
all Protestantism together, but in one way or another it was bringing the large
majority of Protestants into a growing fellowship and was making friendly contacts with thousands in other branches of Christianity.

Moreover, in a distraught world in which colossal suffering and frustrating
fears mingled with daring aspiration, Christianity was the major impelling
motive in healing and relief on a larger scale than had ever before been seen.
Sometimes through frankly Christian channels, such as aid to prisoners of war
by the Young Men's Christian Associations in World War I, the American
Friends Service Committee, Church World Service during and after World
War II, Hilfswerk in Germany, and scores of other agencies, sometimes
through organizations which had their origins in Christian faith and sacrifice
but did not bear the Christian name, such as Near East Relief in and after
World War I and the International Red Cross, aid and hope were brought to
sufferers. The League of Nations and its successor, the United Nations, with
their departments for the peaceful settlement of disputes between nations and
for human welfare, and their dream of an international structure based on law
and coöperation rather than the near-chaos of the day, had as their initial and
chief architects men and women who were moved and sustained by Christian
faith.

By the middle of the twentieth century the age which opened in 1914 was still too near its beginning for adequate appraisal. It was not clear whether it was one of recession or advance in the Christian tide. Evidence could be adduced to support either judgement. Here, as from the beginning of the course of the Christian faith, the words which Paul used to describe himself were applicable to Christianity: ". . . unknown and yet well known, as dying and behold we live." The Christian could find a basis for Paul's confident assertion, "Where sin abounded, grace did much more abound."

To that story we now turn. It must sometime be told in detail. Here we can give it only in inadequate summary.

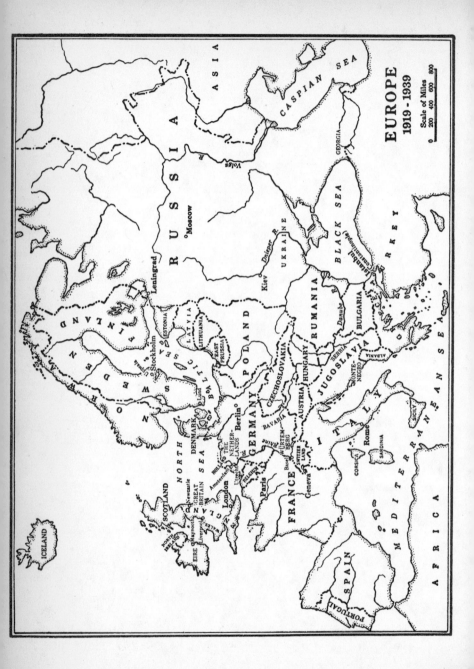

EUROPE
1919 - 1939

Scale of Miles
0   200   400   600   800

ICELAND

RUSSIA

ASIA

CASPIAN SEA

Volga

Moscow

Leningrad

FINLAND

SWEDEN

NORWAY

Stockholm

BALTIC SEA

ESTONIA

LATVIA

LITHUANIA

EAST PRUSSIA

POLAND

Kiev

Dnieper R.

UKRAINE

BLACK SEA

GEORGIA

Istanbul
Constantinople

TURKEY

RUMANIA

BULGARIA

Danube

HUNGARY

AUSTRIA

CZECHOSLOVAKIA

JUGOSLAVIA

SERBIA

MONTE-
NEGRO

ALBANIA

GERMANY

BAVARIA

WÜRTEM-
BERG

BADEN

SWITZER-
LAND

Geneva

Basel

RHINE

Berlin

DENMARK

NORTH SEA

NETHER-
LANDS

THE

Amsterdam
Utrecht

BELGIUM

FRANCE

Paris

ITALY

Rome

CORSICA

SARDINIA

SICILY

MEDITERRANEAN SEA

AFRICA

SPAIN

PORTUGAL

GREAT
BRITAIN

SCOTLAND

ENGLAND

London

Newcastle

Liverpool

WALES

EIRE

Maynooth

NORTH
CHANNEL

ICELAND

Chapter 57

STORM, TESTING, LOSSES, AND VITALITY IN TRADITIONAL CHRISTENDOM AFTER A.D. 1914

As we have suggested, the wars and revolutions which began in the summer of 1914 bore especially heavily on the historic stronghold of Christianity, Europe and Western Asia. Here World War I broke out. Here the revolutions began and the revolutionary ideologies were developed which swept across much of the rest of the world. As was to be expected, they were particularly potent in the region of their origin. Here World War II had its strategic centre and wrought much of its devastation. Here were the scenes of the origin of the main forms of Christianity, whether of the various Eastern Churches, the Roman Catholic Church, or the major expressions of Protestantism. Here had been the chief theological activity and here almost all the varieties of monasticism had had their birth. In Europe and Western Asia, accordingly, after 1914, Christianity faced one of the greatest challenges of its history. In Western Asia it was already suffering from the centuries-long erosion of Islam. In Europe, and particularly in Western Europe, it was being subjected to the continued attrition of the intellectual currents and the industrialization of society which we have noted as menaces in the nineteenth century and earlier.

Would Christianity survive the combination of these older attacks and the added threats of the twentieth century? If it perished or even seriously dwindled in Europe and Western Asia, would it continue on its geographic periphery, where it had displayed so striking an expansion since the fifteenth and especially since the eighteenth century? If it were fatally or even seriously wounded at what had been the centres from which it had spread, would it persist and continue to grow at its extremities? By the middle of the twentieth century it was clear that it was suffering numerical losses in Europe and Western Asia and that in some quarters there were indications of a failure of nerve. On the other hand, fresh expressions of vitality were appearing in all three major branches of Christianity, most strikingly in the one which had displayed the greatest vigour in the nineteenth century, Protestantism, but also in the Roman Catholic Church, and, to a much less extent, in some of the Eastern Churches. Nor did Protestants and Roman Catholics cease their efforts to spread the faith throughout the world. Rather, they redoubled them, and with the result that the momentum seen on the eve of 1914 continued and issued in what we hinted near the close of the preceding chapter.٠

THE ROMAN CATHOLIC CHURCH IN EUROPE AFTER 1914

Following the order which we adopted in our account of the nineteenth century, we turn first of all to the record of the Roman Catholic Church in Europe after 1914. We must remember, however, that simultaneously the developments were in progress in Protestantism and the Eastern Churches which we are to summarize a little later. The three main branches of Christianity did not interact on one another as closely as had the Roman Catholic and the Eastern Churches before 1350 or as had the Roman Catholic Church and Protestantism in the sixteenth and seventeenth centuries. They had about as much influence on one another as in the nineteenth century, perhaps slightly more than then. Protestantism especially affected the other two. Yet they tended to go their separate ways. We will first note, in comprehensive outline, the series of blows to which the Roman Catholic Church was subjected after 1914 and then describe, although with what must be tantalizing brevity, what took place in certain phases of the life of that church and in particular countries and areas.

To those who are at all familiar with the stage in the history of Europe which was ushered in by the events of the summer of 1914, the main blows dealt the Roman Catholic Church in its traditional heart-land require only the briefest mention. First was World War I. It entailed the destruction of what had long been a bulwark of the Roman Catholic Church, the Hapsburg-ruled Austria-Hungarian Empire, serious damage to Belgium, an almost solidly Roman Catholic land, exhausting drains on France, from which more Roman Catholic missionaries had come in the nineteenth century than from any other country, the defeat of Germany, whose Catholic constituency had been increasingly active in the latter part of the nineteenth century, and debilitating efforts by Italy, where was the headquarters of the Roman Catholic Church. There followed, as an aftermath of the war, the triumph of fascism in Italy, with its demand for complete control over the lives of Italians, particularly of youth, with objectives which were not-too-covertly anti-Christian, the domination of Germany and Austria by the Nazis, equally intent upon a totalitarian regime which demanded the subservience of the Church and the complete possession of the minds and souls of youth, and the growing menace of Russian communism, as yet only on the periphery of the Roman Catholic citadel. Civil war in Spain brought further complications, as did the fascist adventure in Ethiopia. Then came World War II with physical destruction and spiritual exhaustion which wounded Europe much more deeply than had World War I and which was followed by the advance of the iron curtain of vigorously totalitarian, emphatically anti-Roman Catholic Russian communism over lands with Roman Catholic majorities and with the threat of a farther westward movement of that curtain into traditionally Roman Catholic territory.

In Europe in general the Roman Catholic Church emerged from World War I with an enhanced prestige and vigour that carried through the troubled period which much of mankind was despairingly hoping would be an introduction to permanent peace but which proved to be a prelude to an even more gigantic war. The Papal throne was occupied by a succession of able men, Benedict XV (Giacomo della Chiesa), who reigned from 1914 to 1922, Pius XI (Achille Ratti), of middle class stock, scholar, mountaineer, and courageous and skilful administrator, who wore the tiara from 1922 to 1939, and Pius XII (Eugenio Pacelli), a scion of the Papal nobility who succeeded him, the first Papal secretary of state to be elevated to that high office since Hildebrand (Gregory VII). Men of experience and initiative, they were vigorous and usually astute.

During and after World War I Benedict XV again and again addressed the world, calling to its attention principles for establishing peace and urging the belligerents to compose their differences. He used the facilities of his church to alleviate the sufferings from the war through negotiating the exchange of prisoners and civilians in occupied countries, aiding the sick, furthering the repatriation of prisoners of war and the correspondence of prisoners with their families, and promoting the relief of devastated areas.

After the war there was a decided revival in the Roman Catholic Church. Youth organizations sprang up, additional episcopal sees were organized, numbers of monastic, educational, and charitable institutions flourished, frequent communion was emphasized, Eucharistic Congresses in various parts of the world stimulated and focused the devotion of clergy and laity, and Catholic Action, begun in the nineteenth century, enlisted more and more of the laity.

The study of theology was quickened. True to the impetus given by Leo XIII, it stressed Thomas Aquinas, and thinkers appeared who commanded respect not only within but also outside Roman Catholic circles. Some of the intellectuals who had regarded Christianity as not worthy of consideration were again willing to examine the claims of Roman Catholic philosophy and theology. Among those who won their attention was Jacques Maritain

(1882——), a Frenchman of Protestant antecedents, a convert in his twenties, who from his personal experience as well as his observation came to believe that the course of the stream from Descartes through Rousseau, Kant, Hegel, Darwin, and Freud had led the modern man away from God to atheism and futility. He found what seemed to him to be the answer in Catholic faith as expressed by Aquinas, sought to interpret it in fresh ways, and hoped that through those who accepted it growing islands of Christian life and sanity would emerge in a culture which he regarded as disintegrating through its abandonment of the principles on which the great spirits of the Middle Ages had sought to build civilization. Étienne Henry Gilson (1884——), another Frenchman, reared a Roman Catholic and not a convert as was Maritain, a specialist on the thought of the Middle Ages, was not so exclusively attached to Aquinas, but regarded him as one of the eminent formulators of Christian theology. The Jesuit Erich Przywara (1889——), of Slavic descent but working in Germany and in German, in opposition to recent and current philosophy which rejected or belittled Christianity, held that logically the only possible metaphysics is Catholic and argued that Aquinas had shown how the Christian revelation apprehended by faith had met the problem of the contradiction between God and the world and had bridged the gap between them.

The trends in Roman Catholic theology, like those which we are to see in Protestant and Orthodox theology, obviously reflected an awareness of the parlous state of the world and especially of Western civilization as revealed by the wars and revolutions of the day. There was a deep conviction that the Occident must have been proceeding on false premises, that the error was in a lack of understanding and in a faulty conception of man and the universe, and that the truth was in the historic Christian faith.

A revival of Roman Catholic piety was furthered by the liturgical movement. Having its inception, as we have seen (Chapter 46), in the nineteenth century, it was given a marked impetus in 1914 in the monastery of Maria Laach in Germany and continued to spread. As we have noted, it was an attempt to deepen and strengthen the corporate life of the Church through a return to the practice of the early centuries of the faith in the intelligent participation of the congregation in the Eucharist. Instead of the members of the congregation being simply spectators and hearers of what was done in the mass by priest and choir, it would have them share in it. The liturgical movement took many forms. In one of its aspects it encouraged the wide distribution of missals, with translations into the vernaculars to enable the congregation to follow what was done at the altar. As a further step it taught the members of the congregation to give the responses to what was said by the priest. In some places it encouraged the congregation to join in singing the mass, often stressing the Gregorian music which had gained fresh favour in the nineteenth century through Papal initiative. In a few localities, notably after World War II, it put the liturgy into the vernacular except for the central formulæ, which were kept in Latin. The movement sought to make of the Roman Catholic Church not merely a huge administrative structure but also and primarily a living organism and wished to penetrate and inspire Catholic Action with a growing sense of the reality of the central mystery of the faith and to reawaken the Church as a community of faith in which both priests and laity had a part. The liturgical movement gained momentum, grew in various countries in Europe, was made a means of winning some from the de-Christianized industrial labourers, and became especially prominent after World War II.

Both the theological developments and the liturgical movement were manifestations of the trend which we noted in the nineteenth century that tended to make the Roman Catholic Church a self-conscious minority in a hostile world and increasingly under centralized control by the Papacy. By the mid-twentieth century that trend was by no means carried through to its logical conclusion. In some countries the traditional particularism continued, even though weakened. In many lands the Roman Catholic faith was officially that of the state and the nation and was accepted by the masses as a social heritage without much intelligent conviction. Yet more and more the Roman Catholic Church was becoming an hierarchical structure directed by the Pope, supported by a loyal, hard-working body of clergy, monks, and nuns, and maintained by an instructed and disciplined laity.

A demonstration of the power of the Supreme Pontiff was given in the proclamation by Pius XII on November 1, 1950, of the bodily assumption to heaven of the Virgin Mary as a dogma to be believed by all the faithful. It was the first instance of a solemn definition of dogma by the Pope since that of the immaculate conception of the Virgin Mary in 1854 and also the first since Papal infallibility had been affirmed by the Vatican Council in 1870. Unlike the action of 1870, it was accepted by the clergy and laity without serious dissent.

The Roman Catholic Church was still the largest of the sects or divisions in the Christian Church. The Popes were unwavering in their insistence that the only true unity of Christians was through obedience to them as the successors of Peter and as therefore entrusted by Christ with the direction of his Church. In face of the growing Ecumenical Movement among Protestants and of invitations from the latter to join in it and thus tacitly or openly to consent to being one among several churches, none with priority over the others or the exclusive possessor and guardian of Christian truth, the Pope (June 5, 1948) forbade Catholics to take part in public discussions of religious questions without the permission of the Holy See. Pius XII, as had others in his office, invited all

Christians to come to what he declared to be the one fold and the one shepherd.

Nor was the Roman Catholic Church content to be on the defensive. Recognizing the hostility of the world and glorying in its heritage of a long line of those who had suffered martyrdom for the faith, it continued to seek to win all men. Never had it had Popes who were more zealous supporters of its global missions than were those of the twentieth century. Increasingly Rome expanded its direction and control of missions. This was partly through able leadership in the Congregation for the Propagation of the Faith. In 1922 the Society for the Propagation of the Faith, an organization French in origin and long French in leadership, was placed more immediately under Papal direction and its headquarters were moved to Rome. Contributions to foreign missions mounted and the staffs of missionaries increased. Moreover, the Popes emphasized the importance of training and recruiting an indigenous clergy and raised to the episcopate more and more natives of Asia and some Negroes of Africa. Thus they sought to root the Church in these areas and to give vivid demonstration of the mankind-embracing scope of the Roman Catholic Church. The number of Roman Catholics mounted in South and East Asia and in Africa south of the Sahara. The growth was especially phenomenal in the Belgian Congo and, until the adverse political conditions which came late in the 1930's, it was very marked in China. While support in personnel and money for the world-wide mission from the United States and Canada mounted rapidly, in the middle of the twentieth century most of it was still from Europe. Beleaguered though it was in Europe, from that, its ancient centre, the Roman Catholic Church continued to push forward its geographic frontiers in all possible quarters of the planet.

In Italy, strangely enough, for both the Roman Catholic Church and the fascist government which came to power in 1922 aspired to control all aspects of the nation's life, the tension was eased which had existed between Church and state since the triumph of the unified Kingdom of Italy in the preceding century. It will be recalled that following the French Revolution and the Napoleonic era anti-clericalism had been prominent. Although almost all Italians were nominally Roman Catholics, the politically united liberal Italy eliminated the Papal States and confiscated the properties of many of the monastic houses. The Popes, in protest, considered themselves "prisoners of the Vatican" and forbade the faithful to take part in the government. Now, by formal agreements, a partial reconciliation was effected between Pius XI and Mussolini, the head of the Fascist regime. At the very outset of his reign Pius XI conferred his initial blessing *urbi et orbi* from the front balcony of St. Peter's, thus breaking the precedent set by his immediate predecessors who, since the absorption of the Papal States in 1870, had given it from within the Vatican. In 1929 by the Lateran Treaty the Pope's temporal power was restored by the creation of the state of Vatican City, a small domain of 109 acres centering about St. Peter's, and by the recognition of the Supreme Pontiff's status as a sovereign prince. The Pope was paid an indemnity to compensate for his loss of revenues from his former domains. A concordat (also in 1929) regularized the relations between the Vatican and the Kingdom of Italy. By it the state recognized the religious ceremony as giving civil status to marriage, and the teaching of the Roman Catholic religion was made obligatory in secondary education, supplementing an earlier act (1923) which introduced religious instruction in the elementary schools. The clergy were accorded special privileges. In return the state was to have a voice in the appointment of clergy and the boundaries of dioceses were to be altered to make them correspond as nearly as possible with those of the civil provinces.

Yet the ink was scarcely dry on these documents when conflict arose, largely over the control of youth and over social and economic issues. Mussolini ordered the church organizations of boys and girls absorbed into the fascist structure and commanded that the young men's organizations connected with Catholic Action be dissolved. The fascists also sought to extend the control of the state over church schools. On his side, the Pope claimed the right to make pronouncements on social and economic issues. This he did in *quadragesimo anno,* May 15, 1931, issued on the fortieth anniversary of Leo XIII's famous *rerum novarum,* in which he sought to apply its principles to current conditions. A partial and uneasy compromise was reached by which the fascists agreed to the renewal of the Roman Catholic youth organizations and the Pope assented to limitations on the functions of those bodies.

When, in 1935, Italy invaded Ethiopia, although Pius XI incurred the displeasure of the fascist press by declaring wars of conquest unjust, the Roman Catholic Church made no clear-cut protest but sought to take advantage of the situation to extend Papal authority over the Ethiopian Church.

World War II and the collapse of the fascist regime and the Kingdom of Italy followed by the coming of a republican form of government worked no basic changes in the relations of Church and state. During World War II Pius XII laboured for peace and sought to protect the suffering. In May, 1940, he incurred the wrath of Mussolini by expressing his sympathy with Belgium, Luxembourg, and the Netherlands at the time of the German invasion. After Italy became a belligerent he exerted himself to have Rome declared an open city by both sides and thus to save it from bombing and pillage. He was so far successful that until the later days of the conflict Rome was spared and then was not as heavily bombed as were several other major cities of Europe. When, in 1946, the monarchy was overturned, the Holy See, true to its established policy of uncompromising condemnation of communism, sought to rouse Italian Catholics to oppose the communists in the elections. In 1948 it mobilized the parish priests, Catholic Action, youth groups, and women's societies and aided in the victory of the Christian Democrats. Already, in 1947, the Lateran Treaty of 1929 had been written into the constitution of the republic. The Pope sought to undercut communism by encouraging measures to improve the conditions of tenant-farmers and other low-income groups.

We must note the revival of Roman Catholic thought among Italians. Papal encyclicals, monastic orders, teachers in the expanding Catholic universities, and various laymen helped to reduce the gap between science and religion and formulated Roman Catholic economics, sociology, political science, and psychology.

Inevitably the Roman Catholic Church was involved in the welter of Spanish politics. In 1931 the monarchy gave way to a republic. The republican government nationalized ecclesiastical property but left it in the hands of the Church. It disestablished the Church, discontinued the salaries paid by the state to the clergy, ordered the Jesuits expelled, and forbade Roman Catholic teaching orders and congregations to continue their educational activities. In several cities mobs destroyed churches and convents. While for a time the moderates were in power and the anti-clerical measures were relaxed, in 1936 radicals again resorted to violence and priests were killed and churches were burned. In 1936 civil war broke out between a confused combination of liberals and radicals, including communists, on the one hand and conservatives on the other. In general Russia supported the radicals and the Nazis the conservatives. The struggle, which did not end until March, 1939, became a prelude to the European phase of World War II. The conservatives were headed by Franco and the *Falange Española Tradicionalista*. Franco, supported by his army, became dictator. Franco's government was an uneasy alliance of the army, the landowners, capitalists, and the Roman Catholic Church. The Roman Catholic faith was again made the state religion, ecclesiastical property was restored to the Church, religious bodies were once more permitted, and religious instruction was resumed in the schools. In general, the support of the Church by the state was continued into the 1950's. The pendulum which in the nineteenth century had swung violently from anti-clericalism to clericalism and again to anti-clericalism, was now pronouncedly at a clerical extreme.

Portugal had a somewhat similar record, although not punctuated by quite as much violence. In its early years the republic which in 1910 had supplanted the monarchy was anti-clerical. Church and state were separated and the religious orders were expelled. The course of the republic was stormy and varied.

A measure of peace was established in 1926 when Carmona became president. He continued in that post into the 1950's. In 1933 Salazar, as prime minister, began what in effect was a dictatorship. A devout Roman Catholic, his regime was pro-clerical. While in principle liberty of worship was assured, by a concordat of 1940 its property was restored to the Roman Catholic Church. In other ways the Salazar regime favoured that church.

In some ways the Roman Catholic Church sank to its nadir in France with its disestablishment in the first decade of the twentieth century. World War I and its immediate aftermath saw a partial recovery. For a variety of reasons the Roman Catholic faith gained in prestige. Several of the most popular generals were known to be devout Catholics and numbers of priests gained fame by their heroism. Diplomatic relations with the Vatican were resumed and religious orders and congregations were permitted to renew their labours. The de-Christianization which had begun in the eighteenth century and which had been proceeding at unequal pace from the time of the Revolution appeared to have been halted. The theological revival and the espousal of the faith by some of the intellectuals of which we spoke a few moments ago continued. The liturgical movement made itself felt.

However, in the 1940's various studies seemed to show that de-Christianization, if halted, was still marked. Slightly more than three-fourths of the population were said to be baptized in the Catholic faith, and it was reported that even in Paris four-fifths of the children born between 1930 and 1943 had been given the rite, but it was contended that for the majority baptism was merely a social convention inherited from earlier ages. It was declared that only about a fourth of the population had regular contact with the Church, and that at most only a tenth could be counted as "observing" Catholics, faithful to their duties to the faith. The "observants" were estimated to vary from 2 per cent. in the cities to 38 per cent. in rural districts. In some cities de-Christianization was comparatively recent and remnants of Christian culture and attitudes survived. In others it had been accomplished so many years before that scarcely a memory of Christian mentality could be found. As part of the aftermath and the sufferings of World War II a form of "existentialism" appeared which was indebted to Kierkegaard but which, with Sartre as its outstanding spokesman, was frankly non-Christian. It enjoyed a wide vogue among intellectuals and pseudo-intellectuals.

Yet after World War II active missionary efforts to win the de-Christianized were noted and here and there priests were working as manual labourers in factories to make understanding contacts with members of the classes who had drifted furthest from the faith.

Belgium remained predominantly Roman Catholic and made surprisingly rapid recovery from the German invasions of the two world wars. All faiths were tolerated and the state paid the salaries not only of Roman Catholic priests but also of Protestant clergy and Jewish pastors. Religious instruction was given in the primary schools. Advanced social legislation was continued. While an anti-clerical trend was sometimes seen in the government, in general Belgium was spared the extremes which were seen in Spain and earlier in France, Italy, and Portugal.

Because of their high birth rate, the proportion of Roman Catholics mounted in the once predominantly and still traditionally Protestant Netherlands.

The decades which followed World War I brought severe trials to the Roman Catholic Church in Germany. The years immediately following the war did not prove as adverse as those of the national socialist (Nazi) regime. Roman Catholics were prominent in the government under the republic which was set up after the overthrow of the Hohenzollern monarchy. Several of the chancellors were of that faith. Communism, for a time a serious threat, ceased to be formidable. A concordat favourable to the Church was entered into between the Vatican and Bavaria. Many schools and monasteries were founded and new parishes were created. The advent to power of Hitler, in 1933, brought increasing adversity. The Centre Party, predominantly Roman Catholic, disbanded in 1933, but the national socialists were distrustful of Catholic Action, fearing that it was the Centre Party under another guise. In 1933 the Vatican entered into a concordat with the German Government which seemed to assure the Church of the large degree of freedom which it had enjoyed under the preceding regime. However, conflicts soon broke out. In 1934 the Nazi state began to act against Roman Catholic labour organizations. Repressive measures were taken against the Roman Catholic press. In 1935 efforts were instituted to indoctrinate children in Roman Catholic schools with the Nazi world view and other attempts followed to curtail Roman Catholic education and to wean youth from the Church and capture it for Hitler. Government officials accused religious houses of being centres of currency smuggling and of sexual irregularities.

The annexation of Austria by Germany in 1938 brought problems to the Church in that prevailingly Roman Catholic country. It was followed by the secularization of most of the schools, the closing of numbers of Church educational institutions, the dissolution of several monasteries and theological seminaries, the imprisonment of many priests, the extensive confiscation of ecclesiastical properties, and the renunciation of the faith by thousands.

In the face of these attacks the German bishops spoke out against the violations of the concordat and against restrictions on freedom and the euthanasia of the insane and incurables. Here and there Roman Catholics united with Protestants in resistance to the Nazi regime.

World War II brought distress, partly through the concentration camps and partly through the destruction by enemy bombing of thousands of civilians and many church buildings. Roman Catholics and Protestants often shared the use of such churches as escaped. After the war the Church rose to the task of relief of the sufferers and the repair and reconstruction of its physical equipment. In the portions of Germany which remained outside the Russian Zone about half the population was Roman Catholic. Better organized than the divided Protestantism, the Roman Catholic Church was making gains and was winning converts.

THE ROMAN CATHOLIC CHURCH AND COMMUNISM IN EUROPE

It was in communism that the Roman Catholic Church discerned its major enemy in the decades which followed World War I and to it that church, led by the Popes, presented sturdy resistance. Communism and the government of the U.S.S.R. paid the Roman Catholic Church the compliment of taking its opposition seriously and seeking in every way in their power to undermine it, either by destroying it completely or by severing its national units from their administrative allegiance to Rome and making them completely submissive to the communist state. Communism could bring to the contest a coherent ideology spread by all the devices of modern propaganda with no regard for the truth and supported by the might of a totalitarian regime. The Roman Catholic Church had as weapons simply its faith and its ecclesiastical organization unsupported by police or armies. The Church entered the struggle handicapped by the losses which it had already suffered and was hampered by the other adverse forces which we have repeatedly described as operating in the nineteenth and twentieth centuries. The contest appeared uneven. The Roman Catholic Church was dealt severe blows, but by the mid-century its main citadels were unshaken. Here was an epic struggle of world-embracing scope which had only begun by the mid-twentieth century and which would require volumes fully to narrate. All that we can hope to do is to mention a few of the main features of its European phases. We must later note it in other parts of the world.

We have already seen the fashion in which the Roman Catholic Church was confronted by communism, usually in association with other movements, in Germany after World War I, in Spain between the two world wars, and in Italy after World War II. Communism was also to be seriously reckoned with in France, especially after World War II. It was, however, in Russia itself and in Central Europe that the Roman Catholic Church chiefly felt the full force of communism. In Russia the Communist Party seized power in 1917, here, in the guise of the U.S.S.R., it fully consolidated itself, and here communism espoused the traditional Russian imperialism, but in new, camouflaged, and more potent forms. In the U.S.S.R. itself Roman Catholics were small minorities. Although the Kremlin took vigorous action against the Roman Catholic Church within what had been its post World War I borders, the numerical losses could not be large. It was in the border lands, especially Hungary, Czechoslovakia, Poland, Latvia, Estonia, and Lithuania, which were brought within the iron curtain, particularly by World War II and its aftermath, that the numerical threat was the most pronounced.

As a consequence of World War I and the break-up of the Hapsburg empire, Hungary became a republic. In it Roman Catholics were a majority, with Protestants constituting substantial minorities. In 1918 that republic was under the communists, led by a Jew, Bela Kun. Many priests and bishops were killed and much ecclesiastical property was confiscated. Roman Catholics and Protestants joined forces, defeated the communists, and in 1920 a monarchical form of government was instituted, but without the Hapsburgs. The former religious situation was largely restored, with Roman Catholics constituting more than two-thirds of the population. In 1928 a concordat was reached with the Vatican and a diplomatic representative was sent to the Holy See. In 1944 German forces occupied the country and set up a regime favourable to the Nazis. The following year Russian troops drove out the Germans, in 1946 a republic was proclaimed, and in February, 1947, a peace treaty was signed with the United Nations. In August, 1946, diplomatic relations were restored with the Vatican. Early in 1949 what was called the People's Independent Front was formed of several parties, with the communists clearly dominant. While the constitution of 1949 separated the Church from the state "to ensure freedom of conscience and the free practice of religion," twice that year the British and American Governments formally declared that the peace treaty was being violated by the denial of human rights and fundamental freedoms. In 1949, in spite of emphatic protests from the Vatican, the primate of the Roman Catholic Church in Hungary, Cardinal Mindszenty, was sentenced to life imprisonment on the charge of treason. The following year fifty-nine orders with more than ten thousand monks and nuns were dissolved and their properties were confiscated. Most church schools, then comprising more than half of the educational institutions, were nationalized in 1948, and in 1950 only eight licensed Roman Catholic schools remained, staffed by members of teaching orders.

In Czechoslovakia, which in 1918 emerged from World War I as an independent republic, nearly three-fourths of the population were Roman Catholics. The first government tended to be socialist and anti-clerical and only strong

Roman Catholic opposition prevented the confiscation of Church property and making civil marriage compulsory. Between 1918 and 1930 several hundred thousand Roman Catholics separated themselves from Rome and, while preserving much of the faith, had a married clergy and a liturgy in the vernacular. More thousands broke entirely with the Church and called themselves agnostics. In the 1920's adjustments were effected between the state and the Vatican through which much of its sequestered land was restored to the Church, the teaching of religion was included in the programmes of the schools, the state was to have a voice in naming the bishops and was to provide the salaries of the clergy, the latter were to be citizens and take the oath of allegiance to the republic, and part of the Church services were to be in the vernacular. In 1939 came the German annexation, but by the outcome of World War II the country was freed from Nazi rule. Then, in 1948, the National Front was formed of several parties, the familiar device by which the communists sought to achieve control, and obtained possession of the government. The orientation was increasingly towards Moscow. In 1949 the state adopted the policy of administering all the churches through a department of ecclesiastical affairs and of paying the salaries of the clergy. By 1950 more than nine-tenths of the clergy were said to have taken the oath of allegiance to the government. Here was an attempt, largely successful, to nullify the administrative control by the Pope of a branch of the Roman Catholic Church.

For the Roman Catholic Church the outcome of World War I brought gains in Poland, gains which were threatened by World War II and its sequel and by ties with Communist Russia. World War I was followed by the independence and re-integration of Poland after its dismemberment in the eighteenth century by its strong neighbours, Russia, Prussia, and Austria. Since Poland was overwhelmingly Roman Catholic, this carried with it the appearance of a strong, unified Roman Catholic bloc, reinforced by nationalist loyalties. In 1925 relations between Poland and the Vatican were regularized by a concordat. With the approval of the Church a dictatorship was set up in Poland and parliamentary government was discontinued. The new Poland had many Orthodox Ukrainians within its borders. The Poles attempted by force to assimilate the Ukrainians and this entailed the attempt to win them to Roman Catholicism by depriving them, by imprisonment, of their Orthodox clergy and the execution of many.

With the coming of World War II to Europe in September, 1939, Poland was invaded from the west by the Germans and from the east by the Russians. Polish resistance was quickly crushed and both the conquerors took measures to erase Polish nationalism, measures which included restraints on the Roman Catholic Church. That church was obviously their enemy, especially since the

Pope maintained close and friendly ties with the Polish government-in-exile and during the latter part of that struggle accorded its ambassador asylum in the Vatican. For nearly four years, from June, 1941, when the Nazi armies moved against Russia, until the fore part of 1945, when the Russians drove them out, the Germans occupied the country and Roman Catholics suffered, although not as much as the Jews.

After the Nazis were expelled, with Russian assistance a Polish government was set up, obviously friendly to Russia and communism. A constitution was adopted for the Republic of Poland. By the standard device of a coalition with friendly groups and parties, in 1947 the communists obtained full control. The coming of the new regime boded ill for the Roman Catholic Church. The Vatican did not give it formal recognition but continued relations with the Polish government-in-exile. The communists attempted to convince the Poles that while they were under the Nazis the Pope had abandoned them. The Ruthenian Uniates, former Orthodox, whom the pressure of the Polish king and nobility had brought into union with Rome in 1596 by the Synod of Brest (Chapter 40), were now encouraged by the Russians to renounce the tie with Rome. Many of their bishops were deported, imprisoned, or killed, a synod of 216 priests seceded from the Union of Brest, praised Stalin for bringing them back into the Orthodox fold, and their church was put under the Patriarch of Moscow. The communist regime attempted to separate the Roman Catholics in Poland from the administrative control of Rome and in 1950 representatives of the episcopate signed an agreement with the government which, while guaranteeing freedom of worship, religious instruction, and participation in charitable activities, was so worded that it could be interpreted by the communists in their favour.

The little countries, Estonia, Latvia, and Lithuania, which had been given their independence as a result of World War I, were forcibly incorporated into the U.S.S.R. in 1940. A considerable proportion of their population was Roman Catholic. Under Soviet rule the Roman Catholic Church was gravely weakened by deportations, many of them to Siberia, and by other measures. The Pope attempted to aid those who had fled to Western Europe and in 1946 set up the Lithuanian Ecclesiastical Institute for exiled Lithuanian priests.

In Rumania, after World War II formally independent but under communist control, action was also taken against Roman Catholics. In 1948 the Uniate priests were constrained to petition the Orthodox Patriarch for readmission to the Orthodox Church. Roman Catholics of the Latin rite were put under pressure and almost all the hierarchy were imprisoned.

The lines continued to be ever more sharply drawn between the Roman Catholic Church and the communists. In July, 1948, a Pan-Orthodox conference held in Moscow in celebration of the five hundredth anniversary of the independence of the Orthodox Church of Russia from Constantinople formally denounced the Pope for his "participation in fratricidal wars against democracy in defense of fascism." On July 1, 1949, Pius XII, through a decree published by the Supreme Congregation of the Holy Office, a body established in 1542 with substantially the same powers as the Spanish Inquisition, declared that it was not permitted to any Catholic to become a member of a communist party or to support or circulate publications which defended the doctrines and practice of communism, and denied the sacraments to those who disobeyed.

Although it broke with Moscow, the communist regime of Tito in Jugoslavia embarrassed the Roman Catholic Church. For centuries the territory embraced by Jugoslavia had been divided between Roman Catholics and Orthodox. Croatia was prevailingly Roman Catholic, the Serbs Orthodox. Under the Italo-German occupation during World War II there were attempts at the forcible conversion of the Orthodox by the puppet regime, although the Vatican formally stood against any form of external pressure and insisted that conversion must be by voluntary adherence to the faith. When Tito drove out the Italians and Germans the tables were turned. The head of the Roman Catholic hierarchy, Archbishop Stepinac, was tried and sentenced to sixteen years of hard labour for alleged collaboration with the invaders and the forcible conversion of Orthodox Serbs. Even after he had severed his ties with the Kremlin, Tito refused to release the archbishop. By the end of 1949 over 4,000 Roman Catholic places of worship had been closed, scores of priests had been executed or imprisoned, and hundreds had gone into exile. As the years passed restrictions were somewhat abated.

THE TESTING OF PROTESTANTISM ON THE CONTINENT OF EUROPE

Serious as were the problems which were presented to the Roman Catholic Church by the post-1914 Europe, they were not as grave as those which Protestantism had to meet. Protestantism had its origin in Germany. Here was the historic centre of Lutheranism. Here the Reformed Churches were also strong. Here the creative ferment in nineteenth century Protestant theology and Biblical scholarship was the most marked. From Germany thousands of Protestant missionaries had gone out to many parts of the world. Yet it was Germany which bore the main brunt of defeat in World War I, it was in Germany that national socialism and Hitler sought to make the Church come to heel in the period between the two wars and during World War II, it was Germany which was crushed and divided by the outcome of World War II, and after that division it was chiefly Protestant portions of Germany which were in the Russian zone and subject to communist pressure. Moreover, millions of the Germans who were forcibly displaced by the westward movement of Poland's boundary at the end of World War II were predominantly Protestant. The

German occupation during World War II of the Netherlands, Denmark, and Norway, all with Protestant majorities, the last two overwhelmingly so, for the time being presented a sharp challenge. The deep involvement of predominantly Protestant Great Britain in the two world wars had repercussions on the Christianity of that realm which were, in general, adverse. We are first of all to sketch the record on the Continent of Europe and then are to summarise that in the British Isles.

Early effects of the defeat in World War I on Germany were spiritual shock and efforts on the part of many to seek the rebirth and strengthening of the nation's life through religion. Several movements arose with this objective, mostly through Protestantism. Some boldly departed from Christianity. The more radical, endeavouring to return to the Teutonic spirit which they asserted had given might to the Germans before the advent of Christianity, declared that the country had been weakened by Jewish-Christian influence. In general they were frankly pagan, and added incentive to the anti-semitism which under the Nazis broke out in the most wholesale persecution of those of Jewish blood which the world had seen in centuries.

Some movements were channelled through the churches. The outcome of World War I with the fall of the Hohenzollern empire loosened the historic bond between Church and state. Under the Republic which followed, Church and state were separated. The state became religiously neutral and while it protected the churches it gave them independence in their inner government. Protestants greatly multiplied their youth organizations and extended their works of charity. In general the financial undergirding of the churches came from a percentage of the members' income collected by the churches or through government agencies on behalf of the churches. There were also subsidies from the civil authorities in return for ecclesiastical property confiscated during the Napoleonic era.

One of the post-war movements sought to mobilize the resources of the churches by uniting the several *Landeskirchen,* the territorial bodies which were a survival of the pre-nineteenth century political divisions. In 1921–1922 it drew together twenty-eight of these churches and the Moravians in the German Evangelical Church Federation. That federation was what its name implied and permitted its members to preserve their autonomy.

The coming to power in 1933 of national socialism under Hitler was even more a menace to Protestantism than to the Roman Catholic Church. The latter was more nearly united and accustomed to oppose itself to the state. Protestants were divided, could not act together, and the Lutheran majority had a tradition of subserviency to the state which boded ill for the future under a totalitarian regime. National socialism, with its emphasis upon the German *volk,* strengthened the hands of those who would accommodate Christianity to what they conceived to be the German spirit or would return to pre-Christian German paganism.

What was called the German Faith Movement attracted several groups who in one way or another expressed this trend. With Jacob Wilhelm Hauer, a former missionary and pastor and a professor of comparative religion in one of the universities as an outstanding representative, it sought the emancipation of the German nation from Christianity. However, it disavowed any intention of restoring the cults of the old German gods.

Much less extreme and having the support of Hitler was the Faith Movement of German Christians. It confined its membership to those of Aryan descent, cut off all Masonic connexions, denounced communism, stressed what it declared to be the spirit of Germany and Luther, and sought, by a nation-wide organization, to make of the Church a united body to parallel national socialism. For a time it seemed successful and effected a centralized nation-wide organization embracing both Lutheran and Reformed which had as its head an ardent supporter of Hitler.

Opposition arose, with the courageous and outspoken Martin Niemöller, a former submarine officer and now pastor of a prominent church in Berlin, as a prominent leader. In 1934 it crystallized in the Confessional Synod, or Church, in which Reformed, Lutherans, and United (Lutheran and Reformed) joined. A complicated struggle ensued. A large proportion of the pastors and a minority of the laity held to the Confessional Church, although rifts appeared in the latter between the Lutheran and Reformed. They stood out against the state. The sales of Bibles mounted.

The government was stern, imprisoned many of the pastors, and, in spite of his release by the court with a comparatively small fine, put Niemöller into a concentration camp. In an effort to win and indoctrinate the rising generation, church youth groups were ordered dissolved and the youth were enrolled in Nazi organizations.

World War II added to the difficulties of Protestants. The national socialist state, embarked on a life and death struggle, strove to crush all opposition, including that in the churches. Church publications were curtailed. Many pastors and laymen were arrested, some for protesting against the cruelties against the Jews, some for opposition to the euthanasia of the aged and infirm and the glorification of the unmarried mother, and some for other criticisms of the government. Further difficulties were placed in the way of giving religious instruction to children and youths. It is said that 85 per cent. of the pastors of the Confessional Church were taken into the armies. As the war progressed, enemy bombings destroyed many church buildings. Fuel shortage reduced the number of services in the structures which survived.

As we have suggested, World War II and its immediate aftermath brought to Protestantism heavy territorial losses in some regions and in several other sections and countries imposed severe handicaps. The blows dealt by the German occupation in the Netherlands, Denmark, and Norway, while serious at the time, were not lasting. However, the Russian annexation in 1940 of Estonia, Latvia, and Lithuania, in each of which Lutherans were in the majority, made for substantial reductions in the Protestant bodies in these lands which the end of the war did not repair. The forced migration of Germans, most of them Protestants, from the territories annexed to Poland on the border between that country and Germany was a major loss. The majority of those who were thus displaced moved into Germany and there for a time constituted undigested, poverty-stricken enclaves. The descent of the iron curtain over Hungary, Czechoslovakia, and much of Eastern Germany brought problems to the Protestants in these areas. Their churches were put under varying restraints and disabilities.

Yet Protestantism, like Roman Catholicism, not only persisted. It also displayed remarkable vigour. The Confessional Church attracted many moderates who were alienated from the state by its anti-Christian actions. Some relief was given to prisoners of war. In German-occupied countries, notably the Netherlands and Norway, much of the opposition was spearheaded by church leaders. In the Netherlands the Reformed Church denounced the Nazi treatment of the Jews and the Nazi view of the soul and the world. The Reformed Church achieved a national synodical structure more effective than it had possessed for several generations. At times Roman Catholics and Protestants coöperated in their resistance. In Germany after World War II hundreds of church buildings wrecked by enemy bombings were repaired or rebuilt, and Protestants did much for relief, especially through *Hilfswerk*. In 1948 and 1949 a national federation of the churches (but not a union, for it respected the autonomy of its members) was achieved under the name of the Evangelical Church in Germany which embraced all but one of the *Landeskirchen,* thus renewing and continuing what had been begun in 1921–1922 and 1933 and making unnecessary the Confessional Synod. For at least the time being, one result of the years of suffering was to lower the barriers that had divided the "liberals" from the "orthodox."

THE GROWTH OF THE ECUMENICAL MOVEMENT AND ITS RELATION TO THE CONTINENT

Between the two world wars and notably during and after World War II the Ecumenical Movement grew. More and more it drew into fellowship with one another the Protestants in Europe and outside Europe, thus strengthening

European Protestantism. To this several agencies contributed. One of them was the World's Committee of the Young Men's Christian Associations, aided by the enlarged activities in Europe of the North American Young Men's Christian Associations. Especially outstanding were the formation and growth of the International Missionary Council and the World Council of Churches.

As we have suggested (Chapter 60), the International Missionary Council was a result of the World Missionary Conference held at Edinburgh in 1910. That gathering had taken steps looking towards the formation of such an organization, but the early coming of World War I delayed it. With the war came a rift between the Protestants of Germany and those of the countries which had fought Germany. Several years were required to heal it and it had not been effaced when, in 1921, a gathering at Lake Mohonk, in New York State, brought the International Missionary Council into being. The International Missionary Council chiefly had as members national and regional bodies, among them at the outset the Foreign Missions Conference of North America and the Conference of Missionary Societies of Great Britain and Ireland, and, eventually, the German Protestant Missions Committee (*Ausschuss*), although this last did not send delegates to Lake Mohonk. Rapidly there were formed such bodies as the National Christian Council of India (1923), the National Christian Council of China (1922), the National Christian Council of Japan (1923), the Congo Protestant Council (1924), and the Near East Christian Council for Missionary Coöperation (1929) which became members of the International Missionary Council. John R. Mott was the first chairman and J. H. Oldham one of the first secretaries. Various functions were undertaken, including the continued publication of *The International Review of Missions* and assistance to German missions and missionaries. Conferences were held at Jerusalem in 1928, late in 1938, on a still larger scale, at Tambaram, on the outskirts of Madras, and with smaller attendances, at Whitby, Ontario, in 1947, and Willingen, Germany, in 1952, which did much to help Protestants in coöperative planning for pursuing their world mission. They were especially significant for the wide range of ecclesiastical and theological convictions represented and for the mounting participation of the "younger churches," a now general designation for the bodies planted by Protestant missions in Latin America, Asia, and the Pacific.

At this particular point in our story, however, we are primarily concerned with the fashion in which during and after World War II the International Missionary Council came to the rescue of most of the Protestant missions of the Continent. The outbreak of the European phase of the war in September, 1939, at once cut off German missionaries from financial support from the Fatherland. An initial gift of £250 was made by a donor in Scotland, a country then at war with Germany. Before long aid was sent from other countries and churches. When in 1940 the German "lightning war" brought France, Belgium, the Netherlands, Denmark, and Norway under the Nazi yoke, the missionaries from these lands were also left without contact with their home constituencies. The International Missionary Council assembled what was soon called the "Orphaned Missions Fund." Contributions came from several countries and denominations, including some of the "younger churches," but were mostly from the United States. Close *liaison* was established with American Lutherans, for they gave generously to maintain the missions of their Continental brethren. Assistance continued after the war. So far as the officers of the International Missionary Council knew, not a single unit of the Continental missionary enterprises was suspended because of lack of funds. Here was a solidarity of mutual help by a Christian fellowship which transcended denominational, national, and warring lines which was unprecedented in all the history of Christianity. It showed a striking gain over the divisions that had marred the Protestant fellowship because of World War I.

The World Council of Churches was slightly younger than the International Missionary Council and grew out of the union of two other bodies, the World Conference on Faith and Order and the Universal Christian Council for Life and Work. The first of these, as we have said (Chapter 60), was in part sprung from the World Missionary Conference of 1910. It was for the purpose of bringing together the representatives of the churches to discuss the issues which had traditionally divided them and to explore the possibility of agreement. It held major conferences at Lausanne in 1927 and at Edinburgh in 1937. The other had as its chief creator Nathan Söderblom (1866–1931), primate of the Church of Sweden, and drew part of its inspiration from the 1910 gathering. It was for the purpose of stimulating thought and action on the application of Christian faith and principles to social and international problems. Its chief meetings were at Stockholm in 1925 and at Oxford in 1937. Before Oxford Söderblom had died and J. H. Oldham had become the leading promoter. It seemed to many that a more inclusive organization was advisable to bring the churches together. In May, 1938, representatives of numbers of these bodies convened in Utrecht and drafted a constitution for the World Council of Churches. This had as its nucleus what were called briefly Faith and Order and Life and Work. It was officially described as "a fellowship of churches which accept our Lord Jesus Christ as God and Saviour." In contrast with the International Missionary Council, whose members were regional and national bodies, its members were churches and it was, accordingly, ecclesiastical in structure and outlook. It could not legislate for the churches, but it was intended to facilitate common study and action. Headquarters were established at Geneva, Switzerland. Although the coming of World War II delayed its formal organization, it began functioning in 1938 under the caption of "the World Council of Churches in process of formation." It was officially constituted in a great assembly at Amsterdam in 1948. By that time well over a hundred churches had become members. They included almost all the major Protestant bodies of the Continent of Europe and the British Isles, the majority of those of the Americas and Australasia, and most of the larger "younger churches" of Asia and Africa. It also embraced several of the Orthodox and Old Catholic Churches. Close working ties were established with the International Missionary Council and the two bodies were officially described as "in association with" each other. Looser, but also friendly relations were had with what were described as "other ecumenical movements," such as the several world denominational or confessional associations, the World Council of Christian Education (formerly the World's Sunday School Association), the World's Student Christian Federation, and the World's Young Men's Christian Association.

We shall later have more to say of the World Council of Churches and the other phases of the Ecumenical Movement. Here we must note that during World War II the World Council of Churches, although still only "in process of formation," did much to cement bonds between churches on both sides of the warring lines and to care for sufferers from the struggle, and that after the fighting ceased it was the major coördinating agency for the extensive relief given by the Protestant Churches of the British Isles, the United States, and other countries to the Christians of the Continent of Europe and their churches.

The Ecumenical Movement made great strides. Here was the new form of unity among Christians which had been begun before 1914 and which had mounted in phenomenal fashion after World War I. Although obtaining most of its financial support and much of its leadership from the United States and drawing in "younger churches" of Latin America, Asia, and Africa and most of the branches of historical Protestant communions in the Dominions of the British Commonwealth, it had its major centre in Europe. This European orientation was especially marked in the World Council of Churches. Here was a body which, with headquarters in Continental Europe, the heart of Christendom, was bringing together in fellowship almost all the hitherto sundered branches of the Protestantism of that part of the world. It embraced not only representatives of all the main and several of the minor families of Protestantism. In one way or another the Ecumenical Movement also took in many non-Protestants. Thus the Young Men's Christian Associations in Poland were predominantly Roman Catholic in membership and in Greece they were overwhelmingly Orthodox. As we have said, the World Council of Churches had in its membership several of the Eastern and Old Catholic bodies. This was accomplished without weakening allegiance to these non-Protestant bodies. Indeed, a concomitant of the Ecumenical Movement was a renewal of confessional consciousness.

Changing Currents in Protestant Scholarship and Thought on the Continent of Europe

The Protestantism of Europe could scarcely pass through the storms which swept over the Continent in the era which began in the summer of 1914 without profound changes in its thought. Had it failed to respond to the stimulus the presumption would have been that it was moribund. That fresh streams of thought issued from it was evidence of continued vitality.

A sobering but quite understandable development was the waning of the leadership which Germany had held in the nineteenth century. This was to be expected, for Germany was defeated in both wars, between them fell victim to the Nazi madness, and in the second suffered not only from exhaustion by reason of the efforts put forth in that struggle, but also from enemy bombing. Following World War II came the political division between the Eastern and the Western Zones, the advance of the Russian-communist iron curtain over Eastern Germany, the "cold war" between Russia and the West, of which Germany was a chief centre, and the long delay in the writing of a peace treaty.

The waning of German leadership did not mean the complete disappearance of theological ferment. Down to the capture of Germany by the national socialists in the 1930's the universities saw an attenuated continuation of the mental activity which had made them outstanding in the nineteenth century. The post World War II years witnessed something of a renewal. Many Germans, some of whom had taken refuge in other countries, commanded the attention and respect of Protestant intellectuals the world over. Yet the number of outstanding German scholars was declining, by mid-century most of them were middle-aged or older, and few younger men were emerging as successors. Much of the theological activity on the Continent which attracted the attention of world-wide Protestantism was in lands which had succeeded in preserving their neutrality during the two wars, Switzerland and Sweden.

In Biblical scholarship a method which gained wide currency was what was known as *Formgeschichte,* or form criticism. It held that records of the life and teaching of Christ in the Four Gospels were largely shaped by the purposes of those who had preserved and handed down what was contained in these brief accounts. These purposes were declared to be missionary and didactic. They were to proclaim the Christian Gospel to non-Christians and instruct catechumens and converts. It was held that they determined to a marked degree the arrangement of what had been transmitted in fragmentary fashion through oral tradition and to some extent modified the phrasing of the incidents and sayings which were reported. So, too, early liturgical use was considered to have modified the accounts of the Last Supper and the interpretations of the meaning of the Eucharist. Form criticism is usually said to have had its inception in *Die Formgeschichte des Evangeliums* by Martin Dibelius (1883-1947), which appeared in 1919, but some of the basic presuppositions were of earlier origin. The method was not universally accepted and those who were more or less committed to it did not fully agree on conclusions reached through it.

Next to form criticism in its influence on the study of the New Testament was the emphasis upon the importance of eschatology in the teachings of Jesus and the letters of Paul. It began before 1914, but was stressed in the period which followed that year. A classic formulation was by Albert Schweitzer (1875——) in the book translated into English under the title *The Quest of the Historical Jesus* and which in its original German edition was published in 1906. An Alsatian, later to become famous as musician, philosopher, theologian, and medical missionary to Africa, in this study Schweitzer held that Jesus had conceived himself as not the founder but the announcer of the kingdom of God and had believed that the kingdom was to be in the future and to be established by the intervention of God. Schweitzer maintained that Jesus regarded "the end of all things" as being close at hand and that he believed that it would be followed by the appearance of himself as Son of Man and the coming of the kingdom. The ethics which Jesus taught, so Schweitzer said, was not intended as universally and always binding on all men, but simply as a "transition-ethics" in preparation for the early climax of history in the coming of the kingdom. Schweitzer also emphasized the eschatological aspects in Paul. Since the death of Jesus was not followed immediately by the intervention of God, so Schweitzer went on to affirm, the Early Church reconstructed its eschatology, or conception of the "last things," the termination of history, and its conviction about Christ. Some other scholars did not accept this view and believed that Jesus expected that the climax of history would be long delayed. However, while by no means fully agreeing with all the conclusions of Schweitzer, a considerable number of scholars saw in the Gospels and Paul more of an expectation of an early end of history than had been often noted. Obviously they ran counter to the assumptions underlying the Social Gospel movement, that the kingdom of God could be built gradually within history by the efforts of man in coöperation with God.

The trend in Protestant thought which attracted the most attention was what was variously known in one or another of its aspects as the theology of crisis, dialectical theology, and neo-orthodoxy. In large part it was at the outset a product of a state of mind induced by World War I and its aftermath. Especially in Germany and the lands immediately around it, men were impressed with the tragedy of life. They saw themselves caught in gigantic forces which were sweeping them to destruction and with which individuals and even nations were unable to cope. They felt themselves powerless in the colossal agony of the years. Sin and evil became real. Did life have meaning? If so, what was it? Where was it to be found? Yet helpless though the individual was to alter the vast and demonic currents about him, he must make decisions. He must say "yes" or "no." He could not be content with abstract, disinterested speculation which had no immediate effect upon him. He could not be merely a spectator. He must make choices between alternatives, between "either" and "or." Those choices might mean for him the difference between life and death.

The results of the struggle were varied. As we have seen, for many the ferment brought the repudiation of Christianity and the search for another answer, often with the dogmatic affirmation of a non-Christian faith. For others who remained within the churches a profound distrust of pre-war philosophy and theology arose. They tended to repudiate the optimism of the nineteenth century and its confidence in the competence of reason and human effort. They lost faith in the idealism which was associated with Kant and Hegel and which saw all the universe, including man, as set in a framework of controlling ideas. They regarded as unsatisfying the theology of Schleiermacher which found validity in the religious experience of the individual, for this was too subjective, and longed for some objective word from God which was not dependent on human feeling. They repudiated the Ritschlianism of the late nineteenth century which believed in the progressive achievement of the kingdom of God through collaboration of men with the divine purpose. Troeltsch himself was badly shaken by the war. Numbers of Christians discovered Kierkegaard (Chapter 47). His existentialism and his dialectical paradoxes spoke to their condition. Many turned again to Luther with renewed interest and found in him, if not the full answer to their quest, at least basic convictions which proved a guide in their darkness.

The theologian who stood out most pronouncedly in this trend and who spoke with a volume and a vigour which commanded the widest hearing, sometimes with assent and sometimes with sharp dissent, was Karl Barth (1886——). Barth was German Swiss by birth, the son of a theological lecturer at Basel. He studied in several German universities and sat at the feet of some of the leading Ritschlians. For a time he was a pronounced liberal. In 1911 he became pastor of a small Reformed church in North-west Switzerland, in that politically neutral land but close to the embattled Germany which was so largely his spiritual home. From that vantage he watched Western Europe pass through the agony of World War I. It was during these years, preaching Sunday after Sunday to a congregation almost within sound of the big guns, that he was forced to think through his faith afresh. It was there that he began the writing which brought him fame. After the war he was in Germany successively on the faculties of Göttingen, Münster, and Bonn. Then, in 1935, because he could not stomach the Nazi regime, he returned to Switzerland and taught at Basel.

The first of his books which brought Barth to the attention of the world was his *Commentary on the Epistle to the Romans,* published in 1918. Coming as it did not far from the climax of World War I and speaking in bold paradoxes and uncompromising denunciation of liberalism and of existing religion and the churches, it provoked controversy. In some quarters it was hailed with enthusiastic approval and in others was emphatically rejected. This and other works which flowed fast from the prolific pen of Barth were the chief source of what became known as the "theology of crisis" or "dialectical theology." By "crisis" was meant what was happening to theology and civilization and also what inevitably overtakes every man and the institutions which man creates when, confident in his own ability, he attempts to solve his problems and finds himself confounded by God. "Dialectical" was intended to signify that man can never by his own reason reach God. When he tries to do so he sees contradictions in his results and can only say "yes" and "no" and wait for a direct word from God, a word which comes not because man deserves it, for this he does not and cannot do, but only through God's grace. Barth maintained that Schleiermacher and those influenced by him had succumbed to subjectivism and that Ritschl, Troeltsch, and others of their ilk had made Christian doctrine contingent on history and therefore as relative to its time and environment and having no absolute, dependable truth. He declared that what we must do is to heed not what other men say about God, but what God has to say to men. Men must listen to the word of God. That word reaches us through the Bible but is not bound by it. He stressed the sinfulness of man. All man's achievements, including religion, so he maintained, are tainted and made worse than futile by man's pride. Man and his works stand under the judgement of God. The world is lost and of themselves men can never find the word which God speaks to it. But, so Barth went on to say, that word has come to us by the direct, sovereign act of God, by revelation through Jesus Christ and his cross and resurrection. Man must humbly accept this revelation. Yet Barth would not have Christians withdraw from the world, but act in it.

Barth thought of himself as formulating nothing new, but as simply again putting into words the unchanging Gospel. In his major work, his several volume *Kirchliche Dogmatik,* he endeavoured to set it forth in full, systematic form. He clearly belonged in the Reformed tradition, with its emphasis upon the sovereignty of God. For a time he was strongly influenced by Kierkegaard, but as the years passed the gloomy Dane was less important in his thinking. However, his orthodoxy was not entirely a repetition of what had gone before. It was "neo-orthodoxy."

Barth was an ardent and often vehement controversialist. Much of his polemic he directed against a fellow and slightly younger Swiss, Emil Brunner (1889——). Brunner was near enough like Barth to be classified with the neo-orthodox, but he differed from him in making a place for "natural theology," namely, man's ability by his searching to arrive at some phases of the truth about God. Born near Zürich, a student there and in Berlin before World War I, for several years a pastor, for a year a student in the United States, during most of his active life Brunner was on the faculty of the University of Zürich. For a time he seemed to agree with Barth, but he came to the conviction that the latter was mistaken in regarding the divine image in man as having been completely destroyed by the fall, in denying that there is a general revelation of God in nature, conscience, and history, and in declaring that there is nothing in human nature which responds to the appeal of God's grace. He affirmed that something of God's will in the "law of nature" is to be found in human institutions. To this Barth made a violently angry retort and from time to time returned to the attack.

Barth's theology helped to give backbone to the Confessional Church in its contest with the Nazi state. A German theologian, Karl Heim (1874——), a native of Württemberg, and for a time secretary of the German Student Christian Movement, led in the intellectual battle against that German Faith Movement which was a frankly pagan and anti-Christian development in the years between the two world wars. He centered his theology around three convictions, namely, Christ as Lord and Leader (the latter in conscious contrast with Hitler and others who were called *Führer,* or leader), Christ as saviour from sin, and Christ as deliverer from the powers of darkness and death.

Differing in many ways from Barth and Heim was Paul Tillich (1886——). Prussian by birth, a chaplain in the German army in World War I, he was successively on the faculties of five German universities, and then, because of his opposition to the Nazis, went to the United States (1933) to the staff of Union Theological Seminary, in New York City. While in Germany, in addition to his writing and teaching in philosophy and theology, he was active in politics. In his later years his thought was especially influential in the United States. Impressed with the urgency of the time and the revolutionary movements, he sought to apply in fresh ways the basic distinctive Protestant principles.

In Sweden, neutral during both world wars, religious life had a somewhat distinct course, by no means indifferent to the storms in the world about it, but without such drastic changes as in Germany. Nathan Söberblom (1866–1931), a distinguished scholar and teacher, who died as Archbishop of Uppsala and thus as primate of the Church of Sweden, in the years which immediately followed World War I was the outstanding personality in Scandinavian religious life. He was best known for his share in the Ecumenical Movement and especially for his part in calling into being the Universal Christian Council for Life and Work and his guiding hand during its earlier years. There was a continuation of the liturgical revival which had become marked in the nineteenth century. In theology two names were especially prominent, Gustaf Emanuel Hildebrand Aulén (1879——) and Anders Nygren (1890——), members of the faculty of the University of Lund. Both men were influenced by Barth and criticized much of the liberalism of nineteenth century German theology from Schleiermacher to Ritschl and Harnack. However, they did not go as far to the extreme of rejecting human reason and its product, natural theology, as did Barth. Moreover, in contrast with Barth, who was clearly in the Reformed tradition, and loyal to their Lutheran rearing and associations, while deploring some of the developments in Lutheranism after Luther, they stressed what they believed that they found in him. They tended to go back to the great theologians of the early Christian centuries and to restore what they regarded as classical Christianity. They did not care for Barth's paradoxes and put in the foreground the wonder and joy of the incarnation of Christ as victor. Nygren especially emphasized *agape,* the self-giving love of God, as central and distinctive in Christianity.

The reaction against nineteenth century liberalism spread to the Reformed Churches in the Netherlands and France, but in neither did it win universal acceptance and in the Netherlands it produced fresh divisions. However, in France reunion was achieved between the two wings of the Reformed Church which had separated in the nineteenth century.

CONTRASTING LOSS AND VIGOUR IN CONTINENTAL PROTESTANTISM

Seen from some angles, after 1914 Protestantism on the Continent of Europe appeared to be declining. The mounting vitality which had been exhibited by many churches in the latter part of the nineteenth century had partly obscured the indifference and even the defection of many which were especially marked in the cities and industrial communities, the storm centres and focal points of the new age. After 1914, accelerated by the world wars and the revolutions which began in that year, the drift away from Christianity continued. The large majority still outwardly conformed to patterns which had become traditional as social customs. They were baptized and confirmed, and usually were married in the Church and buried from it. Yet for the majority active participation in the Church declined. In Germany it was estimated that about 95 per cent. of the population had a formal church membership. Yet, while the proportion varied greatly from section to section and city to city, in the mid-century it was said that only between 5 and 10 per cent. of the Protestants were regular attendants at church.

In the Netherlands an increasing proportion of the population, especially in the cities, was reported to be without a vital church connexion. Even in Sweden, neutral in both wars and where religious instruction was part of the curriculum in the schools, where the overwhelming majority were supposed to be members of the Church of Sweden, and where the tie between Church and state continued, in the 1940's only a small minority, said to be from 4 to 7 per cent., were regular attendants at the services of the Church.

This was only one side of the picture. A minority were deeply committed to the Christian faith and from them new currents of life issued. We have spoken of the Ecumenical Movement and the fashion in which much of the resistance to Nazi domination, both in Germany and in neighbouring lands overrun by the Nazis, came from earnest Christians. Simply as additional instances, by no means exhaustive, we can note that at Sigtuna, in Sweden, there was a folk school which brought together hand workers and brain workers in an effort to further understanding between them on the basis of Christianity, and that in France there came into being in 1939 what was known as CIMADE (*Comité Inter-Mouvements Auprès des Evacués*), a Protestant youth lay movement which began before the German occupation and persisted through and after the occupation to engage in relief and evangelism, first among the refugees and other sufferers from war, and later among the de-Christianized proletariat. After World War II, fresh efforts at evangelism were made in Germany and France, some of them in unique ways, in Germany more laymen became active in the Church, and in the Eastern Zone, behind the iron curtain, church life was maintained in the face of grave hardships and perils.

In the Netherlands in the 1940's an active movement, *Kerk en Wereld* ("Church and World"), was set on foot to effect the re-Christianization of the de-Christianized. Moreover, in 1951, in succession to an *ad interim* organization begun in 1945, the Netherlands Reformed Church achieved a more integrated structure as a means towards reform and renewal. In Continental Protestantism, as in the Roman Catholic Church, the trend appeared to be towards a situation in which convinced Christians were a self-conscious minority set in a pagan and de-Christianized world, but were seeking to reach out into it, serve its needs, and win at least some in it.

Shrinking Numbers but Continuing Vigour in the Protestantism of the British Isles

In the British Isles the course of events was not unlike that on the neighbouring Continent. Britain was deeply involved in the two world wars, an active belligerent throughout the course of the first and from the beginning to the end of the European phase of the second. During World War I she paid a terrific toll in hundreds of thousands of the flower of her young manhood, an incalculable loss in future leadership in Church and state. In World War II the cost in life, although serious, was not as great as in its predecessor. However, in the second, enemy bombings wrought more material damage, and exhaustion from concentrating individual and national effort on the struggle was more marked.

Between the two wars a partial recovery was effected. The churches sought to reinforce their depleted missionary staffs abroad, and at home endeavoured to reach the masses and to permeate the nation's life. A striking example of the latter was what was known as COPEC (Conference on Christian Politics, Economics, and Citizenship), held in 1924, and in which most of the churches joined. There were union movements, part of a wide trend in Protestantism. In 1929 the Church of Scotland and the United Free Church of Scotland came together, thus healing the breach which had existed since the Disruption of 1843. This was the more easily achieved since the practices which had led the Free Church to withdraw had ceased. In 1932 the largest groups of British Methodism were united.

Encouraging symptoms of fresh life were seen. In Scotland a clergyman of aristocratic lineage, George F. MacLeod, inaugurated a movement which had as its object the quickening of the religious life of the country and reaching the unchurched masses through a community enterprise which had as a centre and symbol Iona, the island from which, centuries before, Columba had led in winning much of Scotland and England. There were those who spoke for the life of the spirit. The Keswick conferences continued, a stimulus and fellowship of the theologically conservative Evangelicals of the several denominations. Anglican monastic orders flourished. Evelyn Underhill (1875-1941) wrote extensively on the way of the mystic and with growing feeling and understanding. Congregationalists and Baptists admitted women to their ministry, and at least one of these, Agnes Maude Royden (1876——), became favourably known on both sides of the Atlantic.

Theological thought and Biblical scholarship were vigorous. Neither the Scots nor the English moved as far from nineteenth century patterns as did the Germans and the Swiss. In general they continued, with modifications, late nineteenth century trends. As in the nineteenth century, great variety was seen. Some of the outstanding figures of the period immediately before World War I lived through that struggle, but their principal contributions had been made before it broke out. Thus early in the century the Congregationalist, Peter Taylor Forsyth (1848-1921), wrote books on the place of Christ which some of the next generation held to have made Barth and neo-orthodoxy unnecessary for them. Like Barth, but with less bluntness in repudiating man's natural ability, he emphasized the divine initiative in Christ. The Anglo-Catholic, Charles Gore (1853-1932), in his later years Bishop of Oxford, did much to combine the social message of the Church with theology. In his maturity he is said to have exerted more influence on the theological thought of the Church of England than any other of his contemporaries. After World War II there was a revival of interest in F. D. Maurice. In the evangelical tradition there were liberals and conservatives, and between the two wings much discussion was heard, but not of the dimensions of the "fundamentalist-modernist" controversy which we shall find in the United States of that period. Extreme liberalism was represented by the Unitarian, L. P. Jacks (1860——), editor of *The Hibbert Journal*. Platonism within the Church of England was associated with W. R. Inge (1860——), Dean of St. Paul's Cathedral in London, who, partly because of his Platonic and Neoplatonic bent, contributed to the literature of mysticism. He also took delight in exposing and flaying what he deemed contemporary slogans and shibboleths both among laity and clergy and earned the sobriquet of "the gloomy dean." F. R. Tennant (1866——) of Cambridge, trained in the natural sciences, like Inge an Anglican clergyman, rejected intuition as a road to knowledge, and built his theology on an empirical basis of observed fact through the use of reason. In a sense his was a continuation of the eighteenth century natural theology and he stood in the succession of Butler and Paley.

It is a temptation to give a long list of names, for there were many, Scottish and English, who made what to their contemporaries seemed outstanding contributions, some in theology and some in Biblical studies. In general, the majority conformed to a trait which was said to be characteristically British and did not go to extremes. They stated the historic Christian faith ably and in the language of their day. Much effort was devoted, both in England and Scotland, to putting Christian belief in such a manner that it would be intelligible and convincing to the intellectuals as well as the masses. While recognizing form criticism and eschatology, Biblical experts were not carried away by either school. One of them, the Congregationalist Charles Harold Dodd (1884——), professor of divinity at Cambridge, put forth and persuasively argued for the position known as "realized eschatology," holding that Jesus believed that in his day the kingdom of God had already begun to arrive. Yet to list all the important men in a book as comprehensive and as limited in dimensions as this would issue in a mere catalogue, the chief impression of which would only be the wealth of competent scholars which the churches of Great Britain possessed in these years.

One who rose to prominence in the years between the wars must be more than mentioned, William Temple (1881–1944). He was not to be remembered primarily as a theologian, although he was competent in both philosophy and theology and wrote fairly extensively in those areas, notably in his *Nature, Man and God* (1934). Moving philosophically from an earlier idealism to what he called "dialectical realism," he held to the essential core of the Christain faith as maintained in the Church of England and without aligning himself fully with any one of the particular schools within that communion. He was known, too, as a man of prayer and his *Readings in St. John's Gospel* (1939, 1940), the fruit of many years of meditation, published in his later years, were evidence of a profound devotional life. However, he was noted chiefly for the wide range of his interests and an integrity of character which eventually made him the outstanding British churchman of the 1930's and 1940's and one of the most eminent Englishmen of the century. Born in the palace of the Bishop of Exeter, the son of a man who died as Archbishop of Canterbury, he went, quite naturally, to Rugby and Oxford, had a fellowship in Queen's College, Oxford, and was ordained in the Church of England. Then came the headmastership of a school and a parish in London. He was a leader of the Life and Liberty Movement, designed to inject new life in the Church of England, to free it from some of its encumbrances and abuses, and, while retaining its tie with the state, to give it greater liberty to control its affairs without the interference of government. There followed a canonry at Westminster Abbey (1919), appointment to be Bishop of Manchester (1921), and translation to the Archbishopric of York (1929) and (1942) to the Archbishopric of Canterbury. Temple endeavoured to make the Church a growing force in the nation's life. Born to privilege, he sought to give opportunity to the masses for education and the other good things of life. He was sympathetic with the Labour movement, joined the Labour Party (1918), and worked to eliminate the contrasts, so marked in highly industrialized Britain, between squalor and luxury. Caught up in his youth in the Student Christian Movement, which rose above denominational barriers, he became outstanding in the Ecumenical Movement. He was chairman of COPEC and was prominent in Faith and Order, Life and Work, and the International Missionary Council. He was chairman of the Provisional Committee of the World Council of Churches and laboured until (1942) the British Council of Churches came into being, embracing the Church of England, the Church of Scotland, and the Nonconforming Churches. On his enthronement as Archbishop of Canterbury he declared that the great new fact of the era was that "as though in preparation for such a time as this," God had been building up a Christian fellowship which now extended into every nation, and bound "citizens of them all together in true unity and mutual love." He exerted himself to make that fellowship a growing reality.

The Church of England continued to be inclusive, with a wide range of theological and ecclesiastical convictions. These were all the way from an ultra-conservative Evangelicalism, akin to the fundamentalism of the United States and intensely Protestant, to an Anglo-Catholicism which hoped for "reunion" of the severed branches of the Catholic Church under the Pope, but with the Pope, as Bishop of Rome, being simply *primus inter pares* in the episcopate, without the infallibility and the administrative absolutism which had accrued to him in the Roman Catholic Church.

Various attempts were made to find accord with Catholics of different shades on the one hand and Nonconforming Protestants on the other. From 1921 to 1926 what were known as the Malines Conversations were carried on intermittently between several Anglo-Catholics on the one hand and, on the other, Cardinal Mercier of Belgium and some other members of the Roman Catholic Church. However, they caused uneasiness on both sides, broke down after the death of Mercier, and later (1928) Papal action made their position impossible. More hopeful relations were established with the Orthodox. In 1922 the Ecumenical Patriarch and the Holy Synod of Constantinople declared Anglican orders to have the same validity as those of Rome, the Old Catholics, and the Armenians, a declaration in which two other Orthodox Patriarchs eventually joined. The *Appeal to all Christian People* issued by the Lambeth Conference of 1920 led to extensive conferences with representatives of the Nonconformist Protestant bodies in England, but without the results for which the Anglicans had hoped. An overture of the Archbishop of Canterbury in the 1940's was no more successful, but, in one way and another, friendlier relations were cultivated with the Nonconforming Protestants as well as the Orthodox.

An issue which for a time jeopardized the tie between the state and the Church arose over the revision of the Book of Common Prayer. It was associated with the effort to obtain greater liberty for the Church of England, partly in permitting a variety in public worship which would allow room for those of Catholic as well as Protestant convictions, partly by setting up effective ecclesiastical courts, and partly by allowing the people of the parish an effective voice in choosing their pastor. What was known as the Enabling Act passed by Parliament in 1919 looked in this direction. In 1921 what was known as the Church Assembly came into being, with both lay and clerical membership. It constituted the legislative body for the Church of England. Even before 1914 there had been efforts at a revision of the familiar Book of Common Prayer. During World War I the Eucharist became more prominent. Some Anglo-Catholics used the Roman canon of the mass, either secretly or openly. After long discussion and by actions which represented a substantial majority of the bodies and officials which could speak for the Church of England, a revised prayer book was submitted to Parliament, for that body had the final authority to present it for royal approval. It did not please all in the Church of England. To the extreme Evangelicals it seemed to go too far in the Catholic direction. To the Anglo-Catholics it did not go far enough, especially in restrictions placed on the reserved sacrament which were designed to limit it to giving the communion to the sick and to prevent its adoration. The revised book was approved by the House of Lords but in 1927 was defeated in the House of Commons. The argument against it which proved most potent was that it represented a movement away from Protestantism towards Rome. Some changes were made by the Church to mitigate this objection, but in vain. The House of Commons again (1928) refused its approval. However, the bishops permitted the use of variations from the Book of Common Prayer which did not go beyond those proposed in 1927–1928.

In the 1920's, 1930's, and 1940's a number of factors contributed to bring serious losses to Christianity in the British Isles. One was the continuation of the intellectual trends which, as we have noted, in the nineteenth century questioned Christianity or dismissed it as untenable or irrelevant. For example, the writers who were said to have exerted the widest popular influence in the first half of the century, G. B. Shaw, D. H. Lawrence, and H. G. Wells, all rejected traditional Christian morals. Another adverse factor was the progressive industrialization of the nation with growing aggregations of labourers in factories and mines. There the routine, the attitudes, the conditions of work, the housing conditions, and other patterns of life tended to wean from the faith those caught up in them and presented grave obstacles to those who attempted to reach with the faith either the youth or the elders. The forms of worship and parish organization and activity which had been developed in a different social structure were ill adapted to these phases of an industrialized society. A threat to Christianity, in part related to this last, was the shifts of population. Some suburbs mounted in size, new ones arose, the cities stretched out into the country, and millions changed their places of residence. If they had church connexions in their old homes, effort was required to establish fresh ones in their new ones, and for the majority religious conviction was too mild to provide the needed stimulus. Nor did the churches display sufficient initiative to hold and win more than a minority of the deracinated multitudes. The great depression which began in the United States in 1929 and which spread to the British Isles, as to the larger part of the world, brought other serious problems in unemployment, loss of morale, and declining giving to churches and philanthropic enterprises. The growth of the "welfare state" with its socialistic programme severely handicapped the classes upon which the churches had heavily depended. The hitherto underprivileged were benefited, but the cost was largely defrayed by income and inheritance taxes which bore especially heavily on the middle and upper classes. Other developments also hit these erstwhile privileged groups and reduced their ability to support the churches and the missionary and other organizations related to these bodies.

As if these were not enough, World War II dealt further blows. Many church structures were damaged or destroyed by enemy bombing and because of the difficulty of obtaining building materials after the war were repaired only slowly if at all. Thousands were evacuated from the cities to escape air raids and thus were out of touch with whatever church connexions had once been theirs. Young men were called to the colours and the numbers preparing for the ministry sharply declined. Civilians were caught up in home defense and other war activities on Sundays as well as week days and habits of church attendance were weakened or broken. The prolonged strain of the war left multitudes weary, including the conscientious from whom came much of the leadership of the churches. The impoverishment and the austerity which accompanied and followed the war were additional obstacles. In waging the two wars Britain used up much of the capital accumulated in the halcyon days when it led the world in industry, trade, and finance, and became a debtor rather than a creditor nation. Thus the ability to give to the churches and their agencies was impaired. Moreover, there were the coarsening of morals, the increase in the consumption of alcohol, and the neglect of religion which have been the usual accompaniments of war.

The British Empire which had reached its proud climax in the nineteenth century seemed to be going to pieces. Soon after World War II India, Pakistan, Burma, and Ceylon either became fully independent or self-governing. Increasing restlessness was seen in the African possessions. Young men could no longer be assured of a career in the colonial service. The British West Indies were an economic liability rather than an asset. To be sure, the British Commonwealth, composed of nations bound together by the symbolic tie of the crown, was unique and had strength, but in it the British Isles were not as prominent as formerly and "imperial preference" which gave them a favoured position in the commerce of the dominions was threatened. The larger part of Ireland withdrew from the empire and became an independent republic. Great Britain accorded it dominion status in 1921, and in 1948 and 1949 the last constitutional links were severed between it and the United Kingdom.

Under these circumstances it was not strange that active church membership and church attendance declined. Not far from 1937 it was said that of the potential Protestant constituency in England only about 14 per cent. were communicant members, that only 5 to 10 per cent. were regular attendants at church, and that scarcely one-fourth went to church as often as once in three months. This seems to have been a distinct decline from the beginning of the century. Efforts at mass evangelism of the de-Christianized, some on a local and some on a national scale, yielded only scanty returns. The figures appear to have fallen further by the end of World War II, but to have shown a slight recovery in the years immediately after that struggle. There was reported to be much criticism of the morals and integrity of church members by non-church-goers and disdain for the clergy.

A falling-off in the clergy in numbers and quality from the high point reached on the eve of 1914 was also marked and increasing difficulty was experienced, especially after World War II, in recruiting enough men to fill the vacancies. Part of the cause was the deadening of any inclination towards the ministry by the months and years of service in the armed forces. A few found their vocation to the ministry while in uniform, and immediately after the war there was a sudden and sharp increase in the numbers of those applying for theological training. However, soon after 1950 there was again the cry of a dearth of clergy. Another cause of the shortage of clergy was economic. Stipends did not keep pace with the cost of living and fell behind those of artisans and even, in some instances, of unskilled labourers. The large incomes and pluralism which had been a scandal even as late as the fore part of the nineteenth century had passed, especially after World War II. The huge rectories and episcopal residences which were inherited by the Church of England from an earlier age became a burden which taxed the resources and the energies of those who lived in them. Difficulty was experienced in obtaining funds and personnel to maintain the overseas enterprises which had been an outstanding feature of nineteenth century British Protestantism. Moreover, it was noted that while some of the bishops of the Church of England were national figures with a marked influence in public affairs and on the life of the nation as a whole, and although there were still distinguished preachers and scholars both in England and Scotland, fewer of the clergy of the Nonconformist churches and of the Church of Scotland commanded the attention and respect of the country than in the half century and more before 1914.

Grim though these aspects of the picture undoubtedly were, British Protestantism was by no means dead. Indeed, it displayed marked vigour. We have noted the partial recovery made in the 1920's, after World War I. Although thousands who thought of them at all regarded the churches as irrelevant and as not speaking to their day, little antagonism to Christianity as such was seen. In its ethical standards the nation gave evidence of a Christian heritage, even though that heritage might be fading. In many communities, some of them in the cities, church services were well attended and numbers of congregations maintained an active life. Women constituted a majority of the faithful in the churches, but laymen were not lacking. Among the latter were some in high position in government, business, and education. There was a noticeable hunger for satisfying answers to the riddles of life, with a wistful hope that they might be found in the Christian faith. It was a matter of comment that not a few of the children of nineteenth century agnostics and sceptics were becoming Christians, and from deep conviction. Several outstanding intellectuals, formerly without faith or even scoffers, were converts and in their writing were setting forth Christian convictions and wrestling with the challenge presented by the Gospel to the de-Christianized members of their generation. In the 1950's both faculty members and students in at least some of the universities were increasingly interested in Christianity. The Education Act of 1944 made religious instruction compulsory in the schools, and measures were taken in preparing syllabi and teachers to render the legislation effective. The Religious Affairs Department of the British Broadcasting Corporation arranged programmes which were heard by a larger proportion of the population than attended church and the majority of the listeners were said to be non-church-goers of the working classes. Several of the outstanding intellects among Protestants dealt courageously with the issues presented by the new age with its colossal evils, by the minority position of Christians in what had once been regarded as Christendom, and by what looked like a retreating wave of faith. Out of their straitened resources, British Protestants gave generously to the relief of the suffering on the neighbouring Continent, maintained many of the philanthropies which had been begun at home by their predecessors in a prosperous age, continued the major proportion of their foreign missions, and contributed to the foreign missions of their even more hardly pressed brethren across the Channel. Not only William Temple, but also many men and women of lesser but still significant stature promoted the Ecumenical Movement. British Protestantism was following not only tried methods and historic traditions, but was reaching out in new ways.

Prospering Roman Catholicism in the British Isles

In contrast with the severe blows dealt Protestantism in the British Isles by the events which followed 1914, the Roman Catholic Church prospered.

In England, Scotland, and Wales the advance of the Roman Catholic Church which began in the nineteenth century continued. It will be remembered (Chapter 48) that at the dawn of the nineteenth century there were Roman Catholics, chiefly in Yorkshire, Lancashire, and the Highlands of Scotland, who represented a continuity of the faith from pre-Reformation days. They suffered under political disabilities which were removed in the first half of the century. To them were added, mostly in England, converts, largely from the Anglo-Catholic wing of the Church of England. However, by the year 1914 the large majority of the Roman Catholics in Great Britain were Irish immigrants and their descendants. They or their fathers had come mainly as unskilled labourers to the coal mines of Wales and around Newcastle and to the manufacturing and commercial cities—Liverpool, London, Birmingham, Manchester, Glasgow, and smaller similar centres.

After 1914 this Irish constituency continued to provide the large majority of the Roman Catholics of England, Scotland, and Wales. Converts were made, mainly by marriage, but the gain was chiefly by the excess of births over deaths. In England and Wales the total of Roman Catholics rose from 1,870,000 in 1914 to 2,650,000 in 1950. While there was said to have been some leakage, in general the children of Roman Catholics remained true to the faith of their parents and their attendance at the services of the Church was maintained. No dearth of clergy was experienced. Priests totalled 3,835 in 1910, 5,642 in 1940, and 6,643 in 1950. As the Irish were longer in England, many of them prospered and became members of the middle and professional classes. The rank and file benefited from the social legislation of the period. As a result, funds were obtained, churches and chapels multiplied, and schools, theological seminaries, and monasteries grew. The movements of population to the suburbs in the 1930's and 1940's and the dispersals from the hearts of the cities during World War II brought a wider geographic distribution of the Roman Catholic population and new churches and chapels were erected to care for the Diaspora.

In the Republic of Ireland (Eire) Roman Catholics were predominant. The small Protestant minorities declined after Irish independence. While religious liberty was granted to other denominations, the Roman Catholic Church was officially recognized as the guardian of the faith. As a neutral in World War II, Eire was spared many of the hardships which constituted problems for the churches in Great Britain and on the Continent. The population was enthusiastically Roman Catholic. This may have been because, as earlier, that branch of the faith was identified with Irish nationalism. In the mid-twentieth century almost the entire population were said to be regular in their attendance at church. Priests, monks, and nuns increased, and many went to Great Britain, to the Irish in the Americas and Australasia, and as missionaries to non-Christians. From Maynooth, the Roman Catholic university, were graduated many who became bishops either in Eire or in the Irish communities abroad.

THE COMMUNIST TEST TO RUSSIAN CHRISTIANITY

In 1917, under the stress of World War I, the tsar's regime in Russia collapsed. For a few months the moderate revolutionaries, headed by Kerensky, were in power. Late in 1917 they were swept out by the radicals, and the Bolsheviki, a wing of the communists, took control. Eventually the Union of Soviet Socialist Republics (U.S.S.R.) came into being, with the Communist Party in power, first under Lenin and then under Stalin.

The revolution brought the most searching test that Christianity had known in Russia since the Mongol invasion. In some ways the trial was more severe. To be sure, Christianity was better rooted in Russia in 1917 than in the thirteenth century, but the communists were far more aggressively anti-Christian than the Mongols had been.

The first effect of the liberal stage of the revolution of 1917 was to give the Church greater freedom. In August of that year an all-Russian Sobor, or Synod, of the Russian Orthodox Church met in Moscow, made up of ecclesiastics and laity. In the autumn the Sobor voted to restore the Patriarchate, discontinued under Peter the Great more than two centuries earlier, and in November elected to that post Tikhon, the Metropolitan of Moscow. The Patriarch was made subject to the Sobor and was not much more than its chief executive.

Before the Church could fairly find itself under its new organization the communist storm broke upon it. In December, 1917, the Soviet declared all land to be national property. Ecclesiastical monastic holdings were explicitly included and the Church was deprived of the larger part of its income. That same month all schools, among them theological seminaries and academies, were ordered to be turned over to the state's Commissariat of National Education. Thus the education of youth and even of its own priesthood was taken from the Church. A few days later the state said that it would give legal status only to such marriages as were performed by civil ceremonies and transferred to its bureaus the registration of births and deaths, formerly ecclesiastical functions. Within a few weeks, in January, 1918, the Church was formally separated from the state, state payment of the salaries of the clergy was ordered discontinued, religious vows and oaths were abrogated, instruction in religion was forbidden in both government and private schools, compulsory collection of funds for the support of ecclesiastical institutions was outlawed, the right to hold property was denied to religious associations, and religious rites were no longer to accompany state functions. Citizens were permitted to hold religious convictions or to renounce them, and religious rites might be continued if they did not interfere with public order.

These acts of a communist-dominated government can be easily understood. Communism regarded religion as the "opiate of the people," hindering their full emancipation. Moreover, in the eyes of the communists, who had long been proscribed and hunted down by the old regime, the Church was a tool of the hated oppressor.

It was not to be expected that the Church would tamely submit to the radical changes in its status. Tikhon and the Sobor denounced (January, 1918) the confiscation of ecclesiastical property and appealed to Christians to resist it. Popular outbreaks followed, but they were suppressed and hundreds were shot or otherwise punished.

For a few months the state did not enforce all its ecclesiastical decrees, but in July, 1918, it reaffirmed its position of the preceding December and January, and in the constitution specifically guaranteed to all citizens the right of anti-religious as well as religious propaganda. Associations of citizens might be granted the use of church buildings for worship, but structures not so utilized were ordered seized.

As the resistance of many churchmen continued and a church council of émigrés called for the restoration of the Romanovs, the communist regime, still fighting for its life against the "white" armies which sought to overthrow it, stiffened its anti-Christian measures. Priests and bishops were classified with non-productive elements in the population and were disfranchised. Education for the priesthood was made almost impossible. Divisions in the Church were fomented. About forty bishops and a thousand priests are said to have perished in the civil wars waged with the anti-communist forces. Religious instruction of youths under eighteen years of age in groups of more than four was forbidden. In 1922 church articles were confiscated with the ostensible purpose of applying the proceeds of their sale to famine relief. A Union of the Godless was organized and anti-religious literature was issued.

A five-year programme adopted in 1929 for the progressive conversion of Russia to a communist state included drastic measures against religion. The publication of religious books was made more difficult. Religious societies were forbidden to engage in any social services such as coöperatives, sanatoriums, medical care, relief to their indigent members, associations for recreation, or even meetings for religious instruction. Special theological courses were still allowed, but only by express permission of the state. No believer was permitted to teach in a state school. Itinerant preaching, such as that in which Baptists and Evangelicals engaged, was forbidden. Many of the clergy were arrested and sentenced to hard labour in the North and Siberia. Numbers of church buildings were transformed into moving picture houses. A five-day and then a six-day week was substituted for the seven-day week, and thus the Christian cycle of work and worship was broken. Many church buildings were diverted from their original purpose by the simple expedient of placing on the congregations unbearable burdens for repairs, taxes, rental, and insurance. It is said that in the first year of the five-year plan about two thousand churches were closed, or about as many as had been liquidated in the preceding eleven years. At least two cathedrals in prominent cities were turned into museums of religion which in effect were anti-religious, and other museums were set up to exalt science and defame religion. Anti-religious plays, literature, radio broadcasts, motion pictures, and lectures were employed, and by May, 1932, it is said that the Godless Union numbered 7,000,000 members besides 1,500,000 children who were counted as Godless.

The growth of the cities militated against Christianity. No new churches could be erected and clergy were few, and in the urban environment those coming from the rural districts and the small towns where more of the faith persisted found it difficult to make contact with the Church.

The Russian Orthodox Church was further weakened by divisions within its ranks. What was known as the Living Church was organized, made up of those more in sympathy with the government than was Tikhon. Some of its bishops were from the married clergy rather than the monks, as had been the tradition. In several regions, notably in the Ukraine and Georgia, regional autonomous Orthodox Churches were set up and the one in the Ukraine suffered from additional rifts. Peter, who succeeded to the Patriarchate after the death of Tikhon (1925), was exiled to Siberia and another schism developed.

Beginning in 1936 the anti-religious programme became less severe. Bell-ringing and the collection of funds for churches were permitted. In 1940 the seven-day week was restored and Sunday was made a compulsory holiday. Workers were no longer penalized for absences during the Christmas and Easter festivals. The showing of anti-Christian plays and anti-Christmas and anti-Easter carnivals were prohibited. The franchise was restored to the clergy.

Yet anti-religious measures by no means ceased. Several bishops were shot on the charge of espionage, and more churches, as well as synagogues and mosques, were closed. In 1940 it was estimated that about 90 per cent. of the churches in use in 1917 had been converted to secular purposes or destroyed, that the number of bishops had declined 75 per cent., the number of deacons 80 per cent., and of priests 90 per cent.

Christian bodies outside the Orthodox Church also suffered. This was true of Roman Catholics, the Old Believers, several other sects which had separated from the former state church, and the Baptists and Evangelicals.

In spite of these adversities Christianity persisted. In the 1930's the militant anti-Christian campaign began to decline. It was said that secret monasteries existed and that the training of priests continued, even though surreptitiously. It was reported that numbers of women memorized the New Testament and portions of the prayer book and went from home to home, baptizing the children and giving religious instruction. A substantial proportion of the population, especially in the rural sections, were believers.

In the 1940's relations between Church and state improved. This seems in the first instance to have been because of the need of unity in the face of the German invasion of 1941. The Russian Orthodox Church stood staunchly with the nation and the government in the resistance to the alien armies. In 1943 the state gave permission to the "Old Church," as distinguished from the "New Church," sprung from the Living Church movement, to elect a Patriarch. This it did in September of that year. The following month the government set up a council to maintain official contacts between itself and the Russian Orthodox Church. It also created a council which was to deal with all other religious cults. Another reason for the declining hostility between the Church and the state was said to have been the rise of a generation which had not known the Church in the days of the tsars and so did not share the bitter hostility of the older revolutionaries who had regarded it as an ally of the hated monarchical regime. It was reported, too, that with mounting nationalism there was an awareness of Russian history and of the important part in it which the Church had played. Then, too, it was conjectured that the state regarded the Russian Orthodox Church as useful in cementing relations with the Balkan countries, especially Rumania and Bulgaria, where the Orthodox Churches were strong. Perhaps, too, the Church was deemed to have been sufficiently weakened to be no longer a menace.

Whatever the reasons, at mid-century the antagonism between Church and state was not as acute as in the first years of the communist regime. The Communist Party was still officially antagonistic to religion and called the Church a tool and ally of exploiters, but did not engage in as active persecution as formerly. The episcopate of the Russian Orthodox Church endorsed the peace plans put forward by the communists in their war of nerves with the West and denounced the Central Committee of the World Council of Churches for supporting the action of the United Nations in Korea in the summer of

1950. The Russian Orthodox Church would have no fellowship with the Ecumenical Movement but, presumably in accord with the Kremlin, regarded it as the religious front of Western imperialism and capitalism.

It was clear that at mid-twentieth century Christianity was still very much alive in Russia. In 1945 it was estimated that there were about 20,000 Orthodox churches, 30,000 priests, 10 theological seminaries, 2 theological academies, and 87 monasteries and nunneries. In 1951 it was reported that several famous churches had been restored and were being used for religious purposes, and that the Holy Trinity Monastery near Moscow, long an outstanding centre of the Russian Orthodox Church, had been refurbished and was thronged with pilgrims. There could be no doubt that in at least some of the main cities Orthodox Church services attracted large numbers and that the throngs on the high festivals, notably Easter, were especially large and devout. Some other Christian groups of tsarist days also continued. For example, the Popovsty, or Old Believers who had priests, possessed a supreme council. The Lutherans in Estonia, Latvia, and Lithuania had synods. Those called Baptists, a designation which included Baptists, Evangelicals, and Pentecostals, were numerous and their meetings in Moscow were largely attended. In 1950 they were said to number 3,200,000.

Here and there outside of the U.S.S.R. larger and smaller bodies of Russian Orthodox Christians were found. Some, as in the United States, had been in existence before the Revolution of 1917. Others were made up chiefly of refugees. A major centre of Russian Orthodox thought arose in Paris after World War I. There the most distinguished figure was Nikolai Alexandrovitch Berdyaev (1874–1948). Born in Kiev, of aristocratic and cultured parentage, in his younger days Berdyaev attempted to combine idealistic and Marxist views, but he was never an orthodox Marxist and could not accept the dialectical determination of that ideology. Exiled for a time in his student days for his antagonism to the tsarist regime and his sympathy with the working classes, he early attracted attention in literary and socially radical circles. His wife, deeply mystical and eventually a Roman Catholic, was the daughter of a wealthy lawyer who was religiously a complete sceptic. Berdyaev was much influenced by Soloviev, before World War I was active in religious-philosophical societies, returned to the Church, and had contacts with groups of mystics who wished to see the kingdom of God realized on earth. Grieved by the socially reactionary strain in the Russian Orthodox Church, he criticized it and was threatened with exile to Siberia. When the Revolution brought its adherents to power he was also a critic of Marxism. Yet for a time he held a chair in the University of Moscow and not until 1921 was he deported by the Soviet authorities. In Germany and France he was associated with the Young Men's

Christian Association and the World's Student Christian Federation. It was in the 1920's and 1930's that his writings began to attract wide attention among intellectuals, especially Christian intellectuals, in Western Europe and America. He opposed both the tyranny of the communist regime in Russia and the reactionary attitudes of the Russian *émigrés* and Western *bourgeois* capitalism.

Always courageously independent in his thinking and writing, Berdyaev had his own kind of personalism and existentialism. Never one to conform, he held that knowledge is an activity of a free spirit, that man is a spiritual being, that God is spirit, that spirit is activity, and that God has breathed spirit into man. He maintained that both philosophy and theology must start with the God-man Christ. He believed profoundly in the incarnation. As he saw it, the Trinity, with the historic conviction that the Son was "begotten and not made," showed that while God and man are distinct they are not wholly alien, that there is in God the eternal face of man, and that God is to be known only through Christ, as the God-man through whom He touches man. In the activity of God Berdyaev saw the clue to history, and especially in the liberation of the spirit of man by Christ. He believed that the decay of Western civilization had begun with the Renaissance, when Western man, taking advantage of the freedom and exaltation of man which had come through Christianity, affirmed himself, exalted his reason, ignored the tie between God and man which had brought him this freedom, and paved the way to scepticism and a loss of faith in man's reason. This movement, so he held, culminated in the mechanical age in which the humanism of the Renaissance ended in anti-humanism, making man a mere cog in the machine. History, so he contended, is to be given its final significance by the second coming of Christ.

More limited in his influence, but more nearly in the pattern of the Russian Orthodox Church, was Sergius Bulkagov (1871–1944). The son of a priest, in his youth he was a Marxist and for a time was professor of political economy. Partly through the influence of Soloviev, he returned to the Church, in 1918 was ordained priest, and in 1922 was banished. He became a founder of the Orthodox Theological Institute in Paris and occupied its chair of dogmatic theology. Holding to the Orthodox faith, he wrote extensively.

Storms in the Balkans

In the twentieth century what in its most inclusive sense was the Balkan Peninsula was the scene of storm after storm. The first broke out in 1912 with a war which before it ended in 1913 involved all the countries of the region— Serbia, Montenegro, Bulgaria, Rumania, Greece, and the remnants of the once large possessions of Turkey in Europe. That war was the immediate preliminary to World War I. As a sequel to World War I Greece was defeated in a struggle with Turkey (1921–1923) and nearly a million and a half Greek Orthodox refugees from Anatolia and Asia Minor deluged the country. The Balkans were also engulfed in World War II, with an Italian-German invasion of Greece and Albania, a German invasion of Jugoslavia, the later advance of the Russian armies, the post-war inclusion of Bulgaria and Rumania within the Russian iron curtain, the setting up of the communist regime under Tito in Jugoslavia, and the break of Tito with Moscow. These developments could not but affect the religious scene.

Although they contained Roman Catholic and Moslem minorities, in 1914 in all the Balkan countries except Albania and the remnant of European Turkey through one or another of its branches the Orthodox faith was professed by a majority of the population. This, obviously, was the heritage of the history which we have sketched in earlier chapters. Amid the vicissitudes of the tempestuous post-1914 years the Orthodox Churches continued. They also gave indications of vigour. After World War I the *Zoe* movement enlisted and inspired a number of choice spirits in Greece. Lay initiative was seen in the Orthodox Church both in Greece and Rumania. In Bulgaria the government improved the theological education out of which came the clergy. There was more reading of the Bible than formerly. Several thousand Uniates returned to the Orthodoxy of their fathers.

World War II and its aftermath brought fresh complications. In Greece in the Italian-German invasion and the subsequent civil war in the North hundreds of priests succumbed and many parishes were left vacant. Yet the Orthodox Church remained strong. For a time after 1944 its primate was regent of the country. *Zoe* revived, as did a lay movement, and some of the vacant parishes were re-supplied with priests. The Orthodox Church of Greece adhered to the World Council of Churches and representatives, both lay and clerical, were active in the Ecumenical Movement. In Jugoslavia the Patriarchate which had been suppressed by the Turks in 1766 was reconstituted. Numbers of the clergy, including some of the bishops and the *locum tenens* of the Patriarchate, were imprisoned on the charge of opposition to the Tito regime, but they were subsequently released and in 1952 the churches which had escaped destruction or confiscation were reported to be crowded. In February, 1945, the schism which had separated the Bulgarian Orthodox Church from the Ecumenical Patriarch of Constantinople was healed. In 1949, in accordance with the communist pattern, the Orthodox Church of Bulgaria, while still described as "the traditional Church of the Bulgarian People," was disestablished, churches were forbidden to conduct schools except theological seminaries, or to have youth movements, and their hospitals and relief institutions were taken over by the state. The new constitution of the Bulgarian Orthodox Church provided for a Patriarch to head it, but delay was experienced in filling the post. In Rumania the law of 1948 "concerning the freedom of all religions" placed religions and religious teaching under the control of the state. The Orthodox Church was headed by a Patriarch and a Holy Synod. In 1948 about a million and a third Uniates severed their connexion with Rome and returned to the Orthodox Church.

The Waning Older Churches in Western Asia and North-eastern Africa

The years after 1914 witnessed the further decline of the older churches in Western Asia and North-eastern Africa which had been in process since the Arab and the subsequent Turkish conquests.

In Turkey, shortly before 1914 a quite secular government came into power. It was intent upon making Turkey a strong, unified, Westernized state. To that end it wished to free the nation not only from what it deemed the incubus of Islam but also from the religious minorities, most of them Christian, which by long Turkish policy were distinct political entities. The protection of the Christian minorities had furnished occasion for the intervention of Western governments, a fact intolerable to the nationalists. During and soon after World War I tens of thousands of Armenians and Greek Orthodox perished, many of them massacred, and thousands of Roman Catholics and hundreds of Protestants also succumbed. Early in the 1920's what was euphemistically called on "exchange" moved a few thousand Turks from Greece to Turkey and, as we have seen, a much larger number of Greeks from Asia Minor to Greece. At the mid-century, Turkey, confined by the outcome of World War I and its aftermath to Asia Minor and a slight foothold, including Istanbul (Constantinople), in Europe, had very few Christians. Asia Minor, the first large region to be fairly solidly Christian by faith, now contained only a few of that religion. The constituency over which the Ecumenical Patriarch exercised direct jurisdiction shrank to very small proportions and that office, once vying with the Papacy in power, now had little but the tantalizing memory of a great past.

The Armenian (Gregorian) Church suffered from the communist rule over the portion of its constituency which was in Russian territory south of the Caucasus. The number of monks declined and there was difficulty in electing a successor to the Catholicos who was assassinated in 1937.

During World War I thousands of Nestorians, Chaldeans (Nestorians who had submitted to Rome), Jacobites, and Syrian Uniates in Iran and in what was later Iraq lost their lives. Turks, Kurds, and Moslems took the occasion to fall on them, minorities which were now helpless. The Church of the East, as the Nestorians preferred to call themselves, shrank almost to the vanishing point in scattered remnants.

States, and a few other lands. A great church which had once been represented from Mesopotamia to South India and the China Sea had all but perished.

The coming into being of the state of Israel in 1948 and the ensuing war with the Arabs led to the death of numbers of the Christian Arab minority and to the displacement from their homes of many of the survivors.

In Egypt the Coptic Church continued to suffer from the slow leakage to the dominant Islam which for centuries had been weakening it. Yet because of its birth rate it probably increased in numbers. In the neighbouring Ethiopia the Italian invasion of the 1930's could not but work damage to the church of that land. The Italian masters severed the traditional administrative connexion between the Ethiopian and the Coptic Church and after the restoration of native rule the tie was only in part renewed.

Throughout most of Western Asia and Northern Africa Protestant and Roman Catholic missions persisted. Both drew their converts chiefly from the older Eastern Churches, but to each came a few from Islam. Protestants especially won a few hundred Moslems in Iran and Arabia. The Vatican continued to make much of the Uniate bodies and to enhance their dignity it created (1917) for their special supervision the Congregation for Oriental Churches. Wherever political conditions permitted, both Protestants and Roman Catholics maintained their educational and medical institutions. Both gave extensive relief to the sufferers from the recurrent wars and massacres.

Yet the numerical gains of the Roman Catholic and Protestant communities were not sufficient to offset the losses experienced in the decline of the ancient Eastern Churches. The enterprise of Christians from the West did not halt the slow decline of Christianity which had been under way for over a thousand years in the land of its birth and the region of its initial greatest strength.

SUMMARY

The period of history which opened in the tragic summer of 1914 bore hard on the traditional Christendom and its churches. To the adverse forces which had been present in the nineteenth century and earlier there were added devastating wars and sweeping revolutions, the major one of the latter openly and the others tacitly anti-Christian. In several countries survivals existed from the ages when Christianity was the professed faith of the entire nation and when Church and state were complementary but often rival aspects of an inclusive structure of society. Increasingly, however, the tie between Church and state was either loosened or completely severed. Christians were seemingly in the process of becoming minorities in a frankly or covertly non-Christian society. To many, especially to those whose attention was focused mainly on Europe, mankind appeared to be moving into what some called the post-Christian era.

This interpretation was an over-simplification which ignored other and quite contrary aspects of the world scene. Christianity was by no means dead in what had once been called Christendom. Far from being moribund, it was displaying vigour, especially in its Roman Catholic and Protestant expressions. Moreover, as we have suggested and are to see further in the following chapters, it was gaining outside of Europe, whether in the Americas, Africa, Asia, or the islands which fringe these continents. The gains were partly numerical and partly in the vitality of the churches. Moreover, Protestantism, the most rapidly expanding form of Christianity, was developing a capacity for achieving world-wide unity in ways new in the history of religion. By the mid-century mark that unity by no means included even all Protestants and had drawn in only minorities from Roman Catholics and members of the Eastern Churches. However, it seemed merely at its beginnings. Moreover, in a variety of ways Christianity was making an impression on more of mankind, including those who did not bear the Christian name, than ever before.

The contrast could not help but be provocative to all who sought to understand the history of the race and the place of the Christian Gospel in the course of mankind on the planet.

Selected Bibliography

P. B. Anderson, *People, Church and State in Modern Russia* (New York, The Macmillan Co., 1944, pp. vii, 240). By an expert.

T. Andræ, *Nathan Söderblom,* translated from the Swedish by E. Groening and A. Völklein (Berlin, Alfred Töpelmann, 1938, pp. 232).

K. Barth, *Dogmatics in Outline,* translated by G. T. Thomson (New York, Philosophical Library, 1947, pp. 155). Barth's own summary of his theology.

G. A. Beck, editor, *The English Catholics 1850–1950* (London, Burns, Oates & Washbourne, 1950, pp. xix, 640). Contains some excellent special studies.

G. K. A. Bell, *Randall Davidson, Archbishop of Canterbury* (Oxford University Press, 2 vols., 1935). By a close friend. Valuable not only as a biography but also as a history of the Church of England during Davidson's lifetime.

D. A. Binchy, *Church and State in Fascist Italy* (Oxford University Press, 1941, pp. ix, 774). Excellent. Carefully documented.

W. A. Brown, *Toward a United Church. Three Decades of Ecumenical Christianity* (New York, Charles Scribner's Sons, 1946, pp. xvi, 264). By one long active in the Ecumenical Movement.

R. P. Casey, *Religion in Russia* (New York, Harper & Brothers, 1946, pp. viii, 198). Chiefly on religion under the Communist regime.

O. F. Clarke, *Introduction to Berdyaev* (London, Goeffrey Bles, 1950, pp. 192). Excellent.

J. S. Curtiss, *Church and State in Russia. The Last Years of the Empire 1900–1917* (Columbia University Press, 1940, pp. ix, 442).

A. S. Duncan-Jones, *The Struggle for Religious Freedom in Germany* (London, Victor Gollancz, 1938, pp. 319). By the (Anglican) Dean of Chichester.

C. C. Eckhardt, *The Papacy in World Affairs as Reflected in the Secularization of Politics* (University of Chicago Press, 1937, pp. xiv, 310).

W. C. Emhardt, *Religion in Soviet Russia. Anarchy* (Milwaukee, Morehouse-Gorham, Inc., 1929, pp. xix, 383). By an Episcopalian; well documented.

N. F. S. Ferré, *Swedish Contributions to Modern Theology, with Special Reference to Lundensian Thought* (New York, Harper & Brothers, 1939, pp. x, 250). By a specialist.

P. Guilday, editor, *The Catholic Church in Contemporary Europe, 1919–1931. Papers of the American Catholic Historical Association,* Vol. II (New York, P. J. Kenedy & Sons, 1932, pp. xiv, 354).

O. Halecki, *Eugenio Pacelli: Pope of Peace* (Farrar, Straus & Young, 1951, pp. viii, 355). Sympathetic.

R. d'Harcourt, *The German Catholics,* translated by R. J. Dingle (London, Burns, Oates & Washbourne, 1939, pp. xiii, 274). By a French Roman Catholic cleric.

W. Hauer, K. Heim, and K. Adam, *Germany's New Religion. The German Faith Movement,* translated by T. S. K. Scott-Craig (New York and Nashville, Abingdon-Cokesbury Press, 1937, pp. 168).

S. W. Herman, *It's Your Souls We Want* (New York, Harper & Brothers, 1943, pp. xv, 315). A description of the contemporary religious scene in Germany by one who had been pastor of an American church in Berlin.

W. R. Hogg, *Ecumenical Foundations: A History of the International Missionary Council and Its Nineteenth-century Background* (New York, Harper & Brothers, 1952, pp. viii, 466). The definitive account.

W. M. Horton, *Contemporary Continental Theology. An Interpretation for Anglo-Saxons* (New York, Harper & Brothers, 1938, pp. xxi, 246). By an American specialist.

W. M. Horton, *Contemporary English Theology* (New York, Harper & Brothers, 1936, pp. xix, 186). By a specialist.

F. A. Iremonger, *William Temple, Archbishop of Canterbury, His Life and Letters* (Oxford University Press, 1948, pp. xv, 663). Carefully done.

L. P. Jacks, *The Confessions of an Octogenarian* (London, G. Allen & Unwin, 1942, pp. 272).

A. Keller and G. Stewart, *Protestant Europe: Its Crisis and Outlook* (New York, Harper & Brothers, 1927, pp. 385). By experts.

K. S. Latourette, *A History of the Expansion of Christianity. Volume VII, Advance Through Storm* A.D. *1914 and After, with Concluding Generalizations* (New York, Harper & Brothers, 1945, pp. xiii, 542).

H. Lilje, *The Valley of the Shadow,* translated by O. Wyon (Philadelphia, The Muhlenberg Press, 1950, pp. 128). The autobiographical account of the imprisonment of a German Protestant clergyman under the Nazis.

R. B. Lloyd, *The Church of England in the Twentieth Century* (New York, Longmans, Green & Co., 2 vols., 1947, 1950). By a clergyman of the Church of England. Contains excellent material. Brings the story to 1939.

N. O. Lossky, *History of Russian Philosophy* (New York, International Universities Press, 1951, pp. 416). From a Russian Orthodox viewpoint.

G. MacLeod, *We Shall Rebuild. The Work of the Iona Community on Mainland and on Island* (Glasgow, The Iona Community, 1944, pp. 129).

F. McCullagh, *The Bolshevik Persecution of Christianity* (London, John Murray, 1924, pp. xxi, 401).

A. Manhattan, *The Vatican in World Politics* (New York, Gaer Associates, 1949, pp. 444). Carefully done. Critical of the Vatican.

N. Micklem, *National Socialism and the Roman Catholic Church* (Oxford University Press, 1939, pp. xi, 243). By an English Nonconformist Protestant scholar.

C. Pichon, translated from the French by J. Misrahi, *The Vatican and Its Rôle in World Affairs* (New York, E. P. Dutton & Co., 1950, pp. 382). Very sympathetic.

O. Piper, *Recent Developments in German Protestantism* (London, Student Christian Movement Press, 1934, pp. xvi, 159). By a distinguished German Protestant theologian, an exile from the Hitler regime.

M. Power, *Religion in the Reich* (London, Longmans, Green & Co., 1939, pp. viii, 240). Based largely on visits to Germany. Critical of the Nazis.

J. D. Regester, *Albert Schweitzer, The Man and His Work* (New York and Nashville, Abingdon-Cokesbury Press, 1931, pp. 145). A sympathetic, competent summary.

B. S. Rowntree, *English Life and Leisure. A Social Study* (New York, Longmans, Green & Co., 1951, pp. xvi, 482). An account of contemporary life in England, based upon careful case studies.

A. Schweitzer, *The Quest of the Historical Jesus. A Critical Study of Its Progress from Reimarus to Wrede,* translated by W. Montgomery (2d enlarged ed., London, Adam and Charles Black, 1911, pp. x, 410).

M. Spinka, *The Church and the Russian Revolution* (New York, The Macmillan Co., 1927, pp. xii, 330). By a church historian, competent in Slavic studies.

G. S. Spinks, *Religion in Britain since 1900* (London, Andrew Dakers, 1952, pp. 256). Mostly by Spinks, but with chapters by J. Parkes and E. L. Allen.

N. S. Timasheff, *Religion in Soviet Russia, 1917-1942* (New York, Sheed & Ward, 1942, pp. xii, 171). From a Roman Catholic standpoint. Well documented and, in general, objective.

E. Underhill, *Worship* (New York, Harper & Brothers, 1937, pp. xxi, 350).

M. A. C. Warren, *The Truth of Vision* (London, The Canterbury Press, 1948, pp.

159). Valuable as showing the fashion in which one sensitive, thoughtful English Christian wrestled with the problem presented by the scene in the late 1940's.

The First Assembly of the World Council of Churches, Held at Amsterdam August 22d to September 4th, 1948, edited by W. A. Visser 't Hooft (New York, Harper & Brothers, 1949, pp. 271). The official report.

Chapter 58

THE EXPANDING FAITH IN THE LARGER OCCIDENT: THE AMERICAS AND AUSTRALASIA AFTER A.D. 1914

What did the post-1914 age mean for Christianity in the larger Occident, namely, those nations of European stock which had grown up in the Americas and Australasia in the preceding four centuries? Predominantly Christian by heredity, and, in general, having been held to a profession of the faith, they were also part of what had once been called Christendom. Was the twentieth century course of the faith the same as in the older portion of Christendom?

There could not fail to be similarities. The world was now too closely bound together to permit the complete isolation of one section from another. All but one of the forces which we have noted (Chapter 61) as moulding Western Europe also affected the Americas and Australasia. That one was significant. It was the decline of Western Europe. As a corollary by mid-century the larger Occident, especially the United States, was much more prominent than in 1914. Indeed, by 1950 the United States was generally regarded as the most powerful nation on the planet and its weight was being felt everywhere on the globe. Moreover, in consequence, the pessimism in Western Europe which accompanied the decline of that region was much less marked in the larger Occident.

Since most of the movements which beginning in 1914 shook the world originated in Europe, they had greater effects there than in the Americas and Australasia. Almost all the larger Occident was drawn into the world wars of the century, but they were not fought on its soil and it did not experience physical destruction or as great a loss of life as did Europe. The revolutions which swept across most of that continent, while not without repercussions in the Americas and Australasia, did not plow as deeply in these regions as in the older part of Christendom. Indeed, some were saying that there must be a reversal of traditional designations, that instead of being the Old World, Europe was now the New World, and that the Americas, accustomed to regarding themselves as the New World, were in reality the Old World, for they preserved more of the characteristics of the nineteenth century than did Europe.

Under these circumstances, in the larger Occident Christianity was not dealt as severe blows as it was in Europe. In some ways its course in the one region differed strikingly from that in the other. Several trends knew no boundaries. For instance, the Ecumenical Movement was seen in both, and theological currents in each affected those in the other. Yet in several ways the contrasts were so marked that it became difficult for Christians, particularly Protestant Christians, on the two sides of the Atlantic to understand each other.

We turn, first of all, to the United States, for it was by far the most populous and wealthiest of the countries of the larger Occident. From there we will move on, but more briefly, to the other lands of that region.

The Mounting Vigour of Christianity in the United States of the Twentieth Century: General Movements

The phenomenal growth in population and the even more amazing increase in wealth of the United States in the twentieth century were paralleled by mounting vigour in the Christianity of that country. In this there was a similarity to the British record of the nineteenth century, when the abounding prosperity and power of Great Britain were accompanied by a rising tide in the churches. Here seems to have been more than a coincidence, but in neither land was it certain that the advance of Christianity was chiefly due to that in the other aspects of life or that the latter could be ascribed to the former.

In one respect the gains of Christianity in the United States outstripped those in other phases of the nation's life. Proportionately the increase of church membership was much larger than that of the population as a whole. In 1910 the percentage of the population who were members of some religious body was said to have been 43.4. In the next decade, perhaps because of World War I, it remained stationary. In 1940 it seems to have risen to 47.1. Between 1926 and 1950 the population of Continental United States increased about 28.6 per cent. In the same period the membership of the larger religious bodies grew by 59.8 per cent. In 1950 church membership was about 57 per cent. of the population. This growth was overwhelmingly that of the Christian churches, for the only other religious bodies included in the statistics were Jewish and in 1950 these were only slightly more than 5 per cent. of the whole. Indeed, since from 1926 to 1950 the Jewish congregations increased only about 20 per cent., had they not been included in the figures of religious bodies the gains of the Christian churches would have been seen to have been even greater than 59.8 per cent. What we have called the mass conversion of the population of the United States was obviously continuing, for the percentage of church membership in 1800 has been estimated as 6.9 per cent., in 1850 at 15.5 per cent., and in 1900 at 35.7 per cent. Some of the mass conversion was among previously non-Christian segments, mostly Negroes, Indians, and Asiatics. Most of it was among the partially de-Christianized elements of Christian ancestry.

Whether mass conversion was accompanied by a lowering of the intelligent and whole-hearted commitment of the average church member to the Christian faith would be difficult either to prove or disprove. Nor were there dependable nation-wide figures to disclose whether attendance at church services was increasing or declining. In some sections of the country, mostly in the North and West, the Sunday evening preaching services and the mid-week meetings which in the nineteenth century had been customary among most Protestants were progressively dropped. Life was becoming more complex and the competition of other interests, especially commercialized amusements and various forms of outdoor recreation, proved serious. The older patterns of Protestant church life more nearly survived in the South.

The several aspects of the mass conversion which we have noted (Chapter 50) as characterizing the course of Christianity in the United States in the nineteenth century continued, but with modifications.

The westward movement of population persisted, with the problem of holding to the Church those of its members who were caught up in it and of winning the un-churched. Except for a few pockets, the frontier as such was said to have disappeared late in the nineteenth century, but millions swelled the populations of the westernmost states, especially the three on the Pacific coast. It was clear both that progress was being made and that full success had not been achieved. The proportion of church members remained highest in the older states and while substantial in the newer states was smaller the farther west one went. In 1926 it was 62 and 63 per cent. on the Atlantic seaboard, 51 and 52 per cent. in the central states, 44 per cent. in the Rocky Mountain states, and 35 per cent. on the Pacific coast. The situation varied from locality to locality, but in general these averages gave what seems to have been a correct figure. The churches had been strikingly energetic in dealing with the frontier, but they had not entirely caught up with it.

After 1914 the situation presented by immigration was greatly altered. The coming of World War I all but cut off the stream of immigration which had been pouring across the Atlantic, latterly at the rate of more than a million a year. Following the war drastic legislation kept it from attaining anything approaching its former dimensions. Yet it was still flowing. The numbers of Jews rose sharply, augmented especially by refugees from the ruthless programme of extermination carried out by the Nazis in the 1930's and 1940's. By mid-century more than half the Jews of the entire world were in the United States. After World War II hundreds of thousands of various faiths who had been displaced by that struggle were permitted to enter. More than a million Mexicans, most of them unskilled labourers of the lowest income groups, made their way across the border into the South-west. The hysterical removal of Japanese from the Pacific coast states to what were euphemistically called "relocation camps" after the outbreak of war between the United States and Japan in December, 1941, constituted a further challenge to the churches. For the most part, as before 1914, the immigrants either remained true to the religion of their fathers or drifted away from it into secularism. Not until the second and third generations of their American-born descendants was there much shifting from one denomination to another. Of the effects of the changes in immigration upon the religious history of the United States we shall have something to say when we seek to summarize the developments in the main branches of Christianity.

The Indians, a small minority of the population, tended to fade out of the consciousness of most Americans. In the 1940's only 360,000 were counted as in that category. Yet both Protestant and Roman Catholic mission agencies still sought to serve them. Protestants spent more on them per capita than upon any other racial group. From 1914 to 1939 the proportion of Christians among them rose from between a third and a half to nearly three-fifths.

Negroes constituted a much larger proportion of the population than did the Indians. Although their percentage of the whole slightly declined, in 1950 they were still approximately one-tenth of the total. In general their condition improved, both educationally and economically. They were moving from the farms to the cities, from the South to the North, and from the old South to the South-west. White Protestant churches continued to assist them, mainly through schools. In 1932 they spent more on the Negroes than on any other one group of the population outside their own congregations. Roman Catholics also conducted missions among Negroes.

The large majority of Negro church members were still in purely Negro denominations. This was chiefly by the choice of the Negroes themselves, for here were institutions of which they were in complete control and which were not dominated by the white man. The proportion of Negroes who were church members was slightly larger than that of the whites. As among the whites, more women than men had church membership, but the percentage of women was higher and of men was lower among Negroes than among whites. Baptists still predominated, about two-thirds of the whole, with Methodists second, a little less than a fourth of the total. Roman Catholics remained a small minority, but were growing, especially in the cities.

The movements of population were not confined to those from east to west or of the Negroes. Much of the nation was involved. Villages, towns, and cities continued to grow at the expense of the farming population. In the cities, particularly after the advent of the automobile, suburbs expanded rapidly and in the North-east and parts of the Middle West were made up largely of the older American stock, predominantly Protestant by tradition. Apartment houses multiplied, especially in the centres of the large cities, and in the 1930's, 1940's, and 1950's huge "housing projects" arose, often on sites which had formerly been slums. Migratory elements of the population, subsisting by seasonal employment, were swelled by the great depression of the 1930's, by a devastating drought in the 1930's from the Dakotas southward in what at the time was called the "dust bowl," and by the demand for labour in the "defense industries" of World War II and the rearmament of the 1950's. Many of the migrants were in automobile "trailer camps."

The shifts in population were a threat and a challenge to the churches. Could these largely uprooted and often rootless elements be reached and held? Protestantism had its main strength in the suburban areas and the villages and towns rather than in the hearts of the larger cities, the purely farming areas, and the chronically migratory. In general it lost ground in the congested older sections of the cities. Roman Catholics still seemed to have more success in the crowded portions of the cities, but that was probably because the newer immigration, much of it of that faith and on a lower economic level than the older stock, largely dwelt there. In general, a higher proportion of the city than of the rural population had membership in the churches. In 1926 it was 58 per cent. for the former and 52 per cent. for the latter. Those living on isolated farms were more difficult to gather into congregations than those in villages and towns, where a sense of community was more easily developed.

Ever present were currents of life and thought which were adverse to Christianity. The fevered prosperity of the 1920's led to a neglect of religion. Even after the depression of the 1930's, World War II, and the perilous aftermath of that struggle sobered the nation, the secular spirit was widespread. The sceptical intellectual movements which had been prominent in the nineteenth century and which mounted in the latter part of that period continued. They were reinforced by the philosophy of John Dewey which dominated much of education and penetrated some Protestant circles.

In the United States, displaying as it did more variety than Christianity had ever done elsewhere, in the years following 1914 each main branch of the faith was vigorous and experienced growth.

The Mounting Vigour of Christianity in the United States: The Eastern Churches

The Eastern Churches, planted firmly in constituencies which had sought haven and opportunity in the United States and which were predominantly urban, grew in numbers and wealth. They were a minority and won almost no converts, but they multiplied and were increasingly well-rooted with clergy more and more of whom were American-born. The Patriarch of the Church of the East (Nestorian) found refuge in the United States and there were also congregations of some of the other small Eastern Churches.

The Orthodox were especially prominent. Before 1914 they had been mostly within the structure of the pioneer of their wing of the faith on American soil, the Russian Orthodox Church. After 1914 several churches of national origin achieved distinct ecclesiastical organizations and ultimately became autonomous. They included the Albanian Orthodox Church, the Bulgarian Orthodox Church, the Rumanian Orthodox Church, the Greek Orthodox Church (Hellenic), the Serbian Orthodox Church, and the Ukrainian Orthodox Church. The largest of these was the Greek Orthodox (Hellenic), which in 1943 was said to have 675,000 members. It was dependent on the Ecumenical Patriarch of Constantinople (Istanbul). After 1917 the unity of the Russian Orthodox constituency was broken over the issue of the communist regime and of loyalty to the Patriarchate in Moscow. Several of the other national groups also suffered from fissiparousness. In the 1940's a federation was formed of most of the Orthodox Churches in the United States.

The Mounting Vigour of Christianity in the United States: The Roman Catholic Church

The Roman Catholic Church prospered but was confronted by grave problems. As we have hinted, the stream of immigration to which it owed most of its growth was greatly reduced after 1914. That meant that it was enabled to catch up with its task. We have earlier noted (Chapter 50) the extraordinary record of the nineteenth century. In spite of the extreme poverty of the large majority of its constituency, newly arrived, and primarily through clergy recruited and funds contributed in the United States, the Roman Catholic Church held to its faith the large majority of its hereditary constituency. It erected thousands of churches and chapels, built a vast educational system of parochial and secondary schools, universities, and theological seminaries, developed hundreds of monasteries, and knit very diverse national elements into one national ecclesiastical structure fully loyal to Rome. In 1914 it was by far the largest denomination in the country. Yet this achievement was only by dint of great effort. Now, with the annual immigration only a fraction of what it had been, the Roman Catholic Church consolidated its position, sought to win converts from the population in which it was set, and took an increasing share in foreign missions.

In numbers the Roman Catholic Church registered striking advances. In 1906 its members were said to total 14,210,755, in 1916 15,721,815, in 1926 18,605,003, and in 1950 28,634,878. The increase was due predominantly to immigration and the excess of births over deaths. Several organizations were active in seeking to win converts. Among them were the Paulist Fathers, the Catholic Unity League, the National Converts League, the Catholic Missionary Union, and the League for Prayer for the Conversion of America. In the year 1949 the number of conversions was reported as being 117,130. Many, perhaps the majority of these were through marriage.

Even more marked was the growth of the Roman Catholic Church in material possessions. As its constituency was longer in the United States, it shared more and more in the wealth of the country. By the middle of the century most of its members were still in the lower income groups. Yet Roman Catholics were increasingly in a position to contribute to the various enterprises of the Church and did so. Many new church and school buildings were constructed, numbers of them in much better architectural form than earlier had been general, hundreds of hospitals and orphanages were maintained, enlarged, or founded, and increasing sums were contributed to the Society for the Propagation of the Faith and to other foreign missionary agencies.

Additional organizations were developed and old ones enlarged. In 1919 the National Catholic Welfare Conference was constituted in succession to the National Catholic War Council which had been formed primarily to further the interests of the Church among the members of the armed services. Every bishop in the United States had a voice in it, and it possessed departments and committees which covered a wide range of activities and interests. It was administered by a board of ten bishops elected at the annual meeting of the hierarchy. That annual meeting was in itself a means of achieving a sense of national unity in the Church. The National Catholic Welfare Conference was the chief means of stimulating and coördinating Catholic Action.

Participation in foreign missions rapidly mounted. Some of it was through American provinces of existing orders, such as the Franciscans, the Lazarists, the Jesuits, and the Society of the Divine Word. Much was through new organizations. Notable among the latter was the Catholic Foreign Mission Society of America, better known as Maryknoll from its headquarters on a hill above the Hudson River. It was founded in 1911 and was in close association with the Foreign Mission Sisters of St. Dominic. The Catholic Students' Mission Crusade was begun in 1918, for much the same purpose as the (Protestant) Student Volunteer Movement for Foreign Missions. Indeed, it owed its origin largely to the example given by the latter. Until World War II the region to which the Roman Catholics of the United States directed most of their missionary energy was the Far East, especially China. They also extended their efforts into other areas, among them India and Africa. After World War II they sent more missionaries to Latin America than to any other region.

The growth in numbers, wealth, and participation in the world-wide missions of their church encouraged Roman Catholics, especially the clergy. Official pronouncements and the Roman Catholic press had a note of confidence.

However, the church was confronted by problems, some transient and others persistent. One of its passing perplexities was presented to it by a priest, Charles E. Coughlin (1891——), who rose to nation-wide influence while in charge of the church of the Shrine of the Little Flower at Royal Oak, Michigan, on the outskirts of Detroit. He was among those who early appreciated radio as a vehicle for reaching a wide audience. He began broadcasting in 1926. He addressed himself largely to economic and political issues and, professing to be applying the principles of the *Rerum novarum* (1891) of Leo XIII to the current situation, endeavoured to inject Christianity into the economic system. For several years he won only local attention. Then came the depression which began late in 1929 and which deepened in the 1930's. Millions were unemployed and multitudes lost their savings. They were prepared to listen to a voice which confidently offered a solution. Coughlin quickly attracted a nation-wide radio audience which was most numerous in the Middle West and the North-east. He attacked capitalists and bankers, urged paying off interest-bearing government bonds with non-interest-bearing currency, and was vigorous against national prohibition. From 1932 to 1934 he supported Franklin D. Roosevelt under the slogan, "Roosevelt or ruin," then turned against him and his New Deal, labeling him a "liar" and a "scab President." Becoming more and more violent, he declared that Jewish bankers had made possible Russian communism, advocated the reorganization of the government as a corporate state, and encouraged the formation (1938) of the "Christian Front." To many he seemed to be fomenting a revolt akin to fascism and Nazism. At first some of his superiors defended him, but he became increasingly embarrassing to the hierarchy, was rebuked by the Vatican, and ultimately lapsed into silence.

More chronic and serious were some other problems. One was the fact that, being strongest in the cities, the Roman Catholic Church suffered from the declining birth rate which was a feature of urban life. This was in spite of its vigorously expressed opposition to contraceptive devices. Another was the inroads of secularism. The attraction of the material side of the nation's life diverted many from the claims of the faith. There were also losses to Protestantism. Precisely how large these latter were no one knew. They probably exceeded the gains from Protestantism. Not many were won to the congregations gathered by Protestants specifically for converts from Roman Catholicism. However, many Roman Catholics slipped away through marriage. Numbers became Protestants as part of their assimilation to American life, especially in communities which were predominantly of that wing of the faith. Others sought membership in a Protestant church from profound religious conviction. In New York City there was a mission maintained by former priests to assist priests who wished to leave the Roman Catholic Church.

In general after 1914 the Roman Catholicism of the United States displayed the features which had characterized it in the decades immediately preceding that year. It was activistic. In scholarship it was still behind some Roman Catholic circles in Europe and in academic quality its universities did not yet rank with the best of those on Protestant foundation or supported by the state. No outstanding mystics had emerged from it and no new monastic orders had been formed comparable in size with those which had originated in Europe.

Also as a continuation of nineteenth century trends, the Roman Catholic Church was served by a body of priests and of sisters who were, on the average, well trained, hard-working, and devoted. It had large numbers of bishops and archbishops who were able administrators. So many were there of the latter that even to name the more prominent would unduly lengthen our pages, and to single out two or three for special mention would be to ignore others who were of equal importance.

Skill was shown in utilizing the radio. Through it more than one preacher acquired a national reputation which, while not as spectacular as that of Coughlin, was more nearly in accord with the traditions of the church. Notable among them was Fulton John Sheen (1895——). Highly trained in philosophy and theology in the United States and Europe, he was a member of the faculty of the Catholic University of America, an eloquent preacher, a prolific author, a persuasive apologist and expounder of the Roman Catholic faith, and was eventually honoured with the title of bishop. Through the radio his voice was carried across the nation.

Movements of a novel character were evidence of a vigour which broke out in new ways. Such was that of the Christophers, which sought to enlist both Catholics and non-Catholics in intelligent efforts to "change the world" by making their faith effective in the various lay professions and occupations. The liturgical movement gained headway. Although by the mid-century, as we have seen, only one American had been canonized, and she not native-born, there was much of the kind of prayer and radiant devotion which might well be producing others to whom their church would later accord that recognition.

THE MOUNTING VIGOUR OF CHRISTIANITY IN THE UNITED STATES: PROTESTANTISM

If mounting vigour characterized the Eastern Churches and the Roman Catholic Church in the United States in the generation after 1914, it was even more striking in the Protestantism of the country. As had been true since its beginning, so far as it was affected by any religion the United States was predominantly Protestant. In spite of the secularism which had been present from the inception of the nation, Protestant Christianity had entered decisively into the ideals of the country and continued to do so. The mass conversion to the faith which had been in process in the nineteenth and twentieth centuries was still more through Protestantism than the other two main branches of Christianity. Between 1906 and 1926 the membership of Protestant churches is said to have increased 46 per cent. compared with 25 per cent. in the Roman Catholic Church. Between 1926 and 1950, as against a growth in the population of the country of about 28.6 per cent., Roman Catholic membership seems to have gained 53.9 per cent. and the membership of Protestant denominations 59.7 per cent. The percentage increase in the Eastern Churches in that twenty-four-year period appears to have been very much larger, but that may have been in part because of obviously imperfect estimates. At the most in 1950 these bodies included only a little more than 2 per cent. of the church membership of the country and their growth was due to increasing effectiveness in gathering into their fold their hereditary constituency rather than to conversions. The proportionate gains of Protestantism varied from denomination to denomination. For the most part between 1926 and 1950 the percentage increase of the older and larger denominations, such as the Methodists, the Presbyterians, the Congregationalists, and the Disciples of Christ, was not as large as that of the Roman Catholics, and it was the younger, smaller Protestant bodies which had the most spectacular growth. However, the totals of the three major Baptist bodies, namely, the Southern Baptist Convention and the two main Negro conventions, with a total reported membership in 1950 of over 14,000,000, had risen more than 100 per cent. in that twenty-five year period, and in the three leading Lutheran churches the rise was slightly over 60 per cent. It will be remembered that Baptists were the largest of the denominational families and Lutherans the third largest.

In their general outlines the methods by which the mass conversion and the striking growth of the Protestant bodies were achieved after 1914 did not differ essentially from those employed in the nineteenth century. The Sunday Schools were still the main dependence for the religious education of children and youths. To supplement them more and more moving pictures were filmed. "Evangelistic campaigns" were, as formerly, customary among Baptists, Methodists, and a number of smaller denominational families. Hundreds of itinerant "evangelists" were used in these "special meetings." A few rose to national prominence. Among them was William Ashley ("Billy") Sunday (1863–1935), a Presbyterian, a former professional baseball player, who not far from 1900 began to attract wide attention by his spectacular, informal pulpit mannerisms and by his "sawdust trail" along which converts made their way from their seats to the front of the "tabernacles" which were erected for him. As the radio came into use, it was employed by hundreds of preachers, several of them with nation-wide coverage. Some, notably Harry Emerson Fosdick (1878——), a Baptist, had their audiences chiefly among the educated. The one with the widest hearing was also a Baptist, Charles E. Fuller (1887——), who appealed to the rank and file. He began broadcasting in 1925 and through what he called "The Old-fashioned Revival Hour" by 1942 had what he believed to be a world-wide audience. Soon after World War I a movement grew up around Frank N. D. Buchman (1878——) which was said to have spread to more than sixty countries. By novel means under fresh terminology it sought to win individuals, especially among students, intellectuals, the wealthy, and those influential in political life and labour. Long called "the groups" or the "Oxford groups," a name given it at Christ Church, Oxford, in 1921, in 1938 it was re-named Moral Re-armament, usually "M.R.A."—as "a race in time to re-make men and nations" and sought to effect "personal, social, racial, national, and supernatural change." The Youth for Christ Movement, strong in the 1940's, spread to other countries. It was addressed primarily to those of teen age.

Evangelism was accompanied by a prolific composition of hymns. Most of them were akin to the spirituals, white and Negro, and the Gospel hymns of the previous century and had a widespread popular appeal. They were evidence that the Protestant form of the Christian faith had vitality among the masses.

Theological activity among Protestants was marked. The currents of thought were many and varied. The most widely influential were three. One was the "liberalism" which rose to a crescendo on the eve of 1914. A second was "neo-orthodoxy." The third was "fundamentalism," which repudiated both "liberalism" and "neo-orthodoxy."

"Liberalism" had many and able exponents. They differed among themselves, but in general they had confidence in human reason, applied it to the study of the Bible, using the historical methods that had acquired wide vogue in the nineteenth century, tended to believe that essential Christian doctrines could either be demonstrated by rational processes or could be shown not to be contrary to them, and were hopeful that a society could be achieved by man's effort which would progressively conform to Christian standards. The preacher who did most through the pulpit and pen to present to a wide constituency Christianity as understood by "liberals" was Harry Emerson Fosdick, who exerted his greatest influence while pastor of the Riverside Church in New York City. Earnest, clear, persuasive, stating convictions held by Evangelicals in fresh ways and in terms which took account of current scholarship, he aided many thoughtful souls who in the midst of the challenges of the age were seeking a firm footing to face unafraid and honestly the questions hurled at them by critics and the crises of individual and collective life. He enabled them not only to retain their Christian faith but also to discover that it was richer and more valid than they had once thought possible. A great "liberal" who was best known for his expert knowledge and personal experience in the way of the Christian mystic was the Quaker philosopher, Rufus Matthew Jones (1863–1948). Having a large share in initiating the American Friends Service Committee and serving as its chairman and then its honorary chairman from its inception until his death, he illustrated what had often been earlier demonstrated, that the Christian mystic, by the vision and strength derived from his intimate fellowship with the Unseen, often becomes a man or woman of intense action. The list of outstanding "liberals" in theology, Biblical and historical studies, and action could be greatly prolonged.

"Neo-orthodoxy" had strong kinship with the corresponding movement in Europe. Like the latter, it was in part a reaction against the optimism which was dominant in Western civilization in the latter part of the nineteenth century. It was also a reaffirmation of the uniqueness of the action of God in the revelation of Himself as recorded in the Scriptures and which culminated in what He did through Christ. It was given additional impetus by the financial depression and the deterioration of the international situation in the 1930's with their proof of the insecurity of the civilization which had been so hopefully acclaimed by many in the feverishly prosperous 1920's. It was also a protest against the non-theistic humanism, the confidence in man's ability, which had flourished in the decade after World War I. While willing to accept much of the methods and results of the historical approach to the Scriptures which prevailed in "liberal" circles, "neo-orthodoxy" revolted against a great deal of the theology which went with them. Like "liberalism," it displayed marked variety. Its most prominent exponent and formulator was Reinhold Niebuhr (1892——). He decried what he deemed the utopianism of "liberalism" and its belief that man could achieve an ideal society. He stressed the chronic sinfulness of man and the fashion in which all man's efforts at improvement for himself and his fellows are tainted with sin and therefore can never attain perfection. He made much of the crucifixion as God's way of dealing with man. He thought and spoke in terms of paradoxes. While pouring scorn on utopianism, he laboured prodigiously through many organizations to combat evil and promote righteousness.

The "fundamentalists," many of whom preferred to be called "conservatives" or "evangelicals," denounced what they called "modernism." They sought to maintain the inerrancy of the Bible and the convictions long held by Evangelicals. Among the latter were the deity and virgin birth of Christ, Christ's atoning and substitutionary death, his bodily resurrection, his second coming, the work of the Holy Spirit in the conversion and the sanctification of the sinner, the eternal blessedness of those accounted by God as righteous because of their faith in Christ, and the eternal punishment of the wicked. In doing so they attacked those in the churches who seemed to them to be compromising or corrupting the faith. To many of them Harry Emerson Fosdick became a symbol of what they abhorred. In 1919 the World's Christian Fundamentals Association was organized.

Within several denominations conflicts arose out of the efforts of the "fundamentalists" to obtain the adoption of their convictions and to eliminate those who disagreed with them. In some this led to open division. A redoubtable champion of "fundamentalism" was the intellectually able John Gresham Machen (1881–1937). The failure to retain him on the faculty of the Princeton Theological Seminary became the occasion of a bitter fight and eventual schism in the Presbyterian Church in the U.S.A.

"Evolution" was obnoxious to the "fundamentalists," for it seemed to them to deny the authority of the Scriptures. They attempted to have the states enact legislation to prevent the teaching of it in the schools. In Tennessee, where they succeeded, the trial of a teacher, John Thomas Scopes, in 1925, on the charge of violating the law, attracted world-wide attention, especially since among the attorneys for the prosecution was William Jennings Bryan, former Democratic nominee for the Presidency of the United States and at one time Secretary of State. "Fundamentalist" and "conservative" views were taught in a rapidly growing number of Bible schools and theological seminaries and many evangelists reinforced them through the pulpit, the platform, and the radio.

In spite of the diversity and theological conflicts, Protestantism in the United States moved in the direction of a more conscious and visible unity. Here were some of the most striking phases of the global trend towards Christian unity which was one of the outstanding features of the faith in the post-1914 years.

One of these phases was the fusion of two or more ecclesiastical bodies, sometimes called "organic union." The unions were of churches which were either of the same denominational family or were closely related in polity, creed, and constituency. The largest was that consummated in 1939 through which the Methodist Episcopal Church, the Methodist Episcopal Church, South, and the Methodist Protestant Church came together to form the Methodist Church, which in 1950 numbered nearly 9,000,000 members. Not so large, but totalling approximately 2,000,000 members in 1950, was the United Lutheran Church which, as we have seen (Chapter 50), was formed in 1918 by three groups. In 1919 it was joined by the Slovak Zion Synod. Still smaller, but substantial, was the Norwegian Lutheran Church of America, which came into being in 1917 after a generation or more of negotiation and which in 1946 was re-named the Evangelical Lutheran Church of America. In 1930 the American Lutheran Church resulted from the union of three synods which were chiefly of German stock. In 1934 two other bodies of German origin and of very similar polity and faith, the Evangelical Synod of North America and the Reformed Church in the United States, drew together in the Evangelical and Reformed Church. In the year 1946 there was the union of two denominations of Methodist temper and polity and chiefly of German stock, the Evangelical Church and the United Brethren in Christ, in the Evangelical United Brethren. In 1931 the Congregational Churches and the General Convention of the Christian Church, which was largely congregational in polity, became the Congregational Christian Churches. This partial list embraces the largest of the united bodies, but smaller ones also came into being.

By mid-century attempts at the union of churches of quite distinct polities and traditions had not come to fruition. In two important instances they seemed to be frustrated. These were the prolonged negotiations between the Presbyterian Church in the U.S.A. and the Protestant Episcopal Church and the proposed merger of the Congregational Christian Churches with the Evangelical and Reformed Church.

Looser associations of similar churches were part of the scene, among them the Synodical Conference, of which the Missouri Synod was the main constituent, and the American Lutheran Conference, which embraced the Augustana Lutheran Church, the Lutheran Free Church, the United Evangelical Lutheran Church, the American Lutheran Church, and the Evangelical Lutheran Church. The American Lutheran Conference churches were drawn into a larger but still looser National Lutheran Council which also included the United Lutheran Church and the Finnish and Danish Lutheran Churches.

By the year 1950 there were conversations among outstanding leaders which looked towards an inclusive association and even union of leading denominations.

Much more notable than the progress of organic union was the growth of coöperation among the churches. In 1951 there were said to be over 900 local and state councils of churches, about 2,000 ministerial associations, and over 1,800 councils of United Church Women. Late in 1950 there was formally launched the National Council of the Churches of Christ in the United States of America. By the year 1952 into it had merged twelve bodies through which the majority of Protestants and some of the Orthodox coöperated. These were the Federal Council of the Churches of Christ in America, the Home Missions Council of North America, the Foreign Missions Conference of North America, the Missionary Education Movement, the International Council of Religious Education, the National Protestant Council on Higher Education, the United Council of Church Women, the United Stewardship Council, Church World Service, the Interseminary Committee, the Protestant Radio Commission, and the Protestant Film Commission. In 1951 the National Council could point to a membership of twenty-nine churches which embraced about two-thirds of the Protestant and Orthodox membership of the country. Several other denominations were represented on one or another of the divisions or other units of the National Council.

A still more inclusive organization of Protestant origin was the National Conference of Christians and Jews which came into being between World War I and World War II. It was not made up of religious bodies, but was an association of individuals. Its purpose was to further understanding and remove friction among Protestants, Roman Catholics, and Jews.

Americans were also active in the several world organizations which were global expressions of the Ecumenical Movement. The financial support of these bodies came chiefly from the United States, and while by no means dominant, Americans were prominent in the leadership.

Not all Protestants joined in these coöperative movements. A substantial minority believed that the Federal Council of Churches and its successor, the National Council of the Churches of Christ in the U.S.A., were hopelessly tainted with "modernism." Some of the opposition formed a fellowship called the National Association of Evangelicals. Conservative in theology, it stressed evangelism. Another body which had a Presbyterian core and placed its chief emphasis on doctrine was the American Council of Christian Churches. Each of these reached out to form a global organization, the one the World Evangelical Fellowship and the other the International Council of Christian Churches. There were bodies, several of them large, among them the Southern Baptist Convention and some of the Lutheran churches, which coöperated either very little or not at all with any of these interdenominational organizations.

In spite of dissent and tensions among Protestants there was a growing unity. This was seen not only in organic unions and coöperation but also in other ways. Forms of worship spread from one denomination to another. Among several of the churches which had been opposed to liturgy traditional features of dignified worship began to be taken over from the Catholic (but not necessarily the Roman Catholic) heritage. "Divided chancels" which accorded a central place to the altar or communion table were substituted for the arrangement which focused attention on the pulpit. Ministers and choirs donned vestments. Books of prayer for use in the public services became common, most of them with forms for the communion which were adaptations of the historic liturgies. More and more hymnals, even of the least coöperative denominations, drew from authors who ranged all the way from Unitarians to Roman Catholics. The observance of Lent, Holy Week, Good Friday, and Whitsunday which a generation earlier would have been shunned as "Popery" spread among churches on the extreme wing of Protestantism. Methods of reaching children, young people, and the laity, including summer assemblies, tended to be the same, regardless of the denomination. From time to time, chiefly on the initiative of Protestants, limited coöperation among Protestants, Roman Catholics, and Jews was achieved on special projects.

However, tensions continued between Roman Catholics and Protestants and at times became acute. They were aggravated in the 1940's and in the 1950's by Protestant opposition to proposals for giving aid from the funds of the Federal Government to church schools, which meant primarily Roman Catholic schools, and to the diplomatic representation of the United States Government at the Vatican.

The Protestants of the United States increasingly made their weight felt in questions of global concern and shared in the world-wide spread of the faith. Either through official church channels or through undenominational agencies organized for special emergencies, they contributed hundreds of millions of dollars to the relief of suffering during and after World War I and World War II. This relief was on an ascending scale: it was decidedly greater in the 1940's and 1950's than it had been earlier. Much of it went to former enemy peoples, especially to Germans and Japanese. Such organizations as Near East Relief, which was brought into existence in World War I, the American Friends Service Committee, also an outgrowth of World War I but attaining much larger proportions as the years passed, and Church World Service, through which numbers of churches coöperated during and after World War II, were only a few of the many agencies. With the impoverishment of Western Europe and Britain, the Protestant Churches of the United States undertook an increasing share in the foreign missions of their branch of the faith, and, as we have seen, maintained not only their own representatives, but also because of the vicissitudes of World War II assumed the support of some of the Continental missionaries. For a time after World War I when there was a return to isolationism and what was mistakenly termed "normalcy," a sharp falling off of giving to missions and other benevolences was experienced. The decline was accentuated by the failure of the Interchurch World Movement, an attempt to capitalize on the interest developed in World War I and permanently to increase the contributions to charitable enterprises. The depression which began late in 1929 and which deepened during the fore part of the 1930's brought a further decline of church incomes, and in 1935 the per capita contributions of Protestants to church enterprises, congregational, national, and foreign, was only about half what it had been in 1930. By 1940 it was beginning to recover and in 1951 it was larger by nearly a third than in 1930.

The depression of the 1930's and World War II were not as devastating in the United States as they were across the Atlantic. After the first sharp blow of the depression, the wealth of the United States again mounted. The effect of these two crises proved a stimulus to the Protestantism of the United States. Millions were shocked out of the complacency which had characterized the country in the 1920's and which had so affected impressionable youth that a large proportion of those who were adolescents in that decade were, from the standpoint of the Christian faith, "the lost generation." Realizing the basic and terrifying insecurity of the human race, many turned to the Christian faith for an answer. After World War II, in contrast with what was taking place in Great Britain, hundreds of young men flocked into the ministry of the Protestant churches. Theological seminaries were crowded, and, in general, in native ability and seriousness as well as in numbers the student bodies of these institutions surpassed anything that had been known in the century and possibly in the history of the country.

THE MOUNTING VIGOUR OF THE CHRISTIANITY OF THE UNITED STATES: ITS EFFECT ON THE COUNTRY AND THE WORLD

What effect did this mounting vigour of the Christianity of the United States have upon the United States and upon the world? The answer to that question, important though it is, cannot be fully determined. Nor can we even take the space to summarize all that is known. We can mention only a few facts and be content to regard them as examples of what a full account would disclose.

It was clear that the post-1914 era saw a grave decline in some aspects of the nation's morals which Christianity had not been able to prevent. This was probably the almost inevitable accompaniment and sequel of the wars in which the country engaged and of the deceptive prosperity which it experienced in the 1920's and the 1940's. The prohibition of the manufacture and sale of alcoholic beverages which was written into the Constitution of the United States in 1919 was annulled in the 1930's and subsequently the consumption of alcohol and with it alcoholism reached alarming proportions. The use of narcotics and the attendant addiction to drugs were causes of concern. The divorce rate mounted and the instability of the family was heightened. Psychiatrists rapidly increased in numbers and their offices were thronged with patients. In the 1920's gangsters terrified some of the cities. Corruption was rife in municipal, state, and national governments. In their propaganda communists rang the changes on racial discrimination against the Negroes. The pessimist could easily find evidence to support the thesis that in spite of the progressive mass conversion of the country Christianity was waning in its effect upon the country and its people.

This, however, as often in the past, was only one side of the picture. As heretofore, the scene was one of stark contrasts. Christians were by no means giving up the struggle to make their faith count in the nation and the world. When the divorce rate is mentioned, we must immediately recall the millions of marriages blessed by the Church which were successful amid the strains of a complex and stormy age. When attention is called to political corruption, in the same breath there must be mentioned the thousands of honest, conscientious public servants who were held to integrity by what had come to them through the churches. Race relations, although by no means ideal, were not as bad as formerly, and in no small degree the gain was due to the Christian conscience and initiative. The chief organization for the relief of suffering from natural emergencies, the Red Cross, through its name and symbol witnessed to its Christian origin. In addition to the large sums contributed by individuals for the alleviation of the distresses brought by the wars of the period, vast appropriations were made and disbursed through the national government. Much of this was for former enemies. Never before had a nation given so lavishly for the amelioration of the lot of other peoples. Some was through international organizations, such as UNRRA (United Nations Relief and Rehabilitation Administration), and some through its own bureaus, such as ECA (Economic Coöperation Administration). Much was for prudential reasons, but much was stimulated by the Christian conscience. It was partly because of the pressure put on the Congress by churches and church organizations, for instance, that in 1951 that body voted a large sum to send grain to help cope with famine in India. The chief architect of the League of Nations was Woodrow Wilson, and his vision and persistent labours to make the dream a reality were from his Christian faith. Prolonged education and agitation through the churches had a large share in nullifying the isolationism which kept the United States out of that body and prepared the way for the leadership of that country in the formation of the United Nations. President Franklin D. Roosevelt had a simple but sincere faith about which he said little but which sustained him in the heavy burdens which he bore. During World War II the Federal Council of Churches created a Commission on the Bases of a Just and Durable Peace which was headed by John Foster Dulles. Dulles later declared that his share in that undertaking and his Christian faith were determinative in his negotiation of the peace treaty between the United States and Japan (signed in September, 1951) which was in principle not retaliatory and vindictive, but was intended to make for reconciliation. It was largely from the United States that the impulse came for the Churches Commission on International Affairs, a joint agency of the World Council of Churches and the International Missionary Council, and one of the American officers of the Commission had an outstanding part in the framing of the Declaration of Human Rights and the correlated Covenant of Human Rights put forward through the United Nations.

THE VIGOUR OF CANADIAN CHRISTIANITY

In Canada after 1914 Christianity continued to display the vigour which had marked its course in the nineteenth century. There is space to mention only four of its manifestations.

One of these was the growth of the Roman Catholic Church. This was through a high birth rate rather than immigration or conversions. As we have seen (Chapter 51), the major strength of that church was along the French elements of the population. In contrast with the Roman Catholics of the United States, who were mostly urban and therefore with a declining birth rate, they were predominantly rural and had large families. The Canadian Protestants were increasingly urban and their birth rate reflected that fact. The proportion of Roman Catholics in the population rose from about 40 per cent. in 1911 to approximately 43.8 per cent. in 1941. Between 1931 and 1941 the population of the country mounted by 10.5 per cent., but Roman Catholics added to their numbers by over 16 per cent. Now that immigration from Protestant Great Britain had declined from its nineteenth century dimensions, Roman Catholic leaders were confident that before the century was out they would constitute a majority in the nation. It was not merely in numbers that French Roman Catholicism was increasingly vigorous. In it organizations emerged to deal with social and labour issues. The liturgical movement had adherents. A growing share was taken in the foreign missions of the church.

There were several hundred thousand Orthodox in Canada divided into national churches.

The trend towards unity within Protestantism made itself felt. Its most striking expression was the creation, in 1925, of the United Church of Canada, a merger of the Methodists, Congregationalists, and a majority of the Presbyterians. It and the Church of England were the largest non-Roman Catholic bodies in the Dominion. One of the chief reasons for its formation was to reach more effectively with the faith the burgeoning communities in the West, f r these could be better approached unitedly than by divided and competing churches. In 1944 the Canadian Council of Churches was constituted by bringing together several coöperative interdenominational bodies. In 1951 five Canadian churches had membership in the World Council of Churches. Canadians were also active in the International Missionary Council and other phases of the Ecumenical Movement.

In Canada as in the United States churches which by their enthusiastic, emotional evangelism, the informality of their meetings, and their confidence in the inerrancy of the Scriptures appealed to the lower income groups had a spectacular growth. They were evidence that the larger and older churches, with their tendency towards dignity in worship and intellectual content in their preaching, did not meet the needs of the underprivileged elements of the population.

Weakness and Strength in Latin America

The course of Christianity in Latin America following 1914 was, in the main, one of advance. However, it was advance which was chiefly due to what was injected from abroad rather than to the inherent strength of the Christian communities of the area.

It will be recalled (Chapter 51) that from the beginning the Christianity of the region had been dependent upon continuous infusions of blood from the outside. Until the nineteenth century that Christianity had been Roman Catholic. In Spanish America the Roman Catholic Church had suffered severely from the disturbances which accompanied the achievement of political independence from the mother country. In general it had sided with the elements which sought to preserve the economic and social *status quo*. The struggle between clericals and anti-clericals was a factor in the politics of most Latin American lands. While in the nineteenth century the majority of the clergy were of native stock, their average in character and education left much to be desired. Their numbers were inadequate and they did little for the conversion of the non-Christian Indians who still existed on the fringes of European settlement. Most of the missions to the Indians and some of the care of the nominally Christian population were by clergy from Europe. Protestantism was introduced in the first half of the nineteenth century but did not have much growth until the second half of the century. Then its increase was chiefly through immigration and missionaries from Great Britain and the United States. The Eastern Churches were slimly represented by immigrants.

After 1914 the Roman Catholic Church advanced. This was partly through conversions from non-Christian Indians and chiefly through clergy from Europe and the United States. Until World War II the missionaries were mainly from Europe. That cataclysm cut off much of the help from that continent. It also obstructed the flow of missionaries from the United States to the Far East, until then the area to which had been directed most of the recently awakened missionary interest of the Roman Catholics of that country. Attention was diverted to Latin America and by 1950, as we have seen, that region became the major foreign field of the Roman Catholics of the United States. Some of the missionaries went to non-Christian Indians. Most of them, however, served the nominally Christian population.

In spite of the aid from the outside, the Roman Catholic Church did not fully rid itself of the weaknesses which had plagued it. Many of its nominal adherents and others who had drifted completely away from it sought satisfaction for their religious longings in positivism, theosophy, or one form or another of spiritualism. Many were without religion. A few became communists. In the 1920's and 1930's the Roman Catholic Church was subjected to severe attacks in Mexico by anti-clericals and, latterly, by anti-Christians. By 1935 fourteen states had forbidden priests and had made saying mass or giving the sacraments a criminal offense. However, a reaction occurred, and in the 1940's conditions became less unfavourable.

In some Latin American republics there were indications of fresh vitality in the Roman Catholic Church. Here and there the quality of the indigenous clergy showed improvement. In more than one country Catholic Action enlisted the laity. The revival of the study of Thomas Aquinas came by contagion from Europe and won the respect of some of the intellectuals.

The Eastern Churches were still small and were the result of immigration.

Protestantism displayed more vigour in Latin America than did any other branch of Christianity. It owed its growth chiefly to missionaries from the United States, but by mid-century it was spreading of its own momentum, strikingly so in Brazil. Protestantism increased in numbers in every Latin American country, but was strongest in the largest of them, Brazil, and, next to Brazil, in Mexico. In spite of its many divisions, it showed the trend towards coöperation which it manifested in other regions. Conferences for all Protestants and their missions were held in 1916, 1925, 1929, and 1948. That of 1948 was predominantly indigenous in its initiation and leadership, and this was symptomatic of a general trend. In several of the republics there were national councils and in Brazil there was a Federation of Evangelical Churches. In 1949

Protestant communicants were said to total a million and a third as against about half that in 1938 and less than a fourth that in 1914. In 1949 the Protestant community was estimated as being four and a half millions.

Continued Vigour in Australasia

We can pause for only the briefest of notices of the post-1914 course of Christianity in the predominantly Anglo-Saxon and Protestant nations of Australia and New Zealand. The churches of Australia were less and less dependent for clergy upon the British Isles. They were developing more missions for those of their own land whose connexion with the faith was only nominal and were taking increased responsibility for spreading the Gospel among the aborigines on their frontiers and on the islands in the Pacific to their east and north. Australian Protestants were also showing the trend towards unity which was seen in other countries. Through the National Missionary Council formed in 1927 they had memberhip in the International Missionary Council. Several of their churches were in the World Council of Churches.

Much the same development characterized the post-1914 Christianity of New Zealand. Shifts of population, especially to the cities, were accompanied by the erection of new church buildings. New Zealand Protestants were drawn into the Ecumenical Movement, including both the International Missionary Council and the World Council of Churches. They also reached outside the country in missions in the Pacific.

The vast expanse of islands to the east and north of Australia and New Zealand, all under white control but with predominantly non-white populations, continued to feel the impact of Occidental culture. By 1914, as we have seen (Chapter 51), most of the Polynesians and Micronesians and some of the Melanesians had become Christian. After that year the faith, both Roman Catholic and Protestant, continued its spread among the Melanesians and the Papuans.

Summary

After 1914 in contrast with the de-Christianization of large elements of the populations of what had long been the heart of Christendom, Europe, Christianity was advancing in the nations of European stock in the Americas and Australasia. This was especially notable in the largest of these lands, the United States. It was true of the Eastern Churches and the Roman Catholic Church, but it was even more marked in Protestantism. Protestantism was gaining among the de-Christianized elements and the non-Christian Negroes, Indians, and Orientals in the United States. It was also having a striking growth among the nominally Roman Catholic constituencies in Latin America. Protestants of the United States and Canada were taking an ever larger share in the world outreach of their branch of the faith. They were tending to come together in new expressions of Christian unity and were prominent in the Ecumenical Movement.

SELECTED BIBLIOGRAPHY

A. Abel, *Protestant Home Missions to Catholic Immigrants* (New York, Institute of Social and Religious Research, 1933, pp. xi, 143). Based largely upon careful field work.

P. Blanshard, *American Freedom and Catholic Power* (Boston, The Beacon Press, 1949, pp. 350). Factual, critical of the Roman Catholic Church.

E. Braga and K. G. Grubb, *The Republic of Brazil. A Survey of the Religious Situation* (London, World Dominion Press, 1932, pp. 184).

E. de S. Brunner, *Immigrant Farmers and Their Children* (Garden City, N. Y., Doubleday & Co., 1929, pp. xvii, 277). Carefully done.

E. de S. Brunner, G. S. Hughes, and M. Patten, *American Agricultural Villages* (New York, George H. Doran Co., 1927, pp. 326).

J. W. Burton, *Missionary Survey of the Pacific Islands* (London, World Dominion Movement, 1930, pp. v, 124). By the general secretary of the Methodist Missionary Society of Australia.

La Canada Ecclésiastique. Annuaire du Clergé . . . 1932 (Montreal, Librairie Beauchemin, 1932, pp. 963).

E. T. Clark, *The Small Sects in America* (New York and Nashville, rev. ed., Abingdon-Cokesbury Press, 1949, pp. 256). A standard survey.

W. H. Clark, *The Oxford Group, Its History and Significance* (New York, Bookman Associates, 1951, pp. 268). A doctoral dissertation.

J. J. Considine, *Call for Forty Thousand* (New York, Longmans, Green & Co., 1946, pp. 319). By a Roman Catholic specialist on missions, a survey of the Roman Catholic Church in Latin America with a plea for missionaries from the United States.

H. P. Douglass, *Church Unity Movements in the United States* (New York, Institute of Social and Religious Research, 1934, pp. xxxviii, 576). A careful study based upon extensive research.

Evangelical Handbook of Latin America, 1937 Edition (New York, Committee on Coöperation in Latin America, pp. 119).

H. E. Fosdick, *The Modern Use of the Bible* (New York, The Macmillan Co., 1924, pp. 291). A good example of the writings and general position of the author.

C. L. Fry, *Diagnosing the Rural Church* (New York, Harper & Brothers, 1924, pp. 234).

C. L. Fry, *The U.S. Looks at Its Churches* (New York, Institute of Social and Religious Research, 1930, pp. xiv, 183).

J. T. Gillard, *Colored Catholics in the United States* (Baltimore, The Josephite Press, 1941, pp. x, 298).

W. Halich, *Ukrainians in the United States* (The University of Chicago Press, 1937, pp. xiii, 174). Based upon extensive research and personal knowledge.

D. Hinshaw, *Rufus Jones, Master Quaker* (New York, G. P. Putnam's Sons, 1951, pp. xi, 306). Warmly appreciative, based upon research and personal acquaintance.

J. H. Kolb and E. de S. Brunner, *A Study of Rural Society. Its Organization and Changes* (Boston, Houghton Mifflin Co., 1935, pp. xiv, 642). Objective, scholarly.

K. S. Latourette, *A History of the Expansion of Christianity. Volume VII, Advance Through Storm A.D. 1914 and After, with Concluding Generalizations* (New York, Harper & Brothers, 1945, pp. xiii, 542).

R. S. and H. M. Lynd, *Middletown. A Study in Contemporary American Culture* (New York, Harcourt, Brace and Co., 1929, pp. x, 550). A survey of a midwestern city.

J. G. Machen, *Christianity and Liberalism* (New York, The Macmillan Co., 1930, pp. 189). An excellent example of the author's convictions.

J. A. Mackay, *The Other Spanish Christ. A Study in the Spiritual History of Spain and South America* (London, Student Christian Movement Press, 1932, pp. xv, 288). By a distinguished Protestant scholar and administrator, long a missionary in Latin America.

P. R. Martin, *The First Cardinal of the West. The Story of the Church in the Archdiocese of Chicago under the Administration of His Eminence, George Cardinal Mundelein, Third Archbishop of Chicago and the First Cardinal of the West* (The New World Publishing Co., 1934, pp. 215).

B. E. Mays and J. W. Nicholson, *The Negro's Church* (New York, Institute of Social and Religious Research, 1933, pp. xiii, 321). A dependable, scholarly study.

J. F. Moore, *Will America Become Catholic?* (New York, Harper & Brothers, 1931, pp. x, 252). Objective, by a Protestant.

H. N. Morse, editor, *Home Missions Today and Tomorrow. A Review and Forecast* (New York, Home Missions Council, 1934, pp. xvi, 419). An official study by the Home Missions Council.

R. Niebuhr, *The Nature and Destiny of Man* (New York, Charles Scribner's Sons, 2 vols., 1941, 1943). The major work of a prolific author.

W. Parsons, *Mexican Martyrdom* (New York, The Macmillan Co., 1936, pp. vi, 304). A description of the anti-Catholic movement, by a Jesuit with experience in Mexico.

L. Pope, *Millhands and Preachers. A Study of Gastonia* (Yale University Press, 1942, pp. xvi, 369). A brilliant, competent study of the churches in a Southern mill town.

G. C. Powers, *The Maryknoll Movement* (Maryknoll, Catholic Foreign Mission Society of America, 1920, pp. xix, 167). By a member of the society.

W. S. Rycroft, *On This Foundation. A Study of the Evangelical Witness in Latin*

America (New York, The Friendship Press, 1942, pp. xiii, 210). By a secretary of the Committee on Coöperation in Latin America.

C. E. Silcox, *Church Union in Canada* (New York, Institute of Social and Religious Research, 1933, pp. xvii, 493). Authoritative.

United States Department of Commerce, Bureau of the Census, *Religious Bodies: 1926* (Washington, United States Government Printing Office, 2 vols., 1929).

United States Department of Commerce, Bureau of the Census, *Religious Bodies: 1936* (Washington, United States Government Printing Office, 2 vols., 1941). Not as reliable in its statistics as the one for 1926.

Chapter 59

THE CRUCIAL TEST: THE COURSE OF CHRISTIANITY OUTSIDE THE OCCIDENT AFTER A.D. 1914

While Christianity was facing an extraordinarily formidable combination of enemies in the historic geographic centre of its strength, in the vast portions of the world outside the Occident it was confronted by what in some ways was the most crucial of its tests of the post-1914 era. In the Occident, Christianity, although challenged, was unquestionably vigorous. To be sure, in Europe it was losing in numbers and in fact, although not nominally, convinced Christians were a minority. Yet within that minority there was the vitality which had again and again been displayed by Christians in times of unusual adversity. In the larger Occident, the Americas and Australasia, notably in the most populous and most powerful of its countries, the United States, with some exceptions the Church was gaining. Critics might call this "social lag," and declare that on the geographic periphery of what had once been Christendom the faith was still being carried forward by a momentum gathered in earlier centuries and had not yet felt the full impact of the forces which were so sombrely potent in Europe. Yet advance was being registered.

The situation was different outside the Occident. Here dwelt more than half of mankind. Here, in India and China, were the most populous nations. Here, except on the shores of the Mediterranean, Christians had never been more than a small minority. Christianity had more than once been planted across Asia, but aside from the western fringe of that continent only in India had it gained a continuing foothold, and until late in the nineteenth century the Syrian Christians who there represented it had long ceased to seek to win their non-Christian neighbours. As we have seen, Christianity had been spreading in Asia and Africa south of the Sahara since the latter part of the fifteenth century, but this had been in connexion with European trade and empire-building. Down to 1914 its tide had been mounting, but so also had been that of

European commercial and colonial imperialism. In that year the churches and their associated educational and philanthropic institutions which had been planted in Asia and Africa had been predominantly controlled and financed by missionaries from Europe and North America.

After 1914 the picture rapidly changed. By 1952 burgeoning nationalism had conspired with the declining strength of Western Europe to liquidate Occidental colonial rule from most of Asia and its few remnants might not long be retained. In much of Africa unrest was seething, either openly or under the surface. Russian communism, frankly anti-religious, had taken over China and North Korea, was threatening much of the rest of Asia, and was to be reckoned with in Africa. In some other areas, notably Turkey, secularism was in control of the government, and in India the dominant leader, Nehru, wished to achieve a secular state. Elsewhere secularism was a pervading force.

Under these circumstances could the "younger churches" survive? For the most part they were small minorities. Would they go the way of their predecessors in Asia? The issue was crucial. Christianity had at its heart a Gospel which professed to be for all men. Thus far it had been so largely confined to the Occident that the two had been identified with each other. Were it now to fade in Asia and Africa, the phenomenal spread of the preceding four centuries, and especially of the nineteenth century, would have been ephemeral. Christianity would again be regional, identified with one culture, and that culture and the position of Christianity within it were being so challenged that many observers despaired of them both.

In 1952, when these pages were being composed, the answer was by no means demonstrable. However, in almost every land in Africa south of the Sahara and in South and East Asia and its fringing islands advances were being made in numerical strength, in a firmer rootage through indigenous leadership, and in knitting the Christian communities into the reinforcing strength of one or the other of two world-wide fellowships, the one Roman Catholic and the other Protestant. To a brief summary of these advances and of the menacing forces in the face of which they were made we must now turn.

MADAGASCAR AND AFRICA SOUTH OF THE SAHARA

In that largest congeries of peoples of "primitive" cultures, on the island of Madagascar and in Africa south of the Sahara, the generation which followed 1914 witnessed acceleration in the disintegration of the indigenous cultures which was due to the impact of the Occident. It was also marked by rising restlessness against the white man's rule. At the same time it saw a striking numerical increase of the Christian churches. So rapid was the growth that it might be truthfully said that a mass conversion was in progress which could be compared with that of the Roman Empire in the first five centuries of the faith and of Western Europe between the fifth and twelfth centuries. Indigenous leadership and sects were also emerging, evidence that Christianity was taking root and was not entirely dependent upon continuing stimulus from the churches of Europe and America.

As we have seen (Chapter 53), Christianity, both Roman Catholic and Protestant, had gained a foothold in Madagascar in the nineteenth century and after an initial period of persecution had spread rapidly. Its chief strength was among the Hòva, the enterprising folk whose home was the high interior plateau. After 1914 the numerical growth of both main wings of the Church continued. The proportion of Christians in the population rose from about a fourth in 1914 to about a third in 1950. In the latter year the Protestant and Roman Catholic communities were of about equal size. The latter seems to have increased more than the former. Among the Protestants there were hundreds of Malagasy clergy and still more hundreds of lay preachers, both men and women. In 1925 nine Malagasy were ordained as Roman Catholic priests and in 1939 a Malagasy was consecrated as bishop and appointed to a vicariate apostolic which was entrusted to Malagasy clergy. World War II cut off part of the contacts between missionaries and their home constituencies, but Malagasy Christians rose to meet the emergency. They took a larger share in propagating their faith. Founded by missionaries from several denominations and countries, Protestantism drew together, and in 1934 the majority of the societies agreed to give to the congregations connected with them the common designation "the United Protestant Church of Madagascar."

The wars and revolutions of the twentieth century could not but have repercussions in Africa south of the Sahara. While the region was the scene of little actual fighting, many Africans saw combat service in Europe and Asia. All the area except Liberia was politically under Europeans and administered by them, but German territories passed into other hands and in some sections, notably British, where colonial policy nurtured self-government, there was much restlessness under white rule.

The continued spread of Christianity was furthered by the growing cultural and religious vacuum left by the dissolution of traditional African life. It was more rapid in some sections than in others. In it both Protestants and Roman Catholics shared, but unequally under different political regimes. The Roman Catholic increase was largest in equatorial Africa. In general the Roman Catholic advance was greater than the Protestant. That was in part because Roman Catholics added to their missionary staffs more extensively than did Protestants. Both Roman Catholics and Protestants paid much attention to recruiting and training African leadership for the Church. By mid-century about one-seventh of the priests, more than a fourth of the brothers, and nearly a third of the sisters of the Roman Catholic Church were Africans. In 1952 there were four African bishops. Protestants were also increasing their African ministry. In several colonies Protestants were moving towards a closer integration of their forces. Councils were formed, at least two of which had membership in the International Missionary Council.

As in our description of the course of Christianity in Africa south of the Sahara in the nineteenth century, so for the post-1914 years we must content ourselves with a few brief notes on some of the areas, principally those in which Christianity was making its greatest advances.

In the complex racial structure of the Union of South Africa with its many and growing tensions, Christianity continued its numerical gains in the non-European population. Those bearing the Christian name increased from about one-third of the whole in 1914 to more than half of the whole at the mid-century mark. Although Roman Catholics multiplied their missionaries about fourfold during the period and their constituency grew, in 1950 the large majority of the Christians were still Protestants.

One of the striking developments of the years was the proliferation of Protestant divisions among the Africans. In 1906 what were sometimes called Bantu sects and sometimes separatist churches were said to number fifteen or more, in 1922 sixty-five, in 1932 over three hundred, and in 1947 about one thousand. In the last two years they totalled well over a million members. Nowhere else on the planet was there such a multiplication of independent ecclesiastical bodies. For this fissiparousness several causes were ascribed. One was the desire to be independent of the white man, seen in the fact that several of the separatist churches were secessions from denominations founded and to a greater or less degree controlled by missionaries. The majority of the Bantu sects were fresh divisions from existing separatist bodies. All had African leadership and most of them were the creations of individual "prophets" or preachers. It was suggested that, in a region where the white man was dominant and the Africans were strictly segregated and denied participation in government and many of the professions and occupations, these churches provided an outlet for those ambitious for leadership and were a modern, partly Christian counterpart of the tribe and its chief. Some made much of ritual. Many professed to supply physical healing, and the trend seemed to be towards a syncretism of Christianity with animism.

Just north of the Union of South Africa were Southern and Northern Rhodesia. Here after 1914 the proportion of Christians mounted more rapidly than in the Union of South Africa, but by 1950 it was only about a sixth of the total population.

In Portuguese East and West Africa, or Mozambique and Angola, Roman Catholics were given preference by the colonial administration and accordingly far outnumbered the Protestants. In 1940 about 30 per cent. of the population were classed as Christians, of whom about three-fourths were Roman Catholics and a fourth Protestants.

In Nyasaland, which less than a century earlier had been entered by missionaries in response to the appeal of Livingstone, by 1950 approximately a third of the population were Christians, about half of them Protestants and about half Roman Catholics.

The neighbouring Tanganyika, the former German East Africa, did not have so large a proportion of Christians. Yet here, too, the increase was marked and by mid-century they were about a sixth of the whole, slightly more than half of them Roman Catholics.

Christianity was first introduced to Uganda in the 1870's. There on the relatively salubrious highlands it had flourished. In 1950 more than 40 per cent. of the population were regarded as Christians, about a third of them Protestants and two-thirds Roman Catholics.

In the Belgian Congo and the territory mandated to Belgium after World War I, Ruanda-Urundi, the numerical progress of Christianity after 1914 was phenomenal. Because of the favour shown by the government, which professed to regard them as national and the Protestants as foreign, Roman Catholic missions made much greater gains than did the latter. In 1950 Roman Catholics totalled about 3,500,000, an increase from about 100,000 in 1914. Protestantism also flourished, and in 1946 counted in its community over 1,100,000. This meant that by mid-century about one in three of the population were thought of as Christian.

French Equatorial Africa was made famous in the post-1914 years by the labours of Albert Schweitzer, whom we have already met (Chapter 57) as a distinguished New Testament scholar. Extraordinarily versatile, noted as an organist, an authority on Bach, and a philosopher, from a sense of mission, impelled by the teachings of Jesus, in his late youth, although already on the road to a distinguished career in Europe, Schweitzer studied medicine and went to Africa to devote his skill to the relief of suffering. Dominant in him was reverence for life.

Nigeria, under British rule, and with a population much larger than that of the Belgian Congo, in the mid-1940's counted only slightly more than six out of a hundred of its people as Christians. Of these about two-thirds were Protestants and a third Roman Catholics. The contrast with the Belgian Congo and Uganda was partly due to the fact that, carried across the Sahara on the caravan routes, Islam had preceded Christianity and had won much of the northern portions of the country.

On the Gold Coast, made prosperous by the cacao which was its chief export, the numbers of Christians mounted, mainly in the animistic South rather than the Islam-penetrated North. By 1950 slightly more than 10 per cent. were regarded as Christians, two-fifths of them Roman Catholics and three-fifths Protestants.

In spite of growth in government institutions, Christian schools continued to offer the Africans most of such opportunities as existed to acquire an education of an Occidental kind to prepare them for the white man's world. Christian missionaries also gave much of such medical care and public health safeguards as was available.

It was not only in the Union of South Africa that Christianity was beginning to reflect its environment and thus to root itself in the cultural soil. In some other parts of Africa evidence was appearing of somewhat similar developments. Prophets arose, all bearing the impress of Christianity, some more and some less. Several of them led nationalist or racial movements which gave the white colonial authorities anxious days. At least one, Harris, who came to prominence about 1913, was primarily a Christian itinerant evangelist and prepared the way for mass movements to the Christian faith on the Ivory Coast, the Gold Coast, and in Nigeria. In some areas the Watch Tower Movement, sprung from Jehovah's Witnesses, whom we have met in the United States, took root and stirred thousands of Africans to hope for the day when white supremacy and exploitation would be no more.

THE STRIKING GROWTH OF CHRISTIANITY IN INDIA

In the generation after 1914 revolutionary political change swept across India. At the outbreak of World War I India was still under British rule. Indians were only beginning to have a share in the higher offices of the government. In 1947 as a result of several decades of nationalistic agitation, in which M. K. Gandhi (1869–1948) was the outstanding leader, two self-governing dominions came into being—India, soon to become the Republic of India, and Pakistan. They remained within the Commonwealth to which the name British was usually prefixed, but for all practical purposes were independent nations. The Republic of India was predominantly Hindu, and Pakistan prevailingly Moslem. Although an exodus of Moslems from India to Pakistan and of Hindus from Pakistan to India was accompanied with loss of life, the transition to independence was accomplished with little fighting. By mid-century no such basic cultural revolution was seen as was occurring in China.

In these stirring years the two largest of the Christian communities, the

Roman Catholics and the Protestants, continued to grow, the latter more rapidly than the former. In 1911 the former numbered a little over two and a half millions and in 1950 about three millions. In 1914 the number of baptized Protestants was about one million and in 1936 about two and a half millions. In 1946 the number of Protestant communicants was reported as being 1,865,000. This was an increase from 1,042,000 in 1936, ten years earlier. If in 1946 the proportion of baptized to communicants was the same as in 1936, in that year baptized Protestants totalled nearly four and a half millions. The Christian community—Roman Catholic, Protestant, Syrian, and Mar Thoma—rose from about 1 per cent. of the population in 1914 to about 2½ per cent. in 1950, and that in spite of the fact that the total population of the country had mounted and that the Syrian and Mar Thoma Churches did not have as marked an increase as the Roman Catholics and Protestants. As before 1914, so after that year the majority of Christians were south of an imaginary line from Bombay to Madras.

The Protestant increase was, as earlier, mainly from the depressed classes and the animistic hill tribes and to a large degree by mass movements. Although the overwhelming majority of Protestants were from the lowest rungs of the social and economic ladder, their average death rate was less than that of Moslems and Hindus and their percentage of literacy higher than for India as a whole. Drunkenness, divorce, and polygamy practically disappeared among them.

Among both Roman Catholics and Protestants the growth of Indian leadership was marked. Rome transferred more and more dioceses from foreign to Indian bishops and clergy. Protestants showed a similar trend and some Indians rose high in the Ecumenical Movement. Prominent among the latter was V. S. Azariah (1874–1945), whom we have already met as the first Indian bishop of the Anglican communion, who made his diocese, Dornakal, a model in the quality of its Christian life and its outreach to the non-Christians, and who was a vice-chairman of the International Missionary Council. Outstanding also was Sarah Chakko, as a college president and as a secretary and then a president of the World Council of Churches.

The movement towards unity within Protestantism had striking manifestations in India. This was all the more notable because of the great variety of denominations and nationalities represented in the missionary body. The two most prominent expressions were the National Christian Council and the Church of South India. The National Christian Council was organized in 1923, succeeding the National Missionary Council. The dropping of the word "Missionary" was significant, for it made evident the transition from foreign to indigenous leadership. Missionaries had an important share in the new body, but from the first Indians collaborated and before long were in the fore. The National Christian Council, like its predecessor, was based upon regional councils and through them made for greater coöperation on the local level.

The Church of South India, constituted in 1947, was a union of the South India United Church, which had come into being in 1908 as a fusion of bodies connected with Reformed, Presbyterian, and Congregational churches in Britain and the United States, with Methodists and Anglicans. The Anglicans were the most numerous element. It was the first time that a section of that communion had been drawn into so comprehensive a union. In doing so it had the consent of the Church of India, Burma, and Ceylon, which was the Anglican body in that part of the world. However, led by the Church of England, the Anglican fellowship did not enter into communion with it. The reason for the reluctance was the fact that, while the Church of South India had an episcopate which was regarded by Anglicans as having apostolic succession, some of its clergy, ordained in denominations without that succession, were given full status in the new body. Yet that body, over a million strong, succeeded in establishing a high degree of harmony among its diverse elements and became a member of the World Council of Churches.

One of the features of the course of Christianity in India after 1914 was the growing influence exerted upon the country. Christians were a small, even though rapidly growing minority of the population, yet the Christian faith had effects far outside their circles. These were seen in education, medicine, rural life, and the position of women. Sometimes less tangible but probably more pervasive were the repercussions on religion and morals. Thousands of individuals who had been in Christian schools or who in other ways had come under Christian influence had their beliefs and practices modified, sometimes basically. True to the Hindu tradition, they were quite willing to honour Christ and even to regard him as the greatest of the incarnations of the Divine. Also in accord with their Hindu background, they refused to grant that Christ was uniquely, as the Church firmly declared, *the* way to the Father, rather than one of several ways, all about equally good, to the ultimately Unknowable. Nor were they willing, by being baptized, to sever their connexion with the Hindu community and openly to become members of the Church.

The outstanding single example of the influence of Christianity was in and through Gandhi. Gandhi would not call himself a Christian, but declared himself to be a Hindu. Yet from his student days he was in intimate touch with Christians, mostly Protestants. He had a profound reverence for Christ, was deeply moulded by the Sermon on the Mount, and in such times of crisis as entering upon or concluding one of his fasts would have a Christian as well as a Hindu hymn sung. A favorite of his was: "When I survey the wondrous cross on which the Prince of Glory died." When he was assassinated, the saying was common among non-Christians that he had died a Christ-like death. Thus, perhaps unwittingly, Christ was regarded as the supreme standard. Gandhi had a greater effect on India than any of his fellow-countrymen of his generation. Through him, therefore, the influence of Christ, while by no means dominant, became more widespread in that land than at any previous time. Through Gandhi the teaching and example of Jesus made for non-violent resistance, greater opportunity to the depressed classes, and the positive meaning of un-selfish service rather than the traditional negative connotation to the ancient Indian term *ahimsa,* which may be loosely translated "harmlessness."

THE CHEQUERED COURSE OF CHRISTIANITY IN SOUTH-EAST ASIA

In Ceylon the course of Christianity was but little affected by the wars and revolutions of the first half of the twentieth century. The island saw no fighting, and after World War II the transition to dominion status (1948) within the (British) Commonwealth was made peacefully and without the preliminary conflicts with the British authorities which punctuated Indian history after 1914. Both Roman Catholics and Protestants increased in num-bers, the former about 60 per cent., slightly more rapidly than the rate of growth of the population. Protestants more than doubled their communicant membership. Christians were about one in ten of the population. The Roman Catholic Church, having been on the island much longer than Protestantism, had about five times as many adherents as the latter. Protestants were active in the Ecumenical Movement and at mid-century the three major denominations, Anglicans, Methodists, and Baptists, were in process of merging into one united church. A revival of Buddhism, the dominant religion of Ceylon, and connected with the rising tide of nationalism, brought some anxiety to the Christians, but seemed not greatly to have retarded the latter's growth.

In storm-tossed Burma the course of Christianity was more troubled. Until 1942 it went on much as it had in the latter part of the nineteenth century. Protestants, mainly Baptists, the result of missions from the United States, were more numerous than Roman Catholics. Both had very small constit-uencies among the dominant race, the Burmese, and were strongest among the largest racial minority, the Karens. Until 1942 the numbers of both mounted proportionately much more rapidly than the population as a whole. In-digenous leadership increased and the Baptist churches especially became au-tonomous and progressively less dependent on foreign funds and personnel.

Then, in 1942, the Japanese drove out the British and professed to encourage Burmese independence. The three years of Japanese rule were marked by much fighting. When, in 1945, the Japanese were expelled, the country did no:

quickly achieve domestic peace. Politically it broke away completely from the British Empire (January, 1948). Confused civil war followed. It was particularly acute between the Karens and the Burmese. Bad blood had long existed between the two, for the latter were jealous of the progress made by the Karens, progress due chiefly to the contributions of Christianity, and the Karens were not disposed to submit to the Burmese. In the fighting which accompanied and followed the Japanese occupation, orderly living suffered, and with it the churches and their associated schools and hospitals. However, even during these stormy years the numbers of Christians increased. Between 1942 and 1952 that of the Baptists mounted by about a third.

In the Malay Peninsula and Singapore, it will be remembered (Chapter 54), the chief gains of Christianity were among the Chinese and Indians, mainly the former. Almost none of the Malays were won. Both Roman Catholics and Protestants were present, but were small minorities. Until the Japanese conquest in 1942 both continued to gain. The Japanese conquest brought disruption. After the return of the British there was much banditry, largely communist-inspired. Yet Singapore, where were the strongest churches, was comparatively peaceful under the restored British rule and missions and churches became fairly normal.

Siam (Thailand) was less disturbed by the wars of the era than was any of its neighbours. The Christian communities, both Roman Catholic and Protestant, were small, for the faith found the dominant Buddhism singularly resistant. However, both continued to grow.

As was true of most of South-east Asia, until World War II Indo-China was relatively undisturbed by the storms which were rocking much of the rest of the world. Under French protection, the Roman Catholic Church continued its phenomenal growth. In 1914 it counted about a million members, or about 5 per cent. of the population. In the next twenty years it grew by about 40 per cent. Schools, youth organizations, and literature were used to raise the level of Christian living. Much emphasis was placed on recruiting and training an indigenous clergy and several Indo-Chinese were raised to the episcopate. After the fall of France to the Germans in 1940 the Japanese began to move in and, while the pretense of French rule was maintained, for nearly five years they were increasingly dominant. When, in 1945, they were expelled, strife followed between the French, who were attempting to restore their rule, and Indo-Chinese nationalists. The efforts of the latter to attain independence were led and largely dictated by communists. In the prolonged war which followed the Church inevitably suffered. It seems not to have lost much in numbers, nor does it appear to have gained substantially. The small Protestant communities, the fruits of an American mission, were numerically almost negligible.

Distress and Growth in Indonesia

In the vast area which in 1914 was known as the Netherlands East Indies, until 1942 the onward march of Christianity which had been marked in the nineteenth century was not interrupted. The rapid growth of the Protestant churches continued. Their totals rose from between three-quarters of a million and a million in 1914 to more than a million and a half in 1936. Protestants were strongest among the vigorous Bataks of Sumatra, where by 1939 about a third of that people were Christians, in Celebes, and the Moluccas—almost all formerly animistic folk. There were strong churches among the Chinese. In Java some were won from the dominant Islam. After 1914 there was a growing movement among the Protestant bodies for autonomy and freedom from foreign control. Several churches achieved this status. In 1935 the East Indian Church with nearly half a million members, which had been in existence since the seventeenth century, with clergy appointed and paid by the state, was disestablished, although until a final cash grant in 1950 the government continued its responsibility for the salaries of some of the pastors. It took the name "the Protestant Church of the East Indies." Its separation from the state did not seriously weaken it, but, rather, was followed by sturdy life. Roman Catholics increased proportionately more rapidly than Protestants, a reflexion of the prosperity of that communion in the Netherlands. In 1948 they were said to total about 800,000.

World War II brought strains and distress. When, in 1940, the Nazis invaded the Netherlands, the Dutch authorities interned or imprisoned the German missionaries in the East Indies. Then, in 1942, came the Japanese conquest and the internment of the Dutch personnel. Since almost all the missionaries, whether Protestant or Roman Catholic, were Dutch or German, the Indonesian churches were now without foreign leadership. The Japanese instituted bitter propaganda against Western imperialism and colonialism which augmented Indonesian nationalism. Under Japanese rule some Indonesian Christians, including clergy, suffered.

The downfall of the Japanese in 1945 was followed by resolute efforts by Indonesian nationalists to become completely independent. Attempts to restore Dutch rule brought fighting. While the Dutch eventually yielded (1949) and recognized the independence of the islands, much feeling against the Dutch persisted. The Republic of Indonesia took full control of all Indonesia except the British and Portuguese possessions and wished to extend its rule to the western part of New Guinea, still under Dutch administration.

All these storms worked hardship on the churches of Indonesia. After World War II Dutch missionaries were not welcomed and few Germans were able to come. Help was given by the Protestants of the United States, but the Indonesian Christianity was largely dependent upon its inherent vigour for survival and growth. Yet under these difficult circumstances both Protestants and Roman Catholics registered substantial increases. In the 1940's the Batak Protestants added several scores of thousands to their numbers. Between 1942 and 1948 Roman Catholics were reported to have grown by about 150,000. In 1950 Protestants organized a national council of churches which was a kind of federation of thirty autonomous churches. Contacts were made with both the International Missionary Council and the World Council of Churches.

STORM AND VIGOUR IN THE PHILIPPINES

The record in the Philippines from 1914 until 1942 was one of growth. Protestants multiplied about six-fold, mainly by converts from a nominal Roman Catholicism. Through membership in the International Missionary Council they entered into the Ecumenical Movement. The Roman Catholic Church rapidly increased its Filipino clergy and appointed Filipinos to the majority of its episcopal sees, including the Archbishopric of Manila, its highest ecclesiastical post in the islands. The Philippine Independent Church, the child of Filipino nationalism with Aglipay as its first head, grew slowly, but suffered from inadequate leadership.

The Japanese conquest brought disruption of much of the nation's life. Destruction of life and especially of property accompanied it and the fighting which expelled the Japanese. In 1946 full political independence from the United States came according to a schedule agreed upon before the Japanese invasion, but close ties were maintained with that country.

Following World War II the churches demonstrated by their actions that the vigour displayed before that struggle had not been seriously impaired. Roman Catholics rebuilt or repaired many of their structures and institutions and were active in the relief of suffering. Protestants rebuilt churches, reopened schools, and had more students for the ministry than at any earlier time. In 1948 the United Church of Christ of the Philippines was formed by a fusion of the Presbyterians, Congregational-Christians, Evangelical United Brethren, and some Methodists and Disciples of Christ. That same year the Philippine Independent Church obtained apostolic succession for its episcopate by the consecration of three of its bishops by bishops of the Protestant Episcopal Church. The majority element also adjusted its creeds to eliminate their Unitarian elements and make them conform to the Anglican tradition.

RECURRENT AND MOUNTING STORM IN CHINA

After 1914 China was the scene of as severe a series of trials as Christianity experienced anywhere in those years. That vast country with the largest population of any land on the globe was in the throes of a prolonged revolution which was due to the impact of the Occident. The revolution began in the latter half of the nineteenth century and by the middle of the twentieth century seemed to be only in its early stages. The inherited Chinese culture in all of its aspects was shaken to its foundations and much of it was disappearing. Especially shattering were the blows dealt to Confucianism, the ideology which had been dominant in Chinese civilization. The liquidation of the Confucian monarchy in 1911–1912 was followed by what essayed to be a republic. Civil strife brought increasing chaos. Then, in 1926 and 1927, the Kuomintang, or Nationalist Party, with the teachings of Sun Yat-sen as its ostensible programme and with Chiang Kai-shek as its outstanding leader, brought unity to most of the land. That unity was disputed by the communists and a long struggle ensued between them and the Kuomintang which for a time limited them first to the South-east and then to a section of the North. The Japanese invasion which began in Manchuria in September, 1931, and attained full scale dimensions in July, 1937, by 1941 brought almost all the eastern portions of the country under Japanese-controlled puppet regimes. The defeat of Japan in 1945 was followed by the attempt of the Kuomintang-dominated Nationalist Government to consolidate all the country under its rule. This attempt was contested by the communists and in 1949 they succeeded in taking possession of the entire mainland. With Mao Tse-tung as their outstanding figure, they set up what they called the People's Republic of China. Chiang Kai-shek and the main body of such of the Kuomintang forces as survived took refuge on Formosa, where they were protected by the United States navy. The communists had close ties with Russia and these were strengthened. They set about a comprehensive and resolute campaign for the mass conversion of China to communism through the intensive "re-education" of its millions and their leaders in the Marxist-Lenin interpretation of history and principles of life and action. It was the most gigantic effort at a drastic transformation of the outlook and mores of an entire people that the world had ever seen.

Through all the vicissitudes of these years until the communist triumph Christianity more than held its own. Both the Roman Catholic Church and Protestantism gained in numbers and made rapid progress in developing Chinese leadership. For a brief time after the Revolution of 1911–1912 Christianity was almost popular and seemed to be moving in to fill the vacuum left by the disintegration of Confucianism. In 1914 Roman Catholics were said to number 1,581,430, and in 1924 2,208,880. In 1914 the Protestant communicant membership was reported as being 257,431, and in 1924 402,539. In both years the Protestant constituency was much larger. In the 1920's, beginning in 1922 and coming to a climax in 1926 and 1927, ostensibly an anti-religious but actually anti-Christian movement swept the country. It was encouraged by the communists and was fed by Chinese nationalism, resentful as it was of the "unequal treaties" with their restrictions on China's full autonomy. Missionaries were accused of being "imperialists" and Chinese Christians of being "running dogs" of the foreigners. Many missionaries left the country, government control was extended over Christian educational institutions, and Chinese were given the dominant share in the administration of Christian schools. Late in the 1920's the pressure somewhat abated, but in the 1930's and 1940's the Japanese placed serious restrictions on churches and other Christian institutions in the sections under their rule. Moreover, after the United States and Great Britain entered the war against Japan (December, 1941) American and British missionaries in Japanese-controlled areas were interned. The prolonged fighting of the decades after 1914 brought destruction to much church property and in many regions banditry was a chronic menace.

In spite of all these adversities, Christians increased in numbers and the Church became more deeply rooted. In 1929 Roman Catholics were said to number 2,486,841, in 1937 2,934,175, in 1941 3,262,678, and in 1947 3,251,347. The Chinese clergy multiplied and in 1926 six Chinese priests were consecrated bishops by the Pope himself in a great ceremony in St. Peter's. In later years still more were raised to the episcopacy, and eventually a Chinese was created a cardinal and a hierarchy was created for China (1946). In 1914 a national organization was given the Roman Catholic Church in China. In subsequent years this was strengthened. Catholic Action and other lay activities were encouraged and prospered.

Protestantism also flourished. Between 1924 and 1936 its communicant membership is said to have risen to 567,390, a 40 per cent. increase and proportionately a more rapid growth than that of the Roman Catholic Church. In the next ten years, disturbed by the Japanese occupation as it was, the total continued to mount, but not so strikingly. As heretofore, Protestantism approached the Chinese in a wide variety of ways, seeking to assist them in the time of their painful transition. The most influential Chinese of the century until the triumph of communism, Sun Yat-sen, was a Protestant, and had received most of his formal education through Protestant missionaries. Chiang Kai-shek was baptized by a Protestant after he became master of most of China and seemed to be sincere in his purpose of being true to the faith. Several other outstanding men and women in the Kuomintang regime were Protestants or had been educated in Protestant schools. The majority of Protestants coöperated in the National Christian Council, formed in 1922, and through it were associated with the International Missionary Council. For a brief time a Chinese was one of the presidents of the World Council of Churches. In 1927 what was called the Church of Christ in China came into being. In it were eventually fused the Presbyterians, the United Brethren, the churches associated with the United Church of Canada, and some of the Congregationalists and Baptists. Increasingly Chinese came to the fore as leaders in Protestant churches and institutions. Several indigenous movements akin to churches arose, but not as numerous or as syncretistic as the separatist churches of South Africa.

The triumph of communism brought the greatest reverse which Christianity had suffered in China for at least a century and a half. If threatened the very existence of the faith in that country. Ostensibly the communists granted religious liberty, but only in their sense of that term. They strove to eradicate from the churches all traces of what they deemed foreign imperialism. By the end of 1952 almost all missionaries, Roman Catholic and Protestant, had either voluntarily left the country or had been forcibly expelled. Most of the few who remained were either in prison or were confined to their homes and could not carry on their normal activities. Not for nearly a hundred years had there been so few missionaries in China. The communists sought, but with only scant success, to induce Chinese Roman Catholics to break off all connexions with the Holy See and to form a Chinese Catholic Church. They compelled Protestants to sever all ties with the Occident. Under the specious slogans of self-support, self-government, and self-propagation they constrained Protestant churches and institutions to cease to receive funds and personnel from abroad. After they entered the Korean war against the United Nations the communists required the churches to join in the nation-wide campaign to "resist America" and "aid Korea." Church leaders and Christian constituencies were subjected to indoctrination in communist ideology. The communists sought to constrain all Protestants to join the Church of Christ in China and the National Christian Council, bodies now under the control of those committed to communist theory.

CHRISTIANITY IN BELLIGERENT AND DEFEATED JAPAN

In the 1930's and 1940's Christianity in Japan was submitted to drastic testing, but survived and entered upon a day of opportunity.

From 1914 until early in the 1930's Christians, although a small minority, continued to grow in numbers and were not molested. Between 1912 and 1936 Roman Catholics increased by about a half, to a little over 100,000, and Protestant communicants more than doubled. In the latter year they were more than 200,000. The much smaller Orthodox body suffered from the Russian revolution, for financial aid from Russia ceased and the staff of the mission was reduced. In these years a Japanese, Toyohiko Kagawa (1888——), rose to world-wide fame in Protestantism. Won to the faith in his student days, he received a theological training in Japan and the United States, for a time lived in

Franciscan-like love and poverty in one of the worst slums in the country, espoused the cause of organized labour, encouraged coöperatives, and wrote prolifically. Before many years he became an itinerant preacher, and at one time had as his goal a million converts. Protestants were drawn into the Ecumenical Movement. The National Christian Council was organized in 1923 and had membership in the International Missionary Council.

In the 1930's the government exerted increasing pressure on Christian organizations. Beginning with the Japanese coup in Manchuria in 1931, the condemnation of Japan by the League of Nations in 1933, and the withdrawal of Japan from that body (March, 1933), the war spirit in Japan mounted and nationalism became more and more fevered. When, in 1937, the full scale invasion of China was launched, chauvinism rose to a shrill crescendo. Foreigners, including missionaries, found residence embarrassing and most of them eventually left the country. As a way of reinforcing patriotism the government emphasized state Shinto and required all Japanese, including Christians, to observe its ceremonies. Since the government declared that the ceremonies were purely patriotic and not religious, the Roman Catholic Church permitted its members to comply and the large majority of Japanese Protestants took a similar attitude. The Roman Catholic Church quickened the pace of developing an indigenous clergy and placing administration in the hands of Japanese bishops. A similar process had long been under way among Protestants. In 1940 the Japanese government brought pressure upon all churches to become independent of financial aid from abroad and to complete the transfer of places of responsibility to Japanese. Early in 1941, realizing that if they did not do so voluntarily the government would compel it, the large majority of the Protestants brought about a fusion of the several denominations into what was called the Church of Christ in Japan, in Japanese *Nippon Kirisuto Kyodan,* usually abbreviated as the *Kyodan.*

The outbreak of war with the United States and the British Empire in December, 1941, meant further hardship for the Christians. The pace of the war and of the manufacture of munitions quickened and pastors as well as laymen were forced to join in it. Such British and American missionaries as remained were interned. Christians were urged and some of them were persuaded to establish friendly ties with Christians in lands overrun by the Japanese forces and to induce them to join in building what was euphemistically declared to be the "co-prosperity sphere of East Asia." As the tide turned against Japan, enemy bombing wrought havoc in the cities and a large proportion of the church buildings shared in the general holocaust. Christians, along with non-Christians, came out of the war depleted physically and nervously.

With the defeat and occupation of Japan the door of opportunity once more opened for Christianity. Japanese were willing to listen to the Christian message, for they were spiritually adrift and many wondered whether the reason for the debacle of the empire had not been a false ideology and asked whether the secret of the American victory was to be found in what they deemed the religion of the United States. Both Roman Catholics and Protestants, especially of the United States, sought to take advantage of the opportunity. Numbers of former missionaries returned and hundreds of new ones arrived. Roman Catholics sent more than Protestants. The Orthodox were given an American archbishop for their head. Many church buildings were repaired or rebuilt and new ones were erected. Thousands of converts were gathered, but not as many as the sanguine had hoped. The Church of Christ in Japan continued to have the majority of Protestants, even though the Anglicans, Lutherans, and some others withdrew from it. Contacts were again made by Protestants with the Ecumenical Movement.

TRAGEDY IN KOREA

For Korea and Christianity in Korea the two decades which followed 1914 were comparatively peaceful. The Japanese authorities were suspicious of the Protestant churches as possible centres of disaffection, especially since most Protestant missionaries were from the United States and were known to be critical of Japanese rule. However, in that interval both Roman Catholics and Protestants nearly doubled in numbers.

The 1930's and 1940's brought tragedy. When, in the 1930's, the Japanese embarked on their invasion of China and the opinion of much of the world hardened against them, they became increasingly fearful of possible rebellion in Korea and sought to assimilate that country so far as possible to Japan. Koreans, including Christians, were required to conform to the ceremonies of state Shinto. To Roman Catholics and to some Protestants this did not prove especially embarrassing, but many of the largest Protestant denomination, the Presbyterians, refused to comply. In 1940 most missionaries, especially American Protestant missionaries, left the country.

The defeat of the Japanese was hailed by the Koreans as liberation and an opportunity for national independence. Some missionaries returned and reinforcements were sent. Church life revived.

Disillusion soon came, followed by greater suffering than the nation had known since the Japanese invasion of the sixteenth century. The country was divided at the thirty-eighth parallel between the Russian and the American forces. In the North a communist regime was soon set up and adverse pressure was brought on Christian organizations. In the South under the republic organized through the auspices first of the United States and then of the United Nations, Christians had full liberty. One of their number, a Protestant, was president of the republic and there were Christians in some other high posts in the state. Many Christian refugees from the persecution in the North built churches. Then, in June, 1950, came the invasion from the North which sought to unite the land under communist rule. At first the communist armies seemed triumphant and overran most of the South. Resistance by the United Nations, depending chiefly on the United States, soon rolled back the attackers, but Chinese intervention late that year and Russian supplies led to the establishment of an uneasy front only slightly north of the thirty-eighth parallel. The ebb of the tide of battle to and fro meant intense distress to millions. Yet Christians maintained worship and were active in seeking to win others. Many converts were made among the prisoners taken by the United Nations' forces. Christianity was deeply rooted and vigorous.

SUMMARY

In the brief summaries with which we have had to content ourselves in this chapter statistics, usually dreary, may have seemed too prominent. However, they are indications, even if imperfect ones, of the amazing growth of Christianity in the non-Occidental world in the stormy generation which came on the scene in 1914. Vast revolutions were sweeping across the majority of mankind which lived outside the Occident. The revolutions were largely because of the impact of the Occident. The idealisms and ideologies which they embodied, whether nationalism, liberal democracy of the Anglo-Saxon kind, or communism, were of Occidental origin and were indebted to Christianity, even though in some instances only to a minor degree. In them and in the weakening of the hitherto dominant Western Europe, Christianity faced a major threat and challenge. In general by mid-century it was making striking progress towards meeting it. What the future had in store the historian could not tell. However, as in 1952 he looked back over the little more than a third of a century which covered the tempestuous years since 1914, he could say that, while still minorities, in most countries small ones, Christians had rapidly gained in numbers, leadership was emerging from them, and the churches were being knit into world-wide Christian fellowships. Within the "younger churches" the Gospel was beginning to bear its distinctive fruits in transformed and ennobled lives. Moreover, the Gospel was having effects far outside the circles of those who bore the Christian name. It was by no means dominant but it was more widely potent than at the beginning of the century.

SELECTED BIBLIOGRAPHY

Agenzia Internationale Fides, *Le Missioni Cattoliche* (Rome, Consiglio Superiore della Pontificia Opera della Propagazione della Fide, 1950, pp. xxi, 548). Especially valuable for its statistics.

C. F. Andrews, editor, *Mahatma Gandhi. His Own Story* (New York, The Macmillan Co., 1931, pp. 372). Autobiographical, edited by an Anglican missionary, a close and warmly sympathetic friend of Gandhi.

W. Axling, *Kagawa* (New York, Harper & Brothers, rev. ed., 1946, pp. vii, 195). By a close friend and admirer. Contains selections from Kagawa's writings.

R. T. Baker, *Darkness of the Sun. The Story of Christianity in the Japanese Empire* (New York and Nashville, Abingdon-Cokesbury Press, 1947, pp. 254). An account of Protestant Christianity in Japan from 1941 to 1945.

H. P. Beach and C. H. Fahs, *World Missionary Atlas* (New York, Institute of Social and Religious Research, 1925, pp. 252). A competent statistical survey, mostly of Protestant missions.

B. Chaturvedi and M. Sykes, *C. F. Andrews, a Narrative* (London, George Allen & Unwin, 1949, pp. xiv, 334). A careful biography, by warm admirers, of a unique Anglican missionary to India.

J. J. Considine, *Across a World* (New York, Longmans, Green & Co., 1942, pp. xvi, 400). A popular travelogue of a Maryknoller describing Roman Catholic missions in several lands.

Fides News Service (Rome, c.1926 ff.). News releases on current happenings in Roman Catholic missions. Compiled in close coöperation with the Society for the Propagation of the Faith.

C. Graham, *Azariah of Dornakal* (London, Student Christian Movement Press, 1946, pp. 128). A warmly sympathetic biography.

K. G. Grubb and E. J. Bingle, editors, *World Christian Handbook* (London, World Dominion Press, 1949, pp. xv, 405). A competent statistical survey, mostly of Protestant missions, with interpretative articles.

The International Review of Missions (London, 1912 ff.). The official organ of the International Missionary Council. The standard Protestant journal on foreign missions. Especially valuable for its annual surveys of events in missions, both Protestant and Roman Catholic.

K. S. Latourette, *A History of Christian Missions in China* (New York, The Macmillan Co., 1929, pp. xii, 930).

K. S. Latourette, *A History of the Expansion of Christianity. Volume VII, Advance Through Storm* A.D. *1914 and After, with Concluding Generalizations* (New York, Harper & Brothers, 1945, pp. xiii, 542).

Laymen's Foreign Missions Inquiry, O. A. Petty, editor (New York, Harper & Brothers, 7 vols., 1933). Selections from the factfinders' reports and the appraisers' reports of a comprehensive and elaborate investigation of American Protestant missions in India, Burma, China, and Japan. Contains much valuable information.

J. Mackenzie, editor, *The Christian Task in India* (London, Macmillan & Co., 1929, pp. xvii, 297). By various authors.

N. Macnicol, *India in the Dark Wood* (London, Edinburgh House Press, 1930, pp. 224). A popularly written book by an authority on India and missions in India.

J. I. Parker, *Interpretative Statistical Survey of the World Mission of the Christian Church* (New York, International Missionary Council, 1938, pp. 323). A competent statistical survey of Protestant missions, with interpretative articles.

R. E. Phillips, *The Bantu are Coming. Phases of South Africa's Race Problem* (London, Student Christian Movement Press, 1930, pp. 238). By an American Protestant missionary who devoted his life to the race problem in Johannesburg.

J. W. Pickett, *Christian Mass Movements in India. A Study with Recommendations* (New York and Nashville, Abingdon-Cokesbury Press, 1933, pp. 382). Based upon careful, objective investigation reaching over some years.

J. Rauws *et al., The Netherlands Indies* (London, World Dominion Press, 1935, pp. 186). Authoritative survey of missions in that land.

A. Schweitzer, *Out of My Life and Thought* (New York, Henry Holt and Co., 1933, pp. 288).

B. G. M. Sundkler, *Bantu Prophets in South Africa* (London, Lutterworth Press, 1948, pp. 344). A thoroughly competent study of the Bantu Christian sects in South Africa.

Testo-Atlante Illustrato delle Missioni (Novara, Istituto Geografico de Agostini, 1932, pp. 160). An official atlas and statistical study of Roman Catholic missions.

A. W. Wasson, *Church Growth in Korea* (New York, International Missionary Council, 1934, pp. xii, 175). A scholarly study, chiefly of the part of the Korean Church related to the Methodist Episcopal Church, South.

Chapter 60

VIGOUR IN AN AGE OF STORM:
CONTRASTING WEAKNESS AND
STRENGTH

In a famous letter of a Christian of the first century there is the affirmation: "The weakness of God is stronger than men." It is there applied specifically to Christ crucified, but if it was true the demonstration is to be partly seen in what followed from the crucifixion. The entire course of Christianity since that first Good Friday must be considered if we are to seek to determine whether Paul's triumphant claim is verified by history.

Never was the testing more severe and searching than in the era which opened in the summer of 1914. There then began, in the very heart of the traditional stronghold of Christianity, in the centre of what had been called Christendom, a conflagration which swept across the world. The conflagration did not end with the stilling of the guns in November, 1918. It seemed to die down and men hoped that it had been extinguished, but here and there in the next twenty years it flared up afresh, and that in spite of well-intentioned efforts to guard against it. Outbursts in the 1930's were followed by a holocaust which proved to be even more widespread and devastating than the stage which had its inception in 1914. While this, too, subsided in 1945, in the early 1950's mankind viewed the future with fearful apprehension, wondering whether worse was not still to come. Wars were accompanied and followed by revolutions. Centuries-old forms of government and ruling houses were overthrown. In several countries, including one of the largest and most powerful, Russia, and the most populous on the planet, China, totalitarian regimes more tyrannical than the old took their place. Hundreds of millions of the underprivileged of mankind were stirring to a fierce new hope and demanded access to the good things of life heretofore enjoyed by only the few. The might of Western Europe which had been mounting since at least the fifteenth century and which on the eve of 1914 dominated most of Africa and much of Asia was being shattered.

In the midst of these vast forces the very existence of Christianity seemed threatened. War was notoriously destructive of the moral and spiritual values associated with the faith. Some of the revolutionary movements, including the most extensive, communism, were openly anti-religious and specifically anti-Christian. Geographically even more extensive than communism was a secularism which was undercutting all religions and making them seem irrelevant and outmoded. Whether in Europe, the Americas, Australasia, Africa, Turkey, India, China, or Japan, it was weakening existing faiths and leading to the discontinuance of historic cults and ceremonies. It sprang from a number of sources and was compounded of several elements. To it contributed the scientific method, intellectual currents associated with science and rationalism and which made for religious scepticism, the modern industrial system, the rapid growth of cities and a new type of urban life, and absorption in acquiring the material goods of life accentuated by the exhilarating prospect of obtaining them through the processes made possible by the application of science. Secularism was closely associated with an exaggerated nationalism which for many became a substitute for religion.

It appeared ominous for the future of Christianity that the forces which were menacing Christianity had their rise in Christendom. As we have seen, in varying degree at least some of them were attributable to Christianity. This was true of communism, the scientific method, the machine, the industrial processes of the age, and even of secularism. They would seem, accordingly, to be more destructive of Christianity than of the other religions of mankind.

Moreover, to one not prejudiced in its favour, Christianity appeared singularly handicapped as it was confronted by these foes. The churches which were its vehicles had less backing from armies and governments than at any time since the fourth century. The separation of Church and state which had been in process in the nineteenth century went on more rapidly after 1914. In several lands what had once been support of the faith by civil rulers, even though that had meant control by the government, was supplanted by covert or open hostility. For the most part the churches now depended, not upon taxation levied on all, but upon voluntary contributions. In what had once been Christendom, Christians were increasingly finding themselves moving towards the position of being minorities. As had been true throughout their history, the churches were by no means perfect embodiments of the Gospel. In all of them were features and characteristics which seemed to be a denial of the Gospel.

Here undoubtedly was weakness. Was it simply human weakness? Or was it what Paul called the weakness of God? Would it prove stronger than men and their institutions? Was there what Paul believed to be "the exceeding greatness of His power" and was it, as Paul confidently anticipated, to make Christ 'far above all principality, and power, and might, and dominion and every name that is named . . . in this world," and had God "put all things under" Christ's "feet"? In the first century of the faith *The Epistle to the Hebrews* had said, "We see not yet all things put under him." In the twentieth century that was still true. Was there any indication that progress was being made?

As in attempting to answer these questions we seek to draw together and summarize what has been mentioned in the preceding four chapters we do well to remind ourselves, as we did at the outset of our study of this period, that 1952, when these lines were written, was quite too early to give a final appraisal. In that year the period which opened in 1914 appeared only to have begun. Our narrative must, perforce, pause with a comma or at most a semicolon. At least a generation would need to elapse before perspective could be obtained. Much longer might be required. Yet even as early as 1952 some facts appeared to stand out as significant.

One which we have repeatedly noted was the continued world-wide spread of the faith. Although convinced Christians were becoming a minority in Europe, and in Russia even nominal Christians were far less than half the population, in the United States, the most populous Occidental country outside Europe, the proportion of church members continued the rise which had been in progress since the eighteenth century. It had not declined in most of the rest of the Americas or in Australasia. In all but a few of the non-Occidental parts of the world the numbers of those bearing the Christian name were still mounting. More nearly than at any previous time Christianity was being planted among all the peoples of the globe.

We have also called attention again and again to the fact that in the non-Occidental portions of the earth the faith was rapidly taking root in indigenous leadership and was spreading from the new Christian communities which were springing up. While missionaries were still coming from the Occident, more and more they were assisting rather than directing the "younger churches." As was being said in Protestant circles, they regarded themselves as "colleagues," not masters, and as "partners in obedience" to the command of Christ to make disciples of all nations. In other words, Christianity was ceasing to be as nearly identified with the Occident and Western civilization as it had been for a thousand years or more and was becoming universal.

In a day when through mechanical inventions time distances were shrinking and all men were being drawn into close propinquity with one another, progress was being seen towards a world-wide unity of Christians. This was being achieved through Protestantism, the form of Christianity which by its distinctive principles, salvation by faith and the priesthood of all believers, seemed the most hopelessly divided wing of Christianity.

Here was no sudden or transient movement. It had begun at least as far back as the eighteenth century and had mounted in the nineteenth century. After 1914 it went forward at an accelerated pace. It did not spring from religious indifferentism or from those who had no stake in the distinctive convictions which separated the denominations. Most of its leaders were men and women who were prominent in their respective churches. Nor did it have its source primarily or chiefly in the fear of the forces arrayed against Christianity. It arose, rather, from the desire to spread the faith and to make it more effective in the life of mankind.

The movement towards Christian unity had a multiplicity of expressions. Yet there was a common pattern which was seen in most countries where Protestantism was represented and which had global fellowship as its crowning feature. It was correctly called ecumenical, for it cherished the dream of spreading throughout all mankind and was making headway towards that goal. In some of its expressions individuals coöperated regardless of their denominational affiliations. Others were fusions, or "organic unions," of hitherto distinct denominations. Still others were what were sometimes called "world confessional organizations," global fellowships of denominational families. More numerous were those manifestations through which ecclesiastical bodies, usually churches but many of them missionary societies, coöperated and in doing so found an inclusive fellowship. The organization which loomed largest in 1952 was the World Council of Churches. In that year it had 158 member churches in 43 countries. In close association with it was the International Missionary Council, and in looser association the "world confessional organizations" and what were called "other ecumenical organizations."

The Ecumenical Movement was a new approach towards the attainment of the unity in love which had been the dream of Christians since the very outset of the faith. By the mid-twentieth century it was by no means all-inclusive. Although thousands of Roman Catholic laity were drawn into some of its expressions, notably the Young Men's Christian Associations, officially the Roman Catholic Church held aloof. Some Protestants and the majority of the Eastern Churches did not enter it. Yet the vast majority of Protestants and some of the Eastern Churches were embraced in it. Never before had Christians developed so ecclesiastically inclusive and varied a fellowship. Once before, as we saw near the beginning of our story, a somewhat similar unity had been achieved, but this had been within an existing political structure, that of the Roman Empire. Now it was being made actual in a world which was politically divided and atomistic. At times it was effective across barriers erected by war.

What was this world-wide Christianity doing? What was being accomplished because of the faith, whether through the Ecumenical Movement, the Roman

Catholic Church, the Eastern Churches, or through Christians who were not in any of these bodies? That in the post-1914 world with its wars, revolutions, and blatant display of stark material power Christianity was expanding geographically and was becoming rooted in more peoples than ever before, and that progress was being made towards a fellowship of Christians of unprecedented inclusiveness was evidence of vigour. It could be adduced as proof that the weakness of God was stronger than men and that what to the "wise and the prudent" seemed folly—Christ's course which appeared to end on the cross—was wiser than men.

Was this all? Were there other indications of "the exceeding greatness of His power"? Were these growing, keeping pace or more than keeping pace with the expanding world-wide extent of the visible organizations which bore the Christian name? As we have attempted to follow the course of Christianity across the centuries, we have repeatedly reminded ourselves that much of such evidence could well escape our notice. Even to see the kingdom of God, the indications of God's sovereignty and His "mighty power," we were warned at the very outset of the Good News, requires so drastic a reorientation that it is described as a new birth, a complete "change of mind."

Yet in the preceding four chapters we have here and there called attention to deeds, institutions, and movements which owed their existence at least in part to Christ and which but for him would probably never have been. We have noted the relief given to sufferers from wars and "natural" disasters, such as floods and droughts. Some of it was through churches and bodies connected with churches and clearly bearing the name of Christ. Much was through private organizations, notably the Red Cross, which had their inception in those moved by the Christian faith. More was by governments, in the later years of the period chiefly that of the United States which gave lavishly of its vast resources. State aid was obviously partly from motives of self interest. Much of it, however, was because of pressure from churches or other avowedly Christian organizations, or because of goodwill traceable to Christian sources. We have also seen how, in continuation of what was begun before 1914, thousands of hospitals were founded and maintained both in countries long under Christian influence and in lands where Christianity was a relatively recent arrival. Likewise as a continuation of what had been inaugurated before 1914, the foundations were laid of the modern medical and nursing professions and public health services in China. More important than the technical skills imparted was the inculcation of ideals of self-denying service derived from the Christian faith. In region after region Christian missionaries and those trained in Christian institutions continued to be pioneers in the new forms of education demanded by the age and in better methods of agriculture. In many lands contributions were made to improving the status of women, to the sanctity of marriage, and to the family. Through the Gospel hope of access to more of the good things of life was brought to thousands of the underprivileged, notably among the depressed classes and the animistic hill tribes of India and the Negroes of the United States and Africa. What seems to have been the decisive impulse in calling into being the League of Nations and its successor, the United Nations, was given by the Christian faith operating through some of the creators of these institutions for the achievement of an orderly world. Yet in many of these instances the contribution of Christianity, while undoubted, was difficult to ascertain with precision.

Even less amenable to statistical measurement but, at least from the Christian standpoint, of greater importance was the direct impress of the Gospel upon individuals. In millions who bore the Christian name the effects were slight. Yet in them Christianity was by no means unimportant in providing ethical standards and in giving some gleams of the goal which the Gospel set forth for the individual in maturing as a son of the eternal God. Others whose number no man could know were transformed. To some the change came with dramatic suddenness. In others it was wrought more slowly. Whether abruptly or gradually, it was marked by the appearance of what Paul called the fruits of the Spirit—love, joy, peace, longsuffering, kindness, goodness, faithfulness, meekness, and self-control. In such lives there was a distinctive radiance. They were "the light of the world." That they were found in an increasing number of countries and peoples was of major significance for mankind.

All these were effects within history which the historian could note even if he could not adequately appraise them. The Christian faith holds that of greater consequence were results which transcend history and reach beyond the grave. These the skills of the historian cannot prove. If he is not a Christian he will dismiss them, perhaps wistfully, perhaps impatiently. If he is a Christian he will rejoice in them but only as apprehensible through faith.

Chapter 61

BY WAY OF INCLUSIVE RETROSPECT

Our story is told. It is not completed. As we suggested in the last chapter, it pauses with a comma, for it still goes on. Indeed, it may barely have begun. What we have narrated covers a scant nineteen and a half centuries. This is only a small fraction of the course of mankind on the planet and is merely the latest fifth or sixth of the span thus far of what we call civilization. Because of the date at which these lines must be written, we are discontinuing our narrative when for the first time Christianity was becoming genuinely world-wide, adding universality in fact to what from the beginning had been universality in principle. Yet the historian as historian cannot peer into the future and we have come to the last section to which the scroll has thus far been unrolled.

It may be of help to take a backward glance over what has been traversed. To the reader to whom this book has been the first introduction to the history of Christianity the sixty chapters through which he has made his toilsome way will probably seem so crowded with details, persons, and movements that he comes to their end with a bewildered sigh of relief. Although from time to time we have attempted to pause for perspective, it may be of help to conclude with an attempt at a comprehensive summary which, from the vantage of the mid-twentieth century, will survey the whole road over which we have travelled, point out its main stages, and essay some suggestions of its significance for our knowledge of man and of the universe.

The beginnings of Christianity, it will be remembered, seemed singularly unpromising. To be sure, Jesus had back of him the long religious development which had issued in the Judaism of his day and from which, humanly speaking, he was sprung. Moreover, his brief life was spent in a section of the Mediterranean world at the beginning of a period when the *pax Romana* was bringing administrative unity and material prosperity to that portion of mankind and when a profound and widespread religious ferment gave opportunity for the successful dissemination of a new faith. However, in the few months of his public career Jesus wrote no book and created no elaborate organization to perpetuate his message and his work. His crucifixion appeared to mean complete frustration and his proclamation of the imminence of the kingdom of God seemed to be the futile dream of a well-meaning but quite unpractical visionary. At the outset his followers constituted merely one out of several Jewish sects and one of the feeblest of the many faiths which were competing in the Græco-Roman world. Moreover, the Roman Empire occupied but a small fraction of the earth's surface and embraced only a minority of even the civilized portion of mankind. By the time that Christianity had begun to gain headway, the realm was giving indications of the illnesses which brought its demise. Its inhabitants were ceasing to say or to do much that was really new. The creative impulse seemed to be dying.

Within its first five centuries Christianity won the professed allegiance of the large majority of the population of the Roman Empire and spread beyond it, chiefly but not entirely in contiguous territory. Christianity centered around Christ, but its theology, its organization, and its worship were developments which in part reflected the environment in which they took shape. Without Jesus Christianity would not have been, and while some forms of the faith, especially those known collectively as Gnosticism, tended to belittle his historicity, the one which ultimately prevailed cherished the records of his earthly life and sought to make its theology take full account of it. So much creative vigour did Christianity possess that from it came the various churches. In theory there was only one Church, the "body of Christ," but in actuality there were several churches. One of them, which claimed to be catholic and the custodian of the faith as taught by Jesus and the apostles, was the largest.

There was that about Jesus, his life, teachings, death, and resurrection which stirred men to intense intellectual activity in an attempt to see their meaning and which, while inescapably utilizing some of the thought patterns of the day, issued in conclusions which were essentially new. Christian worship took much from Judaism, but at its core, especially in the Eucharist, it was a fresh creation. By its discipline the Catholic Church as well as some of the bodies which dissented from it attempted to bring the conduct of its members towards an approximation of what Jesus had taught. As hundreds of thousands flocked into the Church and, in spite of the efforts of many zealous clergy, the lives of most Christians were not much if any better than those of the adherents of the surviving remnants of paganism, monasticism arose. Negatively it was a protest against the laxity of the main body of Christians and positively it claimed to offer a way of becoming perfectly conformed to the teachings of Jesus. Although at first the monks on the one hand and many of the bishops and clergy on the other tended to look askance at each other, monasticism soon became an integral part of the life of the Church.

Christianity did not save the Roman Empire. In its first five centuries, except in the area of religion, it did not greatly alter the life and customs of the Græco-Roman community. Nor did it reshape civilization. Death came slowly to the empire. Indeed, it never really arrived. There were prolonged illness and weakness and then transition to later stages of culture which continued much of the Græco-Roman heritage. The decline of the empire was due to internal decay and to invasions from without. Christianity did not prevent either.

From the Christian standpoint the most disastrous of the invasions was that of the Arabs. Inspired by a new religion, Islam, to which both Judaism and Christianity contributed, in the seventh and eighth centuries the Arabs made themselves masters of about half of Christendom, from Syria southward and westward to the Pyrenees. In that stretch of territory Islam was dominant, and while Christianity did not quickly disappear and in most places survived as the faith of a minority, the churches dwindled. In proportion to the area which it covered, through Islam Christianity suffered the greatest defeat in its history. Only in Spain, Portugal, and Sicily did it regain the ground then lost.

For some centuries it seemed that a similar fate might be overtaking Christianity in the territories which remained to it north of the Mediterranean. During five hundred years or more wave after wave of invaders, mostly non-Christian barbarians, poured in from the north and east.

Because of the decay of the realm and the culture with which it had become closely identified—the Roman Empire and its Græco-Roman civilization—Christianity seemed to be on the way out. The churches which were its vehicles were dwindling in numbers and suffering from a loss in morale. A bulwark remained in the remnant of the empire which clustered around Constantinople and in the West Rome was the rallying centre of another wing of the faith. In the East, the Nestorians, although a minority, first under Zoroastrian and then under Moslem rulers, propagated the faith as far as the China Sea and South India. Yet the period roughly bounded by the years 500 and 950 was the most discouraging since the unpromising beginning in the first century. In the West the revival under the Carolingians in the eighth and ninth centuries was followed by a relapse which brought the Church of Rome to the lowest point it had thus far known and by 950 Nestorianism had died out on its easternmost frontier, China.

Out of what looked like hopeless disaster and chiefly in what in the sixth century must have seemed the most unpromising areas and congeries of peoples came fresh achievements which were the preparation for the world-wide rôle which Christianity had in later centuries. The barbarian invaders of Western Europe were won, some of them during the darkest hours of the dark ages. From this apparently discouraging material and in a section of the world from which it seemed most unlikely that light would emerge, a civilization arose on which Christianity made a more profound impress and in which it had a larger creative part than it had had on that of Rome. In the formation of that civilization Christianity was by no means the only element. Pre-Christian Græco-Roman culture, the Moslem Arabs, and Teutonic tradition all had a share. Nor was that civilization fully Christian. Yet it was continually challenged by Christianity and in it were many who were radiant because of the Gospel, who were honoured for their Christlikeness, and who were at once an inspiration and a rebuke to those about them. From Christianity came great theologies, vigorous new monastic movements, universities, noble art and architecture, daring political theories, and haunting ideals of peace. But much in the life of Western Europe from 950 to 1350, as later, was palpably, almost stridently non-Christian and in stark contrast to the faith to which almost all gave lip service.

While this culture was developing in Western Europe, Christianity persisted in the continuation of the Roman Empire which had Constantinople as its capital. From there it permeated some of the barbarians who had settled in the Balkans and spread into the vast plains of the later Russia. However, perhaps because the break with the Græco-Roman past was not as marked, Christianity did not as nearly inform the eastern remnant of the Roman Empire as it did Western Europe, nor did as much creativity issue from it in the Balkans and Russia as in the West.

During the four centuries between 950 and 1350 the faith spread once more across Asia to the China coast, but, as before, it was represented only among small minorities.

There followed, approximately between 1350 and 1500, a period when Christianity again seemed moribund. In Asia it died out except westward from Persia to the Mediterranean and in South India. The Ottoman Turks, bearers of Islam, overwhelmed the remnants of the Byzantine Empire, long the bulwark of Christianity in Eastern Europe and Asia Minor, and turned the chief cathedral of the Greek Orthodox Church, Saint Sophia, into a mosque. They carried the crescent to the very walls of Vienna, threatening Western Europe. In Western Europe, the chief remaining stronghold of Christianity, the major official representative of the faith, the Roman Catholic Church, long suffered from debilitating division between rival Popes, and its hierarchy from the Popes down was shot through and through with moral corruption. The Renaissance came, in part having its source in Christianity. Yet in some of its aspects, notably in phases of humanism, it was in fact even though not ostensibly a departure from the faith. Towards the end of the period Western Europe entered on a breath-taking geographic expansion which at the outset was ruthless in its treatment of non-European peoples and upon which the professed faith of the explorers and conquerors appeared to have little effect.

Then, beginning not far from 1500, there pulsed forth a great resurgence of life. It showed itself first in Western Europe, almost simultaneously in the Protestant and Roman Catholic Reformations. The Protestant Reformation was predominantly in North-western Europe, including the British Isles. It displayed great variety, but in general had as its distinctive principle salvation by faith. The Roman Catholic Church rejected it and Western Christendom was permanently divided. The Roman Catholic Reformation began slightly before the Protestant Reformation. While to a large degree it was independent of the latter, it directed much of its energy against it, defined the position of the Roman Catholic Church on the issues at stake in such fashion as to leave no room for Protestantism, and sought, in some areas with success, to win back the territory which had been lost. By the middle of the seventeenth century it was clear that reconciliation between these two wings of Western Christianity was impossible, and that neither would eliminate the other. While neither was content to accept it as final, thereafter the geographic boundary between the two changed but little.

Somewhat later came movements in Russian Christianity which were indications of rising vigour, but at the outset they were quite distinct from those in Western Europe, nor did they have as widespread repercussions.

The fresh burst of life in European Christianity was followed by a territorial expansion of the faith which for magnitude had never been equalled, either by Christianity or by any other religion. It was closely associated with the amazing geographic discoveries, commerce, conquests, and migrations of European peoples. Precisely to what degree Christianity was responsible for these phenomena has never been determined. Similarly we do not know how far if at all the movements which we call the Protestant and Catholic Reformations and the abounding daring and vitality which led to this spread of European power were due to some factor or factors which were common to them all. However, in the sixteenth, seventeenth, and eighteenth centuries Christianity was planted in the Americas, on the fringes of Africa south of the Sahara, across the northern reaches of Asia, and in much of South and East Asia and its bordering islands. Most of this was by Roman Catholics, chiefly because predominatingly Roman Catholic lands, Spain and Portugal, were the main colonizing powers of the time. Some of it was by Protestants in connexion with the colonies of Protestant peoples, and across Northern Asia it was by the Russian Orthodox.

The Christian communities which arose from this expansion varied greatly in vigour. The largest, in Spanish and Portuguese America, proved anemic and

their continued life depended to no small degree upon unremitting transfusions of blood from Europe in the form of clergy and lay brothers. That in
Canada, Roman Catholic, maintained itself even after the ties with France
were severed. The one in Japan, also Roman Catholic, driven into hiding by
persecution and cut off from the outside world, survived for about two hundred and fifty years with no contact with Christians of other lands. The Russian Orthodox communities, while spread over a large area, were small. The
largest new Protestant communities, those in the British colonies in North
America, were conspicuous for their vitality and propagating power. The small
Protestant community in South Africa was also persistent and later experienced a rapid growth. Protestantism in the West Indies, India, Ceylon, and
the East Indies, like the Roman Catholicism of Spanish and Portuguese
America, was dependent upon that of Europe for its continued existence. In
land after land, the presence of Christianity helped to soften the impact of
European upon non-European peoples and to make the coming of the Occident a blessing rather than a curse.

The latter part of the eighteenth century brought a combination of adversities which to many of the intellectuals seemed to sound the death knell of
Christianity. They were all the more serious because they largely centered in
Western Europe, where Christianity had for several centuries shown its greatest
vigour and because they bore especially heavily upon the Roman Catholic
Church, through which most of the territorial expansion had been accomplished during the preceding several centuries. The dissolution of the Society
of Jesus, the body through which much of the spread of the faith in the preceding two centuries had been made, was crippling. The growth of rationalism,
partly sprung from a one-sided view of the conception of the dignity of man
which had been derived from Christianity, but in which man's creatureliness
and salvation through the act of God in Christ were ignored or discounted,
undercut or destroyed the faith of many. A series of devastating wars and,
above all, the French Revolution and the Wars of Napoleon shook Europe.

Yet, even while thousands were prepared to hail the demise of Christianity,
movements were under way in Great Britain and the United States which were
to issue in one of the most potent revivals that the faith had known. They were
in Protestantism and were to rise to major proportions in the following century.

The nineteenth century presented a combination of contrasts. On the one
hand, much of the traditional Christendom was more prosperous than any
large group of mankind had ever been. Science and the industrial revolution,
to an undetermined degree outgrowths of Christianity, were enriching Western
Europe and North America beyond anything previously seen. Compared with
earlier eras, the age was peaceful. Knowledge of man's physical universe was

expanding by breath-taking leaps and bounds. Optimism was mounting. Revolutionary ideas, partly derived from Christianity, envisioned a human society in which the humblest would share in the good things of life. These ideas contributed to revolutions which from time to time shook much of Christendom. European peoples were continuing at an accelerated pace the expansion which had begun at least as early as the fifteenth century. In that intoxicating atmosphere there were Christians who dreamed and planned for the complete remaking of mankind and civilization to bring them into conformation with the standards of their faith.

On the other hand, some features of the age appeared to threaten the very existence of Christianity. The materialism and secularism which were reinforced by the scientific and mechanical advances of the day dominated thousands and seemed to make Christianity irrelevant or a pleasant but optional adjunct to the good life. The patterns of the burgeoning industrial communities gave little room for the worship and parish life of the churches through which Christianity was perpetuated. At the outset they were a means of exploiting the labourers, with features which were a flat contradiction of Christian precepts and ideals. Some of the programmes offered for the reorganization of society, notably communism, were anti-Christian. Many who worked for better conditions of the labouring classes regarded the Church as one of the bulwarks of entrenched privilege and were critical of it and of the faith which it represented. Numbers of intellectuals and others who followed them believed, some regretfully, some gladly, that science had made Christianity untenable. The association of Christianity with Western imperialism proved a handicap: peoples upon whom that imperialism bore heavily either were critical because of the connexion or were moved by it to look favourably upon Christianity, thus failing to understand the true genius of the faith.

In the face of these adverse factors Christianity displayed striking vitality and came to the end of the century more vigorous and more potent in the affairs of mankind than it had been at the outset of the century or at any previous time. This was true of all three of the main branches of the faith.

The Roman Catholic Church displayed notable resilience in recovering from the blows dealt it in the eighteenth century and especially during the French Revolution and the Napoleonic Wars. Old monastic orders renewed their strength and the Society of Jesus was revived and again became potent. Many new orders came into being. Anti-clericalism led to the separation of Church and state in France and in several other countries brought the confiscation of much ecclesiastical property and various restrictions on the Church. Partly because of the hostility of the governments of states which had once been friendly but which had sought to control the Church within their borders, the

Roman Catholic Church became more tightly integrated under the Popes than ever before. The Pope was now formally declared to be infallible in matters of faith and morals. Administratively his power was markedly enhanced. The Papacy set itself against some of the major trends of the day. This also was in the direction of making the Roman Catholic Church, especially its hierarchy, its monks and nuns, and its more loyal laity as distinguished from those to whom the connexion was mainly a social convention, a self conscious minority in an alien world and closely knit around the Pope. Yet the Roman Catholic Church was not merely on the defensive. It was expanding, both by emigration to the Americas and Australasia and through missions in Asia, Africa, and the Americas.

It was Protestantism which showed the greatest vigour of any of the branches of Christianity. From it issued many new movements and organizations. Within it there was a ferment of theological thought, a large proportion of it fresh and creative. There was also intensive study of the Bible, much of it courageously applying the new methods of historical scholarship. Protestantism moved in on the growing manufacturing and commercialized centres of industrialized Britain. Proportionately it spread more rapidly and widely than either the Roman Catholic Church or the Orthodox Churches. At the outset of the nineteenth century confined almost entirely to North-western Europe and the Atlantic seaboard of North America, by the dawn of the twentieth century it had spanned North America, was making a rapid growth in Latin America, was the dominant religion in Australasia, and had been planted in most of the countries of Africa and Asia.

The Orthodox Churches, especially that of Russia, were also on a rising tide, although not so strikingly as were the Roman Catholic Church and Protestantism. In the Balkans they emerged from under the Moslem Turkish yoke. In Russia there was access of vigour. While geographic expansion was not as spectacular as in the case of the other two major branches of the faith, it took place through migration to the Americas and Siberia and through a notable mission in Japan.

The year 1914 opened a new and stormy stage in the course of Christianity. The contrasts were even greater than in the nineteenth century and the threats to the faith rose to larger proportions. Yet Christianity gave evidence of amazing vigour and continued its geographic spread.

The challenges to Christianity were many. Some were continuations of those of the nineteenth century, among them absorption in the pursuit of wealth, the growing industrialization of society, some of the programmes advocated for collective welfare, and adverse intellectual currents. To them were added two world wars and several lesser wars, the decline of Western Europe, revolutions which destroyed forms of government, social structures, and inherited ethical and religious convictions for at least a third of mankind, rebellion against the supremacy of Western European nations, the advance of pronouncedly anti-Christian communism, and a great groundswell among the masses in many lands demanding more of the good things of life. Significantly, and in the eyes of many observers ominously, most of these challenges originated and attained their most formidable dimensions in what had been regarded as the historic heart of Christendom.

Although it suffered losses, some of them serious, in general Christianity rose to the challenge. The Roman Catholic Church displayed features which had characterized it in the nineteenth century. Many of its hereditary constituency had their allegiance weakened or dissolved, but those who remained were more nearly consolidated under the Papacy. The See of Peter had a succession of able, upright men. There was fresh intellectual activity, especially in theology. The liturgical movement, Eucharistic congresses, and other developments stimulated piety. Catholic Action enlisted more and more of the laity. The geographic spread in Africa and Asia mounted. Also as in the nineteenth century, proportionately Protestantism flourished more pronouncedly than did the Roman Catholic Church. It experienced numerical decline in Europe, but it continued to gain in the United States, in Latin America (where its advance was chiefly among the nominally Roman Catholic population), in Africa, and in South and East Asia and its fringing islands. Even more than the Roman Catholic Church, it was stirred by theological ferment. Through the Ecumenical Movement it developed an expanding fresh approach towards Christian unity. The Eastern Churches were hard hit, especially the Russian Orthodox Church, but none of them died, and some exhibited sturdy vitality in the face of what looked like overwhelming disaster, especially from communism. Christianity came to the mid-twentieth century more nearly world-wide in its extent and influence than either it or any other religion had ever been.

In the relatively brief nineteen and a half centuries of its existence, in spite of its seemingly unpromising beginning, Christianity had spread over most of the earth's surface and was represented by adherents in almost every tribe and nation and in nearly every inhabited land. It had gone forward by pulsations of advance, retreat, and advance. Measured by the criteria of geographic extent, inner vigour as shown by new movements from within it, and the effect on mankind as a whole, each major advance had carried it further into the life of the world than the one before it and each major recession had been less severe than its predecessor. In spite of this spread, in the middle of the twentieth century Christianity was still the professed faith of only a minority of men, in some of the largest countries only a small minority. Of those who bore the

Christian name, especially in lands where they were in the majority, only a minority made the thoroughgoing commitment required by the genius of the faith.

What effect had Christianity had across the centuries, operating as it did through this minority? Again and again in the preceding chapters we have sought to give data towards the answer. Often we cannot know whether Christianity was at all an element in a particular movement or action. In many other instances we can be reasonably sure that it entered as a factor, but so compounded with other causes that we cannot accurately appraise the extent of its responsibility. Among these were the emergence of universities in the Middle Ages, the Renaissance, the rise of the scientific method, the geographic discoveries by Europeans in the fifteenth, sixteenth, and seventeenth centuries, democracy of the Anglo-Saxon kind, and communism. Whether in any of these it was determinative, so that but for it they would not have come into being, we are not and probably cannot be sure. We can be clear that in some movements Christianity was dominant. Such were the appearance and development of the various churches, monasticism in its several manifestations, the Protestant and Catholic Reformations, the formulation of the great creeds of the first few centuries, and the construction of most of the systems of theology. Yet in none of these was Christianity the only cause. Indeed, what we call Christianity changed from time to time. In most of its forms what came from Jesus and his apostles was regarded as primary and determinative, but other contributions entered, among them the cultural background of individuals and groups, the personal experiences of outstanding leaders, and inherited religions and philosophical conceptions.

In spite of these uncertainties and complicating factors, we can be fully assured of some of the fruits of what constitutes the core of the Christian faith and of Christianity, namely, the life, teachings, death, and resurrection of Jesus. We can, of course, be clear that without this core Christianity and the churches would not have been. It is by no means responsible for all that was done in the guise of Christianity or under the ægis of the churches, and much was performed in its name which was quite contrary to it. However, the perversion of the Gospel is one of the facts of which an appraisal of the results of Christianity must take account. It is incontestable that from Christ issued unmeasured and immeasurable power in the life of mankind. We know that because of him across the centuries untold thousands of individuals have borne something of his likeness. Thousands have been so reared in the knowledge of him that from childhood and without striking struggle they have followed him and have increasingly shown the radiance of the faith, hope, and self-giving love which were in him. Other thousands have come to the same path and goal through deep sorrow, initial moral defeat, and soul-wrenching struggles. Some have been famous and have passed on to other thousands the light which has come from him. More have been obscure and have been known only to a limited circle, but within that circle they have been towers of strength.

Through Christ there has come into being the Church. The Church is never fully identical with ecclesiastical organizations. It is to be found in them, but not all of their members belong to it and it is greater than the sum of them all. Yet, though never fully visible as an institution, the Church has been and is a reality, more potent than any one or all of the churches. "The blessed company of all faithful people," it constitutes a fellowship which has been both aided and hampered by the churches, and is both in them and transcends them.

From individuals who have been inspired by Christ and from the Church has issued movement after movement for attaining the Christian ideal. That ideal has centered around the kingdom of God, an order in which God's will is done. It sets infinite value upon the individual. Its goal for the individual is to become a child of God, to "know the love of Christ which passeth knowledge" and to "be filled unto all the fulness of God"—God Who is Creator and Father, Who revealed His true nature, self-giving love, by becoming incarnate in Jesus Christ and permitting the seeming defeat and frustration of the cross, and Who is ever active in history in individuals and the collective life of mankind. Its goal for the individual cannot be completely attained this side of the grave, but is so breath-taking that within history only a beginning is possible. Nor can it be reached in isolation, but only in community. In Christ's teaching love for God, as the duty and privilege of man, is inseparably joined with love for one's neighbour.

The ideal and the goal have determined the character of the movements which have been the fruits of Christianity. Although men can use and often have used knowledge and education to the seeming defeat of the ideal, across the centuries Christianity has been the means of reducing more languages to writing than have all other factors combined. It has created more schools, more theories of education, and more systems than has any other one force. More than any other power in history it has impelled men to fight suffering, whether that suffering has come from disease, war, or natural disasters. It has built thousands of hospitals, inspired the emergence of nursing and medical professions, and furthered movements for public health and the relief and prevention of famine. Although explorations and conquests which were in part its outgrowth led to the enslavement of Africans for the plantations of the Americas, men and women whose consciences were awakened by Christianity and whose wills it nerved brought about the abolition of Negro slavery. Men and women similarly moved and sustained wrote into the laws of Spain and

Portugal provisions to alleviate the ruthless exploitation of the Indians of the New World. Wars have often been waged in the name of Christianity. They have attained their most colossal dimensions through weapons and large scale organization initiated in Christendom. Yet from no other source have there come as many and as strong movements to eliminate or regulate war and to ease the suffering brought by war. From its first centuries the Christian faith has caused many of its adherents to be uneasy about war. It has led minorities to refuse to have any part in it. It has impelled others to seek to limit war by defining what, in their judgement, from the Christian standpoint is a "just war." In the turbulent middle ages of Europe it gave rise to the Truce of God and the Peace of God. In a later era it was the main impulse in the formulation of international law. But for it the League of Nations and the United Nations would not have been. By its name and symbol the most extensive organization ever created for the relief of the suffering caused by war, the Red Cross, bears witness to its Christian origin. The list might go on indefinitely. It includes many another humanitarian project and movement, ideals in government, the reform of prisons and the emergence of criminology, great art and architecture, and outstanding literature. In geographic extent and potency the results were never as marked as in the nineteenth and twentieth centuries.

What meaning does this history of Christianity have? What does it indicate of the nature of man and of the environment in which man finds himself? The answer cannot be given on the basis of facts ascertained by observation and appraised by human reason. It can come only as an act of faith. Yet it need not contradict observation and reason and in it what has been ascertained through them can have a place and intelligibility be given to what otherwise seems confusing and contradictory. The historian is vividly aware that any suggestion which he may essay will not win universal assent. He has seen too many diverse replies given across the centuries, some of them boldly and some hesitantly, to be confident that any which he can offer will have a different fate. He recalls that it was said long ago that "whether there be knowledge it shall be done away" and that we know only in part. Yet the historian owes it to any who may read his pages to state whatever answers his study of the records has brought to him.

First of all, as a conclusion of faith supported by what is deemed to be fact interpreted by reason, is the conviction that we live in a universe which is not unintelligible confusion but is orderly, and that it is created and sustained by One Whom we call God. Next is the conviction, reached in similar fashion, that man, as a part of that universe, is also created by God. The ancient record declares that "God created man in His own image," and that He did so out of the dust of the ground, breathing into him the breath of life. That, too, is partly a conclusion of faith, but it also explains the contradiction of which thoughtful men have long been painfully aware—on the one hand their aspirations to transcend time and space and to have fellowship with God, and on the other hand their earthiness in physical and moral frailty and in their imperfect knowledge.

Faith and reason combine to declare that since God has created man in His own image, He must design him for fellowship with Himself. This means that He desires men to be creatures who are not automata, for robots could not be in His image. They must have freedom of choice, and that freedom must be sufficient to permit them either to rebel against God or voluntarily to seek to know God's will and do it. It is clear that from as far back as men know their own history and presumably further, men have used that freedom to rebel against their Creator and to seek to follow their own, misdirected wills.

Faith declares, and believes that in doing so it rightly interprets the evidence, that God judges men, that through what we may call laws or patterns which He has built into the universe, men's rebellion and perversion of their freedom bring on them misery, corruption of character, and what is painfully obvious in the course of human history—hatred, strife between individuals, classes, races, and nations, physical degeneracy, and moral slavery, so that men, meant to be higher than the animals about them, sink lower than the brutes. Yet faith, also supported by fact, insists that this judgement is in love and mercy and is for the purpose of bringing men back from the perversion of their wills to the purpose which God has for them.

Christian faith declares that because of what Christians call His grace, the love which men can never earn or deserve but can only accept in humble, wondering gratitude, God acted to redeem men and reconcile them to Himself. Still respecting men's wills, He did this by a long preparation through the lawgivers and prophets of Israel and then by the astounding act, without precedent and with no need of repetition, in the incarnation in Jesus of Nazareth, who was both "very God of very God, begotten, not made" and also true man.

The incarnate Word lived, taught, announced the kingdom of God, and was crucified through the self-interest and stupidity of representatives of as high a religion and as good a government as men had thus far known. Thus God at once passed judgement on men's best achievement and sought to save the world which had committed the crime.

Christian faith goes on to declare that the cross did not end all, that through God's power Christ rose, triumphant, and ever lives in what to men is the mystery of his unity with God the Father. Moreover, Christian faith asserts that after these events in history, God continued to act, in enhanced fashion, through what it calls the Holy Spirit, Spirit Who is also God and Who, always present, came in a fresh way because Christ was no longer bodily with men. Christian faith also affirms that in those who "receive Christ" a new birth is wrought by God through His Spirit, that Christ dwells in their hearts by faith, and that they are transformed, becoming lights in a dark world.

The historian, if he shares this faith, believes that in the pattern thus disclosed the facts fit into place. He is certain that, judged by his effect, Jesus Christ has been the most influential life lived on this planet. He sees coming from him the many fruits at which we have hinted in the preceding pages. He believes Christ's influence to be mounting. Yet the historian must also recognize that what has issued from Christ has been the occasion for greater perversions of man's free will than had been witnessed before Christ's appearance. That was seen spectacularly in the crucifixion, in which men whose predecessors had persecuted those of their fellows who had spoken for God now killed the Son Himself. It has been apparent in the centuries since the crucifixion—in the corruption which we have noted in the churches themselves, in the large scale exploitation of other peoples by those bearing the Christian name, in the enslavement of Negroes by nominal Christians, in the slums of the industrial and mining towns and cities which in Christendom were a result of the industrial revolution, in the application of science to mass destruction in war, most highly developed among peoples long under Christian influence, and in the emergence and spread of such tyrannical ideologies as national socialism and communism, both of which arose in Christendom. These and other instances have been the turning of the good gifts of God, in part the fruits of the Gospel, to the misery of men. All of these perversions, however, have been challenges to which earnest Christians have responded. They have been stimulated by them and their faith to use them as an occasion for bringing about a greater good than would have come had they not been stung to action by them. This does not mean that God is responsible for the demonic twistings of His bounty to men's hurt. It may well be evidence, in contrast, that God is sovereign and that, having given men free will, He does not permit its misdirection to defeat His benign purpose. Indeed, it is conceivable that He never allows the abuse of free will to get completely out of hand, but has placed such resources at the disposal of those who, also of their free will, respond to the promptings of His Spirit that they bring good out of evil.

What is to be the end of the story? That the course of Christianity on the planet has only recently begun is evident. Is it only at its beginning? Is history to go on until all human society, within history, and all individuals within it fully conform to God's ideal for men? Or is God to bring history suddenly to an end, perhaps at an early date? Here Christians have not been agreed. Earnest.

intelligent, and devout men, honestly seeking to know God's purpose, have taken what look like diametrically opposing views and have held them with conviction. That was true of the writers of the New Testament, even at times of the same writer. Thus Paul, in his *Letter to the Romans,* speaks of some men as "vessels of wrath fitted to destruction" and declares that God has "mercy on whom He will have mercy and whom He will He hardeneth," and also says that "God hath shut them all up together in unbelief that He might have mercy upon all." Even Jesus both spoke solemnly of the path which leads to destruction and which many enter and in one of his parables pictures the good shepherd as leaving the ninety-nine sheep who are safe in the fold and seeking the one which had gone astray, declaring that it was not the will of God "that one of these little ones should perish." *The Gospel according to John* is emphatic that "God sent not his Son into the world to condemn the world, but that the world through him might be saved." Jesus believed that there would be a dramatic end of history and that until then both the wheat and the weeds would grow together, but for that event he refused to set a date. He advised his disciples to be ready for it at any moment, but warned them, in the parable of the wise and foolish virgins, that it might be long delayed. Here, obviously, we are dealing with a future for which history does not provide a precedent and where the historian must tread humbly and by faith and not by what he has seen.

Yet they who have learned of Jesus reach out in faith and affirm that God is not only sovereign but that He is also love, love as seen in the seeming weakness of the babe in Bethlehem's manger and of the cross, but love which because of "the exceeding greatness of His Power . . . which He wrought in Christ when he raised him from the dead" cannot and will not be defeated. As they are stirred to the depths by the mystery of evil and cry out in anguish "My God, why?" they affirm with Paul that while "the whole creation groaneth and travaileth in pain" God subjected the creation to frustration "in hope," and that it "shall be delivered from the bondage of corruption into the glorious liberty of the children of God." They are convinced that the full course of the Gospel is not and cannot be contained within history, that God has made Christ lord not only in this age but also in that which is to come, and that it is the purpose of God through Christ to reconcile all things unto Himself, whether things upon the earth or things in the heavens. Those who have been taught of Christ have that hope and that faith because of what they know of the love of God in Christ and because that love has been poured into their hearts through His Holy Spirit Whom God has given them.

INCREASING DISESTABLISHMENT,
INCREASING DIVERSITY,
GROWTH AND VITALITY,
A.D. 1950--A.D. 1975

Chapter 62

THE WORLD CHRISTIAN MOVEMENT
1950-1975: AN INTERPRETIVE ESSAY
Ralph D. Winter

In 1975 anyone expecting to live to the year 2000 or even to 1984 would have had to take a very hard look at the unique developments of the 1950-to-1975 period. For the previous two centuries observers with increasing consternation had begun to predict dire events in the future owing to the giddy pace of the acceleration of history. But, by 1975, the voices of doomsday prophets had become a roar, and, at the time, the oil crisis only seemed to confirm man's worst fears. This was a period—if there ever had been one—in which an interpretative treatment of the development of the Christian movement would have to be done, in Latourette's words, "in relation to the total story of mankind." In doing this, a number of traits of the period stood out.

In the first place, during the 1950 to 1975 period the Western world underwent the most astonishing contraction of political empire that had ever been seen in history in so short a period of time. Shortly before the middle of the century, Western man had completed a gradual buildup of control over the rest of the world that was itself unprecedented. But while that control had been achieved during several centuries of time, the collapse of the Western colonial empires took place within the 1945-to-1969 period. Yet this is merely to speak negatively. Positively: never before had so many new nations come into being so suddenly.

In the second place, no account of this period could fail to take note of the great increase in what had been already a noticeable acceleration of history, an increase which distinguished this particular quarter of a century from any other in all the annals of human history. The acceleration that was noticed was only in part because people could travel faster, communicate more readily, and thus collaborate more efficiently. It was in great part because there was a startlingly greater number of people on earth to make things happen. During this twenty-five-year period the *gain* in world population was as great as the entire population of the world in 1875. In the United States, specifically, the total number of human years lived out during the entire nineteenth century was equalled by the same number of people-years for only the fifteen-year period 1960 to 1975. The United States had 5.3 million people in 1800, and, after a very slow buildup for most of the next hundred years, had 76 million by 1900. But by 1960 there were 180 million, and by 1975, 214 million.

But this was not all. Not only was the world population enormously greater—and this meant that history would inevitably seem to speed up simply because there were each year massively more human beings delving, tussling, working at a given time—but an even greater factor in increased acceleration was the fact that in certain parts of the world (the so-called oil-consuming nations) a sudden and immense amount of labor saving, time saving, and effort multiplying had taken place. The almost unbelievable result was that while, as we have seen, United States citizens expended as much human effort between 1960 and 1975 as they had in the nineteenth century, the work performed (measured by Gross National Product adjusted for inflation) during the entire nineteenth century was equalled in just the two years 1973 and 1974.

In the fourth place, no previous twenty-five-year period in history had witnessed so many technological advances. It had been said that the period covered five revolutions and three renaissances. Whatever was intended by that statement, it was during this quarter of a century that the atom was tamed and the cybernetic revolution became prominent in the meteoric rise of the computer. It was the era of jet planes, earth satellites, moon landings, and unmanned travel within the solar system. Microelectronics brought amazing changes including the transistor radio, which found its way to the furthest reaches of the earth. Many of these new achievements remarkably enhanced the spread of Christianity.

In the fifth place, however, while the economic and technological development of the whole world had been a prominent goal for many years, by 1975 it had become clear that there was really no solution, no possible answer to the "rising expectations" of the majority of the population of the earth for development along Western lines. It became plain to all that economic development in the so-called underdeveloped nations was constantly being outrun by the population explosion in those same nations. Thus arose the widespread concern for limitation of population. But before any solution for overpopulation was discovered, it became clear that the Western way of life itself would be unworkable if extended even to the existing, unexpanded world population. If the average American used up twenty-two tons of mineral resources per day, it simply wasn't possible for such a way of life to become standard for all mankind. Neither was anything remotely like the United States diet something other nations could copy. Senator Hatfield remarked in 1975 that "we can get 667 pounds of protein from one acre of soybeans, but we can only get nine pounds of protein from one acre cultivated in feed grain for cattle." Most nations could not afford to use up seventy-four times as much land in order to get animal protein instead of vegetable protein. Thus it turned out that the Western way was sustainable only by a very inefficient use of land for a very few people. By 1975, the impossibility of the orderly continuation of the pattern of past development had become dreadfully obvious.

In the sixth place, a phenomenon somewhat similar to the increasing inefficiency of land use was the increasing inefficiency in the use of fuel to obtain Western man's vastly increased productivity. Just as an animal protein diet was a highly inefficient exploitation of land, in parallel fashion in 1975 United States citizens, in order to produce as much in *two years* as in the entire nineteenth century, were using as much oil in *two months* as was consumed in the entire nineteenth century. That is, fifty times the productivity cost six hundred times as much oil.

In the seventh place, toward the end of this period, Western man finally discovered with acute embarrassment that the Western World itself had become almost irretrievably dependent—"umbilically dependent" was the phrase—upon a single, rapidly shrinking resource: oil. This was one of the main reasons the Western way of life could not be extended to the rest of the earth, but it was also why such a lifestyle could not be perpetuated even in the West at anything like the 1975 level. This sudden awareness threatened that at some future date Western man might appear not as the pioneering technological benefactor of all the earth, but as the bandit that broke into the storehouse and plundered all the world's energy resources before the bulk of mankind had had a chance to enjoy its share. People in 1975 feared that world oil consumption continuing to rise at 1973 rates would exhaust all known reserves in twenty-one years, and that the United States, if it were to use only its own oil, would run out by 1981. Alternative energy sources were believed to be costly, hazardous, delayed, and uncertain, while foreign sources of oil were also uncertain if only because prohibitively expensive.

Thus in early 1975 the outlook for Western man and his way of life was suddenly very bleak. But the hungry, exploding populations of Asia and Africa faced ever so much more serious dangers. Mesarovic and Pestel in *Mankind at the Turning Point: The Second Report to the Club of Rome* described a nearly inevitable scenario in which the number of children dying per year would rise from 10 million to more than 40 million by the year 2000. Probably at no time in the twentieth century had man's achievements loomed smaller in proportion to the real problems he faced. At no time was there greater need for the best possible international understanding. At no time were the values and perspectives of the Christian faith more widely shared. Never before in history had the nations of the world as great a sense of obligation toward each other; superficial though this attitude might be, it was a feeling stemming from the remarkable record of selfless service that had been performed by Christian missions.

In 1975, the world in many ways seemed to be passing into a post-Western period. Would this be a post-Christian period as well? Hopefully the presence of the Christian movement in the world could make a considerable direct and indirect contribution in the troubled times ahead. The movement itself was not in decline. The number of Protestant missionaries from North America more than doubled between 1950 and 1975 and so did the number of mission agencies. The net increase in the number of Christians in the non-Western world by the end of this period was far larger than the total number of Christians in the non-Western world at the beginning of the period. That is to say, in the non-Western world, Christians increased by 140 percent while the general population increased by only 42 percent. Another way to visualize the growth rate of the Christian movement in the non-Western world in 1975 would be to picture at least one thousand new churches opening their doors each Sunday. But we are anticipating the study that follows.

THE WESTERN WORLD

The two areas Latourette spoke of as "traditional Christendom" and "the Larger Occident" are really a single cultural sphere often called the Western world which, for the sake of space, can be discussed as a single unit. One reason this can be done is that during the third quarter of the twentieth century much of this whole area was undergoing the same series of experiences in regard to the breakdown of centuries-old established relations between civil governments and Christian institutional structures.

Thus, the most useful generalization about what happened to Christianity in the Western world between 1950 and 1975 is simply that it continued (and even speeded up) its gradual, painful withdrawal from entrenched legal and cultural establishment. This complex process of disestablishment—and we use the term more broadly than is customary—began much earlier and seemed to move much faster in America. Nevertheless, even as late as 1975 religious properties still escaped taxation in America. Similarly, in Russia, despite the violent disestablishment that occurred in the Communist revolution, the former state church still retained significant cultural influence. But everywhere in the Western world in both Protestant and Roman Catholic areas, and in both

Communist and non-Communist areas, the trend was relentlessly and probably irreversibly away from a Christianity possessing any political power of establishment which could conceivably force its forms upon a whole populace. Latourette stressed that Communism was not the only force hastening the process of disestablishment; he also felt that Communism and the process of disestablishment were partially products of Christianity, even though they might also be anti-Christian.

Thus, while the Communist movement represented the most extensive, single organized force in the trend to disestablishment, it drew much of its inspiration from the social concerns growing out of the Evangelical Awakening in Britain, where it was born amidst the labor pains of the industrial revolution. The Methodist class meeting, borrowed perhaps from the Brethren of the Common Life, was a forerunner of the Communist cell, and the Communistic emphasis on confession also stemmed from Methodism. Going further back in history, Communism's stress on "people governments" and the rights of the people could hardly be distinguished from any number of earlier, more obviously Christian, revolutionary movements such as Wat Tyler's Rebellion, the Bundschuh Revolt, the Peasants' War, etc., except that in these earlier movements the Bible had been appealed to as the source of revolutionary perspective. Since Marx, Engels, and Lenin apparently felt that the Church was forever on the side of the bourgeoise, they saw the rising up of the masses as inevitably requiring the destruction of the Church and, for safety, the elimination of the religion and theology behind the Church. Yet such goals were to some extent incidental to the more profound cause of Communism, the liberation of man— a concept which in turn is a cluster of ideals almost entirely stemming from Christianity. But could such ideals survive as fruits when once separated from their Christian roots? Elton Trueblood felt not and called the society with this kind of secular vision "a cut-flower civilization."

It is not surprising, therefore, that in the 1950's and 1960's many people in the Western world, especially in the United States, confused the somewhat academic tension between capitalism and Communism with the larger issue of Christianity versus atheism. But according to Latourette, even the latter tension did not best describe the major process unfolding in the Revolutionary Age. As Christianity was becoming disestablished, many of the surface evidences of this disestablishment—declining registration of Christians in Germany, declining statistics of baptisms in the areas of state-church traditions, and even declining perfunctory attendance in some of the older church traditions—did not by any means signal the exhaustion of the energy and vitality of the Christian movement. Again and again in Latourette's writings, and in our own observations of the Western world, we are forced to distinguish between the admittedly widespread evidences of the decline of the Christian establishment and the springing up of a vast plethora of new movements, contrasting sharply with the decline of the settled Christian past.

It was, for example, in 1818—early in Latourette's Revolutionary Era—that American churches in Connecticut were finally and dramatically cut off from state support. At that time the eminent church leader, Lyman Beecher, sincerely predicted the fatal demise of the United States Church, only to contradict himself ten years later with relief and exultation when the newly emerging "voluntary church" tradition seemed to offer more hope than ever before for continuity of vigor and vitality despite the absence of the older forms. For Europe, it was under Hitler that German congregations had briefly to face the necessity of direct local support of their pastors when state support was slashed or withdrawn completely. Then for more than a quarter of a century after World War II, the Church in East Germany had to survive in the face of intense opposition by the state. Even earlier in Russia, as we have seen, the Christian movement had proved itself capable of surviving the most extreme opposition of an atheistic government. But the loss of establishment apparently did not mean the emergence of a "post-Christian era."

The thrust of Latourette's blunt, earnest prediction in the 1950's that the use of the phrase "post-Christian era" was "hasty and naive" was eminently confirmed by 1975. A specific case might be the East Germany we have just mentioned. The Protestant community—consistently penalized for church involvement—dropped from 80 percent to 60 percent of the population, and by 1975 there were perhaps at the most only one million people (6 percent) who could be called highly committed Christians. Yet cautious observers suggested that this committed minority was probably larger than at any previous time. Students in Christian groups at the universities of Dresden and Leipzig numbered in the hundreds. It was not uncommon for groups of young people numbering more than one thousand suddenly to materialize for worship and Bible study, coming from all parts of East Germany but especially from the south, brought together by word of mouth alone. The famous Dom (cathedral) across from the Imperial Palace in East Berlin was being reconstructed by the end of the period. A small group of Communist-leaning pastors existed for a time, but had disappeared by 1975.

Thus, for all their trouble, the leaders of the totalitarian Communist regime had through diligent oppression apparently done no more damage to the Christian movement than had the benign neglect of the non-Communist governments in other parts of Europe and the Western world in the same period.

In both the East and West, from Russia west to Australia, the overarching phenomenon was the accelerated disestablishment of the Christian movement. Where was this massive process leading?

Clues to the future could perhaps be seen in the New World where the transformation was more advanced. "The shot heard 'round the world" at the outbreak of the American Revolution had an immediate effect in France but was then heard all down through the Americas. Mainly in the New World the reverberations almost instantly furthered the disestablishment of churches that were for the most part already heading that way. Thus, the churches in the United States were much more extensively disestablished much sooner than in Europe, even though between 1950 and 1975 events were still taking place that further disestablished Christianity even as a semi-official faith. In 1962, the Supreme Court made unlawful even the voluntary recital of a non-denominational prayer written by the New York State Board of Regents. In 1975, the California State Court of Appeal ruled that "the three-hour closing of state offices on Good Friday is unconstitutional and an 'excessive governmental entanglement with religion.'" That same year the California State Legislature appointed a Buddhist priest as chaplain, a move profoundly significant in the disestablishment process. Nevertheless, legal disestablishment meant cultural disestablishment only for a time. Church membership was 6 percent of the population at the time of the American Revolution, but was over 60 percent by 1975.

Latin America, at first glance, may have seemed to many Protestants an area of unrelieved and seemingly permanent Roman Catholic establishment. But by 1975, any such illusions were well-nigh completely shattered. As a matter of fact, the disestablishment of Christendom in Latin America had begun most emphatically over one hundred years earlier as country after country declared its independence both from Europe and from the Church in the years that followed the American Revolution to the north. What had confused Protestants was the apparently close, continued association of the Roman Catholic Church with the various governments. Yet the famous Concordat between the Spanish crown and the Vatican did not consolidate the power of the Vatican in Spain so much as it consolidated the power of the Spanish crown over the Church, and the same shift was true for the Colombian Concordat signed after the wars of independence. Such concordats did mean a continued, prominent role for the Church, but the Church now became subservient to the state—a development which we can see only as the first step in our larger concept of disestablishment. In Mexico, for example, the power of the state over the Church allowed the state eventually to seize all the properties of the Church and progressively to disenfranchise it in many other ways. Legal proscriptions of Roman Catholic activities in Mexico long antedated and perhaps even guided similar measures taken later in Russia by the Bolsheviks as the new era of the USSR came to constitute an even more determined and relentless disestablishment of the Church. In the constitutions of most Latin American countries for over a century there had been provision for both freedom of, and freedom from, religion.

Nevertheless, despite such striking handicaps and limitations, the Roman Catholic Church was able to survive at least as a cultural tradition, and especially following Vatican II it adopted in many places an outright anti-government posture which aligned it with the masses and the downtrodden. Meanwhile, vigorous new thinking, especially in Latin America, championed a "theology of liberation" which boldly assumed the very institution of the Church to be secondary to the larger will of God in society.

Even more estranged from the institutional Roman Catholic tradition were the rising Protestant and Pentecostal movements which flourished in the anti-clerical atmosphere. Pentecostalism was especially prominent in Brazil and Chile, but by 1975 had become a significant force from Mexico to Argentina. Thus Christianity in various forms represented a vigorous and vital element in almost every sector of Latin America despite the fact that the older institutions of the Church by 1975 were more completely disestablished than ever before.

Nevertheless, these traces of final, legal disestablishment in the Western world were accompanied by abundant evidence that legal establishment as such was by no means essential—nor perhaps even desirable—for the best interests of the Christian movement. In America where disestablishment had gone beyond the same process in Europe, it was discovered that when the churches were thrown on their own initiative, this allowed and perhaps even encouraged the development of many striking signs of vitality.

For example, in the 1950's and the 1960's in the United States, and especially in the 1960's as the Vietnam war was escalated, anti-establishment feelings and sometimes militancy were shared by a major sector of the population. Profound doubts about big government and all the established institutions threatened the main-line denominations along with the civil structures. Anti-war dissent bred anti-establishment dissent of many other varieties. The drive for racial integration was in some respects overtaken by the drive for black power, and then brown power, and Indian power, and female power, and youth power, and gay power, and led to a vast convulsion of self-determining subsections of society. The task of assimilating these cause groups into the orderly processes of civil and ecclesiastical government meant a good deal of trauma for many of the ecclesiastical structures which tried hardest to respond to their voices. In the process, the disestablishment of inherited Christian structures seemed to be accelerated, although by 1975 the greatest intensity of most of these storms seemed to have passed.

Meanwhile, a vast profusion of new movements had gained strength. The youth counterculture, which earlier had spurned the entire array of established structures including the Church, had to a considerable extent become the mainspring behind the Christian vitality in the so-called Jesus People movement, which at one extreme was manifested in so radical a movement as the widely reported Children of God, but was also a force behind a new mood and considerable new strength in many traditional seminary student bodies. Of the more than 250 new missionary agencies formed in the period, a significant group were almost exclusively the product of the youth movement, and many more made room for youth divisions; "short-termers" became a third of all missionaries from the United States. Young people, long conspicuous by their absence in both European and mainline church congregations, now became prominent in dozens of unanticipated ventures, both in Europe and in America, which bypassed traditional channels but clearly expressed genuine Christian vitality. One major youth mission originating in the United States, Operation Mobilization, discovered British and Continental young people to be so much more receptive that it virtually abandoned further recruitment in the United States. At the same time the voice of youth became increasingly heard in traditional structures as well, and was characterized by an unprecedented sensitivity to the new common concerns about ecology, hunger, and social justice. But while the most populous American state, California, elected as governor at 37 Edmund G. Brown, Jr., a man who was in his twenties during much of the Vietnam war, it was by 1975 unheard of for there to be any comparable reliance upon youth for formal leadership in the major denominational traditions.

The largest single Christian structure, the Roman Catholic Church, could be the object of a special study of the process of disestablishment. We have briefly touched on it in our references to Latin America, and will be referring to it below in the section on Asia and Africa. For the Roman Catholics, the central event of the third quarter of the twentieth century was clearly Vatican Council II. In a physical sense, this event was simply a four-year-long series of consultations between some two thousand bishops from the world wide domains of the Roman Catholic Church. It was the result of the inspired genius of an elderly man who was elected virtually as an interim pope. Yet in launching this council, Pope John XXIII opened a window which might never be fully closed again.

As a result, in a hundred ways this major ecclesiastical tradition achieved a massive, breath-taking adjustment to modern times—the untranslatable *aggiornamento* in Italian. Pope John's more conservative successor, Pope Paul VI, qualified and tempered but also implemented willingly or unwillingly many of the gains. Long overdue was a readjustment of Roman Catholic theology to the unwaning prominence of the Bible in the Christian movement, a readjustment of Roman Catholic structure to the nearly universal acceptance in the modern world of democratic governmental structure in place of a monarchial pattern of authority, and a readjustment of the Roman Catholic official stance towards Protestantism. In regard to the latter, it seemed that the new attitude of some Catholics simply included Protestantism with other non-Christian religions, welcoming both Protestants and Buddhists on the same ground. But in a new and healthy way, the Catholic charismatic movement fused Protestant, Evangelical, and Pentecostal patterns of informal prayer and worship with a new emphasis on the Bible, including in some quarters in the United States experiments in Christian community living that went beyond the casual fellowship so characteristic of United States church life.

Thus by 1975 in the Western world Christianity was less and less the legally or culturally established religion. In its nominal form it had lost much of the automatic respect it may have had in an earlier era. At the same time, voluntary structures were carrying forward a great deal of what seemed to be, over all, increased vitality in the Christian movement.

The Non-Western World

In 1975 one of the essential differences between the Western and the non-Western worlds insofar as Christianity was concerned was the fact that with some notable exceptions (e.g., the Syrian tradition in India and the Oriental Orthodox Churches in the Middle East and Ethiopia), the Christian movement was relatively young and accordingly less well established in the non-Western sphere. As we have seen, churches in the West were increasingly *disestablished,* while in the non-Western world the churches were to a much greater extent what we may call *unestablished*—that is, they had for the most part not yet attained either a legal or a cultural monopoly. Furthermore, as the nineteenth and twentieth centuries wore on, a significantly increasing percentage of the missionaries working in the non-Western world originated from within the new variety of American disestablished churches of which we have already spoken, and thus tended to implant in non-Western countries that same new type of Christianity which neither sought nor expected to become established. For example, despite the popular stereotype of missionaries being backed by colonial governments, it is likely that as early as 1910 a majority of Protestant missionaries were at work in lands in which their home governments had no control, and this general absence of either government or cultural support tended to modify the very nature of the churches being planted.

We are not surprised therefore to find that by 1975 the overall character of the Christian movement in the non-Western world was extensively different from its Western counterpart. Many Western observers of the so-called younger churches in the non-Western world were so impressed by the unusually high quality of commitment they found overseas that they suggested there ought to be a "reverse flow" of missionaries from the younger churches to help in the work of renewal in the West. This was surely to be welcomed. Ever since Henri Godin and Yvan Daniel had written *La France, Pays de Mission*? the awareness of the need to consider traditional Christendom a mission field had grown apace, and the electrifying phrase of the World Council's new Division of World Mission and Evangelism, "Mission in Six Continents," had become the dominant perspective by 1975.

On the other hand, it would not have been entirely true to suggest that all non-Western Christians belonged to tiny, unestablished, committed minorities any more than to have maintained that all Western Christians belonged to vast nominal masses whose Christianity virtually came with their citizenship. Estimates for 1975 indicated, very roughly, that only about 120 million out of a total of 965 million Western Christians could be considered significantly disestablished, while 80 million out of a total of 214 million non-Western Christians were considered disestablished or unestablished. That is, the ratio was about 1 to 8 in the Western World and 3 to 8 in the non-Western World.

Reminding ourselves that we are speaking of a much broader type of disestablishment than the narrow and technical, conventional meaning of the term, the distinction here drawn is not intended to be invidious but descriptive. We have spoken of Christian communions possessing "legal or cultural monopolies" upon a citizenry, and have suggested that the third quarter of the century witnessed an accelerated shift from an established Christian tradition to a non- or dis-established Christian tradition. While the one form declined, the other was rising. Here is the paradox of weakness and strength referred to in the title of Chapter 60. Here is the distinction the absence of which allows such widely differing assessments of the state of Christianity in the modern world. Here is a perspective which prepares us to evaluate the uniqueness of the Christian movement in the non-Western world. However, our discussion will first turn to the Middle East, which is in some ways a halfway step to the rest of the non-Western world.

THE MIDDLE EAST

Thanks to Alexander the Great, who took Hellenism as far as India, and to Mohammed, whose forces held western Switzerland for over two centuries and parts of Spain for over seven, there was a great deal of inter-penetration between Europe and the Middle East. Furthermore, the Judeo-Christian heritage was by definition a blend of the Indo-European and the Semitic. As a result, the Middle East constitutes a fairly small step away from the Western cultural tradition. We are not surprised therefore to find that the life of the Christian movement in that area has been basically the confrontation of various human traditions, all of which have kinship at some point in the literate past.

In 1975 there were sixteen different kinds of older, culturally established Christian traditions in the Middle East. These groups were in most cases minority enclaves within the overwhelming context of the Muslim tradition, existing as battered survivors of centuries of turmoil. Yet, if North Africa and Ethiopia were included as part of the Middle Eastern museum of the ancient churches, there were by 1975 still nearly 17 million in the various sub-populations of the total Christian community, comprising 7 percent of the whole area, but 77 percent of Cyprus, half the population in Lebanon, 37 percent of Ethiopia, 13 percent of Egypt, 10 percent of Jordan, 9.8 percent of Syria, 5 percent of Sudan, and 4 percent of Iraq. Christians comprised 1 percent or less in all the other countries in this area—Morocco, Algeria, Tunisia, Libya, Turkey, Iran, Saudi Arabia, and the smaller Arabian States. The vast majority of these 17 million Christians represented the tenacious continuation of ancient churches— one million Eastern Orthodox, 13 million Oriental Orthodox (i.e., non-Chalcedonian), and roughly 100,000 Assyrian Church of the East ("Nestorian"), all of whom were at least *culturally* established if not in all cases *legally* established. Then there were almost two million Catholic Christians (of eight different traditions) that recognized the Pope as their supreme authority. These too could be considered culturally established. This left less than one million Protestants and Anglicans who to some considerable extent reflected the characteristically disestablished posture of the Evangelical tradition, but these constituted only 5 percent of the 17 million Christians, and were thus only one-third of 1 percent of the general population of the area.

Curiously, although the scattered elements of this latter group were only tiny minorities wherever they were found, nevertheless because they were relatively committed and were backed by churches in the West, they had a truly immense impact in the area, especially in education and public health.

Between 1950 and 1975 the entire area was drastically shaken by the further withdrawal of colonial forces, by internal revolutions, by wars and tensions with Israel, and in 1974 by the stunning impact of the unexpectedly vast new oil wealth of some of the states. All this turmoil affected the churches in the area. Immediately after withdrawing from Vietnam, the French were determined to hold onto Algeria, but in the ensuing conflict, over a million Algerians lost their lives, and an equal number of French, Spanish, and other foreigners, almost all nominal Roman Catholics, withdrew from Morocco, Algeria, Tunisia, and later Libya.

The impact of the twenty-five-year period on the actual numbers of Christians in the area was extremely difficult to determine, not for the lack of knowledge in 1975 but for the lack of precise figures for the number of Christians in the 1950's with which to make comparisons. Numbers Latourette was forced to quote as estimates diverged so widely from quantities accurately known for 1973 that it was virtually impossible to do more than offer several fairly general observations. By 1950, as colonial protection of the minorities was gradually withdrawn, the Christian populations in the area along with some of the other minorities had been in many cases tragically decimated by nearly genocidal aggression against them in Turkey, Syria, Iraq, and Iran. In the following twenty-five years, however, except for the plight of Christians among the West Bank Jordanians and the southern Sudanese, adversities of this sort were not so extensive. Generally speaking, the Christian communities were able to consolidate and to grow at least as fast as the general population, and thanks to a careful statistical study of the entire area sponsored by the Near East Council of Churches and conducted by Norman Horner, by 1975 there was detailed knowledge of the size and vast complexity of the constituent elements of the 17 million Christians to whom we have referred. Future studies of the area could build on these statistics and keep in closer touch with the growth and life of these churches.

It would be inaccurate to leave a depressing picture of the weakness and division of the Christian movement in the very region where Christianity first began. On the contrary, note the genius of the Eastern Orthodox tradition, for example, that created "autocephalous" branches comprising different ethnic and language communities. The vast bulk of the Christians in the area had early parted ways with the Greek tradition in refusing to accept the Chalcedonian Creed, but their autonomy within their own separate traditions was to a great extent in keeping with the autocephalous concept and was a surprising testimony to the resilience and flexibility of a Christian faith that embraced a widely disparate group of peoples whose diversity was, after all, not created by Christianity but in fact surmounted by it, even if imperfectly. Here was vivid proof that Christianity does not blot out ethnic and cultural uniquenesss, but to an incredible extent is a preserver of such distinctions, even as emigrants from the Middle East carried their distinctive faith with them to other lands. The acid test would be whether ethnic and cultural traditions calling themselves Christian would be known by their love for one another and for all men. Early Protestant attempts to work within and for these ancient churches usually resulted eventually in small Protestant communities outside them. It was a promising fact in 1975 that the Near East Council of Churches, originally a council of missions, was able to number the Antioch Patriarchate of the Syrian Orthodox Church as a member.

In this connection a broad generalization might be hazarded. On the one hand, the Western Roman Catholic tradition developed a monolithic ecclesiastical umbrella that spanned many culturally diverse peoples. But para-ecclesiastical movements such as the Friars and Clerks Regular (e.g., Jesuits) constituted live options for the expression of internal diversity. Such structures by their very nature were voluntary options and thus "unestablished" in the way we are using that word. On the other hand, the Orthodox churches developed decentralized autonomy for each of the ethnic and cultural entities in their region, but possessed very thin overall unity and seriously lacked the profusion of voluntary options presented in the West by the Catholic orders. Protestants, Anglicans, and Western Catholics in modern times brought to the Middle East additional competitive ecclesiastical options, perhaps unintentionally; but they also brought a profusion of non-conflicting para-church structures, ranging from Sunday schools and youth movements of evangelizing societies to major (Catholic) orders. By 1975 it appeared as though these secondary elements in the Western presence were inspiring similar initiatives in the Orthodox churches, especially in Greece and Lebanon. One very influential renewing force which spanned several churches and countries was the Movements of Orthodox Youth, which provided from its ranks the new, young Greek Orthodox Archbishop of Cyprus when Archbishop Makarios was made president of the country. Movements like this had profound implications for renewal and unity in the world of these ancient churches.

Overshadowing all discussion of the Christian movement in the Middle East was the colossus of Islam. It is not our specific purpose to describe non-Christian movements, but it is for several reasons necessary to pause briefly to reflect on the nature and role of Islam. As president of Egypt, Nasser could say, "Islam recognizes Christians as brothers in religion and brothers in God." Contrary to widespread belief among Christians, when Islam overran the Middle East centuries ago, the enforced conversion of Christians to Islam was by far the exception rather than the rule, and nothing in Muslim history approaches the ugliness of the militant opposition to Islam mounted by the warriors calling themselves Crusaders when Europeans fought back five centuries later. Reflections like this are necessary to clear the air.

However, only the most profound reorientation in our Christian thinking about Islam will avoid a harsh and artificial contrast between Islam and the various types of Christianity co-existing in the same area of the world. In some respects Islam was simply one more movement stemming from Judaism and Christianity. The missionary-theologian Arend Th. van Leeuwen suggested that just as Hellenic Christianity resulted from Paul's application of the Christian message to the Greek cultural sphere, so Islam was to a great extent the adaptation of Jewish Christianity into the Arab world. He claimed, in fact, that some forms of Orthodox Christianity in Ethiopia differed more from what the Western world understood by Christianity than did Islam. Whatever the case, the assumption that Islam was as different from Christianity as, say, Hinduism was a gross misunderstanding and perhaps hampered the possibility of Christian growth where Islam was dominant. Nevertheless, by 1975 it was clear that the relatively tiny presence of Western missions in the Middle East had opened a doorway of contact with the Western world which had spectacular influence. A handful of colleges and universities won over a high percentage of the entire new leadership of the area at least to Western science, technology, manners, and morals. This did not produce a Christianized stratum of society in the religious sense, but it did build an enormously significant bridge of understanding across which better religious communication could take place.

By 1975 Islam was the second largest of the world's religions, having about half as many adherents as Christianity. We have already seen Communism as an outgrowth of Christianity; it was far more obvious that Islam was also an outgrowth of the Judeo-Christian tradition. Van Leeuwen would even add that the scientific and technological revolution was still another outgrowth of Christianity. Thus we see that in one way or another the impulse that can be traced back to Jesus had flowed out across the world in the form of the Protestant, Catholic, and Orthodox forms of Christianity proper, plus the various "outgrowths" of Communism, Islam, and science and technology, such that virtually the entire planet had by 1975 been profoundly altered, indirectly at least, by the Gospel of Christ. If to formal Christianity, constituting one-third of mankind in 1975, we were to add the adherents of the profoundly theistic and ethical religion of Islam, constituting one-sixth of mankind, we would find that half of all people on the planet were at least nominal adherents of faiths that recognized Jesus in a very special way. Meanwhile, the other half of mankind was subject to massive cultural, intellectual, educational, medical, political, and moral influences which stemmed from Christianity more than from any other single source.

These statements are not meant to imply that Christians conceived their task to be finished once people had been influenced in the ways we have described. Indeed, Christians would consider the task only begun. Rather, the purpose of such statements is to integrate the massive extent to which the influence of the life of one man has already encompassed the world, and to note the extent to which future efforts have a tremendously significant foundation on which to build. Islam in particular, now that its heartland had come into unbelievable wealth, was by 1975 undergoing the most rapid transition into modern ways, meaning mainly Western ways, and was surely a phenomenon urgently requiring profound, new theological reinterpretation from Christian and Islamic scholars alike.

AFRICA

As we shift our vision to Sub-Saharan Africa, we realize immediately how much further from the Western world we are moving culturally speaking. Unlike the area of the Middle East, North Africa, and Ethiopia which we have just surveyed, in 1975 Sub-Saharan Africa offered no comparably long-standing points of contact with the Western world except in those limited areas that were Semitic or Muslim. The advance of Christianity in Africa in the nineteenth and twentieth centuries thus initiated an abrupt confrontation and interpenetration of cultural systems that were utterly distinct from each other. As a result, the rising interest in the 1970's in the development of African theology raised issues far more profound than did the relatively minor variations involved, for example, in the development of a Latin American theology, a development to a great extent within Western culture. The only parallel in Western experience to the immense impact of Christianity on non-Semitic Africa was the impact a millennium earlier of Latin, Greek, and Celtic Christianity on the pagan tribes of northern Europe—a series of events so far back in history that in the 1970's the lessons seemed not to be readily recoverable.

Between 1950 and 1975 over a century of serious occupation of Africa by colonial nations was abruptly ended. By 1975 forty-one African countries had been granted their freedom and had become members of the United Nations, leaving only a handful of African countries to continue under colonial rule. The largest single sector of these populations were under Portugal, which either partially or fully withdrew from each sector by the end of the period. Speaking in historic terms, a more sudden and complete collapse of external control could hardly have been imagined. Many predictions turned out to be false. Organized Communism was not able to fill the vacuum. Even a man like Kenyatta, whose accession to power was assumed to be equivalent to introducing Communism to Kenya, turned out to be much more pro-Christian and anti-Communist than the reverse. Westerners assumed that the new nations could not manage themselves politically, but the record by 1975 did not involve any instabilities which had not already bedevilled Western countries from the beginnings of the modern nation states. Even the marked trend to dictatorship and totalitarian police states was unfortunately not altogether different from the conditions in many Western countries. As for civil wars in the absence of the colonial powers, leaders in the Nigerian civil war drew comfort and even military guidance from the American experience. The inevitable attempts of resource-rich portions of countries to form separate nations, as in the case of mineral-rich Katanga in Zaire and oil-rich southeastern Nigeria, were direct parallels to the inclination of the cotton-rich American South to rule its own affairs as a separate country.

On the other hand, not everything paralleled contemporary Western experience. In the African nations the dominant social patterns inherited from the colonial era even if relatively secure were nevertheless relatively superficial. Christianity was in many ways becoming culturally established and increasingly nominal. Here the parallel was perhaps with fourth-century Rome when Christians had only recently gained government backing for schools, hospitals, libraries and, most important, public worship. Between 1950 and 1975 as the African states burst into independence it was inevitable that there would be in some measure a resurgence of the cultural substratum. Following the colonial period of nominal Christian ascendance, would a "Julian the Apostate" appear and attempt to reinstate the pagan tradition?

In Chad the Christian movement had brought no effective substitute for the important and impressive indigenous "rites of passage" at puberty, and in 1974 the government sponsored the widespread reintroduction of African puberty ceremonies, even for highly Westernized government officials in adult life, some losing their lives in the austere practice. On the other hand, in Tanzania tribal dress was suppressed in the interests of national unity. But in Zaire in the interests of African "authenticity," beginning in 1972, the government ordered the people to drop European for African names, banned religious youth organizations, church periodicals, and radio programs, seized control of elementary and secondary schools (the vast proportion church-run), and replaced religion courses and wall decorations with teachings that tended to present the president as a saviour. In 1974 Christmas was henceforth to be eliminated in favor of a

June independence celebration, and key theological seminaries were notified of closure at the end of the school year. In December of that year, according to one report, the state press agency announced that the nation's single political party "must henceforth be considered as a church and its founder a messiah." Kwame Nkrumah had already attempted to transfer devotion to the state and to himself in Ghana. He too had problems with the continuing influence of the churches, but was overthrown in 1966.

Christianity and its schools had virtually singlehandedly produced the new leadership of the African nations. But where state power was held by one tribal group and threatened potentially by the leadership of another, the church within the second group often became the enemy of the state. In such a situation, educated leaders of the wrong tribe, as often as not pastors, might be slain by the thousands, as in Burundi. In Uganda, although Muslims constituted only 6 percent of the population, the military dictatorship was held by a Muslim; and Libyan oil money, perhaps with the hope that the number of Muslims could be increased, seemed to provide an external source of power to a government so despotic as to be reminiscent of Caligula's reign. This fact by 1975 might have held grave forebodings for the strong Roman Catholic and Anglican communities in that country had they not constituted two-thirds of the population.

The overall picture in Sub-Saharan Africa seemed to imply that the power of the Church would go unopposed only if it supported political governments, or at least avoided conflict with them. Governments were sometimes rattled by the existence of a pluralism of churches which, though friendly to each other, did not support a centralized church administration for all varieties of Christians. Russia for a long time had attempted to bundle all Protestants under a single Baptist umbrella, and during World War II Japan had attempted the same in the formation of the Kyodan. In Zaire all Protestants were forced into a single council, and in Ghana Nkrumah had moved in the same direction. In Africa, however, the ethnic sub-stratum constituted a mosaic exceedingly more diverse than in Japan, or in the Western world, and the result was an increasingly unmanageable diversity. In particular, what were called the African Independent Churches became prominent. The phrase referred to denominations born in Africa outside missionary initiative. Latourette was well aware of the significant growth of the African Independent Churches even by 1950 (p. 1437). According to estimates by David Barrett, while mission-founded churches were still the majority Christian pattern in less than four hundred denominations, the number of Independent Church denominations had increased by 1975 to five thousand (one thousand in 1950) with a total membership of 7 million adherents (one million in 1950). This kind of church grew about 40 percent faster than the Christian movement in general, which itself grew twice as fast as the population in most areas. The phenomenon of Independent Churches was found in thirty-four African nations and 290 different tribes. Some of these churches were quite orthodox in their theology, others so unorthodox as to have within their midst a "divine" person. Yet each called itself Christian, and most of them looked upon the Bible as their sacred book.

Some observers felt Africa was descending into a chaos of cults. Latourette, had he been alive, would probably have rejoiced cautiously at the luxuriant spontaneity, the apparent overall vitality of a Christian movement which continued despite (perhaps because of) all the tumult of the times. Christianity had not created the immense African diversity but did ultimately bring to it a common denominator. One of the most outstanding indigenous movements, the church resulting from the work of Simon Kimbangu, by 1975 numbered well over one million members, mainly in Zaire, even in the most cautious estimates. Its desire to join the World Council of Churches and its acceptance by that body in some ways hinted that the diversity of the Christian movement worked ultimately for unity rather than disunity.

Between 1950 and 1975 no African nation adopted Christianity as a state religion, and by early 1975 the legal establishment of the Ethiopian Orthodox Church was increasingly tenuous. The prevailing mood did not seem to lead toward a European type of church establishment. For one thing, in most countries Roman Catholic, Anglican, and Protestant traditions were all well represented, and it would have been unlikely that any one tradition would become established in the political sense. Furthermore, even Roman Catholic missionaries from the United States (and certainly all other missions from the New World) arrived without any desire or expectation of becoming established, as noted previously. This was not to say, however, that Christianity was not increasingly established in the cultural sense in many (if not most) African nations south of the Sahara. One significant factor postponing the nominality so often associated with establishment was the continued rapid growth by conversion and the continued high percentage of people in many churches who had elected to become members of the church as adults, especially in the newer and Independent Churches. Even so, by 1975 second- and third-generation Christians dominated the leadership of many denominations, and a remarkable phenomenon called the East African Revival played an important role in renewal. Originating in an Anglican area in the 1930's, it was a movement that deliberately held its meetings outside normal church hours and offered an additional option of fellowship and openness beyond normal church membership. By 1975 it was found in most of East Africa and neighboring countries, touching more than one million lives, and did not show any signs of decline.

This movement and literally hundreds of other para-church phenomena vitally contributed to the overall health of the Christian movement. There was a tendency in the 1960's and 1970's, as the colonial officials disappeared from Africa, for it to be assumed in some quarters that the Western mission agencies also had no further role. A proposal by John Gatu, an East African church leader, for a "moratorium" on Western mission personnel and funds was widely discussed in the 1970's and its meanings and merits were as widely misunderstood. His proposal was eminently reasonable for many situations where a well-founded national church—somewhat parallel to a national political entity—needed to function entirely on its own power. He did not intend his proposal to wipe out all the initiatives of a para-ecclesiastical nature, much less divert attention from population elements that were not yet Christian. On the other hand, while his own church was prepared to send missionaries, very few African denominations had organized their own mission boards. A major exception was the Evangelical Churches of West Africa, which by 1975 had established an autonomous board under which over two hundred Africans served as missionaries.

In any case, the very discussion of a moratorium highlighted the fact that by 1975 the dominant voices in church leadership in Africa (not only in the Independent movement but in the churches which were the direct result of mission agencies) were duly empowered African church leaders. For example, Latourette noted that there were in 1952 only four African Roman Catholic bishops. By 1975 the Roman Catholic Church had consecrated 129 African bishops, 22 African archbishops, and 5 African cardinals. The change in the Protestant sphere was comparable even though not so easily summed up. Christianity, as a movement, was clearly out of the control of the West.

In no other continent during the 1950-to-1975 period had Christianity made a greater apparent advance. Yet the future was not clear. Some signs threatened serious cultural backlash. In many places nationalism seemed to conflict with the power and presence of the Christian churches. Islam was a rising force with new prominence and potential power owing to the oil wealth in its heartland countries. But in 1975 in Sub-Saharan Africa, Christianity was by far the most widespread, potentially unifying religion and was uniquely influential in the formation of most of the other social and cultural forces deriving from the West.

ASIA

By the time Christianity in the 16th century first penetrated to the Far East in force, Asia was by no means a sea of animism as uncontested by any other "higher" religion, as was Sub-Saharan Africa. For the greater part of the first sixteen Christian centuries there was no effective sea route to Asia from Europe, and

Christian missionaries sent overland accomplished relatively little that endured except for the Syrian Orthodox presence in South India. Prior to modern times, Islam had greatly expanded under Muslim rule in many parts of India and even in Southeast Asia. Buddhism, a Hindu reform movement, early had a special appeal where Hinduism was strong, and in expanding into other areas had the advantage of being a religion which originated in the very heart of Asia rather than at its geographically distant Western edge like Christianity and Islam.

Furthermore, when Western colonial powers began to take over many parts of Asia, the two great Protestant colonial powers, the British and the Dutch, never seriously sponsored mission work as did the Portuguese, Spanish, and French. Thus by 1900 Christianity in Asia numbered only 9 million adherents, constituted mostly by the nominal Roman Catholic communities in the Philippines and Indochina. By 1975 Christians had grown to more than 80 million, at an average growth rate of three times that of Asia in general, but this number was still a modest presence compared to the 285 million Muslims just in that part of Asia east of Pakistan. Furthermore, depressed classes in certain parts of India were rapidly becoming Buddhist, and Islam, while not at this time actively missionary in India, had the potential backing of the new wealth of the Middle East. The development of an Islamic way of life—an Islamic basis for civil government—was the serious concern of the new Islamic state, Pakistan, during the entire 1950–1975 period. Nevertheless, neither Buddhism nor Islam possessed a mechanism of outreach remotely comparable to that which had been mounted by Christians in the West and carried to the Far East following the development of sea travel in the sixteenth century. Even so, not until the ninteenth century did the Protestant movement begin participating seriously in this effort, and it was not until the twentieth century that the major growth of Christianity took place.

Between 1950 and 1975 the vast new energy of an industrialized West eclipsed all previous influences on a relatively passive East despite the simultaneous collapse and withdrawl of the formal colonial government apparatus. By 1975 Christianity possessed literally thousands of centers of outreach, mostly new in the twentieth century, which meant that while it was still overshadowed in sheer numbers in most of Asia by the earlier advances of Buddhism and Islam, its overall presence was no longer tenuous but in fact remarkably influential.

On the other hand, its future was by no means assured. One great handicap to a continuation of Western mission efforts was the widespread assumption that the evangelism and missionary outreach of the younger churches, once firmly established, would be relatively automatic. On the contrary, churches in India, for example, showed little ability to evangelize non-Christians. As missionary leadership from the West declined, the churches moved rapidly to co-existence with Hinduism. The vast bulk of what evangelistic efforts there were was evangelism of existing now-nominal Christians. Many of the older missions interpreted the missionary task as "helping the younger churches" rather than communicating the Gospel to unbelievers. Since the main drive of both nation and Church in the post-colonial years was to get rid of foreign domination, the churches showed little ability to use their foreign servants in pioneer evangelism. Consequently huge numbers of the citizens of India, Pakistan, and latterly Bangladesh, growing larger every year, were left untouched. The burgeoning cities, rapidly filling up with immigrants from the countrysides, did not blossom with thousands of new congregations as happened in Africa and Latin America. The main churches remained tied to the cantonments, where the British had lived in the colonial period, and until the mid-1970's few new churches were established in the urban developments which proliferated all over India. On the other hand, in almost no area of India did Christians decrease in their percentage of the population; indeed, they generally increased slightly more rapidly. In the Hill Provinces of northeast India by 1975 Mizoran had become 98 percent Christian, Meghalaya 50 percent Christian, and Nagaland 80 percent Christian.

A word of caution is necessary in regard to these references to percentages of Christians in a given area of the world. For example, of what great value is it to note that the percentage of Christians in Asia was 4 percent or a little more in 1975? As with all averages, there might actually have been no specific area whatsoever where that percentage was actually true. On the one hand, at least a third of the Christians in Asia were those nominally Christian peoples in the Philippines, where practically everyone was Christian but where neither Roman Catholics nor Protestants would claim very many truly committed Christians. On the other hand, there were vast sectors of India, and perhaps virtually the whole of the People's Republic of China, where there was little Christianity, if any, in terms of known numbers of formal adherents. Meanwhile, there were specific areas of Asia where there were not only a large number of Christians, constituting a high percentage of the population, but in fact there was a great deal of fresh, young, vital Christianity. This was spectacularly true in northeast India, as we have mentioned, but was also true for many areas of Indonesia. Burma was not a Christian country, but in northern Burma the vast proportion of the population was Christian. Thailand was not a Christian country, and yet there were areas where there was a strong, virile Christian witness. Roman Catholic Christians had survived in large numbers in South Vietnam, and although the Protestant movement was small, it was healthy and had more than a quarter million adherents, exercising an influence which was considerable. In Hong Kong one out of every ten people was Christian. In Japan a very small proportion of the population, far less than Asia's average, was formally related to Christian churches as such, but more than half of all the marriages taking place in Tokyo followed the Christian pattern. In Japan well over 75 percent of the people answering a government census which asked, "Who is the greatest religious leader in history?" answered "Jesus Christ." In many respects, Korean Christians represented the strongest Christian community in Asia. Over half of all the Protestant theological students in Asia were Koreans studying in one of the many large seminaries there. While only one out of one hundred in the rural areas of South Korea was Christian, one out of ten in the cities was Christian, and one out of seven in the capital city of Seoul. One out of three of the lower-level government officials was Christian, and the proportion of Christians was even higher, close to half, in both the army and the upper echelons of government.

Thus where Christianity had taken root, it had often grown spectacularly. It had proven that it could flourish on almost any soil. But there were many places where it had not taken root at all. It had not necessarily favored any class of society but had demonstrated its ability to give substantial meaning and hope even to the lowest levels of society. In the areas of medicine, in education, and in sacrificial social amelioration, the Christian movement had worked almost without competition.

A few final comments about the meaning of Christianity within so vast a population as Asia, in view of the limitations of space, can perhaps best be focussed on the three largest ethnic-religious groups of non-Christians: the Muslims, the Hindus, and the Chinese. In 1975, by one estimate, they numbered roughly 650 million, 500 million, and 820 million respectively, or about three-fourths of all Asians. It was illuminating to see the potential relationship of the Christian faith to these three major cultural spheres as a parallel to certain new developments in the relationship between Christianity and the Jewish tradition.

In the 1960's and the 1970's there had been increasing interest in certain Christian circles in the possibility that Jews might become "Christians" without calling themselves Christian and without assimilating themselves to what is perhaps basically a Hellenic Christian tradition in the West. "Jews for Jesus" had become well known, although the phrase actually referred to a number of different attempts to reach Jewish people without tearing them out of their cultural tradition. Meanwhile many voices counselled that all evangelistic efforts be given up with regard to the Jews, a view which Gerald Anderson successfully challenged (*Missiology, An International Review*, Vol. II, No. 3). "Messianic Judaism" was the phrase used to refer to the desired result of most of the attempts new in the 1970's and late 1960's, not all of them successful. But it was probably true that the most sensitive attempts along this line avoided many of the admittedly objectional elements of evangelism as it had been practiced toward the Jews in earlier periods.

Of great significance, however, was this approach to the Muslim tradition. The acceptability of the Christian message among the Muslims was hindered by ill-will retained from the age of the Crusaders. There was also the fact that Christianity had approached the Muslims almost invariably from a Hellenic base. The apostle Paul had felt that he should be a Greek to the Greeks and a Jew to the Jews. He might just as well have suggested that he be a Muslim to the Muslims. It was not beyond reason to suppose that Muslims might become truly believers in Jesus Christ as Saviour and Lord without calling themselves Christians, even as the "Messianic Jews" did. Theoretically then what was needed was for the Muslims to become believers without having to abandon their Muslim language and culture. For the most part this was not possible in those areas where the only Christian contact the Muslims had was with enclaves of Christians who had been there for centuries and who represented differing racial, linguistic, or cultural traditions. For Muslims to have to shift from one culture to another, even to a "Christian" culture, seemed to be the kind of proselytism which the Apostle avoided and which all future missions ought assiduously to avoid.

A similar barrier existed to Christian efforts among the Chinese. The very earliest missionaries had felt that the Chinese language and culture could become a vehicle for the Christian faith without, for example, the necessity of destroying the strong cultural traditions in China involving a continuing and abiding respect for one's ancestors. Later missionaries were required by the Pope to reject this inheritance. Communism did everything possible to demolish this trait, and so did the bulk of Protestant missionaries. By 1975 there were fascinating possibilities in recent thinking being done by both Protestants and Catholics with regard to the relations of Chinese to their ancestors and the ways by which Christian truth could be made meaningful to them. Was it possible to encourage the Chinese to adhere to the meaning of the first commandment, that no one but God must be worshipped, and at the same time allow them to honor their elders as is enjoined in the fifth commandment? In early 1975 there was hope that a new era of leadership by Chou En-lai might somehow offer new opportunities for Christian witness in China. This very possibility encouraged a thorough rethinking of the approach.

One of the great practical obstacles to Christian growth in India was the fact that most Christians there—the main exception being the Syrian tradition—

came from the depressed classes, earlier called "untouchables." This fact demonstrated to India more graphically than anything else could have the phenomenal power of the Christian faith to transform and uplift. Yet it also tended to seal off the Christian movement within certain social classes. A few voices were raised in defense of a deliberate "second front" into the higher strata of the former caste system. Asked what receptivity there might be for Christianity on the part of the 500 million middle-caste peoples of India, one Indian leader suggested that at least 100 million of these people would become Christians if it were possible for them to do so without abandoning their entire social inheritance. Yet many Western Christians tended to believe that social evils, seemingly perpetuated by the traditional social structures, could be conquered only by displacing those structures. By 1975 Christian denominations and larger associations bridged many social barriers and impressively demonstrated the unity of all men in Christ; nevertheless, at the same time relatively few local congregations spanned great cultural distances. Many social groups had church traditions within them, but the majority of more than one thousand middle-caste groups, constituting at least 80 percent of the population, had as yet no branch of the Christian Church represented within their communities.

Yet Christian unity across all cultural distances, prejudice barriers, and political boundaries was an accomplished fact in Asia, and the same could be said for other regions of the world, and indeed the world itself. This uniting dimension of the Christian movement was one of its major contributions to international understanding as well as being one of the essential features of Christianity itself. As such it is a fitting subject with which to conclude this interpretive essay.

DIVERSITY AND UNITY

Curiously, during the 1950–1975 period, Christianity as a movement became strikingly more diverse and at the same time remarkably more unified. Its greatest diversity was displayed in Africa, especially in the vast profusion of African Independent Churches, which have already been mentioned. On the other hand, this same period was the era of the World Council of Churches, of new, friendlier attitudes between Catholics and Protestants following upon Vatican Council II, of a remarkable series of local, regional, and world evangelistic crusades and congresses, and finally of the emergence of the neo-pentecostal charismatic movement which by 1975 had penetrated all major Christian traditions.

The diversity was itself unique. Christianity as it expanded across the world displayed the capacity to become clothed in the language and culture of all peoples accepting it, and at the same time to bind those diverse peoples into fellowship with other Christians in other parts of the world. This characteristic was not so well known, nor so widely appreciated, prior to the 1950-to-1975 period, despite the fact that the shift from Semitic to Hellenic culture was one of the central dramas of the New Testament. For example, it was not until Vatican II in the 1960's that the Roman Catholic Mass was extensively translated into other languages, although for Protestants the translation of the Bible had long been a principal task of missions. Nevertheless, the effect of missions had generally been to uplift and enhance the local cultures in which they worked—despite the widespread stereotype to the contrary. Widely diverse types of Christianity were the inevitable result, but that diversity surprisingly did not imply isolation or disunity; rather, it contributed a new richness and renewing balance to the entire world movement.

It was true that centuries earlier as the Roman Empire and later Western Europe had become nominally Christian, wars continued between the nominally Christian peoples of that region, right down to World War II. But the reappearance in modern times of significant movements of relatively disestablished Christianity injected a new and unifying element that became quite powerful by the twentieth century. One of the most significant manifestations of the trend toward this new type of voluntary Christianity was constituted by the various student initiatives at the turn of the century: the college division of the YMCA, the Student Volunteer Movement for Foreign Missions, the various Student Christian Movements, the World's Student Christian Federation, etc. These movements almost immediately leaped ancient barriers, and the impact of this new generation of committed students upon Christian unity world-wide was permanent and incalculable. Latourette had noted that these students, soon church leaders, raised money from the Allied Nations to support German mission efforts during World War I. One of them, J.H. Oldham, made the decisive suggestion at the table of the Treaty of Versailles which prevented expropriation by the Allies of German mission properties. While this new impetus did not prevent World War II, it had by that date forged unbreakable bonds of fellowship and collaboration across warring lines in an unprecedented way (p. 1378). An outgrowth of these student movements had been the trail-blazing World Missionary Conference of 1910. An usher at that conference, William Temple, thirty-two years later (1942) was crowned Archbishop of Canterbury amidst the ruins and deep mood of depression following the Battle of Britain. His oft-quoted remarks at that ceremony (p. 1390) appropriately had as their immediate background the Tambaram (1938) meeting of the International Missionary Council, which had once again demonstrated the long-standing working unity of foreign mission agencies and overseas national church leaders participating in the highly diverse cutting edge of Christianity as it expanded in the non-Western world, a unity which was finally to be realized in the more nominally Christian European and American homeland as the World Council of Churches was formally founded in 1948.

The aftermath of all the students' high-minded aspirations through the 1950–1975 period was a complex and in some ways perplexing story. Voluntary societies, whether denominational or interdenominational, had blazed the trail in the realm of cooperation and in explorations of unity, hoping to renew the older ecclesiastical structures in the process. The resulting ecumenical movement was a gradual transition from the initiatives of para-church structures to the greater and greater prominence of duly constituted church leadership, a phenomenon parallelling in many ways the long-standing process whereby the Catholic order structures had across the centuries lent leadership to the ecclesiastical hierarchy of the Western Roman tradition. In twentieth-century Protestant experience, however, the very voluntary structures which had created the ecumenical movement lacked the centuries of experience and mutual understanding characterizing the abbot-bishop, order-diocese relationship, and gradually gave over and virtually gave up their life to the churches they loved and served. Thus the dozens of councils founded by John R. Mott (and others) around the world generally moved from being consultations between leaders of active voluntary societies to being meetings of leaders of churches—structures passive by comparison. As that happened, the International Missionary Council became increasingly based not on such voluntary societies at all, but (indirectly) on churches (through its national and regional councils) just as the World Council of Churches was (directly) based on churches. The eventual merger of the two organizations in 1961 was in many ways a logical step. The International Missionary Council thus became the Commission on World Mission and Evangelism of the World Council of Churches, the first meeting of which then took place in Mexico in 1963, the second meeting in Bangkok in 1972–1973. At the Bangkok meeting, of the 326 who gathered, 20 percent were World Council and regional council staff, 50 percent were denominational officials, 15 percent theologians, 7 percent Roman Catholic observers, and only 8 percent missionaries or mission directors.

Thus it was equally clear that in the great transition we have described a growing vacuum resulted where once the para-church structures—the voluntary societies—had long held the greater part of the initiative. Let us look at India as an example. The National Christian Council of India, in its decisive constitutional change of 1956, excluded all entities other than churches from direct representation and thus became functionally, from then on, simply a council of churches. But no adequate provision was made or envisioned for continuing consultation specifically between voluntary societies, either (a) those working in India from abroad, or (b) those springing up in India and working in India and/or abroad. (By 1975 there were at least two hundred societies of the latter category.) The resulting vacuum was filled in part by the Evangelical Fellowship of India, which allowed both churches and voluntary societies as members.

To complicate the picture, in 1974 there appeared the Federation of Evangelical Churches of India, the largest member of which, at its founding, was the St. Thomas Evangelical Church, which had in 1961 separated from the Mar Thoma Church. This new structure was for its member churches presumably a substitute for the National Christian Council. Yet, theoretically, a denomination in India could belong simultaneously to the National Christian Council, the Evangelical Fellowship and the Federation of Evangelical Churches as well as to the East Asia Christian Conference (in 1974 renamed Christian Conference of Asia), the World Council of Churches, and the World Evangelical Fellowship. In many cases a church could have regional, national, and international confessional linkage as well, for example with the World Alliance of Reformed Churches, the Lutheran World Federation, the Baptist World Alliance, etc. By contrast, a non-denominational Indian voluntary society could belong only to the Evangelical Fellowship and the World Evangelical Fellowship, and in neither case would the specific role of a society, as distinct from a church, be the dominant concern of the unifying structure. In 1974 the Asia Missions Association was proposed for establishment in 1975. Related to it, hopefully, would be various national associations of Asian-based voluntary societies in mission.

This was still only part of the picture since unity was not expressed merely by the existence of unifying councils, fellowships, and transdenominational voluntary societies (such as the YMCA, the Overseas Missionary Fellowship, the American Bible Society, etc.) Many other types of gatherings also brought Christians together. Beginning in 1966, one society in particular, the Billy Graham Evangelistic Association, sponsored a number of "congresses" on evangelism, which drew representative leaders from a very wide spectrum of the Protestant world. Two of these, Berlin 1966 and Lausanne 1974, were world-level gatherings, the latter spawning a Continuation Committee which in 1975 organized regional committees pledged to the promotion and coordination of evangelism in all six continents.

However, despite the many avenues of unity briefly mentioned, the resulting mechanisms of consultation not only worked for unanimity in some matters but also brought to light seriously different perspectives. Structures of unity, operated by human beings, sometimes tend, against all good intentions, to be monolithic in viewpoint in given subject areas at a given time. Even some denominational structures, in the period under study, tended perceptibly to be fountains of singular emphases, not merely forums of the diverse views of their constituencies. In this respect Protestant and Orthodox communions suffered for the lack of the wide variety of decentralized initiatives represented by the Catholic orders; better said, the Protestant tradition spawned eventually a large variety of mission sodalities, to use the technical term, but Protestant attempts towards unity had not by 1975 achieved any regular, structural way for the churches and the para-church structures to work in constant, responsible reference to each other.

A second area of dispute related to the profound, ultimate question of the destiny of human diversity. In the United States by 1975, owing significantly to the emergence of the Black Power drive for ethnic self-determination, the goal of either racial or cultural integration was for many a thing of the past, and the dominant mood was to allow for and abide all kinds of diversity. This mood ran counter to all forms of imperialism or paternalism or interference, but tended logically to suggest virtual isolation instead. This was not a Christian concept of unity—which assumed interdependence, not independence—yet in an age of new-born nationalism it was difficult to turn away from the new voices pressing for disengagement. An extreme case of the new emphasis stressed mission *in* six continents in place of mission *to* six continents, since it virtually outlawed the sending of missions from one country to another unless, conceivably, the sending structure were internationalized so as at least partially to disguise the national origins of workers from foreign lands.

Yet despite the relative confusion of many clashing views, there seemed to be by 1975 an appreciably greater mutual understanding on the part of all the varied participants. Never before had so many different sectors of the world Church been so well acquainted, so well on the road to even better insights both into self-understanding and into appreciation of the true nature of a multi-cultural world family of faith.

The United Nations gathered together all of the diversity of humanity. But bitter enmities and non-speaking relationships existed in its corridors from the very beginning and without noticeable abatement across the years. Christian circles, on the other hand, gathered people from as wide a spectrum of humanity and did not have anything like the barriers to understanding between them. Furthermore, the success of the movement toward Christian unity was not based on a simple watering down of beliefs and giving up of distinctions, but was in the earliest instances, proposed and carried forward by those members of the world Christian community most committed to their own Christian beliefs, namely the missionaries.

There was a time when Christians fought each other with seeming impunity in much the same way that warring factions within the world Communist movement often found themselves in opposing political polarizations. As late as World War II, Christian nations were locked in massive conflict. Russia and the United States were allies against a country which had contributed much to the Reformation heritage dominant in the U.S. By 1975 there still seemed no hope of resolving the conflict between nominal Protestants and nominal Catholics in Northern Ireland. In the same way, some of the most profound rivals on university campuses were different factions of Communist sympathizers.

Yet, while Christians could not readily find major distinctions between nominal Christian nations and non-Christian nations, there was, nevertheless, no parallel outside of Christendom either to the degree or to the quality of cooperation between Christians. In 1975 consultation, fellowship, and collaboration went on at local, national, regional and world levels in dozens, even hundreds, of ways as Christians conferred, planned and moved earnestly together in worship, conference and united action. It could truly be said that being a Christian in 1975 guaranteed one a profoundly sincere welcome in more countries, among more peoples, in more places than would result from any other allegiance, whether religious, political, ethnic or professional.

Summary

By 1975 Christianity had clearly outpaced and was continuing to outgrow all other religious movements in global size and influence. Insofar as this achievement was largely one of an established nominal membership, along with other older nominal religious movements, Christianity had little power to contribute to the larger human community, and its lukewarm witness in some cases even contributed to its own decline. Insofar as Christianity was able to be manifested in forms that allowed for its highest ideals to be enacted and expressed, it displayed an active, transforming energy which could be traced in the background or the context of a great proportion of the high-minded men and women of integrity in countless circles throughout the world of 1975.

Certainly, in view of the tragic stresses planet earth was sure to face in the days ahead, the developing world unity of the Christian movement could become not only an important aspect of the greatest religious movement in the world but conceivably an essential resource in an ever more necessary civil world community of coordinated action against the age-old problems of hunger, famine, war, and pestilence. By 1975 such goals did not seem more achievable than they had at any earlier time—in some ways less possible. Whatever might come of optimistic hopes for man, it was clearly the hope of the Christian that there might be peace on earth, good will towards all men.

SUPPLEMENTARY
SELECTED BIBLIOGRAPHY

(Books printed since 1950)
I. For the Period 1500 to 1975

Ahlstrom, Sydney. E. *A Religious History of the American People*. New Haven: Yale University Press, 1972.

Anderson, Gerald H. and Thomas F. Stransky, editors. *Mission Trends No. 1*. New York: Paulist Press; Grand Rapids: Eerdmans, 1974.

Bainton, Roland H. *Christendom: A Short History of Christianity and Its Impact on Western Civilization*, (2 vols.). New York: Harper Torchbooks, Cloister Library, 1964 and 1970.

Bates, Margaret, editor. *The Lay Apostolate in Latin America Today. Proceedings of the 1959 Symposium Held under the Auspices of the Institute of Ibero-American Studies of the Catholic University of America*. Washington: Catholic University of America Press. n.d.

Baumgartner, Jakob, S.M.B., editor. *Vermittlun Zwischenkirchlicher Gemeinschaft*. 50 Jahre Missionsgesellschaft Bethlehem Immensee. Neue Zeitschrift für Missionswissen schaft, 6375 Schoneck-Beckenried, Switzerland, 1971. (re: fifty years of brainstorming and decision-making of a Roman Catholic mission society)

Beaver, R. Pierce. *Church, State and the American Indians*. St. Louis: Concordia, 1966.

———. *Ecumenical Beginnings in Protestant World Mission: The History of Comity*. New York: Thomas Nelson, 1962.

———. *Pioneers in Mission, A Source Book on the Rise of American Missions*. Grand Rapids: Eerdmans, 1966.

Bloch-Hoell, Nils. *Pinsebevegelsen*. Oslo: Universitets Forlaget, 1956. (*The Pentecostal Movement*—summary in English).

Brauer, Jerald C. and others, editors. *The Westminster Dictionary of Church History*. Philadelphia: Westminster Press, 1971.

Bridston, Keith and Walter Wagoner. *Unity in Mid Career: an Ecumenical Critique*. New York: Macmillan, 1963.

Brown, Robert McAfee. *The Ecumenical Revolution*. Garden City, N.Y.: Doubleday and Co., 1967.

Burkill, T. A. *The Evolution of Christian Thought*. Ithaca, N.Y.: Cornell University Press, 1971.

Burr, Nelson R. in collaboration with James Ward Smith and A. Leland Jamison. *A Critical Bibliography of Religion in America* (2 vols). Princeton: Princeton University Press, 1961.

Cavert, Samuel McCrea. *The American Churches in the Ecumenical Movement. 1900–1968.* New York: Association Press, 1968.

———. *Church Cooperation and Unity in America: A Historical Review, 1900–1970.* New York: Association Press, 1970.

Cnattingius, Hans. *Bishops and Societies. A Study of Anglican Colonial and Missionary Expansion, 1698–1850.* London: SPCK, 1952.

Costas, Orlando E. *The Church and Its Mission: A Shattering Critique from the Third World.* Wheaton, Ill.: Tyndale House Publishers, 1974.

Cragg, Gerald R. *The Church and the Age of Reason 1648–1790* (Vol. 4 of the Pelican History of the Church). Grand Rapids: Eerdmans, 1962.

Dayton, Edward R., editor. *Mission Handbook: North American Protestant Ministries Overseas.* Monrovia, Calif.: MARC, 1973.

Douglas, J. D., editor. *The New International Dictionary of the Christian Church.* Grand Rapids: Zondervan, 1974.

Fey, Harold E., editor. *The Ecumenical Advance. A History of the Ecumenical Movement.* Vol. II, *1948–1968.* Philadelphia: Westminster Press, 1970.

Forman, Charles W., editor. *Christianity in the Non-Western World.* Englewood Cliffs, N.J.: Prentice-Hall, 1967.

Goddard, B. L., editor. *The Encyclopedia of Modern Christian Missions: The Agencies.* Camden, N.J.: Nelson, 1967.

Goodall, Norman, editor. *The Upsalla Report.* Geneva: World Council of Churches, 1968.

Gutierrez, Gustavo. *A Theology of Liberation.* Maryknoll, N.Y.: Orbis Books, 1973.

Harbison, E. Harris. *The Age of the Reformation.* Ithaca, N.Y.: Cornell University Press, 1955.

Harr, Wilber C., editor. *Frontiers of the Christian World Mission Since 1938.* New York Harper & Row, 1962.

Hogg, William Richey. *Ecumenical Foundations: A History of the International Missionary Council and Its Nineteenth-Century Background.* New York: Harper & Row, 1952.

Jarrett- Kerr, Martin. *Patterns of Christian Acceptance: Individual Responses to the Missionary Import 1550–1950.* London: Oxford University Press, 1972.

Kane, J. Herbert. *A Global View of Christian Missions from Pentecost to the Present.* Grand Rapids: Baker Book House, 1971.

Kempf, Beek, Ewig and Jungwama. *Handbook of Church History* (4 vols.) (trans. by Anselm Biggs). New York: Herder and Herder, 1965.

Küng, Hans. *Structures of the Church.* New York: Nelson, 1964.

Latourette, Kenneth Scott. *The Christian World Mission in Our Day.* New York: Harper & Row, 1954.

————. *Christianity in a Revolutionary Age.* (5 vols.) New York: Harper & Row, 1958–1962.

Littell, Franklin Hamlin. *The Anabaptist View of the Church, A Study in the Origins of Sectarian Protestantism, An Introduction* (rev. and enlarged). Boston, Mass.: Starr King Press, 1958.

Loane, Marcus. *Pioneers of the Reformation in England.* London: Church Book Room Press, 1964.

MacInnes, Donald E. *Religious Policy and Practice in Communist China: A Documentary History.* New York: Hodder, 1972.

Mackay, John A. *Ecumenics; the Science of the Church Universal.* Englewood Cliffs, N.J.: Prentice-Hall, 1964.

Marty, Martin E. *Righteous Empire: The Protestant Experience in America.* New York: Dial Press, 1970.

Mead, Sidney E. *The Lively Experiment: The Shaping of Christianity in America.* New York: Harper & Row, 1963.

Mesarovic, Mihajlo and Edward Pestel. *Mankind at the Turning Point*: The Second Report to the Club of Rome. New York: E.P. Dutton/Reader's Digest Press, 1974.

Mol, J. (edited by Hans Mol in collaboration with Margaret Hetherton and Margaret Henty. *Western Religion: A Country by Country Sociological Inquiry.* The Hague: Mouton, 1972.

Neill, Stephen. *The Church and Christian Union.* London: Oxford University Press, 1968.

————. *Colonialism and Christian Missions.* New York: McGraw-Hill, 1966.

————. *History of Christian Missions.* Baltimore: Penguin, 1964; Grand Rapids: Eerdmans, 1965.

Neill, Stephen and others, editors. *Concise Dictionary of the Christian World Mission.* Nashville: Abingdon, 1971.

Neill, Stephen and Hans-Reudi Weber. *The Layman in Christian History.* London: SCM Press, 1963.

Newbigin, Lesslie. *One Body, One Gospel, One World.* London: International Missionary Council, 1958.

Nichols, James H. *An Interpretative History of Christianity, 1650–1950.* New York: Ronald Press, 1956.

Outler, Albert. *A Methodist Observer at Vatican II.* Philadelphia: Westminster Press, 1967.

Paton, David. *Christian Missions and the Judgment of God.* London: SCM Press, 1953.

Rouse, Ruth and Stephen Neill, editors. *A History of the Ecumenical Movement.* Vol. 2, *1517–1948.* (See Fey above for Vol. 2.) Revised by H. E. Fey. Philadelphia: Westminster Press, 1967.

Scharpff, Paulus. *History of Evangelism* (trans. by Helga Bender Henry). Grand Rapids: Eerdmans, 1964.

Schlink, Edmund. *After the Council: The Meaning of Vatican II for Protestantism and the Ecumenical Dialogue*. Philadelphia: Fortress Press, 1968.

Smith, H. Shelton, Robert T. Handy and Lefferts A. Loetscher. *American Christianity, An Historical Interpretation with Representative Documents*. (2 vols.) New York: Charles Scribner's Sons, 1960, 1963.

Stephenson, George M. *The Puritan Heritage*. New York: Macmillan, 1952.

Sundkler, Bengt. *The World of Mission*. Grand Rapids: Eerdmans, 1965.

Turtas, Raimondo. *L'Attivita' e la Politica Missionaria della Direzione della*. (London Missionary Society, 1795–1820.) Roma: University Gregoriana Editrice, 1971.

Underwood, Joel, editor. *The Future of the Missionary Enterprise Project: In Search of Mission*. New York: IDOC North America, 1974.

Van Dusen, Henry P. *One Great Ground of Hope: Christian Missions and Christian Unity*. Philadelphia: Westminster Press, 1961.

Van Leeuwen, Arent Th. *Christianity in World History: The Meeting of the Faiths of East and West* (transl. by H. H. Hoskins). New York: Charles Scribner's Sons, 1964.

Walker, Williston. *A History of the Christian Church* (revised by Cyril C. Richardson, *et al.*). New York: Charles Scribner's Sons, 1959.

Walsh, H. H. *The Christian Church in Canada*. Toronto: Ryerson Press, 1956.

Warren, Max. *The Missionary Movement from Britain in Modern History*. London: SCM Press, 1965.

———. *Social History and Christian Mission*. London: SCM Press, 1967.

Weber, Hans-Ruedi. *Asia and the Ecumenical Movement*. London: SCM Press, 1966.

Welch, Claude. *Protestant Thought in the 19th Century*. Vol. 1: *1799–1870*. New Haven: Yale University Press, 1972.

Williams, Colin W. *The Church (New Directions in Theology Today, IV)*. London: Lutterworth, 1969.

Winter, Ralph D. *The Twenty-Five Unbelievable Years, 1945–1969*. South Pasadena, Calif.: William Carey Library, rev. ed., 1974.

Winter, Ralph D., editor. *The Evangelical Response to Bangkok*. South Pasadena, Calif.: William Carey Library, 1974.

———. *The Structure of the Christian Movement*. South Pasadena, Calif.: William Carey Library, 1975.

World Development (official report of the Conference on World Co-operation for Development in Beirut, April 1968). Geneva: World Council of Churches, 1968.

Wright, Louis B. *Gold, Glory and the Gospel: The Adventurous Lives and Times of the Renaissance Explorers*. New York: Atheneum, 1970.

II. Works of a General Nature on Various Geographical Areas of the World

AFRICA

Baeta, C. G., editor. *Christianity in Tropical Africa.* London: Oxford University Press, 1968.

Barrett, David B. *Kenya Churches Handbook.* Nairobi: Evangel Press, 1974.

———. *Schism and Renewal in Africa.* Nairobi: Oxford University Press, 1968.

Beckman, David M. *Eden Revival, Spiritual Churches in Ghana.* St. Louis: Concordia, 1975.

Beetham, T. A. *Christianity and the New Africa.* London: Pall Mall Press, 1967.

Blyden, Edward. *Christianity, Islam and the Negro.* Edinburgh: Edinburgh University Press, 1967.

Groves, C. P. *The Planting of Christianity in Africa 1840–1954.* (4 vols.) London: Lutterworth Press, 1948–1958.

Hasting, Adrian. *Church and Mission in Modern Africa.* Bronx, N.Y.: Fordham University Press, 1970.

King, Noel Q. *Christian and Muslim in West Africa.* New York: Harper & Row, 1971.

Lagergren, David. *Mission and State in the Congo.* Lund, Sweden: C. W. K. Gleerup, 1970.

Rubingh, Eugene. *Sons of Tiv.* Grand Rapids: Baker Book House, 1969.

Stephens, Canon R. S. O. *The Church in Urban Nigeria.* London: CMS Press, 1963.

Taylor, John V. and Dorothea Lehman. *Christians of the Copperbelt: The Growth of the Church in Northern Rhodesia.* London: SCM Press, 1961.

Tippett, Alan R. *Peoples of Southwest Ethiopia.* South Pasadena, Calif.: William Carey Library, 1970.

Trimingham, J. Spencer. *Islam in Ethiopia.* London: Oxford University Press, 1952.

Turner, H. W. *African Independent Churches* (2 vols.) London: Oxford University Press, 1967.

Welbourn, F. B. *Religion and Politics in Uganda.* Nairobi: East Africa Publishing House, 1965.

ASIA

Anderson, Gerald H. *Asian Voices in Christian Theology.* Maryknoll, N.Y.: Orbis Books, 1975.

———. *Christianity in South East Asia, A Bibliographical Guide.* New York: Missionary Research Library, 1966.

———. *The Church in Crisis in South East Asia.* New York: Friendship Press, 1968.

Brown, L. W. *The Indian Churches of St. Thomas. An Account of the Ancient Church of Malabar.* New York: Cambridge University Press, 1956.

Bush, Richard C., Jr. *Religion in Communist China.* Nashville: Abingdon, 1970.

Clarke, William H. *The Church in China: Its Vitality; Its Future?* New York: Council Press, 1970.

Cooley, Frank L. *Indonesia Church and Society.* New York: Friendship Press, 1968.

Deats, Richard L. *Nationalism and Christianity in the Philippines.* Dallas: Southern Methodist University Press, 1968.

Drummond, Richard Henry. *A History of Christianity in Japan.* Grand Rapids: Eerdmans, 1971.

Elwood, Douglas J. *Churches and Sects in the Philippines.* Damaguete City, Philippines: Silliman University, 1967.

Gallagher, Louis J., S.J., Editor. *China in the 16th Century: The Journals of Matthew Ricci: 1563–1610* (transl. by editor from Latin). New York: Random House, 1953.

Jennes, Joseph. *A History of the Catholic Church in Japan.* Tokyo: Committee of the Apostolate, 1959.

Lee, Felix George. *The Catholic Church in Malaya.* Singapore: Donald Moore, 1963.

McFarland, H. Neill. *The Rush Hour of the Gods, A Study of New Religious Movements in Japan.* New York: Harper Colophon Books, 1967.

Merwin, Wallace C. *Adventure in Unity: The Church of Christ in China.* Grand Rapids: Eerdmans, 1974.

Neill, Stephen. *The Story of the Christian Church in India and Pakistan.* Grand Rapids: Eerdmans, 1970.

Outerbridge, Leonard M. *The Lost Churches of China.* Philadelphia: Westminster Press, 1952.

Pedersen, Paul B. *Batak Blood and Protestant Soul.* Grand Rapids: Eerdmans, 1970.

Sundkler, Bengt. *Church of South India: The Movement Towards Union, 1900–1947.* New York: Seabury Press, 1954.

EUROPE

Cochrane, Arthur C. *The Church's Confession under Hitler.* Philadelphia: Westminster Press, 1962.

De Grunwald, Constantin. *The Churches and the Soviet Union.* New York: Macmillan, 1962.

Evans, Robert B. *Let Europe Hear.* Chicago: Moody Press, 1970.

Freytag, Justus and Kenji Ozaki. *Nominal Christianity: Studies of Church and People in Hamburg.* ("World Studies of Churches in Mission" series.) London: Lutterworth, 1970.

Hartling, Paul, editor. *The Danish Church.* Copenhagen: Det Danske Selskab, 1964.

Hedlund, Roger E. *The Protestant Movement in Italy.* South Pasadena, Calif.: William Carey Library, 1970.

Hunter, Leslie Stannard, editor. *Scandinavian Churches*. Minneapolis: Augsburg, 1965.

Hutten, Kurt. *Iron Curtain Christians*. Minneapolis: Augsburg, 1967.

Molland, Einar. *Church Life in Norway*. Minneapolis: Augsburg, 1957.

Pollack, J. C. *The Faith of the Russian Evangelicals*. New York: McGraw-Hill, 1965.

Sentze, Geart. *Finland, Its Church and Its People*. Helsinki, 1963.

Solberg, Richard W. *God and Caesar in East Germany*. New York: Macmillan, 1961.

Vought, Dale. *Protestants in Modern Spain: A Struggle for Religious Pluralism*. South Pasadena, Calif.: William Carey Library, 1973.

LATIN AMERICA

D'Epinay, Christian Lalive. *Haven of the Masses* (on Chilean Pentecostals). London: Lutterworth Press, 1969.

Einaudi, Luigi and others. *Latin American Institutional Development: the Changing Catholic Church*. Los Angeles: Rand Corporation, 1969.

Gonzalez, Justo. *The Development of Christianity in the Latin Caribbean*. Grand Rapids: Eerdmans, 1969.

Mutchler, David. *The Church as a Political Factor in Latin America with Particular Reference to Colombia and Chile*. New York: Praeger, 1971.

Nordyke, Quentin. *Animistic Aymaras and Church Growth*. Newburg, Ore.: Barclay Press, 1972.

Read, William R. *New Patterns of Church Growth in Brazil*. Grand Rapids: Eerdmans, 1965.

Read, William R., Victor Monterrosso and Harmon Johnson, *Latin American Church Growth*. Grand Rapids: Eerdmans, 1969.

Read, William R. and Frank A. Ineson. *Brazil 1980: The Protestant Handbook*. Monrovia, Calif.: MARC, 1973.

Ricard, Robert. *The Spiritual Conquest of Mexico, an Essay on the Apostolate and the Evangelizing of the Mendicant Orders in New Spain, 1523–1572*. Los Angeles: University of California Press, 1966.

Sinclair, John H., editor. *Protestantism in Latin America: A Bibliographical Guide*. (revised and enlarged). South Pasadena, Calif.: William Carey Library, 1975.

Taylor, Clyde W. and Wade T. Coggins, editors. *Protestant Missions in Latin America: A Statistical Survey*. Washington, D.C.: Evangelical Foreign Missions Association, 1961.

Vallier, Ivan. *Catholicism, Social Control and Modernization in Latin America*. Englewood Cliffs, N.J.: Prentice-Hall, 1970.

Wagner, C. Peter. *The Protestant Movement in Bolivia*. South Pasadena, California: William Carey Library, 1970.

Willems, Emilio. *Followers of the New Faith: Culture Change and the Rise of Protestantism in Brazil and Chile*. Nashville: Vanderbilt University Press, 1967.

MIDDLE EAST

Atiya, Azia S. *A History of Eastern Christianity*. London: Methuen, 1968.

Attwater, Donald. *The Christian Churches of the East*. Milwaukee: Bruce Publishing Company, 1961.

Downey, Glanville. *A History of Antioch in Syria from Seleucus to the Arab Conquest*. Princeton: Princeton University Press, 1961.

Finnie, David H. *Pioneers East: The Early American Experience in the Middle East*. Cambridge, Mass.: Harvard University Press, 1967.

Fisk, Eric G. *Cross Above the Crescent*. London: Pickering and Inglis, 1971.

Haddad, Robert M. *Syrian Christians in Muslim Society, an Interpretation*. Princeton: Princeton University Press, 1970.

Horner, Norman A. *Rediscovering Christianity Where It Began: A Survey of Contemporary Churches in the Middle East and Ethiopia*. Lebanon: Heidelberg Press, 1974. Distributed by the Near East Council of Churches, P.O. Box 5376, Beirut, Lebanon.

Waterfield, Robin E. *Christians in Persia: Assyrians, Armenians, Roman Catholics and Protestants*. London: Allen and Unwin, 1973.

OCEANIA

Coaldrake, F. W. *Flood Tide in the Pacific*. Sydney, Australia: Australian Board of Missions, c. 1963.

Frerichs, A. C. *Anutu Conquers in New Guinea*. Columbus, Ohio: Wartburn Press, 1957.

Janssen, Fr. H., editor. *Self Study of the Catholic Church in Papua New Guinea: Seminar Handbook*. Goroka, Papua, New Guinea: The Self-Study Secretariat, 1972.

Koschade, Alfred. *New Branches on the Vine: From Mission Field to Church in New Guinea*. Minneapolis: Augsburg Publishing House, 1967.

Reeson, Margaret. *Torn between Two Worlds*. Madang, Papua, New Guinea: Kristen Press, 1972.

Tippett, A. R. *Solomon Islands Christianity* (Second printing), South Pasadena, Calif. William Carey Library, 1975.

Vicedom, G. F. *Church and People in New Guinea*. London: Lutterworth Press for United Society for Christian Literature, 1961.

Williams, Ronald G. *The United Church in Papua, New Guinea and the Solomon Islands*. Rabaul, New Britain, Papua New Guinea: Trinity Press, 1972.

INDEX